"A very important guide. Gives a very clear, very factual picture. I must admit that I carry and use the book like a bible and refer to it often. Thank you *Billboard* and thank you Joel."

**Hy Lit**
Program Director
WSNI RADIO, Philadelphia

"For a number of years I have used a review of music from a specific year as a specialty on my radio show. In those years I've been nicknamed 'The Professor' for my history lessons on music. One of my choice sources for information has been Joel Whitburn's books. Thanks."

**Scott Muni**
WNEW-FM, New York

"There's nothing else like it — only Joel Whitburn could accurately track 7,269 records of the rock era. *The Billboard Book of Top 40 Hits* is worth its weight in solid gold!"

**Arnie "Woo Woo" Ginsburg**
WXKS-FM, Boston

"Don't stay home without it!"

**Bruce Bradley**
WYNY-FM, New York

"Hit records have changed the way we dress, dance, talk, and even perceive ourselves. They make us happy, sad, or just help us to pass the time. Music *is* the message, and with this book Joel has given us a firm platform to catalog those messages and memories."

**Jack Armstrong**
KFRC, San Francisco

"A valuable reference for oldies but goodies — we wouldn't leave home without it!"

**Art Laboe**
Los Angeles radio personality
President, Original Sound
Record Co., Hollywood

"Very informative—takes the guesswork out of pop music."

**Joe Niagara**
WPEN, Philadelphia

"*The Billboard Book of Top 40 Hits* is an invaluable aid to anyone interested in pop music."

**Dick Biondi**
WNMB-FM, North Myrtle Beach
South Carolina

# THE Billboard BOOK OF

# Top 40 Hits

by JOEL WHITBURN/Introduction by CASEY KASEM

BILLBOARD PUBLICATIONS, INC./New York

Photo captions by Jon Young.
Picture sleeves selected from Joel Whitburn's personal collection.
Photography by Malcolm Hjerstedt of Munroe Studios, Inc.
Typography by A-Line and Ries Graphics, Inc. and Intergraphic Technology, Inc.
Edited by Marisa Bulzone and Brooke Dramer
Book design by Bob Fillie
Cover design by Bob Fillie
Cover illustration © 1984 by Andrea Mistretta

First published 1985 by Billboard Publications, Inc., 1515 Broadway,
New York, New York 10036.

**ISBN** 0-8230-7518-4

**Library of Congress Catalog Card Number:** 85-70516

Distributed in the United Kingdom by Guinness Books, 2 Cecil Court,
London Road, Enfield, Middlesex EN2 6DJ, England.

**ISBN** 0-85112-430-5

Manufactured in the United States of America

First Printing, 1985

4  5 6 7 8 9/90 89 88 87 86

This book is dedicated to
the record buffs,
worldwide,
who've supported my work
for the past fifteen years.

The author wishes to give thanks to
the entire staff of RECORD RESEARCH:

Bill Hathaway
Brent Olynick
Kim Whitburn
Fran Whitburn
Doug Lawrence
John Novak
Gary Mueller
Jeff Samp

# CONTENTS

# INTRODUCTION

Everyone who listens to my television and radio shows knows that my source—the only source—of chart data is *Billboard*. As *the* trade paper of the record industry, it's been publishing charts of every size, shape, and significance for more than 40 years, reflecting the popularity of the music and performers that have become part of our lives.

When "American Top 40" began in 1970, our staff had to thumb through back issues of *Billboard* to find the achievement records established by any artist who ever had a hit. But it wasn't too long before we became aware of Joel Whitburn's work.

Joel began collecting popular records in the early '50s, a hobby that not only turned into the world's largest collection of original, mint-condition singles, but also formed the basis for compiling and organizing the data contained in *Billboard*'s weekly surveys. Those surveys themselves are based on radio airplay and retail sales.

This book is the result. You can look up any recording artist or song title in the alphabetical listings. You can identify all the Top 40 hits of a performer's career; the date on which each debuted on the charts; and the number of weeks it spent on them.

You can, of course, check a disc's chart peak, and if it went to Number 1 or Number 2, how many weeks it spent there. Each record's entry includes label name and original record number, and also indicates which were certified gold or platinum by the Recording Industry Association of America.

But music fans cannot live by numbers alone, and that's why you'll find a truckload of trivia from the past three decades: tidbits, essential and otherwise, about the recording artists and their songs, pulled from the pages of history and illustrated with more than 300 photographs of unusual and often rare record sleeves.

For professionals in the record business and in radio, *The Billboard Book of Top 40 Hits* has a practical value that's obvious. For everyone else, it's pop music history—and pure, nostalgic fun.

Casey Kasem

# AUTHOR'S NOTE

Welcome to the second edition of what has become a definitive book of America's popular record/chart history. For the past two decades I have immersed myself amidst pop records and *Billboard's* pop record charts—it seems one can hardly exist without the other—so that this book could be presented to you as a factual account of America's pop music scene of the past 30 years.

If you've ever wondered if one of your favorite songs ever made the top 40, or which version of a particular song was the most popular, or just how many hits your favorite artists have accumulated and which of those made the top 10 or perhaps even No. 1, you hold in your hand the book that will give you all these answers and more. While you'll find that this book can serve as a dictionary that you may refer to on a daily basis, you'll also find that it can be the hit of your next party—you'll find thousands of facts about records and artists that can serve for some great trivia contests.

This book is actually a spin-off of a larger volume, which I have been publishing and selling within the music industry since 1970. Now in its fourth edition, this larger volume details the entire history of *Billboard's* Hot 100 charts (a listing of the top 100, rather than just the top 40). In addition to the Hot 100 charts, I have also written books (most in the same format as this one) dealing with the following *Billboard* charts: *Pop 1940-1955; Top LPs* pop albums); *Country (Country and Western); Black (Soul-Rhythm & Blues); Easy Listening (Adult Contemporary);* and *Bubbling Under the Hot 100.* Although these books are mainly for the music professional, this top 40 volume now gives the average record/music fan a close look into a segment of America's chart history.

I chose 1955 as the beginning year for this look at the popular music scene because it was really the first year of the "rock era." While the roots of rock music go back to perhaps even a decade before 1955, it was in this year that the term "rock and roll" became identifiable to a whole new generation of eager music fans. When Bill Haley's "Rock Around The Clock" topped the charts for the first time in July of 1955, the rock explosion began. Probably at no other time in the history of popular music has such a dramatic change in musical style occurred than at that moment. And when Elvis Presley debuted on the pop charts in March of 1956, rock and roll music found a leader for millions of devoted teenagers worldwide.

Although pop music can include any form of music that captures the public fancy, from dreamy instrumentals to barking dogs, it is rock music that has been the lifeblood of the music industry for the past 30 years. Since the advent of the rock era, the music industry has risen to the top as America's number one source of entertainment. In 1955, the total sales of recorded music was 275 million dollars. By 1980, that figure had risen to over 4 billion dollars!

While critics write of stagnant periods in the pop music industry, it is fresh artists and new styles of music that always seem to pump life into an exciting and ever-changing pop music scene. I hope you will enjoy this book with as much fervor and excitement as I have had in researching and listening to all of the 7,269 titles included herein.

JOEL WHITBURN
January 1985

# ABOUT THE AUTHOR

Considered by many in the music industry to be the foremost authority on charted music, Joel Whitburn began collecting records as a hobby in the early 1950's. Eventually, he started to categorize his records by year according to the highest position each one reached on *Billboard*'s charts. Later, prompted by friends and colleagues who recognized the importance of his research, he published *Top Pop Records 1955–1969*, the first in a series of books based on *Billboard*'s major charts.

Today, Joel Whitburn's *Record Research* books and supplements are used worldwide, and his record collection has grown to be one of the largest and most comprehensive in the country, encompassing every title to appear on *Billboard*'s pop singles and pop albums charts from 1955 on.

Married, with one daughter, Whitburn lives in Menomonee Falls, Wisconsin. An avid sports enthusiast, he especially enjoys water skiing at his lake home in northern Wisconsin, and playing basketball— a game in which the 6'6" Whitburn excels.

For Joel Whitburn, though, there's still no bigger thrill than finding an untouched basement or back room full of old records and simply rummaging to his heart's content.

# RESEARCHING THE CHARTS

Although *Billboard* began publishing in 1894, it wasn't until 1940 that it published its first weekly national pop chart. This first chart was a top 10 listing and the chart fluctuated in size from 10 to 30 positions until 1955, when *Billboard* introduced its first Top 100 chart. The Hot 100 chart, which has become recognized as America's definitive record singles chart, was first published on August 4, 1958.

From 1955 to 1958, before the introduction of the Hot 100, there were a number of charts published by *Billboard*, which were consulted by various members of the music trade. It wasn't until the Hot 100 chart was published in 1958 that the music industry settled down to consulting simply one chart as the definitive source for popular record chart data.

Here are the pop charts that were researched for this book:

| Chart Title | Dates Published | Positions |
| --- | --- | --- |
| Best Sellers in Stores | Jan. 1, 1955 – Oct. 13, 1958 | 25–50 |
| Most Played by Jockeys | Jan. 1, 1955 – July 28, 1958 | 20–25 |
| Most Played in Juke Boxes | Jan. 1, 1955 – June 17, 1957 | 20 |
| Top 100 | Nov. 12, 1955 – July 28, 1958 | 100 |
| Hot 100 | Aug. 4, 1958 – present | 100 |

The record's *date* of chart entry is taken from whichever chart it first appeared on. The date shown is *Billboard*'s actual issue date, and is not taken from the "week ending" dates as shown on the various charts when they were originally published. The issue and week ending dates were different until January 13, 1962, when *Billboard* began using one date system for both the issue and the charts inside.

The record's *highest position* (POS) is taken from the chart on which it achieved a higher ranking.

The record's *weeks charted* (WKS) and weeks at positions No. 1 or No. 2 are taken from the chart on which it achieved its highest total.

# THE ARTISTS

# THE ARTISTS

This section lists, alphabetically by artist name, every single (45 RPM) record release to make the top 40 on *Billboard's* pop charts from 1955 through 1984.

Each artist's charted hits are listed in chronological order. A sequential number is shown in front of each song title to indicate that artist's number of top 40 hits. All top 10 hits are highlighted in dark type.

Columnar headings show the following data:

DATE  Date record first made the top 40

POS  Record's highest charted position (highlighted in dark type)

WKS  Total weeks charted in the top 40

LABEL & NO.  Original record label and number

Other data and symbols:

A number of brackets next to a No. 1 or No. 2 positioned record indicates the total weeks the record held that position.

+ Indicates record peaked in the next year from the year in which it first charted
• RIAA certified gold record (million seller)
★ RIAA certified platinum record (two million seller)

The Record Industry Association of America began certifying gold records in 1958 and platinum records in 1976. Prior to these dates, there are most certainly some hits that would have qualified for these certifications. Also, certain record labels have never requested RIAA certification for records that would have qualified for these awards.

Symbols in brackets after titles indicate the following:
(I)  instrumental
(N)  novelty
(C)  comedy
(S)  spoken word
(F)  foreign language
(X)  Christmas
(R)  reissue of a previously charted single

If both sides of a record made the top 40, a diagonal symbol (/) is shown after the first charted side and the second charted side is indented. The label and number are shown only once—after the second title. In cases where both sides of a record were shown as one listing on the charts, the secondary sides are shown as above, but no date or position is given for the secondary side. Only the weeks it charted as a secondary side are given.

Directly under some artist's names are brief notes about the artist or group that may be of special interest.

Directly under some song titles are brief notes that may be of special interest, such as a record that may have originally charted at an earlier date, or one that may feature a famous singer providing background vocals. If the song is featured in a Broadway musical or film, the title of the show is given under the record title. If the record title and show title are the same, the show title is not given.

| DATE | POS | WKS | ARTIST—Record Title | LABEL & NO. |
|---|---|---|---|---|
| | | | **ABBA** | |
| | | | Swedish: (A)Agnetha (B)Bjorn (B)Benny (A)Anni-Frida | |
| 6/22/74 | 6 | 12 | 1. **Waterloo** | Atlantic 3035 |
| 10/12/74 | 27 | 4 | 2. Honey, Honey | Atlantic 3209 |
| 10/11/75 | 15 | 8 | 3. SOS | Atlantic 3265 |
| 3/27/76 | 15 | 9 | 4. I Do, I Do, I Do, I Do, I Do | Atlantic 3310 |
| 6/19/76 | 32 | 4 | 5. Mamma Mia | Atlantic 3315 |
| 9/25/76 | 13 | 11 | 6. Fernando | Atlantic 3346 |
| 1/22/77 | 1 (1) | 15 | ● 7. **Dancing Queen** | Atlantic 3372 |
| 6/04/77 | 14 | 10 | 8. Knowing Me, Knowing You | Atlantic 3387 |
| 1/28/78 | 12 | 9 | 9. The Name Of The Game | Atlantic 3449 |
| 5/06/78 | 3 | 14 | ● 10. **Take A Chance On Me** | Atlantic 3457 |
| 6/09/79 | 19 | 10 | 11. Does Your Mother Know | Atlantic 3574 |
| 12/08/79 + | 29 | 6 | 12. Chiquitita | Atlantic 3629 |
| 12/27/80 + | 8 | 16 | 13. **The Winner Takes It All** | Atlantic 3776 |
| 2/06/82 | 27 | 8 | 14. When All Is Said And Done | Atlantic 3889 |
| | | | **ABC** | |
| | | | British new wave trio - Martin Fry, lead singer | |
| 10/30/82 + | 18 | 13 | 1. The Look Of Love (Part One) | Mercury 76168 |
| 2/26/83 | 25 | 8 | 2. Poison Arrow | Mercury 810340 |
| | | | **AC/DC** | |
| | | | Australian quintet led by Angus Young (guitar) & Brian Johnson (lead singer) - Bon Scott (former lead singer) died 2/19/80 (30) | |
| 10/25/80 | 35 | 3 | 1. You Shook Me All Night Long | Atlantic 3761 |
| 2/07/81 | 37 | 5 | 2. Back In Black | Atlantic 3787 |
| | | | **ACE** | |
| | | | British pub-rock quintet - Paul Carrack, lead singer | |
| 4/05/75 | 3 | 11 | 1. **How Long** | Anchor 21000 |
| | | | **JOHNNY ACE** | |
| | | | born John Alexander, Jr. on 6/29/29 - died playing Russian roulette on Christmas Eve 1954 (25) | |
| 2/19/55 | 17 | 9 | 1. Pledging My Love | Duke 136 |
| | | | **BARBARA ACKLIN** | |
| | | | R&B singer from Chicago, Illinois | |
| 8/10/68 | 15 | 8 | 1. Love Makes A Woman | Brunswick 55379 |
| | | | **AD LIBS** | |
| | | | New Jersey quintet - Mary Ann Thomas, lead singer | |
| 2/06/65 | 8 | 7 | 1. **The Boy From New York City** | Blue Cat 102 |
| | | | **ADAM & THE ANTS - see ADAM ANT** | |
| | | | **BRYAN ADAMS** | |
| | | | Canadian rock singer/guitarist | |
| 4/16/83 | 10 | 11 | 1. **Straight From The Heart** | A&M 2536 |
| 6/25/83 | 15 | 8 | 2. Cuts Like A Knife | A&M 2553 |
| 10/01/83 | 24 | 6 | 3. This Time | A&M 2574 |

| DATE | POS | WKS | ARTIST—Record Title | LABEL & NO. |
|---|---|---|---|---|
| | | | **JOHNNY ADAMS** | |
| | | | R&B singer from New Orleans | |
| 7/26/69 | 28 | 4 | 1. Reconsider Me | SSS Int'l. 770 |
| | | | **CANNONBALL ADDERLEY** | |
| | | | quintet features Cannonball (alto-sax)-died 8/8/75 (46), brother Nat (cornet), and pianist Joe Zawinul | |
| 1/28/67 | 11 | 8 | 1. Mercy, Mercy, Mercy [I] | Capitol 5798 |
| | | | **ADDRISI BROTHERS** | |
| | | | Dick & Don Addrisi | |
| 2/26/72 | 25 | 7 | 1. We've Got To Get It On Again | Columbia 45521 |
| 5/14/77 | 20 | 8 | 2. Slow Dancin' Don't Turn Me On | Buddah 566 |
| | | | **AEROSMITH** | |
| | | | Boston quintet led by Steve Tyler & Joe Perry | |
| 7/12/75 | 36 | 3 | 1. Sweet Emotion | Columbia 10155 |
| 2/14/76 | 6 | 11 | 2. **Dream On [R]**<br>originally charted in 1973 (Pos. 59) | Columbia 10278 |
| 6/26/76 | 21 | 10 | 3. Last Child | Columbia 10359 |
| 12/18/76 + | 10 | 11 | 4. **Walk This Way** | Columbia 10449 |
| 5/07/77 | 38 | 2 | 5. Back In The Saddle | Columbia 10516 |
| 9/02/78 | 23 | 7 | 6. Come Together | Columbia 10802 |
| | | | **AFTERNOON DELIGHTS** | |
| 9/12/81 | 33 | 5 | 1. General Hospi-Tale [N] | MCA 51148 |
| | | | **AFTER THE FIRE** | |
| | | | English | |
| 3/05/83 | 5 | 14 | 1. **Der Kommissar**<br>Kommissar: a Russian government official | Epic 03559 |
| | | | **AIR SUPPLY** | |
| | | | Australian group led by Graham Russell & Russell Hitchcock | |
| 3/08/80 | 3 | 17 | 1. **Lost In Love** | Arista 0479 |
| 7/19/80 | 2 (4) | 17 | ● 2. **All Out Of Love** | Arista 0520 |
| 11/15/80 + | 5 | 17 | 3. **Every Woman In The World** | Arista 0564 |
| 5/23/81 | 1 (1) | 14 | ● 4. **The One That You Love** | Arista 0604 |
| 10/03/81 | 5 | 15 | 5. **Here I Am (Just When I Thought I Was Over You)** | Arista 0626 |
| 1/09/82 | 5 | 15 | 6. **Sweet Dreams** | Arista 0655 |
| 6/26/82 | 5 | 13 | 7. **Even The Nights Are Better** | Arista 0692 |
| 10/23/82 | 38 | 2 | 8. Young Love | Arista 1005 |
| 12/25/82 + | 38 | 5 | 9. Two Less Lonely People In The World | Arista 1004 |
| 8/13/83 | 2 (3) | 17 | ● 10. **Making Love Out Of Nothing At All** | Arista 9056 |
| | | | **JEWEL AKENS** | |
| 2/06/65 | 3 | 12 | 1. **The Birds And The Bees** | Era 3141 |
| | | | **ALABAMA** | |
| | | | Randy Owen, Jeff Cook, Teddy Gentry (cousins), & Mark Herndo | |
| 7/25/81 | 20 | 8 | 1. Feels So Right | RCA 12236 |
| 1/16/82 | 15 | 10 | 2. Love In The First Degree | RCA 12288 |

**Bryan Adams** is an established force in what's commonly called heavy-metal pop. But just a few years ago, the Canadian had to endure the indignity of scoring a disco hit with "Let Me Take you Dancin'." Today he scoffs at the record, saying, "I sound like a chipmunk."

**Deborah Allen** got a job singing backup for Roy Orbison after accosting the Big O in a restaurant. Then she toured the Soviet Union with Tennessee Ernie Ford. Next, her voice was overdubbed on recordings by the late Jim Reeves. A strange career.

**Herb Alpert,** the "A" in A&M Records, wrote the arrangement for Jan and Dean's first hit, "Baby Talk," way back in 1959. He formed A&M with Jerry Moss three years later, initially operating out of a humble garage in Hollywood.

**The Animals** learned "House of the Rising Sun" from Bob Dylan's first LP. Initially, their British record company refused to release it as a single, considering it too boring and too long to be a hit.

**Louis Armstrong,** the one and only trumpet man, got his first steady job blowing a cornet in New Orleans' red-light district in 1917. He made 15 cents a night, but later got a much-deserved raise, to $1.25 a night.

**Frankie Avalon,** né Avalonne, had credits aplenty—from hits like "Dede Dinah" and "Bobby Sox to Stockings" to movie roles in *The Carpetbaggers* and *Muscle Beach Party*. In 1976 he made a mini-comeback with a four-week summer series titled *Easy Does It . . . Starring Frankie Avalon*—co-starring Annette.

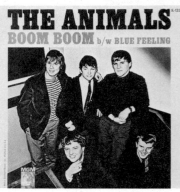

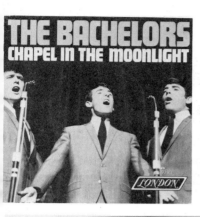

Rock 'n' Roll Fantasy

**The Bachelors** were three silver-throated Irish lads who worked as a harmonica trio before taking up singing. One of their British hits was "The Sounds of Silence," of all things.

**Bad Company,** featuring former members of three classic British bands (Mott the Hoople, Free, and King Crimson), chalked up more hits than all of them combined. They were also the only Top 40 act on Led Zeppelin's Swan Song Records, besides the Zeps themselves.

**The Beach Boys** also tried the names Kenny and the Cadets, and Carl and the Passions. At the height of their sixties popularity, they released a single as the Survivors to see what would happen. It sank.

**The Beatles** entered the studio to cut their first Parlophone single, "Love Me Do," in September 1962. Producer George Martin was unsure of new band member Ringo Starr's skills and used a session musician to play drums on some takes, leaving Mr. Starkey to shake a tambourine.

**The Beatles'** "Ticket to Ride" was a textbook example of the "ping-pong" phenomenon in pop culture. America's Byrds were inspired to trade folk for rock by the Fabs, who in turn incorporated the Byrds' 12-string guitar sound into this 1965 smash.

| DATE | POS | WKS | ARTIST—Record Title | LABEL & NO. |
|---|---|---|---|---|
| 6/05/82 | 18 | 8 | 3. Take Me Down | RCA 13210 |
| 6/04/83 | 38 | 3 | 4. The Closer You Get | RCA 13524 |
| | | | **MORRIS ALBERT** | |
| | | | Brazilian | |
| 8/23/75 | 6 | 16 | ● 1. **Feelings** | RCA 10279 |
| | | | **ARTHUR ALEXANDER** | |
| 3/31/62 | 24 | 6 | 1. You Better Move On | Dot 16309 |
| | | | **ALIVE & KICKING** | |
| 7/04/70 | 7 | 10 | 1. **Tighter, Tighter** | Roulette 7078 |
| | | | produced by Tommy James | |
| | | | **DAVIE ALLAN & THE ARROWS** | |
| 9/09/67 | 37 | 3 | 1. Blue's Theme [I] | Tower 295 |
| | | | for the film "The Wild Angels" | |
| | | | **DEBORAH ALLEN** | |
| | | | country singer | |
| 12/24/83 + | 26 | 7 | 1. Baby I Lied | RCA 13600 |
| | | | **REX ALLEN** | |
| | | | Western movie star | |
| 10/06/62 | 17 | 4 | 1. Don't Go Near The Indians | Mercury 71997 |
| | | | **STEVE ALLEN** | |
| | | | founded TV's "The Tonight Show" in 1954 | |
| 12/03/55 | 35 | 2 | 1. Autumn Leaves [I] | Coral 61485 |
| | | | piano solo by Steve, with George Cates' Orchestra | |
| | | | **GENE ALLISON** | |
| 3/10/58 | 36 | 1 | 1. You Can Make It If You Try | Vee-Jay 256 |
| | | | **ALLMAN BROTHERS BAND** | |
| | | | Duane Allman, founder, died in cycle accident on 10/29/71 (24) - Gregg Allman and Dickey Betts led band after Duane's death | |
| 9/08/73 | 2 (1) | 13 | 1. **Ramblin Man** | Capricorn 0027 |
| 4/07/79 | 29 | 5 | 2. Crazy Love | Capricorn 0320 |
| 9/19/81 | 39 | 2 | 3. Straight From The Heart | Arista 0618 |
| | | | **GREGG ALLMAN** | |
| 1/19/74 | 19 | 8 | 1. Midnight Rider | Capricorn 0035 |
| | | | **HERB ALPERT** | |
| | | | born on 3/31/37 in Los Angeles - co-founder of A&M Records | |
| 5/25/68 | 1 (4) | 12 | ● 1. **This Guy's In Love With You** | A&M 929 |
| 8/25/79 | 1 (2) | 15 | ● 2. **Rise** [I] | A&M 2151 |
| 12/22/79 + | 30 | 6 | 3. Rotation [I] | A&M 2202 |
| 7/31/82 | 37 | 4 | 4. Route 101 [I] | A&M 2422 |
| | | | **HERB ALPERT & THE TIJUANA BRASS** | |
| 11/10/62 | 6 | 11 | 1. **The Lonely Bull** [I] | A&M 703 |
| 10/16/65 | 7 | 13 | 2. **Taste Of Honey** [I] | A&M 775 |

| DATE | POS | WKS | ARTIST—Record Title | LABEL & NO. |
|---|---|---|---|---|
| 1/22/66 | 11 | 7 | 3. Zorba The Greek/ [I] | |
| 2/05/66 | 38 | 2 | 4. Tijuana Taxi [I] | A&M 787 |
| 4/09/66 | 24 | 5 | 5. What Now My Love/ [I] | |
| 4/09/66 | 27 | 4 | 6. Spanish Flea [I] | A&M 792 |
| 7/09/66 | 18 | 6 | 7. The Work Song [I] | A&M 805 |
| 9/17/66 | 28 | 4 | 8. Flamingo [I] | A&M 813 |
| 12/03/66 | 19 | 6 | 9. Mame | A&M 823 |
| 4/01/67 | 37 | 2 | 10. Wade In The Water [I] | A&M 840 |
| 4/29/67 | 27 | 6 | 11. Casino Royale [I] | A&M 850 |
| 7/22/67 | 32 | 3 | 12. The Happening [I] | A&M 860 |
| 9/30/67 | 35 | 3 | 13. A Banda (Ah Bahn-da) [I] | A&M 870 |
| | | | **AMAZING RHYTHM ACES**<br>Memphis-based country/rock sextet - Russell Smith, lead singer | |
| 7/26/75 | 14 | 9 | 1. Third Rate Romance | ABC 12078 |
| | | | **AMBOY DUKES**<br>Detroit rock group led by Ted Nugent | |
| 7/27/68 | 16 | 7 | 1. Journey To The Center Of The Mind | Mainstream 684 |
| | | | **AMBROSIA**<br>Los Angeles trio: Joe Puerta, Burleigh Drummond & David Pack | |
| 7/19/75 | 17 | 8 | 1. Holdin' On To Yesterday | 20th Century 2207 |
| 4/02/77 | 39 | 2 | 2. Magical Mystery Tour<br>from the film "All This & World War II" | 20th Century 2327 |
| 9/30/78 | 3 | 14 | 3. **How Much I Feel** | Warner 8640 |
| 4/19/80 | 3 | 14 | 4. **Biggest Part Of Me** | Warner 49225 |
| 8/02/80 | 13 | 10 | 5. You're The Only Woman (You & I) | Warner 49508 |
| | | | **AMERICA**<br>Dewey Bunnell & Gerry Beckley - with Dan Peek thru 1976 | |
| 3/04/72 | 1 (3) | 12 | ● 1. **A Horse With No Name** | Warner 7555 |
| 5/27/72 | 9 | 9 | 2. **I Need You** | Warner 7580 |
| 11/04/72 | 8 | 9 | 3. **Ventura Highway** | Warner 7641 |
| 2/24/73 | 35 | 2 | 4. Don't Cross The River | Warner 7670 |
| 9/21/74 | 4 | 11 | 5. **Tin Man** | Warner 7839 |
| 1/18/75 | 5 | 10 | 6. **Lonely People** | Warner 8048 |
| 4/26/75 | 1 (1) | 12 | 7. **Sister Golden Hair** | Warner 8086 |
| 8/16/75 | 20 | 7 | 8. Daisy Jane | Warner 8118 |
| 6/12/76 | 23 | 6 | 9. Today's The Day | Warner 8212 |
| 8/21/82 | 8 | 15 | 10. **You Can Do Magic** | Capitol 5142 |
| 7/16/83 | 33 | 6 | 11. The Border | Capitol 5236 |
| | | | **AMERICAN BREED**<br>Chicago rock quartet - Kevin Murphy was a founding member of Rufus | |
| 7/08/67 | 24 | 4 | 1. Step Out Of Your Mind | Acta 804 |
| 12/16/67 + | 5 | 12 | ● 2. **Bend Me, Shape Me** | Acta 811 |
| 3/16/68 | 39 | 3 | 3. Green Light | Acta 821 |

| DATE | POS | WKS | ARTIST—Record Title | LABEL & NO. |
|------|-----|-----|---------------------|-------------|
| | | | **AMES BROTHERS** | |
| | | | Ed, Gene, Joe & Vic Ames - Vic died on 1/23/78 (51) | |
| 11/20/54 + | 3 | 15 | 1. **The Naughty Lady Of Shady Lane** | RCA 5897 |
| 9/24/55 | 11 | 11 | 2. My Bonnie Lassie | RCA 6208 |
| 3/24/56 | 35 | 3 | 3. Forever Darling | RCA 6400 |
| 5/19/56 | 11 | 20 | 4. It Only Hurts For A Little While | RCA 6481 |
| 7/22/57 | 5 | 16 | 5. **Tammy** | RCA 6930 |
| 10/07/57 | 5 | 14 | 6. **Melodie D'Amour** | RCA 7046 |
| 3/31/58 | 23 | 2 | 7. A Very Precious Love<br>from the film "Marjorie Morningstar" | RCA 7167 |
| 9/29/58 | 17 | 10 | 8. Pussy Cat | RCA 7315 |
| 1/19/59 | 37 | 4 | 9. Red River Rose | RCA 7413 |
| 2/22/60 | 38 | 2 | 10. China Doll | RCA 7655 |
| | | | **ED AMES** | |
| | | | played Mingo on the TV series "Daniel Boone" | |
| 2/11/67 | 8 | 10 | 1. **My Cup Runneth Over**<br>from the musical "I Do, I Do" | RCA 9002 |
| 12/30/67 + | 19 | 4 | 2. Who Will Answer? | RCA 9400 |
| | | | **BILL ANDERSON** | |
| | | | host of Nashville Network's TV quiz show "Fandango" | |
| 5/11/63 | 8 | 11 | 1. **Still** | Decca 31458 |
| | | | **LYNN ANDERSON** | |
| | | | daughter of country singer Liz Anderson | |
| 12/19/70 + | 3 | 14 | ● 1. **Rose Garden** | Columbia 45252 |
| | | | **LEE ANDREWS & THE HEARTS** | |
| | | | R&B group from Philadelphia | |
| 12/09/57 | 20 | 10 | 1. Tear Drops | Chess 1675 |
| 6/16/58 | 33 | 1 | 2. Try The Impossible | United Art. 123 |
| | | | **ANGELS** | |
| | | | Peggy Santiglia, lead singer of New Jersey trio | |
| 12/04/61 + | 14 | 7 | 1. 'Til | Caprice 107 |
| 4/07/62 | 38 | 1 | 2. Cry Baby Cry | Caprice 112 |
| 8/10/63 | 1 (3) | 12 | 3. **My Boyfriend's Back** | Smash 1834 |
| 11/09/63 | 25 | 5 | 4. I Adore Him | Smash 1854 |
| | | | **ANIMALS** | |
| | | | British rock quintet led by Eric Burdon | |
| 8/15/64 | 1 (3) | 10 | 1. **The House Of The Rising Sun** | MGM 13264 |
| 10/17/64 | 19 | 6 | 2. I'm Crying | MGM 13274 |
| 3/06/65 | 15 | 6 | 3. Don't Let Me Be Misunderstood | MGM 13311 |
| 5/29/65 | 32 | 4 | 4. Bring It On Home To Me | MGM 13339 |
| 9/04/65 | 13 | 8 | 5. We Gotta Get Out Of This Place | MGM 13382 |
| 12/04/65 + | 23 | 8 | 6. It's My Life | MGM 13414 |
| 4/02/66 | 34 | 1 | 7. Inside-Looking Out | MGM 13468 |
| 6/04/66 | 12 | 8 | 8. Don't Bring Me Down<br>ERIC BURDON & THE ANIMALS: | MGM 13514 |
| 10/01/66 | 10 | 7 | 9. **See See Rider** | MGM 13582 |

| DATE | POS | WKS | ARTIST—Record Title | LABEL & NO. |
|------|-----|-----|---------------------|-------------|
| 12/31/66 | 29 | 4 | 10. Help Me Girl | MGM 13636 |
| 4/22/67 | 15 | 6 | 11. When I Was Young | MGM 13721 |
| 8/19/67 | 9 | 8 | 12. **San Franciscan Nights** | MGM 13769 |
| 12/30/67 + | 15 | 6 | 13. Monterey | MGM 13868 |
| 6/22/68 | 14 | 10 | 14. Sky Pilot (Parts 1 & 2) | MGM 13939 |
| | | | **PAUL ANKA** | |
| | | | born in Ottawa, Canada on July 30, 1941 | |
| 7/29/57 | 1 (1) | 18 | 1. **Diana** | ABC-Para. 9831 |
| 2/03/58 | 7 | 11 | 2. **You Are My Destiny** | ABC-Para. 9880 |
| 4/28/58 | 15 | 10 | 3. Crazy Love/ | |
| 4/28/58 | 18 | 7 | 4. Let The Bells Keep Ringing | ABC-Para. 9907 |
| 1/05/59 | 15 | 13 | 5. (All Of A Sudden) My Heart Sings | ABC-Para. 9987 |
| 4/20/59 | 33 | 3 | 6. I Miss You So | ABC-Para. 10011 |
| 6/08/59 | 1 (4) | 14 | 7. **Lonely Boy** <br> from the film "Girl's Town" | ABC-Para. 10022 |
| 9/14/59 | 2 (3) | 14 | 8. **Put Your Head On My Shoulder** | ABC-Para. 10040 |
| 11/30/59 | 4 | 12 | 9. **It's Time To Cry** | ABC-Para. 10064 |
| 3/07/60 | 2 (2) | 11 | 10. **Puppy Love** | ABC-Para. 10082 |
| 6/06/60 | 8 | 9 | 11. **My Home Town** | ABC-Para. 10106 |
| 8/22/60 | 23 | 6 | 12. Hello Young Lovers/ | |
| 9/12/60 | 40 | 1 | 13. I Love You In The Same Old Way | ABC-Para. 10132 |
| 10/10/60 | 11 | 7 | 14. Summer's Gone | ABC-Para. 10147 |
| 2/06/61 | 16 | 5 | 15. The Story Of My Love | ABC-Para. 10168 |
| 3/27/61 | 13 | 8 | 16. Tonight My Love, Tonight | ABC-Para. 10194 |
| 6/12/61 | 10 | 7 | 17. **Dance On Little Girl** | ABC-Para. 10220 |
| 9/11/61 | 35 | 1 | 18. Kissin' On The Phone | ABC-Para. 10239 |
| 3/17/62 | 12 | 9 | 19. Love Me Warm And Tender | RCA 7977 |
| 6/16/62 | 13 | 7 | 20. A Steel Guitar And A Glass Of Wine | RCA 8030 |
| 11/24/62 | 19 | 5 | 21. Eso Beso (That Kiss!) | RCA 8097 |
| 2/09/63 | 26 | 4 | 22. Love (Makes The World Go 'Round) | RCA 8115 |
| 5/25/63 | 39 | 1 | 23. Remember Diana | RCA 8170 |
| 2/01/69 | 27 | 6 | 24. Goodnight My Love | RCA 9648 |
| 7/27/74 | 1 (3) | 11 | ● 25. **(You're) Having My Baby** | United Art. 454 |
| 11/30/74 + | 7 | 11 | 26. **One Man Woman/One Woman Man** <br> above 2 with Odia Coates (also #28 below) | United Art. 569 |
| 4/05/75 | 8 | 10 | 27. **I Don't Like To Sleep Alone** | United Art. 615 |
| 8/16/75 | 15 | 8 | 28. (I Believe) There's Nothing Stronger <br> Than Our Love | United Art. 685 |
| 11/29/75 + | 7 | 12 | 29. **Times Of Your Life** | United Art. 737 |
| 5/01/76 | 33 | 3 | 30. Anytime (I'll Be There) | United Art. 789 |
| 11/18/78 | 35 | 3 | 31. This Is Love | RCA 11395 |
| 9/03/83 | 40 | 2 | 32. Hold Me 'Til The Mornin' Comes | Columbia 03897 |
| | | | **PAUL ANKA-GEORGE HAMILTON IV-JOHNNY NASH** | |
| 12/15/58 + | 29 | 5 | 1. The Teen Commandments [S] | ABC-Para. 9974 |
| | | | **ANN-MARGRET** | |
| | | | movie starlet Ann-Margret Olson | |
| 8/21/61 | 17 | 6 | 1. I Just Don't Understand | RCA 7894 |

| DATE | POS | WKS | ARTIST—Record Title | LABEL & NO. |
|---|---|---|---|---|
| | | | **ANNETTE** | |
| | | | born Annette Funicello on 10/22/42 - became a Mousketeer in 1955 | |
| 2/02/59 | 7 | 9 | 1. **Tall Paul** | Disneyland 118 |
| 12/14/59 + | 20 | 10 | 2. First Name Initial | Vista 349 |
| 3/07/60 | 10 | 8 | 3. **O Dio Mio** | Vista 354 |
| 6/20/60 | 36 | 3 | 4. Train Of Love | Vista 359 |
| 9/05/60 | 11 | 9 | 5. Pineapple Princess | Vista 362 |
| | | | **ADAM ANT** | |
| | | | British - Adam & The Ants leader | |
| 12/11/82 + | 12 | 14 | 1. Goody Two Shoes | Epic 03367 |
| | | | **RAY ANTHONY & His Orchestra** | |
| | | | trumpet player with the Glenn Miller and Jimmy Dorsey bands | |
| | | | also see Frank Sinatra | |
| 1/19/59 | 8 | 13 | 1. **Peter Gunn [I]** | Capitol 4041 |
| | | | **SUSAN ANTON - see FRED KNOBLOCK** | |
| | | | **APOLLO 100 featuring Tom Parker** | |
| 1/22/72 | 6 | 10 | 1. **Joy [I]** | Mega 0050 |
| | | | based on Bach's "Jesu, Joy of Man's Desiring" | |
| | | | **APPLEJACKS** | |
| | | | Dave Appell, leader | |
| 10/06/58 | 16 | 9 | 1. Mexican Hat Rock [I] | Cameo 149 |
| 1/12/59 | 38 | 3 | 2. Rocka-Conga | Cameo 155 |
| | | | **APRIL WINE** | |
| | | | Canadian rock quintet - Myles Goodwyn, lead singer | |
| 4/29/72 | 32 | 5 | 1. You Could Have Been A Lady | Big Tree 133 |
| 4/14/79 | 34 | 4 | 2. Roller | Capitol 4660 |
| 3/14/81 | 21 | 7 | 3. Just Between You And Me | Capitol 4975 |
| | | | **AQUATONES** | |
| | | | Lond Island, New York group - Barbara Lee, lead singer | |
| 5/05/58 | 21 | 8 | 1. You | Fargo 1001 |
| | | | **ARBORS** | |
| | | | group formed at the University of Michigan in Ann Arbor | |
| 4/05/69 | 20 | 3 | 1. The Letter | Date 1638 |
| | | | **ARCHIES** | |
| | | | studio group created by Don Kirshner—Ron Dante, lead singer | |
| 11/02/68 | 22 | 8 | 1. Bang-Shang-A-Lang | Calendar 1006 |
| 8/16/69 | 1 (4) | 18 | ● 2. **Sugar, Sugar** | Calendar 1008 |
| 12/20/69 + | 10 | 10 | ● 3. **Jingle Jangle** | Kirshner 5002 |
| 3/28/70 | 40 | 2 | 4. Who's Your Baby? | Kirshner 5003 |
| | | | **TONI ARDEN** | |
| 6/02/58 | 13 | 11 | 1. Padre | Decca 30628 |
| | | | **ARGENT** | |
| | | | British rock quartet led by Rod Argent (Zombies) | |
| 7/08/72 | 5 | 11 | 1. **Hold Your Head Up** | Epic 10852 |

| DATE | POS | WKS | ARTIST—Record Title | LABEL & NO. |
|------|-----|-----|---------------------|-------------|
| | | | **RUSSELL ARMS** | |
| | | | star of TV's "Your Hit Parade" | |
| 2/02/57 | 22 | 8 | 1. Cinco Robles (Five Oaks) | Era 1026 |
| | | | with Pete King and Orchestra | |
| | | | **LOUIS ARMSTRONG** | |
| | | | all-time great jazz trumpet player/vocalist - died 7/6/71 (71) | |
| 2/25/56 | 20 | 7 | 1. Mack The Knife (A Theme From The Threepenny Opera) | Columbia 40587 |
| 12/15/56 | 29 | 1 | 2. Blueberry Hill | Decca 30091 |
| | | | originally recorded in 1949 with Gordon Jenkins Orchestra | |
| 2/29/64 | **1** (1) | 19 | 3. **Hello, Dolly!** | Kapp 573 |
| | | | **EDDY ARNOLD** | |
| | | | Country music's all-time #1 artist - born on 5/15/18 near Henderson, Tennessee | |
| 12/01/56 | 22 | 1 | 1. I Wouldn't Know Where To Begin | RCA 6699 |
| 11/13/65 | 6 | 10 | 2. **Make The World Go Away** | RCA 8679 |
| 3/12/66 | 36 | 5 | 3. I Want To Go With You | RCA 8749 |
| 6/18/66 | 40 | 1 | 4. The Last Word In Lonesome Is Me | RCA 8818 |
| | | | **ARROWS - see DAVIE ALLAN** | |
| | | | **ASHFORD & SIMPSON** | |
| | | | Nickolas Ashford & Valerie Simpson (married) | |
| 10/13/79 | 36 | 2 | 1. Found A Cure | Warner 8870 |
| | | | **ASHTON, GARDNER & DYKE** | |
| | | | British: Tony Ashton, Kim Gardner & Roy Dyke | |
| 8/07/71 | 40 | 1 | 1. Resurrection Shuffle | Capitol 3060 |
| | | | **ASIA** | |
| | | | British: Steve Howe, Carl Palmer, Geoff Downes & John Wetton | |
| 5/01/82 | 4 | 12 | 1. **Heat Of The Moment** | Geffen 50040 |
| 8/14/82 | 17 | 8 | 2. Only Time Will Tell | Geffen 29970 |
| 8/06/83 | 10 | 11 | 3. **Don't Cry** | Geffen 29571 |
| 11/12/83 | 34 | 5 | 4. The Smile Has Left Your Eyes | Geffen 29475 |
| | | | **ASSEMBLED MULTITUDE** | |
| 8/01/70 | 16 | 7 | 1. Overture From Tommy (A Rock Opera) [I] | Atlantic 2737 |
| | | | **ASSOCIATION** | |
| | | | California soft-rock sextet | |
| 6/25/66 | 7 | 8 | 1. **Along Comes Mary** | Valiant 741 |
| 9/03/66 | **1** (3) | 12 | ● 2. **Cherish** | Valiant 747 |
| 12/17/66 | 35 | 3 | 3. Pandora's Golden Heebie Jeebies | Valiant 755 |
| 6/03/67 | **1** (4) | 13 | ● 4. **Windy** | Warner 7041 |
| 9/09/67 | **2** (2) | 11 | ● 5. **Never My Love** | Warner 7074 |
| 2/10/68 | 10 | 8 | 6. **Everything That Touches You** | Warner 7163 |
| 6/22/68 | 39 | 2 | 7. Time For Livin' | Warner 7195 |
| | | | **ATLANTA RHYTHM SECTION** | |
| | | | Atlanta studio musicians - Ronnie Hammond, lead singer | |
| 11/09/74 | 35 | 2 | 1. Doraville | Polydor 14248 |
| 2/26/77 | 7 | 14 | 2. **So In To You** | Polydor 14373 |

| DATE | POS | WKS | ARTIST—Record Title | LABEL & NO. |
|---|---|---|---|---|
| 3/25/78 | 7 | 12 | 3. Imaginary Lover | Polydor 14459 |
| 7/08/78 | 14 | 7 | 4. I'm Not Gonna Let It Bother Me Tonight | Polydor 14484 |
| 6/16/79 | 19 | 9 | 5. Do It Or Die | Polydor 14568 |
| 9/08/79 | 17 | 8 | 6. Spooky | Polydor 2001 |
| 10/10/81 | 29 | 4 | 7. Alien | Columbia 02471 |
| | | | **ATLANTIC STARR** | |
| | | | eight-man, one-woman band from Westchester, New York | |
| 5/15/82 | 38 | 3 | 1. Circles | A&M 2392 |
| | | | **JAN AUGUST - see RICHARD HAYMAN** | |
| | | | **PATTI AUSTIN & JAMES INGRAM** | |
| 12/04/82 + | 1 (2) | 18 | ● 1. Baby, Come To Me | Qwest 50036 |
| | | | **SIL AUSTIN** | |
| 11/24/56 | 17 | 7 | 1. Slow Walk [I] | Mercury 70963 |
| | | | **FRANKIE AVALON** | |
| | | | born Francis Avallone on 9/18/40 in Philadelphia | |
| 1/27/58 | 7 | 11 | 1. Dede Dinah | Chancellor 1011 |
| 7/28/58 | 9 | 12 | 2. Ginger Bread | Chancellor 1021 |
| 11/17/58 | 15 | 10 | 3. I'll Wait For You | Chancellor 1026 |
| 2/23/59 | 1 (5) | 14 | 4. Venus | Chancellor 1031 |
| 6/01/59 | 8 | 10 | 5. Bobby Sox To Stockings/ | |
| 6/15/59 | 10 | 9 | 6.  A Boy Without A Girl | Chancellor 1036 |
| 9/14/59 | 7 | 11 | 7. Just Ask Your Heart | Chancellor 1040 |
| 12/07/59 | 1 (1) | 12 | 8. Why/ | |
| 1/04/60 | 39 | 1 | 9.  Swingin' On A Rainbow | Chancellor 1045 |
| 3/28/60 | 22 | 6 | 10. Don't Throw Away All Those Teardrops | Chancellor 1048 |
| 8/01/60 | 32 | 4 | 11. Where Are You | Chancellor 1052 |
| 10/17/60 | 26 | 7 | 12. Togetherness | Chancellor 1056 |
| 5/05/62 | 26 | 4 | 13. You Are Mine | Chancellor 1107 |
| | | | **AVANT-GARDE** | |
| 10/26/68 | 40 | 1 | 1. Naturally Stoned | Columbia 44590 |
| | | | **AVERAGE WHITE BAND** | |
| | | | Scottish 6-man white-soul band | |
| 12/21/74 + | 1 (1) | 13 | ● 1. Pick Up The Pieces [I] | Atlantic 3229 |
| 4/26/75 | 10 | 12 | 2. Cut The Cake | Atlantic 3261 |
| 9/27/75 | 39 | 2 | 3. If I Ever Lose This Heaven | Atlantic 3285 |
| 12/20/75 | 33 | 3 | 4. School Boy Crush | Atlantic 3304 |
| 10/16/76 | 40 | 1 | 5. Queen Of My Soul | Atlantic 3354 |
| | | | **BABYS** | |
| | | | John Waite, lead singer of British foursome | |
| 10/29/77 | 13 | 11 | 1. Isn't It Time | Chrysalis 2173 |
| 2/03/79 | 13 | 10 | 2. Every Time I Think Of You | Chrysalis 2279 |
| 3/08/80 | 33 | 3 | 3. Back On My Feet Again | Chrysalis 2398 |

| DATE | POS | WKS | ARTIST—Record Title | LABEL & NO. |
|---|---|---|---|---|
| | | | **BACHELORS** | |
| | | | trio from Dublin, Ireland | |
| 5/16/64 | 10 | 8 | 1. **Diane** | London 9639 |
| 8/01/64 | 33 | 2 | 2. I Believe | London 9672 |
| 1/30/65 | 27 | 4 | 3. No Arms Can Ever Hold You | London 9724 |
| 7/03/65 | 15 | 7 | 4. Marie | London 9762 |
| 11/06/65 | 32 | 3 | 5. Chapel In The Moonlight | London 9793 |
| 5/14/66 | 38 | 2 | 6. Love Me With All Of Your Heart | London 9828 |
| | | | **BACHMAN-TURNER OVERDRIVE** | |
| | | | Canadian quartet led by Randy Bachman & C.F. Turner | |
| 3/23/74 | 23 | 9 | 1. Let It Ride | Mercury 73457 |
| 6/29/74 | 12 | 10 | 2. Takin' Care Of Business | Mercury 73487 |
| 10/05/74 | 1 (1) | 12 | ● 3. **You Ain't Seen Nothing Yet** | Mercury 73622 |
| 2/01/75 | 14 | 7 | 4. Roll On Down The Highway | Mercury 73656 |
| 6/07/75 | 21 | 7 | 5. Hey You | Mercury 73683 |
| 2/28/76 | 33 | 3 | 6. Take It Like A Man | Mercury 73766 |
| | | | **JIM BACKUS & Friend** | |
| | | | Jim played Thurston Howell III on TV's "Gilligan's Island" | |
| 7/21/58 | 40 | 2 | 1. Delicious! [N] | Jubilee 5330 |
| | | | **BAD COMPANY** | |
| | | | British: Paul Rodgers (vocals), Mick Ralphs (guitar), Simon Kirke (drums), Boz Burrell (bass) | |
| 8/31/74 | 5 | 11 | 1. **Can't Get Enough** | Swan Song 70015 |
| 2/08/75 | 19 | 6 | 2. Movin' On | Swan Song 70101 |
| 5/31/75 | 36 | 2 | 3. Good Lovin' Gone Bad | Swan Song 70103 |
| 7/26/75 | 10 | 11 | 4. **Feel Like Makin' Love** | Swan Song 70106 |
| 4/24/76 | 20 | 7 | 5. Young Blood | Swan Song 70108 |
| 4/14/79 | 13 | 12 | 6. Rock 'N' Roll Fantasy | Swan Song 70119 |
| | | | **BADFINGER** | |
| | | | British quartet originally known as The Iveys - leader Pete Ham committed suicide on 5/1/75 (27) | |
| 3/07/70 | 7 | 11 | 1. **Come And Get It** <br> from the film "The Magic Christian" | Apple 1815 |
| 11/21/70 | 8 | 9 | 2. **No Matter What** | Apple 1822 |
| 12/18/71 + | 4 | 12 | ● 3. **Day After Day** | Apple 1841 |
| 4/08/72 | 14 | 7 | 4. Baby Blue | Apple 1844 |
| | | | **JOAN BAEZ** | |
| | | | folk song stylist born in New York on 1/9/41 | |
| 8/28/71 | 3 | 13 | ● 1. **The Night They Drove Old Dixie Down** | Vanguard 35138 |
| 11/08/75 | 35 | 2 | 2. Diamonds And Rust | A&M 1737 |
| | | | **GEORGE BAKER Selection** | |
| | | | Dutch group led by Hans Bouwens | |
| 4/11/70 | 21 | 10 | 1. Little Green Bag | Colossus 112 |
| 1/10/76 | 26 | 5 | 2. Paloma Blanca | Warner 8115 |
| | | | **LaVERN BAKER** | |
| | | | born on 11/11/29 in Chicago, Illinois | |
| 1/15/55 | 14 | 11 | 1. Tweedlee Dee | Atlantic 1047 |
| 10/13/56 | 22 | 2 | 2. I Can't Love You Enough | Atlantic 1104 |

| DATE | POS | WKS | ARTIST—Record Title | LABEL & NO. |
|---|---|---|---|---|
| 12/29/56 + | 17 | 14 | 3. Jim Dandy | Atlantic 1116 |
| 12/28/58 + | 6 | 15 | 4. I Cried A Tear | Atlantic 2007 |
| 6/01/59 | 33 | 2 | 5. I Waited Too Long | Atlantic 2021 |
| 5/01/61 | 37 | 3 | 6. Saved | Atlantic 2099 |
| 1/05/63 | 34 | 3 | 7. See See Rider | Atlantic 2167 |
| | | | **BALANCE**<br>led by Peppy Castro (Blues Magoos) | |
| 8/15/81 | 22 | 9 | 1. Breaking Away | Portrait 02177 |
| | | | **MARTY BALIN**<br>member of Jefferson Starship | |
| 6/13/81 | 8 | 13 | 1. Hearts | EMI America 8084 |
| 10/10/81 | 27 | 5 | 2. Atlanta Lady (Something About Your Love) | EMI America 8093 |
| | | | **KENNY BALL & His Jazzmen**<br>English dixieland jazz band | |
| 2/17/62 | 2 (1) | 12 | 1. Midnight In Moscow [I] | Kapp 442 |
| | | | **HANK BALLARD & The Midnighters**<br>The Midnighters had 6 top 10 hits on the R&B charts ('54-'55) | |
| 7/18/60 | 7 | 13 | 1. Finger Poppin' Time | King 5341 |
| 8/29/60 | 28 | 6 | 2. The Twist<br>flip of Hank's 1st charted hit "Teardrops On Your Letter" | King 5171 |
| 10/17/60 | 6 | 11 | 3. Let's Go, Let's Go, Let's Go | King 5400 |
| 1/16/61 | 23 | 4 | 4. The Hoochi Coochi Coo | King 5430 |
| 3/20/61 | 39 | 1 | 5. Let's Go Again (Where We Went Last Night) | King 5459 |
| 5/01/61 | 33 | 3 | 6. The Continental Walk | King 5491 |
| 7/17/61 | 26 | 4 | 7. The Switch-A-Roo | King 5510 |
| | | | **BALLOON FARM**<br>New York flower-pop quintet | |
| 3/16/68 | 37 | 4 | 1. A Question Of Temperature | Laurie 3405 |
| | | | **BANANARAMA**<br>female trio from London, England | |
| 8/11/84 | 9 | 11 | 1. Cruel Summer | London 810127 |
| | | | **THE BAND**<br>Robbie Robertson, Levon Helm, Rick Danko, Richard Manuel & Garth Hudson - backing band for Ronnie Hawkins and Bob Dylan | |
| 11/29/69 + | 25 | 7 | 1. Up On Cripple Creek | Capitol 2635 |
| 10/14/72 | 34 | 6 | 2. Don't Do It | Capitol 3433 |
| | | | **DARRELL BANKS** | |
| 9/10/66 | 27 | 4 | 1. Open The Door To Your Heart | Revilot 201 |
| | | | **BAR-KAYS**<br>Otis Redding's backing band - 4 original members killed with him in plane crash on 12/10/67 | |
| 7/01/67 | 17 | 9 | 1. Soul Finger [I] | Volt 148 |
| 12/04/76 + | 23 | 8 | 2. Shake Your Rump To The Funk | Mercury 73833 |

| DATE | POS | WKS | ARTIST—Record Title | LABEL & NO. |
|---|---|---|---|---|
| | | | **CHRIS BARBER'S Jazz Band** | |
| | | | English | |
| 2/02/57 | 5 | 10 | 1. **Petite Fleur (Little Flower) [I]** | Laurie 3022 |
| | | | **KEITH BARBOUR** | |
| 11/01/69 | 40 | 2 | 1. Echo Park | Epic 10486 |
| | | | **EDDIE BARCLAY** | |
| 7/16/55 | 18 | 1 | 1. The Bandit (O'Cangaceiro) [I] | Tico 249 |
| | | | **BOBBY BARE** | |
| | | | born in Ironton, Ohio on 4/7/35 - also see Bill Parsons | |
| 8/18/62 | 23 | 7 | 1. Shame On Me | RCA 8032 |
| 6/29/63 | 16 | 9 | 2. Detroit City | RCA 8183 |
| 10/26/63 | 10 | 7 | 3. **500 Miles Away From Home** | RCA 8238 |
| 3/07/64 | 33 | 2 | 4. Miller's Cave | RCA 8294 |
| | | | **H.B. BARNUM** | |
| 2/06/61 | 35 | 1 | 1. Lost Love [I] | Eldo 111 |
| | | | **RAY BARRETTO** | |
| 5/11/63 | 17 | 7 | 1. El Watusi [F] | Tico 419 |
| | | | **BARRY & THE TAMERLANES** | |
| | | | Barry DeVorzon | |
| 11/16/63 | 21 | 5 | 1. I Wonder What She's Doing Tonight | Valiant 6034 |
| | | | **JOE BARRY** | |
| 5/29/61 | 24 | 5 | 1. I'm A Fool To Care | Smash 1702 |
| | | | **LEN BARRY** | |
| | | | lead singer of The Dovells | |
| 10/23/65 | 2 (1) | 10 | 1. **1-2-3** | Decca 31827 |
| 1/22/66 | 27 | 5 | 2. Like A Baby | Decca 31889 |
| 4/09/66 | 26 | 5 | 3. Somewhere | Decca 31923 |
| | | | **CHRIS BARTLEY** | |
| 8/19/67 | 32 | 2 | 1. The Sweetest Thing This Side Of Heaven | Vando 101 |
| | | | **COUNT BASIE & His Orchestra** | |
| | | | top big-band jazz leader since 1935 - died on 4/26/84 (79) | |
| 2/04/56 | 28 | 3 | 1. April In Paris [I] | Clef 89162 |
| | | | **TONI BASIL** | |
| | | | choreographer/director/dancer | |
| 10/09/82 | 1 (1) | 18 | ★ 1. **Mickey** | Chrysalis 2638 |
| | | | **FONTELLA BASS** | |
| | | | married to jazz trumpeter Lester Bowie | |
| 10/23/65 | 4 | 10 | 1. **Rescue Me** | Checker 1120 |
| 1/29/66 | 37 | 1 | 2. Recovery | Checker 1131 |
| | | | **FONTELLA BASS & BOBBY McCLURE** | |
| 3/27/65 | 33 | 3 | 1. Don't Mess Up A Good Thing | Checker 1097 |

| DATE | POS | WKS | ARTIST—Record Title | LABEL & NO. |
|------|-----|-----|---------------------|-------------|
|  |  |  | **SHIRLEY BASSEY** |  |
|  |  |  | Welsh |  |
| 2/27/65 | **8** | 8 | 1. **Goldfinger** | United Art. 790 |
|  |  |  | **LES BAXTER & His Orchestra** |  |
|  |  |  | musical arranger for Capitol Records in the fifties |  |
| 4/09/55 | **1** (2) | 21 | 1. **Unchained Melody** | Capitol 3055 |
| 8/13/55 | **5** | 12 | 2. **Wake The Town And Tell The People** | Capitol 3120 |
| 2/18/56 | **1** (6) | 20 | 3. **The Poor People Of Paris [I]** | Capitol 3336 |
|  |  |  | **BAY CITY ROLLERS** |  |
|  |  |  | Scottish pop/rock quintet |  |
| 11/08/75 + | **1** (1) | 12 | ● 1. **Saturday Night** | Arista 0149 |
| 2/14/76 | **9** | 11 | 2. **Money Honey** | Arista 0170 |
| 5/22/76 | **28** | 4 | 3. Rock And Roll Love Letter | Arista 0185 |
| 9/18/76 | **12** | 12 | 4. I Only Want To Be With You | Arista 0205 |
| 6/25/77 | **10** | 12 | 5. **You Made Me Believe In Magic** | Arista 0256 |
| 11/19/77 + | **24** | 9 | 6. The Way I Feel Tonight | Arista 0272 |
|  |  |  | **BAZUKA [Tony Camillo's]** |  |
| 6/07/75 | **10** | 11 | 1. **Dynamite - Part 1 [I]** | A&M 1666 |
|  |  |  | **B. BUMBLE & THE STINGERS** |  |
|  |  |  | Billy Bumble |  |
| 4/24/61 | **21** | 5 | 1. Bumble Boogie [I] | Rendezvous 140 |
| 3/31/62 | **23** | 7 | 2. Nut Rocker [I] | Rendezvous 166 |
|  |  |  | **BEACH BOYS** |  |
|  |  |  | California quintet led by Brian Wilson, with brothers Dennis & Carl Wilson, cousin Mike Love, and Alan Jardine - Dennis drowned on 12/28/83 (39) |  |
| 9/15/62 | **14** | 10 | 1. Surfin' Safari | Capitol 4777 |
| 4/13/63 | **3** | 13 | 2. **Surfin' U.S.A./** |  |
| 5/25/63 | **23** | 8 | 3.  Shut Down | Capitol 4932 |
| 8/17/63 | **7** | 11 | 4. **Surfer Girl/** |  |
| 9/07/63 | **15** | 7 | 5.  Little Deuce Coupe | Capitol 5009 |
| 11/23/63 | **6** | 8 | 6. **Be True To Your School/** |  |
| 11/30/63 | **23** | 6 | 7.  In My Room | Capitol 5069 |
| 2/22/64 | **5** | 9 | 8. **Fun, Fun, Fun** | Capitol 5118 |
| 6/06/64 | **1** (2) | 13 | ● 9. **I Get Around/** |  |
| 6/27/64 | **24** | 6 | 10.  Don't Worry Baby | Capitol 5174 |
| 9/19/64 | **9** | 8 | 11. **When I Grow Up (To Be A Man)** | Capitol 5245 |
| 11/21/64 | **8** | 8 | 12. **Dance, Dance, Dance** | Capitol 5306 |
| 3/13/65 | **12** | 7 | 13. Do You Wanna Dance? | Capitol 5372 |
| 5/01/65 | **1** (2) | 11 | 14. **Help Me, Rhonda** | Capitol 5395 |
| 8/07/65 | **3** | 9 | 15. **California Girls** | Capitol 5464 |
| 12/11/65 + | **20** | 5 | 16. The Little Girl I Once Knew | Capitol 5540 |
| 1/15/66 | **2** (2) | 9 | 17. **Barbara Ann** | Capitol 5561 |
| 4/09/66 | **3** | 10 | 18. **Sloop John B** | Capitol 5602 |
| 8/20/66 | **8** | 7 | 19. **Wouldn't It Be Nice/** |  |
| 9/17/66 | **39** | 2 | 20.  God Only Knows | Capitol 5706 |
| 10/29/66 | **1** (1) | 12 | ● 21. Good Vibrations | Capitol 5676 |

| DATE | POS | WKS | ARTIST—Record Title | LABEL & NO. |
|------|-----|-----|---------------------|-------------|
| 8/12/67 | 12 | 5 | 22. Heroes And Villains | Brother 1001 |
| 11/18/67 | 31 | 4 | 23. Wild Honey | Capitol 2028 |
| 1/13/68 | 19 | 6 | 24. Darlin' | Capitol 2068 |
| 8/17/68 | 20 | 7 | 25. Do It Again | Capitol 2239 |
| 4/05/69 | 24 | 6 | 26. I Can Hear Music | Capitol 2432 |
| 9/28/74 | 36 | 1 | 27. Surfin' U.S.A. [R] | Capitol 3924 |
| 6/19/76 | 5 | 13 | 28. **Rock And Roll Music** | Brother 1354 |
| 9/18/76 | 29 | 4 | 29. It's O.K. | Brother 1368 |
| 6/09/79 | 40 | 1 | 30. Good Timin' | Caribou 9029 |
| 8/15/81 | 12 | 11 | 31. The Beach Boys Medley | Capitol 5030 |
| 12/19/81 + | 18 | 8 | 32. Come Go With Me | Caribou 02633 |
| | | | **BEATLES** | |
| | | | #1 recording group of all-time from Liverpool, England: John Lennon, Paul McCartney, George Harrison and Ringo Starr | |
| 1/25/64 | 1 (7) | 14 | ● 1. **I Want To Hold Your Hand/** | |
| 1/25/64 | 14 | 8 | 2. I Saw Her Standing There | Capitol 5112 |
| 2/01/64 | 1 (2) | 14 | 3. **She Loves You** | Swan 4152 |
| 2/22/64 | 3 | 10 | 4. **Please Please Me** | Vee-Jay 581 |
| 3/07/64 | 26 | 2 | 5. My Bonnie | MGM 13213 |
| | | | with Tony Sheridan, lead singer | |
| 3/21/64 | 2 (4) | 9 | 6. **Twist And Shout** | Tollie 9001 |
| 3/28/64 | 1 (5) | 9 | ● 7. **Can't Buy Me Love** | Capitol 5150 |
| 4/11/64 | 2 (1) | 9 | 8. **Do You Want To Know A Secret/** | |
| 4/25/64 | 35 | 3 | 9. Thank You Girl | Vee-Jay 587 |
| 5/02/64 | 1 (1) | 11 | 10. **Love Me Do/** | |
| 5/16/64 | 10 | 7 | 11. **P.S. I Love You** | Tollie 9008 |
| 7/18/64 | 1 (2) | 12 | ● 12. **A Hard Day's Night** | Capitol 5222 |
| 8/01/64 | 19 | 7 | 13. Ain't She Sweet | Atco 6308 |
| 8/08/64 | 12 | 7 | 14. And I Love Her | Capitol 5235 |
| 8/15/64 | 25 | 5 | 15. I'll Cry Instead | Capitol 5234 |
| | | | above 2 songs (plus #12) from the film "A Hard Day's Night" | |
| 9/19/64 | 17 | 5 | 16. Matchbox/ | |
| 9/26/64 | 25 | 4 | 17. Slow Down | Capitol 5255 |
| 12/05/64 | 1 (3) | 11 | ● 18. **I Feel Fine/** | |
| 12/12/64 | 4 | 8 | 19. **She's A Woman** | Capitol 5327 |
| 2/27/65 | 1 (2) | 9 | ● 20. **Eight Days A Week/** | |
| 3/20/65 | 39 | 1 | 21. I Don't Want To Spoil The Party | Capitol 5371 |
| 5/01/65 | 1 (1) | 9 | 22. **Ticket To Ride** | Capitol 5407 |
| 8/14/65 | 1 (3) | 12 | ● 23. **Help!** | Capitol 5476 |
| | | | above 2 songs from the film "Help!" | |
| 10/02/65 | 1 (4) | 9 | ● 24. **Yesterday** | Capitol 5498 |
| 12/18/65 + | 1 (3) | 11 | ● 25. **We Can Work It Out/** | |
| 12/25/65 + | 5 | 8 | 26. **Day Tripper** | Capitol 5555 |
| 3/05/66 | 3 | 9 | ● 27. **Nowhere Man** | Capitol 5587 |
| 6/11/66 | 1 (2) | 10 | ● 28. **Paperback Writer/** | |
| 6/25/66 | 23 | 5 | 29. Rain | Capitol 5651 |
| 8/27/66 | 2 (1) | 8 | ● 30. **Yellow Submarine/** | |
| 9/10/66 | 11 | 6 | 31. Eleanor Rigby | Capitol 5715 |

**The Bee Gees** debuted in America as a fivesome, sounding very much like the Beatles. For the record, the two forgotten members of the group were Colin Petersen and Vince Melouney.

**Harry Belafonte** knows how to change with the times. In 1984, he surfaced as the co-producer of the breakdance movie *Beat Street*. Meanwhile, his daughter advertises Calvin Klein jeans on TV.

**Pat Benatar** prepped for stardom by auditioning at New York's "Catch a Rising Star," a showcase for new talent. She's managed by the guy who started the club.

**Tony Bennett** got started with the help of Bob Hope, who signed him as a support act, and Mitch "Singalong" Miller, who brought him to Columbia Records. Bennett had a cameo role in *The Oscar* (1966).

**George Benson** used to be a "serious" jazz guitarist who recorded with the likes of Miles Davis, and didn't sing. That was before he cut Leon Russell's "This Masquerade" and sang the theme to Muhammad Ali's movie, *The Greatest*.

**Brook Benton** had a number of near-misses before tasting success. He recorded "The Wall" for a soon-to-be-defunct label, and saw Patti Page's cover version enjoy greater success. He also cut a demo of "The Stroll," but the Diamonds made it a hit.

**Berlin's** glossy mixture of glamor and sleaze is the southern California variety, not the German kind. In fact, founder John Crawford admits he's never even been to the fabled city. So much for authenticity.

**Big Country's** chieftan is Stuart Adamson, a veteran of pioneering Scottish punk band, the Skids. Between the two groups, he retired to his hometown Dunfermline and read Celtic history.

**Bill Black** cut his many instrumental hits after backing Elvis Presley during the King's early days. Curiously, The Bill Black Combo played on for many years after the bassist's death in 1965.

**Blondie's** Debbie Harry once guested on an LP by West Coast punk band, the Gun Club, under the pseudonym D. H. Laurence [sic] Jr. Her movie credits include *Union City* and *Videodrome,* cult films at best.

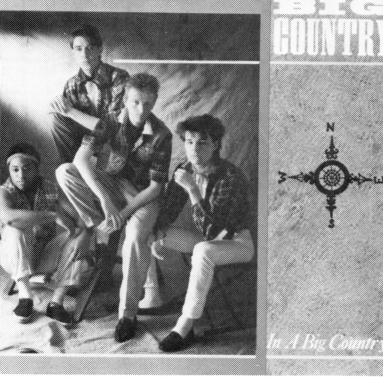

| DATE | POS | WKS | ARTIST—Record Title | LABEL & NO. |
|---|---|---|---|---|
| 3/04/67 | 1 (1) | 9 | ● 32. Penny Lane/ | |
| 3/11/67 | 8 | 7 | 33. Strawberry Fields Forever | Capitol 5810 |
| 7/29/67 | 1 (1) | 9 | ● 34. All You Need Is Love/ | |
| 8/12/67 | 34 | 2 | 35. Baby You're A Rich Man | Capitol 5964 |
| 12/09/67 | 1 (3) | 10 | ● 36. Hello Goodbye | Capitol 2056 |
| 3/23/68 | 4 | 10 | ● 37. Lady Madonna | Capitol 2138 |
| 9/14/68 | 1 (9) | 19 | ● 38. Hey Jude/ | |
| 9/14/68 | 12 | 11 | 39. Revolution | Apple 2276 |
| 5/10/69 | 1 (5) | 12 | ● 40. Get Back/ | |
| 5/10/69 | 35 | 3 | 41. Don't Let Me Down | Apple 2490 |
| | | | above 2 songs with Billy Preston (organ) | |
| 6/21/69 | 8 | 8 | ● 42. The Ballad Of John And Yoko | Apple 2531 |
| 10/18/69 | 1 (1) | 16 | ● 43. Come Together/ | |
| 10/18/69 | 1 | 16 | ● 44. Something | Apple 2654 |
| 3/21/70 | 1 (2) | 13 | ● 45. Let It Be | Apple 2764 |
| 5/23/70 | 1 (2) | 10 | 46. The Long And Winding Road | Apple 2832 |
| | | | above 2 songs from the film "Let It Be" | |
| 6/19/76 | 7 | 11 | 47. Got To Get You Into My Life | Capitol 4274 |
| 4/10/82 | 12 | 8 | 48. The Beatles' Movie Medley: | Capitol 5107 |
| | | | Magical Mystery Tour/All You Need Is Love/ You've Got To Hide Your Love Away/I Should Have Known Better A Hard Day's Night/Ticked To Ride/Get Back | |
| | | | **BEAU BRUMMELS** | |
| | | | San Francisco rock group | |
| 1/30/65 | 15 | 8 | 1. Laugh, Laugh | Autumn 8 |
| 5/08/65 | 8 | 9 | 2. Just A Little | Autumn 10 |
| 8/28/65 | 38 | 1 | 3. You Tell Me Why | Autumn 16 |
| | | | **JEFF BECK - see DONOVAN** | |
| | | | **BOB BECKHAM** | |
| 10/12/59 | 32 | 10 | 1. Just As Much As Ever | Decca 30861 |
| 2/29/60 | 36 | 1 | 2. Crazy Arms | Decca 31029 |
| | | | **BEE GEES** | |
| | | | English/Australian trio of brothers: Robin & Maurice (twins), and Barry Gibb | |
| 6/10/67 | 14 | 5 | 1. New York Mining Disaster 1941 Have You Seen My Wife, Mr. Jones | Atco 6487 |
| 7/29/67 | 17 | 7 | 2. To Love Somebody | Atco 6503 |
| 10/21/67 | 16 | 5 | 3. Holiday | Atco 6521 |
| 11/25/67 | 11 | 6 | 4. (The Lights Went Out In) Massachusetts | Atco 6532 |
| 2/10/68 | 15 | 8 | 5. Words | Atco 6548 |
| 9/07/68 | 8 | 10 | 6. I've Gotta Get A Message To You | Atco 6603 |
| 1/04/69 | 6 | 9 | 7. I Started A Joke | Atco 6639 |
| 4/12/69 | 37 | 3 | 8. First Of May | Atco 6657 |
| 12/26/70 + | 3 | 10 | ● 9. Lonely Days | Atco 6795 |
| 7/03/71 | 1 (4) | 14 | ● 10. How Can You Mend A Broken Heart | Atco 6824 |
| 2/05/72 | 16 | 7 | 11. My World | Atco 6871 |
| 8/26/72 | 16 | 7 | 12. Run To Me | Atco 6896 |

| DATE | POS | WKS | ARTIST—Record Title | LABEL & NO. |
|---|---|---|---|---|
| 12/02/72 | 34 | 4 | 13. Alive | Atco 6909 |
| 6/28/75 | 1 (2) | 12 | ● 14. **Jive Talkin'** | RSO 510 |
| 10/18/75 | 7 | 13 | 15. **Nights On Broadway** | RSO 515 |
| 1/17/76 | 12 | 12 | 16. Fanny (Be Tender With My Love) | RSO 519 |
| 7/17/76 | 1 (1) | 12 | ● 17. **You Should Be Dancing** | RSO 853 |
| 10/02/76 | 3 | 16 | ● 18. **Love So Right** | RSO 859 |
| 1/29/77 | 12 | 9 | 19. Boogie Child | RSO 867 |
| 8/13/77 | 26 | 5 | 20. Edge Of The Universe | RSO 880 |
| 10/08/77 | 1 (3) | 26 | ● 21. **How Deep Is Your Love** | RSO 882 |
| 12/24/77 + | 1 (4) | 22 | ★ 22. **Stayin' Alive** | RSO 885 |
| 2/11/78 | 1 (8) | 18 | ★ 23. **Night Fever** | RSO 889 |
| | | | above 2 tunes from the film "Saturday Night Fever" | |
| 11/18/78 + | 1 (2) | 17 | ★ 24. **Too Much Heaven** | RSO 913 |
| 2/10/79 | 1 (2) | 13 | ★ 25. **Tragedy** | RSO 918 |
| 4/21/79 | 1 (1) | 13 | ● 26. **Love You Inside Out** | RSO 925 |
| 10/10/81 | 30 | 4 | 27. He's A Liar | RSO 1066 |
| 5/28/83 | 24 | 6 | 28. The Woman In You | RSO 813173 |
| | | | **BEGINNING OF THE END** | |
| 6/05/71 | 15 | 10 | 1. Funky Nassau-Part 1 | Alston 4595 |
| | | | **HARRY BELAFONTE** | |
| | | | born in New York City on 3/1/24 | |
| 11/24/56 + | 14 | 16 | 1. Jamaica Farewell | RCA 6663 |
| 12/29/56 | 12 | 3 | 2. Mary's Boy Child [X] | RCA 6735 |
| 1/12/57 | 5 | 17 | 3. **Banana Boat (Day-O)** | RCA 6771 |
| 3/23/57 | 11 | 10 | 4. Mama Look At Bubu | RCA 6830 |
| 7/08/57 | 25 | 3 | 5. Island In The Sun | RCA 6885 |
| | | | **BELL & JAMES** | |
| | | | LeRoy Bell & Casey James | |
| 3/10/79 | 15 | 8 | ● 1. Livin' It Up (Friday Night) | A&M 2069 |
| | | | **BELL NOTES** | |
| | | | Long Island, New York quintet | |
| 2/09/59 | 6 | 11 | 1. **I've Had It** | Time 1004 |
| | | | **ARCHIE BELL & THE DRELLS** | |
| | | | quartet from Houston, Texas | |
| 4/13/68 | 1 (2) | 13 | ● 1. **Tighten Up** | Atlantic 2478 |
| 8/03/68 | 9 | 8 | 2. **I Can't Stop Dancing** | Atlantic 2534 |
| 1/04/69 | 21 | 8 | 3. There's Gonna Be A Showdown | Atlantic 2583 |
| | | | **BENNY BELL** | |
| 4/19/75 | 30 | 4 | 1. Shaving Cream [N-R] | Vanguard 35183 |
| | | | originally released in 1946 - Paul Wynn, vocal | |
| | | | **MADELINE BELL** | |
| | | | lead singer of Blue Mink | |
| 3/09/68 | 26 | 5 | 1. I'm Gonna Make You Love Me | Philips 40517 |
| | | | **VINCENT BELL** | |
| 4/25/70 | 31 | 5 | 1. Airport Love Theme [I] | Decca 32659 |

| DATE | POS | WKS | ARTIST—Record Title | LABEL & NO. |
|---|---|---|---|---|
| | | | **WILLIAM BELL** | |
| 3/12/77 | 10 | 9 | ● 1. **Tryin' To Love Two** | Mercury 73839 |
| | | | **BELLAMY BROTHERS** | |
| | | | David & Howard Bellamy | |
| 3/06/76 | **1** (1) | 12 | 1. **Let Your Love Flow** | Warner 8169 |
| 7/14/79 | 39 | 2 | 2. If I Said You Have A Beautiful Body Would You Hold It Against Me | Warner 8790 |
| | | | **BELLS** | |
| | | | Jacki Ralph & Cliff Edwards, lead singers of Canadian quinte | |
| 3/27/71 | 7 | 11 | ● 1. **Stay Awhile** | Polydor 15023 |
| | | | **TONY BELLUS** | |
| 6/29/59 | 25 | 11 | 1. Robbin' The Cradle | NRC 023 |
| | | | **BELMONTS** | |
| | | | former trio with Dion | |
| 6/19/61 | 18 | 6 | 1. Tell Me Why | Sabrina 500 |
| 8/25/62 | 28 | 8 | 2. Come On Little Angel | Sabina 505 |
| | | | **JESSE BELVIN** | |
| | | | died in an auto crash on 2/6/60 (26) | |
| 4/13/59 | 31 | 9 | 1. Guess Who | RCA 7469 |
| | | | **PAT BENATAR** | |
| | | | hard-rock singer from Brooklyn, New York - real name: Patricia Andrzejewski | |
| 2/09/80 | 23 | 10 | 1. Heartbreaker | Chrysalis 2395 |
| 5/17/80 | 27 | 6 | 2. We Live For Love | Chrysalis 2419 |
| 10/18/80 | 9 | 15 | ● 3. **Hit Me With Your Best Shot** | Chrysalis 2464 |
| 1/31/81 | 18 | 10 | 4. Treat Me Right | Chrysalis 2487 |
| 8/01/81 | 17 | 9 | 5. Fire And Ice | Chrysalis 2529 |
| 10/31/81 | 38 | 2 | 6. Promises In The Dark | Chrysalis 2555 |
| 11/06/82 | 13 | 10 | 7. Shadows Of The Night | Chrysalis 2647 |
| 3/05/83 | 20 | 7 | 8. Little Too Late | Chrysalis 03536 |
| 5/21/83 | 39 | 3 | 9. Looking For A Stranger | Chrysalis 42688 |
| 10/15/83 | 5 | 14 | 10. **Love Is A Battlefield** | Chrysalis 42732 |
| 11/03/84 | 5 | 14 | 11. **We Belong** | Chrysalis 42826 |
| | | | **BOYD BENNETT & His Rockets** | |
| 7/09/55 | 5 | 17 | 1. **Seventeen** | King 1470 |
| 11/12/55 | 39 | 1 | 2. My Boy - Flat Top | King 1494 |
| | | | vocal by Big Moe on above 2 songs | |
| | | | **JOE BENNETT & THE SPARKLETONES** | |
| 9/23/57 | 17 | 9 | 1. Black Slacks | ABC-Para. 9837 |
| | | | **TONY BENNETT** | |
| | | | born in Queens, New York on 8/3/26 | |
| 5/05/56 | 16 | 11 | 1. Can You Find It In Your Heart | Columbia 40667 |
| 8/18/56 | 11 | 7 | 2. From The Candy Store On The Corner To The Chapel On The Hill/ | |

| DATE | POS | WKS | ARTIST—Record Title | LABEL & NO. |
|---|---|---|---|---|
| 11/17/56 | 18 | 4 | 4. The Autumn Waltz | Columbia 40770 |
| 8/12/57 | 9 | 14 | 5. **In The Middle Of An Island** | Columbia 40965 |
| 11/18/57 | 22 | 1 | 6. Ca, C'est L'amour<br>from the film "Les Girls" | Columbia 41032 |
| 6/30/58 | 23 | 1 | 7. Young And Warm And Wonderful | Columbia 41172 |
| 9/22/58 | 20 | 8 | 8. Firefly | Columbia 41237 |
| 9/29/62 | 19 | 10 | 9. I Left My Heart In San Francisco | Columbia 42332 |
| 2/16/63 | 14 | 10 | 10. I Wanna Be Around | Columbia 42634 |
| 6/01/63 | 18 | 6 | 11. The Good Life | Columbia 42779 |
| 10/31/64 | 33 | 6 | 12. Who Can I Turn To (When Nobody Needs Me)<br>from the musical "The Roar Of The Greasepaint" | Columbia 43141 |
| 3/20/65 | 34 | 4 | 13. If I Ruled The World<br>from the musical "Pickwick" | Columbia 43220 |
| | | | **GEORGE BENSON**<br>jazz/pop guitarist, vocalist | |
| 7/17/76 | 10 | 11 | 1. **This Masquerade** | Warner 8209 |
| 9/03/77 | 24 | 7 | 2. The Greatest Love Of All<br>from the film "The Greatest" | Arista 0251 |
| 4/22/78 | 7 | 10 | 3. **On Broadway** | Warner 8542 |
| 3/24/79 | 18 | 8 | 4. Love Ballad | Warner 8759 |
| 8/02/80 | 4 | 14 | 5. **Give Me The Night** | Warner 49505 |
| 11/21/81 + | 5 | 16 | 6. **Turn Your Love Around** | Warner 49846 |
| 8/27/83 | 30 | 6 | 7. Lady Love Me (One More Time) | Warner 29563 |
| | | | **BROOK BENTON**<br>born Benjamin Peay on 9/19/31 in Camden, South Carolina | |
| 2/09/59 | 3 | 14 | 1. **It's Just A Matter Of Time** | Mercury 71394 |
| 5/04/59 | 12 | 9 | 2. Endlessly/ | |
| 6/08/59 | 38 | 1 | 3. So Close | Mercury 71443 |
| 8/03/59 | 16 | 9 | 4. Thank You Pretty Baby | Mercury 71478 |
| 10/26/59 | 6 | 13 | 5. **So Many Ways** | Mercury 71512 |
| 5/09/60 | 37 | 1 | 6. The Ties That Bind | Mercury 71566 |
| 8/22/60 | 7 | 13 | 7. **Kiddio/** | |
| 8/29/60 | 16 | 10 | 8. The Same One | Mercury 71652 |
| 11/21/60 | 24 | 7 | 9. Fools Rush In | Mercury 71722 |
| 2/27/61 | 11 | 9 | 10. Think Twice/ | |
| 3/20/61 | 28 | 1 | 11. For My Baby | Mercury 71774 |
| 6/05/61 | 2 (3) | 12 | 12. **The Boll Weevil Song [N]** | Mercury 71820 |
| 9/04/61 | 20 | 4 | 13. Frankie And Johnny | Mercury 71859 |
| 12/18/61 + | 15 | 5 | 14. Revenge | Mercury 71903 |
| 1/27/62 | 19 | 5 | 15. Shadrack | Mercury 71912 |
| 9/15/62 | 13 | 6 | 16. Lie To Me | Mercury 72024 |
| 12/08/62 + | 3 | 10 | 17. **Hotel Happiness** | Mercury 72055 |
| 4/06/63 | 28 | 4 | 18. I Got What I Wanted | Mercury 72099 |
| 7/13/63 | 22 | 4 | 19. My True Confession | Mercury 72135 |
| 10/05/63 | 32 | 5 | 20. Two Tickets To Paradise | Mercury 72177 |
| 2/15/64 | 35 | 3 | 21. Going Going Gone | Mercury 72230 |
| 1/31/70 | 4 | 12 | ● 22. **Rainy Night In Georgia** | Cotillion 44057 |

| DATE | POS | WKS | ARTIST—Record Title | LABEL & NO. |
|------|-----|-----|---------------------|-------------|
| | | | **BROOK BENTON & DINAH WASHINGTON** | |
| 2/08/60 | 5 | 12 | 1. **Baby (You've Got What It Takes)** | Mercury 71565 |
| 6/06/60 | 7 | 10 | 2. **A Rockin' Good Way (To Mess Around And Fall In Love)** | Mercury 71629 |
| | | | **BERLIN** | |
| | | | Los Angeles electro-pop trio | |
| 4/07/84 | 23 | 8 | 1. No More Words | Geffen 29360 |
| | | | **ROD BERNARD** | |
| 3/23/59 | 20 | 9 | 1. This Should Go On Forever | Argo 5327 |
| | | | **ELMER BERNSTEIN & Orchestra** | |
| | | | composer/conductor | |
| 4/07/56 | 16 | 9 | 1. Main Title From "The Man With The Golden Arm" [I] | Decca 29869 |
| | | | **CHUCK BERRY** | |
| | | | legendary rock & roller - born in St. Louis on 10/18/31 | |
| 8/20/55 | 5 | 11 | 1. **Maybellene** | Chess 1604 |
| 6/30/56 | 29 | 1 | 2. Roll Over Beethoven | Chess 1626 |
| 4/20/57 | 3 | 15 | 3. **School Day** | Chess 1653 |
| 11/11/57 | 8 | 13 | 4. **Rock & Roll Music** | Chess 1671 |
| 2/24/58 | 2 (3) | 11 | 5. **Sweet Little Sixteen** | Chess 1683 |
| 5/05/58 | 8 | 11 | 6. **Johnny B. Goode** | Chess 1691 |
| 9/15/58 | 18 | 5 | 7. Carol | Chess 1700 |
| 4/20/59 | 32 | 7 | 8. Almost Grown | Chess 1722 |
| 7/13/59 | 37 | 1 | 9. Back In The U.S.A. | Chess 1729 |
| 4/04/64 | 23 | 5 | 10. Nadine (Is It You?) | Chess 1883 |
| 6/13/64 | 10 | 7 | 11. **No Particular Place To Go** | Chess 1898 |
| 8/22/64 | 14 | 5 | 12. You Never Can Tell | Chess 1906 |
| 9/09/72 | 1 (2) | 12 | ● 13. **My Ding-A-Ling [N]** | Chess 2131 |
| 1/06/73 | 27 | 7 | 14. Reelin' & Rockin' | Chess 2136 |
| | | | live version of tune originally issued as the 'B' side of Chess 1683 | |
| | | | **BIG BOPPER** | |
| | | | J.P. Richardson (the Big Bopper) died with Buddy Holly and Ritchie Valens in a plane crash on 2/3/59 (28) | |
| 8/04/58 | 6 | 22 | 1. **Chantilly Lace [N]** | Mercury 71343 |
| 12/22/58 | 38 | 1 | 2. Big Bopper's Wedding [N] | Mercury 71375 |
| | | | **BIG BROTHER & THE HOLDING COMPANY** | |
| | | | Janis Joplin, lead singer | |
| 9/28/68 | 12 | 8 | 1. Piece Of My Heart | Columbia 44626 |
| | | | **BIG COUNTRY** | |
| | | | Scottish four-man rock band | |
| 11/12/83 | 17 | 9 | 1. In A Big Country | Mercury 814467 |
| | | | **MR. ACKER BILK** | |
| | | | English clarinetist - with the Leon Young String Chorale | |
| 4/07/62 | 1 (1) | 15 | ● 1. **Stranger On The Shore [I]** | Atco 6217 |

| DATE | POS | WKS | ARTIST—Record Title | LABEL & NO. |
|---|---|---|---|---|
| | | | **BILLY & LILLIE** | |
| | | | Billy Ford & Lillie Bryant | |
| 1/13/58 | 9 | 10 | 1. **La Dee Dah** | Swan 4002 |
| 1/05/59 | 14 | 8 | 2. Lucky Ladybug | Swan 4020 |
| | | | **BILLY & THE BEATERS** | |
| | | | Billy Vera | |
| 6/06/81 | 39 | 2 | 1. I Can Take Care Of Myself | Alfa 7002 |
| | | | **BILLY JOE & THE CHECKMATES** | |
| | | | Billy Joe Hunter | |
| 2/17/62 | 10 | 7 | 1. **Percolator (Twist) [I]** | Dore 620 |
| | | | **ELVIN BISHOP** | |
| | | | guitarist with the Paul Butterfield Blues Band | |
| 4/03/76 | 3 | 12 | ● 1. **Fooled Around And Fell In Love** | Capricorn 0252 |
| | | | **STEPHEN BISHOP** | |
| | | | pop-rock singer/songwriter | |
| 1/22/77 | 22 | 7 | 1. Save It For A Rainy Day | ABC 12232 |
| 7/23/77 | 11 | 15 | 2. On And On | ABC 12260 |
| 10/28/78 | 32 | 5 | 3. Everybody Needs Love | ABC 12406 |
| 4/02/83 | 25 | 8 | 4. It Might Be You | Warner 29791 |
| | | | theme from the film "Tootsie" | |
| | | | **BLACKBYRDS** | |
| | | | pop/soul group founded by Donald Byrd | |
| 3/15/75 | 6 | 12 | 1. **Walking In Rhythm** | Fantasy 736 |
| 4/17/76 | 19 | 6 | 2. Happy Music | Fantasy 762 |
| | | | **BLACKFOOT** | |
| | | | Rick "Rattlesnake" Medlocke, lead singer | |
| 8/04/79 | 26 | 6 | 1. Highway Song | Atco 7104 |
| 12/22/79 | 38 | 4 | 2. Train, Train | Atco 7207 |
| | | | **BLACK OAK ARKANSAS** | |
| | | | Southern rock sextet led by Jim "Dandy" Mangrum | |
| 1/26/74 | 25 | 6 | 1. Jim Dandy | Atco 6948 |
| | | | **BILL BLACK'S Combo** | |
| | | | Bill, of "Scotty & Bill" on Elvis Presley's Sun recordings - died on 10/21/65 (39) | |
| 12/21/59 + | 17 | 8 | 1. Smokie - Part 2 [I] | Hi 2018 |
| 3/21/60 | 9 | 11 | 2. **White Silver Sands [I]** | Hi 2021 |
| 7/04/60 | 18 | 8 | 3. Josephine [I] | Hi 2022 |
| 10/03/60 | 11 | 9 | 4. Don't Be Cruel [I] | Hi 2026 |
| 12/12/60 | 16 | 7 | 5. Blue Tango [I] | Hi 2027 |
| 3/06/61 | 20 | 4 | 6. Hearts Of Stone [I] | Hi 2028 |
| 6/26/61 | 25 | 4 | 7. Ole Buttermilk Sky [I] | Hi 2036 |
| 1/20/62 | 26 | 4 | 8. Twist-Her [I] | Hi 2042 |
| | | | **CILLA BLACK** | |
| | | | born Priscilla White on 5/27/43 in Liverpool, England | |
| 7/25/64 | 26 | 4 | 1. You're My World | Capitol 5196 |

| DATE | POS | WKS | ARTIST—Record Title | LABEL & NO. |
|---|---|---|---|---|
| | | | **JEANNE BLACK** | |
| 5/02/60 | 4 | 10 | 1. **He'll Have To Stay** | Capitol 4368 |
| | | | **JACK BLANCHARD & MISTY MORGAN** | |
| | | | husband and wife | |
| 3/28/70 | 23 | 8 | 1. Tennessee Bird Walk [N] | Wayside 010 |
| | | | **BILLY BLAND** | |
| 3/28/60 | 7 | 13 | 1. **Let The Little Girl Dance** | Old Town 1076 |
| | | | **BOBBY BLAND** | |
| | | | born in Rosemark, Tennessee on 1/27/30 | |
| 1/20/62 | 28 | 3 | 1. Turn On Your Love Light | Duke 344 |
| 2/02/63 | 22 | 7 | 2. Call On Me/ | |
| 2/09/63 | 33 | 5 | 3.  That's The Way Love Is | Duke 360 |
| 3/28/64 | 20 | 6 | 4. Ain't Nothing You Can Do | Duke 375 |
| | | | **MARCIE BLANE** | |
| 11/10/62 | 3 | 13 | 1. **Bobby's Girl** | Seville 120 |
| | | | **ARCHIE BLEYER** | |
| | | | founder of Cadence Records | |
| 12/04/54 + | 17 | 6 | 1. The Naughty Lady Of Shady Lane | Cadence 1254 |
| | | | **BLONDIE** | |
| | | | New York rock group led by Debbie Harry | |
| 3/17/79 | 1 (1) | 14 | ● 1. **Heart Of Glass** | Chrysalis 2295 |
| 6/30/79 | 24 | 7 | 2. One Way Or Another | Chrysalis 2336 |
| 11/03/79 | 27 | 6 | 3. Dreaming | Chrysalis 2379 |
| 3/08/80 | 1 (6) | 19 | ● 4. **Call Me** | Chrysalis 2414 |
| | | | from the film "American Gigolo" | |
| 6/21/80 | 39 | 3 | 5. Atomic | Chrysalis 2410 |
| 11/29/80 + | 1 (1) | 17 | ● 6. **The Tide Is High** | Chrysalis 2465 |
| 2/14/81 | 1 (2) | 14 | ● 7. **Rapture** | Chrysalis 2485 |
| 6/26/82 | 37 | 3 | 8. Island Of Lost Souls | Chrysalis 2603 |
| | | | **BLOODROCK** | |
| | | | rock group from Fort Worth, Texas | |
| 2/27/71 | 36 | 2 | 1. D.O.A. | Capitol 3009 |
| | | | **BLOODSTONE** | |
| | | | soul group from Kansas City, Missouri | |
| 6/09/73 | 10 | 12 | ● 1. **Natural High** | London 1046 |
| 4/06/74 | 34 | 4 | 2. Outside Woman | London 1052 |
| | | | **BLOOD, SWEAT & TEARS** | |
| | | | New York jazz-rock group formed by Al Kooper, Steve Katz & Bobby Colomby - David Clayton-Thomas, lead singer | |
| 3/15/69 | 2 (3) | 11 | ● 1. **You've Made Me So Very Happy** | Columbia 44776 |
| 6/07/69 | 2 (3) | 12 | ● 2. **Spinning Wheel** | Columbia 44871 |
| 10/25/69 | 2 (1) | 12 | ● 3. **And When I Die** | Columbia 45008 |
| 8/15/70 | 14 | 6 | 4. Hi-De-Ho | Columbia 45204 |
| 10/10/70 | 29 | 6 | 5. Lucretia Mac Evil | Columbia 45235 |
| 8/14/71 | 32 | 5 | 6. Go Down Gamblin' | Columbia 45427 |

| DATE | POS | WKS | ARTIST—Record Title | LABEL & NO. |
|---|---|---|---|---|
| | | | **BOBBY BLOOM** | |
| | | | died as a result of an accidental shooting on 2/28/74 | |
| 10/17/70 | 8 | 11 | 1. **Montego Bay** | L&R/MGM 157 |
| | | | **BLUE-BELLES** | |
| | | | group later changed name to Patti LaBelle & The Blue Belles | |
| 5/12/62 | 15 | 7 | 1. I Sold My Heart To The Junkman | Newtown 5000 |
| | | | **BLUE CHEER** | |
| | | | San Francisco heavy-metal band | |
| 3/23/68 | 14 | 10 | 1. Summertime Blues | Philips 40516 |
| | | | **BLUE HAZE** | |
| | | | English | |
| 12/23/72 + | 27 | 7 | 1. Smoke Gets In Your Eyes | A&M 1357 |
| | | | **BLUE JAYS** | |
| | | | Leon Peels, lead singer | |
| 9/04/61 | 31 | 4 | 1. Lover's Island | Milestone 2008 |
| | | | **BLUE MAGIC** | |
| | | | Philadelphia soul quintet | |
| 6/08/74 | 8 | 15 | ● 1. **Sideshow** | Atco 6961 |
| 11/23/74 | 36 | 2 | 2. Three Ring Circus | Atco 7004 |
| | | | **BLUE OYSTER CULT** | |
| | | | U.S. rock quintet led by Donald "Buck Dharma" Roeser & Eric Bloom | |
| 9/04/76 | 12 | 14 | 1. (Don't Fear) The Reaper | Columbia 10384 |
| 10/03/81 | 40 | 3 | 2. Burnin' For You | Columbia 02415 |
| | | | **BLUE RIDGE RANGERS** | |
| | | | John Fogerty (of CCR) - one man band | |
| 1/06/73 | 16 | 10 | 1. Jambalaya (On The Bayou) | Fantasy 689 |
| 5/19/73 | 37 | 2 | 2. Hearts Of Stone | Fantasy 700 |
| | | | **BLUE STARS** | |
| 2/04/56 | 16 | 7 | 1. Lullaby Of Birdland [F] | Mercury 70742 |
| | | | **BLUE SWEDE** | |
| | | | Swedish sextet | |
| 3/02/74 | 1 (1) | 14 | ● 1. **Hooked On A Feeling** | EMI 3627 |
| 9/07/74 | 7 | 8 | 2. **Never My Love** | EMI 3938 |
| | | | **BLUES BROTHERS** | |
| | | | John Belushi (died on 3/5/82-33) & Dan Aykroyd | |
| 1/06/79 | 14 | 9 | 1. Soul Man | Atlantic 3545 |
| 3/31/79 | 37 | 3 | 2. Rubber Biscuit [N] | Atlantic 3564 |
| 6/21/80 | 18 | 8 | 3. Gimme Some Lovin' | Atlantic 3666 |
| 1/31/81 | 39 | 2 | 4. Who's Making Love | Atlantic 3785 |
| | | | **BLUES IMAGE** | |
| | | | Tampa, Florida quintet led by Mike Pinera | |
| 5/23/70 | 4 | 12 | ● 1. **Ride Captain Ride** | Atco 6746 |
| | | | **BLUES MAGOOS** | |
| | | | Bronx, New York rock quintet led by Peppy Castro | |
| 1/07/67 | 5 | 10 | 1. **(We Ain't Got) Nothin' Yet** | Mercury 72622 |

| DATE | POS | WKS | ARTIST—Record Title | LABEL & NO. |
|------|-----|-----|---------------------|-------------|
| | | | **BOB B. SOXX & The Blue Jeans** | |
| | | | Bobby Sheen (Bob B. Soxx), Darlene Love, & Fanita James | |
| 12/08/62 + | 8 | 7 | 1. **Zip-A-Dee Doo-Dah** | Philles 107 |
| 3/23/63 | 38 | 3 | 2. Why Do Lovers Break Each Other's Heart? | Philles 110 |
| | | | **BOBBETTES** | |
| | | | "doo-wop" quintet of girls (ages 11-15) from New York | |
| 8/12/57 | 6 | 14 | 1. **Mr. Lee** | Atlantic 1144 |
| | | | **BON JOVI** | |
| | | | Jon Bon Jovi, lead singer of East Coast quintet | |
| 4/21/84 | 39 | 1 | 1. Runaway | Mercury 818309 |
| | | | **JOHNNY BOND** | |
| | | | died on 6/12/78 (63) | |
| 8/22/60 | 26 | 7 | 1. Hot Rod Lincoln [N] | Republic 2005 |
| | | | **GARY "U.S." BONDS** | |
| | | | real name: Gary Anderson | |
| 10/31/60 | 6 | 11 | 1. **New Orleans** | Legrand 1003 |
| 6/05/61 | 1 (2) | 12 | 2. **Quarter To Three** | Legrand 1008 |
| | | | music taken from "A Night With Daddy G" (Church Street Five) | |
| 7/31/61 | 5 | 9 | 3. **School Is Out** | Legrand 1009 |
| 11/06/61 | 28 | 2 | 4. School Is In | Legrand 1012 |
| 1/13/62 | 9 | 11 | 5. **Dear Lady Twist** | Legrand 1015 |
| 4/07/62 | 9 | 9 | 6. **Twist, Twist Senora** | Legrand 1018 |
| 7/07/62 | 27 | 4 | 7. Seven Day Weekend | Legrand 1019 |
| | | | from the film "It's Trad-Dad" | |
| 5/02/81 | 11 | 13 | 8. This Little Girl | EMI America 8079 |
| 7/10/82 | 21 | 9 | 9. Out Of Work | EMI America 8117 |
| | | | above 2 titles produced by Bruce Springstein | |
| | | | **BONEY M** | |
| | | | German disco quartet | |
| 7/22/78 | 30 | 6 | 1. Rivers Of Babylon | Sire 1027 |
| | | | **BONNIE SISTERS** | |
| 2/25/56 | 18 | 3 | 1. Cry Baby | Rainbow 328 |
| | | | **KARLA BONOFF** | |
| | | | songwriter/singer from Los Angeles | |
| 6/05/82 | 19 | 12 | 1. Personally | Columbia 02805 |
| | | | **BOOKER T. & THE MG's** | |
| | | | MG's (Memphis Group): Booker T. Jones, Steve Cropper, Duck Dunn & Al Jackson (died 10/1/75-39) | |
| 9/01/62 | 3 | 12 | ● 1. **Green Onions [I]** | Stax 127 |
| 5/20/67 | 37 | 3 | 2. Hip Hug-Her [I] | Stax 211 |
| 9/02/67 | 21 | 7 | 3. Groovin' [I] | Stax 224 |
| 8/03/68 | 17 | 7 | 4. Soul-Limbo [I] | Stax 0001 |
| 12/28/68 + | 9 | 11 | 5. **Hang 'Em High [I]** | Stax 0013 |
| 4/05/69 | 6 | 10 | 6. **Time Is Tight [I]** | Stax 0028 |
| | | | from the soundtrack "Uptight" | |
| 7/05/69 | 37 | 3 | 7. Mrs. Robinson [I] | Stax 0037 |

| DATE | POS | WKS | ARTIST—Record Title | LABEL & NO. |
|---|---|---|---|---|
| | | | **DANIEL BOONE** | |
| | | | English - real name: Peter Lee Stirling | |
| 8/05/72 | 15 | 11 | 1. Beautiful Sunday | Mercury 73281 |
| | | | **DEBBY BOONE** | |
| | | | Pat Boone's daughter | |
| 9/17/77 | 1(10) | 21 | ★ 1. **You Light Up My Life** | Warner 8455 |
| | | | **PAT BOONE** | |
| | | | born Charles Eugene Boone on 6/1/34; son-in-law of Red Foley | |
| 4/02/55 | 16 | 12 | 1. Two Hearts | Dot 15338 |
| 7/09/55 | 1 (2) | 20 | 2. **Ain't That A Shame** | Dot 15377 |
| 10/29/55 | 7 | 10 | 3. **At My Front Door (Crazy Little Mama)**/ | |
| 11/19/55 | 26 | 5 | 4. No Other Arms (No Arms Can Ever Hold You) | Dot 15422 |
| 12/24/55 + | 19 | 5 | 5. Gee Whittakers! | Dot 15435 |
| 2/04/56 | 4 | 18 | 6. **I'll Be Home**/ | |
| 2/04/56 | 12 | 10 | 7. Tutti' Frutti | Dot 15443 |
| 4/28/56 | 8 | 9 | 8. **Long Tall Sally** | Dot 15457 |
| 6/09/56 | 1 (4) | 19 | 9. **I Almost Lost My Mind** | Dot 15472 |
| 9/22/56 | 5 | 17 | 10. **Friendly Persuasion (Thee I Love)**/ | |
| 9/29/56 | 20 | 8 | 11. Chains Of Love | Dot 15490 |
| 12/22/56 + | 1 (1) | 19 | 12. **Don't Forbid Me**/ | |
| 1/26/57 | 37 | 2 | 13. Anastasia | Dot 15521 |
| 3/23/57 | 5 | 13 | 14. **Why Baby Why**/ | |
| 3/23/57 | 27 | 5 | 15. I'm Waiting Just For You | Dot 15545 |
| 5/13/57 | 1 (7) | 24 | 16. **Love Letters In The Sand**/ | |
| 5/20/57 | 14 | 13 | 17. Bernardine | Dot 15570 |
| | | | above 2 tunes from the film "Bernardine" | |
| 8/12/57 | 6 | 14 | 18. **Remember You're Mine**/ | |
| 8/19/57 | 20 | 8 | 19. There's A Gold Mine In The Sky | Dot 15602 |
| 10/28/57 | 1 (6) | 19 | 20. **April Love** | Dot 15660 |
| 2/17/58 | 4 | 15 | 21. **A Wonderful Time Up There**/ | |
| 2/17/58 | 11 | 12 | 22. It's Too Soon To Know | Dot 15690 |
| 5/12/58 | 5 | 12 | 23. **Sugar Moon** | Dot 15750 |
| 7/14/58 | 7 | 10 | 24. **If Dreams Came True**/ | |
| 8/04/58 | 39 | 1 | 25. That's How Much I Love You | Dot 15785 |
| 10/06/58 | 21 | 4 | 26. For My Good Fortune/ | |
| 10/06/58 | 31 | 2 | 27. Gee, But It's Lonely | Dot 15825 |
| 11/17/58 | 34 | 5 | 28. I'll Remember Tonight | Dot 15840 |
| | | | from the film "Mardi Gras" | |
| 1/26/59 | 21 | 8 | 29. With The Wind And The Rain In Your Hair | Dot 15888 |
| 4/06/59 | 23 | 7 | 30. For A Penny | Dot 15914 |
| 6/29/59 | 17 | 6 | 31. Twixt Twelve And Twenty | Dot 15955 |
| 9/28/59 | 29 | 4 | 32. Fools Hall Of Fame | Dot 15982 |
| 3/07/60 | 18 | 7 | 33. (Welcome) New Lovers | Dot 16048 |
| 5/22/61 | 1 (1) | 12 | 34. **Moody River** | Dot 16209 |
| 9/04/61 | 19 | 5 | 35. Big Cold Wind | Dot 16244 |

**Blood, Sweat and Tears** brought together members with a wealth of experience. Their credits included: the Blues Project, Mothers of Invention, Eric Andersen, Buffalo Springfield, Odetta, and the Even Dozen Jug Band.

**Blue Cheer's** first album contained these suitably freaked-out liner notes: "Subtle color of the MIND/BLUE/Call the figure of the SOUL/CHEER." Turn on, tune in, drop out.

**Pat Boone** was the establishment's bland alternative to the energy of rock-'n'roll. Among the great r&b songs he covered were "Long Tall Sally," "Tutti Frutti," "Ain't That a Shame," and "At My Front Door."

**Laura Branigan** was a Broadway hopeful when Leonard Cohen enlisted her for his 1977 tour. Afterwards, she was signed to Atlantic Records by label head Ahmet Ertegun himself.

**Bread** co-founders David Gates and Robb Royer met in a Los Angeles group called Pleasure Faire. Under the names Arthur James and Robb Wilson they wrote the theme for *Lovers and Other Strangers*, receiving a 1969 Oscar for their troubles.

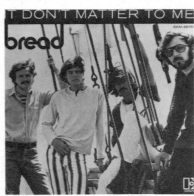

**James Brown.** When Little Richard suddenly abandoned rock'n'roll for The Lord, the struggling Brown was the beneficiary. He inherited Richard's 40-date tour, his backing singers, and his band.

**Jackson Browne** deserves a good guy award for helping others, producing Warren Zevon's self-titled 1976 LP and Greg Copeland's 1982 premiere, *Revenge Will Come.*

**Lindsey Buckingham** likes to work. He wrote the theme song for *National Lampoon's Vacation,* played on John Stewart's hit "Gold," and has the majority vote in producing Fleetwood Mac.

**Eric Burdon,** the former Animals leader, linked up with War in 1970. The group began as an instrumental band in California, working under names like the Creators, the Romeos, and Señor Soul and the Night Shift.

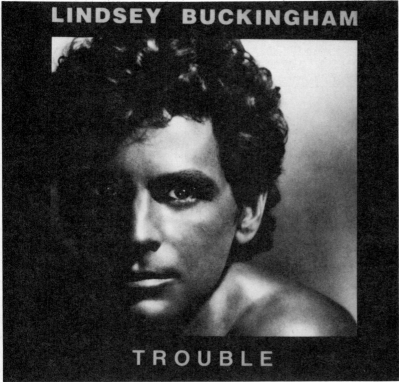

| DATE | POS | WKS | ARTIST—Record Title | LABEL & NO. |
|---|---|---|---|---|
| 12/25/61 + | 35 | 3 | 36. Johnny Will | Dot 16284 |
| 2/24/62 | 32 | 3 | 37. I'll See You In My Dreams | Dot 16312 |
| 6/30/62 | 6 | 10 | 38. **Speedy Gonzales [N]** | Dot 16368 |
| | | | **BOSTON** | |
| | | | rock quintet from Boston - led by Tom Scholz & Brad Delp | |
| 10/16/76 | 5 | 14 | 1. **More Than A Feeling** | Epic 50266 |
| 2/12/77 | 22 | 6 | 2. Long Time | Epic 50329 |
| 6/18/77 | 38 | 2 | 3. Peace Of Mind | Epic 50381 |
| 8/26/78 | 4 | 10 | 4. **Don't Look Back** | Epic 50590 |
| 12/23/78 + | 31 | 5 | 5. A Man I'll Never Be | Epic 50638 |
| | | | **PERRY BOTKIN JR. - see BARRY DeVORZON** | |
| | | | **JIMMY BOWEN with the Rhythm Orchids** | |
| | | | Buddy Knox was a member of the Rhythm Orchids | |
| 3/09/57 | 14 | 12 | 1. I'm Stickin' With You | Roulette 4001 |
| | | | **DAVID BOWIE** | |
| | | | English "glitter rock" star - also see Queen | |
| 2/24/73 | 15 | 10 | 1. Space Oddity | RCA 0876 |
| 4/19/75 | 28 | 4 | 2. Young Americans | RCA 10152 |
| 8/02/75 | 1 (2) | 14 | ● 3. **Fame** | RCA 10320 |
| 1/10/76 | 10 | 16 | 4. **Golden Years** | RCA 10441 |
| 4/09/83 | 1 (1) | 14 | ● 5. **Let's Dance** | EMI America 8158 |
| 7/09/83 | 10 | 11 | 6. **China Girl** | EMI America 8165 |
| 10/01/83 | 14 | 9 | 7. Modern Love | EMI America 8177 |
| 9/29/84 | 8 | 10 | 8. **Blue Jean** | EMI America 8231 |
| | | | **BOX TOPS** | |
| | | | quintet from Memphis area - Alex Chilton, lead singer | |
| 8/26/67 | 1 (4) | 13 | ● 1. **The Letter** | Mala 565 |
| 12/02/67 | 24 | 5 | 2. Neon Rainbow | Mala 580 |
| 3/16/68 | 2 (2) | 12 | ● 3. **Cry Like A Baby** | Mala 593 |
| 6/08/68 | 26 | 6 | 4. Choo Choo Train | Mala 12005 |
| 10/12/68 | 37 | 1 | 5. I Met Her In Church | Mala 12017 |
| 2/08/69 | 28 | 9 | 6. Sweet Cream Ladies, Forward March | Mala 12035 |
| 8/23/69 | 18 | 7 | 7. Soul Deep | Mala 12040 |
| | | | **TOMMY BOYCE & BOBBY HART** | |
| | | | pop songwriting team | |
| 8/05/67 | 39 | 2 | 1. Out & About | A&M 858 |
| 1/20/68 | 8 | 9 | 2. **I Wonder What She's Doing Tonite** | A&M 893 |
| 8/03/68 | 27 | 6 | 3. Alice Long (You're Still My Favorite Girlfriend) | A&M 948 |
| | | | **JAN BRADLEY** | |
| 2/02/63 | 14 | 9 | 1. Mama Didn't Lie | Chess 1845 |
| | | | **OWEN BRADLEY Quintet** | |
| 7/29/57 | 18 | 4 | 1. White Silver Sands<br>vocal by the Anita Kerr Quartet | Decca 30363 |

| DATE | POS | WKS | ARTIST—Record Title | LABEL & NO. |
|---|---|---|---|---|
| | | | **BRAM TCHAIKOVSKY** | |
| | | | rock quartet led by Bram (real name Peter Bramall) | |
| 8/18/79 | 37 | 3 | 1. Girl Of My Dreams | Polydor 14575 |
| | | | **LAURA BRANIGAN** | |
| 9/04/82 | **2** (3) | 22 | ● 1. **Gloria** | Atlantic 4048 |
| 4/02/83 | 7 | 13 | 2. **Solitaire** | Atlantic 89868 |
| 8/13/83 | 12 | 12 | 3. How Am I Supposed To Live Without You | Atlantic 89805 |
| 5/05/84 | 4 | 15 | 4. **Self Control** | Atlantic 89676 |
| 8/25/84 | 20 | 8 | 5. The Lucky One | Atlantic 89636 |
| | | | from the TV program "An Uncommon Love" | |
| | | | **BRASS CONSTRUCTION** | |
| | | | 9-man disco ensemble | |
| 5/08/76 | 14 | 9 | 1. Movin' [I] | United Art. 775 |
| | | | **BRASS RING featuring Phil Bodner** | |
| 4/16/66 | 32 | 4 | 1. The Phoenix Love Theme [I] | Dunhill 4023 |
| | | | from the film "The Flight Of The Phoenix" | |
| 3/04/67 | 36 | 2 | 2. The Dis-Advantages Of You [I] | Dunhill 4065 |
| | | | melody taken from a Benson & Hedges cigarette jingle | |
| | | | **BOB BRAUN** | |
| 8/18/62 | 26 | 4 | 1. Till Death Do Us Part [S] | Decca 31355 |
| | | | **BREAD** | |
| | | | David Gates, leader - James Griffin, Larry Knechtel, Mike Botts | |
| 7/11/70 | **1** (1) | 13 | ● 1. **Make It With You** | Elektra 45686 |
| 10/10/70 | 10 | 9 | 2. **It Don't Matter To Me** | Elektra 45701 |
| 1/30/71 | 28 | 4 | 3. Let Your Love Go | Elektra 45711 |
| 4/03/71 | 4 | 11 | 4. **If** | Elektra 45720 |
| 8/14/71 | 37 | 2 | 5. Mother Freedom | Elektra 45740 |
| 11/06/71 | 3 | 10 | ● 6. **Baby I'm-A Want You** | Elektra 45751 |
| 2/05/72 | 5 | 11 | 7. **Everything I Own** | Elektra 45765 |
| 5/06/72 | 15 | 8 | 8. Diary | Elektra 45784 |
| 8/05/72 | 11 | 9 | 9. The Guitar Man | Elektra 45803 |
| 11/18/72 | 15 | 8 | 10. Sweet Surrender | Elektra 45818 |
| 2/17/73 | 15 | 8 | 11. Aubrey | Elektra 45832 |
| 12/04/76 + | 9 | 13 | 12. **Lost Without Your Love** | Elektra 45365 |
| | | | **BEVERLY BREMERS** | |
| 1/22/72 | 15 | 10 | 1. Don't Say You Don't Remember | Scepter 12315 |
| 7/22/72 | 40 | 2 | 2. We're Free | Scepter 12348 |
| | | | **BRENDA & THE TABULATIONS** | |
| | | | Philadelphian Brenda Payton & male trio | |
| 3/25/67 | 20 | 6 | 1. Dry Your Eyes | Dionn 500 |
| 5/01/71 | 23 | 9 | 2. Right On The Tip Of My Tongue | Top & Bottom 407 |

| DATE | POS | WKS | ARTIST—Record Title | LABEL & NO. |
|------|-----|-----|---------------------|-------------|
| | | | **WALTER BRENNAN** | |
| | | | Grandpa of TV series "The Real McCoys" - died on 9/21/74 (80) | |
| 5/30/60 | 30 | 3 | 1. Dutchman's Gold [S]<br>with Billy Vaughn's Orchestra | Dot 16066 |
| 4/21/62 | 5 | 9 | 2. **Old Rivers** [S] | Liberty 55436 |
| 12/01/62 | 38 | 1 | 3. Mama Sang A Song [S] | Liberty 55508 |
| | | | **BREWER & SHIPLEY** | |
| | | | Mike Brewer & Tom Shipley | |
| 3/13/71 | 10 | 10 | 1. **One Toke Over The Line** | Kama Sutra 516 |
| | | | **TERESA BREWER** | |
| 12/18/54 + | 6 | 12 | 1. **Let Me Go, Lover!**<br>with the Lancers | Coral 61315 |
| 3/19/55 | 17 | 3 | 2. Pledging My Love | Coral 61362 |
| 6/04/55 | 20 | 1 | 3. Silver Dollar | Coral 61394 |
| 7/30/55 | 15 | 4 | 4. The Banjo's Back In Town | Coral 61448 |
| 3/03/56 | 5 | 17 | 5. **A Tear Fell/** | |
| 3/10/56 | 17 | 10 | 6. Bo Weevil | Coral 61590 |
| 6/16/56 | 7 | 16 | 7. **A Sweet Old Fashioned Girl** | Coral 61636 |
| 11/17/56 | 21 | 8 | 8. Mutual Admiration Society<br>from the musical "Happy Hunting" | Coral 61737 |
| 4/27/57 | 13 | 9 | 9. Empty Arms | Coral 61805 |
| 11/11/57 | 8 | 11 | 10. **You Send Me** | Coral 61898 |
| 10/20/58 | 38 | 1 | 11. The Hula Hoop Song | Coral 62033 |
| 4/06/59 | 40 | 1 | 12. Heavenly Lover | Coral 62084 |
| 9/12/60 | 31 | 6 | 13. Anymore | Coral 62219 |
| | | | **BRICK** | |
| | | | Atlanta-based disco/jazz quintet | |
| 11/20/76 + | 3 | 15 | 1. **Dazz** | Bang 727 |
| 10/01/77 | 18 | 10 | 2. Dusic | Bang 734 |
| | | | **ALICIA BRIDGES** | |
| 9/09/78 | 5 | 19 | ● 1. **I Love The Nightlife (Disco 'Round)** | Polydor 14483 |
| | | | **LILLIAN BRIGGS** | |
| 9/17/55 | 18 | 3 | 1. I Want You To Be My Baby | Epic 9115 |
| | | | **BRIGHTER SIDE OF DARKNESS** | |
| 1/06/73 | 16 | 8 | ● 1. Love Jones | 20th Century 2002 |
| | | | **MARTIN BRILEY** | |
| | | | British | |
| 7/16/83 | 36 | 3 | 1. The Salt In My Tears | Mercury 812165 |
| | | | **JOHNNY BRISTOL** | |
| 7/20/74 | 8 | 13 | 1. **Hang On In There Baby** | MGM 14715 |
| | | | **HERMAN BROOD** | |
| 9/01/79 | 35 | 3 | 1. Saturdaynight | Ariola 7754 |

| DATE | POS | WKS | ARTIST—Record Title | LABEL & NO. |
|---|---|---|---|---|
| | | | **BROOKLYN BRIDGE** | |
| | | | Johnny Maestro (Crests), lead singer | |
| 1/04/69 | 3 | 10 | ● 1. **Worst That Could Happen** | Buddah 75 |
| | | | **DONNIE BROOKS** | |
| 7/11/60 | 7 | 15 | 1. **Mission Bell** | Era 3018 |
| 12/26/60 | 31 | 3 | 2. Doll House | Era 3028 |
| | | | **BROTHERHOOD OF MAN** | |
| | | | British - a Tony Hiller production | |
| 5/23/70 | 13 | 10 | 1. United We Stand | Deram 85059 |
| 6/19/76 | 27 | 4 | 2. Save Your Kisses For Me | Pye 71066 |
| | | | **BROTHERS FOUR** | |
| | | | Dick Foley, Bob Flick, John Paine, Mike Kirkland - fraternity brothers at the University of Washington | |
| 3/21/60 | 2 (4) | 15 | 1. **Greenfields** | Columbia 41571 |
| 4/24/61 | 32 | 3 | 2. Frogg [N] | Columbia 41958 |
| | | | **BROTHERS JOHNSON** | |
| | | | funk guitarists George & Louis Johnson | |
| 5/22/76 | 3 | 12 | ● 1. **I'll Be Good To You** | A&M 1806 |
| 9/18/76 | 30 | 6 | 2. Get The Funk Out Ma Face | A&M 1851 |
| 7/30/77 | 5 | 13 | ● 3. **Strawberry Letter 23** | A&M 1949 |
| 4/12/80 | 7 | 13 | 4. **Stomp!** | A&M 2216 |
| | | | **AL BROWN'S Tunetoppers** | |
| 5/02/60 | 23 | 5 | 1. The Madison | Amy 804 |
| | | | dance calls by Cookie Brown | |
| | | | **ARTHUR BROWN [The Crazy World Of]** | |
| | | | British | |
| 9/21/68 | 2 (1) | 11 | ● 1. **Fire** | Atlantic 2556 |
| | | | **BOOTS BROWN & His Blockbusters** | |
| 9/15/58 | 23 | 3 | 1. Cerveza [I] | RCA 7269 |
| | | | an imitation of the tune "Tequila" | |
| | | | **BUSTER BROWN** | |
| | | | died on 1/31/76 (61) | |
| 3/28/60 | 38 | 3 | 1. Fannie Mae | Fire 1008 |
| | | | **CHUCK BROWN & The Soul Searchers** | |
| 3/17/79 | 34 | 5 | ● 1. Bustin' Loose, Part 1 | Source 40967 |
| | | | **JAMES BROWN** | |
| | | | Black music's all-time #1 artist - born on 5/3/33 near Augusta, Georgia | |
| 5/30/60 | 33 | 2 | 1. Think | Federal 12370 |
| 4/03/61 | 40 | 2 | 2. Bewildered | King 5442 |
| 5/19/62 | 35 | 4 | 3. Night Train [I] | King 5614 |
| 5/18/63 | 18 | 7 | 4. Prisoner Of Love | King 5739 |
| 2/15/64 | 23 | 7 | 5. Oh Baby Don't You Weep (Part 1) | King 5842 |
| 9/12/64 | 24 | 5 | 6. Out Of Sight | Smash 1919 |
| 8/07/65 | 8 | 9 | 7. **Papa's Got A Brand New Bag (Part 1)** | King 5999 |

| DATE | POS | WKS | ARTIST—Record Title | LABEL & NO. |
|---|---|---|---|---|
| 11/20/65 | 3 | 10 | 8. **I Got You (I Feel Good)** | King 6015 |
| 5/07/66 | 8 | 8 | 9. **It's A Man's Man's Man's World** | King 6035 |
| 1/28/67 | 29 | 4 | 10. Bring It Up | King 6071 |
| 8/12/67 | 7 | 8 | 11. **Cold Sweat (Part 1)** | King 6110 |
| 11/25/67 | 40 | 1 | 12. Get It Together (Part 1) | King 6122 |
| 12/30/67 + | 28 | 5 | 13. I Can't Stand Myself (When You Touch Me)/ | |
| 2/17/68 | 36 | 4 | 14.   There Was A Time | King 6144 |
| 3/23/68 | 6 | 10 | 15. **I Got The Feelin'** | King 6155 |
| 6/01/68 | 14 | 7 | 16. Licking Stick - Licking Stick | King 6166 |
| | | | above King hits labeled as James Brown & The Famous Flames | |
| 9/14/68 | 10 | 10 | 17. **Say It Loud - I'm Black And I'm Proud** | King 6187 |
| 12/07/68 | 31 | 2 | 18. Goodbye My Love | King 6198 |
| 2/08/69 | 15 | 7 | 19. Give It Up Or Turnit A Loose | King 6213 |
| 4/19/69 | 20 | 6 | 20. I Don't Want Nobody To Give Me Nothing (Open Up The Door, I'll Get It Myself) | King 6224 |
| 6/21/69 | 11 | 10 | 21. Mother Popcorn (You Got To Have A Mother For Me) (Part 1) | King 6245 |
| 6/28/69 | 30 | 5 | 22. The Popcorn [I] | King 6240 |
| 9/27/69 | 37 | 2 | 23. World (Part 1) | King 6258 |
| 11/01/69 | 21 | 5 | 24. Let A Man Come In And Do The Popcorn (Part One) | King 6255 |
| 12/13/69 + | 24 | 8 | 25. Ain't It Funky Now (Part 1) [I] | King 6280 |
| 1/24/70 | 40 | 2 | 26. Let A Man Come In And Do The Popcorn (Part Two) | King 6275 |
| 2/28/70 | 32 | 6 | 27. It's A New Day (Part 1 & Part 2) | King 6292 |
| 5/23/70 | 32 | 2 | 28. Brother Rapp (Part 1 & Part 2) | King 6310 |
| 8/01/70 | 15 | 7 | 29. Get Up I Feel Like Being Like A Sex Machine (Part 1) | King 6318 |
| 10/17/70 | 13 | 8 | 30. Super Bad (Part 1 & Part 2) | King 6329 |
| 1/16/71 | 34 | 5 | 31. Get Up, Get Into It, Get Involved | King 6347 |
| 3/13/71 | 29 | 6 | 32. Soul Power (Part 1) | King 6368 |
| 6/26/71 | 35 | 3 | 33. Escape-ism (Part 1) [S] | People 2500 |
| 7/17/71 | 15 | 9 | 34. Hot Pants (She Got To Use What She Got, To Get What She Wants) (Part 1) | People 2501 |
| 9/11/71 | 22 | 6 | 35. Make It Funky (Part 1) | Polydor 14088 |
| 12/04/71 | 35 | 3 | 36. I'm A Greedy Man (Part 1) | Polydor 14100 |
| 2/26/72 | 27 | 4 | 37. Talking Loud And Saying Nothing | Polydor 14109 |
| 4/01/72 | 40 | 2 | 38. King Heroin [S] | Polydor 14116 |
| 9/09/72 | 18 | 8 | ● 39. Get On The Good Foot (Part 1) | Polydor 14139 |
| 2/10/73 | 27 | 4 | 40. I Got Ants In My Pants (and i want to dance) (Part 1) | Polydor 14162 |
| 4/13/74 | 26 | 9 | ● 41. The Payback (Part 1) | Polydor 14223 |
| 8/03/74 | 29 | 4 | 42. My Thang | Polydor 14244 |
| 9/21/74 | 31 | 3 | 43. Papa Don't Take No Mess (Part 1) | Polydor 14255 |

| DATE | POS | WKS | ARTIST—Record Title | LABEL & NO. |
|---|---|---|---|---|
| | | | **MAXINE BROWN** | |
| 1/30/61 | 19 | 6 | 1. All In My Mind | Nomar 103 |
| 4/24/61 | 25 | 5 | 2. Funny | Nomar 106 |
| 12/05/64 + | 24 | 7 | 3. Oh No Not My Baby | Wand 162 |
| | | | **NAPPY BROWN** | |
| 4/30/55 | 25 | 4 | 1. Don't Be Angry | Savoy 1155 |
| | | | **PETER BROWN** | |
| 10/08/77 | 18 | 8 | 1. Do Ya Wanna Get Funky With Me | Drive 6258 |
| 5/06/78 | 8 | 14 | 2. **Dance With Me** <br> with Betty Wright | Drive 6269 |
| | | | **POLLY BROWN** <br> lead singer of Pickettywitch | |
| 2/08/75 | 16 | 7 | 1. Up In A Puff Of Smoke | GTO 1002 |
| | | | **ROY BROWN** <br> New Orleans R&B singer - died on 5/25/81 (55) | |
| 7/01/57 | 29 | 1 | 1. Let The Four Winds Blow | Imperial 5439 |
| | | | **RUTH BROWN** <br> Atlantic Records' top selling artist of the fifties | |
| 3/02/57 | 25 | 5 | 1. Lucky Lips | Atlantic 1125 |
| 10/13/58 | 24 | 2 | 2. This Little Girl's Gone Rockin' <br> sax solo by King Curtis | Atlantic 1197 |
| | | | **SHIRLEY BROWN** | |
| 11/23/74 | 22 | 6 | 1. Woman To Woman | Truth 3206 |
| | | | **JACKSON BROWNE** <br> born in West Germany on 10/9/48 | |
| 4/08/72 | 8 | 9 | 1. **Doctor My Eyes** | Asylum 11004 |
| 2/19/77 | 23 | 6 | 2. Here Come Those Tears Again | Asylum 45379 |
| 3/04/78 | 11 | 12 | 3. Running On Empty | Asylum 45460 |
| 7/08/78 | 20 | 7 | 4. Stay/ | |
| | | 4 | 5. **The Load-Out** | Asylum 45485 |
| 7/26/80 | 19 | 10 | 6. Boulevard | Asylum 47003 |
| 10/18/80 | 22 | 5 | 7. That Girl Could Sing | Asylum 47036 |
| 8/21/82 | 7 | 12 | 8. **Somebody's Baby** <br> from the soundtrack "Fast Times At Ridgemont High" | Asylum 69982 |
| 7/16/83 | 13 | 12 | 9. Lawyers In Love | Asylum 69826 |
| 10/22/83 | 25 | 7 | 10. Tender Is The Night | Asylum 69791 |
| | | | **BROWNS** <br> Jim Ed Brown and his sisters Maxine & Bonnie | |
| 8/03/59 | 1 (4) | 14 | 1. **The Three Bells** | RCA 7555 |
| 11/23/59 | 13 | 9 | 2. Scarlet Ribbons (For Her Hair) | RCA 7614 |
| 3/28/60 | 5 | 12 | 3. **The Old Lamplighter** | RCA 7700 |
| | | | **BROWNSVILLE STATION** <br> Ann Arbor, Michigan trio led by Michael Lutz | |
| 12/08/73 + | 3 | 13 | ● 1. **Smokin' In The Boy's Room** | Big Tree 16011 |
| 10/05/74 | 31 | 3 | 2. Kings Of The Party | Big Tree 16001 |

| DATE | POS | WKS | ARTIST—Record Title | LABEL & NO. |
|------|-----|-----|---------------------|-------------|
| | | | **DAVE BRUBECK Quartet** | |
| | | | jazz quartet featuring Dave (piano) & Paul Desmond (alto sax) | |
| 9/25/61 | 25 | 6 | 1. Take Five [I] | Columbia 41479 |
| | | | **ANITA BRYANT** | |
| | | | 2nd runner-up to Miss America in 1958 | |
| 7/27/59 | 30 | 7 | 1. Till There Was You | Carlton 512 |
| | | | from the musical "The Music Man" | |
| 5/02/60 | 5 | 12 | 2. **Paper Roses** | Carlton 528 |
| 8/08/60 | 10 | 9 | 3. **In My Little Corner Of The World** | Carlton 530 |
| 12/26/60 + | 18 | 6 | 4. Wonderland By Night | Carlton 537 |
| | | | **RAY BRYANT Combo** | |
| | | | combo led by jazz pianist Bryant | |
| 5/09/60 | 30 | 4 | 1. The Madison Time - Part I [S-I] | Columbia 41628 |
| | | | dance calls by Eddie Morrison | |
| | | | **PEABO BRYSON** | |
| | | | soul ballad singer from South Carolina | |
| 6/30/84 | 10 | 13 | 1. **If Ever You're In My Arms Again** | Elektra 69728 |
| | | | **PEABO BRYSON/ROBERTA FLACK** | |
| 9/03/83 | 16 | 15 | 1. Tonight, I Celebrate My Love | Capitol 5242 |
| | | | **B.T. EXPRESS** | |
| | | | Brooklyn, New York disco ensemble | |
| 10/05/74 | 2 (2) | 14 | ● 1. **Do It ('Til You're Satisfied)** | Roadshow 12395 |
| 2/08/75 | 4 | 11 | ● 2. **Express [I]** | Roadshow 7001 |
| 9/06/75 | 40 | 2 | 3. Give It What You Got/ | |
| 11/01/75 | 31 | 3 | 4. Peace Pipe | Roadshow 7003 |
| | | | **BUBBLE PUPPY** | |
| | | | psychedelic rock band from Austin, Texas | |
| 3/15/69 | 14 | 7 | 1. Hot Smoke & Sasafrass | Int. Artists 128 |
| | | | **BUCHANAN & GOODMAN** | |
| | | | Bill Buchanan & Dickie Goodman | |
| 8/11/56 | 3 | 10 | 1. **The Flying Saucer (Parts 1 & 2) [N]** | Luniverse 101 |
| 7/29/57 | 18 | 8 | 2. Flying Saucer The 2nd [N] | Luniverse 105 |
| 12/30/57 | 32 | 2 | 3. Santa & The Satellite (Parts 1 & 2) [X-N] | Luniverse 107 |
| | | | **BUCHANAN BROTHERS** | |
| | | | Terry Cashman, Gene Pistilli, & Tommy West | |
| 5/31/69 | 22 | 7 | 1. Medicine Man (Part 1) | Event 3302 |
| | | | **LINDSEY BUCKINGHAM** | |
| | | | member of Fleetwood Mac | |
| 11/07/81 + | 9 | 14 | 1. Trouble | Asylum 47223 |
| 8/25/84 | 23 | 9 | 2. Go Insane | Elektra 69714 |
| | | | **BUCKINGHAMS** | |
| | | | Chicago quintet led by Dennis Tufano & Carl Giammarese | |
| 1/21/67 | 1 (2) | 10 | 1. **Kind Of A Drag** | U.S.A. 860 |
| 4/08/67 | 6 | 10 | 2. **Don't You Care** | Columbia 44053 |
| 7/01/67 | 5 | 10 | 3. **Mercy, Mercy, Mercy** | Columbia 44182 |

| DATE | POS | WKS | ARTIST—Record Title | LABEL & NO. |
|------|-----|-----|---------------------|-------------|
| 9/30/67 | 12 | 7 | 4. Hey Baby (They're Playing Our Song) | Columbia 44254 |
| 12/23/67 + | 11 | 10 | 5. Susan | Columbia 44378 |
| | | | **BUCKNER & GARCIA** | |
| | | | Jerry Buckner & Gary Garcia | |
| 1/30/82 | 9 | 14 | ● 1. **Pac-Man Fever [N]** | Columbia 02673 |
| | | | **BUFFALO SPRINGFIELD** | |
| | | | Stephen Stills, Neil Young, Richie Furay, Dewey Martin, and Bruce Palmer (replaced Jim Messina) | |
| 2/18/67 | 7 | 11 | 1. **For What It's Worth (Stop, Hey What's That Sound)** | Atco 6459 |
| | | | **JIMMY BUFFETT** | |
| | | | backed by The Coral Reefer Band | |
| 6/29/74 | 30 | 5 | 1. Come Monday | Dunhill 4385 |
| 5/07/77 | 8 | 15 | 2. **Margaritaville** | ABC 12254 |
| 10/22/77 | 37 | 3 | 3. Changes In Latitudes, Changes In Attitudes | ABC 12305 |
| 5/27/78 | 32 | 4 | 4. Cheeseburger In Paradise [N] | ABC 12358 |
| 10/20/79 | 35 | 3 | 5. Fins | MCA 41109 |
| | | | **BUGGLES** | |
| | | | British - Geoff Downes & Trevor Horne joined "Yes" in 1980 | |
| 12/15/79 | 40 | 1 | 1. Video Killed The Radio Star | Island 49114 |
| | | | **BULL & THE MATADORS** | |
| 11/16/68 | 39 | 1 | 1. The Funky Judge | Toddlin' Town 108 |
| | | | **BULLET** | |
| 12/25/71 + | 28 | 5 | 1. White Lies, Blue Eyes | Big Tree 123 |
| | | | **BUOYS** | |
| 4/17/71 | 17 | 8 | 1. Timothy | Scepter 12275 |
| | | | **ERIC BURDON & WAR** | |
| | | | also see Animals, and War | |
| 7/11/70 | 3 | 13 | ● 1. **Spill The Wine** | MGM 14118 |
| | | | **SOLOMON BURKE** | |
| | | | soul singer from Philadelphia | |
| 11/13/61 | 24 | 7 | 1. Just Out Of Reach (Of My Two Open Arms) | Atlantic 2114 |
| 5/25/63 | 37 | 2 | 2. If You Need Me | Atlantic 2185 |
| 5/23/64 | 33 | 4 | 3. Goodbye Baby (Baby Goodbye) | Atlantic 2226 |
| 4/03/65 | 22 | 5 | 4. Got To Get You Off My Mind | Atlantic 2276 |
| 7/03/65 | 28 | 5 | 5. Tonight's The Night | Atlantic 2288 |
| | | | **DORSEY BURNETTE** | |
| | | | Dorsey & brother Johnny were members of the rockabilly "Rock 'n Roll trio" - Dorsey died on 8/19/79 (46) | |
| 2/22/60 | 23 | 9 | 1. (There Was A) Tall Oak Tree | Era 3012 |
| | | | **JOHNNY BURNETTE** | |
| | | | brother of Dorsey and father of Rocky - drowned on 8/1/64 (30) | |
| 8/15/60 | 11 | 11 | 1. Dreamin' | Liberty 55258 |
| 11/21/60 | 8 | 11 | 2. **You're Sixteen** | Liberty 55285 |

| DATE | POS | WKS | ARTIST—Record Title | LABEL & NO. |
|------|-----|-----|--------------------|-------------|
| 2/20/61 | 17 | 6 | 3. Little Boy Sad | Liberty 55298 |
| 11/06/61 | 18 | 4 | 4. God, Country And My Baby | Liberty 55379 |
| | | | **ROCKY BURNETTE** | |
| | | | Johnny Burnette's son | |
| 6/07/80 | 8 | 12 | 1. **Tired Of Toein' The Line** | EMI America 8043 |
| | | | **LOU BUSCH & His Orchestra** | |
| | | | died on 9/19/79 (69) - also see Joe "Fingers" Carr | |
| 3/24/56 | 35 | 2 | 1. 11th Hour Melody | Capitol 3349 |
| | | | **BUSTERS** | |
| 9/28/63 | 25 | 5 | 1. Bust Out [I] | Arlen 735 |
| | | | **JERRY BUTLER** | |
| | | | Chicago-bred soul singer born on 12/8/39 | |
| 6/16/58 | 11 | 9 | 1. For Your Precious Love | Abner/Falcon 1013 |
| | | | with The Impressions | |
| 11/07/60 | 7 | 13 | 2. **He Will Break Your Heart** | Vee-Jay 354 |
| 4/03/61 | 27 | 4 | 3. Find Another Girl | Vee-Jay 375 |
| 8/07/61 | 25 | 4 | 4. I'm A Telling You | Vee-Jay 390 |
| 10/30/61 | 11 | 11 | 5. Moon River | Vee-Jay 405 |
| | | | from the film "Breakfast At Tiffany's" | |
| 8/18/62 | 20 | 4 | 6. Make It Easy On Yourself | Vee-Jay 451 |
| 12/28/63 + | 31 | 5 | 7. Need To Belong | Vee-Jay 567 |
| 11/25/67 | 38 | 2 | 8. Mr. Dream Merchant | Mercury 72721 |
| 6/08/68 | 20 | 9 | 9. Never Give You Up | Mercury 72798 |
| 10/05/68 | 16 | 8 | 10. Hey, Western Union Man | Mercury 72850 |
| 1/18/69 | 39 | 2 | 11. Are You Happy | Mercury 72876 |
| 3/08/69 | 4 | 12 | • 12. **Only The Strong Survive** | Mercury 72898 |
| 6/21/69 | 24 | 7 | 13. Moody Woman | Mercury 72929 |
| 9/06/69 | 20 | 9 | 14. What's The Use Of Breaking Up | Mercury 72960 |
| | | | **JERRY BUTLER & BRENDA LEE EAGER** | |
| 2/05/72 | 21 | 10 | • 1. Ain't Understanding Mellow | Mercury 73255 |
| | | | **JERRY BUTLER & BETTY EVERETT** | |
| 9/19/64 | 5 | 11 | 1. **Let It Be Me** | Vee-Jay 613 |
| | | | **CHARLIE BYRD - see STAN GETZ** | |
| | | | **BYRDS** | |
| | | | original Los Angeles-based folk/rock group: Roger McGuinn, Gene Clark, Chris Hillman, Mike Clarke, and David Crosby | |
| 6/05/65 | 1 (1) | 10 | 1. **Mr. Tambourine Man** | Columbia 43271 |
| 8/21/65 | 40 | 1 | 2. All I Really Want To Do | Columbia 43332 |
| 11/06/65 | 1 (3) | 11 | 3. **Turn! Turn! Turn!** | Columbia 43424 |
| | | | from the Book of Ecclesiastes | |
| 4/30/66 | 14 | 6 | 4. Eight Miles High | Columbia 43578 |
| 10/22/66 | 36 | 2 | 5. Mr. Spaceman | Columbia 43766 |
| 2/18/67 | 29 | 3 | 6. So You Want To Be A Rock 'N' Roll Star | Columbia 43987 |
| 4/29/67 | 30 | 3 | 7. My Back Pages | Columbia 44054 |

| DATE | POS | WKS | ARTIST—Record Title | LABEL & NO. |
|------|-----|-----|---------------------|-------------|
| | | | **EDWARD BYRNES** | |
| | | | Kookie of TVs "77 Sunset Strip" | |
| 4/27/59 | 4 | 11 | 1. **Kookie, Kookie (Lend Me Your Comb) [N]** | Warner 5047 |
| | | | with Connie Stevens | |
| | | | **CADETS** | |
| | | | also recorded as The Jacks | |
| 7/21/56 | 15 | 7 | 1. Stranded In The Jungle [N] | Modern 994 |
| | | | **CADILLACS** | |
| | | | New York R&B quintet - Earl Carroll, lead singer | |
| 2/04/56 | 17 | 5 | 1. Speedo | Josie 785 |
| 1/12/59 | 28 | 3 | 2. Peek-A-Boo | Josie 846 |
| | | | **JOHN CAFFERTY & THE BEAVER BROWN BAND** | |
| | | | rock sextet from Rhode Island | |
| 9/15/84 | 7 | 11 | 1. **On The Dark Side** | Scotti Br. 04594 |
| | | | originally charted on 10/8/83 (Pos. 64) - from the film "Eddie And The Cruisers" | |
| | | | **TANE CAIN** | |
| | | | wife of Journey's Jonathan Cain | |
| 9/18/82 | 37 | 3 | 1. Holdin' On | RCA 13287 |
| | | | **AL CAIOLA & His Orchestra** | |
| 1/16/61 | 35 | 4 | 1. The Magnificent Seven [I] | United Art. 261 |
| 5/01/61 | 19 | 5 | 2. Bonanza [I] | United Art. 302 |
| | | | **BOBBY CALDWELL** | |
| | | | formerly with Johnny Winter, Captain Beyond and Armageddon | |
| 2/03/79 | 9 | 12 | 1. **What You Won't Do For Love** | Clouds 11 |
| | | | **J.J. CALE** | |
| | | | laid-back rock singer/songwriter | |
| 3/11/72 | 22 | 8 | 1. Crazy Mama | Shelter 7314 |
| | | | **GLEN CAMPBELL** | |
| | | | born in Arkansas on 3/22/36 | |
| 11/25/67 | 26 | 7 | 1. By The Time I Get To Phoenix | Capitol 2015 |
| 5/25/68 | 36 | 2 | 2. I Wanna Live | Capitol 2146 |
| 8/03/68 | 32 | 3 | 3. Dreams Of The Everyday Housewife | Capitol 2224 |
| 11/02/68 | 39 | 1 | 4. Gentle On My Mind [R] | Capitol 5939 |
| | | | originally charted in 1967 (Pos. 62) | |
| 11/16/68 + | 3 | 13 | ● 5. **Wichita Lineman** | Capitol 2302 |
| 3/15/69 | 4 | 10 | ● 6. **Galveston** | Capitol 2428 |
| 5/17/69 | 26 | 5 | 7. Where's The Playground Susie | Capitol 2494 |
| 8/23/69 | 35 | 2 | 8. True Grit | Capitol 2573 |
| 11/01/69 | 23 | 7 | 9. Try A Little Kindness | Capitol 2659 |
| 1/31/70 | 19 | 7 | 10. Honey Come Back | Capitol 2718 |
| 5/09/70 | 40 | 2 | 11. Oh Happy Day | Capitol 2787 |
| 9/26/70 | 10 | 9 | 12. **It's Only Make Believe** | Capitol 2905 |
| 3/27/71 | 31 | 4 | 13. Dream Baby (How Long Must I Dream) | Capitol 3062 |
| 6/21/75 | 1 (2) | 18 | ● 14. **Rhinestone Cowboy** | Capitol 4095 |

| DATE | POS | WKS | ARTIST—Record Title | LABEL & NO. |
|---|---|---|---|---|
| 11/22/75 + | 11 | 11 | 15. Country Boy (You Got Your Feet In L.A.) | Capitol 4155 |
| 4/17/76 | 27 | 5 | 16. Don't Pull Your Love/Then You Can Tell Me Goodbye | Capitol 4245 |
| 3/05/77 | 1 (1) | 15 | ● 17. **Southern Nights** | Capitol 4376 |
| 8/13/77 | 39 | 2 | 18. Sunflower | Capitol 4445 |
| 12/09/78 | 38 | 2 | 19. Can You Fool | Capitol 4584 |
| | | | **GLEN CAMPBELL & BOBBIE GENTRY** | |
| 3/08/69 | 36 | 1 | 1. Let It Be Me | Capitol 2387 |
| 3/14/70 | 27 | 6 | 2. All I Have To Do Is Dream | Capitol 2745 |
| | | | **JO ANN CAMPBELL** | |
| 9/08/62 | 38 | 3 | 1. (I'm The Girl On) Wolverton Mountain | Cameo 223 |
| | | | **CANNED HEAT** | |
| | | | Los Angeles group formed by Bob "The Bear" Hite (died 4/6/81-36) & Alan Wilson (died 9/3/70-27) | |
| 9/07/68 | 16 | 7 | 1. On The Road Again | Liberty 56038 |
| 12/21/68 + | 11 | 9 | 2. Going Up The Country | Liberty 56077 |
| 11/07/70 | 26 | 6 | 3. Let's Work Together | Liberty 56151 |
| | | | **CANNIBAL & THE HEADHUNTERS** | |
| | | | four Mexican-American youths | |
| 4/17/65 | 30 | 6 | 1. Land Of 1000 Dances | Rampart 642 |
| | | | **ACE CANNON** | |
| | | | alto saxophonist | |
| 1/27/62 | 17 | 11 | 1. Tuff [I] | Hi 2040 |
| 5/19/62 | 36 | 1 | 2. Blues (Stay Away From Me) [I] | Hi 2051 |
| | | | **FREDDY CANNON** | |
| | | | born Frederick Picariello on 12/4/40 in Lynn, Massachusetts | |
| 5/25/59 | 6 | 10 | 1. **Tallahassee Lassie** | Swan 4031 |
| 12/07/59 + | 3 | 11 | 2. **Way Down Yonder In New Orleans** | Swan 4043 |
| 3/07/60 | 34 | 3 | 3. Chattanooga Shoe Shine Boy | Swan 4050 |
| 5/30/60 | 28 | 4 | 4. Jump Over | Swan 4053 |
| 9/04/61 | 35 | 1 | 5. Transistor Sister | Swan 4078 |
| 5/26/62 | 3 | 12 | 6. **Palisades Park** | Swan 4106 |
| 2/15/64 | 16 | 6 | 7. Abigail Beecher | Warner 5409 |
| 8/28/65 | 13 | 6 | 8. Action | Warner 5645 |
| | | | from TV's "Where The Action Is" | |
| | | | **JIM CAPALDI** | |
| | | | English - original member of Traffic | |
| 5/28/83 | 28 | 5 | 1. That's Love | Atlantic 89849 |
| | | | **CAPITOLS** | |
| | | | Detroit trio | |
| 5/21/66 | 7 | 11 | 1. **Cool Jerk** | Karen 1524 |
| | | | **CAPRIS** | |
| | | | Italian quartet from New York City | |
| 1/23/61 | 3 | 10 | 1. **There's A Moon Out Tonight** | Old Town 1094 |

| DATE | POS | WKS | ARTIST—Record Title | LABEL & NO. |
|---|---|---|---|---|
| | | | **CAPTAIN & TENNILLE** | |
| | | | Daryl Dragon & Toni Tennille (married) | |
| 5/24/75 | 1 (4) | 16 | ● 1. **Love Will Keep Us Together** | A&M 1672 |
| 10/04/75 | 4 | 14 | ● 2. **The Way I Want To Touch You** | A&M 1725 |
| 2/07/76 | 3 | 13 | ● 3. **Lonely Night (Angel Face)** | A&M 1782 |
| 5/08/76 | 4 | 12 | ● 4. **Shop Around** | A&M 1817 |
| 10/09/76 | 4 | 15 | ● 5. **Muskrat Love** | A&M 1870 |
| 4/02/77 | 13 | 8 | 6. Can't Stop Dancin' | A&M 1912 |
| 9/09/78 | 10 | 14 | 7. **You Never Done It Like That** | A&M 2063 |
| 1/27/79 | 40 | 1 | 8. You Need A Woman Tonight | A&M 2106 |
| 11/10/79 + | 1 (1) | 22 | ● 9. **Do That To Me One More Time** | Casablanca 2215 |
| | | | **IRENE CARA** | |
| | | | star of the film "Fame" | |
| 7/26/80 | 4 | 12 | 1. **Fame** | RSO 1034 |
| 9/27/80 | 19 | 9 | 2. Out Here On My Own | RSO 1048 |
| | | | above 2 tunes from the film "Fame" | |
| 4/16/83 | 1 (6) | 20 | ● 3. **Flashdance...What A Feeling** | Casablanca 811440 |
| | | | from the film "Flashdance" | |
| 11/05/83 | 13 | 10 | 4. Why Me? | Geffen 29464 |
| 1/28/84 | 37 | 3 | 5. The Dream (Hold On To Your Dream) | Geffen 29396 |
| | | | from the film "D.C. Cab" | |
| 4/14/84 | 8 | 11 | 6. **Breakdance** | Geffen 29328 |
| | | | **CARAVELLES** | |
| | | | English duo: Andrea Simpson & Lois Wilkinson | |
| 11/23/63 | 3 | 10 | 1. **You Don't Have To Be A Baby To Cry** | Smash 1852 |
| | | | **CAREFREES** | |
| 4/11/64 | 39 | 1 | 1. We Love You Beatles [N] | London Int. 10614 |
| | | | **TONY CAREY** | |
| | | | former keyboardist with Rainbow - leader of Planet P | |
| 3/31/84 | 22 | 8 | 1. A Fine Fine Day | MCA 52343 |
| 7/14/84 | 33 | 2 | 2. The First Day Of Summer | MCA 52388 |
| | | | **HENSON CARGILL** | |
| 1/20/68 | 25 | 7 | 1. Skip A Rope | Monument 1041 |
| | | | **CARL CARLTON** | |
| | | | originally recorded as Little Carl Carlton | |
| 10/12/74 | 6 | 10 | 1. **Everlasting Love** | Back Beat 27001 |
| 9/26/81 | 22 | 7 | ● 2. She's A Bad Mama Jama (She's Built, She's Stacked) | 20th Century 2488 |
| | | | **ERIC CARMEN** | |
| | | | lead singer of The Raspberries | |
| 1/17/76 | 2 (3) | 14 | ● 1. **All By Myself** | Arista 0165 |
| 5/22/76 | 11 | 10 | 2. Never Gonna Fall In Love Again | Arista 0184 |
| 9/18/76 | 34 | 3 | 3. Sunrise | Arista 0200 |
| 9/24/77 | 23 | 8 | 4. She Did It | Arista 0266 |
| 10/28/78 | 19 | 7 | 5. Change Of Heart | Arista 0354 |

| DATE | POS | WKS | ARTIST—Record Title | LABEL & NO. |
|---|---|---|---|---|
| | | | **KIM CARNES** | |
| | | | singer/songwriter from Los Angeles - also see Gene Cotton/Kenny Rogers | |
| 6/14/80 | **10** | 15 | 1. **More Love** | EMI America 8045 |
| 4/11/81 | **1** (9) | 20 | ● 2. **Bette Davis Eyes** | EMI America 8077 |
| 8/29/81 | **28** | 6 | 3. Draw Of The Cards | EMI America 8087 |
| 9/11/82 | **29** | 6 | 4. Voyeur | EMI America 8127 |
| 12/25/82 + | **36** | 4 | 5. Does It Make You Remember | EMI America 8147 |
| 11/26/83 | **40** | 2 | 6. Invisible Hands | EMI America 8181 |
| | | | **RENATO CAROSONE** | |
| | | | Italian | |
| 5/12/58 | **18** | 9 | 1. Torero [F] | Capitol 71080 |
| | | | **CARPENTERS** | |
| | | | Karen and brother Richard Carpenter - Karen died on 2/4/83 (32) | |
| 6/27/70 | **1** (4) | 15 | ● 1. **(They Long To Be) Close To You** | A&M 1183 |
| 10/03/70 | **2** (4) | 14 | ● 2. **We've Only Just Begun** | A&M 1217 |
| 2/13/71 | **3** | 12 | ● 3. **For All We Know** | A&M 1243 |
| | | | from the film "Lovers & Other Strangers" | |
| 5/22/71 | **2** (2) | 11 | ● 4. **Rainy Days And Mondays** | A&M 1260 |
| 9/11/71 | **2** (2) | 12 | ● 5. **Superstar** | A&M 1289 |
| 1/22/72 | **2** (2) | 11 | ● 6. **Hurting Each Other** | A&M 1322 |
| 5/13/72 | **12** | 8 | 7. It's Going To Take Some Time | A&M 1351 |
| 7/22/72 | **7** | 9 | 8. **Goodbye To Love** | A&M 1367 |
| 3/10/73 | **3** | 11 | ● 9. **Sing** | A&M 1413 |
| 6/16/73 | **2** (1) | 12 | ● 10. **Yesterday Once More** | A&M 1446 |
| 10/20/73 | **1** (2) | 16 | ● 11. **Top Of The World** | A&M 1468 |
| 4/27/74 | **11** | 9 | 12. I Won't Last A Day Without You | A&M 1521 |
| 12/07/74 + | **1** (1) | 12 | ● 13. **Please Mr. Postman** | A&M 1646 |
| 4/12/75 | **4** | 9 | 14. **Only Yesterday** | A&M 1677 |
| 8/16/75 | **17** | 7 | 15. Solitaire | A&M 1721 |
| 3/13/76 | **12** | 8 | 16. There's A Kind Of Hush (All Over The World) | A&M 1800 |
| 7/04/76 | **25** | 5 | 17. I Need To Be In Love | A&M 1828 |
| 6/18/77 | **35** | 3 | 18. All You Get From Love Is A Love Song | A&M 1940 |
| 11/05/77 | **32** | 4 | 19. Calling Occupants Of Interplanetary Craft | A&M 1978 |
| 7/04/81 | **16** | 9 | 20. Touch Me When We're Dancing | A&M 2344 |
| | | | **CATHY CARR** | |
| 4/07/56 | **2** (1) | 18 | 1. **Ivory Tower** | Fraternity 734 |
| | | | **JOE "FINGERS" CARR** | |
| | | | real name: Lou Busch | |
| 6/16/56 | **19** | 10 | 1. Portuguese Washerwomen [I] | Capitol 3418 |
| | | | **VALERIE CARR** | |
| | | | English | |
| 6/09/58 | **19** | 2 | 1. When The Boys Talk About The Girls | Roulette 4066 |

| DATE | POS | WKS | ARTIST—Record Title | LABEL & NO. |
|---|---|---|---|---|
| | | | **VIKKI CARR** | |
| | | | real name: Florencia Cardona | |
| 9/30/67 | 3 | 11 | 1. **It Must Be Him** | Liberty 55986 |
| 1/27/68 | 34 | 1 | 2. The Lesson | Liberty 56012 |
| 6/28/69 | 35 | 4 | 3. With Pen In Hand | Liberty 56092 |
| | | | **PAUL CARRACK** | |
| | | | formerly with Ace, and Squeeze | |
| 10/30/82 | 37 | 2 | 1. I Need You | Epic 03146 |
| | | | **KEITH CARRADINE** | |
| | | | son of actor John Carradine | |
| 6/12/76 | 17 | 12 | 1. I'm Easy | ABC 12117 |
| | | | from the soundtrack "Nashville" | |
| | | | **DAVID CARROLL & His Orchestra** | |
| | | | real name: Nook Schrier | |
| 1/08/55 | 8 | 17 | 1. **Melody Of Love [I]** | Mercury 70516 |
| 12/17/55 | 20 | 1 | 2. It's Almost Tomorrow | Mercury 70717 |
| | | | vocal by the Jack Halloran Singers | |
| | | | **CARS** | |
| | | | Boston-area quintet led by Ric Ocasek | |
| 8/12/78 | 27 | 7 | 1. Just What I Needed | Elektra 45491 |
| 12/09/78 | 35 | 5 | 2. My Best Friend's Girl | Elektra 45537 |
| 7/28/79 | 14 | 9 | 3. Let's Go | Elektra 46063 |
| 10/11/80 | 37 | 3 | 4. Touch And Go | Elektra 47039 |
| 12/12/81 + | 4 | 17 | 5. **Shake It Up** | Elektra 47250 |
| 3/24/84 | 7 | 11 | 6. You Might Think | Electra 69744 |
| 5/26/84 | 12 | 11 | 7. Magic | Electra 69724 |
| 8/11/84 | 3 | 14 | 8. Drive | Electra 69706 |
| | | | lead vocal by bassist Ben Orr | |
| | | | **KIT CARSON** | |
| | | | real name: Liza Morrow | |
| 12/31/55 + | 11 | 11 | 1. Band Of Gold | Capitol 3283 |
| | | | **MINDY CARSON** | |
| 8/27/55 | 13 | 8 | 1. Wake The Town And Tell The People | Columbia 40537 |
| 1/05/57 | 34 | 2 | 2. Since I Met You Baby | Columbia 40789 |
| | | | **CARLENE CARTER - see ROBERT ELLIS ORRALL** | |
| | | | **CLARENCE CARTER** | |
| | | | blind since childhood - formerly married to Candi Staton | |
| 8/17/68 | 6 | 11 | ● 1. **Slip Away** | Atlantic 2508 |
| 11/30/68 + | 13 | 11 | ● 2. Too Weak To Fight | Atlantic 2569 |
| 3/29/69 | 31 | 5 | 3. Snatching It Back | Atlantic 2605 |
| 8/01/70 | 4 | 12 | ● 4. **Patches** | Atlantic 2748 |
| | | | **MEL CARTER** | |
| | | | born on 4/22/43 in Cincinnati, Ohio | |
| 7/24/65 | 8 | 11 | 1. **Hold Me, Thrill Me, Kiss Me** | Imperial 66113 |
| 11/27/65 | 38 | 2 | 2. (All Of A Sudden) My Heart Sings | Imperial 66138 |
| 5/21/66 | 32 | 2 | 3. Band Of Gold | Imperial 66165 |

| DATE | POS | WKS | ARTIST—Record Title | LABEL & NO. |
|---|---|---|---|---|
| | | | **CASCADES** | |
| | | | quintet from San Diego | |
| 1/26/63 | 3 | 13 | 1. **Rhythm Of The Rain** | Valiant 6026 |
| | | | **ALVIN CASH & THE CRAWLERS** | |
| | | | brothers Alvin, Robert & George Cash | |
| 1/30/65 | 14 | 7 | 1. Twine Time [I] | Mar-V-Lus 6002 |
| | | | **JOHNNY CASH** | |
| | | | born in Dyess, Arkansas on 2/26/32 | |
| 10/20/56 | 17 | 11 | 1. I Walk The Line | Sun 241 |
| 2/10/58 | 14 | 13 | 2. Ballad Of A Teenage Queen | Sun 283 |
| 6/09/58 | 11 | 13 | 3. Guess Things Happen That Way | Sun 295 |
| 9/01/58 | 24 | 6 | 4. The Ways Of A Woman In Love | Sun 302 |
| 11/10/58 | 38 | 1 | 5. All Over Again | Columbia 41251 |
| 2/02/59 | 32 | 6 | 6. Don't Take Your Guns To Town | Columbia 41313 |
| 6/22/63 | 17 | 10 | 7. Ring Of Fire | Columbia 42788 |
| 3/14/64 | 35 | 3 | 8. Understand Your Man | Columbia 42964 |
| 6/29/68 | 32 | 6 | 9. Folsom Prison Blues | Columbia 44513 |
| | | | original version released in 1956 on Sun 232 | |
| 8/02/69 | 2 (3) | 11 | ● 10. **A Boy Named Sue [N]** | Columbia 44944 |
| 4/25/70 | 19 | 6 | 11. What Is Truth | Columbia 45134 |
| 5/15/76 | 29 | 3 | 12. One Piece At A Time [N] | Columbia 10321 |
| | | | **JOHNNY CASH & JUNE CARTER** | |
| 2/21/70 | 36 | 2 | 1. If I Were A Carpenter | Columbia 45064 |
| | | | **ROSANNE CASH** | |
| | | | Johnny Cash's daughter - married to Rodney Crowell | |
| 6/13/81 | 22 | 7 | 1. Seven Year Ache | Columbia 11426 |
| | | | **CASHMAN & WEST** | |
| | | | Terry Cashman & Tommy West - also see Buchanan Brothers | |
| 10/21/72 | 27 | 7 | 1. American City Suite: | Dunhill 4324 |
| | | | Sweet City Song/All Around The Town/A Friend Is Dying | |
| | | | **CASINOS** | |
| | | | 9-man group from Cincinnati led by Gene Hughes | |
| 1/28/67 | 6 | 10 | 1. **Then You Can Tell Me Goodbye** | Fraternity 977 |
| | | | **DAVID CASSIDY** | |
| | | | played Keith and was lead singer for TV's "The Partridge Family" | |
| 11/13/71 | 9 | 11 | ● 1. **Cherish** | Bell 45150 |
| 3/25/72 | 37 | 2 | 2. Could It Be Forever | Bell 45187 |
| 6/10/72 | 25 | 5 | 3. How Can I Be Sure | Bell 45220 |
| 10/14/72 | 38 | 2 | 4. Rock Me Baby | Bell 45260 |
| | | | **SHAUN CASSIDY** | |
| | | | Shaun & David are half-brothers | |
| 6/04/77 | 1 (1) | 12 | ● 1. **Da Doo Ron Ron** | Warner 8365 |
| 8/20/77 | 3 | 15 | ● 2. **That's Rock 'N' Roll** | Warner 8423 |
| 11/26/77 + | 7 | 12 | ● 3. **Hey Deanie** | Warner 8488 |
| 4/22/78 | 31 | 5 | 4. Do You Believe In Magic | Warner 8533 |

| DATE | POS | WKS | ARTIST—Record Title | LABEL & NO. |
|---|---|---|---|---|
| | | | **CASTAWAYS** | |
| | | | Minneapolis quintet | |
| 9/18/65 | 12 | 9 | 1. Liar, Liar | Soma 1433 |
| | | | **CASTELLS** | |
| | | | quartet from Santa Rosa, California | |
| 7/03/61 | 20 | 7 | 1. Sacred | Era 3048 |
| 5/26/62 | 21 | 5 | 2. So This Is Love | Era 3073 |
| | | | **BOOMER CASTLEMAN** | |
| | | | Clarke of Lewis & Clarke Expedition | |
| 5/31/75 | 33 | 3 | 1. Judy Mae | Mums 6038 |
| | | | **JIMMY CASTOR Bunch** | |
| 2/04/67 | 31 | 3 | 1. Hey, Leroy, Your Mama's Callin' You [I] | Smash 2069 |
| 5/27/72 | 6 | 10 | ● 2. **Troglodyte (Cave Man) [N]** | RCA 1029 |
| 3/22/75 | 16 | 8 | 3. The Bertha Butt Boogie (Part 1) [N] | Atlantic 3232 |
| | | | **CAT MOTHER & the ALL NIGHT NEWS BOYS** | |
| | | | New York rock quintet produced by Jimi Hendrix | |
| 7/12/69 | 21 | 6 | 1. Good Old Rock 'N Roll: | Polydor 14002 |
| | | | Sweet Little Sixteen/Long Tall Sally/Chantilly Lace/ Whole Lotta Shakin' Goin On/Blue Suede Shoes/Party Doll | |
| | | | **CATE BROS.** | |
| | | | twins Earl & Ernie Cate | |
| 4/17/76 | 24 | 8 | 1. Union Man | Asylum 45294 |
| | | | **GEORGE CATES** | |
| | | | Lawrence Welk's musical director - also see Steve Allen | |
| 4/21/56 | 4 | 19 | 1. **Moonglow And Theme From "Picnic" [I]** | Coral 61618 |
| | | | with The Stan Wrightsman Quartet - from the film "Picnic" | |
| | | | **CATHY JEAN & THE ROOMMATES** | |
| 3/06/61 | 12 | 10 | 1. Please Love Me Forever | Valmor 007 |
| | | | **FELIX CAVALIERE** | |
| | | | lead singer of the Rascals | |
| 4/12/80 | 36 | 3 | 1. Only A Lonely Heart Sees | Epic 50829 |
| | | | **C COMPANY Featuring TERRY NELSON** | |
| 5/01/71 | 37 | 3 | ● 1. Battle Hymn Of Lt. Calley [S] | Plantation 73 |
| | | | **CELEBRATION featuring MIKE LOVE** | |
| | | | Mike is one of the Beach Boys | |
| 6/03/78 | 28 | 4 | 1. Almost Summer | MCA 40891 |
| | | | **CERRONE** | |
| | | | French disco production by Jean-Marc Cerrone | |
| 3/26/77 | 36 | 3 | 1. Love In 'C' Minor (Part 1) [I] | Cotillion 44215 |
| | | | **CHAD & JEREMY** | |
| | | | English - Chad Stuart & Jeremy Clyde | |
| 6/13/64 | 21 | 6 | 1. Yesterday's Gone | World Art. 1021 |
| 9/19/64 | 7 | 9 | 2. **A Summer Song** | World Art. 1027 |
| 12/12/64 + | 15 | 8 | 3. Willow Weep For Me | World Art. 1034 |
| 3/13/65 | 23 | 5 | 4. If I Loved You | World Art. 1041 |
| 5/29/65 | 17 | 6 | 5. Before And After | Columbia 43277 |

| DATE | POS | WKS | ARTIST—Record Title | LABEL & NO. |
|---|---|---|---|---|
| 8/28/65 | 35 | 3 | 6. I Don't Wanna Lose You Baby | Columbia 43339 |
| 8/13/66 | 30 | 2 | 7. Distant Shores | Columbia 43682 |
| | | | **CHAIRMEN OF THE BOARD** | |
| | | | General Johnson, lead singer | |
| 2/07/70 | 3 | 12 | ● 1. **Give Me Just A Little More Time** | Invictus 9074 |
| 6/06/70 | 38 | 2 | 2. (You've Got Me) Dangling On A String | Invictus 9078 |
| 9/12/70 | 38 | 2 | 3. Everything's Tuesday | Invictus 9079 |
| 12/12/70 + | 13 | 9 | 4. Pay To The Piper | Invictus 9081 |
| | | | **CHAKACHAS** | |
| 2/19/72 | 8 | 10 | ● 1. **Jungle Fever [I]** | Polydor 15030 |
| | | | **RICHARD CHAMBERLAIN** | |
| | | | TV's "Dr. Kildare" | |
| 6/23/62 | 10 | 10 | 1. **Theme From Dr. Kildare (Three Stars Will Shine Tonight)** | MGM 13075 |
| 10/27/62 | 21 | 5 | 2. Love Me Tender | MGM 13097 |
| 3/09/63 | 14 | 7 | 3. All I Have To Do Is Dream | MGM 13121 |
| | | | **CHAMBERS BROTHERS** | |
| | | | four brothers from Mississippi | |
| 9/14/68 | 11 | 9 | 1. Time Has Come Today | Columbia 44414 |
| 12/21/68 | 37 | 2 | 2. I Can't Turn You Loose | Columbia 44679 |
| | | | **CHAMPAIGN** | |
| | | | from Champaign, Illinois | |
| 3/28/81 | 12 | 13 | 1. How 'Bout Us | Columbia 11433 |
| 5/14/83 | 23 | 9 | 2. Try Again | Columbia 03563 |
| | | | **CHAMPS** | |
| | | | rock instrumental quintet led by Dave Burgess (guitar) & Chuck Rio (sax) - Seals & Crofts were members after "Tequila" | |
| 3/03/58 | 1 (5) | 16 | 1. **Tequila [I]** | Challenge 1016 |
| 6/02/58 | 30 | 5 | 2. El Rancho Rock [I] | Challenge 59007 |
| 2/08/60 | 30 | 5 | 3. Too Much Tequila [I] | Challenge 59063 |
| 7/14/62 | 40 | 1 | 4. Limbo Rock [I] | Challenge 9131 |
| | | | **GENE CHANDLER** | |
| | | | born in Chicago on 7/6/37 | |
| 1/27/62 | 1 (3) | 11 | 1. **Duke Of Earl** | Vee-Jay 416 |
| 8/01/64 | 19 | 7 | 2. Just Be True | Constellation 130 |
| 11/14/64 | 39 | 1 | 3. Bless Our Love | Constellation 136 |
| 1/16/65 | 40 | 1 | 4. What Now | Constellation 141 |
| 5/22/65 | 18 | 6 | 5. Nothing Can Stop Me | Constellation 149 |
| 8/08/70 | 12 | 11 | ● 6. Groovy Situation | Mercury 73083 |
| | | | **CHANGE** | |
| | | | Italian disco production | |
| 7/19/80 | 40 | 1 | 1. A Lover's Holiday | RFC 49208 |
| | | | **BRUCE CHANNEL** | |
| 2/10/62 | 1 (3) | 12 | 1. **Hey! Baby** | Smash 1731 |
| | | | harmonica player: Delbert McClinton | |
| | | | **CHANSON** | |
| 12/16/78 + | 21 | 9 | 1. Don't Hold Back | Ariola 7717 |

| DATE | POS | WKS | ARTIST—Record Title | LABEL & NO. |
|---|---|---|---|---|
| | | | **CHANTAY'S** | |
| | | | Southern California surf/rock quintet (ages 17-18) | |
| 4/06/63 | 4 | 11 | 1. **Pipeline [I]** | Dot 16440 |
| | | | **CHANTELS** | |
| | | | female quintet from the Bronx, New York | |
| 1/27/58 | 15 | 12 | 1. Maybe | End 1005 |
| 4/07/58 | 39 | 3 | 2. Every Night (I Pray) | End 1015 |
| 9/11/61 | 14 | 8 | 3. Look In My Eyes | Carlton 555 |
| 12/11/61 | 29 | 3 | 4. Well, I Told You | Carlton 564 |
| | | | **HARRY CHAPIN** | |
| | | | folk-rock storyteller - died in an auto accident on 7/16/81 (38) | |
| 4/22/72 | 24 | 9 | 1. Taxi | Elektra 45770 |
| 3/16/74 | 36 | 2 | 2. W-O-L-D | Elektra 45874 |
| 11/02/74 | 1 (1) | 12 | ● 3. **Cat's In The Cradle** | Elektra 45203 |
| 11/22/80 | 23 | 7 | 4. Sequel | Boardwalk 5700 |
| | | | sequel to his 1972 hit "Taxi" | |
| | | | **CHARLENE** | |
| | | | Charlene Duncan | |
| 3/27/82 | 3 | 14 | 1. **I've Never Been To Me [R]** | Motown 1611 |
| | | | re-entry of 1977 hit (Pos. 97) | |
| | | | **JIMMY CHARLES & The Revelletts** | |
| 9/05/60 | 5 | 11 | 1. **A Million To One** | Promo 1002 |
| | | | **RAY CHARLES** | |
| | | | born Ray Charles Robinson in Albany, Georgia on 9/23/32 | |
| 11/25/57 | 34 | 1 | 1. Swanee River Rock (Talkin' 'Bout That River) | Atlantic 1154 |
| 7/20/59 | 6 | 11 | 2. **What'd I Say (Part 1)** | Atlantic 2031 |
| 12/14/59 | 40 | 1 | 3. I'm Movin' On | Atlantic 2043 |
| 8/08/60 | 40 | 1 | 4. Sticks And Stones | ABC-Para. 10118 |
| 10/10/60 | 1 (1) | 10 | 5. **Georgia On My Mind** | ABC-Para. 10135 |
| 12/12/60 | 28 | 5 | 6. Ruby | ABC-Para. 10164 |
| 3/27/61 | 8 | 9 | 7. **One Mint Julep [I]** | Impulse 200 |
| 9/18/61 | 1 (2) | 11 | 8. **Hit The Road Jack** | ABC-Para. 10244 |
| 12/04/61 + | 9 | 10 | 9. Unchain My Heart | ABC-Para. 10266 |
| 4/21/62 | 20 | 4 | 10. Hide 'Nor Hair | ABC-Para. 10314 |
| 5/19/62 | 1 (5) | 14 | ● 11. **I Can't Stop Loving You** | ABC-Para. 10330 |
| 8/04/62 | 2 (1) | 9 | 12. **You Don't Know Me** | ABC-Para. 10345 |
| 12/01/62 | 7 | 9 | 13. **You Are My Sunshine/** | |
| 12/08/62 | 29 | 5 | 14. Your Cheating Heart | ABC-Para. 10375 |
| 3/16/63 | 20 | 4 | 15. Don't Set Me Free | ABC-Para. 10405 |
| 4/27/63 | 8 | 8 | 16. **Take These Chains From My Heart** | ABC-Para. 10435 |
| 7/06/63 | 21 | 5 | 17. No One/ | |
| 7/06/63 | 29 | 4 | 18.  Without Love (There Is Nothing) | ABC-Para. 10453 |
| 9/14/63 | 4 | 11 | 19. **Busted** | ABC-Para. 10481 |
| 12/21/63 + | 20 | 7 | 20. That Lucky Old Sun | ABC-Para. 10509 |
| 3/21/64 | 38 | 2 | 21. My Heart Cries For You/ | |
| 3/21/64 | 39 | 1 | 22.  Baby, Don't You Cry | ABC-Para. 10530 |

**Canned Heat** was one of the most credible blues bands of the later sixties. This was primarily due to singer Bob "The Bear" Hite, who had a massive record collection, and guitarist Al "Blind Owl" Wilson, a music major from Boston University.

**Jim Capaldi** of Traffic fame grew up in Birmingham, England, where he played in the local r&b groups the Sapphires and Deep Feeling. The latter band included future members of Mott the Hoople and Family, as well as Dave Mason, another Traffic star.

**The Captain and Tennille.** The Captain is Daryl Dragon, son of Los Angeles symphony conductor Carmen Dragon. He played keyboards with the Beach Boys for many years, collaborating on a single credited to Dennis Wilson and Rumbo. (Rumbo was Dumbo the Elephant's son.)

**Irene Cara** has become known for movie music, thanks to *Fame, D.C. Cab,* and *Flashdance.* She won an Oscar for co-authoring "Flashdance. . .What a Feeling."

**The Cars** took five months to record 1984's *Heartbeat City* LP. The video for "You Might Think," the album's first single, won MTV's award for video of the year, edging out Michael Jackson and Cyndi Lauper.

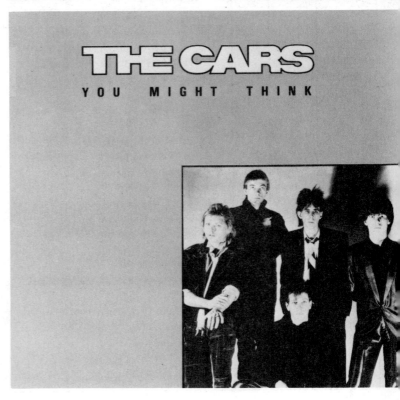

**Shaun Cassidy** followed in half-brother David's footsteps and became a lightweight teen idol. Later, he attempted to add credibility, cutting a hard-edged rock'n'roll LP with producer Todd Rundgren. Too late.

**The Carpenters.** With Richard on piano, Karen on drums, and a friend on bass, the jazzy Carpenter Trio won a talent contest at the Hollywood Bowl. However, record company indifference required a shift in direction, so Karen tried singing.

**Richard Chamberlain** wasn't much of a singer, but addicts of the "Dr. Kildare" TV series didn't really care. At least he had the good judgment not to sing songs from "Shōgun."

**The Chambers Brothers** were a busy California gospel group a good decade before they took up rock'n'roll. The electrification of folk and the rise of soul music prompted them to make the switch in 1967.

**Cheech and Chong** are rooted in music. Tommy Chong once played guitar with Motown's Bobby Taylor and the Vancouvers. The duo actually booked its first date as a rock band, but started the show with comedy and never got to the songs.

| DATE | POS | WKS | ARTIST—Record Title | LABEL & NO. |
|------|-----|-----|---------------------|-------------|
| 1/15/66 | 6 | 9 | 23. **Crying Time** | ABC-Para. 10739 |
| 4/16/66 | 19 | 5 | 24. Together Again | ABC-Para. 10785 |
| 6/25/66 | 31 | 4 | 25. Let's Go Get Stoned | ABC 10808 |
| 10/01/66 | 32 | 2 | 26. I Chose To Sing The Blues | ABC 10840 |
| 6/10/67 | 15 | 9 | 27. Here We Go Again | ABC/TRC 10938 |
| 9/23/67 | 33 | 3 | 28. In The Heat Of The Night | ABC/TRC 10970 |
| 12/02/67 | 25 | 3 | 29. Yesterday | ABC/TRC 11009 |
| 7/20/68 | 35 | 3 | 30. Eleanor Rigby | ABC/TRC 11090 |
| 4/17/71 | 36 | 4 | 31. Don't Change On Me | ABC/TRC 11291 |
| 5/15/71 | 36 | 2 | 32. Booty Butt [I] | Tangerine 1015 |
| | | | **RAY CHARLES Singers** | |
| 5/02/64 | 3 | 12 | 1. **Love Me With All Your Heart** | Command 4046 |
| 7/25/64 | 29 | 4 | 2. Al-Di-La | Command 4049 |
| 12/19/64 + | 32 | 5 | 3. One More Time | Command 4057 |
| | | | **SONNY CHARLES** | |
| | | | also see Checkmates, Ltd. | |
| 1/22/83 | 40 | 2 | 1. Put It In A Magazine | Highrise 2001 |
| | | | **CHARLIE** | |
| | | | five-man British group | |
| 8/06/83 | 38 | 2 | 1. It's Inevitable | Mirage 99862 |
| | | | **CHARMS** | |
| | | | R&B quintet from Cincinnati, Ohio | |
| 11/27/54 + | 15 | 15 | 1. Hearts Of Stone | DeLuxe 6062 |
| 1/15/55 | 26 | 3 | 2. Ling, Ting, Tong | DeLuxe 6076 |
| | | | OTIS WILLIAMS & HIS CHARMS: | |
| 4/14/56 | 11 | 15 | 3. Ivory Tower | DeLuxe 6093 |
| | | | **CHARTBUSTERS** | |
| | | | Washington, D.C. rock group | |
| 8/15/64 | 33 | 3 | 1. She's The One | Mutual 502 |
| | | | **CHASE** | |
| | | | Bill Chase and 3 other members killed in plane crash on 8/9/74 | |
| 6/26/71 | 24 | 8 | 1. Get It On | Epic 10738 |
| | | | **CHEAP TRICK** | |
| | | | Chicago rock quartet: Rick Nielsen, Bun E. Carlos, Robin Zander, Tom Petersson - replaced by Jon Brant | |
| 5/26/79 | 7 | 13 | ● 1. **I Want You To Want Me** | Epic 50680 |
| 9/15/79 | 35 | 3 | 2. Ain't That A Shame | Epic 50743 |
| 10/27/79 | 26 | 5 | 3. Dream Police | Epic 50774 |
| 1/19/80 | 32 | 3 | 4. Voices | Epic 50814 |
| | | | **CHUBBY CHECKER** | |
| | | | born Ernest Evans on 10/3/41 in Philadelphia - also see Bobby Rydell | |
| 6/15/59 | 38 | 2 | 1. The Class [N] imitations of Fats Domino, The Coasters, Elvis Presley, The Chipmunks | Parkway 804 |
| 8/08/60 | 1 (1) | 15 | 2. **The Twist** | Parkway 811 |
| 10/31/60 | 14 | 9 | 3. The Hucklebuck | Parkway 813 |

| DATE | POS | WKS | ARTIST—Record Title | LABEL & NO. |
|---|---|---|---|---|
| 1/30/61 | **1** (3) | 14 | 4. **Pony Time** | Parkway 818 |
| 5/01/61 | 24 | 4 | 5. Dance The Mess Around | Parkway 822 |
| 7/03/61 | 8 | 15 | 6. **Let's Twist Again** | Parkway 824 |
| 10/02/61 | 7 | 11 | 7. **The Fly** | Parkway 830 |
| 11/20/61 + | **1** (2) | 18 | 8. **The Twist [R]** | Parkway 811 |
| 3/10/62 | **3** | 12 | 9. **Slow Twistin'**<br>with Dee Dee Sharp | Parkway 835 |
| 7/07/62 | 12 | 7 | 10. **Dancin' Party** | Parkway 842 |
| 9/29/62 | **2** (2) | 17 | 11. **Limbo Rock/** | |
| 9/29/62 | 10 | 9 | 12.   **Popeye The Hitchhiker** | Parkway 849 |
| 2/23/63 | 20 | 8 | 13. Let's Limbo Some More/ | |
| 3/23/63 | 15 | 7 | 14.   Twenty Miles | Parkway 862 |
| 6/01/63 | 12 | 7 | 15. Birdland | Parkway 873 |
| 8/03/63 | 25 | 5 | 16. Twist It Up | Parkway 879 |
| 11/23/63 | 12 | 9 | 17. Loddy Lo/ | |
| 1/11/64 | 17 | 8 | 18.   Hooka Tooka | Parkway 890 |
| 4/04/64 | 23 | 5 | 19. Hey, Bobba Needle | Parkway 907 |
| 7/11/64 | 40 | 1 | 20. Lazy Elsie Molly | Parkway 920 |
| 5/22/65 | 40 | 1 | 21. Let's Do The Freddie | Parkway 949 |
| | | | **CHECKMATES, LTD. featuring SONNY CHARLES**<br>quintet from Fort Wayne, Indiana | |
| 5/31/69 | 13 | 10 | 1. Black Pearl | A&M 1053 |
| | | | **CHEECH & CHONG**<br>Richard Marin & Thomas Chong | |
| 9/29/73 | 15 | 7 | 1. Basketball Jones Featuring Tyrone Shoelaces [N] | Ode 66038 |
| 12/29/73 + | 24 | 5 | 2. Sister Mary Elephant (Shudd-Up!) [C] | Ode 66041 |
| 8/31/74 | 9 | 8 | 3. **Earache My Eye Featuring Alice Bowie [C]** | Ode 66102 |
| | | | **CHEERS**<br>actor Bert Convy was a member | |
| 9/24/55 | 6 | 11 | 1. **Black Denim Trousers** | Capitol 3219 |
| | | | **CHER**<br>real name: Cherilyn LaPierre - also see Sonny & Cher | |
| 8/07/65 | 15 | 6 | 1. All I Really Want To Do | Imperial 66114 |
| 11/06/65 | 25 | 3 | 2. Where Do You Go | Imperial 66136 |
| 3/26/66 | **2** (1) | 9 | 3. **Bang Bang (My Baby Shot Me Down)** | Imperial 66160 |
| 8/20/66 | 32 | 3 | 4. Alfie | Imperial 66192 |
| 11/18/67 | 9 | 9 | 5. **You Better Sit Down Kids** | Imperial 66261 |
| 10/02/71 | **1** (2) | 14 | ● 6. **Gypsys, Tramps & Thieves** | Kapp 2146 |
| 2/12/72 | 7 | 10 | 7. **The Way Of Love** | Kapp 2158 |
| 6/03/72 | 22 | 6 | 8. Living In A House Divided | Kapp 2171 |
| 9/01/73 | **1** (2) | 14 | ● 9. **Half-Breed** | MCA 40102 |
| 2/02/74 | **1** (1) | 12 | ● 10. **Dark Lady** | MCA 40161 |
| 6/15/74 | 27 | 4 | 11. Train Of Thought | MCA 40245 |
| 3/17/79 | 8 | 11 | ● 12. **Take Me Home** | Casablanca 965 |

| DATE | POS | WKS | ARTIST—Record Title | LABEL & NO. |
|---|---|---|---|---|
| | | | **CHERI** | |
| | | | Canadian duo | |
| 6/05/82 | 39 | 2 | 1. Murphy's Law [N] | Venture 149 |
| | | | **DON CHERRY** | |
| | | | born in Wichita, Texas on 1/11/24 | |
| 12/10/55 + | 4 | 18 | 1. **Band Of Gold** | Columbia 40597 |
| 4/14/56 | 29 | 6 | 2. Wild Cherry | Columbia 40665 |
| 8/11/56 | 22 | 6 | 3. Ghost Town | Columbia 40705 |
| | | | **CHI-LITES** | |
| | | | Eugene Record, leader of soul group from Chicago | |
| 5/08/71 | 26 | 6 | 1. (For God's Sake) Give More Power To The People | Brunswick 55450 |
| 10/30/71 | 3 | 13 | 2. **Have You Seen Her** | Brunswick 55462 |
| 4/15/72 | 1 (1) | 14 | 3. **Oh Girl** | Brunswick 55471 |
| 3/24/73 | 33 | 5 | 4. A Letter To Myself | Brunswick 55491 |
| 9/01/73 | 30 | 5 | 5. Stoned Out Of My Mind | Brunswick 55500 |
| | | | **CHIC** | |
| | | | disco production of Nile Rodgers & Bernard Edwards | |
| 12/10/77 + | 6 | 17 | ● 1. **Dance, Dance, Dance (Yowsah, Yowsah, Yowsah)** | Atlantic 3435 |
| 6/17/78 | 38 | 1 | 2. Everybody Dance | Atlantic 3469 |
| 11/18/78 | 1 (6) | 19 | ★ 3. **Le Freak** | Atlantic 3519 |
| 3/10/79 | 7 | 12 | ● 4. **I Want Your Love** | Atlantic 3557 |
| 7/07/79 | 1 (1) | 14 | ● 5. **Good Times** | Atlantic 3584 |
| | | | **CHICAGO** | |
| | | | original band: Terry Kath (died 1/23/78-31), Robert Lamm, Peter Cetera, James Pankow, Danny Seraphine, Lee Loughnane, Walter Parazaider | |
| 4/25/70 | 9 | 11 | 1. **Make Me Smile** | Columbia 45127 |
| 8/01/70 | 4 | 11 | 2. **25 Or 6 To 4** | Columbia 45194 |
| 11/21/70 + | 7 | 11 | 3. **Does Anybody Really Know What Time It Is?** | Columbia 45264 |
| 3/06/71 | 20 | 6 | 4. Free | Columbia 45331 |
| 5/29/71 | 35 | 4 | 5. Lowdown | Columbia 45370 |
| 7/10/71 | 7 | 11 | 6. **Beginnings/** | |
| | | 10 | 7. **Colour My World** | Columbia 45417 |
| 10/30/71 | 24 | 6 | 8. Questions 67 And 68/ [R] | |
| | | | re-entry of 1969 hit (Pos. 71) | |
| | | 6 | 9. **I'm A Man** | Columbia 45467 |
| 8/12/72 | 3 | 10 | ● 10. **Saturday In The Park** | Columbia 45657 |
| 11/18/72 | 24 | 6 | 11. Dialogue (Part I & II) | Columbia 45717 |
| 7/07/73 | 10 | 12 | 12. **Feelin' Stronger Every Day** | Columbia 45880 |
| 10/20/73 | 4 | 14 | ● 13. **Just You 'N' Me** | Columbia 45933 |
| 4/06/74 | 9 | 12 | 14. **(I've Been) Searchin' So Long** | Columbia 46020 |
| 7/13/74 | 6 | 8 | 15. **Call On Me** | Columbia 46062 |
| 10/26/74 | 11 | 10 | 16. Wishing You Were Here | Columbia 10049 |
| | | | backing vocals by 3 of the Beach Boys | |
| 3/08/75 | 13 | 7 | 17. Harry Truman | Columbia 10092 |
| 5/10/75 | 5 | 7 | 18. **Old Days** | Columbia 10131 |

| DATE | POS | WKS | ARTIST—Record Title | LABEL & NO. |
|---|---|---|---|---|
| 7/17/76 | 32 | 4 | 19. Another Rainy Day In New York City | Columbia 10360 |
| 8/21/76 | 1 (2) | 17 | ● 20. **If You Leave Me Now** | Columbia 10390 |
| 10/15/77 | 4 | 13 | 21. **Baby, What A Big Surprise** | Columbia 10620 |
| 10/28/78 | 14 | 8 | 22. Alive Again | Columbia 10845 |
| 1/13/79 | 14 | 9 | 23. No Tell Lover | Columbia 10879 |
| 6/26/82 | 1 (2) | 18 | ● 24. **Hard To Say I'm Sorry**<br>from the film "Summer Lovers" | Full Moon 29979 |
| 10/23/82 | 22 | 8 | 25. Love Me Tomorrow | Full Moon 29911 |
| 5/12/84 | 16 | 10 | 26. Stay The Night | Full Moon 29306 |
| 8/25/84 | 3 | 15 | 27. **Hard Habit To Break** | Full Moon 29214 |
| | | | **CHICAGO LOOP** | |
| 11/26/66 | 37 | 3 | 1. (When She Needs Good Lovin') She Comes To Me | DynoVoice 226 |
| | | | **CHIFFONS**<br>female quartet from the Bronx, New York | |
| 3/09/63 | 1 (4) | 12 | 1. **He's So Fine** | Laurie 3152 |
| 6/08/63 | 5 | 9 | 2. **One Fine Day** | Laurie 3179 |
| 10/19/63 | 40 | 1 | 3. A Love So Fine | Laurie 3195 |
| 1/04/64 | 36 | 2 | 4. I Have A Boyfriend | Laurie 3212 |
| 5/28/66 | 10 | 7 | 5. **Sweet Talkin' Guy** | Laurie 3340 |
| | | | **CHILLIWACK**<br>Canadian | |
| 10/31/81 | 22 | 11 | 1. My Girl (Gone, Gone, Gone) | Millennium 11813 |
| 2/27/82 | 33 | 3 | 2. I Believe | Millennium 13102 |
| | | | **CHIMES**<br>Brooklyn, New York quintet | |
| 1/16/61 | 11 | 6 | 1. Once In Awhile | Tag 444 |
| 5/15/61 | 38 | 1 | 2. I'm In The Mood For Love | Tag 445 |
| | | | **CHIPMUNKS**<br>David Seville (Alvin, Simon & Theodore's creator) died on<br>1/16/72 (52) | |
| 12/08/58 | 1 (4) | 11 | 1. **The Chipmunk Song [N-X]** | Liberty 55168 |
| 2/23/59 | 3 | 9 | 2. **Alvin's Harmonica [N]** | Liberty 55179 |
| 7/13/59 | 16 | 6 | 3. Ragtime Cowboy Joe [N] | Liberty 55200 |
| 3/07/60 | 33 | 2 | 4. Alvin's Orchestra [N] | Liberty 55233 |
| 12/26/60 | 21 | 1 | 5. Rudolph The Red Nosed Reindeer [N-X] | Liberty 55289 |
| 1/06/62 + | 39 | 1 | 6. The Chipmunk Song [R-X] | Liberty 55250 |
| 3/31/62 | 40 | 1 | 7. The Alvin Twist [N] | Liberty 55424 |
| 12/29/62 | 40 | 1 | 8. The Chipmunk Song [R-X] | Liberty 55250 |
| | | | **CHORDETTES**<br>quartet from Sheboygan, Wisconsin | |
| 3/10/56 | 14 | 9 | 1. Eddie My Love | Cadence 1284 |
| 6/02/56 | 5 | 17 | 2. **Born To Be With You** | Cadence 1291 |
| 10/13/56 | 16 | 10 | 3. Lay Down Your Arms | Cadence 1299 |
| 9/16/57 | 8 | 8 | 4. **Just Between You And Me** | Cadence 1330 |

| DATE | POS | WKS | ARTIST—Record Title | LABEL & NO. |
|---|---|---|---|---|
| 3/10/58 | 2 (2) | 12 | 5. **Lollipop** | Cadence 1345 |
| 5/26/58 | 17 | 7 | 6. Zorro | Cadence 1349 |
| 3/30/59 | 27 | 4 | 7. No Other Arms, No Other Lips | Cadence 1361 |
| 7/03/61 | 13 | 8 | 8. Never On Sunday | Cadence 1402 |
| | | | **CHRIS CHRISTIAN** | |
| 11/14/81 | 37 | 3 | 1. I Want You, I Need You | Boardwalk 126 |
| | | | **CHRISTIE** | |
| | | | English trio - Jeff Christie, leader | |
| 10/24/70 | 23 | 8 | 1. Yellow River | Epic 10626 |
| | | | **LOU CHRISTIE** | |
| | | | born Lugee Geno Sacco on 2/19/43 in Glen Willard, Pennsylvania | |
| 2/16/63 | 24 | 6 | 1. The Gypsy Cried | Roulette 4457 |
| 4/27/63 | 6 | 10 | 2. **Two Faces Have I** | Roulette 4481 |
| 1/22/66 | 1 (1) | 10 | ● 3. **Lightnin' Strikes** | MGM 13412 |
| 4/23/66 | 16 | 4 | 4. Rhapsody In The Rain | MGM 13473 |
| 9/13/69 | 10 | 9 | 5. **I'm Gonna Make You Mine** | Buddah 116 |
| | | | **EUGENE CHURCH & The Fellows** | |
| 2/23/59 | 36 | 2 | 1. Pretty Girls Everywhere | Class 235 |
| | | | **CITY BOY** | |
| | | | British rock sextet | |
| 9/09/78 | 27 | 6 | 1. 5.7.0.5. | Mercury 73999 |
| | | | **C.J. & CO.** | |
| | | | Detroit disco/soul band | |
| 7/09/77 | 36 | 2 | 1. Devil's Gun | Westbound 55400 |
| | | | **JIMMY CLANTON** | |
| | | | born on 9/2/40 in Baton Rouge, Louisiana | |
| 7/21/58 | 4 | 15 | 1. **Just A Dream** | Ace 546 |
| 11/17/58 | 25 | 5 | 2. A Letter To An Angel/ | |
| 12/01/58 | 38 | 2 | 3.  A Part Of Me | Ace 551 |
| 8/17/59 | 33 | 6 | 4. My Own True Love | Ace 567 |
| 12/21/59 + | 5 | 11 | 5. **Go, Jimmy, Go** | Ace 575 |
| 5/30/60 | 22 | 6 | 6. Another Sleepless Night | Ace 585 |
| 9/01/62 | 7 | 10 | 7. **Venus In Blue Jeans** | Ace 8001 |
| | | | **ERIC CLAPTON** | |
| | | | Britain's premier rock guitarist - formerly with The Yardbirds, John Mayall's Bluesbreakers, Cream, and Blind Faith - also see Derek & The Dominos | |
| 11/14/70 | 18 | 8 | 1. After Midnight | Atco 6784 |
| 8/03/74 | 1 (1) | 10 | ● 2. **I Shot The Sheriff** | RSO 409 |
| 11/23/74 | 26 | 5 | 3. Willie And The Hand Jive | RSO 503 |
| 11/13/76 | 24 | 6 | 4. Hello Old Friend | RSO 861 |
| 2/04/78 | 3 | 17 | ● 5. **Lay Down Sally** | RSO 886 |
| 6/10/78 | 16 | 7 | 6. Wonderful Tonight | RSO 895 |
| | | | ERIC CLAPTON & HIS BAND: | |
| 11/25/78 + | 9 | 11 | 7. **Promises**/ | |
| 3/24/79 | 40 | 2 | 8.  Watch Out For Lucy | RSO 910 |

| DATE | POS | WKS | ARTIST—Record Title | LABEL & NO. |
|---|---|---|---|---|
| 7/26/80 | 30 | 5 | 9. Tulsa Time/ | |
| | | 5 | 10. **Cocaine** | RSO 1039 |
| 3/14/81 | 10 | 12 | 11. **I Can't Stand It** | RSO 1060 |
| 2/19/83 | 18 | 10 | 12. I've Got A Rock N' Roll Heart | Duck 29780 |
| | | | **CLAUDINE CLARK** | |
| 7/21/62 | 5 | 10 | 1. **Party Lights** | Chancellor 1113 |
| | | | **DAVE CLARK FIVE** | |
| | | | British: Dave Clark, Mike Smith, Lenny Davidson, Rick Huxley, Denny Payton | |
| 3/07/64 | 6 | 11 | 1. **Glad All Over** | Epic 9656 |
| 4/11/64 | 4 | 10 | 2. **Bits And Pieces** | Epic 9671 |
| 5/09/64 | 11 | 9 | 3. Do You Love Me | Epic 9678 |
| 6/20/64 | 4 | 9 | 4. **Can't You See That She's Mine** | Epic 9692 |
| 8/08/64 | 3 | 9 | 5. **Because** | Epic 9704 |
| 10/17/64 | 15 | 6 | 6. Everybody Knows (I Still Love You) | Epic 9722 |
| 12/05/64 + | 14 | 9 | 7. Any Way You Want It | Epic 9739 |
| 2/27/65 | 14 | 6 | 8. Come Home | Epic 9763 |
| 5/08/65 | 23 | 5 | 9. Reelin' And Rockin' | Epic 9786 |
| 7/10/65 | 7 | 8 | 10. **I Like It Like That** | Epic 9811 |
| 9/04/65 | 4 | 9 | 11. **Catch Us If You Can** | Epic 9833 |
| 11/20/65 | 1 (1) | 11 | 12. **Over And Over** | Epic 9863 |
| 2/19/66 | 18 | 5 | 13. At The Scene | Epic 9882 |
| 4/23/66 | 12 | 5 | 14. Try Too Hard | Epic 10004 |
| 7/02/66 | 28 | 4 | 15. Please Tell Me Why | Epic 10031 |
| 4/15/67 | 7 | 7 | 16. **You Got What It Takes** | Epic 10144 |
| 7/01/67 | 35 | 2 | 17. You Must Have Been A Beautiful Baby | Epic 10179 |
| | | | **DEE CLARK** | |
| | | | performed on Red Saunders' 1952 pop chart hit "Hambone" | |
| 1/12/59 | 21 | 6 | 1. Nobody But You | Abner 1019 |
| 5/25/59 | 18 | 9 | 2. Just Keep It Up | Abner 1026 |
| 9/14/59 | 20 | 9 | 3. Hey Little Girl | Abner 1029 |
| 1/04/60 | 33 | 5 | 4. How About That | Abner 1032 |
| 3/06/61 | 34 | 4 | 5. Your Friends | Vee-Jay 372 |
| 5/22/61 | 2 (1) | 12 | 6. **Raindrops** | Vee-Jay 383 |
| | | | **PETULA CLARK** | |
| | | | English - born on 11/15/33 | |
| 1/02/65 | 1 (2) | 13 | ● 1. **Downtown** | Warner 5494 |
| 4/03/65 | 3 | 9 | 2. **I Know A Place** | Warner 5612 |
| 7/31/65 | 22 | 5 | 3. You'd Better Come Home | Warner 5643 |
| 10/30/65 | 21 | 4 | 4. Round Every Corner | Warner 5661 |
| 1/15/66 | 1 (2) | 10 | 5. **My Love** | Warner 5684 |
| 4/02/66 | 11 | 7 | 6. A Sign Of The Times | Warner 5802 |
| 7/30/66 | 9 | 7 | 7. **I Couldn't Live Without Your Love** | Warner 5835 |
| 10/29/66 | 21 | 6 | 8. Who Am I | Warner 5863 |
| 12/31/66 + | 16 | 7 | 9. Color My World | Warner 5882 |

| DATE | POS | WKS | ARTIST—Record Title | LABEL & NO. |
|---|---|---|---|---|
| 3/18/67 | 3 | 9 | 10. **This Is My Song**<br>from the film "A Countess From Hong Kong" | Warner 7002 |
| 6/17/67 | 5 | 7 | 11. **Don't Sleep In The Subway** | Warner 7049 |
| 9/16/67 | 26 | 4 | 12. The Cat In The Window (The Bird In The Sky) | Warner 7073 |
| 12/30/67 | 31 | 2 | 13. The Other Man's Grass Is Always Greener | Warner 7097 |
| 3/02/68 | 15 | 9 | 14. Kiss Me Goodbye | Warner 7170 |
| 8/24/68 | 37 | 1 | 15. Don't Give Up | Warner 7216 |
| | | | **ROY CLARK**<br>co-host of TV's "Hee-Haw" | |
| 7/12/69 | 19 | 6 | 1. Yesterday, When I Was Young | Dot 17246 |
| | | | **SANFORD CLARK** | |
| 8/11/56 | 7 | 15 | 1. **The Fool**<br>backing guitarist: Al Casey | Dot 15481 |
| | | | **STANLEY CLARKE/GEORGE DUKE**<br>jazz bassist/keyboardist | |
| 6/13/81 | 19 | 9 | 1. Sweet Baby | Epic 01052 |
| | | | **TONY CLARKE** | |
| 5/08/65 | 31 | 2 | 1. The Entertainer | Chess 1924 |
| | | | **CLASH**<br>leader of Great Britain's new music wave: Joe Strummer,<br>Mick Jones, Paul Simonon, Topper Headon | |
| 4/26/80 | 23 | 7 | 1. Train In Vain (Stand By Me) | Epic 50851 |
| 11/13/82 + | 8 | 15 | 2. **Rock The Casbah** | Epic 03245 |
| | | | **CLASSICS**<br>Brooklyn, New York quartet | |
| 7/20/63 | 20 | 5 | 1. Till Then | Musicnote 1116 |
| | | | **CLASSICS IV**<br>Atlanta, Georgia quartet led by Dennis Yost | |
| 1/13/68 | 3 | 12 | 1. **Spooky** | Imperial 66259 |
| 11/16/68 | 5 | 12 | ● 2. **Stormy** | Imperial 66328 |
| 2/22/69 | 2 (1) | 10 | 3. Traces | Imperial 66352 |
| 5/31/69 | 19 | 7 | 4. Everyday With You Girl | Imperial 66378 |
| 12/09/72 | 39 | 3 | 5. What Am I Crying For? | MGM South 7002 |
| | | | **TOM CLAY** | |
| 7/24/71 | 8 | 7 | 1. **What The World Needs Now Is<br>Love/Abraham, Martin And John [S]**<br>vocal accompaniment by The Blackberries | Mowest 5002 |
| | | | **CLEFTONES**<br>quintet from Queens, New York | |
| 6/19/61 | 18 | 4 | 1. Heart And Soul | Gee 1064 |
| | | | **JIMMY CLIFF**<br>Jamaican reggae singer/composer | |
| 12/27/69 + | 25 | 7 | 1. Wonderful World, Beautiful People | A&M 1146 |

| DATE | POS | WKS | ARTIST—Record Title | LABEL & NO. |
|---|---|---|---|---|
| | | | **BUZZ CLIFFORD** | |
| 1/30/61 | 6 | 10 | 1. **Baby Sittin' Boogie [N]** | Columbia 41876 |
| | | | **MIKE CLIFFORD** | |
| 10/13/62 | 12 | 8 | 1. Close To Cathy | United Art. 489 |
| | | | **CLIMAX** | |
| | | | Sonny Geraci, lead singer (formerly with The Outsiders) | |
| 1/22/72 | 3 | 12 | ● 1. **Precious And Few** | Carousel 30055 |
| | | | **CLIMAX BLUES BAND** | |
| | | | English quartet led by Colin Cooper & Peter Haycock | |
| 3/26/77 | 3 | 14 | 1. **Couldn't Get It Right** | Sire 736 |
| 4/04/81 | 12 | 17 | 2. I Love You | Warner 49669 |
| | | | **PATSY CLINE** | |
| | | | killed in a plane crash on 3/5/63 (30) with Cowboy Copas and Hawkshaw Hawkins | |
| 3/02/57 | 12 | 11 | 1. Walkin' After Midnight | Decca 30221 |
| 7/24/61 | 12 | 10 | 2. I Fall To Pieces | Decca 31205 |
| 11/06/61 | 9 | 7 | 3. **Crazy** | Decca 31317 |
| 2/24/62 | 14 | 8 | 4. She's Got You | Decca 31354 |
| | | | **CLIQUE** | |
| 9/27/69 | 22 | 7 | 1. Sugar On Sunday | White Whale 323 |
| | | | **ROSEMARY CLOONEY** | |
| | | | Rosemary, along with Patti Page and Jo Stafford, were the top female singers of the early fifties - also see Benny Goodman | |
| 4/13/57 | 10 | 9 | 1. **Mangos** | Columbia 40835 |
| | | | **CLOVERS** | |
| | | | quintet had 13 consecutive Top 10 R&B hits from 1951 thru 1954 | |
| 7/28/56 | 30 | 3 | 1. Love, Love, Love | Atlantic 1094 |
| 11/02/59 | 23 | 5 | 2. Love Potion No. 9 | United Art. 180 |
| | | | **COASTERS** | |
| | | | quintet formed in Los Angeles as The Robins - Leiber/Stoller wrote and produced nearly all their hits | |
| 5/20/57 | 3 | 22 | 1. **Searchin'/** | |
| 5/20/57 | 8 | 11 | 2. **Young Blood** | Atco 6087 |
| 6/09/58 | 1 (1) | 15 | 3. **Yakety Yak** | Atco 6116 |
| 2/09/59 | 2 (3) | 12 | 4. **Charlie Brown [N]** | Atco 6132 |
| 6/01/59 | 9 | 8 | 5. **Along Came Jones [N]** | Atco 6141 |
| 9/07/59 | 7 | 11 | 6. **Poison Ivy/** | |
| 9/21/59 | 38 | 1 | 7. I'm A Hog For You | Atco 6146 |
| 1/25/60 | 36 | 1 | 8. Run Red Run | Atco 6153 |
| 2/27/61 | 37 | 2 | 9. Wait A Minute | Atco 6186 |
| 5/29/61 | 23 | 6 | 10. Little Egypt (Ying-Yang) [N] | Atco 6192 |
| | | | **ODIA COATES - see PAUL ANKA** | |

| DATE | POS | WKS | ARTIST—Record Title | LABEL & NO. |
|------|-----|-----|---------------------|-------------|
| | | | **EDDIE COCHRAN** | |
| | | | died in an auto accident in England on 4/17/60 (21) - Gene Vincent was seriously injured in the accident | |
| 3/30/57 | 18 | 8 | 1. Sittin' In The Balcony | Liberty 55056 |
| 8/25/58 | 8 | 12 | 2. **Summertime Blues** | Liberty 55144 |
| 1/05/59 | 35 | 1 | 3. C'mon Everybody | Liberty 55166 |
| | | | **BRUCE COCKBURN** | |
| | | | Canadian | |
| 5/03/80 | 21 | 9 | 1. Wondering Where The Lions Are | Millennium 11786 |
| | | | **JOE COCKER** | |
| | | | English white blues singer | |
| 1/10/70 | 30 | 7 | 1. She Came In Through The Bathroom Window | A&M 1147 |
| 5/09/70 | 7 | 9 | 2. **The Letter** with Leon Russell & The Shelter People | A&M 1174 |
| 10/24/70 | 11 | 7 | 3. Cry Me A River | A&M 1200 |
| 6/19/71 | 22 | 6 | 4. High Time We Went | A&M 1258 |
| 1/29/72 | 33 | 5 | 5. Feeling Alright [R] re-entry of 1969 hit (Pos. 69) | A&M 1063 |
| 10/07/72 | 27 | 5 | 6. Midnight Rider with the Chris Stainton Band | A&M 1370 |
| 2/15/75 | 5 | 10 | 7. **You Are So Beautiful** | A&M 1641 |
| | | | **JOE COCKER & JENNIFER WARNES** | |
| 10/02/82 | 1 (3) | 15 | 1. **Up Where We Belong** love theme from the film "An Officer & A Gentleman" | Island 99996 |
| | | | **DENNIS COFFEY & The Detroit Guitar Band** | |
| 11/13/71 + | 6 | 15 | ● 1. **Scorpio [I]** | Sussex 226 |
| 3/11/72 | 18 | 8 | 2. Taurus [I] | Sussex 233 |
| | | | **COZY COLE** | |
| | | | drummer with Jelly Roll Morton, Cab Calloway and Louis Armstrong - died of cancer on 1/29/81 (73) | |
| 9/29/58 | 3 | 14 | 1. **Topsy II/ [I]** | |
| 10/27/58 | 27 | 3 | 2. Topsy I [I] | Love 5004 |
| 12/28/58 | 36 | 1 | 3. Turvy II [I] | Love 5014 |
| | | | **NAT KING COLE** | |
| | | | formed King Cole Trio in 1939 - died of cancer on 2/15/65 (45) | |
| 3/05/55 | 7 | 16 | 1. **Darling Je Vous Aime Beaucoup/** | |
| 3/05/55 | 23 | 4 | 2. The Sand And The Sea | Capitol 3027 |
| 5/07/55 | 2 (1) | 20 | 3. **A Blossom Fell/** | |
| 5/21/55 | 8 | 10 | 4. If I May with The Four Knights | Capitol 3095 |
| 7/16/55 | 24 | 2 | 5. My One Sin | Capitol 3136 |
| 10/22/55 | 13 | 8 | 6. Someone You Love/ | |
| 11/12/55 | 21 | 5 | 7. Forgive My Heart | Capitol 3234 |
| 3/03/56 | 18 | 3 | 8. Ask Me | Capitol 3328 |
| 4/21/56 | 21 | 6 | 9. Too Young To Go Steady from the musical "Strip For Action" | Capitol 3390 |
| 7/21/56 | 16 | 12 | 10. That's All There Is To That with The Four Knights | Capitol 3456 |

| DATE | POS | WKS | ARTIST—Record Title | LABEL & NO. |
|---|---|---|---|---|
| 11/03/56 | 11 | 10 | 11. Night Lights/ | |
| 11/10/56 | 25 | 2 | 12.   To The Ends Of The Earth | Capitol 3551 |
| 2/23/57 | 18 | 5 | 13. Ballerina | Capitol 3619 |
| 7/01/57 | 6 | 18 | 14. **Send For Me/** | |
| 8/05/57 | 21 | 1 | 15.   My Personal Possession<br>with The Four Knights | Capitol 3737 |
| 10/21/57 | 30 | 4 | 16. With You On My Mind | Capitol 3782 |
| 2/24/58 | 33 | 3 | 17. Angel Smile | Capitol 3860 |
| 4/14/58 | 5 | 16 | 18. **Looking Back** | Capitol 3939 |
| 7/28/58 | 38 | 2 | 19. Come Closer To Me | Capitol 4004 |
| 2/15/60 | 30 | 3 | 20. Time And The River | Capitol 4325 |
| 8/18/62 | 2 (2) | 13 | 21. **Ramblin' Rose** | Capitol 4804 |
| 12/01/62 | 13 | 8 | 22. Dear Lonely Hearts | Capitol 4870 |
| 5/25/63 | 6 | 9 | 23. **Those Lazy-Hazy-Crazy Days Of Summer** | Capitol 4965 |
| 9/28/63 | 12 | 9 | 24. That Sunday, That Summer | Capitol 5027 |
| 5/16/64 | 22 | 6 | 25. I Don't Want To Be Hurt Anymore | Capitol 5155 |
| 10/24/64 | 34 | 4 | 26. I Don't Want To See Tomorrow | Capitol 5261 |
| | | | **NATALIE COLE**<br>Nat King Cole's daughter | |
| 10/04/75 | 6 | 11 | 1. **This Will Be** | Capitol 4109 |
| 2/28/76 | 32 | 5 | 2. Inseparable | Capitol 4193 |
| 6/26/76 | 25 | 7 | 3. Sophisticated Lady (She's A Different Lady) | Capitol 4259 |
| 2/26/77 | 5 | 14 | ● 4. **I've Got Love On My Mind** | Capitol 4360 |
| 2/11/78 | 10 | 15 | ● 5. **Our Love** | Capitol 4509 |
| 8/09/80 | 21 | 9 | 6. Someone That I Used To Love | Capitol 4869 |
| | | | **DAVE & ANSIL COLLINS**<br>Jamaican | |
| 7/03/71 | 22 | 8 | 1. Double Barrel | Big Tree 115 |
| | | | **DOROTHY COLLINS**<br>star of TV's "Your Hit Parade" | |
| 12/03/55 | 16 | 2 | 1. My Boy - Flat Top | Coral 61510 |
| 2/11/56 | 17 | 2 | 2. Seven Days | Coral 61562 |
| | | | **JUDY COLLINS**<br>folksinger born in Denver, Colorado on 5/1/39 | |
| 11/23/68 | 8 | 9 | 1. **Both Sides Now** | Elektra 45639 |
| 1/09/71 | 15 | 11 | 2. Amazing Grace | Elektra 45709 |
| 3/17/73 | 32 | 5 | 3. Cook With Honey | Elektra 45831 |
| 7/26/75 | 36 | 3 | 4. Send In The Clowns | Elektra 45253 |
| 10/15/77 | 19 | 8 | 5. Send In The Clowns [R] | Elektra 45253 |
| | | | **PHIL COLLINS**<br>drummer and leader of Genesis | |
| 4/11/81 | 19 | 9 | 1. I Missed Again | Atlantic 3790 |
| 7/11/81 | 19 | 8 | 2. In The Air Tonight | Atlantic 3824 |
| 11/27/82 + | 10 | 16 | 3. **You Can't Hurry Love** | Atlantic 89933 |

**David Seville and the Chipmunks**
were born when Ross Bagdasarian began experimenting with tape speeds. He named squeaky-voiced Alvin and Simon after the heads of his record company.

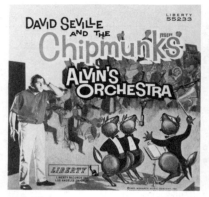

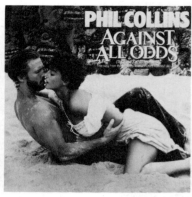

**Phil Collins** never stops. He's produced Adam Ant and Abba's Frida, drummed with progressive Brand X and Led Zeppelin's Robert Plant, and recorded a chart-topping theme song for *Against All Odds*. Plus, he's still singing for Genesis.

**John Cougar Mellencamp** acquired his unusual middle name through an association with David Bowie's ex-manager. Tony De Fries attempted to launch the young Indiana lad in England as a modern James Dean, and the name Cougar was thought to enhance the effect.

**Johnny Crawford** parlayed a starring role on "The Rifleman" (playing tough Chuck Connors' son) into a successful recording career. The liner notes to his greatest hits LP claimed that on "Rumors" the lad "definitely reached a new plateau."

**Culture Club's** George O'Dowd (a.k.a. Boy George) appeared on the stage, but never recorded with Bow Wow Wow, who were managed by Sex Pistols mastermind Malcolm McLaren. At the time "Boy" was known as Lieutenant Lush.

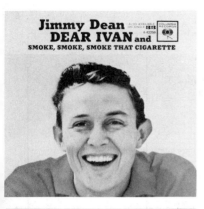

**Jimmy Dean** is known for a successful TV series and a mighty tasty brand of sausage, as well as all-American hits like "Big Bad John" and "P.T. 109." To boot, he was once named an honorary colonel by the governor of Tennessee.

**Joey Dee and the Starliters** used hits like "Peppermint Twist" as a springboard to appearances in the movies *Hey Let's Twist* and *Vive Le Twist.* "Shout" was just one of many covers of the Isley Brothers' classic.

**Neil Diamond** paid plenty of dues before tasting success. He worked as a staff songwriter for Tin Pan Alley's Sunbeam Music, sang in coffee houses, and recorded as half of Jack and Neil.

**Dion and the Belmonts** were part of the ill-fated 1959 tour that ended with the plane-crash deaths of Buddy Holly, the Big Bopper, and Richie Valens.

**Fats Domino,** born one of nine children in New Orleans, began playing in local honky tonks at age 10. He cut "The Fat Man," his first single, a decade later.

**The Doobie Brothers,** all unrelated, evolved from a band with the unappealing name Pud. A later infusion of Steely Dan vets Jeff "Skunk" Baxter and Michael McDonald kept the group running strong until 1982.

| DATE | POS | WKS | ARTIST—Record Title | LABEL & NO. |
|------|-----|-----|---------------------|-------------|
| 3/26/83 | 39 | 3 | 4. I Don't Care Anymore | Atlantic 89877 |
| 3/10/84 | 1 (3) | 16 | ● 5. **Against All Odds (Take A Look At Me Now)**<br>title song from the film "Against All Odds" | Atlantic 89700 |
| | | | **JESSI COLTER**<br>Waylon Jenning's wife | |
| 4/26/75 | 4 | 14 | 1. **I'm Not Lisa** | Capitol 4009 |
| | | | **CHI COLTRANE** | |
| 9/30/72 | 17 | 9 | 1. Thunder And Lightning | Columbia 45640 |
| | | | **COMMANDER CODY & His Lost Planet Airmen**<br>George Frayne is Commander Cody | |
| 4/15/72 | 9 | 11 | 1. **Hot Rod Lincoln [N]** | Paramount 0146 |
| | | | **COMMODORES**<br>Tuskegee, Alabama soul group led by Lionel Richie | |
| 7/06/74 | 22 | 6 | 1. Machine Gun [I] | Motown 1307 |
| 6/28/75 | 19 | 7 | 2. Slippery When Wet | Motown 1338 |
| 2/14/76 | 5 | 14 | 3. **Sweet Love** | Motown 1381 |
| 10/09/76 | 7 | 11 | 4. **Just To Be Close To You** | Motown 1402 |
| 2/19/77 | 39 | 1 | 5. Fancy Dancer | Motown 1408 |
| 6/25/77 | 4 | 13 | 6. **Easy** | Motown 1418 |
| 9/17/77 | 5 | 11 | 7. **Brick House** | Motown 1425 |
| 1/14/78 | 24 | 7 | 8. Too Hot Ta Trot | Motown 1432 |
| 7/08/78 | 1 (2) | 16 | 9. **Three Times A Lady** | Motown 1443 |
| 11/04/78 | 38 | 2 | 10. Flying High | Motown 1452 |
| 8/18/79 | 4 | 12 | 11. **Sail On** | Motown 1466 |
| 10/13/79 | 1 (1) | 15 | 12. **Still** | Motown 1474 |
| 1/26/80 | 25 | 6 | 13. Wonderland | Motown 1479 |
| 7/12/80 | 20 | 11 | 14. Old-Fashion Love | Motown 1489 |
| 7/11/81 | 8 | 15 | 15. **Lady (You Bring Me Up)** | Motown 1514 |
| 10/10/81 | 4 | 15 | 16. **Oh No** | Motown 1527 |
| | | | **PERRY COMO**<br>vocalist with Ted Weems' band from 1936 to 1942 | |
| 2/05/55 | 2 (3) | 14 | 1. **Ko Ko Mo (I Love You So)** | RCA 5994 |
| 8/13/55 | 5 | 14 | 2. **Tina Marie/** | |
| 8/20/55 | 20 | 1 | 3. Fooled | RCA 6192 |
| 11/19/55 + | 11 | 11 | 4. All At Once You Love Her<br>from the musical "Pipe Dream" | RCA 6294 |
| 3/10/56 | 1 (1) | 20 | 5. **Hot Diggity (Dog Ziggity Boom)/** | |
| 3/10/56 | 10 | 10 | 6. **Juke Box Baby** | RCA 6427 |
| 6/16/56 | 4 | 14 | 7. **More/** | |
| 6/23/56 | 8 | 12 | 8. **Glendora** | RCA 6554 |
| 8/25/56 | 18 | 3 | 9. Somebody Up There Likes Me | RCA 6590 |
| 3/02/57 | 1 (2) | 19 | 10. **Round And Round** | RCA 6815 |
| 5/27/57 | 13 | 7 | 11. The Girl With The Golden Braids | RCA 6904 |
| 10/14/57 | 12 | 14 | 12. Just Born (To Be Your Baby)/ | |
| 10/21/57 | 18 | 8 | 13. Ivy Rose | RCA 7050 |

| DATE | POS | WKS | ARTIST—Record Title | LABEL & NO. |
|---|---|---|---|---|
| 1/13/58 | 1 (1) | 16 | ● 14. **Catch A Falling Star/** | |
| 1/20/58 | 4 | 12 | 15. **Magic Moments** | RCA 7128 |
| 4/21/58 | 6 | 11 | 16. **Kewpie Doll/** | |
| 5/05/58 | 19 | 1 | 17. Dance Only With Me<br>from the musical "Say Darling" | RCA 7202 |
| 8/04/58 | 28 | 6 | 18. Moon Talk | RCA 7274 |
| 11/17/58 | 33 | 2 | 19. Love Makes The World Go 'Round | RCA 7353 |
| 3/23/59 | 29 | 3 | 20. Tomboy | RCA 7464 |
| 2/22/60 | 22 | 6 | 21. Delaware [N] | RCA 7670 |
| 4/28/62 | 23 | 6 | 22. Caterina | RCA 8004 |
| 7/20/63 | 39 | 1 | 23. (I Love You) Don't You Forget It | RCA 8186 |
| 5/01/65 | 25 | 6 | 24. Dream On Little Dreamer | RCA 8533 |
| 5/31/69 | 38 | 1 | 25. Seattle<br>from TV's "Here Come The Brides" | RCA 9722 |
| 12/05/70 + | 10 | 13 | 26. **It's Impossible** | RCA 0387 |
| 5/19/73 | 29 | 8 | 27. And I Love You So | RCA 0906 |
| | | | **PERRY COMO & JAYE P. MORGAN** | |
| 6/11/55 | 12 | 5 | 1. Chee Chee-Oo-Chee (Sang The Little Bird)/ | |
| 6/25/55 | 18 | 1 | 2. Two Lost Souls<br>from the musical "Damn Yankees" | RCA 6137 |
| | | | **CON FUNK SHUN**<br>7-man funk/soul band led by Michael Cooper | |
| 1/21/78 | 23 | 6 | 1. Ffun | Mercury 73959 |
| 2/28/81 | 40 | 1 | 2. Too Tight | Mercury 76089 |
| | | | **ARTHUR CONLEY**<br>discovered and produced by Otis Redding | |
| 4/01/67 | 2 (1) | 11 | ● 1. **Sweet Soul Music** | Atco 6463 |
| 7/01/67 | 31 | 3 | 2. Shake, Rattle & Roll | Atco 6494 |
| 4/06/68 | 14 | 9 | 3. Funky Street | Atco 6563 |
| | | | **RAY CONNIFF & The Singers**<br>arranger/conductor for Columbia's leading singers | |
| 7/09/66 | 9 | 9 | 1. **Somewhere, My Love**<br>Lara's Theme from the film "Dr. Zhivago" | Columbia 43626 |
| | | | **CHRIS CONNOR**<br>singer with Stan Kenton's band from 1952-53 | |
| 2/16/57 | 34 | 3 | 1. I Miss You So | Atlantic 1105 |
| | | | **NORMAN CONNORS**<br>jazz/soul drummer | |
| 10/02/76 | 27 | 10 | 1. You Are My Starship<br>featuring vocalist Michael Henderson | Buddah 542 |
| | | | **BILL CONTI** | |
| 5/07/77 | 1 (1) | 13 | ● 1. **Gonna Fly Now (Theme From "Rocky") [I]** | United Art. 940 |
| | | | **CONTOURS**<br>Detroit sextet | |
| 9/22/62 | 3 | 11 | 1. **Do You Love Me** | Gordy 7005 |

| DATE | POS | WKS | ARTIST—Record Title | LABEL & NO. |
|---|---|---|---|---|
| | | | **SAM COOKE** | |
| | | | born in Chicago, Illinois on 1/22/35 - died in a shooting incident on 12/11/64 (29) | |
| 10/28/57 | **1** (3) | 17 | 1. **You Send Me** | Keen 34013 |
| 12/23/57 + | **18** | 10 | 2. I'll Come Running Back To You | Specialty 619 |
| 1/06/58 | **17** | 7 | 3. (I Love You) For Sentimental Reasons | Keen 4002 |
| 3/24/58 | **26** | 5 | 4. Lonely Island/ | |
| 3/31/58 | **39** | 1 | 5. You Were Made For Me | Keen 4009 |
| 9/08/58 | **22** | 6 | 6. Win Your Love For Me | Keen 2006 |
| 12/15/58 | **26** | 7 | 7. Love You Most Of All | Keen 2008 |
| 3/30/59 | **31** | 5 | 8. Everybody Likes To Cha Cha Cha | Keen 2018 |
| 7/06/59 | **28** | 4 | 9. Only Sixteen | Keen 2022 |
| 5/23/60 | **12** | 11 | 10. Wonderful World | Keen 2112 |
| 8/29/60 | **2** (2) | 13 | 11. **Chain Gang** | RCA 7783 |
| 12/19/60 | **29** | 2 | 12. Sad Mood | RCA 7816 |
| 3/20/61 | **31** | 4 | 13. That's It-I Quit-I'm Movin' On | RCA 7853 |
| 6/26/61 | **17** | 9 | 14. Cupid | RCA 7883 |
| 2/17/62 | **9** | 13 | 15. **Twistin' The Night Away** | RCA 7983 |
| 6/16/62 | **17** | 9 | 16. Having A Party/ | |
| 8/04/62 | **13** | 5 | 17. Bring It On Home To Me<br>backing vocals by Lou Rawls | RCA 8036 |
| 10/20/62 | **12** | 8 | 18. Nothing Can Change This Love | RCA 8088 |
| 2/02/63 | **13** | 8 | 19. Send Me Some Lovin' | RCA 8129 |
| 5/04/63 | **10** | 9 | 20. **Another Saturday Night** | RCA 8164 |
| 8/17/63 | **14** | 7 | 21. Frankie And Johnny | RCA 8215 |
| 11/09/63 | **11** | 8 | 22. Little Red Rooster | RCA 8247 |
| 2/15/64 | **11** | 7 | 23. Good News | RCA 8299 |
| 6/27/64 | **11** | 7 | 24. Good Times/ | |
| 7/04/64 | **35** | 4 | 25. Tennessee Waltz | RCA 8368 |
| 10/24/64 | **31** | 4 | 26. Cousin Of Mine | RCA 8426 |
| 1/16/65 | **7** | 9 | 27. **Shake**/ | |
| 2/13/65 | **31** | 4 | 28. A Change Is Gonna Come | RCA 8486 |
| 8/28/65 | **32** | 3 | 29. Sugar Dumpling | RCA 8631 |
| | | | **COOKIES** | |
| | | | female backing trio for Little Eva, Carole King and others - also see Earl-Jean | |
| 12/01/62 | **17** | 8 | 1. Chains | Dimension 1002 |
| 3/23/63 | **7** | 9 | 2. **Don't Say Nothin' Bad (About My Baby)** | Dimension 1008 |
| 1/18/64 | **33** | 4 | 3. Girls Grow Up Faster Than Boys | Dimension 1020 |
| | | | **EDDIE COOLEY & The Dimples** | |
| 11/24/56 | **20** | 8 | 1. Priscilla | Royal Roost 621 |
| | | | **RITA COOLIDGE** | |
| | | | began career as one of the Friends of Delaney & Bonnie | |
| 6/11/77 | **2** (1) | 17 | ● 1. **(Your Love Has Lifted Me) Higher And Higher** | A&M 1922 |
| 10/15/77 | **7** | 13 | ● 2. **We're All Alone** | A&M 1965 |

| DATE | POS | WKS | ARTIST—Record Title | LABEL & NO. |
|------|-----|-----|---------------------|-------------|
| 2/04/78 | **20** | 7 | 3. The Way You Do The Things You Do | A&M 2004 |
| 7/29/78 | **25** | 6 | 4. You | A&M 2058 |
| 1/05/80 | **38** | 2 | 5. I'd Rather Leave While I'm In Love | A&M 2199 |
| 8/06/83 | **36** | 4 | 6. All Time High<br>from the film "Octopussy" | A&M 2551 |
| | | | **ALICE COOPER**<br>real name: Vincent Furnier - stage show known as Theatre Of The Absurd | |
| 3/20/71 | **21** | 8 | 1. Eighteen | Warner 7449 |
| 6/24/72 | **7** | 10 | 2. **School's Out** | Warner 7596 |
| 10/21/72 | **26** | 6 | 3. Elected | Warner 7631 |
| 3/10/73 | **35** | 3 | 4. Hello Hurray | Warner 7673 |
| 5/12/73 | **25** | 8 | 5. No More Mr. Nice Guy | Warner 7691 |
| 5/03/75 | **12** | 11 | 6. Only Women | Atlantic 3254 |
| 10/30/76 + | **12** | 14 | ● 7. I Never Cry | Warner 8228 |
| 6/11/77 | **9** | 13 | 8. **You And Me** | Warner 8349 |
| 11/11/78 | **12** | 11 | 9. How You Gonna See Me Now | Warner 8695 |
| 7/05/80 | **40** | 1 | 10. Clones (We're All) | Warner 49204 |
| | | | **LES COOPER & The Soul Rockers** | |
| 11/17/62 + | **22** | 11 | 1. Wiggle Wobble [I] | Everlast 5019 |
| | | | **KEN COPELAND** | |
| 4/20/57 | **12** | 8 | 1. Pledge Of Love | Imperial 5432 |
| | | | **JILL COREY**<br>real name: Norma Jean Speranza | |
| 2/02/57 | **21** | 5 | 1. I Love My Baby (My Baby Loves Me) | Columbia 40794 |
| 8/05/57 | **11** | 9 | 2. Love Me To Pieces | Columbia 40955 |
| | | | **CORNELIUS BROTHERS & SISTER ROSE**<br>Edward, Carter & Rose Cornelius | |
| 5/15/71 | **3** | 13 | ● 1. **Treat Her Like A Lady** | United Art. 50721 |
| 6/17/72 | **2** (2) | 11 | ● 2. **Too Late To Turn Back Now** | United Art. 50910 |
| 9/23/72 | **23** | 7 | 3. Don't Ever Be Lonely (A Poor Little Fool Like Me) | United Art. 50954 |
| 2/03/73 | **37** | 2 | 4. I'm Never Gonna Be Alone Anymore | United Art. 50996 |
| | | | **DON CORNELL**<br>vocalist with Sammy Kaye's band (1942-49) | |
| 5/14/55 | **14** | 6 | 1. Most Of All | Coral 61393 |
| 9/10/55 | **7** | 13 | 2. **The Bible Tells Me So/** | |
| 11/05/55 | **26** | 3 | 3.  Love Is A Many-Splendored Thing | Coral 61467 |
| 11/12/55 | **25** | 1 | 4. Young Abe Lincoln | Coral 61521 |
| | | | **CORSAIRS**<br>featuring Jay "Bird" Uzzell (artist trivia) | |
| 1/27/62 | **12** | 10 | 1. Smoky Places | Tuff 1808 |
| | | | **DAVE "BABY" CORTEZ**<br>rock and roll organist | |
| 3/30/59 | **1** (1) | 14 | 1. **The Happy Organ [I]** | Clock 1009 |
| 8/11/62 | **10** | 9 | 2. **Rinky Dink [I]** | Chess 1829 |

| DATE | POS | WKS | ARTIST—Record Title | LABEL & NO. |
|---|---|---|---|---|
| | | | **BILL COSBY** | |
| | | | Comedian - played Alexander Scott on TV series "I Spy" -<br>star of new NBC-TV series "The Cosby Show" | |
| 9/16/67 | 4 | 8 | 1. **Little Ole Man (Uptight-Everything's<br>Alright) [N]** | Warner 7072 |
| | | | **DON COSTA & His Orchestra** | |
| | | | founded DCP Records (Don Costa Productions) - died 1/19/83 (57) | |
| 6/27/60 | 27 | 4 | 1. Theme From "The Unforgiven" (The Need<br>For Love) [I] | United Art. 221 |
| 8/29/60 | 19 | 14 | 2. Never On Sunday [I] | United Art. 234 |
| | | | **ELVIS COSTELLO & The Attractions** | |
| | | | born Declan McManus in Liverpool, England | |
| 10/15/83 | 36 | 2 | 1. Everyday I Write The Book | Columbia 04045 |
| | | | **GENE COTTON** | |
| | | | singer/songwriter from Columbus, Ohio | |
| 1/22/77 | 33 | 3 | 1. You've Got Me Runnin' | ABC 12227 |
| 3/04/78 | 23 | 7 | 2. Before My Heart Finds Out | Ariola 7675 |
| 11/11/78 | 40 | 2 | 3. Like A Sunday In Salem (The Amos &<br>Andy Song) | Ariola 7723 |
| | | | **GENE COTTON with KIM CARNES** | |
| 8/05/78 | 36 | 3 | 1. You're A Part Of Me | Ariola 7704 |
| | | | **JOHN COUGAR** | |
| | | | born John Cougar Mellencamp on 10/7/51 in Seymour, Indiana | |
| 11/10/79 | 28 | 8 | 1. I Need A Lover | Riva 202 |
| 11/08/80 | 27 | 7 | 2. This Time | Riva 205 |
| 3/14/81 | 17 | 12 | 3. Ain't Even Done With The Night | Riva 207 |
| 5/22/82 | 2 (4) | 22 | ● 4. **Hurts So Good** | Riva 209 |
| 8/07/82 | 1 (4) | 17 | ● 5. **Jack & Diane** | Riva 210 |
| 11/27/82 + | 19 | 11 | 6. Hand To Hold On To | Riva 211 |
| 10/22/83 | 9 | 11 | 7. **Crumblin' Down** | Riva 214 |
| 12/17/83 + | 8 | 11 | 8. **Pink Houses** | Riva 215 |
| 3/31/84 | 15 | 9 | 9. Authority Song | Riva 216 |
| | | | **COUNT FIVE** | |
| | | | 5 teenagers from San Jose, California | |
| 9/24/66 | 5 | 9 | 1. **Psychotic Reaction** | Double Shot 104 |
| | | | **DON COVAY** | |
| 10/03/64 | 35 | 5 | 1. Mercy, Mercy<br>Don Covay & The Goodtimers | Rosemart 801 |
| 8/11/73 | 29 | 5 | 2. I Was Checkin' Out She Was<br>Checkin' In | Mercury 73385 |
| | | | **COVEN** | |
| 10/30/71 | 26 | 6 | 1. One Tin Soldier [The Legend Of Billy Jack] | Warner 7509 |
| | | | **COWBOY CHURCH SUNDAY SCHOOL** | |
| 1/01/55 | 8 | 21 | 1. **Open Up Your Heart (And Let The<br>Sunshine In) [N]** | Decca 29367 |

| DATE | POS | WKS | ARTIST—Record Title | LABEL & NO. |
|---|---|---|---|---|
| | | | **COWSILLS** | |
| | | | Newport, Rhode Island family | |
| 10/21/67 | 2 (2) | 12 | ● 1. **The Rain, The Park & Other Things** | MGM 13810 |
| 2/03/68 | 21 | 6 | 2. We Can Fly | MGM 13886 |
| 6/22/68 | 10 | 9 | 3. Indian Lake | MGM 13944 |
| 3/29/69 | 2 (2) | 13 | ● 4. **Hair** | MGM 14026 |
| | | | **CRABBY APPLETON** | |
| | | | West Coast rock quintet led by Michael Fennelly | |
| 6/27/70 | 36 | 5 | 1. Go Back | Elektra 45687 |
| | | | **BILLY "CRASH" CRADDOCK** | |
| | | | country/rock singer from Greensboro, North Carolina | |
| 7/27/74 | 16 | 9 | 1. Rub It In | ABC 12013 |
| 12/28/74 + | 33 | 2 | 2. Ruby, Baby | ABC 12036 |
| | | | **FLOYD CRAMER** | |
| | | | Nashville's top session pianist | |
| 10/31/60 | 2 (4) | 15 | 1. **Last Date [I]** | RCA 7775 |
| 3/13/61 | 4 | 11 | 2. **On The Rebound [I]** | RCA 7840 |
| 6/26/61 | 8 | 8 | 3. **San Antonio Rose [I]** | RCA 7893 |
| 2/24/62 | 36 | 2 | 4. Chattanooga Choo Choo [I] | RCA 7978 |
| | | | **LES CRANE** | |
| | | | TV talk-show host from San Francisco | |
| 10/23/71 | 8 | 10 | 1. **Desiderata [S]** | Warner 7520 |
| | | | **JOHNNY CRAWFORD** | |
| | | | Mark McCain of TV's "The Rifleman" | |
| 6/02/62 | 8 | 9 | 1. **Cindy's Birthday** | Del-Fi 4178 |
| 8/25/62 | 14 | 6 | 2. Your Nose Is Gonna Grow | Del-Fi 4181 |
| 11/24/62 | 12 | 7 | 3. Rumors | Del-Fi 4188 |
| 1/26/63 | 29 | 4 | 4. Proud | Del-Fi 4193 |
| | | | **CRAZY ELEPHANT** | |
| 4/05/69 | 12 | 8 | 1. Gimme Gimme Good Lovin' | Bell 763 |
| | | | **CRAZY OTTO** | |
| | | | German pianist Fritz Schulz-Reichel - also see Johnny Maddox | |
| 2/26/55 | 19 | 5 | 1. Glad Rag Doll/ [I] | |
| 2/26/55 | 21 | 3 | 2.  Smiles [I] | Decca 29403 |
| | | | **CREAM** | |
| | | | British: Eric Clapton, Ginger Baker and Jack Bruce | |
| 2/24/68 | 5 | 12 | ● 1. **Sunshine Of Your Love** | Atco 6544 |
| 10/19/68 | 6 | 9 | 2. **White Room** | Atco 6617 |
| 2/08/69 | 28 | 6 | 3. Crossroads | Atco 6646 |
| | | | **CREEDENCE CLEARWATER REVIVAL** | |
| | | | four-man group from San Francisco, led by John Fogerty | |
| 9/28/68 | 11 | 9 | 1. Suzie Q. (Part One) | Fantasy 616 |
| 2/08/69 | 2 (3) | 12 | ● 2. **Proud Mary** | Fantasy 619 |
| 5/17/69 | 2 (1) | 12 | ● 3. **Bad Moon Rising** | Fantasy 622 |
| 8/09/69 | 2 (1) | 11 | 4. **Green River/** | |

| DATE | POS | WKS | ARTIST—Record Title | LABEL & NO. |
|------|-----|-----|---------------------|-------------|
| 8/09/69 | 30 | 7 | 5.  Commotion | Fantasy 625 |
| 11/08/69 | 3 | 13 | ● 6. **Down On The Corner/** | |
| | | 13 | 7. **Fortunate Son** | Fantasy 634 |
| 2/07/70 | 2 (2) | 9 | ● 8. **Travelin' Band/** | |
| | | 9 | 9. **Who'll Stop The Rain** | Fantasy 637 |
| 5/02/70 | 4 | 10 | ● 10. **Up Around The Bend** | Fantasy 641 |
| 8/15/70 | 2 (1) | 12 | ● 11. **Lookin' Out My Back Door** | Fantasy 645 |
| 2/06/71 | 8 | 9 | ● 12. **Have You Ever Seen The Rain** | Fantasy 655 |
| 7/24/71 | 6 | 8 | 13. **Sweet Hitch-Hiker** | Fantasy 665 |
| 5/20/72 | 25 | 5 | 14. Someday Never Comes | Fantasy 676 |
| | | | **MARSHALL CRENSHAW** | |
| 8/14/82 | 36 | 4 | 1. Someday, Someway | Warner 29974 |
| | | | **CRESCENDOS** | |
| | | | quartet from Nashville - Dale Ward, lead singer | |
| 1/20/58 | 5 | 14 | 1. **Oh Julie** | Nasco 6005 |
| | | | **CRESTS** | |
| | | | New York quartet - Johnny Maestro, lead singer | |
| 12/22/58 + | 2 (2) | 14 | 1. **16 Candles** | Coed 506 |
| 4/13/59 | 28 | 7 | 2. Six Nights A Week | Coed 509 |
| 9/14/59 | 22 | 9 | 3. The Angels Listened In | Coed 515 |
| 4/04/60 | 14 | 8 | 4. Step By Step | Coed 525 |
| 7/18/60 | 20 | 8 | 5. Trouble In Paradise | Coed 531 |
| | | | **CREW-CUTS** | |
| | | | Canadian quartet | |
| 1/29/55 | 3 | 13 | 1. **Earth Angel/** | |
| 1/29/55 | 6 | 12 | 2.  **Ko Ko Mo (I Love You So)** | Mercury 70529 |
| 4/30/55 | 14 | 8 | 3. Don't Be Angry | Mercury 70597 |
| 6/25/55 | 16 | 7 | 4. A Story Untold | Mercury 70634 |
| 8/27/55 | 10 | 8 | 5. **Gum Drop** | Mercury 70668 |
| 12/17/55 + | 11 | 15 | 6. Angels In The Sky/ | |
| 1/07/56 | 31 | 8 | 7.  Mostly Martha | Mercury 70741 |
| 2/18/56 | 18 | 5 | 8. Seven Days | Mercury 70782 |
| 1/26/57 | 17 | 3 | 9. Young Love | Mercury 71022 |
| | | | **BOB CREWE Generation** | |
| | | | Bob produced many of the Four Seasons' hits | |
| 1/21/67 | 15 | 7 | 1. Music To Watch Girls By [I] | DynoVoice 229 |
| | | | **CRICKETS** | |
| | | | Lubbock, Texas quartet: Buddy Holly, Jerry Allison, Joe Mauldin, & Niki Sullivan (left Nov. '57) | |
| 8/19/57 | 1 (1) | 16 | ● 1. **That'll Be The Day** | Brunswick 55009 |
| 12/02/57 + | 10 | 13 | 2. **Oh, Boy!** | Brunswick 55035 |
| 3/10/58 | 17 | 8 | 3. Maybe Baby | Brunswick 55053 |
| 8/04/58 | 27 | 4 | 4. Think It Over | Brunswick 55072 |
| | | | **CRITTERS** | |
| | | | New Jersey quintet | |
| 9/03/66 | 17 | 8 | 1. Mr. Dieingly Sad | Kapp 769 |
| 8/05/67 | 39 | 3 | 2. Don't Let The Rain Fall Down On Me | Kapp 838 |

| DATE | POS | WKS | ARTIST—Record Title | LABEL & NO. |
|------|-----|-----|---------------------|-------------|
| | | | **JIM CROCE** | |
| | | | killed in a plane crash on 9/20/73 (30) | |
| 7/22/72 | 8 | 10 | 1. **You Don't Mess Around With Jim** | ABC 11328 |
| 11/04/72 | 17 | 8 | 2. Operator (That's Not The Way It Feels) | ABC 11335 |
| 3/17/73 | 37 | 3 | 3. One Less Set Of Footsteps | ABC 11346 |
| 6/02/73 | 1 (2) | 16 | ● 4. **Bad, Bad Leroy Brown** | ABC 11359 |
| 10/13/73 | 10 | 13 | 5. **I Got A Name** | ABC 11389 |
| | | | from the film "Last American Hero" | |
| 12/01/73 | 1 (2) | 12 | ● 6. **Time In A Bottle** | ABC 11405 |
| 3/16/74 | 9 | 11 | 7. **I'll Have To Say I Love You In A Song** | ABC 11424 |
| 6/29/74 | 32 | 6 | 8. Workin' At The Car Wash Blues | ABC 11447 |
| | | | **BING CROSBY** | |
| | | | Harry Lillis Crosby - began career with Paul Whiteman in 1926- died on 10/14/77 (76) | |
| 12/31/55 | 7 | 2 | 1. **White Christmas [R-X]** | Decca 29342 |
| | | | originally charted December, 1942, and re-entered the pop charts for 18 more seasons | |
| 10/21/57 | 25 | 1 | 2. Around The World (In Eighty Days) | Decca 30262 |
| 12/23/57 | 34 | 2 | 3. White Christmas [R-X] | Decca 29342 |
| 12/19/60 | 26 | 2 | 4. White Christmas [R-X] | Decca 23778 |
| 12/18/61 | 12 | 3 | 5. White Christmas [R-X] | Decca 23778 |
| 12/29/62 | 38 | 1 | 6. White Christmas [R-X] | Decca 23778 |
| | | | **BING CROSBY & GRACE KELLY** | |
| | | | Grace died in an auto accident on 9/14/82 (52) | |
| 10/06/56 | 3 | 22 | 1. **True Love** | Capitol 3507 |
| | | | from the film "High Society" | |
| | | | **DAVID CROSBY/GRAHAM NASH** | |
| 6/10/72 | 36 | 4 | 1. Immigration Man | Atlantic 2873 |
| | | | **CROSBY, STILLS & NASH** | |
| | | | David Crosby/Stephen Stills/Graham Nash | |
| 8/02/69 | 28 | 6 | 1. Marrakesh Express | Atlantic 2652 |
| 10/25/69 | 21 | 9 | 2. Suite: Judy Blue Eyes | Atlantic 2676 |
| 7/02/77 | 7 | 12 | 3. **Just A Song Before I Go** | Atlantic 3401 |
| 7/03/82 | 9 | 12 | 4. **Wasted On The Way** | Atlantic 4058 |
| 10/09/82 | 18 | 9 | 5. Southern Cross | Atlantic 89969 |
| | | | **CROSBY, STILLS, NASH & YOUNG** | |
| | | | David Crosby/Stephen Stills/Graham Nash/Neil Young | |
| 4/04/70 | 11 | 10 | 1. Woodstock | Atlantic 2723 |
| 6/20/70 | 16 | 9 | 2. Teach Your Children | Atlantic 2735 |
| 7/11/70 | 14 | 7 | 3. Ohio | Atlantic 2740 |
| 10/10/70 | 30 | 6 | 4. Our House | Atlantic 2760 |
| | | | **CROSS COUNTRY** | |
| | | | group evolved from The Tokens | |
| 9/22/73 | 30 | 4 | 1. In The Midnight Hour | Atco 6934 |
| | | | **CHRISTOPHER CROSS** | |
| | | | real name: Christopher Geppert | |
| 3/01/80 | 2 (4) | 17 | 1. **Ride Like The Wind** | Warner 49184 |
| 7/05/80 | 1 (1) | 13 | 2. **Sailing** | Warner 49507 |

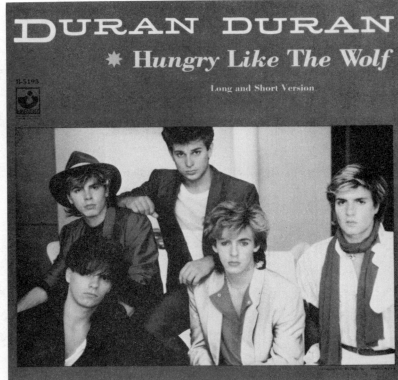

**The Dovells,** residents of Philadelphia, spawned Len Barry, singer of the 1965 smash "1–2–3". Their name came from a Florida hotel (the Dovel) frequented by their record company president.

**Patty Duke** sure covered a lot of ground. She had an Oscar-winning performance in the 1962 movie *The Miracle Worker,* a popular TV sitcom (with guests like Chad and Jeremy, and Bobby Vinton), and melodramatic pop records.

**Duran Duran** took their name from a character in the comic-strip movie *Barbarella,* which indicated vision for a band from the grimy industrial city of Birmingham, England. Today they hold the world's record for number of unrelated members named Taylor (three).

**Bob Dylan's** 1966 single "I Want You" is prized by collectors because the B-side is a live version of "Just Like Tom Thumb's Blues," recorded in Liverpool with the Band and unavailable on any LP.

**The Eagles** began with an impressive list of credentials. Various members had played with such heavies as Linda Ronstadt, the Flying Burrito Bros., and Poco, not to mention obscure bands Shiloh and Longbranch Pennywhistle.

**Sheena Easton** wanted to title her first American single "Nine to Five" the way she had in England, but Dolly Parton had already released a song with the same name. "Morning Train (Nine to Five)" went to Number One anyway.

**Duane Eddy** unveiled a twangy guitar sound on his very first single, 1958's "Moovin' N' Groovin'." The first record executive approached said it sounded like someone trying "to string telephone wire across the Grand Canyon" and turned it down. His mistake.

**Eurythmics'** Annie Lennox and Dave Stewart were the driving force behind the Tourists, who reached the Top 83 in 1980 with a remake of the Dusty Springfield/Bay City Rollers classic "I Only Want to Be With You."

**The Everly Brothers** became fast friends with Buddy Holly during a 1958 tour. Holly subsequently presented the Brothers with demos of two of his own songs—"Love's Made a Fool of You" and "Wishing"—but they never recorded either of them.

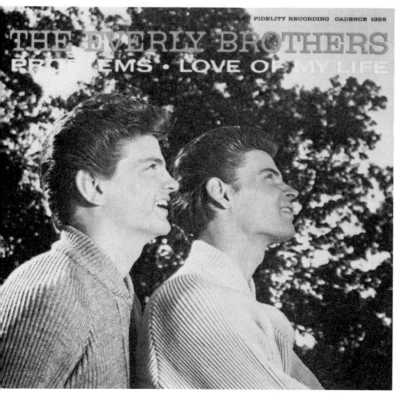

| DATE | POS | WKS | ARTIST—Record Title | LABEL & NO. |
|---|---|---|---|---|
| 10/25/80 | 15 | 12 | 3. Never Be The Same | Warner 49580 |
| 4/25/81 | 20 | 7 | 4. Say You'll Be Mine | Warner 49705 |
| 8/29/81 | 1 (3) | 17 | ● 5. **Arthur's Theme (Best That You Can Do)** | Warner 49787 |
| 1/22/83 | 12 | 13 | 6. All Right | Warner 29843 |
| 5/21/83 | 33 | 5 | 7. No Time For Talk | Warner 29662 |
| 12/24/83 + | 9 | 11 | 8. **Think Of Laura** | Warner 29658 |
| | | | popularized through play on TV's "General Hospital" | |
| | | | **CROW** | |
| | | | rock/blues quintet - Dave Wagner, lead singer | |
| 11/29/69 + | 19 | 10 | 1. Evil Woman Don't Play Your Games With Me | Amaret 112 |
| | | | **RODNEY CROWELL** | |
| | | | Rosanne Cash's husband | |
| 6/28/80 | 37 | 2 | 1. Ashes By Now | Warner 49224 |
| | | | **CRUSADERS** | |
| | | | contemporary jazz group led by Wilton Felder (reeds), Joe Sample (keyboards) & Stix Hooper (drums) | |
| 10/27/79 | 36 | 3 | 1. Street Life | MCA 41054 |
| | | | vocal by Randy Crawford | |
| | | | **CRYSTALS** | |
| | | | Brooklyn female quintet produced by Phil Spector | |
| 12/11/61 + | 20 | 7 | 1. There's No Other (Like My Baby) | Philles 100 |
| 4/28/62 | 13 | 8 | 2. Uptown | Philles 102 |
| 10/06/62 | 1 (2) | 12 | 3. He's A Rebel | Philles 106 |
| 1/19/63 | 11 | 8 | 4. He's Sure The Boy I Love | Philles 109 |
| 5/11/63 | 3 | 10 | 5. **Da Doo Ron Ron (When He Walked Me Home)** | Philles 112 |
| 8/31/63 | 6 | 9 | 6. **Then He Kissed Me** | Philles 115 |
| | | | **CUFF LINKS** | |
| | | | featuring the vocals of Ron Dante (Archies) | |
| 10/04/69 | 9 | 9 | 1. **Tracy** | Decca 32533 |
| | | | **CULTURE CLUB** | |
| | | | English quartet led by Boy George (real name: George O'Dowd) | |
| 1/15/83 | 2 (3) | 18 | 1. **Do You Really Want To Hurt Me** | Epic 03368 |
| 4/30/83 | 2 (2) | 13 | 2. **Time (Clock Of The Heart)** | Epic 03796 |
| 7/16/83 | 9 | 12 | 3. **I'll Tumble 4 Ya** | Epic 03912 |
| 10/29/83 | 10 | 12 | 4. **Church Of The Poison Mind** | Epic 04144 |
| 12/10/83 + | 1 (3) | 16 | ● 5. **Karma Chameleon** | Virgin 04221 |
| 3/03/84 | 5 | 12 | 6. **Miss Me Blind** | Virgin 04388 |
| 5/19/84 | 13 | 8 | 7. It's A Miracle | Virgin 04457 |
| 10/20/84 | 17 | 0 | 8. The War Song | Virgin 04638 |
| | | | **BURTON CUMMINGS** | |
| | | | lead singer of The Guess Who | |
| 11/06/76 + | 10 | 15 | ● 1. **Stand Tall** | Portrait 70001 |
| 10/24/81 | 37 | 2 | 2. You Saved My Soul | Alfa 7008 |
| | | | **MIKE CURB Congregation** | |
| 2/27/71 | 34 | 4 | 1. Burning Bridges | MGM 14151 |
| | | | from the film "Kelly's Heroes" | |

| DATE | POS | WKS | ARTIST—Record Title | LABEL & NO. |
|---|---|---|---|---|
| | | | **CYMARRON** | |
| | | | group name taken from the TV series "Cimarron Strip" | |
| 7/17/71 | 17 | 7 | 1. Rings | Entrance 7500 |
| | | | **JOHNNY CYMBAL** | |
| | | | also see Derek | |
| 3/16/63 | 16 | 8 | 1. Mr. Bass Man [N] | Kapp 503 |
| | | | bass singer: Ronnie Bright (Coasters) | |
| | | | **CYRKLE** | |
| | | | American group managed by The Beatles' manager Brian Epstein | |
| 6/04/66 | 2 (1) | 11 | 1. **Red Rubber Ball** | Columbia 43589 |
| 8/27/66 | 16 | 5 | 2. Turn-Down Day | Columbia 43729 |
| | | | **DADDY DEWDROP** | |
| | | | Richard Monda | |
| 4/10/71 | 9 | 11 | 1. **Chick-A-Boom (Don't Ya Jes' Love It)** | Sunflower 105 |
| | | | **DADDY-O'S** | |
| | | | a Billy Mure production | |
| 6/23/58 | 39 | 3 | 1. Got A Match? [I] | Cabot 122 |
| | | | **DALE & GRACE** | |
| | | | Dale Houston & Grace Broussard | |
| 10/26/63 | 1 (2) | 12 | 1. **I'm Leaving It Up To You** | Montel 921 |
| 2/08/64 | 8 | 7 | 2. **Stop And Think It Over** | Montel 922 |
| | | | **ALAN DALE** | |
| 4/30/55 | 14 | 7 | 1. Cherry Pink (And Apple Blossom White) | Coral 61373 |
| | | | from the film "Under Water!" | |
| 7/02/55 | 10 | 7 | 2. **Sweet And Gentle** | Coral 61435 |
| | | | **ROGER DALTREY** | |
| | | | lead singer of The Who - star of rock opera film "Tommy" | |
| 10/25/80 | 20 | 8 | 1. Without Your Love | Polydor 2121 |
| | | | **LIZ DAMON'S Orient Express** | |
| | | | Hawaiian | |
| 1/30/71 | 33 | 3 | 1. 1900 Yesterday | White Whale 368 |
| | | | **VIC DAMONE** | |
| | | | born Vito Farinola on 6/12/28 in Brooklyn, New York | |
| 6/02/56 | 4 | 16 | 1. **On The Street Where You Live** | Columbia 40654 |
| | | | from the musical "My Fair Lady" | |
| 9/30/57 | 16 | 4 | 2. An Affair To Remember (Our Love Affair) | Columbia 40945 |
| 5/22/65 | 30 | 4 | 3. You Were Only Fooling (While I Was Falling In Love) | Warner 5616 |
| | | | **VIC DANA** | |
| | | | born on 8/26/42 in Buffalo, New York | |
| 4/25/64 | 27 | 5 | 1. Shangri-La | Dolton 92 |
| 3/06/65 | 10 | 8 | 2. **Red Roses For A Blue Lady** | Dolton 304 |
| 6/04/66 | 30 | 4 | 3. I Love You Drops | Dolton 319 |
| | | | **DANCER, PRANCER & NERVOUS** | |
| 12/28/59 | 34 | 1 | 1. The Happy Reindeer [X-N] | Capitol 4300 |

| DATE | POS | WKS | ARTIST—Record Title | LABEL & NO. |
|---|---|---|---|---|
| | | | **CHARLIE DANIELS Band** | |
| | | | Southern rock/boogie band | |
| 7/21/73 | **9** | 9 | 1. **Uneasy Rider [N]** | Kama Sutra 576 |
| 3/15/75 | **29** | 3 | 2. The South's Gonna Do It | Kama Sutra 598 |
| 7/21/79 | **3** | 12 | ● 3. **The Devil Went Down To Georgia** | Epic 50700 |
| 6/28/80 | **11** | 8 | 4. In America | Epic 50888 |
| 9/27/80 | **31** | 4 | 5. The Legend Of Wooley Swamp | Epic 50921 |
| 4/17/82 | **22** | 8 | 6. Still In Saigon | Epic 02828 |
| | | | **DANLEERS** | |
| | | | R&B quartet from Brooklyn, New York - Jimmy Weston, lead singer | |
| 6/30/58 | **7** | 10 | 1. **One Summer Night** | Mercury 71322 |
| | | | **DANNY & THE JUNIORS** | |
| | | | Danny Rapp, lead singer of quartet from Philadelphia, died on 4/5/83 (42) | |
| 12/09/57 + | **1** (7) | 18 | 1. **At The Hop** | ABC-Para. 9871 |
| 3/10/58 | **19** | 7 | 2. Rock And Roll Is Here To Stay | ABC-Para. 9888 |
| 7/21/58 | **39** | 1 | 3. Dottie | ABC-Para. 9926 |
| 10/10/60 | **27** | 3 | 4. Twistin' U.S.A. | Swan 4060 |
| | | | **DANTE & The EVERGREENS** | |
| | | | Dante Drowty, lead singer of quartet from Los Angeles | |
| 6/13/60 | **15** | 8 | 1. Alley-Oop [N] | Madison 130 |
| | | | **BOBBY DARIN** | |
| | | | born Walden Robert Cassotto on 5/14/36 in the Bronx, New York - died on 12/20/73 (37) - also see Rinky-Dinks | |
| 6/30/58 | **3** | 13 | 1. **Splish Splash** | Atco 6117 |
| 10/27/58 | **9** | 14 | 2. **Queen Of The Hop** | Atco 6127 |
| 2/23/59 | **38** | 2 | 3. Plain Jane | Atco 6133 |
| 5/04/59 | **2** (1) | 13 | 4. **Dream Lover** | Atco 6140 |
| 9/07/59 | **1** (9) | 22 | 5. **Mack The Knife** | Atco 6147 |
| 1/25/60 | **6** | 11 | 6. **Beyond The Sea** | Atco 6158 |
| 4/04/60 | **21** | 6 | 7. Clementine | Atco 6161 |
| 6/20/60 | **19** | 5 | 8. Won't You Come Home Bill Bailey | Atco 6167 |
| 10/17/60 | **20** | 8 | 9. Artificial Flowers | Atco 6179 |
| | | | from the musical "Tenderloin" | |
| 2/20/61 | **14** | 7 | 10. Lazy River | Atco 6188 |
| 7/10/61 | **40** | 1 | 11. Nature Boy | Atco 6196 |
| 9/11/61 | **5** | 9 | 12. **You Must Have Been A Beautiful Baby** | Atco 6206 |
| 1/13/62 | **15** | 8 | 13. Irresistible You/ | |
| 1/20/62 | **30** | 5 | 14. Multiplication | Atco 6214 |
| | | | from the film "Come September" | |
| 4/14/62 | **24** | 5 | 15. What'd I Say (Part 1) | Atco 6221 |
| 7/21/62 | **3** | 9 | 16. **Things** | Atco 6229 |
| 10/27/62 | **32** | 3 | 17. If A Man Answers | Capitol 4837 |
| 2/02/63 | **3** | 12 | 18. **You're The Reason I'm Living** | Capitol 4897 |
| 5/25/63 | **10** | 7 | 19. **18 Yellow Roses** | Capitol 4970 |
| 10/08/66 | **8** | 9 | 20. **If I Were A Carpenter** | Atlantic 2350 |
| 2/11/67 | **32** | 3 | 21. Lovin' You | Atlantic 2376 |

| DATE | POS | WKS | ARTIST—Record Title | LABEL & NO. |
|------|-----|-----|---------------------|-------------|
| | | | **JAMES DARREN** | |
| | | | born James Ercolani on 10/3/36 in Philadelphia | |
| 11/06/61 | 3 | 12 | 1. **Goodbye Cruel World** | Colpix 609 |
| 2/17/62 | 6 | 8 | 2. **Her Royal Majesty** | Colpix 622 |
| 5/05/62 | 11 | 7 | 3. Conscience | Colpix 630 |
| 8/04/62 | 39 | 1 | 4. Mary's Little Lamb | Colpix 644 |
| 2/18/67 | 35 | 2 | 5. All | Warner 5874 |
| | | | from the film "Run For Your Wife" | |
| | | | **DARTELLS** | |
| | | | 6-man band from Oxnard, California | |
| 4/27/63 | 11 | 9 | 1. Hot Pastrami | Dot 16453 |
| | | | **DAVID & JONATHAN** | |
| | | | English - Roger Greenaway & Roger Cook | |
| 1/29/66 | 18 | 5 | 1. Michelle | Capitol 5563 |
| | | | **MAC DAVIS** | |
| | | | born in Lubbock, Texas on 1/21/42 | |
| 8/05/72 | 1 (3) | 13 | ● 1. **Baby Don't Get Hooked On Me** | Columbia 45618 |
| 5/25/74 | 11 | 14 | 2. One Hell Of A Woman | Columbia 46004 |
| 9/07/74 | 9 | 10 | 3. **Stop And Smell The Roses** | Columbia 10018 |
| 12/21/74 + | 15 | 8 | 4. Rock N' Roll (I Gave You The Best Years Of My Life) | Columbia 10070 |
| | | | **PAUL DAVIS** | |
| | | | born in Meridian, Mississippi on 4/21/48 | |
| 12/07/74 + | 23 | 8 | 1. Ride 'Em Cowboy | Bang 712 |
| 9/11/76 | 35 | 3 | 2. Superstar | Bang 726 |
| 10/29/77 + | 7 | 25 | 3. **I Go Crazy** | Bang 733 |
| 10/07/78 | 17 | 13 | 4. Sweet Life | Bang 738 |
| 4/12/80 | 23 | 6 | 5. Do Right | Bang 4808 |
| 11/28/81 + | 11 | 13 | 6. Cool Night | Arista 0645 |
| 3/20/82 | 6 | 13 | 7. **'65 Love Affair** | Arista 0661 |
| 8/28/82 | 40 | 2 | 8. Love Or Let Me Be Lonely | Arista 0697 |
| | | | **SAMMY DAVIS, JR.** | |
| | | | Sammy lost his left eye in an auto crash on 11/19/54 | |
| 5/28/55 | 9 | 12 | 1. **Something's Gotta Give/** | |
| | | | from the film "Daddy Long Legs" | |
| 6/25/55 | 20 | 1 | 2.  Love Me Or Leave Me | Decca 29484 |
| 7/02/55 | 13 | 6 | 3. That Old Black Magic | Decca 29541 |
| 10/06/62 | 17 | 10 | 4. What Kind Of Fool Am I | Reprise 20048 |
| | | | from the musical "Stop The World-I Want To Get Off" | |
| 2/01/64 | 17 | 9 | 5. The Shelter Of Your Arms | Reprise 20216 |
| 6/24/67 | 37 | 4 | 6. Don't Blame The Children [S] | Reprise 0566 |
| 1/18/69 | 11 | 11 | 7. I've Gotta Be Me | Reprise 0779 |
| | | | from the musical "Golden Rainbow" | |
| 4/15/72 | 1 (3) | 16 | ● 8. **The Candy Man** | MGM 14320 |
| | | | from the film "Willy Wonka And The Chocolate Factory" | |

| DATE | POS | WKS | ARTIST—Record Title | LABEL & NO. |
|------|-----|-----|---------------------|-------------|
| | | | **SKEETER DAVIS** | |
| | | | real name: Mary Frances Penick | |
| 9/05/60 | 39 | 1 | 1. (I Can't Help You) I'm Falling Too | RCA 7767 |
| 1/16/61 | 26 | 2 | 2. My Last Date (With You) | RCA 7825 |
| 2/16/63 | 2 (1) | 13 | 3. **The End Of The World** | RCA 8098 |
| 9/21/63 | 7 | 11 | 4. **I Can't Stay Mad At You** | RCA 8219 |
| | | | **SPENCER DAVIS Group** | |
| | | | British quartet - Steve Winwood, lead singer | |
| 1/28/67 | 7 | 9 | 1. **Gimme Some Lovin'** | United Art. 50108 |
| 4/08/67 | 10 | 7 | 2. **I'm A Man** | United Art. 50144 |
| | | | **TYRONE DAVIS** | |
| | | | blues singer from Chicago | |
| 1/04/69 | 5 | 11 | ● 1. **Can I Change My Mind** | Dakar 602 |
| 4/12/69 | 34 | 2 | 2. Is It Something You've Got | Dakar 605 |
| 4/04/70 | 3 | 11 | ● 3. **Turn Back The Hands Of Time** | Dakar 616 |
| 8/25/73 | 32 | 3 | 4. There It Is | Dakar 4523 |
| 10/30/76 | 38 | 4 | 5. Give It Up (Turn It Loose) | Columbia 10388 |
| | | | **DAWN** | |
| | | | Tony Orlando, Joyce Vincent Wilson & Telma Hopkins | |
| 8/29/70 | 3 | 13 | ● 1. **Candida** | Bell 903 |
| 12/05/70 + | 1 (3) | 16 | ● 2. **Knock Three Times** | Bell 938 |
| 4/10/71 | 25 | 5 | 3. I Play And Sing | Bell 970 |
| 7/10/71 | 33 | 6 | 4. Summer Sand | Bell 45107 |
| | | | DAWN featuring TONY ORLANDO: | |
| 11/13/71 | 39 | 1 | 5. What Are You Doing Sunday | Bell 45141 |
| 3/17/73 | 1 (4) | 17 | ● 6. **Tie A Yellow Ribbon Round The Ole Oak Tree** | Bell 45318 |
| 7/28/73 | 3 | 13 | ● 7. **Say, Has Anybody Seen My Sweet Gypsy Rose** | Bell 45374 |
| | | | TONY ORLANDO & DAWN: | |
| 12/01/73 | 27 | 7 | 8. Who's In The Strawberry Patch With Sally | Bell 45424 |
| 9/07/74 | 7 | 9 | 9. **Steppin' Out (Gonna Boogie Tonight)** | Bell 45601 |
| 1/11/75 | 11 | 8 | 10. Look In My Eyes Pretty Woman | Bell 45620 |
| 3/29/75 | 1 (3) | 10 | ● 11. **He Don't Love You (Like I Love You)** | Elektra 45240 |
| 7/12/75 | 14 | 6 | 12. Mornin' Beautiful | Elektra 45260 |
| 9/20/75 | 34 | 3 | 13. You're All I Need To Get By | Elektra 45275 |
| 2/21/76 | 22 | 6 | 14. Cupid | Elektra 45302 |
| | | | **BOBBY DAY** | |
| | | | real name: Robert Byrd - lead singer of the Hollywood Flames | |
| 8/04/58 | 2 (2) | 19 | 1. **Rock-In Robin** | Class 229 |
| | | | **DORIS DAY** | |
| | | | born Doris Kappelhoff on 4/3/24 - vocalist with Les Brown's band (1943-1946) | |
| 7/23/55 | 13 | 9 | 1. **I'll Never Stop Loving You** <br> from the film "Love Me Or Leave Me" | Columbia 40505 |
| 7/07/56 | 2 (3) | 22 | 2. **Whatever Will Be, Will Be (Que Sera, Sera)** <br> from the film "The Man Who Knew Too Much" | Columbia 40704 |
| 7/21/58 | 6 | 12 | 3. **Everybody Loves A Lover** | Columbia 41195 |

| DATE | POS | WKS | ARTIST—Record Title | LABEL & NO. |
|---|---|---|---|---|
| | | | **DAZZ BAND** | |
| | | | 8-man ultrafunk band - formerly known as Kinsman Dazz | |
| 5/15/82 | 5 | 16 | 1. **Let It Whip** | Motown 1609 |
| | | | **BILL DEAL & THE RHONDELS** | |
| | | | 8-man New York City band | |
| 3/15/69 | 39 | 1 | 1. May I | Heritage 803 |
| 5/31/69 | 35 | 3 | 2. I've Been Hurt | Heritage 812 |
| 9/13/69 | 23 | 5 | 3. What Kind Of Fool Do You Think I Am | Heritage 817 |
| | | | **DEAN & JEAN** | |
| | | | Welton Young & Brenda Lee Jones | |
| 3/21/64 | 32 | 3 | 1. Hey Jean, Hey Dean | Rust 5075 |
| 12/14/68 + | 35 | 2 | 2. Tra La La La Suzy | Rust 5067 |
| | | | **JIMMY DEAN** | |
| | | | born Seth Ward in Plainview, Texas on 8/10/28 | |
| 1/06/58 + | 32 | 1 | 1. Little Sandy Sleighfoot [X-N] | Columbia 41025 |
| 10/09/61 | 1 (5) | 13 | ● 2. **Big Bad John** | Columbia 42175 |
| 1/20/62 | 24 | 3 | 3. Dear Ivan [S] | Columbia 42259 |
| 2/10/62 | 22 | 5 | 4. The Cajun Queen/ [S] | |
| 2/10/62 | 26 | 5 | 5. To A Sleeping Beauty [S] | Columbia 42282 |
| | | | background music: "Memories" | |
| 4/14/62 | 8 | 9 | 6. P.T. 109 | Columbia 42338 |
| 10/06/62 | 29 | 5 | 7. Little Black Book | Columbia 42529 |
| 5/22/76 | 35 | 2 | ● 8. I.O.U. [S] | Casino 052 |
| | | | **DeBARGE** | |
| | | | 5-member DeBarge family | |
| 3/26/83 | 31 | 6 | 1. I Like It | Gordy 1645 |
| 5/28/83 | 17 | 10 | 2. All This Love | Gordy 1660 |
| 11/26/83 + | 18 | 11 | 3. Time Will Reveal | Gordy 1705 |
| | | | **CHRIS DE BURGH** | |
| | | | British | |
| 6/11/83 | 34 | 4 | 1. Don't Pay The Ferryman | A&M 2511 |
| | | | **DE CASTRO SISTERS** | |
| | | | Peggy, Babette & Cherie | |
| 5/07/55 | 17 | 4 | 1. Boom Boom Boomerang | Abbott 3003 |
| | | | bass voice: Thurl Ravenscroft | |
| | | | **JOEY DEE & The Starliters** | |
| 12/04/61 + | 1 (3) | 14 | 1. **Peppermint Twist - Part 1** | Roulette 4401 |
| | | | inspired by New York's Peppermint Lounge | |
| 3/03/62 | 20 | 4 | 2. Hey, Let's Twist | Roulette 4408 |
| 3/31/62 | 6 | 9 | 3. **Shout - Part 1** | Roulette 4416 |
| 9/15/62 | 18 | 6 | 4. What Kind Of Love Is This | Roulette 4438 |
| | | | from the film "Two Tickets To Paris" | |
| 6/01/63 | 36 | 1 | 5. Hot Pastrami With Mashed Potatoes - Part I | Roulette 4488 |
| | | | **JOHNNY DEE** | |
| | | | John D. Loudermilk | |
| 4/06/57 | 38 | 1 | 1. Sittin' In The Balcony | Colonial 430 |

| DATE | POS | WKS | ARTIST—Record Title | LABEL & NO. |
|---|---|---|---|---|
| | | | **KIKI DEE** | |
| | | | English - also see Elton John | |
| 10/19/74 | **12** | 10 | 1. I've Got The Music In Me | Rocket 40293 |
| | | | **LENNY DEE** | |
| | | | organist | |
| 2/12/55 | **19** | 15 | 1. Plantation Boogie [I] | Decca 29360 |
| | | | **TOMMY DEE with Carol Kay & the Teen-Aires** | |
| 4/13/59 | **11** | 8 | 1. Three Stars [S] | Crest 1057 |
| | | | dedicated to Buddy Holly/Ritchie Valens/the Big Bopper | |
| | | | **DEEP PURPLE** | |
| | | | British heavy-metal band led by Ritchie Blackmore (lead guitar | |
| 8/24/68 | **4** | 9 | 1. **Hush** | Tetragramm. 1503 |
| 12/07/68 | **38** | 3 | 2. Kentucky Woman | Tetragramm. 1508 |
| 6/16/73 | **4** | 12 | ● 3. **Smoke On The Water** | Warner 7710 |
| | | | **RICK DEES & His Cast Of Idiots** | |
| | | | popular television and radio disc jockey | |
| 9/04/76 | **1** (1) | 16 | ★ 1. **Disco Duck (Part 1) [N]** | RSO 857 |
| | | | **DEF LEPPARD** | |
| | | | British heavy-metal quintet; Joe Elliott, lead singer | |
| 4/16/83 | **12** | 9 | 1. Photograph | Mercury 811215 |
| 7/09/83 | **16** | 9 | 2. Rock Of Ages | Mercury 812604 |
| 10/08/83 | **28** | 5 | 3. Foolin' | Mercury 814178 |
| | | | **DeFRANCO FAMILY featuring Tony DeFranco** | |
| | | | 5-member family from Canada | |
| 9/29/73 | **3** | 14 | ● 1. **Heartbeat - It's A Lovebeat** | 20th Century 2030 |
| 1/26/74 | **32** | 4 | 2. Abra-Ca-Dabra | 20th Century 2070 |
| 5/25/74 | **18** | 6 | 3. Save The Last Dance For Me | 20th Century 2088 |
| | | | **DE JOHN SISTERS** | |
| | | | Julie & Dux DeGiovanni | |
| 12/25/54 + | **6** | 13 | 1. **(My Baby Don't Love Me) No More** | Epic 9085 |
| | | | **DESMOND DEKKER & THE ACES** | |
| | | | Jamaican | |
| 6/07/69 | **9** | 7 | 1. **Israelites** | Uni 55129 |
| | | | **DELANEY & BONNIE & FRIENDS** | |
| | | | Delaney & Bonnie (Lynn) Bramlett | |
| 6/26/71 | **13** | 10 | 1. Never Ending Song Of Love | Atco 6804 |
| 10/09/71 | **20** | 7 | 2. Only You Know And I Know | Atco 6838 |
| | | | **DELEGATES** | |
| 11/04/72 | **8** | 6 | 1. **Convention '72 [N]** | Mainstream 5525 |
| | | | **DELFONICS** | |
| | | | Philadelphia trio | |
| 2/24/68 | **4** | 12 | 1. **La - La - Means I Love You** | Philly Groove 150 |
| 10/05/68 | **35** | 4 | 2. Break Your Promise | Philly Groove 152 |
| 1/25/69 | **35** | 1 | 3. Ready Or Not Here I Come (Can't Hide From Love) | Philly Groove 154 |

| DATE | POS | WKS | ARTIST—Record Title | LABEL & NO. |
|---|---|---|---|---|
| 10/04/69 | 40 | 2 | 4. You Got Yours And I'll Get Mine | Philly Groove 157 |
| 2/07/70 | 10 | 10 | ● 5. **Didn't I (Blow Your Mind This Time)** | Philly Groove 161 |
| 7/25/70 | 40 | 1 | 6. Trying To Make A Fool Of Me | Philly Groove 162 |
| | | | **DELL-VIKINGS** | |
| | | | racially integrated quintet - formed while in the Air Force in Pittsburgh | |
| 3/02/57 | 4 | 22 | 1. **Come Go With Me** | Dot 15538 |
| 7/15/57 | 9 | 13 | 2. **Whispering Bells** | Dot 15592 |
| 7/15/57 | 12 | 1 | 3. Cool Shake | Mercury 71132 |
| | | | **DELLS** | |
| | | | Chicago-area quintet formed in 1953 | |
| 2/17/68 | 20 | 7 | 1. There Is | Cadet 5590 |
| 7/20/68 | 10 | 10 | 2. **Stay In My Corner** | Cadet 5612 |
| | | | originally released in 1965 | |
| 11/02/68 | 18 | 5 | 3. Always Together | Cadet 5621 |
| 2/08/69 | 38 | 2 | 4. Does Anybody Know I'm Here | Cadet 5631 |
| 6/21/69 | 22 | 6 | 5. I Can Sing A Rainbow/Love Is Blue | Cadet 5641 |
| 8/23/69 | 10 | 10 | 6. **Oh, What A Night** | Cadet 5649 |
| | | | original version made the R&B charts in 1956 | |
| 9/18/71 | 30 | 6 | 7. The Love We Had (Stays On My Mind) | Cadet 5683 |
| 6/23/73 | 34 | 2 | ● 8. Give Your Baby A Standing Ovation | Cadet 5696 |
| | | | **DEMENSIONS** | |
| | | | quartet from the Bronx, New York | |
| 8/08/60 | 16 | 9 | 1. Over The Rainbow | Mohawk 116 |
| | | | **MARTIN DENNY** | |
| | | | exotic sounds featuring Martin (piano) & Julius Wechter (vibes) | |
| 4/27/59 | 4 | 13 | 1. **Quiet Village [I]** | Liberty 55162 |
| 11/16/59 | 28 | 2 | 2. The Enchanted Sea [I] | Liberty 55212 |
| | | | **JOHN DENVER** | |
| | | | born Henry John Deutchendorf on 12/31/43 in Roswell, New Mexico | |
| 6/26/71 | 2 (1) | 14 | ● 1. **Take Me Home, Country Roads** | RCA 0445 |
| | | | with Fat City | |
| 1/06/73 | 9 | 12 | 2. **Rocky Mountain High** | RCA 0829 |
| 2/16/74 | 1 (1) | 13 | ● 3. **Sunshine On My Shoulders** | RCA 0213 |
| 6/15/74 | 1 (2) | 11 | ● 4. **Annie's Song** | RCA 0295 |
| 10/05/74 | 5 | 10 | ● 5. **Back Home Again** | RCA 10065 |
| 1/11/75 | 13 | 8 | 6. Sweet Surrender | RCA 10148 |
| 4/05/75 | 1 (1) | 15 | ● 7. **Thank God I'm A Country Boy** | RCA 10239 |
| 8/30/75 | 1 (1) | 13 | ● 8. **I'm Sorry/** | RCA 10239 |
| | | 7 | 9. **Calypso** | RCA 10353 |
| | | | inspired by Jacques Cousteau's ship "Calypso" | |
| 12/13/75 + | 13 | 9 | 10. Fly Away | RCA 10517 |
| | | | backing vocals by Olivia Newton-John | |
| 3/20/76 | 29 | 4 | 11. Looking For Space | RCA 10586 |
| 10/02/76 | 36 | 2 | 12. Like A Sad Song | RCA 10774 |
| 4/30/77 | 32 | 3 | 13. My Sweet Lady | RCA 10911 |
| | | | also the flip side of RCA 10239 | |
| 9/05/81 | 36 | 4 | 14. Some Days Are Diamonds (Some Days Are Stone) | RCA 12246 |
| 4/24/82 | 31 | 5 | 15. Shanghai Breezes | RCA 13071 |

| DATE | POS | WKS | ARTIST—Record Title | LABEL & NO. |
|---|---|---|---|---|
| | | | **DEODATO** | |
| | | | Eumir Deodato - Brazilian keyboardist | |
| 2/17/73 | **2 (1)** | 10 | 1. **Also Sprach Zarathustra (2001) [I]** | CTI 12 |
| | | | **DEREK** | |
| | | | Derek is Johnny Cymbal | |
| 11/23/68 + | **11** | 11 | 1. **Cinnamon** | Bang 558 |
| | | | **DEREK & THE DOMINOS** | |
| | | | Eric Clapton, Bobby Whitlock, Jim Gordon, Carl Radle | |
| 6/17/72 | **10** | 10 | 1. **Layla [R]** | Atco 6809 |
| | | | re-entry of 1971 hit (Pos. 51) | |
| | | | **RICK DERRINGER** | |
| | | | member of The McCoys, and Johnny and Edgar Winter's bands | |
| 3/02/74 | **23** | 6 | 1. **Rock And Roll, Hoochie Koo** | Blue Sky 2751 |
| | | | **TERI DeSARIO with K.C.** | |
| | | | K.C. of KC & The Sunshine Band | |
| 12/22/79 + | **2 (2)** | 16 | ● 1. **Yes, I'm Ready** | Casablanca 2227 |
| | | | **JACKIE DeSHANNON** | |
| | | | born in Kentucky on 8/21/44 | |
| 6/19/65 | **7** | 9 | 1. **What The World Needs Now Is Love** | Imperial 66110 |
| 7/26/69 | **4** | 10 | ● 2. **Put A Little Love In Your Heart** | Imperial 66385 |
| 12/06/69 | **40** | 1 | 3. **Love Will Find A Way** | Imperial 66419 |
| | | | **JOHNNY DESMOND** | |
| 3/26/55 | **6** | 11 | 1. **Play Me Hearts And Flowers (I Wanna Cry)** | Coral 61379 |
| 8/13/55 | **3** | 16 | 2. **The Yellow Rose Of Texas** | Coral 61476 |
| 12/03/55 | **17** | 1 | 3. **Sixteen Tons** | Coral 61529 |
| | | | **DETERGENTS** | |
| | | | Ron Dante/Tommy Wynn/Danny Jordan | |
| 12/19/64 + | **19** | 6 | 1. **Leader Of The Laundromat [N]** | Roulette 4590 |
| | | | parody of the Shangri-Las' "Leader Of The Pack" | |
| | | | **DETROIT EMERALDS** | |
| | | | brothers Abe & Ivory Tillmon and James Mitchell | |
| 2/19/72 | **36** | 4 | 1. **You Want It, You Got It** | Westbound 192 |
| 7/29/72 | **24** | 7 | 2. **Baby Let Me Take You (In My Arms)** | Westbound 203 |
| | | | **WILLIAM DeVAUGHN** | |
| 5/18/74 | **4** | 10 | ● 1. **Be Thankful For What You Got** | Roxbury 0236 |
| | | | **DEVO** | |
| | | | Akron, Ohio quintet specializing in robotic rock rhythms | |
| 10/04/80 | **14** | 15 | ● 1. **Whip It** | Warner 49550 |
| | | | **BARRY DeVORZON & PERRY BOTKIN, JR.** | |
| | | | also see Barry & The Tamerlanes | |
| 10/02/76 | **8** | 16 | ● 1. **Nadia's Theme (The Young And The Restless) [I]** | A&M 1856 |
| | | | previously entitled "Cotton's Dream" Nadia: gymnast Nadia Comaneci of Romania | |
| | | | **DEVOTIONS** | |
| 4/04/64 | **36** | 1 | 1. **Rip Van Winkle [N]** | Roulette 4541 |

| DATE | POS | WKS | ARTIST—Record Title | LABEL & NO. |
|---|---|---|---|---|
| | | | **DEXYS MIDNIGHT RUNNERS** | |
| | | | Kevin Rowland, leader of 8-piece Birmingham, England band | |
| 2/26/83 | **1** (1) | 14 | 1. **Come On Eileen** | Mercury 76189 |
| | | | **CLIFF DeYOUNG** | |
| 2/16/74 | 17 | 8 | 1. My Sweet Lady | MCA 40156 |
| | | | from the TV soundtrack "Sunshine" | |
| | | | **DENNIS DeYOUNG** | |
| | | | lead singer of Styx | |
| 9/22/84 | 10 | 12 | 1. **Desert Moon** | A&M 2666 |
| | | | **LEO DIAMOND** | |
| | | | harmonica player | |
| 2/19/55 | 30 | 1 | 1. Melody Of Love [I] | RCA 5973 |
| | | | **NEIL DIAMOND** | |
| | | | born in Brooklyn on 1/24/41 - also see Barbra Streisand | |
| 9/10/66 | **6** | 9 | 1. **Cherry, Cherry** | Bang 528 |
| 11/26/66 | **16** | 6 | 2. I Got The Feelin' (Oh No No) | Bang 536 |
| 2/11/67 | **18** | 5 | 3. You Got To Me | Bang 540 |
| 4/29/67 | **10** | 8 | 4. **Girl, You'll Be A Woman Soon** | Bang 542 |
| 8/05/67 | **13** | 7 | 5. I Thank The Lord For The Night Time | Bang 547 |
| 10/28/67 | **22** | 6 | 6. Kentucky Woman | Bang 551 |
| 3/29/69 | **22** | 7 | 7. Brother Love's Travelling Salvation Show | Uni 55109 |
| 7/12/69 | **4** | 12 | ● 8. **Sweet Caroline (Good Times Never Seemed So Good)** | Uni 55136 |
| 11/15/69 | **6** | 12 | ● 9. **Holly Holy** | Uni 55175 |
| 3/21/70 | **24** | 8 | 10. Shilo | Bang 575 |
| 5/16/70 | **30** | 4 | 11. Soolaimon (African Trilogy II) | Uni 55224 |
| 8/15/70 | **21** | 7 | 12. Solitary Man [R] | Bang 578 |
| | | | re-entry of Neil's first hit (Pos. 55-'66) | |
| 8/29/70 | **1** (1) | 14 | ● 13. **Cracklin' Rosie** | Uni 55250 |
| 11/21/70 | **20** | 9 | 14. He Ain't Heavy...He's My Brother | Uni 55264 |
| 12/05/70 | **36** | 5 | 15. Do It | Bang 580 |
| 4/03/71 | **4** | 8 | 16. **I Am...I Said** | Uni 55278 |
| 11/27/71 | **14** | 7 | 17. Stones | Uni 55310 |
| 5/13/72 | **1** (1) | 12 | ● 18. **Song Sung Blue** | Uni 55326 |
| 9/02/72 | **11** | 7 | 19. Play Me | Uni 55346 |
| 11/25/72 | **17** | 8 | 20. Walk On Water | Uni 55352 |
| 4/21/73 | **31** | 4 | 21. "Cherry Cherry" from Hot August Night | MCA 40017 |
| | | | live version of 1966 hit | |
| 11/24/73 | **34** | 3 | 22. Be | Columbia 45942 |
| | | | from the film "Jonathan Livingston Seagull" | |
| 10/19/74 | **5** | 10 | 23. **Longfellow Serenade** | Columbia 10043 |
| 3/01/75 | **34** | 2 | 24. I've Been This Way Before | Columbia 10084 |
| 6/26/76 | **11** | 8 | 25. If You Know What I Mean | Columbia 10366 |
| 12/24/77 + | **16** | 9 | 26. Desiree | Columbia 10657 |
| 2/17/79 | **20** | 6 | 27. Forever In Blue Jeans | Columbia 10897 |
| 1/19/80 | **17** | 10 | 28. September Morn' | Columbia 11175 |
| 11/01/80 + | **2** (3) | 17 | 29. **Love On The Rocks** | Capitol 4939 |
| 1/31/81 | **6** | 12 | 30. **Hello Again** | Capitol 4960 |

Remixed Edited Version                    MCA-5226

**Fabian** was discovered sitting on his South Philadelphia doorstep by the head of Chancellor Records who believed Fabian looked like a teen idol. Questions about his singing ability came later.

**Agnetha Fältskog,** a Swedish solo star in her pre-ABBA days, chose Mike Chapman (Blondie, the Knack) to produce her first American outing, and didn't do half bad.

**The Fifth Dimension,** originally known as the Versatiles, debuted on Johnny Rivers' Soul City label in 1966. They recorded hits by major songwriters like Laura Nyro ("Stoned Soul Picnic") and Jim Webb ("Up, Up and Away").

**The Fixx** (formerly the Portraits) distinguished themselves from Duran Duran and other so-called "New Romantics" by adopting a harder edge and singing about serious matters like nuclear war.

**Roberta Flack's** rendition of "The First Time Ever I Saw Your Face," a charttopper in 1972, was originally released as part of her debut LP three years earlier. Atlantic Records decided to release the song as a single after it was featured in Clint Eastwood's *Play Misty For Me*.

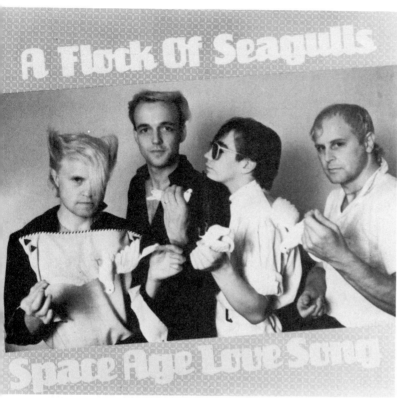

GYPSY

Produced by Peter Frampton. From The Forthcoming A&M Album "I'm In You"

HOLLYWOOD
(HE'S MY)
DREAMBOAT

Connie Francis

MGM

**Fleetwood Mac.** Hard to believe today, but Fleetwood Mac were once one of the premier British blues bands. They even cut an LP in Chicago with blues greats Otis Spann, Walter Horton, and Willie Dixon.

**A Flock of Seagulls** began in Liverpool, England (just like you know who), taking their name from the best seller *Jonathan Livingston Seagull.* Lyricist Mike Score says "I Ran (So Far Away)" was inspired by *Close Encounters of the Third Kind.*

**The Four Lads** were one of many similarly named quartets to chart in the fifties. The others: the Four Aces, Four Coins, Four Esquires, Four Freshmen, Four Preps, Four Voices, Four Tunes, and Four Knights.

**Peter Frampton** must have seemed a fresh new face to many who bought his multi-platinum *Framptom Comes Alive* in 1975. In fact, he had nearly a decade of experience, first with teenybopper band, the Herd, and then with raunchy blues-rockers, Humble Pie.

**Connie Francis,** born Concetta Rosa Maria Franconero, provided the singing voice for Tuesday Weld in the 1956 movie *Rock, Rock, Rock.* Later, she got her own chances in film, most notably *Where the Boys Are.*

| DATE | POS | WKS | ARTIST—Record Title | LABEL & NO. |
|---|---|---|---|---|
| 5/02/81 | 8 | 13 | 31. **America** | Capitol 4994 |
| | | | above 3 tunes are from the film "The Jazz Singer" | |
| 11/14/81 + | 11 | 12 | 32. Yesterday's Songs | Columbia 02604 |
| 3/06/82 | 27 | 5 | 33. On The Way To The Sky | Columbia 02712 |
| 6/19/82 | 35 | 4 | 34. Be Mine Tonight | Columbia 02928 |
| 10/02/82 | 5 | 11 | 35. **Heartlight** | Columbia 03219 |
| | | | inspired by the film "E.T." | |
| 2/19/83 | 35 | 4 | 36. I'm Alive | Columbia 03503 |
| | | | **DIAMONDS** | |
| | | | Dave Somerville, lead singer of Canadian quartet | |
| 3/17/56 | 12 | 11 | 1. Why Do Fools Fall In Love | Mercury 70790 |
| 5/12/56 | 14 | 11 | 2. The Church Bells May Ring | Mercury 70835 |
| 7/28/56 | 30 | 2 | 3. Love, Love, Love | Mercury 70889 |
| 9/29/56 | 34 | 1 | 4. Soft Summer Breeze/ | |
| 9/29/56 | 35 | 2 | 5. Ka-Ding-Dong | Mercury 70934 |
| 3/16/57 | 2 (8) | 21 | 6. **Little Darlin'** | Mercury 71060 |
| 7/15/57 | 13 | 2 | 7. Words Of Love | Mercury 71128 |
| 9/30/57 | 16 | 1 | 8. Zip Zip | Mercury 71165 |
| 11/04/57 | 10 | 8 | 9. **Silhouettes** | Mercury 71197 |
| 1/06/58 | 4 | 14 | 10. **The Stroll** | Mercury 71242 |
| 5/19/58 | 37 | 1 | 11. High Sign | Mercury 71291 |
| 7/28/58 | 16 | 1 | 12. Kathy-O | Mercury 71330 |
| 11/17/58 | 29 | 6 | 13. Walking Along | Mercury 71366 |
| 2/09/59 | 18 | 10 | 14. She Say (Oom Dooby Doom) | Mercury 71404 |
| 8/07/61 | 22 | 4 | 15. One Summer Night | Mercury 71831 |
| | | | **MANU DIBANGO** | |
| | | | African | |
| 7/21/73 | 35 | 3 | 1. Soul Makossa [I] | Atlantic 2971 |
| | | | **DICK & DEEDEE** | |
| | | | Dick St. John & DeeDee Sperling | |
| 8/28/61 | 2 (2) | 10 | 1. **The Mountain's High** | Liberty 55350 |
| 5/12/62 | 22 | 5 | 2. Tell Me | Liberty 55412 |
| 4/06/63 | 17 | 6 | 3. Young And In Love | Warner 5342 |
| 12/21/63 + | 27 | 4 | 4. Turn Around | Warner 5396 |
| 12/12/64 + | 13 | 10 | 5. Thou Shalt Not Steal | Warner 5482 |
| | | | **"LITTLE" JIMMY DICKENS** | |
| 11/13/65 | 15 | 5 | 1. May The Bird Of Paradise Fly Up Your Nose [N] | Columbia 43388 |
| | | | **DICKY DOO & THE DON'TS** | |
| | | | Dicky Doo's real name: Gerry Granahan | |
| 2/17/58 | 28 | 6 | 1. Click-Clack | Swan 4001 |
| 5/12/58 | 40 | 1 | 2. Nee Nee Na Na Na Na Nu Nu [I] | Swan 4006 |
| | | | **BO DIDDLEY** | |
| | | | legendary early rock & roller - real name: Ellas McDaniel | |
| 10/05/59 | 20 | 7 | 1. Say Man [N] | Checker 931 |
| | | | **DIESEL** | |
| | | | rock quartet from Holland | |
| 10/17/81 | 25 | 6 | 1. Sausalito Summernight | Regency 7339 |

| DATE | POS | WKS | ARTIST—Record Title | LABEL & NO. |
|------|-----|-----|---------------------|-------------|
| | | | **MARK DINNING** | |
| | | | brother of the Dinning Sisters trio | |
| 1/04/60 | 1 (2) | 14 | 1. **Teen Angel** | MGM 12845 |
| | | | **DINO, DESI & BILLY** | |
| | | | Jr.'s: Dean Martin & Desi Arnaz - with Billy Hinsche | |
| 7/24/65 | 17 | 7 | 1. I'm A Fool | Reprise 0367 |
| 10/16/65 | 25 | 5 | 2. Not The Lovin' Kind | Reprise 0401 |
| | | | **KENNY DINO** | |
| 12/04/61 | 24 | 6 | 1. Your Ma Said You Cried In Your Sleep Last Night | Musicor 1013 |
| | | | **PAUL DINO** | |
| 4/10/61 | 38 | 1 | 1. Ginnie Bell | Promo 2180 |
| | | | **DION** | |
| | | | Dion Di Muci - born 7/18/38 in the Bronx, New York | |
| 11/14/60 | 12 | 11 | 1. Lonely Teenager | Laurie 3070 |
| 10/02/61 | 1 (2) | 12 | 2. **Runaround Sue** | Laurie 3110 |
| 12/18/61 + | 2 (1) | 13 | 3. **The Wanderer/** | |
| 12/18/61 | 36 | 1 | 4. The Majestic | Laurie 3115 |
| 5/05/62 | 3 | 9 | 5. **Lovers Who Wander** | Laurie 3123 |
| 7/21/62 | 8 | 8 | 6. **Little Diane** | Laurie 3134 |
| 11/24/62 | 10 | 9 | 7. **Love Came To Me** | Laurie 3145 |
| 1/26/63 | 2 (3) | 11 | 8. **Ruby Baby** | Columbia 42662 |
| 3/30/63 | 21 | 6 | 9. Sandy | Laurie 3153 |
| 5/04/63 | 21 | 6 | 10. This Little Girl | Columbia 42776 |
| 7/27/63 | 31 | 3 | 11. Be Careful Of Stones That You Throw | Columbia 42810 |
| 9/28/63 | 6 | 8 | 12. **Donna The Prima Donna** | Columbia 42852 |
| 11/23/63 | 6 | 9 | 13. **Drip Drop** | Columbia 42917 |
| 11/02/68 | 4 | 12 | ● 14. **Abraham, Martin And John** | Laurie 3464 |
| | | | **DION & THE BELMONTS** | |
| | | | Belmonts: Angelo D'Aleo, Freddie Milano and Carlo Mastrangelo-also see the Belmonts | |
| 5/26/58 | 22 | 10 | 1. I Wonder Why | Laurie 3013 |
| 9/15/58 | 19 | 8 | 2. No One Knows | Laurie 3015 |
| 1/05/59 | 40 | 1 | 3. Don't Pity Me | Laurie 3021 |
| 4/27/59 | 5 | 13 | 4. **A Teenager In Love** | Laurie 3027 |
| 1/11/60 | 3 | 11 | 5. **Where Or When** | Laurie 3044 |
| 5/16/60 | 30 | 2 | 6. When You Wish Upon A Star | Laurie 3052 |
| 8/15/60 | 38 | 1 | 7. In The Still Of The Night | Laurie 3059 |
| | | | **DIRE STRAITS** | |
| | | | English quintet led by Mark Knopfler | |
| 2/17/79 | 4 | 12 | 1. **Sultans Of Swing** | Warner 8736 |
| | | | **SENATOR EVERETT McKINLEY DIRKSEN** | |
| | | | Senator from Illinois ('50-'69) - died on 9/7/69 (73) | |
| 1/07/67 | 29 | 3 | 1. Gallant Men [S] | Capitol 5805 |
| | | | **DIRT BAND - see NITTY GRITTY DIRT BAND** | |

| DATE | POS | WKS | ARTIST—Record Title | LABEL & NO. |
|---|---|---|---|---|
| | | | **DISCO TEX & THE SEX-O-LETTES** | |
| | | | featuring Sir Monti Rock III | |
| 12/28/74 + | 10 | 9 | 1. **Get Dancin'** | Chelsea 3004 |
| 5/17/75 | 23 | 5 | 2. I Wanna Dance Wit' Choo (Doo Dat Dance), Part 1 | Chelsea 3015 |
| | | | **DIXIEBELLES** | |
| | | | female trio from Memphis | |
| 10/26/63 | 9 | 8 | 1. **(Down At) Papa Joe's** | Sound Stage 2507 |
| 2/08/64 | 15 | 5 | 2. Southtown, U.S.A. | Sound Stage 2517 |
| | | | **DIXIE CUPS** | |
| | | | female trio from New Orleans | |
| 5/16/64 | 1 (3) | 11 | 1. **Chapel Of Love** | Red Bird 001 |
| 8/01/64 | 12 | 7 | 2. People Say | Red Bird 006 |
| 11/21/64 | 39 | 1 | 3. You Should Have Seen The Way He Looked At Me | Red Bird 012 |
| 5/01/65 | 20 | 5 | 4. Iko Iko | Red Bird 024 |
| | | | **CARL DOBKINS, JR.** | |
| 6/01/59 | 3 | 16 | 1. **My Heart Is An Open Book** | Decca 30803 |
| 1/18/60 | 25 | 8 | 2. Lucky Devil | Decca 31020 |
| | | | **DR. BUZZARD'S ORIGINAL "SAVANNAH" BAND** | |
| | | | '30s-style group - evolved into Kid Creole | |
| 12/11/76 + | 27 | 8 | 1. Whispering/Cherchez La Femme/Se Si Bon | RCA 10827 |
| | | | **DR. HOOK** | |
| | | | 7-man band led by Ray (eye patch) Sawyer & Dennis Locorriere | |
| 5/06/72 | 5 | 10 | ● 1. **Sylvia's Mother** | Columbia 45562 |
| 2/03/73 | 6 | 11 | ● 2. **The Cover Of "Rolling Stone" [N]** | Columbia 45732 |
| | | | above 2 shown as Dr. Hook & The Medicine Show | |
| 2/07/76 | 6 | 14 | ● 3. **Only Sixteen** | Capitol 4171 |
| 7/31/76 | 11 | 14 | 4. A Little Bit More | Capitol 4280 |
| 10/14/78 + | 6 | 16 | ● 5. **Sharing The Night Together** | Capitol 4621 |
| 6/02/79 | 6 | 16 | ● 6. **When You're In Love With A Beautiful Woman** | Capitol 4705 |
| 11/03/79 + | 12 | 14 | 7. Better Love Next Time | Capitol 4785 |
| 3/15/80 | 5 | 15 | ● 8. **Sexy Eyes** | Capitol 4831 |
| 11/29/80 | 34 | 6 | 9. Girls Can Get It | Casablanca 2314 |
| 3/27/82 | 25 | 6 | 10. Baby Makes Her Blue Jeans Talk | Casablanca 2347 |
| | | | **DR. JOHN** | |
| | | | real name: Malcolm Rebennack | |
| 5/12/73 | 9 | 13 | 1. **Right Place Wrong Time** | Atco 6914 |
| | | | **BILL DOGGETT** | |
| | | | pianist/organist | |
| 8/25/56 | 2 (3) | 22 | 1. **Honky Tonk (Parts 1 & 2) [I]** | King 4950 |
| | | | sax player: Clifford Scott | |
| 12/15/56 + | 26 | 5 | 2. Slow Walk [I] | King 5000 |
| 12/02/57 | 35 | 1 | 3. Soft [I] | King 5080 |
| | | | **THOMAS DOLBY** | |
| | | | British | |
| 3/19/83 | 5 | 15 | 1. **She Blinded Me With Science** | Capitol 5204 |

| DATE | POS | WKS | ARTIST—Record Title | LABEL & NO. |
|---|---|---|---|---|
| | | | **FATS DOMINO** | |
| | | | born Antoine Domino on 2/26/28 in New Orleans | |
| 7/16/55 | 10 | 13 | 1. **Ain't That A Shame** | Imperial 5348 |
| 4/07/56 | 35 | 1 | 2. Bo Weevil | Imperial 5375 |
| 5/05/56 | 3 | 18 | 3. **I'm In Love Again/** | |
| 5/19/56 | 21 | 10 | 4. My Blue Heaven | Imperial 5386 |
| 7/28/56 | 14 | 8 | 5. When My Dreamboat Comes Home | Imperial 5396 |
| 10/13/56 + | 2 (3) | 21 | 6. **Blueberry Hill** | Imperial 5407 |
| 1/12/57 | 5 | 12 | 7. **Blue Monday** | Imperial 5417 |
| | | | from the film "The Girl Can't Help It" | |
| 3/09/57 | 4 | 14 | 8. **I'm Walkin'** | Imperial 5428 |
| 5/27/57 | 6 | 13 | 9. **Valley Of Tears/** | |
| 7/22/57 | 22 | 4 | 10. It's You I Love | Imperial 5442 |
| 8/26/57 | 29 | 2 | 11. When I See You | Imperial 5454 |
| 10/21/57 | 23 | 6 | 12. Wait And See | Imperial 5467 |
| | | | from the film "Jamboree" | |
| 12/23/57 + | 26 | 9 | 13. The Big Beat | Imperial 5477 |
| 5/05/58 | 22 | 7 | 14. Sick And Tired | Imperial 5515 |
| 12/01/58 + | 6 | 12 | 15. **Whole Lotta Loving** | Imperial 5553 |
| 5/25/59 | 16 | 7 | 16. I'm Ready | Imperial 5585 |
| 8/10/59 | 8 | 10 | 17. **I Want To Walk You Home/** | |
| 8/10/59 | 17 | 9 | 18. I'm Gonna Be A Wheel Some Day | Imperial 5606 |
| 11/09/59 | 8 | 10 | 19. **Be My Guest/** | |
| 11/09/59 | 33 | 2 | 20. I've Been Around | Imperial 5629 |
| 2/15/60 | 25 | 5 | 21. Country Boy | Imperial 5645 |
| 7/04/60 | 6 | 11 | 22. **Walking To New Orleans/** | |
| 7/18/60 | 21 | 7 | 23. Don't Come Knockin' | Imperial 5675 |
| 9/12/60 | 15 | 9 | 24. Three Nights A Week | Imperial 5687 |
| 11/14/60 | 14 | 11 | 25. My Girl Josephine/ | |
| 12/05/60 | 38 | 3 | 26. Natural Born Lover | Imperial 5704 |
| 2/06/61 | 22 | 6 | 27. What A Price/ | |
| 2/13/61 | 33 | 4 | 28. Ain't That Just Like A Woman | Imperial 5723 |
| 4/03/61 | 32 | 2 | 29. Fell In Love On Monday/ | |
| 4/17/61 | 32 | 2 | 30. Shu Rah | Imperial 5734 |
| 6/19/61 | 23 | 5 | 31. It Keeps Rainin' | Imperial 5753 |
| 7/31/61 | 15 | 6 | 32. Let The Four Winds Blow | Imperial 5764 |
| 10/23/61 | 22 | 4 | 33. What A Party | Imperial 5779 |
| 12/25/61 + | 30 | 3 | 34. Jambalaya (On The Bayou) | Imperial 5796 |
| 3/17/62 | 22 | 5 | 35. You Win Again | Imperial 5816 |
| 10/26/63 | 35 | 1 | 36. Red Sails In The Sunset | ABC-Para. 10484 |
| | | | **DON & JUAN** | |
| | | | Roland Trone & Claude Johnson of The Genies | |
| 2/24/62 | 7 | 9 | 1. **What's Your Name** | Big Top 3079 |
| | | | **BO DONALDSON & THE HEYWOODS** | |
| | | | Cincinnati, Ohio septet | |
| 5/11/74 | 1 (2) | 12 | ● 1. **Billy, Don't Be A Hero** | ABC 11435 |
| 8/24/74 | 15 | 7 | 2. Who Do You Think You Are | ABC 12006 |
| 12/14/74 | 39 | 1 | 3. The Heartbreak Kid | ABC 12039 |

| DATE | POS | WKS | ARTIST—Record Title | LABEL & NO. |
|---|---|---|---|---|
| | | | **LONNIE DONEGAN & His Skiffle Group** | |
| | | | Scottish | |
| 3/31/56 | 8 | 11 | 1. **Rock Island Line** | London 1650 |
| 8/14/61 | 5 | 9 | 2. **Does Your Chewing Gum Lose It's Flavor** **(On The Bedpost Over Night) [N]** | Dot 15911 |
| | | | **RAL DONNER** | |
| | | | Ral was narrator and Elvis' voice in the film "This Is Elvis"- died of cancer on 4/6/84 (41) | |
| 5/01/61 | 19 | 8 | 1. Girl Of My Best Friend | Gone 5102 |
| | | | with the Starfires | |
| 7/24/61 | 4 | 9 | 2. **You Don't Know What You've Got (Until** **You Lose It)** | Gone 5108 |
| 11/13/61 | 39 | 1 | 3. Please Don't Go | Gone 5114 |
| 2/03/62 | 18 | 4 | 4. She's Everything (I Wanted You To Be) | Gone 5121 |
| | | | **DONNIE & THE DREAMERS** | |
| | | | Donnie is Louis Bugio | |
| 6/12/61 | 35 | 3 | 1. Count Every Star | Whale 500 |
| | | | **DONOVAN** | |
| | | | born Donovan Leitch in Glasgow, Scotland on 2/10/46 | |
| 6/12/65 | 23 | 5 | 1. Catch The Wind | Hickory 1309 |
| 8/13/66 | 1 (1) | 10 | 2. **Sunshine Superman** | Epic 10045 |
| 11/19/66 | 2 (3) | 10 | ● 3. **Mellow Yellow** | Epic 10098 |
| 2/25/67 | 19 | 5 | 4. Epistle To Dippy | Epic 10127 |
| 8/26/67 | 11 | 6 | 5. There Is A Mountain | Epic 10212 |
| 12/09/67 | 23 | 5 | 6. Wear Your Love Like Heaven | Epic 10253 |
| 3/30/68 | 26 | 5 | 7. Jennifer Juniper | Epic 10300 |
| 6/29/68 | 5 | 10 | 8. **Hurdy Gurdy Man** | Epic 10345 |
| 10/19/68 | 33 | 4 | 9. Lalena | Epic 10393 |
| 3/01/69 | 35 | 2 | 10. To Susan On The West Coast Waiting/ | |
| 4/26/69 | 7 | 10 | 11. **Atlantis** | Epic 10434 |
| 8/30/69 | 36 | 2 | 12. Goo Goo Barabajagal (Love Is Hot) | Epic 10510 |
| | | | with the Jeff Beck Group | |
| | | | **DOOBIE BROTHERS** | |
| | | | California group - lead singers: Tom Johnston ('71-'78), Patrick Simmons ('71-'81) and Michael McDonald ('76-'81) | |
| 9/23/72 | 11 | 10 | 1. Listen To The Music | Warner 7619 |
| 2/17/73 | 35 | 2 | 2. Jesus Is Just Alright | Warner 7661 |
| 5/26/73 | 8 | 11 | 3. **Long Train Runnin'** | Warner 7698 |
| 9/15/73 | 15 | 8 | 4. China Grove | Warner 7728 |
| 6/01/74 | 32 | 2 | 5. Another Park, Another Sunday | Warner 7795 |
| 1/11/75 | 1 (1) | 12 | ● 6. **Black Water** | Warner 8062 |
| | | | originally the flip side of Warner 7795 | |
| 5/17/75 | 11 | 9 | 7. Take Me In Your Arms (Rock Me) | Warner 8092 |
| 8/30/75 | 40 | 1 | 8. Sweet Maxine | Warner 8126 |
| 5/15/76 | 13 | 8 | 9. Takin' It To The Streets | Warner 8196 |
| 1/22/77 | 37 | 2 | 10. It Keeps You Runnin' | Warner 8282 |
| 2/10/79 | 1 (1) | 14 | ● 11. **What A Fool Believes** | Warner 8725 |
| 5/19/79 | 14 | 9 | 12. Minute By Minute | Warner 8828 |

| DATE | POS | WKS | ARTIST—Record Title | LABEL & NO. |
|------|-----|-----|---------------------|-------------|
| 9/15/79 | 25 | 6 | 13. Dependin' On You | Warner 49029 |
| 9/06/80 | 5 | 11 | 14. **Real Love** | Warner 49503 |
| 12/06/80 + | 24 | 7 | 15. One Step Closer | Warner 49622 |
| | | | **DOORS** | |
| | | | Jim Morrison (vocals - died 7/3/71-27), Robby Krieger (guitar), Ray Manzarek (keyboards), John Densmore (drums) | |
| 6/24/67 | 1 (3) | 14 | ● 1. **Light My Fire** | Elektra 45615 |
| 10/07/67 | 12 | 7 | 2. People Are Strange | Elektra 45621 |
| 12/30/67 + | 25 | 4 | 3. Love Me Two Times | Elektra 45624 |
| 5/04/68 | 39 | 3 | 4. The Unknown Soldier | Elektra 45628 |
| 7/13/68 | 1 (2) | 11 | ● 5. **Hello, I Love You** | Elektra 45635 |
| 1/04/69 | 3 | 12 | ● 6. **Touch Me** | Elektra 45646 |
| 4/24/71 | 11 | 9 | 7. Love Her Madly | Elektra 45726 |
| 7/24/71 | 14 | 9 | 8. Riders On The Storm | Elektra 45738 |
| | | | **CHARLIE DORE** | |
| | | | British female vocalist | |
| 3/22/80 | 13 | 10 | 1. Pilot Of The Airwaves | Island 49166 |
| | | | **HAROLD DORMAN** | |
| 4/18/60 | 21 | 9 | 1. Mountain Of Love | Rita 1003 |
| | | | **JIMMY DORSEY Orchestra & Chorus** | |
| | | | alto sax & clarinet soloist and bandleader beginning in 1935 - died on 6/12/57 (53) | |
| 4/13/57 | 2 (4) | 26 | 1. **So Rare** | Fraternity 755 |
| 9/09/57 | 21 | 2 | 2. June Night | Fraternity 777 |
| | | | featuring Dick Stabile on sax | |
| | | | **LEE DORSEY** | |
| | | | former professional boxer from New Orleans | |
| 9/25/61 | 7 | 10 | 1. **Ya Ya** | Fury 1053 |
| 1/20/62 | 27 | 5 | 2. Do-Re-Mi | Fury 1056 |
| 7/31/65 | 28 | 4 | 3. Ride Your Pony | Amy 927 |
| 8/13/66 | 8 | 9 | 4. **Working In The Coal Mine** | Amy 958 |
| 11/19/66 | 23 | 5 | 5. Holy Cow | Amy 965 |
| | | | **TOMMY DORSEY Orchestra** | |
| | | | trombone soloist and bandleader beginning in 1934 - died on 11/26/56 (51) | |
| 9/15/58 | 7 | 14 | 1. **Tea For Two Cha Cha [I]** | Decca 30704 |
| | | | featuring Warren Covington (conductor/musician) | |
| | | | **CARL DOUGLAS** | |
| | | | Jamaican | |
| 11/09/74 | 1 (2) | 12 | ● 1. **Kung Fu Fighting** | 20th Century 2140 |
| | | | **CAROL DOUGLAS** | |
| 12/21/74 + | 11 | 11 | 1. Doctor's Orders | Midland I. 10113 |
| | | | **MIKE DOUGLAS** | |
| | | | TV talk show host - vocalist with Kay Kyser's band ('45-'49) | |
| 1/08/66 | 6 | 7 | 1. **The Men In My Little Girl's Life** | Epic 9876 |

| DATE | POS | WKS | ARTIST—Record Title | LABEL & NO. |
|---|---|---|---|---|
| | | | **RONNIE DOVE** | |
| | | | born on 9/7/40 in Baltimore, Maryland | |
| 9/26/64 | **40** | 1 | 1. Say You | Diamond 167 |
| 11/14/64 | **14** | 7 | 2. Right Or Wrong | Diamond 173 |
| 4/10/65 | **14** | 7 | 3. One Kiss For Old Times' Sake | Diamond 179 |
| 6/26/65 | **16** | 6 | 4. A Little Bit Of Heaven | Diamond 184 |
| 9/18/65 | **21** | 5 | 5. I'll Make All Your Dreams Come True | Diamond 188 |
| 11/27/65 | **25** | 4 | 6. Kiss Away | Diamond 191 |
| 2/05/66 | **18** | 7 | 7. When Liking Turns To Loving | Diamond 195 |
| 5/07/66 | **20** | 5 | 8. Let's Start All Over Again | Diamond 198 |
| 7/09/66 | **27** | 4 | 9. Happy Summer Days | Diamond 205 |
| 9/24/66 | **22** | 5 | 10. I Really Don't Want To Know | Diamond 208 |
| 12/10/66 | **18** | 6 | 11. Cry | Diamond 214 |
| | | | **DOVELLS** | |
| | | | Len Barry, lead singer of Philadelphia quartet | |
| 9/18/61 | **2** (2) | 14 | 1. **Bristol Stomp** | Parkway 827 |
| 3/03/62 | **37** | 2 | 2. Do The New Continental | Parkway 833 |
| 6/23/62 | **27** | 5 | 3. Bristol Twistin' Annie | Parkway 838 |
| 9/15/62 | **25** | 7 | 4. Hully Gully Baby | Parkway 845 |
| 5/11/63 | **3** | 11 | 5. **You Can't Sit Down** | Parkway 867 |
| | | | **JOE DOWELL** | |
| 7/17/61 | **1** (1) | 12 | 1. **Wooden Heart** | Smash 1708 |
| 7/28/62 | **23** | 4 | 2. Little Red Rented Rowboat | Smash 1759 |
| | | | **LAMONT DOZIER** | |
| | | | 1/3 of songwriting team Holland-Dozier-Holland | |
| 2/16/74 | **15** | 9 | 1. Trying To Hold On To My Woman | ABC 11407 |
| 7/06/74 | **26** | 6 | 2. Fish Ain't Bitin' | ABC 11438 |
| | | | **CHARLIE DRAKE** | |
| | | | British | |
| 2/17/62 | **21** | 6 | 1. My Boomerang Won't Come Back [N] | United Art. 398 |
| | | | **PETE DRAKE & His Talking Steel Guitar** | |
| | | | Grand Ole Opry steel guitarist | |
| 4/11/64 | **25** | 5 | 1. Forever | Smash 1867 |
| | | | **DRAMATICS** | |
| | | | Detroit quintet - Ron Banks, lead singer | |
| 7/31/71 | **9** | 11 | 1. **Whatcha See Is Whatcha Get** | Volt 4058 |
| 3/04/72 | **5** | 11 | 2. **In The Rain** | Volt 4075 |
| | | | **RUSTY DRAPER** | |
| 8/20/55 | **18** | 4 | 1. Seventeen | Mercury 70651 |
| 10/01/55 | **3** | 16 | 2. **The Shifting, Whispering Sands** | Mercury 70696 |
| 12/31/55 + | **11** | 12 | 3. Are You Satisfied? | Mercury 70757 |
| 9/22/56 | **20** | 8 | 4. In The Middle Of The House [N] | Mercury 70921 |
| 5/27/57 | **6** | 12 | 5. **Freight Train** | Mercury 71102 |

| DATE | POS | WKS | ARTIST—Record Title | LABEL & NO. |
|------|-----|-----|---------------------|-------------|
| | | | **DREAMLOVERS** | |
| | | | backup vocal group for Chubby Checker's "The Twist" | |
| 8/28/61 | **10** | 6 | 1. **When We Get Married** | Heritage 102 |
| | | | **DREAM WEAVERS** | |
| | | | Wade Buff, lead singer of trio from Miami, Florida | |
| 11/12/55 + | **7** | 21 | 1. **It's Almost Tomorrow** | Decca 29683 |
| 5/19/56 | **33** | 1 | 2. A Little Love Can Go A Long, Long Way | Decca 29905 |
| | | | from the Goodyear TV show "Joey" | |
| | | | **DRIFTERS** | |
| | | | trend setting R&B vocal group formed in 1953 | |
| 6/29/59 | **2** (1) | 14 | 1. **There Goes My Baby** | Atlantic 2025 |
| 11/02/59 | **15** | 9 | 2. Dance With Me/ | |
| 11/23/59 | **33** | 5 | 3.  (If You Cry) True Love, True Love | Atlantic 2040 |
| 3/14/60 | **16** | 6 | 4. This Magic Moment | Atlantic 2050 |
| 9/19/60 | **1** (3) | 14 | 5. **Save The Last Dance For Me** | Atlantic 2071 |
| 12/31/60 + | **17** | 7 | 6. I Count The Tears | Atlantic 2087 |
| | | | Ben E. King, lead singer on above songs (except #3) | |
| 4/10/61 | **32** | 6 | 7. Some Kind Of Wonderful | Atlantic 2096 |
| 6/26/61 | **14** | 8 | 8. Please Stay | Atlantic 2105 |
| 9/25/61 | **16** | 9 | 9. Sweets For My Sweet | Atlantic 2117 |
| 3/24/62 | **28** | 4 | 10. When My Little Girl Is Smiling | Atlantic 2134 |
| 12/29/62 + | **5** | 11 | 11. **Up On The Roof** | Atlantic 2162 |
| 4/06/63 | **9** | 8 | 12. **On Broadway** | Atlantic 2182 |
| 10/05/63 | **25** | 5 | 13. I'll Take You Home | Atlantic 2201 |
| 7/11/64 | **4** | 12 | 14. **Under The Boardwalk** | Atlantic 2237 |
| 10/10/64 | **33** | 5 | 15. I've Got Sand In My Shoes | Atlantic 2253 |
| 11/28/64 | **18** | 7 | 16. Saturday Night At The Movies | Atlantic 2260 |
| | | | **ROY DRUSKY** | |
| 6/26/61 | **35** | 1 | 1. Three Hearts In A Tangle | Decca 31193 |
| | | | **DUALS** | |
| | | | Henry Bellinger & Johnny Lageman | |
| 10/02/61 | **25** | 6 | 1. Stick Shift [I] | Sue 745 |
| | | | **DUBS** | |
| | | | R&B quintet - Richard Blandon, lead singer | |
| 11/18/57 | **23** | 8 | 1. Could This Be Magic | Gone 5011 |
| | | | **DAVE DUDLEY** | |
| 7/20/63 | **32** | 4 | 1. Six Days On The Road | Golden Wing 3020 |
| | | | **GEORGE DUKE - see STANLEY CLARKE** | |
| | | | **PATTY DUKE** | |
| | | | star of TV's "Patty Duke Show" | |
| 7/17/65 | **8** | 8 | 1. **Don't Just Stand There** | United Art. 875 |
| 10/30/65 | **22** | 4 | 2. Say Something Funny | United Art. 915 |
| | | | **DAVID DUNDAS** | |
| | | | English | |
| 11/27/76 + | **17** | 13 | 1. Jeans On | Chrysalis 2094 |

| DATE | POS | WKS | ARTIST—Record Title | LABEL & NO. |
|------|-----|-----|---------------------|-------------|
| | | | **ROBBIE DUPREE** | |
| 5/03/80 | **6** | 15 | 1. **Steal Away** | Elektra 46621 |
| 8/09/80 | **15** | 12 | 2. Hot Rod Hearts | Elektra 47005 |
| | | | **DUPREES** | |
| | | | Jersey City quintet - Joseph Canzano, lead singer | |
| 8/25/62 | **7** | 9 | 1. **You Belong To Me** | Coed 569 |
| 11/10/62 | **13** | 6 | 2. My Own True Love | Coed 571 |
| | | | Tara's Theme from "Gone With The Wind" | |
| 9/14/63 | **37** | 3 | 3. Why Don't You Believe Me | Coed 584 |
| 11/30/63 | **18** | 6 | 4. Have You Heard | Coed 585 |
| | | | **DURAN DURAN** | |
| | | | British: Simon Le Bon (vocals), Andy Taylor (guitar), John Taylor (bass), Roger Taylor (drums), Nick Rhodes (keyboards) | |
| 1/22/83 | **3** | 16 | 1. **Hungry Like The Wolf** | Harvest 5195 |
| 4/09/83 | **14** | 9 | 2. Rio | Capitol 5215 |
| 6/18/83 | **4** | 12 | 3. **Is There Something I Should Know** | Capitol 5233 |
| 11/19/83 | **3** | 12 | 4. **Union Of The Snake** | Capitol 5290 |
| 1/28/84 | **10** | 10 | 5. **New Moon On Monday** | Capitol 5309 |
| 4/28/84 | **1** (2) | 15 | 6. **The Reflex** | Capitol 5345 |
| 11/03/84 | **2** (4) | 14 | 7. **The Wild Boys** | Capitol 5417 |
| | | | **DYKE & THE BLAZERS** | |
| | | | Dyke is Arlester Christian | |
| 7/05/69 | **35** | 3 | 1. We Got More Soul | Original Sound 86 |
| 11/01/69 | **36** | 1 | 2. Let A Woman Be A Woman - Let A Man Be A Man | Original Sound 89 |
| | | | **BOB DYLAN** | |
| | | | born Robert Allen Zimmerman on 5/24/41 in Duluth, Minnesota - Bob was the spokesman of the folk-protest movement | |
| 5/15/65 | **39** | 1 | 1. Subterranean Homesick Blues | Columbia 43242 |
| 8/14/65 | **2** (2) | 9 | 2. **Like A Rolling Stone** | Columbia 43346 |
| 10/09/65 | **7** | 7 | 3. **Positively 4th Street** | Columbia 43389 |
| 4/23/66 | **2** (1) | 9 | 4. **Rainy Day Women #12 & 35** | Columbia 43592 |
| 7/16/66 | **20** | 4 | 5. I Want You | Columbia 43683 |
| 10/01/66 | **33** | 3 | 6. Just Like A Woman | Columbia 43792 |
| 8/02/69 | **7** | 11 | 7. **Lay Lady Lay** | Columbia 44926 |
| 12/25/71 + | **33** | 4 | 8. George Jackson | Columbia 45516 |
| 9/29/73 | **12** | 11 | 9. Knockin' On Heaven's Door | Columbia 45913 |
| 3/29/75 | **31** | 3 | 10. Tangled Up In Blue | Columbia 10106 |
| 1/03/76 | **33** | 3 | 11. Hurricane (Part 1) | Columbia 10245 |
| | | | dedicated to boxer Rubin Carter | |
| 10/06/79 | **24** | 6 | 12. Gotta Serve Somebody | Columbia 11072 |
| | | | **RONNIE DYSON** | |
| | | | starred in the Broadway musical "Hair" | |
| 7/25/70 | **8** | 9 | 1. **(If You Let Me Make Love To You Then) Why Can't I Touch You?** | Columbia 45110 |
| | | | from the musical "Salvation" | |
| 4/07/73 | **28** | 4 | 2. One Man Band (Plays All Alone) | Columbia 45776 |

| DATE | POS | WKS | ARTIST—Record Title | LABEL & NO. |
|---|---|---|---|---|
| | | | **EAGLES** | |
| | | | Don Henley, Glen Frey, Randy Meisner (1-11), Bernie Leadon (1-8), Don Felder (5-16), Joe Walsh (9-16), Timothy B. Schmit (13-16) | |
| 6/24/72 | 12 | 8 | 1. Take It Easy | Asylum 11005 |
| 9/30/72 | 9 | 10 | 2. **Witchy Woman** | Asylum 11008 |
| 2/03/73 | 22 | 6 | 3. Peaceful Easy Feeling | Asylum 11013 |
| 6/22/74 | 32 | 3 | 4. Already Gone | Asylum 11036 |
| 12/28/74 + | 1 (1) | 14 | 5. **Best Of My Love** | Asylum 45218 |
| 6/14/75 | 1 (1) | 14 | 6. **One Of These Nights** | Asylum 45257 |
| 9/27/75 | 2 (2) | 11 | 7. **Lyin' Eyes** | Asylum 45279 |
| 1/17/76 | 4 | 14 | 8. **Take It To The Limit** | Asylum 45293 |
| 12/25/76 + | 1 (1) | 13 | ● 9. **New Kid In Town** | Asylum 45373 |
| 3/12/77 | 1 (1) | 15 | ● 10. **Hotel California** | Asylum 45386 |
| 5/28/77 | 11 | 8 | 11. Life In The Fast Lane | Asylum 45403 |
| 12/23/78 | 18 | 5 | 12. Please Come Home For Christmas [X] | Asylum 45555 |
| 10/13/79 | 1 (1) | 13 | ● 13. **Heartache Tonight** | Asylum 46545 |
| 12/08/79 + | 8 | 12 | 14. **The Long Run** | Asylum 46569 |
| 3/01/80 | 8 | 12 | 15. **I Can't Tell You Why** | Asylum 46608 |
| 1/10/81 | 21 | 7 | 16. Seven Bridges Road | Asylum 47100 |
| | | | **EARL-JEAN** | |
| | | | Earl-Jean McCree of The Cookies | |
| 8/08/64 | 38 | 1 | 1. I'm Into Somethin' Good | Colpix 729 |
| | | | **EARLS** | |
| | | | Bronx quartet - Larry Chance, lead singer | |
| 1/12/63 | 24 | 4 | 1. Remember Then | Old Town 1130 |
| | | | **EARTH, WIND & FIRE** | |
| | | | Chicago group, led by vocalists Maurice White and Philip Bailey | |
| 4/27/74 | 29 | 7 | 1. Mighty Mighty | Columbia 46007 |
| 10/12/74 | 33 | 2 | 2. Devotion | Columbia 10026 |
| 3/22/75 | 1 (1) | 14 | ● 3. **Shining Star** | Columbia 10090 |
| 7/26/75 | 12 | 11 | 4. That's The Way Of The World | Columbia 10172 |
| 12/13/75 + | 5 | 12 | ● 5. **Sing A Song** | Columbia 10251 |
| 4/24/76 | 39 | 2 | 6. Can't Hide Love | Columbia 10309 |
| 8/14/76 | 12 | 12 | ● 7. Getaway | Columbia 10373 |
| 12/11/76 + | 21 | 10 | 8. Saturday Nite | Columbia 10439 |
| 11/26/77 + | 13 | 13 | 9. Serpentine Fire | Columbia 10625 |
| 4/01/78 | 32 | 5 | 10. Fantasy | Columbia 10688 |
| 8/05/78 | 9 | 9 | ● 11. **Got To Get You Into My Life** | Columbia 10796 |
| 12/16/78 + | 8 | 11 | ● 12. **September** | ARC 10854 |
| 7/28/79 | 2 (2) | 13 | ● 13. **After The Love Has Gone** | ARC 11033 |
| 10/31/81 | 3 | 16 | ● 14. **Let's Groove** | ARC 02536 |
| 2/12/83 | 17 | 10 | 15. Fall In Love With Me | Columbia 03375 |
| | | | **EARTH, WIND & FIRE with THE EMOTIONS** | |
| 5/26/79 | 6 | 12 | ● 1. **Boogie Wonderland** | ARC 10956 |

| DATE | POS | WKS | ARTIST—Record Title | LABEL & NO. |
|---|---|---|---|---|
| | | | **SHEENA EASTON** | |
| | | | born Sheena Orr on 4/27/59 in Glasgow, Scotland - also see Kenny Rogers | |
| 2/28/81 | **1** (2) | 15 | ● 1. **Morning Train (Nine To Five)** | EMI America 8071 |
| 6/06/81 | **18** | 9 | 2. Modern Girl | EMI America 8080 |
| 8/22/81 | **4** | 14 | 3. **For Your Eyes Only** | Liberty 1418 |
| 12/19/81 + | **15** | 12 | 4. You Could Have Been With Me | EMI America 8101 |
| 5/08/82 | **30** | 6 | 5. When He Shines | EMI America 8113 |
| 9/10/83 | **9** | 14 | 6. **Telefone (Long Distance Love Affair)** | EMI America 8172 |
| 2/11/84 | **25** | 6 | 7. Almost Over You | EMI America 8186 |
| 9/22/84 | **7** | 15 | 8. **Strut** | EMI America 8227 |
| | | | **EASYBEATS** | |
| | | | Australian quintet - members George Young & Harry Vanda formed "Flash & The Pan" | |
| 4/22/67 | **16** | 8 | 1. Friday On My Mind | United Art. 50106 |
| | | | **EASY RIDERS - see TERRY GILKYSON** | |
| | | | **ECHOES** | |
| | | | Brooklyn trio | |
| 3/27/61 | **12** | 9 | 1. Baby Blue | Seg-Way 103 |
| | | | **DUANE EDDY** | |
| | | | born in Corning, New York on 4/26/38 - Duane, with his "twangy" guitar, is rock and roll's #1 instrumentalist | |
| 7/07/58 | **6** | 12 | 1. **Rebel-'Rouser [I]** | Jamie 1104 |
| 9/15/58 | **27** | 5 | 2. Ramrod [I] | Jamie 1109 |
| 11/17/58 | **15** | 9 | 3. Cannonball [I] | Jamie 1111 |
| 2/02/59 | **23** | 8 | 4. The Lonely One [I] | Jamie 1117 |
| 4/20/59 | **30** | 2 | 5. "Yep!" [I] | Jamie 1122 |
| 6/29/59 | **9** | 11 | 6. **Forty Miles Of Bad Road [I]** | Jamie 1126 |
| 10/26/59 | **37** | 3 | 7. Some Kind-A Earthquake [I] | Jamie 1130 |
| 1/11/60 | **26** | 5 | 8. Bonnie Came Back [I] | Jamie 1144 |
| 6/06/60 | **4** | 12 | 9. **Because They're Young [I]** | Jamie 1156 |
| 10/31/60 | **27** | 4 | 10. Peter Gunn [I] | Jamie 1168 |
| 1/16/61 | **18** | 7 | 11. "Pepe" [I] | Jamie 1175 |
| 4/17/61 | **39** | 1 | 12. Theme From Dixie [I] | Jamie 1183 |
| 8/11/62 | **33** | 3 | 13. The Ballad Of Paladin [I] theme from TV's "Have Gun-Will Travel" | RCA 8047 |
| 11/03/62 | **12** | 10 | 14. (Dance With The) Guitar Man | RCA 8087 |
| 2/23/63 | **28** | 5 | 15. Boss Guitar | RCA 8131 |
| | | | **EDISON LIGHTHOUSE** | |
| | | | English studio group | |
| 2/28/70 | **5** | 12 | ● 1. **Love Grows (Where My Rosemary Goes)** | Bell 858 |
| | | | **DAVE EDMUNDS** | |
| | | | Welsh - leader of Rockpile | |
| 1/16/71 | **4** | 9 | 1. **I Hear You Knocking** | MAM 3601 |
| 7/30/83 | **39** | 1 | 2. Slipping Away | Columbia 03877 |

| DATE | POS | WKS | ARTIST—Record Title | LABEL & NO. |
|------|-----|-----|---------------------|-------------|
| | | | **EDSELS** | |
| | | | quintet from Youngstown, Ohio | |
| 6/05/61 | **21** | 5 | 1. Rama Lama Ding Dong | Twin 700 |
| | | | originally released on the Dub label in 1958 | |
| | | | **EDWARD BEAR** | |
| | | | Canadian trio led by Larry Evoy | |
| 1/27/73 | **3** | 12 | ● 1. **Last Song** | Capitol 3452 |
| 5/26/73 | **37** | 2 | 2. Close Your Eyes | Capitol 3581 |
| | | | **BOBBY EDWARDS** | |
| 10/16/61 | **11** | 9 | 1. You're The Reason | Crest 1075 |
| | | | **JONATHAN EDWARDS** | |
| 12/04/71 + | **4** | 12 | ● 1. **Sunshine** | Capricorn 8021 |
| | | | **TOMMY EDWARDS** | |
| | | | died on 10/22/69 (47) | |
| 8/25/58 | **1** (6) | 19 | 1. **It's All In The Game** | MGM 12688 |
| | | | written by U.S. Vice President Charles Dawes | |
| | | | original version charted in 1951 (Pos. 18) | |
| 11/17/58 | **15** | 9 | 2. Love Is All We Need | MGM 12722 |
| 3/02/59 | **11** | 8 | 3. Please Mr. Sun/ | |
| | | | original version charted in 1952 (Pos. 22) | |
| 3/23/59 | **27** | 4 | 4. The Morning Side Of The Mountain | MGM 12757 |
| | | | original version charted in 1951 (Pos. 24) | |
| 6/08/59 | **26** | 4 | 5. My Melancholy Baby | MGM 12794 |
| 6/06/60 | **18** | 7 | 6. I Really Don't Want To Know | MGM 12890 |
| | | | **WALTER EGAN** | |
| 7/01/78 | **8** | 13 | ● 1. **Magnet And Steel** | Columbia 10719 |
| | | | **8TH DAY** | |
| | | | Detroit session musicians | |
| 6/05/71 | **11** | 10 | ● 1. She's Not Just Another Woman | Invictus 9087 |
| 10/16/71 | **28** | 6 | 2. You've Got To Crawl (Before You Walk) | Invictus 9098 |
| | | | **EL CHICANO** | |
| | | | Mexican-American band led by Bobby Espinosa | |
| 5/02/70 | **28** | 5 | 1. Viva Tirado - Part I [I] | Kapp 2085 |
| 12/22/73 | **40** | 1 | 2. Tell Her She's Lovely | MCA 40104 |
| | | | **EL DORADOS** | |
| | | | Chicago R&B quintet - Pirkle Lee Moses, lead singer | |
| 10/15/55 | **17** | 6 | 1. At My Front Door | Vee-Jay 147 |
| | | | **DONNIE ELBERT** | |
| 11/20/71 | **15** | 8 | 1. Where Did Our Love Go | All Platinum 2330 |
| 2/12/72 | **22** | 6 | 2. I Can't Help Myself (Sugar Pie, Honey Bunch) | Avco 4587 |
| | | | **ELECTRIC INDIAN** | |
| 8/23/69 | **16** | 8 | 1. Keem-O-Sabe [I] | United Art. 50563 |

| DATE | POS | WKS | ARTIST—Record Title | LABEL & NO. |
|---|---|---|---|---|
| | | | **ELECTRIC LIGHT ORCHESTRA** | |
| | | | British symphonic rock band led by Jeff Lynne - also see Olivia Newton-John | |
| 1/25/75 | 9 | 10 | 1. **Can't Get It Out Of My Head** | United Art. 573 |
| 12/13/75 + | 10 | 12 | 2. **Evil Woman** | United Art. 729 |
| 4/10/76 | 14 | 9 | 3. Strange Magic | United Art. 770 |
| 11/13/76 + | 13 | 14 | 4. Livin' Thing | United Art. 888 |
| 3/05/77 | 24 | 6 | 5. Do Ya | United Art. 939 |
| | | | originally charted by the Move (forerunner of ELO) in 1972 | |
| 7/09/77 | 7 | 16 | ● 6. **Telephone Line** | United Art. 1000 |
| 12/10/77 + | 13 | 10 | 7. Turn To Stone | Jet 1099 |
| 3/11/78 | 17 | 12 | 8. Sweet Talkin' Woman | Jet 1145 |
| 7/29/78 | 35 | 3 | 9. Mr. Blue Sky | Jet 5050 |
| 6/02/79 | 8 | 11 | 10. **Shine A Little Love** | Jet 5057 |
| 8/11/79 | 4 | 11 | ● 11. **Don't Bring Me Down** | Jet 5060 |
| 11/17/79 | 37 | 2 | 12. Confusion | Jet 5064 |
| 1/26/80 | 39 | 2 | 13. Last Train To London | Jet 5067 |
| 6/14/80 | 16 | 8 | ● 14. I'm Alive | MCA 41246 |
| 8/16/80 | 13 | 9 | 15. All Over The World | MCA 41289 |
| | | | above 2 are from the film "Xanadu" | |
| 8/08/81 | 10 | 13 | 16. **Hold On Tight** | Jet 02408 |
| 11/28/81 | 38 | 2 | 17. Twilight | Jet 02559 |
| 7/09/83 | 19 | 9 | 18. Rock 'N' Roll Is King | Jet 03964 |
| | | | **ELECTRIC PRUNES** | |
| | | | Seattle rock quartet led by James Lowe | |
| 1/21/67 | 11 | 8 | 1. I Had Too Much To Dream (Last Night) | Reprise 0532 |
| 4/22/67 | 27 | 5 | 2. Get Me To The World On Time | Reprise 0564 |
| | | | **ELEGANTS** | |
| | | | Italian doo-wop quintet from Staten Island, New York - Vito Picone, lead singer | |
| 7/28/58 | 1 (1) | 16 | 1. **Little Star** | Apt 25005 |
| | | | **LARRY ELGART & his Manhattan Swing Orchestra** | |
| | | | big band leader of the '40's | |
| 7/03/82 | 31 | 5 | 1. Hooked On Swing (medley) [I] | RCA 13219 |
| | | | **JIMMY ELLEDGE** | |
| 12/25/61 + | 22 | 7 | 1. Funny How Time Slips Away | RCA 7946 |
| | | | **YVONNE ELLIMAN** | |
| | | | Hawaiian - portrayed Mary Magdalene in "Jesus Christ Superstar" | |
| 5/22/71 | 28 | 6 | 1. I Don't Know How To Love Him | Decca 32785 |
| | | | from the rock opera "Jesus Christ Superstar" | |
| 11/06/76 | 14 | 12 | 2. Love Me | RSO 858 |
| 4/16/77 | 15 | 9 | 3. Hello Stranger | RSO 871 |
| 2/25/78 | 1 (1) | 16 | ● 4. **If I Can't Have You** | RSO 884 |
| | | | from the film "Saturday Night Fever" | |
| 12/01/79 | 34 | 3 | 5. Love Pains | RSO 1007 |

| DATE | POS | WKS | ARTIST—Record Title | LABEL & NO. |
|---|---|---|---|---|
| | | | **SHIRLEY ELLIS** | |
| 12/07/63 + | 8 | 10 | 1. **The Nitty Gritty** | Congress 202 |
| 1/09/65 | 3 | 10 | 2. **The Name Game** | Congress 230 |
| 4/03/65 | 8 | 7 | 3. **The Clapping Song (Clap Pat Clap Slap)** | Congress 234 |
| | | | **EMERSON, LAKE & PALMER** | |
| | | | English: Keith Emerson (keyboards), Greg Lake (guitar, vocals), & Carl Palmer (drums) | |
| 10/21/72 | 39 | 2 | 1. From The Beginning | Cotillion 44158 |
| | | | **EMOTIONS** | |
| | | | sisters Wanda, Sheila, & Jeanette Hutchinson from Chicago - also see Earth, Wind & Fire | |
| 7/19/69 | 39 | 1 | 1. So I Can Love You | Volt 4010 |
| 7/02/77 | 1 (5) | 17 | ● 2. **Best Of My Love** | Columbia 10544 |
| | | | **ENCHANTMENT** | |
| | | | Detroit soul quintet | |
| 3/05/77 | 25 | 5 | 1. Gloria | United Art. 912 |
| 3/11/78 | 33 | 4 | 2. It's You That I Need | Roadshow 1124 |
| | | | **ENGLAND DAN & JOHN FORD COLEY** | |
| | | | Texas duo - Dan Seals is Jim Seals (Seals & Crofts) brother | |
| 7/10/76 | 2 (2) | 17 | ● 1. **I'd Really Love To See You Tonight** | Big Tree 16069 |
| 10/30/76 | 10 | 12 | 2. **Nights Are Forever Without You** | Big Tree 16079 |
| 6/18/77 | 21 | 8 | 3. It's Sad To Belong | Big Tree 16088 |
| 11/05/77 | 23 | 6 | 4. Gone Too Far | Big Tree 16102 |
| 3/11/78 | 9 | 8 | 5. **We'll Never Have To Say Goodbye Again** | Big Tree 16110 |
| 4/07/79 | 10 | 10 | 6. **Love Is The Answer** | Big Tree 16131 |
| | | | **ENGLISH CONGREGATION** | |
| 2/19/72 | 29 | 5 | 1. Softly Whispering I Love You | Atco 6865 |
| | | | **PRESTON EPPS** | |
| 6/01/59 | 14 | 9 | 1. Bongo Rock [I] | Original Sound 4 |
| | | | **EQUALS** | |
| | | | English/Jamaican band led by Eddy Grant | |
| 9/28/68 | 32 | 6 | 1. Baby, Come Back | RCA 9583 |
| | | | **ERNIE** | |
| | | | Ernie is one of Jim Henson's Muppets - also see Kermit | |
| 8/29/70 | 16 | 7 | 1. Rubber Duckie [N] | Columbia 45207 |
| | | | **ERUPTION** | |
| | | | Jamaican band featuring Precious Wilson | |
| 6/10/78 | 18 | 6 | 1. I Can't Stand The Rain | Ariola 7686 |
| | | | **ESQUIRES** | |
| | | | soul quartet from Milwaukee, Wisconsin | |
| 9/16/67 | 11 | 10 | 1. Get On Up | Bunky 7750 |
| 12/16/67 | 22 | 5 | 2. And Get Away | Bunky 7752 |
| | | | **ESSEX** | |
| | | | formed quintet at the U.S. Marine Corps. Camp LeJune | |
| 6/22/63 | 1 (2) | 10 | 1. **Easier Said Than Done** | Roulette 4494 |
| 9/14/63 | 12 | 6 | 2. A Walkin' Miracle | Roulette 4515 |

| DATE | POS | WKS | ARTIST—Record Title | LABEL & NO. |
|------|-----|-----|---------------------|-------------|
| | | | **DAVID ESSEX** | |
| | | | British - leading actor in London's "Godspell" musical | |
| 1/12/74 | 5 | 14 | ● 1. **Rock On** | Columbia 45940 |
| | | | **EURYTHMICS** | |
| | | | British: Annie Lennox & David Stewart (formerly The Tourists) | |
| 6/18/83 | 1 (1) | 17 | ● 1. **Sweet Dreams (Are Made of This)** | RCA 13533 |
| 10/15/83 | 23 | 6 | 2. Love Is A Stranger | RCA 13618 |
| 2/04/84 | 4 | 14 | 3. **Here Comes The Rain Again** | RCA 13725 |
| 5/19/84 | 21 | 7 | 4. Who's That Girl? | RCA 13800 |
| 8/11/84 | 29 | 5 | 5. Right By Your Side | RCA 13695 |
| | | | **PAUL EVANS** | |
| | | | writer of "When" (Kalin Twins) & "Roses Are Red" (Bobby Vinton) | |
| 10/05/59 | 9 | 11 | 1. **Seven Little Girls Sitting In The Back Seat** | Guaranteed 200 |
| | | | with the Curls (female backing duo) | |
| 2/15/60 | 16 | 7 | 2. Midnite Special | Guaranteed 205 |
| 5/30/60 | 10 | 8 | 3. **Happy-Go-Lucky-Me** | Guaranteed 208 |
| | | | **BETTY EVERETT** | |
| | | | also see Jerry Butler | |
| 3/21/64 | 6 | 10 | 1. **The Shoop Shoop Song (It's In His Kiss)** | Vee-Jay 585 |
| 2/15/69 | 26 | 6 | 2. There'll Come A Time | Uni 55100 |
| | | | **EVERLY BROTHERS** | |
| | | | born in Brownie, Kentucky - Don on 2/1/37; Phil on 1/19/39 | |
| 5/27/57 | 2 (4) | 22 | 1. **Bye Bye Love** | Cadence 1315 |
| 9/30/57 | 1 (4) | 20 | 2. **Wake Up Little Susie** | Cadence 1337 |
| 2/17/58 | 26 | 3 | 3. This Little Girl Of Mine | Cadence 1342 |
| 4/28/58 | 1 (5) | 16 | 4. **All I Have To Do Is Dream/** | |
| 5/12/58 | 30 | 2 | 5. Claudette | Cadence 1348 |
| 8/11/58 | 1 (1) | 15 | 6. **Bird Dog/** | |
| 8/18/58 | 10 | 11 | 7. **Devoted To You** | Cadence 1350 |
| 11/24/58 | 2 (1) | 11 | 8. **Problems/** | |
| 12/15/58 | 40 | 1 | 9. Love Of My Life | Cadence 1355 |
| 4/20/59 | 16 | 8 | 10. Take A Message To Mary/ | |
| 4/20/59 | 22 | 6 | 11. Poor Jenny | Cadence 1364 |
| 8/24/59 | 4 | 13 | 12. **('Til) I Kissed You** | Cadence 1369 |
| 1/25/60 | 7 | 11 | 13. **Let It Be Me** | Cadence 1376 |
| 5/02/60 | 1 (5) | 13 | 14. **Cathy's Clown** | Warner 5151 |
| 6/27/60 | 8 | 9 | 15. **When Will I Be Loved** | Cadence 1380 |
| 9/12/60 | 7 | 10 | 16. **So Sad (To Watch Good Love Go Bad)/** | |
| 9/12/60 | 21 | 7 | 17. Lucille | Warner 5163 |
| 11/28/60 | 22 | 4 | 18. Like Strangers | Cadence 1388 |
| 2/13/61 | 7 | 10 | 19. **Walk Right Back/** | |
| 2/13/61 | 8 | 9 | 20. Ebony Eyes | Warner 5199 |
| 6/12/61 | 27 | 3 | 21. Temptation | Warner 5220 |
| 10/09/61 | 20 | 6 | 22. Don't Blame Me | Warner 5501 |
| 2/03/62 | 6 | 9 | 23. **Crying In The Rain** | Warner 5250 |

| DATE | POS | WKS | ARTIST—Record Title | LABEL & NO. |
|------|-----|-----|---------------------|-------------|
| 6/02/62 | 9 | 7 | 24. **That's Old Fashioned (That's The Way Love Should Be)** | Warner 5273 |
| 12/05/64 | 31 | 2 | 25. Gone, Gone, Gone | Warner 5478 |
| 7/08/67 | 40 | 2 | 26. Bowling Green | Warner 7020 |
| | | | **EVERY MOTHERS' SON** | |
| | | | New York quintet | |
| 5/27/67 | 6 | 12 | 1. **Come On Down To My Boat** | MGM 13733 |
| | | | **EXCITERS** | |
| | | | New York quartet led by Herb Rooney and his wife Brenda Reid | |
| 12/15/62 + | 4 | 10 | 1. **Tell Him** | United Art. 544 |
| | | | **EXILE** | |
| | | | 6-man group from Lexington, Kentucky | |
| 8/05/78 | 1 (4) | 17 | ● 1. **Kiss You All Over** | Warner 8589 |
| 2/03/79 | 40 | 1 | 2. You Thrill Me | Warner 8711 |
| | | | **EYE TO EYE** | |
| | | | duo: Deborah Berg & Julian Marshall (of Marshall Hain) | |
| 7/17/82 | 37 | 3 | 1. Nice Girls | Warner 50050 |
| | | | **SHELLEY FABARES** | |
| | | | Nanette Fabray's niece | |
| 3/17/62 | 1 (2) | 13 | 1. **Johnny Angel** | Colpix 621 |
| 6/30/62 | 21 | 6 | 2. Johnny Loves Me | Colpix 636 |
| | | | **FABIAN** | |
| | | | Fabian Forte - born in Philadelphia on 2/6/43 | |
| 2/02/59 | 31 | 3 | 1. I'm A Man | Chancellor 1029 |
| 4/06/59 | 9 | 11 | 2. **Turn Me Loose** | Chancellor 1033 |
| 6/22/59 | 3 | 10 | 3. **Tiger** | Chancellor 1037 |
| 9/28/59 | 29 | 3 | 4. Come On And Get Me | Chancellor 1041 |
| 11/30/59 | 9 | 11 | 5. **Hound Dog Man**/ | |
| 12/07/59 | 12 | 9 | 6. This Friendly World | Chancellor 1044 |
| | | | above 2 from the film "Hound Dog Man" | |
| 3/14/60 | 31 | 3 | 7. About This Thing Called Love/ | |
| 3/14/60 | 39 | 2 | 8. String Along | Chancellor 1047 |
| | | | **BENT FABRIC & His Piano** | |
| | | | Bent Fabricius-Bierre - from Denmark | |
| 8/25/62 | 7 | 12 | 1. **Alley Cat [I]** | Atco 6226 |
| | | | **FACE TO FACE** | |
| | | | Boston rock quintet - lead singer Laurie Sargent (featured in the film "Streets Of Fire") | |
| 7/21/84 | 38 | 3 | 1. 10-9-8 | Epic 04430 |
| | | | **TOMMY FACENDA** | |
| 11/09/59 | 28 | 3 | 1. High School U.S.A. [N] | Atlantic 51 - 78 |
| | | | Atlantic released 28 different versions of this record, each mentioning the names of high schools in various cities | |
| | | | **FACES** | |
| | | | Rod Stewart, lead singer of British group descended from the Small Faces | |
| 1/15/72 | 17 | 8 | 1. Stay With Me | Warner 7545 |

| DATE | POS | WKS | ARTIST—Record Title | LABEL & NO. |
|------|-----|-----|---------------------|-------------|
| | | | **FACTS OF LIFE** | |
| 4/09/77 | 31 | 4 | 1. Sometimes | Kayvette 5128 |
| | | | **DONALD FAGEN** | |
| | | | member of Steely Dan | |
| 10/30/82 | 26 | 7 | 1. I.G.Y. (What A Beautiful World) | Warner 29900 |
| | | | I.G.Y.: International Geo-physical Year (Jul '57-Dec '58) | |
| | | | **BARBARA FAIRCHILD** | |
| 5/12/73 | 32 | 5 | 1. Teddy Bear Song | Columbia 45743 |
| | | | **ADAM FAITH** | |
| | | | British | |
| 2/20/65 | 31 | 2 | 1. It's Alright | Amy 913 |
| | | | with The Roulettes | |
| | | | **PERCY FAITH & His Orchestra** | |
| | | | Canadian conductor-arranger - died on 2/9/76 (67) | |
| 1/25/60 | 1 (9) | 17 | ● 1. **The Theme From "A Summer Place" [I]** | Columbia 41490 |
| 6/27/60 | 35 | 1 | 2. Theme For Young Lovers [I] | Columbia 41655 |
| | | | **MARIANNE FAITHFULL** | |
| | | | English | |
| 12/19/64 + | 22 | 6 | 1. As Tears Go By | London 9697 |
| 3/27/65 | 26 | 5 | 2. Come And Stay With Me | London 9731 |
| 6/26/65 | 32 | 5 | 3. This Little Bird | London 9759 |
| 9/04/65 | 24 | 5 | 4. Summer Nights | London 9780 |
| | | | **FALCONS** | |
| | | | Detroit R&B quintet - Eddie Floyd, lead singer | |
| 6/08/59 | 17 | 10 | 1. You're So Fine | Unart 2013 |
| | | | **AGNETHA FALTSKOG** | |
| | | | member of Abba | |
| 10/08/83 | 29 | 5 | 1. Can't Shake Loose | Polydor 815230 |
| | | | **GEORGIE FAME** | |
| | | | English | |
| 2/27/65 | 21 | 6 | 1. Yeh, Yeh | Imperial 66086 |
| | | | with The Blue Flames | |
| 3/02/68 | 7 | 12 | 2. **The Ballad Of Bonnie And Clyde** | Epic 10283 |
| | | | **FANCY** | |
| | | | English rock group - Helen Court, lead singer | |
| 8/03/74 | 14 | 8 | 1. Wild Thing | Big Tree 15004 |
| 11/16/74 | 19 | 4 | 2. Touch Me | Big Tree 16026 |
| | | | **FANNY** | |
| | | | female rock quartet | |
| 11/06/71 | 40 | 1 | 1. Charity Ball | Reprise 1033 |
| 3/15/75 | 29 | 4 | 2. Butter Boy | Casablanca 814 |
| | | | **FANTASTIC JOHNNY C** | |
| | | | Johnny Corley | |
| 11/04/67 | 7 | 12 | 1. **Boogaloo Down Broadway** | Phil. L.A. 305 |
| 8/10/68 | 34 | 2 | 2. Hitch It To The Horse | Phil. L.A. 315 |

| DATE | POS | WKS | ARTIST—Record Title | LABEL & NO. |
|---|---|---|---|---|
| | | | **DON FARDON** | |
| | | | British | |
| 9/21/68 | 20 | 6 | 1. (The Lament Of The Cherokee) Indian Reservation | GNP Crescendo 405 |
| | | | **DONNA FARGO** | |
| | | | Donna was stricken with multiple sclerosis in 1979 | |
| 7/08/72 | 11 | 9 | ● 1. The Happiest Girl In The Whole U.S.A. | Dot 17409 |
| 11/11/72 + | 5 | 14 | ● 2. Funny Face | Dot 17429 |
| | | | **JOSE FELICIANO** | |
| | | | Puerto Rican - born blind on 9/8/45 | |
| 8/03/68 | 3 | 11 | 1. Light My Fire | RCA 9550 |
| 10/26/68 | 25 | 7 | 2. Hi-Heel Sneakers | RCA 9641 |
| | | | **FREDDY FENDER** | |
| | | | Mexican-American - real name: Baldemar Huerta | |
| 3/08/75 | 1 (1) | 15 | ● 1. Before The Next Teardrop Falls | ABC/Dot 17540 |
| 7/19/75 | 8 | 14 | ● 2. Wasted Days And Wasted Nights | ABC/Dot 17558 |
| 11/08/75 | 20 | 6 | 3. Secret Love | ABC/Dot 17585 |
| 3/20/76 | 32 | 4 | 4. You'll Lose A Good Thing | ABC/Dot 17607 |
| | | | **FENDERMEN** | |
| | | | Phil Humphrey & Jim Sundquist | |
| 6/13/60 | 5 | 13 | 1. Mule Skinner Blues | Soma 1137 |
| | | | **JAY FERGUSON** | |
| | | | lead singer of Spirit & Jo Jo Gunne | |
| 1/28/78 | 9 | 12 | 1. Thunder Island | Asylum 45444 |
| 6/09/79 | 31 | 4 | 2. Shakedown Cruise | Asylum 46041 |
| | | | **JOHNNY FERGUSON** | |
| 4/18/60 | 27 | 3 | 1. Angela Jones | MGM 12855 |
| | | | **MAYNARD FERGUSON** | |
| | | | Canadian - played trumpet for Stan Kenton's band ('50-'53) | |
| 5/28/77 | 28 | 6 | 1. Gonna Fly Now (Theme From "Rocky") [I] | Columbia 10468 |
| | | | **FERKO STRING BAND** | |
| 6/18/55 | 14 | 6 | 1. Alabama Jubilee [I] | Media 1010 |
| | | | **FERRANTE & TEICHER** | |
| | | | piano duo: Arthur Ferrante & Louis Teicher | |
| 8/08/60 | 10 | 18 | 1. Theme From The Apartment [I] | United Art. 231 |
| 11/28/60 + | 2 (1) | 18 | 2. Exodus [I] | United Art. 274 |
| 4/17/61 | 37 | 1 | 3. Love Theme From One Eyed Jacks [I] | United Art. 300 |
| 11/13/61 | 8 | 8 | 4. Tonight [I]<br>from the film "West Side Story" | United Art. 373 |
| 11/29/69 + | 10 | 11 | 5. Midnight Cowboy [I] | United Art. 50554 |
| | | | **ERNIE FIELDS Orchestra** | |
| 10/12/59 | 4 | 14 | 1. In The Mood [I] | Rendezvous 110 |
| | | | **FIESTAS** | |
| | | | Newark, New Jersey quartet | |
| 4/27/59 | 11 | 11 | 1. So Fine | Old Town 1062 |

**Marvin Gaye** worked as a member of the Moonglows, post-"Ten Commandments of Love," before joining Berry Gordy's Motown label. His first chores with Gordy were session drummer and background singer.

**J. Geils Band** lead singer Peter Wolf used to be married to actress Faye Dunaway. A few years after their divorce, he parted ways with the group, too.

**Lesley Gore** not only cut sixties hits with famed producer Quincy Jones (*Thriller,* et al.), but also appeared in such teen-oriented movies as *Girls on the Beach, Ski Party,* and *The T.A.M.I. Show.*

**Larry Graham** took the hard-funk bass playing he pioneered with Sly and the Family Stone and used it as the cornerstone of his own Graham Central Station. Later he became a sweet crooner and cut "One in a Million You."

**The Guess Who** were one of Canada's leading exports from 1969 to 1974. They complained about the difficulty of getting U.S. work permits, but managed to score a dozen Top 40 hits during that period, despite the obstacles.

**Corey Hart** was no doubt flattered to have Eric Clapton guest on his debut LP. Concerning his hit single "Sunglasses at Night," the young Canadian said the tune had been "busting my brain to get on vinyl." Ouch!

**Bobby Hebb.** Along with Charley Pride, Hebb was one of the few black artists to sing country music in the sixties. He followed up "Sunny" with "A Satisifed Mind," a country hit for three different acts: Jean Shepard, Porter Wagoner, and Red and Betty Foley.

**Don Henley.** How many drummers double as a lead vocalist? Henley did for the Eagles. His first recorded effort, with obscure country rockers Shiloh, now fetches a high price from collectors.

**Herman's Hermits.** Peter Noone (a.k.a. Herman) cut his first single with Herman's Hermits at the tender age of 16. The baby-faced singer attempted a comeback in the early eighties leading a band called the Tremblers, to no avail.

**The Hollies** enjoyed their first British chart hit in 1963. They took a stab at Hollywood when they cut the theme song for Peter Sellers' 1966 movie *After the Fox* (script by Neil Simon).

**The Human League** once lost a chance to tour with the Talking Heads when they informed the promoter they planned to devote their part of the show to a 30-minute film. They subsequently opted for more conventional live performances and prospered.

| DATE | POS | WKS | ARTIST—Record Title | LABEL & NO. |
|------|-----|-----|--------------------|-------------|
| | | | **5TH DIMENSION** | |
| | | | Marilyn McCoo, Billy Davis Jr., Lamonte McLemore, Florence LaRue, & Ron Townson | |
| 2/04/67 | 16 | 7 | 1. Go Where You Wanna Go | Soul City 753 |
| 6/17/67 | 7 | 10 | 2. **Up-Up And Away** | Soul City 756 |
| 12/09/67 | 34 | 1 | 3. Paper Cup | Soul City 760 |
| 2/24/68 | 29 | 5 | 4. Carpet Man | Soul City 762 |
| 6/22/68 | 3 | 12 | ● 5. **Stoned Soul Picnic** | Soul City 766 |
| 10/26/68 | 13 | 6 | 6. Sweet Blindness | Soul City 768 |
| 1/11/69 | 25 | 6 | 7. California Soul | Soul City 770 |
| 3/15/69 | 1 (6) | 16 | ● 8. **Aquarius/Let The Sunshine In** <br> from the musical "Hair" | Soul City 772 |
| 8/09/69 | 20 | 7 | 9. Workin' On A Groovy Thing | Soul City 776 |
| 10/04/69 | 1 (3) | 14 | ● 10. **Wedding Bell Blues** | Soul City 779 |
| 1/24/70 | 21 | 6 | 11. Blowing Away | Soul City 780 |
| 5/02/70 | 24 | 5 | 12. Puppet Man | Bell 880 |
| 6/27/70 | 27 | 5 | 13. Save The Country | Bell 895 |
| 11/21/70 | 2 (2) | 15 | ● 14. **One Less Bell To Answer** | Bell 940 |
| 3/13/71 | 19 | 8 | 15. Love's Lines, Angles And Rhymes | Bell 965 |
| 10/02/71 | 12 | 9 | 16. Never My Love | Bell 45134 |
| 1/29/72 | 37 | 3 | 17. Together Let's Find Love | Bell 45170 |
| 4/22/72 | 8 | 13 | ● 18. **(Last Night) I Didn't Get To Sleep At All** | Bell 45195 |
| 9/30/72 | 10 | 12 | 19. **If I Could Reach You** | Bell 45261 |
| 2/10/73 | 32 | 4 | 20. Living Together, Growing Together <br> from the film "Lost Horizon" | Bell 45310 |
| | | | **FIFTH ESTATE** | |
| 6/10/67 | 11 | 6 | 1. Ding Dong! The Witch Is Dead <br> from "The Wizard Of Oz" | Jubilee 5573 |
| | | | **LARRY FINNEGAN** | |
| 3/31/62 | 11 | 8 | 1. Dear One | Old Town 1113 |
| | | | **FIREBALLS** | |
| | | | quartet led by George Tomsco (lead guitar) & Jimmy Gilmer (vocals on #4) - also see Jimmy Gilmer & The Fireballs | |
| 10/26/59 | 39 | 2 | 1. Torquay [I] | Top Rank 2008 |
| 2/01/60 | 24 | 6 | 2. Bulldog [I] | Top Rank 2026 |
| 8/07/61 | 27 | 3 | 3. Quite A Party [I] | Warwick 644 |
| 1/27/68 | 9 | 10 | 4. **Bottle Of Wine** | Atco 6491 |
| | | | **FIREFALL** | |
| | | | Denver quintet - Rick Roberts, lead singer | |
| 9/25/76 | 9 | 15 | 1. **You Are The Woman** | Atlantic 3335 |
| 4/30/77 | 34 | 3 | 2. Cinderella | Atlantic 3392 |
| 9/17/77 | 11 | 12 | 3. Just Remember I Love You | Atlantic 3420 |
| 10/28/78 | 11 | 10 | 4. Strange Way | Atlantic 3518 |
| 5/10/80 | 35 | 3 | 5. Headed For A Fall | Atlantic 3657 |
| 2/28/81 | 37 | 3 | 6. Staying With It <br> with Lisa Nemzo | Atlantic 3791 |

| DATE | POS | WKS | ARTIST—Record Title | LABEL & NO. |
|---|---|---|---|---|
| | | | **FIREFLIES** | |
| | | | Ritchie Adams, lead singer (wrote "Tossin' And Turnin'") | |
| 9/28/59 | 21 | 10 | 1. You Were Mine | Ribbon 6901 |
| | | | **FIRST CHOICE** | |
| | | | Philadelphia trio | |
| 4/28/73 | 28 | 5 | 1. Armed And Extremely Dangerous | Philly Groove 175 |
| | | | **FIRST CLASS** | |
| | | | English studio group | |
| 8/17/74 | 4 | 11 | 1. **Beach Baby** | UK 49022 |
| | | | **FIRST EDITION - see KENNY ROGERS** | |
| | | | **EDDIE FISHER** | |
| | | | born in Philadelphia on 8/10/28 | |
| 3/05/55 | 16 | 2 | 1. A Man Chases A Girl/ | |
| | | | from the film "There's No Business Like Show Business" | |
| 4/02/55 | 20 | 1 | 2. (I'm Always Hearing) Wedding Bells | RCA 6015 |
| 5/14/55 | 6 | 13 | 3. **Heart** | RCA 6097 |
| | | | from the musical "Damn Yankees" | |
| 8/27/55 | 11 | 8 | 4. Song Of The Dreamer | RCA 6196 |
| 12/24/55 + | 7 | 16 | 5. **Dungaree Doll/** | |
| 12/31/55 | 20 | 1 | 6. Everybody's Got A Home But Me | RCA 6337 |
| | | | from Broadway's "Pipe Dream" | |
| 6/30/56 | 18 | 7 | 7. On The Street Where You Live | RCA 6529 |
| | | | from the musical "My Fair Lady" | |
| 10/20/56 | 10 | 17 | 8. **Cindy, Oh Cindy** | RCA 6677 |
| | | | **MISS TONI FISHER** | |
| 11/23/59 | 3 | 14 | 1. **The Big Hurt** | Signet 275 |
| 7/14/62 | 37 | 1 | 2. West Of The Wall | Big Top 3097 |
| | | | **ELLA FITZGERALD** | |
| | | | 1st lady of Jazz - born in Newport News, Virginia on 4/25/18 | |
| 5/30/60 | 27 | 7 | 1. Mack The Knife | Verve 10209 |
| | | | live recording with the Paul Smith Quartet | |
| | | | **FIVE AMERICANS** | |
| | | | Dallas quintet | |
| 2/12/66 | 26 | 5 | 1. I See The Light | HBR 454 |
| 3/18/67 | 5 | 9 | 2. **Western Union** | Abnak 118 |
| 6/17/67 | 36 | 2 | 3. Sound Of Love | Abnak 120 |
| 9/16/67 | 36 | 1 | 4. Zip Code | Abnak 123 |
| | | | **FIVE BLOBS** | |
| | | | Bernie Nee - one man group | |
| 11/03/58 | 33 | 3 | 1. The Blob | Columbia 41250 |
| | | | from the film of the same title | |
| | | | **FIVE FLIGHTS UP** | |
| 10/03/70 | 37 | 5 | 1. Do What You Wanna Do | T-A 202 |
| | | | **FIVE KEYS** | |
| | | | R&B group from Newport News, Virginia led by Rudy West & Maryland Pierce | |
| 12/25/54 + | 28 | 2 | 1. Ling, Ting, Tong | Capitol 2945 |
| 10/06/56 | 23 | 6 | 2. Out Of Sight, Out Of Mind | Capitol 3502 |
| 1/12/57 | 35 | 2 | 3. Wisdom Of A Fool | Capitol 3597 |

| DATE | POS | WKS | ARTIST—Record Title | LABEL & NO. |
|------|-----|-----|---------------------|-------------|
| | | | **FIVE MAN ELECTRICAL BAND** | |
| | | | Canadian - Les Emmerson, lead singer | |
| 7/10/71 | 3 | 12 | ● 1. **Signs** | Lionel 3213 |
| 10/30/71 | 26 | 6 | 2. Absolutely Right | Lionel 3220 |
| | | | **FIVE SATINS** | |
| | | | doo-wop group from New Haven, Connecticut - Fred Parris, leader | |
| 9/29/56 | 24 | 6 | 1. In The Still Of The Nite | Ember 1005 |
| 8/12/57 | 25 | 8 | 2. To The Aisle | Ember 1019 |
| | | | **FIVE STAIRSTEPS** | |
| | | | Chicago family group | |
| 6/20/70 | 8 | 11 | ● 1. **O-o-h Child** | Buddah 165 |
| | | | **5000 VOLTS** | |
| | | | British | |
| 11/15/75 | 26 | 5 | 1. I'm On Fire | Philips 40801 |
| | | | **FIXX** | |
| | | | London-based techno-pop group - Cy Curnin, lead singer | |
| 7/09/83 | 20 | 8 | 1. Saved By Zero | MCA 52213 |
| 9/10/83 | 4 | 13 | 2. **One Thing Leads To Another** | MCA 52264 |
| 12/17/83 + | 32 | 7 | 3. The Sign Of Fire | MCA 52316 |
| 9/08/84 | 15 | 8 | 4. Are We Ourselves? | MCA 52444 |
| | | | **ROBERTA FLACK** | |
| | | | born on 2/10/39 in Asheville, North Carolina - also see Peabo Bryson | |
| 3/25/72 | 1 (6) | 15 | ● 1. **The First Time Ever I Saw Your Face** | Atlantic 2864 |
| | | | popularized because of inclusion in the film "Play Misty For Me" | |
| 2/03/73 | 1 (5) | 13 | ● 2. **Killing Me Softly With His Song** | Atlantic 2940 |
| 10/13/73 | 30 | 5 | 3. Jesse | Atlantic 2982 |
| 7/06/74 | 1 (1) | 13 | ● 4. **Feel Like Makin' Love** | Atlantic 3025 |
| 6/24/78 | 24 | 5 | 5. If Ever I See You Again | Atlantic 3483 |
| 4/17/82 | 13 | 11 | 6. Making Love | Atlantic 4005 |
| | | | **ROBERTA FLACK & DONNY HATHAWAY** | |
| | | | Donny died on 1/13/79 (33) | |
| 7/03/71 | 29 | 9 | 1. You've Got A Friend | Atlantic 2808 |
| 6/24/72 | 5 | 11 | ● 2. **Where Is The Love** | Atlantic 2879 |
| 3/18/78 | 2 (2) | 14 | ● 3. **The Closer I Get To You** | Atlantic 3463 |
| | | | **FLAMING EMBER** | |
| | | | Detroit rock quartet | |
| 11/15/69 | 26 | 6 | 1. Mind, Body And Soul | Hot Wax 6902 |
| 6/20/70 | 24 | 10 | 2. Westbound # 9 | Hot Wax 7003 |
| 11/28/70 | 34 | 6 | 3. I'm Not My Brothers Keeper | Hot Wax 7006 |
| | | | **FLAMINGOS** | |
| | | | Chicago R&B quintet led by Nate Nelson (died on 6/1/84-52) and cousins Zeke & Jake Carey | |
| 6/08/59 | 11 | 11 | 1. I Only Have Eyes For You | End 1046 |
| 5/23/60 | 30 | 3 | 2. Nobody Loves Me Like You | End 1068 |

| DATE | POS | WKS | ARTIST—Record Title | LABEL & NO. |
|------|-----|-----|---------------------|-------------|
| | | | **FLARES** | |
| 10/09/61 | 25 | 9 | 1. Foot Stomping - Part 1 | Felsted 8624 |
| | | | **FLASH** | |
| | | | English quartet led by Peter Banks (guitar) & Colin Carter (vocals) | |
| 7/29/72 | 29 | 6 | 1. Small Beginnings | Capitol 3345 |
| | | | **FLASH CADILLAC & THE CONTINENTAL KIDS** | |
| | | | formed by 6 students at the University of Colorado | |
| 10/02/76 | 29 | 6 | 1. Did You Boogie (With Your Baby) with Wolfman Jack | Private S. 45079 |
| | | | **FLEETWOOD MAC** | |
| | | | English-American band: Mick Fleetwood, Christine McVie, John McVie, Stevie Nicks, & Lindsey Buckingham | |
| 12/13/75 + | 20 | 7 | 1. Over My Head | Reprise 1339 |
| 4/10/76 | 11 | 11 | 2. Rhiannon (Will You Ever Win) | Reprise 1345 |
| 7/31/76 | 11 | 13 | 3. Say You Love Me | Reprise 1356 |
| 1/22/77 | 10 | 11 | 4. **Go Your Own Way** | Warner 8304 |
| 4/30/77 | 1 (1) | 13 | ● 5. **Dreams** | Warner 8371 |
| 7/23/77 | 3 | 14 | 6. **Don't Stop** | Warner 8413 |
| 10/29/77 | 9 | 10 | 7. **You Make Loving Fun** | Warner 8483 |
| 10/13/79 | 8 | 10 | 8. **Tusk** | Warner 49077 |
| 12/22/79 + | 7 | 11 | 9. **Sara** | Warner 49150 |
| 3/29/80 | 20 | 7 | 10. Think About Me | Warner 49196 |
| 6/19/82 | 4 | 15 | 11. **Hold Me** | Warner 29966 |
| 9/25/82 | 12 | 8 | 12. Gypsy | Warner 29918 |
| 12/11/82 + | 22 | 8 | 13. Love In Store | Warner 29848 |
| | | | **FLEETWOODS** | |
| | | | Gary Troxel, Barbara Ellis and Gretchen Christopher - met while attending high school in Olympia, Washington | |
| 3/16/59 | 1 (4) | 12 | 1. **Come Softly To Me** | Dolphin 1 |
| 6/22/59 | 39 | 1 | 2. Graduation's Here | Dolton 3 |
| 9/14/59 | 1 (1) | 12 | 3. **Mr. Blue** | Dolton 5 |
| 2/29/60 | 28 | 3 | 4. Outside My Window | Dolton 15 |
| 6/27/60 | 23 | 4 | 5. Runaround | Dolton 22 |
| 5/08/61 | 10 | 8 | 6. **Tragedy** | Dolton 40 |
| 10/02/61 | 30 | 4 | 7. (He's) The Great Impostor | Dolton 45 |
| 11/24/62 | 36 | 2 | 8. Lovers By Night, Strangers By Day | Dolton 62 |
| 7/13/63 | 32 | 4 | 9. Goodnight My Love | Dolton 75 |
| | | | **SHELBY FLINT** | |
| 2/06/61 | 22 | 5 | 1. Angel On My Shoulder | Valiant 6001 |
| | | | **FLIRTATIONS** | |
| 5/24/69 | 34 | 2 | 1. Nothing But A Heartache | Deram 85038 |
| | | | **FLOATERS** | |
| | | | four-man soul group from Detroit | |
| 7/30/77 | 2 (2) | 11 | ● 1. **Float On** | ABC 12284 |

| DATE | POS | WKS | ARTIST—Record Title | LABEL & NO. |
|---|---|---|---|---|
| | | | **FLOCK OF SEAGULLS** | |
| | | | British techno-rock quartet - Mike Score, lead singer | |
| 9/04/82 | 9 | 10 | 1. **I Ran (So Far Away)** | Jive 102 |
| 1/08/83 | 30 | 7 | 2. Space Age Love Song | Jive 2003 |
| 6/11/83 | 26 | 7 | 3. Wishing (If I Had A Photograph Of You) | Jive 2006 |
| | | | **DICK FLOOD** | |
| 9/14/59 | 23 | 4 | 1. The Three Bells (The Jimmy Brown Story) | Monument 408 |
| | | | **EDDIE FLOYD** | |
| | | | lead singer on The Falcons' "You're So Fine" | |
| 11/19/66 | 28 | 6 | 1. Knock On Wood | Stax 194 |
| 9/07/68 | 40 | 2 | 2. I've Never Found A Girl (To Love Me Like You Do) | Stax 0002 |
| 11/16/68 | 17 | 9 | 3. Bring It On Home To Me | Stax 0012 |
| | | | **FLYING MACHINE** | |
| | | | English quartet | |
| 10/18/69 | 5 | 12 | ● 1. **Smile A Little Smile For Me** | Congress 6000 |
| | | | **FOCUS** | |
| | | | Dutch rock quartet led by guitar virtuoso Jan Akkerman | |
| 4/21/73 | 9 | 11 | 1. **Hocus Pocus [I]** | Sire 704 |
| | | | **DAN FOGELBERG** | |
| | | | born in Peoria, Illinois on 8/13/51 | |
| 3/01/75 | 31 | 3 | 1. Part Of The Plan | Epic 50055 |
| 1/19/80 | 2 (2) | 13 | 2. **Longer** | Full Moon 50824 |
| 4/19/80 | 21 | 6 | 3. Heart Hotels | Full Moon 50862 |
| 12/27/80 + | 9 | 13 | 4. **Same Old Lang Syne** | Full Moon 50961 |
| 9/19/81 | 7 | 10 | 5. **Hard To Say** | Full Moon 02488 |
| 12/19/81 + | 9 | 16 | 6. **Leader Of The Band** | Full Moon 02647 |
| 4/24/82 | 18 | 8 | 7. Run For The Roses | Full Moon 02821 |
| 11/13/82 | 23 | 9 | 8. Missing You | Full Moon 03289 |
| 3/05/83 | 29 | 6 | 9. Make Love Stay | Full Moon 03525 |
| 2/11/84 | 13 | 10 | 10. The Language Of Love | Full Moon 04314 |
| | | | **DAN FOGELBERG/TIM WEISBERG** | |
| 11/04/78 | 24 | 7 | 1. The Power Of Gold | Full Moon 50606 |
| | | | **JOHN FOGERTY** | |
| | | | leader of Creedence Clearwater Revival, & the Blue Ridge Rangers | |
| 10/04/75 | 27 | 6 | 1. Rockin' All Over The World | Asylum 45274 |
| | | | **FOGHAT** | |
| | | | British quartet led by Lonesome Dave Peverett - formerly with Savoy Brown | |
| 1/10/76 | 20 | 12 | 1. Slow Ride | Bearsville 0306 |
| 12/25/76 + | 34 | 4 | 2. Drivin' Wheel | Bearsville 0313 |
| 10/15/77 | 33 | 3 | 3. I Just Want To Make Love To You<br>live version of 1972 hit (Pos. 83) | Bearsville 0319 |
| 6/24/78 | 36 | 2 | 4. Stone Blue | Bearsville 0325 |
| 12/08/79 + | 23 | 10 | 5. Third Time Lucky (First Time I Was A Fool) | Bearsville 49125 |

| DATE | POS | WKS | ARTIST—Record Title | LABEL & NO. |
|------|-----|-----|---------------------|-------------|
| | | | **WAYNE FONTANA** - see MINDBENDERS | |
| | | | **FONTANE SISTERS** | |
| | | | Marge, Bea & Geri - featuring Billy Vaughn's Orchestra | |
| 12/11/54 + | 1 (3) | 20 | 1. **Hearts Of Stone** | Dot 15265 |
| 2/26/55 | 13 | 8 | 2. Rock Love | Dot 15333 |
| 6/04/55 | 13 | 6 | 3. Rollin' Stone | Dot 15370 |
| 8/20/55 | 3 | 15 | 4. **Seventeen** | Dot 15386 |
| 11/26/55 | 11 | 11 | 5. Daddy-O | Dot 15428 |
| 12/31/55 | 36 | 1 | 6. Nuttin' For Christmas [N] | Dot 15434 |
| 3/17/56 | 11 | 11 | 7. Eddie My Love | Dot 15450 |
| 7/14/56 | 38 | 1 | 8. I'm In Love Again | Dot 15462 |
| 1/12/57 | 13 | 10 | 9. The Banana Boat Song | Dot 15527 |
| 4/28/58 | 12 | 9 | 10. Chanson D'Amour (Song Of Love) | Dot 15736 |
| | | | **STEVE FORBERT** | |
| 1/05/80 | 11 | 12 | 1. Romeo's Tune | Nemperor 7525 |
| | | | **FRANKIE FORD** | |
| 3/09/59 | 14 | 12 | 1. Sea Cruise | Ace 554 |
| | | | with Huey "Piano" Smith and The Clowns | |
| | | | **TENNESSEE ERNIE FORD** | |
| | | | host of his own TV show from 1956-1961 | |
| 3/19/55 | 5 | 17 | 1. **Ballad Of Davy Crockett** | Capitol 3058 |
| 11/12/55 | 1 (8) | 19 | 2. **Sixteen Tons** | Capitol 3262 |
| 3/10/56 | 17 | 1 | 3. That's All | Capitol 3343 |
| 9/23/57 | 23 | 1 | 4. In The Middle Of An Island | Capitol 3762 |
| | | | **FOREIGNER** | |
| | | | English-American rock group led by Mick Jones (guitar) and Lou Gramm (vocals) | |
| 4/23/77 | 4 | 13 | 1. **Feels Like The First Time** | Atlantic 3394 |
| 8/13/77 | 6 | 15 | 2. **Cold As Ice** | Atlantic 3410 |
| 1/14/78 | 20 | 8 | 3. Long, Long Way From Home | Atlantic 3439 |
| 7/08/78 | 3 | 14 | ● 4. **Hot Blooded** | Atlantic 3488 |
| 9/30/78 | 2 (2) | 12 | ● 5. **Double Vision** | Atlantic 3514 |
| 1/20/79 | 15 | 8 | 6. Blue Morning, Blue Day | Atlantic 3543 |
| 9/22/79 | 12 | 9 | 7. Dirty White Boy | Atlantic 3618 |
| 11/24/79 | 14 | 9 | 8. Head Games | Atlantic 3633 |
| 7/11/81 | 4 | 17 | 9. **Urgent** | Atlantic 3831 |
| 10/17/81 | 2(10) | 19 | ● 10. **Waiting For A Girl Like You** | Atlantic 3868 |
| 3/06/82 | 26 | 6 | 11. Juke Box Hero | Atlantic 4017 |
| 6/05/82 | 26 | 6 | 12. Break It Up | Atlantic 4044 |
| | | | **FORTUNES** | |
| | | | British | |
| 9/11/65 | 7 | 8 | 1. **You've Got Your Troubles** | Press 9773 |
| 11/27/65 | 27 | 4 | 2. Here It Comes Again | Press 9798 |
| 6/19/71 | 15 | 9 | 3. Here Comes That Rainy Day Feeling Again | Capitol 3086 |

| DATE | POS | WKS | ARTIST—Record Title | LABEL & NO. |
|---|---|---|---|---|
| | | | **FOUNDATIONS** | |
| | | | English - Clem Curtis, leader | |
| 1/13/68 | 11 | 10 | 1. Baby, Now That I've Found You | Uni 55038 |
| 1/18/69 | 3 | 13 | ● 2. **Build Me Up Buttercup** | Uni 55101 |
| | | | **FOUR ACES** | |
| | | | Al Alberts, Dave Mahoney, Lou Silvestri, Sod Vocarro | |
| 1/15/55 | 3 | 21 | 1. **Melody Of Love** | Decca 29395 |
| 5/28/55 | 13 | 6 | 2. Heart | Decca 29476 |
| | | | from the musical "Damn Yankees" | |
| 8/27/55 | 1 (6) | 21 | 3. **Love Is A Many-Splendored Thing** | Decca 29625 |
| 12/03/55 | 14 | 12 | 4. A Woman In Love | Decca 29725 |
| | | | from the film "Guys And Dolls" | |
| 8/04/56 | 22 | 5 | 5. I Only Know I Love You | Decca 29989 |
| 10/20/56 | 20 | 2 | 6. You Can't Run Away From It | Decca 30041 |
| | | | **FOUR COINS** | |
| | | | George Mantalis, Jim Gregorakis, Michael & George James | |
| 1/15/55 | 28 | 1 | 1. I Love You Madly | Epic 9082 |
| 12/10/55 | 22 | 8 | 2. Memories Of You | Epic 9129 |
| | | | from the film "The Benny Goodman Story" | |
| 6/17/57 | 11 | 14 | 3. Shangri-La | Epic 9213 |
| 10/14/57 | 28 | 4 | 4. My One Sin | Epic 9229 |
| 11/17/58 | 21 | 8 | 5. The World Outside | Epic 9295 |
| | | | adapted from the "Warsaw Concerto" | |
| | | | **FOUR ESQUIRES** | |
| | | | formed group at Boston University | |
| 12/16/57 | 25 | 1 | 1. Love Me Forever | Paris 509 |
| 11/03/58 | 21 | 6 | 2. Hideaway | Paris 520 |
| | | | **FOUR FRESHMEN** | |
| | | | formed in Indianapolis at Butler University | |
| 6/09/56 | 17 | 7 | 1. Graduation Day | Capitol 3410 |
| | | | **FOUR JACKS AND A JILL** | |
| | | | South African quintet - Jill: Glenys Lynne | |
| 5/18/68 | 18 | 7 | 1. Master Jack | RCA 9473 |
| | | | **FOUR KNIGHTS - see NAT KING COLE** | |
| | | | **FOUR LADS** | |
| | | | Canadian - background vocalists on Johnnie Ray's hit "Cry" | |
| 9/03/55 | 2 (6) | 25 | 1. **Moments To Remember** | Columbia 40539 |
| 1/28/56 | 2 (4) | 19 | 2. **No, Not Much!** | Columbia 40629 |
| 4/28/56 | 3 | 18 | 3. **Standing On The Corner/** | |
| | | | from Broadway's "The Most Happy Fella" | |
| 4/28/56 | 24 | 6 | 4. My Little Angel | Columbia 40674 |
| 9/15/56 | 16 | 6 | 5. The Bus Stop Song (A Paper Of Pins)/ | |
| | | | from the film "Bus Stop" | |
| 9/15/56 | 20 | 6 | 6. A House With Love In It | Columbia 40736 |
| 2/02/57 | 9 | 15 | 7. **Who Needs You** | Columbia 40811 |
| 5/20/57 | 17 | 4 | 8. I Just Don't Know | Columbia 40914 |

| DATE | POS | WKS | ARTIST—Record Title | LABEL & NO. |
|---|---|---|---|---|
| 12/09/57 + | 8 | 9 | 9. **Put A Light In The Window** | Columbia 41058 |
| 4/07/58 | 10 | 7 | 10. **There's Only One Of You** | Columbia 41136 |
| 7/14/58 | 12 | 6 | 11. Enchanted Island | Columbia 41194 |
| 11/24/58 | 32 | 3 | 12. The Mocking Bird<br>new version of their 1952 and 1956 hits | Columbia 41266 |
| | | | **FOUR PREPS**<br>Bruce, Glen, Ed & Marv formed group at Hollywood High School | |
| 1/20/58 | 2 (3) | 14 | 1. **26 Miles (Santa Catalina)** | Capitol 3845 |
| 5/05/58 | 3 | 14 | 2. **Big Man** | Capitol 3960 |
| 9/01/58 | 21 | 6 | 3. Lazy Summer Night<br>from the film "Andy Hardy Comes Home" | Capitol 4023 |
| 1/11/60 | 13 | 11 | 4. Down By The Station | Capitol 4312 |
| 5/16/60 | 24 | 3 | 5. Got A Girl [N] | Capitol 4362 |
| 9/11/61 | 17 | 4 | 6. More Money For You And Me: [N]<br>Mr. Blue/Alley Oop/Smoke Gets In Your Eyes/In This Whole<br>Wide World/A Worried Man/Tom Dooley/A Teenager In Love | Capitol 4599 |
| | | | **FOUR SEASONS**<br>formed in Newark, New Jersey in 1956 as The Four Lovers -<br>group's success was mainly due to the "sound" of Frankie Valli -<br>also see Wonder Who | |
| 9/01/62 | 1 (5) | 12 | 1. **Sherry** | Vee-Jay 456 |
| 10/27/62 | 1 (5) | 14 | 2. **Big Girls Don't Cry** | Vee-Jay 465 |
| 12/22/62 | 23 | 2 | 3. Santa Claus Is Coming To Town [X] | Vee-Jay 478 |
| 1/26/63 | 1 (3) | 12 | 4. **Walk Like A Man** | Vee-Jay 485 |
| 5/04/63 | 22 | 6 | 5. Ain't That A Shame! | Vee-Jay 512 |
| 7/20/63 | 3 | 10 | 6. **Candy Girl/** | |
| 8/10/63 | 36 | 3 | 7. Marlena | Vee-Jay 539 |
| 11/02/63 | 36 | 2 | 8. New Mexican Rose | Vee-Jay 562 |
| 2/08/64 | 3 | 11 | 9. **Dawn (Go Away)** | Philips 40166 |
| 3/07/64 | 16 | 8 | 10. Stay | Vee-Jay 582 |
| 4/18/64 | 6 | 8 | 11. **Ronnie** | Philips 40185 |
| 6/27/64 | 1 (2) | 11 | ● 12. **Rag Doll** | Philips 40211 |
| 6/27/64 | 28 | 5 | 13. Alone | Vee-Jay 597 |
| 9/05/64 | 10 | 6 | 14. **Save It For Me** | Philips 40225 |
| 11/21/64 | 20 | 5 | 15. Big Man In Town | Philips 40238 |
| 1/30/65 | 12 | 6 | 16. Bye, Bye, Baby (Baby Goodbye) | Philips 40260 |
| 7/10/65 | 30 | 3 | 17. Girl Come Running | Philips 40305 |
| 10/30/65 | 3 | 12 | 18. **Let's Hang On!** | Philips 40317 |
| 2/12/66 | 9 | 6 | 19. **Working My Way Back To You** | Philips 40350 |
| 5/28/66 | 13 | 7 | 20. Opus 17 (Don't You Worry 'Bout Me) | Philips 40370 |
| 9/17/66 | 9 | 8 | 21. **I've Got You Under My Skin** | Philips 40393 |
| 12/24/66 + | 10 | 8 | 22. **Tell It To The Rain** | Philips 40412 |
| 3/18/67 | 16 | 7 | 23. Beggin' | Philips 40433 |
| 6/17/67 | 9 | 8 | 24. **C'mon Marianne** | Philips 40460 |
| 11/18/67 | 30 | 4 | 25. Watch The Flowers Grow | Philips 40490 |
| 3/09/68 | 24 | 5 | 26. Will You Love Me Tomorrow | Philips 40523 |

| DATE | POS | WKS | ARTIST—Record Title | LABEL & NO. |
|---|---|---|---|---|
| 9/20/75 | 3 | 12 | 27. **Who Loves You** | Warner 8122 |
| 1/31/76 | 1 (3) | 15 | ● 28. **December, 1963 (Oh, What A Night)** | Warner 8168 |
| 7/04/76 | 38 | 2 | 29. Silver Star | Warner 8203 |
| | | | **FOUR TOPS** | |
| | | | Detroit quartet: Levi Stubbs, Duke Fakir, Lawrence Payton, Obie Benson - also see the Supremes | |
| 8/29/64 | 11 | 10 | 1. Baby I Need Your Loving | Motown 1062 |
| 2/20/65 | 24 | 6 | 2. Ask The Lonely | Motown 1073 |
| 5/22/65 | 1 (2) | 13 | 3. **I Can't Help Myself** | Motown 1076 |
| 8/07/65 | 5 | 8 | 4. **It's The Same Old Song** | Motown 1081 |
| 11/20/65 | 19 | 6 | 5. Something About You | Motown 1084 |
| 3/12/66 | 18 | 6 | 6. Shake Me, Wake Me (When It's Over) | Motown 1090 |
| 9/17/66 | 1 (2) | 12 | 7. **Reach Out I'll Be There** | Motown 1098 |
| 12/24/66 + | 6 | 9 | 8. **Standing In The Shadows Of Love** | Motown 1102 |
| 3/18/67 | 4 | 8 | 9. **Bernadette** | Motown 1104 |
| 6/03/67 | 14 | 6 | 10. 7 Rooms Of Gloom | Motown 1110 |
| 9/30/67 | 19 | 5 | 11. You Keep Running Away | Motown 1113 |
| 2/17/68 | 14 | 6 | 12. Walk Away Renee | Motown 1119 |
| 5/11/68 | 20 | 6 | 13. If I Were A Carpenter | Motown 1124 |
| 5/30/70 | 24 | 8 | 14. It's All In The Game | Motown 1164 |
| 9/26/70 | 11 | 10 | 15. Still Water (Love) | Motown 1170 |
| 2/27/71 | 40 | 2 | 16. Just Seven Numbers (Can Straighten Out My Life) | Motown 1175 |
| 10/02/71 | 38 | 3 | 17. Mac Arthur Park (Part II) | Motown 1189 |
| 12/02/72 + | 10 | 9 | 18. **Keeper Of The Castle** | Dunhill 4330 |
| 2/24/73 | 4 | 12 | ● 19. **Ain't No Woman (Like The One I've Got)** | Dunhill 4339 |
| 7/28/73 | 15 | 8 | 20. Are You Man Enough <br> from the film "Shaft In Africa" | Dunhill 4354 |
| 11/17/73 | 33 | 3 | 21. Sweet Understanding Love | Dunhill 4366 |
| 9/19/81 | 11 | 11 | 22. When She Was My Girl | Casablanca 2338 |
| | | | **FOUR VOICES** | |
| 3/17/56 | 20 | 4 | 1. Lovely One | Columbia 40643 |
| | | | **INEZ FOXX** | |
| 8/03/63 | 7 | 10 | 1. **Mockingbird** <br> vocal accompaniment by her brother Charlie Foxx | Symbol 919 |
| | | | **FOXY** | |
| | | | Miami Latino dance band | |
| 8/26/78 | 9 | 13 | 1. **Get Off** | Dash 5046 |
| 4/28/79 | 21 | 9 | 2. Hot Number | Dash 5050 |
| | | | **PETER FRAMPTON** | |
| | | | guitarist/vocalist with English bands The Herd and Humble Pie | |
| 3/13/76 | 6 | 14 | 1. **Show Me The Way** | A&M 1795 |
| 7/17/76 | 12 | 11 | 2. **Baby, I Love Your Way** | A&M 1832 |
| 10/09/76 | 10 | 10 | 3. **Do You Feel Like We Do** | A&M 1867 |
| 6/11/77 | 2 (3) | 13 | 4. **I'm In You** | A&M 1941 |
| 9/10/77 | 18 | 10 | 5. Signed, Sealed, Delivered (I'm Yours) | A&M 1972 |
| 6/09/79 | 14 | 9 | 6. I Can't Stand It No More | A&M 2148 |

| DATE | POS | WKS | ARTIST—Record Title | LABEL & NO. |
|---|---|---|---|---|
| | | | **CONNIE FRANCIS** | |
| | | | born Concetta Franconero on 12/12/38 in Newark, New Jersey | |
| 3/03/58 | 4 | 15 | 1. **Who's Sorry Now** | MGM 12588 |
| 6/09/58 | 36 | 2 | 2. I'm Sorry I Made You Cry | MGM 12647 |
| 8/04/58 | 14 | 11 | 3. **Stupid Cupid** | MGM 12683 |
| 11/17/58 | 30 | 1 | 4. Fallin' | MGM 12713 |
| 12/15/58 + | 2 (2) | 14 | 5. **My Happiness** | MGM 12738 |
| 3/30/59 | 22 | 4 | 6. If I Didn't Care | MGM 12769 |
| 6/01/59 | 5 | 12 | 7. **Lipstick On Your Collar/** | |
| 6/01/59 | 9 | 11 | 8.  **Frankie** | MGM 12793 |
| 9/21/59 | 34 | 4 | 9. You're Gonna Miss Me | MGM 12824 |
| 12/07/59 | 7 | 11 | 10. **Among My Souvenirs/** | |
| 12/21/59 | 36 | 2 | 11.  God Bless America | MGM 12841 |
| 3/14/60 | 8 | 9 | 12. **Mama/** | |
| 3/28/60 | 17 | 6 | 13.  Teddy | MGM 12878 |
| 5/16/60 | 1 (2) | 16 | 14. **Everybody's Somebody's Fool/** | |
| 6/06/60 | 19 | 8 | 15.  Jealous Of You [F] | MGM 12899 |
| 8/22/60 | 1 (2) | 14 | 16. **My Heart Has A Mind Of Its Own** | MGM 12923 |
| 11/21/60 | 7 | 10 | 17. **Many Tears Ago** | MGM 12964 |
| 1/30/61 | 4 | 12 | 18. **Where The Boys Are/** | |
| 2/20/61 | 34 | 2 | 19.  No One | MGM 12971 |
| 4/24/61 | 7 | 9 | 20. **Breakin' In A Brand New Broken Heart** | MGM 12995 |
| 7/03/61 | 6 | 9 | 21. **Together** | MGM 13019 |
| 10/09/61 | 14 | 7 | 22. (He's My) Dreamboat | MGM 13039 |
| 12/04/61 + | 10 | 9 | 23. **When The Boy In Your Arms (Is The Boy In Your Heart)/** | |
| 1/06/62 + | 26 | 1 | 24.  Baby's First Christmas [X] | MGM 13051 |
| 2/24/62 | 1 (1) | 10 | 25. **Don't Break The Heart That Loves You** | MGM 13059 |
| 5/19/62 | 7 | 7 | 26. **Second Hand Love** | MGM 13074 |
| 8/11/62 | 9 | 6 | 27. **Vacation** | MGM 13087 |
| 11/03/62 | 24 | 4 | 28. I Was Such A Fool (To Fall In Love With You) | MGM 13096 |
| 1/05/63 | 18 | 6 | 29. I'm Gonna' Be Warm This Winter | MGM 13116 |
| 3/16/63 | 17 | 7 | 30. Follow The Boys | MGM 13127 |
| 6/08/63 | 23 | 5 | 31. If My Pillow Could Talk | MGM 13143 |
| 8/31/63 | 36 | 3 | 32. Drownin' My Sorrows | MGM 13160 |
| 11/09/63 | 28 | 4 | 33. Your Other Love | MGM 13176 |
| 3/07/64 | 24 | 6 | 34. Blue Winter | MGM 13214 |
| 5/30/64 | 25 | 5 | 35. Be Anything (But Be Mine) | MGM 13237 |
| | | | **FRANKE & THE KNOCKOUTS** | |
| | | | East Coast quintet led by Frankie Previte | |
| 3/21/81 | 10 | 14 | 1. **Sweetheart** | Millennium 11801 |
| 8/01/81 | 27 | 5 | 2. You're My Girl | Millennium 11808 |
| 5/08/82 | 24 | 7 | 3. Without You (Not Another Lonely Night) | Millennium 13105 |
| | | | **ARETHA FRANKLIN** | |
| | | | born on 3/25/42 in Memphis, Tennessee | |
| 11/20/61 | 37 | 2 | 1. Rock-A-Bye Your Baby With A Dixie Melody | Columbia 42157 |
| 3/18/67 | 9 | 9 | ● 2. **I Never Loved A Man (The Way I Love You)** | Atlantic 2386 |

| DATE | POS | WKS | ARTIST—Record Title | LABEL & NO. |
|---|---|---|---|---|
| 5/06/67 | 1 (2) | 11 | ● 3. **Respect** | Atlantic 2403 |
| 8/05/67 | 4 | 8 | ● 4. **Baby I Love You** | Atlantic 2427 |
| 10/07/67 | 8 | 8 | 5. **A Natural Woman (You Make Me Feel Like)** | Atlantic 2441 |
| 12/16/67 + | 2 (2) | 11 | ● 6. **Chain Of Fools** | Atlantic 2464 |
| 3/02/68 | 5 | 12 | ● 7. **(Sweet Sweet Baby) Since You've Been Gone/** | |
| 4/13/68 | 16 | 7 | 8. Ain't No Way | Atlantic 2486 |
| 5/25/68 | 7 | 9 | ● 9. **Think** | Atlantic 2518 |
| 8/24/68 | 6 | 8 | 10. **The House That Jack Built/** | |
| 8/24/68 | 10 | 10 | ● 11. **I Say A Little Prayer** | Atlantic 2546 |
| 11/23/68 | 14 | 8 | ● 12. See Saw/ | |
| 12/28/68 + | 31 | 2 | 13. My Song | Atlantic 2574 |
| 3/01/69 | 19 | 6 | 14. The Weight | Atlantic 2603 |
| 4/26/69 | 28 | 6 | 15. I Can't See Myself Leaving You | Atlantic 2619 |
| 8/09/69 | 13 | 9 | 16. Share Your Love With Me | Atlantic 2650 |
| 11/15/69 | 17 | 7 | 17. Eleanor Rigby | Atlantic 2683 |
| 2/28/70 | 13 | 9 | 18. Call Me | Atlantic 2706 |
| 6/13/70 | 23 | 5 | 19. Spirit In The Dark | Atlantic 2731 |
| 8/22/70 | 11 | 8 | ● 20. Don't Play That Song | Atlantic 2751 |
| 12/19/70 | 37 | 2 | 21. Border Song (Holy Moses) | Atlantic 2772 |
| 3/06/71 | 19 | 7 | 22. You're All I Need To Get By | Atlantic 2787 |
| 4/24/71 | 6 | 11 | ● 23. **Bridge Over Troubled Water** | Atlantic 2796 |
| 8/07/71 | 2 (2) | 11 | ● 24. **Spanish Harlem** | Atlantic 2817 |
| 11/06/71 | 9 | 8 | ● 25. **Rock Steady** | Atlantic 2838 |
| 3/25/72 | 5 | 11 | ● 26. **Day Dreaming** | Atlantic 2866 |
| 6/17/72 | 26 | 6 | 27. All The King's Horses | Atlantic 2883 |
| 3/10/73 | 33 | 5 | 28. Master Of Eyes (The Deepness Of Your Eyes) | Atlantic 2941 |
| 7/21/73 | 20 | 10 | 29. Angel | Atlantic 2969 |
| 12/15/73 + | 3 | 17 | ● 30. **Until You Come Back To Me (That's What I'm Gonna Do)** | Atlantic 2995 |
| 5/04/74 | 19 | 8 | 31. I'm In Love | Atlantic 2999 |
| 7/10/76 | 28 | 6 | 32. Something He Can Feel | Atlantic 3326 |
| 9/11/82 | 24 | 6 | 33. Jump To It | Arista 0699 |
| | | | **STAN FREBERG** | |
| | | | master-satirist | |
| 10/22/55 | 16 | 2 | 1. The Yellow Rose Of Texas [C] | Capitol 3249 |
| 4/27/57 | 25 | 1 | 2. Banana Boat (Day-O) [C] | Capitol 3687 |
| | | | interruptions by Peter Leeds | |
| 11/18/57 | 32 | 3 | 3. Wun'erful, Wun'erful! (Parts 1 & 2) [C] | Capitol 3815 |
| | | | with Peggy Taylor & Daws Butler | |
| | | | **JOHN FRED & His Playboy Band** | |
| | | | John Fred Gourrier from Baton Rouge, Louisiana | |
| 12/16/67 + | 1 (2) | 13 | ● 1. **Judy In Disguise (With Glasses)** | Paula 282 |
| | | | **FREDDIE & THE DREAMERS** | |
| | | | Freddie Garrity, leader of quintet from Manchester, England | |
| 3/27/65 | 1 (2) | 8 | 1. **I'm Telling You Now** | Tower 125 |
| 4/24/65 | 36 | 2 | 2. I Understand (Just How You Feel) | Mercury 72377 |

| DATE | POS | WKS | ARTIST—Record Title | LABEL & NO. |
|------|-----|-----|---------------------|-------------|
| 5/15/65 | 18 | 5 | 3. Do The Freddie | Mercury 72428 |
| 5/15/65 | 21 | 5 | 4. You Were Made For Me | Tower 127 |
| | | | **FREE** | |
| | | | British quartet - Paul Rodgers (vocals) & Simon Kirke (drums) retired group in 1973 to form Bad Company | |
| 9/05/70 | 4 | 13 | 1. **All Right Now** | A&M 1206 |
| | | | **FREE MOVEMENT** | |
| 9/18/71 | 5 | 11 | 1. **I've Found Someone Of My Own** | Decca 32818 |
| | | | **BOBBY FREEMAN** | |
| | | | born on 6/13/40 in San Francisco | |
| 5/26/58 | 5 | 12 | 1. **Do You Want To Dance** | Josie 835 |
| 8/18/58 | 37 | 1 | 2. Betty Lou Got A New Pair Of Shoes | Josie 841 |
| 9/26/60 | 37 | 3 | 3. (I Do The) Shimmy Shimmy | King 5373 |
| 7/25/64 | 5 | 10 | 4. **C'mon And Swim** | Autumn 2 |
| | | | **ERNIE FREEMAN** | |
| | | | producer/arranger - died on 5/15/81 (57) | |
| 11/18/57 | 4 | 12 | 1. **Raunchy [I]** | Imperial 5474 |
| | | | **ACE FREHLEY** | |
| | | | Kiss' lead guitarist | |
| 12/02/78 + | 13 | 12 | 1. New York Groove | Casablanca 941 |
| | | | **GLENN FREY** | |
| | | | Eagles' guitarist | |
| 7/17/82 | 31 | 5 | 1. I Found Somebody | Asylum 47466 |
| 9/11/82 | 15 | 11 | 2. The One You Love | Asylum 69974 |
| 7/14/84 | 20 | 9 | 3. Sexy Girl | MCA 52413 |
| | | | **FRIDA** | |
| | | | member of Abba | |
| 2/12/83 | 13 | 12 | 1. I Know There's Something Going On | Atlantic 89984 |
| | | | **DEAN FRIEDMAN** | |
| | | | New Jersey vocalist | |
| 5/21/77 | 26 | 10 | 1. Ariel | Lifesong 45022 |
| | | | **FRIEND AND LOVER** | |
| | | | James & wife Cathy Post | |
| 6/01/68 | 10 | 11 | 1. **Reach Out Of The Darkness** | Verve Fore. 5069 |
| | | | **FRIENDS OF DISTINCTION** | |
| | | | Los Angeles-based pop/soul quartet | |
| 4/26/69 | 3 | 13 | ● 1. **Grazing In The Grass** | RCA 0107 |
| 10/11/69 | 15 | 12 | ● 2. **Going In Circles** | RCA 0204 |
| 3/21/70 | 6 | 11 | 3. **Love Or Let Me Be Lonely** | RCA 0319 |
| | | | **FRIJID PINK** | |
| | | | Michigan rock quartet | |
| 2/21/70 | 7 | 11 | ● 1. **House Of The Rising Sun** | Parrot 341 |
| | | | **MAX FROST & THE TROOPERS** | |
| 9/28/68 | 22 | 9 | 1. Shape Of Things To Come | Tower 419 |
| | | | from the film "Wild In The Streets" | |

| DATE | POS | WKS | ARTIST—Record Title | LABEL & NO. |
|---|---|---|---|---|
| | | | **BOBBY FULLER Four** | |
| | | | El Paso, Texas rock band - Bobby died on 7/18/66 (22) | |
| 2/12/66 | 9 | 8 | 1. **I Fought The Law** | Mustang 3014 |
| 5/07/66 | 26 | 3 | 2. Love's Made A Fool Of You | Mustang 3016 |
| | | | **FUNKADELIC** | |
| | | | part of George Clinton's "P.Funk" battalion - also see Parliaments | |
| 11/04/78 | 28 | 5 | ● 1. One Nation Under A Groove (Part 1) | Warner 8618 |
| | | | **RICHIE FURAY** | |
| | | | member of Buffalo Springfield, Poco, and Souther, Hillman, Furay Band | |
| 12/15/79 | 39 | 3 | 1. I Still Have Dreams | Asylum 46534 |
| | | | **FUZZ** | |
| | | | Washington, D.C. female soul trio | |
| 4/17/71 | 21 | 8 | 1. I Love You For All Seasons | Calla 174 |
| | | | **PETER GABRIEL** | |
| | | | English - leader of Genesis from 1966-1975 | |
| 12/04/82 + | 29 | 10 | 1. Shock The Monkey | Geffen 29883 |
| | | | **GADABOUTS** | |
| | | | featuring Wild Bill Putnam | |
| 8/04/56 | 39 | 1 | 1. Stranded In The Jungle [N] | Mercury 70898 |
| | | | **SUNNY GALE** | |
| 1/08/55 | 17 | 1 | 1. Let Me Go, Lover! | RCA 5952 |
| | | | **GALLERY** | |
| | | | Jim Gold, leader of Detroit sextet | |
| 4/29/72 | 4 | 13 | ● 1. **Nice To Be With You** | Sussex 232 |
| 10/07/72 | 22 | 8 | 2. I Believe In Music | Sussex 239 |
| 2/10/73 | 23 | 8 | 3. Big City Miss Ruth Ann | Sussex 248 |
| | | | **FRANK GALLOP** | |
| | | | radio & TV announcer | |
| 5/07/66 | 34 | 5 | 1. The Ballad Of Irving [C] | Kapp 745 |
| | | | **GAP BAND** | |
| | | | brothers Charles, Ronnie, and Robert Wilson from Tulsa | |
| 7/03/82 | 24 | 6 | 1. Early In The Morning | Total Exp. 8201 |
| 9/11/82 | 31 | 7 | 2. You Dropped A Bomb On Me | Total Exp. 8203 |
| | | | **DAVE GARDNER** | |
| | | | comedian "Brother" Dave Gardner | |
| 7/22/57 | 22 | 4 | 1. White Silver Sands | OJ 1002 |
| | | | **DON GARDNER & DEE DEE FORD** | |
| 7/07/62 | 20 | 7 | 1. I Need Your Loving | Fire 508 |
| | | | **ART GARFUNKEL** | |
| | | | born on 10/13/42 in New York City - also see Simon & Garfunkel | |
| 10/06/73 | 9 | 10 | 1. **All I Know** | Columbia 45926 |
| 2/09/74 | 38 | 1 | 2. I Shall Sing | Columbia 45983 |

| DATE | POS | WKS | ARTIST—Record Title | LABEL & NO. |
|------|-----|-----|---------------------|-------------|
| 10/19/74 | 34 | 3 | 3. Second Avenue | Columbia 10020 |
| 9/27/75 | 18 | 12 | 4. I Only Have Eyes For You | Columbia 10190 |
| 1/31/76 | 39 | 2 | 5. Break Away | Columbia 10273 |
| | | | **ART GARFUNKEL with JAMES TAYLOR & PAUL SIMON** | |
| 2/11/78 | 17 | 7 | 1. (What A) Wonderful World | Columbia 10676 |
| | | | **FRANK GARI** | |
| 2/13/61 | 27 | 5 | 1. Utopia | Crusade 1020 |
| 5/15/61 | 23 | 6 | 2. Lullaby Of Love | Crusade 1021 |
| 8/14/61 | 30 | 3 | 3. Princess | Crusade 1022 |
| | | | **GALE GARNETT** | |
| 9/05/64 | 4 | 13 | 1. **We'll Sing In The Sunshine** | RCA 8388 |
| | | | **LEIF GARRETT** | |
| | | | born on 11/8/61 in Hollywood, California | |
| 9/17/77 | 20 | 8 | 1. Surfin' USA | Atlantic 3423 |
| 12/03/77 + | 13 | 9 | 2. Runaround Sue | Atlantic 3440 |
| 12/09/78 + | 10 | 15 | 3. **I Was Made For Dancin'** | Scotti Br. 403 |
| | | | **DAVID GATES** | |
| | | | lead singer of Bread | |
| 2/15/75 | 29 | 5 | 1. Never Let Her Go | Elektra 45223 |
| 2/18/78 | 15 | 12 | 2. Goodbye Girl | Elektra 45450 |
| 10/07/78 | 30 | 5 | 3. Took The Last Train | Elektra 45500 |
| | | | **MARVIN GAYE** | |
| | | | born in Washington, D.C. on 4/2/39 - shot to death by his father on 4/1/84 (44) | |
| 3/02/63 | 30 | 3 | 1. Hitch Hike | Tamla 54075 |
| 6/15/63 | 10 | 10 | 2. **Pride And Joy** | Tamla 54079 |
| 11/23/63 | 22 | 10 | 3. Can I Get A Witness | Tamla 54087 |
| 3/28/64 | 15 | 7 | 4. You're A Wonderful One | Tamla 54093 |
| 6/27/64 | 15 | 8 | 5. Try It Baby | Tamla 54095 |
| 10/10/64 | 27 | 6 | 6. Baby Don't You Do It | Tamla 54101 |
| 12/12/64 + | 6 | 11 | 7. **How Sweet It Is To Be Loved By You** | Tamla 54107 |
| 4/10/65 | 8 | 8 | 8. **I'll Be Doggone** | Tamla 54112 |
| 7/24/65 | 25 | 5 | 9. Pretty Little Baby | Tamla 54117 |
| 10/23/65 | 8 | 9 | 10. **Ain't That Peculiar** | Tamla 54122 |
| 3/12/66 | 29 | 4 | 11. One More Heartache | Tamla 54129 |
| 7/22/67 | 33 | 3 | 12. Your Unchanging Love | Tamla 54153 |
| 2/03/68 | 34 | 3 | 13. You | Tamla 54160 |
| 10/19/68 | 32 | 4 | 14. Chained | Tamla 54170 |
| 11/23/68 | 1 (7) | 15 | 15. **I Heard It Through The Grapevine** | Tamla 54176 |
| 5/10/69 | 4 | 13 | 16. **Too Busy Thinking About My Baby** | Tamla 54181 |
| 9/13/69 | 7 | 9 | 17. **That's The Way Love Is** | Tamla 54185 |
| 7/11/70 | 40 | 2 | 18. The End Of Our Road | Tamla 54195 |
| 3/06/71 | 2 (3) | 13 | 19. **What's Going On** | Tamla 54201 |

**Janis Ian** received an unusual endorsement when Leonard Bernstein praised her in a 1967 TV special. She was only 16 when "Society's Child" entered the charts. Interestingly, her next Top 40 song was "At Seventeen," which didn't appear until 1975.

**Billy Idol** (born William Broad) earned his spurs singing for Generation X, one of the most respected bands of the British punk movement. Then he moved to America, hooked up with Kiss manager Bill Aucoin, and hit the jackpot.

**Julio Iglesias** and **Diana Ross.** By August 1984, Julio Iglesias had sold an estimated 100 million albums and given over 2,200 live concerts. And he was just getting started in the U.S.

**Jackson 5.** Diana Ross is most often given credit for the discovery of the superstar family from Gary, Indiana, but other claimants include Gladys Knight, Bobby Taylor of the Vancouvers, and Richard Hatcher, who was the mayor of the boys' hometown.

**Jermaine Jackson** wanted to release "Tell Me I'm Not Dreamin' (Too Good to Be True)," his electrifying duet with brother Michael, as a single. But Michael's label wouldn't grant Jermaine's label permission, so a potential chart-topper went down the drain.

Michael Jackson autograph: *Michael Jackson P.Y.T. (Pretty Young Thing)*

**M J**

Taken from the Epic LP
"Thriller" (QE 3811)

**Michael Jackson.** Amidst all the excitement over *Thriller's* unprecedented seven Top Ten singles, it was sometimes forgotten that Jackson's prior LP *Off the Wall,* had produced four Top Tens, sharing the old record with *Grease, Saturday Night Fever,* and Fleetwood Mac's *Rumours.*

**Joe Jackson** stuck his neck out and attacked the video revolution in 1984. Writing in *Billboard,* he characterized videos as a "shallow, tasteless and formularized way of selling music," but conceded, "If I could dance like Michael Jackson I might be making a video right now."

**Jan and Dean's** third original member was Arnie Ginsburg. Dean was in the army when "Jennie Lee" came out in 1958, so the record was credited to Jan and Arnie.

**Al Jarreau.** Besides possessing an exceptionally dextrous voice, Al Jarreau is also the proud owner of a Masters degree in psychology.

**Joan Jett.** Next to rock'n'roll, Jett loves baseball best. A die-hard Baltimore Orioles fan, she once broke an ankle sliding hard into second in a softball game.

JOE JACKSON
steppin' out
b/w
chinatown

THE NEW GIRL IN SCHOOL
b/w DEAD MAN'S CURVE
JAN & DEAN   *LIBERTY*   #55672

You can use these photos for bookmarks. Just cut on dotted lines.

JARREAU
*MORNIN'*

Joan Jett and the Blackhearts
Fake Friends

| DATE | POS | WKS | ARTIST—Record Title | LABEL & NO. |
|------|-----|-----|---------------------|-------------|
| 7/17/71 | 4 | 10 | 20. **Mercy Mercy Me (The Ecology)** | Tamla 54207 |
| 10/16/71 | 9 | 8 | 21. **Inner City Blues (Make Me Wanna Holler)** | Tamla 54209 |
| 12/30/72 + | 7 | 9 | 22. **Trouble Man** | Tamla 54228 |
| 7/28/73 | 1 (2) | 17 | 23. **Let's Get It On** | Tamla 54234 |
| 11/17/73 | 21 | 8 | 24. Come Get To This | Tamla 54241 |
| 10/26/74 | 28 | 3 | 25. Distant Lover | Tamla 54253 |
| 5/08/76 | 15 | 9 | 26. I Want You | Tamla 54264 |
| 4/23/77 | 1 (1) | 15 | 27. **Got To Give It Up - Pt. 1** | Tamla 54280 |
| 11/20/82 + | 3 | 15 | ● 28. **Sexual Healing** | Columbia 03302 |
|  |  |  | **MARVIN GAYE & DIANA ROSS** |  |
| 10/13/73 | 12 | 10 | 1. You're A Special Part Of Me | Motown 1280 |
| 3/30/74 | 19 | 10 | 2. My Mistake (Was To Love You) | Motown 1269 |
|  |  |  | **MARVIN GAYE & TAMMI TERRELL** |  |
|  |  |  | Tammi died on 3/16/70 (23) |  |
| 6/03/67 | 19 | 9 | 1. Ain't No Mountain High Enough | Tamla 54149 |
| 9/30/67 | 5 | 10 | 2. **Your Precious Love** | Tamla 54156 |
| 12/16/67 + | 10 | 9 | 3. **If I Could Build My Whole World Around You** | Tamla 54161 |
| 4/27/68 | 8 | 11 | 4. **Ain't Nothing Like The Real Thing** | Tamla 54163 |
| 8/10/68 | 7 | 10 | 5. **You're All I Need To Get By** | Tamla 54169 |
| 10/19/68 | 24 | 6 | 6. Keep On Lovin' Me Honey | Tamla 54173 |
| 2/15/69 | 30 | 4 | 7. Good Lovin' Ain't Easy To Come By | Tamla 54179 |
|  |  |  | **MARVIN GAYE & MARY WELLS** |  |
| 5/23/64 | 19 | 6 | 1. Once Upon A Time/ |  |
| 6/13/64 | 17 | 6 | 2.  What's The Matter With You Baby | Motown 1057 |
|  |  |  | **MARVIN GAYE & KIM WESTON** |  |
| 2/04/67 | 14 | 7 | 1. It Takes Two | Tamla 54141 |
|  |  |  | **CRYSTAL GAYLE** |  |
|  |  |  | younger sister of Loretta Lynn - also see Eddie Rabbitt |  |
| 9/24/77 | 2 (3) | 18 | ● 1. **Don't It Make My Brown Eyes Blue** | United Art. 1016 |
| 9/02/78 | 18 | 11 | 2. Talking In Your Sleep | United Art. 1214 |
| 11/03/79 | 15 | 10 | 3. Half The Way | Columbia 11087 |
|  |  |  | **GLORIA GAYNOR** |  |
|  |  |  | Newark, New Jersey disco queen |  |
| 12/07/74 + | 9 | 10 | 1. **Never Can Say Goodbye** | MGM 14748 |
| 1/20/79 | 1 (3) | 17 | ★ 2. **I Will Survive** | Polydor 14508 |
|  |  |  | **G-CLEFS** |  |
|  |  |  | 4 brothers and a friend from Roxbury, Massachusetts |  |
| 9/15/56 | 24 | 1 | 1. Ka-Ding Dong | Pilgrim 715 |
| 10/16/61 | 9 | 11 | 2. **I Understand (Just How You Feel)** | Terrace 7500 |
|  |  |  | backing tune is "Auld Lang Syne" |  |
|  |  |  | **DAVID GEDDES** |  |
| 8/23/75 | 4 | 9 | 1. **Run Joey Run** | Big Tree 16044 |
| 11/22/75 | 18 | 6 | 2. The Last Game Of The Season (A Blind Man In The Bleachers) | Big Tree 16052 |

| DATE | POS | WKS | ARTIST—Record Title | LABEL & NO. |
|------|-----|-----|---------------------|-------------|
| | | | **J. GEILS BAND** | |
| | | | Boston sextet led by Peter Wolf (vocals), Seth Justman (keyboards), & Jerome Geils (guitar) | |
| 1/15/72 | 39 | 2 | 1. Looking For A Love | Atlantic 2844 |
| 5/26/73 | 30 | 6 | 2. Give It To Me | Atlantic 2953 |
| 11/23/74 + | 12 | 7 | 3. Must Of Got Lost | Atlantic 3214 |
| 1/20/79 | 35 | 3 | 4. One Last Kiss | EMI America 8007 |
| 3/08/80 | 32 | 5 | 5. Come Back | EMI America 8032 |
| 5/24/80 | 38 | 3 | 6. Love Stinks | EMI America 8039 |
| 11/28/81 + | 1 (6) | 20 | • 7. **Centerfold** | EMI America 8102 |
| 3/06/82 | 4 | 12 | • 8. **Freeze-Frame** | EMI America 8108 |
| 7/03/82 | 40 | 2 | 9. Angel In Blue | EMI America 8100 |
| 12/11/82 + | 24 | 7 | 10. I Do | EMI America 8148 |
| | | | **GENE & DEBBE** | |
| | | | Gene Thomas & Debbe Nevills | |
| 3/09/68 | 17 | 12 | 1. Playboy | TRX 5006 |
| | | | **GENESIS** | |
| | | | English group formed in 1966 featuring Phil Collins, Peter Gabriel, Mike Rutherford, Tony Banks & Steve Hackett | |
| 6/03/78 | 23 | 5 | 1. Follow You Follow Me | Atlantic 3474 |
| 6/21/80 | 14 | 11 | 2. Misunderstanding | Atlantic 3662 |
| 11/07/81 | 29 | 6 | 3. No Reply At All | Atlantic 3858 |
| 1/23/82 | 26 | 6 | 4. Abacab | Atlantic 3891 |
| 5/08/82 | 40 | 2 | 5. Man On The Corner | Atlantic 4025 |
| 7/24/82 | 32 | 5 | 6. Paperlate | Atlantic 4053 |
| 12/10/83 + | 6 | 14 | 7. **That's All!** | Atlantic 89724 |
| | | | **BOBBIE GENTRY** | |
| | | | born in Chickasaw County, Mississippi on 7/27/44 - also see Glen Campbell | |
| 8/12/67 | 1 (4) | 12 | • 1. **Ode To Billie Joe** | Capitol 5950 |
| 1/31/70 | 31 | 4 | 2. Fancy | Capitol 2675 |
| | | | **GENTRYS** | |
| | | | Memphis-based 7-man band - Larry Raspberry, leader | |
| 9/25/65 | 4 | 11 | 1. **Keep On Dancing** | MGM 13379 |
| | | | **BARBARA GEORGE** | |
| 12/18/61 + | 3 | 11 | 1. **I Know (You Don't Love Me No More)** | A.F.O. 302 |
| | | | **GERRY & THE PACEMAKERS** | |
| | | | quartet from Liverpool, England - led by Gerry Marsden | |
| 6/06/64 | 4 | 9 | 1. **Don't Let The Sun Catch You Crying** | Laurie 3251 |
| 8/08/64 | 9 | 7 | 2. **How Do You Do It?** | Laurie 3261 |
| 10/17/64 | 17 | 6 | 3. I Like It | Laurie 3271 |
| 1/09/65 | 14 | 5 | 4. I'll Be There | Laurie 3279 |
| 2/13/65 | 6 | 9 | 5. **Ferry Across The Mersey** | Laurie 3284 |
| 4/24/65 | 23 | 5 | 6. It's Gonna Be Alright | Laurie 3293 |
| | | | above 2 from the film "Ferry Cross The Mersey" | |
| 10/08/66 | 28 | 4 | 7. Girl On A Swing | Laurie 3354 |
| | | | **GET WET** | |
| 5/23/81 | 39 | 2 | 1. Just So Lonely | Boardwalk 02018 |

| DATE | POS | WKS | ARTIST—Record Title | LABEL & NO. |
|---|---|---|---|---|
| | | | **STAN GETZ/CHARLIE BYRD** | |
| | | | Getz: jazz tenor saxophonist/Byrd: jazz guitarist | |
| 10/27/62 | **15** | 10 | 1. Desafinado [I] | Verve 10260 |
| | | | **STAN GETZ/ASTRUD GILBERTO** | |
| | | | Gilberto: Brazilian vocalist | |
| 6/20/64 | **5** | 10 | 1. **The Girl From Ipanema** | Verve 10323 |
| | | | **ANDY GIBB** | |
| | | | Bee Gees' younger brother - also see Olivia Newton-John | |
| 5/28/77 | **1** (4) | 23 | ● 1. **I Just Want To Be Your Everything** | RSO 872 |
| 12/10/77 + | **1** (2) | 22 | ● 2. **(Love Is) Thicker Than Water** | RSO 883 |
| 4/22/78 | **1** (7) | 19 | ★ 3. **Shadow Dancing** | RSO 893 |
| 7/22/78 | **5** | 13 | ● 4. **An Everlasting Love** | RSO 904 |
| 11/04/78 | **9** | 13 | ● 5. **(Our Love) Don't Throw It All Away** | RSO 911 |
| 2/02/80 | **4** | 12 | 6. **Desire** | RSO 1019 |
| 12/06/80 + | **15** | 11 | 7. Time Is Time | RSO 1059 |
| 4/11/81 | **40** | 1 | 8. Me (Without You) | RSO 1056 |
| | | | **BARRY GIBB** | |
| | | | eldest brother of the Bee Gees - also see Samantha Sang and Barbra Streisand | |
| 9/29/84 | **37** | 3 | 1. Shine Shine | MCA 52443 |
| | | | **ROBIN GIBB** | |
| | | | twin brother of the Bee Gees' Maurice Gibb | |
| 8/19/78 | **15** | 9 | 1. Oh! Darling | RSO 907 |
| | | | from the film "Sgt. Pepper's Lonely Hearts Club Band" | |
| 7/07/84 | **37** | 4 | 2. Boys Do Fall In Love | Mirage 99743 |
| | | | **GEORGIA GIBBS** | |
| | | | real name: Fredda Lipson | |
| 1/29/55 | **2** (1) | 19 | 1. **Tweedle Dee** | Mercury 70517 |
| 3/26/55 | **1** (3) | 20 | 2. **Dance With Me Henry (Wallflower)** | Mercury 70572 |
| 7/09/55 | **12** | 4 | 3. Sweet And Gentle | Mercury 70647 |
| 9/17/55 | **14** | 4 | 4. I Want You To Be My Baby | Mercury 70685 |
| 4/14/56 | **36** | 1 | 5. Rock Right | Mercury 70811 |
| 5/26/56 | **30** | 4 | 6. Kiss Me Another | Mercury 70850 |
| 8/25/56 | **20** | 8 | 7. Happiness Street | Mercury 70920 |
| 12/22/56 | **24** | 1 | 8. Tra La La | Mercury 70998 |
| 10/20/58 | **32** | 1 | 9. The Hula Hoop Song | Roulette 4106 |
| | | | **TERRI GIBBS** | |
| | | | Terri, blind since birth, is from Augusta, Georgia | |
| 2/28/81 | **13** | 12 | 1. Somebody's Knockin' | MCA 41309 |
| | | | **DON GIBSON** | |
| | | | born on 3/3/28 in Shelby, North Carolina | |
| 3/31/58 | **7** | 17 | 1. **Oh Lonesome Me** | RCA 7133 |
| 7/14/58 | **20** | 8 | 2. Blue Blue Day | RCA 7010 |
| 3/28/60 | **29** | 6 | 3. Just One Time | RCA 7690 |
| 7/10/61 | **21** | 8 | 4. Sea Of Heartbreak | RCA 7890 |
| | | | **ASTRUD GILBERTO - see STAN GETZ** | |

| DATE | POS | WKS | ARTIST—Record Title | LABEL & NO. |
|------|-----|-----|---------------------|-------------|
| | | | **NICK GILDER** | |
| | | | Canadian - member of Sweeny Todd | |
| 8/05/78 | **1** (1) | 18 | ★ 1. **Hot Child In The City** | Chrysalis 2226 |
| | | | **TERRY GILKYSON & THE EASY RIDERS** | |
| | | | Terry, Rich Dehr & Frank Miller | |
| | | | also see Frankie Laine and Dean Martin | |
| 2/09/57 | **4** | 14 | 1. **Marianne** | Columbia 40817 |
| | | | **MICKEY GILLEY** | |
| | | | owner of "Gilleys" club in Pasadena, Texas | |
| 6/28/80 | **22** | 9 | 1. Stand By Me | Full Moon 46640 |
| | | | from the soundtrack "Urban Cowboy" | |
| | | | **JIMMY GILMER & THE FIREBALLS** | |
| | | | Amarillo, Texas native - also see Fireballs | |
| 9/28/63 | **1** (5) | 13 | ● 1. **Sugar Shack** | Dot 16487 |
| 1/04/64 | **15** | 8 | 2. Daisy Petal Pickin' | Dot 16539 |
| | | | **JAMES GILREATH** | |
| 4/27/63 | **21** | 6 | 1. Little Band Of Gold | Joy 274 |
| | | | **GINO & GINA** | |
| 6/09/58 | **20** | 1 | 1. (It's Been A Long Time) Pretty Baby | Mercury 71283 |
| | | | **WILL GLAHE & His Orchestra & Chorus** | |
| 11/25/57 | **16** | 15 | 1. Liechtensteiner Polka [F] | London 1755 |
| | | | **GLASS BOTTLE** | |
| 9/18/71 | **36** | 3 | 1. I Ain't Got Time Anymore | Avco Embassy 4575 |
| | | | **TOM GLAZER & The Do-Re-Mi Children's Chorus** | |
| 6/15/63 | **14** | 7 | 1. On Top Of Spaghetti [N] | Kapp 526 |
| | | | based on the tune "On Top Of Old Smokey" | |
| | | | **GLENCOVES** | |
| 7/27/63 | **38** | 2 | 1. Hootenanny | Select 724 |
| | | | **GARY GLITTER** | |
| | | | British - real name: Paul Gadd | |
| 8/05/72 | **7** | 9 | 1. **Rock And Roll Part 2 [I]** | Bell 45237 |
| 12/02/72 | **35** | 3 | 2. I Didn't Know I Loved You (Till I Saw You Rock And Roll) | Bell 45276 |
| | | | **GO-GO'S** | |
| | | | Belinda Carlisle, lead singer of Los Angeles female quintet | |
| 10/24/81 | **20** | 13 | 1. **Our Lips Are Sealed** | I.R.S. 9901 |
| 2/13/82 | **2** (3) | 15 | ● 2. **We Got The Beat** | I.R.S. 9903 |
| 7/17/82 | **8** | 9 | 3. **Vacation** | I.R.S. 9907 |
| 3/31/84 | **11** | 10 | 4. **Head Over Heels** | I.R.S. 9926 |
| 7/14/84 | **32** | 5 | 5. Turn To You | I.R.S. 9928 |
| | | | **GODSPELL** | |
| | | | original Broadway cast of "Godspell" | |
| 6/24/72 | **13** | 9 | 1. Day By Day | Bell 45210 |
| | | | lead vocal by Robin Lamont | |

| DATE | POS | WKS | ARTIST—Record Title | LABEL & NO. |
|---|---|---|---|---|
| | | | **ANDREW GOLD** | |
| | | | son of composer Ernest Gold ("Exodus") & singer Marni Nixon | |
| 4/16/77 | 7 | 13 | 1. **Lonely Boy** | Asylum 45384 |
| 3/04/78 | 25 | 9 | 2. Thank You For Being A Friend | Asylum 45456 |
| | | | **GOLDEN EARRING** | |
| | | | Dutch rock quartet | |
| 6/22/74 | 13 | 10 | 1. Radar Love | Track 40202 |
| 1/22/83 | 10 | 15 | 2. **Twilight Zone** | 21 Records 103 |
| | | | **BOBBY GOLDSBORO** | |
| | | | born 1/18/41 in Marianna, Florida | |
| 2/15/64 | 9 | 8 | 1. **See The Funny Little Clown** | United Art. 672 |
| 5/23/64 | 39 | 2 | 2. Whenever He Holds You | United Art. 710 |
| 2/20/65 | 13 | 8 | 3. Little Things | United Art. 810 |
| 6/05/65 | 27 | 6 | 4. Voodoo Woman | United Art. 862 |
| 3/12/66 | 23 | 5 | 5. It's Too Late | United Art. 980 |
| 1/14/67 | 35 | 3 | 6. Blue Autumn | United Art. 50087 |
| 3/30/68 | 1 (5) | 13 | ● 7. **Honey** | United Art. 50283 |
| 7/13/68 | 19 | 7 | 8. Autumn Of My Life | United Art. 50318 |
| 11/30/68 | 36 | 2 | 9. The Straight Life | United Art. 50461 |
| 1/09/71 | 11 | 11 | 10. Watching Scotty Grow | United Art. 50727 |
| 10/06/73 | 21 | 8 | 11. Summer (The First Time) | United Art. 251 |
| | | | **IAN GOMM** | |
| | | | English - member of Brinsley Schwarz | |
| 10/06/79 | 18 | 5 | 1. Hold On | Stiff/Epic 50747 |
| | | | **GONE ALL STARS** | |
| 3/03/58 | 30 | 4 | 1. "7-11" [I] | Gone 5016 |
| | | | Mambo No. 5 | |
| | | | **GONZALEZ** | |
| | | | English disco band | |
| 2/10/79 | 26 | 5 | 1. Haven't Stopped Dancing Yet | Capitol 4674 |
| | | | **BENNY GOODMAN Trio with ROSEMARY CLOONEY** | |
| 3/17/56 | 20 | 1 | 1. Memories Of You | Columbia 40616 |
| | | | from the film "The Benny Goodman Story" | |
| | | | **DICKIE GOODMAN** | |
| | | | also see Buchanan & Goodman | |
| 2/23/74 | 33 | 4 | 1. Energy Crisis '74 [N] | Rainy Wed. 206 |
| 9/13/75 | 4 | 7 | ● 2. **Mr. Jaws [N]** | Cash 451 |
| | | | **BARRY GORDON** | |
| | | | 7-year-old boy | |
| 12/17/55 | 6 | 4 | 1. **Nuttin' For Christmas [X-N]** | MGM 12092 |
| | | | backed by Art Mooney & his orchestra | |
| | | | **LESLEY GORE** | |
| | | | born on 5/2/46 in New York City | |
| 5/18/63 | 1 (2) | 11 | 1. **It's My Party** | Mercury 72119 |
| 7/20/63 | 5 | 9 | 2. Judy's Turn To Cry | Mercury 72143 |

| DATE | POS | WKS | ARTIST—Record Title | LABEL & NO. |
|------|-----|-----|---------------------|-------------|
| 10/19/63 | 5 | 11 | 3. **She's A Fool** | Mercury 72180 |
| 1/11/64 | 2 (3) | 10 | 4. **You Don't Own Me** | Mercury 72206 |
| 4/04/64 | 12 | 7 | 5. That's The Way Boys Are | Mercury 72259 |
| 6/20/64 | 37 | 1 | 6. I Don't Wanna Be A Loser | Mercury 72270 |
| 8/15/64 | 14 | 6 | 7. Maybe I Know | Mercury 72309 |
| 1/23/65 | 27 | 5 | 8. Look Of Love | Mercury 72372 |
| 7/17/65 | 13 | 7 | 9. Sunshine, Lollipops And Rainbows<br>from the film "Ski Party" | Mercury 72433 |
| 10/09/65 | 32 | 3 | 10. My Town, My Guy And Me | Mercury 72475 |
| 3/04/67 | 16 | 9 | 11. California Nights | Mercury 72649 |
| | | | **EYDIE GORME**<br>also see Steve & Eydie | |
| 6/16/56 | 39 | 1 | 1. Too Close For Comfort<br>from the musical "Mr. Wonderful" | ABC-Para. 9684 |
| 9/01/56 | 34 | 3 | 2. Mama, Teach Me To Dance | ABC-Para. 9722 |
| 12/30/57 | 24 | 1 | 3. Love Me Forever | ABC-Para. 9863 |
| 5/26/58 | 11 | 9 | 4. You Need Hands | ABC-Para. 9925 |
| 2/09/63 | 7 | 11 | 5. **Blame It On The Bossa Nova** | Columbia 42661 |
| | | | **ROBERT GOULET**<br>played Sir Lancelot in Broadway's "Camelot" | |
| 11/28/64 + | 16 | 9 | 1. My Love, Forgive Me (Amore, Scusami) | Columbia 43131 |
| | | | **GQ**<br>Bronx, New York soul trio | |
| 4/14/79 | 12 | 11 | ● 1. Disco Nights (Rock-Freak) | Arista 0388 |
| 8/11/79 | 20 | 8 | 2. I Do Love You | Arista 0426 |
| | | | **CHARLIE GRACIE**<br>born on 1/12/36 in Philadelphia, Pennsylvania | |
| 2/23/57 | 1 (2) | 14 | 1. **Butterfly** | Cameo 105 |
| 5/20/57 | 16 | 6 | 2. Fabulous | Cameo 107 |
| | | | **GRAHAM CENTRAL STATION**<br>soul-dance band led by Larry Graham | |
| 9/13/75 | 38 | 2 | 1. Your Love | Warner 8105 |
| | | | **LARRY GRAHAM**<br>former bass player with Sly & The Family Stone | |
| 8/09/80 | 9 | 9 | ● 1. **One In A Million You** | Warner 49221 |
| | | | **BILLY GRAMMER** | |
| 12/08/58 + | 4 | 15 | 1. **Gotta Travel On** | Monument 400 |
| | | | **GERRY GRANAHAN**<br>also see Dicky Doo & The Don'ts | |
| 6/16/58 | 23 | 8 | 1. No Chemise, Please | Sunbeam 102 |
| | | | **ROCCO GRANATA**<br>Belgian | |
| 11/23/59 | 31 | 7 | 1. Marina [F] | Laurie 3041 |

| DATE | POS | WKS | ARTIST—Record Title | LABEL & NO. |
|---|---|---|---|---|
| | | | **GRAND FUNK RAILROAD** | |
| | | | Flint, Michigan hard-rock band: Mark Farner, Don Brewer & Mel Schacher | |
| 9/05/70 | 22 | 8 | 1. Closer To Home | Capitol 2877 |
| 2/05/72 | 29 | 5 | 2. Footstompin' Music | Capitol 3255 |
| 11/04/72 | 29 | 6 | 3. Rock 'N Roll Soul | Capitol 3363 |
| | | | GRAND FUNK: | |
| 8/18/73 | 1 (1) | 13 | ● 4. **We're An American Band** | Capitol 3660 |
| 12/29/73 + | 19 | 6 | 5. Walk Like A Man | Capitol 3760 |
| 3/30/74 | 1 (2) | 14 | ● 6. **The Loco-Motion** | Capitol 3840 |
| 7/20/74 | 11 | 8 | 7. Shinin' On | Capitol 3917 |
| 12/21/74 + | 3 | 12 | 8. **Some Kind Of Wonderful** | Capitol 4002 |
| 4/19/75 | 4 | 12 | 9. **Bad Time** | Capitol 4046 |
| | | | **EARL GRANT** | |
| | | | organist-pianist-vocalist - died on 6/10/70 (39) | |
| 9/29/58 | 7 | 13 | 1. **The End** | Decca 30719 |
| | | | **EDDY GRANT** | |
| | | | native of Guyana - former leader of The Equals | |
| 5/21/83 | 2 (5) | 15 | ● 1. **Electric Avenue** | Portrait 03793 |
| 6/30/84 | 26 | 6 | 2. **Romancing The Stone** | Portrait 04433 |
| | | | written for the film but not included in it | |
| | | | **GOGI GRANT** | |
| | | | real name: Audrey Brown | |
| 10/01/55 | 9 | 10 | 1. **Suddenly There's A Valley** | Era 1003 |
| 5/05/56 | 1 (8) | 22 | 2. **The Wayward Wind** | Era 1013 |
| | | | **JANIE GRANT** | |
| 5/15/61 | 29 | 5 | 1. Triangle | Caprice 104 |
| | | | **GRASS ROOTS** | |
| | | | Los Angeles-based group - original members: Warren Entner, Rob Grill, Creed Bratton & Rick Coonce | |
| 7/16/66 | 28 | 4 | 1. Where Were You When I Needed You | Dunhill 4029 |
| 6/03/67 | 8 | 9 | 2. **Let's Live For Today** | Dunhill 4084 |
| 9/02/67 | 23 | 4 | 3. Things I Should Have Said | Dunhill 4094 |
| 9/21/68 | 5 | 12 | ● 4. **Midnight Confessions** | Dunhill 4144 |
| 1/11/69 | 28 | 2 | 5. Bella Linda | Dunhill 4162 |
| 5/17/69 | 31 | 5 | 6. The River Is Wide | Dunhill 4187 |
| 8/09/69 | 15 | 10 | 7. I'd Wait A Million Years | Dunhill 4198 |
| 11/22/69 | 24 | 7 | 8. Heaven Knows | Dunhill 4217 |
| 6/13/70 | 35 | 3 | 9. Baby Hold On | Dunhill 4237 |
| 2/13/71 | 15 | 11 | 10. Temptation Eyes | Dunhill 4263 |
| 6/19/71 | 9 | 9 | 11. **Sooner Or Later** | Dunhill 4279 |
| 10/30/71 | 16 | 8 | 12. Two Divided By Love | Dunhill 4289 |
| 3/18/72 | 34 | 3 | 13. Glory Bound | Dunhill 4302 |
| 7/22/72 | 39 | 2 | 14. The Runway | Dunhill 4316 |
| | | | **DOBIE GRAY** | |
| | | | born Leonard Ainsworth, Jr. on 7/26/42 in Brookshire, Texas | |
| 1/23/65 | 13 | 7 | 1. The "In" Crowd | Charger 105 |
| 3/31/73 | 5 | 15 | ● 2. **Drift Away** | Decca 33057 |
| 2/10/79 | 37 | 2 | 3. You Can Do It | Infinity 50003 |

| DATE | POS | WKS | ARTIST—Record Title | LABEL & NO. |
|------|-----|-----|---------------------|-------------|
| | | | **CHARLES RANDOLPH GREAN Sounde** | |
| | | | former artist & repertoire director at RCA & Dot Records | |
| 7/05/69 | 13 | 8 | 1. Quentin's Theme [I] | Ranwood 840 |
| | | | from the TV series "Dark Shadows" | |
| | | | **R.B. GREAVES** | |
| | | | full name: Ronald Bertram Aloysius Greaves, III | |
| 10/25/69 | 2 (1) | 13 | ● 1. **Take A Letter Maria** | Atco 6714 |
| 2/14/70 | 27 | 5 | 2. Always Something There To Remind Me | Atco 6726 |
| | | | **CYNDI GRECCO** | |
| 6/12/76 | 25 | 5 | 1. Making Our Dreams Come True | Private S. 45086 |
| | | | theme from TV's "LaVerne & Shirley" | |
| | | | **AL GREEN** | |
| | | | born in Forrest City, Arkansas on 4/13/46 | |
| 8/21/71 | 11 | 15 | ● 1. Tired Of Being Alone | Hi 2194 |
| 12/11/71 + | 1 (1) | 15 | ● 2. **Let's Stay Together** | Hi 2202 |
| 4/08/72 | 4 | 11 | ● 3. **Look What You Done For Me** | Hi 2211 |
| 7/15/72 | 3 | 11 | ● 4. **I'm Still In Love With You** | Hi 2216 |
| 11/04/72 | 3 | 12 | ● 5. **You Ought To Be With Me** | Hi 2227 |
| 3/03/73 | 10 | 9 | ● 6. **Call Me (Come Back Home)** | Hi 2235 |
| 7/21/73 | 10 | 12 | ● 7. **Here I Am (Come And Take Me)** | Hi 2247 |
| 12/22/73 + | 19 | 8 | 8. Livin' For You | Hi 2257 |
| 5/11/74 | 32 | 3 | 9. Let's Get Married | Hi 2262 |
| 11/02/74 | 7 | 11 | ● 10. **Sha-La-La (Make Me Happy)** | Hi 2274 |
| 3/22/75 | 13 | 8 | 11. L-O-V-E (Love) | Hi 2282 |
| 11/29/75 | 28 | 6 | 12. Full Of Fire | Hi 2300 |
| 12/18/76 + | 37 | 4 | 13. Keep Me Cryin' | Hi 2319 |
| | | | **GARLAND GREEN** | |
| 10/18/69 | 20 | 4 | 1. Jealous Kind Of Fella | Uni 55143 |
| | | | **NORMAN GREENBAUM** | |
| 3/07/70 | 3 | 14 | ● 1. **Spirit In The Sky** | Reprise 0885 |
| | | | **LORNE GREENE** | |
| | | | Ben Cartwright of TV's "Bonanza" | |
| 11/07/64 | 1 (1) | 10 | 1. **Ringo [S]** | RCA 8444 |
| | | | **BOBBY GREGG & His Friends** | |
| 4/14/62 | 29 | 5 | 1. The Jam - Part 1 [I] | Cotton 1003 |
| | | | **ANDY GRIFFITH** | |
| | | | Sheriff Andy Taylor of "The Andy Griffith Show" | |
| 4/02/55 | 26 | 1 | 1. Make Yourself Comfortable [C] | Capitol 3057 |
| | | | vocal by Jean Wilson | |
| | | | **LARRY GROCE** | |
| 2/07/76 | 9 | 9 | 1. **Junk Food Junkie [N]** | Warner 8165 |
| | | | recorded live at McCabe's in Santa Monica | |
| | | | **HENRY GROSS** | |
| | | | original lead guitarist of Sha-Na-Na | |
| 4/03/76 | 6 | 13 | ● 1. **Shannon** | Lifesong 45002 |
| 8/21/76 | 37 | 2 | 2. Springtime Mama | Lifesong 45008 |

| DATE | POS | WKS | ARTIST—Record Title | LABEL & NO. |
|------|-----|-----|---------------------|-------------|
| | | | **VINCE GUARALDI Trio** | |
| | | | jazz trio led by Vince on piano - died on 2/6/76 (43) | |
| 2/09/63 | 22 | 6 | 1. Cast Your Fate To The Wind [I] | Fantasy 563 |
| | | | **GUESS WHO** | |
| | | | Canadian group featuring Burton Cummings (lead singer) and Randy Bachman (lead guitar - left group after "American Woman") | |
| 6/05/65 | 22 | 7 | 1. Shakin' All Over | Scepter 1295 |
| | | | Chad Allan, lead singer | |
| 4/26/69 | 6 | 11 | ● 2. These Eyes | RCA 0102 |
| 7/26/69 | 10 | 9 | ● 3. Laughing/ | |
| 11/08/69 | 22 | 6 | 4. Undun | RCA 0195 |
| 1/17/70 | 5 | 10 | 5. No Time | RCA 0300 |
| 3/28/70 | 1 (3) | 14 | ● 6. American Woman/ | |
| | | 13 | 7. No Sugar Tonight | RCA 0325 |
| 8/08/70 | 17 | 8 | 8. Hand Me Down World | RCA 0367 |
| 11/07/70 | 10 | 8 | 9. Share The Land | RCA 0388 |
| 6/12/71 | 29 | 4 | 10. Albert Flasher | RCA 0458 |
| 9/04/71 | 19 | 8 | 11. Rain Dance | RCA 0522 |
| 4/20/74 | 39 | 1 | 12. Star Baby | RCA 0217 |
| 8/10/74 | 6 | 11 | 13. Clap For The Wolfman | RCA 0324 |
| | | | with Wolfman Jack | |
| 12/14/74 + | 28 | 4 | 14. Dancin' Fool | RCA 10075 |
| | | | **GREG GUIDRY** | |
| 3/20/82 | 17 | 10 | 1. Goin' Down | Columbia 02691 |
| | | | **BONNIE GUITAR** | |
| 4/27/57 | 6 | 10 | 1. Dark Moon | Dot 15550 |
| | | | **GUNHILL ROAD** | |
| 6/02/73 | 40 | 1 | 1. Back When My Hair Was Short | Kama Sutra 569 |
| | | | **ARLO GUTHRIE** | |
| | | | Woody Guthrie's son | |
| 9/09/72 | 18 | 9 | 1. The City Of New Orleans | Reprise 1103 |
| | | | **SAMMY HAGAR** | |
| | | | lead singer of Montrose (1973-1975) | |
| 12/25/82 + | 13 | 13 | 1. Your Love Is Driving Me Crazy | Geffen 29816 |
| 8/18/84 | 38 | 3 | 2. Two Sides Of Love | Geffen 29246 |
| 10/27/84 | 26 | 6 | 3. I Can't Drive 55 | Geffen 29173 |
| | | | **MERLE HAGGARD** | |
| | | | born in Bakersville, California on 4/6/37 | |
| 1/05/74 | 28 | 3 | 1. If We Make It Through December | Capitol 3746 |
| | | | **HAIRCUT ONE HUNDRED** | |
| | | | British sextet led by Nick Heyward | |
| 7/17/82 | 37 | 4 | 1. Love Plus One | Arista 0672 |
| | | | **BILL HALEY & His Comets** | |
| | | | Bill, a rock and roll pioneer, died on 2/9/81 (55) | |
| 11/20/54 + | 11 | 15 | 1. Dim, Dim The Lights (I Want Some Atmosphere) | Decca 29317 |
| 3/05/55 | 17 | 8 | 2. Mambo Rock/ | |
| 3/19/55 | 26 | 2 | 3. Birth Of The Boogie | Decca 29418 |

| DATE | POS | WKS | ARTIST—Record Title | LABEL & NO. |
|---|---|---|---|---|
| 5/14/55 | 1 (8) | 24 | 4. **Rock Around The Clock**<br>featured in the film "Blackboard Jungle" | Decca 29124 |
| 7/23/55 | 15 | 4 | 5. Razzle-Dazzle | Decca 29552 |
| 11/19/55 | 9 | 13 | 6. **Burn That Candle** | Decca 29713 |
| 1/14/56 | 6 | 15 | 7. **See You Later, Alligator** | Decca 29791 |
| 4/07/56 | 16 | 5 | 8. R-O-C-K/<br>featured in the film "Rock Around The Clock" | |
| 4/07/56 | 18 | 5 | 9.  The Saints Rock 'N Roll | Decca 29870 |
| 9/01/56 | 25 | 4 | 10. Rip It Up | Decca 30028 |
| 11/24/56 | 34 | 3 | 11. Rudy's Rock [I]<br>sax solo by Rudy Pompilli (died on 2/5/76 - 47) | Decca 30085 |
| 4/21/58 | 22 | 6 | 12. Skinny Minnie | Decca 30592 |
| 5/25/74 | 39 | 1 | 13. Rock Around The Clock [R] | MCA 60025 |
| | | | **DARYL HALL & JOHN OATES**<br>Daryl: born on 10/11/49 in Pottstown, Pennsylvania;<br>John: born on 4/7/49 in New York City | |
| 4/03/76 | 4 | 17 | ● 1. **Sara Smile** | RCA 10530 |
| 8/14/76 | 7 | 16 | 2. **She's Gone [R]**<br>re-entry of 1974 hit (Pos. 60) | Atlantic 3332 |
| 12/25/76 | 39 | 3 | 3. Do What You Want, Be What You Are | RCA 10808 |
| 2/05/77 | 1 (2) | 14 | ● 4. **Rich Girl** | RCA 10860 |
| 5/28/77 | 28 | 4 | 5. Back Together Again | RCA 10970 |
| 9/30/78 | 20 | 7 | 6. It's A Laugh | RCA 11371 |
| 12/01/79 + | 18 | 10 | 7. Wait For Me | RCA 11747 |
| 8/30/80 | 30 | 4 | 8. How Does It Feel To Be Back | RCA 12048 |
| 10/11/80 | 12 | 14 | 9. You've Lost That Lovin' Feeling | RCA 12103 |
| 2/14/81 | 1 (3) | 17 | ● 10. **Kiss On My List** | RCA 12142 |
| 5/16/81 | 5 | 14 | 11. **You Make My Dreams** | RCA 12217 |
| 9/12/81 | 1 (2) | 17 | ● 12. **Private Eyes** | RCA 12296 |
| 11/21/81 + | 1 (1) | 17 | ● 13. **I Can't Go For That (No Can Do)** | RCA 12357 |
| 4/03/82 | 9 | 11 | 14. **Did It In A Minute** | RCA 13065 |
| 7/24/82 | 33 | 5 | 15. Your Imagination | RCA 13252 |
| 11/06/82 | 1 (4) | 17 | ● 16. **Maneater** | RCA 13354 |
| 2/05/83 | 7 | 15 | 17. **One On One** | RCA 13421 |
| 5/07/83 | 6 | 12 | 18. **Family Man** | RCA 13507 |
| 10/29/83 | 2 (4) | 15 | 19. **Say It Isn't So** | RCA 13654 |
| 2/25/84 | 8 | 11 | 20. **Adult Education** | RCA 13714 |
| 10/06/84 | 1 (2) | 16 | 21. **Out Of Touch** | RCA 13916 |
| | | | **JIMMY HALL**<br>former member of Wet Willie | |
| 11/01/80 | 27 | 4 | 1. I'm Happy That Love Has Found You | Epic 50931 |
| | | | **LARRY HALL** | |
| 12/07/59 + | 15 | 11 | 1. Sandy | Strand 25007 |
| | | | **TOM T. HALL**<br>country music storyteller | |
| 1/19/74 | 12 | 9 | 1. I Love | Mercury 73436 |

| DATE | POS | WKS | ARTIST—Record Title | LABEL & NO. |
|---|---|---|---|---|
| | | | **HALOS** | |
| | | | backing vocal group on Curtis Lee's "Pretty Little Angel Eyes" | |
| 8/28/61 | 25 | 4 | 1. "Nag" | 7 Arts 709 |
| | | | **HAMILTON, JOE FRANK & REYNOLDS** | |
| | | | Dan Hamilton, Joe Frank Carollo & Tom Reynolds | |
| 6/12/71 | 4 | 11 | ● 1. **Don't Pull Your Love** | Dunhill 4276 |
| 7/19/75 | 1 (1) | 12 | ● 2. **Fallin' In Love** | Playboy 6024 |
| 12/13/75 + | 21 | 8 | 3. Winners And Losers | Playboy 6054 |
| | | | **BOBBY HAMILTON** | |
| 8/04/58 | 40 | 1 | 1. Crazy Eyes For You | Apt 25002 |
| | | | **GEORGE HAMILTON IV** | |
| | | | born on 7/19/37 in Winston Salem, North Carolina - also see Paul Anka | |
| 11/17/56 | 6 | 14 | 1. **A Rose And A Baby Ruth** | ABC-Para. 9765 |
| 3/09/57 | 33 | 4 | 2. Only One Love | ABC-Para. 9782 |
| 12/09/57 + | 10 | 12 | 3. **Why Don't They Understand** | ABC-Para. 9862 |
| 4/07/58 | 25 | 1 | 4. Now And For Always | ABC-Para. 9898 |
| 7/20/63 | 15 | 7 | 5. Abilene | RCA 8181 |
| | | | **ROY HAMILTON** | |
| | | | born on 4/16/29 in Leesburg, Georgia - died on 7/20/69 (40) | |
| 4/23/55 | 6 | 16 | 1. **Unchained Melody** | Epic 9102 |
| | | | from the film "Unchained" | |
| 1/27/58 | 13 | 11 | 2. Don't Let Go | Epic 9257 |
| 2/13/61 | 12 | 7 | 3. You Can Have Her | Epic 9434 |
| | | | **RUSS HAMILTON** | |
| | | | English | |
| 8/05/57 | 4 | 17 | 1. **Rainbow** | Kapp 184 |
| | | | **MARVIN HAMLISCH** | |
| | | | pianist/composer/conductor for numerous soundtracks | |
| 4/20/74 | 3 | 12 | ● 1. **The Entertainer [I]** | MCA 40174 |
| | | | a Scott Joplin song from the film "The Sting" | |
| | | | **ALBERT HAMMOND** | |
| | | | English | |
| 11/04/72 | 5 | 13 | ● 1. **It Never Rains In Southern California** | Mums 6011 |
| 4/13/74 | 31 | 4 | 2. I'm A Train | Mums 6026 |
| | | | **HAPPENINGS** | |
| | | | Paterson, New Jersey quartet | |
| 7/30/66 | 3 | 11 | 1. **See You In September** | B.T. Puppy 520 |
| 10/22/66 | 12 | 5 | 2. Go Away Little Girl | B.T. Puppy 522 |
| 4/29/67 | 3 | 9 | 3. **I Got Rhythm** | B.T. Puppy 527 |
| 7/22/67 | 13 | 6 | 4. My Mammy | B.T. Puppy 530 |
| | | | **JOE HARNELL & His Orchestra** | |
| 1/26/63 | 14 | 8 | 1. Fly Me To The Moon-Bossa Nova [I] | Kapp 497 |
| | | | **HARPERS BIZARRE** | |
| | | | Santa Cruz, California quintet | |
| 3/18/67 | 13 | 7 | 1. The 59th Street Bridge Song (Feelin' Groovy) | Warner 5890 |
| 6/17/67 | 37 | 3 | 2. Come To The Sunshine | Warner 7028 |

| DATE | POS | WKS | ARTIST—Record Title | LABEL & NO. |
|---|---|---|---|---|
| | | | **SLIM HARPO** | |
| | | | real name: James Moore - died on 1/31/70 (46) | |
| 7/10/61 | 34 | 2 | 1. Rainin' In My Heart | Excello 2194 |
| 3/05/66 | 16 | 8 | 2. Baby Scratch My Back [I] | Excello 2273 |
| | | | **BETTY HARRIS** | |
| 10/26/63 | 23 | 6 | 1. Cry To Me | Jubilee 5456 |
| | | | **EDDIE HARRIS** | |
| | | | jazz tenor saxophonist | |
| 5/29/61 | 36 | 3 | 1. Exodus [I] | Vee-Jay 378 |
| | | | **EMMYLOU HARRIS** | |
| | | | contemporary country vocalist | |
| 4/11/81 | 37 | 3 | 1. Mister Sandman | Warner 49684 |
| | | | **MAJOR HARRIS** | |
| | | | member of the Delfonics (1971-1973) | |
| 4/19/75 | 5 | 14 | ● 1. **Love Won't Let Me Wait** | Atlantic 3248 |
| | | | **RICHARD HARRIS** | |
| | | | British actor | |
| 5/25/68 | 2 (1) | 10 | 1. **MacArthur Park** | Dunhill 4134 |
| | | | **ROLF HARRIS** | |
| | | | Australian | |
| 6/22/63 | 3 | 9 | 1. **Tie Me Kangaroo Down, Sport** [N] | Epic 9596 |
| | | | **SAM HARRIS** | |
| | | | winner of TV's "Star Search" male vocalist category in 1984 | |
| 11/03/84 | 36 | 3 | 1. Sugar Don't Bite | Motown 1743 |
| | | | **THURSTON HARRIS** | |
| | | | member of R&B groups the 5 Royales and the Lamplighters | |
| 10/28/57 | 6 | 13 | 1. **Little Bitty Pretty One** | Aladdin 3398 |
| | | | **GEORGE HARRISON** | |
| | | | Beatles' lead guitarist - born on 2/25/43 in Liverpool, England | |
| 12/05/70 | 1 (4) | 13 | ● 1. **My Sweet Lord**/ | |
| | | 13 | 2.  **Isn't It A Pity** | Apple 2995 |
| 3/06/71 | 10 | 8 | 3. **What Is Life** | Apple 1828 |
| 8/28/71 | 23 | 5 | 4. Bangla-Desh | Apple 1836 |
| 5/26/73 | 1 (1) | 11 | 5. **Give Me Love (Give Me Peace On Earth)** | Apple 1862 |
| 12/14/74 + | 15 | 6 | 6. Dark Horse | Apple 1877 |
| 2/01/75 | 36 | 2 | 7. Ding Dong; Ding Dong | Apple 1879 |
| 10/11/75 | 20 | 6 | 8. You | Apple 1884 |
| 12/11/76 + | 25 | 7 | 9. This Song | Dark Horse 8294 |
| 2/12/77 | 19 | 7 | 10. Crackerbox Palace | Dark Horse 8313 |
| 3/31/79 | 16 | 8 | 11. Blow Away | Dark Horse 8763 |
| 5/23/81 | 2 (3) | 11 | 12. **All Those Years Ago** | Dark Horse 49725 |
| | | | **WILBERT HARRISON** | |
| | | | born on 1/6/29 in Charlotte, North Carolina | |
| 4/27/59 | 1 (2) | 12 | 1. **Kansas City** | Fury 1023 |
| 1/24/70 | 32 | 4 | 2. Let's Work Together (Part 1) | Sue 11 |

| DATE | POS | WKS | ARTIST—Record Title | LABEL & NO. |
|---|---|---|---|---|
| | | | **COREY HART** | |
| | | | Canadian rock singer/songwriter | |
| 6/23/84 | **7** | 15 | 1. **Sunglasses At Night** | EMI America 8203 |
| 10/20/84 | **17** | 19 | 2. **It Ain't Enough** | EMI America 8236 |
| | | | **FREDDIE HART** | |
| 9/25/71 | **17** | 12 | ● 1. Easy Loving | Capitol 3115 |
| | | | **DAN HARTMAN** | |
| | | | member of the Edgar Winter Group (1972-76) | |
| 12/02/78 + | **29** | 7 | ● 1. Instant Replay | Blue Sky 2772 |
| 6/02/84 | **6** | 16 | 2. **I Can Dream About You** | MCA 52378 |
| | | | from the film "Streets Of Fire" | |
| 11/03/84 | **25** | 9 | 3. **We Are The Young** | MCA 52471 |
| | | | **HARVEY & THE MOONGLOWS** | |
| | | | also see the Moonglows | |
| 10/20/58 | **22** | 4 | 1. Ten Commandments Of Love | Chess 1705 |
| | | | **DONNY HATHAWAY - see ROBERTA FLACK** | |
| | | | **RICHIE HAVENS** | |
| | | | black folksinger/guitarist | |
| 4/24/71 | **16** | 9 | 1. Here Comes The Sun | Stormy F. 656 |
| | | | **DALE HAWKINS** | |
| | | | rockabilly singer/guitarist from Louisiana | |
| 7/01/57 | **27** | 5 | 1. Susie-Q | Checker 863 |
| 10/13/58 | **32** | 3 | 2. La-Do-Dada | Checker 900 |
| | | | **EDWIN HAWKINS Singers** | |
| | | | formerly the Northern California State Youth Choir - also see Melanie | |
| 5/03/69 | **4** | 9 | ● 1. **Oh Happy Day** | Pavilion 20001 |
| | | | featuring vocalist Dorothy Morrison | |
| | | | **RONNIE HAWKINS & The Hawks** | |
| | | | also see The Band | |
| 9/21/59 | **26** | 7 | 1. Mary Lou | Roulette 4177 |
| | | | **DEANE HAWLEY** | |
| 7/04/60 | **29** | 5 | 1. Look For A Star | Dore 554 |
| | | | from the film "Circus Of Horrors" | |
| | | | **BILL HAYES** | |
| | | | Doug Williams of the TV soap "Days Of Our Lives" | |
| 2/26/55 | **1** (5) | 20 | 1. **The Ballad Of Davy Crockett** | Cadence 1256 |
| 2/16/57 | **33** | 3 | 2. Wringle, Wrangle | ABC-Para. 9785 |
| | | | from the movie "Westward Ho, The Wagons" | |
| | | | **ISAAC HAYES** | |
| | | | born on 8/6/38 in Covington, Tennessee | |
| 9/27/69 | **37** | 4 | 1. By The Time I Get To Phoenix/ | |
| 10/18/69 | **30** | 5 | 2.  Walk On By | Enterprise 9003 |
| 6/12/71 | **22** | 5 | 3. Never Can Say Goodbye | Enterprise 9031 |
| 10/23/71 | **1** (2) | 12 | 4. **Theme From Shaft** | Enterprise 9038 |

| DATE | POS | WKS | ARTIST—Record Title | LABEL & NO. |
|---|---|---|---|---|
| 3/25/72 | 30 | 5 | 5. Do Your Thing | Enterprise 9042 |
| 12/02/72 | 38 | 2 | 6. Theme From The Men [I] | Enterprise 9058 |
| 1/12/74 | 30 | 5 | 7. Joy - Pt. 1 | Enterprise 9085 |
| 12/08/79 + | 18 | 12 | 8. Don't Let Go | Polydor 2011 |
| | | | **RICHARD HAYMAN & JAN AUGUST** | |
| | | | Jan died on 1/17/76 (71) | |
| 2/11/56 | 11 | 11 | 1. A Theme from "The Three Penny Opera" (Moritat) [I] | Mercury 70781 |
| | | | **LEON HAYWOOD** | |
| 11/01/75 | 15 | 8 | 1. I Want'a Do Something Freaky To You | 20th Century 2228 |
| | | | **LEE HAZLEWOOD - see NANCY SINATRA** | |
| | | | **MURRAY HEAD With The Trinidad Singers** | |
| | | | from "Jesus Christ Superstar - A Rock Opera" | |
| 5/08/71 | 14 | 8 | 1. Superstar [R] | Decca 32603 |
| | | | re-entry of 1970 hit (Pos. 74) | |
| | | | **ROY HEAD** | |
| | | | from San Marcus, Texas | |
| 9/18/65 | 2 (2) | 9 | 1. **Treat Her Right** | Back Beat 546 |
| 12/04/65 | 39 | 1 | 2. Just A Little Bit | Scepter 12116 |
| 12/18/65 | 32 | 2 | 3. Apple Of My Eye | Back Beat 555 |
| | | | **HEART** | |
| | | | Seattle-based group led by Ann Wilson (vocals) & sister Nancy (guitar) - also see Mike Reno & Ann Wilson | |
| 5/29/76 | 35 | 2 | 1. Crazy On You | Mushroom 7021 |
| 9/04/76 | 9 | 14 | 2. **Magic Man** | Mushroom 7011 |
| 7/02/77 | 11 | 12 | 3. Barracuda | Portrait 70004 |
| 5/13/78 | 24 | 7 | 4. Heartless | Mushroom 7031 |
| 10/28/78 | 15 | 10 | 5. Straight On | Portrait 70020 |
| 3/17/79 | 34 | 3 | 6. Dog & Butterfly | Portrait 70025 |
| 3/15/80 | 33 | 4 | 7. Even It Up | Epic 50847 |
| 11/29/80 + | 8 | 11 | 8. **Tell It Like It Is** | Epic 50950 |
| 6/19/82 | 33 | 4 | 9. This Man Is Mine | Epic 02925 |
| | | | **JOEY HEATHERTON** | |
| | | | movie/TV actress | |
| 7/15/72 | 24 | 7 | 1. Gone | MGM 14387 |
| | | | **HEATWAVE** | |
| | | | multinational London-based disco band | |
| 8/27/77 | 2 (2) | 17 | ★ 1. **Boogie Nights** | Epic 50370 |
| 2/04/78 | 18 | 11 | ● 2. Always And Forever | Epic 50490 |
| 6/03/78 | 7 | 11 | ● 3. **The Groove Line** | Epic 50524 |
| | | | **BOBBY HEBB** | |
| | | | one of the first black artists to perform at the Grand Ole Opry | |
| 7/23/66 | 2 (2) | 11 | ● 1. **Sunny** | Philips 40365 |
| 11/05/66 | 39 | 1 | 2. A Satisfied Mind | Philips 40400 |
| | | | **NEAL HEFTI** | |
| 3/05/66 | 35 | 4 | 1. Batman Theme [I] | RCA 8755 |

| DATE | POS | WKS | ARTIST—Record Title | LABEL & NO. |
|---|---|---|---|---|
| | | | **BOBBY HELMS** | |
| | | | born on 8/15/35 in Bloomington, Indiana | |
| 10/14/57 | 7 | 15 | 1. **My Special Angel** | Decca 30423 |
| 10/14/57 | 36 | 2 | 2. Fraulein | Decca 30194 |
| 12/23/57 | 6 | 4 | 3. **Jingle Bell Rock** [X] | Decca 30513 |
| 12/28/58 | 35 | 1 | 4. Jingle Bell Rock [X-R] | Decca 30513 |
| 12/26/60 | 36 | 1 | 5. Jingle Bell Rock [X-R] | Decca 30513 |
| | | | **JOE HENDERSON** | |
| 6/02/62 | 8 | 10 | 1. **Snap Your Fingers** | Todd 1072 |
| | | | **MICHAEL HENDERSON - see NORMAN CONNORS** | |
| | | | **BOBBY HENDRICKS** | |
| | | | member of the Drifters & the Swallows | |
| 9/01/58 | 25 | 4 | 1. Itchy Twitchy Feeling | Sue 706 |
| | | | **JIMI HENDRIX** | |
| | | | psychedelic-blues guitarist - died 9/18/70 (27) | |
| 9/28/68 | 20 | 8 | 1. All Along The Watchtower | Reprise 0767 |
| | | | **HENHOUSE FIVE PLUS TOO** | |
| | | | a Ray Stevens creation | |
| 2/05/77 | 40 | 1 | 1. In The Mood [N] | Warner 8301 |
| | | | **DON HENLEY** | |
| | | | drummer/vocalist with The Eagles - also see Stevie Nicks | |
| 11/13/82 + | 3 | 14 | ● 1. **Dirty Laundry** | Asylum 69894 |
| | | | **CLARENCE "Frogman" HENRY** | |
| | | | born on 3/19/37 near New Orleans, Louisiana | |
| 1/12/57 | 20 | 3 | 1. **Ain't Got No Home** [N] | Argo 5259 |
| 3/20/61 | 4 | 11 | 2. **But I Do** | Argo 5378 |
| | | | also titled "I Don't Know Why" | |
| 5/29/61 | 12 | 7 | 3. You Always Hurt The One You Love | Argo 5388 |
| | | | **JIM HENSON - see ERNIE / KERMIT** | |
| | | | **HERMAN'S HERMITS** | |
| | | | Manchester, England quintet led by Peter Noone | |
| 11/14/64 | 13 | 9 | 1. I'm Into Something Good | MGM 13280 |
| 2/20/65 | 2 (2) | 11 | 2. **Can't You Hear My Heartbeat** | MGM 13310 |
| 4/17/65 | 1 (3) | 11 | ● 3. **Mrs. Brown You've Got A Lovely Daughter** | MGM 13341 |
| 4/17/65 | 5 | 10 | 4. Silhouettes | MGM 13332 |
| 6/05/65 | 4 | 8 | 5. **Wonderful World** | MGM 13354 |
| 7/10/65 | 1 (1) | 8 | ● 6. **I'm Henry VIII, I Am** | MGM 13367 |
| 9/25/65 | 7 | 8 | 7. **Just A Little Bit Better** | MGM 13398 |
| 1/01/66 | 8 | 8 | 8. **A Must To Avoid** | MGM 13437 |
| | | | from the film "Hold On!" | |
| 2/26/66 | 3 | 7 | 9. **Listen People** | MGM 13462 |
| | | | from the film "When The Boys Meet The Girls" | |
| 4/16/66 | 9 | 7 | 10. **Leaning On The Lamp Post** | MGM 13500 |
| | | | from the film "Hold On!" | |

| DATE | POS | WKS | ARTIST—Record Title | LABEL & NO. |
|------|-----|-----|---------------------|-------------|
| 7/23/66 | 12 | 5 | 11. This Door Swings Both Ways | MGM 13548 |
| 10/15/66 | 5 | 8 | 12. **Dandy** | MGM 13603 |
| 12/24/66 | 27 | 5 | 13. East West | MGM 13639 |
| 3/04/67 | 4 | 9 | ● 14. **There's A Kind Of Hush/** | |
| 3/18/67 | 35 | 4 | 15.  No Milk Today | MGM 13681 |
| 7/08/67 | 18 | 4 | 16. Don't Go Out Into The Rain (You're Going To Melt) | MGM 13761 |
| 9/16/67 | 39 | 2 | 17. Museum | MGM 13787 |
| 2/03/68 | 22 | 6 | 18. I Can Take Or Leave Your Loving | MGM 13885 |
| | | | **PATRICK HERNANDEZ** | |
| | | | Belgian disco artist | |
| 8/04/79 | 16 | 11 | ● 1. Born To Be Alive | Columbia 10986 |
| | | | **HESITATIONS** | |
| | | | Cleveland 7-man soul group | |
| 2/17/68 | 38 | 2 | 1. Born Free | Kapp 878 |
| | | | **EDDIE HEYWOOD** | |
| | | | jazz pianist/composer - also see Hugo Winterhalter | |
| 7/21/56 | 11 | 18 | 1. Soft Summer Breeze [I] | Mercury 70863 |
| | | | **AL HIBBLER** | |
| | | | born blind - vocalist with Duke Ellington 1943-1951 | |
| 4/09/55 | 3 | 19 | 1. **Unchained Melody** from the film "Unchained" | Decca 29441 |
| 10/15/55 | 4 | 22 | 2. **He** | Decca 29660 |
| 2/25/56 | 21 | 5 | 3. 11th Hour Melody | Decca 29789 |
| 7/14/56 | 22 | 2 | 4. Never Turn Back | Decca 29950 |
| 8/25/56 | 10 | 12 | 5. **After The Lights Go Down Low** | Decca 29982 |
| | | | **BERTIE HIGGINS** | |
| 1/16/82 | 8 | 18 | 1. **Key Largo** | Kat Family 02524 |
| | | | **HIGH INERGY** | |
| | | | Pasadena, Calif. soul quartet - Barbara Mitchell, lead singer | |
| 11/19/77 | 12 | 11 | 1. You Can't Turn Me Off (In The Middle Of Turning Me On) | Gordy 7155 |
| | | | **HIGHLIGHTS** | |
| | | | Frank Pizani, lead singer | |
| 11/10/56 | 19 | 5 | 1. City Of Angels | Bally 1016 |
| | | | **HIGHWAYMEN** | |
| | | | folk quintet formed at Wesleyan University, Connecticut | |
| 7/31/61 | 1 (2) | 11 | 1. **Michael** | United Art. 258 |
| 12/25/61 + | 13 | 13 | 2. Cotton Fields | United Art. 370 |
| | | | **BUNKER HILL** | |
| 10/13/62 | 33 | 3 | 1. Hide & Go Seek, Part 1 | Mala 451 |
| | | | **DAN HILL** | |
| | | | Canadian | |
| 12/24/77 + | 3 | 15 | ● 1. **Sometimes When We Touch** | 20th Century 2355 |

**Damita Jo (DuBlanc)** answered the Drifters by singing "I'll Save the Last Dance for You." A later single, "Dance With a Dolly (With a Hole in Her Stocking)," failed to find a comparable audience.

**Billy Joel's** record as an amateur boxer wasn't bad—22 wins out of 28 decisions. A broken nose played a major role in his switch to music.

**Elton John** (born Reginald Dwight) took his name from two legends who helped him get started, bandleader Long John Baldry and saxophonist Elton Dean. He also produced one side of Baldry's late-sixties comeback LP; Rod Stewart handled the other half.

**Howard Jones** studied classical piano for over a decade before turning to pop. He bought his synthesizers with the cash settlement from a car accident.

**Jack Jones.** Rockabilly fans gasped when they heard what Jack had done to George Jones' down-home rocker "The Race Is On." Of course, it's only to be expected from the son of the man who recorded "Donkey Serenade."

**Tom Jones** began as a Welsh Elvis Presley, but manager Gordon Mills soon discovered that kids were intimidated by his aggressive style. Jones subsequently concentrated on the "mature" market instead and enjoys boundless popularity.

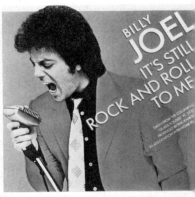

**Keith.** James Barry Keefer took a cue from Donovan and became Keith, enjoying fair to middling record sales. His biggest hit, "98.6," featured vocal backing by the Tokens.

**Chaka Khan** has impressively expanded her range since cutting ties with Rufus. She has sung a duet with George Benson, appeared on a Ry Cooder album, and participated in *Echoes of an Era,* an LP of jazz from the fifties.

**B.B. King.** Born Riley King in Itta Bena, Mississippi, he became B.B., or "Blues Boy," while working as a DJ in Memphis. At the time of his biggest Top 40 hit, "The Thrill Is Gone," King had been a favorite of black audiences for two decades.

**Evelyn "Champagne" King** was discovered singing in the hallway of a Philadelphia recording studio where she worked as a cleaning lady. She was barely 18 when her first hit, "Shame," moved into the Top Ten.

**Kiss** debuted in 1974 with a disrespectful cover version of Bobby Rydell's "Kissin' Time," which missed the Top 40 by 43 spots. Legions of detractors aside, they thunder on today, without their trademark makeup.

| DATE | POS | WKS | ARTIST—Record Title | LABEL & NO. |
|---|---|---|---|---|
| | | | **JESSIE HILL** | |
| | | | New Orleans pianist | |
| 5/09/60 | 28 | 4 | 1. Ooh Poo Pah Doo - Part II [I] | Minit 607 |
| | | | **HILLSIDE SINGERS** | |
| 12/11/71 + | 13 | 10 | 1. I'd Like To Teach The World To Sing (In Perfect Harmony) | Metromedia 231 |
| | | | adapted from a "Coca-Cola" jingle | |
| | | | **HILLTOPPERS** | |
| | | | quartet formed at Western Kentucky College in Bowling Green | |
| 7/30/55 | 20 | 4 | 1. The Kentuckian Song | Dot 15375 |
| 11/12/55 | 8 | 13 | 2. **Only You (And You Alone)** | Dot 15423 |
| 1/21/56 | 31 | 1 | 3. My Treasure | Dot 15437 |
| 10/06/56 | 38 | 2 | 4. Ka-Ding-Dong | Dot 15489 |
| 2/09/57 | 3 | 13 | 5. **Marianne** | Dot 15537 |
| 11/25/57 | 22 | 4 | 6. The Joker (That's What They Call Me) | Dot 15662 |
| | | | **JOE HINTON** | |
| | | | died on 8/13/68 | |
| 9/05/64 | 13 | 9 | 1. Funny | Back Beat 541 |
| | | | **AL HIRT** | |
| | | | New Orleans "Trumpet King" | |
| 1/25/64 | 4 | 13 | 1. **Java [I]** | RCA 8280 |
| 5/02/64 | 15 | 8 | 2. Cotton Candy [I] | RCA 8346 |
| 8/01/64 | 30 | 4 | 3. Sugar Lips [I] | RCA 8391 |
| | | | **EDDIE HODGES** | |
| | | | played Frank Sinatra's son in the film "A Hole In The Head" | |
| 7/24/61 | 12 | 8 | 1. I'm Gonna Knock On Your Door | Cadence 1397 |
| 7/07/62 | 14 | 8 | 2. (Girls, Girls, Girls) Made To Love | Cadence 1421 |
| | | | **RON HOLDEN with The Thunderbirds** | |
| 4/25/60 | 7 | 13 | 1. **Love You So** | Donna 1315 |
| | | | **AMY HOLLAND** | |
| | | | daughter of country singer Esmeraldy & opera singer Harry Boersma | |
| 9/13/80 | 22 | 6 | 1. How Do I Survive | Capitol 4884 |
| | | | **EDDIE HOLLAND** | |
| | | | 1/3 of Holland-Dozier-Holland production/songwriting team | |
| 3/10/62 | 30 | 4 | 1. Jamie | Motown 1021 |
| | | | **JENNIFER HOLLIDAY** | |
| | | | Tony award winner for Best Actress in Broadway's "Dreamgirls" | |
| 7/31/82 | 22 | 7 | 1. And I Am Telling You I'm Not Going | Geffen 29983 |
| | | | from the Broadway cast "Dreamgirls" | |
| | | | **HOLLIES** | |
| | | | Manchester, England quintet formed by Allan Clarke (vocals) & Graham Nash (guitar) | |
| 1/08/66 | 32 | 4 | 1. Look Through Any Window | Imperial 66134 |
| 8/20/66 | 5 | 9 | 2. **Bus Stop** | Imperial 66186 |
| 11/12/66 | 7 | 7 | 3. **Stop Stop Stop** | Imperial 66214 |

| DATE | POS | WKS | ARTIST—Record Title | LABEL & NO. |
|------|-----|-----|---------------------|-------------|
| 4/15/67 | **11** | 9 | 4. On A Carousel | Imperial 66231 |
| 6/24/67 | **28** | 3 | 5. Pay You Back With Interest | Imperial 66240 |
| 7/08/67 | **9** | 10 | 6. **Carrie-Anne** | Epic 10180 |
| 5/18/68 | **40** | 1 | 7. Jennifer Eccles | Epic 10298 |
| 2/07/70 | **7** | 11 | 8. **He Ain't Heavy, He's My Brother** | Epic 10532 |
| 7/08/72 | **2** (2) | 13 | ● 9. **Long Cool Woman (In A Black Dress)** | Epic 10871 |
| 12/02/72 | **26** | 5 | 10. Long Dark Road | Epic 10920 |
| 6/08/74 | **6** | 11 | ● 11. **The Air That I Breathe** | Epic 11100 |
| 7/02/83 | **29** | 6 | 12. Stop In The Name Of Love | Atlantic 89819 |
| | | | **BRENDA HOLLOWAY** | |
| 5/23/64 | **13** | 6 | 1. Every Little Bit Hurts | Tamla 54094 |
| 3/27/65 | **25** | 5 | 2. When I'm Gone | Tamla 54111 |
| 11/04/67 | **39** | 1 | 3. You've Made Me So Very Happy | Tamla 54155 |
| | | | **BUDDY HOLLY** | |
| | | | Lubbock, Texas rock and roll legend - died on 2/3/59 (22) - also see the Crickets | |
| 11/11/57 | **3** | 16 | 1. **Peggy Sue** | Coral 61885 |
| 6/09/58 | **37** | 2 | 2. Rave On | Coral 61985 |
| 8/11/58 | **32** | 4 | 3. Early In The Morning | Coral 62006 |
| 3/09/59 | **13** | 9 | 4. It Doesn't Matter Anymore | Coral 62074 |
| | | | **HOLLYWOOD ARGYLES** | |
| | | | Los Angeles-based quintet formed by Gary Paxton and Bobby Rey | |
| 6/13/60 | **1** (1) | 11 | 1. **Alley-Oop [N]** | Lute 5905 |
| | | | **HOLLYWOOD FLAMES** | |
| | | | formerly Bobby Day's backing group The Satellites | |
| 12/02/57 + | **11** | 12 | 1. Buzz-Buzz-Buzz | Ebb 119 |
| | | | **EDDIE HOLMAN** | |
| | | | Norfolk, Virginia soul singer | |
| 1/10/70 | **2** (1) | 12 | ● 1. **Hey There Lonely Girl** | ABC 11240 |
| | | | **CLINT HOLMES** | |
| 5/05/73 | **2** (2) | 15 | ● 1. **Playground In My Mind** | Epic 10891 |
| | | | **RUPERT HOLMES** | |
| | | | pop songwriter/arranger - also see Street People | |
| 11/10/79 | **1** (3) | 16 | ● 1. **Escape (The Pina Colada Song)** | Infinity 50035 |
| 2/09/80 | **6** | 12 | 2. **Him** | MCA 41173 |
| 6/14/80 | **32** | 3 | 3. Answering Machine | MCA 41235 |
| | | | **HOMBRES** | |
| | | | Memphis, Tennessee foursome | |
| 10/07/67 | **12** | 10 | 1. Let It Out (Let It All Hang Out) | Verve Fore. 5058 |
| | | | **HOMER & JETHRO** | |
| | | | Henry Haynes & Kenneth Burns - Homer (Henry) died on 8/7/71 (54) | |
| 9/14/59 | **14** | 7 | 1. The Battle Of Kookamonga [C] <br> a parody of "The Battle Of New Orleans" | RCA 7585 |
| | | | **HONDELLS** | |
| | | | Southern California quartet led by Ritchie Burns | |
| 10/03/64 | **9** | 9 | 1. **Little Honda** | Mercury 72324 |

| DATE | POS | WKS | ARTIST—Record Title | LABEL & NO. |
|---|---|---|---|---|
| | | | **HONEYCOMBS** | |
| | | | English quintet - Dennis D'ell, lead singer | |
| 10/10/64 | 5 | 9 | 1. **Have I The Right?** | Interphon 7707 |
| | | | **HONEY CONE** | |
| | | | West Coast black female background vocal trio | |
| 5/01/71 | 1 (1) | 13 | ● 1. **Want Ads** | Hot Wax 7011 |
| 8/21/71 | 11 | 10 | ● 2. **Stick-Up** | Hot Wax 7106 |
| 12/11/71 + | 15 | 8 | 3. One Monkey Don't Stop No Show - Part 1 | Hot Wax 7110 |
| 3/25/72 | 23 | 6 | 4. The Day I Found Myself | Hot Wax 7113 |
| | | | **HONEYDRIPPERS** | |
| | | | Robert Plant, Jimmy Page, Jeff Beck, Nile Rodgers | |
| 10/27/84 | 3 | 14 | 1. **Sea Of Love** | Es Paranza 99701 |
| | | | **MARY HOPKIN** | |
| | | | British | |
| 10/12/68 | 2 (3) | 12 | ● 1. **Those Were The Days** | Apple 1801 |
| 5/03/69 | 13 | 7 | 2. Goodbye | Apple 1806 |
| | | | above 2 produced by Paul McCartney | |
| 3/28/70 | 39 | 2 | 3. Temma Harbour | Apple 1816 |
| | | | **JIMMY "BO" HORNE** | |
| 6/24/78 | 38 | 1 | 1. Dance Across The Floor | Sunshine S. 1003 |
| | | | **LENA HORNE** | |
| | | | legendary singer/actress/Broadway star | |
| 7/09/55 | 19 | 1 | 1. Love Me Or Leave Me | RCA 6073 |
| | | | **JOHNNY HORTON** | |
| | | | killed in an auto crash on 11/5/60 (33) | |
| 5/04/59 | 1 (6) | 18 | ● 1. **The Battle Of New Orleans** | Columbia 41339 |
| 3/14/60 | 3 | 13 | 2. **Sink The Bismarck** | Columbia 41568 |
| | | | inspired by the film of the same title | |
| 10/17/60 | 4 | 18 | 3. **North To Alaska** | Columbia 41782 |
| | | | **HOT** | |
| | | | female soul/pop trio | |
| 4/02/77 | 6 | 19 | ● 1. **Angel In Your Arms** | Big Tree 16085 |
| | | | **HOT BUTTER** | |
| | | | Stan Free plays the Moog synthesizer | |
| 8/19/72 | 9 | 12 | 1. **Popcorn [I]** | Musicor 1458 |
| | | | **HOT CHOCOLATE** | |
| | | | Errol Brown, lead singer of British interracial rock/soul group | |
| 3/08/75 | 8 | 9 | 1. **Emma** | Big Tree 16031 |
| 7/05/75 | 28 | 4 | 2. Disco Queen | Big Tree 16038 |
| 12/06/75 + | 3 | 15 | ● 3. **You Sexy Thing** | Big Tree 16047 |
| 8/13/77 | 31 | 5 | 4. So You Win Again | Big Tree 16096 |
| 12/02/78 + | 6 | 13 | ● 5. **Every 1's A Winner** | Infinity 50002 |
| | | | **HOTLEGS** | |
| | | | also see 10cc | |
| 9/05/70 | 22 | 6 | 1. Neanderthal Man | Capitol 2886 |

| DATE | POS | WKS | ARTIST—Record Title | LABEL & NO. |
|---|---|---|---|---|
| | | | **DAVID HOUSTON** | |
| | | | country singer from Shreveport, Louisiana | |
| 8/27/66 | 24 | 8 | 1. Almost Persuaded | Epic 10025 |
| | | | **THELMA HOUSTON** | |
| 1/29/77 | **1** (1) | 17 | 1. **Don't Leave Me This Way** | Tamla 54278 |
| 5/19/79 | 34 | 3 | 2. Saturday Night, Sunday Morning | Tamla 54297 |
| | | | **HUDSON BROTHERS** | |
| | | | Bill, Brett & Mark Hudson from Portland, Oregon | |
| 10/26/74 | 21 | 5 | 1. So You Are A Star | Casablanca 0108 |
| 8/02/75 | 26 | 4 | 2. Rendezvous | Rocket 40417 |
| | | | **HUES CORPORATION** | |
| | | | Los Angeles black disco/soul trio | |
| 6/15/74 | **1** (1) | 10 | ● 1. **Rock The Boat** | RCA 0232 |
| 10/26/74 | 18 | 5 | 2. Rockin' Soul | RCA 10066 |
| | | | **FRED HUGHES** | |
| 6/19/65 | 23 | 6 | 1. Oo Wee Baby, I Love You | Vee-Jay 684 |
| | | | **JIMMY HUGHES** | |
| 7/11/64 | 17 | 9 | 1. Steal Away | Fame 6401 |
| | | | **HUGO & LUIGI Chorus** | |
| | | | producers Hugo Peretti & Luigi Creatore | |
| 1/04/60 | 35 | 3 | 1. Just Come Home | RCA 7639 |
| | | | **HUMAN BEINZ** | |
| | | | Cleveland bar band | |
| 1/06/68 | 8 | 11 | 1. **Nobody But Me** | Capitol 5990 |
| | | | **HUMAN LEAGUE** | |
| | | | British 6-member electronic pop band, led by Philip Oakey | |
| 4/10/82 | **1** (3) | 21 | ● 1. **Don't You Want Me** | A&M 2397 |
| 7/02/83 | 8 | 13 | 2. **(Keep Feeling) Fascination** | A&M 2547 |
| 10/29/83 | 30 | 5 | 3. Mirror Man | A&M 2587 |
| | | | **ENGELBERT HUMPERDINCK** | |
| | | | real name: Arnold Dorsey - born in India and raised in England | |
| 4/29/67 | 4 | 10 | 1. **Release Me (And Let Me Love Again)** | Parrot 40011 |
| 7/15/67 | 20 | 4 | 2. There Goes My Everything | Parrot 40015 |
| 10/14/67 | 25 | 5 | 3. The Last Waltz | Parrot 40019 |
| 1/06/68 | 18 | 7 | 4. Am I That Easy To Forget | Parrot 40023 |
| 6/01/68 | 19 | 5 | 5. A Man Without Love | Parrot 40027 |
| 11/23/68 | 31 | 3 | 6. Les Bicyclettes De Belsize | Parrot 40032 |
| 9/27/69 | 38 | 1 | 7. I'm A Better Man | Parrot 40040 |
| 1/03/70 | 16 | 8 | 8. Winter World Of Love | Parrot 40044 |
| 11/20/76 + | 8 | 14 | ● 9. **After The Lovin'** | Epic 50270 |
| | | | **PAUL HUMPHREY & His Cool Aid Chemists** | |
| | | | West Coast session drummer | |
| 5/15/71 | 29 | 7 | 1. Cool Aid [I] | Lizard 21006 |

| DATE | POS | WKS | ARTIST—Record Title | LABEL & NO. |
|------|-----|-----|---------------------|-------------|
| | | | **IVORY JOE HUNTER** | |
| | | | R&B singer/pianist - died on 11/8/74 (60) | |
| 12/01/56 | **12** | 15 | 1. Since I Met You Baby | Atlantic 1111 |
| | | | **TAB HUNTER** | |
| | | | movie/TV star of the '50's - real name: Art Gelien | |
| 1/19/57 | **1** (6) | 17 | 1. **Young Love** | Dot 15533 |
| 3/30/57 | **11** | 8 | 2. Ninety-Nine Ways | Dot 15548 |
| 2/23/59 | **31** | 4 | 3. (I'll Be With You In) Apple Blossom Time | Warner 5032 |
| | | | **FERLIN HUSKY** | |
| | | | country singer - also recorded as his alter ego Simon Crum | |
| 3/09/57 | **4** | 19 | 1. **Gone** | Capitol 3628 |
| 12/26/60 + | **12** | 13 | 2. Wings Of A Dove | Capitol 4406 |
| | | | **BRIAN HYLAND** | |
| | | | born in Queens, New York on 11/12/43 | |
| 7/11/60 | **1** (1) | 13 | 1. **Itsy Bitsy Teenie Weenie Yellow Polkadot Bikini [N]** | Leader 805 |
| 9/04/61 | **20** | 5 | 2. Let Me Belong To You | ABC-Para. 10236 |
| 4/07/62 | **21** | 6 | 3. Ginny Come Lately | ABC-Para. 10294 |
| 6/30/62 | **3** | 11 | 4. **Sealed With A Kiss** | ABC-Para. 10336 |
| 10/13/62 | **25** | 4 | 5. Warmed Over Kisses (Left Over Love) | ABC-Para. 10359 |
| 8/06/66 | **20** | 8 | 6. The Joker Went Wild | Philips 40377 |
| 11/26/66 | **25** | 3 | 7. Run, Run, Look And See | Philips 40405 |
| 10/24/70 | **3** | 13 | ● 8. **Gypsy Woman** | Uni 55240 |
| | | | **DICK HYMAN Trio** | |
| | | | arranger/conductor/pianist/organist | |
| 1/28/56 | **8** | 15 | 1. **Moritat - A Theme from "The Three Penny Opera" [I]** | MGM 12149 |
| | | | **DICK HYMAN & His Electric Eclectics** | |
| 7/05/69 | **38** | 2 | 1. The Minotaur [I] | Command 4126 |
| | | | **JANIS IAN** | |
| | | | real name: Janis Fink - born in New York City on 5/7/51 | |
| 6/17/67 | **14** | 8 | 1. Society's Child (Baby I've Been Thinking) | Verve 5027 |
| 7/12/75 | **3** | 14 | 2. **At Seventeen** | Columbia 10154 |
| | | | **ICICLE WORKS** | |
| | | | Liverpool rock trio - Ian McNabb, leader | |
| 5/26/84 | **37** | 4 | 1. Whisper To A Scream (Birds Fly) | Arista 9155 |
| | | | **IDES OF MARCH** | |
| | | | Chicago group led by Jim Peterik (Survivor) | |
| 4/11/70 | **2** (1) | 10 | 1. **Vehicle** | Warner 7378 |
| | | | **BILLY IDOL** | |
| | | | English - born William Broad - former leader of British punk group Generation X | |
| 8/07/82 | **23** | 9 | 1. Hot In The City | Chrysalis 2605 |
| 6/25/83 | **36** | 3 | 2. White Wedding | Chrysalis 42697 |
| | | | originally "Bubbled Under" on 11/27/82 (Pos. 108) | |
| 5/19/84 | **4** | 14 | 3. **Eyes Without A Face** | Chrysalis 42786 |
| 9/15/84 | **29** | 6 | 4. Flesh For Fantasy | Chrysalis 42809 |

| DATE | POS | WKS | ARTIST—Record Title | LABEL & NO. |
|---|---|---|---|---|
| | | | **FRANK IFIELD** | |
| | | | British | |
| 9/22/62 | 5 | 8 | 1. **I Remember You** | Vee-Jay 457 |
| | | | **JULIO IGLESIAS & WILLIE NELSON** | |
| | | | Julio is the #1 male vocalist of Spanish countries | |
| 3/31/84 | 5 | 12 | ● 1. **To All The Girls I've Loved Before** | Columbia 04217 |
| | | | **JULIO IGLESIAS & DIANA ROSS** | |
| 8/04/84 | 19 | 8 | 1. All Of You | Columbia 04507 |
| | | | **IKETTES** | |
| | | | Ike & Tina Turner's backing vocal group | |
| 2/03/62 | 19 | 8 | 1. I'm Blue (The Gong-Gong Song) | Atco 6212 |
| 4/10/65 | 36 | 4 | 2. Peaches "N" Cream | Modern 1005 |
| | | | **ILLUSION** | |
| | | | rock quintet led by John Vinci | |
| 8/23/69 | 32 | 6 | 1. Did You See Her Eyes | Steed 718 |
| | | | **IMPALAS** | |
| | | | Brooklyn quartet - Joe "Speedo" Frazier, lead singer | |
| 4/13/59 | 2 (2) | 11 | 1. **Sorry (I Ran All The Way Home)** | Cub 9022 |
| | | | **IMPRESSIONS** | |
| | | | Chicago-based soul group led by Curtis Mayfield ('61-'70) - also see Jerry Butler | |
| 11/20/61 | 20 | 8 | 1. Gypsy Woman | ABC-Para. 10241 |
| 10/12/63 | 4 | 11 | 2. **It's All Right** | ABC-Para. 10487 |
| 1/25/64 | 12 | 7 | 3. Talking About My Baby | ABC-Para. 10511 |
| 4/18/64 | 14 | 9 | 4. I'm So Proud | ABC-Para. 10544 |
| 6/27/64 | 10 | 10 | 5. **Keep On Pushing** | ABC-Para. 10554 |
| 9/19/64 | 15 | 8 | 6. You Must Believe Me | ABC-Para. 10581 |
| 12/12/64 + | 7 | 7 | 7. **Amen** | ABC-Para. 10602 |
| 3/06/65 | 14 | 5 | 8. People Get Ready | ABC-Para. 10622 |
| 4/24/65 | 29 | 4 | 9. Woman's Got Soul | ABC-Para. 10647 |
| 1/01/66 | 33 | 2 | 10. You've Been Cheatin' | ABC-Para. 10750 |
| 2/03/68 | 14 | 8 | 11. We're A Winner | ABC 11022 |
| 10/05/68 | 22 | 7 | 12. Fool For You | Curtom 1932 |
| 12/28/68 + | 25 | 6 | 13. This Is My Country | Curtom 1934 |
| 7/12/69 | 21 | 9 | 14. Choice Of Colors | Curtom 1943 |
| 6/13/70 | 28 | 8 | 15. Check Out Your Mind | Curtom 1951 |
| 6/29/74 | 17 | 6 | 16. Finally Got Myself Together (I'm A Changed Man) | Curtom 1997 |
| | | | **INDEPENDENTS** | |
| | | | Chicago-based soul trio | |
| 4/28/73 | 21 | 9 | ● 1. Leaving Me | Wand 11252 |
| | | | **JORGEN INGMANN & His Guitar** | |
| | | | Danish | |
| 2/20/61 | 2 (2) | 13 | 1. **Apache [I]** | Atco 6184 |

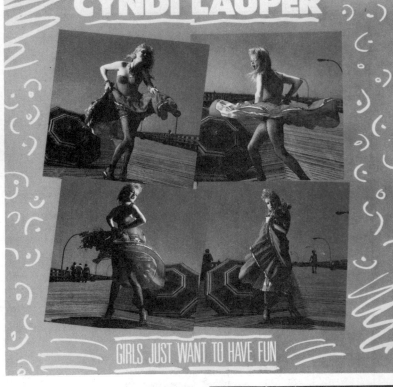

**Major Lance** cut "Mama Didn't Know" as an answer song to Jan Bradley's "Mama Didn't Lie," but DJs quickly gravitated to the B-side instead. The song, "The Monkey Time," was the Major's first of six Top 40 entries.

**Cyndi Lauper** fronted a band called Blue Angel before going solo. For her video of "Girls Just Want to Have Fun," she cast her mom and brother in supporting roles. Nice kid.

**Brenda Lee,** dubbed "Little Miss Dynamite," had just turned 15 when her first Top 40 hit entered the charts. Today the diminutive singer confines herself to the country market.

**John Lennon** tried his hand as producer on old buddy Harry Nilsson's *Pussy Cats* album in 1974. Their revamped version of oldies like "Rock Around the Clock" and "Subterranean Homesick Blues" failed to catch the public's fancy.

**Little Richard** reportedly wrote "Tutti Frutti" while working as a dishwasher in Macon, Georgia. According to the story, he'd shout "awompbomalooma-balomp-bompbomp—tutti frutti!" or words to that effect, while performing his chores.

**The Lovin' Spoonful** took their name from a song by Mississippi John Hurt. The band was founded by John Sebastian and Zal Yanovsky, both of whom had previously worked in the Mugwumps with two future Mamas and Papas—Cass Eliot and Denny Doherty.

**Huey Lewis** was a member of Clover, the West Coast bar band that contributed (uncredited) backup to Elvis Costello's first LP, *My Aim is True*. Listen for Huey's harmonica.

**Jerry Lee Lewis,** aptly nicknamed "The Killer," is considered by many to be the finest rock'n'roll singer ever, bar none. He's got interesting relatives, too. His cousins include TV evangelist Jimmy Swaggert and country crooner Mickey Gilley.

**Kenny Loggins** planned to become a solo artist in the early seventies, but got along so well with producer Jim Messina that the two formed a duo instead. Thus, Loggins' first solo hit had to wait until 1978.

**Bob Luman** came from Nacogdoches, Texas, made some wicked rockabilly records for Imperial in the late fifties, appeared in the movie *Carnival Rock*, slowed down to cut the hit "Let's Think About Living," and died in 1978.

| DATE | POS | WKS | ARTIST—Record Title | LABEL & NO. |
|------|-----|-----|---------------------|-------------|
| | | | **JAMES INGRAM** | |
| 9/19/81 | 17 | 10 | 1. Just Once | A&M 2357 |
| 2/13/82 | 14 | 11 | 2. One Hundred Ways | A&M 2387 |
| | | | above 2 shown as Quincy Jones featuring James Ingram | |
| 1/14/84 | 19 | 9 | 3. Yah Mo B There | Qwest 29394 |
| | | | with Michael McDonald | |
| | | | **LUTHER INGRAM** | |
| 6/24/72 | 3 | 13 | 1. **(If Loving You Is Wrong) I Don't Want To Be Right** | KoKo 2111 |
| 1/20/73 | 40 | 2 | 2. I'll Be Your Shelter (In Time Of Storm) | KoKo 2113 |
| | | | **INNOCENCE** | |
| | | | Pete Anders & Vinnie Poncia - also recorded as the Trade Winds | |
| 1/07/67 | 34 | 3 | 1. There's Got To Be A Word! | Kama Sutra 214 |
| | | | **INNOCENTS** | |
| | | | Kathy Young's backup vocal group | |
| 9/19/60 | 28 | 3 | 1. Honest I Do | Indigo 105 |
| 1/09/61 | 28 | 3 | 2. Gee Whiz | Indigo 111 |
| | | | **INSTANT FUNK** | |
| | | | 9-man funk ensemble led by James Carmichael | |
| 3/31/79 | 20 | 8 | ● 1. I Got My Mind Made Up (You Can Get It Girl) | Salsoul 2078 |
| | | | **INTRIGUES** | |
| 10/04/69 | 31 | 4 | 1. In A Moment | Yew 1001 |
| | | | **INTRUDERS** | |
| | | | Philadelphia quartet led by "Little Sonny" Brown | |
| 4/06/68 | 6 | 11 | ● 1. **Cowboys To Girls** | Gamble 214 |
| 8/10/68 | 26 | 4 | 2. (Love Is Like A) Baseball Game | Gamble 217 |
| 6/30/73 | 36 | 6 | 3. I'll Always Love My Mama (Part 1) | Gamble 2506 |
| | | | **INXS** | |
| | | | Australian quintet - Michael Hutchence, lead singer | |
| 5/14/83 | 30 | 5 | 1. The One Thing | Atco 99905 |
| | | | **DONNIE IRIS** | |
| | | | leader of The Jaggerz | |
| 2/07/81 | 29 | 6 | 1. Ah! Leah! | MCA 51025 |
| 2/13/82 | 37 | 2 | 2. Love Is Like A Rock | MCA 51223 |
| 5/01/82 | 25 | 6 | 3. My Girl | MCA 52031 |
| | | | **IRISH ROVERS** | |
| | | | Irish-born folk quintet - group formed in Canada | |
| 4/06/68 | 7 | 9 | 1. **The Unicorn** | Decca 32254 |
| 4/18/81 | 37 | 4 | 2. Wasn't That A Party | Epic 51007 |
| | | | shown as The Rovers | |
| | | | **IRON BUTTERFLY** | |
| | | | San Diego heavy-metal rock band led by Doug Ingle | |
| 9/28/68 | 30 | 7 | 1. In-A-Gadda-Da-Vida | Atco 6606 |
| | | | **IRONHORSE** | |
| | | | Randy Bachman (BTO), leader | |
| 4/21/79 | 36 | 3 | 1. Sweet Lui-Louise | Scotti Br. 406 |

| DATE | POS | WKS | ARTIST—Record Title | LABEL & NO. |
|---|---|---|---|---|
| | | | **BIG DEE IRWIN** | |
| | | | also see the Pastels | |
| 7/13/63 | 38 | 2 | 1. Swinging On A Star<br>vocal duet with Little Eva | Dimension 1010 |
| | | | **ISLANDERS** | |
| | | | Randy Starr, leader | |
| 10/19/59 | 15 | 8 | 1. The Enchanted Sea [I] | Mayflower 16 |
| | | | **ISLEY BROTHERS** | |
| | | | family group from Cincinnati led by Ronald, Rudolph & O'Kelly | |
| 6/30/62 | 17 | 11 | 1. Twist And Shout | Wand 124 |
| 3/19/66 | 12 | 8 | 2. This Old Heart Of Mine (Is Weak For You) | Tamla 54128 |
| 3/29/69 | 2 (1) | 12 | ● 3. **It's Your Thing** | T-Neck 901 |
| 6/21/69 | 23 | 7 | 4. I Turned You On | T-Neck 902 |
| 7/03/71 | 18 | 9 | 5. Love The One You're With | T-Neck 930 |
| 8/19/72 | 24 | 7 | 6. Pop That Thang | T-Neck 935 |
| 8/18/73 | 6 | 15 | ● 7. **That Lady (Part 1)** | T-Neck 2251 |
| 7/12/75 | 4 | 13 | ● 8. **Fight The Power - Part 1** | T-Neck 2256 |
| 11/22/75 | 22 | 9 | 9. For The Love Of You (Part 1 & 2) | T-Neck 2259 |
| 8/06/77 | 40 | 1 | 10. Livin' In The Life | T-Neck 2264 |
| 5/24/80 | 39 | 2 | 11. Don't Say Goodnight (It's Time For Love<br>(Parts 1 & 2) | T-Neck 2290 |
| | | | **BURL IVES** | |
| | | | folk singer/actor | |
| 1/06/62 | 9 | 11 | 1. **A Little Bitty Tear** | Decca 31330 |
| 4/21/62 | 10 | 8 | 2. **Funny Way Of Laughin'** | Decca 31371 |
| 8/11/62 | 19 | 4 | 3. Call Me Mr. In-Between | Decca 31405 |
| 12/08/62 | 39 | 1 | 4. Mary Ann Regrets | Decca 31433 |
| | | | **IVY THREE** | |
| 8/29/60 | 8 | 7 | 1. **Yogi [N]**<br>based on a character from TV's "Huckleberry Hound" show | Shell 720 |
| | | | **TERRY JACKS** | |
| | | | Canadian - Terry and wife Susan were The Poppy Family | |
| 2/09/74 | 1 (3) | 15 | ● 1. **Seasons In The Sun** | Bell 45432 |
| | | | **CHUCK JACKSON** | |
| | | | born on 7/22/37 in Winston Salem, South Carolina | |
| 3/13/61 | 36 | 2 | 1. I Don't Want To Cry | Wand 106 |
| 6/02/62 | 23 | 6 | 2. Any Day Now (My Wild Beautiful Bird) | Wand 122 |
| | | | **DEON JACKSON** | |
| 2/19/66 | 11 | 9 | 1. Love Makes The World Go Round | Carla 2526 |
| | | | **JERMAINE JACKSON** | |
| | | | member of the Jackson 5 (1970-1975) | |
| 1/13/73 | 9 | 13 | 1. **Daddy's Home** | Motown 1216 |
| 5/03/80 | 9 | 14 | 2. **Let's Get Serious** | Motown 1469 |
| 8/30/80 | 34 | 4 | 3. You're Supposed To Keep Your Love For Me | Motown 1490 |
| 8/21/82 | 18 | 7 | 4. Let Me Tickle Your Fancy<br>backing vocals by Devo | Motown 1628 |
| 8/04/84 | 15 | 10 | 5. Dynamite | Arista 9190 |

| DATE | POS | WKS | ARTIST—Record Title | LABEL & NO. |
|---|---|---|---|---|
| | | | **J.J. JACKSON** | |
| 11/05/66 | 22 | 7 | 1. But It's Alright | Calla 119 |
| | | | **JOE JACKSON** | |
| | | | English | |
| 7/07/79 | 21 | 8 | 1. Is She Really Going Out With Him? | A&M 2132 |
| 10/16/82 | 6 | 15 | 2. **Steppin' Out** | A&M 2428 |
| 2/05/83 | 18 | 10 | 3. Breaking Us In Two | A&M 2510 |
| 5/05/84 | 15 | 9 | 4. You Can't Get What You Want (Till You Know What You Want) | A&M 2628 |
| | | | **MICHAEL JACKSON** | |
| | | | member of the Jacksons - born in Gary, Indiana on 8/29/58 - also see Paul McCartney | |
| 11/06/71 | 4 | 13 | 1. **Got To Be There** | Motown 1191 |
| 3/18/72 | 2 (2) | 11 | 2. **Rockin' Robin** | Motown 1197 |
| 6/10/72 | 16 | 9 | 3. I Wanna Be Where You Are | Motown 1202 |
| 9/09/72 | 1 (1) | 11 | 4. **Ben** | Motown 1207 |
| 7/12/75 | 23 | 6 | 5. Just A Little Bit Of You | Motown 1349 |
| 9/01/79 | 1 (1) | 12 | ● 6. **Don't Stop 'Til You Get Enough** | Epic 50742 |
| 11/24/79 + | 1 (4) | 19 | ● 7. **Rock With You** | Epic 50797 |
| 2/23/80 | 10 | 11 | 8. **Off The Wall** | Epic 50838 |
| 5/10/80 | 10 | 11 | 9. **She's Out Of My Life** | Epic 50871 |
| 1/29/83 | 1 (7) | 17 | ● 10. **Billie Jean** | Epic 03509 |
| 3/19/83 | 1 (3) | 18 | ● 11. **Beat It** | Epic 03759 |
| 6/04/83 | 5 | 11 | 12. **Wanna Be Startin' Somethin'** | Epic 03914 |
| 7/30/83 | 7 | 11 | 13. **Human Nature** | Epic 04026 |
| 10/22/83 | 10 | 9 | 14. **P.Y.T. (Pretty Young Thing)** | Epic 04165 |
| 2/11/84 | 4 | 9 | 15. **Thriller** | Epic 04364 |
| | | | above 6 are from the "Thriller" LP | |
| 6/23/84 | 38 | 3 | 16. Farewell My Summer Love | Motown 1739 |
| | | | re-mix of a recording from 8/31/73 | |
| | | | **MILLIE JACKSON** | |
| | | | raunchy soul singer from Georgia | |
| 5/13/72 | 27 | 6 | 1. Ask Me What You Want | Spring 123 |
| 9/29/73 | 24 | 8 | 2. Hurts So Good | Spring 139 |
| | | | from the film "Cleopatra Jones" | |
| | | | **STONEWALL JACKSON** | |
| | | | country singer named after the Confederate general | |
| 6/08/59 | 4 | 12 | 1. **Waterloo** | Columbia 41393 |
| | | | **WANDA JACKSON** | |
| | | | born on 10/20/37 in Maud, Oklahoma | |
| 10/10/60 | 37 | 1 | 1. Let's Have A Party | Capitol 4397 |
| 8/14/61 | 29 | 3 | 2. Right Or Wrong | Capitol 4553 |
| 11/27/61 | 27 | 3 | 3. In The Middle Of A Heartache | Capitol 4635 |
| | | | **JACKSONS** | |
| | | | brothers Jackie, Tito, Jermaine, Marlon, Michael & Randy (Randy replaced Jermaine in 1975) JACKSON 5: | |
| 12/06/69 + | 1 (1) | 16 | 1. **I Want You Back** | Motown 1157 |
| 3/21/70 | 1 (2) | 12 | 2. **ABC** | Motown 1163 |
| 6/06/70 | 1 (2) | 12 | 3. **The Love You Save** | Motown 1166 |

| DATE | POS | WKS | ARTIST—Record Title | LABEL & NO. |
|------|-----|-----|---------------------|-------------|
| 9/19/70 | **1** (5) | 16 | 4. **I'll Be There** | Motown 1171 |
| 2/06/71 | **2** (2) | 9 | 5. **Mama's Pearl** | Motown 1177 |
| 4/10/71 | **2** (3) | 11 | 6. **Never Can Say Goodbye** | Motown 1179 |
| 7/31/71 | **20** | 6 | 7. Maybe Tomorrow | Motown 1186 |
| 12/25/71 + | **10** | 8 | 8. **Sugar Daddy** | Motown 1194 |
| 4/29/72 | **13** | 8 | 9. Little Bitty Pretty One | Motown 1199 |
| 7/29/72 | **16** | 8 | 10. Lookin' Through The Windows | Motown 1205 |
| 11/18/72 | **18** | 8 | 11. Corner Of The Sky<br>from the Broadway musical "Pippin" | Motown 1214 |
| 4/14/73 | **28** | 4 | 12. Hallelujah Day | Motown 1224 |
| 9/22/73 | **28** | 7 | 13. Get It Together | Motown 1277 |
| 3/30/74 | **2** (2) | 16 | 14. **Dancing Machine** | Motown 1286 |
| 11/30/74 | **38** | 2 | 15. Whatever You Got, I Want | Motown 1308 |
| 2/22/75 | **15** | 7 | 16. I Am Love (Parts I & II)<br>JACKSONS: | Motown 1310 |
| 12/11/76 + | ● **6** | 15 | 17. **Enjoy Yourself** | Epic 50289 |
| 5/07/77 + | **28** | 3 | 18. Show You The Way To Go | Epic 50350 |
| 3/31/79 | ★ **7** | 14 | 19. **Shake Your Body (Down To The Ground)** | Epic 50656 |
| 10/11/80 | **12** | 9 | 20. Lovely One | Epic 50938 |
| 1/10/81 + | **22** | 8 | 21. Heartbreak Hotel | Epic 50959 |
| 6/30/84 | ● **3** | 11 | 22. **State Of Shock**<br>lead vocals: Michael Jackson & Mick Jagger | Epic 04503 |
| 8/25/84 | **17** | 8 | 23. Torture<br>lead vocals: Jermanie & Michael Jackson | Epic 04575 |
| | | | **DICK JACOBS & His Chorus & Orchestra** | |
| 4/07/56 | **22** | 7 | 1. "Main Title" And "Molly-O"<br>from the film "The Man With The Golden Arm" | Coral 61606 |
| 11/03/56 | **16** | 9 | 2. Petticoats Of Portugal | Coral 61724 |
| 9/16/57 | **17** | 4 | 3. Fascination<br>from the film "Love In The Afternoon" | Coral 61864 |
| | | | **JAGGERZ**<br>Donnie Iris, leader of Pittsburgh sextet | |
| 2/14/70 | **2** (1) | 11 | ● 1. **The Rapper** | Kama Sutra 502 |
| | | | **ETTA JAMES**<br>top R&B singer discovered by Johnny Otis in 1955 | |
| 6/06/60 | **33** | 4 | 1. All I Could Do Was Cry | Argo 5359 |
| 11/21/60 | **34** | 3 | 2. My Dearest Darling | Argo 5368 |
| 4/03/61 | **30** | 4 | 3. Trust In Me | Argo 5385 |
| 9/04/61 | **39** | 2 | 4. Don't Cry, Baby | Argo 5393 |
| 3/31/62 | **37** | 4 | 5. Something's Got A Hold On Me | Argo 5409 |
| 9/08/62 | **34** | 2 | 6. Stop The Wedding | Argo 5418 |
| 5/11/63 | **25** | 6 | 7. Pushover | Argo 5437 |
| 12/30/67 + | **23** | 7 | 8. Tell Mama | Cadet 5578 |
| 4/06/68 | **35** | 4 | 9. Security | Cadet 5594 |
| | | | **JONI JAMES**<br>born Joan Babbo on 9/22/30 in Chicago, Illinois | |
| 2/19/55 | **2** (1) | 16 | 1. **How Important Can It Be?** | MGM 11919 |
| 10/22/55 | **6** | 10 | 2. **You Are My Love** | MGM 12066 |

| DATE | POS | WKS | ARTIST—Record Title | LABEL & NO. |
|---|---|---|---|---|
| 8/11/56 | 30 | 2 | 3. Give Us This Day | MGM 12288 |
| 10/20/58 | 19 | 8 | 4. There Goes My Heart | MGM 12706 |
| 2/16/59 | 33 | 4 | 5. There Must Be A Way | MGM 12746 |
| 1/25/60 | 35 | 3 | 6. Little Things Mean A Lot | MGM 12849 |
| 1/23/61 | 38 | 1 | 7. My Last Date (With You) | MGM 12933 |
| | | | **RICK JAMES** | |
| | | | Buffalo, New York "punk-funk" rocker | |
| 8/05/78 | 13 | 10 | 1. You And I | Gordy 7156 |
| 7/18/81 | 40 | 2 | 2. Give It To Me Baby | Gordy 7197 |
| 9/05/81 | 16 | 10 | 3. Super Freak (Part 1) | Gordy 7205 |
| 9/24/83 | 40 | 1 | 4. Cold Blooded | Gordy 1687 |
| 8/18/84 | 36 | 3 | 5. 17 | Gordy 1730 |
| | | | **SONNY JAMES** | |
| | | | real name: Jimmy Loden - Sonny had 16 consecutive #1 country singles from 1967-1971 | |
| 1/05/57 | 1 (1) | 17 | 1. **Young Love** | Capitol 3602 |
| 4/20/57 | 25 | 1 | 2. First Date, First Kiss, First Love | Capitol 3674 |
| | | | **TOMMY JAMES** | |
| | | | lead singer of The Shondells - born in Dayton, Ohio on 4/29/47 | |
| 6/26/71 | 4 | 11 | 1. **Draggin' The Line** | Roulette 7103 |
| 10/23/71 | 40 | 1 | 2. I'm Comin' Home | Roulette 7110 |
| 2/23/80 | 19 | 9 | 3. Three Times In Love | Millennium 11785 |
| | | | **TOMMY JAMES & THE SHONDELLS** | |
| | | | Tommy formed the group in 1960 in Niles, Michigan | |
| 6/18/66 | 1 (2) | 10 | ● 1. **Hanky Panky** | Roulette 4686 |
| 8/20/66 | 21 | 5 | 2. Say I Am (What I Am) | Roulette 4695 |
| 12/10/66 | 31 | 4 | 3. It's Only Love | Roulette 4710 |
| 3/11/67 | 4 | 12 | 4. **I Think We're Alone Now** | Roulette 4720 |
| 5/06/67 | 10 | 8 | 5. **Mirage** | Roulette 4736 |
| 7/15/67 | 25 | 5 | 6. I Like The Way | Roulette 4756 |
| 9/02/67 | 18 | 6 | 7. Gettin' Together | Roulette 4762 |
| 5/04/68 | 3 | 13 | 8. **Mony Mony** | Roulette 7008 |
| 11/23/68 | 38 | 2 | 9. Do Something To Me | Roulette 7024 |
| 12/21/68 + | 1 (2) | 15 | 10. **Crimson And Clover** | Roulette 7028 |
| 4/05/69 | 7 | 8 | 11. **Sweet Cherry Wine** | Roulette 7039 |
| 6/28/69 | 2 (3) | 12 | 12. **Crystal Blue Persuasion** | Roulette 7050 |
| 10/25/69 | 19 | 5 | 13. Ball Of Fire | Roulette 7060 |
| 12/20/69 + | 23 | 7 | 14. She | Roulette 7066 |
| | | | **JAMIES** | |
| | | | quartet from Dorchester, Massachusetts, led by Tom Jameson and his sister Serena Jameson | |
| 9/15/58 | 26 | 4 | 1. Summertime, Summertime | Epic 9281 |
| 8/04/62 | 38 | 1 | 2. Summertime, Summertime [R] | Epic 9281 |
| | | | **JAN & ARNIE** | |
| | | | Jan Berry & Arnie Ginsburg - actually recorded by Jan & Dean with Arnie in background (Dean in Army at time of release) | |
| 5/26/58 | 8 | 11 | 1. **Jennie Lee** | Arwin 108 |

| DATE | POS | WKS | ARTIST—Record Title | LABEL & NO. |
|------|-----|-----|---------------------|-------------|
| | | | **JAN & DEAN** | |
| | | | Jan Berry & Dean Torrence - Jan was partially paralyzed in a car accident, April 1966 | |
| 8/10/59 | 10 | 9 | 1. **Baby Talk** | Dore 522 |
| 7/10/61 | 25 | 4 | 2. Heart And Soul | Challenge 9111 |
| 4/20/63 | 28 | 5 | 3. Linda | Liberty 55531 |
| 6/22/63 | 1 (2) | 11 | 4. **Surf City** | Liberty 55580 |
| 9/21/63 | 11 | 8 | 5. Honolulu Lulu | Liberty 55613 |
| 12/21/63 + | 10 | 9 | 6. **Drag City** | Liberty 55641 |
| 3/28/64 | 8 | 11 | 7. **Dead Man's Curve** | |
| 4/04/64 | 37 | 4 | 8. The New Girl In School | Liberty 55672 |
| 7/04/64 | 3 | 10 | 9. **The Little Old Lady (From Pasadena)** | Liberty 55704 |
| 10/10/64 | 16 | 5 | 10. Ride The Wild Surf | Liberty 55724 |
| 11/21/64 | 25 | 5 | 11. Sidewalk Surfin' | Liberty 55727 |
| 6/26/65 | 27 | 4 | 12. You Really Know How To Hurt A Guy | Liberty 55792 |
| 11/13/65 | 30 | 2 | 13. I Found A Girl | Liberty 55833 |
| 6/18/66 | 21 | 6 | 14. Popsicle | Liberty 55886 |
| | | | **HORST JANKOWSKI** | |
| | | | German pianist/arranger | |
| 6/05/65 | 12 | 9 | 1. A Walk In The Black Forest [I] | Mercury 72425 |
| | | | **JARMELS** | |
| | | | R&B quintet from Richmond, Virginia | |
| 8/28/61 | 12 | 6 | 1. A Little Bit Of Soap | Laurie 3098 |
| | | | **AL JARREAU** | |
| | | | Grammy winning jazz vocalist from Milwaukee | |
| 9/12/81 | 15 | 11 | 1. We're In This Love Together | Warner 49746 |
| 4/23/83 | 21 | 6 | 2. Mornin' | Warner 29720 |
| | | | **JAY & THE AMERICANS** | |
| | | | Jay Black, lead singer of Brooklyn group | |
| 4/07/62 | 5 | 11 | 1. **She Cried** | United Art. 415 |
| | | | Jay Traynor, lead singer | |
| 9/21/63 | 25 | 4 | 2. Only In America | United Art. 626 |
| 10/03/64 | 3 | 11 | 3. **Come A Little Bit Closer** | United Art. 759 |
| 1/16/65 | 11 | 7 | 4. Let's Lock The Door (And Throw Away The Key) | United Art. 805 |
| 6/19/65 | 4 | 11 | 5. **Cara, Mia** | United Art. 881 |
| 9/25/65 | 13 | 6 | 6. Some Enchanted Evening | United Art. 919 |
| 12/04/65 | 18 | 6 | 7. Sunday And Me | United Art. 948 |
| 6/11/66 | 25 | 4 | 8. Crying | United Art. 50016 |
| 1/25/69 | 6 | 10 | ● 9. **This Magic Moment** | United Art. 50475 |
| 1/17/70 | 19 | 7 | 10. Walkin' In The Rain | United Art. 50605 |
| | | | **JAY & THE TECHNIQUES** | |
| | | | Jay Proctor, lead singer of Allentown, Pennsylvania group | |
| 8/19/67 | 6 | 11 | 1. **Apples, Peaches, Pumpkin Pie** | **Smash 2086** |
| 11/11/67 | 14 | 9 | 2. Keep The Ball Rollin' | **Smash 2124** |
| 2/10/68 | 39 | 2 | 3. Strawberry Shortcake | **Smash 2142** |

| DATE | POS | WKS | ARTIST—Record Title | LABEL & NO. |
|---|---|---|---|---|
| | | | **JERRY JAYE** | |
| | | | country/rock singer from Manilla, Arkansas | |
| 5/06/67 | 29 | 6 | 1. My Girl Josephine | Hi 2120 |
| | | | **JAYHAWKS** | |
| | | | also recorded as the Marathons and the Vibrations | |
| 7/28/56 | 18 | 2 | 1. Stranded In The Jungle [N] | Flash 109 |
| | | | **JAYNETTS** | |
| 9/07/63 | 2 (2) | 10 | 1. **Sally, Go 'Round The Roses** | Tuff 369 |
| | | | **J.B.'s** | |
| | | | James Brown's super-funk backup band - Fred Wesley, leader | |
| 6/23/73 | 22 | 6 | ● 1. Doing It To Death | People 621 |
| | | | **JEFFERSON** | |
| | | | English | |
| 1/24/70 | 23 | 6 | 1. Baby Take Me In Your Arms | Janus 106 |
| | | | **JEFFERSON AIRPLANE** | |
| | | | formed in San Francisco by Marty Balin & Paul Kantner - featuring lead singer Grace Slick - evolved into Jefferson Starship | |
| 5/06/67 | 5 | 9 | 1. **Somebody To Love** | RCA 9140 |
| 7/01/67 | 8 | 9 | 2. **White Rabbit** | RCA 9248 |
| | | | **JEFFERSON STARSHIP** | |
| 9/13/75 | 3 | 13 | 1. **Miracles** | Grunt 10367 |
| 8/14/76 | 12 | 11 | 2. With Your Love | Grunt 10746 |
| 3/25/78 | 8 | 11 | 3. **Count On Me** | Grunt 11196 |
| 6/24/78 | 12 | 8 | 4. Runaway | Grunt 11274 |
| 11/24/79 + | 14 | 11 | 5. Jane | Grunt 11750 |
| 5/02/81 | 29 | 6 | 6. Find Your Way Back | Grunt 12211 |
| 11/13/82 | 28 | 6 | 7. Be My Lady | Grunt 13350 |
| 3/19/83 | 38 | 2 | 8. Winds Of Change | Grunt 13439 |
| 6/09/84 | 23 | 8 | 9. No Way Out | Grunt 13811 |
| | | | **JOE JEFFREY Group** | |
| 7/05/69 | 14 | 8 | 1. My Pledge Of Love | Wand 11200 |
| | | | **JELLY BEANS** | |
| 7/18/64 | 9 | 7 | 1. **I Wanna Love Him So Bad** | Red Bird 10003 |
| | | | **WAYLON JENNINGS** | |
| | | | outlaw country singer - bass player with Buddy Holly 1958-59 - also see Waylon & Willie | |
| 6/11/77 | 25 | 7 | 1. Luckenbach, Texas (Back To The Basics Of Love) | RCA 10924 |
| 11/01/80 | 21 | 10 | ● 2. Theme From The Dukes Of Hazzard (Good Ol' Boys) | RCA 12067 |
| | | | **KRIS JENSEN** | |
| 10/06/62 | 20 | 6 | 1. Torture | Hickory 1173 |
| | | | **JETHRO TULL** | |
| | | | English progressive rock group led by Ian Anderson | |
| 11/25/72 + | 11 | 10 | 1. Living In The Past | Chrysalis 2006 |
| 11/30/74 + | 12 | 10 | 2. Bungle In The Jungle | Chrysalis 2101 |

| DATE | POS | WKS | ARTIST—Record Title | LABEL & NO. |
|---|---|---|---|---|
| | | | **JOAN JETT & THE BLACKHEARTS** | |
| | | | Joan was former leader of Los Angeles girl band The Runaways | |
| 2/13/82 | 1 (7) | 16 | ★ 1. **I Love Rock 'N Roll** | Boardwalk 135 |
| 5/15/82 | 7 | 10 | 2. **Crimson And Clover** | Boardwalk 144 |
| 8/28/82 | 20 | 7 | 3. Do You Wanna Touch Me (Oh Yeah) | Boardwalk 150 |
| 7/30/83 | 35 | 4 | 4. Fake Friends | Blackheart 52240 |
| 10/15/83 | 37 | 2 | 5. Everyday People | Blackheart 52272 |
| | | | **JIGSAW** | |
| | | | Australian quartet | |
| 10/11/75 | 3 | 14 | 1. **Sky High** | Chelsea 3022 |
| | | | from the movie "The Dragon Flies" | |
| 3/13/76 | 30 | 5 | 2. Love Fire | Chelsea 3037 |
| | | | **JOSE JIMENEZ** | |
| | | | Jose is comedian Bill Dana | |
| 9/18/61 | 19 | 4 | 1. The Astronaut (Parts 1 & 2) [C] | Kapp 409 |
| | | | interviewed by Don Hinckley | |
| | | | **JIVE BOMBERS** | |
| 3/16/57 | 36 | 1 | 1. Bad Boy | Savoy 1508 |
| | | | featuring Clarence Palmer, vocal | |
| | | | **JIVE FIVE** | |
| | | | Brooklyn, New York R&B group - Eugene Pitt, lead singer | |
| 8/14/61 | 3 | 12 | 1. **My True Story** | Beltone 1006 |
| 9/11/65 | 36 | 3 | 2. I'm A Happy Man | United Art. 853 |
| | | | **JO JO GUNNE** | |
| | | | Los Angeles quartet formed by Jay Ferguson (Spirit) | |
| 4/15/72 | 27 | 6 | 1. Run Run Run | Asylum 11003 |
| | | | **DAMITA JO** | |
| | | | Damita Jo DeBlanc - former lead singer of Steve Gibson's Red Caps | |
| 11/07/60 | 22 | 8 | 1. I'll Save The Last Dance For You | Mercury 71690 |
| 7/17/61 | 12 | 7 | 2. I'll Be There | Mercury 71840 |
| | | | **SAMI JO** | |
| 3/23/74 | 21 | 7 | 1. Tell Me A Lie | MGM South 7029 |
| | | | **JoBOXERS** | |
| | | | Dig Wayne, leader of British quintet | |
| 11/05/83 | 36 | 4 | 1. Just Got Lucky | RCA 13601 |
| | | | **BILLY JOEL** | |
| | | | born in Long Island, New York on 5/9/49 | |
| 4/06/74 | 25 | 4 | 1. Piano Man | Columbia 45963 |
| 12/28/74 + | 34 | 5 | 2. The Entertainer | Columbia 10064 |
| 12/10/77 + | 3 | 18 | ● 3. **Just The Way You Are** | Columbia 10646 |
| 4/15/78 | 17 | 8 | 4. Movin' Out (Anthony's Song) | Columbia 10708 |
| 6/17/78 | 24 | 5 | 5. Only The Good Die Young | Columbia 10750 |
| 9/09/78 | 17 | 9 | 6. She's Always A Woman | Columbia 10788 |
| 11/11/78 + | 3 | 16 | ● 7. **My Life** | Columbia 10853 |
| 3/03/79 | 14 | 6 | 8. Big Shot | Columbia 10913 |

| DATE | POS | WKS | ARTIST—Record Title | LABEL & NO. |
|---|---|---|---|---|
| 5/12/79 | 24 | 4 | 9. Honesty | Columbia 10959 |
| 3/22/80 | 7 | 11 | 10. **You May Be Right** | Columbia 11231 |
| 5/24/80 | 1 (2) | 19 | ● 11. **It's Still Rock And Roll To Me** | Columbia 11276 |
| 8/16/80 | 19 | 9 | 12. Don't Ask Me Why | Columbia 11331 |
| 11/01/80 | 36 | 3 | 13. Sometimes A Fantasy | Columbia 11379 |
| 9/26/81 | 17 | 8 | 14. Say Goodbye To Hollywood | Columbia 02518 |
| 12/12/81 + | 23 | 9 | 15. She's Got A Way | Columbia 02628 |
| 10/16/82 | 20 | 8 | 16. Pressure | Columbia 03244 |
| 12/18/82 + | 17 | 16 | 17. Allentown | Columbia 03413 |
| 7/30/83 | 1 (1) | 15 | 18. **Tell Her About It** | Columbia 04012 |
| 10/08/83 | 3 | 16 | ● 19. **Uptown Girl** | Columbia 04149 |
| 1/07/84 | 10 | 11 | 20. **An Innocent Man** | Columbia 04259 |
| 4/07/84 | 14 | 11 | 21. The Longest Time | Columbia 04400 |
| 8/04/84 | 27 | 7 | 22. Leave A Tender Moment Alone | Columbia 04514 |

**JOHN & ERNEST**
John Free & Ernest Smith - a Dickie Goodman production

| DATE | POS | WKS | ARTIST—Record Title | LABEL & NO. |
|---|---|---|---|---|
| 5/12/73 | 31 | 4 | 1. Super Fly Meets Shaft [N] | Rainy Wed. 201 |

**ELTON JOHN**
born Reginald Kenneth Dwight on 3/25/47 in Pinner, England

| DATE | POS | WKS | ARTIST—Record Title | LABEL & NO. |
|---|---|---|---|---|
| 12/19/70 + | 8 | 11 | 1. **Your Song** | Uni 55265 |
| 4/10/71 | 34 | 4 | 2. Friends | Uni 55277 |
| 1/01/72 | 24 | 7 | 3. Levon | Uni 55314 |
| 5/27/72 | 6 | 12 | 4. **Rocket Man** | Uni 55328 |
| 8/26/72 | 8 | 7 | 5. **Honky Cat** | Uni 55343 |
| 12/23/72 + | 1 (3) | 14 | ● 6. **Crocodile Rock** | MCA 40000 |
| 4/21/73 | 2 (1) | 12 | 7. **Daniel** | MCA 40046 |
| 8/11/73 | 12 | 9 | 8. Saturday Night's Alright For Fighting | MCA 40105 |
| 11/03/73 | 2 (3) | 14 | ● 9. **Goodbye Yellow Brick Road** | MCA 40148 |
| 3/02/74 | 1 (1) | 16 | ● 10. **Bennie And The Jets** | MCA 40198 |
| 7/06/74 | 2 (2) | 9 | ● 11. **Don't Let The Sun Go Down On Me** | MCA 40259 |
| 9/21/74 | 4 | 9 | 12. **The Bitch Is Back** | MCA 40297 |
| 12/07/74 + | 1 (2) | 10 | ● 13. **Lucy In The Sky With Diamonds** <br> with the reggae guitars of Dr. Winston O'Boogie (John Lennon) | MCA 40344 |
| 3/15/75 | 1 (2) | 17 | ● 14. **Philadelphia Freedom** | MCA 40364 |
| 7/12/75 | 4 | 10 | ● 15. **Someone Saved My Life Tonight** | MCA 40421 |
| 10/18/75 | 1 (3) | 12 | ● 16. **Island Girl** | MCA 40461 |
| 1/31/76 | 14 | 5 | 17. Grow Some Funk Of Your Own/ | |
| | | 5 | 18. **I Feel Like A Bullet (In The Gun Of Robert Ford)** | MCA 40505 |
| 11/20/76 | 6 | 11 | ● 19. **Sorry Seems To Be The Hardest Word** | MCA/Rocket 40645 |
| 2/26/77 | 28 | 3 | 20. Bite Your Lip (Get up and dance!) | MCA/Rocket 40677 |
| 4/29/78 | 34 | 3 | 21. Ego | MCA 40892 |
| 11/18/78 | 22 | 7 | 22. Part-Time Love | MCA 40973 |
| 6/23/79 | 9 | 14 | ● 23. **Mama Can't Buy You Love** | MCA 41042 |
| 10/27/79 | 31 | 4 | 24. Victim Of Love | MCA 41126 |
| 5/10/80 | 3 | 17 | ● 25. **Little Jeannie** | MCA 41236 |

| DATE | POS | WKS | ARTIST—Record Title | LABEL & NO. |
|---|---|---|---|---|
| 9/20/80 | 39 | 2 | 26. (Sartorial Eloquence) Don't Ya Wanna Play This Game No More? | MCA 41293 |
| 5/30/81 | 21 | 6 | 27. Nobody Wins | Geffen 49722 |
| 9/05/81 | 34 | 3 | 28. Chloe | Geffen 49788 |
| 4/17/82 | 13 | 10 | 29. Empty Garden (Hey Hey Johnny) | Geffen 50049 |
| 8/14/82 | 12 | 10 | 30. Blue Eyes | Geffen 29954 |
| 5/14/83 | 12 | 12 | 31. I'm Still Standing | Geffen 29639 |
| 8/20/83 | 25 | 8 | 32. Kiss The Bride | Geffen 29568 |
| 11/19/83 + | 4 | 15 | 33. I Guess That's Why They Call It The Blues | Geffen 29460 |
| 6/16/84 | 5 | 13 | 34. Sad Songs (Say So Much) | Geffen 29292 |
| 9/15/84 | 16 | 10 | 35. Who Wears These Shoes? | Geffen 29189 |
| | | | **ELTON JOHN & KIKI DEE** | Rocket 40585 |
| 7/17/76 | 1 (4) | 15 | ● 1. **Don't Go Breaking My Heart** | |
| | | | **LITTLE WILLIE JOHN** | |
| | | | died in prison on 5/26/68 (30) | |
| 7/14/56 | 24 | 9 | 1. Fever | King 4935 |
| 4/21/58 | 20 | 7 | 2. Talk To Me, Talk To Me | King 5108 |
| 7/25/60 | 38 | 1 | 3. Heartbreak (It's Hurtin' Me) | King 5356 |
| 10/10/60 | 13 | 10 | 4. Sleep | King 5394 |
| | | | **ROBERT JOHN** | |
| | | | real name: Robert Pedrick, Jr. | |
| 1/29/72 | 3 | 13 | ● 1. **The Lion Sleeps Tonight** | Atlantic 2846 |
| 6/30/79 | 1 (1) | 19 | ● 2. **Sad Eyes** | EMI America 8015 |
| 8/23/80 | 31 | 4 | 3. Hey There Lonely Girl | EMI America 8049 |
| | | | **JOHNNIE & JOE** | |
| | | | Johnnie Richardson & Joe Rivers | |
| 5/27/57 | 8 | 15 | 1. **Over The Mountain; Across The Sea** | Chess 1654 |
| | | | **JOHNNY & THE HURRICANES** | |
| | | | Toledo, Ohio rock instrumental quintet, led by Johnny Paris | |
| 6/01/59 | 23 | 6 | 1. Crossfire [I] | Warwick 502 |
| 8/17/59 | 5 | 13 | 2. **Red River Rock** [I] rock version of "Red River Valley" | Warwick 509 |
| 11/16/59 | 25 | 6 | 3. Reveille Rock [I] adaptation of the Army Bugle Call | Warwick 513 |
| 2/22/60 | 15 | 10 | 4. Beatnik Fly [I] adaptation of "Blue Tail Fly" | Warwick 520 |
| | | | **SAMMY JOHNS** | |
| 3/01/75 | 5 | 12 | ● 1. **Chevy Van** | Grc 2046 |
| | | | **BETTY JOHNSON** | |
| | | | married to Charles Randolph Grean | |
| 12/15/56 + | 9 | 18 | 1. **I Dreamed** | Bally 1020 |
| 6/24/57 | 25 | 1 | 2. Little White Lies | Bally 1033 |
| 2/24/58 | 17 | 11 | 3. The Little Blue Man [N] | Atlantic 1169 |
| 6/30/58 | 19 | 1 | 4. Dream | Atlantic 1186 |

**Madness.** Along with the English Beat and the Specials, Madness led the British "two-tone" movement that combines reggae, ska, and pop. They were major stars in England and Europe long before their first American hit.

**Herbie Mann** is a talented flautist who might have made a bid for serious jazz credibility. Instead he chose to tread the disco and fusion waters with Billy Cobham, the Bee Gees, Roy Ayers, and the like.

**Mantovani.** Born in Venice, Annunzio Paola Mantovani specialized in recording themes from movies like *Around the World in 80 Days, Exodus,* and *The Sundowners*.

**Little Peggy March,** winner of a Philadelphia talent contest at age five, was recommended to RCA after singing at a cousin's wedding. She was 15 when "I Will Follow Him" climbed the charts.

**The Marvelettes** lacked the strong image of the Supremes or Martha and the Vandellas, but boasted a fine lead singer in Gladys Horton. They gave Motown one of its first mega-hits in "Please Mr. Postman."

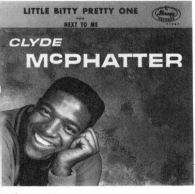

**Johnny Mathis** was a track star at San Francisco State College, practicing for the 1956 Olympics, when Columbia Records signed him to a contract. His greatest hits LP stayed on the charts for over 400 weeks.

**Paul McCartney** and **Michael Jackson's** duet "Say Say Say" debuted on the *Billboard* charts at Number 26, the highest initial placement since John Lennon's "Imagine" in 1971.

**Clyde McPhatter** gained widespread attention singing with Billy Ward's Dominoes in the early fifties. When Ward fired McPhatter, Ahmet Ertegun of Atlantic Records snapped him up to lead the Drifters.

**Christine McVie.** Before joining Fleetwood Mac at the start of the seventies, Christine McVie (then Christine Perfect) paid her dues as keyboardist for the British blues band Chicken Shack. Her first solo album, "The Legendary Christine Perfect," dates from this period.

**Men At Work** were criticized by some for sounding like the Police. The Australians weathered their overwhelming success with good humor. Once the initial hysteria had passed, they released a single called "Overkill."

| DATE | POS | WKS | ARTIST—Record Title | LABEL & NO. |
|---|---|---|---|---|
| | | | **MARV JOHNSON** | |
| | | | born on 10/15/38 in Detroit, Michigan | |
| 4/20/59 | 30 | 6 | 1. Come To Me | United Art. 160 |
| 11/16/59 + | 10 | 16 | 2. **You Got What It Takes** | United Art. 185 |
| 3/21/60 | 9 | 10 | 3. **I Love The Way You Love** | United Art. 208 |
| 10/10/60 | 20 | 4 | 4. (You've Got To) Move Two Mountains | United Art. 241 |
| | | | **MICHAEL JOHNSON** | |
| 5/27/78 | 12 | 10 | 1. Bluer Than Blue | EMI America 8001 |
| 9/23/78 | 32 | 5 | 2. Almost Like Being In Love | EMI America 8004 |
| 9/29/79 | 19 | 9 | 3. This Night Won't Last Forever | EMI America 8019 |
| | | | **TOM JOHNSTON** | |
| | | | lead singer of the Doobie Brothers (1971-78) | |
| 1/12/80 | 34 | 2 | 1. Savannah Nights | Warner 49096 |
| | | | **FRANCE JOLI** | |
| | | | 16-year-old French Canadian singer | |
| 9/29/79 | 15 | 8 | 1. Come To Me | Prelude 8001 |
| | | | **JON & ROBIN & The In Crowd** | |
| | | | Jon & Robin Abnor | |
| 5/27/67 | 18 | 6 | 1. Do It Again A Little Bit Slower | Abnak 119 |
| | | | **JONES GIRLS** | |
| | | | sisters Shirley, Brenda & Valorie | |
| 8/18/79 | 38 | 1 | ● 1. You Gonna Make Me Love Somebody Else | Phil. Int. 3680 |
| | | | **ETTA JONES** | |
| | | | singer with Earl Hines orchestra (1949-52) | |
| 12/12/60 | 36 | 1 | 1. Don't Go To Strangers | Prestige 180 |
| | | | **HOWARD JONES** | |
| | | | British synth wizard | |
| 2/25/84 | 27 | 6 | 1. New Song | Elektra 69766 |
| 6/02/84 | 33 | 4 | 2. What Is Love? | Elektra 69737 |
| | | | **JACK JONES** | |
| | | | son of actor Allan Jones & actress Irene Hervey | |
| 11/30/63 + | 14 | 10 | 1. Wives And Lovers | Kapp 551 |
| 12/26/64 + | 30 | 5 | 2. Dear Heart | Kapp 635 |
| 3/20/65 | 15 | 7 | 3. The Race Is On | Kapp 651 |
| 7/16/66 | 35 | 4 | 4. The Impossible Dream | Kapp 755 |
| | | | from the musical "Man Of La Mancha" | |
| 3/25/67 | 39 | 2 | 5. Lady | Kapp 800 |
| | | | **JIMMY JONES** | |
| | | | born on 6/2/37 in Birmingham, Alabama | |
| 1/18/60 | 2 (1) | 15 | 1. **Handy Man** | Cub 9049 |
| 5/09/60 | 3 | 10 | 2. **Good Timin'** | Cub 9067 |
| | | | **JOE JONES** | |
| 10/10/60 | 3 | 9 | 1. **You Talk Too Much** | Roulette 4304 |

| DATE | POS | WKS | ARTIST—Record Title | LABEL & NO. |
|---|---|---|---|---|
| | | | **LINDA JONES** | |
| | | | died on 3/24/72 (26) | |
| 7/22/67 | 21 | 7 | 1. Hypnotized | Loma 2070 |
| | | | **QUINCY JONES** | |
| | | | jazz musician - arranger/producer/writer - president of Qwest Records - also see James Ingram | |
| 7/22/78 | 21 | 7 | 1. Stuff Like That | A&M 2043 |
| | | | vocals: Ashford & Simpson, and Chaka Khan | |
| 5/09/81 | 28 | 4 | 2. Ai No Corrida | A&M 2309 |
| | | | featuring vocals by Dune | |
| | | | **RICKIE LEE JONES** | |
| 5/12/79 | 4 | 12 | 1. **Chuck E.'s In Love** | Warner 8825 |
| 9/01/79 | 40 | 1 | 2. Young Blood | Warner 49018 |
| | | | **TOM JONES** | |
| | | | Welsh - born Thomas Jones Woodward on 6/7/42 | |
| 5/01/65 | 10 | 9 | 1. **It's Not Unusual** | Parrot 9737 |
| 7/03/65 | 3 | 10 | 2. **What's New Pussycat?** | Parrot 9765 |
| 9/18/65 | 27 | 5 | 3. With These Hands | Parrot 9787 |
| 1/01/66 | 25 | 6 | 4. Thunderball | Parrot 9801 |
| 1/21/67 | 11 | 7 | 5. Green, Green Grass Of Home | Parrot 40009 |
| 4/01/67 | 27 | 4 | 6. Detroit City | Parrot 40012 |
| 4/13/68 | 15 | 11 | 7. Delilah | Parrot 40025 |
| 10/05/68 | 35 | 2 | 8. Help Yourself | Parrot 40029 |
| 6/07/69 | 13 | 9 | 9. Love Me Tonight | Parrot 40038 |
| 8/09/69 | 6 | 14 | ● 10. **I'll Never Fall In Love Again [R]** | Parrot 40018 |
| | | | re-entry of 1967 hit (Pos. 49) | |
| 1/03/70 | 5 | 10 | ● 11. **Without Love (There Is Nothing)** | Parrot 40045 |
| 5/09/70 | 13 | 7 | 12. Daughter Of Darkness | Parrot 40048 |
| 8/29/70 | 14 | 7 | 13. I (Who Have Nothing) | Parrot 40051 |
| 11/28/70 | 25 | 7 | 14. Can't Stop Loving You | Parrot 40056 |
| 2/20/71 | 2 (1) | 12 | ● 15. **She's A Lady** | Parrot 40058 |
| 6/12/71 | 26 | 6 | 16. Puppet Man/ | |
| | | 3 | 17.   Resurrection Shuffle | Parrot 40064 |
| 2/12/77 | 15 | 10 | 18. Say You'll Stay Until Tomorrow | Epic 50308 |
| | | | **JANIS JOPLIN** | |
| | | | "Pearl", lead singer of Big Brother & The Holding Company, died on 10/4/70 (27) | |
| 2/20/71 | 1 (2) | 12 | 1. **Me And Bobby McGee** | Columbia 45314 |
| | | | **JOURNEY** | |
| | | | San Francisco rock group led by Steve Perry (vocals) & Neal Schon (guitar) | |
| 8/25/79 | 16 | 12 | 1. Lovin', Touchin', Squeezin' | Columbia 11036 |
| 3/29/80 | 23 | 6 | 2. Any Way You Want It | Columbia 11213 |
| 7/05/80 | 32 | 4 | 3. Walks Like A Lady | Columbia 11275 |
| 4/04/81 | 34 | 4 | 4. The Party's Over (Hopelessly In Love) | Columbia 60505 |
| 8/01/81 | 4 | 14 | 5. **Who's Crying Now** | Columbia 02241 |
| 11/07/81 | 9 | 13 | 6. **Don't Stop Believin'** | Columbia 02567 |

| DATE | POS | WKS | ARTIST—Record Title | LABEL & NO. |
|---|---|---|---|---|
| 1/23/82 | 2 (6) | 14 | 7. **Open Arms** | Columbia 02687 |
| 6/12/82 | 19 | 9 | 8. Still They Ride | Columbia 02883 |
| 2/05/83 | 8 | 16 | 9. **Separate Ways (Worlds Apart)** | Columbia 03513 |
| 4/30/83 | 12 | 11 | 10. Faithfully | Columbia 03840 |
| 7/23/83 | 23 | 8 | 11. After The Fall | Columbia 04004 |
| 10/22/83 | 23 | 7 | 12. Send Her My Love | Columbia 04151 |
| | | | **JUMP 'N THE SADDLE**<br>Chicago-based band - Peter Quinn, lead singer | |
| 12/24/83 + | 15 | 7 | 1. The Curly Shuffle [N]<br>a Three Stooges parody | Atlantic 89718 |
| | | | **JUNIOR**<br>British - Junior Giscombe | |
| 4/10/82 | 30 | 3 | 1. Mama Used To Say | Mercury 76132 |
| | | | **JUST US** | |
| 5/07/66 | 34 | 2 | 1. I Can't Grow Peaches On A Cherry Tree | Colpix 803 |
| | | | **BILL JUSTIS**<br>Sun Records' musical director in the '50s - died on 7/15/82 (55) | |
| 11/18/57 | 2 (1) | 14 | 1. **Raunchy [I]**<br>sax: Bill Justis; guitar: Sid Manker | Phillips 3519 |
| | | | **BERT KAEMPFERT & His Orchestra**<br>German - produced 1st Beatles' recording - died on 6/21/80 (56). | |
| 11/21/60 + | 1 (3) | 15 | 1. **Wonderland By Night [I]** | Decca 31141 |
| 4/10/61 | 31 | 4 | 2. Tenderly [I] | Decca 31236 |
| 2/13/65 | 11 | 10 | 3. Red Roses For A Blue Lady [I] | Decca 31722 |
| 5/29/65 | 33 | 3 | 4. Three O'Clock In The Morning [I] | Decca 31778 |
| | | | **KAJAGOOGOO**<br>English quintet led by Limahl | |
| 5/21/83 | 5 | 12 | 1. **Too Shy** | EMI America 8161 |
| | | | **KALIN TWINS**<br>Herbie & Hal | |
| 6/30/58 | 5 | 13 | 1. **When** | Decca 30642 |
| 10/20/58 | 12 | 9 | 2. Forget Me Not | Decca 30745 |
| | | | **KITTY KALLEN**<br>vocalist with Jimmy Dorsey and Harry James' bands | |
| 11/09/59 | 34 | 3 | 1. If I Give My Heart To You | Columbia 41473 |
| 1/12/63 | 18 | 6 | 2. My Coloring Book | RCA 8124 |
| | | | **KITTY KALLEN & GEORGIE SHAW** | |
| 2/11/56 | 39 | 1 | 1. Go On With The Wedding | Decca 29776 |
| | | | **KANSAS**<br>progressive rock group from Topeka led by Steve Walsh & Kerry Livgren | |
| 2/05/77 | 11 | 13 | 1. Carry On Wayward Son | Kirshner 4267 |
| 12/17/77 + | 28 | 6 | 2. Point Of Know Return | Kirshner 4273 |
| 2/18/78 | 6 | 15 | ● 3. **Dust In The Wind** | Kirshner 4274 |

| DATE | POS | WKS | ARTIST—Record Title | LABEL & NO. |
|------|-----|-----|---------------------|-------------|
| 6/23/79 | 23 | 8 | 4. People Of The South Wind | Kirshner 4284 |
| 11/08/80 | 40 | 1 | 5. Hold On | Kirshner 4291 |
| 5/29/82 | 17 | 9 | 6. Play The Game Tonight | Kirshner 02903 |
| | | | **KASENETZ-KATZ Singing Orchestral Circus** | |
| | | | producers Jerry Kasenetz & Jeff Katz | |
| 11/09/68 | 25 | 6 | 1. Quick Joey Small (Run Joey Run) | Buddah 64 |
| | | | **SAMMY KAYE & His Orchestra** | |
| | | | leader of dance band since 1932 | |
| 5/02/64 | 36 | 2 | 1. Charade [I] | Decca 31589 |
| | | | **KC** | |
| | | | Harry Wayne Casey - leader of The Sunshine Band - also see Teri DeSario | |
| 2/04/84 | 18 | 10 | 1. Give It Up | Meca 1001 |
| | | | **KC & THE SUNSHINE BAND** | |
| | | | Florida disco band led by KC (Harry Wayne Casey) | |
| 8/02/75 | 1 (1) | 9 | 1. **Get Down Tonight** | T.K. 1009 |
| 11/01/75 | 1 (2) | 13 | 2. **That's The Way (I Like It)** | T.K. 1015 |
| 7/31/76 | 1 (1) | 16 | 3. **(Shake, Shake, Shake) Shake Your Booty** | T.K. 1019 |
| 1/29/77 | 37 | 2 | 4. I Like To Do It | T.K. 1020 |
| 4/02/77 | 1 (1) | 16 | 5. **I'm Your Boogie Man** | T.K. 1022 |
| 8/13/77 | 2 (3) | 14 | 6. **Keep It Comin' Love** | T.K. 1023 |
| 3/25/78 | 35 | 3 | 7. Boogie Shoes | T.K. 1025 |
| 6/24/78 | 35 | 2 | 8. It's The Same Old Song | T.K. 1028 |
| 9/29/79 + | 1 (1) | 18 | 9. **Please Don't Go** | T.K. 1035 |
| | | | **ERNIE K-DOE** | |
| | | | real name: Ernest Kador, Jr. | |
| 4/03/61 | 1 (1) | 12 | 1. **Mother-In-Law** | Minit 623 |
| | | | bass vocal by Benny Spellman | |
| | | | **KEITH** | |
| | | | James Barry Keefer from Philadelphia | |
| 11/12/66 | 39 | 1 | 1. Ain't Gonna Lie | Mercury 72596 |
| 1/07/67 | 7 | 9 | 2. **98.6** | Mercury 72639 |
| 4/08/67 | 37 | 2 | 3. Tell Me To My Face | Mercury 72652 |
| | | | **JERRY KELLER** | |
| 7/20/59 | 14 | 8 | 1. Here Comes Summer | Kapp 277 |
| | | | **GRACE KELLY - see BING CROSBY** | |
| | | | **MONTY KELLY & His Orchestra** | |
| 4/04/60 | 30 | 3 | 1. Summer Set [I] | Carlton 527 |
| | | | **EDDIE KENDRICKS** | |
| | | | lead singer of the Temptations thru 1971 | |
| 9/15/73 | 1 (2) | 16 | 1. **Keep On Truckin' (Part 1)** | Tamla 54238 |
| 1/26/74 | 2 (2) | 13 | 2. **Boogie Down** | Tamla 54243 |
| 6/01/74 | 28 | 4 | 3. Son Of Sagittarius | Tamla 54247 |
| 4/05/75 | 18 | 10 | 4. Shoeshine Boy | Tamla 54257 |
| 3/20/76 | 36 | 3 | 5. He's A Friend | Tamla 54266 |

| DATE | POS | WKS | ARTIST—Record Title | LABEL & NO. |
|---|---|---|---|---|
| | | | **JOYCE KENNEDY & JEFFREY OSBORNE** | |
| | | | Kennedy (Mother's Finest)/Osborne (L.T.D.) | |
| 10/06/84 | 40 | 2 | 1. The Last Time I Made Love | A&M 2656 |
| | | | **CHRIS KENNER** | |
| | | | died on 1/25/76 (46) | |
| 7/03/61 | 2 (3) | 10 | 1. **I Like It Like That, Part 1** | Instant 3229 |
| | | | **STAN KENTON** | |
| | | | progressive jazz big band leader - died on 8/25/79 (67) | |
| 11/17/62 | 32 | 4 | 1. Mama Sang A Song [S] | Capitol 4847 |
| | | | **KERMIT** | |
| | | | Kermit is one of Jim Henson's Muppets - also see Ernie | |
| 10/20/79 | 25 | 7 | 1. Rainbow Connection | Atlantic 3610 |
| | | | from "The Muppet Movie" | |
| | | | **CHAKA KHAN** | |
| | | | lead singer of Rufus - real name: Yvette Marie Stevens | |
| 11/18/78 | 21 | 8 | 1. I'm Every Woman | Warner 8683 |
| 9/29/84 | 3 | 17 | 2. **I Feel For You** | Warner 29195 |
| | | | with Grandmaster Melle Mel (rap); Stevie Wonder (harmonica) | |
| | | | **GREG KIHN Band** | |
| | | | group formed in Berkeley, California | |
| 7/11/81 | 15 | 13 | 1. The Breakup Song (They Don't Write 'Em) | Beserkley 47149 |
| 3/05/83 | 2 (1) | 14 | 2. **Jeopardy** | Beserkley 69847 |
| | | | **THEOLA KILGORE** | |
| 5/11/63 | 21 | 8 | 1. The Love Of My Man | Serock 2004 |
| | | | **ANDY KIM** | |
| | | | Canadian - real name: Andrew Joachim | |
| 6/01/68 | 21 | 8 | 1. How'd We Ever Get This Way | Steed 707 |
| 10/19/68 | 31 | 3 | 2. Shoot'em Up, Baby | Steed 710 |
| 6/21/69 | 9 | 12 | ● 3. **Baby, I Love You** | Steed 716 |
| 11/08/69 | 36 | 1 | 4. So Good Together | Steed 720 |
| 11/28/70 | 17 | 8 | 5. Be My Baby | Steed 729 |
| 7/20/74 | 1 (1) | 13 | ● 6. **Rock Me Gently** | Capitol 3895 |
| 11/23/74 | 28 | 4 | 7. Fire, Baby I'm On Fire | Capitol 3962 |
| | | | **ADRIAN KIMBERLY** | |
| 7/10/61 | 34 | 1 | 1. The Graduation Song...Pomp And Circumstance [I] | Calliope 6501 |
| | | | **KING CURTIS** | |
| | | | R&B saxophonist Curtis Ousley - died on 8/14/71 (37) | |
| 4/07/62 | 17 | 8 | 1. Soul Twist [I] | Enjoy 1000 |
| 9/23/67 | 33 | 4 | 2. Memphis Soul Stew [I] | Atco 6511 |
| 10/07/67 | 28 | 4 | 3. Ode To Billie Joe [I] | Atco 6516 |
| | | | shown only as The Kingpins | |
| | | | **KING FLOYD** | |
| 12/12/70 + | 6 | 13 | ● 1. **Groove Me** | Chimneyville 435 |
| 4/03/71 | 29 | 7 | 2. Baby Let Me Kiss You | Chimneyville 437 |

| DATE | POS | WKS | ARTIST—Record Title | LABEL & NO. |
|---|---|---|---|---|
| | | | **KING HARVEST** | |
| 1/06/73 | 13 | 11 | 1. Dancing In The Moonlight | Perception 515 |
| | | | **B.B. KING** | |
| | | | Riley B. ("Blues Boy") King - "King of The Blues" | |
| 6/13/64 | 34 | 3 | 1. Rock Me Baby | Kent 393 |
| 5/25/68 | 39 | 1 | 2. Paying The Cost To Be The Boss | BluesWay 61015 |
| 1/31/70 | 15 | 8 | 3. The Thrill Is Gone | BluesWay 61032 |
| 4/03/71 | 40 | 1 | 4. Ask Me No Questions | ABC 11290 |
| 9/22/73 | 38 | 2 | 5. To Know You Is To Love You | ABC 11373 |
| 2/09/74 | 28 | 6 | 6. I Like To Live The Love | ABC 11406 |
| | | | **BEN E. KING** | |
| | | | real name: Benjamin Nelson - lead singer of the Drifters ('59-'60) | |
| 1/30/61 | 10 | 10 | 1. **Spanish Harlem** | Atco 6185 |
| 5/22/61 | 4 | 11 | 2. **Stand By Me** | Atco 6194 |
| 8/21/61 | 18 | 5 | 3. Amor | Atco 6203 |
| 5/19/62 | 11 | 7 | 4. Don't Play That Song (You Lied) | Atco 6222 |
| 8/03/63 | 29 | 6 | 5. I (Who Have Nothing) | Atco 6267 |
| 3/08/75 | 5 | 9 | 6. **Supernatural Thing - Part 1** | Atlantic 3241 |
| | | | **CAROLE KING** | |
| | | | Carole Klein - one of pop music's most prolific songwriters | |
| 9/22/62 | 22 | 4 | 1. It Might As Well Rain Until September | Dimension 2000 |
| 5/22/71 | 1 (5) | 15 | ● 2. **It's Too Late/** | |
| | | 12 | 3. **I Feel The Earth Move** | Ode 66015 |
| 9/04/71 | 14 | 9 | 4. So Far Away | Ode 66019 |
| 2/05/72 | 9 | 8 | 5. **Sweet Seasons** | Ode 66022 |
| 12/09/72 + | 24 | 7 | 6. Been To Canaan | Ode 66031 |
| 8/11/73 | 28 | 5 | 7. Believe In Humanity | Ode 66035 |
| 12/08/73 | 37 | 2 | 8. Corazon [I] | Ode 66039 |
| 9/14/74 | 2 (1) | 12 | 9. **Jazzman** | Ode 66101 |
| 1/18/75 | 9 | 8 | 10. **Nightingale** | Ode 66106 |
| 3/06/76 | 28 | 6 | 11. Only Love Is Real | Ode 66119 |
| 8/20/77 | 30 | 5 | 12. Hard Rock Cafe | Capitol 4455 |
| 6/14/80 | 12 | 10 | 13. One Fine Day | Capitol 4864 |
| | | | **CLAUDE KING** | |
| | | | country singer from Shreveport, Louisiana | |
| 6/16/62 | 6 | 11 | 1. **Wolverton Mountain** | Columbia 42352 |
| | | | **EVELYN "CHAMPAGNE" KING** | |
| | | | born in the Bronx, New York on 6/29/60 | |
| 7/22/78 | 9 | 10 | ● 1. **Shame** | RCA 11122 |
| 3/03/79 | 23 | 8 | ● 2. I Don't Know If It's Right | RCA 11386 |
| 9/12/81 | 40 | 2 | 3. I'm In Love | RCA 12243 |
| 10/02/82 | 17 | 8 | 4. Love Come Down | RCA 13273 |
| | | | **FREDDY KING** | |
| | | | blues guitarist - died on 12/27/76 (42) | |
| 4/03/61 | 29 | 4 | 1. Hide Away [I] | Federal 12401 |

| DATE | POS | WKS | ARTIST—Record Title | LABEL & NO. |
|------|-----|-----|---------------------|-------------|
| | | | **JONATHAN KING** | |
| | | | English - founder of the U.K. record label | |
| 10/23/65 | 17 | 7 | 1. Everyone's Gone To The Moon | Parrot 9774 |
| | | | **PEGGY KING** | |
| 2/05/55 | 30 | 1 | 1. Make Yourself Comfortable | Columbia 40363 |
| | | | **TEDDI KING** | |
| | | | died on 11/18/77 (48) | |
| 3/03/56 | 18 | 2 | 1. Mr. Wonderful | RCA 6392 |
| | | | **KINGSMEN** | |
| | | | Bill Haley's Comets (without Haley) | |
| 9/22/58 | 35 | 2 | 1. Week End [I] | East West 115 |
| | | | **KINGSMEN** | |
| | | | Portland quintet led by Lynn Easton | |
| 11/30/63 | 2 (6) | 13 | 1. **Louie Louie** | Wand 143 |
| 4/04/64 | 16 | 8 | 2. Money | Wand 150 |
| 1/30/65 | 4 | 9 | 3. **The Jolly Green Giant** | Wand 172 |
| | | | **KINGSTON TRIO** | |
| | | | Bob Shane, Nick Reynolds & Dave Guard (replaced by John Stewart) | |
| 10/06/58 | 1 (1) | 18 | ● 1. **Tom Dooley** | Capitol 4049 |
| 3/30/59 | 12 | 9 | 2. The Tijuana Jail | Capitol 4167 |
| 6/29/59 | 15 | 6 | 3. M.T.A. [N] | Capitol 4221 |
| 9/21/59 | 20 | 8 | 4. A Worried Man | Capitol 4271 |
| 3/14/60 | 32 | 5 | 5. El Matador | Capitol 4338 |
| 8/08/60 | 37 | 2 | 6. Bad Man Blunder [N] | Capitol 4379 |
| 3/03/62 | 21 | 7 | 7. Where Have All The Flowers Gone | Capitol 4671 |
| 2/23/63 | 21 | 5 | 8. Greenback Dollar | Capitol 4898 |
| 4/20/63 | 8 | 8 | 9. **Reverend Mr. Black** | Capitol 4951 |
| 8/31/63 | 33 | 4 | 10. Desert Pete | Capitol 5005 |
| | | | **KINKS** | |
| | | | English group led by brothers Ray & Dave Davies | |
| 10/24/64 | 7 | 10 | 1. **You Really Got Me** | Reprise 0306 |
| 1/16/65 | 7 | 10 | 2. **All Day And All Of The Night** | Reprise 0334 |
| 3/27/65 | 6 | 8 | 3. **Tired Of Waiting For You** | Reprise 0347 |
| 7/10/65 | 23 | 4 | 4. Set Me Free | Reprise 0379 |
| 9/04/65 | 34 | 3 | 5. Who'll Be The Next In Line | Reprise 0366 |
| 1/08/66 | 13 | 9 | 6. A Well Respected Man | Reprise 0420 |
| 6/18/66 | 36 | 1 | 7. Dedicated Follower Of Fashion | Reprise 0471 |
| 8/27/66 | 14 | 7 | 8. Sunny Afternoon | Reprise 0497 |
| 9/12/70 | 9 | 12 | 9. Lola | Reprise 0930 |
| 8/19/78 | 30 | 5 | 10. A Rock 'N' Roll Fantasy | Arista 0342 |
| 5/28/83 | 6 | 12 | 11. **Come Dancing** | Arista 1054 |
| 9/17/83 | 29 | 4 | 12. Don't Forget To Dance | Arista 9075 |
| | | | **KISS** | |
| | | | Gene Simmons, Paul Stanley, Ace Frehley & Peter Criss | |
| 11/29/75 + | 12 | 10 | 1. Rock And Roll All Nite | Casablanca 850 |
| 4/17/76 | 31 | 4 | 2. Shout It Out Loud | Casablanca 854 |

| DATE | POS | WKS | ARTIST—Record Title | LABEL & NO. |
|---|---|---|---|---|
| 9/25/76 | 7 | 13 | ●   3. **Beth** | Casablanca 863 |
| 1/15/77 | 15 | 8 | 4. Hard Luck Woman | Casablanca 873 |
| 4/09/77 | 16 | 8 | 5. Calling Dr. Love | Casablanca 880 |
| 7/30/77 | 25 | 7 | 6. Christine Sixteen | Casablanca 889 |
| 4/15/78 | 39 | 2 | 7. Rocket Ride | Casablanca 915 |
| 6/16/79 | 11 | 11 | ●   8. I Was Made For Lovin' You | Casablanca 983 |
| | | | **MAC & KATIE KISSOON** | |
| | | | brother and sister from Trinidad | |
| 9/04/71 | 20 | 9 | 1. Chirpy Chirpy Cheep Cheep | ABC 11306 |
| | | | **KNACK** | |
| | | | Los Angeles rock quartet led by Doug Fieger (vocals) & Berton Averre (guitar) | |
| 7/21/79 | 1 (6) | 16 | ●   1. **My Sharona** | Capitol 4731 |
| 9/22/79 | 11 | 11 | 2. Good Girls Don't | Capitol 4771 |
| 3/08/80 | 38 | 2 | 3. Baby Talks Dirty | Capitol 4822 |
| | | | **KNICKERBOCKERS** | |
| | | | New Jersey rock quartet - Buddy Randell, leader | |
| 1/01/66 | 20 | 9 | 1. Lies | Challenge 59321 |
| | | | **FREDERICK KNIGHT** | |
| 5/27/72 | 27 | 9 | 1. I've Been Lonely For So Long | Stax 0117 |
| | | | **GLADYS KNIGHT & THE PIPS** | |
| | | | The Pips: Gladys' brother Merald, and cousins William Guest and Edward Patten | |
| 6/05/61 | 6 | 10 | 1. **Every Beat Of My Heart**<br>shown only as the Pips | Vee-Jay 386 |
| 1/20/62 | 19 | 6 | 2. Letter Full Of Tears | Fury 1054 |
| 7/04/64 | 38 | 1 | 3. Giving Up | Maxx 326 |
| 8/19/67 | 39 | 2 | 4. Everybody Needs Love | Soul 35034 |
| 11/04/67 | 2 (3) | 14 | 5. **I Heard It Through The Grapevine** | Soul 35039 |
| 2/17/68 | 15 | 8 | 6. The End Of Our Road | Soul 35042 |
| 7/06/68 | 40 | 1 | 7. It Should Have Been Me | Soul 35045 |
| 8/09/69 | 19 | 8 | 8. The Nitty Gritty | Soul 35063 |
| 11/15/69 | 17 | 10 | 9. Friendship Train | Soul 35068 |
| 4/04/70 | 25 | 5 | 10. You Need Love Like I Do (Don't You) | Soul 35071 |
| 12/19/70 + | 9 | 12 | 11. **If I Were Your Woman** | Soul 35078 |
| 6/19/71 | 17 | 9 | 12. I Don't Want To Do Wrong | Soul 35083 |
| 1/08/72 | 27 | 5 | 13. Make Me The Woman That You Go Home To | Soul 35091 |
| 4/08/72 | 33 | 6 | 14. Help Me Make It Through The Night | Soul 35094 |
| 2/17/73 | 2 (2) | 12 | 15. **Neither One Of Us (Wants To Be The First To Say Goodbye)** | Soul 35098 |
| 6/02/73 | 19 | 8 | 16. Daddy Could Swear, I Declare | Soul 35105 |
| 7/07/73 | 28 | 7 | 17. Where Peaceful Waters Flow | Buddah 363 |
| 9/15/73 | 1 (2) | 16 | ●   18. **Midnight Train To Georgia** | Buddah 383 |
| 12/08/73 + | 4 | 13 | ●   19. **I've Got To Use My Imagination** | Buddah 393 |
| 3/09/74 | 3 | 13 | ●   20. **Best Thing That Ever Happened To Me** | Buddah 403 |

| DATE | POS | WKS | ARTIST—Record Title | LABEL & NO. |
|---|---|---|---|---|
| 6/01/74 | 5 | 11 | ● 21. **On And On**<br>from the film "Claudine" | Buddah 423 |
| 11/16/74 | 21 | 9 | 22. I Feel A Song (In My Heart) | Buddah 433 |
| 5/24/75 | 11 | 12 | 23. The Way We Were/Try To Remember | Buddah 463 |
| 11/29/75 | 22 | 7 | 24. Part Time Love | Buddah 513 |
| | | | **JEAN KNIGHT** | |
| 6/19/71 | 2 (2) | 13 | 1. **Mr. Big Stuff** | Stax 0088 |
| | | | **ROBERT KNIGHT** | |
| 10/28/67 | 13 | 8 | 1. Everlasting Love | Rising Sons 705 |
| | | | **SONNY KNIGHT** | |
| 11/24/56 | 17 | 9 | 1. Confidential | Dot 15507 |
| | | | **FRED KNOBLOCK** | |
| 7/26/80 | 18 | 7 | 1. Why Not Me | Scotti Br. 518 |
| | | | **FRED KNOBLOCK & SUSAN ANTON** | |
| 12/27/80 + | 28 | 9 | 1. Killin' Time | Scotti Br. 609 |
| | | | **BUDDY KNOX**<br>born on 4/14/33 in Happy, Texas - also see Jimmy Bowen | |
| 3/02/57 | 1 (1) | 15 | 1. **Party Doll** | Roulette 4002 |
| 6/03/57 | 17 | 7 | 2. Rock Your Little Baby To Sleep | Roulette 4009 |
| 9/09/57 | 9 | 15 | 3. **Hula Love** | Roulette 4018 |
| 8/04/58 | 22 | 11 | 4. Somebody Touched Me<br>above hits with the Rhythm Orchids | Roulette 4082 |
| 1/09/61 | 25 | 4 | 5. Lovey Dovey | Liberty 55290 |
| | | | **MOE KOFFMAN Quartette**<br>Canadian | |
| 2/10/58 | 23 | 5 | 1. The Swingin' Shepherd Blues [I] | Jubilee 5311 |
| | | | **KOKOMO**<br>Jimmy Wisner | |
| 3/06/61 | 8 | 11 | 1. **Asia Minor [I]** | Felsted 8612 |
| | | | **KOOL & THE GANG**<br>Jersey City group led by Robert "Kool" Bell (bass) & James Taylor | |
| 10/06/73 | 29 | 6 | 1. Funky Stuff | De-Lite 557 |
| 1/05/74 | 4 | 16 | ● 2. **Jungle Boogie** | De-Lite 559 |
| 5/18/74 | 6 | 11 | ● 3. **Hollywood Swinging** | De-Lite 561 |
| 10/12/74 | 37 | 2 | 4. Higher Plane | De-Lite 1562 |
| 6/28/75 | 35 | 3 | 5. Spirit Of The Boogie | De-Lite 1567 |
| 11/10/79 + | 8 | 14 | ● 6. **Ladies Night** | De-Lite 801 |
| 2/09/80 | 5 | 13 | 7. **Too Hot** | De-Lite 802 |
| 11/22/80 + | 1 (2) | 21 | ★ 8. **Celebration** | De-Lite 807 |
| 6/27/81 | 39 | 2 | 9. Jones Vs. Jones | De-Lite 813 |
| 11/07/81 | 17 | 12 | 10. Take My Heart (You Can Have It If You Want It) | De-Lite 815 |
| 4/03/82 | 10 | 9 | 11. **Get Down On It** | De-Lite 818 |
| 9/11/82 | 21 | 7 | 12. Big Fun | De-Lite 822 |

| DATE | POS | WKS | ARTIST—Record Title | LABEL & NO. |
|------|-----|-----|---------------------|-------------|
| 12/04/82 + | 30 | 7 | 13. Let's Go Dancin' (Ooh La, La, La) | De-Lite 824 |
| 12/03/83 + | 2 (1) | 16 | 14. **Joanna** | De-Lite 829 |
| 3/17/84 | 13 | 10 | 15. Tonight | De-Lite 830 |
| | | | **KORGIS** | |
| | | | British trio | |
| 11/08/80 | 18 | 11 | 1. Everybody's Got To Learn Sometime | Asylum 47055 |
| | | | **KRAFTWERK** | |
| | | | German duo specializing in synthesized robotic rock | |
| 4/12/75 | 25 | 5 | 1. Autobahn [I] | Vertigo 203 |
| | | | **BILLY J. KRAMER with the Dakotas** | |
| | | | English - managed by Brian Epstein; produced by George Martin | |
| 5/02/64 | 7 | 12 | 1. **Little Children/** | |
| 6/13/64 | 9 | 8 | 2. **Bad To Me** | Imperial 66027 |
| 8/15/64 | 30 | 3 | 3. I'll Keep You Satisfied | Imperial 66048 |
| 9/19/64 | 23 | 5 | 4. From A Window | Imperial 66051 |
| | | | **KRIS KRISTOFFERSON** | |
| | | | songwriter/vocalist/actor | |
| 10/02/71 | 26 | 7 | 1. Loving Her Was Easier (Than Anything I'll Ever Do Again) | Monument 8525 |
| 7/07/73 | 16 | 19 | ● 2. Why Me | Monument 8571 |
| | | | **BOB KUBAN & the In-Men** | |
| | | | 8-man St. Louis band - Walter Scott, lead singer | |
| 2/19/66 | 12 | 7 | 1. The Cheater | Musicland 20001 |
| | | | **PATTI LABELLE & The Blue Belles** | |
| | | | Patti Labelle, Sarah Dash & Nona Hendryx - formerly the Blue-Belles | |
| 11/02/63 | 37 | 3 | 1. Down The Aisle (Wedding Song) | Newtown 5777 |
| 2/08/64 | 34 | 1 | 2. You'll Never Walk Alone | Parkway 896 |
| | | | LABELLE: | |
| 2/01/75 | 1 (1) | 13 | ● 3. **Lady Marmalade** | Epic 50048 |
| | | | **CHERYL LADD** | |
| | | | Kris Monroe of TV's "Charlie's Angels" | |
| 8/26/78 | 34 | 3 | 1. Think It Over | Capitol 4599 |
| | | | **LADY FLASH** | |
| | | | Barry Manilow's back-up singers | |
| 8/14/76 | 27 | 6 | 1. Street Singin' | RSO 852 |
| | | | **FRANCIS LAI & His Orchestra** | |
| 2/27/71 | 31 | 4 | 1. Theme From Love Story [I] | Paramount 0064 |
| | | | piano Solo by Georges Pludermacher | |
| | | | **LAID BACK** | |
| | | | Danish duo: Tim Stahl and John Guldberg | |
| 4/28/84 | 26 | 4 | 1. White Horse | Sire 29346 |
| | | | **FRANKIE LAINE** | |
| | | | born Frank LoVecchio in Chicago on 3/30/13 | |
| 9/03/55 | 17 | 3 | 1. Humming Bird | Columbia 40526 |
| 12/17/55 | 19 | 10 | 2. A Woman In Love | Columbia 40583 |
| | | | from the film "Guys And Dolls" | |

| DATE | POS | WKS | ARTIST—Record Title | LABEL & NO. |
|---|---|---|---|---|
| 12/08/56 + | 3 | 18 | 3. **Moonlight Gambler** | Columbia 40780 |
| 4/20/57 | 10 | 8 | 4. **Love Is A Golden Ring**<br>with The Easy Riders | Columbia 40856 |
| 3/04/67 | 39 | 2 | 5. I'll Take Care Of Your Cares | ABC 10891 |
| 5/06/67 | 35 | 3 | 6. Making Memories | ABC 10924 |
| 3/01/69 | 24 | 7 | 7. You Gave Me A Mountain | ABC 11174 |
| | | | **MAJOR LANCE**<br>born on 4/4/41 in Chicago, Illinois | |
| 8/10/63 | 8 | 10 | 1. **The Monkey Time** | Okeh 7175 |
| 11/02/63 | 13 | 8 | 2. Hey Little Girl | Okeh 7181 |
| 1/11/64 | 5 | 10 | 3. **Um, Um, Um, Um, Um, Um** | Okeh 7187 |
| 4/11/64 | 20 | 6 | 4. The Matador | Okeh 7191 |
| 9/19/64 | 24 | 5 | 5. Rhythm | Okeh 7203 |
| 4/03/65 | 40 | 1 | 6. Come See | Okeh 7216 |
| | | | **MICKEY LEE LANE** | |
| 11/28/64 | 38 | 1 | 1. Shaggy Dog | Swan 4183 |
| | | | **SNOOKY LANSON**<br>star of TV's "Your Hit Parade" | |
| 12/03/55 | 20 | 6 | 1. It's Almost Tomorrow | Dot 15424 |
| | | | **LARKS**<br>Don Julian, Charles Morrison & Ted Walters | |
| 11/28/64 + | 7 | 11 | 1. **The Jerk** | Money 106 |
| | | | **JULIUS LaROSA**<br>born on 1/2/30 in Brooklyn, New York | |
| 7/23/55 | 13 | 7 | 1. Domani (Tomorrow) | Cadence 1265 |
| 10/08/55 | 20 | 5 | 2. Suddenly There's A Valley | Cadence 1270 |
| 2/18/56 | 15 | 7 | 3. Lipstick And Candy And Rubbersole Shoes | RCA 6416 |
| 6/16/58 | 21 | 1 | 4. Torero | RCA 7227 |
| | | | **LARSEN/FEITEN BAND**<br>Neil Larsen (keyboards) & Buzz Feiten (guitar) | |
| 9/13/80 | 29 | 6 | 1. Who'll Be The Fool Tonight | Warner 49282 |
| | | | **NICOLETTE LARSON**<br>former backup harmony singer with Neil Young | |
| 12/23/78 + | 8 | 14 | 1. **Lotta Love** | Warner 8664 |
| 2/16/80 | 35 | 3 | 2. Let Me Go, Love<br>duet with Michael McDonald | Warner 49130 |
| | | | **DENISE LaSALLE** | |
| 9/25/71 | 13 | 9 | ● 1. Trapped By A Thing Called Love | Westbound 182 |
| | | | **DAVID LASLEY**<br>backup singer and songwriter | |
| 4/24/82 | 36 | 4 | 1. If I Had My Wish Tonight | EMI America 8111 |
| | | | **JAMES LAST**<br>German producer/arranger | |
| 4/26/80 | 28 | 6 | 1. The Seduction (Love Theme From<br>"American Gigolo") [I] | Polydor 2071 |

| DATE | POS | WKS | ARTIST—Record Title | LABEL & NO. |
|---|---|---|---|---|
| | | | **LATIMORE** | |
| | | | Benny Latimore | |
| 11/23/74 | 31 | 3 | 1. Let's Straighten It Out | Glades 1722 |
| 3/26/77 | 37 | 2 | 2. Somethin' 'Bout 'Cha | Glades 1739 |
| | | | **STACY LATTISAW** | |
| | | | born on 11/25/66 in Washington, D.C. | |
| 10/04/80 | 21 | 10 | 1. Let Me Be Your Angel | Cotillion 46001 |
| 8/01/81 | 26 | 7 | 2. Love On A Two Way Street | Cotillion 46015 |
| 10/22/83 | 40 | 1 | 3. Miracles | Cotillion 99855 |
| | | | **CYNDI LAUPER** | |
| | | | pop/rock singer/songwriter from Brooklyn, New York | |
| 1/28/84 | 2 (2) | 14 | • 1. **Girls Just Want To Have Fun** | Portrait 04120 |
| 4/21/84 | 1 (2) | 14 | 2. **Time After Time** | Portrait 04432 |
| 7/28/84 | 3 | 14 | 3. **She Bop** | Portrait 04516 |
| 10/13/84 | 5 | 14 | 4. **All Through The Night** | Portrait 04639 |
| | | | **ROD LAUREN** | |
| 1/11/60 | 31 | 5 | 1. If I Had A Girl | RCA 7645 |
| | | | **LAURIE SISTERS** | |
| 4/16/55 | 30 | 1 | 1. Dixie Danny | Mercury 70548 |
| | | | **EDDIE LAWRENCE** | |
| 9/01/56 | 34 | 1 | 1. The Old Philosopher [C] | Coral 61671 |
| | | | **STEVE LAWRENCE** | |
| | | | a charter member of Steve Allen's "Tonight" show - also see Steve & Eydie | |
| 1/19/57 | 18 | 8 | 1. The Banana Boat Song | Coral 61761 |
| 3/09/57 | 5 | 12 | 2. **Party Doll** | Coral 61792 |
| 12/14/59 + | 9 | 13 | 3. **Pretty Blue Eyes** | ABC-Para. 10058 |
| 3/28/60 | 7 | 9 | 4. **Footsteps** | ABC-Para. 10085 |
| 4/03/61 | 9 | 10 | 5. **Portrait Of My Love** | United Art. 291 |
| 12/08/62 + | 1 (2) | 12 | 6. **Go Away Little Girl** | Columbia 42601 |
| 3/30/63 | 26 | 6 | 7. Don't Be Afraid, Little Darlin' | Columbia 42699 |
| 6/15/63 | 27 | 3 | 8. Poor Little Rich Girl | Columbia 42795 |
| 11/09/63 | 26 | 4 | 9. Walking Proud | Columbia 42865 |
| | | | **VICKI LAWRENCE** | |
| | | | star of TV's "Mama's Family" | |
| 3/17/73 | 1 (2) | 14 | • 1. **The Night The Lights Went Out In Georgia** | Bell 45303 |
| | | | **JOY LAYNE** | |
| 2/16/57 | 20 | 5 | 1. Your Wild Heart | Mercury 71038 |
| | | | **LE ROUX** | |
| | | | 6-man Louisiana rock band - Jeff Pollard, lead singer | |
| 3/20/82 | 18 | 6 | 1. Nobody Said It Was Easy (Lookin' For The Lights) | RCA 13059 |
| | | | **LEAPY LEE** | |
| 11/09/68 | 16 | 8 | 1. Little Arrows | Decca 32380 |

| DATE | POS | WKS | ARTIST—Record Title | LABEL & NO. |
|---|---|---|---|---|
| | | | **LEAVES** | |
| | | | Los Angeles rock quintet - John Beck, lead singer | |
| 6/18/66 | **31** | 4 | 1. Hey Joe | Mira 222 |
| | | | **LeBLANC & CARR** | |
| | | | Lenny LeBlanc & Pete Carr | |
| 2/04/78 | **13** | 10 | 1. Falling | Big Tree 16100 |
| | | | **LED ZEPPELIN** | |
| | | | British: Robert Plant (vocals), Jimmy Page (guitar), John Paul Jones (bass/keyboards) & John Bonham (drums) - Bonham died on 9/25/80 (33) | |
| 12/06/69 + | **4** | 13 | ● 1. **Whole Lotta Love** | Atlantic 2690 |
| 12/12/70 + | **16** | 10 | 2. Immigrant Song | Atlantic 2777 |
| 1/15/72 | **15** | 8 | 3. Black Dog | Atlantic 2849 |
| 11/24/73 | **20** | 8 | 4. D'yer Mak'er | Atlantic 2986 |
| 5/17/75 | **38** | 2 | 5. Trampled Under Foot | Swan Song 70102 |
| 1/12/80 | **21** | 8 | 6. Fool In The Rain<br>the classic "Stairway To Heaven" was released only on the album "Led Zeppelin IV" in November, 1971 | Swan Song 71003 |
| | | | **BRENDA LEE** | |
| | | | born Brenda Mae Tarpley on 12/11/44 in Atlanta, Georgia | |
| 2/15/60 | **4** | 15 | 1. **Sweet Nothin's** | Decca 30967 |
| 6/06/60 | **1** (3) | 18 | 2. **I'm Sorry/** | |
| 6/20/60 | **6** | 9 | 3. **That's All You Gotta Do** | Decca 31093 |
| 9/19/60 | **1** (1) | 13 | 4. **I Want To Be Wanted/** | |
| 10/31/60 | **40** | 1 | 5. Just A Little | Decca 31149 |
| 12/19/60 | **14** | 3 | 6. Rockin' Around The Christmas Tree [X]<br>recorded in 1958 | Decca 30776 |
| 1/16/61 | **7** | 9 | 7. **Emotions/** | |
| 2/06/61 | **33** | 2 | 8. I'm Learning About Love | Decca 31195 |
| 4/03/61 | **6** | 10 | 9. **You Can Depend On Me** | Decca 31231 |
| 6/26/61 | **4** | 10 | 10. **Dum Dum** | Decca 31272 |
| 10/09/61 | **3** | 12 | 11. **Fool #1/** | |
| 10/16/61 | **31** | 3 | 12. Anybody But Me | Decca 31309 |
| 1/20/62 | **4** | 12 | 13. **Break It To Me Gently** | Decca 31348 |
| 4/28/62 | **6** | 8 | 14. **Everybody Loves Me But You** | Decca 31379 |
| 7/21/62 | **15** | 7 | 15. Heart In Hand/ | |
| 7/21/62 | **29** | 4 | 16. It Started All Over Again | Decca 31407 |
| 10/06/62 | **3** | 12 | 17. **All Alone Am I** | Decca 31424 |
| 2/16/63 | **32** | 3 | 18. Your Used To Be | Decca 31454 |
| 4/20/63 | **6** | 10 | 19. **Losing You** | Decca 31478 |
| 7/27/63 | **24** | 6 | 20. My Whole World Is Falling Down/ | |
| 7/27/63 | **25** | 5 | 21. I Wonder | Decca 31510 |
| 10/12/63 | **17** | 5 | 22. The Grass Is Greener | Decca 31539 |
| 12/28/63 + | **12** | 8 | 23. As Usual | Decca 31570 |
| 3/28/64 | **25** | 5 | 24. Think | Decca 31599 |
| 10/31/64 | **17** | 7 | 25. Is It True | Decca 31690 |
| 6/26/65 | **13** | 8 | 26. Too Many Rivers | Decca 31792 |
| 11/13/65 | **33** | 3 | 27. Rusty Bells | Decca 31849 |

| DATE | POS | WKS | ARTIST—Record Title | LABEL & NO. |
|---|---|---|---|---|
| 10/29/66 | 11 | 8 | 28. Coming On Strong | Decca 32018 |
| 2/11/67 | 37 | 2 | 29. Ride, Ride, Ride | Decca 32079 |
| | | | **CURTIS LEE** | |
| 7/17/61 | 7 | 8 | 1. **Pretty Little Angel Eyes**<br>backing vocals by the Halos | Dunes 2007 |
| | | | **DICKEY LEE**<br>born Dick Lipscomb on 9/21/41 in Memphis | |
| 9/08/62 | 6 | 11 | 1. **Patches** | Smash 1758 |
| 12/29/62 + | 14 | 8 | 2. I Saw Linda Yesterday | Smash 1791 |
| 6/19/65 | 14 | 7 | 3. Laurie (Strange Things Happen) | TCF Hall 102 |
| | | | **JACKIE LEE**<br>member of the Hollywood Flames - also recorded as Earl Cosby<br>for Bob & Earl | |
| 12/18/65 + | 14 | 9 | 1. The Duck | Mirwood 5502 |
| | | | **JOHNNY LEE**<br>performed with Mickey Gilley at his club in Pasadena, Texas | |
| 8/02/80 | 5 | 13 | ● 1. **Lookin' For Love**<br>from the movie "Urban Cowboy" | Full Moon 47004 |
| | | | **LAURA LEE** | |
| 10/16/71 | 36 | 4 | 1. Women's Love Rights | Hot Wax 7105 |
| | | | **PEGGY LEE**<br>born Norma Jean Egstrom on 5/26/20 in Jamestown, North<br>Dakota - vocalist with Benny Goodman from 1941-1943 | |
| 3/24/56 | 14 | 10 | 1. Mr. Wonderful | Decca 29834 |
| 7/21/58 | 8 | 13 | 2. **Fever** | Capitol 3998 |
| 10/11/69 | 11 | 8 | 3. Is That All There Is | Capitol 2602 |
| | | | **RAYMOND LEFEVRE & His Orchestra**<br>French | |
| 11/03/58 | 30 | 5 | 1. The Day The Rains Came [I] | Kapp 231 |
| 4/06/68 | 37 | 5 | 2. Ame Caline (Soul Coaxing) [I] | Four Corners 147 |
| | | | **LEFT BANKE**<br>New York quintet - Steve Martin, lead singer | |
| 9/24/66 | 5 | 10 | 1. **Walk Away Renee** | Smash 2041 |
| 2/04/67 | 15 | 6 | 2. Pretty Ballerina | Smash 2074 |
| | | | **LEMON PIPERS**<br>Cincinnati quintet - Ivan Browne, lead singer | |
| 12/23/67 + | 1 (1) | 12 | ● 1. **Green Tambourine** | Buddah 23 |
| | | | **LENNON SISTERS**<br>Dianne, Peggy, Kathy & Janet | |
| 9/29/56 | 15 | 10 | 1. Tonight You Belong To Me<br>with Lawrence Welk's Orchestra | Coral 61701 |
| | | | **JOHN LENNON**<br>The Beatles' guitarist/lyricist - born on 10/9/40 in Liverpool,<br>England - murdered on 12/8/80 (40) in New York City | |
| 8/09/69 | 14 | 6 | 1. Give Peace A Chance<br>shown as Plastic Ono Band (also on 2, 4, 5 & 7) | Apple 1809 |
| 12/13/69 + | 30 | 7 | 2. Cold Turkey | Apple 1813 |

| DATE | POS | WKS | ARTIST—Record Title | LABEL & NO. |
|------|-----|-----|---------------------|-------------|
| 3/07/70 | 3 | 12 | ●   3. **Instant Karma (We All Shine On)** | Apple 1818 |
| 4/10/71 | 11 | 8 | 4. Power To The People | Apple 1830 |
| 10/23/71 | 3 | 9 | 5. **Imagine** | Apple 1840 |
| 12/01/73 | 18 | 8 | 6. Mind Games | Apple 1868 |
| 10/05/74 | 1 (1) | 11 | 7. **Whatever Gets You Thru The Night**<br>backing vocals by Elton John | Apple 1874 |
| 1/11/75 | 9 | 8 | 8. **#9 Dream** | Apple 1878 |
| 4/05/75 | 20 | 5 | 9. Stand By Me | Apple 1881 |
| 11/01/80 | 1 (5) | 19 | ● 10. **(Just Like) Starting Over** | Geffen 49604 |
| 1/17/81 | 2 (3) | 17 | ● 11. **Woman** | Geffen 49644 |
| 4/11/81 | 10 | 10 | 12. Watching The Wheels | Geffen 49695 |
| 1/21/84 | 5 | 11 | 13. **Nobody Told Me** | Polydor 817254 |
| | | | **TOMMY LEONETTI** | |
| | | | died on 9/15/79 (50) | |
| 7/07/56 | 23 | 2 | 1. Free | Capitol 3442 |
| | | | **KETTY LESTER** | |
| 3/10/62 | 5 | 11 | 1. **Love Letters** | Era 3068 |
| | | | **LETTERMEN** | |
| | | | original trio: Tony Butala, Jim Pike and Bob Engemann -<br>Gary Pike (Jim's brother) replaced Bob Engemann in 1968 | |
| 9/25/61 | 13 | 9 | 1. The Way You Look Tonight | Capitol 4586 |
| 12/04/61 + | 7 | 11 | 2. **When I Fall In Love** | Capitol 4658 |
| 3/10/62 | 17 | 7 | 3. Come Back Silly Girl | Capitol 4699 |
| 7/17/65 | 16 | 5 | 4. Theme From "A Summer Place" | Capitol 5437 |
| 1/06/68 | 7 | 11 | 5. **Goin' Out Of My Head/Can't Take My Eyes Off You** | Capitol 2054 |
| 8/16/69 | 12 | 10 | 6. Hurt So Bad | Capitol 2482 |
| | | | **BARBARA LEWIS** | |
| | | | born on 2/9/44 in Detroit, Michigan | |
| 5/25/63 | 3 | 10 | 1. **Hello Stranger** | Atlantic 2184 |
| 3/14/64 | 38 | 1 | 2. Puppy Love | Atlantic 2214 |
| 7/17/65 | 11 | 9 | 3. Baby, I'm Yours | Atlantic 2283 |
| 10/09/65 | 11 | 8 | 4. Make Me Your Baby | Atlantic 2300 |
| 8/13/66 | 28 | 4 | 5. Make Me Belong To You | Atlantic 2346 |
| | | | **BOBBY LEWIS** | |
| | | | born on 2/17/33 in Indianapolis, Indiana | |
| 5/29/61 | 1 (7) | 17 | 1. **Tossin' And Turnin'** | Beltone 1002 |
| 9/11/61 | 9 | 7 | 2. **One Track Mind** | Beltone 1012 |
| | | | **GARY LEWIS & The Playboys** | |
| | | | Gary is the eldest son of comedian Jerry Lewis | |
| 1/23/65 | 1 (2) | 11 | ● 1. **This Diamond Ring** | Liberty 55756 |
| 4/17/65 | 2 (2) | 9 | 2. **Count Me In** | Liberty 55778 |
| 7/17/65 | 2 (1) | 9 | 3. **Save Your Heart For Me** | Liberty 55809 |
| 10/09/65 | 4 | 8 | 4. **Everybody Loves A Clown** | Liberty 55818 |
| 12/18/65 + | 3 | 11 | 5. **She's Just My Style** | Liberty 55846 |
| 3/19/66 | 9 | 7 | 6. **Sure Gonna Miss Her** | Liberty 55865 |

| DATE | POS | WKS | ARTIST—Record Title | LABEL & NO. |
|------|-----|-----|---------------------|-------------|
| 5/21/66 | 8 | 7 | 7. **Green Grass** | Liberty 55880 |
| 8/13/66 | 13 | 5 | 8. My Heart's Symphony | Liberty 55898 |
| 10/22/66 | 15 | 6 | 9. (You Don't Have To) Paint Me A Picture | Liberty 55914 |
| 1/07/67 | 21 | 6 | 10. Where Will The Words Come From | Liberty 55933 |
| 6/10/67 | 39 | 2 | 11. Girls In Love | Liberty 55971 |
| 7/27/68 | 19 | 9 | 12. Sealed With A Kiss | Liberty 56037 |
| | | | **HUEY LEWIS & THE NEWS** | |
| | | | San Francisco 6-man rock band | |
| 2/20/82 | 7 | 13 | 1. **Do You Believe In Love** | Chrysalis 2589 |
| 6/12/82 | 36 | 4 | 2. Hope You Love Me Like You Say You Do | Chrysalis 2604 |
| 10/08/83 | 8 | 13 | 3. **Heart And Soul** | Chrysalis 42726 |
| 1/28/84 | 6 | 13 | 4. **I Want A New Drug** | Chrysalis 42766 |
| 4/28/84 | 6 | 14 | 5. **The Heart Of Rock & Roll** | Chrysalis 42782 |
| 7/28/84 | 6 | 13 | 6. **If This Is It** | Chrysalis 42803 |
| 10/27/84 | 18 | 10 | 7. **Walking On A Thin Line** | Chrysalis 42825 |
| | | | **JERRY LEWIS** | |
| | | | popular comedian/actor | |
| 11/24/56 | 10 | 15 | 1. **Rock-A-Bye Your Baby With A Dixie Melody** | Decca 30124 |
| | | | **JERRY LEE LEWIS** | |
| | | | one of the Fifties leading rockers - born on 9/29/35 in Ferriday, Louisiana | |
| 7/15/57 | 3 | 20 | 1. **Whole Lot Of Shakin' Going On** | Sun 267 |
| 12/02/57 + | 2 (4) | 13 | 2. **Great Balls Of Fire** | Sun 281 |
| 3/10/58 | 7 | 9 | 3. **Breathless** | Sun 288 |
| 6/02/58 | 21 | 8 | 4. High School Confidential | Sun 296 |
| 4/24/61 | 30 | 4 | 5. What'd I Say | Sun 356 |
| 1/15/72 | 40 | 1 | 6. Me And Bobby McGee | Mercury 73248 |
| | | | **RAMSEY LEWIS** | |
| | | | keyboardist born on 5/27/35 in Chicago, Illinois | |
| 8/21/65 | 5 | 12 | 1. **The "In" Crowd [I]** | Argo 5506 |
| 11/27/65 | 11 | 6 | 2. Hang On Sloopy [I] | Cadet 5522 |
| 2/05/66 | 29 | 4 | 3. A Hard Day's Night [I] | Cadet 5525 |
| | | | above 3 shown as Ramsey Lewis Trio | |
| 8/20/66 | 19 | 6 | 4. Wade In The Water [I] | Cadet 5541 |
| | | | **GORDON LIGHTFOOT** | |
| | | | born on 11/17/38 in Orillia, Ontario, Canada | |
| 1/23/71 | 5 | 11 | 1. **If You Could Read My Mind** | Reprise 0974 |
| 5/11/74 | 1 (1) | 11 | ● 2. **Sundown** | Reprise 1194 |
| 10/05/74 | 10 | 7 | 3. **Carefree Highway** | Reprise 1309 |
| 5/03/75 | 26 | 4 | 4. **Rainy Day People** | Reprise 1328 |
| 9/25/76 | 2 (2) | 13 | 5. **Wreck Of The Edmund Fitzgerald** | Reprise 1369 |
| 3/25/78 | 33 | 3 | 6. The Circle Is Small (I Can See It In Your Eyes) | Warner 8518 |
| | | | **LIGHTHOUSE** | |
| | | | Canadian rock band - Bob McBride, lead singer | |
| 10/09/71 | 24 | 8 | 1. One Fine Morning | Evolution 1048 |
| 11/25/72 | 34 | 5 | 2. Sunny Days | Evolution 1069 |

| DATE | POS | WKS | ARTIST—Record Title | LABEL & NO. |
|------|-----|-----|---------------------|-------------|
| | | | **BOB LIND** | |
| 2/12/66 | 5 | 9 | 1. **Elusive Butterfly** | World Pac. 77808 |
| | | | **KATHY LINDEN** | |
| 3/31/58 | 7 | 11 | 1. **Billy** | Felsted 8510 |
| 4/27/59 | 11 | 10 | 2. Goodbye Jimmy, Goodbye | Felsted 8571 |
| | | | **LINDISFARNE** | |
| 11/25/78 | 33 | 4 | 1. Run For Home | Atco 7093 |
| | | | **MARK LINDSAY** | |
| | | | lead singer of Paul Revere & The Raiders | |
| 1/10/70 | 10 | 11 | ● 1. **Arizona** | Columbia 45037 |
| 7/11/70 | 25 | 5 | 2. Silver Bird | Columbia 45180 |
| | | | **LIPPS, INC.** | |
| | | | a Steve Greenberg production with vocals by Cynthia Johnson | |
| 4/19/80 | 1 (4) | 15 | ★ 1. **Funkytown** | Casablanca 2233 |
| | | | **LITTLE ANTHONY & THE IMPERIALS** | |
| | | | Anthony Gourdine, lead singer of Brooklyn doo-wop quartet | |
| 8/18/58 | 4 | 14 | 1. **Tears On My Pillow** | End 1027 |
| 1/18/60 | 24 | 7 | 2. Shimmy, Shimmy, Ko-Ko-Bop | End 1060 |
| 9/05/64 | 15 | 8 | 3. I'm On The Outside (Looking In) | DCP 1104 |
| 11/21/64 | 6 | 12 | 4. **Goin' Out Of My Head** | DCP 1119 |
| 2/13/65 | 10 | 8 | 5. **Hurt So Bad** | DCP 1128 |
| 7/17/65 | 16 | 7 | 6. Take Me Back | DCP 1136 |
| 11/06/65 | 34 | 1 | 7. I Miss You So | DCP 1149 |
| | | | **LITTLE CAESAR & THE ROMANS** | |
| | | | Little Caesar is Carl Burnett | |
| 5/29/61 | 9 | 9 | 1. **Those Oldies But Goodies (Remind Me Of You)** | Del-Fi 4158 |
| | | | **LITTLE DIPPERS** | |
| | | | Anita Kerr Singers | |
| 2/08/60 | 9 | 10 | 1. **Forever** | University 210 |
| | | | **LITTLE EVA** | |
| | | | Eva Boyd - discovered while baby sitting at Carole King & Gerry Goffin's home - also see Big Dee Irwin | |
| 7/21/62 | 1 (1) | 12 | 1. **The Loco-Motion** | Dimension 1000 |
| 11/24/62 | 12 | 8 | 2. Keep Your Hands Off My Baby | Dimension 1003 |
| 2/23/63 | 20 | 6 | 3. Let's Turkey Trot | Dimension 1006 |
| | | | **LITTLE JOE & THE THRILLERS** | |
| | | | Joe Cook and quartet from Philadelphia | |
| 10/07/57 | 22 | 9 | 1. Peanuts | Okeh 7088 |
| | | | **LITTLE JOEY & THE FLIPS** | |
| | | | Joey Hall | |
| 7/14/62 | 33 | 3 | 1. Bongo Stomp | Joy 262 |
| | | | **LITTLE MILTON** | |
| | | | Milton Campbell, Jr. from Leland, Mississippi | |
| 4/24/65 | 25 | 7 | 1. We're Gonna Make It | Checker 1105 |

| DATE | POS | WKS | ARTIST—Record Title | LABEL & NO. |
|---|---|---|---|---|
| | | | **LITTLE RICHARD** | |
| | | | Richard Penniman - born on 12/25/35 in Macon, Georgia | |
| 1/28/56 | 17 | 5 | 1. Tutti-Frutti | Specialty 561 |
| 4/07/56 | 6 | 12 | 2. **Long Tall Sally/** | |
| 6/30/56 | 33 | 1 | 3. Slippin' And Slidin' (Peepin' And Hidin') | Specialty 572 |
| 7/14/56 | 17 | 7 | 4. Rip It Up | Specialty 579 |
| 4/06/57 | 21 | 7 | 5. Lucille | Specialty 598 |
| 6/24/57 | 10 | 13 | 6. **Jenny, Jenny** | Specialty 606 |
| 10/07/57 | 8 | 12 | 7. **Keep A Knockin'** | Specialty 611 |
| | | | from the film "Mr. Rock 'n' Roll" | |
| 2/24/58 | 10 | 10 | 8. **Good Golly, Miss Molly** | Specialty 624 |
| 6/23/58 | 31 | 3 | 9. Ooh! My Soul | Specialty 633 |
| | | | **LITTLE RIVER BAND** | |
| | | | Australian - Glenn Shorrock, lead singer | |
| 11/06/76 | 28 | 6 | 1. It's A Long Way There | Harvest 4318 |
| 9/24/77 | 14 | 11 | 2. Help Is On Its Way | Harvest 4428 |
| 1/21/78 | 16 | 9 | 3. Happy Anniversary | Harvest 4524 |
| 8/12/78 | 3 | 14 | 4. **Reminiscing** | Harvest 4605 |
| 1/27/79 | 10 | 14 | 5. **Lady** | Harvest 4667 |
| 8/04/79 | 6 | 14 | 6. **Lonesome Loser** | Capitol 4748 |
| 11/10/79 + | 10 | 13 | 7. **Cool Change** | Capitol 4789 |
| 9/05/81 | 6 | 14 | 8. **The Night Owls** | Capitol 5033 |
| 12/26/81 + | 10 | 15 | 9. **Take It Easy On Me** | Capitol 5057 |
| 4/24/82 | 14 | 9 | 10. Man On Your Mind | Capitol 5061 |
| 12/04/82 + | 11 | 13 | 11. The Other Guy | Capitol 5185 |
| 5/28/83 | 22 | 6 | 12. We Two | Capitol 5231 |
| | | | John Farnham replaces Shorrock as lead singer | |
| 8/27/83 | 35 | 3 | 13. You're Driving Me Out Of My Mind | Capitol 5256 |
| | | | **LITTLE SISTER** | |
| | | | Vanetta Stewart, sister of Sly Stone | |
| 3/28/70 | 22 | 6 | 1. You're The One - Part I | Stone Flower 9000 |
| 1/30/71 | 32 | 3 | 2. Somebody's Watching You | Stone Flower 9001 |
| | | | **LOBO** | |
| | | | Kent LaVoie from Florida | |
| 4/24/71 | 5 | 10 | 1. **Me And You And A Dog Named Boo** | Big Tree 112 |
| 10/14/72 | 2 (2) | 10 | ● 2. **I'd Love You To Want Me** | Big Tree 147 |
| 1/13/73 | 8 | 10 | 3. **Don't Expect Me To Be Your Friend** | Big Tree 158 |
| 5/05/73 | 27 | 5 | 4. It Sure Took A Long, Long Time | Big Tree 16001 |
| 7/21/73 | 22 | 8 | 5. How Can I Tell Her | Big Tree 16004 |
| 5/11/74 | 37 | 2 | 6. Standing At The End Of The Line | Big Tree 15001 |
| 4/26/75 | 27 | 4 | 7. Don't Tell Me Goodnight | Big Tree 16033 |
| 9/08/79 | 23 | 8 | 8. Where Were You When I Was Falling In Love | MCA 41065 |
| | | | **HANK LOCKLIN** | |
| 6/13/60 | 8 | 15 | 1. **Please Help Me, I'm Falling** | RCA 7692 |

| DATE | POS | WKS | ARTIST—Record Title | LABEL & NO. |
|---|---|---|---|---|
| | | | **LOGGINS & MESSINA** | |
| | | | Kenny Loggins & Jim Messina | |
| 12/02/72 + | 4 | 13 | ● 1. **Your Mama Don't Dance** | Columbia 45719 |
| 4/28/73 | 18 | 8 | 2. Thinking Of You | Columbia 45815 |
| 11/24/73 | 16 | 8 | 3. My Music | Columbia 45952 |
| | | | **DAVE LOGGINS** | |
| 7/13/74 | 5 | 10 | 1. **Please Come To Boston** | Epic 11115 |
| | | | **KENNY LOGGINS** | |
| | | | born on 1/7/48 in Everett, Washington | |
| 8/19/78 | 5 | 15 | 1. **Whenever I Call You "Friend"** | Columbia 10794 |
| | | | harmony vocal by Stevie Nicks | |
| 11/24/79 + | 11 | 16 | 2. This Is It | Columbia 11109 |
| 4/05/80 | 36 | 2 | 3. Keep The Fire | Columbia 11215 |
| 8/23/80 | 7 | 12 | 4. **I'm Alright** | Columbia 11317 |
| | | | theme from the film "Caddyshack" | |
| 12/11/82 + | 15 | 13 | 5. Heart To Heart | Columbia 03377 |
| 4/02/83 | 24 | 7 | 6. Welcome To Heartlight | Columbia 03555 |
| | | | inspired by writings of the children of Heartlight School | |
| 2/11/84 | 1 (3) | 16 | ● 7. **Footloose** | Columbia 04310 |
| 6/23/84 | 22 | 8 | 8. I'm Free (Heaven Helps The Man) | Columbia 04452 |
| | | | above 2 from the film "Footloose" | |
| | | | **KENNY LOGGINS with STEVE PERRY** | |
| | | | Steve is lead singer of Journey | |
| 9/25/82 | 17 | 6 | 1. Don't Fight It | Columbia 03192 |
| | | | **LOLITA** | |
| | | | Lolita Ditta - German | |
| 11/14/60 | 5 | 14 | 1. **Sailor (Your Home Is The Sea) [F]** | Kapp 349 |
| | | | **LONDON SYMPHONY ORCHESTRA -** **see JOHN WILLIAMS** | |
| | | | **JULIE LONDON** | |
| | | | Dixie McCall of TV's "Emergency" - former wife of Jack Webb | |
| 12/03/55 | 9 | 13 | 1. **Cry Me A River** | Liberty 55006 |
| | | | **LAURIE LONDON** | |
| | | | English lad - age 13 | |
| 3/24/58 | 1 (4) | 14 | ● 1. **He's Got The Whole World (In His Hands)** | Capitol 3891 |
| | | | **SHORTY LONG** | |
| | | | drowned on 6/29/69 | |
| 6/15/68 | 8 | 8 | 1. **Here Comes The Judge [N]** | Soul 35044 |
| | | | **LOOKING GLASS** | |
| | | | New Jersey quartet | |
| 7/01/72 | 1 (1) | 14 | ● 1. **Brandy (You're A Fine Girl)** | Epic 10874 |
| 9/29/73 | 33 | 3 | 2. Jimmy Loves Mary-Anne | Epic 11001 |
| | | | **TRINI LOPEZ** | |
| | | | born on 5/15/37 in Dallas, Texas | |
| 8/10/63 | 3 | 11 | 1. **If I Had A Hammer** | Reprise 20198 |
| 12/14/63 + | 23 | 6 | 2. Kansas City | Reprise 20236 |

| DATE | POS | WKS | ARTIST—Record Title | LABEL & NO. |
|---|---|---|---|---|
| 2/06/65 | 20 | 5 | 3. Lemon Tree | Reprise 0336 |
| 5/07/66 | 39 | 3 | 4. I'm Comin' Home, Cindy | Reprise 0455 |
| | | | **LOS BRAVOS** | |
| | | | rock quintet from Spain - Mike Kogel (Kennedy), lead singer | |
| 9/10/66 | 4 | 8 | 1. **Black Is Black** | Press 60002 |
| | | | **LOS INDIOS TABAJARAS** | |
| | | | Brazilian brothers: Natalicio & Antenor Moreyra Lima | |
| 10/12/63 | 6 | 10 | 1. **Maria Elena [I]** | RCA 8216 |
| | | | **LOST GENERATION** | |
| 8/01/70 | 30 | 5 | 1. The Sly, Slick, And The Wicked | Brunswick 55436 |
| | | | **BONNIE LOU** | |
| 11/26/55 | 14 | 3 | 1. Daddy-O | King 4835 |
| | | | **JOHN D. LOUDERMILK** | |
| | | | also see Johnny Dee | |
| 12/04/61 | 32 | 3 | 1. Language Of Love | RCA 7938 |
| | | | **LOVE** | |
| | | | Los Angeles rock group led by Arthur Lee | |
| 9/10/66 | 33 | 3 | 1. 7 And 7 Is | Elektra 45605 |
| | | | **LOVE & KISSES** | |
| | | | disco production by Alec Costandinos | |
| 6/24/78 | 22 | 6 | 1. Thank God It's Friday | Casablanca 925 |
| | | | **LOVE UNLIMITED** | |
| | | | Barry White's vocal back-up trio | |
| 5/06/72 | 14 | 9 | ● 1. Walkin' In The Rain With The One I Love | Uni 55319 |
| 1/04/75 | 27 | 7 | 2. I Belong To You | 20th Century 2141 |
| | | | **LOVE UNLIMITED ORCHESTRA** | |
| | | | studio orchestra conducted by Barry White | |
| 12/22/73 + | 1 (1) | 16 | ● 1. **Love's Theme [I]** | 20th Century 2069 |
| 3/15/75 | 22 | 5 | 2. Satin Soul [I] | 20th Century 2162 |
| | | | **DARLENE LOVE** | |
| | | | recorded with the Blossoms, the Crystals, and Bob B. Soxx & The Blue Jeans | |
| 5/11/63 | 39 | 1 | 1. (Today I Met) The Boy I'm Gonna Marry | Philles 111 |
| 8/24/63 | 26 | 4 | 2. Wait Til' My Bobby Gets Home | Philles 114 |
| | | | **LOVERBOY** | |
| | | | Canadian quintet led by Mike Reno (vocals) & Paul Dean (guitar) | |
| 3/21/81 | 35 | 6 | 1. Turn Me Loose | Columbia 11421 |
| 1/09/82 | 29 | 8 | 2. Working For The Weekend | Columbia 02589 |
| 5/15/82 | 26 | 6 | 3. When It's Over | Columbia 02814 |
| | | | backing vocals by Nancy Nash | |
| 7/02/83 | 11 | 11 | 4. Hot Girls In Love | Columbia 03941 |
| 10/29/83 | 34 | 3 | 5. Queen Of The Broken Hearts | Columbia 04096 |

| DATE | POS | WKS | ARTIST—Record Title | LABEL & NO. |
|---|---|---|---|---|
| | | | **LOVIN' SPOONFUL** | |
| | | | John Sebastian, lead singer and co-founder with Zal Yanovsky, Steve Boone & Joe Butler | |
| 9/18/65 | 9 | 8 | 1. **Do You Believe In Magic** | Kama Sutra 201 |
| 12/11/65 + | 10 | 9 | 2. **You Didn't Have To Be So Nice** | Kama Sutra 205 |
| 3/12/66 | 2 (2) | 10 | 3. **Daydream** | Kama Sutra 208 |
| 5/14/66 | 2 (2) | 9 | 4. **Did You Ever Have To Make Up Your Mind?** | Kama Sutra 209 |
| 7/23/66 | 1 (3) | 10 | ● 5. **Summer In The City** | Kama Sutra 211 |
| 10/22/66 | 10 | 8 | 6. **Rain On The Roof** | Kama Sutra 216 |
| 12/31/66 + | 8 | 8 | 7. **Nashville Cats** | Kama Sutra 219 |
| 2/25/67 | 15 | 5 | 8. Darling Be Home Soon | Kama Sutra 220 |
| | | | from the film "You're A Big Boy Now" | |
| 5/20/67 | 18 | 5 | 9. Six O'Clock | Kama Sutra 225 |
| 11/11/67 | 27 | 3 | 10. She Is Still A Mystery | Kama Sutra 239 |
| | | | **JIM LOWE** | |
| | | | disc jockey | |
| 9/29/56 | 1 (3) | 22 | 1. **The Green Door** | Dot 15486 |
| 5/13/57 | 15 | 6 | 2. Four Walls/ | |
| 5/13/57 | 20 | 5 | 3. Talkin' To The Blues | Dot 15569 |
| | | | **NICK LOWE** | |
| | | | English - member of Brinsley Schwarz ('70-'75) | |
| 8/18/79 | 12 | 10 | 1. Cruel To Be Kind | Columbia 11018 |
| | | | **L.T.D.** | |
| | | | Jeffrey Osborne, lead singer of 10 man R&B/funk band | |
| 11/06/76 | 20 | 9 | 1. Love Ballad | A&M 1847 |
| 11/12/77 | 4 | 12 | ● 2. **(Every Time I Turn Around) Back In Love Again** | A&M 1974 |
| 1/31/81 | 40 | 1 | 3. Shine On | A&M 2283 |
| | | | **ROBIN LUKE** | |
| 8/18/58 | 5 | 15 | 1. **Susie Darlin'** | Dot 15781 |
| | | | **LULU** | |
| | | | British - real name Marie Lawrie - formerly married to Maurice Gibb (Bee Gees) | |
| 9/23/67 | 1 (5) | 15 | ● 1. **To Sir With Love** | Epic 10187 |
| 1/06/68 | 32 | 3 | 2. Best Of Both Worlds | Epic 10260 |
| 2/07/70 | 22 | 8 | 3. Oh Me Oh My (I'm A Fool For You Baby) | Atco 6722 |
| 8/22/81 | 18 | 10 | 4. I Could Never Miss You (More Than I Do) | Alfa 7006 |
| | | | **BOB LUMAN** | |
| | | | died on 12/27/78 (40) | |
| 9/26/60 | 7 | 9 | 1. **Let's Think About Living [N]** | Warner 5172 |
| | | | **VICTOR LUNDBERG** | |
| 11/25/67 | 10 | 4 | 1. **An Open Letter To My Teenage Son [S]** | Liberty 55996 |
| | | | **ARTHUR LYMAN Group** | |
| | | | percussionist (vibes/marimba) from Hawaii | |
| 6/12/61 | 4 | 10 | 1. **Yellow Bird [I]** | Hi Fi 5024 |

| DATE | POS | WKS | ARTIST—Record Title | LABEL & NO. |
|------|-----|-----|---------------------|-------------|
| | | | **FRANKIE LYMON & The Teenagers** | |
| | | | Frankie was born on 9/30/42 in New York City - died 2/28/68 (25) | |
| 2/18/56 | 6 | 16 | 1. **Why Do Fools Fall In Love** | Gee 1002 |
| 5/12/56 | 13 | 11 | 2. I Want You To Be My Girl | Gee 1012 |
| 8/26/57 | 20 | 7 | 3. Goody Goody | Gee 1039 |
| | | | **BARBARA LYNN** | |
| | | | born Barbara Lynn Ozone on 1/16/42 in Beaumont, Texas | |
| 7/14/62 | 8 | 8 | 1. **You'll Lose A Good Thing** | Jamie 1220 |
| | | | **CHERYL LYNN** | |
| | | | discovered on TV's "Gong Show" | |
| 1/06/79 | 12 | 12 | ● 1. Got To Be Real | Columbia 10808 |
| | | | **GLORIA LYNNE** | |
| | | | jazz singer from New York City | |
| 2/29/64 | 28 | 4 | 1. I Wish You Love | Everest 2036 |
| | | | **LYNYRD SKYNYRD** | |
| | | | Jacksonville, Florida Southern rock band - plane crash on 10/20/77 killed leader Ronnie Van Zant (28) and members Steve & Cassie Gaines | |
| 8/24/74 | 8 | 11 | 1. **Sweet Home Alabama** | MCA 40258 |
| 1/04/75 | 19 | 5 | 2. Free Bird | MCA 40328 |
| 7/19/75 | 27 | 3 | 3. Saturday Night Special | MCA 40416 |
| 1/08/77 | 38 | 2 | 4. Free Bird | MCA 40665 |
| | | | live version of #2 above | |
| 1/07/78 | 13 | 11 | 5. What's Your Name | MCA 40819 |
| | | | **M** | |
| | | | M is Robin Scott | |
| 8/25/79 | 1 (1) | 20 | ● 1. **Pop Muzik** | Sire 49033 |
| | | | **MOMS MABLEY** | |
| | | | comedienne - real name: Loretta Mary Aiken - died 5/23/75 (78) | |
| 7/19/69 | 35 | 2 | 1. Abraham, Martin And John | Mercury 72935 |
| | | | **BYRON MacGREGOR** | |
| | | | news director of CKLW Radio in Detroit | |
| 1/12/74 | 4 | 9 | ● 1. **Americans [S]** | Westbound 222 |
| | | | **MARY MacGREGOR** | |
| | | | pop singer from St. Paul, Minnesota | |
| 12/25/76 + | 1 (2) | 16 | ● 1. **Torn Between Two Lovers** | Ariola Am. 7638 |
| 10/06/79 | 39 | 2 | 2. Good Friend | RSO 938 |
| | | | from the movie "Meatballs" | |
| | | | **LONNIE MACK** | |
| | | | full name: Lonnie McIntosh | |
| 6/22/63 | 5 | 10 | 1. **Memphis [I]** | Fraternity 906 |
| 9/21/63 | 24 | 4 | 2. Wham! [I] | Fraternity 912 |
| | | | **GISELE MacKENZIE** | |
| | | | star of TV's "Your Hit Parade" | |
| 6/04/55 | 4 | 19 | 1. **Hard To Get** | X 0137 |

| DATE | POS | WKS | ARTIST—Record Title | LABEL & NO. |
|---|---|---|---|---|
| | | | **GORDON MacRAE** | |
| | | | starred in the film musicals "Oklahoma" and "Carousel" | |
| 10/06/58 | **18** | 6 | 1. The Secret | Capitol 4033 |
| | | | **JOHNNY MADDOX & The Rhythm Masters** | |
| 2/05/55 | **2** (7) | 20 | 1. **The Crazy Otto (Medley) [I]** | Dot 15325 |
| | | | cover of orginal version by the honky tonk piano player Crazy Otto | |
| | | | **BETTY MADIGAN** | |
| 9/08/58 | **31** | 3 | 1. Dance Everyone Dance | Coral 62007 |
| | | | based on the Israeli harvest song "Hava Nagila" | |
| | | | **MADNESS** | |
| | | | septet from London, England | |
| 5/28/83 | **7** | 13 | 1. **Our House** | Geffen 29668 |
| 9/17/83 | **33** | 5 | 2. It Must Be Love | Geffen 29562 |
| | | | **MADONNA** | |
| | | | Madonna Ciccone from Detroit | |
| 12/10/83 + | **16** | 11 | 1. Holiday | Sire 29478 |
| 4/14/84 | **10** | 15 | 2. **Borderline** | Sire 29354 |
| 9/01/84 | **4** | 12 | 3. **Lucky Star** | Sire 29177 |
| | | | **JOHNNY MAESTRO** | |
| | | | lead singer of the Crests and Brooklyn Bridge | |
| 3/20/61 | **20** | 5 | 1. Model Girl | Coed 545 |
| 5/22/61 | **33** | 4 | 2. What A Surprise | Coed 549 |
| | | | **CLEDUS MAGGARD & The Citizen's Band** | |
| | | | Cledus' real name: Jay Huguely | |
| 1/24/76 | **19** | 9 | 1. The White Knight [N] | Mercury 73751 |
| | | | **MAGIC LANTERNS** | |
| | | | English rock quintet | |
| 11/30/68 | **29** | 5 | 1. Shame, Shame | Atlantic 2560 |
| | | | **GEORGE MAHARIS** | |
| | | | Buz Murdock of TV's "Route 66" | |
| 5/26/62 | **25** | 5 | 1. Teach Me Tonight | Epic 9504 |
| | | | **MAIN INGREDIENT** | |
| | | | New York soul trio - original lead singer, Don McPherson, died 7/4/71 (29) - replaced by Cuba Gooding | |
| 9/02/72 | **3** | 10 | ● 1. **Everybody Plays The Fool** | RCA 0731 |
| 3/16/74 | **10** | 14 | ● 2. **Just Don't Want To Be Lonely** | RCA 0205 |
| 8/10/74 | **35** | 2 | 3. Happiness Is Just Around The Bend | RCA 0305 |
| | | | **MAJORS** | |
| | | | quintet from Philadelphia - Ricky Cordo, lead singer | |
| 9/08/62 | **22** | 5 | 1. A Wonderful Dream | Imperial 5855 |
| | | | **MIRIAM MAKEBA** | |
| | | | native of South Africa - married to Hugh Masekela | |
| 10/28/67 | **12** | 8 | 1. Pata Pata [F] | Reprise 0606 |

| DATE | POS | WKS | ARTIST—Record Title | LABEL & NO. |
|---|---|---|---|---|
| | | | **MALO** | |
| | | | latin-rock band formed by Jorge Santana (brother of Carlos) | |
| 4/01/72 | 18 | 8 | 1. Suavecito | Warner 7559 |
| | | | **RICHARD MALTBY & his Orchestra** | |
| 3/31/56 | 14 | 8 | 1. Themes From "The Man With The Golden Arm" [I] | Vik 0196 |
| | | | **MAMA CASS** | |
| | | | Cass Elliot of The Mamas & The Papas - died on 7/29/74 (30) | |
| 7/27/68 | 12 | 8 | 1. Dream A Little Dream Of Me | Dunhill 4145 |
| | | | with The Mamas & The Papas | |
| 8/02/69 | 30 | 7 | 2. It's Getting Better | Dunhill 4195 |
| 11/15/69 | 36 | 3 | 3. Make Your Own Kind Of Music | Dunhill 4214 |
| | | | **MAMAS & THE PAPAS** | |
| | | | Cass Elliot, Michelle Phillips, John Phillips & Denny Doherty | |
| 2/05/66 | 4 | 13 | ● 1. **California Dreamin'** | Dunhill 4020 |
| 4/16/66 | 1 (3) | 10 | ● 2. **Monday, Monday** | Dunhill 4026 |
| 7/09/66 | 5 | 8 | 3. **I Saw Her Again** | Dunhill 4031 |
| 11/05/66 | 24 | 4 | 4. Look Through My Window | Dunhill 4050 |
| 12/17/66 + | 5 | 9 | 5. **Words Of Love** | Dunhill 4057 |
| 3/04/67 | 2 (3) | 9 | 6. **Dedicated To The One I Love** | Dunhill 4077 |
| 5/13/67 | 5 | 7 | 7. **Creeque Alley** | Dunhill 4083 |
| 9/02/67 | 20 | 5 | 8. Twelve Thirty (Young Girls Are Coming To The Canyon) | Dunhill 4099 |
| 11/04/67 | 26 | 5 | 9. Glad To Be Unhappy | Dunhill 4107 |
| | | | **MELISSA MANCHESTER** | |
| | | | singer/songwriter/pianist - born 2/15/51 in the Bronx, New York | |
| 6/14/75 | 6 | 11 | 1. **Midnight Blue** | Arista 0116 |
| 10/18/75 | 30 | 5 | 2. Just Too Many People | Arista 0146 |
| 2/28/76 | 27 | 4 | 3. Just You And I | Arista 0168 |
| 1/06/79 | 10 | 14 | 4. **Don't Cry Out Loud** | Arista 0373 |
| 11/24/79 | 39 | 2 | 5. Pretty Girls | Arista 0456 |
| 4/05/80 | 32 | 5 | 6. Fire In The Morning | Arista 0485 |
| 7/10/82 | 5 | 15 | 7. **You Should Hear How She Talks About You** | Arista 0676 |
| | | | **HENRY MANCINI & His Orchestra** | |
| | | | top movie-TV composer/arranger/conductor | |
| 4/18/60 | 21 | 8 | 1. Mr. Lucky [I] | RCA 7705 |
| 11/13/61 | 11 | 16 | 2. Moon River | RCA 7916 |
| | | | from the film "Breakfast At Tiffany's" | |
| 3/02/63 | 33 | 10 | 3. Days Of Wine And Roses | RCA 8120 |
| 1/25/64 | 36 | 4 | 4. Charade | RCA 8256 |
| 5/09/64 | 31 | 2 | 5. The Pink Panther Theme [I] | RCA 8286 |
| 5/24/69 | 1 (2) | 12 | ● 6. **Love Theme From Romeo & Juliet [I]** | RCA 0131 |
| 2/06/71 | 13 | 8 | 7. Theme From Love Story [I] | RCA 9927 |
| | | | **BARBARA MANDRELL** | |
| | | | born on 12/25/48 in Houston, Texas | |
| 5/12/79 | 31 | 5 | 1. (If Loving You Is Wrong) I Don't Want To Be Right | ABC 12451 |

| DATE | POS | WKS | ARTIST—Record Title | LABEL & NO. |
|---|---|---|---|---|
| | | | **MANFRED MANN** | |
| | | | British band led by keyboardist Manfred Mann | |
| 9/12/64 | **1** (2) | 12 | 1. **Do Wah Diddy Diddy** | Ascot 2157 |
| 11/28/64 + | **12** | 9 | 2. Sha La La | Ascot 2165 |
| 7/23/66 | **29** | 5 | 3. Pretty Flamingo | United Art. 50040 |
| 3/09/68 | **10** | 10 | 4. **Mighty Quinn (Quinn The Eskimo)** | Mercury 72770 |
| | | | **MANFRED MANN'S EARTH BAND** | |
| 12/18/76 + | **1** (1) | 15 | ● 1. **Blinded By The Light** | Warner 8252 |
| 6/04/77 | **40** | 1 | 2. Spirit In The Night [R] | Warner 8355 |
| | | | re-entry of 1976 hit (Pos. 97) | |
| 2/18/84 | **22** | 8 | 3. Runner | Arista 9143 |
| | | | **CHUCK MANGIONE** | |
| | | | pop-jazz flugelhornist/composer | |
| 3/18/78 | **4** | 16 | 1. **Feels So Good [I]** | A&M 2001 |
| 2/16/80 | **18** | 9 | 2. Give It All You Got [I] | A&M 2211 |
| | | | featured song by ABC Sports for the 1980 Winter Olympics | |
| | | | **MANHATTAN TRANSFER** | |
| | | | versatile vocal harmony quartet | |
| 11/01/75 | **22** | 5 | 1. Operator | Atlantic 3292 |
| 5/31/80 | **30** | 4 | 2. Twilight Zone/Twilight Tone | Atlantic 3649 |
| 6/13/81 | **7** | 13 | 3. **Boy From New York City** | Atlantic 3816 |
| 11/05/83 | **40** | 2 | 4. Spice Of Life | Atlantic 89786 |
| | | | **MANHATTANS** | |
| | | | soul ballad quartet formed in 1962 | |
| 2/15/75 | **37** | 2 | 1. Don't Take Your Love | Columbia 10045 |
| 5/29/76 | **1** (2) | 17 | ★ 2. **Kiss And Say Goodbye** | Columbia 10310 |
| 5/31/80 | **5** | 14 | ● 3. **Shining Star** | Columbia 11222 |
| | | | **BARRY MANILOW** | |
| | | | pop singer/songwriter born on 6/17/46 in Brooklyn, New York | |
| 12/07/74 + | **1** (1) | 12 | ● 1. **Mandy** | Bell 45613 |
| 3/29/75 | **12** | 8 | 2. It's A Miracle | Arista 0108 |
| 7/26/75 | **6** | 12 | 3. **Could It Be Magic** | Arista 0126 |
| 11/22/75 + | **1** (1) | 16 | ● 4. **I Write The Songs** | Arista 0157 |
| 4/10/76 | **10** | 10 | 5. **Tryin' To Get The Feeling Again** | Arista 0172 |
| 10/09/76 | **29** | 5 | 6. This One's For You | Arista 0206 |
| 12/25/76 + | **10** | 13 | 7. **Weekend In New England** | Arista 0212 |
| 5/28/77 | **1** (1) | 13 | ● 8. **Looks Like We Made It** | Arista 0244 |
| 10/22/77 | **23** | 5 | 9. Daybreak | Arista 0273 |
| 2/18/78 | **3** | 16 | ● 10. **Can't Smile Without You** | Arista 0305 |
| 6/10/78 | **19** | 4 | 11. Even Now | Arista 0330 |
| 7/08/78 | **8** | 9 | ● 12. **Copacabana (At The Copa)** | Arista 0339 |
| 10/07/78 | **11** | 10 | 13. Ready To Take A Chance Again | Arista 0357 |
| | | | above 2 from the movie "Foul Play" | |
| 1/06/79 | **9** | 10 | 14. **Somewhere In The Night** | Arista 0382 |
| 10/20/79 | **9** | 11 | 15. **Ships** | Arista 0464 |
| 2/02/80 | **20** | 7 | 16. When I Wanted You | Arista 0481 |

| DATE | POS | WKS | ARTIST—Record Title | LABEL & NO. |
|------|-----|-----|---------------------|-------------|
| 5/17/80 | 36 | 4 | 17. I Don't Want To Walk Without You | Arista 0501 |
| 12/06/80 + | 10 | 11 | 18. **I Made It Through The Rain** | Arista 0566 |
| 10/17/81 | 15 | 10 | 19. The Old Songs | Arista 0633 |
| 1/23/82 | 21 | 7 | 20. Somewhere Down The Road | Arista 0658 |
| 4/24/82 | 32 | 4 | 21. Let's Hang On | Arista 0675 |
| 9/18/82 | 38 | 2 | 22. Oh Julie | Arista 0698 |
| 1/15/83 | 39 | 2 | 23. Memory<br>theme from the musical "Cats" | Arista 1025 |
| 4/09/83 | 26 | 7 | 24. Some Kind Of Friend | Arista 1046 |
| 11/26/83 + | 18 | 10 | 25. Read 'Em And Weep | Arista 9101 |
| | | | **BARRY MANN**<br>one of pop music's most prolific songwriters | |
| 8/21/61 | 7 | 9 | 1. **Who Put The Bomp (In The Bomp, Bomp, Bomp) [N]** | ABC-Para. 10237 |
| | | | **CARL MANN**<br>16-year-old from Jackson, Tennessee | |
| 7/27/59 | 25 | 6 | 1. Mona Lisa | Phillips 3539 |
| | | | **GLORIA MANN** | |
| 2/12/55 | 18 | 2 | 1. Earth Angel (Will You Be Mine) | Sound 109 |
| 12/24/55 + | 19 | 8 | 2. Teen Age Prayer | Sound 126 |
| | | | **HERBIE MANN**<br>jazz flautist - born on 4/16/30 in Brooklyn, New York | |
| 4/26/75 | 14 | 6 | 1. Hijack | Atlantic 3246 |
| 3/17/79 | 26 | 6 | 2. Superman | Atlantic 3547 |
| | | | **MANTOVANI & His Orchestra**<br>Annunzio Paolo Mantovani, born in Venice, Italy -<br>died on 3/29/80 (74) | |
| 7/22/57 | 12 | 14 | 1. Around The World (In Eighty Days) [I]<br>trumpet solo by Stan Newsome | London 1746 |
| 1/23/61 | 31 | 2 | 2. Main Theme From Exodus [I] | London 1953 |
| | | | **MARATHONS**<br>also recorded as The Jayhawks and The Vibrations | |
| 5/22/61 | 20 | 7 | 1. Peanut Butter | Arvee 5027 |
| | | | **MARCELS**<br>quintet from Pittsburgh - Cornelius Harp, lead singer;<br>Fred Johnson, bass singer | |
| 3/20/61 | 1 (3) | 11 | 1. **Blue Moon** | Colpix 186 |
| 10/30/61 | 7 | 9 | 2. **Heartaches** | Colpix 612 |
| | | | **LITTLE PEGGY MARCH**<br>Philadelphian - born on 3/7/48 | |
| 4/06/63 | 1 (3) | 11 | 1. **I Will Follow Him** | RCA 8139 |
| 6/29/63 | 32 | 3 | 2. I Wish I Were A Princess | RCA 8189 |
| 9/28/63 | 26 | 4 | 3. Hello Heartache, Goodbye Love | RCA 8221 |
| | | | **BOBBY MARCHAN**<br>member of Huey Smith's Clowns | |
| 7/11/60 | 31 | 4 | 1. There's Something On Your Mind, Part 2 [N] | Fire 1022 |

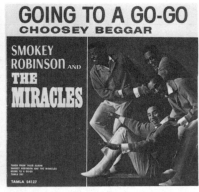

**Steve Miller's** early days as a blues-band leader were highlighted by a live album with Chuck Berry. Later incarnations of his group featured Boz Scaggs and keyboard ace Nicky Hopkins.

**Smokey Robinson and the Miracles** failed a 1957 audition for one of Jackie Wilson's managers. But Berry Gordy liked Smokey's original material and recorded their first single ("Got a Job") shortly thereafter.

**Eddie Money** is a versatile guy. He used to be a New York City cop named Eddie Mahoney; in the video for "Think I'm in Love" he plays a vampire.

**The Monkees** were a concoction of music biz mogul Don Kirshner. He previously employed Brill Building songwriters like Carole King and Neil Sedaka, and later inflicted the Archies upon the world.

**Lou Monte.** Sure, you love New Jersey's Lou Monte for "Pepino the Italian Mouse." But do you know "Please Mr. Columbus (Turn the Ship Around)" or "Bossa Nova Italiano"?

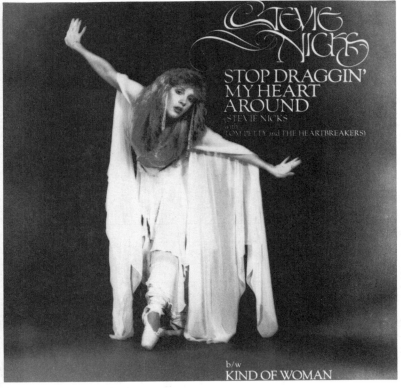

**Ricky Nelson,** so legend has it, began recording to save face. When a date gushed over Elvis, young Rick bragged that he was about to make a record, too. And he did!

**Willie Nelson.** Back in his struggling, short-haired days, Houston-based songwriter Willie Nelson sold his composition "Family Bible" outright for $50. Shortly thereafter, Claude Gray had a Top Ten country hit with the very same song, which must have given Willie ulcers.

**Olivia Newton-John** didn't let the box-office failure of *Two of a Kind* prevent her from scoring a hit with "Twist of Fate," a song from the movie. It was a rerun of 1980's commercial flop *Xanadu,* from which she extracted an impressive total of three hits.

**Stevie Nicks** takes her mythology seriously. Her first Fleetwood Mac hit, "Rhiannon (Will You Ever Win)," concerns a Welsh witch, and the name of her publishing company is Welsh Witch.

**Aldo Nova's** heavy hit "Fantasy" contains the following lyric: "See the girls with dresses so tight/Give you love if the price is right." Pure poetry!

| DATE | POS | WKS | ARTIST—Record Title | LABEL & NO. |
|---|---|---|---|---|
| | | | **BENNY MARDONES** | |
| | | | Savage, Maryland native | |
| 7/12/80 | 11 | 12 | 1. Into The Night | Polydor 2091 |
| | | | **ERNIE MARESCA** | |
| | | | wrote "Runaround Sue" & "The Wanderer" for Dion | |
| 4/21/62 | 6 | 9 | 1. **Shout! Shout! (Knock Yourself Out)** | Seville 117 |
| | | | **TEENA MARIE** | |
| | | | white soul singer from California - real name: Mary Brocker | |
| 1/17/81 | 37 | 3 | 1. I Need Your Lovin' | Gordy 7189 |
| | | | **MARK IV** | |
| | | | Chicago quartet | |
| 2/09/59 | 24 | 7 | 1. I Got A Wife [N] | Mercury 71403 |
| | | | **MARKETTS** | |
| | | | West Coast instrumental surf group | |
| 2/17/62 | 31 | 3 | 1. Surfer's Stomp [I] | Liberty 55401 |
| 12/28/63 + | 3 | 11 | 2. **Out Of Limits [I]** | Warner 5391 |
| 2/26/66 | 17 | 5 | 3. Batman Theme [I] | Warner 5696 |
| | | | **MAR-KEYS** | |
| | | | 7-man group from Memphis featuring Steve Cropper & Duck Dunn | |
| 7/17/61 | 3 | 12 | 1. **Last Night [I]** | Satellite 107 |
| | | | **PIGMEAT MARKHAM** | |
| | | | vaudeville comedian - died on 12/13/81 | |
| 7/06/68 | 19 | 4 | 1. Here Comes The Judge [N] | Chess 2049 |
| | | | **MARION MARLOWE** | |
| 7/16/55 | 14 | 2 | 1. The Man In The Raincoat | Cadence 1266 |
| | | | **MARMALADE** | |
| | | | British quintet - Dean Ford, lead singer | |
| 4/04/70 | 10 | 11 | 1. **Reflections Of My Life** | London 20058 |
| | | | **MARSHALL TUCKER BAND** | |
| | | | South Carolina Southern rock band - Doug Gray, lead singer; Toy Caldwell, lead guitar | |
| 12/20/75 | 38 | 2 | 1. Fire On The Mountain | Capricorn 0244 |
| 4/16/77 | 14 | 13 | 2. Heard It In A Love Song | Capricorn 0270 |
| | | | **RALPH MARTERIE & His Orchestra** | |
| | | | died on 10/8/78 (63) | |
| 3/30/57 | 25 | 3 | 1. Tricky [I] | Mercury 71050 |
| 5/13/57 | 10 | 6 | 2. **Shish-Kebab [I]** | Mercury 71092 |
| | | | **MARTHA & THE VANDELLAS** | |
| | | | Detroit trio led by Martha Reeves | |
| 5/18/63 | 29 | 8 | 1. Come And Get These Memories | Gordy 7014 |
| 8/17/63 | 4 | 11 | 2. **Heat Wave** | Gordy 7022 |
| 12/07/63 + | 8 | 9 | 3. **Quicksand** | Gordy 7025 |
| 9/05/64 | 2 (2) | 11 | 4. **Dancing In The Street** | Gordy 7033 |
| 12/26/64 + | 34 | 4 | 5. Wild One | Gordy 7036 |

| DATE | POS | WKS | ARTIST—Record Title | LABEL & NO. |
|------|-----|-----|---------------------|-------------|
| 3/13/65 | **8** | 8 | 6. **Nowhere To Run** | Gordy 7039 |
| 9/11/65 | **36** | 2 | 7. You've Been In Love Too Long | Gordy 7045 |
| 2/19/66 | **22** | 7 | 8. My Baby Loves Me | Gordy 7048 |
| 11/12/66 | **9** | 7 | 9. **I'm Ready For Love** | Gordy 7056 |
| 3/18/67 | **10** | 10 | 10. **Jimmy Mack** | Gordy 7058 |
| 9/09/67 | **25** | 6 | 11. Love Bug Leave My Heart Alone | Gordy 7062 |
| | | | MARTHA REEVES & THE VANDELLAS: | |
| 12/02/67 | **11** | 9 | 12. Honey Chile | Gordy 7067 |
| | | | **BOBBI MARTIN** | |
| 1/02/65 | **19** | 7 | 1. Don't Forget I Still Love You | Coral 62426 |
| 4/11/70 | **13** | 10 | 2. For The Love Of Him | United Art. 50602 |
| | | | **DEAN MARTIN** | |
| | | | born Dino Crocetti in Steubenville, Ohio on 6/7/17 | |
| 12/03/55 + | **1** (6) | 19 | 1. **Memories Are Made Of This** | Capitol 3295 |
| | | | with The Easy Riders | |
| 4/07/56 | **27** | 4 | 2. Innamorata | Capitol 3352 |
| | | | from the film "Artists & Models" | |
| 5/26/56 | **22** | 6 | 3. Standing On The Corner | Capitol 3414 |
| | | | from the musical "The Most Happy Fella" | |
| 4/07/58 | **4** | 18 | 4. **Return To Me** | Capitol 3894 |
| 8/04/58 | **30** | 3 | 5. Angel Baby | Capitol 3988 |
| 8/11/58 | **12** | 10 | 6. Volare (Nel Blu Dipinto Di Blu) | Capitol 4028 |
| 7/11/64 | **1** (1) | 13 | ● 7. **Everybody Loves Somebody** | Reprise 0281 |
| 10/17/64 | **6** | 8 | 8. **The Door Is Still Open To My Heart** | Reprise 0307 |
| 1/09/65 | **25** | 5 | 9. You're Nobody Till Somebody Loves You | Reprise 0333 |
| 3/13/65 | **22** | 5 | 10. Send Me The Pillow You Dream On | Reprise 0344 |
| 6/12/65 | **32** | 3 | 11. (Remember Me) I'm The One Who Loves You | Reprise 0369 |
| 8/21/65 | **21** | 7 | 12. Houston | Reprise 0393 |
| 11/13/65 | **10** | 8 | 13. **I Will** | Reprise 0415 |
| 3/05/66 | **32** | 4 | 14. Somewhere There's A Someone | Reprise 0443 |
| 6/11/66 | **35** | 1 | 15. Come Running Back | Reprise 0466 |
| 7/22/67 | **25** | 4 | 16. In The Chapel In The Moonlight | Reprise 0601 |
| 9/09/67 | **38** | 2 | 17. Little Ole Wine Drinker, Me | Reprise 0608 |
| | | | **MOON MARTIN** | |
| 9/22/79 | **30** | 4 | 1. Rolene | Capitol 4765 |
| | | | **STEVE MARTIN** | |
| | | | popular television and film comedian | |
| 7/08/78 | **17** | 7 | ● 1. King Tut [N] | Warner 8577 |
| | | | with The Toot Uncommons | |
| | | | **TONY MARTIN** | |
| | | | real name: Alvin Morris, Jr. | |
| 5/26/56 | **10** | 11 | 1. **Walk Hand In Hand** | RCA 6493 |
| | | | **TRADE MARTIN** | |
| 11/17/62 | **28** | 4 | 1. That Stranger Used To Be My Girl | Coed 570 |
| | | | **VINCE MARTIN with The Tarriers** | |
| | | | also see Tarriers | |
| 10/13/56 | **9** | 15 | 1. **Cindy, Oh Cindy** | Glory 247 |

| DATE | POS | WKS | ARTIST—Record Title | LABEL & NO. |
|---|---|---|---|---|
| | | | **WINK MARTINDALE** | |
| | | | TV game show host | |
| 9/28/59 | 7 | 12 | 1. **Deck Of Cards [S]** | Dot 15968 |
| | | | **AL MARTINO** | |
| | | | born Alfred Cini in Philadelphia on 10/7/27 | |
| 5/04/63 | 3 | 11 | 1. **I Love You Because** | Capitol 4930 |
| 8/17/63 | 15 | 8 | 2. Painted, Tainted Rose | Capitol 5000 |
| 11/16/63 | 22 | 6 | 3. Living A Lie | Capitol 5060 |
| 2/15/64 | 9 | 8 | 4. **I Love You More And More Every Day** | Capitol 5108 |
| 5/30/64 | 20 | 6 | 5. Tears And Roses | Capitol 5183 |
| 9/12/64 | 33 | 4 | 6. Always Together | Capitol 5239 |
| 12/18/65 + | 15 | 9 | 7. Spanish Eyes | Capitol 5542 |
| 4/02/66 | 30 | 4 | 8. Think I'll Go Somewhere And Cry Myself To Sleep | Capitol 5598 |
| 6/17/67 | 27 | 5 | 9. Mary In The Morning | Capitol 5904 |
| 2/08/75 | 17 | 8 | 10. To The Door Of The Sun (Alle Porte Del Sole) | Capitol 3987 |
| 12/06/75 | 33 | 4 | 11. Volare | Capitol 4134 |
| | | | **MARVELETTES** | |
| | | | Detroit trio led by Gladys Horton | |
| 10/16/61 | 1 (1) | 15 | 1. **Please Mr. Postman** | Tamla 54046 |
| 3/03/62 | 34 | 1 | 2. Twistin' Postman | Tamla 54054 |
| 5/26/62 | 7 | 11 | 3. **Playboy** | Tamla 54060 |
| 9/01/62 | 17 | 7 | 4. Beechwood 4-5789 | Tamla 54065 |
| 12/05/64 + | 25 | 8 | 5. Too Many Fish In The Sea | Tamla 54105 |
| 7/03/65 | 34 | 1 | 6. I'll Keep Holding On | Tamla 54116 |
| 1/29/66 | 7 | 8 | 7. **Don't Mess With Bill** | Tamla 54126 |
| 2/18/67 | 13 | 7 | 8. The Hunter Gets Captured By The Game | Tamla 54143 |
| 5/20/67 | 23 | 5 | 9. When You're Young And In Love | Tamla 54150 |
| 1/06/68 | 17 | 8 | 10. My Baby Must Be A Magician | Tamla 54158 |
| | | | **MARVELOWS** | |
| | | | quintet from Chicago, Illinois | |
| 7/03/65 | 37 | 1 | 1. I Do | ABC-Para. 10629 |
| | | | **HUGH MASEKELA** | |
| | | | native of South Africa - married to Miriam Makeba | |
| 6/22/68 | 1 (2) | 10 | • 1. **Grazing In The Grass [I]** | Uni 55066 |
| | | | **MASHMAKHAN** | |
| 11/07/70 | 31 | 4 | 1. As The Years Go By | Epic 10634 |
| | | | **BARBARA MASON** | |
| | | | born on 8/9/47 in Philadelphia | |
| 6/12/65 | 5 | 10 | 1. **Yes, I'm Ready** | Arctic 105 |
| 9/04/65 | 27 | 5 | 2. Sad, Sad Girl | Arctic 108 |
| 2/24/73 | 31 | 5 | 3. Give Me Your Love | Buddah 331 |
| 12/28/74 + | 28 | 4 | 4. From His Woman To You | Buddah 441 |

| DATE | POS | WKS | ARTIST—Record Title | LABEL & NO. |
|---|---|---|---|---|
| | | | **DAVE MASON** | |
| | | | English - original member of Traffic | |
| 10/08/77 | 12 | 10 | 1. We Just Disagree | Columbia 10575 |
| 7/08/78 | 39 | 2 | 2. Will You Still Love Me Tomorrow | Columbia 10749 |
| | | | **TOBIN MATHEWS & Co.** | |
| 11/14/60 | 30 | 4 | 1. Ruby Duby Du [I]<br>from the movie "Key Witness" | Chief 7022 |
| | | | **JOHNNY MATHIS** | |
| | | | born in San Francisco on 9/30/35 | |
| 5/06/57 | 14 | 20 | 1. Wonderful! Wonderful! | Columbia 40784 |
| 5/20/57 | 5 | 23 | 2. **It's Not For Me To Say**<br>from the movie "Lizzie" | Columbia 40851 |
| 9/16/57 | 1 (1) | 22 | 3. **Chances Are**/ | |
| 10/14/57 | 9 | 14 | 4. **The Twelfth Of Never** | Columbia 40993 |
| 12/16/57 | 22 | 7 | 5. Wild Is The Wind/ | |
| 1/06/58 | 21 | 1 | 6. No Love (But Your Love) | Columbia 41060 |
| 2/10/58 | 22 | 1 | 7. Come To Me | Columbia 41082 |
| 5/05/58 | 21 | 7 | 8. All The Time/<br>from the musical "Oh Captain!" | |
| 5/19/58 | 21 | 2 | 9. Teacher, Teacher | Columbia 41152 |
| 7/14/58 | 14 | 11 | 10. A Certain Smile | Columbia 41193 |
| 10/20/58 | 21 | 8 | 11. Call Me | Columbia 41253 |
| 5/04/59 | 35 | 3 | 12. Someone | Columbia 41355 |
| 7/20/59 | 20 | 8 | 13. Small World<br>from the Broadway musical "Gypsy" | Columbia 41410 |
| 10/19/59 | 12 | 12 | 14. Misty | Columbia 41483 |
| 3/28/60 | 25 | 5 | 15. Starbright | Columbia 41583 |
| 10/13/62 | 6 | 9 | 16. **Gina** | Columbia 42582 |
| 2/09/63 | 9 | 10 | 17. **What Will Mary Say** | Columbia 42666 |
| 6/08/63 | 30 | 4 | 18. Every Step Of The Way | Columbia 42799 |
| | | | **JOHNNY MATHIS & DIONNE WARWICK** | |
| 5/29/82 | 38 | 3 | 1. Friends In Love | Arista 0673 |
| | | | **JOHNNY MATHIS & DENIECE WILLIAMS** | |
| 4/22/78 | 1 (1) | 11 | ● 1. **Too Much, Too Little, Too Late** | Columbia 10693 |
| | | | **MATTHEWS' SOUTHERN COMFORT** | |
| | | | English sextet - Ian Matthews, lead singer | |
| 4/24/71 | 23 | 9 | 1. Woodstock | Decca 32774 |
| | | | **IAN MATTHEWS** | |
| | | | English - founder of Fairport Convention and<br>Matthews' Southern Comfort | |
| 12/16/78 + | 13 | 12 | 1. Shake It | Mushroom 7039 |
| | | | **PAUL MAURIAT & His Orchestra** | |
| | | | French conductor/arranger | |
| 1/27/68 | 1 (5) | 15 | ● 1. **Love Is Blue [I]** | Philips 40495 |
| | | | **ROBERT MAXWELL His Harp & Orchestra** | |
| 4/18/64 | 15 | 7 | 1. Shangri-La [I] | Decca 25622 |

| DATE | POS | WKS | ARTIST—Record Title | LABEL & NO. |
|------|-----|-----|---------------------|-------------|
| | | | **NATHANIEL MAYER & The Fabulous Twilights** | |
| 5/26/62 | 22 | 6 | 1. Village Of Love | Fortune 449 |
| | | | **CURTIS MAYFIELD** | |
| | | | lead singer of The Impressions from 1961-1970 | |
| 1/02/71 | 29 | 4 | 1. (Don't Worry) If There's A Hell Below We're All Going To Go | Curtom 1955 |
| 9/23/72 | 4 | 11 | ● 2. **Freddie's Dead** | Curtom 1975 |
| | | | Theme from the film "Superfly" | |
| 11/25/72 + | 8 | 13 | ● 3. **Superfly** | Curtom 1978 |
| 8/25/73 | 39 | 2 | 4. Future Shock | Curtom 1987 |
| 8/03/74 | 40 | 1 | 5. Kung Fu | Curtom 1999 |
| | | | **MAC McANALLY** | |
| 8/13/77 | 37 | 2 | 1. It's A Crazy World | Ariola Am. 7665 |
| | | | **C.W. McCALL** | |
| | | | real name: Bill Fries - an advertising agent from Omaha | |
| 3/22/75 | 40 | 1 | 1. Wolf Creek Pass [N] | MGM 14764 |
| 12/13/75 + | 1 (1) | 11 | ● 2. **Convoy [N]** | MGM 14839 |
| | | | **PETER McCANN** | |
| | | | staffwriter with ABC Music | |
| 5/21/77 | 5 | 16 | ● 1. **Do You Wanna Make Love** | 20th Century 2335 |
| | | | **PAUL McCARTNEY** | |
| | | | Beatles' bass guitarist/songwriter - born on 6/18/42 in Liverpool, England | |
| 3/13/71 | 5 | 11 | 1. **Another Day** | Apple 1829 |
| 8/21/71 | 1 (1) | 12 | ● 2. **Uncle Albert/Admiral Halsey** | Apple 1837 |
| 3/25/72 | 21 | 6 | 3. Give Ireland Back To The Irish | Apple 1847 |
| 7/08/72 | 28 | 3 | 4. Mary Had A Little Lamb | Apple 1851 |
| 12/30/72 + | 10 | 9 | 5. **Hi, Hi, Hi** | Apple 1857 |
| 4/28/73 | 1 (4) | 15 | ● 6. **My Love** | Apple 1861 |
| 7/21/73 | 2 (3) | 12 | ● 7. **Live And Let Die** | Apple 1863 |
| 12/08/73 + | 10 | 10 | 8. **Helen Wheels** | Apple 1869 |
| 2/23/74 | 7 | 10 | 9. **Jet** | Apple 1871 |
| 5/04/74 | 1 (1) | 13 | ● 10. **Band On The Run** | Apple 1873 |
| 11/23/74 + | 3 | 10 | 11. **Junior's Farm/** | |
| 2/22/75 | 39 | 1 | 12.  Sally G | Apple 1875 |
| 6/07/75 | 1 (1) | 11 | ● 13. **Listen To What The Man Said** | Capitol 4091 |
| 10/25/75 | 39 | 2 | 14. Letting Go | Capitol 4145 |
| 11/15/75 | 12 | 6 | 15. Venus And Mars Rock Show | Capitol 4175 |
| 4/17/76 | 1 (5) | 15 | ● 16. **Silly Love Songs** | Capitol 4256 |
| 7/17/76 | 3 | 11 | ● 17. **Let 'Em In** | Capitol 4293 |
| 2/19/77 | 10 | 11 | 18. **Maybe I'm Amazed** | Capitol 4385 |
| 12/24/77 + | 33 | 4 | 19. Girls' School | Capitol 4504 |
| 4/08/78 | 1 (2) | 12 | 20. **With A Little Luck** | Capitol 4559 |
| 7/15/78 | 25 | 5 | 21. I've Had Enough | Capitol 4594 |
| 10/14/78 | 39 | 2 | 22. London Town | Capitol 4625 |

| DATE | POS | WKS | ARTIST—Record Title | LABEL & NO. |
|---|---|---|---|---|
| 3/31/79 | 5 | 13 | ● 23. **Goodnight Tonight** | Columbia 10939 |
| 6/30/79 | 20 | 6 | 24. Getting Closer | Columbia 11020 |
| 9/22/79 | 29 | 4 | 25. Arrow Through Me | Columbia 11070 |
| 5/10/80 | 1 (3) | 16 | ● 26. **Coming Up (Live at Glasgow)** | Columbia 11263 |
| 7/17/82 | 10 | 11 | 27. **Take It Away** | Columbia 03018 |
| 1/07/84 | 23 | 8 | 28. So Bad | Columbia 04296 |
| 10/20/84 | 6 | 14 | 29. **No More Lonely Nights**<br>from the film "Give My Regards To Broad Street" | Columbia 04581 |
| | | | **PAUL McCARTNEY & MICHAEL JACKSON** | |
| 11/13/82 + | 2 (3) | 14 | ● 1. **The Girl Is Mine** | Epic 03288 |
| 10/15/83 | 1 (6) | 18 | ● 2. **Say Say Say** | Columbia 04168 |
| | | | **PAUL McCARTNEY & STEVIE WONDER** | |
| 4/10/82 | 1 (7) | 15 | ● 1. **Ebony And Ivory** | Columbia 02860 |
| | | | **ALTON McCLAIN & DESTINY** | |
| 5/19/79 | 32 | 4 | 1. It Must Be Love | Polydor 14532 |
| | | | **DELBERT McCLINTON**<br>played harmonica on Bruce Channel's hit "Hey Baby" | |
| 12/20/80 + | 8 | 14 | 1. **Giving It Up For Your Love** | Capitol 4948 |
| | | | **BOBBY McCLURE - see FONTELLA BASS** | |
| | | | **MARILYN McCOO & BILLY DAVIS, JR.**<br>Marilyn & husband Billy were members of the 5th Dimension | |
| 10/23/76 + | 1 (1) | 18 | ● 1. **You Don't Have To Be A Star (To Be In My Show)** | ABC 12208 |
| 4/02/77 | 15 | 8 | 2. Your Love | ABC 12262 |
| | | | **VAN McCOY**<br>session keyboardist/composer/producer - died on 7/6/79 (35) | |
| 5/31/75 | 1 (1) | 12 | ● 1. **The Hustle [I]**<br>with The Soul City Symphony | Avco 4653 |
| | | | **McCOYS**<br>Rick Derringer, lead singer/guitarist | |
| 9/04/65 | 1 (1) | 11 | 1. **Hang On Sloopy** | Bang 506 |
| 11/27/65 | 7 | 8 | 2. **Fever** | Bang 511 |
| 5/14/66 | 22 | 6 | 3. Come On Let's Go | Bang 522 |
| | | | **JIMMY McCRACKLIN** | |
| 3/03/58 | 7 | 10 | 1. **The Walk** | Checker 885 |
| | | | **GEORGE McCRAE** | |
| 6/15/74 | 1 (2) | 10 | 1. **Rock Your Baby** | T.K. 1004 |
| 3/01/75 | 37 | 2 | 2. I Get Lifted | T.K. 1007 |
| | | | **GWEN McCRAE**<br>formerly married to George McCrae | |
| 6/21/75 | 9 | 8 | 1. **Rockin' Chair** | Cat 1996 |

| DATE | POS | WKS | ARTIST—Record Title | LABEL & NO. |
|------|-----|-----|---------------------|-------------|
| | | | **GENE McDANIELS** | |
| | | | born on 2/12/35 in Kansas City, Missouri | |
| 4/03/61 | 3 | 12 | 1. **A Hundred Pounds Of Clay** | Liberty 55308 |
| 8/07/61 | 31 | 2 | 2. A Tear | Liberty 55344 |
| 10/16/61 | 5 | 10 | 3. **Tower Of Strength** | Liberty 55371 |
| 2/10/62 | 10 | 7 | 4. **Chip Chip** | Liberty 55405 |
| 9/01/62 | 21 | 5 | 5. Point Of No Return | Liberty 55480 |
| 12/15/62 | 31 | 2 | 6. Spanish Lace | Liberty 55510 |
| | | | **CHAS. McDEVITT Skiffle Group** | |
| 6/10/57 | 40 | 1 | 1. Freight Train<br>vocal by Nancy Wiskey | Chic 1008 |
| | | | **MICHAEL McDONALD** | |
| | | | former lead singer of The Doobie Brothers | |
| 8/28/82 | 4 | 13 | 1. **I Keep Forgettin' (Every Time You're Near)** | Warner 29933 |
| | | | **RONNIE McDOWELL** | |
| 9/17/77 | 13 | 9 | ● 1. The King Is Gone<br>a tribute to Elvis Presley | Scorpion 135 |
| | | | **McFADDEN & WHITEHEAD** | |
| | | | songwriting duo Gene McFadden & John Whitehead | |
| 6/02/79 | 13 | 11 | ★ 1. Ain't No Stoppin' Us Now | Phil. Int. 3681 |
| | | | **BOB McFADDEN & DOR** | |
| 9/14/59 | 39 | 1 | 1. The Mummy [N]<br>with spoken comments by Rod McKuen | Brunswick 55140 |
| | | | **MAUREEN McGOVERN** | |
| | | | born on 7/27/49 in Youngstown, Ohio | |
| 7/14/73 | 1 (2) | 11 | ● 1. **The Morning After**<br>from the film "The Poseidon Adventure" | 20th Century 2010 |
| 8/11/79 | 18 | 9 | 2. Different Worlds<br>theme from the TV series "Angie" | Warner 8835 |
| | | | **JIMMY McGRIFF** | |
| | | | jazz organist | |
| 10/27/62 | 20 | 7 | 1. I've Got A Woman, Part I [I] | Sue 770 |
| | | | **McGUINN, CLARK & HILLMAN** | |
| | | | Roger McGuinn, Gene Clark & Chris Hillman of the Byrds | |
| 4/28/79 | 33 | 4 | 1. Don't You Write Her Off | Capitol 4693 |
| | | | **McGUIRE SISTERS** | |
| | | | Phyllis, Dorothy & Christine from Middletown, Ohio | |
| 1/08/55 | 1(10) | 21 | 1. **Sincerely/** | |
| 1/29/55 | 17 | 6 | 2. No More | Coral 61323 |
| 3/26/55 | 11 | 7 | 3. It May Sound Silly | Coral 61369 |
| 6/04/55 | 5 | 14 | 4. **Something's Gotta Give**<br>from the film "Daddy Long Legs" | Coral 61423 |
| 10/29/55 | 10 | 13 | 5. **He** | Coral 61501 |
| 5/19/56 | 13 | 12 | 6. Picnic/ | |
| 6/02/56 | 37 | 1 | 7. Delilah Jones<br>from the film "The Man With The Golden Arm" | Coral 61627 |

| DATE | POS | WKS | ARTIST—Record Title | LABEL & NO. |
|---|---|---|---|---|
| 8/11/56 | 32 | 3 | 8. Weary Blues<br>with Lawrence Welk & his champagne music | Coral 61670 |
| 10/27/56 | 37 | 3 | 9. Ev'ry Day Of My Life | Coral 61703 |
| 12/22/56 + | 32 | 3 | 10. Goodnight My Love, Pleasant Dreams | Coral 61748 |
| 1/06/58 | 1 (4) | 19 | 11. **Sugartime** | Coral 61924 |
| 6/09/58 | 25 | 1 | 12. Ding Dong | Coral 61991 |
| 1/19/59 | 11 | 12 | 13. May You Always | Coral 62059 |
| 4/17/61 | 20 | 7 | 14. Just For Old Time's Sake | Coral 62249 |
| | | | **BARRY McGUIRE**<br>member of the New Christy Minstrels | |
| 8/28/65 | 1 (1) | 10 | 1. **Eve Of Destruction** | Dunhill 4009 |
| | | | **BOB & DOUG McKENZIE**<br>Rick Moranis & Dave Thomas of 'SCTV' | |
| 2/20/82 | 16 | 9 | 1. Take Off [N]<br>with vocals by Geddy Lee of Rush | Mercury 76134 |
| | | | **SCOTT McKENZIE** | |
| 6/10/67 | 4 | 10 | 1. **San Francisco (Be Sure To Wear Flowers In Your Hair)** | Ode 103 |
| 11/11/67 | 24 | 3 | 2. Like An Old Time Movie | Ode 105 |
| | | | **TOMMY McLAIN** | |
| 7/23/66 | 15 | 7 | 1. Sweet Dreams | MSL 197 |
| | | | **DON McLEAN**<br>born on 10/2/45 in New Rochelle, New York | |
| 12/04/71 + | 1 (4) | 17 | • 1. **American Pie - Parts I & II** | United Art. 50856 |
| 4/01/72 | 12 | 10 | 2. Vincent/<br>a tribute to artist Van Gogh | |
| | | 7 | 3. **Castles In The Air** | United Art. 50887 |
| 1/20/73 | 21 | 8 | 4. Dreidel | United Art. 51100 |
| 1/24/81 | 5 | 15 | 5. **Crying** | Millennium 11799 |
| 5/02/81 | 23 | 6 | 6. Since I Don't Have You | Millennium 11804 |
| 12/12/81 | 36 | 5 | 7. Castles In The Air<br>new version of 1972 hit | Millennium 11819 |
| | | | **PHIL McLEAN**<br>disc jockey | |
| 12/18/61 + | 21 | 6 | 1. Small Sad Sam [S-N]<br>a parody of "Big Bad John" | Versatile 107 |
| | | | **ROBIN McNAMARA**<br>one of the original cast members of "Hair" | |
| 7/18/70 | 11 | 8 | 1. Lay A Little Lovin' On Me | Steed 724 |
| | | | **CLYDE McPHATTER**<br>former lead singer of the Dominoes and the Drifters<br>died on 6/13/72 (38) | |
| 6/09/56 | 16 | 12 | 1. Treasure Of Love | Atlantic 1092 |
| 2/23/57 | 19 | 2 | 2. Without Love (There Is Nothing) | Atlantic 1117 |
| 7/08/57 | 26 | 3 | 3. Just To Hold My Hand | Atlantic 1133 |
| 10/20/58 + | 6 | 20 | 4. **A Lover's Question** | Atlantic 1199 |
| 8/03/59 | 38 | 2 | 5. Since You've Been Gone | Atlantic 2028 |

| DATE | POS | WKS | ARTIST—Record Title | LABEL & NO. |
|---|---|---|---|---|
| 8/22/60 | 23 | 5 | 6. Ta Ta | Mercury 71660 |
| 3/24/62 | 7 | 10 | 7. **Lover Please** | Mercury 71941 |
| 6/30/62 | 25 | 5 | 8. Little Bitty Pretty One | Mercury 71987 |
| | | | **CHRISTINE McVIE** | |
| | | | English - vocalist with Fleetwood Mac since 1970 | |
| 2/04/84 | 10 | 12 | 1. **Got A Hold On Me** | Warner 29372 |
| 5/12/84 | 30 | 6 | 2. Love Will Show Us How | Warner 29313 |
| | | | **SISTER JANET MEAD** | |
| | | | Australian nun | |
| 3/09/74 | 4 | 11 | ● 1. **The Lord's Prayer** | A&M 1491 |
| | | | **MEAT LOAF** | |
| | | | real name: Marvin Lee Aday - played Eddie in the film "The Rocky Horror Picture Show" | |
| 4/29/78 | 11 | 13 | ● 1. Two Out Of Three Ain't Bad | Epic 50513 |
| 9/16/78 | 39 | 2 | 2. Paradise By The Dashboard Light [N] | Epic 50588 |
| | | | female vocal: Ellen Foley; baseball announcer: Phil Rizzuto | |
| 1/20/79 | 39 | 1 | 3. You Took The Words Right Out Of My Mouth | Epic 50634 |
| | | | **MECO** | |
| | | | discofied instrumentals by producer Meco Monardo | |
| 8/27/77 | 1 (2) | 13 | ★ 1. **Star Wars Theme/Cantina Band [I]** | Millennium 604 |
| 1/21/78 | 25 | 6 | 2. Theme From Close Encounters [I] | Millennium 608 |
| 10/21/78 | 35 | 3 | 3. Themes From The Wizard Of Oz [N] | Millennium 620 |
| 7/05/80 | 18 | 8 | 4. Empire Strikes Back (Medley) [I] | RSO 1038 |
| 4/03/82 | 35 | 3 | 5. Pop Goes The Movies, Part 1 [I] | Arista 0660 |
| | | | **RANDY MEISNER** | |
| | | | member of Poco and the Eagles | |
| 11/08/80 | 22 | 7 | 1. Deep Inside My Heart | Epic 50939 |
| 2/07/81 | 19 | 9 | 2. Hearts On Fire | Epic 50964 |
| 8/28/82 | 28 | 6 | 3. Never Been In Love | Epic 03032 |
| | | | **MEL & TIM** | |
| | | | cousins Mel Harden & Tim McPherson | |
| 11/08/69 | 10 | 11 | ● 1. **Backfield In Motion** | Bamboo 107 |
| 9/16/72 | 19 | 9 | 2. Starting All Over Again | Stax 0127 |
| | | | **MELANIE** | |
| | | | born Melanie Safka on 2/3/47 in Queens, New York | |
| 5/16/70 | 6 | 14 | 1. **Lay Down (Candles In The Rain)** | Buddah 167 |
| | | | with the Edwin Hawkins Singers | |
| 9/05/70 | 32 | 4 | 2. Peace Will Come (According To Plan) | Buddah 186 |
| 11/27/71 | 1 (3) | 14 | ● 3. **Brand New Key** | Neighborhood 4201 |
| 2/19/72 | 31 | 5 | 4. Ring The Living Bell | Neighborhood 4202 |
| 2/26/72 | 35 | 3 | 5. The Nickel Song | Buddah 268 |
| 4/07/73 | 36 | 2 | 6. Bitter Bad | Neighborhood 4210 |
| | | | **MELLO-TONES** | |
| 5/13/57 | 24 | 1 | 1. Rosie Lee | Gee 1037 |

| DATE | POS | WKS | ARTIST—Record Title | LABEL & NO. |
|---|---|---|---|---|
| | | | **HAROLD MELVIN & THE BLUE NOTES** | |
| | | | Philadelphia soul quintet - Teddy Pendergrass, lead singer | |
| 10/28/72 | 3 | 11 | ● 1. **If You Don't Know Me By Now** | Phil. Int. 3520 |
| 10/20/73 | 7 | 12 | ● 2. **The Love I Lost (Part 1)** | Phil. Int. 3533 |
| 5/03/75 | 15 | 10 | 3. Bad Luck (Part 1) | Phil. Int. 3562 |
| 12/20/75 + | 12 | 12 | 4. Wake Up Everybody (Part 1) | Phil. Int. 3579 |
| | | | **MEN AT WORK** | |
| | | | Australian quintet, led by Colin Hay | |
| 8/07/82 | 1 (1) | 17 | 1. **Who Can It Be Now?** | Columbia 02888 |
| 11/27/82 + | 1 (4) | 19 | ● 2. **Down Under** | Columbia 03303 |
| 4/09/83 | 3 | 13 | 3. **Overkill** | Columbia 03795 |
| 7/09/83 | 6 | 12 | 4. **It's A Mistake** | Columbia 03959 |
| 10/08/83 | 28 | 5 | 5. Dr. Heckyll & Mr. Jive | Columbia 04111 |
| | | | **MEN WITHOUT HATS** | |
| | | | trio from Montreal, Canada | |
| 7/30/83 | 3 | 16 | 1. **The Safety Dance** | Backstreet 52232 |
| | | | **SERGIO MENDES** | |
| 5/14/83 | 4 | 16 | 1. **Never Gonna Let You Go** | A&M 2540 |
| | | | vocals: Joe Pizzulo & Leza Miller | |
| 7/07/84 | 29 | 7 | 2. Alibis | A&M 2639 |
| | | | vocal by Joe Pizzulo | |
| | | | **SERGIO MENDES & BRASIL '66** | |
| | | | Latin stylists led by pianist Sergio Mendes | |
| 6/01/68 | 4 | 11 | 1. **The Look Of Love** | A&M 924 |
| | | | from the film "Casino Royale" | |
| 8/24/68 | 6 | 10 | 2. **The Fool On The Hill** | A&M 961 |
| 12/07/68 | 16 | 6 | 3. Scarborough Fair | A&M 986 |
| | | | **MERCY** | |
| 5/03/69 | 2 (2) | 10 | ● 1. **Love (Can Make You Happy)** | Sundi 6811 |
| | | | **JIM MESSINA - see LOGGINS & MESSINA** | |
| | | | **METERS** | |
| | | | New Orleans' funk band led by Art Neville (Aaron's brother) | |
| 3/22/69 | 34 | 1 | 1. Sophisticated Cissy [I] | Josie 1001 |
| 5/24/69 | 23 | 3 | 2. Cissy Strut [I] | Josie 1005 |
| | | | **MFSB featuring The Three Degrees** | |
| | | | MFSB = Mother Father Sister Brother - studio musicians | |
| 3/16/74 | 1 (2) | 14 | ● 1. **TSOP (The Sound Of Philadelphia) [I]** | Phil. Int. 3540 |
| | | | theme from the TV show "Soul Train" | |
| | | | **LEE MICHAELS** | |
| | | | rock organist/vocalist from Los Angeles | |
| 9/04/71 | 6 | 12 | 1. **Do You Know What I Mean** | A&M 1262 |
| 12/25/71 | 39 | 1 | 2. Can I Get A Witness | A&M 1303 |
| | | | **MICKEY & SYLVIA** | |
| | | | Mickey Baker & Sylvia Robinson - also see Sylvia | |
| 1/12/57 | 11 | 14 | 1. Love Is Strange | Groove 0175 |

**Roy Orbison.** Troubador Don McLean, of "American Pie" fame, revived his career by recording Orbison's 1961 smash "Crying" in 1981. Just six months earlier, Orbison had made his first chart entry (#55) in thirteen years, dueting with Emmylou Harris on "That Lovin' You Feelin' Again."

**Tony Orlando** reluctantly added the lead vocal to a demo tape of "Candida" at the request of producer Hank Medress (ex-Tokens). In a flash, the song shot to the top of the charts and Dawn was a hot property.

**Marie Osmond** recorded six Top 40 duets with her brother Donny. Their biggest hit was a remake of Dale & Grace's 1963 chart-topper "I'm Leaving It (All) Up to You."

**Jeffrey Osborne** got his start with funk group L.T.D. almost by chance. When the band's regular drummer failed to show for a Providence, Rhode Island, date, local talent Osborne stepped in and won the job.

**The Outsiders** put Cleveland on the rock'n'roll map in 1966 with the blistering "Time Won't Let Me" (later recorded by the infamous Iggy Pop). One of their members had the very un-Cleveland name of Merdin Prince Gunnar Madsen.

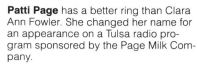

**Patti Page** has a better ring than Clara Ann Fowler. She changed her name for an appearance on a Tulsa radio program sponsored by the Page Milk Company.

**Ray Parker Jr.** would have been a success even if he'd never written "Ghostbusters." Before debuting his band Raydio in 1978, he'd already worked as a backup guitarist for such notables as Stevie Wonder, Gladys Knight, and the Temptations.

**The Partridge Family** came from the TV series of the same name starring Shirley Jones and David Cassidy. Unlike the Monkees, who were dogged by charges of fraud, the Partridges were never expected to be anything but good, clean, manufactured fun.

**Bernadette Peters** was a singer first, recording flops like "We'll Start the Party Again" and "When I Hear Our Song" in the sixties. Later, she became a movie star, appearing in *The Jerk* and *Pennies From Heaven.*

**Tom Petty** returned the favor to one of his inspirations by producing Del Shannon's 1982 comeback LP *Drop Down and Get Me,* which spawned the hit "Sea of Love." In addition, most of his Heartbreakers chipped in as backup musicians.

| DATE | POS | WKS | ARTIST—Record Title | LABEL & NO. |
|---|---|---|---|---|
| | | | **BETTE MIDLER** | |
| | | | born on 12/1/45 in Paterson, New Jersey | |
| 1/20/73 | **17** | 11 | 1. Do You Want To Dance? | Atlantic 2928 |
| 6/09/73 | **8** | 11 | 2. **Boogie Woogie Bugle Boy** | Atlantic 2964 |
| 11/10/73 | **40** | 1 | 3. Friends | Atlantic 2980 |
| 7/07/79 | **40** | 2 | 4. Married Men | Atlantic 3582 |
| 3/01/80 | **35** | 3 | 5. When A Man Loves A Woman | Atlantic 3643 |
| 4/26/80 | **3** | 16 | ● 6. **The Rose** | Atlantic 3656 |
| | | | above 2 from the film "The Rose" | |
| 1/17/81 | **39** | 2 | 7. My Mother's Eyes | Atlantic 3771 |
| | | | from the film "Divine Madness" | |
| | | | **GARRY MILES** | |
| | | | real name: Buzz Cason - also see Garry Mills (different artist with a different version of the same song) | |
| 7/18/60 | **16** | 6 | 1. Look For A Star | Liberty 55261 |
| | | | from the film "Circus Of Horrors" | |
| | | | **JOHN MILES** | |
| | | | English | |
| 5/14/77 | **34** | 5 | 1. Slowdown | London 20092 |
| | | | **CHUCK MILLER** | |
| 6/18/55 | **9** | 14 | 1. **The House Of Blue Lights** | Mercury 70627 |
| | | | **JODY MILLER** | |
| | | | born in Phoenix, Arizona on 11/29/41 | |
| 5/15/65 | **12** | 5 | 1. Queen Of The House | Capitol 5402 |
| 9/25/65 | **25** | 5 | 2. Home Of The Brave | Capitol 5483 |
| | | | **MITCH MILLER & His Orchestra** | |
| | | | producer/conductor/arranger for the male sing-along chorus | |
| 8/06/55 | **1** (6) | 19 | 1. **The Yellow Rose Of Texas** | Columbia 40540 |
| 2/18/56 | **19** | 3 | 2. Lisbon Antigua [I] | Columbia 40635 |
| 8/11/56 | **8** | 12 | 3. **Song For A Summer Night (Parts 1 & 2) [I]** | Columbia 40730 |
| | | | part 1: instrumental; part 2: vocal | |
| 1/27/58 | **20** | 11 | 4. March From The River Kwai And Colonel Bogey [I] | Columbia 41066 |
| | | | from the film "The Bridge On The River Kwai" | |
| 1/26/59 | **16** | 10 | 5. The Children's Marching Song [N] | Columbia 41317 |
| | | | from the film "The Inn of The Sixth Happiness" | |
| | | | **NED MILLER** | |
| 1/26/63 | **6** | 8 | 1. **From A Jack To A King** | Fabor 114 |
| | | | **ROGER MILLER** | |
| | | | born in Fort Worth, Texas on 1/2/36 | |
| 7/04/64 | **7** | 8 | 1. **Dang Me [N]** | Smash 1881 |
| 10/03/64 | **9** | 8 | 2. **Chug-A-Lug [N]** | Smash 1926 |
| 1/02/65 | **31** | 3 | 3. Do-Wacka-Do [N] | Smash 1947 |
| 2/06/65 | **4** | 12 | ● 4. **King Of The Road** | Smash 1965 |
| 5/22/65 | **7** | 7 | 5. **Engine Engine #9** | Smash 1983 |
| 8/07/65 | **34** | 2 | 6. One Dyin' And A Buryin' | Smash 1994 |
| 10/02/65 | **31** | 3 | 7. Kansas City Star [N] | Smash 1998 |
| 11/27/65 | **8** | 8 | 8. **England Swings** | Smash 2010 |

| DATE | POS | WKS | ARTIST—Record Title | LABEL & NO. |
|------|-----|-----|---------------------|-------------|
| 3/05/66 | 26 | 5 | 9. Husbands And Wives [N] | Smash 2024 |
| 7/23/66 | 40 | 1 | 10. You Can't Roller Skate In A Buffalo Herd [N] | Smash 2043 |
| 5/06/67 | 37 | 1 | 11. Walkin' In The Sunshine | Smash 2081 |
| 3/16/68 | 39 | 6 | 12. Little Green Apples | Smash 2148 |
| | | | **STEVE MILLER Band** | |
| | | | rock band formed in 1966 in San Francisco | |
| 11/17/73 + | 1 (1) | 16 | ● 1. **The Joker** | Capitol 3732 |
| 6/05/76 | 11 | 9 | 2. Take The Money And Run | Capitol 4260 |
| 9/04/76 | 1 (1) | 14 | 3. **Rock'n Me** | Capitol 4323 |
| 1/08/77 | 2 (2) | 15 | ● 4. **Fly Like An Eagle** | Capitol 4372 |
| 5/14/77 | 8 | 13 | 5. **Jet Airliner** | Capitol 4424 |
| 9/03/77 | 23 | 7 | 6. Jungle Love | Capitol 4466 |
| 11/12/77 | 17 | 9 | 7. Swingtown | Capitol 4496 |
| 11/14/81 | 24 | 9 | 8. Heart Like A Wheel | Capitol 5068 |
| 6/19/82 | 1 (2) | 19 | ● 9. **Abracadabra** | Capitol 5126 |
| | | | **MILLS BROTHERS** | |
| | | | Harry, Herbert & Donald - formed vocal group in 1930 - Harry died on 6/28/82 (68) | |
| 6/17/57 | 39 | 1 | 1. Queen Of The Senior Prom | Decca 30299 |
| 3/03/58 | 21 | 2 | 2. Get A Job | Dot 15695 |
| 3/02/68 | 23 | 10 | 3. Cab Driver | Dot 17041 |
| | | | **FRANK MILLS** | |
| | | | pianist/composer/producer/arranger | |
| 3/03/79 | 3 | 12 | ● 1. **Music Box Dancer** [I] | Polydor 14517 |
| | | | **GARRY MILLS** | |
| | | | also see Garry Miles | |
| 7/04/60 | 26 | 5 | 1. Look For A Star - Part I | Imperial 5674 |
| | | | from the film "Circus Of Horrors" | |
| | | | **HAYLEY MILLS** | |
| | | | 15-year-old English actress | |
| 9/18/61 | 8 | 11 | 1. **Let's Get Together** | Vista 385 |
| | | | from the film "The Parent Trap" | |
| 4/14/62 | 21 | 6 | 2. Johnny Jingo | Vista 395 |
| | | | **STEPHANIE MILLS** | |
| | | | starred in the Broadway show "The Wiz" | |
| 9/01/79 | 22 | 6 | 1. What Cha Gonna Do With My Lovin' | 20th Century 2403 |
| 8/30/80 | 6 | 16 | ● 2. **Never Knew Love Like This Before** | 20th Century 2460 |
| | | | **STEPHANIE MILLS & TEDDY PENDERGRASS** | |
| 7/04/81 | 40 | 2 | 1. Two Hearts | 20th Century 2492 |
| | | | **RONNIE MILSAP** | |
| | | | born blind in Robbinsville, North Carolina on 1/16/46 | |
| 8/27/77 | 16 | 10 | 1. It Was Almost Like A Song | RCA 10976 |
| 1/24/81 | 24 | 9 | 2. Smoky Mountain Rain | RCA 12084 |
| 7/11/81 | 5 | 15 | 3. **(There's) No Gettin' Over Me** | RCA 12264 |
| 11/28/81 + | 20 | 11 | 4. I Wouldn't Have Missed It For The World | RCA 12342 |
| 5/29/82 | 14 | 9 | 5. Any Day Now | RCA 13216 |
| 4/23/83 | 23 | 8 | 6. Stranger In My House | RCA 13470 |

| DATE | POS | WKS | ARTIST—Record Title | LABEL & NO. |
|---|---|---|---|---|
| | | | **GARNET MIMMS** | |
| 5/07/66 | 30 | 3 | 1. I'll Take Good Care Of You | United Art. 995 |
| | | | **GARNET MIMMS & The Enchanters** | |
| | | | Enchanters: soul trio from Philadelphia | |
| 9/07/63 | 4 | 11 | 1. **Cry Baby** | United Art. 629 |
| 12/07/63 + | 26 | 5 | 2. For Your Precious Love/ | |
| 12/07/63 | 30 | 4 | 3. Baby Don't You Weep | United Art. 658 |
| | | | **MINDBENDERS** | |
| | | | Manchester, England group | |
| 3/27/65 | 1 (1) | 10 | 1. **Game Of Love** | Fontana 1509 |
| | | | Wayne Fontana & The Mindbenders | |
| 4/30/66 | 2 (2) | 10 | 2. **A Groovy Kind Of Love** | Fontana 1541 |
| | | | **SAL MINEO** | |
| | | | Broadway/Hollywood actor - died on 2/12/76 (37) | |
| 5/20/57 | 9 | 13 | 1. **Start Movin' (In My Direction)** | Epic 9216 |
| 9/23/57 | 27 | 3 | 2. Lasting Love | Epic 9227 |
| | | | **MIRACLES** | |
| | | | led by singer/songwriter/producer Smokey Robinson, The Miracles were Motown's first successful recording group | |
| 12/31/60 + | 2 (1) | 13 | 1. **Shop Around** | Tamla 54034 |
| 2/17/62 | 35 | 2 | 2. What's So Good About Good-By | Tamla 54053 |
| 6/30/62 | 39 | 1 | 3. I'll Try Something New | Tamla 54059 |
| 1/12/63 | 8 | 10 | 4. **You've Really Got A Hold On Me** | Tamla 54073 |
| 5/04/63 | 31 | 3 | 5. A Love She Can Count On | Tamla 54078 |
| 8/31/63 | 8 | 9 | 6. **Mickey's Monkey** | Tamla 54083 |
| 1/04/64 | 35 | 3 | 7. I Gotta Dance To Keep From Crying | Tamla 54089 |
| 7/25/64 | 27 | 4 | 8. I Like It Like That | Tamla 54098 |
| 10/10/64 | 35 | 1 | 9. That's What Love Is Made Of | Tamla 54102 |
| 4/17/65 | 16 | 7 | 10. Ooo Baby Baby | Tamla 54113 |
| 8/07/65 | 16 | 8 | 11. The Tracks Of My Tears | Tamla 54118 |
| 11/06/65 | 14 | 6 | 12. My Girl Has Gone | Tamla 54123 |
| 1/22/66 | 11 | 7 | 13. Going To A Go-Go | Tamla 54127 |
| 11/26/66 | 17 | 6 | 14. (Come 'Round Here) I'm The One You Need | Tamla 54140 |
| | | | SMOKEY ROBINSON & THE MIRACLES: | |
| 3/11/67 | 20 | 7 | 15. The Love I Saw In You Was Just A Mirage | Tamla 54145 |
| 7/08/67 | 23 | 8 | 16. More Love | Tamla 54152 |
| 11/25/67 | 4 | 12 | 17. **I Second That Emotion** | Tamla 54159 |
| 3/09/68 | 11 | 10 | 18. If You Can Want | Tamla 54162 |
| 6/29/68 | 31 | 3 | 19. Yester Love | Tamla 54167 |
| 8/31/68 | 26 | 6 | 20. Special Occasion | Tamla 54172 |
| 1/25/69 | 8 | 11 | 21. **Baby, Baby Don't Cry** | Tamla 54178 |
| 7/19/69 | 33 | 2 | 22. Abraham, Martin And John | Tamla 54184 |
| 7/26/69 | 32 | 4 | 23. Doggone Right/ | |
| 10/04/69 | 37 | 3 | 24. Here I Go Again | Tamla 54183 |
| 12/27/69 + | 37 | 4 | 25. Point It Out | Tamla 54189 |
| 10/31/70 | 1 (2) | 14 | 26. **The Tears Of A Clown** | Tamla 54199 |

| DATE | POS | WKS | ARTIST—Record Title | LABEL & NO. |
|---|---|---|---|---|
| 4/17/71 | 18 | 8 | 27. I Don't Blame You At All | Tamla 54205 |
| | | | MIRACLES: | |
| 9/14/74 | 13 | 9 | 28. Do It Baby | Tamla 54248 |
| 12/13/75 + | 1 (1) | 19 | 29. **Love Machine (Part 1)** | Tamla 54262 |
| | | | **GUY MITCHELL** | |
| | | | born Al Cernik on 2/28/27 in Detroit | |
| 2/25/56 | 23 | 4 | 1. Ninety Nine Years (Dead Or Alive) | Columbia 40631 |
| 11/03/56 | 1(10) | 22 | 2. **Singing The Blues** | Columbia 40769 |
| 2/02/57 | 16 | 8 | 3. Knee Deep In The Blues | Columbia 40820 |
| 4/13/57 | 10 | 12 | 4. **Rock-A-Billy** | Columbia 40877 |
| 10/19/59 | 1 (2) | 16 | 5. **Heartaches By The Number** | Columbia 41476 |
| | | | **JONI MITCHELL** | |
| | | | born Roberta Joan Anderson on 11/7/43 in Alberta, Canada - also see James Taylor | |
| 12/30/72 + | 25 | 8 | 1. You Turn Me On, I'm A Radio | Asylum 11010 |
| 4/20/74 | 7 | 11 | 2. **Help Me** | Asylum 11034 |
| 8/24/74 | 22 | 7 | 3. Free Man In Paris | Asylum 11041 |
| 1/25/75 | 24 | 4 | 4. Big Yellow Taxi | Asylum 45221 |
| | | | live version of 1970 studio hit | |
| | | | **WILLIE MITCHELL** | |
| | | | soul trumpeter/arranger/conductor of combo | |
| 10/03/64 | 31 | 5 | 1. 20-75 [I] | Hi 2075 |
| 4/13/68 | 23 | 10 | 2. Soul Serenade [I] | Hi 2140 |
| | | | **MOCEDADES** | |
| | | | sextet from Bilbao, Spain featuring the Amezaga sisters | |
| 2/16/74 | 9 | 11 | 1. **Eres Tu (Touch The Wind) [F]** | Tara 100 |
| | | | **DOMENICO MODUGNO** | |
| | | | native of Sicily | |
| 8/04/58 | 1 (5) | 13 | 1. **Nel Blu Dipinto Di Blu (Volare) [F]** | Decca 30677 |
| | | | **MOJO MEN** | |
| 3/18/67 | 36 | 3 | 1. Sit Down, I Think I Love You | Reprise 0539 |
| | | | **MOMENTS** | |
| | | | also see Ray, Goodman & Brown | |
| 4/18/70 | 3 | 14 | ● 1. **Love On A Two-Way Street** | Stang 5012 |
| 2/02/74 | 17 | 9 | 2. Sexy Mama | Stang 5052 |
| 8/02/75 | 39 | 3 | 3. Look At Me (I'm In Love) | Stang 5060 |
| | | | **EDDIE MONEY** | |
| | | | real name: Edward Mahoney | |
| 4/08/78 | 11 | 11 | 1. Baby Hold On | Columbia 10663 |
| 7/29/78 | 22 | 8 | 2. Two Tickets To Paradise | Columbia 10765 |
| 2/24/79 | 22 | 8 | 3. Maybe I'm A Fool | Columbia 10900 |
| 7/24/82 | 16 | 12 | 4. Think I'm In Love | Columbia 02964 |
| | | | **MONKEES** | |
| | | | Davy Jones, Michael Nesmith, Micky Dolenz & Peter Tork | |
| 9/24/66 | 1 (1) | 12 | ● 1. **Last Train To Clarksville** | Colgems 1001 |
| 12/17/66 | 1 (7) | 13 | ● 2. **I'm A Believer/** | |
| 12/31/66 + | 20 | 6 | 3. (I'm Not Your) Steppin' Stone | Colgems 1002 |

| DATE | POS | WKS | ARTIST—Record Title | LABEL & NO. |
|---|---|---|---|---|
| 3/25/67 | 2 (1) | 10 | ● 4. **A Little Bit Me, A Little Bit You/** | |
| 4/15/67 | 39 | 1 | 5. The Girl I Knew Somewhere | Colgems 1004 |
| 7/29/67 | 3 | 9 | ● 6. **Pleasant Valley Sunday/** | |
| 8/05/67 | 11 | 7 | 7. Words | Colgems 1007 |
| 11/18/67 | 1 (4) | 12 | ● 8. **Daydream Believer** | Colgems 1012 |
| 3/09/68 | 3 | 7 | ● 9. **Valleri/** | |
| 3/30/68 | 34 | 1 | 10. Tapioca Tundra | Colgems 1019 |
| 6/22/68 | 19 | 6 | 11. D. W. Washburn | Colgems 1023 |
| | | | **MONOTONES** | |
| | | | "doo-wop" sextet from Newark, New Jersey | |
| 4/07/58 | 5 | 12 | 1. **Book Of Love** | Argo 5290 |
| | | | **MATT MONRO** | |
| | | | English | |
| 6/26/61 | 18 | 9 | 1. My Kind Of Girl | Warwick 636 |
| 12/26/64 + | 23 | 5 | 2. Walk Away | Liberty 55745 |
| | | | **VAUGHN MONROE** | |
| | | | died on 5/21/73 (6l) | |
| 11/12/55 | 38 | 1 | 1. Black Denim Trousers And Motorcycle Boots | RCA 6260 |
| 2/18/56 | 38 | 1 | 2. Don't Go To Strangers | RCA 6358 |
| 9/08/56 | 11 | 8 | 3. In The Middle Of The House [N] | RCA 6619 |
| | | | **LOU MONTE** | |
| 3/17/58 | 12 | 11 | 1. Lazy Mary (Luna Mezzo Mare) [F] | RCA 7160 |
| 12/15/62 + | 5 | 9 | 2. **Pepino The Italian Mouse** [N] | Reprise 20106 |
| | | | **HUGO MONTENEGRO & His Orchestra** | |
| | | | conductor-arranger-composer - died on 2/6/81 (55) | |
| 4/06/68 | 2 (1) | 14 | 1. **The Good, The Bad And The Ugly** [I] | RCA 9423 |
| | | | **CHRIS MONTEZ** | |
| | | | protege of Ritchie Valens | |
| 9/08/62 | 4 | 9 | 1. **Let's Dance** | Monogram 505 |
| 2/12/66 | 22 | 5 | 2. Call Me | A&M 780 |
| 5/28/66 | 16 | 7 | 3. The More I See You | A&M 796 |
| 9/10/66 | 33 | 2 | 4. There Will Never Be Another You | A&M 810 |
| 12/03/66 | 36 | 2 | 5. Time After Time | A&M 822 |
| | | | **MELBA MONTGOMERY** | |
| 6/08/74 | 39 | 1 | 1. No Charge [N] | Elektra 45883 |
| | | | **MOODY BLUES** | |
| | | | English classical-rock group: Justin Hayward, John Lodge, Graeme Edge, Mike Pinder & Ray Thomas | |
| 3/27/65 | 10 | 8 | 1. **Go Now!** | London 9726 |
| 8/24/68 | 24 | 6 | 2. Tuesday Afternoon (Forever Afternoon) | Deram 85028 |
| 5/30/70 | 21 | 8 | 3. Question | Threshold 67004 |
| 9/04/71 | 23 | 7 | 4. The Story In Your Eyes | Threshold 67006 |
| 5/13/72 | 29 | 7 | 5. Isn't Life Strange | Threshold 67009 |
| 9/02/72 | 2 (2) | 14 | ● 6. **Nights In White Satin** | Deram 85023 |

| DATE | POS | WKS | ARTIST—Record Title | LABEL & NO. |
|------|-----|-----|---------------------|-------------|
| 2/17/73 | 12 | 8 | 7. I'm Just A Singer (In A Rock And Roll Band) | Threshold 67012 |
| 9/02/78 | 39 | 2 | 8. Steppin' In A Slide Zone | London 270 |
| 6/13/81 | 12 | 9 | 9. Gemini Dream | Threshold 601 |
| 8/15/81 | 15 | 11 | 10. The Voice | Threshold 602 |
| 9/17/83 | 27 | 6 | 11. Sitting At The Wheel | Threshold 604 |
| | | | **ART MOONEY & His Orchestra** | |
| | | | also see Barry Gordon | |
| 4/23/55 | 6 | 17 | 1. **Honey-Babe** | MGM 11900 |
| | | | from the film "Battle Cry" | |
| | | | **MOONGLOWS** | |
| | | | classic fifties R&B group led by Harvey Fuqua - also see Harvey & The Moonglows | |
| 3/26/55 | 20 | 1 | 1. Sincerely | Chess 1581 |
| 10/13/56 | 25 | 1 | 2. See Saw | Chess 1629 |
| | | | **BOB MOORE & His Orchestra** | |
| 9/11/61 | 7 | 10 | 1. **Mexico** [I] | Monument 446 |
| | | | **BOBBY MOORE & The Rhythm Aces** | |
| 7/30/66 | 27 | 4 | 1. Searching For My Love | Checker 1129 |
| | | | **DOROTHY MOORE** | |
| | | | lead singer of The Poppies | |
| 4/10/76 | 3 | 16 | 1. **Misty Blue** | Malaco 1029 |
| 9/10/77 | 27 | 7 | 2. I Believe You | Malaco 1042 |
| | | | **JACKIE MOORE** | |
| 1/23/71 | 30 | 7 | ● 1. Precious, Precious | Atlantic 2681 |
| | | | **JANE MORGAN** | |
| 9/09/57 | 7 | 21 | 1. **Fascination** | Kapp 191 |
| | | | with the Troubadors -- from the film "Love In The Afternoon" | |
| 10/13/58 | 21 | 10 | 2. The Day The Rains Came | Kapp 235 |
| 8/31/59 | 39 | 1 | 3. With Open Arms | Kapp 284 |
| | | | **JAYE P. MORGAN** | |
| | | | real name: Mary Margaret Morgan - also see Perry Como | |
| 11/27/54 + | 3 | 21 | 1. **That's All I Want From You** | RCA 5896 |
| 3/12/55 | 12 | 8 | 2. Danger! Heartbreak Ahead | RCA 6016 |
| 8/20/55 | 6 | 14 | 3. **The Longest Walk** | RCA 6182 |
| 11/12/55 | 12 | 8 | 4. Pepper-Hot Baby/ | |
| 12/10/55 | 40 | 1 | 5.  If You Don't Want My Love | RCA 6282 |
| | | | **RUSS MORGAN & His Orchestra** | |
| | | | Russ died on 8/8/69 (65) | |
| 11/12/55 | 30 | 4 | 1. Dogface Soldier | Decca 29703 |
| | | | from the movie "From Hell And Back" | |
| 3/17/56 | 19 | 3 | 2. The Poor People Of Paris [I] | Decca 29835 |
| | | | **MORMON TABERNACLE CHOIR** | |
| | | | Richard P. Condie directs the 375-voice choir | |
| 9/21/59 | 13 | 11 | 1. Battle Hymn Of The Republic | Columbia 41459 |
| | | | with the Philadelphia Orchestra, Eugene Ormandy, conductor | |

| DATE | POS | WKS | ARTIST—Record Title | LABEL & NO. |
|---|---|---|---|---|
| | | | **GIORGIO MORODER** | |
| | | | electronic composer/conductor for numerous soundtracks | |
| 3/10/79 | 33 | 4 | 1. Chase [I] | Casablanca 956 |
| | | | from the film "Midnight Express" | |
| | | | **VAN MORRISON** | |
| | | | Irish blue-eyed soul singer/songwriter - leader of Them | |
| 8/19/67 | 10 | 10 | 1. **Brown Eyed Girl** | Bang 545 |
| 4/25/70 | 39 | 2 | 2. Come Running | Warner 7383 |
| 12/05/70 + | 9 | 9 | 3. **Domino** | Warner 7434 |
| 3/06/71 | 23 | 8 | 4. Blue Money | Warner 7462 |
| 11/20/71 | 28 | 4 | 5. Wild Night | Warner 7518 |
| | | | **MOTELS** | |
| | | | Martha Davis, lead singer of quintet from Los Angeles | |
| 5/29/82 | 9 | 15 | 1. **Only The Lonely** | Capitol 5114 |
| 9/17/83 | 9 | 13 | 2. **Suddenly Last Summer** | Capitol 5271 |
| 1/14/84 | 36 | 3 | 3. Remember The Nights | Capitol 5246 |
| | | | **MOTHERLODE** | |
| | | | Canadian pop quartet led by "Smitty" Smith | |
| 9/13/69 | 18 | 7 | 1. When I Die | Buddah 131 |
| | | | **MOTT THE HOOPLE** | |
| | | | British rock group led by Ian Hunter | |
| 11/04/72 | 37 | 3 | 1. All The Young Dudes | Columbia 45673 |
| | | | **MOUNTAIN** | |
| | | | New York power-rock group led by Leslie West & Felix Pappalardi (shot to death on 4/17/83-44) | |
| 6/13/70 | 21 | 9 | 1. Mississippi Queen | Windfall 532 |
| | | | **MOUTH & MacNEAL** | |
| | | | Dutch duo: Willem Duyn & Maggie MacNeal | |
| 6/17/72 | 8 | 12 | ● 1. **How Do You Do?** | Philips 40715 |
| | | | **MOVING PICTURES** | |
| | | | Alex Smith, lead singer of Australian 6-man group | |
| 11/27/82 + | 29 | 13 | 1. What About Me | Network 69952 |
| | | | **MICKEY MOZART Quintet** | |
| 6/08/59 | 30 | 6 | 1. Little Dipper [I] | Roulette 4148 |
| | | | **MARIA MULDAUR** | |
| | | | Maria and former husband Geoff Muldaur were members of Jim Kweskin's Jug Band | |
| 4/13/74 | 6 | 14 | 1. **Midnight At The Oasis** | Reprise 1183 |
| 1/25/75 | 12 | 8 | 2. I'm A Woman | Reprise 1319 |
| | | | **MUNGO JERRY** | |
| | | | British skiffle quartet - Ray Dorset, lead singer | |
| 7/25/70 | 3 | 11 | ● 1. **In The Summertime** | Janus 125 |
| | | | **MURMAIDS** | |
| | | | female trio from Los Angeles | |
| 12/07/63 + | 3 | 11 | 1. **Popsicles And Icicles** | Chattahoochee 628 |

| DATE | POS | WKS | ARTIST—Record Title | LABEL & NO. |
|---|---|---|---|---|
| | | | **MICHAEL MURPHEY** | |
| | | | progressive country singer/songwriter from Austin, Texas | |
| 10/07/72 | 37 | 2 | 1. Geronimo's Cadillac | A&M 1368 |
| 5/03/75 | 3 | 13 | ● 2. **Wildfire** | Epic 50084 |
| 9/13/75 | 21 | 7 | 3. Carolina In The Pines | Epic 50131 |
| 2/21/76 | 39 | 2 | 4. Renegade | Epic 50184 |
| 8/28/82 | 19 | 11 | 5. What's Forever For | Liberty 1466 |
| | | | **WALTER MURPHY & The Big Apple Band** | |
| | | | keyboardist, composer and arranger of disco music | |
| 7/04/76 | 1 (1) | 22 | ● 1. **A Fifth Of Beethoven [I]** | Private S. 45073 |
| | | | based on Beethoven's Fifth Symphony | |
| | | | **ANNE MURRAY** | |
| | | | born in Springhill, Nova Scotia, Canada on 6/20/46 | |
| 8/22/70 | 8 | 11 | ● 1. **Snowbird** | Capitol 2738 |
| 2/10/73 | 7 | 13 | 2. **Danny's Song** | Capitol 3481 |
| | | | written by Kenny Loggins for his nephew | |
| 1/19/74 | 12 | 10 | 3. Love Song | Capitol 3776 |
| 5/25/74 | 8 | 10 | 4. **You Won't See Me** | Capitol 3867 |
| 8/19/78 | 1 (1) | 17 | ● 5. **You Needed Me** | Capitol 4574 |
| 2/10/79 | 12 | 12 | 6. I Just Fall In Love Again | Capitol 4675 |
| 6/23/79 | 25 | 7 | 7. Shadows In The Moonlight | Capitol 4716 |
| 10/20/79 | 12 | 11 | 8. Broken Hearted Me | Capitol 4773 |
| 1/19/80 | 12 | 12 | 9. Daydream Believer | Capitol 4813 |
| 10/18/80 | 33 | 4 | 10. Could I Have This Dance | Capitol 4920 |
| 5/02/81 | 34 | 4 | 11. Blessed Are The Believers | Capitol 4987 |
| | | | **MUSIC EXPLOSION** | |
| | | | Jamie Lyons, lead singer of pop/rock quintet from Ohio | |
| 5/27/67 | 2 (2) | 13 | ● 1. **Little Bit O'Soul** | Laurie 3380 |
| | | | **MUSIC MACHINE** | |
| | | | Los Angeles rock quintet - Sean Bonniwell, lead singer | |
| 12/10/66 + | 15 | 8 | 1. Talk Talk | Original Sound 61 |
| | | | **MUSICAL YOUTH** | |
| | | | 5 English boys (ages 11 to 16) | |
| 1/15/83 | 10 | 10 | 1. **Pass The Dutchie** | MCA 52149 |
| | | | Dutchie: a Jamaican cooking pot | |
| | | | **BILLY MYLES** | |
| 11/25/57 | 25 | 6 | 1. The Joker (That's What They Call Me) | Ember 1026 |
| | | | **MYSTICS** | |
| | | | Brooklyn, New York quintet - Phil Cracolici, lead singer | |
| 6/15/59 | 20 | 9 | 1. Hushabye | Laurie 3028 |
| | | | **NAKED EYES** | |
| | | | English duo: Pete Byrne (vocals) & Rob Fisher (keyboards) | |
| 4/23/83 | 8 | 13 | 1. **Always Something There To Remind Me** | EMI America 8155 |
| 8/13/83 | 11 | 12 | 2. Promises, Promises | EMI America 8170 |
| 12/17/83 | 37 | 3 | 3. When The Lights Go Out | EMI America 8183 |
| 9/29/84 | 39 | 2 | 4. (What) In The Name Of Love | EMI America 8219 |

| DATE | POS | WKS | ARTIST—Record Title | LABEL & NO. |
|---|---|---|---|---|
| | | | **NAPOLEON XIV** | |
| | | | Napoleon is Jerry Samuels | |
| 7/30/66 | 3 | 5 | 1. **They're Coming To Take Me Away, Ha-Haaa! [N]** | Warner 5831 |
| | | | **GRAHAM NASH** | |
| | | | English - co-founder of the Hollies - also see Crosby/Nash and Crosby, Stills & Nash | |
| 7/10/71 | 35 | 4 | 1. Chicago | Atlantic 2804 |
| | | | **JOHNNY NASH** | |
| | | | reggae/R&B singer from Houston, Texas - also see Paul Anka | |
| 2/03/58 | 23 | 1 | 1. A Very Special Love | ABC-Para. 9874 |
| 10/05/68 | 5 | 12 | 2. **Hold Me Tight** | JAD 207 |
| 1/24/70 | 39 | 1 | 3. Cupid | JAD 220 |
| 10/07/72 | 1 (4) | 14 | ● 4. **I Can See Clearly Now** | Epic 10902 |
| 3/03/73 | 12 | 10 | 5. Stir It Up | Epic 10949 |
| | | | **NASHVILLE TEENS** | |
| | | | British rock sextet - Arthur Sharp, lead singer | |
| 10/10/64 | 14 | 6 | 1. Tobacco Road | London 9689 |
| | | | **NATURAL FOUR** | |
| | | | soul foursome from San Francisco | |
| 2/09/74 | 31 | 4 | 1. Can This Be Real | Curtom 1990 |
| | | | **DAVID NAUGHTON** | |
| | | | star of TV's "Makin' It" | |
| 5/12/79 | 5 | 16 | ● 1. **Makin' It** <br> from the film "Meatballs" | RSO 916 |
| | | | **NAZARETH** | |
| | | | hard-rock group from Scotland - Dan McCafferty, lead singer | |
| 1/03/76 | 8 | 14 | ● 1. **Love Hurts** | A&M 1671 |
| | | | **SAM NEELY** | |
| | | | singer/songwriter from Corpus Christi, Texas | |
| 10/07/72 | 29 | 6 | 1. Loving You Just Crossed My Mind | Capitol 3381 |
| 11/09/74 | 34 | 2 | 2. You Can Have Her | A&M 1612 |
| | | | **NEIGHBORHOOD** | |
| 8/08/70 | 29 | 4 | 1. Big Yellow Taxi | Big Tree 102 |
| | | | **RICKY NELSON** | |
| | | | born Eric Hilliard Nelson on 5/8/40 in Teaneck, New Jersey | |
| 5/06/57 | 17 | 9 | 1. I'm Walking/ | |
| 5/27/57 | 2 (1) | 15 | 2. **A Teenager's Romance** | Verve 10047 |
| 9/16/57 | 14 | 7 | 3. You're My One And Only Love | Verve 10070 |
| 10/07/57 | 3 | 18 | 4. Be-Bop Baby/ | |
| 10/28/57 | 29 | 3 | 5. Have I Told You Lately That I Love You | Imperial 5463 |
| 12/30/57 + | 2 (3) | 14 | 6. **Stood Up/** | |
| 12/30/57 + | 18 | 9 | 7. Waitin' In School | Imperial 5483 |
| 4/07/58 | 4 | 10 | 8. **Believe What You Say/** | |
| 4/07/58 | 18 | 8 | 9. My Bucket's Got A Hole In It | Imperial 5503 |
| 7/07/58 | 1 (2) | 15 | 10. **Poor Little Fool** | Imperial 5528 |

| DATE | POS | WKS | ARTIST—Record Title | LABEL & NO. |
|---|---|---|---|---|
| 10/20/58 | 7 | 16 | 11. **Lonesome Town**/ | |
| 10/20/58 | 10 | 13 | 12.  **I Got A Feeling** | Imperial 5545 |
| 3/09/59 | 6 | 12 | 13. **Never Be Anyone Else But You**/ | |
| 3/16/59 | 9 | 10 | 14.  **It's Late** | Imperial 5565 |
| 7/13/59 | 9 | 9 | 15. **Just A Little Too Much**/ | |
| 7/13/59 | 9 | 8 | 16.  **Sweeter Than You** | Imperial 5595 |
| 12/07/59 | 20 | 8 | 17. I Wanna Be Loved/ | |
| 12/21/59 | 38 | 1 | 18.  Mighty Good | Imperial 5614 |
| 5/09/60 | 12 | 9 | 19. Young Emotions | Imperial 5663 |
| 9/19/60 | 27 | 4 | 20. I'm Not Afraid/ | |
| 9/26/60 | 34 | 2 | 21.  Yes Sir, That's My Baby | Imperial 5685 |
| 1/09/61 | 25 | 4 | 22. You Are The Only One | Imperial 5707 |
| 5/01/61 | 1 (2) | 15 | ● 23. **Travelin' Man**/ | |
| 5/08/61 | 9 | 13 | 24.  **Hello Mary Lou**<br>RICK NELSON: | Imperial 5741 |
| 10/09/61 | 11 | 9 | 25. A Wonder Like You/ | |
| 10/09/61 | 16 | 8 | 26.  Everlovin' | Imperial 5770 |
| 3/17/62 | 5 | 10 | 27. **Young World** | Imperial 5805 |
| 8/25/62 | 5 | 9 | 28. **Teen Age Idol** | Imperial 5864 |
| 12/29/62 + | 6 | 9 | 29. **It's Up To You** | Imperial 5901 |
| 6/15/63 | 25 | 5 | 30. String Along | Decca 31495 |
| 10/05/63 | 12 | 9 | 31. Fools Rush In | Decca 31533 |
| 1/11/64 | 6 | 9 | 32. **For You** | Decca 31574 |
| 5/09/64 | 26 | 5 | 33. The Very Thought Of You<br>RICK NELSON & THE STONE CANYON BAND: | Decca 31612 |
| 1/03/70 | 33 | 6 | 34. She Belongs To Me | Decca 32550 |
| 9/16/72 | 6 | 12 | ● 35. **Garden Party** | Decca 32980 |
| | | | **SANDY NELSON**<br>drummer - born on 12/1/38 in Santa Monica, California | |
| 9/14/59 | 4 | 12 | 1. **Teen Beat [I]** | Original Sound 5 |
| 11/20/61 | 7 | 12 | 2. **Let There Be Drums [I]** | Imperial 5775 |
| 3/03/62 | 29 | 4 | 3. **Drums Are My Beat [I]** | Imperial 5809 |
| | | | **WILLIE NELSON**<br>prolific country singer/songwriter from Austin, Texas -<br>born on 4/30/33 - also see Waylon & Willie/Julio Iglesias | |
| 10/11/75 | 21 | 9 | 1. Blue Eyes Crying In The Rain | Columbia 10176 |
| 9/27/80 | 20 | 10 | 2. On The Road Again<br>from the film "Honeysuckle Rose" | Columbia 11351 |
| 4/10/82 | 5 | 15 | 3. **Always On My Mind** | Columbia 02741 |
| 9/18/82 | 40 | 3 | 4. Let It Be Me | Columbia 03073 |
| | | | **NENA**<br>German - real name: Gabriele Kerner | |
| 1/21/84 | 2 (1) | 13 | ● 1. **99 Luftballons [F]** | Epic 04108 |
| | | | **NEON PHILHARMONIC**<br>Nashville session musicians | |
| 5/10/69 | 17 | 7 | 1. Morning Girl | Warner 7261 |

| DATE | POS | WKS | ARTIST—Record Title | LABEL & NO. |
|---|---|---|---|---|
| | | | **PETER NERO** | |
| | | | pop/jazz/classical pianist from Brooklyn | |
| 11/20/71 | 21 | 8 | 1. Theme From "Summer Of '42" [I] | Columbia 45399 |
| | | | **NERVOUS NORVUS** | |
| | | | real name: Jimmy Drake | |
| 6/09/56 | 8 | 9 | 1. **Transfusion [N]** | Dot 15470 |
| 8/11/56 | 24 | 4 | 2. Ape Call [N] | Dot 15485 |
| | | | ape calls by Red Blanchard | |
| | | | **MICHAEL NESMITH & The First National Band** | |
| | | | Michael was a member of The Monkees | |
| 9/05/70 | 21 | 7 | 1. Joanne | RCA 0368 |
| | | | **AARON NEVILLE** | |
| | | | brother of The Meters' Art Neville | |
| 12/17/66 + | 2 (1) | 11 | 1. **Tell It Like It Is** | Par-Lo 101 |
| | | | **NEWBEATS** | |
| | | | Larry Henley (lead singer) with Dean & Marc Mathis | |
| 8/22/64 | 2 (2) | 11 | 1. **Bread And Butter** | Hickory 1269 |
| 11/07/64 | 16 | 7 | 2. Everything's Alright | Hickory 1282 |
| 2/20/65 | 40 | 1 | 3. Break Away (From That Boy) | Hickory 1290 |
| 10/30/65 | 12 | 9 | 4. Run, Baby Run (Back Into My Arms) | Hickory 1332 |
| | | | **NEW BIRTH** | |
| | | | 12 member soul-funk band founded by Harvey Fuqua | |
| 5/05/73 | 35 | 4 | 1. I Can Understand It | RCA 0912 |
| 8/23/75 | 36 | 2 | 2. Dream Merchant | Buddah 470 |
| | | | **NEW CHRISTY MINSTRELS** | |
| | | | folk/balladeer troupe named after the Christy Minstrels formed in 1842 by Edwin P. Christy | |
| 7/27/63 | 14 | 7 | 1. Green, Green | Columbia 42805 |
| 11/16/63 | 29 | 3 | 2. Saturday Night | Columbia 42887 |
| 5/16/64 | 17 | 9 | 3. Today | Columbia 43000 |
| | | | from the film: "Advance To The Rear" | |
| | | | **NEW COLONY SIX** | |
| | | | soft-rock group from Chicago | |
| 5/11/68 | 22 | 6 | 1. I Will Always Think About You | Mercury 72775 |
| 2/15/69 | 16 | 9 | 2. Things I'd Like To Say | Mercury 72858 |
| | | | **NEW EDITION** | |
| | | | teen quintet from Boston - Ralph Tresvant, lead singer | |
| 10/27/84 | 4 | 14 | 1. **Cool It Now** | MCA 52455 |
| | | | **NEW ENGLAND** | |
| | | | East Coast melodic rock quartet | |
| 6/16/79 | 40 | 1 | 1. Don't Ever Wanna Lose Ya | Infinity 50013 |
| | | | **NEW SEEKERS** | |
| | | | group formed by Keith Potger after disbandment of The Seekers | |
| 9/19/70 | 14 | 9 | 1. Look What They've Done To My Song Ma | Elektra 45699 |
| 12/18/71 + | 7 | 9 | ● 2. **I'd Like To Teach The World To Sing (In Perfect Harmony)** | Elektra 45762 |
| 4/14/73 | 29 | 4 | 3. Pinball Wizard/See Me, Feel Me | Verve 10709 |
| | | | from the rock opera "Tommy" | |

| DATE | POS | WKS | ARTIST—Record Title | LABEL & NO. |
|---|---|---|---|---|
| | | | **NEW VAUDEVILLE BAND** | |
| | | | English - Geoff Stevens, vocals | |
| 11/05/66 | **1** (3) | 13 | ● 1. **Winchester Cathedral** | Fontana 1562 |
| | | | **NEW YORK CITY** | |
| | | | R&B quartet - first tenor John Brown was a member of the Five Satins | |
| 4/28/73 | **17** | 12 | 1. I'm Doin' Fine Now | Chelsea 0113 |
| | | | **MICKEY NEWBURY** | |
| 12/04/71 + | **26** | 7 | 1. An American Trilogy | Elektra 45750 |
| | | | **JIMMY NEWMAN** | |
| 7/22/57 | **23** | 1 | 1. A Fallen Star | Dot 15574 |
| | | | **RANDY NEWMAN** | |
| | | | nephew of composers Alfred, Emil, & Lionel Newman | |
| 12/10/77 + | **2** (3) | 13 | ● 1. **Short People [N]** | Warner 8492 |
| | | | **JUICE NEWTON** | |
| | | | country-pop singer born in Virginia Beach, Virginia | |
| 3/07/81 | **4** | 16 | ● 1. **Angel Of The Morning** | Capitol 4976 |
| 6/20/81 | **2** (2) | 19 | ● 2. **Queen Of Hearts** | Capitol 4997 |
| 11/07/81 + | **7** | 18 | 3. **The Sweetest Thing (I've Ever Known)** | Capitol 5046 |
| 5/22/82 | **7** | 13 | 4. **Love's Been A Little Bit Hard On Me** | Capitol 5120 |
| 9/11/82 | **11** | 10 | 5. Break It To Me Gently | Capitol 5148 |
| 12/18/82 + | **25** | 10 | 6. Heart Of The Night | Capitol 5192 |
| 9/03/83 | **27** | 5 | 7. Tell Her No | Capitol 5265 |
| | | | **WAYNE NEWTON** | |
| | | | Las Vegas's #1 entertainer - born on 4/3/42 in Roanoke, Virginia | |
| 8/03/63 | **13** | 8 | 1. Danke Schoen | Capitol 4989 |
| 3/27/65 | **23** | 5 | 2. Red Roses For A Blue Lady | Capitol 5366 |
| 6/10/72 | **4** | 13 | ● 3. **Daddy Don't You Walk So Fast** | Chelsea 0100 |
| 3/22/80 | **35** | 3 | 4. Years | Aries II 108 |
| | | | **OLIVIA NEWTON-JOHN** | |
| | | | born on 9/26/48 in Cambridge, England - raised in Melbourne, Australia - also see John Denver | |
| 7/17/71 | **25** | 10 | 1. If Not For You | Uni 55281 |
| 12/15/73 + | **6** | 14 | ● 2. **Let Me Be There** | MCA 40101 |
| 5/11/74 | **5** | 12 | ● 3. **If You Love Me (Let Me Know)** | MCA 40209 |
| 8/24/74 | **1** (2) | 10 | ● 4. **I Honestly Love You** | MCA 40280 |
| 2/08/75 | **1** (1) | 11 | ● 5. **Have You Never Been Mellow** | MCA 40349 |
| 6/21/75 | **3** | 12 | ● 6. **Please Mr. Please** | MCA 40418 |
| 10/11/75 | **13** | 7 | 7. Something Better To Do | MCA 40459 |
| 1/03/76 | **30** | 4 | 8. Let It Shine | MCA 40495 |
| 4/17/76 | **23** | 6 | 9. Come On Over | MCA 40525 |
| 9/04/76 | **33** | 4 | 10. Don't Stop Believin' | MCA 40600 |
| 2/19/77 | **20** | 9 | 11. Sam | MCA 40670 |
| 7/22/78 | **3** | 15 | ● 12. **Hopelessly Devoted To You** | RSO 903 |
| | | | from the film "Grease" | |
| 12/09/78 + | **3** | 17 | ● 13. **A Little More Love** | MCA 40975 |

| DATE | POS | WKS | ARTIST—Record Title | LABEL & NO. |
|---|---|---|---|---|
| 5/05/79 | 11 | 8 | 14. Deeper Than The Night | MCA 41009 |
| 6/14/80 | 1 (4) | 16 | ● 15. **Magic**<br>from the film "Xanadu" | MCA 41247 |
| 10/17/81 | 1(10) | 21 | ★ 16. **Physical** | MCA 51182 |
| 2/27/82 | 5 | 10 | 17. **Make A Move On Me** | MCA 52000 |
| 9/25/82 | 3 | 13 | 18. **Heart Attack** | MCA 52100 |
| 2/19/83 | 38 | 3 | 19. Tied Up | MCA 52155 |
| 11/12/83 + | 5 | 14 | 20. **Twist Of Fate** | MCA 52284 |
| 2/25/84 | 31 | 5 | 21. Livin' In Desperate Times<br>above 2 from the film "Two Of A Kind" | MCA 52341 |
| | | | **OLIVIA NEWTON-JOHN/ELECTRIC LIGHT ORCHESTRA** | |
| 8/30/80 | 8 | 10 | 1. **Xanadu** | MCA 41285 |
| | | | **OLIVIA NEWTON-JOHN & ANDY GIBB** | |
| 4/19/80 | 12 | 8 | 1. I Can't Help It | RSO 1026 |
| | | | **OLIVIA NEWTON-JOHN & CLIFF RICHARD** | |
| 11/22/80 + | 20 | 11 | 1. **Suddenly**<br>from the film "Xanadu" | MCA 51007 |
| | | | **OLIVIA NEWTON-JOHN & JOHN TRAVOLTA** | |
| 4/08/78 | 1 (1) | 16 | ★ 1. **You're The One That I Want** | RSO 891 |
| 8/19/78 | 5 | 12 | ● 2. **Summer Nights**<br>above 2 from the film "Grease" | RSO 906 |
| | | | **PAUL NICHOLAS**<br>English | |
| 9/17/77 | 6 | 16 | ● 1. **Heaven On The 7th Floor** | RSO 878 |
| | | | **STEVIE NICKS**<br>lead singer of Fleetwood Mac | |
| 8/01/81 | 3 | 15 | 1. **Stop Draggin' My Heart Around**<br>with Tom Petty & The Heartbreakers | Modern 7336 |
| 11/07/81 + | 6 | 15 | 2. **Leather And Lace**<br>with Don Henley | Modern 7341 |
| 3/06/82 | 11 | 11 | 3. Edge Of Seventeen (Just Like The White Winged Dove) | Modern 7401 |
| 6/12/82 | 32 | 4 | 4. After The Glitter Fades | Modern 7405 |
| 6/18/83 | 5 | 14 | 5. **Stand Back** | Modern 99863 |
| 9/24/83 | 14 | 9 | 6. If Anyone Falls | Modern 99832 |
| 1/21/84 | 33 | 4 | 7. Nightbird<br>with Sandy Stewart | Modern 99799 |
| | | | **NIELSEN/PEARSON**<br>Reid Nielsen/Mark Pearson | |
| 11/15/80 | 38 | 2 | 1. If You Should Sail | Capitol 4910 |
| | | | **NIGHT**<br>Stevie Lange & Chris Thompson (Manfred Mann), lead singers - also see Chris Thompson | |
| 8/04/79 | 18 | 8 | 1. Hot Summer Nights | Planet 45903 |

| DATE | POS | WKS | ARTIST—Record Title | LABEL & NO. |
|------|-----|-----|---------------------|-------------|
| | | | **MAXINE NIGHTINGALE** | |
| | | | English | |
| 3/13/76 | **2** (2) | 15 | ● 1. **Right Back Where We Started From** | United Art. 752 |
| 7/07/79 | **5** | 14 | ● 2. **Lead Me On** | Windsong 11530 |
| | | | **NIGHT RANGER** | |
| | | | rock quintet from California | |
| 2/26/83 | **40** | 3 | 1. Don't Tell Me You Love Me | Boardwalk 171 |
| 4/21/84 | **5** | 12 | 2. **Sister Christian** | MCA 52350 |
| 8/04/84 | **14** | 11 | 3. When You Close Your Eyes | MCA 52420 |
| | | | **NILSSON** | |
| | | | Harry Nilsson - born on 6/15/41 in Brooklyn, New York | |
| 9/06/69 | **6** | 9 | 1. **Everybody's Talkin'** | RCA 0161 |
| | | | from the film "Midnight Cowboy" | |
| 11/29/69 | **34** | 2 | 2. I Guess The Lord Must Be In New York City | RCA 0261 |
| 5/08/71 | **34** | 4 | 3. Me And My Arrow | RCA 0443 |
| 1/15/72 | **1** (4) | 14 | ● 4. **Without You** | RCA 0604 |
| 4/08/72 | **27** | 6 | 5. Jump Into The Fire | RCA 0673 |
| 7/08/72 | **8** | 10 | 6. **Coconut** | RCA 0718 |
| 10/14/72 | **23** | 6 | 7. Spaceman | RCA 0788 |
| 5/25/74 | **39** | 2 | 8. Daybreak | RCA 0246 |
| | | | from the film "Son Of Dracula" | |
| | | | **1910 FRUITGUM CO.** | |
| | | | bubblegum group assembled by producers Jerry Kasenetz & Jeff Katz | |
| 2/10/68 | **4** | 11 | ● 1. **Simon Says** | Buddah 24 |
| 8/10/68 | **5** | 11 | ● 2. **1, 2, 3, Red Light** | Buddah 54 |
| 12/07/68 | **37** | 3 | 3. Goody Goody Gumdrops | Buddah 71 |
| 2/08/69 | **5** | 11 | ● 4. **Indian Giver** | Buddah 91 |
| 6/14/69 | **38** | 2 | 5. Special Delivery | Buddah 114 |
| | | | **NITE-LITERS** | |
| | | | funk 'n' roll band produced by Harvey Fuqua | |
| 9/11/71 | **39** | 1 | 1. K-Jee [I] | RCA 0461 |
| | | | **NITEFLYTE** | |
| 11/24/79 | **37** | 2 | 1. If You Want It | Ariola 7747 |
| | | | **NITTY GRITTY DIRT BAND** | |
| | | | country-rock-folk group led by Jeff Hanna & John McEuen | |
| 1/02/71 | **9** | 13 | 1. **Mr. Bojangles** | Liberty 56197 |
| | | | prologue: Uncle Charlie & his dog Teddy | |
| 1/12/80 | **13** | 11 | 2. An American Dream | United Art. 1330 |
| | | | harmony vocal: Linda Ronstadt | |
| 7/12/80 | **25** | 9 | 3. Make A Little Magic | United Art. 1356 |
| | | | **JACK NITZSCHE** | |
| | | | arranger for many of Phil Spector's productions | |
| 9/07/63 | **39** | 2 | 1. The Lonely Surfer [I] | Reprise 20202 |
| | | | **NICK NOBLE** | |
| 8/20/55 | **22** | 3 | 1. The Bible Tells Me So | Wing 90003 |
| 3/24/56 | **27** | 6 | 2. To You, My Love | Mercury 70821 |

| DATE | POS | WKS | ARTIST—Record Title | LABEL & NO. |
|---|---|---|---|---|
| 7/15/57 | **20** | 1 | 3. A Fallen Star | Mercury 71124 |
| 9/30/57 | **37** | 1 | 4. Moonlight Swim | Mercury 71169 |
| | | | **CLIFF NOBLES & Co.** | |
| 6/08/68 | **2** (3) | 12 | ● 1. **The Horse [I]** | Phil. L.A. 313 |
| | | | **JACKY NOGUEZ & His Musette Orchestra** | |
| | | | French | |
| 7/27/59 | **24** | 5 | 1. Ciao, Ciao Bambina [I] | Jamie 1127 |
| | | | **KENNY NOLAN** | |
| 12/11/76 + | **3** | 20 | ● 1. **I Like Dreamin'** | 20th Century 2287 |
| 5/07/77 | **20** | 11 | 2. Love's Grown Deep | 20th Century 2331 |
| | | | **CHRIS NORMAN - see SUZI QUATRO** | |
| | | | **FREDDIE NORTH** | |
| 11/27/71 | **39** | 1 | 1. She's All I Got | Mankind 12004 |
| | | | **ALDO NOVA** | |
| | | | rock singer/songwriter from Montreal, Canada | |
| 5/01/82 | **23** | 7 | 1. Fantasy | Portrait 02799 |
| | | | **NU TORNADOS** | |
| 12/15/58 | **26** | 6 | 1. Philadelphia U.S.A. | Carlton 492 |
| | | | **TED NUGENT** | |
| | | | heavy-metal rock guitarist from Detroit - also see Amboy Dukes | |
| 9/10/77 | **30** | 6 | 1. Cat Scratch Fever | Epic 50425 |
| | | | **GARY NUMAN** | |
| | | | British synthesized techno-rock artist | |
| 3/29/80 | **9** | 17 | 1. **Cars** | Atco 7211 |
| | | | **NUTTY SQUIRRELS** | |
| | | | creators: Don Elliot & Sascha Burland | |
| 11/30/59 | **14** | 7 | 1. Uh! Oh! Part 2 [N] | Hanover 4540 |
| | | | **OAK** | |
| 7/12/80 | **36** | 3 | 1. King Of The Hill | Mercury 76049 |
| | | | shown as Rick Pinette & Oak | |
| | | | **OAK RIDGE BOYS** | |
| | | | formed in Oak Ridge, Tennessee in 1957 as a gospel quartet | |
| 6/06/81 | **5** | 14 | ★ 1. **Elvira** | MCA 51084 |
| 2/13/82 | **12** | 9 | 2. Bobbie Sue | MCA 51231 |
| | | | **JOHN O'BANION** | |
| | | | from Kokomo, Indiana | |
| 4/18/81 | **24** | 7 | 1. Love You Like I Never Loved Before | Elektra 47125 |
| | | | **OCEAN** | |
| | | | Canadian quintet | |
| 3/27/71 | **2** (1) | 12 | ● 1. **Put Your Hand In The Hand** | Kama Sutra 519 |

| DATE | POS | WKS | ARTIST—Record Title | LABEL & NO. |
|---|---|---|---|---|
| | | | **BILLY OCEAN** | |
| | | | born in Trinidad - raised in London | |
| 5/01/76 | 22 | 6 | 1. Love Really Hurts Without You | Ariola 7621 |
| 9/08/84 | 1 (2) | 15 | ● 2. **Caribbean Queen (No More Love On The Run)** | Jive 9199 |
| | | | **ALAN O'DAY** | |
| | | | wrote Helen Reddy's #1 hit "Angie Baby" | |
| 5/07/77 | 1 (1) | 17 | ● 1. **Undercover Angel** | Pacific 001 |
| | | | **KENNY O'DELL** | |
| | | | real name: Kenneth Gist, Jr. | |
| 12/16/67 | 38 | 2 | 1. Beautiful People | Vegas 718 |
| | | | **ODYSSEY** | |
| | | | lead vocals by sisters Lillian & Louise Lopez | |
| 12/17/77 + | 21 | 12 | 1. Native New Yorker | RCA 11129 |
| | | | **OHIO EXPRESS** | |
| | | | bubblegum group assembled by producers Jerry Kasenetz & Jeff Katz | |
| 11/18/67 | 29 | 5 | 1. Beg, Borrow And Steal | Cameo 483 |
| 5/18/68 | 4 | 11 | ● 2. **Yummy Yummy Yummy** | Buddah 38 |
| 8/31/68 | 33 | 5 | 3. Down At Lulu's | Buddah 56 |
| 11/02/68 | 15 | 10 | ● 4. Chewy Chewy | Buddah 70 |
| 4/26/69 | 30 | 4 | 5. Mercy | Buddah 102 |
| | | | **OHIO PLAYERS** | |
| | | | R&B/funk group originally formed in Dayton, Ohio in 1959 as the Ohio Untouchables | |
| 4/14/73 | 15 | 9 | ● 1. Funky Worm [N] | Westbound 214 |
| 9/22/73 | 31 | 6 | 2. Ecstasy | Westbound 216 |
| 9/14/74 | 13 | 7 | ● 3. Skin Tight | Mercury 73609 |
| 12/28/74 + | 1 (1) | 12 | ● 4. **Fire** | Mercury 73643 |
| 10/11/75 | 33 | 3 | 5. Sweet Sticky Thing | Mercury 73713 |
| 11/22/75 + | 1 (1) | 14 | ● 6. **Love Rollercoaster** | Mercury 73734 |
| 3/27/76 | 30 | 5 | 7. Fopp | Mercury 73775 |
| 7/31/76 | 18 | 10 | 8. Who'd She Coo? | Mercury 73814 |
| | | | **O'JAYS** | |
| | | | soul group formed in Canton, Ohio in 1958: Eddie Levert, Walt Williams, William Powell (died 5/26/77) - replaced by Sam Strain | |
| 8/12/72 | 3 | 12 | ● 1. **Back Stabbers** | Phil. Int. 3517 |
| 1/27/73 | 1 (1) | 13 | ● 2. **Love Train** | Phil. Int. 3524 |
| 6/30/73 | 33 | 2 | 3. Time To Get Down | Phil. Int. 3531 |
| 1/12/74 | 10 | 11 | 4. **Put Your Hands Together** | Phil. Int. 3535 |
| 5/04/74 | 9 | 10 | ● 5. **For The Love Of Money** | Phil. Int. 3544 |
| 11/15/75 + | 5 | 14 | ● 6. **I Love Music (Part 1)** | Phil. Int. 3577 |
| 3/27/76 | 20 | 6 | 7. Livin' For The Weekend | Phil. Int. 3587 |
| 6/03/78 | 4 | 11 | ● 8. **Use Ta Be My Girl** | Phil. Int. 3642 |
| 1/05/80 | 28 | 5 | 9. Forever Mine | Phil. Int. 3727 |
| | | | **O'KAYSIONS** | |
| | | | white soul group from North Carolina - Donny Weaver, lead singer | |
| 9/07/68 | 5 | 11 | ● 1. **Girl Watcher** | ABC 11094 |

robert plant
in the mood

I'LL NEVER SMILE AGAIN
AND
YOU DON'T SAY
the platters

Mercury
RECORDS
71847

POINTER SISTERS
Fire

FROM THE ALBUM

THE POLICE

SYNCHRONICITY II

**Robert Plant.** According to myth, when Jimmy Page set out to form the New Yardbirds (later known as Led Zeppelin), his first choice for singer was Terry Reid. However, Reid declined the offer, recommending powerful blues shouter Plant instead.

**The Platters** were working as parking lot attendants when they were discovered by manager Buck Ram. He signed the group with Federal Records, where they faltered, and then Mercury, where they hit the jackpot.

**The Pointer Sisters** had to overcome the objections of their parents, both of whom were ministers, to embark on a singing career. Before making their own records, the Pointers sang backup for the likes of Elvin Bishop, Dave Mason, Boz Scaggs, and Dr. Hook.

**The Police** flew to America for their first club tour via Freddy Laker's budget airline, checking their equipment as luggage.

**Mike Post,** formerly the producer of Kenny Rogers and the First Edition, and Mason Williams, has become king of TV theme songs with his work for "Magnum, P.I.," "The Rockford Files," and "Hill Street Blues."

**Elvis Presley's** contract was purchased from Sam Phillips of Sun Records in 1955 for the then-unheard-of sum of $35,000. RCA Records' investment was quickly recouped when his label debut, "Heartbreak Hotel," went straight to Number One.

MIKE POST
Theme From
MAGNUM P.I.

A "New Orthophonic" High Fidelity Recording
RCA VICTOR
47-6800

PLAYING FOR KEEPS
and
TOO MUCH

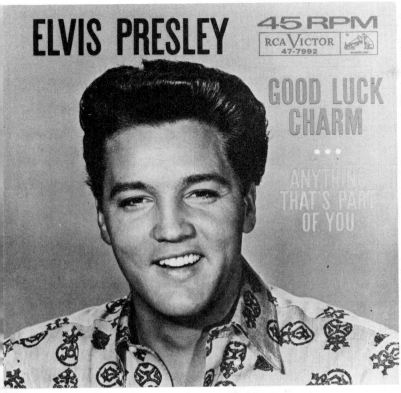

ELVIS PRESLEY

45 RPM

RCA VICTOR
47-7992

GOOD LUCK
CHARM

• • •

ANYTHING
THAT'S PART
OF YOU

BILLY PRESTON

NOTHING
FROM
NOTHING

Delirious

**Elvis Presley.** From a $35-a-week truck driver for the Crown Electric Company to Graceland and undisputed dominance of the music world. Is this a great country, or what?

**Billy Preston's** been around. He appeared in the movie *St. Louis Blues* (starring Nat "King" Cole and Eartha Kitt) in 1958. He also toured with Ray Charles, Little Richard, and the Rolling Stones, cut "Let It Be" with the Beatles, and sang with Syreeta, the former Mrs. Stevie Wonder.

**Prince's** third single from the *1999* LP followed its predecessors into the Top Ten, but even that success couldn't secure airplay for the B-side. Title? "Horny Toad."

**Prince** might have been unleashed on the world much sooner. Numerous A&R men offered the talented Minnesotan record deals, but none would guarantee him the right to produce himself. He held out until he found someone who did.

| DATE | POS | WKS | ARTIST—Record Title | LABEL & NO. |
|------|-----|-----|---------------------|-------------|
| | | | **DANNY O'KEEFE** | |
| 9/23/72 | 9 | 10 | 1. **Good Time Charlie's Got The Blues** | Signpost 70006 |
| | | | **MIKE OLDFIELD** | |
| | | | English electronic prodigy | |
| 3/30/74 | 7 | 10 | 1. **Tubular Bells [I]** | Virgin 55100 |
| | | | theme from the film "The Exorcist" | |
| | | | **OLIVER** | |
| | | | William Oliver Swofford - from North Carolina | |
| 6/07/69 | 3 | 11 | 1. **Good Morning Starshine** | Jubilee 5659 |
| | | | from the Broadway musical "Hair" | |
| 8/30/69 | 2 (2) | 12 | ● 2. **Jean** | Crewe 334 |
| | | | from the film "The Prime Of Miss Jean Brodie" | |
| 12/20/69 | 35 | 2 | 3. Sunday Mornin' | Crewe 337 |
| | | | **OLLIE & JERRY** | |
| | | | Ollie Brown & Jerry Knight (Raydio) | |
| 6/16/84 | 9 | 11 | 1. **Breakin'...There's No Stopping Us** | Polydor 821708 |
| | | | from the film "Breakin'" | |
| | | | **NIGEL OLSSON** | |
| | | | drummer for Elton John's band | |
| 1/27/79 | 18 | 9 | 1. Dancin' Shoes | Bang 740 |
| 5/19/79 | 34 | 4 | 2. Little Bit Of Soap | Bang 4800 |
| | | | **OLYMPICS** | |
| | | | Walter Ward, founder & leader of Los Angeles R&B quartet | |
| 8/04/58 | 8 | 11 | 1. **Western Movies [N]** | Demon 1508 |
| 6/08/63 | 40 | 2 | 2. The Bounce | Tri Disc 106 |
| | | | **100 PROOF Aged In Soul** | |
| 10/03/70 | 8 | 10 | ● 1. **Somebody's Been Sleeping** | Hot Wax 7004 |
| | | | **ROY ORBISON** | |
| | | | born in Wink, Texas on 4/23/36 | |
| 6/20/60 | 2 (1) | 15 | 1. **Only The Lonely (Know How I Feel)** | Monument 421 |
| 10/17/60 | 9 | 8 | 2. **Blue Angel** | Monument 425 |
| 12/31/60 + | 27 | 3 | 3. I'm Hurtin | Monument 433 |
| 4/24/61 | 1 (1) | 15 | 4. **Running Scared** | Monument 438 |
| 8/28/61 | 2 (1) | 14 | 5. **Crying/** | |
| 10/09/61 | 25 | 5 | 6. Candy Man | Monument 447 |
| 3/03/62 | 4 | 9 | 7. **Dream Baby (How Long Must I Dream)** | Monument 456 |
| 6/23/62 | 26 | 6 | 8. The Crowd | Monument 461 |
| 10/27/62 | 25 | 5 | 9. Leah/ | |
| 10/27/62 | 33 | 4 | 10. Workin' For The Man | Monument 467 |
| 2/23/63 | 7 | 10 | 11. **In Dreams** | Monument 806 |
| 6/22/63 | 22 | 5 | 12. Falling | Monument 815 |
| 9/28/63 | 5 | 10 | 13. **Mean Woman Blues/** | |
| 10/12/63 | 29 | 5 | 14. Blue Bayou | Monument 824 |
| 12/21/63 + | 15 | 5 | 15. Pretty Paper [X] | Monument 830 |
| 4/25/64 | 9 | 9 | 16. **It's Over** | Monument 837 |

| DATE | POS | WKS | ARTIST—Record Title | LABEL & NO. |
|---|---|---|---|---|
| 9/05/64 | **1** (3) | 14 | ● 17. **Oh, Pretty Woman**<br>with the Candymen | Monument 851 |
| 2/20/65 | **21** | 6 | 18. Goodnight | Monument 873 |
| 8/07/65 | **39** | 2 | 19. (Say) You're My Girl | Monument 891 |
| 9/18/65 | **25** | 5 | 20. Ride Away | MGM 13386 |
| 2/12/66 | **31** | 4 | 21. Breakin' Up Is Breakin' My Heart | MGM 13446 |
| 5/21/66 | **39** | 2 | 22. Twinkle Toes | MGM 13498 |
| | | | **ORIGINAL CASTE** | |
| 2/07/70 | **34** | 2 | 1. One Tin Soldier<br>from the film "Billy Jack" | T-A 186 |
| | | | **ORIGINALS**<br>Detroit soul quartet | |
| 10/18/69 | **14** | 13 | 1. Baby, I'm For Real | Soul 35066 |
| 3/07/70 | **12** | 9 | 2. The Bells | Soul 35069 |
| | | | **TONY ORLANDO**<br>also see Dawn, and Wind | |
| 5/29/61 | **39** | 2 | 1. Halfway To Paradise | Epic 9441 |
| 9/04/61 | **15** | 7 | 2. Bless You | Epic 9452 |
| | | | **ORLEANS**<br>rock group founded by John Hall | |
| 8/30/75 | **6** | 11 | 1. **Dance With Me** | Asylum 45261 |
| 8/14/76 | **5** | 12 | 2. **Still The One** | Asylum 45336 |
| 4/07/79 | **11** | 9 | 3. Love Takes Time | Infinity 50006 |
| | | | **ORLONS**<br>Philadelphia quartet - Shirley Brickley, lead singer | |
| 6/23/62 | **2** (2) | 11 | 1. **The Wah Watusi** | Cameo 218 |
| 11/03/62 | **4** | 11 | 2. **Don't Hang Up** | Cameo 231 |
| 3/02/63 | **3** | 10 | 3. **South Street** | Cameo 243 |
| 7/06/63 | **12** | 7 | 4. Not Me | Cameo 257 |
| 10/19/63 | **19** | 5 | 5. Cross Fire! | Cameo 273 |
| | | | **ROBERT ELLIS ORRALL with CARLENE CARTER** | |
| 5/07/83 | **32** | 3 | 1. I Couldn't Say No | RCA 13431 |
| | | | **JEFFREY OSBORNE**<br>former lead singer of L.T.D. | |
| 8/14/82 | **39** | 2 | 1. I Really Don't Need No Light | A&M 2410 |
| 11/20/82 | **29** | 7 | 2. On The Wings Of Love | A&M 2434 |
| 8/20/83 | **25** | 6 | 3. Don't You Get So Mad | A&M 2561 |
| 12/17/83 + | **30** | 8 | 4. Stay With Me Tonight | A&M 2591 |
| | | | **DONNY OSMOND**<br>born on 12/9/57 in Ogden, Utah | |
| 5/01/71 | **7** | 11 | ● 1. **Sweet And Innocent** | MGM 14227 |
| 8/21/71 | **1** (3) | 13 | ● 2. **Go Away Little Girl** | MGM 14285 |
| 12/04/71 + | **9** | 9 | ● 3. **Hey Girl** | MGM 14322 |
| 3/04/72 | **3** | 10 | ● 4. **Puppy Love** | MGM 14367 |
| 6/17/72 | **13** | 8 | 5. Too Young | MGM 14407 |

| DATE | POS | WKS | ARTIST—Record Title | LABEL & NO. |
|---|---|---|---|---|
| 9/16/72 | 13 | 9 | 6. Why/ | |
| | | 9 | 7. **Lonely Boy** | MGM 14424 |
| 3/24/73 | 8 | 9 | ● 8. **The Twelfth Of Never** | MGM 14503 |
| 8/04/73 | 23 | 7 | 9. A Million To One/ | |
| | | 7 | 10. Young Love | MGM 14583 |
| 12/15/73 + | 14 | 8 | 11. Are You Lonesome Tonight | MGM 14677 |
| 7/24/76 | 38 | 3 | 12. C'mon Marianne | Polydor 14320 |
| | | | **DONNY & MARIE OSMOND** | |
| | | | co-hosts of a musical/variety TV show, 1976-1978 | |
| 7/27/74 | 4 | 10 | ● 1. **I'm Leaving It (All) Up To You** | MGM 14735 |
| 12/14/74 + | 8 | 10 | 2. **Morning Side Of The Mountain** | MGM 14765 |
| 1/24/76 | 14 | 13 | 3. Deep Purple | MGM 14840 |
| 12/25/76 + | 21 | 8 | 4. Ain't Nothing Like The Real Thing | Polydor 14363 |
| 1/07/78 | 38 | 3 | 5. (You're My) Soul And Inspiration | Polydor 14439 |
| 11/18/78 | 38 | 2 | 6. On The Shelf | Polydor 14510 |
| | | | **LITTLE JIMMY OSMOND** | |
| | | | born on 4/16/63 in Canoga Park, California | |
| 6/03/72 | 38 | 3 | 1. Long Haired Lover From Liverpool | MGM 14376 |
| | | | **MARIE OSMOND** | |
| | | | born on 10/13/59 in Odgen, Utah | |
| 10/06/73 | 5 | 12 | ● 1. **Paper Roses** | MGM 14609 |
| 4/05/75 | 40 | 2 | 2. Who's Sorry Now | MGM 14786 |
| 6/04/77 | 39 | 1 | 3. This Is The Way That I Feel | Polydor 14385 |
| | | | **OSMONDS** | |
| | | | Alan, Wayne, Merrill, Jay & Donny | |
| 1/23/71 | 1 (5) | 12 | ● 1. **One Bad Apple** | MGM 14193 |
| 5/29/71 | 14 | 7 | 2. Double Lovin' | MGM 14259 |
| 9/18/71 | 3 | 12 | ● 3. **Yo-Yo** | MGM 14295 |
| 1/29/72 | 4 | 12 | ● 4. **Down By The Lazy River** | MGM 14324 |
| 7/08/72 | 14 | 6 | 5. Hold Her Tight | MGM 14405 |
| 11/11/72 | 14 | 8 | 6. Crazy Horses | MGM 14450 |
| 7/07/73 | 36 | 2 | 7. Goin' Home | MGM 14562 |
| 10/06/73 | 36 | 3 | 8. Let Me In | MGM 14617 |
| 9/21/74 | 10 | 7 | 9. **Love Me For A Reason** | MGM 14746 |
| 8/23/75 | 22 | 6 | 10. The Proud One | MGM 14791 |
| | | | **GILBERT O'SULLIVAN** | |
| | | | Irish | |
| 7/01/72 | 1 (6) | 15 | ● 1. **Alone Again (Naturally)** | MAM 3619 |
| 11/11/72 | 2 (2) | 14 | ● 2. **Clair** | MAM 3626 |
| 4/07/73 | 17 | 8 | 3. Out Of The Question | MAM 3628 |
| 7/14/73 | 7 | 11 | ● 4. **Get Down** | MAM 3629 |
| 11/10/73 | 25 | 4 | 5. Ooh Baby | MAM 3633 |
| | | | **OTIS & CARLA** | |
| | | | Otis Redding & Carla Thomas | |
| 6/03/67 | 26 | 4 | 1. Tramp | Stax 216 |
| 9/23/67 | 30 | 2 | 2. Knock On Wood | Stax 228 |

| DATE | POS | WKS | ARTIST—Record Title | LABEL & NO. |
|---|---|---|---|---|
| | | | **JOHNNY OTIS Show** | |
| | | | Johnny's R&B Caravan featured the top R&B artists of the Fifties | |
| 6/30/58 | 9 | 15 | 1. **Willie And The Hand Jive** | Capitol 3966 |
| | | | **OUTLAWS** | |
| | | | Southern rock band from Tampa, Florida | |
| 10/11/75 | 34 | 3 | 1. There Goes Another Love Song | Arista 0150 |
| 2/14/81 | 31 | 4 | 2. (Ghost) Riders In The Sky | Arista 0582 |
| | | | **OUTSIDERS** | |
| | | | Cleveland rock quintet - Sonny Geraci, lead singer | |
| 3/26/66 | 5 | 10 | 1. **Time Won't Let Me** | Capitol 5573 |
| 6/04/66 | 21 | 5 | 2. Girl In Love | Capitol 5646 |
| 8/20/66 | 15 | 6 | 3. Respectable | Capitol 5701 |
| 12/10/66 | 37 | 2 | 4. Help Me Girl | Capitol 5759 |
| | | | **REG OWEN & His Orchestra** | |
| 12/22/58 + | 10 | 13 | 1. **Manhattan Spiritual [I]** | Palette 5005 |
| | | | **BUCK OWENS** | |
| | | | country singer from Bakersfield, California - co-host of "Hee-Haw" since 1969 | |
| 2/13/65 | 25 | 5 | 1. I've Got A Tiger By The Tail | Capitol 5336 |
| | | | **DONNIE OWENS** | |
| 11/03/58 | 25 | 8 | 1. Need You | Guyden 2001 |
| | | | **OXO** | |
| | | | West Coast quartet led by former Foxy member, Ish Angel | |
| 4/02/83 | 28 | 6 | 1. Whirly Girl | Geffen 29765 |
| | | | **OZARK MOUNTAIN DAREDEVILS** | |
| | | | country-rock group from Springfield, Missouri | |
| 6/08/74 | 25 | 5 | 1. If You Wanna Get To Heaven | A&M 1515 |
| 3/22/75 | 3 | 12 | 2. **Jackie Blue** | A&M 1654 |
| | | | **PABLO CRUISE** | |
| | | | San Francisco quartet led by Dave Jenkins (Stoneground) | |
| 6/11/77 | 6 | 14 | 1. **Whatcha Gonna Do?** | A&M 1920 |
| 7/01/78 | 6 | 12 | 2. **Love Will Find A Way** | A&M 2048 |
| 10/21/78 | 21 | 8 | 3. Don't Want To Live Without It | A&M 2076 |
| 11/10/79 | 19 | 10 | 4. I Want You Tonight | A&M 2195 |
| 7/25/81 | 13 | 11 | 5. Cool Love | A&M 2349 |
| | | | **PACIFIC GAS & ELECTRIC** | |
| | | | West Coast blues-rock quintet - Charlie Allen, lead singer | |
| 6/20/70 | 14 | 9 | 1. Are You Ready? | Columbia 45158 |
| | | | vocal backing by The Blackberries | |
| | | | **PATTI PAGE** | |
| | | | born Clara Ann Fowler in Claremore, Oklahoma on 11/8/27 | |
| 12/18/54 + | 8 | 7 | 1. **Let Me Go, Lover!** | Mercury 70511 |
| 11/12/55 | 16 | 8 | 2. Croce Di Oro (Cross Of Gold) | Mercury 70713 |
| 1/14/56 | 11 | 8 | 3. Go On With The Wedding | Mercury 70766 |
| 6/16/56 | 2 (2) | 22 | 4. **Allegheny Moon** | Mercury 70878 |

| DATE | POS | WKS | ARTIST—Record Title | LABEL & NO. |
|---|---|---|---|---|
| 11/03/56 | 11 | 12 | 5. Mama From The Train | Mercury 70971 |
| 3/23/57 | 14 | 6 | 6. A Poor Man's Roses (Or A Rich Man's Gold) | Mercury 71059 |
| 6/03/57 | 3 | 17 | 7. **Old Cape Cod/** | |
| 6/03/57 | 12 | 5 | 8. Wondering | Mercury 71101 |
| 11/11/57 | 23 | 3 | 9. I'll Remember Today | Mercury 71189 |
| 2/10/58 | 13 | 8 | 10. Belonging To Someone | Mercury 71247 |
| 5/05/58 | 20 | 1 | 11. Another Time, Another Place | Mercury 71294 |
| 6/30/58 | 9 | 10 | 12. **Left Right Out Of Your Heart** | Mercury 71331 |
| 10/20/58 | 39 | 1 | 13. Fibbin' | Mercury 71355 |
| 7/04/60 | 31 | 5 | 14. One Of Us (Will Weep Tonight) | Mercury 71639 |
| 5/12/62 | 27 | 4 | 15. Most People Get Married | Mercury 71950 |
| 5/22/65 | 8 | 9 | 16. **Hush, Hush, Sweet Charlotte** | Columbia 43251 |
| | | | **ROBERT PALMER** | |
| | | | British blue-eyed soul singer | |
| 5/06/78 | 16 | 9 | 1. Every Kinda People | Island 100 |
| 8/11/79 | 14 | 10 | 2. Bad Case Of Loving You (Doctor, Doctor) | Island 49016 |
| | | | **PAPER LACE** | |
| | | | English quintet - Phil Wright, lead singer | |
| 7/13/74 | 1 (1) | 11 | ● 1. **The Night Chicago Died** | Mercury 73492 |
| | | | **PARADE** | |
| | | | Los Angeles pop-rock group - Jerry Riopelle, leader | |
| 5/06/67 | 20 | 5 | 1. Sunshine Girl | A&M 841 |
| | | | **PARADONS** | |
| | | | quartet from Bakersfield, California | |
| 9/26/60 | 18 | 7 | 1. Diamonds And Pearls | Milestone 2003 |
| | | | **PARIS SISTERS** | |
| | | | Albeth, Priscilla & Sherrell from San Francisco | |
| 10/02/61 | 5 | 11 | 1. **I Love How You Love Me** | Gregmark 6 |
| 3/03/62 | 34 | 3 | 2. He Knows I Love Him Too Much | Gregmark 10 |
| | | | **FESS PARKER** | |
| | | | starred in the movie "Davy Crockett" and TV's "Daniel Boone" | |
| 3/12/55 | 5 | 17 | 1. **Ballad Of Davy Crockett** | Columbia 40449 |
| 2/09/57 | 12 | 6 | 2. Wringle Wrangle | Disneyland 43 |
| | | | from the film "Westward Ho, The Wagons" | |
| | | | **RAY PARKER JR.** | |
| | | | originally a session guitarist for Marvin Gaye and Stevie Wonder | |
| 4/10/82 | 4 | 14 | 1. **The Other Woman** | Arista 0669 |
| 8/21/82 | 38 | 3 | 2. Let Me Go | Arista 0695 |
| 1/15/83 | 35 | 4 | 3. Bad Boy | Arista 1030 |
| 12/10/83 + | 12 | 11 | 4. I Still Can't Get Over Loving You | Arista 9116 |
| 6/30/84 | 1 (3) | 14 | ● 5. **Ghostbusters** | Arista 9212 |
| | | | **RAY PARKER JR. & RAYDIO** | |
| 2/11/78 | 8 | 16 | ● 1. **Jack And Jill** | Arista 0283 |
| 6/09/79 | 9 | 14 | 2. **You Can't Change That** | Arista 0399 |
| | | | above 2 shown only as Raydio | |

| DATE | POS | WKS | ARTIST—Record Title | LABEL & NO. |
|---|---|---|---|---|
| 6/07/80 | 30 | 5 | 3. Two Places At The Same Time | Arista 0494 |
| 4/25/81 | 4 | 15 | 4. **A Woman Needs Love (Just Like You Do)** | Arista 0592 |
| 8/08/81 | 21 | 6 | 5. That Old Song | Arista 0616 |
| | | | **ROBERT PARKER** | |
| | | | New Orleans session musician | |
| 5/21/66 | 7 | 9 | 1. **Barefootin'** | Nola 721 |
| | | | **MICHAEL PARKS** | |
| | | | portrayed Jim Bronson on TV's "Then Came Bronson" | |
| 3/28/70 | 20 | 8 | 1. Long Lonesome Highway | MGM 14104 |
| | | | **PARLIAMENT** | |
| | | | Parliament and Funkadelic head George Clinton's funk empire | |
| 6/12/76 | 15 | 10 | ● 1. Tear The Roof Off The Sucker (Give Up The Funk) | Casablanca 856 |
| 2/25/78 | 16 | 12 | ● 2. Flash Light | Casablanca 909 |
| | | | **PARLIAMENTS** | |
| | | | George Clinton's original group -later evolved into Parliament and Funkadelic | |
| 8/05/67 | 20 | 7 | 1. (I Wanna) Testify | Revilot 207 |
| | | | **ALAN PARSONS Project** | |
| | | | English session musicians headed by producer/engineer Parsons, and his partner Eric Woolfson | |
| 9/11/76 | 37 | 2 | 1. (The System Of) Doctor Tarr And Professor Fether | 20th Century 2297 |
| 9/24/77 | 36 | 3 | 2. I Wouldn't Want To Be Like You | Arista 0260 |
| 11/17/79 | 27 | 8 | 3. Damned If I Do | Arista 0454 |
| 1/24/81 | 16 | 10 | 4. Games People Play | Arista 0573 |
| 6/06/81 | 15 | 12 | 5. Time | Arista 0598 |
| 7/31/82 | 3 | 17 | 6. **Eye In The Sky** | Arista 0696 |
| 3/24/84 | 15 | 8 | 7. Don't Answer Me | Arista 9160 |
| 6/23/84 | 34 | 3 | 8. Prime Time | Arista 9208 |
| | | | **BILL PARSONS** | |
| 12/28/58 + | 2 (1) | 13 | 1. **The All American Boy [N]**<br>Bobby Bare is the real vocalist on this song (label error listed Parsons as the artist) | Fraternity 835 |
| | | | **DOLLY PARTON** | |
| | | | born on 1/19/46 in Sevierville, Tennessee - also see Kenny Rogers | |
| 11/12/77 + | 3 | 13 | ● 1. **Here You Come Again** | RCA 11123 |
| 4/08/78 | 19 | 8 | 2. Two Doors Down | RCA 11240 |
| 9/23/78 | 37 | 4 | 3. Heartbreaker | RCA 11296 |
| 1/13/79 | 25 | 7 | 4. Baby I'm Burnin' | RCA 11420 |
| 5/03/80 | 36 | 3 | 5. Starting Over Again | RCA 11926 |
| 12/20/80 + | 1 (2) | 18 | ● 6. **9 To 5** | RCA 12133 |
| | | | **PARTRIDGE FAMILY** | |
| | | | David Cassidy, lead singer; with stepmother Shirley Jones | |
| 10/31/70 | 1 (3) | 16 | ● 1. **I Think I Love You** | Bell 910 |
| 2/20/71 | 6 | 11 | ● 2. **Doesn't Somebody Want To Be Wanted** | Bell 963 |
| 5/15/71 | 9 | 8 | 3. **I'll Meet You Halfway** | Bell 996 |

| DATE | POS | WKS | ARTIST—Record Title | LABEL & NO. |
|------|-----|-----|---------------------|-------------|
| 8/21/71 | 13 | 10 | 4. I Woke Up In Love This Morning | Bell 45130 |
| 1/01/72 | 20 | 6 | 5. It's One Of Those Nights (Yes Love) | Bell 45160 |
| 7/29/72 | 28 | 4 | 6. Breaking Up Is Hard To Do | Bell 45235 |
| 1/27/73 | 39 | 2 | 7. Looking Through The Eyes Of Love | Bell 45301 |
| | | | **PASTEL SIX** | |
| 1/19/63 | 25 | 5 | 1. The Cinnamon Cinder (It's A Very Nice Dance) | Zen 102 |
| | | | **PASTELS** | |
| | | | Big Dee Irwin, lead singer | |
| 3/03/58 | 24 | 3 | 1. Been So Long | Argo 5287 |
| | | | **PATIENCE & PRUDENCE** | |
| | | | McIntyre sisters - ages II & I4 | |
| 8/25/56 | 4 | 17 | 1. **Tonight You Belong To Me** | Liberty 55022 |
| 12/01/56 | 11 | 12 | 2. Gonna Get Along Without Ya Now | Liberty 55040 |
| | | | **ROBBIE PATTON** | |
| | | | English | |
| 8/01/81 | 26 | 6 | 1. Don't Give It Up | Liberty 1420 |
| | | | **PATTY & THE EMBLEMS** | |
| 8/15/64 | 37 | 3 | 1. Mixed-Up, Shook-Up, Girl | Herald 590 |
| | | | **PAUL & PAULA** | |
| | | | Ray Hildebrand & Jill Jackson | |
| 1/12/63 | 1 (3) | 12 | ● 1. **Hey Paula** | Philips 40084 |
| 3/23/63 | 6 | 8 | 2. **Young Lovers** | Philips 40096 |
| 6/22/63 | 27 | 4 | 3. First Quarrel | Philips 40114 |
| | | | **BILLY PAUL** | |
| | | | born Paul Williams on 12/1/34 in Philadelphia | |
| 11/18/72 | 1 (3) | 14 | ● 1. **Me And Mrs. Jones** | Phil. Int. 3521 |
| 4/20/74 | 37 | 3 | 2. Thanks For Saving My Life | Phil. Int. 3538 |
| | | | **LES PAUL & MARY FORD** | |
| | | | husband & wife (separated May, 1963) - Mary died on 9/30/77 (53) | |
| 7/09/55 | 7 | 13 | 1. **Hummingbird** | Capitol 3165 |
| 11/12/55 | 38 | 2 | 2. Amukiriki (The Lord Willing) | Capitol 3248 |
| 2/23/57 | 35 | 2 | 3. Cinco Robles | Capitol 3612 |
| 9/08/58 | 32 | 4 | 4. Put A Ring On My Finger | Columbia 41222 |
| 7/03/61 | 37 | 1 | 5. Jura (I Swear I Love You) | Columbia 41994 |
| | | | **RITA PAVONE** | |
| | | | pop singer from Italy | |
| 7/04/64 | 26 | 4 | 1. Remember Me | RCA 8365 |
| | | | **FREDA PAYNE** | |
| | | | sang with Duke Ellington in the late '60's | |
| 5/30/70 | 3 | 15 | ● 1. **Band Of Gold** | Invictus 9075 |
| 10/10/70 | 24 | 8 | 2. Deeper & Deeper | Invictus 9080 |
| 6/26/71 | 12 | 10 | ● 3. Bring The Boys Home | Invictus 9092 |

| DATE | POS | WKS | ARTIST—Record Title | LABEL & NO. |
|---|---|---|---|---|
| | | | **PEACHES & HERB** | |
| | | | Francine Barker (replaced by Linda Greene in '78) & Herb Fame | |
| 2/25/67 | 21 | 6 | 1. Let's Fall In Love | Date 1523 |
| 4/15/67 | 8 | 9 | 2. **Close Your Eyes** | Date 1549 |
| 7/08/67 | 20 | 5 | 3. For Your Love | Date 1563 |
| 10/14/67 | 13 | 7 | 4. Love Is Strange | Date 1574 |
| 1/13/68 | 31 | 3 | 5. Two Little Kids | Date 1586 |
| 1/27/79 | 5 | 13 | ● 6. **Shake Your Groove Thing** | Polydor 14514 |
| 3/31/79 | 1 (4) | 15 | ★ 7. **Reunited** | Polydor 14547 |
| 3/15/80 | 19 | 8 | 8. I Pledge My Love | Polydor 2053 |
| | | | **LESLIE PEARL** | |
| 7/10/82 | 28 | 7 | 1. If The Love Fits Wear It | RCA 13235 |
| | | | **ANN PEEBLES** | |
| 12/22/73 | 38 | 1 | 1. I Can't Stand The Rain | Hi 2248 |
| | | | **TEDDY PENDERGRASS** | |
| | | | lead singer of Harold Melvin & The Blue Notes (1970-1976) - paralyzed in an auto crash on 3/18/82 - also see Stephanie Mills | |
| 8/12/78 | 25 | 6 | ● 1. Close The Door | Phil. Int. 3648 |
| | | | **PENGUINS** | |
| | | | Los Angeles R&B quartet - Cleveland Duncan, lead singer | |
| 12/25/54 + | 8 | 15 | 1. **Earth Angel (Will You Be Mine)** | DooTone 348 |
| | | | **PEOPLE** | |
| | | | San Jose, California pop-rock sextet | |
| 5/25/68 | 14 | 10 | 1. I Love You | Capitol 2078 |
| | | | **PEOPLE'S CHOICE** | |
| | | | soul/disco group led by Frankie Brunson | |
| 9/04/71 | 38 | 2 | 1. I Likes To Do It [I] | Phil. L.A. 349 |
| 9/13/75 | 11 | 11 | ● 2. Do It Any Way You Wanna [I] | TSOP 4769 |
| | | | **PEPPERMINT RAINBOW** | |
| 4/12/69 | 32 | 5 | 1. Will You Be Staying After Sunday | Decca 32410 |
| | | | **EMILIO PERICOLI** | |
| | | | Italian | |
| 6/09/62 | 6 | 10 | 1. **Al Di La' [F]** | Warner 5259 |
| | | | from the film "Rome Adventure" | |
| | | | **CARL PERKINS** | |
| | | | born on 4/9/32 in Lake City, Tennessee | |
| 3/10/56 | 2 (4) | 17 | 1. **Blue Suede Shoes** | Sun 234 |
| | | | **TONY PERKINS** | |
| | | | movie actor | |
| 10/07/57 | 24 | 1 | 1. Moon-Light Swim | RCA 7020 |
| | | | **STEVE PERRY** | |
| | | | lead singer of Journey - also see Kenny Loggins | |
| 4/14/84 | 3 | 13 | 1. **Oh Sherrie** | Columbia 04391 |
| 7/07/84 | 21 | 8 | 2. She's Mine | Columbia 04496 |
| 10/27/84 | 40 | 1 | 3. Strung Out | Columbia 04598 |

**Queen** caught the public's fancy with a crafty combination of Led Zeppelin's muscle and David Bowie's glamor. Early supporters included Mott the Hoople, who booked Freddie Mercury and crew as the opening act for their U.S. dates.

**Quiet Riot** achieved massive popularity in 1983 with "Cum On Feel the Noize," originally a 1973 British hit for hot'n-'nasty rockers Slade. They tried to repeat the trick in '84 with another Slade classic, "Mama Weer All Crazee Now," but the public wasn't having any. They missed the Top 40 entirely. Meanwhile, Slade took advantage of the situation and secured *their* first Top 40 entry ever with "Run Runaway."

**The Rascals'** drummer Dino Danelli was a true prodigy. By the time the band debuted in 1965, he'd already worked as a teenager with Lionel Hampton and r&b great Little Willie John.

**Chris Rea** once seemed headed for Elton John–level stardom, thanks to a big, husky voice, catchy tunes, and production by Elton's associate Gus Dudgeon. However, his string of Top 40 hits stopped at one.

**REO Speedwagon** rolled out of Champaign, Illinois, to become Midwest headliners without a hit single. Before their first Top 40 entry, they'd already sold six million records and headlined 20,000-seat halls in the heartland.

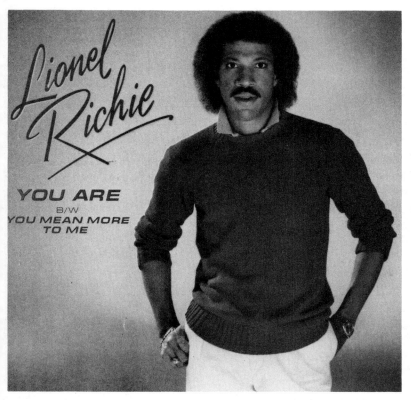

**Lionel Richie** wrote the Commodores' romantic hit "Three Times a Lady" after a talk with his dad about the importance of love. The song later won the ASCAP Nashville Country Songwriter Award, confirming his crossover potential.

**The Righteous Brothers.** After parting ways with genius producer Phil Spector, singers Bill Medley and Bobby Hatfield did their darndest to recreate that famous Wall of Sound—and succeeded magnificently. Their first post-Spector single, "Soul and Inspiration," went straight to Number One.

**Marty Robbins** grew up in Arizona listening to the tall tales of his grandfather, Texas Bob Heckle, a veteran medicine show salesman. As a young adult, he appeared in B-movie westerns like *Buffalo Guns* and *The Gun and the Gavel*.

**The Rocky Fellers,** Pop and four sons, hailed from the Philippines. Their non-hits included "Ching-A-Ling Baby," "Don't Throw My Toys Away" and "Rented Tuxedo."

**Kenny Rogers** broke in with light folk groups like the Kirby Stone Four and the New Christy Minstrels. In the late sixties, he and other Minstrels broke away to form the First Edition. This sometimes psychedelic group recorded "Just Dropped In (To See What Condition My Condition Was In)."

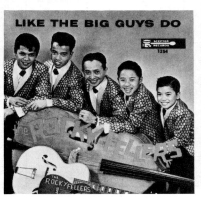

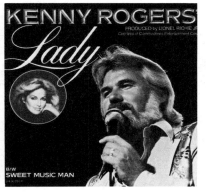

| DATE | POS | WKS | ARTIST—Record Title | LABEL & NO. |
|---|---|---|---|---|
| | | | **PERSUADERS** | |
| 9/18/71 | 15 | 9 | ● 1. Thin Line Between Love & Hate | Atco 6822 |
| 12/08/73 | 39 | 3 | 2. Some Guys Have All The Luck | Atco 6943 |
| | | | **PETER & GORDON** | |
| | | | British: Peter Asher & Gordon Waller | |
| 5/16/64 | 1 (1) | 11 | 1. **A World Without Love** | Capitol 5175 |
| 7/11/64 | 12 | 6 | 2. Nobody I Know | Capitol 5211 |
| 10/24/64 | 16 | 6 | 3. I Don't Want To See You Again | Capitol 5272 |
| 1/23/65 | 9 | 9 | 4. **I Go To Pieces** | Capitol 5335 |
| 5/08/65 | 14 | 8 | 5. True Love Ways | Capitol 5406 |
| 7/24/65 | 24 | 5 | 6. To Know You Is To Love You | Capitol 5461 |
| 3/12/66 | 14 | 8 | 7. Woman | Capitol 5579 |
| 11/05/66 | 6 | 10 | 8. **Lady Godiva** | Capitol 5740 |
| 1/14/67 | 15 | 5 | 9. Knight In Rusty Armour | Capitol 5808 |
| 4/15/67 | 31 | 3 | 10. Sunday For Tea | Capitol 5864 |
| | | | **PETER, PAUL & MARY** | |
| | | | folk trio formed at Greenwich Village, New York: Peter Yarrow, Paul Stookey & Mary Travers | |
| 6/09/62 | 35 | 2 | 1. Lemon Tree | Warner 5274 |
| 9/08/62 | 10 | 8 | 2. **If I Had A Hammer** | Warner 5296 |
| 3/30/63 | 2 (1) | 11 | 3. **Puff The Magic Dragon** | Warner 5348 |
| 7/13/63 | 2 (1) | 12 | 4. **Blowin' In The Wind** | Warner 5368 |
| 9/28/63 | 9 | 8 | 5. **Don't Think Twice, It's All Right** | Warner 5385 |
| 12/28/63 | 35 | 2 | 6. Stewball | Warner 5399 |
| 4/04/64 | 33 | 3 | 7. Tell It On The Mountain | Warner 5418 |
| 2/13/65 | 30 | 4 | 8. For Lovin' Me | Warner 5496 |
| 9/02/67 | 9 | 8 | 9. **I Dig Rock And Roll Music** | Warner 7067 |
| 12/23/67 | 35 | 2 | 10. Too Much Of Nothing | Warner 7092 |
| 5/17/69 | 21 | 7 | 11. Day Is Done | Warner 7279 |
| 11/08/69 | 1 (1) | 15 | ● 12. **Leaving On A Jet Plane** | Warner 7340 |
| | | | **BERNADETTE PETERS** | |
| | | | film comedienne | |
| 5/10/80 | 31 | 5 | 1. Gee Whiz | MCA 41210 |
| | | | **PAUL PETERSEN** | |
| | | | Jeff Stone of TV's "Donna Reed Show" | |
| 3/31/62 | 19 | 7 | 1. She Can't Find Her Keys | Colpix 620 |
| 12/15/62 + | 6 | 10 | 2. **My Dad** | Colpix 663 |
| | | | **RAY PETERSON** | |
| | | | born on 4/23/39 in Denton, Texas | |
| 6/15/59 | 25 | 7 | 1. The Wonder Of You | RCA 7513 |
| 6/27/60 | 7 | 11 | 2. **Tell Laura I Love Her** | RCA 7745 |
| 12/19/60 + | 9 | 9 | 3. **Corinna, Corinna** | Dunes 2002 |
| 9/25/61 | 29 | 3 | 4. Missing You | Dunes 2006 |
| | | | **PETS** | |
| 6/09/58 | 34 | 1 | 1. Cha-Hua-Hua [I] | Arwin 109 |

| DATE | POS | WKS | ARTIST—Record Title | LABEL & NO. |
|---|---|---|---|---|
| | | | **TOM PETTY & The HEARTBREAKERS** | |
| | | | rock quintet formed in Los Angeles - also see Stevie Nicks | |
| 2/18/78 | 40 | 1 | 1. Breakdown | Shelter 62008 |
| 12/08/79 + | 10 | 13 | 2. **Don't Do Me Like That** | Backstreet 41138 |
| 2/09/80 | 15 | 10 | 3. Refugee | Backstreet 41169 |
| 5/16/81 | 19 | 7 | 4. The Waiting | Backstreet 51100 |
| 12/04/82 + | 20 | 11 | 5. You Got Lucky | Backstreet 52144 |
| 3/12/83 | 21 | 7 | 6. Change Of Heart | Backstreet 52181 |
| | | | **JOHN PHILLIPS** | |
| | | | co-founder of The Mamas & The Papas | |
| 6/20/70 | 32 | 7 | 1. Mississippi | Dunhill 4236 |
| | | | **LITTLE ESTHER PHILLIPS** | |
| | | | "Little Esther" had 5 top ten singles on the R&B charts in 1950 (with Johnny Otis) - died on 8/7/84 (48) | |
| 11/17/62 | 8 | 10 | 1. **Release Me** | Lenox 5555 |
| 9/20/75 | 20 | 9 | 2. What A Diff'rence A Day Makes | Kudu 925 |
| | | | **PHIL PHILLIPS with The Twilights** | |
| | | | real name: Phil Baptiste | |
| 7/20/59 | 2 (2) | 14 | 1. **Sea Of Love** | Mercury 71465 |
| | | | **JIM PHOTOGLO** | |
| 5/31/80 | 31 | 4 | 1. We Were Meant To Be Lovers<br>shown only as Photoglo | 20th Century 2446 |
| 5/30/81 | 25 | 7 | 2. Fool In Love With You | 20th Century 2487 |
| | | | **BOBBY (BORIS) PICKETT & The Crypt-Kickers** | |
| 9/15/62 | 1 (2) | 12 | ● 1. **Monster Mash [N]** | Garpax 44167 |
| 12/22/62 | 30 | 4 | 2. Monsters' Holiday [X-N] | Garpax 44171 |
| 6/30/73 | 10 | 12 | 3. **Monster Mash [N-R]** | Parrot 348 |
| | | | **WILSON PICKETT** | |
| | | | born on 3/18/41 in Prattville, Alabama | |
| 8/14/65 | 21 | 6 | 1. In The Midnight Hour | Atlantic 2289 |
| 3/05/66 | 13 | 8 | 2. 634-5789 (Soulsville, U.S.A.) | Atlantic 2320 |
| 8/13/66 | 6 | 8 | 3. **Land Of 1000 Dances** | Atlantic 2348 |
| 12/10/66 | 23 | 6 | 4. Mustang Sally | Atlantic 2365 |
| 2/25/67 | 29 | 3 | 5. Everybody Needs Somebody To Love | Atlantic 2381 |
| 4/22/67 | 32 | 2 | 6. I Found A Love - Part 1 | Atlantic 2394 |
| 8/26/67 | 8 | 9 | 7. **Funky Broadway** | Atlantic 2430 |
| 11/11/67 | 22 | 5 | 8. Stag-O-Lee | Atlantic 2448 |
| 5/11/68 | 15 | 6 | 9. She's Lookin' Good | Atlantic 2504 |
| 7/06/68 | 24 | 4 | 10. I'm A Midnight Mover | Atlantic 2528 |
| 1/04/69 | 23 | 6 | 11. Hey Jude | Atlantic 2591 |
| 5/23/70 | 25 | 9 | 12. Sugar Sugar | Atlantic 2722 |
| 10/24/70 | 14 | 9 | 13. Engine Number 9 | Atlantic 2765 |
| 2/06/71 | 17 | 8 | ● 14. Don't Let The Green Grass Fool You | Atlantic 2781 |
| 5/15/71 | 13 | 9 | ● 15. Don't Knock My Love - Pt. 1 | Atlantic 2797 |
| 1/15/72 | 24 | 8 | 16. Fire And Water | Atlantic 2852 |

| DATE | POS | WKS | ARTIST—Record Title | LABEL & NO. |
|---|---|---|---|---|
| | | | **WEBB PIERCE** | |
| | | | Webb's first 20 releases hit the Top 10 on the Country charts | |
| 8/31/59 | 24 | 7 | 1. I Ain't Never | Decca 30923 |
| | | | **PILOT** | |
| | | | Scottish trio | |
| 5/10/75 | 5 | 12 | ● 1. **Magic** | EMI 3992 |
| | | | **PINK FLOYD** | |
| | | | English progressive rock band: David Gilmour (guitar), Roger Waters (bass), Nick Mason (drums), Rick Wright (keyboards) | |
| 6/23/73 | 13 | 9 | 1. Money | Harvest 3609 |
| 2/09/80 | 1 (4) | 19 | ● 2. **Another Brick In The Wall (Part II)** | Columbia 11187 |
| | | | **PINK LADY** | |
| | | | Japanese - Mie & Kei | |
| 7/21/79 | 37 | 3 | 1. Kiss In The Dark | Elektra 46040 |
| | | | **PIPKINS** | |
| | | | British studio group - Tony Burrows, lead singer | |
| 6/06/70 | 9 | 10 | 1. **Gimme Dat Ding [N]** | Capitol 2819 |
| | | | **PIPS - see GLADYS KNIGHT** | |
| | | | **GENE PITNEY** | |
| | | | born on 2/17/41 in Hartford, Connecticut | |
| 2/27/61 | 39 | 1 | 1. (I Wanna) Love My Life Away | Musicor 1002 |
| 12/18/61 + | 13 | 10 | 2. Town Without Pity | Musicor 1009 |
| 5/19/62 | 4 | 8 | 3. **(The Man Who Shot) Liberty Valance** | Musicor 1020 |
| 9/29/62 | 2 (1) | 11 | 4. **Only Love Can Break A Heart** | Musicor 1022 |
| 1/05/63 | 12 | 8 | 5. Half Heaven - Half Heartache | Musicor 1026 |
| 4/13/63 | 12 | 7 | 6. Mecca | Musicor 1028 |
| 8/03/63 | 21 | 6 | 7. True Love Never Runs Smooth | Musicor 1032 |
| 11/16/63 | 17 | 6 | 8. Twenty Four Hours From Tulsa | Musicor 1034 |
| 8/29/64 | 7 | 10 | 9. **It Hurts To Be In Love** | Musicor 1040 |
| 11/07/64 | 9 | 9 | 10. **I'm Gonna Be Strong** | Musicor 1045 |
| 3/20/65 | 31 | 4 | 11. I Must Be Seeing Things | Musicor 1070 |
| 5/22/65 | 13 | 7 | 12. Last Chance To Turn Around | Musicor 1093 |
| 8/21/65 | 28 | 4 | 13. Looking Through The Eyes Of Love | Musicor 1103 |
| 12/18/65 | 37 | 2 | 14. Princess In Rags | Musicor 1130 |
| 5/14/66 | 25 | 5 | 15. Backstage | Musicor 1171 |
| 6/15/68 | 16 | 8 | 16. She's A Heartbreaker | Musicor 1306 |
| | | | **PIXIES THREE** | |
| 10/05/63 | 40 | 1 | 1. Birthday Party | Mercury 72130 |
| | | | **ROBERT PLANT** | |
| | | | lead singer of Led Zeppelin/Honeydrippers | |
| 9/03/83 | 20 | 9 | 1. Big Log | Atlantic 99844 |
| 12/24/83 + | 39 | 5 | 2. In The Mood | Esparanza 99820 |
| | | | **PLASTIC ONO BAND - see JOHN LENNON** | |

| DATE | POS | WKS | ARTIST—Record Title | LABEL & NO. |
|---|---|---|---|---|
| | | | **EDDIE PLATT & His Orchestra** | |
| 3/10/58 | 20 | 4 | 1. Tequila [I] | ABC-Para. 9899 |
| | | | **PLATTERS** | |
| | | | Los Angeles-based R&B quintet - Tony Williams, lead singer through 1961 (replaced by Sonny Turner) | |
| 10/01/55 | 5 | 20 | 1. **Only You (And You Alone)** | Mercury 70633 |
| 12/24/55 + | 1 (2) | 19 | 2. **The Great Pretender** | Mercury 70753 |
| 3/31/56 | 4 | 16 | 3. **(You've Got) The Magic Touch** | Mercury 70819 |
| 7/07/56 | 1 (5) | 20 | 4. **My Prayer**/ | Mercury 70893 |
| 8/11/56 | 39 | 1 | 5.  Heaven On Earth | |
| 10/06/56 | 11 | 12 | 6. You'll Never Never Know/ | Mercury 70948 |
| 10/13/56 | 23 | 9 | 7.  It Isn't Right | |
| 1/12/57 | 20 | 6 | 8. On My Word Of Honor/ | Mercury 71011 |
| 1/26/57 | 31 | 2 | 9.  One In A Million | |
| 3/23/57 | 11 | 11 | 10. I'm Sorry/ | Mercury 71032 |
| 4/06/57 | 23 | 9 | 11.  He's Mine | |
| 6/10/57 | 24 | 7 | 12. My Dream | Mercury 71093 |
| 4/07/58 | 1 (1) | 14 | 13. **Twilight Time** | Mercury 71289 |
| 12/01/58 + | 1 (3) | 16 | 14. **Smoke Gets In Your Eyes** | Mercury 71383 |
| 4/06/59 | 12 | 11 | 15. Enchanted | Mercury 71427 |
| 2/15/60 | 8 | 11 | 16. **Harbor Lights** | Mercury 71563 |
| 8/22/60 | 36 | 1 | 17. Red Sails In The Sunset | Mercury 71656 |
| 10/24/60 | 21 | 8 | 18. To Each His Own | Mercury 71697 |
| 1/30/61 | 30 | 2 | 19. If I Didn't Care | Mercury 71749 |
| 8/21/61 | 25 | 4 | 20. I'll Never Smile Again | Mercury 71847 |
| 6/04/66 | 31 | 5 | 21. I Love You 1000 Times | Musicor 1166 |
| 3/25/67 | 14 | 7 | 22. With This Ring | Musicor 1229 |
| | | | **PLAYER** | |
| | | | pop/rock group formed in Los Angeles - Peter Beckett, lead singer | |
| 11/19/77 + | 1 (3) | 16 | ● 1. **Baby Come Back** | RSO 879 |
| 4/01/78 | 10 | 12 | 2. **This Time I'm In It For Love** | RSO 890 |
| 10/21/78 | 27 | 3 | 3. Prisoner Of Your Love | RSO 908 |
| | | | **PLAYMATES** | |
| | | | Donny Conn, Morey Carr & Chic Hetti | |
| 1/27/58 | 19 | 7 | 1. Jo-Ann | Roulette 4037 |
| 6/09/58 | 22 | 2 | 2. Don't Go Home | Roulette 4072 |
| 11/10/58 | 4 | 12 | 3. **Beep Beep [N]** | Roulette 4115 |
| 7/27/59 | 15 | 9 | 4. What Is Love? | Roulette 4160 |
| 11/21/60 | 37 | 2 | 5. Wait For Me | Roulette 4276 |
| | | | **POCO** | |
| | | | Los Angeles country-rock band formed by Rusty Young and Buffalo Springfield members Richie Furay & Jim Messina | |
| 2/10/79 | 17 | 9 | 1. Crazy Love | ABC 12439 |
| 6/16/79 | 20 | 7 | 2. Heart Of The Night | MCA 41023 |
| | | | **POINT BLANK** | |
| | | | 6-man rock band from Texas | |
| 8/29/81 | 39 | 2 | 1. Nicole | MCA 51132 |

| DATE | POS | WKS | ARTIST—Record Title | LABEL & NO. |
|---|---|---|---|---|
| | | | **POINTER SISTERS** | |
| | | | Ruth, Anita, June & Bonnie Pointer - from Oakland, California - Bonnie left group in 1978 | |
| 9/08/73 | 11 | 12 | 1. Yes We Can Can | Blue Thumb 229 |
| 11/09/74 | 13 | 8 | 2. Fairytale | Blue Thumb 254 |
| 8/23/75 | 20 | 8 | 3. How Long (Betcha' Got A Chick On The Side) | Blue Thumb 265 |
| 12/16/78 + | 2 (2) | 16 | ● 4. **Fire** | Planet 45901 |
| 4/14/79 | 30 | 4 | 5. Happiness | Planet 45902 |
| 8/30/80 | 3 | 17 | ● 6. **He's So Shy** | Planet 47916 |
| 6/27/81 | 2 (3) | 16 | ● 7. **Slow Hand** | Planet 47929 |
| 2/13/82 | 13 | 10 | 8. Should I Do It | Planet 47960 |
| 7/24/82 | 16 | 8 | 9. American Music | Planet 13254 |
| 10/30/82 | 30 | 6 | 10. I'm So Excited | Planet 13327 |
| 2/11/84 | 5 | 14 | 11. **Automatic** | Planet 13730 |
| 5/12/84 | 3 | 15 | 12. **Jump (For My Love)** | Planet 13780 |
| 9/08/84 | 9 | 12 | 13. **I'm So Excited [R]** | Planet 13857 |
| | | | **BONNIE POINTER** | |
| | | | one of the Pointer Sisters | |
| 7/28/79 | 11 | 15 | 1. Heaven Must Have Sent You | Motown 1459 |
| 2/16/80 | 40 | 2 | 2. I Can't Help Myself (Sugar Pie, Honey Bunch) | Motown 1478 |
| | | | **POLICE** | |
| | | | English/U.S. trio: Sting (Gordon Sumner - lead singer), Andy Summers (guitar), Stewart Copeland (drums - from U.S.) | |
| 4/07/79 | 32 | 5 | 1. Roxanne | A&M 2096 |
| 11/22/80 + | 10 | 13 | 2. **De Do Do Do, De Da Da Da** | A&M 2275 |
| 2/21/81 | 10 | 13 | 3. **Don't Stand So Close To Me** | A&M 2301 |
| 10/10/81 | 3 | 15 | 4. **Every Little Thing She Does Is Magic** | A&M 2371 |
| 1/30/82 | 11 | 10 | 5. Spirits In The Material World | A&M 2390 |
| 6/04/83 | 1 (8) | 20 | ● 6. **Every Breath You Take** | A&M 2542 |
| 8/27/83 | 3 | 13 | 7. **King Of Pain** | A&M 2569 |
| 11/19/83 | 16 | 9 | 8. Synchronicity II | A&M 2571 |
| 1/21/84 | 8 | 10 | 9. **Wrapped Around Your Finger** | A&M 2614 |
| | | | **PONI-TAILS** | |
| | | | female trio from Cleveland, Ohio | |
| 7/28/58 | 7 | 12 | 1. **Born Too Late** | ABC-Para. 9934 |
| | | | **POPPY FAMILY featuring Susan Jacks** | |
| | | | Canadian - Susan & Terry Jacks | |
| 4/25/70 | 2 (2) | 13 | ● 1. **Which Way You Goin' Billy?** | London 129 |
| 9/19/70 | 29 | 6 | 2. That's Where I Went Wrong | London 139 |
| | | | **SANDY POSEY** | |
| | | | formerly a session vocalist in Memphis and Nashville | |
| 8/06/66 | 12 | 12 | 1. Born A Woman | MGM 13501 |
| 12/10/66 | 12 | 8 | 2. Single Girl | MGM 13612 |
| 4/08/67 | 31 | 2 | 3. What A Woman In Love Won't Do | MGM 13702 |
| 7/01/67 | 12 | 8 | 4. I Take It Back | MGM 13744 |

| DATE | POS | WKS | ARTIST—Record Title | LABEL & NO. |
|------|-----|-----|---------------------|-------------|
| | | | **MIKE POST** | |
| | | | composer of numerous television and film scores | |
| 6/21/75 | **10** | 10 | 1. **The Rockford Files [I]** | MGM 14772 |
| 10/03/81 | **10** | 10 | 2. **The Theme From Hill Street Blues [I]** | Elektra 47186 |
| | | | featuring guitarist Larry Carlton | |
| 4/03/82 | **25** | 7 | 3. Theme From Magnum P.I. [I] | Elektra 47400 |
| | | | **FRANCK POURCEL'S French Fiddles** | |
| 4/27/59 | **9** | 11 | 1. **Only You [I]** | Capitol 4165 |
| | | | **JANE POWELL** | |
| | | | movie actress | |
| 10/06/56 | **15** | 9 | 1. True Love | Verve 2018 |
| | | | **JOEY POWERS** | |
| 12/07/63 + | **10** | 9 | 1. **Midnight Mary** | Amy 892 |
| | | | **POZO-SECO SINGERS** | |
| | | | country singer Don Williams was a member of this Texas trio | |
| 10/08/66 | **32** | 6 | 1. I Can Make It With You | Columbia 43784 |
| 1/14/67 | **32** | 4 | 2. Look What You've Done | Columbia 43927 |
| | | | **PEREZ PRADO & His Orchestra** | |
| | | | Cuban-born mambo band leader - died on 12/4/83 (57) | |
| 3/05/55 | **1**(10) | 26 | 1. **Cherry Pink And Apple Blossom White [I]** | RCA 5965 |
| | | | trumpet solo by Billy Regis -- from the film "Under Water!" | |
| 6/23/58 | **1** (1) | 17 | ● 2. **Patricia [I]** | RCA 7245 |
| | | | **PRATT & McCLAIN** | |
| | | | Truett Pratt & Jerry McClain | |
| 4/24/76 | **5** | 10 | 1. **Happy Days** | Reprise 1351 |
| | | | **PRELUDE** | |
| | | | English folk-based trio | |
| 11/02/74 | **22** | 5 | 1. After The Goldrush | Island 002 |
| | | | **PREMIERS** | |
| | | | Latin-rock band from San Gabriel, California | |
| 7/04/64 | **19** | 6 | 1. Farmer John | Warner 5443 |
| | | | **PRESIDENTS** | |
| | | | soul trio, produced by Van McCoy | |
| 11/14/70 | **11** | 9 | 1. 5-10-15-20 (25-30 Years Of Love) | Sussex 207 |
| | | | **ELVIS PRESLEY** | |
| | | | Elvis - the #1 artist of the rock era, was born in Tupelo, Mississippi on 1/8/35, and died in Memphis, Tennessee on 8/16/77 at the age of 42 | |
| 3/10/56 | **1** (8) | 22 | 1. **Heartbreak Hotel/** | |
| 3/17/56 | **19** | 10 | 2.  I Was The One | RCA 47-6420 |
| 4/28/56 | **20** | 5 | 3. Blue Suede Shoes | RCA EPA-747 |
| | | | from the E.P. "Elvis Presley" | |
| 6/02/56 | **1** (1) | 19 | 4. **I Want You, I Need You, I Love You/** | |
| 6/09/56 | **31** | 3 | 5.  My Baby Left Me | RCA 47-6540 |
| 8/04/56 | **1**(11) | 24 | 6. **Don't Be Cruel/** | |
| 8/04/56 | **1** | 23 | 7. **Hound Dog** | RCA 47-6604 |

| DATE | POS | WKS | ARTIST—Record Title | LABEL & NO. |
|------|-----|-----|---------------------|-------------|
| 10/20/56 | 1 (5) | 19 | 8. **Love Me Tender/**<br>from Elvis' first movie -- tune adapted from "Aura Lee" | |
| 11/10/56 | 20 | 4 | 9.  Anyway You Want Me (That's How I Will Be) | RCA 47-6643 |
| 11/24/56 + | 2 (2) | 14 | 10. **Love Me/** | |
| 12/29/56 | 19 | 4 | 11.  When My Blue Moon Turns To Gold Again | RCA EPA-992 |
| 1/05/57 | 24 | 3 | 12. Poor Boy<br>from the film/E.P. "Love Me Tender" | RCA EPA-4006 |
| 1/26/57 | 1 (3) | 14 | 13. **Too Much/** | |
| 2/09/57 | 21 | 4 | 14.  Playing For Keeps | RCA 47-6800 |
| 4/06/57 | 1 (9) | 22 | 15. **All Shook Up** | RCA 47-6870 |
| 4/29/57 | 25 | 1 | 16. (There'll Be) Peace In The Valley (For Me)<br>from the E.P. "Peace In The Valley" | RCA EPA-4054 |
| 6/24/57 | 1 (7) | 18 | 17. **(Let Me Be Your) Teddy Bear/** | |
| 7/08/57 | 20 | 13 | 18.  Loving You<br>above 2 from the film "Loving You" | RCA 47-7000 |
| 10/14/57 | 1 (7) | 19 | 19. **Jailhouse Rock/** | |
| 10/21/57 | 18 | 6 | 20.  Treat Me Nice<br>above 2 from the film "Jailhouse Rock" | RCA 47-7035 |
| 1/27/58 | 1 (5) | 16 | ● 21. **Don't/** | |
| 2/03/58 | 8 | 7 | 22.  **I Beg Of You** | RCA 47-7150 |
| 4/21/58 | 2 (1) | 13 | ● 23. **Wear My Ring Around Your Neck/** | |
| 5/05/58 | 15 | 2 | 24.  Doncha' Think It's Time | RCA 47-7240 |
| 6/30/58 | 1 (2) | 14 | ● 25. **Hard Headed Woman/** | |
| 7/14/58 | 25 | 4 | 26.  Don't Ask Me Why<br>above 2 from the film "King Creole" | RCA 47-7280 |
| 11/10/58 | 4 | 14 | 27. **One Night/** | |
| 11/10/58 | 8 | 12 | ● 28.  **I Got Stung** | RCA 47-7410 |
| 3/30/59 | 2 (1) | 11 | ● 29. **(Now And Then There's) A Fool Such As I/** | |
| 3/30/59 | 4 | 10 | 30.  **I Need Your Love Tonight** | RCA 47-7506 |
| 7/13/59 | 1 (2) | 10 | 31. **A Big Hunk O' Love/** | |
| 7/13/59 | 12 | 10 | 32.  My Wish Came True | RCA 47-7600 |
| 4/11/60 | 1 (4) | 13 | 33. **Stuck On You/** | |
| 4/25/60 | 17 | 7 | 34.  Fame And Fortune | RCA 47-7740 |
| 7/25/60 | 1 (5) | 16 | ● 35. **It's Now Or Never/**<br>adapted from "O Sole Mio" | |
| 8/01/60 | 32 | 2 | 36.  A Mess Of Blues | RCA 47-7777 |
| 11/14/60 | 1 (6) | 14 | ● 37. **Are You Lonesome To-night?/**<br>written in 1926 | |
| 11/28/60 | 20 | 8 | 38.  I Gotta Know | RCA 47-7810 |
| 2/20/61 | 1 (2) | 11 | 39. **Surrender/**<br>adapted from "Come Back To Sorrento" | |
| 3/13/61 | 32 | 2 | 40.  Lonely Man<br>from the film "Wild In The Country" | RCA 47-7850 |
| 4/24/61 | 14 | 5 | 41. Flaming Star<br>from the E.P. "Elvis By Request" | RCA LPC-128 |
| 5/22/61 | 5 | 7 | 42. **I Feel So Bad/** | |
| 6/19/61 | 26 | 2 | 43.  Wild In The Country | RCA 47-7880 |
| 8/28/61 | 5 | 10 | 44. **Little Sister/** | |
| 9/04/61 | 4 | 7 | 45.  (Marie's the Name) His Latest Flame | RCA 47-7908 |
| 12/18/61 + | 2 (1) | 12 | ● 46. **Can't Help Falling In Love/** | |
| 12/18/61 + | 23 | 5 | 47.  Rock-A-Hula Baby<br>above 2 from the film "Blue Hawaii" | RCA 47-7968 |

| DATE | POS | WKS | ARTIST—Record Title | LABEL & NO. |
|------|-----|-----|---------------------|-------------|
| 3/24/62 | 1 (2) | 11 | 48. **Good Luck Charm/** | |
| 4/07/62 | 31 | 5 | 49.  Anything That's Part Of You | RCA 47-7992 |
| 5/19/62 | 15 | 7 | 50. Follow That Dream <br> from the film/E.P. of same title | RCA EPA-4368 |
| 8/11/62 | 5 | 9 | 51. **She's Not You** | RCA 47-8041 |
| 10/06/62 | 30 | 4 | 52. King Of The Whole Wide World <br> from the film/E.P. "Kid Galahad" | RCA EPA-4371 |
| 10/27/62 | 2 (5) | 14 | ● 53. **Return To Sender** <br> from the film "Girls! Girls! Girls!" | RCA 47-8100 |
| 2/23/63 | 11 | 7 | 54. One Broken Heart For Sale <br> from the film "It Happened At The World's Fair" | RCA 47-8134 |
| 7/13/63 | 3 | 8 | 55. **(You're the) Devil In Disguise** | RCA 47-8188 |
| 11/02/63 | 8 | 7 | 56. **Bossa Nova Baby/** <br> from the film "Fun In Acapulco" | |
| 11/09/63 | 32 | 3 | 57.  Witchcraft | RCA 47-8243 |
| 3/07/64 | 12 | 7 | 58. Kissin' Cousins/ | |
| 3/14/64 | 29 | 4 | 59.  It Hurts Me | RCA 47-8307 |
| 5/23/64 | 34 | 2 | 60. Kiss Me Quick <br> recorded June 25, 1961 | RCA 447-0639 |
| 5/30/64 | 21 | 5 | 61. What'd I Say/ | |
| 5/30/64 | 29 | 4 | 62.  Viva Las Vegas <br> above 2 from the film "Viva Las Vegas" | RCA 47-8360 |
| 8/08/64 | 16 | 6 | 63. Such A Night <br> recorded April 4, 1960 | RCA 47-8400 |
| 10/24/64 | 12 | 8 | 64. Ask Me/ | |
| 10/24/64 | 16 | 8 | 65.  Ain't That Loving You Baby <br> recorded June 10, 1958 | RCA 47-8440 |
| 3/13/65 | 21 | 6 | 66. Do The Clam <br> from the film "Girl Happy" | RCA 47-8500 |
| 5/08/65 | 3 | 11 | 67. **Crying In The Chapel** <br> recorded October 31, 1960 | RCA 447-0643 |
| 7/03/65 | 11 | 6 | 68. (Such An) Easy Question <br> recorded March 18, 1962 -- from the film "Tickle Me" | RCA 47-8585 |
| 9/18/65 | 11 | 7 | 69. I'm Yours <br> recorded June 26, 1961 | RCA 47-8657 |
| 12/04/65 | 14 | 6 | 70. Puppet On A String <br> from the film "Girl Happy" | RCA 447-0650 |
| 1/22/66 | 33 | 3 | 71. Tell Me Why <br> recorded January 12, 1957 | RCA 47-8740 |
| 4/09/66 | 25 | 5 | 72. Frankie And Johnny | RCA 47-8780 |
| 7/09/66 | 19 | 5 | 73. Love Letters | RCA 47-8870 |
| 11/05/66 | 40 | 2 | 74. Spinout | RCA 47-8941 |
| 2/18/67 | 33 | 4 | 75. Indescribably Blue | RCA 47-9056 |
| 11/04/67 | 38 | 2 | 76. Big Boss Man | RCA 47-9341 |
| 4/20/68 | 28 | 4 | 77. U.S. Male | RCA 47-9465 |
| 12/14/68 + | 12 | 11 | 78. If I Can Dream | RCA 47-9670 |
| 4/12/69 | 35 | 2 | 79. Memories <br> from the TV special "Elvis" | RCA 47-9731 |
| 5/17/69 | 3 | 11 | ● 80. **In The Ghetto** | RCA 47-9741 |
| 8/02/69 | 35 | 4 | 81. Clean Up Your Own Back Yard <br> from the film "The Trouble With Girls" | RCA 47-9747 |
| 9/20/69 | 1 (1) | 13 | ● 82. **Suspicious Minds** | RCA 47-9764 |
| 12/13/69 + | 6 | 11 | ● 83. **Don't Cry Daddy** | RCA 47-9768 |

| DATE | POS | WKS | ARTIST—Record Title | LABEL & NO. |
|---|---|---|---|---|
| 2/21/70 | 16 | 8 | 84. Kentucky Rain | RCA 47-9791 |
| 5/23/70 | 9 | 11 | ● 85. **The Wonder Of You**<br>recorded live at Las Vegas | RCA 47-9835 |
| 8/22/70 | 32 | 3 | 86. I've Lost You/ | |
| | | 3 | 87. **The Next Step Is Love** | RCA 47-9873 |
| 11/07/70 | 11 | 8 | 88. You Don't Have To Say You Love Me | RCA 47-9916 |
| 1/02/71 | 21 | 8 | 89. I Really Don't Want To Know/ | |
| | | 8 | 90. **There Goes My Everything** | RCA 47-9960 |
| 3/27/71 | 33 | 4 | 91. Where Did They Go, Lord/ | |
| | | 4 | 92. **Rags To Riches** | RCA 47-9980 |
| 8/14/71 | 36 | 2 | 93. I'm Leavin' | RCA 47-9998 |
| 3/11/72 | 40 | 1 | 94. Until It's Time For You To Go | RCA 74-0619 |
| 9/09/72 | 2 (1) | 12 | ● 95. **Burning Love** | RCA 74-0769 |
| 12/23/72 + | 20 | 8 | 96. Separate Ways<br>featured in the film "Elvis On Tour" | RCA 74-0815 |
| 5/05/73 | 17 | 7 | 97. Steamroller Blues<br>recorded live in Hawaii | RCA 74-0910 |
| 3/23/74 | 39 | 2 | 98. I've Got A Thing About You Baby | RCA APBO-0196 |
| 6/29/74 | 17 | 7 | 99. If You Talk In Your Sleep | RCA APBO-0280 |
| 11/09/74 | 14 | 9 | 100. Promised Land | RCA PB-10074 |
| 2/15/75 | 20 | 6 | 101. My Boy | RCA PB-10191 |
| 6/07/75 | 35 | 3 | 102. T-R-O-U-B-L-E | RCA PB-10278 |
| 5/01/76 | 28 | 5 | 103. Hurt | RCA PB-10601 |
| 2/05/77 | 31 | 5 | 104. Moody Blue | RCA PB-10857 |
| 7/16/77 | 18 | 12 | ●105. Way Down | RCA PB-10998 |
| 12/03/77 | 22 | 7 | ●106. My Way<br>recorded live from Elvis' tour | RCA PB-11165 |
| 2/28/81 | 28 | 5 | 107. Guitar Man [R]<br>re-entry/re-mix of 1968 hit (Pos. 43) | RCA PB-12158 |
| | | | **BILLY PRESTON**<br>organist - played with the Beatles and the Rolling Stones | |
| 5/13/72 | 2 (1) | 14 | ● 1. **Outa-Space [I]** | A&M 1320 |
| 5/19/73 | 1 (2) | 14 | ● 2. **Will It Go Round In Circles** | A&M 1411 |
| 10/13/73 | 4 | 13 | ● 3. **Space Race [I]** | A&M 1463 |
| 8/03/74 | 1 (1) | 14 | ● 4. **Nothing From Nothing** | A&M 1544 |
| 1/04/75 | 22 | 6 | 5. Struttin' [I] | A&M 1644 |
| | | | **BILLY PRESTON & SYREETA**<br>Syreeta Wright - formerly married to Stevie Wonder | |
| 3/01/80 | 4 | 15 | 1. **With You I'm Born Again** | Motown 1477 |
| | | | **JOHNNY PRESTON**<br>born on 8/18/30 in Port Arthur, Texas | |
| 12/21/59 + | 1 (3) | 14 | 1. **Running Bear**<br>Indian sounds by the Big Bopper | Mercury 71474 |
| 4/04/60 | 7 | 12 | 2. **Cradle Of Love** | Mercury 71598 |
| 7/25/60 | 14 | 7 | 3. Feel So Fine | Mercury 71651 |
| | | | **PRETENDERS**<br>new wave quartet - 3 Englishmen and an American woman (Chrissie Hynde) | |
| 4/12/80 | 14 | 12 | 1. Brass In Pocket (I'm Special) | Sire 49181 |
| 1/29/83 | 5 | 14 | 2. **Back On The Chain Gang** | Sire 29840 |

| DATE | POS | WKS | ARTIST—Record Title | LABEL & NO. |
|------|-----|-----|---------------------|-------------|
| 1/07/84 | 19 | 9 | 3. Middle Of The Road | Sire 29444 |
| 4/07/84 | 28 | 6 | 4. Show Me | Sire 29317 |
| | | | **LLOYD PRICE** | |
| | | | born on 3/9/34 in New Orleans, Louisiana | |
| 4/06/57 | 29 | 6 | 1. Just Because | ABC-Para. 9792 |
| 1/05/59 | 1 (4) | 15 | 2. **Stagger Lee** | ABC-Para. 9972 |
| 3/30/59 | 23 | 4 | 3. Where Were You (On Our Wedding Day)? | ABC-Para. 9997 |
| 5/11/59 | 2 (3) | 14 | 4. **Personality** | ABC-Para. 10018 |
| 8/17/59 | 3 | 12 | 5. **I'm Gonna Get Married** | ABC-Para. 10032 |
| 11/23/59 | 20 | 9 | 6. Come Into My Heart | ABC-Para. 10062 |
| 2/15/60 | 14 | 8 | 7. Lady Luck | ABC-Para. 10075 |
| 5/30/60 | 40 | 1 | 8. No If's - No And's | ABC-Para. 10102 |
| 7/18/60 | 19 | 7 | 9. Question | ABC-Para. 10123 |
| 10/26/63 | 21 | 6 | 10. Misty | Double-L 722 |
| | | | **RAY PRICE** | |
| | | | country singer born on 1/12/26 in Perryville, Texas | |
| 11/07/70 + | 11 | 14 | 1. For The Good Times | Columbia 45178 |
| | | | **CHARLEY PRIDE** | |
| | | | country singer born on 3/18/38 in Sledge, Mississippi - Charley's had 29 #1 hits on the Country charts (1969-83) | |
| 12/18/71 + | 21 | 11 | ● 1. Kiss An Angel Good Mornin' | RCA 0550 |
| | | | **LOUIS PRIMA** | |
| | | | jazz trumpeter - band/combo leader since mid-30s - died on 8/24/78 (67) | |
| 12/12/60 + | 15 | 9 | 1. Wonderland By Night [I] | Dot 16151 |
| | | | **LOUIS PRIMA & KEELY SMITH** | |
| | | | husband & wife (divorced in '62) - back-up band: Sam Butera & The Witnesses | |
| 11/24/58 | 18 | 7 | 1. That Old Black Magic | Capitol 4063 |
| | | | ∗ from the film "Senior Prom" | |
| | | | **PRINCE** | |
| | | | born Prince Rogers Nelson on 6/7/60 in Minneapolis | |
| 12/08/79 + | 11 | 12 | ● 1. I Wanna Be Your Lover | Warner 49050 |
| 3/19/83 | 6 | 15 | 2. **Little Red Corvette** | Warner 29746 |
| 6/18/83 | 12 | 10 | 3. 1999 | Warner 29896 |
| 9/17/83 | 8 | 11 | 4. **Delirious** | Warner 29503 |
| 6/09/84 | 1 (5) | 16 | ★ 5. **When Doves Cry** | Warner 29286 |
| 8/11/84 | 1 (2) | 14 | 6. **Let's Go Crazy** | Warner 29216 |
| 10/06/84 | 2 (2) | 11 | 7. **Purple Rain** | Warner 29174 |
| | | | above 3 from the film "Purple Rain" | |
| | | | **PRISM** | |
| | | | Canadian rock group | |
| 3/13/82 | 39 | 2 | 1. Don't Let Him Know | Capitol 5082 |
| | | | **P.J. PROBY** | |
| | | | real name: James Marcus Smith | |
| 2/25/67 | 23 | 5 | 1. Niki Hoeky | Liberty 55936 |

| DATE | POS | WKS | ARTIST—Record Title | LABEL & NO. |
|---|---|---|---|---|
| | | | **PROCOL HARUM** | |
| | | | British rock group led by Gary Brooker (vocals/piano) & Robin Trower (guitar) | |
| 7/01/67 | 5 | 10 | 1. **A Whiter Shade Of Pale** | Deram 7507 |
| 11/11/67 | 34 | 2 | 2. Homburg | A&M 885 |
| 6/24/72 | 16 | 8 | 3. Conquistador | A&M 1347 |
| | | | **JEANNE PRUETT** | |
| | | | country singer/songwriter | |
| 6/23/73 | 28 | 5 | 1. Satin Sheets | MCA 40015 |
| | | | **GARY PUCKETT & THE UNION GAP** | |
| | | | formed in San Diego - named after the town of Union Gap, Wash. | |
| 12/02/67 + | 4 | 15 | ● 1. **Woman, Woman** | Columbia 44297 |
| 3/16/68 | 2 (3) | 13 | ● 2. **Young Girl** | Columbia 44450 |
| 6/22/68 | 2 (2) | 11 | ● 3. **Lady Willpower** | Columbia 44547 |
| 9/28/68 | 7 | 10 | ● 4. **Over You** | Columbia 44644 |
| 3/22/69 | 15 | 8 | 5. Don't Give In To Him | Columbia 44788 |
| 9/06/69 | 9 | 9 | 6. **This Girl Is A Woman Now** | Columbia 44967 |
| | | | **PURE PRAIRIE LEAGUE** | |
| | | | country-rock group formed in Cincinnati | |
| 4/12/75 | 27 | 3 | 1. Amie | RCA 10184 |
| 5/24/80 | 10 | 11 | 2. **Let Me Love You Tonight** | Casablanca 2266 |
| 10/04/80 | 34 | 4 | 3. I'm Almost Ready | Casablanca 2294 |
| 5/23/81 | 28 | 6 | 4. Still Right Here In My Heart | Casablanca 2332 |
| | | | **JAMES & BOBBY PURIFY** | |
| | | | James Purify & cousin Bobby Dicky | |
| 10/22/66 | 6 | 10 | 1. **I'm Your Puppet** | Bell 648 |
| 2/25/67 | 38 | 1 | 2. Wish You Didn't Have To Go | Bell 660 |
| 5/13/67 | 25 | 5 | 3. Shake A Tail Feather | Bell 669 |
| 10/07/67 | 23 | 5 | 4. Let Love Come Between Us | Bell 685 |
| | | | **BILL PURSELL** | |
| | | | pianist from Tulare, California | |
| 2/16/63 | 9 | 10 | 1. **Our Winter Love [I]** | Columbia 42619 |
| | | | **PYRAMIDS** | |
| | | | West Coast surf band | |
| 2/22/64 | 18 | 6 | 1. Penetration [I] | Best 13002 |
| | | | **Q** | |
| 4/09/77 | 23 | 7 | 1. Dancin' Man | Epic 50335 |
| | | | **QUAKER CITY BOYS** | |
| 1/26/59 | 39 | 1 | 1. Teasin' | Swan 4023 |
| | | | **QUARTERFLASH** | |
| | | | rock group from Portland area originally known as Seafood Mama | |
| 11/07/81 + | 3 | 19 | 1. **Harden My Heart** | Geffen 49824 |
| 3/13/82 | 16 | 7 | 2. Find Another Fool | Geffen 50006 |
| 7/02/83 | 14 | 11 | 3. Take Me To Heart | Geffen 29603 |

| DATE | POS | WKS | ARTIST—Record Title | LABEL & NO. |
|------|-----|-----|---------------------|-------------|
| | | | **SUZI QUATRO & CHRIS NORMAN** Chris is lead singer of Smokie | |
| 2/24/79 | 4 | 15 | ● 1. **Stumblin' In** | RSO 917 |
| | | | **QUEEN** British: Freddie Mercury (vocals), Brian May (guitar), John Deacon (bass), Roger Taylor (drums) | |
| 3/29/75 | 12 | 11 | 1. Killer Queen | Elektra 45226 |
| 2/07/76 | 9 | 17 | ● 2. **Bohemian Rhapsody** | Elektra 45297 |
| 6/12/76 | 16 | 11 | 3. You're My Best Friend | Elektra 45318 |
| 12/04/76 + | 13 | 12 | 4. Somebody To Love | Elektra 45362 |
| 11/26/77 + | 4 | 17 | ★ 5. **We Are The Champions/** | |
| | | 10 | 6. **We Will Rock You** | Elektra 45441 |
| 12/09/78 + | 24 | 6 | 7. Bicycle Race/ | |
| | | 6 | 8. **Fat Bottomed Girls** | Elektra 45541 |
| 1/12/80 | 1 (4) | 17 | ● 9. **Crazy Little Thing Called Love** | Elektra 46579 |
| 8/30/80 | 1 (3) | 21 | ★ 10. **Another One Bites The Dust** | Elektra 47031 |
| 5/15/82 | 11 | 8 | 11. Body Language | Elektra 47452 |
| 3/03/84 | 16 | 8 | 12. Radio Ga-Ga | Capitol 5317 |
| | | | **QUEEN & DAVID BOWIE** | |
| 12/05/81 + | 29 | 8 | 1. Under Pressure | Elektra 47235 |
| | | | **? (QUESTION MARK) & THE MYSTERIANS** Mexican-born quintet - formed group in Detroit | |
| 9/17/66 | 1 (1) | 12 | ● 1. **96 Tears** | Cameo 428 |
| 12/10/66 | 22 | 6 | 2. I Need Somebody | Cameo 441 |
| | | | **QUIET RIOT** heavy-metal rock quartet from L.A. - Kevin DuBrow, lead singer | |
| 10/15/83 | 5 | 14 | ● 1. **Cum On Feel The Noize** | Pasha 04005 |
| 1/28/84 | 31 | 4 | 2. Bang Your Head (Metal Health) | Pasha 04267 |
| | | | **QUIN-TONES** Philadelphia quintet | |
| 9/08/58 | 18 | 6 | 1. Down The Aisle Of Love | Hunt 321 |
| | | | **EDDIE RABBITT** born Edward Thomas on 11/27/44 in Brooklyn, New York | |
| 3/03/79 | 30 | 4 | 1. Every Which Way But Loose | Elektra 45554 |
| 7/14/79 | 13 | 10 | 2. Suspicions | Elektra 46053 |
| 7/26/80 | 5 | 15 | ● 3. **Drivin' My Life Away** from the film "Roadie" | Elektra 46656 |
| 12/06/80 + | 1 (2) | 18 | ● 4. **I Love A Rainy Night** | Elektra 47066 |
| 8/08/81 | 5 | 15 | 5. **Step By Step** | Elektra 47174 |
| 12/05/81 + | 15 | 10 | 6. Someone Could Lose A Heart Tonight | Elektra 47239 |
| 5/22/82 | 35 | 4 | 7. I Don't Know Where To Start | Elektra 47435 |
| | | | **EDDIE RABBITT & CRYSTAL GAYLE** | |
| 11/13/82 + | 7 | 21 | 1. **You And I** | Elektra 69936 |

**Rolling Stones.** One of Mick Jagger's lesser-known efforts is a 1964 single with The Andrew Loog Oldham Orchestra, singing Phil Spector's "Da Doo Ron Ron." For collectors only.

**Linda Ronstadt** can certainly be called a quintessential stylist. Her long career had its beginnings in folk music, and since then she has recorded tunes by a variety of songwriters, including Hank Williams, Chuck Berry, Elvis Costello, Rodgers and Hart, and even Gilbert and Sullivan.

**The Romantics** claim to have held their first rehearsal in Detroit on Valentine's Day. Worthy heirs to the Motor City rock-'n'roll tradition forged by Mitch Ryder and Bob Seger, they just missed hitting Top 40 in 1980 with "What I like About You."

**Bobby Rydell,** known to his mother as Robert Ridarelli, was one of many teen idols of the early sixties who called Philadelphia their home town. Others included Frankie Avalon and Fabian. In 1957, Rydell played drums and Avalon trumpet in a local band called Rocco and his Saints.

**Mitch Ryder,** formerly Billy Levise, was one of the sixties leading white soul shouters. In the eighties, he attempted a comeback with an LP produced by number one fan, John Cougar Mellencamp.

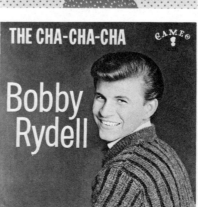

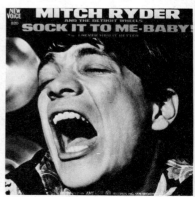

**The Searchers** took their name from John Ford's classic 1956 western, and distinguished themselves by being the first successful Liverpool band not managed by Brian Epstein.

**Bob Seger** retired from music in the late sixties to go back to college, but returned to the fray two years later when he joined forces with Teegarden and Van Winkle ("God, Love and Rock & Roll").

**The Shocking Blue** were part of a mini-Dutch invasion that included the Tee Set and George Baker. The Who were no doubt shocked to hear their intro to "Pinball Wizard" turn up undisguised at the beginning of "Venus."

**Tommy James and the Shondells** first hit with "Hanky Panky" in 1966, but the song had actually been recorded and released four years earlier. It was only after an enterprising Pittsburgh DJ discovered the song that the moldy flop began a belated trek to the top of the charts.

**Simon & Garfunkel.** What a difference a few years makes: In 1966's "The Dangling Conversation," Paul Simon talked of reading Emily Dickinson and Robert Frost; three years before, under the name Jerry Landis, he sang about life as "The Lone Teen Ranger."

| DATE | POS | WKS | ARTIST—Record Title | LABEL & NO. |
|---|---|---|---|---|
| | | | **GERRY RAFFERTY** | |
| | | | Scottish - co-leader of Stealers Wheel | |
| 5/13/78 | **2** (6) | 15 | ● 1. **Baker Street** | United Art. 1192 |
| | | | sax solo by Raphael Ravenscroft | |
| 8/26/78 | **12** | 11 | 2. Right Down The Line | United Art. 1233 |
| 1/06/79 | **28** | 6 | 3. Home And Dry | United Art. 1266 |
| 6/16/79 | **17** | 7 | 4. Days Gone Down (Still Got The Light In Your Eyes) | United Art. 1298 |
| 9/08/79 | **21** | 8 | 5. Get It Right Next Time | United Art. 1316 |
| | | | **RAIDERS - see PAUL REVERE & THE RAIDERS** | |
| | | | **RAINBOW** | |
| | | | hard-rock band led by British guitarist Ritchie Blackmore & bassist Roger Glover, both members of Deep Purple | |
| 6/19/82 | **40** | 1 | 1. Stone Cold | Mercury 76146 |
| | | | **RAINDROPS** | |
| | | | Jeff Barry & his wife Ellie Greenwich | |
| 8/31/63 | **17** | 7 | 1. The Kind Of Boy You Can't Forget | Jubilee 5455 |
| | | | **MARVIN RAINWATER** | |
| | | | American Indian from Wichita, Kansas | |
| 6/10/57 | **18** | 12 | 1. Gonna Find Me A Bluebird | MGM 12412 |
| | | | **RAM JAM** | |
| | | | East Coast rock quartet led by Bill Bartlett (Lemon Pipers) | |
| 7/23/77 | **18** | 8 | 1. Black Betty | Epic 50357 |
| | | | **EDDIE RAMBEAU** | |
| | | | singer/songwriter from Hazleton, Pennsylvania | |
| 6/05/65 | **35** | 2 | 1. Concrete And Clay | DynoVoice 204 |
| | | | **RAMRODS** | |
| | | | instrumental rock quartet from Connecticut | |
| 2/20/61 | **30** | 1 | 1. (Ghost) Riders In The Sky [I] | Amy 813 |
| | | | **RAN-DELLS** | |
| | | | cousins Steve Rappaport & John Spirt from New Jersey | |
| 8/31/63 | **16** | 8 | 1. Martian Hop | Chairman 4403 |
| | | | **BOOTS RANDOLPH** | |
| | | | premier Nashville session saxophonist | |
| 3/30/63 | **35** | 3 | 1. Yakety Sax [I] | Monument 804 |
| | | | **RANDY & THE RAINBOWS** | |
| | | | Randy Safuto, lead singer of quintet from New York | |
| 7/27/63 | **10** | 10 | 1. **Denise** | Rust 5059 |
| | | | **RARE EARTH** | |
| | | | Detroit rock group | |
| 4/04/70 | **4** | 17 | 1. **Get Ready** | Rare Earth 5012 |
| 8/22/70 | **7** | 11 | 2. **(I Know) I'm Losing You** | Rare Earth 5017 |
| 1/02/71 | **17** | 8 | 3. Born To Wander | Rare Earth 5021 |
| 8/07/71 | **7** | 10 | 4. **I Just Want To Celebrate** | Rare Earth 5031 |
| 12/18/71 + | **19** | 7 | 5. Hey Big Brother | Rare Earth 5038 |
| 6/17/78 | **39** | 2 | 6. Warm Ride | Prodigal 0640 |

| DATE | POS | WKS | ARTIST—Record Title | LABEL & NO. |
|------|-----|-----|---------------------|-------------|
| | | | **RASCALS** | |
| | | | Felix Cavaliere, Dino Danelli, Eddie Brigati, Gene Cornish<br>YOUNG RASCALS: | |
| 3/26/66 | **1** (1) | 12 | 1. **Good Lovin'** | Atlantic 2321 |
| 7/09/66 | **20** | 4 | 2. You Better Run | Atlantic 2338 |
| 2/25/67 | **16** | 9 | 3. I've Been Lonely Too Long | Atlantic 2377 |
| 5/06/67 | **1** (4) | 11 | ● 4. **Groovin'** | Atlantic 2401 |
| 7/22/67 | **10** | 8 | 5. **A Girl Like You** | Atlantic 2424 |
| 9/23/67 | **4** | 9 | 6. **How Can I Be Sure** | Atlantic 2438 |
| 12/23/67 + | **20** | 5 | 7. It's Wonderful<br>RASCALS: | Atlantic 2463 |
| 4/20/68 | **3** | 11 | ● 8. **A Beautiful Morning** | Atlantic 2493 |
| 7/27/68 | **1** (5) | 13 | ● 9. **People Got To Be Free** | Atlantic 2537 |
| 12/14/68 + | **24** | 6 | 10. A Ray Of Hope | Atlantic 2584 |
| 3/01/69 | **39** | 2 | 11. Heaven | Atlantic 2599 |
| 6/07/69 | **27** | 5 | 12. See | Atlantic 2634 |
| 9/20/69 | **26** | 6 | 13. Carry Me Back | Atlantic 2664 |
| | | | **RASPBERRIES** | |
| | | | Cleveland, Ohio pop/rock quartet - Eric Carmen, lead singer | |
| 8/19/72 | **5** | 11 | ● 1. **Go All The Way** | Capitol 3348 |
| 12/09/72 + | **16** | 9 | 2. I Wanna Be With You | Capitol 3473 |
| 5/12/73 | **35** | 7 | 3. Let's Pretend | Capitol 3546 |
| 10/12/74 | **18** | 6 | 4. Overnight Sensation (Hit Record) | Capitol 3946 |
| | | | **RATT** | |
| | | | hard-rock quintet from Los Angeles - Stephen Pearcy, lead singer | |
| 7/14/84 | **12** | 10 | 1. Round And Round | Atlantic 89693 |
| | | | **LOU RAWLS** | |
| | | | born on 12/1/35 in Chicago, Illinois - also see Sam Cooke | |
| 10/15/66 | **13** | 8 | 1. Love Is A Hurtin' Thing | Capitol 5709 |
| 5/06/67 | **29** | 4 | 2. Dead End Street | Capitol 5869 |
| 8/30/69 | **18** | 8 | 3. Your Good Thing (Is About To End) | Capitol 2550 |
| 10/16/71 | **17** | 11 | 4. A Natural Man | MGM 14262 |
| 7/10/76 | **2** (2) | 13 | ● 5. **You'll Never Find Another Love Like Mine** | Phil. Int. 3592 |
| 2/25/78 | **24** | 8 | 6. Lady Love | Phil. Int. 3634 |
| | | | **RAY, GOODMAN & BROWN** | |
| | | | Harry Ray, Al Goodman & William Brown - formerly known as<br>The Moments | |
| 2/16/80 | **5** | 14 | ● 1. **Special Lady** | Polydor 2033 |
| | | | **DIANE RAY** | |
| 9/07/63 | **31** | 3 | 1. Please Don't Talk To The Lifeguard | Mercury 72117 |
| | | | **JAMES RAY** | |
| 12/25/61 + | **22** | 7 | 1. If You Gotta Make A Fool Of Somebody | Caprice 110 |
| | | | **JOHNNIE RAY** | |
| | | | born in Roseburg, Oregon on 1/10/27 | |
| 9/08/56 | **2** (1) | 23 | 1. **Just Walking In The Rain** | Columbia 40729 |
| 1/19/57 | **10** | 10 | 2. **You Don't Owe Me A Thing/** | |
| 2/02/57 | **36** | 2 | 3. Look Homeward, Angel | Columbia 40803 |
| 5/06/57 | **12** | 5 | 4. Yes Tonight, Josephine | Columbia 40893 |

| DATE | POS | WKS | ARTIST—Record Title | LABEL & NO. |
|---|---|---|---|---|
| | | | **MARGIE RAYBURN** | |
| 11/11/57 | 9 | 13 | 1. I'm Available | Liberty 55102 |
| | | | **RAYDIO - see RAY PARKER JR.** | |
| | | | **RAYS** | |
| | | | Hal Miller, lead singer of New York R&B quartet | |
| 10/21/57 | 3 | 17 | 1. Silhouettes | Cameo 117 |
| | | | **CHRIS REA** | |
| | | | English | |
| 7/29/78 | 12 | 10 | 1. Fool (If You Think It's Over) | United Art. 1198 |
| | | | **REAL LIFE** | |
| | | | Australian quartet | |
| 1/14/84 | 29 | 6 | 1. Send Me An Angel | Curb 52287 |
| 5/05/84 | 40 | 1 | 2. Catch Me I'm Falling | Curb 52362 |
| | | | **REBELS** | |
| | | | also recorded as the Rockin' Rebels | |
| 1/26/63 | 8 | 12 | 1. Wild Weekend [I] | Swan 4125 |
| | | | **REDBONE** | |
| | | | American Indian rock group led by brothers Pat & Lolly Vegas | |
| 1/08/72 | 21 | 7 | 1. The Witch Queen Of New Orleans | Epic 10749 |
| 2/09/74 | 5 | 18 | ● 2. Come And Get Your Love | Epic 11035 |
| | | | **GENE REDDING** | |
| 7/06/74 | 24 | 5 | 1. This Heart | Haven 7000 |
| | | | **OTIS REDDING** | |
| | | | soulful blues singer - born 9/9/41 in Dawson, Georgia; killed in a plane crash on 12/10/67 (26) - also see Otis & Carla | |
| 6/19/65 | 21 | 6 | 1. I've Been Loving You Too Long (To Stop Now) | Volt 126 |
| 10/23/65 | 35 | 3 | 2. Respect | Volt 128 |
| 4/02/66 | 31 | 3 | 3. Satisfaction | Volt 132 |
| 10/29/66 | 29 | 4 | 4. Fa-Fa-Fa-Fa-Fa (Sad Song) | Volt 138 |
| 12/31/66 + | 25 | 6 | 5. Try A Little Tenderness | Volt 141 |
| 2/10/68 | 1 (4) | 14 | ● 6. (Sittin' On) The Dock Of The Bay | Volt 157 |
| 5/11/68 | 25 | 5 | 7. The Happy Song (Dum-Dum) | Volt 163 |
| 7/27/68 | 36 | 1 | 8. Amen | Atco 6592 |
| 12/14/68 + | 21 | 5 | 9. Papa's Got A Brand New Bag | Atco 6636 |
| | | | **HELEN REDDY** | |
| | | | born on 10/4/42 in Melbourne, Australia | |
| 5/08/71 | 13 | 9 | 1. I Don't Know How To Love Him | Capitol 3027 |
| | | | from the rock opera "Jesus Christ Superstar" | |
| 10/14/72 | 1 (1) | 14 | ● 2. I Am Woman | Capitol 3350 |
| 3/10/73 | 12 | 10 | 3. Peaceful | Capitol 3527 |
| 7/28/73 | 1 (1) | 14 | ● 4. Delta Dawn | Capitol 3645 |
| 11/17/73 | 3 | 13 | ● 5. Leave Me Alone (Ruby Red Dress) | Capitol 3768 |
| 3/30/74 | 15 | 9 | 6. Keep On Singing | Capitol 3845 |
| 7/20/74 | 9 | 12 | 7. You And Me Against The World | Capitol 3897 |

| DATE | POS | WKS | ARTIST—Record Title | LABEL & NO. |
|---|---|---|---|---|
| 11/02/74 | **1** (1) | 13 | ● 8. **Angie Baby** | Capitol 3972 |
| 3/01/75 | **22** | 5 | 9. Emotion | Capitol 4021 |
| 7/26/75 | **35** | 2 | 10. Bluebird | Capitol 4108 |
| 8/30/75 | **8** | 9 | 11. **Ain't No Way To Treat A Lady** | Capitol 4128 |
| 12/27/75 + | **19** | 9 | 12. Somewhere In The Night | Capitol 4192 |
| 8/21/76 | **29** | 5 | 13. I Can't Hear You No More | Capitol 4312 |
| 6/11/77 | **18** | 12 | 14. You're My World | Capitol 4418 |
| | | | **REDEYE** | |
| | | | rock quartet led by Dave Hodgkins & Douglas "Red" Mark | |
| 12/26/70 + | **27** | 7 | 1. Games | Pentagram 204 |
| | | | **JERRY REED** | |
| | | | born Jerry Hubbard on 3/20/37 in Atlanta, Georgia | |
| 1/09/71 | **8** | 14 | ● 1. **Amos Moses [N]** | RCA 9904 |
| 5/29/71 | **9** | 9 | 2. **When You're Hot, You're Hot [N]** | RCA 9976 |
| | | | **JIMMY REED** | |
| | | | blues singer, guitarist, harmonica player - died on 8/29/76 (50) | |
| 11/04/57 | **32** | 3 | 1. Honest I Do | Vee-Jay 253 |
| 2/29/60 | **37** | 2 | 2. Baby What You Want Me To Do | Vee-Jay 333 |
| | | | **LOU REED** | |
| | | | lead singer of New York seminal rock band, the Velvet Underground | |
| 3/31/73 | **16** | 8 | 1. Walk On The Wild Side | RCA 0887 |
| | | | **DELLA REESE** | |
| | | | born Dellareese Taliaferro on 7/6/32 in Detroit, Michigan | |
| 9/09/57 | **12** | 13 | 1. And That Reminds Me | Jubilee 5292 |
| 10/05/59 | **2** (1) | 15 | 2. **Don't You Know** | RCA 7591 |
| 12/28/59 + | **16** | 8 | 3. Not One Minute More | RCA 7644 |
| | | | **JIM REEVES** | |
| | | | Country Music Hall Of Famer - born on 8/20/24 in Galloway, Texas - killed in a plane crash on 7/31/64 (39) | |
| 5/06/57 | **11** | 14 | 1. Four Walls | RCA 6874 |
| 1/11/60 | **2** (3) | 20 | 2. **He'll Have To Go** | RCA 7643 |
| 7/11/60 | **37** | 1 | 3. I'm Gettin' Better | RCA 7756 |
| 11/28/60 | **31** | 4 | 4. Am I Losing You | RCA 7800 |
| | | | **REFLECTIONS** | |
| | | | Detroit quartet | |
| 5/02/64 | **6** | 9 | 1. **(Just Like) Romeo & Juliet** | Golden World 9 |
| | | | **RE-FLEX** | |
| | | | British techno-rock quartet | |
| 2/18/84 | **24** | 5 | 1. The Politics Of Dancing | Capitol 5301 |
| | | | **REGENTS** | |
| | | | Bronx quintet - Guy Villari, lead singer | |
| 5/22/61 | **13** | 7 | 1. Barbara-Ann | Gee 1065 |
| 7/31/61 | **28** | 4 | 2. Runaround | Gee 1071 |
| | | | **CLARENCE REID** | |
| 9/13/69 | **40** | 2 | 1. Nobody But You Babe | Alston 4574 |

| DATE | POS | WKS | ARTIST—Record Title | LABEL & NO. |
|---|---|---|---|---|
| | | | **DIANE RENAY** | |
| | | | Philadelphian Renee Diane Kushner | |
| 2/15/64 | 6 | 8 | 1. **Navy Blue** | 20th Century 456 |
| 4/25/64 | 29 | 4 | 2. Kiss Me Sailor | 20th Century 477 |
| | | | **RENE & RENE** | |
| | | | Rene Ornelas & Rene Herrera | |
| 12/14/68 + | 14 | 9 | 1. Lo Mucho Que Te Quiero (The More I Love You) | White Whale 287 |
| | | | **MIKE RENO & ANN WILSON** | |
| | | | lead singers of Loverboy and Heart respectively | |
| 5/19/84 | 7 | 13 | 1. **Almost Paradise...Love Theme From Footloose** | Columbia 04418 |
| | | | **REO SPEEDWAGON** | |
| | | | Champaign, Illinois rock quintet led by Kevin Kronin (vocals) & Gary Richrath (guitar) | |
| 12/27/80 + | 1 (1) | 20 | ● 1. **Keep On Loving You** | Epic 50953 |
| 3/28/81 | 5 | 15 | 2. **Take It On The Run** | Epic 01054 |
| 7/04/81 | 24 | 6 | 3. **Don't Let Him Go** | Epic 02127 |
| 8/29/81 | 20 | 7 | 4. In Your Letter | Epic 02457 |
| 6/19/82 | 7 | 13 | 5. **Keep The Fire Burnin'** | Epic 02967 |
| 10/02/82 | 26 | 6 | 6. Sweet Time | Epic 03175 |
| | | | **REUNION** | |
| | | | Joey (Ohio Express) Levine, lead singer | |
| 9/28/74 | 8 | 10 | 1. **Life Is A Rock (But The Radio Rolled Me) [N]** | RCA 10056 |
| | | | **REVELS** | |
| 11/23/59 | 35 | 2 | 1. Midnight Stroll | Norgolde 103 |
| | | | **PAUL REVERE & THE RAIDERS** | |
| | | | Portland, Oregon pop/rock quintet led by Paul Revere (organ) & Mark Lindsay (vocals) | |
| 4/17/61 | 38 | 1 | 1. Like, Long Hair [I] | Gardena 116 |
| 12/25/65 + | 11 | 11 | 2. Just Like Me | Columbia 43461 |
| 3/26/66 | 4 | 12 | 3. **Kicks** | Columbia 43556 |
| 7/09/66 | 6 | 7 | 4. **Hungry** | Columbia 43678 |
| 10/15/66 | 20 | 5 | 5. The Great Airplane Strike | Columbia 43810 |
| 12/17/66 + | 4 | 10 | 6. **Good Thing** | Columbia 43907 |
| 3/04/67 | 22 | 6 | 7. Ups And Downs | Columbia 44018 |
| 5/06/67 | 5 | 8 | 8. **Him Or Me - What's It Gonna Be?** | Columbia 44094 |
| 9/02/67 | 17 | 5 | 9. I Had A Dream | Columbia 44227 |
| 2/24/68 | 19 | 6 | 10. Too Much Talk | Columbia 44444 |
| 7/13/68 | 27 | 6 | 11. Don't Take It So Hard | Columbia 44553 |
| 3/08/69 | 18 | 9 | 12. Mr. Sun, Mr. Moon | Columbia 44744 |
| 6/14/69 | 20 | 8 | 13. Let Me | Columbia 44854 |
| | | | RAIDERS: | |
| 5/29/71 | 1 (1) | 15 | ● 14. **Indian Reservation (The Lament Of The Cherokee Reservation Indian)** | Columbia 45332 |
| 10/02/71 | 23 | 6 | 15. Birds Of A Feather | Columbia 45453 |

| DATE | POS | WKS | ARTIST—Record Title | LABEL & NO. |
|---|---|---|---|---|
| | | | **DEBBIE REYNOLDS** | |
| | | | movie actress - mother of actress Carrie Fisher (Eddie Fisher, father) | |
| 7/22/57 | **1** (5) | 23 | 1. **Tammy** | Coral 61851 |
| | | | from the film: "Tammy & The Bachelor" | |
| 1/20/58 | **20** | 1 | 2. A Very Special Love | Coral 61897 |
| 2/22/60 | **25** | 8 | 3. Am I That Easy To Forget | Dot 15985 |
| | | | **JODY REYNOLDS** | |
| 5/26/58 | **5** | 14 | 1. **Endless Sleep** | Demon 1507 |
| | | | **LAWRENCE REYNOLDS** | |
| 10/11/69 | **28** | 6 | 1. Jesus Is A Soul Man | Warner 7322 |
| | | | **RHYTHM HERITAGE** | |
| | | | a disco production by Steve Barri & Michael Omartian | |
| 1/10/76 | **1** (1) | 12 | ● 1. **Theme From S.W.A.T. [I]** | ABC 12135 |
| 5/08/76 | **20** | 8 | 2. Barretta's Theme ("Keep Your Eye On The Sparrow") | ABC 12177 |
| | | | **CHARLIE RICH** | |
| | | | originally signed by Sam Phillips' Sun label as a rockabilly artist | |
| 5/02/60 | **22** | 9 | 1. Lonely Weekends | Phillips 3552 |
| 9/25/65 | **21** | 7 | 2. Mohair Sam | Smash 1993 |
| 6/09/73 | **15** | 12 | ● 3. Behind Closed Doors | Epic 10950 |
| 10/27/73 | **1** (2) | 17 | ● 4. **The Most Beautiful Girl** | Epic 11040 |
| 2/23/74 | **18** | 8 | 5. There Won't Be Anymore | RCA 0195 |
| 3/09/74 | **11** | 9 | 6. A Very Special Love Song | Epic 11091 |
| 8/24/74 | **24** | 7 | 7. I Love My Friend | Epic 20006 |
| 6/28/75 | **19** | 6 | 8. Every Time You Touch Me (I Get High) | Epic 50103 |
| | | | **CLIFF RICHARD** | |
| | | | born Harry Webb in India on 10/14/40 - Britain's most popular solo vocalist - also see Olivia Newton-John | |
| 11/02/59 | **30** | 4 | 1. Living Doll | ABC-Para. 10042 |
| | | | with the Drifters - from the film "Serious Charge" | |
| 1/18/64 | **25** | 7 | 2. It's All In The Game | Epic 9633 |
| 8/14/76 | **6** | 12 | ● 3. **Devil Woman** | Rocket 40574 |
| 11/17/79 + | **7** | 14 | 4. **We Don't Talk Anymore** | EMI America 8025 |
| 4/05/80 | **34** | 3 | 5. Carrie | EMI America 8035 |
| 9/27/80 | **10** | 13 | 6. **Dreaming** | EMI America 8057 |
| 1/24/81 | **17** | 11 | 7. A Little In Love | EMI America 8068 |
| 2/06/82 | **23** | 8 | 8. Daddy's Home | EMI America 8103 |
| | | | **LIONEL RICHIE** | |
| | | | singer/songwriter/producer - Commodores' lead singer ('74-'81) - also see Diana Ross | |
| 10/23/82 | **1** (2) | 13 | ● 1. **Truly** | Motown 1644 |
| 1/22/83 | **4** | 16 | 2. **You Are** | Motown 1657 |
| 4/16/83 | **5** | 12 | 3. **My Love** | Motown 1677 |
| 10/01/83 | **1** (4) | 17 | ● 4. **All Night Long (All Night)** | Motown 1698 |
| 12/03/83 + | **7** | 14 | 5. **Running With The Night** | Motown 1710 |
| 3/10/84 | **1** (2) | 17 | ● 6. **Hello** | Motown 1722 |
| 7/07/84 | **3** | 14 | 7. **Stuck On You** | Motown 1746 |
| 10/13/84 | **8** | 13 | 8. **Penny Lover** | Motown 1762 |

| DATE | POS | WKS | ARTIST—Record Title | LABEL & NO. |
|---|---|---|---|---|
| | | | **NELSON RIDDLE & His Orchestra** | |
| | | | leading pop/jazz arranger/conductor since 1940 | |
| 12/31/55 + | **1** (4) | 24 | 1. **Lisbon Antigua [I]** | Capitol 3287 |
| 3/31/56 | **20** | 4 | 2. Port Au Prince [I] | Capitol 3374 |
| 8/04/56 | **39** | 2 | 3. Theme From "The Proud Ones" [I] | Capitol 3472 |
| 8/04/62 | **30** | 3 | 4. Route 66 Theme [I] | Capitol 4741 |
| | | | **RIGHTEOUS BROTHERS** | |
| | | | Southern California blue-eyed soul duo - Bill Medley & Bobby Hatfield | |
| 12/26/64 + | **1** (2) | 13 | 1. **You've Lost That Lovin' Feelin'** | Philles 124 |
| 4/17/65 | **9** | 10 | 2. **Just Once In My Life** | Philles 127 |
| 7/31/65 | **4** | 11 | 3. **Unchained Melody** | Philles 129 |
| 12/11/65 + | **5** | 8 | 4. **Ebb Tide** | Philles 130 |
| 3/19/66 | **1** (3) | 11 | ● 5. **(You're My) Soul And Inspiration** | Verve 10383 |
| 6/18/66 | **18** | 5 | 6. He | Verve 10406 |
| 8/27/66 | **30** | 3 | 7. Go Ahead And Cry | Verve 10430 |
| 6/15/74 | **3** | 10 | 8. **Rock And Roll Heaven** | Haven 7002 |
| 10/05/74 | **20** | 4 | 9. Give It To The People | Haven 7004 |
| 12/07/74 | **32** | 3 | 10. Dream On | Haven 7006 |
| | | | **JEANNIE C. RILEY** | |
| | | | born on 10/19/45 in Anson, Texas | |
| 8/31/68 | **1** (1) | 12 | ● 1. **Harper Valley P.T.A.** | Plantation 3 |
| | | | **RINKY-DINKS** | |
| | | | group is actually Bobby Darin | |
| 8/11/58 | **24** | 5 | 1. Early In The Morning | Atco 6121 |
| | | | **MIGUEL RIOS** | |
| | | | native of Granada, Spain | |
| 6/20/70 | **14** | 8 | 1. A Song Of Joy | A&M 1193 |
| | | | based on the last movement of Beethoven's 9th Symphony - Waldo de los Rios, conductor | |
| | | | **RIP CHORDS** | |
| | | | Southern California quartet | |
| 1/04/64 | **4** | 11 | 1. **Hey Little Cobra** | Columbia 42921 |
| 5/23/64 | **28** | 5 | 2. Three Window Coupe | Columbia 43035 |
| | | | **MINNIE RIPERTON** | |
| | | | lead singer of Rotary Connection - Minnie died on 7/12/79 (30) | |
| 2/15/75 | **1** (1) | 13 | ● 1. **Lovin' You** | Epic 50057 |
| | | | **RITCHIE FAMILY** | |
| | | | female disco trio produced by Jacques Morali | |
| 9/06/75 | **11** | 12 | 1. Brazil [I] | 20th Century 2218 |
| 10/02/76 | **17** | 11 | 2. The Best Disco In Town | Marlin 3306 |
| | | | **LEE RITENOUR** | |
| | | | jazz-fusion guitar virtuoso | |
| 5/23/81 | **15** | 9 | 1. Is It You | Elektra 47124 |
| | | | vocal by Eric Tagg | |

| DATE | POS | WKS | ARTIST—Record Title | LABEL & NO. |
|---|---|---|---|---|
| | | | **TEX RITTER** | |
| | | | father of TV star John Ritter - Tex died on 1/2/74 (67) | |
| 7/07/56 | 28 | 6 | 1. The Wayward Wind | Capitol 3430 |
| 8/14/61 | 20 | 4 | 2. I Dreamed Of A Hill-Billy Heaven [S] | Capitol 4567 |
| | | | **JOHNNY RIVERS** | |
| | | | born John Ramistella on 11/7/42 in New York City | |
| 6/13/64 | 2 (2) | 10 | 1. **Memphis** | Imperial 66032 |
| 8/22/64 | 12 | 7 | 2. **Maybelline** | Imperial 66056 |
| 11/14/64 | 9 | 9 | 3. **Mountain Of Love** | Imperial 66075 |
| 2/27/65 | 20 | 4 | 4. Midnight Special | Imperial 66087 |
| 6/19/65 | 7 | 8 | 5. **Seventh Son** | Imperial 66112 |
| 10/30/65 | 26 | 4 | 6. Where Have All The Flowers Gone | Imperial 66133 |
| 1/15/66 | 35 | 3 | 7. Under Your Spell Again | Imperial 66144 |
| 3/26/66 | 3 | 10 | 8. **Secret Agent Man** | Imperial 66159 |
| 6/25/66 | 19 | 6 | 9. (I Washed My Hands In) Muddy Water | Imperial 66175 |
| 10/08/66 | 1 (1) | 12 | 10. **Poor Side Of Town** | Imperial 66205 |
| 2/18/67 | 3 | 8 | 11. **Baby I Need Your Lovin'** | Imperial 66227 |
| 6/17/67 | 10 | 6 | 12. **The Tracks Of My Tears** | Imperial 66244 |
| 12/02/67 + | 14 | 8 | 13. Summer Rain | Imperial 66267 |
| 11/11/72 + | 6 | 14 | ● 14. **Rockin' Pneumonia - Boogie Woogie Flu** | United Art. 50960 |
| 5/05/73 | 38 | 2 | 15. Blue Suede Shoes | United Art. 198 |
| 8/09/75 | 22 | 5 | 16. Help Me Rhonda | Epic 50121 |
| 7/30/77 | 10 | 15 | ● 17. **Swayin' To The Music (Slow Dancin')** | Big Tree 16094 |
| | | | **RIVIERAS** | |
| | | | rock sextet from Indiana - Bill Dobslaw, lead singer | |
| 2/01/64 | 5 | 9 | 1. **California Sun** | Riviera 1401 |
| | | | **ROAD APPLES** | |
| 12/27/75 + | 35 | 4 | 1. Let's Live Together | Polydor 14285 |
| | | | **MARTY ROBBINS** | |
| | | | born in Glendale, Arizona on 9/26/25, and died on 12/8/82 (57) - Marty's had hits on the Country charts every year since 1956 | |
| 11/24/56 | 17 | 7 | 1. Singing The Blues | Columbia 21545 |
| 4/27/57 | 2 (1) | 21 | 2. **A White Sport Coat (And A Pink Carnation)** | Columbia 40864 |
| 12/09/57 + | 15 | 9 | 3. The Story Of My Life | Columbia 41013 |
| 5/05/58 | 26 | 5 | 4. Just Married | Columbia 41143 |
| 8/25/58 | 27 | 5 | 5. She Was Only Seventeen (He Was One Year More) | Columbia 41208 |
| 3/16/59 | 38 | 3 | 6. The Hanging Tree | Columbia 41325 |
| 11/30/59 + | 1 (2) | 16 | 7. **El Paso** | Columbia 41511 |
| 4/11/60 | 26 | 4 | 8. Big Iron | Columbia 41589 |
| 8/01/60 | 31 | 3 | 9. Is There Any Chance | Columbia 41686 |
| 12/05/60 | 34 | 5 | 10. Ballad Of The Alamo | Columbia 41809 |
| 2/13/61 | 3 | 12 | 11. **Don't Worry** | Columbia 41922 |
| 8/18/62 | 16 | 7 | 12. Devil Woman | Columbia 42486 |
| 12/08/62 | 18 | 5 | 13. Ruby Ann | Columbia 42614 |
| | | | **ROBERT & JOHNNY** | |
| | | | Robert Carr & Johnny Mitchell from the Bronx, New York | |
| 3/03/58 | 32 | 6 | 1. We Belong Together | Old Town 1047 |

| DATE | POS | WKS | ARTIST—Record Title | LABEL & NO. |
|---|---|---|---|---|
| | | | **AUSTIN ROBERTS** | |
| 11/11/72 | 12 | 10 | 1. Something's Wrong With Me | Chelsea 0101 |
| 8/30/75 | 9 | 9 | 2. **Rocky** | Private S. 45020 |
| | | | **DON ROBERTSON** | |
| 5/05/56 | 6 | 14 | 1. **The Happy Whistler [I]** | Capitol 3391 |
| | | | **IVO ROBIC** | |
| | | | Yugoslavian | |
| 8/31/59 | 13 | 11 | 1. Morgen [F] | Laurie 3033 |
| | | | **FLOYD ROBINSON** | |
| 8/03/59 | 20 | 12 | 1. Makin' Love | RCA 7529 |
| | | | **SMOKEY ROBINSON** | |
| | | | black music's all-time great singer/songwriter/producer - currently vice-president of Motown Records - also see Miracles | |
| 1/19/74 | 27 | 6 | 1. Baby Come Close | Tamla 54239 |
| 5/31/75 | 26 | 6 | 2. Baby That's Backatcha | Tamla 54258 |
| 10/18/75 | 36 | 3 | 3. The Agony And The Ecstasy | Tamla 54261 |
| 11/17/79 + | 4 | 17 | 4. **Cruisin'** | Tamla 54306 |
| 5/03/80 | 31 | 4 | 5. Let Me Be The Clock | Tamla 54311 |
| 3/21/81 | 2 (3) | 16 | ● 6. **Being With You** | Tamla 54321 |
| 2/27/82 | 33 | 5 | 7. Tell Me Tomorrow - Part 1 | Tamla 1601 |
| | | | **VICKI SUE ROBINSON** | |
| | | | performed on Broadway in "Hair" & "Jesus Christ Superstar" | |
| 6/19/76 | 10 | 13 | 1. **Turn The Beat Around** | RCA 10562 |
| | | | **ROCHELL & THE CANDLES** | |
| | | | Rochell Henderson with lead singer Johnny Wyatt | |
| 3/27/61 | 26 | 4 | 1. Once Upon A Time | Swingin' 623 |
| | | | **ROCK-A-TEENS** | |
| 10/12/59 | 16 | 9 | 1. Woo-Hoo [I] | Roulette 4192 |
| | | | **ROCKETS** | |
| | | | rock band from Detroit led by David Gilbert (vocals) & Jim McCarty (guitar) | |
| 8/11/79 | 30 | 6 | 1. Oh Well | RSO 935 |
| | | | **ROCKWELL** | |
| | | | Motown chairman Berry Gordy's son, Kennedy Gordy | |
| 2/11/84 | 2 (3) | 14 | ● 1. **Somebody's Watching Me** | Motown 1702 |
| | | | background vocals by Michael Jackson | |
| 6/23/84 | 35 | 2 | 2. Obscene Phone Caller | Motown 1731 |
| | | | **ROCKY FELLERS** | |
| | | | father and his four sons from Manila, The Philippines | |
| 4/27/63 | 16 | 8 | 1. Killer Joe | Scepter 1246 |
| | | | **EILEEN RODGERS** | |
| 9/08/56 | 18 | 10 | 1. Miracle Of Love | Columbia 40708 |
| 9/29/58 | 26 | 4 | 2. Treasure Of Your Love | Columbia 41214 |

| DATE | POS | WKS | ARTIST—Record Title | LABEL & NO. |
|------|-----|-----|---------------------|-------------|
| | | | **JIMMIE RODGERS** | |
| | | | born on 9/18/33 in Camus, Washington | |
| 8/19/57 | 1 (4) | 23 | 1. **Honeycomb** | Roulette 4015 |
| 11/18/57 | 3 | 14 | 2. **Kisses Sweeter Than Wine** | Roulette 4031 |
| 2/24/58 | 7 | 9 | 3. **Oh-Oh, I'm Falling In Love Again** | Roulette 4045 |
| 5/19/58 | 3 | 15 | 4. **Secretly/** | |
| 5/26/58 | 16 | 1 | 5.  Make Me A Miracle | Roulette 4070 |
| 8/11/58 | 10 | 10 | 6. **Are You Really Mine** | Roulette 4090 |
| 12/01/58 | 11 | 10 | 7. Bimbombey | Roulette 4116 |
| 3/30/59 | 36 | 3 | 8. I'm Never Gonna Tell | Roulette 4129 |
| 6/15/59 | 32 | 4 | 9. Ring-A-Ling-A-Lario/ | |
| 7/06/59 | 40 | 1 | 10.  Wonderful You | Roulette 4158 |
| 10/12/59 | 32 | 3 | 11. Tucumcari | Roulette 4191 |
| 2/01/60 | 24 | 5 | 12. Tender Love And Care (T.L.C.) | Roulette 4218 |
| 6/18/66 | 37 | 2 | 13. It's Over | Dot 16861 |
| 10/14/67 | 31 | 4 | 14. Child Of Clay | A&M 871 |
| | | | **TOMMY ROE** | |
| | | | born on 5/9/42 in Atlanta, Georgia | |
| 8/11/62 | 1 (2) | 11 | ● 1. **Sheila** | ABC-Para. 10329 |
| 11/03/62 | 35 | 2 | 2. Susie Darlin' | ABC-Para. 10362 |
| 10/26/63 | 3 | 11 | 3. **Everybody** | ABC-Para. 10478 |
| 2/08/64 | 36 | 4 | 4. Come On | ABC-Para. 10515 |
| 7/02/66 | 8 | 10 | ● 5. **Sweet Pea** | ABC-Para. 10762 |
| 10/01/66 | 6 | 11 | 6. **Hooray For Hazel** | ABC 10852 |
| 1/28/67 | 23 | 5 | 7. It's Now Winters Day | ABC 10888 |
| 2/15/69 | 1 (4) | 13 | ● 8. **Dizzy** | ABC 11164 |
| 5/17/69 | 29 | 3 | 9. Heather Honey | ABC 11211 |
| 12/06/69 + | 8 | 11 | ● 10. **Jam Up Jelly Tight** | ABC 11247 |
| 9/25/71 | 25 | 7 | 11. Stagger Lee | ABC 11307 |
| | | | **JULIE ROGERS** | |
| 12/05/64 + | 10 | 9 | 1. **The Wedding** | Mercury 72332 |
| | | | **KENNY ROGERS** | |
| | | | born on 8/21/41 in Houston, Texas - also see Dottie West | |
| 4/23/77 | 5 | 13 | ● 1. **Lucille** | United Art. 929 |
| 9/10/77 | 28 | 4 | 2. Daytime Friends | United Art. 1027 |
| 7/15/78 | 32 | 3 | 3. Love Or Something Like It | United Art. 1210 |
| 12/23/78 + | 16 | 13 | 4. The Gambler | United Art. 1250 |
| 5/12/79 | 5 | 13 | ● 5. **She Believes In Me** | United Art. 1273 |
| 9/22/79 | 7 | 12 | 6. **You Decorated My Life** | United Art. 1315 |
| 12/01/79 + | 3 | 15 | ● 7. **Coward Of The County** | United Art. 1327 |
| 6/28/80 | 14 | 8 | 8. Love The World Away<br>from the film "Urban Cowboy" | United Art. 1359 |
| 10/04/80 | 1 (6) | 19 | ● 9. **Lady** | Liberty 1380 |
| 6/13/81 | 3 | 14 | 10. **I Don't Need You** | Liberty 1415 |
| 9/12/81 | 14 | 10 | 11. Share Your Love With Me | Liberty 1430 |
| 1/16/82 | 13 | 11 | 12. Through The Years | Liberty 1444 |

| DATE | POS | WKS | ARTIST—Record Title | LABEL & NO. |
|------|-----|-----|---------------------|-------------|
| 7/24/82 | **13** | 10 | 13. Love Will Turn You Around<br>from the film "Six Pack" | Liberty 1471 |
| 5/28/83 | **37** | 3 | 14. All My Life | Liberty 1495 |
| 2/04/84 | **23** | 6 | 15. This Woman | RCA 13710 |
| | | | **KENNY ROGERS & KIM CARNES** | |
| 4/12/80 | **4** | 14 | 1. **Don't Fall In Love With A Dreamer** | United Art. 1345 |
| | | | **KENNY ROGERS with KIM CARNES & JAMES INGRAM** | |
| 10/13/84 | **15** | 9 | 1. What About Me? | RCA 13899 |
| | | | **KENNY ROGERS & SHEENA EASTON** | |
| 1/29/83 | **6** | 15 | 1. **We've Got Tonight** | Liberty 1492 |
| | | | **KENNY ROGERS with DOLLY PARTON** | |
| 9/10/83 | **1** (2) | 18 | ★ 1. **Islands In The Stream** | RCA 13615 |
| | | | **KENNY ROGERS & THE FIRST EDITION**<br>Kenny and 3 other members were with The New Christy Minstrels<br>THE FIRST EDITION: | |
| 2/24/68 | **5** | 8 | 1. **Just Dropped In (To See What Condition My Condition Was In)** | Reprise 0655 |
| 2/08/69 | **19** | 8 | 2. But You Know I Love You<br>KENNY ROGERS & THE FIRST EDITION: | Reprise 0799 |
| 7/05/69 | **6** | 9 | 3. **Ruby, Don't Take Your Love To Town** | Reprise 0829 |
| 10/25/69 | **26** | 6 | 4. Ruben James | Reprise 0854 |
| 3/14/70 | **11** | 12 | 5. **Something's Burning** | Reprise 0888 |
| 7/25/70 | **17** | 8 | 6. Tell It All Brother | Reprise 0923 |
| 11/14/70 | **33** | 5 | 7. Heed The Call | Reprise 0953 |
| | | | **TIMMIE "Oh Yeah" ROGERS** | |
| 11/04/57 | **36** | 4 | 1. Back To School Again | Cameo 116 |
| | | | **ROLLING STONES**<br>English: Mick Jagger (vocals), Keith Richards (guitar), Bill Wyman (bass), Charlie Watts (drums), Brian Jones (guitar - died 7/3/69-27), replaced by Mick Taylor, who was replaced in 1975 by Ron Wood | |
| 8/01/64 | **24** | 5 | 1. Tell Me (You're Coming Back) | London 9682 |
| 8/22/64 | **26** | 6 | 2. It's All Over Now | London 9687 |
| 11/07/64 | **6** | 9 | 3. **Time Is On My Side** | London 9708 |
| 1/30/65 | **19** | 5 | 4. Heart Of Stone | London 9725 |
| 4/10/65 | **9** | 8 | 5. **The Last Time** | London 9741 |
| 6/19/65 | **1** (4) | 12 | ● 6. **(I Can't Get No) Satisfaction** | London 9766 |
| 10/16/65 | **1** (2) | 11 | 7. **Get Off Of My Cloud** | London 9792 |
| 1/08/66 | **6** | 6 | 8. **As Tears Go By** | London 9808 |
| 3/05/66 | **2** (3) | 9 | 9. **19th Nervous Breakdown** | London 9823 |
| 5/21/66 | **1** (2) | 10 | 10. **Paint It, Black** | London 901 |
| 7/16/66 | **8** | 8 | 11. **Mothers Little Helper/** | |
| 8/06/66 | **24** | 4 | 12. Lady Jane | London 902 |
| 10/08/66 | **9** | 6 | 13. **Have You Seen Your Mother, Baby, Standing In The Shadow?** | London 903 |

| DATE | POS | | WKS | ARTIST—Record Title | LABEL & NO. |
|---|---|---|---|---|---|
| 2/04/67 | 1 | (1) | 9 | ● 14. **Ruby Tuesday** | London 904 |
| 9/23/67 | 14 | | 6 | 15. Dandelion | London 905 |
| 1/13/68 | 25 | | 4 | 16. She's A Rainbow | London 906 |
| 6/15/68 | 3 | | 11 | 17. **Jumpin' Jack Flash** | London 908 |
| 7/26/69 | 1 | (4) | 14 | ● 18. **Honky Tonk Women** | London 910 |
| 5/01/71 | 1 | (2) | 12 | 19. **Brown Sugar** | Rolling S. 19100 |
| 7/03/71 | 28 | | 5 | 20. Wild Horses | Rolling S. 19101 |
| 5/06/72 | 7 | | 9 | 21. **Tumbling Dice** | Rolling S. 19103 |
| 7/29/72 | 22 | | 4 | 22. Happy | Rolling S. 19104 |
| 9/22/73 | 1 | (1) | 13 | ● 23. **Angie** | Rolling S. 19105 |
| 2/02/74 | 15 | | 6 | 24. Doo Doo Doo Doo Doo (Heartbreaker) | Rolling S. 19109 |
| 8/17/74 | 16 | | 7 | 25. It's Only Rock 'N Roll (But I Like It) | Rolling S. 19301 |
| 11/16/74 | 17 | | 7 | 26. Ain't Too Proud To Beg | Rolling S. 19302 |
| 5/08/76 | 10 | | 7 | 27. **Fool To Cry** | Rolling S. 19304 |
| 6/10/78 | 1 | (1) | 16 | ● 28. **Miss You** | Rolling S. 19307 |
| 9/23/78 | 8 | | 9 | 29. **Beast Of Burden** | Rolling S. 19309 |
| 1/13/79 | 31 | | 4 | 30. Shattered | Rolling S. 19310 |
| 7/05/80 | 3 | | 14 | 31. **Emotional Rescue** | Rolling S. 20001 |
| 10/18/80 | 26 | | 5 | 32. She's So Cold | Rolling S. 21001 |
| 8/29/81 | 2 | (3) | 19 | 33. **Start Me Up** | Rolling S. 21003 |
| 12/12/81 + | 13 | | 12 | 34. Waiting On A Friend | Rolling S. 21004 |
| 4/10/82 | 20 | | 6 | 35. Hang Fire | Rolling S. 21300 |
| 7/03/82 | 25 | | 5 | 36. Going To A Go-Go | Rolling S. 21301 |
| 11/19/83 | 9 | | 10 | 37. **Undercover Of The Night** | Rolling S. 99813 |
| | | | | **ROMANTICS** | |
| | | | | rock quartet from Detroit | |
| 12/03/83 + | 3 | | 15 | 1. **Talking In Your Sleep** | Nemperor 04135 |
| 3/31/84 | 37 | | 3 | 2. One In A Million | Nemperor 04373 |
| | | | | **ROMEO VOID** | |
| | | | | San Francisco new-wave quintet - Debora Iyall, lead singer | |
| 10/20/84 | 35 | | 2 | 1. A Girl In Trouble (Is A Temporary Thing) | Columbia 04534 |
| | | | | **RONALD & RUBY** | |
| 3/24/58 | 20 | | 3 | 1. Lollipop | RCA 7174 |
| | | | | **DON RONDO** | |
| 11/03/56 | 11 | | 12 | 1. Two Different Worlds | Jubilee 5256 |
| 7/29/57 | 7 | | 15 | 2. **White Silver Sands** | Jubilee 5288 |
| | | | | **RONETTES** | |
| | | | | New York trio: Veronica Bennett (Ronnie Spector), & sister Estelle Bennett, with cousin Nedra Talley | |
| 9/14/63 | 2 | (3) | 10 | 1. **Be My Baby** | Philles 116 |
| 1/11/64 | 24 | | 6 | 2. Baby, I Love You | Philles 118 |
| 5/16/64 | 39 | | 1 | 3. (The Best Part Of) Breakin' Up | Philles 120 |
| 7/18/64 | 34 | | 4 | 4. Do I Love You? | Philles 121 |
| 11/21/64 | 23 | | 7 | 5. Walking In The Rain | Philles 123 |

| DATE | POS | WKS | ARTIST—Record Title | LABEL & NO. |
|---|---|---|---|---|
| | | | **RONNIE & THE HI-LITES** | |
| | | | Ronnie Goodson died on 11/4/80 (33) | |
| 4/21/62 | 16 | 8 | 1. I Wish That We Were Married | Joy 260 |
| | | | **RONNY & THE DAYTONAS** | |
| | | | Ronny is Bucky Wilkin | |
| 8/22/64 | 4 | 10 | 1. **G.T.O.** | Mala 481 |
| 1/08/66 | 27 | 5 | 2. Sandy | Mala 513 |
| | | | **LINDA RONSTADT** | |
| | | | born 7/15/46 in Tucson, Arizona - also see Nitty Gritty Dirt Band | |
| 12/09/67 + | 13 | 13 | 1. Different Drum | Capitol 2004 |
| | | | shown as Stone Poneys featuring Linda Ronstadt | |
| 9/12/70 | 25 | 7 | 2. Long Long Time | Capitol 2846 |
| 1/04/75 | 1 (1) | 10 | 3. **You're No Good** | Capitol 3990 |
| 4/26/75 | 2 (2) | 13 | 4. **When Will I Be Loved** | Capitol 4050 |
| 10/04/75 | 5 | 10 | 5. **Heat Wave/** | |
| | | 8 | 6.  **Love Is A Rose** | Asylum 45282 |
| 1/24/76 | 25 | 6 | 7. Tracks Of My Tears | Asylum 45295 |
| 9/04/76 | 11 | 11 | 8. That'll Be The Day | Asylum 45340 |
| 10/08/77 | 3 | 16 | ● 9. **Blue Bayou** | Asylum 45431 |
| 10/29/77 | 5 | 12 | 10. It's So Easy | Asylum 45438 |
| 2/25/78 | 31 | 3 | 11. Poor Poor Pitiful Me | Asylum 45462 |
| 5/20/78 | 32 | 3 | 12. Tumbling Dice | Asylum 45479 |
| 9/09/78 | 16 | 8 | 13. Back In The U.S.A. | Asylum 45519 |
| 11/18/78 + | 7 | 13 | 14. **Ooh Baby Baby** | Asylum 45546 |
| 2/09/80 | 10 | 12 | 15. **How Do I Make You** | Asylum 46602 |
| 4/19/80 | 8 | 11 | 16. **Hurt So Bad** | Asylum 46624 |
| 7/19/80 | 31 | 4 | 17. I Can't Let Go | Asylum 46654 |
| 10/23/82 | 29 | 5 | 18. Get Closer | Asylum 69948 |
| 1/29/83 | 37 | 3 | 19. I Knew You When | Asylum 69853 |
| | | | **ROOFTOP SINGERS** | |
| | | | Erik Darling, leader (founder of the Tarriers and a member of the Weavers) | |
| 1/12/63 | 1 (2) | 11 | 1. **Walk Right In** | Vanguard 35017 |
| 4/20/63 | 20 | 5 | 2. Tom Cat | Vanguard 35019 |
| | | | **ROSE GARDEN** | |
| | | | West Virginia quintet - Diana Di Rose, lead singer | |
| 12/09/67 | 17 | 7 | 1. Next Plane To London | Atco 6510 |
| | | | **ROSE ROYCE** | |
| | | | former backing band for the Temptations and Undisputed Truth | |
| 12/11/76 + | 1 (1) | 14 | ★ 1. **Car Wash** | MCA 40615 |
| 3/19/77 | 10 | 10 | 2. **I Wanna Get Next To You** | MCA 40662 |
| | | | above 2 from the film "Car Wash" | |
| 10/22/77 | 39 | 2 | 3. Do Your Dance - Part 1 | Whitfield 8440 |
| 1/13/79 | 32 | 4 | 4. Love Don't Live Here Anymore | Whitfield 8712 |
| | | | **DAVID ROSE & His Orchestra** | |
| | | | born in London, England - orchestra leader/composer/arranger for films and TV | |
| 6/02/62 | 1 (1) | 13 | 1. **The Stripper [I]** | MGM 13064 |

| DATE | POS | WKS | ARTIST—Record Title | LABEL & NO. |
|---|---|---|---|---|
| | | | **ROSIE & The Originals** | |
| | | | Rosie Hamlin | |
| 12/12/60 + | 5 | 12 | 1. **Angel Baby** | Highland 1011 |
| | | | **DIANA ROSS** | |
| | | | born on 3/26/44 in Detroit - also see Supremes/Marvin Gaye/ Julio Iglesias | |
| 5/02/70 | 20 | 8 | 1. Reach Out And Touch (Somebody's Hand) | Motown 1165 |
| 8/15/70 | 1 (3) | 13 | 2. **Ain't No Mountain High Enough** | Motown 1169 |
| 1/09/71 | 16 | 8 | 3. Remember Me | Motown 1176 |
| 5/15/71 | 29 | 5 | 4. Reach Out I'll Be There | Motown 1184 |
| 9/11/71 | 38 | 3 | 5. Surrender | Motown 1188 |
| 3/03/73 | 34 | 4 | 6. Good Morning Heartache | Motown 1211 |
| | | | from the film "Lady Sings The Blues" | |
| 7/07/73 | 1 (1) | 16 | 7. **Touch Me In The Morning** | Motown 1239 |
| 1/26/74 | 14 | 8 | 8. Last Time I Saw Him | Motown 1278 |
| 11/22/75 + | 1 (1) | 13 | 9. **Theme From Mahogany (Do You Know Where You're Going To)** | Motown 1377 |
| 4/24/76 | 1 (2) | 13 | 10. **Love Hangover** | Motown 1392 |
| 8/21/76 | 25 | 8 | 11. One Love In My Lifetime | Motown 1398 |
| 12/03/77 + | 27 | 7 | 12. Gettin' Ready For Love | Motown 1427 |
| 8/18/79 | 19 | 9 | 13. The Boss | Motown 1462 |
| 8/09/80 | 1 (4) | 17 | ● 14. **Upside Down** | Motown 1494 |
| 10/04/80 | 5 | 14 | 15. **I'm Coming Out** | Motown 1491 |
| 11/15/80 + | 9 | 15 | 16. **It's My Turn** | Motown 1496 |
| 10/24/81 | 7 | 14 | 17. **Why Do Fools Fall In Love** | RCA 12349 |
| 1/30/82 | 8 | 10 | 18. **Mirror, Mirror** | RCA 13021 |
| 10/16/82 | 10 | 10 | 19. **Muscles** | RCA 13348 |
| 3/19/83 | 40 | 2 | 20. So Close | RCA 13424 |
| 7/23/83 | 31 | 3 | 21. Pieces Of Ice | RCA 13549 |
| 9/22/84 | 19 | 8 | 22. Swept Away | RCA 13864 |
| | | | produced by Daryl Hall | |
| | | | **DIANA ROSS & LIONEL RICHIE** | |
| 7/18/81 | 1 (9) | 19 | ★ 1. **Endless Love** | Motown 1519 |
| | | | **JACK ROSS** | |
| | | | died on 12/16/82 (66) | |
| 4/07/62 | 16 | 6 | 1. Cinderella [C] | Dot 16333 |
| | | | **JACKIE ROSS** | |
| 8/15/64 | 11 | 8 | 1. Selfish One | Chess 1903 |
| | | | **SPENCER ROSS** | |
| 1/18/60 | 13 | 10 | 1. Tracy's Theme [I] | Columbia 41532 |
| | | | from the TV production "Philadelphia Story" | |
| | | | **ROUTERS** | |
| | | | rock instrumental quintet | |
| 11/24/62 | 19 | 7 | 1. Let's Go (pony) [I] | Warner 5283 |
| | | | **ROVER BOYS** | |
| | | | Canadian group featuring Billy Albert, lead singer | |
| 5/19/56 | 16 | 7 | 1. Graduation Day | ABC-Para. 9700 |

| DATE | POS | WKS | ARTIST—Record Title | LABEL & NO. |
|------|-----|-----|---------------------|-------------|
| | | | **ROVERS - see IRISH ROVERS** | |
| | | | **ROXY MUSIC** | |
| | | | English art-rock band led by Bryan Ferry (vocals/keyboards) | |
| 2/21/76 | 30 | 5 | 1. Love Is The Drug | Atco 7042 |
| | | | **ROYAL GUARDSMEN** | |
| | | | Florida sextet led by Barry Winslow and Chris Nunley | |
| 12/17/66 | 2 (4) | 11 | ● 1. **Snoopy Vs. The Red Baron** [N] | Laurie 3366 |
| 3/11/67 | 15 | 5 | 2. The Return Of The Red Baron [N] | Laurie 3379 |
| 1/04/69 | 35 | 5 | 3. Baby Let's Wait | Laurie 3461 |
| | | | **ROYAL PHILHARMONIC ORCHESTRA** | |
| | | | British - Louis Clark, conductor (arranger for ELO) | |
| 11/28/81 + | 10 | 12 | 1. **Hooked On Classics** [I] | RCA 12304 |
| | | | **ROYAL SCOTS DRAGOON GUARDS** | |
| | | | The Pipes and Drums and Military Band of Scotland's armoured Regiment | |
| 5/27/72 | 11 | 8 | 1. Amazing Grace [I] | RCA 0709 |
| | | | **ROYAL TEENS** | |
| | | | member Bob Gaudio was an original Four Seasons member | |
| 2/03/58 | 3 | 12 | 1. **Short Shorts** | ABC-Para. 9882 |
| 11/16/59 | 26 | 6 | 2. Believe Me | Capitol 4261 |
| | | | **ROYALTONES** | |
| | | | Detroit instrumental rock quartet | |
| 11/10/58 | 17 | 10 | 1. Poor Boy [I] | Jubilee 5338 |
| | | | **BILLY JOE ROYAL** | |
| | | | native of Atlanta, Georgia | |
| 7/31/65 | 9 | 8 | 1. **Down In The Boondocks** | Columbia 43305 |
| 10/09/65 | 14 | 8 | 2. I Knew You When | Columbia 43390 |
| 1/15/66 | 38 | 1 | 3. I've Got To Be Somebody | Columbia 43465 |
| 11/01/69 | 15 | 10 | 4. Cherry Hill Park | Columbia 44902 |
| | | | **RUBETTES** | |
| 8/31/74 | 37 | 2 | 1. Sugar Baby Love | Polydor 15089 |
| | | | **RUBICON** | |
| | | | Jerry Martini, leader (member of Sly & The Family Stone '66-'76) | |
| 4/08/78 | 28 | 3 | 1. I'm Gonna Take Care Of Everything | 20th Century 2362 |
| | | | **RUBY & THE ROMANTICS** | |
| | | | Akron, Ohio quintet featuring Ruby Nash | |
| 2/23/63 | 1 (1) | 10 | 1. **Our Day Will Come** | Kapp 501 |
| 6/15/63 | 16 | 6 | 2. My Summer Love | Kapp 525 |
| 8/31/63 | 27 | 5 | 3. Hey There Lonely Boy | Kapp 544 |
| | | | **DAVID RUFFIN** | |
| | | | lead singer of the Temptations from 1964-1968 | |
| 2/22/69 | 9 | 9 | 1. **My Whole World Ended (The Moment You Left Me)** | Motown 1140 |
| 11/29/75 + | 9 | 11 | 2. **Walk Away From Love** | Motown 1376 |

| DATE | POS | WKS | ARTIST—Record Title | LABEL & NO. |
|---|---|---|---|---|
| | | | **JIMMY RUFFIN** | |
| | | | brother of David Ruffin | |
| 9/10/66 | 7 | 14 | 1. **What Becomes Of The Brokenhearted** | Soul 35022 |
| 12/24/66 + | 17 | 8 | 2. I've Passed This Way Before | Soul 35027 |
| 4/08/67 | 29 | 3 | 3. Gonna Give Her All The Love I've Got | Soul 35032 |
| 3/22/80 | 10 | 9 | 4. **Hold On To My Love** | RSO 1021 |
| | | | **RUFUS featuring Chaka Khan** | |
| | | | soul group formed in Chicago - Chaka Khan, lead singer | |
| 7/13/74 | 3 | 12 | ● 1. **Tell Me Something Good** | ABC 11427 |
| | | | shown only as Rufus | |
| 11/02/74 | 11 | 11 | 2. You Got The Love | ABC 12032 |
| 3/08/75 | 10 | 7 | 3. **Once You Get Started** | ABC 12066 |
| 2/14/76 | 5 | 12 | ● 4. **Sweet Thing** | ABC 12149 |
| 6/12/76 | 39 | 1 | 5. Dance Wit Me | ABC 12179 |
| 3/12/77 | 30 | 6 | 6. At Midnight (My Love Will Lift You Up) | ABC 12239 |
| 6/04/77 | 32 | 3 | 7. Hollywood | ABC 12269 |
| 5/27/78 | 38 | 3 | 8. Stay | ABC 12349 |
| 1/19/80 | 30 | 4 | 9. Do You Love What You Feel | MCA 41131 |
| 11/12/83 | 22 | 8 | 10. Ain't Nobody | Warner 29555 |
| | | | **RUGBYS** | |
| 9/20/69 | 24 | 7 | 1. You, I | Amazon 1 |
| | | | **TODD RUNDGREN** | |
| | | | virtuoso musician, songwriter, producer, engineer - also see Utopia | |
| 12/26/70 + | 20 | 9 | 1. We Gotta Get You A Woman | Ampex 31001 |
| 5/06/72 | 16 | 9 | 2. I Saw The Light | Bearsville 0003 |
| 11/10/73 | 5 | 12 | 3. **Hello It's Me** | Bearsville 0009 |
| | | | original version by Nazz in 1969 | |
| 6/26/76 | 34 | 3 | 4. Good Vibrations | Bearsville 0309 |
| 7/08/78 | 29 | 5 | 5. Can We Still Be Friends | Bearsville 0324 |
| | | | **RUSH** | |
| | | | Candian power-rock trio: Geddy Lee (vocals/bass), Alex Lifeson (guitar), Neil Peart (drums) - also see Bob & Doug McKenzie | |
| 10/09/82 | 21 | 6 | 1. New World Man | Mercury 76179 |
| | | | **MERRILEE RUSH & The Turnabouts** | |
| | | | Seattle, Washington native | |
| 6/01/68 | 7 | 12 | 1. **Angel Of The Morning** | Bell 705 |
| | | | **PATRICE RUSHEN** | |
| | | | singer, composer, keyboardist from Los Angeles | |
| 6/05/82 | 23 | 7 | 1. Forget Me Nots | Elektra 47427 |
| | | | **BOBBY RUSSELL** | |
| | | | songwriter of "Honey" and "Little Green Apples" | |
| 11/23/68 | 36 | 2 | 1. 1432 Franklin Pike Circle Hero | Elf 90020 |
| 8/28/71 | 28 | 7 | 2. Saturday Morning Confusion [N] | United Art. 50788 |
| | | | **BRENDA RUSSELL** | |
| | | | Canadian | |
| 10/13/79 | 30 | 6 | 1. So Good, So Right | Horizon 123 |

| DATE | POS | WKS | ARTIST—Record Title | LABEL & NO. |
|---|---|---|---|---|
| | | | **LEON RUSSELL** | |
| | | | top multi-instrumentalist sessionman - also see Joe Cocker | |
| 9/23/72 | 11 | 7 | 1. Tight Rope | Shelter 7325 |
| 9/13/75 | 14 | 10 | 2. Lady Blue | Shelter 40378 |
| | | | **CHARLIE RYAN & the Timberline Riders** | |
| 8/08/60 | 33 | 4 | 1. Hot Rod Lincoln [S-N] | 4 Star 7047 |
| | | | **BOBBY RYDELL** | |
| | | | born Robert Ridarelli on 4/26/42 in Philadelphia | |
| 8/10/59 | 11 | 9 | 1. Kissin' Time | Cameo 167 |
| 10/26/59 | 6 | 14 | 2. **We Got Love** | Cameo 169 |
| 2/08/60 | 2 (1) | 13 | 3. **Wild One/** | |
| 2/22/60 | 19 | 10 | 4.  Little Bitty Girl | Cameo 171 |
| 5/16/60 | 5 | 8 | 5. **Swingin' School/** | |
| | | | from the film "Because They're Young" | |
| 5/16/60 | 18 | 8 | 6.  Ding-A-Ling | Cameo 175 |
| 8/01/60 | 4 | 11 | 7. **Volare** | Cameo 179 |
| 11/14/60 | 14 | 10 | 8. Sway | Cameo 182 |
| 2/06/61 | 11 | 8 | 9. Good Time Baby | Cameo 186 |
| 5/08/61 | 21 | 5 | 10. That Old Black Magic | Cameo 190 |
| 7/10/61 | 25 | 5 | 11. The Fish | Cameo 192 |
| 11/06/61 | 21 | 6 | 12. I Wanna Thank You | Cameo 201 |
| 3/10/62 | 18 | 7 | 13. I've Got Bonnie | Cameo 209 |
| 6/23/62 | 14 | 7 | 14. I'll Never Dance Again | Cameo 217 |
| 10/27/62 | 10 | 8 | 15. **The Cha-Cha-Cha** | Cameo 228 |
| 2/23/63 | 23 | 6 | 16. Butterfly Baby | Cameo 242 |
| 6/01/63 | 17 | 5 | 17. Wildwood Days | Cameo 252 |
| 12/07/63 + | 4 | 12 | 18. **Forget Him** | Cameo 280 |
| | | | **BOBBY RYDELL & CHUBBY CHECKER** | |
| 12/25/61 | 21 | 3 | 1. Jingle Bell Rock [X] | Cameo 205 |
| | | | **MITCH RYDER** | |
| | | | white soul singer from Detroit - real name William Levise, Jr. | |
| 9/30/67 | 30 | 4 | 1. What Now My Love | DynoVoice 901 |
| | | | **MITCH RYDER & The Detroit Wheels** | |
| 1/08/66 | 10 | 8 | 1. **Jenny Take A Ride!** | New Voice 806 |
| 3/26/66 | 17 | 6 | 2. Little Latin Lupe Lu | New Voice 808 |
| 10/22/66 | 4 | 14 | 3. **Devil With A Blue Dress On & Good Golly Miss Molly (medley)** | New Voice 817 |
| 2/18/67 | 6 | 9 | 4. **Sock It To Me-Baby!** | New Voice 820 |
| 5/13/67 | 24 | 4 | 5. Too Many Fish In The Sea & Three Little Fishes (medley) | New Voice 822 |
| | | | **SSgt BARRY SADLER** | |
| | | | Staff Sergeant of the U.S. Army Special Forces | |
| 2/19/66 | 1 (5) | 11 | ● 1. **The Ballad Of The Green Berets** | RCA 8739 |
| 5/14/66 | 28 | 4 | 2. The "A" Team | RCA 8804 |

| DATE | POS | WKS | ARTIST—Record Title | LABEL & NO. |
|------|-----|-----|---------------------|-------------|
| | | | **SAFARIS** | |
| | | | Los Angeles quartet - Jim Stephens, lead singer | |
| 7/11/60 | 6 | 11 | 1. **Image Of A Girl** | Eldo 101 |
| | | | with The Phantom's Band | |
| | | | **SAGA** | |
| | | | Canadian rock quintet - Michael Sadler, lead singer | |
| 1/29/83 | 26 | 8 | 1. On The Loose | Portrait 03359 |
| | | | **CAROLE BAYER SAGER** | |
| | | | pop songwriter - married Burt Bacharach in 1982 | |
| 6/13/81 | 30 | 7 | 1. Stronger Than Before | Boardwalk 02054 |
| | | | **SAILCAT** | |
| | | | country-rock duo: Court Pickett & John Wyker | |
| 7/15/72 | 12 | 10 | 1. Motorcycle Mama | Elektra 45782 |
| | | | **BUFFY SAINTE-MARIE** | |
| | | | folk singer - born of Cree Indian parents | |
| 4/29/72 | 38 | 2 | 1. Mister Can't You See | Vanguard 35151 |
| | | | **CRISPIAN ST. PETERS** | |
| | | | English | |
| 7/09/66 | 4 | 8 | 1. **The Pied Piper** | Jamie 1320 |
| 7/22/67 | 36 | 2 | 2. You Were On My Mind | Jamie 1310 |
| | | | **KYU SAKAMOTO** | |
| | | | from Kawasaki, Japan | |
| 5/25/63 | 1 (3) | 12 | 1. **Sukiyaki [F]** | Capitol 4945 |
| | | | **SALSOUL ORCHESTRA** | |
| | | | disco orchestra conducted by Vincent Montana, Jr. | |
| 2/14/76 | 18 | 9 | 1. Tangerine [I] | Salsoul 2004 |
| 10/30/76 | 30 | 5 | 2. Nice 'N' Naasty | Salsoul 2011 |
| | | | **SAMMY SALVO** | |
| 3/03/58 | 23 | 1 | 1. Oh Julie | RCA 7097 |
| | | | **SAM & DAVE** | |
| | | | Sam Moore & Dave Prater | |
| 6/04/66 | 21 | 7 | 1. Hold On! I'm A Comin' | Stax 189 |
| 9/30/67 | 2 (3) | 11 | ● 2. **Soul Man** | Stax 231 |
| 2/17/68 | 9 | 9 | 3. **I Thank You** | Stax 242 |
| | | | **SAM THE SHAM & The Pharaohs** | |
| | | | Sam is Domingo Samudio from Dallas, Texas | |
| 5/01/65 | 2 (2) | 14 | ● 1. **Wooly Bully** | MGM 13322 |
| 8/21/65 | 26 | 4 | 2. Ju Ju Hand | MGM 13364 |
| 11/13/65 | 33 | 3 | 3. Ring Dang Doo | MGM 13397 |
| 7/02/66 | 2 (2) | 11 | ● 4. **Lil' Red Riding Hood** | MGM 13506 |
| 10/15/66 | 22 | 5 | 5. The Hair On My Chinny Chin Chin | MGM 13581 |
| 1/21/67 | 27 | 4 | 6. How Do You Catch A Girl | MGM 13649 |
| | | | **SAN REMO GOLDEN STRINGS** | |
| 10/09/65 | 27 | 5 | 1. Hungry For Love [I] | Ric-Tic 104 |

**Frank Sinatra** inadvertently inspired the name of one of 1984's most outrageous groups, Frankie Goes to Hollywood. The British band came up with the monicker after seeing a newspaper clipping on Sinatra's first movie venture.

**Sly and the Family Stone.** Sylvester Stewart enjoyed his first chart successes working behind the scenes at San Francisco's Vault Records. He produced hits for the Beau Brummels ("Laugh, Laugh") and Bobby Freeman ("C'mon and Swim").

**Spandau Ballet** flourished amidst the trendy, fashion-conscious London club scene. Says leader Gary Kemp, "We just wanted to relate to kids who were into the kind of clothes we were into." That's rock'n'roll?

**Bruce Springsteen** is reputed to have an aversion to making videos, but when he took the plunge in 1984, he went first class. His "Dancing in the Dark" clip is directed by Brian De Palma (*Scarface, Dressed to Kill*).

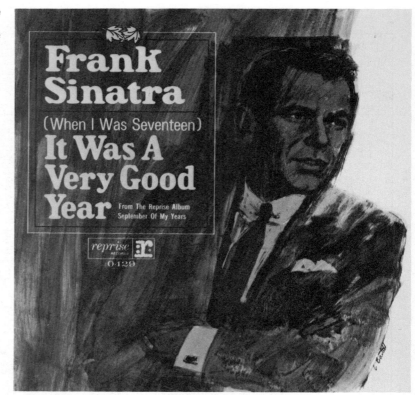

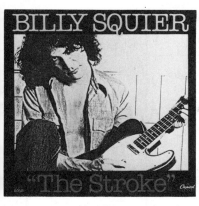

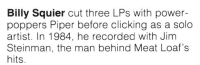

**Billy Squier** cut three LPs with power-poppers Piper before clicking as a solo artist. In 1984, he recorded with Jim Steinman, the man behind Meat Loaf's hits.

**Van Stephenson's** dues-paying days saw him tour, with little reward, everywhere from Sweden to Oklahoma. A true rock'n'roll yeoman.

**Rod Stewart** is an experienced grave-digger, banjo player, and soccer enthusiast, not to mention one of the world's most durable rockers. He cites Sam Cooke and Al Jolson as significant influences.

**Barbra Streisand** has caught duet fever in recent years, teaming with Barry Gibb, Donna Summer, and Neil Diamond, and reaching the "Top Three" each time.

**Donna Summer** warmed up for her pop music career with eight years on the European stage, performing in productions of *Hair, Godspell, Porgy and Bess, Showboat,* and *The Me Nobody Knows.*

**The Supremes,** who came out of Detroit's Brewster Housing Project, began as The Primettes. They received the queenly sum of $2.50 per session to back up Marvin Gaye and Mary Wells. Times changed fast.

| DATE | POS | WKS | ARTIST—Record Title | LABEL & NO. |
|------|-----|-----|---------------------|-------------|
| | | | **FELICIA SANDERS** | |
| | | | died on 2/7/75 | |
| 5/28/55 | 29 | 3 | 1. Blue Star | Columbia 40508 |
| | | | the "Medic" theme | |
| | | | **SANDPEBBLES** | |
| 1/06/68 | 22 | 6 | 1. Love Power | Calla 141 |
| | | | **SANDPIPERS** | |
| | | | Los Angeles-based trio - met in the Mitchell Boys Choir | |
| 8/13/66 | 9 | 9 | 1. Guantanamera [F] | A&M 806 |
| 11/12/66 | 30 | 4 | 2. Louie, Louie [F] | A&M 819 |
| 5/02/70 | 17 | 8 | 3. Come Saturday Morning | A&M 1134 |
| | | | from the film "The Sterile Cuckoo" | |
| | | | **JODIE SANDS** | |
| 6/10/57 | 15 | 9 | 1. With All My Heart | Chancellor 1003 |
| | | | **TOMMY SANDS** | |
| | | | singer/actor - married to Nancy Sinatra ('60-'65) | |
| 2/23/57 | 2 (2) | 12 | 1. Teen-Age Crush | Capitol 3639 |
| 5/27/57 | 16 | 8 | 2. Goin' Steady | Capitol 3723 |
| 2/24/58 | 24 | 2 | 3. Sing Boy Sing | Capitol 3867 |
| | | | **SANFORD/TOWNSEND Band** | |
| | | | Ed Sanford/John Townsend | |
| 7/16/77 | 9 | 12 | 1. Smoke From A Distant Fire | Warner 8370 |
| | | | **SAMANTHA SANG** | |
| | | | Australian | |
| 1/07/78 | 3 | 17 | ★ 1. Emotion | Private S. 45178 |
| | | | backing vocal by Barry Gibb | |
| | | | **SANTA ESMERALDA** | |
| | | | Spanish-flavored disco band featuring Leroy Gomez | |
| 12/10/77 + | 15 | 12 | 1. Don't Let Me Be Misunderstood | Casablanca 902 |
| | | | **MONGO SANTAMARIA** | |
| | | | Cuban-born band leader and bongo player | |
| 4/13/63 | 10 | 6 | 1. Watermelon Man [I] | Battle 45909 |
| 3/08/69 | 32 | 2 | 2. Cloud Nine [I] | Columbia 44740 |
| | | | **SANTANA** | |
| | | | Latin-rock band formed in San Francisco, led by guitarist/vocalist Carlos Santana | |
| 2/07/70 | 9 | 11 | 1. Evil Ways | Columbia 45069 |
| 11/21/70 + | 4 | 12 | 2. Black Magic Woman | Columbia 45270 |
| 3/06/71 | 13 | 8 | 3. Oye Como Va [F] | Columbia 45330 |
| 10/30/71 | 12 | 8 | 4. Everybody's Everything | Columbia 45472 |
| 3/11/72 | 36 | 4 | 5. No One To Depend On | Columbia 45552 |
| 11/19/77 | 27 | 5 | 6. She's Not There | Columbia 10616 |
| 2/17/79 | 32 | 3 | 7. Stormy | Columbia 10873 |
| 1/19/80 | 35 | 3 | 8. You Know That I Love You | Columbia 11144 |
| 5/16/81 | 17 | 11 | 9. Winning | Columbia 01050 |
| 8/28/82 | 15 | 10 | 10. Hold On | Columbia 03160 |

| DATE | POS | WKS | ARTIST—Record Title | LABEL & NO. |
|------|-----|-----|---------------------|-------------|
| | | | **SANTO & JOHNNY** | |
| | | | Santo (steel guitar) & brother Johnny (rhythm guitar) Farina from Brooklyn | |
| 8/17/59 | **1** (2) | 13 | 1. **Sleep Walk [I]** | Canadian A. 103 |
| 12/14/59 | **23** | 7 | 2. Tear Drop [I] | Canadian A. 107 |
| | | | **LARRY SANTOS** | |
| 4/03/76 | **36** | 2 | 1. We Can't Hide It Anymore | Casablanca 844 |
| | | | **SAPPHIRES** | |
| | | | Philadelphia R&B quartet - Carol Jackson, lead singer | |
| 2/22/64 | **25** | 5 | 1. Who Do You Love | Swan 4162 |
| | | | **LEO SAYER** | |
| | | | English singer/songwriter | |
| 3/22/75 | **9** | 9 | 1. **Long Tall Glasses (I Can Dance)** | Warner 8043 |
| 11/06/76 + | **1** (1) | 17 | ● 2. **You Make Me Feel Like Dancing** | Warner 8283 |
| 3/26/77 | **1** (1) | 14 | ● 3. **When I Need You** | Warner 8332 |
| 7/23/77 | **17** | 10 | 4. How Much Love | Warner 8319 |
| 11/05/77 | **38** | 2 | 5. Thunder In My Heart | Warner 8465 |
| 1/28/78 | **36** | 2 | 6. Easy To Love | Warner 8502 |
| 10/18/80 | **2** (5) | 15 | ● 7. **More Than I Can Say** | Warner 49565 |
| 2/14/81 | **23** | 6 | 8. Living In A Fantasy | Warner 49657 |
| | | | **BOZ SCAGGS** | |
| | | | singer/songwriter from Ohio - original member of the Steve Miller Band | |
| 5/22/76 | **38** | 3 | 1. It's Over | Columbia 10319 |
| 8/07/76 | **3** | 15 | ● 2. **Lowdown** | Columbia 10367 |
| 3/19/77 | **11** | 12 | 3. Lido Shuffle | Columbia 10491 |
| 4/19/80 | **15** | 9 | 4. Breakdown Dead Ahead | Columbia 11241 |
| 7/12/80 | **17** | 9 | 5. JoJo | Columbia 11281 |
| 9/06/80 | **14** | 10 | 6. Look What You've Done To Me | Columbia 11349 |
| 12/27/80 + | **14** | 9 | 7. Miss Sun<br>backing vocal: Lisa Dal Bello | Columbia 11406 |
| | | | **SCANDAL featuring Patty Smyth** | |
| | | | New York-based rock band | |
| 7/21/84 | **7** | 15 | 1. **The Warrior** | Columbia 04424 |
| | | | **JOEY SCARBURY** | |
| 6/13/81 | **2** (2) | 18 | ● 1. **Theme From "Greatest American Hero"<br>(Believe It Or Not)** | Elektra 47147 |
| | | | **PETER SCHILLING** | |
| | | | German singer/songwriter | |
| 11/12/83 | **14** | 10 | 1. Major Tom (Coming Home) | Elektra 69811 |
| | | | **JOHN SCHNEIDER** | |
| | | | Bo Duke of TV's "The Dukes Of Hazzard" | |
| 6/27/81 | **14** | 11 | 1. It's Now Or Never | Scotti Br. 02105 |
| | | | **WALTER SCHUMANN [The Voices of]** | |
| 4/09/55 | **14** | 6 | 1. The Ballad Of Davy Crockett | RCA 6041 |

| DATE | POS | WKS | ARTIST—Record Title | LABEL & NO. |
|------|-----|-----|---------------------|-------------|
| | | | **EDDIE SCHWARTZ** | |
| | | | Canadian singer/songwriter | |
| 1/16/82 | 28 | 7 | 1. All Our Tomorrows | Atco 7342 |
| | | | **SCORPIONS** | |
| | | | German heavy-metal rock quintet led by Rudolf Schenker (guitar - Michael's brother), & Klaus Meine (vocals) | |
| 4/28/84 | 25 | 7 | 1. Rock You Like A Hurricane | Mercury 818440 |
| | | | **BOBBY SCOTT** | |
| 1/21/56 | 13 | 10 | 1. Chain Gang | ABC-Para. 9658 |
| | | | **FREDDIE SCOTT** | |
| 8/10/63 | 10 | 9 | 1. **Hey, Girl** | Colpix 692 |
| 2/18/67 | 39 | 2 | 2. Are You Lonely For Me | Shout 207 |
| | | | **JACK SCOTT** | |
| | | | born Jack Scafone, Jr. on 1/24/36 in Ontario, Canada | |
| 6/16/58 | 25 | 7 | 1. Leroy/ | |
| 7/07/58 | 3 | 15 | 2. **My True Love** | Carlton 462 |
| 10/20/58 | 28 | 4 | 3. With Your Love | Carlton 483 |
| 12/28/58 + | 8 | 13 | 4. **Goodbye Baby** | Carlton 493 |
| 8/03/59 | 35 | 4 | 5. The Way I Walk | Carlton 514 |
| 1/18/60 | 5 | 12 | 6. **What In The World's Come Over You** | Top Rank 2028 |
| 5/09/60 | 3 | 12 | 7. **Burning Bridges/** | |
| 5/30/60 | 34 | 2 | 8. Oh, Little One | Top Rank 2041 |
| 9/05/60 | 38 | 2 | 9. It Only Happened Yesterday | Top Rank 2055 |
| | | | **LINDA SCOTT** | |
| | | | born Linda Joy Sampson on 6/1/45 in Queens, New York | |
| 4/03/61 | 3 | 10 | 1. **I've Told Every Little Star** | Canadian A. 123 |
| 7/24/61 | 9 | 10 | 2. **Don't Bet Money Honey** | Canadian A. 127 |
| 11/27/61 | 12 | 8 | 3. I Don't Know Why | Canadian A. 129 |
| | | | **PEGGY SCOTT & JO JO BENSON** | |
| 7/06/68 | 31 | 7 | 1. Lover's Holiday | SSS Int'l. 736 |
| 11/30/68 | 27 | 4 | 2. Pickin' Wild Mountain Berries | SSS Int'l. 748 |
| 2/15/69 | 37 | 3 | 3. Soul Shake | SSS Int'l. 761 |
| | | | **JOHNNY SEA** | |
| 6/25/66 | 35 | 2 | 1. Day For Decision [S] | Warner 5820 |
| | | | patriotic answer to "Eve Of Destruction" | |
| | | | **SEALS & CROFTS** | |
| | | | Jim Seals & Dash Crofts - both from Texas | |
| 10/21/72 | 6 | 11 | 1. **Summer Breeze** | Warner 7606 |
| 2/17/73 | 20 | 9 | 2. Hummingbird | Warner 7671 |
| 6/16/73 | 6 | 12 | 3. **Diamond Girl** | Warner 7708 |
| 10/13/73 | 21 | 8 | 4. We May Never Pass This Way (Again) | Warner 7740 |
| 5/17/75 | 18 | 8 | 5. I'll Play For You | Warner 8075 |
| 6/05/76 | 6 | 15 | 6. **Get Closer** | Warner 8190 |
| | | | featuring Carolyn Willis | |

| DATE | POS | WKS | ARTIST—Record Title | LABEL & NO. |
|------|-----|-----|---------------------|-------------|
| 10/22/77 | 28 | 5 | 7. My Fair Share<br>Love Theme from the film "One On One" | Warner 8405 |
| 5/27/78 | 18 | 7 | 8. You're The Love | Warner 8551 |
| | | | **SEARCHERS**<br>rock quartet from Liverpool, England | |
| 3/21/64 | 13 | 8 | 1. Needles And Pins | Kapp 577 |
| 6/20/64 | 16 | 8 | 2. Don't Throw Your Love Away | Kapp 593 |
| 9/12/64 | 34 | 3 | 3. Some Day We're Gonna Love Again | Kapp 609 |
| 11/14/64 | 35 | 2 | 4. When You Walk In The Room | Kapp 618 |
| 12/19/64 + | 3 | 11 | 5. **Love Potion Number Nine** | Kapp 27 |
| 2/20/65 | 29 | 3 | 6. What Have They Done To The Rain | Kapp 644 |
| 4/10/65 | 21 | 4 | 7. Bumble Bee | Kapp 49 |
| | | | **JOHN SEBASTIAN**<br>lead singer of the Lovin' Spoonful | |
| 4/10/76 | 1 (1) | 11 | ● 1. **Welcome Back**<br>from TV's "Welcome Back Kotter" | Reprise 1349 |
| | | | **SECRETS**<br>female quartet from Cleveland, Ohio | |
| 12/07/63 | 18 | 6 | 1. The Boy Next Door | Philips 40146 |
| | | | **NEIL SEDAKA**<br>born on 3/13/39 in Brooklyn, New York | |
| 12/28/58 + | 14 | 9 | 1. The Diary | RCA 7408 |
| 10/26/59 | 9 | 13 | 2. **Oh! Carol** | RCA 7595 |
| 4/18/60 | 9 | 9 | 3. **Stairway To Heaven** | RCA 7709 |
| 8/29/60 | 17 | 9 | 4. You Mean Everything To Me/ | RCA 7781 |
| 10/03/60 | 28 | 3 | 5.  Run Samson Run | |
| 12/31/60 + | 4 | 12 | 6. **Calendar Girl** | RCA 7829 |
| 5/08/61 | 11 | 7 | 7. Little Devil | RCA 7874 |
| 11/27/61 + | 6 | 11 | 8. **Happy Birthday, Sweet Sixteen** | RCA 7957 |
| 7/07/62 | 1 (2) | 12 | 9. **Breaking Up Is Hard To Do** | RCA 8046 |
| 10/20/62 | 5 | 9 | 10. **Next Door To An Angel** | RCA 8086 |
| 2/16/63 | 17 | 7 | 11. Alice In Wonderland | RCA 8137 |
| 5/18/63 | 26 | 5 | 12. Let's Go Steady Again | RCA 8169 |
| 12/07/63 | 33 | 4 | 13. Bad Girl | RCA 8254 |
| 11/16/74 + | 1 (1) | 15 | 14. **Laughter In The Rain** | Rocket 40313 |
| 4/26/75 | 22 | 5 | 15. The Immigrant | Rocket 40370 |
| 8/02/75 | 27 | 4 | 16. That's When The Music Takes Me | Rocket 40426 |
| 9/20/75 | 1 (3) | 12 | ● 17. **Bad Blood**<br>background vocals: Elton John | Rocket 40460 |
| 12/27/75 + | 8 | 11 | 18. **Breaking Up Is Hard To Do**<br>slow version of the 1962 hit | Rocket 40500 |
| 5/01/76 | 16 | 7 | 19. Love In The Shadows | Rocket 40543 |
| 7/24/76 | 36 | 2 | 20. Steppin' Out | Rocket 40582 |
| | | | **NEIL & DARA SEDAKA**<br>father and daughter | |
| 5/10/80 | 19 | 10 | 1. Should've Never Let You Go | Elektra 46615 |

| DATE | POS | WKS | ARTIST—Record Title | LABEL & NO. |
|------|-----|-----|---------------------|-------------|
| | | | **SEEDS** | |
| | | | Los Angeles psychedelic rock quartet - Sky Saxon, lead singer | |
| 2/11/67 | 36 | 3 | 1. Pushin' Too Hard | GNP Crescendo 372 |
| | | | **SEEKERS** | |
| | | | pop-folk Australian-born quartet: Judith Durham, lead singer - also see New Seekers | |
| 4/10/65 | 4 | 10 | 1. **I'll Never Find Another You** | Capitol 5383 |
| 6/26/65 | 19 | 7 | 2. A World Of Our Own | Capitol 5430 |
| 12/31/66 + | 2 (2) | 12 | ● 3. **Georgy Girl** | Capitol 5756 |
| | | | **BOB SEGER** | |
| | | | born on 5/6/45 in Ann Arbor, Michigan - featuring backing by the Silver Bullet Band | |
| 1/25/69 | 17 | 9 | 1. Ramblin' Gamblin' Man | Capitol 2297 |
| | | | shown as Bob Seger System | |
| 1/15/77 | 4 | 13 | 2. **Night Moves** | Capitol 4369 |
| 5/14/77 | 24 | 4 | 3. Mainstreet | Capitol 4422 |
| 6/03/78 | 4 | 11 | 4. **Still The Same** | Capitol 4581 |
| 8/19/78 | 12 | 10 | 5. Hollywood Nights | Capitol 4618 |
| 11/25/78 + | 13 | 11 | 6. We've Got Tonite | Capitol 4653 |
| 5/05/79 | 28 | 5 | 7. Old Time Rock & Roll | Capitol 4702 |
| 3/01/80 | 6 | 12 | 8. **Fire Lake** | Capitol 4836 |
| 5/10/80 | 5 | 11 | 9. **Against The Wind** | Capitol 4863 |
| 8/16/80 | 14 | 9 | 10. You'll Accomp'ny Me | Capitol 4904 |
| 9/26/81 | 5 | 12 | 11. **Tryin' To Live My Life Without You** | Capitol 5042 |
| 12/18/82 + | 2 (4) | 19 | 12. **Shame On The Moon** | Capitol 5187 |
| 3/26/83 | 12 | 9 | 13. Even Now | Capitol 5213 |
| 6/11/83 | 27 | 6 | 14. Roll Me Away | Capitol 5235 |
| | | | **MARILYN SELLARS** | |
| 9/28/74 | 37 | 2 | 1. One Day At A Time | Mega 1205 |
| | | | **MICHAEL SEMBELLO** | |
| | | | session guitarist/producer/composer/arranger/vocalist | |
| 7/02/83 | 1 (2) | 16 | 1. **Maniac** | Casablanca 812516 |
| | | | from the film "Flashdance" | |
| 10/29/83 | 34 | 2 | 2. Automatic Man | Warner 29485 |
| | | | **SENATOR BOBBY** | |
| | | | Senator Bobby is Bill Minkin | |
| 1/21/67 | 20 | 4 | 1. Wild Thing [C] | Parkway 127 |
| | | | **SENSATIONS** | |
| | | | Yvonne Baker, lead singer of R&B quartet from Philadelphia | |
| 2/10/62 | 4 | 12 | 1. **Let Me In** | Argo 5405 |
| | | | **SERENDIPITY SINGERS** | |
| | | | pop-folk group organized at the University of Colorado | |
| 3/21/64 | 6 | 11 | 1. **Don't Let The Rain Come Down (Crooked Little Man)** | Philips 40175 |
| 6/13/64 | 30 | 5 | 2. Beans In My Ears [N] | Philips 40198 |

| DATE | POS | WKS | ARTIST—Record Title | LABEL & NO. |
|------|-----|-----|---------------------|-------------|
| | | | **DAVID SEVILLE** | |
| | | | real name: Ross Bagdasarian - died on 1/16/72 (52) - also see Chipmunks | |
| 4/14/58 | **1** (3) | 18 | 1. **Witch Doctor** [N] | Liberty 55132 |
| 7/14/58 | **34** | 2 | 2. The Bird On My Head [N] | Liberty 55140 |
| | | | **PHIL SEYMOUR** | |
| | | | vocalist/drummer with the Dwight Twilley Band | |
| 2/21/81 | **22** | 7 | 1. Precious To Me | Boardwalk 5703 |
| | | | **SHADES OF BLUE** | |
| 5/28/66 | **12** | 8 | 1. Oh How Happy | Impact 1007 |
| | | | **SHADOWS OF KNIGHT** | |
| | | | Chicago-area "garage band" - Jim Sohns, lead singer | |
| 4/16/66 | **10** | 8 | 1. **Gloria** | Dunwich 116 |
| 7/02/66 | **39** | 1 | 2. Oh Yeah | Dunwich 122 |
| | | | **SHALAMAR** | |
| | | | soul/dance trio: Howard Hewett, Jeffrey Daniel, Jody Watley | |
| 4/16/77 | **25** | 8 | 1. Uptown Festival (Motown Medley) [N] | Soul Train 10885 |
| 2/02/80 | **8** | 13 | ● 2. **The Second Time Around** | Solar 11709 |
| 8/06/83 | **22** | 10 | 3. Dead Giveaway | Solar 69819 |
| 4/14/84 | **17** | 10 | 4. Dancing In The Sheets | Columbia 04372 |
| | | | from the film "Footloose" | |
| | | | **SHANGRI-LAS** | |
| | | | Queens, New York "girl group" - Mary Weiss, lead singer | |
| 9/05/64 | **5** | 9 | 1. **Remember (Walkin' In The Sand)** | Red Bird 008 |
| 10/24/64 | **1** (1) | 10 | 2. **Leader Of The Pack** | Red Bird 014 |
| 1/16/65 | **18** | 5 | 3. Give Him A Great Big Kiss | Red Bird 018 |
| 6/19/65 | **29** | 4 | 4. Give Us Your Blessings | Red Bird 030 |
| 11/20/65 | **6** | 8 | 5. **I Can Never Go Home Anymore** | Red Bird 043 |
| 2/26/66 | **33** | 2 | 6. Long Live Our Love | Red Bird 048 |
| | | | **SHANNON** | |
| | | | New Yorker Shannon Greene | |
| 1/07/84 | **8** | 12 | ● 1. **Let The Music Play** | Mirage 99810 |
| | | | **DEL SHANNON** | |
| | | | born Charles Westover on 12/30/39 in Coopersville, Michigan | |
| 3/27/61 | **1** (4) | 12 | 1. **Runaway** | Big Top 3067 |
| 6/19/61 | **5** | 11 | 2. **Hats Off To Larry** | Big Top 3075 |
| 10/09/61 | **28** | 5 | 3. So Long Baby | Big Top 3083 |
| 1/06/62 | **38** | 2 | 4. Hey! Little Girl | Big Top 3091 |
| 1/26/63 | **12** | 7 | 5. Little Town Flirt | Big Top 3131 |
| 7/25/64 | **22** | 7 | 6. Handy Man | Amy 905 |
| 12/19/64 + | **9** | 10 | 7. **Keep Searchin' (We'll Follow The Sun)** | Amy 915 |
| 3/13/65 | **30** | 4 | 8. Stranger In Town | Amy 919 |
| 1/23/82 | **33** | 4 | 9. Sea Of Love | Network 47951 |
| | | | **DEE DEE SHARP** | |
| | | | born Dione LaRue on 9/9/45 in Philadelphia - also see Chubby Checker | |
| 3/17/62 | **2** (2) | 15 | 1. **Mashed Potato Time** | Cameo 212 |
| 6/23/62 | **9** | 9 | 2. **Gravy (For My Mashed Potatoes)** | Cameo 219 |

| DATE | POS | WKS | ARTIST—Record Title | LABEL & NO. |
|------|-----|-----|---------------------|-------------|
| 11/10/62 | 5 | 9 | 3. **Ride!** | Cameo 230 |
| 3/09/63 | 10 | 9 | 4. **Do The Bird** | Cameo 244 |
| 11/02/63 | 33 | 5 | 5. **Wild!** | Cameo 274 |
| | | | **GEORGIE SHAW** | |
| | | | also see Kitty Kallen | |
| 11/12/55 | 23 | 6 | 1. No Arms Can Ever Hold You (Like These Arms Of Mine | Decca 29679 |
| | | | **TOMMY SHAW** | |
| | | | lead guitarist of Styx | |
| 11/03/84 | 33 | 3 | 1. Girls With Guns | A&M 2676 |
| | | | **SHEILA E.** | |
| | | | Sheila Escovedo - daughter of Pete Escovedo (Santana/Azteca) | |
| 7/21/84 | 7 | 16 | 1. **The Glamorous Life** | Warner 29285 |
| | | | **SHELLS** | |
| | | | Brooklyn R&B quintet - Nate Bouknight, lead singer | |
| 12/31/60 + | 21 | 5 | 1. Baby Oh Baby | Johnson 104 |
| | | | **SHEP & THE LIMELITES** | |
| | | | James (Shep) Sheppard, leader of R&B trio from New York, died on 1/24/70 | |
| 4/10/61 | 2 (1) | 11 | 1. **Daddy's Home** <br> answer to the Heartbeats "A Thousand Miles Away" | Hull 740 |
| | | | **SHEPHERD SISTERS** | |
| 11/04/57 | 18 | 7 | 1. Alone (Why Must I Be Alone) | Lance 125 |
| | | | **T.G. SHEPPARD** | |
| | | | born Bill Browder in Humbolt, Tennessee - T.G.: The Good | |
| 5/16/81 | 37 | 2 | 1. I Loved 'Em Every One | Warner 49690 |
| | | | **ALLAN SHERMAN** | |
| | | | comedy writer-producer of TV's "I've Got A Secret" - died on 11/21/73 (48) | |
| 8/10/63 | 2 (3) | 8 | 1. **Hello Mudduh, Hello Fadduh! (A Letter From Camp) [C]** <br> adaptation of Ponchielli's "Dance Of The Hours" | Warner 5378 |
| 5/08/65 | 40 | 1 | 2. Crazy Downtown [C] <br> adapted from "Downtown" | Warner 5614 |
| | | | **BOBBY SHERMAN** | |
| | | | regular on TV's "Shindig" - Jeremy Bolt on TV's "Here Come The Brides" | |
| 9/06/69 | 3 | 11 | ● 1. **Little Woman** | Metromedia 121 |
| 12/06/69 + | 9 | 9 | ● 2. **La La La (If I Had You)** | Metromedia 150 |
| 2/28/70 | 9 | 11 | ● 3. **Easy Come, Easy Go** | Metromedia 177 |
| 6/06/70 | 24 | 5 | 4. Hey, Mister Sun | Metromedia 188 |
| 8/15/70 | 5 | 13 | ● 5. **Julie, Do Ya Love Me** | Metromedia 194 |
| 2/27/71 | 16 | 7 | 6. Cried Like A Baby | Metromedia 206 |
| 5/15/71 | 29 | 5 | 7. The Drum | Metromedia 217 |
| | | | **SHERRYS** | |
| | | | female R&B quartet from Philadelphia | |
| 11/10/62 | 35 | 2 | 1. Pop Pop Pop-Pie | Guyden 2068 |

| DATE | POS | WKS | ARTIST—Record Title | LABEL & NO. |
|------|-----|-----|---------------------|-------------|
| | | | **SHIELDS** | |
| 9/15/58 | 12 | 9 | 1. You Cheated | Dot 15805 |
| | | | **SHIRELLES** | |
| | | | female quartet from Passaic, New Jersey - Shirley Alston, lead singer - Micki Harris died on 6/10/82 (42) | |
| 10/17/60 | 39 | 3 | 1. Tonights The Night | Scepter 1208 |
| 12/12/60 + | 1 (2) | 15 | 2. **Will You Love Me Tomorrow** | Scepter 1211 |
| 2/06/61 | 3 | 14 | 3. **Dedicated To The One I Love [R]** re-entry of 1959 hit (Pos. 83) | Scepter 1203 |
| 5/01/61 | 4 | 8 | 4. **Mama Said** | Scepter 1217 |
| 10/23/61 | 21 | 5 | 5. Big John | Scepter 1223 |
| 1/06/62 | 8 | 11 | 6. **Baby It's You** | Scepter 1227 |
| 3/31/62 | 1 (3) | 13 | 7. **Soldier Boy** | Scepter 1228 |
| 7/07/62 | 22 | 6 | 8. Welcome Home Baby | Scepter 1234 |
| 10/06/62 | 36 | 3 | 9. Stop The Music | Scepter 1237 |
| 12/15/62 + | 19 | 9 | 10. Everybody Loves A Lover | Scepter 1243 |
| 4/20/63 | 4 | 9 | 11. **Foolish Little Girl** | Scepter 1248 |
| 7/13/63 | 26 | 4 | 12. Don't Say Goodnight And Mean Goodbye | Scepter 1255 |
| | | | **SHIRLEY and COMPANY** | |
| | | | Shirley Goodman of Shirley & Lee | |
| 2/22/75 | 12 | 8 | 1. Shame, Shame, Shame | Vibration 532 |
| | | | **SHIRLEY & LEE** | |
| | | | Shirley Goodman & Leonard Lee | |
| 9/08/56 | 20 | 9 | 1. Let The Good Times Roll | Aladdin 3325 |
| 1/05/57 | 38 | 1 | 2. I Feel Good | Aladdin 3338 |
| | | | **DON SHIRLEY Trio** | |
| | | | pianist - born in Kingston, Jamaica on 1/27/27 | |
| 10/09/61 | 40 | 1 | 1. Water Boy [I] | Cadence 1392 |
| | | | **SHOCKING BLUE** | |
| | | | Dutch quartet - Mariska Veres, lead singer | |
| 12/20/69 + | 1 (1) | 13 | ● 1. **Venus** | Colossus 108 |
| | | | **TROY SHONDELL** | |
| 9/25/61 | 6 | 12 | 1. **This Time** | Liberty 55353 |
| | | | **DINAH SHORE** | |
| | | | born Frances Shore on 3/1/17 in Winchester, Tennessee | |
| 5/21/55 | 12 | 2 | 1. Whatever Lola Wants from Broadway's "Damn Yankees" | RCA 6077 |
| 12/10/55 | 20 | 1 | 2. Love And Marriage | RCA 6266 |
| 2/23/57 | 19 | 10 | 3. Chantez-Chantez | RCA 6792 |
| 9/09/57 | 15 | 7 | 4. Fascination from the film "Love In The Afternoon" | RCA 6980 |
| 12/02/57 | 24 | 1 | 5. I'll Never Say "Never Again" Again | RCA 7056 |
| | | | **BUNNY SIGLER** | |
| | | | songwriter/producer from Philadelphia | |
| 7/22/67 | 22 | 7 | 1. Let The Good Times Roll & Feel So Good | Parkway 153 |

| DATE | POS | WKS | ARTIST—Record Title | LABEL & NO. |
|---|---|---|---|---|
| | | | **SILHOUETTES** | |
| | | | Philadelphia "doo-wop" quartet - Billy Horton, lead singer | |
| 1/20/58 | **1** (2) | 13 | 1. **Get A Job** | Ember 1029 |
| | | | **SILKIE** | |
| | | | English | |
| 11/06/65 | **10** | 7 | 1. **You've Got To Hide Your Love Away** | Fontana 1525 |
| | | | **SILVER** | |
| | | | country-rock quintet led by John Batdorf (Batdorf & Rodney) | |
| 8/07/76 | **16** | 12 | 1. Wham Bam (Shang-A-Lang) | Arista 0189 |
| | | | **SILVER CONDOR** | |
| | | | rock quintet led by Joe Cerisano (vocals) & Earl Slick (guitar) | |
| 8/29/81 | **32** | 4 | 1. You Could Take My Heart Away | Columbia 02268 |
| | | | **SILVER CONVENTION** | |
| | | | female disco trio from Munich, Germany | |
| 10/25/75 | **1** (3) | 13 | ● 1. **Fly, Robin, Fly [I]** | Midland I. 10339 |
| 4/17/76 | **2** (3) | 15 | ● 2. **Get Up And Boogie (That's Right)** | Midland I. 10571 |
| | | | **SILVETTI** | |
| | | | Bebu Silvetti | |
| 3/19/77 | **39** | 3 | 1. Spring Rain [I] | Salsoul 2014 |
| | | | **HARRY SIMEONE Chorale** | |
| 12/28/58 | **13** | 6 | 1. The Little Drummer Boy [X] | 20th Fox 121 |
| 12/28/59 | **15** | 3 | 2. The Little Drummer Boy [X-R] | 20th Fox 121 |
| 12/19/60 | **24** | 3 | 3. The Little Drummer Boy [X-R] | 20th Fox 121 |
| 12/25/61 | **22** | 2 | 4. The Little Drummer Boy [X-R] | 20th Fox 121 |
| 12/15/62 | **28** | 3 | 5. The Little Drummer Boy [X-R] | 20th Fox 121 |
| | | | **GENE SIMMONS** | |
| 8/29/64 | **11** | 8 | 1. Haunted House | Hi 2076 |
| | | | **PATRICK SIMMONS** | |
| | | | original member of the Doobie Brothers | |
| 4/16/83 | **30** | 5 | 1. So Wrong | Elektra 69839 |
| | | | **SIMON & GARFUNKEL** | |
| | | | Paul Simon & Art Garfunkel | |
| 12/04/65 + | **1** (2) | 12 | ● 1. **The Sounds Of Silence** | Columbia 43396 |
| 2/26/66 | **5** | 10 | 2. **Homeward Bound** | Columbia 43511 |
| 5/14/66 | **3** | 10 | 3. **I Am A Rock** | Columbia 43617 |
| 8/27/66 | **25** | 4 | 4. The Dangling Conversation | Columbia 43728 |
| 11/19/66 | **13** | 6 | 5. A Hazy Shade Of Winter | Columbia 43873 |
| 4/01/67 | **16** | 7 | 6. At The Zoo | Columbia 44046 |
| 8/12/67 | **23** | 5 | 7. Fakin' It | Columbia 44232 |
| 3/16/68 | **11** | 9 | 8. Scarborough Fair/Canticle | Columbia 44465 |
| 5/04/68 | **1** (3) | 12 | ● 9. **Mrs. Robinson** | Columbia 44511 |
| | | | above 2 from the film "The Graduate" | |
| 4/19/69 | **7** | 9 | 10. **The Boxer** | Columbia 44785 |

| DATE | POS | WKS | ARTIST—Record Title | LABEL & NO. |
|---|---|---|---|---|
| 2/14/70 | 1 (6) | 13 | ● 11. **Bridge Over Troubled Water** | Columbia 45079 |
| 4/18/70 | 4 | 12 | ● 12. **Cecilia** | Columbia 45133 |
| 9/26/70 | 18 | 8 | 13. El Condor Pasa | Columbia 45237 |
| 11/01/75 | 9 | 9 | 14. **My Little Town** | Columbia 10230 |
| 5/01/82 | 27 | 6 | 15. Wake Up Little Susie<br>recorded live in New York's Central Park on 9/19/81 | Warner 50053 |
| | | | **CARLY SIMON**<br>born on 6/25/45 in New York City - recorded with sister Lucy<br>as the Simon Sisters | |
| 6/05/71 | 10 | 10 | 1. **That's The Way I've Always Heard It Should Be** | Elektra 45724 |
| 1/01/72 | 13 | 10 | 2. Anticipation | Elektra 45759 |
| 12/16/72 + | 1 (3) | 14 | ● 3. **You're So Vain** | Elektra 45824 |
| 4/21/73 | 17 | 9 | 4. The Right Thing To Do | Elektra 45843 |
| 6/01/74 | 14 | 6 | 5. Haven't Got Time For The Pain | Elektra 45887 |
| 5/24/75 | 21 | 5 | 6. Attitude Dancing | Elektra 45246 |
| 8/27/77 | 2 (3) | 15 | ● 7. **Nobody Does It Better**<br>from the film "The Spy Who Loved Me" | Elektra 45413 |
| 5/06/78 | 6 | 11 | 8. **You Belong To Me** | Elektra 45477 |
| 8/23/80 | 11 | 13 | ● 9. Jesse | Warner 49518 |
| | | | **CARLY SIMON & JAMES TAYLOR**<br>husband & wife | |
| 2/16/74 | 5 | 13 | ● 1. **Mockingbird** | Elektra 45880 |
| 9/23/78 | 36 | 3 | 2. Devoted To You | Elektra 45506 |
| | | | **JOE SIMON**<br>soul singer - born on 9/2/43 in Simmesport, Louisiana | |
| 6/08/68 | 25 | 7 | 1. (You Keep Me) Hangin' On | Sound Stage 2608 |
| 3/29/69 | 13 | 11 | ● 2. The Chokin' Kind | Sound Stage 2628 |
| 2/06/71 | 40 | 3 | 3. Your Time To Cry | Spring 108 |
| 12/11/71 + | 11 | 11 | ● 4. Drowning In The Sea Of Love | Spring 120 |
| 8/19/72 | 11 | 8 | ● 5. Power Of Love | Spring 128 |
| 4/14/73 | 37 | 2 | 6. Step By Step | Spring 133 |
| 8/25/73 | 18 | 8 | 7. Theme From Cleopatra Jones<br>featuring the Mainstreeters | Spring 138 |
| 5/10/75 | 8 | 11 | 8. **Get Down, Get Down (Get On The Floor)** | Spring 156 |
| | | | **PAUL SIMON**<br>born on 10/13/42 in Newark, New Jersey - also see Art Garfunkel | |
| 2/19/72 | 4 | 11 | 1. **Mother And Child Reunion** | Columbia 45547 |
| 4/22/72 | 22 | 8 | 2. Me And Julio Down By The Schoolyard | Columbia 45585 |
| 6/02/73 | 2 (2) | 11 | 3. **Kodachrome** | Columbia 45859 |
| 8/18/73 | 2 (1) | 14 | ● 4. **Loves Me Like A Rock**<br>with The Dixie Hummingbirds | Columbia 45907 |
| 1/05/74 | 35 | 3 | 5. American Tune | Columbia 45900 |
| 1/03/76 | 1 (3) | 13 | ● 6. **50 Ways To Leave Your Lover** | Columbia 10270 |
| 5/29/76 | 40 | 2 | 7. Still Crazy After All These Years | Columbia 10332 |
| 11/05/77 + | 5 | 14 | 8. **Slip Slidin' Away** | Columbia 10630 |
| 8/16/80 | 6 | 12 | 9. **Late In The Evening** | Warner 49511 |
| 11/22/80 | 40 | 2 | 10. One-Trick Pony | Warner 49601 |

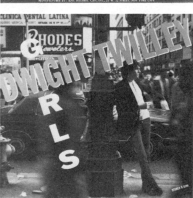

**B. J. Thomas,** from Houston, first hit with a version of Hank Williams' "I'm So Lonesome I Could Cry" in 1966. His 1972 hit "Rock and Roll Lullabye" features imitation "Beach Boy" voices and the real Duane Eddy on guitar.

**The Thompson Twins** are neither related nor a twosome, just three friends. At one time, they numbered seven and handed out hubcaps for the audience to keep time on.

**The Tremeloes.** England's Tremeloes were formed by a butcher's son, Brian Poole, in 1959. In those early days, his act included a painstaking Buddy Holly imitation complete with Holly's trademark glasses. The Trems' U.S. hits came after Poole left the band.

**Tina Turner,** born Annie Mae Bullock, met husband Ike in the fifties, divorced him in the seventies, and finally earned her first chart-topper in 1984, "What's Love Got to Do With It."

**Dwight Twilley** waited nine years for his second hit, "Girls," which features backing vocals by old pal Tom Petty and Susan Cowsill. (Remember the Cowsill Family?)

**Tracey Ullman** would have scored a hit with the winsome "They Don't Know" anyway, but it couldn't have hurt that Paul McCartney made a cameo appearance in the video.

**The Unifics** were paragons of classy New York soul. Their biggest hit, "Court of Love," was arranged by Donny Hathaway, best known for his duets with Roberta Flack.

**Van Halen's** startling switch from heavy metal to straight pop on "Jump" isn't the only surprising thing about the band. Guitar whiz Eddie Van Halen added a sizzling guitar solo to Michael Jackson's "Beat It" and even joined the gloved one onstage once in the summer of '84.

**Gene Vincent** was Capitol Record's answer to Elvis Presley. A navy vet, Vincent was left partially crippled, reportedly by a motorbike accident (others said a bullet wound). He was later seriously injured in the 1960 car crash that killed Eddie Cochran.

**John Waite** was the lead singer for the Baby's, a moderately successful band carefully calculated to hit the teen audience. Their impact was mild compared to his solo smash "Missing You," of course.

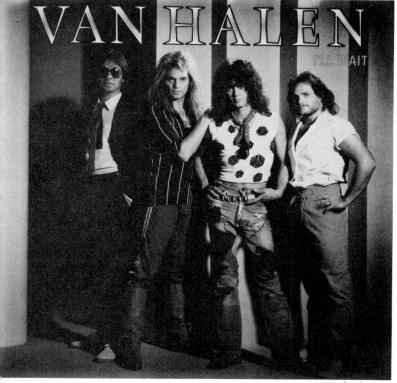

| DATE | POS | WKS | ARTIST—Record Title | LABEL & NO. |
|---|---|---|---|---|
| | | | **PAUL SIMON/PHOEBE SNOW** | |
| 9/06/75 | 23 | 6 | 1. Gone At Last<br>with The Jessy Dixon Singers | Columbia 10197 |
| | | | **NINA SIMONE** | |
| | | | born Eunice Waymon on 2/21/33 in Tryon, North Carolina | |
| 8/24/59 | 18 | 11 | 1. I Loves You, Porgy<br>from the film "Porgy And Bess" | Bethlehem 11021 |
| | | | **FRANK SINATRA** | |
| | | | Francis Albert Sinatra was born on 12/12/15 in Hoboken, New Jersey - vocalist with Harry James' Band ('39) and Tommy Dorsey's Band ('40-'42) - also see Nancy & Frank Sinatra | |
| 5/07/55 | 1 (2) | 21 | 1. **Learnin' The Blues** | Capitol 3102 |
| 9/24/55 | 13 | 5 | 2. Same Old Saturday Night | Capitol 3218 |
| 11/05/55 | 5 | 15 | 3. **Love And Marriage**<br>from the TV production "Our Town" | Capitol 3260 |
| 12/17/55 + | 7 | 9 | 4. **(Love Is) The Tender Trap** | Capitol 3290 |
| 3/24/56 | 21 | 3 | 5. Flowers Mean Forgiveness | Capitol 3350 |
| 6/02/56 | 13 | 6 | 6. (How Little It Matters) How Little We Know | Capitol 3423 |
| 11/03/56 + | 3 | 17 | 7. **Hey! Jealous Lover** | Capitol 3552 |
| 2/09/57 | 15 | 6 | 8. Can I Steal A Little Love<br>from the film "Rock Pretty Baby" | Capitol 3608 |
| 7/22/57 | 25 | 1 | 9. You're Cheatin' Yourself (If You're<br>Cheatin' On Me) | Capitol 3744 |
| 10/28/57 + | 2 (1) | 17 | 10. **All The Way**<br>from the film "The Joker Is Wild" | Capitol 3793 |
| 1/20/58 | 6 | 14 | 11. **Witchcraft** | Capitol 3859 |
| 9/07/59 | 30 | 1 | 12. High Hopes<br>from the film "A Hole In The Head" | Capitol 4214 |
| 11/16/59 | 38 | 3 | 13. Talk To Me | Capitol 4284 |
| 11/28/60 | 25 | 2 | 14. Ol' Mac Donald | Capitol 4466 |
| 1/20/62 | 34 | 3 | 15. Pocketful Of Miracles | Reprise 20040 |
| 10/10/64 | 27 | 6 | 16. Softly, As I Leave You | Reprise 0301 |
| 1/30/65 | 32 | 3 | 17. Somewhere In Your Heart | Reprise 0332 |
| 1/15/66 | 28 | 4 | 18. It Was A Very Good Year | Reprise 0429 |
| 5/28/66 | 1 (1) | 11 | 19. **Strangers In The Night**<br>from the film "A Man Could Get Killed" | Reprise 0470 |
| 9/17/66 | 25 | 5 | 20. Summer Wind | Reprise 0509 |
| 12/03/66 | 4 | 9 | 21. **That's Life** | Reprise 0531 |
| 8/26/67 | 30 | 4 | 22. The World We Knew (Over And Over) | Reprise 0610 |
| 11/16/68 | 23 | 5 | 23. Cycles | Reprise 0764 |
| 4/12/69 | 27 | 6 | 24. My Way | Reprise 0817 |
| 5/31/80 | 32 | 6 | 25. Theme From New York, New York | Reprise 49233 |
| | | | **FRANK SINATRA & RAY ANTHONY** | |
| 1/22/55 | 19 | 4 | 1. Melody Of Love | Capitol 3018 |
| | | | **FRANK SINATRA & KEELY SMITH** | |
| 5/12/58 | 22 | 1 | 1. How Are Ya' Fixed For Love? | Capitol 3952 |

| DATE | POS | WKS | ARTIST—Record Title | LABEL & NO. |
|------|-----|-----|---------------------|-------------|
| | | | **NANCY SINATRA** | |
| | | | daughter of Frank Sinatra | |
| 2/05/66 | **1** (1) | 12 | ● 1. **These Boots Are Made For Walkin'** | Reprise 0432 |
| 4/30/66 | 7 | 7 | 2. **How Does That Grab You, Darlin'?** | Reprise 0461 |
| 7/30/66 | 36 | 2 | 3. Friday's Child | Reprise 0491 |
| 12/10/66 | **5** | 9 | ● 4. **Sugar Town** | Reprise 0527 |
| 4/08/67 | 15 | 5 | 5. Love Eyes | Reprise 0559 |
| 10/07/67 | 24 | 4 | 6. Lightning's Girl | Reprise 0620 |
| | | | **NANCY & FRANK SINATRA** | |
| 3/25/67 | **1** (4) | 11 | ● 1. **Somethin' Stupid** | Reprise 0561 |
| | | | **NANCY SINATRA & LEE HAZLEWOOD** | |
| 7/08/67 | **14** | 7 | 1. Jackson | Reprise 0595 |
| 11/04/67 | 20 | 4 | 2. Lady Bird | Reprise 0629 |
| 1/27/68 | 26 | 5 | 3. Some Velvet Morning | Reprise 0651 |
| | | | **GORDON SINCLAIR** | |
| | | | Canadian broadcaster - died on 5/17/84 (83) | |
| 1/26/74 | **24** | 4 | 1. The Americans (A Canadian's Opinion) | Avco 4628 |
| | | | originally broadcast on 6/5/73 on CFRB Radio in Toronto | |
| | | | **SINGING DOGS [Don Charles Presents]** | |
| 12/17/55 | **22** | 2 | 1. Oh! Susanna [N] | RCA 6344 |
| | | | featuring the barking of 5 dogs | |
| | | | **SINGING NUN** | |
| | | | Soeur Sourire, from the Fichermont, Belgium nuns convent | |
| 11/16/63 | **1** (4) | 12 | 1. **Dominique [F]** | Philips 40152 |
| | | | **SIR DOUGLAS QUINTET** | |
| | | | 'Tex-Mex' rock band led by Doug Sahm from San Antonio | |
| 4/17/65 | **13** | 9 | 1. She's About A Mover | Tribe 8308 |
| 3/05/66 | 31 | 5 | 2. The Rains Came | Tribe 8314 |
| 3/15/69 | 27 | 6 | 3. Mendocino | Smash 2191 |
| | | | **SISTER SLEDGE** | |
| | | | Kathy, Debbie, Kim and Joni Sledge | |
| 3/10/79 | **9** | 13 | 1. **He's The Greatest Dancer** | Cotillion 44245 |
| 5/12/79 | **2** (2) | 11 | ● 2. **We Are Family** | Cotillion 44251 |
| 3/06/82 | 23 | 6 | 3. My Guy | Cotillion 47000 |
| | | | **SIX TEENS** | |
| | | | Los Angeles sextet - Trudy Williams, lead singer | |
| 9/01/56 | **25** | 1 | 1. A Casual Look | Flip 315 |
| | | | **SKIP & FLIP** | |
| | | | Clyde Battin & Gary Paxton (classmates at the Univ. of Arizona) | |
| 7/27/59 | **11** | 9 | 1. It Was I | Brent 7002 |
| 4/25/60 | **11** | 10 | 2. Cherry Pie | Brent 7010 |
| | | | **SKYLARK** | |
| | | | Canadian quartet - Donny Gerrard & Ms. B.J. Cook, lead singers | |
| 3/31/73 | **9** | 14 | 1. **Wildflower** | Capitol 3511 |

| DATE | POS | WKS | ARTIST—Record Title | LABEL & NO. |
|---|---|---|---|---|
| | | | **SKYLINERS** | |
| | | | 4 boys and a girl from Pittsburgh - Jimmy Beaumont, lead singer | |
| 3/23/59 | 12 | 10 | 1. Since I Don't Have You | Calico 103 |
| 6/15/59 | 26 | 7 | 2. This I Swear | Calico 106 |
| 6/20/60 | 24 | 6 | 3. Pennies From Heaven | Calico 117 |
| | | | **SKYY** | |
| | | | New York City-based 8-piece dance/funk band | |
| 2/20/82 | 26 | 4 | 1. Call Me | Salsoul 2152 |
| | | | **SLADE** | |
| | | | English hard-rock quartet, Noddy Holder, lead singer | |
| 5/05/84 | 20 | 8 | 1. Run Runaway | CBS Assoc. 04398 |
| 8/11/84 | 37 | 3 | 2. My Oh My | CBS Assoc. 04528 |
| | | | **SLAVE** | |
| | | | Dayton, Ohio 8-man funk band | |
| 7/23/77 | 32 | 6 | 1. Slide [I] | Cotillion 44218 |
| | | | **PERCY SLEDGE** | |
| | | | soul singer from Leighton, Alabama | |
| 4/30/66 | 1 (2) | 10 | ● 1. **When A Man Loves A Woman** | Atlantic 2326 |
| 8/06/66 | 17 | 6 | 2. Warm And Tender Love | Atlantic 2342 |
| 11/19/66 | 20 | 7 | 3. It Tears Me Up | Atlantic 2358 |
| 7/22/67 | 40 | 1 | 4. Love Me Tender | Atlantic 2414 |
| 4/06/68 | 11 | 11 | 5. Take Time To Know Her | Atlantic 2490 |
| | | | **SLY & THE FAMILY STONE** | |
| | | | San Francisco funk/rock band featuring Sly Stone (Sylvester Stewart), brother Freddie Stone, sister Rose Stone, & Larry Graham | |
| 3/02/68 | 8 | 12 | 1. **Dance To The Music** | Epic 10256 |
| 1/04/69 | 1 (4) | 14 | ● 2. **Everyday People** | Epic 10407 |
| 4/26/69 | 22 | 6 | 3. Stand! | Epic 10450 |
| 8/30/69 | 2 (2) | 13 | 4. **Hot Fun In The Summertime** | Epic 10497 |
| 1/10/70 | 1 (2) | 12 | ● 5. **Thank You (Falettinme Be Mice Elf Agin)**/ | Epic 10555 |
| | | 12 | 6. **Everybody Is A Star** | |
| 6/20/70 | 38 | 3 | 7. I Want To Take You Higher [R] | Epic 10450 |
| | | | re-entry of 1969 hit (Pos. 60 - flip side of "Stand!") | |
| 11/13/71 | 1 (3) | 13 | ● 8. **Family Affair** | Epic 10805 |
| 2/26/72 | 23 | 6 | 9. Runnin' Away | Epic 10829 |
| 7/14/73 | 12 | 13 | ● 10. **If You Want Me To Stay** | Epic 11017 |
| 8/17/74 | 32 | 3 | 11. Time For Livin' | Epic 11140 |
| | | | **SMALL FACES** | |
| | | | British: Steve Marriott (guitar). Ronnie Lane (bass), Ian MacLagan (organ), Kenny Jones (drums) - also see Faces | |
| 1/13/68 | 16 | 8 | 1. Itchycoo Park | Immediate 501 |
| | | | **MILLIE SMALL** | |
| | | | 16-year-old from Jamaica | |
| 6/06/64 | 2 (1) | 9 | 1. **My Boy Lollipop** | Smash 1893 |
| 9/05/64 | 40 | 2 | 2. Sweet William | Smash 1920 |

| DATE | POS | WKS | ARTIST—Record Title | LABEL & NO. |
|---|---|---|---|---|
| | | | **SMITH** | |
| | | | Gayle McCormick, lead singer | |
| 10/04/69 | 5 | 11 | 1. **Baby It's You** | Dunhill 4206 |
| | | | **FRANKIE SMITH** | |
| 7/11/81 | 30 | 7 | ● 1. Double Dutch Bus | WMOT 5356 |
| | | | certified gold for both 7" and 12" singles | |
| | | | **HUEY "PIANO" SMITH & The Clowns** | |
| | | | New Orleans R&B session pianist - also see Frankie Ford | |
| 3/31/58 | 9 | 9 | 1. **Don't You Just Know It** | Ace 545 |
| | | | Bobby Marchan, lead singer | |
| | | | **HURRICANE SMITH** | |
| | | | English producer (Pink Floyd) and engineer (Beatles) - real name: Norman Smith | |
| 12/23/72 + | 3 | 12 | 1. **Oh, Babe, What Would You Say?** | Capitol 3383 |
| | | | **JIMMY SMITH** | |
| | | | jazz organist from Philadelphia - born on 12/8/25 | |
| 6/09/62 | 21 | 7 | 1. Walk On The Wild Side - Part 1 [I] | Verve 10255 |
| | | | **KEELY SMITH - see LOUIS PRIMA/FRANK SINATRA** | |
| | | | **O.C. SMITH** | |
| | | | Ocie Lee Smith - replaced Joe Williams as lead singer with Count Basie | |
| 4/20/68 | 40 | 2 | 1. The Son Of Hickory Holler's Tramp | Columbia 44425 |
| 9/21/68 | 2 (1) | 12 | ● 2. **Little Green Apples** | Columbia 44616 |
| 9/20/69 | 34 | 2 | 3. Daddy's Little Man | Columbia 44948 |
| | | | **PATTI SMITH Group** | |
| | | | punk-rocker from Chicago | |
| 5/13/78 | 13 | 9 | 1. Because The Night | Arista 0318 |
| | | | **RAY SMITH** | |
| | | | died on 11/29/79 (41) | |
| 2/01/60 | 22 | 8 | 1. Rockin' Little Angel | Judd 1016 |
| | | | **REX SMITH** | |
| | | | starred in several Broadway musicals | |
| 5/12/79 | 10 | 10 | ● 1. **You Take My Breath Away** | Columbia 10908 |
| | | | from the TV film "Sooner Or Later" | |
| | | | **REX SMITH/RACHEL SWEET** | |
| 8/08/81 | 32 | 4 | 1. Everlasting Love | Columbia 02169 |
| | | | **SAMMI SMITH** | |
| 2/20/71 | 8 | 11 | ● 1. **Help Me Make It Through The Night** | Mega 0015 |
| | | | **SOMETHIN' SMITH & THE REDHEADS** | |
| | | | trio formed at UCLA | |
| 4/02/55 | 7 | 23 | 1. **It's A Sin To Tell A Lie** | Epic 9093 |
| 7/14/56 | 27 | 3 | 2. In A Shanty In Old Shanty Town | Epic 9168 |
| | | | **VERDELLE SMITH** | |
| 8/13/66 | 38 | 2 | 1. Tar And Cement | Capitol 5632 |

| DATE | POS | WKS | ARTIST—Record Title | LABEL & NO. |
|---|---|---|---|---|
| | | | **WHISTLING JACK SMITH** | |
| 5/13/67 | 20 | 5 | 1. I Was Kaiser Bill's Batman [I] | Deram 85005 |
| | | | **SMOKIE** | |
| | | | Chris Norman, lead singer of pop/rock quartet - also see Suzi Quatro | |
| 1/22/77 | 25 | 8 | 1. Living Next Door To Alice | RSO 860 |
| | | | **SNEAKER** | |
| | | | Los Angeles-based sextet | |
| 12/19/81 + | 34 | 6 | 1. More Than Just The Two Of Us | Handshake 02557 |
| | | | **SNIFF 'n' the TEARS** | |
| | | | British - Paul Roberts, lead singer | |
| 8/18/79 | 15 | 9 | 1. Driver's Seat | Atlantic 3604 |
| | | | **PHOEBE SNOW** | |
| | | | born Phoebe Laub on 7/17/52 in New York City - also see Paul Simon | |
| 2/08/75 | 5 | 11 | 1. **Poetry Man** | Shelter 40353 |
| | | | **SOFT CELL** | |
| | | | British electro-rock duo: Marc Almond & David Ball | |
| 5/22/82 | 8 | 15 | 1. **Tainted Love** | Sire 49855 |
| | | | **JOANIE SOMMERS** | |
| | | | first heard as the vocalist for "Pepsi-Cola" jingles | |
| 6/16/62 | 7 | 11 | 1. **Johnny Get Angry** | Warner 5275 |
| | | | **SONNY** | |
| | | | Sonny Bono of Sonny & Cher | |
| 9/04/65 | 10 | 8 | 1. **Laugh At Me** | Atco 6369 |
| | | | **SONNY & CHER** | |
| | | | Salvatore Bono & Cherilyn LaPier (married 1964-1974) - hosts of their own TV comedy/musical variety series (1971-1977) | |
| 7/31/65 | 1 (3) | 10 | ● 1. **I Got You Babe** | Atco 6359 |
| 9/11/65 | 8 | 9 | 2. **Baby Don't Go** | Reprise 0309 |
| 9/25/65 | 20 | 4 | 3. Just You | Atco 6345 |
| 10/23/65 | 15 | 6 | 4. But You're Mine | Atco 6381 |
| 2/12/66 | 14 | 6 | 5. What Now My Love | Atco 6395 |
| 10/15/66 | 21 | 4 | 6. Little Man | Atco 6440 |
| 1/28/67 | 6 | 8 | 7. **The Beat Goes On** | Atco 6461 |
| 11/13/71 | 7 | 11 | 8. **All I Ever Need Is You** | Kapp 2151 |
| 3/11/72 | 8 | 11 | 9. **A Cowboys Work Is Never Done** | Kapp 2163 |
| 8/05/72 | 32 | 5 | 10. When You Say Love<br>adapted from the "Budweiser" jingle | Kapp 2176 |
| | | | **SOPWITH CAMEL** | |
| | | | San Francisco quintet | |
| 1/28/67 | 26 | 4 | 1. Hello Hello | Kama Sutra 217 |
| | | | **S.O.S. BAND** | |
| | | | Atlanta funk/R&B band - Mary Davis, lead singer | |
| 6/28/80 | 3 | 14 | ★ 1. **Take Your Time (Do It Right) Part 1** | Tabu 5522 |

| DATE | POS | WKS | ARTIST—Record Title | LABEL & NO. |
|------|-----|-----|---------------------|-------------|
| | | | **SOUL CHILDREN** | |
| 3/23/74 | 36 | 2 | 1. I'll Be The Other Woman | Stax 0182 |
| | | | **SOUL SURVIVORS** | |
| | | | white-soul band from New York City and Philadelphia | |
| 9/23/67 | 4 | 12 | 1. **Expressway To Your Heart** | Crimson 1010 |
| 1/20/68 | 33 | 3 | 2. Explosion In My Soul | Crimson 1012 |
| | | | **DAVID SOUL** | |
| | | | Ken Hutchinson of TV's "Starsky & Hutch" | |
| 2/19/77 | 1 (1) | 13 | ● 1. **Don't Give Up On Us** | Private S. 45129 |
| | | | **JIMMY SOUL** | |
| | | | real name: Jimmy McCleese | |
| 5/05/62 | 22 | 8 | 1. Twistin' Matilda | S.P.Q.R. 3300 |
| 4/20/63 | 1 (2) | 11 | 2. **If You Wanna Be Happy** | S.P.Q.R. 3305 |
| | | | **SOUNDS OF SUNSHINE** | |
| 7/24/71 | 39 | 2 | 1. Love Means (You Never Have To Say You're Sorry) | Ranwood 896 |
| | | | **SOUNDS ORCHESTRAL** | |
| | | | English - Johnny Pearson on piano | |
| 4/10/65 | 10 | 11 | 1. **Cast Your Fate To The Wind [I]** | Parkway 942 |
| | | | **JOE SOUTH** | |
| | | | singer/songwriter from Atlanta, Georgia | |
| 2/01/69 | 12 | 9 | 1. Games People Play | Capitol 2248 |
| 1/17/70 | 12 | 9 | 2. Walk A Mile In My Shoes | Capitol 2704 |
| | | | **SOUTHER, HILLMAN, FURAY Band** | |
| | | | J.D. Souther, Chris Hillman, Richie Furay | |
| 9/21/74 | 27 | 4 | 1. Fallin' In Love | Asylum 45201 |
| | | | **J.D. SOUTHER** | |
| | | | John David Souther - also see James Taylor | |
| 10/20/79 | 7 | 13 | 1. **You're Only Lonely** | Columbia 11079 |
| | | | **RED SOVINE** | |
| | | | full name: Woodrow Wilson Sovine - died on 4/4/80 (61) | |
| 8/28/76 | 40 | 1 | ● 1. Teddy Bear [S] | Starday 142 |
| | | | **SPANDAU BALLET** | |
| | | | English quintet - Tony Hadley, lead singer | |
| 8/27/83 | 4 | 13 | 1. **True** | Chrysalis 42720 |
| 12/17/83 + | 29 | 6 | 2. Gold | Chrysalis 42743 |
| 9/01/84 | 34 | 4 | 3. Only When You Leave | Chrysalis 42792 |
| | | | **SPANKY & OUR GANG** | |
| | | | Elaine "Spanky" McFarlane, lead singer | |
| 6/03/67 | 9 | 5 | 1. **Sunday Will Never Be The Same** | Mercury 72679 |
| 9/16/67 | 31 | 2 | 2. Making Every Minute Count | Mercury 72714 |
| 10/28/67 | 14 | 9 | 3. Lazy Day | Mercury 72732 |
| 2/03/68 | 30 | 4 | 4. Sunday Mornin' | Mercury 72765 |
| 5/18/68 | 17 | 7 | 5. Like To Get To Know You | Mercury 72795 |

| DATE | POS | WKS | ARTIST—Record Title | LABEL & NO. |
|---|---|---|---|---|
| | | | **SPIDER** | |
| | | | Amanda Blue, lead singer of New York-based quintet | |
| 6/07/80 | 39 | 2 | 1. New Romance (It's A Mystery) | Dreamland 100 |
| | | | **SPINNERS** | |
| | | | R&B quintet founded by Harvey Fuqua in Detroit in 1957 - Philippe Wynne, lead singer ('72-'77) died 7/14/84 (43) - also see Dionne Warwick | |
| 7/17/61 | 27 | 5 | 1. That's What Girls Are Made For | Tri-Phi 1001 |
| 8/14/65 | 35 | 2 | 2. I'll Always Love You | Motown 1078 |
| 8/22/70 | 14 | 10 | 3. It's A Shame | V.I.P. 25057 |
| 10/07/72 | 3 | 11 | ● 4. **I'll Be Around** | Atlantic 2904 |
| 1/20/73 | 4 | 12 | ● 5. **Could It Be I'm Falling In Love** | Atlantic 2927 |
| 5/19/73 | 11 | 11 | ● 6. One Of A Kind (Love Affair) | Atlantic 2962 |
| 9/08/73 | 29 | 3 | 7. Ghetto Child | Atlantic 2973 |
| 2/23/74 | 20 | 8 | 8. Mighty Love - Pt. 1 | Atlantic 3006 |
| 6/08/74 | 18 | 6 | 9. I'm Coming Home | Atlantic 3027 |
| 10/26/74 | 15 | 5 | 10. Love Don't Love Nobody - Pt. I | Atlantic 3206 |
| 4/05/75 | 37 | 2 | 11. Living A Little, Laughing A Little | Atlantic 3252 |
| 8/30/75 | 5 | 13 | ● 12. **They Just Can't Stop It the (Games People Play)** | Atlantic 3284 |
| 1/24/76 | 36 | 3 | 13. Love Or Leave | Atlantic 3309 |
| 10/02/76 | 2 (3) | 17 | ● 14. **The Rubberband Man** | Atlantic 3355 |
| 1/26/80 | 2 (2) | 16 | ● 15. **Working My Way Back To You/Forgive Me, Girl** | Atlantic 3637 |
| 5/24/80 | 4 | 14 | 16. **Cupid/I've Loved You For A Long Time** | Atlantic 3664 |
| | | | **SPIRAL STARECASE** | |
| | | | pop/rock quintet from Sacramento, California - Pat Upton, lead singer | |
| 5/03/69 | 12 | 11 | 1. More Today Than Yesterday | Columbia 44741 |
| | | | **SPIRIT** | |
| | | | Los Angeles rock fusion group - Jay Ferguson, lead singer | |
| 3/08/69 | 25 | 5 | 1. I Got A Line On You | Ode 115 |
| | | | **SPOKESMEN** | |
| 10/09/65 | 36 | 3 | 1. The Dawn Of Correction<br>answer to "Eve Of Destruction" | Decca 31844 |
| | | | **DUSTY SPRINGFIELD** | |
| | | | born Mary O'Brien on 4/16/39 in London, England | |
| 2/15/64 | 12 | 7 | 1. I Only Want To Be With You | Philips 40162 |
| 5/02/64 | 38 | 2 | 2. Stay Awhile | Philips 40180 |
| 7/11/64 | 6 | 10 | 3. **Wishin' And Hopin'** | Philips 40207 |
| 6/04/66 | 4 | 10 | 4. **You Don't Have To Say You Love Me** | Philips 40371 |
| 10/01/66 | 20 | 5 | 5. All I See Is You | Philips 40396 |
| 4/22/67 | 40 | 2 | 6. I'll Try Anything | Philips 40439 |
| 10/14/67 | 22 | 5 | 7. The Look Of Love<br>from the film "Casino Royale" | Philips 40465 |
| 12/14/68 + | 10 | 10 | 8. **Son-Of-A Preacher Man** | Atlantic 2580 |
| 5/24/69 | 31 | 4 | 9. The Windmills Of Your Mind | Atlantic 2623 |
| 11/29/69 | 24 | 9 | 10. A Brand New Me | Atlantic 2685 |

| DATE | POS | WKS | ARTIST—Record Title | LABEL & NO. |
|---|---|---|---|---|
| | | | **RICK SPRINGFIELD** | |
| | | | Australian - played Noah Drake on TV's "General Hospital" | |
| 9/02/72 | 14 | 9 | 1. Speak To The Sky | Capitol 3340 |
| 5/09/81 | 1 (2) | 22 | ● 2. Jessie's Girl | RCA 12201 |
| 9/12/81 | 8 | 12 | 3. I've Done Everything For You | RCA 12166 |
| 12/26/81 + | 20 | 10 | 4. Love Is Alright Tonite | RCA 13008 |
| 3/13/82 | 2 (4) | 16 | 5. Don't Talk To Strangers | RCA 13070 |
| 6/19/82 | 21 | 9 | 6. What Kind Of Fool Am I | RCA 13245 |
| 10/09/82 | 32 | 5 | 7. I Get Excited | RCA 13303 |
| 4/23/83 | 9 | 13 | 8. Affair Of The Heart | RCA 13497 |
| 7/23/83 | 18 | 11 | 9. Human Touch | RCA 13576 |
| 11/12/83 | 23 | 6 | 10. Souls | RCA 13650 |
| 3/17/84 | 5 | 12 | 11. Love Somebody | RCA 13738 |
| 6/09/84 | 26 | 6 | 12. Don't Walk Away | RCA 13813 |
| 9/08/84 | 20 | 9 | 13. Bop 'Til You Drop | RCA 13861 |
| | | | above 3 from the film "Hard To Hold" | |
| | | | **SPRINGFIELDS** | |
| | | | English folk trio featuring Dusty & brother Tom Springfield | |
| 9/01/62 | 20 | 6 | 1. Silver Threads And Golden Needles | Philips 40038 |
| | | | **BRUCE SPRINGSTEEN** | |
| | | | born on 9/23/49 in Freehold, New Jersey | |
| 10/11/75 | 23 | 5 | 1. Born To Run | Columbia 10209 |
| 7/15/78 | 33 | 2 | 2. Prove It All Night | Columbia 10763 |
| 11/08/80 | 5 | 14 | 3. Hungry Heart | Columbia 11391 |
| 2/21/81 | 20 | 6 | 4. Fade Away | Columbia 11431 |
| 5/26/84 | 2 (4) | 15 | 5. Dancing In The Dark | Columbia 04463 |
| 8/18/84 | 7 | 13 | 6. Cover Me | Columbia 04561 |
| | | | **SPYRO GYRA** | |
| | | | Buffalo-based jazz/pop band led by sax man Jay Beckenstein | |
| 7/28/79 | 24 | 8 | 1. Morning Dance [I] | Infinity 50011 |
| | | | **BILLY SQUIER** | |
| | | | Boston-bred heavy-metal rock guitarist | |
| 6/20/81 | 17 | 11 | 1. The Stroke | Capitol 5005 |
| 10/17/81 | 35 | 3 | 2. In The Dark | Capitol 5040 |
| 11/27/82 | 32 | 6 | 3. Everybody Wants You | Capitol 5163 |
| 7/14/84 | 15 | 12 | 4. Rock Me Tonite | Capitol 5370 |
| | | | **JIM STAFFORD** | |
| | | | host of a summer variety TV show in 1975 | |
| 7/14/73 | 39 | 1 | 1. Swamp Witch [N] | MGM 14496 |
| 12/29/73 + | 3 | 15 | ● 2. Spiders & Snakes | MGM 14648 |
| 5/04/74 | 12 | 9 | 3. My Girl Bill [N] | MGM 14718 |
| 7/20/74 | 7 | 11 | 4. Wildwood Weed [N] | MGM 14737 |
| 1/18/75 | 24 | 5 | 5. Your Bulldog Drinks Champagne [N] | MGM 14775 |
| 9/27/75 | 37 | 2 | 6. I Got Stoned And I Missed It [N] | MGM 14819 |

| DATE | POS | WKS | ARTIST—Record Title | LABEL & NO. |
|------|-----|-----|---------------------|-------------|
| | | | **JO STAFFORD** | |
| | | | member of Tommy Dorsey's vocal group, the Pied Pipers | |
| 10/15/55 | **13** | 7 | 1. Suddenly There's A Valley | Columbia 40559 |
| 12/03/55 + | **14** | 14 | 2. It's Almost Tomorrow | Columbia 40595 |
| 12/22/56 | **38** | 1 | 3. On London Bridge | Columbia 40782 |
| | | | **TERRY STAFFORD** | |
| | | | from Amarillo, Texas | |
| 3/21/64 | **3** | 10 | 1. **Suspicion** | Crusader 101 |
| 6/06/64 | **25** | 6 | 2. I'll Touch A Star | Crusader 105 |
| | | | **STALLION** | |
| 4/23/77 | **37** | 2 | 1. Old Fashioned Boy (You're The One) | Casablanca 877 |
| | | | **FRANK STALLONE** | |
| | | | Sylvester Stallone's brother | |
| 8/20/83 | **10** | 10 | 1. **Far From Over** <br> from the film "Staying Alive" | RSO 815023 |
| | | | **STAMPEDERS** | |
| | | | Canadian country-rock trio | |
| 9/11/71 | **8** | 10 | 1. **Sweet City Woman** | Bell 45120 |
| 4/03/76 | **40** | 2 | 2. Hit The Road Jack <br> with Wolfman Jack | Quality 501 |
| | | | **JOE STAMPLEY** | |
| | | | country singer - was lead singer of the Uniques | |
| 3/03/73 | **37** | 3 | 1. Soul Song | Dot 17442 |
| | | | **STANDELLS** | |
| | | | Los Angeles-area punk rock quintet - Dick Todd, lead singer | |
| 6/11/66 | **11** | 9 | 1. Dirty Water | Tower 185 |
| | | | **MICHAEL STANLEY Band** | |
| | | | rock group from Cleveland, Ohio | |
| 1/10/81 | **33** | 5 | 1. He Can't Love You | EMI America 8063 |
| 11/12/83 | **39** | 1 | 2. My Town | EMI America 8178 |
| | | | **STAPLE SINGERS** | |
| | | | Roebuck 'Pop' Staples and daughters Mavis, Cleo & Yvonne | |
| 3/20/71 | **27** | 5 | 1. Heavy Makes You Happy (Sha-Na-Boom Boom) | Stax 0083 |
| 11/13/71 | **12** | 10 | 2. Respect Yourself | Stax 0104 |
| 4/15/72 | **1** (1) | 14 | 3. **I'll Take You There** | Stax 0125 |
| 8/26/72 | **38** | 3 | 4. This World | Stax 0137 |
| 4/14/73 | **33** | 3 | 5. Oh La De Da | Stax 0156 |
| 11/10/73 | **9** | 11 | ● 6. **If You're Ready (Come Go With Me)** | Stax 0179 |
| 3/23/74 | **23** | 7 | 7. Touch A Hand, Make A Friend | Stax 0196 |
| 11/01/75 | **1** (1) | 12 | ● 8. **Let's Do It Again** | Curtom 0109 |
| | | | **CYRIL STAPLETON & His Orchestra** | |
| 9/29/56 | **25** | 2 | 1. The Italian Theme [I] | London 1672 |
| 1/19/59 | **13** | 10 | 2. The Children's Marching Song [N] <br> featuring the children from film "The Inn Of The Sixth Happiness" | London 1851 |

| DATE | POS | WKS | ARTIST—Record Title | LABEL & NO. |
|---|---|---|---|---|
| | | | **STARBUCK** | |
| | | | Atlanta septet - Bruce Blackman, lead singer | |
| 5/29/76 | 3 | 14 | 1. **Moonlight Feels Right** | Private S. 45039 |
| 5/21/77 | 38 | 2 | 2. Everybody Be Dancin' | Private S. 45144 |
| | | | **BUDDY STARCHER** | |
| 5/14/66 | 39 | 1 | 1. History Repeats Itself [S] | Boone 1038 |
| | | | **STARGARD** | |
| | | | disco-funk female trio | |
| 3/04/78 | 21 | 7 | 1. Theme Song From "Which Way Is Up" | MCA 40825 |
| | | | **STARLAND VOCAL BAND** | |
| | | | quartet led by Bill Danoff and his wife Taffy | |
| 6/05/76 | 1 (2) | 14 | ● 1. **Afternoon Delight** | Windsong 10588 |
| | | | **STARLETS** | |
| 6/12/61 | 38 | 2 | 1. Better Tell Him No | Pam 1003 |
| | | | **EDWIN STARR** | |
| | | | born Charles Hatcher on 1/21/42 in Nashville | |
| 9/04/65 | 21 | 6 | 1. Agent Double-O-Soul | Ric-Tic 103 |
| 3/22/69 | 6 | 9 | 2. **Twenty-Five Miles** | Gordy 7083 |
| 7/25/70 | 1 (3) | 13 | 3. **War** | Gordy 7101 |
| 1/02/71 | 26 | 4 | 4. Stop The War Now | Gordy 7104 |
| | | | **KAY STARR** | |
| | | | born Kay Stark on 7/21/22 in Dougherty, Oklahoma | |
| 8/06/55 | 17 | 1 | 1. Good And Lonesome | RCA 6146 |
| 1/07/56 | 1 (6) | 20 | 2. **Rock And Roll Waltz** | RCA 6359 |
| 6/30/56 | 40 | 1 | 3. Second Fiddle | RCA 6541 |
| 9/16/57 | 9 | 10 | 4. **My Heart Reminds Me** | RCA 6981 |
| | | | **RANDY STARR** | |
| | | | leader of the Islanders | |
| 5/06/57 | 32 | 2 | 1. After School | Dale 100 |
| | | | **RINGO STARR** | |
| | | | born Richard Starkey on 7/7/40 in Liverpool, England - he replaced Pete Best as the Beatles' drummer, August, 1962 | |
| 5/08/71 | 4 | 11 | ● 1. **It Don't Come Easy** | Apple 1831 |
| 4/15/72 | 9 | 7 | 2. **Back Off Boogaloo** | Apple 1849 |
| 10/20/73 | 1 (1) | 12 | ● 3. **Photograph** | Apple 1865 |
| 12/29/73 + | 1 (1) | 12 | ● 4. **You're Sixteen** | Apple 1870 |
| 3/23/74 | 5 | 11 | 5. **Oh My My** | Apple 1872 |
| 11/30/74 + | 6 | 10 | 6. **Only You** | Apple 1876 |
| 2/22/75 | 3 | 10 | 7. **No No Song** | Apple 1880 |
| 7/05/75 | 31 | 3 | 8. It's All Down To Goodnight Vienna | Apple 1882 |
| 10/16/76 | 26 | 6 | 9. A Dose Of Rock 'N' Roll | Atlantic 3361 |
| 12/05/81 | 38 | 2 | 10. Wrack My Brain | Boardwalk 130 |

**Dinah Washington** sang with Lionel Hampton before striking out on her own. A major influence on Aretha Franklin, Washington died of an overdose of sleeping pills in 1963.

**The Who's** Peter Townshend and John Entwistle first played together as youths in a Dixieland band. Pete strummed banjo; John blew trumpet.

**Deniece Williams** toured and recorded with Stevie Wonder in the early seventies. She got a chance to record solo when Maurice White of Earth, Wind and Fire admired her demo tapes and signed her up.

**Jackie Wilson** replaced Clyde McPhatter as the lead singer of Billy Ward's Dominoes. Going solo in 1957, Wilson went on to chalk up an incredible 24 Top 40 hits in ten years.

**Stevie Wonder.** Young Steveland Morris came to the attention of Motown through Ronnie White, a member of Smokey Robinson's Miracles. Early singles like "Mother Thank You" and "I Call It Pretty Music" gave little hint of what was to come.

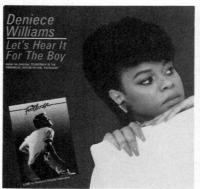

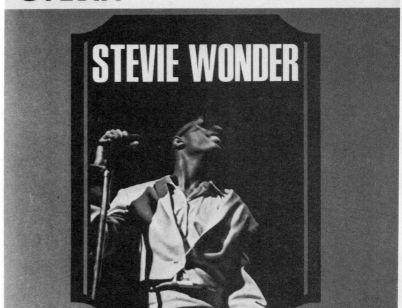

Kim Wilde's records are family affairs. Brother Ricky produces and co-authors the songs with dad Marty (né Reginald Smith), a British teen idol himself in the early sixties.

Andy Williams. "Anthony September" was the composer credit on Andy's most successful single, "Butterfly." It was the pseudonym for Tony Mammarella, producer of Dick Clark's "American Bandstand" TV show — although the song was actually written by Philadelphia's Kal Mann and Bernie Lowe.

Paul Young, who grew up idolizing American soul singers like Otis Redding and Al Green, learned his craft fronting the Q-Tips, a British soul band that played 700 live shows in less than three years.

"Weird Al" Yankovic's parody of Michael Jackson's "Beat It" was just the latest in a series of good-natured satires. He'd previously turned the Knack's "My Sharona" into "My Bologna" and Queen's "Another One Bites the Dust" into "Another One Rides the Bus."

The Yardbirds were known as the Metropolis Blues Quartet before Eric Clapton joined up in 1963. He split just two years later, disgusted by the pop direction of "For Your Love."

| DATE | POS | WKS | ARTIST—Record Title | LABEL & NO. |
|---|---|---|---|---|
| | | | **STARS ON 45** | |
| | | | session musicians from Holland | |
| 5/02/81 | **1** (1) | 14 | ● 1. **Stars On 45 [Medley]** | Radio 3810 |
| | | | primarily a Beatles' medley | |
| 4/17/82 | **28** | 5 | 2. Stars On 45 III | Radio 4019 |
| | | | a tribute to Stevie Wonder | |
| | | | **STARZ** | |
| | | | New York-based rock quintet - Michael Lee Smith, lead singer | |
| 4/30/77 | **33** | 2 | 1. Cherry Baby | Capitol 4399 |
| | | | **STATLER BROTHERS** | |
| | | | Harold & Don Reid (brothers), Lew DeWitt, Phil Balsley | |
| 12/11/65 + | **4** | 9 | 1. **Flowers On The Wall** | Columbia 43315 |
| | | | **CANDI STATON** | |
| | | | formerly married to Clarence Carter | |
| 10/03/70 | **24** | 9 | 1. Stand By Your Man | Fame 1472 |
| 6/26/76 | **20** | 11 | 2. Young Hearts Run Free | Warner 8181 |
| | | | **STATUS QUO** | |
| | | | English rock quartet | |
| 6/29/68 | **12** | 11 | 1. Pictures Of Matchstick Men | Cadet Con. 7001 |
| | | | **STEALERS WHEEL** | |
| | | | English group featuring Gerry Rafferty & Joe Egan | |
| 3/31/73 | **6** | 13 | 1. **Stuck In The Middle With You** | A&M 1416 |
| 3/09/74 | **29** | 3 | 2. Star | A&M 1483 |
| | | | **STEAM** | |
| | | | New York City session musicians | |
| 11/08/69 | **1** (2) | 13 | ● 1. **Na Na Hey Hey Kiss Him Goodbye** | Fontana 1667 |
| | | | **STEEL BREEZE** | |
| | | | Ric Jacobs, lead singer of 6-man pop band from California | |
| 9/18/82 | **16** | 11 | 1. You Don't Want Me Anymore | RCA 13283 |
| 2/19/83 | **30** | 6 | 2. Dreamin' Is Easy | RCA 13427 |
| | | | **STEELY DAN** | |
| | | | sophisticated pop/jazz group, reduced to a duo (Donald Fagen & Walter Becker) beginning with "Black Friday" | |
| 12/30/72 + | **6** | 11 | 1. **Do It Again** | ABC 11338 |
| 4/07/73 | **11** | 11 | 2. Reeling In The Years | ABC 11352 |
| 6/08/74 | **4** | 11 | 3. **Rikki Don't Lose That Number** | ABC 11439 |
| 6/21/75 | **37** | 2 | 4. Black Friday | ABC 12101 |
| 1/07/78 | **11** | 11 | 5. Peg | ABC 12320 |
| 5/06/78 | **19** | 8 | 6. Deacon Blues | ABC 12355 |
| 7/01/78 | **22** | 5 | 7. FM (No Static At All) | MCA 40894 |
| | | | from the film "FM" | |
| 9/23/78 | **26** | 5 | 8. Josie | ABC 12404 |
| 12/13/80 + | **10** | 13 | 9. **Hey Nineteen** | MCA 51036 |
| 3/28/81 | **22** | 7 | 10. Time Out Of Mind | MCA 51082 |
| | | | **LOU STEIN** | |
| | | | pianist | |
| 3/30/57 | **31** | 3 | 1. Almost Paradise [I] | RKO Unique 385 |
| | | | with Bill Fontaine's orchestra | |

| DATE | POS | WKS | ARTIST—Record Title | LABEL & NO. |
|------|-----|-----|---------------------|-------------|
| | | | **JIM STEINMAN** | |
| | | | writer & producer for Meat Loaf | |
| 7/18/81 | 32 | 6 | 1. Rock And Roll Dreams Come Through | Epic 02111 |
| | | | **VAN STEPHENSON** | |
| | | | singer/songwriter from Nashville | |
| 5/12/84 | 22 | 10 | 1. Modern Day Delilah | MCA 52376 |
| | | | **STEPPENWOLF** | |
| | | | hard-rock quintet led by John Kay | |
| 7/20/68 | 2 (3) | 12 | ● 1. **Born To Be Wild** | Dunhill 4138 |
| 10/26/68 | 3 | 13 | ● 2. **Magic Carpet Ride** | Dunhill 4161 |
| 3/15/69 | 10 | 8 | 3. **Rock Me** | Dunhill 4182 |
| 9/06/69 | 31 | 5 | 4. Move Over | Dunhill 4205 |
| 2/07/70 | 39 | 1 | 5. Monster | Dunhill 4221 |
| 5/09/70 | 35 | 3 | 6. Hey Lawdy Mama | Dunhill 4234 |
| 10/05/74 | 29 | 3 | 7. Straight Shootin' Woman | Mums 6031 |
| | | | **STEREOS** | |
| | | | Steubenville, Ohio quintet | |
| 10/16/61 | 29 | 3 | 1. I Really Love You | Cub 9095 |
| | | | **STEVE & EYDIE** | |
| | | | Steve Lawrence & Eydie Gorme | |
| 8/24/63 | 28 | 5 | 1. I Want To Stay Here | Columbia 42815 |
| 1/25/64 | 35 | 3 | 2. I Can't Stop Talking About You | Columbia 42932 |
| | | | **CAT STEVENS** | |
| | | | English - born Stephen Georgiou on 7/21/48 - currently a Muslim living in London | |
| 3/06/71 | 11 | 10 | 1. Wild World | A&M 1231 |
| 7/10/71 | 30 | 7 | 2. Moon Shadow | A&M 1265 |
| 10/09/71 | 7 | 10 | 3. **Peace Train** | A&M 1291 |
| 4/22/72 | 6 | 11 | 4. **Morning Has Broken** | A&M 1335 |
| 12/02/72 + | 16 | 9 | 5. Sitting | A&M 1396 |
| 8/04/73 | 31 | 5 | 6. The Hurt | A&M 1418 |
| 4/20/74 | 10 | 11 | 7. **Oh Very Young** | A&M 1503 |
| 8/24/74 | 6 | 9 | 8. **Another Saturday Night** | A&M 1602 |
| 1/11/75 | 26 | 4 | 9. Ready | A&M 1645 |
| 8/16/75 | 33 | 4 | 10. Two Fine People | A&M 1700 |
| 7/23/77 | 33 | 3 | 11. (Remember The Days Of The) Old Schoolyard | A&M 1948 |
| | | | **CONNIE STEVENS** | |
| | | | Cricket Blake of TV's "Hawaiian Eye" - real name: Concetta Ingolia - also see Edward Byrnes | |
| 3/14/60 | 3 | 17 | 1. **Sixteen Reasons** | Warner 5137 |
| | | | **DODIE STEVENS** | |
| | | | real name: Geraldine Pasquale | |
| 3/09/59 | 3 | 14 | 1. **Pink Shoe Laces** | Crystalette 724 |

| DATE | POS | WKS | ARTIST—Record Title | LABEL & NO. |
|---|---|---|---|---|
| | | | **RAY STEVENS** | |
| | | | born on 1/24/41 in Clarkdale, Georgia - also see Henhouse Five Plus Too | |
| 9/18/61 | 35 | 1 | 1. Jeremiah Peabody's Poly Unsaturated Quick Dissolving Fast Acting Pleasant Tasting Green & Purple Pills [N] | Mercury 71843 |
| 7/14/62 | 5 | 9 | 2. **Ahab, The Arab [N]** | Mercury 71966 |
| 6/29/63 | 17 | 6 | 3. Harry The Hairy Ape [N] | Mercury 72125 |
| 8/31/68 | 28 | 3 | 4. Mr. Businessman | Monument 1083 |
| 4/26/69 | 8 | 10 | ● 5. **Gitarzan [N]** | Monument 1131 |
| 7/26/69 | 27 | 4 | 6. Along Came Jones [N] | Monument 1150 |
| 4/18/70 | 1 (2) | 13 | ● 7. **Everything Is Beautiful** | Barnaby 2011 |
| 4/27/74 | 1 (3) | 12 | ● 8. **The Streak [N]** | Barnaby 600 |
| 5/24/75 | 14 | 10 | 9. Misty | Barnaby 614 |
| | | | **B.W. STEVENSON** | |
| | | | Austin, Texas native | |
| 8/25/73 | 9 | 12 | 1. **My Maria** | RCA 0030 |
| | | | **AL STEWART** | |
| | | | born on 9/5/45 in Glasgow, Scotland | |
| 1/22/77 | 8 | 10 | 1. **Year Of The Cat** | Janus 266 |
| 10/21/78 | 7 | 13 | 2. **Time Passages** | Arista 0362 |
| 2/17/79 | 29 | 4 | 3. Song On The Radio | Arista 0389 |
| 9/27/80 | 24 | 6 | 4. Midnight Rocks | Arista 0552 |
| | | | **AMII STEWART** | |
| | | | cabaret star from Washington, D.C. | |
| 2/24/79 | 1 (1) | 14 | ★ 1. **Knock On Wood** | Ariola 7736 |
| | | | **BILLY STEWART** | |
| | | | killed in an auto crash on 1/17/70 (32) | |
| 5/01/65 | 26 | 4 | 1. I Do Love You | Chess 1922 |
| 7/10/65 | 24 | 5 | 2. Sitting In The Park | Chess 1932 |
| 8/06/66 | 10 | 7 | 3. **Summertime** | Chess 1966 |
| 11/05/66 | 29 | 5 | 4. Secret Love | Chess 1978 |
| | | | **JOHN STEWART** | |
| | | | member of the Kingston Trio 1961-1967 | |
| 6/02/79 | 5 | 13 | 1. **Gold** | RSO 931 |
| 9/29/79 | 28 | 5 | 2. Midnight Wind | RSO 1000 |
| | | | above 2 with Stevie Nicks & Lindsey Buckingham | |
| 1/26/80 | 34 | 4 | 3. Lost Her In The Sun | RSO 1016 |
| | | | **ROD STEWART** | |
| | | | born on 1/10/45 in London, England - lead singer with the Jeff Beck Group ('68-'69), and with Faces ('69-'75) | |
| 8/28/71 | 1 (5) | 15 | ● 1. **Maggie May** | Mercury 73224 |
| 11/27/71 | 24 | 6 | 2. (I Know) I'm Losing You | Mercury 73244 |
| | | | with Faces | |
| 9/16/72 | 13 | 7 | 3. You Wear It Well | Mercury 73330 |
| 12/16/72 | 40 | 1 | 4. Angel | Mercury 73344 |
| 10/23/76 | 1 (8) | 17 | ● 5. **Tonight's The Night (Gonna Be Alright)** | Warner 8262 |

| DATE | POS | WKS | ARTIST—Record Title | LABEL & NO. |
|---|---|---|---|---|
| 2/26/77 | 21 | 9 | 6. The First Cut Is The Deepest | Warner 8321 |
| 7/02/77 | 30 | 4 | 7. The Killing Of Georgie (Part 1 & 2) | Warner 8396 |
| 11/26/77 + | 4 | 15 | ● 8. **You're In My Heart (The Final Acclaim)** | Warner 8475 |
| 3/11/78 | 28 | 4 | 9. Hot Legs | Warner 8535 |
| 5/27/78 | 22 | 6 | 10. I Was Only Joking | Warner 8568 |
| 12/23/78 + | 1 (4) | 18 | ★ 11. **Da Ya Think I'm Sexy?** | Warner 8724 |
| 5/12/79 | 22 | 6 | 12. Ain't Love A Bitch | Warner 8810 |
| 11/29/80 + | 5 | 17 | 13. **Passion** | Warner 49617 |
| 10/31/81 | 5 | 15 | 14. **Young Turks** | Warner 49843 |
| 2/13/82 | 20 | 8 | 15. Tonight I'm Yours (Don't Hurt Me) | Warner 49886 |
| 6/11/83 | 14 | 9 | 16. Baby Jane | Warner 29608 |
| 10/01/83 | 35 | 3 | 17. What Am I Gonna Do (I'm So In Love With You) | Warner 29564 |
| 6/02/84 | 6 | 13 | 18. **Infatuation** | Warner 29256 |
| 9/15/84 | 10 | 10 | 19. **Some Guys Have All The Luck** | Warner 29215 |
| | | | **SANDY STEWART**<br>Sandy was a regular on Eddie Fisher's and Perry Como's TV shows | |
| 1/12/63 | 20 | 6 | 1. My Coloring Book | Colpix 669 |
| | | | **STEPHEN STILLS**<br>member of Buffalo Springfield - also see Crosby, Stills & Nash | |
| 12/19/70 + | 14 | 10 | 1. Love The One You're With | Atlantic 2778 |
| 3/27/71 | 37 | 2 | 2. Sit Yourself Down | Atlantic 2790 |
| | | | **GARY STITES** | |
| 5/18/59 | 24 | 5 | 1. Lonely For You | Carlton 508 |
| | | | **MORRIS STOLOFF/Columbia Pictures Orchestra**<br>Morris died on 4/16/80 (84) | |
| 4/21/56 | 1 (3) | 22 | 1. **Moonglow And Theme From "Picnic" [I]** | Decca 29888 |
| | | | **STONE PONEYS - see LINDA RONSTADT** | |
| | | | **CLIFFIE STONE & His Orchestra** | |
| 8/13/55 | 14 | 4 | 1. The Popcorn Song [N]<br>vocal by Bob Roubian | Capitol 3131 |
| | | | **KIRBY STONE Four**<br>Kirby Stone, Eddie Hall, Larry Foster, Mike Gardner | |
| 7/28/58 | 25 | 1 | 1. Baubles, Bangles And Beads<br>from Broadway's "Kismet" | Columbia 41183 |
| | | | **STONEBOLT**<br>Pacific Northwest pop/rock quintet | |
| 9/30/78 | 29 | 5 | 1. I Will Still Love You | Parachute 512 |
| | | | **PAUL STOOKEY**<br>Paul of Peter, Paul & Mary | |
| 9/04/71 | 24 | 9 | 1. Wedding Song (There Is Love) | Warner 7511 |
| | | | **STORIES**<br>New York rock quartet led by Michael Brown (keyboards) & Ian Lloyd (vocals) | |
| 7/14/73 | 1 (2) | 15 | ● 1. **Brother Louie** | Kama Sutra 577 |

| DATE | POS | WKS | ARTIST—Record Title | LABEL & NO. |
|---|---|---|---|---|
| | | | **BILLY STORM** | |
| | | | lead singer of the Valiants | |
| 5/18/59 | 28 | 6 | 1. I've Come Of Age | Columbia 41356 |
| | | | **GALE STORM** | |
| | | | Margie Albright of TV's "My Little Margie" | |
| 10/22/55 | 2 (3) | 17 | 1. **I Hear You Knocking** | Dot 15412 |
| 12/24/55 + | 6 | 12 | 2. **Teen Age Prayer/** | |
| 12/31/55 + | 5 | 9 | 3. **Memories Are Made Of This** | Dot 15436 |
| 3/03/56 | 9 | 14 | 4. **Why Do Fools Fall In Love** | Dot 15448 |
| 5/05/56 | 6 | 14 | 5. **Ivory Tower** | Dot 15458 |
| 4/29/57 | 4 | 18 | 6. **Dark Moon** | Dot 15558 |
| | | | **STRANGELOVES** | |
| | | | producers Bob Feldman, Jerry Goldstein, Richard Gottehrer | |
| 7/10/65 | 11 | 8 | 1. I Want Candy | Bang 501 |
| 10/23/65 | 39 | 1 | 2. Cara-Lin | Bang 508 |
| 2/05/66 | 30 | 4 | 3. Night Time | Bang 514 |
| | | | **STRAWBERRY ALARM CLOCK** | |
| | | | west coast psychedelic rock sextet | |
| 10/14/67 | 1 (1) | 14 | ● 1. **Incense And Peppermints** | Uni 55018 |
| 1/27/68 | 23 | 6 | 2. Tomorrow | Uni 55046 |
| | | | **STRAY CATS** | |
| | | | rockabilly trio from Long Island, New York led by Brian Setzer | |
| 10/23/82 | 9 | 13 | 1. **Rock This Town** | EMI America 8132 |
| 1/08/83 | 3 | 14 | 2. **Stray Cat Strut** | EMI America 8122 |
| 8/20/83 | 5 | 12 | 3. **(She's) Sexy + 17** | EMI America 8168 |
| 12/03/83 | 35 | 3 | 4. I Won't Stand In Your Way | EMI America 8185 |
| | | | **STREET PEOPLE** | |
| | | | studio group - Rupert Holmes, member | |
| 2/21/70 | 36 | 5 | 1. Jennifer Tomkins | Musicor 1365 |
| | | | **BARBRA STREISAND** | |
| | | | born on 4/24/42 in Brooklyn, New York - leading stage and screen actress since 1962 | |
| 5/23/64 | 5 | 12 | 1. **People** | Columbia 42965 |
| | | | from Broadway's "Funny Girl" | |
| 1/22/66 | 32 | 3 | 2. Second Hand Rose | Columbia 43469 |
| 12/12/70 + | 6 | 12 | 3. **Stoney End** | Columbia 45236 |
| 8/28/71 | 40 | 1 | 4. Where You Lead | Columbia 45414 |
| 8/12/72 | 37 | 4 | 5. Sweet Inspiration/Where You Lead | Columbia 45626 |
| 12/22/73 + | 1 (3) | 17 | ● 6. **The Way We Were** | Columbia 45944 |
| 1/08/77 | 1 (3) | 18 | ● 7. **Evergreen** | Columbia 10450 |
| | | | Love Theme from "A Star Is Born" | |
| 5/28/77 | 4 | 14 | 8. **My Heart Belongs To Me** | Columbia 10555 |
| 7/01/78 | 25 | 5 | 9. Songbird | Columbia 10756 |
| 8/26/78 | 21 | 6 | 10. Love Theme From "Eyes Of Laura Mars" (Prisoner) | Columbia 10777 |
| 7/07/79 | 3 | 13 | ● 11. **The Main Event/Fight** | Columbia 11008 |
| 2/23/80 | 37 | 3 | 12. Kiss Me In The Rain | Columbia 11179 |

| DATE | POS | WKS | ARTIST—Record Title | LABEL & NO. |
|---|---|---|---|---|
| 9/13/80 | **1** (3) | 19 | ● 13. **Woman In Love** | Columbia 11364 |
| 11/28/81 + | **11** | 11 | 14. Comin' In And Out Of Your Life | Columbia 02621 |
| 12/10/83 | **40** | 2 | 15. The Way He Makes Me Feel<br>from the film "Yentl" | Columbia 04177 |
| | | | **BARBRA STREISAND & NEIL DIAMOND** | |
| 11/04/78 | **1** (2) | 15 | ● 1. **You Don't Bring Me Flowers** | Columbia 10840 |
| | | | **BARBRA STREISAND & BARRY GIBB** | |
| 11/15/80 + | **3** | 15 | ● 1. **Guilty** | Columbia 11390 |
| 2/14/81 | **10** | 10 | 2. **What Kind Of Fool** | Columbia 11430 |
| | | | **BARBRA STREISAND & DONNA SUMMER** | |
| 10/27/79 | **1** (2) | 13 | ● 1. **No More Tears (Enough Is Enough)** | Columbia 11125 |
| | | | **STRING-A-LONGS**<br>quintet signed by Buddy Holly's producer, Norman Petty | |
| 1/23/61 | **3** | 13 | 1. Wheels [I] | Warwick 603 |
| 4/17/61 | **35** | 2 | 2. Brass Buttons [I] | Warwick 625 |
| | | | **BARRETT STRONG**<br>Barrett and Nolan Strong (Diablos' lead singer) are cousins | |
| 3/21/60 | **23** | 8 | 1. Money (That's What I Want) | Anna 1111 |
| | | | **JUD STRUNK**<br>killed in a plane crash on 10/15/81 (45) | |
| 3/24/73 | **14** | 10 | 1. Daisy A Day | MGM 14463 |
| | | | **STYLE COUNCIL**<br>English duo: Paul Weller (The Jam) & Mick Talbot | |
| 5/12/84 | **29** | 6 | 1. My Ever Changing Moods | Geffen 29359 |
| | | | **STYLISTICS**<br>Philadelphia soul quintet - Russell Thompkins, Jr., lead singer | |
| 7/17/71 | **39** | 1 | 1. Stop, Look, Listen (To Your Heart) | Avco Embassy 4572 |
| 11/27/71 + | **9** | 13 | ● 2. **You Are Everything** | Avco 4581 |
| 3/11/72 | **3** | 14 | ● 3. **Betcha By Golly, Wow** | Avco 4591 |
| 7/01/72 | **25** | 6 | 4. People Make The World Go Round | Avco 4595 |
| 11/11/72 | **10** | 8 | ● 5. **I'm Stone In Love With You** | Avco 4603 |
| 3/03/73 | **5** | 9 | ● 6. **Break Up To Make Up** | Avco 4611 |
| 6/09/73 | **23** | 5 | 7. You'll Never Get To Heaven (If You<br>Break My Heart) | Avco 4618 |
| 11/17/73 | **14** | 11 | 8. Rockin' Roll Baby | Avco 4625 |
| 4/13/74 | **2** (2) | 14 | ● 9. **You Make Me Feel Brand New** | Avco 4634 |
| 8/17/74 | **18** | 7 | 10. Let's Put It All Together | Avco 4640 |
| | | | **STYX**<br>Chicago-based rock quintet: Dennis DeYoung (vocals/keyboards),<br>Tommy Shaw (lead guitar), James Young (guitar), and<br>John (drums) & brother Chuck Panozzo (bass) | |
| 1/18/75 | **6** | 11 | 1. **Lady** | Wooden N. 10102 |
| 3/27/76 | **27** | 5 | 2. Lorelei | A&M 1786 |
| 12/18/76 | **36** | 3 | 3. Mademoiselle | A&M 1877 |
| 10/29/77 + | **8** | 15 | 4. **Come Sail Away** | A&M 1977 |

| DATE | POS | WKS | ARTIST—Record Title | LABEL & NO. |
|------|-----|-----|---------------------|-------------|
| 4/01/78 | 29 | 4 | 5. Fooling Yourself (The Angry Young Man) | A&M 2007 |
| 10/21/78 | 21 | 7 | 6. Blue Collar Man (Long Nights) | A&M 2087 |
| 4/07/79 | 16 | 13 | 7. Renegade | A&M 2110 |
| 10/20/79 | 1 (2) | 14 | ● 8. **Babe** | A&M 2188 |
| 1/19/80 | 26 | 5 | 9. Why Me | A&M 2206 |
| 1/24/81 | 3 | 15 | 10. **The Best Of Times** | A&M 2300 |
| 3/28/81 | 9 | 13 | 11. **Too Much Time On My Hands** | A&M 2323 |
| 2/12/83 | 3 | 16 | ● 12. **Mr. Roboto** | A&M 2525 |
| 4/30/83 | 6 | 13 | 13. **Don't Let It End** | A&M 2543 |
| 6/02/84 | 40 | 2 | 14. Music Time | A&M 2625 |

**SUGARHILL GANG**
New York City rap/funk trio

| DATE | POS | WKS | ARTIST—Record Title | LABEL & NO. |
|------|-----|-----|---------------------|-------------|
| 1/05/80 | 36 | 2 | 1. Rapper's Delight | Sugar Hill 542 |

**SUGARLOAF**
rock quartet from Denver, Colorado - Jerry Corbetta, lead singer

| DATE | POS | WKS | ARTIST—Record Title | LABEL & NO. |
|------|-----|-----|---------------------|-------------|
| 9/19/70 | 3 | 12 | 1. **Green-Eyed Lady** | Liberty 56183 |
| 2/01/75 | 9 | 11 | 2. **Don't Call Us, We'll Call You** | Claridge 402 |

**DONNA SUMMER**
born LaDonna Gaines on 12/31/48 in Boston, Massachusetts - also see Barbra Streisand

| DATE | POS | WKS | ARTIST—Record Title | LABEL & NO. |
|------|-----|-----|---------------------|-------------|
| 12/20/75 + | 2 (2) | 14 | ● 1. **Love To Love You Baby** | Oasis 401 |
| 9/03/77 | 6 | 14 | ● 2. **I Feel Love** | Casablanca 884 |
| 1/28/78 | 37 | 3 | 3. I Love You | Casablanca 907 |
| 6/03/78 | 3 | 14 | ● 4. **Last Dance** <br> from the film "Thank God It's Friday" | Casablanca 926 |
| 9/30/78 | 1 (3) | 15 | ● 5. **Mac Arthur Park** | Casablanca 939 |
| 1/20/79 | 4 | 14 | ● 6. **Heaven Knows** <br> with Brooklyn Dreams | Casablanca 959 |
| 4/28/79 | 1 (3) | 17 | ★ 7. **Hot Stuff** | Casablanca 978 |
| 6/09/79 | 1 (5) | 15 | ★ 8. **Bad Girls** | Casablanca 988 |
| 9/15/79 | 2 (2) | 14 | ● 9. **Dim All The Lights** | Casablanca 2201 |
| 1/26/80 | 5 | 12 | ● 10. **On The Radio** | Casablanca 2236 |
| 9/27/80 | 3 | 13 | ● 11. **The Wanderer** | Geffen 49563 |
| 10/11/80 | 36 | 3 | 12. Walk Away | Casablanca 2300 |
| 1/10/81 | 33 | 3 | 13. Cold Love | Geffen 49634 |
| 3/28/81 | 40 | 2 | 14. Who Do You Think You're Foolin' | Geffen 49664 |
| 7/17/82 | 10 | 11 | 15. **Love Is In Control (Finger On The Trigger)** | Geffen 29982 |
| 2/05/83 | 33 | 6 | 16. The Woman In Me | Geffen 29805 |
| 6/18/83 | 3 | 17 | 17. **She Works Hard For The Money** | Mercury 812370 |
| 9/01/84 | 21 | 8 | 18. There Goes My Baby <br> revival of the Drifters 1959 hit | Geffen 29291 |

**SUNNY & The Sunglows**
San Antonio, Texas band led by Sunny Ozuna

| DATE | POS | WKS | ARTIST—Record Title | LABEL & NO. |
|------|-----|-----|---------------------|-------------|
| 9/28/63 | 11 | 9 | 1. Talk To Me | Tear Drop 3014 |

**SUNNYSIDERS**

| DATE | POS | WKS | ARTIST—Record Title | LABEL & NO. |
|------|-----|-----|---------------------|-------------|
| 5/21/55 | 12 | 10 | 1. Hey, Mr. Banjo | Kapp 113 |

| DATE | POS | WKS | ARTIST—Record Title | LABEL & NO. |
|------|-----|-----|---------------------|-------------|
| | | | **SUNSHINE COMPANY** Mary Nance, lead singer of Southern California quintet | |
| 11/18/67 | 36 | 3 | 1. Back On The Street Again | Imperial 66260 |
| | | | **SUPERTRAMP** British rock quintet: Rick Davies (vocals/keyboards), Roger Hodgson (guitar), John Helliwell (sax), Dougie Thomson (bass), & Bob Benberg (drums) | |
| 5/17/75 | 35 | 2 | 1. Bloody Well Right | A&M 1660 |
| 7/02/77 | 15 | 11 | 2. Give A Little Bit | A&M 1938 |
| 4/28/79 | 6 | 13 | 3. **The Logical Song** | A&M 2128 |
| 8/04/79 | 15 | 8 | 4. Goodbye Stranger | A&M 2162 |
| 11/03/79 | 10 | 11 | 5. **Take The Long Way Home** | A&M 2193 |
| 10/04/80 | 15 | 8 | 6. Dreamer | A&M 2269 |
| 10/30/82 | 11 | 11 | 7. It's Raining Again | A&M 2502 |
| 2/26/83 | 31 | 5 | 8. My Kind Of Lady | A&M 2517 |
| | | | **SUPREMES** Diana Ross, lead singer; Mary Wilson & Florence Ballard (died 2/21/76-32) - Cindy Birdsong replaced Flo in 1967, and Jean Terrell replaced Diana in 1970 | |
| 12/28/63 + | 23 | 7 | 1. When The Lovelight Starts Shining Through His Eyes | Motown 1051 |
| 7/18/64 | 1 (2) | 13 | 2. **Where Did Our Love Go** | Motown 1060 |
| 10/10/64 | 1 (4) | 12 | 3. **Baby Love** | Motown 1066 |
| 11/21/64 | 1 (2) | 13 | 4. **Come See About Me** | Motown 1068 |
| 3/06/65 | 1 (2) | 10 | 5. **Stop! In The Name Of Love** | Motown 1074 |
| 5/08/65 | 1 (1) | 10 | 6. **Back In My Arms Again** | Motown 1075 |
| 8/14/65 | 11 | 7 | 7. Nothing But Heartaches | Motown 1080 |
| 10/30/65 | 1 (2) | 10 | 8. **I Hear A Symphony** | Motown 1083 |
| 1/29/66 | 5 | 8 | 9. **My World Is Empty Without You** | Motown 1089 |
| 5/07/66 | 9 | 7 | 10. **Love Is Like An Itching In My Heart** | Motown 1094 |
| 8/20/66 | 1 (2) | 11 | 11. **You Can't Hurry Love** | Motown 1097 |
| 11/05/66 | 1 (2) | 10 | 12. **You Keep Me Hangin' On** | Motown 1101 |
| 2/04/67 | 1 (1) | 10 | 13. **Love Is Here And Now You're Gone** | Motown 1103 |
| 4/15/67 | 1 (1) | 10 | 14. **The Happening** DIANA ROSS & THE SUPREMES: | Motown 1107 |
| 8/19/67 | 2 (2) | 10 | 15. **Reflections** | Motown 1111 |
| 11/25/67 | 9 | 6 | 16. **In And Out Of Love** | Motown 1116 |
| 4/06/68 | 28 | 5 | 17. Forever Came Today | Motown 1122 |
| 7/06/68 | 30 | 3 | 18. Some Things You Never Get Used To | Motown 1126 |
| 10/26/68 | 1 (2) | 15 | 19. **Love Child** | Motown 1135 |
| 2/01/69 | 10 | 7 | 20. **I'm Livin' In Shame** | Motown 1139 |
| 4/26/69 | 27 | 5 | 21. The Composer | Motown 1146 |
| 6/14/69 | 31 | 4 | 22. No Matter What Sign You Are | Motown 1148 |
| 11/15/69 | 1 (1) | 15 | 23. **Someday We'll Be Together** SUPREMES: | Motown 1156 |
| 3/14/70 | 10 | 10 | 24. **Up The Ladder To The Roof** | Motown 1162 |
| 8/01/70 | 21 | 8 | 25. Everybody's Got The Right To Love | Motown 1167 |
| 11/21/70 | 7 | 12 | 26. **Stoned Love** | Motown 1172 |

| DATE | POS | WKS | ARTIST—Record Title | LABEL & NO. |
|------|-----|-----|---------------------|-------------|
| 5/22/71 | 16 | 8 | 27. Nathan Jones | Motown 1182 |
| 1/29/72 | 16 | 9 | 28. Floy Joy | Motown 1195 |
| 6/03/72 | 37 | 3 | 29. Automatically Sunshine | Motown 1200 |
| 8/07/76 | 40 | 1 | 30. I'm Gonna Let My Heart Do The Walking | Motown 1391 |
| | | | **SUPREMES & FOUR TOPS** | |
| 12/12/70 + | 14 | 8 | 1. River Deep - Mountain High | Motown 1173 |
| | | | **SUPREMES & TEMPTATIONS** | |
| 12/14/68 + | 2 (2) | 12 | 1. **I'm Gonna Make You Love Me** | Motown 1137 |
| 3/22/69 | 25 | 6 | 2. I'll Try Something New | Motown 1142 |
| | | | **SURFARIS** | |
| | | | surf band from Glendora, California | |
| 7/06/63 | 2 (1) | 10 | 1. **Wipe Out [I]** | Dot 16479 |
| 8/27/66 | 16 | 10 | 2. Wipe Out [I-R] | Dot 144 |
| | | | **SURVIVOR** | |
| | | | midwest rock quintet led by Dave Bickler & Jim Peterik | |
| 11/21/81 | 33 | 4 | 1. Poor Man's Son | Scotti Br. 02560 |
| 6/26/82 | 1 (6) | 18 | ★ 2. **Eye Of The Tiger** <br> from the film "Rocky III" | Scotti Br. 02912 |
| 10/16/82 | 17 | 7 | 3. American Heartbeat | Scotti Br. 03213 |
| 10/20/84 | 13 | 13 | 4. **I Can't Hold Back** | Scotti Br. 04603 |
| | | | **BILLY SWAN** | |
| 10/26/74 | 1 (2) | 12 | ● 1. **I Can Help** | Monument 8621 |
| | | | **BETTYE SWANN** | |
| | | | soul singer from Louisiana - real name: Betty Champion | |
| 7/01/67 | 21 | 7 | 1. Make Me Yours | Money 126 |
| 4/19/69 | 38 | 2 | 2. Don't Touch Me | Capitol 2382 |
| | | | **SWEATHOG** | |
| 12/11/71 | 33 | 4 | 1. Hallelujah | Columbia 45492 |
| | | | **SWEET** | |
| | | | English rock band - Brian Connolly, lead singer | |
| 3/17/73 | 3 | 15 | ● 1. **Little Willy** | Bell 45251 |
| 8/02/75 | 5 | 14 | 2. **Ballroom Blitz** | Capitol 4055 |
| 11/22/75 + | 5 | 11 | ● 3. **Fox On The Run** | Capitol 4157 |
| 3/06/76 | 20 | 7 | 4. Action | Capitol 4220 |
| 4/15/78 | 8 | 14 | 5. **Love Is Like Oxygen** | Capitol 4549 |
| | | | **SWEET INSPIRATIONS** | |
| | | | studio vocal group led by Cissy Houston | |
| 3/30/68 | 18 | 10 | 1. Sweet Inspiration | Atlantic 2476 |
| | | | **SWEET SENSATION** | |
| | | | 8-man British soul band - Marcel King, lead singer | |
| 2/15/75 | 14 | 8 | 1. Sad Sweet Dreamer | Pye 71002 |
| | | | **RACHEL SWEET - see REX SMITH** | |

| DATE | POS | WKS | ARTIST—Record Title | LABEL & NO. |
|---|---|---|---|---|
| | | | **SWINGING BLUE JEANS** | |
| | | | rock quartet from Liverpool, England | |
| 3/28/64 | 24 | 5 | 1. Hippy Hippy Shake | Imperial 66021 |
| | | | **SWINGIN' MEDALLIONS** | |
| | | | 8-man rock band from South Carolina | |
| 6/04/66 | 17 | 6 | 1. Double Shot (Of My Baby's Love) | Smash 2033 |
| | | | **SWITCH** | |
| | | | 6-member soul/funk band from Detroit, discovered by Jermaine Jackson | |
| 12/02/78 | 36 | 3 | 1. There'll Never Be | Gordy 7159 |
| | | | **SYLVERS** | |
| | | | Memphis family of 9 brothers and sisters | |
| 3/13/76 | 1 (1) | 15 | ● 1. **Boogie Fever** | Capitol 4179 |
| 11/13/76 + | 5 | 17 | ● 2. **Hot Line** | Capitol 4336 |
| 5/21/77 | 17 | 10 | 3. High School Dance | Capitol 4405 |
| | | | **FOSTER SYLVERS** | |
| | | | member of The Sylvers (age 11 in '73) | |
| 6/30/73 | 22 | 8 | 1. Misdemeanor | MGM 14580 |
| | | | **SYLVESTER** | |
| | | | San Francisco disco star Sylvester James | |
| 9/30/78 | 19 | 10 | 1. Dance (Disco Heat) | Fantasy 827 |
| 2/17/79 | 36 | 3 | 2. You Make Me Feel (Mighty Real) | Fantasy 846 |
| 5/05/79 | 40 | 2 | 3. I (Who Have Nothing) | Fantasy 855 |
| | | | **SYLVIA** | |
| | | | Sylvia Kirby Allen from Kokomo, Indiana | |
| 10/09/82 | 15 | 9 | ● 1. **Nobody** | RCA 13223 |
| | | | **SYLVIA** | |
| | | | Sylvia Robinson of Mickey & Sylvia | |
| 4/21/73 | 3 | 13 | ● 1. **Pillow Talk** | Vibration 521 |
| | | | **SYLVIA SYMS** | |
| 6/16/56 | 20 | 2 | 1. I Could Have Danced All Night | Decca 29903 |
| | | | from the musical "My Fair Lady" | |
| 9/01/56 | 21 | 3 | 2. English Muffins And Irish Stew | Decca 29969 |
| | | | **SYNDICATE OF SOUND** | |
| | | | rock quintet from San Jose, California | |
| 6/25/66 | 8 | 6 | 1. **Little Girl** | Bell 640 |
| | | | **SYREETA - see BILLY PRESTON** | |
| | | | **TACO** | |
| | | | Taco Ockerse - Indonesian/Dutch | |
| 7/23/83 | 4 | 14 | ● 1. **Puttin' On The Ritz** | RCA 13574 |
| | | | written in 1929 by Irving Berlin | |
| | | | **TALK TALK** | |
| | | | rock quartet from Britain - Mark Hollis, lead singer | |
| 4/21/84 | 31 | 10 | 1. It's My Life | EMI America 8195 |

| DATE | POS | WKS | ARTIST—Record Title | LABEL & NO. |
|------|-----|-----|---------------------|-------------|
| | | | **TALKING HEADS** | |
| | | | New York City new-wave quartet led by David Byrne - also see Tom Tom Club | |
| 12/23/78 + | 26 | 9 | 1. Take Me To The River | Sire 1032 |
| 9/03/83 | 9 | 11 | 2. **Burning Down The House** | Sire 29565 |
| | | | **TAMS** | |
| | | | Atlanta soul quintet | |
| 1/18/64 | 9 | 9 | 1. **What Kind Of Fool (Do You Think I Am)** | ABC-Para. 10502 |
| | | | **NORMA TANEGA** | |
| 3/19/66 | 22 | 6 | 1. Walkin' My Cat Named Dog | New Voice 807 |
| | | | **TARRIERS** | |
| | | | movie actor Alan Arkin was an original member - also see Vince Martin | |
| 12/22/56 + | 4 | 16 | 1. **The Banana Boat Song** | Glory 249 |
| | | | **TASTE OF HONEY** | |
| | | | Janice Marie Johnson & Hazel Payne | |
| 7/22/78 | 1 (3) | 17 | ★ 1. **Boogie Oogie Oogie** | Capitol 4565 |
| 4/11/81 | 3 | 16 | ● 2. **Sukiyaki** | Capitol 4953 |
| | | | **TAVARES** | |
| | | | five Tavares brothers from New Bedford, Massachusetts | |
| 11/03/73 | 35 | 3 | 1. Check It Out | Capitol 3674 |
| 5/17/75 | 25 | 5 | 2. Remember What I Told You To Forget | Capitol 4010 |
| 8/23/75 | 10 | 13 | 3. **It Only Takes A Minute** | Capitol 4111 |
| 7/10/76 | 15 | 12 | ● 4. Heaven Must Be Missing An Angel | Capitol 4270 |
| 12/11/76 | 34 | 2 | 5. Don't Take Away The Music | Capitol 4348 |
| 4/23/77 | 22 | 7 | 6. Whodunit | Capitol 4398 |
| 4/15/78 | 32 | 4 | 7. More Than A Woman<br>from the film "Saturday Night Fever" | Capitol 4500 |
| 11/20/82 | 33 | 9 | 8. A Penny For Your Thoughts | RCA 13292 |
| | | | **BOBBY TAYLOR & THE VANCOUVERS** | |
| | | | Thomas Chong (of Cheech & Chong) was lead guitarist | |
| 5/18/68 | 29 | 5 | 1. Does Your Mama Know About Me | Gordy 7069 |
| | | | **JAMES TAYLOR** | |
| | | | born on 3/12/48 in Boston - married to Carly Simon ('72-'82) - also see Carly Simon and Art Garfunkel | |
| 9/26/70 | 3 | 14 | 1. **Fire And Rain** | Warner 7423 |
| 3/20/71 | 37 | 1 | 2. Country Road | Warner 7460 |
| 6/19/71 | 1 (1) | 12 | ● 3. **You've Got A Friend** | Warner 7498 |
| 10/16/71 | 31 | 5 | 4. Long Ago And Far Away<br>backing vocals on above 2 by Joni Mitchell | Warner 7521 |
| 12/16/72 + | 14 | 9 | 5. Don't Let Me Be Lonely Tonight | Warner 7655 |
| 7/19/75 | 5 | 10 | 6. **How Sweet It Is (To Be Loved By You)** | Warner 8109 |
| 8/07/76 | 22 | 8 | 7. Shower The People | Warner 8222 |
| 7/09/77 | 4 | 13 | 8. **Handy Man** | Columbia 10557 |
| 11/05/77 | 20 | 9 | 9. Your Smiling Face | Columbia 10602 |
| 6/30/79 | 28 | 5 | 10. Up On The Roof | Columbia 11005 |

| DATE | POS | WKS | ARTIST—Record Title | LABEL & NO. |
|---|---|---|---|---|
| | | | **JAMES TAYLOR & J.D. SOUTHER** | |
| 3/14/81 | 11 | 10 | 1. Her Town Too | Columbia 60514 |
| | | | **JOHNNIE TAYLOR** | |
| | | | replaced Sam Cooke as lead singer of the Soul Stirrers gospel group | |
| 11/02/68 | 5 | 13 | ● 1. **Who's Making Love** | Stax 0009 |
| 1/25/69 | 20 | 8 | 2. Take Care Of Your Homework | Stax 0023 |
| 5/31/69 | 36 | 5 | 3. Testify (I Wonna) | Stax 0033 |
| 7/18/70 | 37 | 2 | 4. Steal Away | Stax 0068 |
| 11/14/70 | 39 | 2 | 5. I Am Somebody, Part II | Stax 0078 |
| 2/13/71 | 28 | 5 | 6. Jody's Got Your Girl And Gone | Stax 0085 |
| 7/14/73 | 11 | 12 | ● 7. I Believe In You (You Believe In Me) | Stax 0161 |
| 10/27/73 | 15 | 8 | 8. Cheaper To Keep Her | Stax 0176 |
| 3/16/74 | 34 | 2 | 9. We're Getting Careless With Our Love | Stax 0193 |
| 3/06/76 | 1 (4) | 13 | ★ 10. **Disco Lady** | Columbia 10281 |
| 6/26/76 | 33 | 3 | 11. Somebody's Gettin' It | Columbia 10334 |
| | | | **LITTLE JOHNNY TAYLOR** | |
| 9/14/63 | 19 | 8 | 1. Part Time Love | Galaxy 722 |
| | | | **LIVINGSTON TAYLOR** | |
| | | | James Taylor's younger brother | |
| 12/16/78 + | 30 | 5 | 1. I Will Be In Love With You | Epic 50604 |
| 9/13/80 | 38 | 2 | 2. First Time Love | Epic 50894 |
| | | | **R. DEAN TAYLOR** | |
| | | | Canadian | |
| 9/19/70 | 5 | 13 | 1. **Indiana Wants Me** | Rare Earth 5013 |
| | | | **T-BONES** | |
| | | | a Joe Saraceno studio production | |
| 12/25/65 + | 3 | 11 | 1. **No Matter What Shape (Your Stomach's In) [I]** | Liberty 55836 |
| | | | tune is from an "Alka Seltzer" jingle | |
| | | | **TECHNIQUES** | |
| 11/25/57 | 29 | 2 | 1. Hey! Little Girl | Roulette 4030 |
| | | | **TEDDY BEARS** | |
| | | | Los Angeles trio featuring producer Phil Spector | |
| 10/13/58 | 1 (3) | 18 | 1. **To Know Him, Is To Love Him** | Dore 503 |
| | | | **TEE SET** | |
| | | | Dutch quintet | |
| 2/07/70 | 5 | 10 | 1. **Ma Belle Amie** | Colossus 107 |
| | | | **TEEGARDEN & VAN WINKLE** | |
| | | | David Teegarden & Skip Knape | |
| 10/17/70 | 22 | 5 | 1. God, Love And Rock & Roll | Westbound 170 |
| | | | **TEEN QUEENS** | |
| | | | sisters Betty & Rosie Collins | |
| 3/10/56 | 14 | 8 | 1. Eddie My Love | RPM 453 |

| DATE | POS | WKS | ARTIST—Record Title | LABEL & NO. |
|---|---|---|---|---|
| | | | **NINO TEMPO & APRIL STEVENS** | |
| | | | brother & sister | |
| 10/05/63 | **1** (1) | 12 | 1. **Deep Purple** | Atco 6273 |
| 12/28/63 + | **11** | 7 | 2. Whispering | Atco 6281 |
| 3/14/64 | **32** | 3 | 3. Stardust | Atco 6286 |
| 10/01/66 | **26** | 5 | 4. All Strung Out | White Whale 236 |
| | | | **TEMPOS** | |
| | | | Pittsburgh quartet - Mike Lazo, lead singer | |
| 8/10/59 | **23** | 6 | 1. See You In September | Climax 102 |
| | | | **TEMPTATIONS** | |
| | | | white group | |
| 5/09/60 | **29** | 3 | 1. Barbara | Goldisc 3001 |
| | | | **TEMPTATIONS** | |
| | | | original group: David Ruffin, Eddie Kendricks, Otis Williams, Mel Franklin & Paul Williams (died 8/17/73-34) - David left in '68 & Eddie in '71 - also see the Supremes | |
| 3/21/64 | **11** | 8 | 1. The Way You Do The Things You Do | Gordy 7028 |
| 7/04/64 | **33** | 4 | 2. I'll Be In Trouble | Gordy 7032 |
| 9/26/64 | **26** | 6 | 3. Girl (Why You Wanna Make Me Blue) | Gordy 7035 |
| 1/30/65 | **1** (1) | 11 | 4. **My Girl** | Gordy 7038 |
| 4/17/65 | **18** | 7 | 5. It's Growing | Gordy 7040 |
| 8/07/65 | **17** | 7 | 6. Since I Lost My Baby | Gordy 7043 |
| 11/06/65 | **13** | 6 | 7. My Baby | Gordy 7047 |
| 3/26/66 | **29** | 3 | 8. Get Ready | Gordy 7049 |
| 6/11/66 | **13** | 10 | 9. Ain't Too Proud To Beg | Gordy 7054 |
| 9/03/66 | **3** | 9 | 10. **Beauty Is Only Skin Deep** | Gordy 7055 |
| 12/03/66 | **8** | 8 | 11. **(I Know) I'm Losing You** | Gordy 7057 |
| 5/13/67 | **8** | 8 | 12. **All I Need** | Gordy 7061 |
| 8/12/67 | **6** | 9 | 13. **You're My Everything** | Gordy 7063 |
| 10/21/67 | **14** | 8 | 14. (Loneliness Made Me Realize) It's You That I Need | Gordy 7065 |
| 1/27/68 | **4** | 11 | 15. **I Wish It Would Rain** | Gordy 7068 |
| 5/18/68 | **13** | 8 | 16. I Could Never Love Another (After Loving You) | Gordy 7072 |
| 8/17/68 | **26** | 5 | 17. Please Return Your Love To Me | Gordy 7074 |
| 11/23/68 + | **6** | 11 | 18. **Cloud Nine** | Gordy 7081 |
| 2/22/69 | **6** | 11 | 19. **Run Away Child, Running Wild** | Gordy 7084 |
| 5/31/69 | **20** | 6 | 20. Don't Let The Joneses Get You Down | Gordy 7086 |
| 8/30/69 | **1** (2) | 15 | 21. **I Can't Get Next To You** | Gordy 7093 |
| 1/24/70 | **7** | 10 | 22. **Psychedelic Shack** | Gordy 7096 |
| 6/06/70 | **3** | 13 | 23. **Ball Of Confusion (That's What The World Is Today)** | Gordy 7099 |
| 10/17/70 | **33** | 4 | 24. Ungena Za Ulimwengu (Unite The World) | Gordy 7102 |
| 2/20/71 | **1** (2) | 13 | 25. **Just My Imagination (Running Away With Me)** | Gordy 7105 |
| 11/20/71 | **18** | 8 | 26. Superstar (Remember How You Got Where You Are) | Gordy 7111 |
| 3/18/72 | **30** | 4 | 27. Take A Look Around | Gordy 7115 |
| 10/28/72 | **1** (1) | 12 | 28. **Papa Was A Rollin' Stone** | Gordy 7121 |

| DATE | POS | WKS | ARTIST—Record Title | LABEL & NO. |
|---|---|---|---|---|
| 3/10/73 | 7 | 11 | 29. **Masterpiece** | Gordy 7126 |
| 7/07/73 | 40 | 2 | 30. The Plastic Man | Gordy 7129 |
| 9/08/73 | 35 | 4 | 31. Hey Girl (I Like Your Style) | Gordy 7131 |
| 1/12/74 | 27 | 4 | 32. Let Your Hair Down | Gordy 7133 |
| 2/01/75 | 40 | 1 | 33. Happy People | Gordy 7138 |
| 4/19/75 | 26 | 9 | 34. Shakey Ground | Gordy 7142 |
| 8/23/75 | 37 | 2 | 35. Glasshouse | Gordy 7144 |
| | | | **10cc** | |
| | | | English art-rock group which evolved from Hotlegs | |
| 6/14/75 | 2 (3) | 11 | 1. **I'm Not In Love** | Mercury 73678 |
| 1/29/77 | 5 | 14 | ● 2. **The Things We Do For Love** | Mercury 73875 |
| 6/25/77 | 40 | 1 | 3. People In Love | Mercury 73917 |
| | | | **TEN YEARS AFTER** | |
| | | | British blues-rock group led by guitarist/vocalist Alvin Lee | |
| 11/20/71 | 40 | 2 | 1. I'd Love To Change The World | Columbia 45457 |
| | | | **JOE TEX** | |
| | | | born Joseph Arrington in Rogers, Texas - died on 8/13/82 (49) | |
| 1/02/65 | 5 | 8 | 1. **Hold What You've Got** | Dial 4001 |
| 10/16/65 | 23 | 5 | 2. I Want To (Do Everything For You) | Dial 4016 |
| 1/01/66 | 29 | 4 | 3. A Sweet Woman Like You | Dial 4022 |
| 6/18/66 | 39 | 1 | 4. S.Y.S.L.J.F.M. (The Letter Song) | Dial 4028 |
| 4/08/67 | 35 | 3 | 5. Show Me | Dial 4055 |
| 11/25/67 | 10 | 10 | ● 6. **Skinny Legs And All** | Dial 4063 |
| 3/02/68 | 33 | 3 | 7. Men Are Gettin' Scarce | Dial 4069 |
| 2/26/72 | 2 (2) | 16 | ● 8. **I Gotcha** | Dial 1010 |
| 4/23/77 | 12 | 10 | ● 9. **Ain't Gonna Bump No More (With No Big Fat Woman)** | Epic 50313 |
| | | | **THEM** | |
| | | | Irish rock quintet led by Van Morrison | |
| 6/26/65 | 24 | 6 | 1. Here Comes The Night | Parrot 9749 |
| 12/04/65 | 33 | 2 | 2. Mystic Eyes [I] | Parrot 9796 |
| | | | **THIN LIZZY** | |
| | | | Irish rock quartet led by Phil Lynott | |
| 6/05/76 | 12 | 9 | 1. The Boys Are Back In Town | Mercury 73786 |
| | | | **THINK** | |
| | | | studio group assembled by producer Lou Stallman | |
| 1/01/72 | 23 | 5 | 1. Once You Understand [N] | Laurie 3583 |
| | | | **38 SPECIAL** | |
| | | | Donnie Van Zant, leader - younger brother of Lynyrd Skynyrd's Ronnie Van Zant | |
| 4/18/81 | 27 | 6 | 1. Hold On Loosely | A&M 2316 |
| 5/22/82 | 10 | 12 | 2. **Caught Up In You** | A&M 2412 |
| 10/02/82 | 38 | 2 | 3. You Keep Runnin' Away | A&M 2431 |
| 12/03/83 + | 19 | 9 | 4. If I'd Been The One | A&M 2594 |
| 2/18/84 | 20 | 8 | 5. Back Where You Belong | A&M 2615 |
| 10/27/84 | 25 | 5 | 6. Teacher Teacher<br>from the film "Teachers" | Capitol 5405 |

| DATE | POS | WKS | ARTIST—Record Title | LABEL & NO. |
|---|---|---|---|---|
| | | | **B.J. THOMAS** | |
| | | | born Billy Joe Thomas on 8/7/42 in Hugo, Oklahoma | |
| 3/12/66 | 8 | 10 | 1. **I'm So Lonesome I Could Cry** | Scepter 12129 |
| | | | with the Triumphs (also on #3) | |
| 6/04/66 | 22 | 5 | 2. Mama | Scepter 12139 |
| 7/23/66 | 34 | 4 | 3. Billy And Sue | Hickory 1395 |
| 8/03/68 | 28 | 7 | 4. The Eyes Of A New York Woman | Scepter 12219 |
| 12/14/68 + | 5 | 12 | ● 5. **Hooked On A Feeling** | Scepter 12230 |
| 11/22/69 + | 1 (4) | 19 | ● 6. **Raindrops Keep Fallin' On My Head** | Scepter 12265 |
| | | | from the film "Butch Cassidy & The Sundance Kid" | |
| 4/11/70 | 26 | 6 | 7. Everybody's Out Of Town | Scepter 12277 |
| 7/11/70 | 9 | 10 | 8. **I Just Can't Help Believing** | Scepter 12283 |
| 1/09/71 | 38 | 3 | 9. Most Of All | Scepter 12299 |
| 3/13/71 | 16 | 9 | 10. No Love At All | Scepter 12307 |
| 8/14/71 | 34 | 3 | 11. Mighty Clouds Of Joy | Scepter 12320 |
| 2/26/72 | 15 | 9 | 12. Rock And Roll Lullaby | Scepter 12344 |
| | | | featuring Duane Eddy on guitar | |
| 3/01/75 | 1 (1) | 14 | ● 13. **(Hey Won't You Play) Another Somebody Done Somebody Wrong Song** | ABC 12054 |
| 8/06/77 | 17 | 10 | 14. Don't Worry Baby | MCA 40735 |
| | | | **CARLA THOMAS** | |
| | | | daughter of Rufus Thomas - also see Otis & Carla | |
| 2/20/61 | 10 | 10 | 1. **Gee Whiz (Look At His Eyes)** | Atlantic 2086 |
| 9/24/66 | 14 | 10 | 2. B-A-B-Y | Stax 195 |
| | | | **IAN THOMAS** | |
| | | | Canadian | |
| 12/29/73 + | 34 | 3 | 1. Painted Ladies | Janus 224 |
| | | | **IRMA THOMAS** | |
| | | | R&B vocalist from Panchatla, Louisiana | |
| 4/25/64 | 17 | 7 | 1. Wish Someone Would Care | Imperial 66013 |
| | | | **RUFUS THOMAS** | |
| | | | R&B singer, dance creator, disc jockey | |
| 11/02/63 | 10 | 9 | 1. **Walking The Dog** | Stax 140 |
| 2/28/70 | 28 | 8 | 2. Do The Funky Chicken | Stax 0059 |
| 1/23/71 | 25 | 8 | 3. (Do The) Push And Pull, Part I | Stax 0079 |
| 9/18/71 | 31 | 4 | 4. The Breakdown (Part I) | Stax 0098 |
| | | | **TIMMY THOMAS** | |
| | | | native of Evansville, Indiana | |
| 12/23/72 + | 3 | 11 | 1. **Why Can't We Live Together** | Glades 1703 |
| | | | **THOMPSON TWINS** | |
| | | | Tom Bailey (English), Alannah Currie (New Zealand), Joe Leeway (South Africa) | |
| 3/12/83 | 30 | 5 | 1. Lies | Arista 1024 |
| 2/25/84 | 3 | 15 | 2. **Hold Me Now** | Arista 9164 |
| 6/09/84 | 11 | 9 | 3. Doctor! Doctor! | Arista 9209 |
| | | | **CHRIS THOMPSON & Night** | |
| | | | member of Manfred Mann ('76-'79) - also see Night | |
| 10/20/79 | 17 | 8 | 1. If You Remember Me | Planet 45909 |

| DATE | POS | WKS | ARTIST—Record Title | LABEL & NO. |
|------|-----|-----|---------------------|-------------|
| | | | **KAY THOMPSON** | |
| 3/17/56 | 39 | 2 | 1. Eloise [N] | Cadence 3 |
| | | | **SUE THOMPSON** | |
| | | | born Eva Sue McKee on 7/19/26 in Nevada, Missouri | |
| 9/25/61 | 5 | 11 | 1. **Sad Movies (Make Me Cry)** | Hickory 1153 |
| 1/13/62 | 3 | 11 | 2. **Norman** | Hickory 1159 |
| 7/21/62 | 31 | 5 | 3. Have A Good Time | Hickory 1174 |
| 10/20/62 | 17 | 6 | 4. James (Hold The Ladder Steady) | Hickory 1183 |
| 2/06/65 | 23 | 4 | 5. Paper Tiger | Hickory 1284 |
| | | | **ALI THOMSON** | |
| | | | Scottish - younger brother of Supertramp's Dougie Thomson | |
| 7/12/80 | 15 | 9 | 1. Take A Little Rhythm | A&M 2243 |
| | | | **THREE DEGREES** | |
| | | | Fayette Pinkney, Sheila Ferguson & Valerie Holiday - also see MFSB | |
| 7/25/70 | 29 | 4 | 1. Maybe | Roulette 7079 |
| 10/19/74 | 2 (1) | 13 | ● 2. **When Will I See You Again** | Phil. Int. 3550 |
| | | | **THREE DOG NIGHT** | |
| | | | Danny Hutton, Chuck Negron & Cory Wells | |
| 3/29/69 | 29 | 4 | 1. Try A Little Tenderness | Dunhill 4177 |
| 5/31/69 | 5 | 12 | ● 2. **One** | Dunhill 4191 |
| 8/16/69 | 4 | 12 | 3. **Easy To Be Hard** | Dunhill 4203 |
| 11/08/69 | 10 | 12 | 4. **Eli's Coming** | Dunhill 4215 |
| 3/07/70 | 15 | 8 | 5. Celebrate | Dunhill 4229 |
| 6/06/70 | 1 (2) | 13 | ● 6. **Mama Told Me (Not To Come)** | Dunhill 4239 |
| 9/12/70 | 15 | 8 | 7. Out In The Country | Dunhill 4250 |
| 12/05/70 + | 19 | 9 | 8. One Man Band | Dunhill 4262 |
| 3/27/71 | 1 (6) | 15 | ● 9. **Joy To The World** | Dunhill 4272 |
| 7/17/71 | 7 | 11 | 10. **Liar** | Dunhill 4282 |
| 11/20/71 | 4 | 10 | ● 11. **An Old Fashioned Love Song** | Dunhill 4294 |
| 1/08/72 | 5 | 10 | 12. **Never Been To Spain** | Dunhill 4299 |
| 4/01/72 | 12 | 8 | 13. The Family Of Man | Dunhill 4306 |
| 8/26/72 | 1 (1) | 9 | ● 14. **Black & White** | Dunhill 4317 |
| 12/09/72 + | 19 | 9 | 15. Pieces Of April | Dunhill 4331 |
| 6/02/73 | 3 | 13 | ● 16. **Shambala** | Dunhill 4352 |
| 11/17/73 | 17 | 6 | 17. Let Me Serenade You | Dunhill 4370 |
| 4/13/74 | 4 | 12 | ● 18. **The Show Must Go On** | Dunhill 4382 |
| 7/13/74 | 16 | 8 | 19. Sure As I'm Sittin' Here | Dunhill 15001 |
| 11/02/74 | 33 | 3 | 20. Play Something Sweet (Brickyard Blues) | Dunhill 15013 |
| 8/09/75 | 32 | 3 | 21. Til The World Ends | ABC 12114 |
| | | | **JOHNNY THUNDER** | |
| 1/05/63 | 4 | 9 | 1. **Loop De Loop** | Diamond 129 |
| | | | **THUNDERCLAP NEWMAN** | |
| | | | British trio: Andy Newman, Speedy Keen, Jimmy McCulloch | |
| 10/25/69 | 37 | 2 | 1. Something In The Air | Track 2656 |
| | | | from the film "The Magic Christian" | |

| DATE | POS | WKS | ARTIST—Record Title | LABEL & NO. |
|---|---|---|---|---|
| | | | **TIERRA** | |
| | | | Los Angeles septet - 3 members were formerly with El Chicano | |
| 12/13/80 + | 18 | 15 | 1. Together | Boardwalk 5702 |
| | | | **JOHNNY TILLOTSON** | |
| | | | born on 4/20/39 in Jacksonville, Florida | |
| 10/24/60 | 2 (1) | 12 | 1. **Poetry In Motion** | Cadence 1384 |
| 2/06/61 | 25 | 5 | 2. Jimmy's Girl | Cadence 1391 |
| 8/28/61 | 7 | 8 | 3. **Without You** | Cadence 1404 |
| 1/20/62 | 35 | 1 | 4. Dreamy Eyes [R] | Cadence 1409 |
| | | | re-entry of 1958 hit (Pos. 63) | |
| 5/19/62 | 3 | 12 | 5. **It Keeps Right On A-Hurtin'** | Cadence 1418 |
| 8/25/62 | 17 | 6 | 6. Send Me The Pillow You Dream On | Cadence 1424 |
| 11/17/62 | 24 | 5 | 7. I Can't Help It (If I'm Still In Love With You) | Cadence 1432 |
| 3/23/63 | 24 | 6 | 8. Out Of My Mind | Cadence 1434 |
| 8/24/63 | 18 | 7 | 9. You Can Never Stop Me Loving You | Cadence 1437 |
| 11/30/63 + | 7 | 10 | 10. **Talk Back Trembling Lips** | MGM 13181 |
| 3/14/64 | 37 | 2 | 11. Worried Guy | MGM 13193 |
| 6/06/64 | 36 | 2 | 12. I Rise, I Fall | MGM 13232 |
| 11/28/64 | 31 | 6 | 13. She Understands Me | MGM 13284 |
| 10/02/65 | 35 | 2 | 14. Heartaches By The Number | MGM 13376 |
| | | | **TIN TIN** | |
| | | | Australian duo: Steve Kipner & Steve Groves | |
| 5/08/71 | 20 | 6 | 1. Toast And Marmalade For Tea | Atco 6794 |
| | | | **TINY TIM** | |
| | | | born Herbert Khaury on 4/12/25 in New York City | |
| 6/08/68 | 17 | 6 | 1. Tip-Toe Thru' The Tulips With Me [N] | Reprise 0679 |
| | | | **TOBY BEAU** | |
| 7/01/78 | 13 | 12 | 1. My Angel Baby | RCA 11250 |
| | | | **ART & DOTTY TODD** | |
| | | | husband and wife from Rhode Island | |
| 4/21/58 | 6 | 11 | 1. **Chanson D'Amour (Song Of Love)** | Era 1064 |
| | | | **NICK TODD** | |
| | | | Pat Boone's younger brother | |
| 2/10/58 | 21 | 2 | 1. At The Hop | Dot 15675 |
| | | | **TOKENS** | |
| | | | Brooklyn quartet - former backup group for Neil Sedaka | |
| 4/24/61 | 15 | 6 | 1. Tonight I Fell In Love | Warwick 615 |
| 11/27/61 | 1 (3) | 13 | ● 2. **The Lion Sleeps Tonight** | RCA 7954 |
| 4/09/66 | 30 | 5 | 3. I Hear Trumpets Blow | B.T. Puppy 518 |
| 5/20/67 | 36 | 2 | 4. Portrait Of My Love | Warner 5900 |
| | | | **TOM TOM CLUB** | |
| | | | group formed by Chris Frantz & Tina Weymouth of Talking Heads | |
| 4/10/82 | 31 | 4 | 1. Genius Of Love | Sire 49882 |
| | | | **TOMMY TUTONE** | |
| | | | San Francisco rock band led by Tommy Heath | |
| 6/21/80 | 38 | 2 | 1. Angel Say No | Columbia 11278 |
| 3/13/82 | 4 | 16 | 2. **867-5309/Jenny** | Columbia 02646 |

| DATE | POS | WKS | ARTIST—Record Title | LABEL & NO. |
|---|---|---|---|---|
| | | | **OSCAR TONEY, JR.** | |
| 6/17/67 | 23 | 5 | 1. For Your Precious Love | Bell 672 |
| | | | **TONY & JOE** | |
| | | | Tony Savonne & Joe Saraceno | |
| 8/04/58 | 33 | 1 | 1. The Freeze | Era 1075 |
| | | | **MEL TORME** | |
| | | | born Melvin Howard on 9/13/25 in Chicago | |
| 12/15/62 | 36 | 3 | 1. Comin' Home Baby | Atlantic 2165 |
| | | | **TORNADOES** | |
| | | | English quintet | |
| 11/17/62 | 1 (3) | 13 | 1. **Telstar [I]** | London 9561 |
| | | | **MITCHELL TOROK** | |
| 4/29/57 | 25 | 3 | 1. Pledge Of Love | Decca 30230 |
| 8/31/59 | 27 | 6 | 2. Caribbean | Guyden 2018 |
| | | | **TOTO** | |
| | | | Los Angeles-based studio musicians | |
| 11/11/78 + | 5 | 14 | ● 1. **Hold The Line** | Columbia 10830 |
| 2/09/80 | 26 | 8 | 2. 99 | Columbia 11173 |
| 5/08/82 | 2 (5) | 18 | 3. **Rosanna** | Columbia 02811 |
| 9/11/82 | 30 | 5 | 4. Make Believe | Columbia 03143 |
| 11/20/82 + | 1 (1) | 16 | 5. **Africa** | Columbia 03335 |
| 3/26/83 | 10 | 12 | 6. **I Won't Hold You Back** | Columbia 03597 |
| | | | **TOWER OF POWER** | |
| | | | brass oriented Oakland-area R&B/funk band | |
| 8/26/72 | 29 | 5 | 1. You're Still A Young Man | Warner 7612 |
| 6/16/73 | 17 | 11 | 2. So Very Hard To Go | Warner 7687 |
| 8/24/74 | 26 | 4 | 3. Don't Change Horses (In The Middle Of A Stream) | Warner 7828 |
| | | | **ED TOWNSEND** | |
| 4/28/58 | 13 | 13 | 1. For Your Love | Capitol 3926 |
| | | | **PETE TOWNSHEND** | |
| | | | English - lead guitarist/songwriter of The Who | |
| 7/05/80 | 9 | 12 | 1. **Let My Love Open The Door** | Atco 7217 |
| | | | **TOYS** | |
| | | | New York trio: Barbara Harris, Barbara Parritt, June Monteiro | |
| 10/02/65 | 2 (3) | 11 | ● 1. **A Lover's Concerto** | DynoVoice 209 |
| | | | adapted from Bach: Minuet In G | |
| 1/01/66 | 18 | 6 | 2. Attack | DynoVoice 214 |
| | | | **TRADE WINDS** | |
| | | | also see Innocence | |
| 2/27/65 | 32 | 4 | 1. New York's A Lonely Town | Red Bird 020 |
| | | | **TRAMMPS** | |
| | | | originally session musicians and singers from Philadelphia | |
| 2/21/76 | 35 | 4 | 1. Hold Back The Night | Buddah 507 |
| 6/05/76 | 27 | 5 | 2. That's Where The Happy People Go | Atlantic 3306 |
| 3/25/78 | 11 | 13 | 3. Disco Inferno | Atlantic 3389 |
| | | | in the film "Saturday Night Fever" | |

| DATE | POS | WKS | ARTIST—Record Title | LABEL & NO. |
|---|---|---|---|---|
| | | | **TRASHMEN** | |
| | | | Minneapolis/St. Paul surf quartet | |
| 12/28/63 + | 4 | 10 | 1. **Surfin' Bird** | Garrett 4002 |
| 2/29/64 | 30 | 4 | 2. Bird Dance Beat | Garrett 4003 |
| | | | **TRAVIS & BOB** | |
| | | | Travis Pritchett & Bob Weaver | |
| 4/06/59 | 8 | 9 | 1. **Tell Him No** | Sandy 1017 |
| | | | **JOHN TRAVOLTA** | |
| | | | starred in "Saturday Night Fever", "Grease" & "Urban Cowboy" - also see Olivia Newton-John | |
| 6/12/76 | 10 | 10 | 1. **Let Her In** | Midland I. 10623 |
| 11/27/76 | 38 | 2 | 2. Whenever I'm Away From You | Midland I. 10780 |
| 3/19/77 | 34 | 3 | 3. All Strung Out On You | Midland I. 10907 |
| | | | **TREMELOES** | |
| | | | British quartet | |
| 5/06/67 | 13 | 8 | 1. Here Comes My Baby | Epic 10139 |
| 7/15/67 | 11 | 10 | 2. Silence Is Golden | Epic 10184 |
| 10/21/67 | 36 | 4 | 3. Even The Bad Times Are Good | Epic 10233 |
| | | | **T. REX** | |
| | | | British group led by Marc Bolan - died on 9/16/77 (28) | |
| 1/29/72 | 10 | 11 | 1. **Bang A Gong (Get It On)** | Reprise 1032 |
| | | | **TRIUMPH** | |
| | | | Gil Moore, Rik Emmett, & Mike Levine - from Toronto, Canada | |
| 8/25/79 | 38 | 3 | 1. Hold On | RCA 11569 |
| | | | **TROGGS** | |
| | | | British foursome - Reg Presley, lead singer | |
| 7/09/66 | 1 (2) | 9 | 1. **Wild Thing** | Fontana 1548 |
| 9/03/66 | 29 | 2 | 2. With A Girl Like You | Fontana 1552 |
| | | | above 2 also on Atco 6415 | |
| 3/23/68 | 7 | 12 | 3. **Love Is All Around** | Fontana 1607 |
| | | | **DORIS TROY** | |
| | | | backing vocalist for Solomon Burke and Chuck Jackson | |
| 7/06/63 | 10 | 8 | . 1. **Just One Look** | Atlantic 2188 |
| | | | **ANDREA TRUE Connection** | |
| | | | disco singer/actress from Nashville | |
| 4/24/76 | 4 | 16 | ● 1. **More, More, More (Pt. 1)** | Buddah 515 |
| 3/26/77 | 27 | 5 | 2. N.Y., You Got Me Dancing | Buddah 564 |
| | | | **TUBES** | |
| | | | San Francisco theatre rock troupe - Fee Waybill, lead singer | |
| 8/01/81 | 35 | 3 | 1. Don't Want To Wait Anymore | Capitol 5007 |
| 5/07/83 | 10 | 12 | 2. She's A Beauty | Capitol 5217 |
| | | | **TANYA TUCKER** | |
| | | | born on 10/10/58 in Seminole, Texas | |
| 6/07/75 | 37 | 2 | 1. Lizzie And The Rainman | MCA 40402 |

| DATE | POS | WKS | ARTIST—Record Title | LABEL & NO. |
|---|---|---|---|---|
| | | | **TOMMY TUCKER** | |
| | | | died of poisoning on 1/17/82 (48) | |
| 2/29/64 | 11 | 8 | 1. Hi-Heel Sneakers | Checker 1067 |
| | | | **TUNE WEAVERS** | |
| | | | Boston R&B quintet - Margo Sylvia, lead singer | |
| 9/23/57 | 5 | 14 | 1. **Happy, Happy Birthday Baby** | Checker 872 |
| | | | **TURBANS** | |
| | | | Philadelphia R&B quartet - Al Banks, lead singer | |
| 1/14/56 | 33 | 1 | 1. When You Dance | Herald 458 |
| | | | **IKE & TINA TURNER** | |
| | | | R&B/rock duo (married '58-'76) - Ike was an A&R man/ producer/session guitarist in the Fifties | |
| 10/03/60 | 27 | 6 | 1. A Fool In Love | Sue 730 |
| 9/04/61 | 14 | 5 | 2. It's Gonna Work Out Fine | Sue 749 |
| 1/13/62 | 38 | 2 | 3. Poor Fool | Sue 753 |
| 8/08/70 | 34 | 6 | 4. I Want To Take You Higher | Liberty 56177 |
| 2/13/71 | 4 | 11 | ● 5. **Proud Mary** | Liberty 56216 |
| 10/27/73 | 22 | 7 | 6. Nutbush City Limits | United Art. 298 |
| | | | **JESSE LEE TURNER** | |
| 1/26/59 | 20 | 6 | 1. The Little Space Girl [N] | Carlton 496 |
| | | | **SAMMY TURNER** | |
| | | | born on 6/2/32 in Paterson, New Jersey | |
| 7/06/59 | 3 | 14 | 1. **Lavender-Blue** | Big Top 3016 |
| 11/16/59 | 19 | 7 | 2. Always | Big Top 3029 |
| | | | **SPYDER TURNER** | |
| | | | born Dwight Turner in Beckley, West Virginia | |
| 1/14/67 | 12 | 8 | 1. Stand By Me [N] vocal impressions of Jackie Wilson, David Ruffin, Billy Stewart, Smokey Robinson, and Chuck Jackson | MGM 13617 |
| | | | **TINA TURNER** | |
| | | | born Annie Mae Bullock on 11/26/38 in Nutbush, Tennessee | |
| 2/18/84 | 26 | 7 | 1. Let's Stay Together | Capitol 5322 |
| 6/23/84 | 1 (3) | 18 | ● 2. **What's Love Got To Do With It** | Capitol 5354 |
| 10/06/84 | 5 | 13 | 3. **Better Be Good To Me** | Capitol 5387 |
| | | | **TURTLES** | |
| | | | Los Angeles-based pop group featuring Mark Volman & Howard Kaylan (Flo & Eddie) | |
| 8/21/65 | 8 | 8 | 1. **It Ain't Me Babe** | White Whale 222 |
| 11/20/65 | 29 | 4 | 2. Let Me Be | White Whale 224 |
| 2/19/66 | 20 | 9 | 3. You Baby | White Whale 227 |
| 3/04/67 | 1 (3) | 12 | ● 4. **Happy Together** | White Whale 244 |
| 5/27/67 | 3 | 8 | 5. **She'd Rather Be With Me** | White Whale 249 |
| 8/26/67 | 12 | 7 | 6. You Know What I Mean | White Whale 254 |
| 12/02/67 | 14 | 7 | 7. She's My Girl | White Whale 260 |
| 10/12/68 | 6 | 9 | 8. Elenore | White Whale 276 |
| 1/25/69 | 6 | 9 | 9. **You Showed Me** | White Whale 292 |

| DATE | POS | WKS | ARTIST—Record Title | LABEL & NO. |
|------|-----|-----|---------------------|-------------|
| | | | **TUXEDO JUNCTION** | |
| 7/01/78 | 32 | 2 | 1. Chattanooga Choo Choo | Butterfly 1205 |
| | | | **DWIGHT TWILLEY** | |
| | | | rock singer/songwriter from Tulsa, Oklahoma | |
| 6/21/75 | 16 | 8 | 1. I'm On Fire | Shelter 40380 |
| | | | Dwight Twilley Band (with Phil Seymour) | |
| 3/03/84 | 16 | 10 | 2. Girls | EMI America 8196 |
| | | | **TWISTED SISTER** | |
| | | | Long Island, N.Y. heavy-metal quintet - Dee Snider, lead singer | |
| 8/18/84 | 21 | 7 | 1. We're Not Gonna Take It | Atlantic 89641 |
| | | | **CONWAY TWITTY** | |
| | | | born Harold Jenkins on 9/1/33 in Friars Point, Mississippi - Conway had 36 consecutive Top 5 hits on the Country Singles charts ('68-'77) | |
| 9/29/58 | 1 (2) | 17 | 1. **It's Only Make Believe** | MGM 12677 |
| 2/16/59 | 28 | 7 | 2. The Story Of My Love | MGM 12748 |
| 8/24/59 | 29 | 3 | 3. Mona Lisa | MGM 12804 |
| 10/12/59 | 10 | 13 | 4. **Danny Boy** | MGM 12826 |
| 1/18/60 | 6 | 10 | 5. **Lonely Blue Boy** | MGM 12857 |
| 4/25/60 | 26 | 5 | 6. What Am I Living For | MGM 12886 |
| 7/11/60 | 35 | 5 | 7. Is A Blue Bird Blue | MGM 12911 |
| 1/16/61 | 22 | 5 | 8. C'est Si Bon (It's So Good) | MGM 12969 |
| 9/15/73 | 22 | 7 | 9. You've Never Been This Far Before | MCA 40094 |
| | | | **TYCOON** | |
| 4/28/79 | 26 | 5 | 1. Such A Woman | Arista 0398 |
| | | | **BONNIE TYLER** | |
| | | | British songstress | |
| 4/22/78 | 3 | 15 | ● 1. **It's A Heartache** | RCA 11249 |
| 8/13/83 | 1 (4) | 18 | ● 2. **Total Eclipse Of The Heart** | Columbia 03906 |
| 4/07/84 | 34 | 4 | 3. Holding Out For A Hero | Columbia 04370 |
| | | | from the film "Footloose" | |
| | | | **TYMES** | |
| | | | sweet soul quintet from Philadelphia | |
| 6/22/63 | 1 (1) | 12 | 1. **So Much In Love** | Parkway 871 |
| 8/31/63 | 7 | 8 | 2. **Wonderful! Wonderful!** | Parkway 884 |
| 1/04/64 | 19 | 6 | 3. Somewhere | Parkway 891 |
| 12/28/68 | 39 | 1 | 4. People | Columbia 44630 |
| | | | from the film "Funny Girl" | |
| 9/07/74 | 12 | 8 | 5. You Little Trustmaker | RCA 10022 |
| | | | **UB40** | |
| | | | British reggae octet - UB40 = British unemployment benefit form | |
| 3/17/84 | 34 | 4 | 1. Red Red Wine | A&M 2600 |
| | | | **TRACEY ULLMAN** | |
| | | | British singer/actress | |
| 3/17/84 | 8 | 11 | 1. **They Don't Know** | MCA 52347 |

| DATE | POS | WKS | ARTIST—Record Title | LABEL & NO. |
|---|---|---|---|---|
| | | | **UNDERGROUND SUNSHINE** | |
| | | | rock quartet - 2 members from Wisconsin; 2 from Germany | |
| 8/23/69 | 26 | 5 | 1. Birthday | Intrepid 75002 |
| | | | **UNDISPUTED TRUTH** | |
| | | | soul group founded and produced by Norman Whitfield | |
| 7/31/71 | 3 | 13 | 1. **Smiling Faces Sometimes** | Gordy 7108 |
| | | | **UNIFICS** | |
| | | | New York soul quartet | |
| 10/19/68 | 25 | 5 | 1. Court Of Love | Kapp 935 |
| 1/18/69 | 36 | 4 | 2. The Beginning Of My End | Kapp 957 |
| | | | **UNION GAP - see GARY PUCKETT** | |
| | | | **UNIT FOUR plus TWO** | |
| | | | English sextet | |
| 5/29/65 | 28 | 4 | 1. Concrete And Clay | London 9751 |
| | | | **PHILIP UPCHURCH Combo** | |
| 6/26/61 | 29 | 3 | 1. You Can't Sit Down, Part 2 [I] | Boyd 3398 |
| | | | **URIAH HEEP** | |
| | | | British heavy-metal rock quintet led by David Byron (lead singer) & Mick Box (lead guitar) | |
| 9/16/72 | 39 | 3 | 1. Easy Livin | Mercury 73307 |
| | | | **UTOPIA** | |
| | | | Todd Rundgren, leader | |
| 3/29/80 | 27 | 5 | 1. Set Me Free | Bearsville 49180 |
| | | | **JERRY VALE** | |
| | | | born Genaro Vitaliano on 7/8/32 in the Bronx, New York | |
| 3/24/56 | 30 | 5 | 1. Innamorata (Sweetheart) | Columbia 40634 |
| | | | from the film "Artists & Models" | |
| 7/28/56 | 14 | 17 | 2. You Don't Know Me | Columbia 40710 |
| 1/23/65 | 24 | 4 | 3. Have You Looked Into Your Heart | Columbia 43181 |
| | | | **RITCHIE VALENS** | |
| | | | real name: Richard Valenzuela - died in a plane crash with Buddy Holly & the Big Bopper on 2/3/59 (17) | |
| 12/15/58 + | 2 (2) | 18 | 1. **Donna**/ | |
| 1/19/59 | 22 | 8 | 2. La Bamba [F] | Del-Fi 4110 |
| | | | **CATERINA VALENTE** | |
| 4/09/55 | 8 | 14 | 1. **The Breeze And I** | Decca 29467 |
| | | | **JOHN VALENTI** | |
| 10/30/76 | 37 | 2 | 1. Anything You Want | Ariola Am. 7625 |
| | | | **MARK VALENTINO** | |
| | | | real name: Anthony Busillo | |
| 12/08/62 | 27 | 3 | 1. The Push And Kick | Swan 4121 |
| | | | **JOE VALINO** | |
| 10/27/56 | 12 | 14 | 1. Garden Of Eden | Vik 0226 |

**Neil Young.** The way slick Rick James tells it, Neil Young and he once shared an apartment and a band, the Mynah Birds. They even recorded for Motown, he says, although nothing was released.

**The Youngbloods** started out as a mid '60s house band at New York's Cafe A Go-Go, comprising a couple of folkies (Jesse Colin Young and Jerry Corbitt) and a bluegrass musician (Banana Lowell Levinger). One hit was to be their fate.

Neil Young — Comes A Time

47-9015

THE YOUNGBLOODS
GRIZZLY BEAR/TEARS ARE FALLING

RCA VICTOR

**ZZ Top** guitarist Billy Gibbons got his start with the Houston-based psychedelic band 99th Floor, who once opened for Jimi Hendrix. Gibbons' playing so impressed Hendrix that he later praised the Texan on the "Tonight Show."

**Frank Zappa.**   Although the Mothers of Invention first began charting with albums in 1967, Frank Zappa himself had to wait until 1982 for his first top 40 single. Even then, he had to share the glory with daughter Moon Unit.

**The Zombies**   and Laurence Olivier once appeared in the same movie, Otto Preminger's *Bunny Lake Is Missing*. Watch for it on television. Late.

| DATE | POS | WKS | ARTIST—Record Title | LABEL & NO. |
|---|---|---|---|---|
| | | | **VALJEAN** | |
| | | | pianist Valjean Johns from Shattuck, Oklahoma | |
| 6/16/62 | 28 | 4 | 1. Theme From Ben Casey [I] | Carlton 573 |
| | | | **FRANKIE VALLI** | |
| | | | born Frank Castelluccio on 5/3/37 - also see the Four Seasons | |
| 2/12/66 | 39 | 1 | 1. (You're Gonna) Hurt Yourself | Smash 2015 |
| 6/03/67 | 2 (1) | 14 | ● 2. **Can't Take My Eyes Off You** | Philips 40446 |
| 9/16/67 | 18 | 5 | 3. I Make A Fool Of Myself | Philips 40484 |
| 1/20/68 | 29 | 4 | 4. To Give (The Reason I Live) | Philips 40510 |
| 1/18/75 | 1 (1) | 14 | ● 5. **My Eyes Adored You** | Private S. 45003 |
| 6/14/75 | 6 | 9 | 6. **Swearin' To God** | Private S. 45021 |
| 11/08/75 | 11 | 8 | 7. Our Day Will Come | Private S. 45043 |
| 5/08/76 | 36 | 2 | 8. Fallen Angel | Private S. 45074 |
| 6/17/78 | 1 (2) | 15 | ★ 9. **Grease** | RSO 897 |
| | | | **JUNE VALLI** | |
| | | | married to Chicago disc jockey Howard Miller | |
| 5/14/55 | 29 | 1 | 1. Unchained Melody<br>from the film "Unchained" | RCA 6078 |
| 4/18/60 | 29 | 4 | 2. Apple Green | Mercury 71588 |
| | | | **LEROY VAN DYKE** | |
| 12/08/56 + | 19 | 7 | 1. Auctioneer [N] | Dot 15503 |
| 11/20/61 | 5 | 12 | 2. **Walk On By** | Mercury 71834 |
| 3/31/62 | 35 | 2 | 3. If A Woman Answers (Hang Up The Phone) | Mercury 71926 |
| | | | **VAN HALEN** | |
| | | | heavy-metal rock band formed in Pasadena, California:<br>David Lee Roth (vocals), Edward (guitar) & Alex Van Halen<br>(drums), and Michael Anthony (bass) | |
| 3/11/78 | 36 | 3 | 1. You Really Got Me | Warner 8515 |
| 5/26/79 | 15 | 9 | 2. Dance The Night Away | Warner 8823 |
| 3/13/82 | 12 | 10 | 3. (Oh) Pretty Woman | Warner 50003 |
| 6/26/82 | 38 | 3 | 4. Dancing In The Street | Warner 29986 |
| 1/21/84 | 1 (5) | 15 | ● 5. **Jump** | Warner 29384 |
| 4/21/84 | 13 | 10 | 6. I'll Wait | Warner 29307 |
| 6/30/84 | 13 | 10 | 7. Panama | Warner 29250 |
| | | | **VANDENBERG** | |
| | | | Dutch hard-rock quartet led by Adrian Vandenberg & Bert Heerink | |
| 3/12/83 | 39 | 2 | 1. Burning Heart | Atco 99947 |
| | | | **LUTHER VANDROSS** | |
| | | | soul singer/producer/songwriter from New York -<br>also see Dionne Warwick | |
| 11/14/81 | 33 | 4 | 1. Never Too Much | Epic 02409 |
| | | | **VANGELIS** | |
| | | | Greek keyboardist - real name: Evangelos Papathanassiou | |
| 2/20/82 | 1 (1) | 15 | 1. **Chariots Of Fire - Titles [I]** | Polydor 2189 |
| | | | **VANILLA FUDGE** | |
| | | | New York psychedelic rock quartet - Mark Stein, lead singer | |
| 8/03/68 | 6 | 8 | 1. **You Keep Me Hangin' On** | Atco 6590 |
| 10/26/68 | 38 | 4 | 2. Take Me For A Little While | Atco 6616 |

| DATE | POS | WKS | ARTIST—Record Title | LABEL & NO. |
|---|---|---|---|---|
| | | | **VANITY FARE** | |
| | | | British quintet | |
| 12/20/69 + | 12 | 9 | 1. Early In The Morning | Page One 21027 |
| 5/16/70 | 5 | 14 | ● 2. **Hitchin' A Ride** | Page One 21029 |
| | | | **GINO VANNELLI** | |
| | | | Canadian singer/songwriter | |
| 10/26/74 | 22 | 5 | 1. People Gotta Move | A&M 1614 |
| 10/14/78 | 4 | 13 | 2. **I Just Wanna Stop** | A&M 2072 |
| 4/04/81 | 6 | 14 | 3. **Living Inside Myself** | Arista 0588 |
| | | | **RANDY VANWARMER** | |
| 4/21/79 | 4 | 14 | ● 1. **Just When I Needed You Most** | Bearsville 0334 |
| | | | **VAPORS** | |
| | | | British pub-rock quartet - David Fenton, lead singer | |
| 11/15/80 | 36 | 3 | 1. Turning Japanese | Liberty 1364 |
| | | | **FRANKIE VAUGHAN** | |
| | | | English | |
| 7/28/58 | 22 | 1 | 1. Judy | Epic 9273 |
| | | | **SARAH VAUGHAN** | |
| | | | jazz-styled singer from Newark, New Jersey | |
| 11/27/54 + | 6 | 15 | 1. **Make Yourself Comfortable** | Mercury 70469 |
| 2/26/55 | 12 | 9 | 2. How Important Can It Be? | Mercury 70534 |
| 4/23/55 | 6 | 11 | 3. **Whatever Lola Wants** <br> from Broadway's "Damn Yankees" | Mercury 70595 |
| 7/16/55 | 14 | 1 | 4. Experience Unnecessary | Mercury 70646 |
| 12/03/55 | 11 | 7 | 5. C'est La Vie | Mercury 70727 |
| 3/03/56 | 13 | 7 | 6. Mr. Wonderful | Mercury 70777 |
| 7/21/56 | 19 | 6 | 7. Fabulous Character | Mercury 70885 |
| 1/12/57 | 19 | 5 | 8. The Banana Boat Song | Mercury 71020 |
| 8/17/59 | 7 | 11 | 9. **Broken-Hearted Melody** | Mercury 71477 |
| | | | **BILLY VAUGHN & His Orchestra** | |
| | | | Dot Records musical director - arranger/conductor for Pat Boone <br> and other Dot artists - also see Walter Brennan/Fontane Sisters | |
| 12/11/54 + | 2 (1) | 27 | 1. **Melody Of Love [I]** | Dot 15247 |
| 9/24/55 | 5 | 15 | 2. **The Shifting Whispering Sands (Parts 1 & 2) [S]** <br> narration by Ken Nordine | Dot 15409 |
| 2/25/56 | 37 | 2 | 3. A Theme From "The Three Penny Opera" <br> (Moritat) [I] | Dot 15444 |
| 9/08/56 | 18 | 6 | 4. When The White Lilacs Bloom Again [I] | Dot 15491 |
| 12/16/57 | 10 | 7 | 5. **Raunchy/ [I]** | |
| 1/13/58 | 5 | 18 | 6. **Sail Along Silvery Moon [I]** | Dot 15661 |
| 4/14/58 | 30 | 4 | 7. Tumbling Tumbleweeds [I] | Dot 15710 |
| 8/25/58 | 20 | 8 | 8. La Paloma [I] | Dot 15795 |
| 2/02/59 | 37 | 1 | 9. Blue Hawaii [I] | Dot 15879 |
| 7/18/60 | 19 | 7 | 10. Look For A Star [I] <br> from the film "Circus Of Horrors" | Dot 16106 |
| 3/06/61 | 28 | 3 | 11. Wheels [I] | Dot 16174 |
| 8/11/62 | 13 | 8 | 12. A Swingin' Safari [I] | Dot 16374 |

| DATE | POS | WKS | ARTIST—Record Title | LABEL & NO. |
|---|---|---|---|---|
| | | | **BOBBY VEE** | |
| | | | born Robert Velline on 4/30/43 in Fargo, North Dakota | |
| 9/05/60 | 6 | 13 | 1. **Devil Or Angel** | Liberty 55270 |
| 12/12/60 + | 6 | 11 | 2. **Rubber Ball** | Liberty 55287 |
| 2/27/61 | 33 | 3 | 3. Stayin' In | Liberty 55296 |
| 8/21/61 | 1 (3) | 11 | 4. **Take Good Care Of My Baby** | Liberty 55354 |
| 11/20/61 | 2 (1) | 13 | 5. **Run To Him** | Liberty 55388 |
| 3/17/62 | 15 | 6 | 6. Please Don't Ask About Barbara | Liberty 55419 |
| 6/09/62 | 15 | 6 | 7. Sharing You | Liberty 55451 |
| 9/15/62 | 20 | 6 | 8. Punish Her | Liberty 55479 |
| 12/22/62 + | 3 | 11 | 9. **The Night Has A Thousand Eyes** | Liberty 55521 |
| 4/13/63 | 13 | 7 | 10. Charms | Liberty 55530 |
| 7/20/63 | 34 | 2 | 11. Be True To Yourself | Liberty 55581 |
| 8/12/67 | 3 | 13 | ● 12. **Come Back When You Grow Up** | Liberty 55964 |
| 12/16/67 | 37 | 2 | 13. Beautiful People | Liberty 56009 |
| | | | above 2 with The Strangers | |
| 5/18/68 | 35 | 4 | 14. My Girl/My Guy (medley) | Liberty 56033 |
| | | | **VELVETS** | |
| | | | R&B quintet from Odessa, Texas - Virgil Johnson, lead singer | |
| 6/26/61 | 26 | 4 | 1. Tonight (Could Be The Night) | Monument 441 |
| | | | **VENTURES** | |
| | | | instrumental quartet from Tacoma, Washington featuring guitarists Bob Bogle (bass), Don Wilson (rhythm), & Nokie Edwards (lead) | |
| 7/25/60 | 2 (1) | 14 | 1. **Walk--Don't Run [I]** | Dolton 25 |
| 11/14/60 | 15 | 10 | 2. Perfidia [I] | Dolton 28 |
| 2/13/61 | 29 | 5 | 3. Ram-Bunk-Shush [I] | Dolton 32 |
| 8/01/64 | 8 | 7 | 4. **Walk-Don't Run '64 [I]** | Dolton 96 |
| | | | new version of 1960 hit | |
| 11/21/64 | 35 | 3 | 5. Slaughter On Tenth Avenue [I] | Dolton 300 |
| 4/12/69 | 4 | 9 | 6. **Hawaii Five-O [I]** | Liberty 56068 |
| | | | **VIK VENUS** | |
| 7/26/69 | 38 | 3 | 1. Moonflight [N] | Buddah 118 |
| | | | **BILLY VERA & JUDY CLAY** | |
| | | | also see Billy & The Beaters | |
| 3/23/68 | 36 | 1 | 1. Country Girl - City Man | Atlantic 2480 |
| | | | **LARRY VERNE** | |
| 9/05/60 | 1 (1) | 10 | 1. **Mr. Custer [N]** | Era 3024 |
| | | | **VIBRATIONS** | |
| | | | also recorded as The Jayhawks and The Marathons | |
| 3/13/61 | 25 | 4 | 1. The Watusi | Checker 969 |
| 4/25/64 | 26 | 5 | 2. My Girl Sloopy | Atlantic 2221 |
| | | | **VILLAGE PEOPLE** | |
| | | | New York campy disco act | |
| 7/29/78 | 25 | 6 | ● 1. Macho Man | Casablanca 922 |
| 11/11/78 + | 2 (3) | 20 | ★ 2. **Y.M.C.A.** | Casablanca 945 |
| 3/31/79 | 3 | 13 | ● 3. **In The Navy** | Casablanca 973 |

| DATE | POS | WKS | ARTIST—Record Title | LABEL & NO. |
|------|-----|-----|--------------------|-------------|
| | | | **VILLAGE STOMPERS** | |
| | | | Greenwich Village, New York dixieland band | |
| 10/05/63 | 2 (1) | 12 | 1. **Washington Square [I]** | Epic 9617 |
| | | | **GENE VINCENT & His Blue Caps** | |
| | | | born Eugene Vincent Craddock on 2/11/35 - died on 10/12/71 (36) | |
| 6/23/56 | 7 | 15 | 1. **Be-Bop-A-Lula** | Capitol 3450 |
| 9/16/57 | 13 | 12 | 2. Lotta Lovin' | Capitol 3763 |
| 1/13/58 | 23 | 1 | 3. Dance To The Bop | Capitol 3839 |
| | | | **BOBBY VINTON** | |
| | | | born Stanley Robert Vinton on 4/16/41 in Canonsburg, Penn. | |
| 6/16/62 | 1 (4) | 13 | ● 1. **Roses Are Red (My Love)** | Epic 9509 |
| 9/15/62 | 12 | 7 | 2. Rain Rain Go Away | Epic 9532 |
| 9/22/62 | 38 | 2 | 3. I Love You The Way You Are | Diamond 121 |
| 1/05/63 | 33 | 3 | 4. Trouble Is My Middle Name/ | |
| 1/12/63 | 38 | 2 | 5.  Let's Kiss And Make Up | Epic 9561 |
| 3/30/63 | 21 | 6 | 6. Over The Mountain (Across The Sea) | Epic 9577 |
| 6/01/63 | 3 | 10 | 7. **Blue On Blue** | Epic 9593 |
| 8/24/63 | 1 (3) | 12 | 8. **Blue Velvet** | Epic 9614 |
| 12/07/63 + | 1 (4) | 12 | 9. **There! I've Said It Again** | Epic 9638 |
| 3/07/64 | 9 | 8 | 10. **My Heart Belongs To Only You** | Epic 9662 |
| 5/30/64 | 13 | 6 | 11. Tell Me Why | Epic 9687 |
| 8/22/64 | 17 | 6 | 12. Clinging Vine | Epic 9705 |
| 11/07/64 | 1 (1) | 14 | 13. **Mr. Lonely** | Epic 9730 |
| 3/20/65 | 17 | 5 | 14. Long Lonely Nights | Epic 9768 |
| 5/22/65 | 22 | 6 | 15. L-O-N-E-L-Y | Epic 9791 |
| 10/16/65 | 38 | 1 | 16. What Color (Is A Man) | Epic 9846 |
| 12/25/65 + | 23 | 6 | 17. Satin Pillows | Epic 9869 |
| 5/28/66 | 40 | 1 | 18. Dum-De-Da | Epic 10014 |
| | | | aka "She Understands Me" | |
| 12/17/66 + | 11 | 8 | 19. Coming Home Soldier | Epic 10090 |
| 10/14/67 | 6 | 11 | 20. **Please Love Me Forever** | Epic 10228 |
| 1/27/68 | 24 | 4 | 21. Just As Much As Ever | Epic 10266 |
| 4/13/68 | 33 | 6 | 22. Take Good Care Of My Baby | Epic 10305 |
| 8/03/68 | 23 | 5 | 23. Halfway To Paradise | Epic 10350 |
| 11/16/68 | 9 | 12 | ● 24. **I Love How You Love Me** | Epic 10397 |
| 5/03/69 | 34 | 2 | 25. To Know You Is To Love You | Epic 10461 |
| 7/12/69 | 34 | 2 | 26. The Days Of Sand And Shovels | Epic 10485 |
| 3/18/72 | 24 | 8 | 27. Every Day Of My Life | Epic 10822 |
| 7/08/72 | 19 | 10 | 28. Sealed With A Kiss | Epic 10861 |
| 10/12/74 | 3 | 11 | ● 29. **My Melody Of Love** | ABC 12022 |
| 4/19/75 | 33 | 2 | 30. Beer Barrel Polka | ABC 12056 |
| | | | **VIRTUES** | |
| | | | Frank Virtue, lead guitarist of Philadelphia quartet | |
| 3/23/59 | 5 | 12 | 1. **Guitar Boogie Shuffle [I]** | Hunt 324 |

| DATE | POS | WKS | ARTIST—Record Title | LABEL & NO. |
|---|---|---|---|---|
| | | | **VISCOUNTS** | |
| | | | New Jersey instrumental quintet led by brothers Bobby & Joe Spievak | |
| 1/01/66 | 39 | 1 | 1. Harlem Nocturne [I-R]<br>re-release of 1960 hit (Pos. 52) | Amy 940 |
| | | | **VOGUES** | |
| | | | quartet from Turtle Creek, Pennsylvania | |
| 10/09/65 | 4 | 9 | 1. **You're The One** | Co & Ce 229 |
| 12/11/65 + | 4 | 12 | 2. **Five O'Clock World** | Co & Ce 232 |
| 3/19/66 | 21 | 6 | 3. Magic Town | Co & Ce 234 |
| 6/25/66 | 29 | 4 | 4. The Land Of Milk And Honey | Co & Ce 238 |
| 7/13/68 | 7 | 11 | ● 5. **Turn Around, Look At Me** | Reprise 0686 |
| 9/21/68 | 7 | 8 | 6. **My Special Angel** | Reprise 0766 |
| 12/07/68 | 27 | 4 | 7. Till | Reprise 0788 |
| 3/29/69 | 34 | 2 | 8. No, Not Much | Reprise 0803 |
| | | | **VOLUME'S** | |
| | | | R&B quintet from Detroit - Ed Union, lead singer | |
| 6/02/62 | 22 | 6 | 1. I Love You | Chex 1002 |
| | | | **ROGER VOUDOURIS** | |
| | | | Sacramento, California vocalist/guitarist | |
| 4/28/79 | 21 | 10 | 1. Get Used To It | Warner 8762 |
| | | | **VOXPOPPERS** | |
| 5/05/58 | 18 | 1 | 1. Wishing For Your Love | Mercury 71282 |
| | | | **ADAM WADE** | |
| | | | born on 3/17/37 in Pittsburgh, Pennsylvania | |
| 3/27/61 | 7 | 10 | 1. **Take Good Care Of Her** | Coed 546 |
| 5/29/61 | 5 | 9 | 2. **The Writing On The Wall** | Coed 550 |
| 8/07/61 | 10 | 7 | 3. **As If I Didn't Know** | Coed 553 |
| | | | **WADSWORTH MANSION** | |
| 2/13/71 | 7 | 7 | 1. **Sweet Mary** | Sussex 209 |
| | | | **WAIKIKIS** | |
| | | | Belgian instrumental group | |
| 1/09/65 | 33 | 3 | 1. Hawaii Tattoo [I] | Kapp 30 |
| | | | **WAILERS** | |
| | | | teenage quintet (in 1959) from Tacoma, Washington | |
| 6/01/59 | 36 | 2 | 1. Tall Cool One [I] | Golden Crest 518 |
| 5/30/64 | 38 | 1 | 2. Tall Cool One [I-R] | Golden Crest 518 |
| | | | **LOUDON WAINWRIGHT III** | |
| | | | satirical folksinger/songwriter | |
| 2/24/73 | 16 | 9 | 1. **Dead Skunk** [N] | Columbia 45726 |
| | | | **JOHN WAITE** | |
| | | | British - lead singer of the Babys | |
| 7/21/84 | 1 (1) | 16 | 1. **Missing You** | EMI America 8212 |

| DATE | POS | WKS | ARTIST—Record Title | LABEL & NO. |
|---|---|---|---|---|
| | | | **JOHNNY WAKELIN & The Kinshasa Band** | |
| | | | British | |
| 8/16/75 | 21 | 6 | 1. Black Superman - "Muhammad Ali" [N] | Pye 71012 |
| | | | **WALKER BROS.** | |
| | | | Scott Engel, Gary Leeds & John Maus - from Los Angeles | |
| 11/13/65 | 16 | 6 | 1. Make It Easy On Yourself | Smash 2009 |
| 4/30/66 | 13 | 7 | 2. The Sun Ain't Gonna Shine (Anymore) | Smash 2032 |
| | | | **JR. WALKER & THE ALL STARS** | |
| | | | Jr. (born Autry DeWalt, Jr.) began as a session tenor sax player | |
| 3/06/65 | 4 | 10 | 1. **Shotgun** | Soul 35008 |
| 7/03/65 | 36 | 2 | 2. Do The Boomerang | Soul 35012 |
| 8/21/65 | 29 | 5 | 3. Shake And Fingerpop | Soul 35013 |
| 5/21/66 | 20 | 6 | 4. (I'm A) Road Runner | Soul 35015 |
| 9/03/66 | 18 | 5 | 5. How Sweet It Is (To Be Loved By You) | Soul 35024 |
| 3/11/67 | 31 | 4 | 6. Pucker Up Buttercup | Soul 35030 |
| 12/23/67 + | 24 | 6 | 7. Come See About Me | Soul 35041 |
| 9/14/68 | 31 | 6 | 8. Hip City - Pt. 2 | Soul 35048 |
| 6/21/69 | 4 | 11 | 9. **What Does It Take (To Win Your Love)** | Soul 35062 |
| 11/22/69 | 16 | 9 | 10. These Eyes | Soul 35067 |
| 2/28/70 | 21 | 9 | 11. Gotta Hold On To This Feeling | Soul 35070 |
| 8/01/70 | 32 | 4 | 12. Do You See My Love (For You Growing) | Soul 35073 |
| | | | **JERRY WALLACE** | |
| | | | born on 12/15/38 in Kansas City, Missouri | |
| 9/15/58 | 11 | 9 | 1. How The Time Flies | Challenge 59013 |
| 9/07/59 | 8 | 15 | 2. **Primrose Lane** | Challenge 59047 |
| | | | with the Jewels | |
| 2/01/60 | 36 | 2 | 3. Little Coco Palm | Challenge 59060 |
| 1/09/61 | 26 | 4 | 4. There She Goes | Challenge 59098 |
| 12/22/62 + | 24 | 7 | 5. Shutters And Boards | Challenge 9171 |
| 8/22/64 | 19 | 7 | 6. In The Misty Moonlight | Challenge 59246 |
| 9/30/72 | 38 | 2 | 7. If You Leave Me Tonight I'll Cry | Decca 32989 |
| | | | from TV's Night Gallery: "The Tune In Dan's Cafe" | |
| | | | **JOE WALSH** | |
| | | | rock guitarist - member of the James Gang and the Eagles | |
| 9/22/73 | 23 | 7 | 1. Rocky Mountain Way | Dunhill 4361 |
| 7/01/78 | 12 | 9 | 2. Life's Been Good | Asylum 45493 |
| 6/14/80 | 19 | 8 | 3. All Night Long | Full Moon 46639 |
| | | | from the film "Urban Cowboy" | |
| 6/27/81 | 34 | 4 | 4. A Life Of Illusion | Asylum 47144 |
| | | | **TRAVIS WAMMACK** | |
| 8/09/75 | 38 | 2 | 1. (Shu-Doo-Pa-Poo-Poop) Love Being Your Fool | Capricorn 0239 |
| | | | **WALTER WANDERLEY** | |
| | | | Brazilian Bossa Nova organist | |
| 10/01/66 | 26 | 4 | 1. Summer Samba (So Nice) [I] | Verve 10421 |
| | | | **WANG CHUNG** | |
| | | | British rock trio - formerly Huang Chung | |
| 3/10/84 | 38 | 3 | 1. Don't Let Go | Geffen 29377 |
| 5/26/84 | 16 | 10 | 2. Dance Hall Days | Geffen 29310 |

| DATE | POS | WKS | ARTIST—Record Title | LABEL & NO. |
|---|---|---|---|---|
| | | | **WAR** | |
| | | | Latin jazz/funk band from Long Beach, California - also see Eric Burdon | |
| 9/25/71 | 35 | 2 | 1. All Day Music | United Art. 50815 |
| 4/01/72 | 16 | 10 | ● 2. Slippin' Into Darkness | United Art. 50867 |
| 12/30/72 + | 7 | 9 | ● 3. **The World Is A Ghetto** | United Art. 50975 |
| 3/24/73 | 2 (2) | 12 | ● 4. **The Cisco Kid** | United Art. 163 |
| 8/04/73 | 8 | 10 | 5. **Gypsy Man** | United Art. 281 |
| 12/08/73 + | 15 | 10 | 6. Me And Baby Brother | United Art. 350 |
| 7/13/74 | 33 | 2 | 7. Ballero [I] | United Art. 432 |
| 6/14/75 | 6 | 13 | ● 8. **Why Can't We Be Friends?** | United Art. 629 |
| 10/11/75 | 7 | 11 | 9. **Low Rider** | United Art. 706 |
| 7/31/76 | 7 | 12 | ● 10. **Summer** | United Art. 834 |
| 2/11/78 | 39 | 2 | 11. Galaxy | MCA 40820 |
| | | | **ANITA WARD** | |
| 5/26/79 | 1 (2) | 15 | 1. **Ring My Bell** | Juana 3422 |
| | | | **BILLY WARD & His Dominoes** | |
| | | | R&B quintet - originally known as the Dominoes, with Clyde McPhatter, lead singer (1950-52) | |
| 9/15/56 | 13 | 6 | 1. St. Therese Of The Roses | Decca 29933 |
| | | | Jackie Wilson, lead singer | |
| 7/15/57 | 12 | 17 | 2. Star Dust | Liberty 55071 |
| 10/07/57 | 20 | 8 | 3. Deep Purple | Liberty 55099 |
| | | | **DALE WARD** | |
| | | | lead singer of the Crescendos | |
| 2/01/64 | 25 | 5 | 1. Letter From Sherry | Dot 16520 |
| | | | **JOE WARD** | |
| 12/24/55 | 20 | 3 | 1. Nuttin For Xmas [N-X] | King 4854 |
| | | | **ROBIN WARD** | |
| 11/16/63 | 14 | 7 | 1. Wonderful Summer | Dot 16530 |
| | | | **JENNIFER WARNES** | |
| | | | lead part in the Los Angeles production of "Hair" - also see Joe Cocker | |
| 2/26/77 | 6 | 14 | 1. **Right Time Of The Night** | Arista 0223 |
| 9/22/79 | 19 | 8 | 2. I Know A Heartache When I See One | Arista 0430 |
| | | | **DIONNE WARWICK** | |
| | | | born on 12/12/41 in East Orange, New Jersey - also see Johnny Mathis | |
| 1/05/63 | 21 | 7 | 1. Don't Make Me Over | Scepter 1239 |
| 1/04/64 | 8 | 9 | 2. **Anyone Who Had A Heart** | Scepter 1262 |
| 5/09/64 | 6 | 11 | 3. **Walk On By** | Scepter 1274 |
| 9/19/64 | 34 | 3 | 4. You'll Never Get To Heaven (If You Break My Heart) | Scepter 1282 |
| 11/07/64 | 20 | 6 | 5. Reach Out For Me | Scepter 1285 |
| 1/22/66 | 39 | 1 | 6. Are You There (With Another Girl) | Scepter 12122 |
| 4/23/66 | 8 | 8 | 7. **Message To Michael** | Scepter 12133 |

| DATE | POS | WKS | ARTIST—Record Title | LABEL & NO. |
|------|-----|-----|---------------------|-------------|
| 7/16/66 | 22 | 5 | 8. Trains And Boats And Planes | Scepter 12153 |
| 10/22/66 | 26 | 5 | 9. I Just Don't Know What To Do With Myself | Scepter 12167 |
| 5/27/67 | 15 | 9 | 10. Alfie | Scepter 12187 |
| 8/26/67 | 32 | 3 | 11. The Windows Of The World | Scepter 12196 |
| 11/04/67 | 4 | 10 | ● 12. **I Say A Little Prayer/** | |
| 2/03/68 | 2 (4) | 11 | 13. **(Theme From) Valley Of The Dolls** | Scepter 12203 |
| 4/27/68 | 10 | 9 | 14. **Do You Know The Way To San Jose** | Scepter 12216 |
| 9/21/68 | 33 | 4 | 15. Who Is Gonna Love Me? | Scepter 12226 |
| 11/23/68 | 19 | 6 | 16. Promises, Promises | Scepter 12231 |
| 2/08/69 | 7 | 11 | 17. **This Girl's In Love With You** | Scepter 12241 |
| 6/07/69 | 37 | 3 | 18. The April Fools | Scepter 12249 |
| 10/11/69 | 16 | 7 | 19. You've Lost That Lovin' Feeling | Scepter 12262 |
| 1/03/70 | 6 | 10 | 20. **I'll Never Fall In Love Again**<br>from Broadways "Promises, Promises" | Scepter 12273 |
| 5/09/70 | 32 | 3 | 21. Let Me Go To Him | Scepter 12276 |
| 10/31/70 | 37 | 2 | 22. Make It Easy On Yourself | Scepter 12294 |
| 7/28/79 | 5 | 17 | ● 23. **I'll Never Love This Way Again** | Arista 0419 |
| 12/15/79 + | 15 | 11 | 24. Deja Vu | Arista 0459 |
| 9/06/80 | 23 | 6 | 25. No Night So Long | Arista 0527 |
| 11/06/82 + | 10 | 13 | 26. **Heartbreaker**<br>backing vocals: Barry Gibb | Arista 1015 |
| | | | **DIONNE WARWICK & SPINNERS** | |
| 8/03/74 | 1 (1) | 15 | ● 1. **Then Came You** | Atlantic 3202 |
| | | | **DIONNE WARWICK & LUTHER VANDROSS** | |
| 10/29/83 | 27 | 5 | 1. How Many Times Can We Say Goodbye | Arista 9073 |
| | | | **BABY WASHINGTON**<br>lead singer of the Hearts | |
| 6/01/63 | 40 | 1 | 1. That's How Heartaches Are Made | Sue 783 |
| | | | **DINAH WASHINGTON**<br>born Ruth Jones - renown as the "Queen Of The Blues" -<br>died on 12/14/63 (39) - also see Brook Benton | |
| 6/22/59 | 8 | 14 | 1. **What A Diff'rence A Day Makes** | Mercury 71435 |
| 10/26/59 | 17 | 8 | 2. Unforgettable | Mercury 71508 |
| 7/18/60 | 24 | 6 | 3. This Bitter Earth | Mercury 71635 |
| 11/07/60 | 30 | 2 | 4. Love Walked In | Mercury 71696 |
| 11/06/61 | 23 | 6 | 5. September In The Rain | Mercury 71876 |
| 6/23/62 | 36 | 3 | 6. Where Are You | Roulette 4424 |
| | | | **GROVER WASHINGTON, JR.**<br>jazz/R&B saxophonist from Buffalo, New York | |
| 3/07/81 | 2 (3) | 16 | 1. **Just The Two Of Us**<br>vocal by Bill Withers | Elektra 47103 |
| | | | **WATTS 103RD STREET RHYTHM BAND -<br>see CHARLES WRIGHT** | |
| | | | **WAYLON & WILLIE**<br>Waylon Jennings & Willie Nelson | |
| 3/06/76 | 25 | 5 | 1. Good Hearted Woman | RCA 10529 |

| DATE | POS | WKS | ARTIST—Record Title | LABEL & NO. |
|---|---|---|---|---|
| | | | **THOMAS WAYNE** | |
| | | | died in a car cash on 8/15/71 (29) | |
| 2/16/59 | **5** | 13 | 1. **Tragedy** | Fernwood 109 |
| | | | with The DeLons | |
| | | | **WE FIVE** | |
| | | | quintet led by John Stewart's brother, Mike Stewart | |
| 8/07/65 | **3** | 13 | 1. **You Were On My Mind** | A&M 770 |
| 12/25/65 | **31** | 2 | 2. Let's Get Together | A&M 784 |
| | | | **JIM WEATHERLY** | |
| | | | pop/country songwriter and singer | |
| 10/12/74 | **11** | 8 | 1. The Need To Be | Buddah 420 |
| | | | **JOAN WEBER** | |
| | | | died on 5/13/81 (45) | |
| 12/04/54 + | **1 (4)** | 16 | 1. **Let Me Go Lover** | Columbia 40366 |
| | | | from a "Studio One" TV production | |
| | | | **WEDNESDAY** | |
| 2/16/74 | **34** | 4 | 1. Last Kiss | Sussex 507 |
| | | | **TIM WEISBERG - see DAN FOGELBERG** | |
| | | | **ERIC WEISSBERG & STEVE MANDELL** | |
| 2/03/73 | **2 (4)** | 11 | ● 1. **Dueling Banjos [I]** | Warner 7659 |
| | | | from the film "Deliverance" | |
| | | | **BOB WELCH** | |
| | | | guitarist with Fleetwood Mac ('71-'74) | |
| 11/19/77 + | **8** | 12 | 1. **Sentimental Lady** | Capitol 4479 |
| | | | backing vocals: Christine McVie & Lindsey Buckingham | |
| 2/25/78 | **14** | 10 | 2. Ebony Eyes | Capitol 4543 |
| 7/01/78 | **31** | 3 | 3. Hot Love, Cold World | Capitol 4588 |
| 3/17/79 | **19** | 8 | 4. Precious Love | Capitol 4685 |
| | | | **LENNY WELCH** | |
| | | | born on 5/15/38 in Asbury Park, New Jersey | |
| 11/23/63 | **4** | 12 | 1. **Since I Fell For You** | Cadence 1439 |
| 4/11/64 | **25** | 5 | 2. Ebb Tide | Cadence 1422 |
| | | | from the film "Sweet Bird Of Youth" | |
| 2/14/70 | **34** | 4 | 3. Breaking Up Is Hard To Do | Common. U. 3004 |
| | | | **LAWRENCE WELK** | |
| | | | leader of polka and dance bands since mid 1920's - began his TV show in 1955 | |
| 3/03/56 | **17** | 2 | 1. Moritat (A Theme From "The Threepenny Opera") [I] | Coral 61574 |
| 4/07/56 | **17** | 2 | 2. The Poor People Of Paris [I] | Coral 61592 |
| 12/05/60 | **21** | 3 | 3. Last Date [I] | Dot 16145 |
| 12/31/60 + | **1 (2)** | 13 | ● 4. Calcutta [I] | Dot 16161 |
| | | | **MARY WELLS** | |
| | | | born on 5/13/43 in Detroit, Michigan - also see Marvin Gaye | |
| 8/21/61 | **33** | 3 | 1. I Don't Want To Take A Chance | Motown 1011 |
| 5/05/62 | **8** | 10 | 2. **The One Who Really Loves You** | Motown 1024 |

| DATE | POS | WKS | ARTIST—Record Title | LABEL & NO. |
|---|---|---|---|---|
| 8/25/62 | 9 | 9 | 3. **You Beat Me To The Punch** | Motown 1032 |
| 12/15/62 + | 7 | 10 | 4. **Two Lovers** | Motown 1035 |
| 3/09/63 | 15 | 6 | 5. Laughing Boy | Motown 1039 |
| 7/06/63 | 40 | 1 | 6. Your Old Stand By | Motown 1042 |
| 10/12/63 | 22 | 7 | 7. You Lost The Sweetest Boy/ | |
| 1/25/64 | 29 | 6 | 8.   What's Easy For Two Is So Hard For One | Motown 1048 |
| 4/11/64 | 1 (2) | 13 | 9. **My Guy** | Motown 1056 |
| 1/30/65 | 34 | 2 | 10. Use Your Head | 20th Century 555 |
| | | | **FRED WESLEY - see J.B.'s** | |
| | | | **DOTTIE WEST** | |
| 4/25/81 | 14 | 12 | 1. What Are We Doin' In Love | Liberty 1404 |
| | | | with backing vocals by Kenny Rogers | |
| | | | **KIM WESTON - see MARVIN GAYE** | |
| | | | **WET WILLIE** | |
| | | | Southern rock band led by brothers Jimmy & Jack Hall | |
| 7/06/74 | 10 | 11 | 1. **Keep On Smilin'** | Capricorn 0043 |
| 1/28/78 | 30 | 4 | 2. Street Corner Serenade | Epic 50478 |
| 6/30/79 | 29 | 5 | 3. Weekend | Epic 50714 |
| | | | **WHAM!** | |
| | | | English duo: George Michael & Andrew Ridgely | |
| 10/06/84 | 1 (3) | 14 | 1. **Wake Me Up Before You Go-Go** | Columbia 04552 |
| | | | **WHISPERS** | |
| | | | soul quintet led by twin brothers Wallace & Walter Scott | |
| 3/15/80 | 19 | 8 | ● 1. And The Beat Goes On | Solar 11894 |
| 5/24/80 | 28 | 4 | 2. Lady | Solar 11928 |
| 3/28/81 | 28 | 5 | 3. It's A Love Thing | Solar 12154 |
| | | | **IAN WHITCOMB** | |
| | | | English | |
| 6/19/65 | 8 | 8 | 1. **You Turn Me On (Turn On Song)** | Tower 134 |
| | | | with backing band Bluesville | |
| | | | **WHITE PLAINS** | |
| | | | English production by Roger Greenaway & Roger Cook | |
| 5/23/70 | 13 | 10 | 1. My Baby Loves Lovin' | Deram 85058 |
| | | | **BARRY WHITE** | |
| | | | producer of Love Unlimited (his female backing trio) and Love Unlimited Orchestra | |
| 5/05/73 | 3 | 12 | ● 1. **I'm Gonna Love You Just A Little More Baby** | 20th Century 2018 |
| 9/01/73 | 32 | 6 | 2. I've Got So Much To Give | 20th Century 2042 |
| 11/17/73 + | 7 | 15 | ● 3. **Never, Never Gonna Give Ya Up** | 20th Century 2058 |
| 8/10/74 | 1 (1) | 9 | ● 4. **Can't Get Enough Of Your Love, Babe** | 20th Century 2120 |
| 11/16/74 + | 2 (2) | 12 | ● 5. **You're The First, The Last, My Everything** | 20th Century 2133 |
| 3/22/75 | 8 | 7 | 6. **What Am I Gonna Do With You** | 20th Century 2177 |
| 6/21/75 | 40 | 2 | 7. I'll Do For You Anything You Want Me To | 20th Century 2208 |
| 1/24/76 | 32 | 4 | 8. Let The Music Play | 20th Century 2265 |
| 10/01/77 | 4 | 12 | ● 9. **It's Ecstasy When You Lay Down Next To Me** | 20th Century 2350 |
| 5/27/78 | 24 | 5 | 10. Oh What A Night For Dancing | 20th Century 2365 |

| DATE | POS | WKS | ARTIST—Record Title | LABEL & NO. |
|---|---|---|---|---|
| | | | **TONY JOE WHITE** | |
| | | | "swamp rock" singer from the Louisiana Bayous | |
| 7/26/69 | 8 | 8 | 1. **Polk Salad Annie** | Monument 1104 |
| | | | **MARGARET WHITING** | |
| | | | one of the most popular female vocalists of the forties | |
| 12/08/56 | 20 | 5 | 1. The Money Tree | Capitol 3586 |
| 11/19/66 | 26 | 5 | 2. The Wheel Of Hurt | London 101 |
| | | | **ROGER WHITTAKER** | |
| | | | English MOR singer - born in Nairobi, Africa | |
| 5/10/75 | 19 | 9 | 1. The Last Farewell | RCA 50030 |
| | | | **WHO** | |
| | | | English: Roger Daltrey (vocals), Pete Townshend (guitar/songwriter), John Entwistle (bass), Keith Moon (drums - died 9/7/78-32) - replaced by Kenny Jones | |
| 5/20/67 | 24 | 4 | 1. Happy Jack | Decca 32114 |
| 10/28/67 | 9 | 9 | 2. **I Can See For Miles** | Decca 32206 |
| 5/04/68 | 40 | 2 | 3. Call Me Lightning | Decca 32288 |
| 8/31/68 | 25 | 6 | 4. Magic Bus | Decca 32362 |
| 5/03/69 | 19 | 5 | 5. Pinball Wizard | Decca 32465 |
| 8/23/69 | 37 | 2 | 6. I'm Free | Decca 32519 |
| 8/01/70 | 27 | 6 | 7. Summertime Blues | Decca 32708 |
| 10/17/70 | 12 | 9 | 8. See Me, Feel Me | Decca 32729 |
| 8/07/71 | 15 | 10 | 9. Won't Get Fooled Again from the film "Lifehouse" | Decca 32846 |
| 12/04/71 | 34 | 5 | 10. Behind Blue Eyes | Decca 32888 |
| 8/05/72 | 17 | 8 | 11. Join Together | Decca 32983 |
| 1/13/73 | 39 | 2 | 12. The Relay | Track 33041 |
| 1/03/76 | 16 | 10 | 13. Squeeze Box | MCA 40475 |
| 9/16/78 | 14 | 9 | 14. Who Are You | MCA 40948 |
| 4/04/81 | 18 | 10 | 15. You Better You Bet | Warner 49698 |
| 10/09/82 | 28 | 6 | 16. Athena | Warner 29905 |
| | | | **HARLOW WILCOX & the Oakies** | |
| 11/22/69 | 30 | 6 | 1. Groovy Grubworm [I] | Plantation 28 |
| | | | **WILD CHERRY** | |
| | | | Cleveland, Ohio electrified funk band - Bob Parissi, lead singer | |
| 7/31/76 | 1 (3) | 18 | ★ 1. **Play That Funky Music** | Epic 50225 |
| | | | **KIM WILDE** | |
| | | | English - daughter of Marty Wilde ("Bad Boy") | |
| 7/17/82 | 25 | 8 | 1. Kids In America | EMI America 8110 |
| | | | **MATTHEW WILDER** | |
| | | | New York City native | |
| 11/26/83 + | 5 | 14 | 1. **Break My Stride** | Private I 04113 |
| 3/24/84 | 33 | 4 | 2. The Kid's American | Private I 04363 |

| DATE | POS | WKS | ARTIST—Record Title | LABEL & NO. |
|---|---|---|---|---|
| | | | **ANDY WILLIAMS** | |
| | | | born on 12/3/30 in Wall Lake, Iowa - host of his own NBC-TV musical/variety series (1962-1971) | |
| 8/18/56 | 7 | 17 | 1. **Canadian Sunset** | Cadence 1297 |
| 12/22/56 | 33 | 3 | 2. Baby Doll | Cadence 1303 |
| 3/02/57 | 1 (3) | 14 | 3. **Butterfly** | Cadence 1308 |
| 6/03/57 | 8 | 14 | 4. **I Like Your Kind Of Love** | Cadence 1323 |
| | | | female vocal by Peggy Powers | |
| 10/14/57 | 17 | 3 | 5. Lips Of Wine | Cadence 1336 |
| 2/24/58 | 3 | 14 | 6. **Are You Sincere** | Cadence 1340 |
| 9/22/58 | 17 | 6 | 7. Promise Me, Love | Cadence 1351 |
| 1/12/59 | 11 | 15 | 8. The Hawaiian Wedding Song | Cadence 1358 |
| 9/28/59 | 5 | 11 | 9. **Lonely Street** | Cadence 1370 |
| 12/28/59 + | 7 | 9 | 10. **The Village Of St. Bernadette** | Cadence 1374 |
| 6/05/61 | 37 | 2 | 11. The Bilbao Song | Cadence 1398 |
| 7/14/62 | 38 | 1 | 12. Stranger On The Shore | Columbia 42451 |
| 11/03/62 | 39 | 1 | 13. Don't You Believe It | Columbia 42523 |
| 3/23/63 | 2 (4) | 12 | 14. **Can't Get Used To Losing You/** | |
| 4/13/63 | 26 | 7 | 15. Days Of Wine And Roses | Columbia 42674 |
| 7/06/63 | 13 | 8 | 16. Hopeless | Columbia 42784 |
| 1/25/64 | 13 | 8 | 17. A Fool Never Learns | Columbia 42950 |
| 5/16/64 | 34 | 4 | 18. Wrong For Each Other | Columbia 43015 |
| 10/03/64 | 28 | 5 | 19. On The Street Where You Live | Columbia 43128 |
| | | | from the musical "My Fair Lady" | |
| 12/19/64 + | 24 | 7 | 20. Dear Heart | Columbia 43180 |
| 4/24/65 | 36 | 3 | 21. And Roses And Roses | Columbia 43257 |
| 10/16/65 | 40 | 1 | 22. Ain't It True | Columbia 43358 |
| 4/22/67 | 34 | 3 | 23. Music To Watch Girls By | Columbia 44065 |
| 11/30/68 | 33 | 4 | 24. Battle Hymn Of The Republic | Columbia 44650 |
| | | | with the St. Charles Borromeo Choir | |
| 5/03/69 | 22 | 7 | 25. Happy Heart | Columbia 44818 |
| 2/27/71 | 9 | 10 | 26. **(Where Do I Begin) Love Story** | Columbia 45317 |
| | | | from the film "Love Story" | |
| 5/20/72 | 34 | 4 | 27. Love Theme From "The Godfather" (Speak Softly Love) | Columbia 45579 |
| | | | **BILLY WILLIAMS** | |
| | | | member of black vocal group, the Charioteers (1935-1949) - died on 7/16/84 (74) | |
| 6/17/57 | 3 | 18 | 1. **I'm Gonna Sit Right Down And Write Myself A Letter** | Coral 61830 |
| 2/16/59 | 39 | 3 | 2. Nola | Coral 62069 |
| | | | **DANNY WILLIAMS** | |
| | | | native of Port Elizabeth, South Africa | |
| 4/04/64 | 9 | 10 | 1. **White On White** | United Art. 685 |
| | | | **DENIECE WILLIAMS** | |
| | | | member of Stevie Wonder's back-up group, Wonderlove (1971-76) - also see Johnny Mathis | |
| 3/05/77 | 25 | 7 | 1. Free | Columbia 10429 |
| 5/01/82 | 10 | 9 | 2. It's Gonna Take A Miracle | ARC 02812 |
| 4/14/84 | 1 (2) | 14 | ● 3. **Let's Hear It For The Boy** | Columbia 04417 |
| | | | from the film "Footloose" | |

| DATE | POS | WKS | ARTIST—Record Title | LABEL & NO. |
|---|---|---|---|---|
| | | | **DON WILLIAMS** | |
| | | | leader of the Pozo-Seco Singers | |
| 11/15/80 | 24 | 9 | 1. I Believe In You | MCA 41304 |
| | | | **JOHN WILLIAMS** | |
| | | | noted composer/conductor of many top box-office film hits | |
| 9/13/75 | 32 | 4 | 1. Theme From "Jaws" (Main Title) [I] | MCA 40439 |
| 8/13/77 | 10 | 7 | 2. **Star Wars (Main Title) [I]** | 20th Century 2345 |
| | | | performed by The London Symphony Orchestra | |
| 1/21/78 | 13 | 8 | 3. Theme From "Close Encounters Of The Third Kind" [I] | Arista 0300 |
| | | | **LARRY WILLIAMS** | |
| | | | began as a session pianist for Lloyd Price - commited suicide on 1/2/80 (44) | |
| 7/08/57 | 5 | 17 | 1. **Short Fat Fannie** | Specialty 608 |
| 11/11/57 | 14 | 14 | 2. Bony Moronie | Specialty 615 |
| | | | **MASON WILLIAMS** | |
| | | | one of the writers for the Smothers Brothers TV show | |
| 7/13/68 | 2 (2) | 11 | 1. **Classical Gas [I]** | Warner 7190 |
| | | | **MAURICE WILLIAMS & The Zodiacs** | |
| | | | Maurice, a native of Lancaster, South Carolina, was lead singer of the Gladiolas | |
| 10/10/60 | 1 (1) | 14 | 1. **Stay** | Herald 552 |
| | | | **OTIS WILLIAMS - see CHARMS** | |
| | | | **ROGER WILLIAMS** | |
| | | | America's #1 selling popular pianist in history | |
| 8/20/55 | 1 (4) | 26 | 1. **Autumn Leaves [I]** | Kapp 116 |
| 1/14/56 | 38 | 1 | 2. Wanting You [I] | Kapp 127 |
| 3/24/56 | 37 | 1 | 3. La Mer (Beyond The Sea) [I] | Kapp 138 |
| 3/16/57 | 15 | 10 | 4. Almost Paradise [I] | Kapp 175 |
| 11/11/57 | 22 | 7 | 5. Till | Kapp 197 |
| 9/08/58 | 10 | 11 | 6. **Near You [I]** | Kapp 233 |
| 10/15/66 | 7 | 14 | 7. **Born Free** | Kapp 767 |
| | | | **CHUCK WILLIS** | |
| | | | R&B singer/songwriter - died in a car accident on 4/10/58 (30) | |
| 5/13/57 | 12 | 8 | 1. C. C. Rider | Atlantic 1130 |
| 3/10/58 | 33 | 3 | 2. Betty And Dupree | Atlantic 1168 |
| 5/12/58 | 9 | 17 | 3. **What Am I Living For/** | |
| 5/26/58 | 24 | 2 | 4. Hang Up My Rock And Roll Shoes | Atlantic 1179 |
| | | | **AL WILSON** | |
| | | | member of The Jewels, and The Rollers | |
| 9/21/68 | 27 | 5 | 1. The Snake | Soul City 767 |
| 11/24/73 + | 1 (1) | 16 | ● 2. **Show And Tell** | Rocky Road 30073 |
| 11/09/74 | 30 | 3 | 3. La La Peace Song | Rocky Road 30200 |
| 5/01/76 | 29 | 4 | 4. I've Got A Feeling (We'll Be Seeing Each Other Again) | Playboy 6062 |
| | | | **ANN WILSON - see MIKE RENO** | |

| DATE | POS | WKS | ARTIST—Record Title | LABEL & NO. |
|------|-----|-----|---------------------|-------------|
| | | | **BRIAN WILSON** | |
| | | | leader of the Beach Boys | |
| 4/23/66 | 32 | 3 | 1. Caroline, No | Capitol 5610 |
| | | | **J. FRANK WILSON & The Cavaliers** | |
| | | | band formed in San Angelo, Texas | |
| 9/26/64 | 2 (1) | 12 | 1. **Last Kiss** | Josie 923 |
| | | | **JACKIE WILSON** | |
| | | | replaced Clyde McPhatter in Billy Ward & The Dominoes (1953-56) - died on 1/21/84 (49) | |
| 4/21/58 | 22 | 10 | 1. To Be Loved | Brunswick 55052 |
| 12/08/58 + | 7 | 16 | 2. **Lonely Teardrops** | Brunswick 55105 |
| 4/13/59 | 13 | 9 | 3. That's Why (I Love You So) | Brunswick 55121 |
| 7/06/59 | 20 | 6 | 4. I'll Be Satisfied | Brunswick 55136 |
| 10/12/59 | 37 | 1 | 5. You Better Know It | Brunswick 55149 |
| | | | from the film "Go Johnny Go" | |
| 1/04/60 | 34 | 3 | 6. Talk That Talk | Brunswick 55165 |
| 4/11/60 | 4 | 12 | 7. **Night/** | |
| 4/25/60 | 15 | 9 | 8.  Doggin' Around | Brunswick 55166 |
| 8/01/60 | 12 | 9 | 9. (You Were Made For) All My Love/ | |
| 8/01/60 | 15 | 8 | 10.  A Woman, A Lover, A Friend | Brunswick 55167 |
| 10/24/60 | 8 | 12 | 11. **Alone At Last/** | |
| 11/28/60 | 32 | 2 | 12.  Am I The Man | Brunswick 55170 |
| 1/16/61 | 9 | 6 | 13. **My Empty Arms** | Brunswick 55201 |
| 3/27/61 | 20 | 5 | 14. Please Tell Me Why/ | |
| 3/27/61 | 40 | 1 | 15.  Your One And Only Love | Brunswick 55208 |
| 6/26/61 | 19 | 5 | 16. I'm Comin' On Back To You | Brunswick 55216 |
| 9/11/61 | 37 | 2 | 17. Years From Now | Brunswick 55219 |
| 2/03/62 | 34 | 4 | 18. The Greatest Hurt | Brunswick 55221 |
| 3/23/63 | 5 | 9 | 19. **Baby Workout** | Brunswick 55239 |
| 8/10/63 | 33 | 1 | 20. Shake! Shake! Shake! | Brunswick 55246 |
| 11/19/66 | 11 | 8 | 21. Whispers (Gettin' Louder) | Brunswick 55300 |
| 9/02/67 | 6 | 9 | 22. **(Your Love Keeps Lifting Me) Higher And Higher** | Brunswick 55336 |
| 12/16/67 | 32 | 2 | 23. Since You Showed Me How To Be Happy | Brunswick 55354 |
| 8/31/68 | 34 | 2 | 24. I Get The Sweetest Feeling | Brunswick 55381 |
| | | | **MERI WILSON** | |
| 7/02/77 | 18 | 10 | ● 1. Telephone Man [N] | GRT 127 |
| | | | **NANCY WILSON** | |
| | | | jazz stylist from Columbus, Ohio | |
| 7/18/64 | 11 | 7 | 1. (You Don't Know) How Glad I Am | Capitol 5198 |
| 6/15/68 | 29 | 9 | 2. Face It Girl, It's Over | Capitol 2136 |
| | | | **WILTON PLACE STREET BAND** | |
| 3/12/77 | 24 | 7 | 1. Disco Lucy (I Love Lucy Theme) [I] | Island 078 |
| | | | **JESSE WINCHESTER** | |
| | | | Canadian citizen, originally from Shreveport, Louisiana | |
| 5/30/81 | 32 | 5 | 1. Say What | Bearsville 49711 |

| DATE | POS | WKS | ARTIST—Record Title | LABEL & NO. |
|---|---|---|---|---|
| | | | **WIND** | |
| | | | studio group featuring Tony Orlando as lead singer | |
| 10/04/69 | 28 | 4 | 1. Make Believe | Life 200 |
| | | | **KAI WINDING & Orchestra** | |
| | | | Danish - trombonist with Stan Kenton - died on 5/6/83 (60) | |
| 7/27/63 | 8 | 9 | 1. **More [I]** | Verve 10295 |
| | | | theme from the film "Mondo Cane" | |
| | | | **WING & A PRAYER FIFE & DRUM CORPS.** | |
| | | | New York studio disco production | |
| 12/20/75 + | 14 | 12 | 1. Baby Face | Wing & Prayer 103 |
| | | | **PETE WINGFIELD** | |
| | | | English | |
| 10/25/75 | 15 | 8 | 1. Eighteen With A Bullet | Island 026 |
| | | | hit #18 with a bullet on the 11/22/75 "Hot 100" | |
| | | | **WINGS - see PAUL McCARTNEY** | |
| | | | **WINSTONS** | |
| | | | soul sextet from Washington, D.C. | |
| 6/14/69 | 7 | 10 | ● 1. **Color Him Father** | Metromedia 117 |
| | | | **EDGAR WINTER Group** | |
| | | | born in Beaumont, Texas on 12/28/46 - younger brother of Johnny Winter - group features Rick Derringer, Ronnie Montrose & Dan Hartman | |
| 4/21/73 | 1 (1) | 14 | ● 1. **Frankenstein [I]** | Epic 10967 |
| 9/08/73 | 14 | 9 | 2. Free Ride | Epic 11024 |
| 8/10/74 | 33 | 2 | 3. River's Risin' | Epic 11143 |
| | | | **HUGO WINTERHALTER & his Orchestra** | |
| | | | conductor/arranger for RCA Records - died of cancer 9/17/73 (64) | |
| 7/28/56 | 2 (2) | 23 | 1. **Canadian Sunset [I]** | RCA 6537 |
| | | | piano solo by Eddie Heywood | |
| | | | **STEVE WINWOOD** | |
| | | | lead singer of Spencer Davis Group, Blind Faith, and Traffic | |
| 2/28/81 | 7 | 12 | 1. **While You See A Chance** | Island 49656 |
| | | | **BILL WITHERS** | |
| | | | born in Slab Fork, West Virginia on 7/4/38 - also see Grover Washington, Jr. | |
| 8/14/71 | 3 | 12 | ● 1. **Ain't No Sunshine** | Sussex 219 |
| 5/27/72 | 1 (3) | 14 | ● 2. **Lean On Me** | Sussex 235 |
| 9/09/72 | 2 (2) | 10 | ● 3. **Use Me** | Sussex 241 |
| 3/03/73 | 31 | 5 | 4. Kissing My Love | Sussex 250 |
| 1/21/78 | 30 | 4 | 5. Lovely Day | Columbia 10627 |
| | | | **PETER WOLF** | |
| | | | former lead singer of J. Geils Band | |
| 7/28/84 | 12 | 10 | 1. Lights Out | EMI America 8208 |
| | | | **WOLFMAN JACK - see GUESS WHO / STAMPEDERS** | |

| DATE | POS | WKS | ARTIST—Record Title | LABEL & NO. |
|------|-----|-----|---------------------|-------------|
| | | | **BOBBY WOMACK** | |
| | | | top session guitarist - Bobby and his four brothers formed the Valentinos | |
| 1/08/72 | 27 | 7 | 1. That's The Way I Feel About Cha | United Art. 50847 |
| 1/13/73 | 31 | 6 | ● 2. Harry Hippie | United Art. 50946 |
| 8/11/73 | 29 | 6 | 3. Nobody Wants You When You're Down And Out | United Art. 255 |
| 3/09/74 | 10 | 11 | ● 4. **Lookin' For A Love** | United Art. 375 |
| | | | **WONDER WHO?** | |
| | | | group is actually The 4 Seasons | |
| 11/27/65 | 12 | 8 | 1. Don't Think Twice | Philips 40324 |
| | | | **STEVIE WONDER** | |
| | | | born Steveland Morris on 5/13/50 in Saginaw, Michigan - also see Paul McCartney | |
| 7/06/63 | 1 (3) | 12 | 1. **Fingertips - Pt 2** | Tamla 54080 |
| 10/19/63 | 33 | 4 | 2. Workout Stevie, Workout | Tamla 54086 |
| | | | above 2 shown as Little Stevie Wonder | |
| 7/11/64 | 29 | 4 | 3. Hey Harmonica Man | Tamla 54096 |
| 1/22/66 | 3 | 9 | 4. **Uptight (Everything's Alright)** | Tamla 54124 |
| 5/07/66 | 20 | 4 | 5. Nothing's Too Good For My Baby | Tamla 54130 |
| 7/30/66 | 9 | 8 | 6. **Blowin In The Wind** | Tamla 54136 |
| 11/26/66 | 9 | 8 | 7. **A Place In The Sun** | Tamla 54139 |
| 4/01/67 | 32 | 3 | 8. Travlin' Man | Tamla 54147 |
| 6/24/67 | 2 (2) | 12 | 9. **I Was Made To Love Her** | Tamla 54151 |
| 10/21/67 | 12 | 5 | 10. I'm Wondering | Tamla 54157 |
| 4/27/68 | 9 | 9 | 11. **Shoo-Be-Doo-Be-Doo-Da-Day** | Tamla 54165 |
| 8/17/68 | 35 | 3 | 12. You Met Your Match | Tamla 54168 |
| 11/09/68 | 2 (2) | 13 | 13. **For Once In My Life** | Tamla 54174 |
| 3/22/69 | 39 | 1 | 14. I Don't Know Why/ | |
| 6/21/69 | 4 | 11 | 15.  **My Cherie Amour** | Tamla 54180 |
| 11/01/69 | 7 | 12 | 16. Yester-Me, Yester-You, Yesterday | Tamla 54188 |
| 2/21/70 | 26 | 5 | 17. Never Had A Dream Come True | Tamla 54191 |
| 7/04/70 | 3 | 13 | 18. **Signed, Sealed, Delivered I'm Yours** | Tamla 54196 |
| 10/31/70 | 9 | 8 | 19. **Heaven Help Us All** | Tamla 54200 |
| 3/27/71 | 13 | 9 | 20. We Can Work It Out | Tamla 54202 |
| 9/04/71 | 8 | 11 | 21. **If You Really Love Me** | Tamla 54208 |
| 6/24/72 | 33 | 5 | 22. Superwoman (Where Were You When I Needed You) | Tamla 54216 |
| 12/09/72 + | 1 (1) | 13 | 23. **Superstition** | Tamla 54226 |
| 3/31/73 | 1 (1) | 13 | 24. **You Are The Sunshine Of My Life** | Tamla 54232 |
| 9/01/73 | 4 | 12 | 25. **Higher Ground** | Tamla 54235 |
| 11/24/73 + | 8 | 14 | 26. **Living For The City** | Tamla 54242 |
| 4/27/74 | 16 | 9 | 27. Don't You Worry 'Bout A Thing | Tamla 54245 |
| 8/17/74 | 1 (1) | 14 | 28. **You Haven't Done Nothin** | Tamla 54252 |
| | | | background vocals by the Jackson 5 | |
| 11/30/74 + | 3 | 14 | 29. **Boogie On Reggae Woman** | Tamla 54254 |
| 12/04/76 + | 1 (1) | 15 | 30. **I Wish** | Tamla 54274 |
| 4/16/77 | 1 (3) | 13 | 31. **Sir Duke** | Tamla 54281 |
| | | | a tribute to Duke Ellington | |

| DATE | POS | WKS | ARTIST—Record Title | LABEL & NO. |
|------|-----|-----|---------------------|-------------|
| 9/17/77 | 32 | 4 | 32. Another Star | Tamla 54286 |
| 12/03/77 + | 36 | 5 | 33. As | Tamla 54291 |
| 11/10/79 | 4 | 14 | 34. **Send One Your Love** | Tamla 54303 |
| 10/04/80 | 5 | 16 | 35. **Master Blaster (Jammin')** | Tamla 54317 |
| 1/17/81 | 11 | 11 | 36. I Ain't Gonna Stand For It | Tamla 54320 |
| 1/30/82 | 4 | 13 | 37. **That Girl** | Tamla 1602 |
| 6/19/82 | 13 | 9 | 38. Do I Do | Tamla 1612 |
| 9/01/84 | 1 (3) | 15 | 39. **I Just Called To Say I Love You**<br>from the film "The Woman In Red" | Motown 1745 |
| | | | **BRENTON WOOD** | |
| 6/24/67 | 34 | 1 | 1. The Oogum Boogum Song | Double Shot 111 |
| 9/09/67 | 9 | 9 | 2. **Gimme Little Sign** | Double Shot 116 |
| 12/16/67 | 34 | 3 | 3. Baby You Got It | Double Shot 121 |
| | | | **LAUREN WOOD** | |
| 10/27/79 | 24 | 6 | 1. Please Don't Leave<br>harmony vocals by Michael McDonald | Warner 49043 |
| | | | **STEVIE WOODS** | |
| 11/14/81 | 25 | 10 | 1. Steal The Night | Cotillion 46016 |
| 3/20/82 | 38 | 3 | 2. Just Can't Win 'Em All | Cotillion 46030 |
| | | | **SHEB WOOLEY** | |
| | | | played Pete Nolan in the TV series "Rawhide" - also did<br>comical recordings as Ben Colder | |
| 6/02/58 | 1 (6) | 14 | 1. **The Purple People Eater [N]** | MGM 12651 |
| | | | **LINK WRAY & His Ray Men** | |
| | | | rock guitarist - American Indian from North Carolina | |
| 5/12/58 | 16 | 10 | 1. Rumble [I] | Cadence 1347 |
| 3/16/59 | 23 | 3 | 2. Raw-Hide [I] | Epic 9300 |
| | | | **BETTY WRIGHT** | |
| | | | background singer with KC, and Peter Brown | |
| 9/07/68 | 33 | 2 | 1. Girls Can't Do What The Guys Do | Alston 4569 |
| 12/11/71 + | 6 | 12 | ● 2. **Clean Up Woman** | Alston 4601 |
| | | | **CHARLES WRIGHT & THE WATTS 103rd STREET RHYTHM BAND** | |
| | | | Los Angeles-based funk group - originally known as the<br>Soul Runners | |
| 3/22/69 | 11 | 10 | 1. Do Your Thing | Warner 7250 |
| 5/30/70 | 16 | 10 | 2. Love Land | Warner 7365 |
| 9/12/70 | 12 | 10 | 3. Express Yourself | Warner 7417 |
| | | | **DALE WRIGHT** | |
| 2/24/58 | 38 | 2 | 1. She's Neat<br>with the Rock-Its | Fraternity 792 |
| | | | **GARY WRIGHT** | |
| | | | keyboardist/vocalist with Spooky Tooth | |
| 1/31/76 | 2 (3) | 14 | ● 1. **Dream Weaver** | Warner 8167 |
| 5/15/76 | 2 (2) | 18 | 2. **Love Is Alive** | Warner 8143 |
| 8/01/81 | 16 | 10 | 3. Really Wanna Know You | Warner 49769 |

| DATE | POS | WKS | ARTIST—Record Title | LABEL & NO. |
|---|---|---|---|---|
| 6/25/55 | 16 | 9 | **PRISCILLA WRIGHT**<br>1. The Man In The Raincoat<br>with Don Wright & The Septette | Unique 303 |
| 12/28/68 + | 19 | 9 | **TAMMY WYNETTE**<br>born Wynette Pugh on 5/5/42 near Tupelo, Mississippi<br>1. Stand By Your Man | Epic 10398 |
| 3/17/84 | 12 | 7 | **"WEIRD AL" YANKOVIC**<br>comical accordionist, specializing in parodies<br>1. Eat It [N]<br>parody of Michael Jackson's "Beat It" - guitar: Rick Derringer | Rock 'n' R. 04374 |
| 3/14/81 | 19 | 7 | **YARBROUGH & PEOPLES**<br>Cavin Yarbrough & Alisa Peoples<br>● 1. Don't Stop The Music | Mercury 76085 |
| 4/17/65 | 12 | 9 | **GLENN YARBROUGH**<br>lead singer of the Limeliters (1959-63)<br>1. Baby The Rain Must Fall | RCA 8498 |
| | | | **YARDBIRDS**<br>British legendary rock band featuring Eric Clapton & Jeff Beck, evolved into Led Zeppelin - Keith Relf (original lead singer) died on 5/14/76 (33) | |
| 6/05/65 | 6 | 9 | 1. **For Your Love** | Epic 9790 |
| 8/21/65 | 9 | 8 | 2. **Heart Full Of Soul** | Epic 9823 |
| 11/20/65 | 17 | 7 | 3. I'm A Man | Epic 9857 |
| 4/09/66 | 11 | 8 | 4. Shapes Of Things | Epic 10006 |
| 7/16/66 | 13 | 7 | 5. Over Under Sideways Down | Epic 10035 |
| 12/24/66 | 30 | 4 | 6. Happenings Ten Years Time Ago | Epic 10094 |
| 4/29/67 | 25 | 5 | **YELLOW BALLOON**<br>quintet from Oregon and Arizona formed by Don Grady of TV's "My Three Sons"<br>1. Yellow Balloon | Canterbury 508 |
| | | | **YES**<br>British progressive rock band - original lineup: Jon Anderson (vocals), Steve Howe (guitars), Chris Squire (bass), Bill Bruford (drums), Tony Kaye (keyboards) | |
| 12/04/71 | 40 | 2 | 1. Your Move | Atlantic 2819 |
| 3/04/72 | 13 | 10 | 2. Roundabout | Atlantic 2854 |
| 11/19/83 + | 1 (2) | 17 | 3. **Owner Of A Lonely Heart** | Atco 99817 |
| 3/24/84 | 24 | 7 | 4. Leave It | Atco 99787 |
| | | | **DENNIS YOST - see CLASSICS IV** | |
| 8/02/69 | 5 | 12 | **YOUNGBLOODS**<br>folk-rock group led by Jesse Colin Young<br>● 1. **Get Together [R]**<br>re-release of 1967 hit (Pos. 62) | RCA 9752 |
| | | | **YOUNG-HOLT UNLIMITED**<br>Eldee Young & Isaac "Red" Holt - 2/3 of the Ramsey Lewis Trio | |
| 1/21/67 | 40 | 2 | 1. Wack Wack [I]<br>shown as the Young Holt Trio | Brunswick 55305 |
| 12/07/68 + | 3 | 12 | ● 2. **Soulful Strut [I]** | Brunswick 55391 |

| DATE | POS | WKS | ARTIST—Record Title | LABEL & NO. |
|---|---|---|---|---|
| | | | **YOUNG RASCALS - see RASCALS** | |
| | | | **BARRY YOUNG** | |
| 12/04/65 + | **13** | 7 | 1. One Has My Name (The Other Has My Heart) | Dot 16756 |
| | | | **FARON YOUNG** | |
| | | | country singer - born in Shreveport, Louisiana on 2/25/32 | |
| 5/01/61 | **12** | 11 | 1. Hello Walls | Capitol 4533 |
| | | | **JOHN PAUL YOUNG** | |
| | | | Australian | |
| 8/05/78 | **7** | 15 | 1. **Love Is In The Air** | Scotti Br. 402 |
| | | | **KATHY YOUNG with The Innocents** | |
| | | | Kathy was born on 10/21/45 in Santa Ana, California | |
| 10/31/60 | **3** | 15 | 1. **A Thousand Stars** | Indigo 108 |
| 3/06/61 | **30** | 6 | 2. Happy Birthday Blues | Indigo 115 |
| | | | **NEIL YOUNG** | |
| | | | Canadian-born - member of Buffalo Springfield and Crosby, Stills, Nash & Young - featuring backup band, Crazy Horse | |
| 12/05/70 | **33** | 3 | 1. Only Love Can Break Your Heart | Reprise 0958 |
| 2/12/72 | **1** (1) | 13 | ● 2. **Heart Of Gold** | Reprise 1065 |
| 5/20/72 | **31** | 4 | 3. Old Man | Reprise 1084 |
| | | | **PAUL YOUNG** | |
| | | | English | |
| 3/03/84 | **22** | 8 | 1. Come Back And Stay | Columbia 04313 |
| | | | **VICTOR YOUNG & Orchestra** | |
| | | | composer/conductor - died on 11/11/56 (56) | |
| 7/08/57 | **13** | 9 | 1. Around The World In 80 Days [I] | Decca 30262 |
| | | | flip side is Bing Crosby's vocal version | |
| | | | **TIMI YURO** | |
| | | | born Rosemarie Yuro on 8/4/41 in Chicago | |
| 7/31/61 | **4** | 10 | 1. **Hurt** | Liberty 55343 |
| 8/11/62 | **12** | 6 | 2. What's A Matter Baby (Is It Hurting You) | Liberty 55469 |
| 8/10/63 | **24** | 7 | 3. Make The World Go Away | Liberty 55587 |
| | | | **HELMUT ZACHARIAS & His Magic Violins** | |
| | | | German | |
| 9/08/56 | **12** | 7 | 1. When The White Lilacs Bloom Again [I] | Decca 30039 |
| | | | **JOHN ZACHERLE "The Cool Ghoul"** | |
| 3/10/58 | **6** | 7 | 1. **Dinner With Drac - Part 1 [N]** | Cameo 130 |
| | | | **PIA ZADORA** | |
| | | | actress | |
| 2/12/83 | **36** | 3 | 1. The Clapping Song | Elektra 69889 |
| | | | **ZAGER & EVANS** | |
| | | | Denny Zager & Rick Evans | |
| 6/28/69 | **1** (6) | 12 | ● 1. **In The Year 2525 (Exordium & Terminus)** | RCA 0174 |

| DATE | POS | WKS | ARTIST—Record Title | LABEL & NO. |
|---|---|---|---|---|
| | | | **MICHAEL ZAGER Band** | |
| | | | keyboardist with Ten Wheel Drive | |
| 4/29/78 | **36** | 4 | 1. Let's All Chant [I] | Private S. 45184 |
| | | | **RICKY ZAHND & The Blue Jeaners** | |
| 12/24/55 | **21** | 2 | 1. (I'm Gettin') Nuttin' For Christmas [N-X] | Columbia 40576 |
| | | | **FRANK ZAPPA** | |
| | | | rock music's leading satirist - formed The Mothers Of Invention in 1966 | |
| 9/04/82 | **32** | 3 | 1. Valley Girl [N] | Barking P. 02972 |
| | | | featuring Frank's daughter: Moon Unit Zappa | |
| | | | **WARREN ZEVON** | |
| | | | Canadian-born singer/songwriter | |
| 4/22/78 | **21** | 6 | 1. Werewolves Of London | Asylum 45472 |
| | | | **ZOMBIES** | |
| | | | British rock quintet featuring Rod Argent (keyboards) & Colin Blunstone (vocals) | |
| 11/07/64 | **2** (1) | 12 | 1. **She's Not There** | Parrot 9695 |
| 1/30/65 | **6** | 8 | 2. **Tell Her No** | Parrot 9723 |
| 2/22/69 | **3** | 11 | ● 3. **Time Of The Season** | Date 1628 |
| | | | **ZZ TOP** | |
| | | | rock trio from El Paso, Texas: Billy Gibbons (guitar), Dusty Hill (bass), & Frank Beard (drums) | |
| 8/16/75 | **20** | 4 | 1. Tush | London 220 |
| 3/01/80 | **34** | 3 | 2. I Thank You | Warner 49163 |
| 5/07/83 | **37** | 3 | 3. Gimme All Your Lovin | Warner 29693 |
| 6/02/84 | **8** | 12 | 4. **Legs** | Warner 29272 |

# THE SONGS

# THE SONGS

This section lists, alphabetically, all titles from the artist section. The artist's name is listed below each title, along with the highest position attained (POS) and year of peak popularity (YR). Some titles show the letter F as a position, indicating the title was listed as a flip side and did not chart on its own.

A song with more than one charted version is listed once, with the artist's names listed below in chronological order. Many songs that have the same title, but are different tunes, are listed separately, with the most popular title listed first. This will make it easy to determine if songs are indeed the same, the amount of charted versions of a particular song, and the most popular version.

Cross references have been used throughout to aid in finding a title. If you have trouble, please keep in mind the following: Titles in which an apostrophe is used within a word will come before a title using the complete spelling (Lovin' comes before Loving). A title with dashes between words will follow titles of similar wording (Mother-In-Law follows Mother Popcorn). Titles such as I.O.U., D.O.A., and SOS will be found at the beginning of each letter.

| POS/YR | RECORD TITLE/ARTIST |
|---|---|

**A**

| POS/YR | RECORD TITLE/ARTIST |
|---|---|
| 28/66 | "A" Team<br>SSgt Barry Sadler |
| 1/70 | ABC<br>Jacksons |
| 26/82 | Abacab<br>Genesis |
| 16/64 | Abigail Beecher<br>Freddy Cannon |
| 15/63 | Abilene<br>George Hamilton IV |
| 31/60 | About This Thing Called Love<br>Fabian |
| 32/74 | Abra-Ca-Dabra<br>DeFranco Family featuring Tony DeFranco |
| 1/82 | Abracadabra<br>Steve Miller Band |
| | Abraham, Martin And John |
| 4/68 | Dion |
| 33/69 | Miracles |
| 35/69 | Moms Mabley |
| 8/71 | Tom Clay (medley) |
| 26/71 | Absolutely Right<br>Five Man Electrical Band |
| 13/65 | Action<br>Freddy Cannon |
| 20/76 | Action<br>Sweet |
| | Admiral Halsey...see: Uncle Albert |
| 8/84 | Adult Education<br>Daryl Hall & John Oates |
| 9/83 | Affair Of The Heart<br>Rick Springfield |
| 16/57 | Affair To Remember (Our Love Affair)<br>Vic Damone |
| 1/83 | Africa<br>Toto |
| 18/70 | After Midnight<br>Eric Clapton |

| POS/YR | RECORD TITLE/ARTIST |
|---|---|
| 32/57 | After School<br>Randy Starr |
| 23/83 | After The Fall<br>Journey |
| 32/82 | After The Glitter Fades<br>Stevie Nicks |
| 22/74 | After The Goldrush<br>Prelude |
| 10/56 | After The Lights Go Down Low<br>Al Hibbler |
| 2/79 | After The Love Has Gone<br>Earth, Wind & Fire |
| 8/77 | After The Lovin'<br>Engelbert Humperdinck |
| 1/76 | Afternoon Delight<br>Starland Vocal Band |
| 1/84 | Against All Odds (Take A Look At Me Now)<br>Phil Collins |
| 5/80 | Against The Wind<br>Bob Seger |
| 21/65 | Agent Double-O-Soul<br>Edwin Starr |
| 36/75 | Agony And The Ecstasy<br>Smokey Robinson |
| 29/81 | Ah! Leah!<br>Donnie Iris |
| 5/62 | Ahab, The Arab<br>Ray Stevens |
| 28/81 | Ai No Corrida<br>Quincy Jones |
| 17/81 | Ain't Even Done With The Night<br>John Cougar |
| 12/77 | Ain't Gonna Bump No More (With No Big Fat Woman)<br>Joe Tex |
| 39/66 | Ain't Gonna Lie<br>Keith |
| 20/57 | Ain't Got No Home<br>Clarence "Frogman" Henry |
| 24/70 | Ain't It Funky Now<br>James Brown |
| 40/65 | Ain't It True<br>Andy Williams |

| POS/YR | RECORD TITLE/ARTIST |
|---|---|
| 22/79 | **Ain't Love A Bitch**<br>Rod Stewart |
| 19/67<br>1/70 | **Ain't No Mountain High Enough**<br>Marvin Gaye & Tammi Terrell<br>Diana Ross |
| 13/79 | **Ain't No Stoppin' Us Now**<br>McFadden & Whitehead |
| 3/71 | **Ain't No Sunshine**<br>Bill Withers |
| 16/68 | **Ain't No Way**<br>Aretha Franklin |
| 8/75 | **Ain't No Way To Treat A Lady**<br>Helen Reddy |
| 4/73 | **Ain't No Woman (Like The One I've Got)**<br>Four Tops |
| 22/83 | **Ain't Nobody**<br>Rufus featuring Chaka Khan |
| 8/68<br>21/77 | **Ain't Nothing Like The Real Thing**<br>Marvin Gaye & Tammi Terrell<br>Donny & Marie Osmond |
| 20/64 | **Ain't Nothing You Can Do**<br>Bobby Bland |
| 19/64 | **Ain't She Sweet**<br>Beatles |
| 1/55<br>10/55<br>22/63<br>35/79 | **Ain't That A Shame**<br>Pat Boone<br>Fats Domino<br>Four Seasons<br>Cheap Trick |
| 33/61 | **Ain't That Just Like A Woman**<br>Fats Domino |
| 16/64 | **Ain't That Loving You Baby**<br>Elvis Presley |
| 8/65 | **Ain't That Peculiar**<br>Marvin Gaye |
| 13/66<br>17/74 | **Ain't Too Proud To Beg**<br>Temptations<br>Rolling Stones |
| 21/72 | **Ain't Understanding Mellow**<br>Jerry Butler & Brenda Lee Eager |
| 6/74 | **Air That I Breathe**<br>Hollies |
| 31/70 | **Airport Love Theme**<br>Vincent Bell |

| POS/YR | RECORD TITLE/ARTIST |
|---|---|
| 6/62<br>29/64 | **Al Di La'**<br>Emilio Pericoli<br>Ray Charles Singers |
| 14/55 | **Alabama Jubilee**<br>Ferko String Band |
|  | **Alamo**...see: Ballad Of |
| 29/71 | **Albert Flasher**<br>Guess Who |
| 32/66<br>15/67 | **Alfie**<br>Cher<br>Dionne Warwick |
| 29/84 | **Alibis**<br>Sergio Mendes |
| 17/63 | **Alice In Wonderland**<br>Neil Sedaka |
| 27/68 | **Alice Long (You're Still My Favorite Girlfriend)**<br>Tommy Boyce & Bobby Hart |
| 29/81 | **Alien**<br>Atlanta Rhythm Section |
| 34/72 | **Alive**<br>Bee Gees |
| 14/78 | **Alive Again**<br>Chicago |
| 35/67 | **All**<br>James Darren |
| 3/62 | **All Alone Am I**<br>Brenda Lee |
| 20/68 | **All Along The Watchtower**<br>Jimi Hendrix |
| 2/59 | **All American Boy**<br>Bill Parsons |
| 11/56 | **All At Once You Love Her**<br>Perry Como |
| 2/76 | **All By Myself**<br>Eric Carmen |
| 7/65 | **All Day And All Of The Night**<br>Kinks |
| 35/71 | **All Day Music**<br>War |
| 33/60 | **All I Could Do Was Cry**<br>Etta James |
| 7/71 | **All I Ever Need Is You**<br>Sonny & Cher |

| POS/YR | RECORD TITLE/ARTIST |
|--------|---------------------|
| | **All I Have To Do Is Dream** |
| 1/58 | Everly Brothers |
| 14/63 | Richard Chamberlain |
| 27/70 | Glen Campbell & Bobbie Gentry |
| | **All I Know** |
| 9/73 | Art Garfunkel |
| | **All I Need** |
| 8/67 | Temptations |
| | **All I Really Want To Do** |
| 15/65 | Cher |
| 40/65 | Byrds |
| | **All I See Is You** |
| 20/66 | Dusty Springfield |
| | **All In My Mind** |
| 19/61 | Maxine Brown |
| | **All My Life** |
| 37/83 | Kenny Rogers |
| | **All Night Long** |
| 19/80 | Joe Walsh |
| | **All Night Long (All Night)** |
| 1/83 | Lionel Richie |
| | **(All Of A Sudden) My Heart Sings** |
| 15/59 | Paul Anka |
| 38/65 | Mel Carter |
| | **All Of You** |
| 19/84 | Julio Iglesias & Diana Ross |
| | **All Our Tomorrows** |
| 28/82 | Eddie Schwartz |
| | **All Out Of Love** |
| 2/80 | Air Supply |
| | **All Over Again** |
| 38/58 | Johnny Cash |
| | **All Over The World** |
| 13/80 | Electric Light Orchestra |
| | **All Right** |
| 12/83 | Christopher Cross |
| | **All Right Now** |
| 4/70 | Free |
| | **All Shook Up** |
| 1/57 | Elvis Presley |
| | **All Strung Out** |
| 26/66 | Nino Tempo & April Stevens |
| 34/77 | John Travolta |
| | **All The King's Horses** |
| 26/72 | Aretha Franklin |

| POS/YR | RECORD TITLE/ARTIST |
|--------|---------------------|
| | **All The Time** |
| 21/58 | Johnny Mathis |
| | **All The Way** |
| 2/58 | Frank Sinatra |
| | **All The Young Dudes** |
| 37/72 | Mott The Hoople |
| | **All This Love** |
| 17/83 | DeBarge |
| | **All Those Years Ago** |
| 2/81 | George Harrison |
| | **All Through The Night** |
| 5/84 | Cyndi Lauper |
| | **All Time High** |
| 36/83 | Rita Coolidge |
| | **All You Get From Love Is A Love Song** |
| 35/77 | Carpenters |
| | **All You Need Is Love** |
| 1/67 | Beatles |
| | **Allegheny Moon** |
| 2/56 | Patti Page |
| | **Allentown** |
| 17/83 | Billy Joel |
| | **Alley Cat** |
| 7/62 | Bent Fabric & His Piano |
| | **Alley-Oop** |
| 1/60 | Hollywood Argyles |
| 15/60 | Dante & The Evergreens |
| | **Almost Grown** |
| 32/59 | Chuck Berry |
| | **Almost Like Being In Love** |
| 32/78 | Michael Johnson |
| | **Almost Over You** |
| 25/84 | Sheena Easton |
| | **Almost Paradise** |
| 15/57 | Roger Williams |
| 31/57 | Lou Stein |
| | **Almost Paradise...Love Theme From Footloose** |
| 7/84 | Mike Reno & Ann Wilson |
| | **Almost Persuaded** |
| 24/66 | David Houston |
| | **Almost Summer** |
| 28/78 | Celebration featuring Mike Love |

| POS/YR | RECORD TITLE/ARTIST |
|--------|---------------------|
| 1/72 | **Alone Again (Naturally)** <br> Gilbert O'Sullivan |
| 8/60 | **Alone At Last** <br> Jackie Wilson |
| 18/57 <br> 28/64 | **Alone (Why Must I Be Alone)** <br> Shepherd Sisters <br> Four Seasons |
| 9/59 <br> 27/69 | **Along Came Jones** <br> Coasters <br> Ray Stevens |
| 7/66 | **Along Comes Mary** <br> Association |
| 32/74 | **Already Gone** <br> Eagles |
| 2/73 | **Also Sprach Zarathustra (2001)** <br> Deodato |
| 40/62 | **Alvin Twist** <br> Chipmunks |
| 3/59 | **Alvin's Harmonica** <br> Chipmunks |
| 33/60 | **Alvin's Orchestra** <br> Chipmunks |
| 19/59 | **Always** <br> Sammy Turner |
| 18/78 | **Always And Forever** <br> Heatwave |
| 5/82 | **Always On My Mind** <br> Willie Nelson |
| | **Always Something There To Remind Me**...*see: (There's)* |
| 18/68 | **Always Together** <br> Dells |
| 33/64 | **Always Together** <br> Al Martino |
| 31/60 | **Am I Losing You** <br> Jim Reeves |
| 25/60 <br> 18/68 | **Am I That Easy To Forget** <br> Debbie Reynolds <br> Engelbert Humperdinck |
| 32/60 | **Am I The Man** <br> Jackie Wilson |
| 15/71 <br> 11/72 | **Amazing Grace** <br> Judy Collins <br> Royal Scots Dragoon Guards |

| POS/YR | RECORD TITLE/ARTIST |
|--------|---------------------|
| 37/68 | **Ame Caline (Soul Coaxing)** <br> Raymond Lefevre & His Orchestra |
| 7/65 <br> 36/68 | **Amen** <br> Impressions <br> Otis Redding |
| 8/81 | **America** <br> Neil Diamond |
| 27/72 | **American City Suite** <br> Cashman & West |
| 13/80 | **American Dream** <br> Nitty Gritty Dirt Band |
| 17/82 | **American Heartbeat** <br> Survivor |
| 16/82 | **American Music** <br> Pointer Sisters |
| 1/72 | **American Pie** <br> Don McLean |
| 26/72 | **American Trilogy** <br> Mickey Newbury |
| 35/74 | **American Tune** <br> Paul Simon |
| 1/70 | **American Woman** <br> Guess Who |
| 4/74 <br> 24/74 | **Americans** <br> Byron MacGregor <br> Gordon Sinclair |
| 27/75 | **Amie** <br> Pure Prairie League |
| 7/59 | **Among My Souvenirs** <br> Connie Francis |
| 18/61 | **Amor** <br> Ben E. King |
| | **(Amos & Andy Song)**...*see: Like A Sunday In Salem* |
| 8/71 | **Amos Moses** <br> Jerry Reed |
| 38/55 | **Amukiriki (The Lord Willing)** <br> Les Paul & Mary Ford |
| 37/57 | **Anastasia** <br> Pat Boone |
| 22/67 | **And Get Away** <br> Esquires |
| 22/82 | **And I Am Telling You I'm Not Going** <br> Jennifer Holliday |

| POS/YR | RECORD TITLE/ARTIST |
|--------|---------------------|
| 12/64 | **And I Love Her (Him)** Beatles |
| 29/73 | **And I Love You So** Perry Como |
| 36/65 | **And Roses And Roses** Andy Williams |
| 9/57 12/57 | **And That Reminds Me** Kay Starr Della Reese |
| 19/80 | **And The Beat Goes On** Whispers |
| 2/69 | **And When I Die** Blood, Sweat & Tears |
| 20/73 | **Angel** Aretha Franklin |
| 40/72 | **Angel** Rod Stewart |
| 5/61 | **Angel Baby** Rosie & The Originals |
| 30/58 | **Angel Baby** Dean Martin |
| 40/82 | **Angel In Blue** J. Geils Band |
| 6/77 | **Angel In Your Arms** Hot |
| 7/68 4/81 | **Angel Of The Morning** Merrilee Rush & The Turnabouts Juice Newton |
| 22/61 | **Angel On My Shoulder** Shelby Flint |
| 38/80 | **Angel Say No** Tommy Tutone |
| 33/58 | **Angel Smile** Nat King Cole |
| 27/60 | **Angela Jones** Johnny Ferguson |
| 11/56 | **Angels In The Sky** Crew-Cuts |
| 22/59 | **Angels Listened In** Crests |
| 1/73 | **Angie** Rolling Stones |
| | **Angie**...see: *Different Worlds* |

| POS/YR | RECORD TITLE/ARTIST |
|--------|---------------------|
| 1/74 | **Angie Baby** Helen Reddy |
| | **(Angry Young Man)**...see:*Fooling Yourself* |
| 1/74 | **Annie's Song** John Denver |
| 1/80 | **Another Brick In The Wall (Part II)** Pink Floyd |
| 5/71 | **Another Day** Paul McCartney |
| 1/80 | **Another One Bites The Dust** Queen |
| 32/74 | **Another Park, Another Sunday** Doobie Brothers |
| 32/76 | **Another Rainy Day In New York City** Chicago |
| 10/63 6/74 | **Another Saturday Night** Sam Cooke Cat Stevens |
| 22/60 | **Another Sleepless Night** Jimmy Clanton |
| 32/77 | **Another Star** Stevie Wonder |
| 20/58 | **Another Time, Another Place** Patti Page |
| 32/80 | **Answering Machine** Rupert Holmes |
| | **(Anthony's Song)**...see: *Movin' Out* |
| 13/72 | **Anticipation** Carly Simon |
| 23/62 14/82 | **Any Day Now** Chuck Jackson Ronnie Milsap |
| 14/65 | **Any Way You Want It** Dave Clark Five |
| 23/80 | **Any Way You Want It** Journey |
| 31/61 | **Anybody But Me** Brenda Lee |
| 31/60 | **Anymore** Teresa Brewer |
| 8/64 | **Anyone Who Had A Heart** Dionne Warwick |

| POS/YR | RECORD TITLE/ARTIST |
|---|---|
| 31/62 | **Anything That's Part Of You**<br>Elvis Presley |
| 37/76 | **Anything You Want**<br>John Valenti |
| 33/76 | **Anytime (I'll Be There)**<br>Paul Anka |
| 20/56 | **Anyway You Want Me (That's How I Will Be)**<br>Elvis Presley |
| 2/61 | **Apache**<br>Jorgen Ingmann & His Guitar |
| | **Apartment**...see: *Theme From The* |
| 24/56 | **Ape Call**<br>Nervous Norvus |
| 29/60 | **Apple Green**<br>June Valli |
| 32/65 | **Apple Of My Eye**<br>Roy Head |
| 6/67 | **Apples, Peaches, Pumpkin Pie**<br>Jay & The Techniques |
| 37/69 | **April Fools**<br>Dionne Warwick |
| 28/56 | **April In Paris**<br>Count Basie & His Orchestra |
| 1/57 | **April Love**<br>Pat Boone |
| 1/69 | **Aquarius**<br>5th Dimension |
| 15/84 | **Are We Ourselves?**<br>Fixx |
| 39/69 | **Are You Happy**<br>Jerry Butler |
| 39/67 | **Are You Lonely For Me**<br>Freddie Scott |
| 1/60<br>14/74 | **Are You Lonesome Tonight?**<br>Elvis Presley<br>Donny Osmond |
| 15/73 | **Are You Man Enough**<br>Four Tops |
| 14/70 | **Are You Ready?**<br>Pacific Gas & Electric |
| 10/58 | **Are You Really Mine**<br>Jimmie Rodgers |

| POS/YR | RECORD TITLE/ARTIST |
|---|---|
| 11/56 | **Are You Satisfied?**<br>Rusty Draper |
| 3/58 | **Are You Sincere**<br>Andy Williams |
| 39/66 | **Are You There (With Another Girl)**<br>Dionne Warwick |
| 26/77 | **Ariel**<br>Dean Friedman |
| 10/70 | **Arizona**<br>Mark Lindsay |
| 28/73 | **Armed And Extremely Dangerous**<br>First Choice |
| 12/57<br>13/57<br>25/57 | **Around The World In 80 Days**<br>Mantovani & His Orchestra<br>Victor Young & Orchestra<br>Bing Crosby |
| 29/79 | **Arrow Through Me**<br>Paul McCartney |
| 1/81 | **Arthur's Theme (Best That You Can Do)**<br>Christopher Cross |
| 20/60 | **Artificial Flowers**<br>Bobby Darin |
| 36/78 | **As**<br>Stevie Wonder |
| 10/61 | **As If I Didn't Know**<br>Adam Wade |
| 22/65<br>6/66 | **As Tears Go By**<br>Marianne Faithfull<br>Rolling Stones |
| 31/70 | **As The Years Go By**<br>Mashmakhan |
| 12/64 | **As Usual**<br>Brenda Lee |
| 37/80 | **Ashes By Now**<br>Rodney Crowell |
| 8/61 | **Asia Minor**<br>Kokomo |
| 12/64 | **Ask Me**<br>Elvis Presley |
| 18/56 | **Ask Me**<br>Nat King Cole |
| 40/71 | **Ask Me No Questions**<br>B.B. King |

| POS/YR | RECORD TITLE/ARTIST |
|--------|---------------------|
| 27/72 | **Ask Me What You Want**<br>Millie Jackson |
| 24/65 | **Ask The Lonely**<br>Four Tops |
| 19/61 | **Astronaut (Parts 1 & 2)**<br>Jose Jimenez |
| 30/77 | **At Midnight (My Love Will Lift You Up)**<br>Rufus featuring Chaka Khan |
| 7/55<br>17/55 | **At My Front Door**<br>Pat Boone<br>El Dorados |
| 3/75 | **At Seventeen**<br>Janis Ian |
|  | **(At The Copa)**...see: Copacabana |
| 1/58<br>21/58 | **At The Hop**<br>Danny & The Juniors<br>Nick Todd |
| 18/66 | **At The Scene**<br>Dave Clark Five |
| 16/67 | **At The Zoo**<br>Simon & Garfunkel |
| 28/82 | **Athena**<br>Who |
| 27/81 | **Atlanta Lady (Something About Your Love)**<br>Marty Balin |
| 7/69 | **Atlantis**<br>Donovan |
| 39/80 | **Atomic**<br>Blondie |
| 18/66 | **Attack**<br>Toys |
| 21/75 | **Attitude Dancing**<br>Carly Simon |
| 15/73 | **Aubrey**<br>Bread |
| 19/57 | **Auctioneer**<br>Leroy Van Dyke |
| 15/84 | **Authority Song**<br>John Cougar |
| 25/75 | **Autobahn**<br>Kraftwerk |
| 5/84 | **Automatic**<br>Pointer Sisters |

| POS/YR | RECORD TITLE/ARTIST |
|--------|---------------------|
| 34/83 | **Automatic Man**<br>Michael Sembello |
| 37/72 | **Automatically Sunshine**<br>Supremes |
| 1/55<br>35/55 | **Autumn Leaves**<br>Roger Williams<br>Steve Allen |
| 19/68 | **Autumn Of My Life**<br>Bobby Goldsboro |
| 18/56 | **Autumn Waltz**<br>Tony Bennett |

# B

| POS/YR | RECORD TITLE/ARTIST |
|--------|---------------------|
| 1/79 | **Babe**<br>Styx |
| 14/66 | **B-A-B-Y**<br>Carla Thomas |
| 8/69 | **Baby, Baby Don't Cry**<br>Miracles |
| 12/61 | **Baby Blue**<br>Echoes |
| 14/72 | **Baby Blue**<br>Badfinger |
| 1/78 | **Baby Come Back**<br>Player |
| 32/68 | **Baby, Come Back**<br>Equals |
| 27/74 | **Baby Come Close**<br>Smokey Robinson |
| 1/83 | **Baby, Come To Me**<br>Patti Austin & James Ingram |
| 33/56 | **Baby Doll**<br>Andy Williams |
| 1/72 | **Baby Don't Get Hooked On Me**<br>Mac Davis |
| 8/65 | **Baby Don't Go**<br>Sonny & Cher |
| 39/64 | **Baby, Don't You Cry**<br>Ray Charles |
| 27/64 | **Baby Don't You Do It**<br>Marvin Gaye |

| POS/YR | RECORD TITLE/ARTIST |
|--------|---------------------|
| 30/63 | **Baby Don't You Weep**<br>Garnet Mimms & The Enchanters |
| 14/76 | **Baby Face**<br>Wing & A Prayer Fife & Drum Corps. |
| 11/78 | **Baby Hold On**<br>Eddie Money |
| 35/70 | **Baby Hold On**<br>Grass Roots |
| 26/84 | **Baby I Lied**<br>Deborah Allen |
| 4/67 | **Baby I Love You**<br>Aretha Franklin |
| 24/64<br>9/69 | **Baby, I Love You**<br>Ronettes<br>Andy Kim |
| 12/76 | **Baby, I Love Your Way**<br>Peter Frampton |
| 11/64<br>3/67 | **Baby I Need Your Loving**<br>Four Tops<br>Johnny Rivers |
| 3/71 | **Baby I'm-A Want You**<br>Bread |
| 25/79 | **Baby I'm Burnin'**<br>Dolly Parton |
| 14/69 | **Baby, I'm For Real**<br>Originals |
| 11/65 | **Baby, I'm Yours**<br>Barbara Lewis |
| 8/62<br>5/69 | **Baby It's You**<br>Shirelles<br>Smith |
| 14/83 | **Baby Jane**<br>Rod Stewart |
| 29/71 | **Baby Let Me Kiss You**<br>King Floyd |
| 24/72 | **Baby Let Me Take You (In My Arms)**<br>Detroit Emeralds |
| 35/69 | **Baby Let's Wait**<br>Royal Guardsmen |
| 1/64 | **Baby Love**<br>Supremes |
| 25/82 | **Baby Makes Her Blue Jeans Talk**<br>Dr. Hook |
| 11/68 | **Baby, Now That I've Found You**<br>Foundations |
| 21/61 | **Baby Oh Baby**<br>Shells |
| 16/66 | **Baby Scratch My Back**<br>Slim Harpo |
| 6/61 | **Baby Sittin' Boogie**<br>Buzz Clifford |
| 23/70 | **Baby Take Me In Your Arms**<br>Jefferson |
| 10/59 | **Baby Talk**<br>Jan & Dean |
| 38/80 | **Baby Talks Dirty**<br>Knack |
| 26/75 | **Baby That's Backatcha**<br>Smokey Robinson |
| 12/65 | **Baby The Rain Must Fall**<br>Glenn Yarbrough |
| 4/77 | **Baby, What A Big Surprise**<br>Chicago |
| 37/60 | **Baby What You Want Me To Do**<br>Jimmy Reed |
| 5/63 | **Baby Workout**<br>Jackie Wilson |
| 34/67 | **Baby You Got It**<br>Brenton Wood |
| 34/67 | **Baby You're A Rich Man**<br>Beatles |
| 5/60 | **Baby (You've Got What It Takes)**<br>Brook Benton & Dinah Washington |
| 26/61 | **Baby's First Christmas**<br>Connie Francis |
| 5/74 | **Back Home Again**<br>John Denver |
| 37/81 | **Back In Black**<br>AC/DC |
| 1/65 | **Back In My Arms Again**<br>Supremes |
| 38/77 | **Back In The Saddle**<br>Aerosmith |
| 37/59<br>16/78 | **Back In The U.S.A.**<br>Chuck Berry<br>Linda Ronstadt |
| 9/72 | **Back Off Boogaloo**<br>Ringo Starr |

| POS/YR | RECORD TITLE/ARTIST |
|--------|---------------------|
| 33/80 | **Back On My Feet Again**<br>Babys |
| 5/83 | **Back On The Chain Gang**<br>Pretenders |
| 36/67 | **Back On The Street Again**<br>Sunshine Company |
| 3/72 | **Back Stabbers**<br>O'Jays |
| 36/57 | **Back To School Again**<br>Timmie "Oh Yeah" Rogers |
| 28/77 | **Back Together Again**<br>Daryl Hall & John Oates |
| 40/73 | **Back When My Hair Was Short**<br>Gunhill Road |
| 20/84 | **Back Where You Belong**<br>38 Special |
| 10/69 | **Backfield In Motion**<br>Mel & Tim |
| 25/66 | **Backstage**<br>Gene Pitney |
| 1/73 | **Bad, Bad Leroy Brown**<br>Jim Croce |
| 1/75 | **Bad Blood**<br>Neil Sedaka |
| 35/83 | **Bad Boy**<br>Ray Parker Jr. |
| 36/57 | **Bad Boy**<br>Jive Bombers |
| 14/79 | **Bad Case Of Loving You (Doctor, Doctor)**<br>Robert Palmer |
| 33/63 | **Bad Girl**<br>Neil Sedaka |
| 1/79 | **Bad Girls**<br>Donna Summer |
| 15/75 | **Bad Luck**<br>Harold Melvin & The Blue Notes |
| 37/60 | **Bad Man Blunder**<br>Kingston Trio |
| 2/69 | **Bad Moon Rising**<br>Creedence Clearwater Revival |
| 4/75 | **Bad Time**<br>Grand Funk Railroad |
| 9/64 | **Bad To Me**<br>Billy J. Kramer with the Dakotas |

| POS/YR | RECORD TITLE/ARTIST |
|--------|---------------------|
| 2/78 | **Baker Street**<br>Gerry Rafferty |
| 3/70 | **Ball Of Confusion (That's What The World Is Today)**<br>Temptations |
| 19/69 | **Ball Of Fire**<br>Tommy James & The Shondells |
| 14/58 | **Ballad Of A Teenage Queen**<br>Johnny Cash |
| 7/68 | **Ballad Of Bonnie And Clyde**<br>Georgie Fame |
| 1/55<br>5/55<br>5/55<br>14/55 | **Ballad Of Davy Crockett**<br>Bill Hayes<br>Tennessee Ernie Ford<br>Fess Parker<br>Walter Schumann [The Voices of] |
| 34/66 | **Ballad Of Irving**<br>Frank Gallop |
| 8/69 | **Ballad Of John And Yoko**<br>Beatles |
| 33/62 | **Ballad Of Paladin**<br>Duane Eddy |
| 34/60 | **Ballad Of The Alamo**<br>Marty Robbins |
| 1/66 | **Ballad Of The Green Berets**<br>SSgt Barry Sadler |
| 18/57 | **Ballerina**<br>Nat King Cole |
| 33/74 | **Ballero**<br>War |
| 5/75 | **Ballroom Blitz**<br>Sweet |
| 5/57<br>25/57 | **Banana Boat (Day-O)**<br>Harry Belafonte<br>Stan Freberg |
| 4/57<br>13/57<br>18/57<br>19/57 | **Banana Boat Song**<br>Tarriers<br>Fontane Sisters<br>Steve Lawrence<br>Sarah Vaughan |
| 3/70 | **Band Of Gold**<br>Freda Payne |
| 4/56<br>11/56<br>32/66 | **Band Of Gold**<br>Don Cherry<br>Kit Carson<br>Mel Carter |

| POS/YR | RECORD TITLE/ARTIST |
|---|---|
| 1/74 | **Band On The Run** <br> Paul McCartney |
| 35/67 | **Banda, A** <br> Herb Alpert & The Tijuana Brass |
| 18/55 | **Bandit (O'Cangaceiro)** <br> Eddie Barclay |
| 10/72 | **Bang A Gong (Get It On)** <br> T. Rex |
| 2/66 | **Bang Bang (My Baby Shot Me Down)** <br> Cher |
| 22/68 | **Bang-Shang-A-Lang** <br> Archies |
| 31/84 | **Bang Your Head (Metal Health)** <br> Quiet Riot |
| 23/71 | **Bangla-Desh** <br> George Harrison |
| 15/55 | **Banjo's Back In Town** <br> Teresa Brewer |
| 29/60 | **Barbara** <br> Temptations |
| 13/61 <br> 2/66 | **Barbara Ann** <br> Regents <br> Beach Boys |
| 7/66 | **Barefootin'** <br> Robert Parker |
| 20/76 | **Baretta's Theme ("Keep Your Eye On The Sparrow")** <br> Rhythm Heritage |
| 11/77 | **Barracuda** <br> Heart |
|  | **Baseball Game** . . . *see: (Love Is Like A)* |
| 15/73 | **Basketball Jones Featuring Tyrone Shoelaces** <br> Cheech & Chong <br> *(also see: Love Jones)* |
| 17/66 <br> 35/66 | **Batman Theme** <br> Marketts <br> Neal Hefti |
| 37/71 | **Battle Hymn Of Lt. Calley** <br> C Company Featuring Terry Nelson |
| 13/59 <br> 33/68 | **Battle Hymn Of The Republic** <br> Mormon Tabernacle Choir <br> Andy Williams |
| 14/59 | **Battle Of Kookamonga** <br> Homer & Jethro |

| POS/YR | RECORD TITLE/ARTIST |
|---|---|
| 1/59 | **Battle Of New Orleans** <br> Johnny Horton |
| 25/58 | **Baubles, Bangles And Beads** <br> Kirby Stone Four |
| 34/73 | **Be** <br> Neil Diamond |
| 25/64 | **Be Anything (But Be Mine)** <br> Connie Francis |
| 7/56 | **Be-Bop-A-Lula** <br> Gene Vincent & His Blue Caps |
| 3/57 | **Be-Bop Baby** <br> Ricky Nelson |
| 31/63 | **Be Careful Of Stones That You Throw** <br> Dion |
| 35/82 | **Be Mine Tonight** <br> Neil Diamond |
| 2/63 <br> 17/70 | **Be My Baby** <br> Ronettes <br> Andy Kim |
| 8/59 | **Be My Guest** <br> Fats Domino |
| 28/82 | **Be My Lady** <br> Jefferson Starship |
| 4/74 | **Be Thankful For What You Got** <br> William DeVaughn |
| 6/63 | **Be True To Your School** <br> Beach Boys |
| 34/63 | **Be True To Yourself** <br> Bobby Vee |
| 4/74 | **Beach Baby** <br> First Class |
| 12/81 | **Beach Boys Medley** <br> Beach Boys |
| 30/64 | **Beans In My Ears** <br> Serendipity Singers |
| 8/78 | **Beast Of Burden** <br> Rolling Stones |
| 6/67 | **Beat Goes On** <br> Sonny & Cher |
| 1/83 | **Beat It** <br> Michael Jackson <br> *(also see: Eat It)* |
| 12/82 | **Beatles' Movie Medley** <br> Beatles |

| POS/YR | RECORD TITLE/ARTIST |
|--------|---------------------|
| 15/60 | **Beatnik Fly**<br>Johnny & The Hurricanes |
| 3/68 | **Beautiful Morning**<br>Rascals |
| 37/67<br>38/67 | **Beautiful People**<br>Bobby Vee<br>Kenny O'Dell |
| 15/72 | **Beautiful Sunday**<br>Daniel Boone |
| 3/66 | **Beauty Is Only Skin Deep**<br>Temptations |
| 3/64 | **Because**<br>Dave Clark Five |
| 13/78 | **Because The Night**<br>Patti Smith Group |
| 4/60 | **Because They're Young**<br>Duane Eddy |
| 17/62 | **Beechwood 4-5789**<br>Marvelettes |
| 24/58 | **Been So Long**<br>Pastels |
| 24/73 | **Been To Canaan**<br>Carole King |
| 4/58 | **Beep Beep**<br>Playmates |
| 33/75 | **Beer Barrel Polka**<br>Bobby Vinton |
| 17/65 | **Before And After**<br>Chad & Jeremy |
| 23/78 | **Before My Heart Finds Out**<br>Gene Cotton |
| 1/75 | **Before The Next Teardrop Falls**<br>Freddy Fender |
| 29/67 | **Beg, Borrow And Steal**<br>Ohio Express |
| 16/67 | **Beggin'**<br>Four Seasons |
| 36/69 | **Beginning Of My End**<br>Unifics |
| 7/71 | **Beginnings**<br>Chicago |
| 34/71 | **Behind Blue Eyes**<br>Who |

| POS/YR | RECORD TITLE/ARTIST |
|--------|---------------------|
| 15/73 | **Behind Closed Doors**<br>Charlie Rich |
| 2/81 | **Being With You**<br>Smokey Robinson |
| 28/73 | **Believe In Humanity**<br>Carole King |
| 26/59 | **Believe Me**<br>Royal Teens |
| 4/58 | **Believe What You Say**<br>Ricky Nelson |
| 28/69 | **Bella Linda**<br>Grass Roots |
| 12/70 | **Bells, The**<br>Originals |
| 13/58 | **Belonging To Someone**<br>Patti Page |
| 1/72 | **Ben**<br>Michael Jackson |
| | **Ben Casey**. . .*see: Theme From* |
| 5/68 | **Bend Me, Shape Me**<br>American Breed |
| 1/74 | **Bennie And The Jets**<br>Elton John |
| 4/67 | **Bernadette**<br>Four Tops |
| 14/57 | **Bernardine**<br>Pat Boone |
| 16/75 | **Bertha Butt Boogie**<br>Jimmy Castor Bunch |
| 17/76 | **Best Disco In Town**<br>Ritchie Family |
| 32/68 | **Best Of Both Worlds**<br>Lulu |
| 1/77 | **Best Of My Love**<br>Emotions |
| 1/75 | **Best Of My Love**<br>Eagles |
| 3/81 | **Best Of Times**<br>Styx |
| 39/64 | **(Best Part Of) Breakin' Up**<br>Ronettes |
| 3/74 | **Best Thing That Ever Happened To Me**<br>Gladys Knight & The Pips |

| POS/YR | RECORD TITLE/ARTIST |
|---|---|
| 3/72 | **Betcha By Golly, Wow** <br> Stylistics |
| | **(Betcha Got A Chick On The Side)**...*see:* <br> *How Long* |
| 7/76 | **Beth** <br> Kiss |
| 1/81 | **Bette Davis Eyes** <br> Kim Carnes |
| 5/84 | **Better Be Good To Me** <br> Tina Turner |
| 12/80 | **Better Love Next Time** <br> Dr. Hook |
| 38/61 | **Better Tell Him No** <br> Starlets |
| 33/58 | **Betty And Dupree** <br> Chuck Willis |
| 37/58 | **Betty Lou Got A New Pair Of Shoes** <br> Bobby Freeman |
| 40/61 | **Bewildered** <br> James Brown |
| 37/56 <br> 6/60 | **Beyond The Sea** <br> Roger Williams <br> Bobby Darin |
| 7/55 <br> 22/55 | **Bible Tells Me So** <br> Don Cornell <br> Nick Noble |
| 24/79 | **Bicycle Race** <br> Queen |
| 1/61 | **Big Bad John** <br> Jimmy Dean |
| 26/58 | **Big Beat** <br> Fats Domino |
| 38/58 | **Big Bopper's Wedding** <br> Big Bopper |
| 38/67 | **Big Boss Man** <br> Elvis Presley |
| 23/73 | **Big City Miss Ruth Ann** <br> Gallery |
| 19/61 | **Big Cold Wind** <br> Pat Boone |
| 21/82 | **Big Fun** <br> Kool & The Gang |
| 1/62 | **Big Girls Don't Cry** <br> Four Seasons |

| POS/YR | RECORD TITLE/ARTIST |
|---|---|
| 1/59 | **Big Hunk O' Love** <br> Elvis Presley |
| 3/59 | **Big Hurt** <br> Miss Toni Fisher |
| 26/60 | **Big Iron** <br> Marty Robbins |
| 21/61 | **Big John** <br> Shirelles |
| 20/83 | **Big Log** <br> Robert Plant |
| 3/58 | **Big Man** <br> Four Preps |
| 20/64 | **Big Man In Town** <br> Four Seasons |
| 14/79 | **Big Shot** <br> Billy Joel |
| 29/70 <br> 24/75 | **Big Yellow Taxi** <br> Neighborhood <br> Joni Mitchell |
| 3/80 | **Biggest Part Of Me** <br> Ambrosia |
| 37/61 | **Bilbao Song** <br> Andy Williams |
| 1/83 | **Billie Jean** <br> Michael Jackson |
| 7/58 | **Billy** <br> Kathy Linden |
| 34/66 | **Billy And Sue** <br> B.J. Thomas |
| 1/74 | **Billy, Don't Be A Hero** <br> Bo Donaldson & The Heywoods |
| | **Billy Jack**...*see: One Tin Soldier* |
| 11/58 | **Bimbombey** <br> Jimmie Rodgers |
| | **Bird**...*see: Do The* |
| 30/64 | **Bird Dance Beat** <br> Trashmen |
| 1/58 | **Bird Dog** <br> Everly Brothers |
| 34/58 | **Bird On My Head** <br> David Seville |
| 12/63 | **Birdland** <br> Chubby Checker |

| POS/YR | RECORD TITLE/ARTIST |
|---|---|
| 3/65 | **Birds And The Bees**<br>Jewel Akens |
| 23/71 | **Birds Of A Feather**<br>Paul Revere & The Raiders |
| 26/55 | **Birth Of The Boogie**<br>Bill Haley & His Comets |
| 26/69 | **Birthday**<br>Underground Sunshine |
| 40/63 | **Birthday Party**<br>Pixies Three |
| 4/74 | **Bitch Is Back**<br>Elton John |
| 28/77 | **Bite Your Lip (Get up and dance!)**<br>Elton John |
| 4/64 | **Bits And Pieces**<br>Dave Clark Five |
| 36/73 | **Bitter Bad**<br>Melanie |
| 1/72 | **Black & White**<br>Three Dog Night |
| 18/77 | **Black Betty**<br>Ram Jam |
| 6/55<br>38/55 | **Black Denim Trousers**<br>Cheers<br>Vaughn Monroe |
| 15/72 | **Black Dog**<br>Led Zeppelin |
| 37/75 | **Black Friday**<br>Steely Dan |
| 4/66 | **Black Is Black**<br>Los Bravos |
| 4/71 | **Black Magic Woman**<br>Santana |
| 13/69 | **Black Pearl**<br>Checkmates, Ltd. featuring Sonny Charles |
| 17/57 | **Black Slacks**<br>Joe Bennett & The Sparkletones |
| 21/75 | **Black Superman - "Muhammad Ali"**<br>Johnny Wakelin & The Kinshasa Band |
| 1/75 | **Black Water**<br>Doobie Brothers |
| 7/63 | **Blame It On The Bossa Nova**<br>Eydie Gorme |

| POS/YR | RECORD TITLE/ARTIST |
|---|---|
| 39/64 | **Bless Our Love**<br>Gene Chandler |
| 15/61 | **Bless You**<br>Tony Orlando |
| 34/81 | **Blessed Are The Believers**<br>Anne Murray |
| | **Blind Man In The Bleachers**...see: Last<br>*Game Of The Season* |
| 1/77 | **Blinded By The Light**<br>Manfred Mann's Earth Band |
| 33/58 | **Blob, The**<br>Five Blobs |
| 35/75 | **Bloody Well Right**<br>Supertramp |
| 2/55 | **Blossom Fell**<br>Nat King Cole |
| 16/79 | **Blow Away**<br>George Harrison |
| 2/63<br>9/66 | **Blowin' In The Wind**<br>Peter, Paul & Mary<br>Stevie Wonder |
| 21/70 | **Blowing Away**<br>5th Dimension |
| 9/60 | **Blue Angel**<br>Roy Orbison |
| 35/67 | **Blue Autumn**<br>Bobby Goldsboro |
| 29/63<br>3/77 | **Blue Bayou**<br>Roy Orbison<br>Linda Ronstadt |
| 20/58 | **Blue Blue Day**<br>Don Gibson |
| 21/78 | **Blue Collar Man (Long Nights)**<br>Styx |
| 12/82 | **Blue Eyes**<br>Elton John |
| 21/75 | **Blue Eyes Crying In The Rain**<br>Willie Nelson |
| 37/59 | **Blue Hawaii**<br>Billy Vaughn & His Orchestra |
| 8/84 | **Blue Jean**<br>David Bowie |
| 5/57 | **Blue Monday**<br>Fats Domino |

| POS/YR | RECORD TITLE/ARTIST |
|---|---|
| 23/71 | **Blue Money**<br>Van Morrison |
| 1/61 | **Blue Moon**<br>Marcels |
| 15/79 | **Blue Morning, Blue Day**<br>Foreigner |
| 3/63 | **Blue On Blue**<br>Bobby Vinton |
| 29/55 | **Blue Star**<br>Felicia Sanders |
| | **Blue Suede Shoes** |
| 2/56 | Carl Perkins |
| 20/56 | Elvis Presley |
| 38/73 | Johnny Rivers |
| 16/60 | **Blue Tango**<br>Bill Black's Combo |
| 1/63 | **Blue Velvet**<br>Bobby Vinton |
| 24/64 | **Blue Winter**<br>Connie Francis |
| | **Blueberry Hill** |
| 29/56 | Louis Armstrong |
| 2/57 | Fats Domino |
| 35/75 | **Bluebird**<br>Helen Reddy |
| 12/78 | **Bluer Than Blue**<br>Michael Johnson |
| 36/62 | **Blues (Stay Away From Me)**<br>Ace Cannon |
| 37/67 | **Blue's Theme**<br>Davie Allan & The Arrows |
| | **Bo Weevil** |
| 17/56 | Teresa Brewer |
| 35/56 | Fats Domino<br>*(also see: Boll Weevil)* |
| 12/82 | **Bobbie Sue**<br>Oak Ridge Boys |
| 8/59 | **Bobby Sox To Stockings**<br>Frankie Avalon |
| 3/62 | **Bobby's Girl**<br>Marcie Blane |
| 11/82 | **Body Language**<br>Queen |
| 9/76 | **Bohemian Rhapsody**<br>Queen |

| POS/YR | RECORD TITLE/ARTIST |
|---|---|
| 2/61 | **Boll Weevil Song**<br>Brook Benton |
| 19/61 | **Bonanza**<br>Al Caiola & His Orchestra |
| 14/59 | **Bongo Rock**<br>Preston Epps |
| 33/62 | **Bongo Stomp**<br>Little Joey & The Flips |
| | **Bonnie And Clyde**...*see: Ballad* |
| 26/60 | **Bonnie Came Back**<br>Duane Eddy<br>*(also see: My Bonnie)* |
| 14/57 | **Bony Moronie**<br>Larry Williams |
| 7/67 | **Boogaloo Down Broadway**<br>Fantastic Johnny C |
| 12/77 | **Boogie Child**<br>Bee Gees |
| 2/74 | **Boogie Down**<br>Eddie Kendricks |
| 1/76 | **Boogie Fever**<br>Sylvers |
| 2/77 | **Boogie Nights**<br>Heatwave |
| 3/75 | **Boogie On Reggae Woman**<br>Stevie Wonder |
| 1/78 | **Boogie Oogie Oogie**<br>Taste Of Honey |
| 35/78 | **Boogie Shoes**<br>KC & The Sunshine Band |
| 6/79 | **Boogie Wonderland**<br>Earth, Wind & Fire with The Emotions |
| 8/73 | **Boogie Woogie Bugle Boy**<br>Bette Midler |
| 5/58 | **Book Of Love**<br>Monotones |
| 17/55 | **Boom Boom Boomerang**<br>De Castro Sisters |
| | **Boomerang**...*see: Do The* |
| 36/71 | **Booty Butt**<br>Ray Charles |
| 20/84 | **Bop 'Til You Drop**<br>Rick Springfield |

| POS/YR | RECORD TITLE/ARTIST |
|---|---|
| 33/83 | **Border, The**<br>America |
| 37/70 | **Border Song**<br>Aretha Franklin |
| 10/84 | **Borderline**<br>Madonna |
| 12/66 | **Born A Woman**<br>Sandy Posey |
| 7/66<br>38/68 | **Born Free**<br>Roger Williams<br>Hesitations |
| 16/79 | **Born To Be Alive**<br>Patrick Hernandez |
| 2/68 | **Born To Be Wild**<br>Steppenwolf |
| 5/56 | **Born To Be With You**<br>Chordettes |
| 23/75 | **Born To Run**<br>Bruce Springsteen |
| 17/71 | **Born To Wander**<br>Rare Earth |
| 7/58 | **Born Too Late**<br>Poni-Tails |
| 19/79 | **Boss**<br>Diana Ross |
| 28/63 | **Boss Guitar**<br>Duane Eddy |
| 8/63 | **Bossa Nova Baby**<br>Elvis Presley |
| 8/68 | **Both Sides Now**<br>Judy Collins |
| 9/68 | **Bottle Of Wine**<br>Fireballs |
| 19/80 | **Boulevard**<br>Jackson Browne |
| 40/63 | **Bounce, The**<br>Olympics |
| 40/67 | **Bowling Green**<br>Everly Brothers |
| 7/69 | **Boxer, The**<br>Simon & Garfunkel |
| 8/65<br>7/81 | **Boy From New York City**<br>Ad Libs<br>Manhattan Transfer |

| POS/YR | RECORD TITLE/ARTIST |
|---|---|
|  | **Boy I'm Gonna Marry**...*see: (Today I Met)* |
| 2/69 | **Boy Named Sue**<br>Johnny Cash |
| 18/63 | **Boy Next Door**<br>Secrets |
| 10/59 | **Boy Without A Girl**<br>Frankie Avalon |
| 12/76 | **Boys Are Back In Town**<br>Thin Lizzy |
| 37/84 | **Boys Do Fall In Love**<br>Robin Gibb |
| 1/71 | **Brand New Key**<br>Melanie |
| 24/69 | **Brand New Me**<br>Dusty Springfield |
| 1/72 | **Brandy (You're A Fine Girl)**<br>Looking Glass |
| 35/61 | **Brass Buttons**<br>String-A-Longs |
| 14/80 | **Brass In Pocket (I'm Special)**<br>Pretenders |
| 11/75 | **Brazil**<br>Ritchie Family |
| 2/64 | **Bread And Butter**<br>Newbeats |
| 39/76 | **Break Away**<br>Art Garfunkel |
| 40/65 | **Break Away (From That Boy)**<br>Newbeats |
| 4/62<br>11/82 | **Break It To Me Gently**<br>Brenda Lee<br>Juice Newton |
| 26/82 | **Break It Up**<br>Foreigner |
| 5/84 | **Break My Stride**<br>Matthew Wilder |
| 5/73 | **Break Up To Make Up**<br>Stylistics |
| 35/68 | **Break Your Promise**<br>Delfonics |
| 8/84 | **Breakdance**<br>Irene Cara |

| POS/YR | RECORD TITLE/ARTIST |
|---|---|
| 31/71 | **Breakdown, The**<br>Rufus Thomas |
| 40/78 | **Breakdown, The**<br>Tom Petty & The Heartbreakers |
| 15/80 | **Breakdown Dead Ahead**<br>Boz Scaggs |
| 7/61 | **Breakin' In A Brand New Broken Heart**<br>Connie Francis |
| 9/84 | **Breakin'...There's No Stopping Us**<br>Ollie & Jerry |
| | **Breakin' Up**...*see: (Best Part Of)* |
| 31/66 | **Breakin' Up Is Breakin' My Heart**<br>Roy Orbison |
| 22/81 | **Breaking Away**<br>Balance |
| 1/62<br>34/70<br>28/72<br>8/76 | **Breaking Up Is Hard To Do**<br>Neil Sedaka<br>Lenny Welch<br>Partridge Family<br>Neil Sedaka |
| 18/83 | **Breaking Us In Two**<br>Joe Jackson |
| 15/81 | **Breakup Song (They Don't Write 'Em)**<br>Greg Kihn Band |
| 7/58 | **Breathless**<br>Jerry Lee Lewis |
| 8/55 | **Breeze And I**<br>Caterina Valente |
| 5/77 | **Brick House**<br>Commodores |
| 1/70<br>6/71 | **Bridge Over Troubled Water**<br>Simon & Garfunkel<br>Aretha Franklin |
| 13/62<br>32/65<br>17/68 | **Bring It On Home To Me**<br>Sam Cooke<br>Animals<br>Eddie Floyd |
| 29/67 | **Bring It Up**<br>James Brown |
| 12/71 | **Bring The Boys Home**<br>Freda Payne |
| 2/61 | **Bristol Stomp**<br>Dovells |
| 27/62 | **Bristol Twistin' Annie**<br>Dovells |

| POS/YR | RECORD TITLE/ARTIST |
|---|---|
| 12/79 | **Broken Hearted Me**<br>Anne Murray |
| 7/59 | **Broken-Hearted Melody**<br>Sarah Vaughan |
| 1/73 | **Brother Louie**<br>Stories |
| 22/69 | **Brother Love's Travelling Salvation Show**<br>Neil Diamond |
| 32/70 | **Brother Rapp**<br>James Brown |
| 10/67 | **Brown Eyed Girl**<br>Van Morrison |
| 1/71 | **Brown Sugar**<br>Rolling Stones |
| 3/69 | **Build Me Up Buttercup**<br>Foundations |
| 24/60 | **Bulldog**<br>Fireballs |
| 21/65 | **Bumble Bee**<br>Searchers |
| 21/61 | **Bumble Boogie**<br>B. Bumble & The Stingers |
| 12/75 | **Bungle In The Jungle**<br>Jethro Tull |
| 9/55 | **Burn That Candle**<br>Bill Haley & His Comets |
| 40/81 | **Burnin' For You**<br>Blue Oyster Cult |
| 3/60 | **Burning Bridges**<br>Jack Scott |
| 34/71 | **Burning Bridges**<br>Mike Curb Congregation |
| 9/83 | **Burning Down The House**<br>Talking Heads |
| 39/83 | **Burning Heart**<br>Vandenberg |
| 2/72 | **Burning Love**<br>Elvis Presley |
| 5/66 | **Bus Stop**<br>Hollies |
| 16/56 | **Bus Stop Song (A Paper Of Pins)**<br>Four Lads |

| POS/YR | RECORD TITLE/ARTIST |
|---|---|
| 25/63 | **Bust Out**<br>Busters |
| 4/63 | **Busted**<br>Ray Charles |
| 34/79 | **Bustin' Loose**<br>Chuck Brown & The Soul Searchers |
| 4/61 | **But I Do**<br>Clarence "Frogman" Henry |
| 22/66 | **But It's Alright**<br>J.J. Jackson |
| 19/69 | **But You Know I Love You**<br>Kenny Rogers & The First Edition |
| 15/65 | **But You're Mine**<br>Sonny & Cher |
| 29/75 | **Butter Boy**<br>Fanny |
| 1/57<br>1/57 | **Butterfly**<br>Charlie Gracie<br>Andy Williams |
| 23/63 | **Butterfly Baby**<br>Bobby Rydell |
| 11/58 | **Buzz-Buzz-Buzz**<br>Hollywood Flames |
| 26/67<br>37/69 | **By The Time I Get To Phoenix**<br>Glen Campbell<br>Isaac Hayes |
| 12/65 | **Bye, Bye, Baby (Baby Goodbye)**<br>Four Seasons |
| 2/57 | **Bye Bye Love**<br>Everly Brothers |

**C**

| POS/YR | RECORD TITLE/ARTIST |
|---|---|
| 12/57<br>34/63<br>10/66 | **C.C. Rider**<br>Chuck Willis<br>LaVern Baker<br>Animals<br>*(also see: Jenny Take A Ride)* |
| 11/55 | **C'est La Vie**<br>Sarah Vaughan |
| 22/61 | **C'est Si Bon (It's So Good)**<br>Conway Twitty |

| POS/YR | RECORD TITLE/ARTIST |
|---|---|
| 22/57 | **Ca, C'est L'amour**<br>Tony Bennett |
| 23/68 | **Cab Driver**<br>Mills Brothers |
| 22/62 | **Cajun Queen**<br>Jimmy Dean |
| 1/61 | **Calcutta**<br>Lawrence Welk |
| 4/61 | **Calendar Girl**<br>Neil Sedaka |
| 4/66 | **California Dreamin'**<br>Mamas & The Papas |
| 3/65 | **California Girls**<br>Beach Boys |
| 16/67 | **California Nights**<br>Lesley Gore |
| 25/69 | **California Soul**<br>5th Dimension |
| 5/64 | **California Sun**<br>Rivieras |
| 1/80 | **Call Me**<br>Blondie |
| 13/70 | **Call Me**<br>Aretha Franklin |
| 21/58 | **Call Me**<br>Johnny Mathis |
| 22/66 | **Call Me**<br>Chris Montez |
| 26/82 | **Call Me**<br>Skyy |
| 10/73 | **Call Me (Come Back Home)**<br>Al Green |
| 40/68 | **Call Me Lightning**<br>Who |
| 19/62 | **Call Me Mr. In-Between**<br>Burl Ives |
| 6/74 | **Call On Me**<br>Chicago |
| 22/63 | **Call On Me**<br>Bobby Bland |
| 16/77 | **Calling Dr. Love**<br>Kiss |

| POS/YR | RECORD TITLE/ARTIST |
|---|---|
| 32/77 | **Calling Occupants Of Interplanetary Craft** <br> Carpenters |
| F/75 | **Calypso** <br> John Denver |
| 5/69 | **Can I Change My Mind** <br> Tyrone Davis |
| 22/63 <br> 39/71 | **Can I Get A Witness** <br> Marvin Gaye <br> Lee Michaels |
| 15/57 | **Can I Steal A Little Love** <br> Frank Sinatra |
| 31/74 | **Can This Be Real** <br> Natural Four |
| 29/78 | **Can We Still Be Friends** <br> Todd Rundgren |
| 16/56 | **Can You Find It In Your Heart** <br> Tony Bennett |
| 38/78 | **Can You Fool** <br> Glen Campbell |
| 1/64 | **Can't Buy Me Love** <br> Beatles |
| 5/74 | **Can't Get Enough** <br> Bad Company |
| 1/74 | **Can't Get Enough Of Your Love, Babe** <br> Barry White |
| 9/75 | **Can't Get It Out Of My Head** <br> Electric Light Orchestra |
| 2/63 | **Can't Get Used To Losing You** <br> Andy Williams |
| 2/62 | **Can't Help Falling In Love** <br> Elvis Presley |
| 39/76 | **Can't Hide Love** <br> Earth, Wind & Fire |
| 29/83 | **Can't Shake Loose** <br> Agnetha Faltskog |
| 3/78 | **Can't Smile Without You** <br> Barry Manilow |
| 13/77 | **Can't Stop Dancin'** <br> Captain & Tennille |
| 25/70 | **Can't Stop Loving You** <br> Tom Jones |
| 2/67 <br> 7/68 | **Can't Take My Eyes Off You** <br> Frankie Valli <br> Lettermen (medley) |

| POS/YR | RECORD TITLE/ARTIST |
|---|---|
| 2/65 | **Can't You Hear My Heartbeat** <br> Herman's Hermits |
| 4/64 | **Can't You See That She's Mine** <br> Dave Clark Five |
| 2/56 <br> 7/56 | **Canadian Sunset** <br> Hugo Winterhalter & his Orchestra <br> Andy Williams |
| 3/70 | **Candida** <br> Dawn |
| | **(Candles In The Rain)** . . . *see: Lay Down* |
| 3/63 | **Candy Girl** <br> Four Seasons |
| 25/61 | **Candy Man** <br> Roy Orbison |
| 1/72 | **Candy Man** <br> Sammy Davis, Jr. |
| 15/58 | **Cannonball** <br> Duane Eddy |
| 1/77 | **Car Wash** <br> Rose Royce |
| 39/65 | **Cara-Lin** <br> Strangeloves |
| 4/65 | **Cara, Mia** <br> Jay & The Americans |
| 10/74 | **Carefree Highway** <br> Gordon Lightfoot |
| 27/59 | **Caribbean** <br> Mitchell Torok |
| 1/84 | **Caribbean Queen (No More Love On The Run)** <br> Billy Ocean |
| 18/58 | **Carol** <br> Chuck Berry |
| 21/75 | **Carolina In The Pines** <br> Michael Murphey |
| 32/66 | **Caroline, No** <br> Brian Wilson |
| 29/68 | **Carpet Man** <br> 5th Dimension |
| 34/80 | **Carrie** <br> Cliff Richard |
| 9/67 | **Carrie-Anne** <br> Hollies |

| POS/YR | RECORD TITLE/ARTIST |
|--------|---------------------|
| 26/69 | **Carry Me Back**<br>Rascals |
| 11/77 | **Carry On Wayward Son**<br>Kansas |
| 9/80 | **Cars**<br>Gary Numan |
| 27/67 | **Casino Royale**<br>Herb Alpert & The Tijuana Brass |
| 22/63<br>10/65 | **Cast Your Fate To The Wind**<br>Vince Guaraldi Trio<br>Sounds Orchestral |
| F/72<br>36/81 | **Castles In The Air**<br>Don McLean<br>Don McLean |
| 25/56 | **Casual Look**<br>Six Teens |
| 26/67 | **Cat In The Window (The Bird In The Sky)**<br>Petula Clark |
| 30/77 | **Cat Scratch Fever**<br>Ted Nugent |
| 1/74 | **Cat's In The Cradle**<br>Harry Chapin |
| 1/58 | **Catch A Falling Star**<br>Perry Como |
| 40/84 | **Catch Me I'm Falling**<br>Real Life |
| 23/65 | **Catch The Wind**<br>Donovan |
| 4/65 | **Catch Us If You Can**<br>Dave Clark Five |
| 23/62 | **Caterina**<br>Perry Como |
| 1/60 | **Cathy's Clown**<br>Everly Brothers |
| 10/82 | **Caught Up In You**<br>38 Special |
| | **(Cave Man)**...see: Troglodyte |
| 4/70 | **Cecilia**<br>Simon & Garfunkel |
| 15/70 | **Celebrate**<br>Three Dog Night |
| 1/81 | **Celebration**<br>Kool & The Gang |

| POS/YR | RECORD TITLE/ARTIST |
|--------|---------------------|
| 1/82 | **Centerfold**<br>J. Geils Band |
| 14/58 | **Certain Smile**<br>Johnny Mathis |
| 23/58 | **Cerveza**<br>Boots Brown |
| 10/62 | **Cha-Cha-Cha**<br>Bobby Rydell |
| 34/58 | **Cha-Hua-Hua**<br>Pets |
| 2/60 | **Chain Gang**<br>Sam Cooke |
| 13/56 | **Chain Gang**<br>Bobby Scott |
| 2/68 | **Chain Of Fools**<br>Aretha Franklin |
| 32/68 | **Chained**<br>Marvin Gaye |
| 17/62 | **Chains**<br>Cookies |
| 20/56 | **Chains Of Love**<br>Pat Boone |
| 1/57 | **Chances Are**<br>Johnny Mathis |
| 31/65 | **Change Is Gonna Come**<br>Sam Cooke |
| 19/78 | **Change Of Heart**<br>Eric Carmen |
| 21/83 | **Change Of Heart**<br>Tom Petty & The Heartbreakers |
| 37/77 | **Changes In Latitudes, Changes In Attitudes**<br>Jimmy Buffett |
| 6/58<br>12/58 | **Chanson D'Amour (Song Of Love)**<br>Art & Dotty Todd<br>Fontane Sisters |
| 19/57 | **Chantez-Chantez**<br>Dinah Shore |
| 6/58 | **Chantilly Lace**<br>Big Bopper |
| 32/65<br>25/67 | **Chapel In The Moonlight**<br>Bachelors<br>Dean Martin |

| POS/YR | RECORD TITLE/ARTIST |
|--------|---------------------|
| 1/64 | **Chapel Of Love**<br>Dixie Cups |
| 36/64<br>36/64 | **Charade**<br>Sammy Kaye & His Orchestra<br>Henry Mancini & His Orchestra |
| 1/82 | **Chariots Of Fire - Titles**<br>Vangelis |
| 40/71 | **Charity Ball**<br>Fanny |
| 2/59 | **Charlie Brown**<br>Coasters |
| 13/63 | **Charms**<br>Bobby Vee |
| 33/79 | **Chase**<br>Giorgio Moroder |
| 36/62<br>32/78 | **Chattanooga Choo Choo**<br>Floyd Cramer<br>Tuxedo Junction |
| 34/60 | **Chattanooga Shoe Shine Boy**<br>Freddy Cannon |
| 15/73 | **Cheaper To Keep Her**<br>Johnnie Taylor |
| 12/66 | **Cheater, The**<br>Bob Kuban & the In-Men |
| 35/73 | **Check It Out**<br>Tavares |
| 28/70 | **Check Out Your Mind**<br>Impressions |
| 12/55 | **Chee Chee-Oo-Chee (Sang The Little Bird)**<br>Perry Como & Jaye P. Morgan |
| 32/78 | **Cheeseburger In Paradise**<br>Jimmy Buffett |
|  | **Cherchez La Femme**...*see:Whispering* |
| 1/66<br>9/71 | **Cherish**<br>Association<br>David Cassidy |
| 33/77 | **Cherry Baby**<br>Starz |
| 6/66<br>31/73 | **Cherry, Cherry**<br>Neil Diamond<br>Neil Diamond |
| 15/69 | **Cherry Hill Park**<br>Billy Joe Royal |

| POS/YR | RECORD TITLE/ARTIST |
|--------|---------------------|
| 11/60 | **Cherry Pie**<br>Skip & Flip |
| 1/55<br>14/55 | **Cherry Pink And Apple Blossom White**<br>Perez Prado & His Orchestra<br>Alan Dale |
| 5/75 | **Chevy Van**<br>Sammy Johns |
| 15/68 | **Chewy Chewy**<br>Ohio Express |
| 35/71 | **Chicago**<br>Graham Nash |
| 9/71 | **Chick-A-Boom (Don't Ya Jes' Love It)**<br>Daddy Dewdrop |
| 31/67 | **Child Of Clay**<br>Jimmie Rodgers |
| 13/59<br>16/59 | **Children's Marching Song**<br>Cyril Stapleton & His Orchestra<br>Mitch Miller & His Orchestra |
| 38/60 | **China Doll**<br>Ames Brothers |
| 10/83 | **China Girl**<br>David Bowie |
| 15/73 | **China Grove**<br>Doobie Brothers |
| 10/62 | **Chip Chip**<br>Gene McDaniels |
| 1/58<br>39/61<br>40/62 | **Chipmunk Song**<br>Chipmunks<br>Chipmunks<br>Chipmunks |
| 29/80 | **Chiquitita**<br>Abba |
| 20/71 | **Chirpy Chirpy Cheep Cheep**<br>Mac & Katie Kissoon |
| 34/81 | **Chloe**<br>Elton John |
| 21/69 | **Choice Of Colors**<br>Impressions |
| 13/69 | **Chokin' Kind**<br>Joe Simon |
| 26/68 | **Choo Choo Train**<br>Box Tops |
| 25/77 | **Christine Sixteen**<br>Kiss |

| POS/YR | RECORD TITLE/ARTIST |
|--------|---------------------|
| 4/79 | **Chuck E.'s In Love**<br>Rickie Lee Jones |
| 9/64 | **Chug-A-Lug**<br>Roger Miller |
| 14/56 | **Church Bells May Ring**<br>Diamonds |
| 10/83 | **Church Of The Poison Mind**<br>Culture Club |
| 24/59 | **Ciao, Ciao Bambina**<br>Jacky Noguez & His Musette Orchestra |
| 22/57<br>35/57 | **Cinco Robles (Five Oaks)**<br>Russell Arms<br>Les Paul & Mary Ford |
| 16/62 | **Cinderella**<br>Jack Ross |
| 34/77 | **Cinderella**<br>Firefall |
| 9/56<br>10/56 | **Cindy, Oh Cindy**<br>Vince Martin with The Tarriers<br>Eddie Fisher |
| 8/62 | **Cindy's Birthday**<br>Johnny Crawford |
| 11/69 | **Cinnamon**<br>Derek |
| 25/63 | **Cinnamon Cinder (It's A Very Nice Dance)**<br>Pastel Six |
| 33/78 | **Circle Is Small (I Can See It In Your Eyes)**<br>Gordon Lightfoot |
| 38/82 | **Circles**<br>Atlantic Starr |
| 2/73 | **Cisco Kid**<br>War |
| 23/69 | **Cissy Strut**<br>Meters |
| 19/56 | **City Of Angels**<br>Highlights |
| 18/72 | **City Of New Orleans**<br>Arlo Guthrie |
| 2/72 | **Clair**<br>Gilbert O'Sullivan |
|  | **Clam**...see: Do The |
| 6/74 | **Clap For The Wolfman**<br>Guess Who |

| POS/YR | RECORD TITLE/ARTIST |
|--------|---------------------|
| 36/83 | **Clapping Song**<br>Pia Zadora |
| 8/65 | **Clapping Song (Clap Pat Clap Slap)**<br>Shirley Ellis |
| 38/59 | **Class, The**<br>Chubby Checker |
| 2/68 | **Classical Gas**<br>Mason Williams |
| 30/58 | **Claudette**<br>Everly Brothers |
| 6/72 | **Clean Up Woman**<br>Betty Wright |
| 35/69 | **Clean Up Your Own Back Yard**<br>Elvis Presley |
| 21/60 | **Clementine**<br>Bobby Darin |
|  | **Cleopatra Jones**...see: Theme From |
| 28/58 | **Click-Clack**<br>Dicky Doo & The Don'ts |
| 17/64 | **Clinging Vine**<br>Bobby Vinton |
| 40/80 | **Clones (We're All)**<br>Alice Cooper |
|  | **Close Encounters**...see: Theme From |
| 25/78 | **Close The Door**<br>Teddy Pendergrass |
| 12/62 | **Close To Cathy**<br>Mike Clifford |
| 8/67 | **Close Your Eyes**<br>Peaches & Herb |
| 37/73 | **Close Your Eyes**<br>Edward Bear |
| 2/78 | **Closer I Get To You**<br>Roberta Flack & Donny Hathaway |
| 22/70 | **Closer To Home**<br>Grand Funk Railroad |
| 38/83 | **Closer You Get**<br>Alabama |
| 6/69<br>32/69 | **Cloud Nine**<br>Temptations<br>Mongo Santamaria |
|  | **C'mon**...see: Come On |

| POS/YR | RECORD TITLE/ARTIST |
|---|---|
| F/80 | **Cocaine**<br>Eric Clapton |
| 8/72 | **Coconut**<br>Nilsson |
| 6/77 | **Cold As Ice**<br>Foreigner |
| 40/83 | **Cold Blooded**<br>Rick James |
| 33/81 | **Cold Love**<br>Donna Summer |
| 7/67 | **Cold Sweat**<br>James Brown |
| 30/70 | **Cold Turkey**<br>John Lennon |
| | **Colonel Bogey**...see: March From The River Kwai |
| 7/69 | **Color Him Father**<br>Winstons |
| 16/67 | **Color My World**<br>Petula Clark |
| F/71 | **Colour My World**<br>Chicago |
| | **Come**...also see: Cum |
| 3/64 | **Come A Little Bit Closer**<br>Jay & The Americans |
| 7/70 | **Come And Get It**<br>Badfinger |
| 29/63 | **Come And Get These Memories**<br>Martha & The Vandellas |
| 5/74 | **Come And Get Your Love**<br>Redbone |
| 26/65 | **Come And Stay With Me**<br>Marianne Faithfull |
| 32/80 | **Come Back**<br>J. Geils Band |
| 22/84 | **Come Back And Stay**<br>Paul Young |
| 17/62 | **Come Back Silly Girl**<br>Lettermen |
| 3/67 | **Come Back When You Grow Up**<br>Bobby Vee |
| 38/58 | **Come Closer To Me**<br>Nat King Cole |

| POS/YR | RECORD TITLE/ARTIST |
|---|---|
| 6/83 | **Come Dancing**<br>Kinks |
| 21/73 | **Come Get To This**<br>Marvin Gaye |
| 4/57<br>18/82 | **Come Go With Me**<br>Dell-Vikings<br>Beach Boys |
| 14/65 | **Come Home**<br>Dave Clark Five |
| 20/59 | **Come Into My Heart**<br>Lloyd Price |
| 30/74 | **Come Monday**<br>Jimmy Buffett |
| 36/64 | **Come On**<br>Tommy Roe |
| 29/59 | **Come On And Get Me**<br>Fabian |
| 5/64 | **C'mon And Swim**<br>Bobby Freeman |
| 6/67 | **Come On Down To My Boat**<br>Every Mothers' Son |
| 1/83 | **Come On Eileen**<br>Dexys Midnight Runners |
| 35/59 | **C'mon Everybody**<br>Eddie Cochran |
| 22/66 | **Come On Let's Go**<br>McCoys |
| 28/62 | **Come On Little Angel**<br>Belmonts |
| 9/67<br>38/76 | **C'mon Marianne**<br>Four Seasons<br>Donny Osmond |
| 23/76 | **Come On Over**<br>Olivia Newton-John |
| 17/66 | **(Come 'Round Here) I'm The One You Need**<br>Miracles |
| 39/70 | **Come Running**<br>Van Morrison |
| 35/66 | **Come Running Back**<br>Dean Martin |
| 8/78 | **Come Sail Away**<br>Styx |

| POS/YR | RECORD TITLE/ARTIST |
|---|---|
| 17/70 | **Come Saturday Morning** <br> Sandpipers |
| 40/65 | **Come See** <br> Major Lance |
| 1/64 <br> 24/68 | **Come See About Me** <br> Supremes <br> Jr. Walker & The All Stars |
| 1/59 | **Come Softly To Me** <br> Fleetwoods |
| 15/79 | **Come To Me** <br> France Joli |
| 22/58 | **Come To Me** <br> Johnny Mathis |
| 30/59 | **Come To Me** <br> Marv Johnson |
| 37/67 | **Come To The Sunshine** <br> Harpers Bizarre |
| 1/69 <br> 23/78 | **Come Together** <br> Beatles <br> Aerosmith |
| 36/62 | **Comin' Home Baby** <br> Mel Torme |
| 11/82 | **Comin' In And Out Of Your Life** <br> Barbra Streisand |
| 11/67 | **Coming Home Soldier** <br> Bobby Vinton |
| 11/66 | **Coming On Strong** <br> Brenda Lee |
| 1/80 | **Coming Up (Live at Glasgow)** <br> Paul McCartney |
| 30/69 | **Commotion** <br> Creedence Clearwater Revival |
| 27/69 | **Composer, The** <br> Supremes |
| 28/65 <br> 35/65 | **Concrete And Clay** <br> Unit Four plus Two <br> Eddie Rambeau |
| 17/56 | **Confidential** <br> Sonny Knight |
| 37/79 | **Confusion** <br> Electric Light Orchestra |
| 16/72 | **Conquistador** <br> Procol Harum |
| 11/62 | **Conscience** <br> James Darren |

| POS/YR | RECORD TITLE/ARTIST |
|---|---|
| 33/61 | **Continental Walk** <br> Hank Ballard & The Midnighters <br> *(also see: Do The & Do The New)* |
| 8/72 | **Convention '72** <br> Delegates |
| 1/76 | **Convoy** <br> C.W. McCall |
| 32/73 | **Cook With Honey** <br> Judy Collins |
| 29/71 | **Cool Aid** <br> Paul Humphrey |
| 10/80 | **Cool Change** <br> Little River Band |
| 4/85 | **Cool It Now** <br> New Edition |
| 7/66 | **Cool Jerk** <br> Capitols |
| 13/81 | **Cool Love** <br> Pablo Cruise |
| 11/82 | **Cool Night** <br> Paul Davis |
| 12/57 | **Cool Shake** <br> Dell-Vikings |
| 8/78 | **Copacabana (At The Copa)** <br> Barry Manilow |
| 37/73 | **Corazon** <br> Carole King |
| 9/61 | **Corinna, Corinna** <br> Ray Peterson |
| 18/72 | **Corner Of The Sky** <br> Jacksons |
| 15/64 | **Cotton Candy** <br> Al Hirt |
| 13/62 | **Cotton Fields** <br> Highwaymen |
| 33/80 | **Could I Have This Dance** <br> Anne Murray |
| 37/72 | **Could It Be Forever** <br> David Cassidy |
| 4/73 | **Could It Be I'm Falling In Love** <br> Spinners |
| 6/75 | **Could It Be Magic** <br> Barry Manilow |

| POS/YR | RECORD TITLE/ARTIST |
|--------|---------------------|
| 23/57 | **Could This Be Magic** <br> Dubs |
| 3/77 | **Couldn't Get It Right** <br> Climax Blues Band |
| 35/61 | **Count Every Star** <br> Donnie & The Dreamers |
| 2/65 | **Count Me In** <br> Gary Lewis & The Playboys |
| 8/78 | **Count On Me** <br> Jefferson Starship |
| 25/60 | **Country Boy** <br> Fats Domino |
| 11/76 | **Country Boy (You Got Your Feet In L.A.)** <br> Glen Campbell |
| 36/68 | **Country Girl - City Man** <br> Billy Vera & Judy Clay |
| 37/71 | **Country Road** <br> James Taylor |
| 25/68 | **Court Of Love** <br> Unifics |
| 31/64 | **Cousin Of Mine** <br> Sam Cooke |
| 7/84 | **Cover Me** <br> Bruce Springsteen |
| 6/73 | **Cover Of "Rolling Stone"** <br> Dr. Hook |
| 3/80 | **Coward Of The County** <br> Kenny Rogers |
| 6/68 | **Cowboys To Girls** <br> Intruders |
| 8/72 | **Cowboys Work Is Never Done** <br> Sonny & Cher |
| 19/77 | **Crackerbox Palace** <br> George Harrison |
| 1/70 | **Cracklin' Rosie** <br> Neil Diamond |
| 7/60 | **Cradle Of Love** <br> Johnny Preston |
| 9/61 | **Crazy** <br> Patsy Cline |
| 36/60 | **Crazy Arms** <br> Bob Beckham |
|  | **Crazy Downtown**...see: *Downtown* |

| POS/YR | RECORD TITLE/ARTIST |
|--------|---------------------|
| 40/58 | **Crazy Eyes For You** <br> Bobby Hamilton |
| 14/72 | **Crazy Horses** <br> Osmonds |
|  | **Crazy Little Mama**...see:*At My Front Door* |
| 1/80 | **Crazy Little Thing Called Love** <br> Queen |
| 15/58 | **Crazy Love** <br> Paul Anka |
| 17/79 | **Crazy Love** <br> Poco |
| 29/79 | **Crazy Love** <br> Allman Brothers Band |
| 22/72 | **Crazy Mama** <br> J.J. Cale |
| 35/76 | **Crazy On You** <br> Heart |
| 2/55 | **Crazy Otto (Medley)** <br> Johnny Maddox & The Rhythmasters |
| 5/67 | **Creeque Alley** <br> Mamas & The Papas |
| 16/71 | **Cried Like A Baby** <br> Bobby Sherman |
| 1/69 <br> 7/82 | **Crimson And Clover** <br> Tommy James & The Shondells <br> Joan Jett & The Blackhearts |
| 16/55 | **Croce Di Oro (Cross Of Gold)** <br> Patti Page |
| 1/73 | **Crocodile Rock** <br> Elton John |
|  | **Crooked Little Man**...see: *Don't Let The Rain Come Down* |
| 19/63 | **Cross Fire!** <br> Orlons |
|  | **Cross Of Gold**...see: *Croce Di Oro* |
| 23/59 | **Crossfire** <br> Johnny & The Hurricanes |
| 28/69 | **Crossroads** <br> Cream |
| 26/62 | **Crowd, The** <br> Roy Orbison |

| POS/YR | RECORD TITLE/ARTIST |
|--------|---------------------|
| 9/84 | **Cruel Summer**<br>Bananarama |
| 12/79 | **Cruel To Be Kind**<br>Nick Lowe |
| 4/80 | **Cruisin'**<br>Smokey Robinson |
| 9/83 | **Crumblin' Down**<br>John Cougar |
| 18/66 | **Cry**<br>Ronnie Dove |
| 4/63 | **Cry Baby**<br>Garnet Mimms & The Enchanters |
| 18/56 | **Cry Baby**<br>Bonnie Sisters |
| 38/62 | **Cry Baby Cry**<br>Angels |
| 2/68 | **Cry Like A Baby**<br>Box Tops |
| 9/55<br>11/70 | **Cry Me A River**<br>Julie London<br>Joe Cocker |
| 23/63 | **Cry To Me**<br>Betty Harris |
| 2/61<br>25/66<br>5/81 | **Crying**<br>Roy Orbison<br>Jay & The Americans<br>Don McLean |
| 3/65 | **Crying In The Chapel**<br>Elvis Presley |
| 6/62 | **Crying In The Rain**<br>Everly Brothers |
| 6/66 | **Crying Time**<br>Ray Charles |
| 2/69 | **Crystal Blue Persuasion**<br>Tommy James & The Shondells |
| 5/83 | **Cum On Feel The Noize**<br>Quiet Riot |
| 17/61<br>39/70<br>22/76<br>4/80 | **Cupid**<br>Sam Cooke<br>Johnny Nash<br>Dawn<br>Spinners |
| | **Curious Mind**...see: Um, Um, Um, Um, Um, Um |
| 15/84 | **Curly Shuffle**<br>Jump 'n The Saddle |

| POS/YR | RECORD TITLE/ARTIST |
|--------|---------------------|
| 10/75 | **Cut The Cake**<br>Average White Band |
| 15/83 | **Cuts Like A Knife**<br>Bryan Adams |
| 23/68 | **Cycles**<br>Frank Sinatra |

# D

| POS/YR | RECORD TITLE/ARTIST |
|--------|---------------------|
| 36/71 | **D.O.A.**<br>Bloodrock |
| 19/68 | **D.W. Washburn**<br>Monkees |
| 20/73 | **D'yer Mak'er**<br>Led Zeppelin |
| 3/63<br>1/77 | **Da Doo Ron Ron**<br>Crystals<br>Shaun Cassidy |
| 1/79 | **Da Ya Think I'm Sexy?**<br>Rod Stewart |
| 19/73 | **Daddy Could Swear, I Declare**<br>Gladys Knight & The Pips |
| 4/72 | **Daddy Don't You Walk So Fast**<br>Wayne Newton |
| 11/55<br>14/55 | **Daddy-O**<br>Fontane Sisters<br>Bonnie Lou |
| 2/61<br>9/73<br>23/82 | **Daddy's Home**<br>Shep & The Limelites<br>Jermaine Jackson<br>Cliff Richard |
| 34/69 | **Daddy's Little Man**<br>O.C. Smith |
| 14/73 | **Daisy A Day**<br>Jud Strunk |
| 20/75 | **Daisy Jane**<br>America |
| 15/64 | **Daisy Petal Pickin'**<br>Jimmy Gilmer & The Fireballs |
| 27/79 | **Damned If I Do**<br>Alan Parsons Project |
| 38/78 | **Dance Across The Floor**<br>Jimmy "Bo" Horne |

**The American Breed.** Kevin Murphy and Andre Fischer are remembered not so much for their snappy, clean-cut hits with the American Breed, but for the fact that they went on to form Rufus, Chaka Khan's starting point.

**Paul Anka** began performing professionally at age 11. Singing in Quebec nightclubs for $15 a night, he did a mean impression of singer Johnnie Ray, which enabled him to win a talent contest the next year.

**The Association** attempted to follow up the chart-topping romanticism of "Cherish" with the unexpectedly psychedelic "Pandora's Golden Heebie Jeebies." Instead of Number One, they had to settle for 35.

**Badfinger,** recording for the Beatles' Apple Records in a similar style, emerged from that huge shadow with a brilliant string of singles. Later years were marked by tragedy, with two of the four members committing suicide.

**The Beatles'** *Let It Be* album was the only one not produced solely by George Martin. Actually, he did supervise the original sessions. Phil Spector was brought in later to "re-produce," adding overdubs and remixing.

**The Beatles'** double-sided 1965–66 smash provided fertile ground for other artists. Stevie Wonder recorded "We Can Work It Out" and had a Top 20 hit, while artists as diverse as Otis Redding and Cheap Trick covered "Day Tripper" with excellent results.

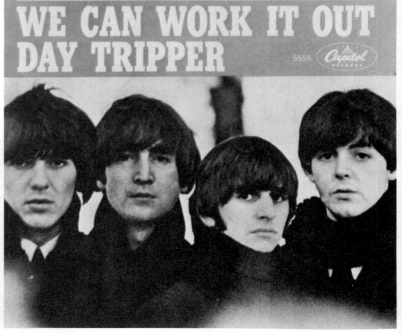

| POS/YR | RECORD TITLE/ARTIST |
|---|---|
| 8/64 | **Dance, Dance, Dance**<br>Beach Boys |
| 6/78 | **Dance, Dance, Dance (Yowsah, Yowsah, Yowsah)**<br>Chic |
| 19/78 | **Dance (Disco Heat)**<br>Sylvester |
| 31/58 | **Dance Everyone Dance**<br>Betty Madigan |
| 16/84 | **Dance Hall Days**<br>Wang Chung |
| 10/61 | **Dance On Little Girl**<br>Paul Anka |
| 19/58 | **Dance Only With Me**<br>Perry Como |
| 24/61 | **Dance The Mess Around**<br>Chubby Checker |
| 15/79 | **Dance The Night Away**<br>Van Halen |
| 23/58 | **Dance To The Bop**<br>Gene Vincent & His Blue Caps |
| 8/68 | **Dance To The Music**<br>Sly & The Family Stone |
| 39/76 | **Dance Wit Me**<br>Rufus featuring Chaka Khan |
| 6/75 | **Dance With Me**<br>Orleans |
| 8/78 | **Dance With Me**<br>Peter Brown |
| 15/59 | **Dance With Me**<br>Drifters |
| 1/55 | **Dance With Me Henry (Wallflower)**<br>Georgia Gibbs |
| 12/62 | **(Dance With The) Guitar Man**<br>Duane Eddy |
| 28/75 | **Dancin' Fool**<br>Guess Who |
| 23/77 | **Dancin' Man**<br>Q |
| 12/62 | **Dancin' Party**<br>Chubby Checker |
| 18/79 | **Dancin' Shoes**<br>Nigel Olsson |

| POS/YR | RECORD TITLE/ARTIST |
|---|---|
| 2/84 | **Dancing In The Dark**<br>Bruce Springsteen |
| 13/73 | **Dancing In The Moonlight**<br>King Harvest |
| 17/84 | **Dancing In The Sheets**<br>Shalamar |
| 2/64<br>38/82 | **Dancing In The Street**<br>Martha & The Vandellas<br>Van Halen |
| 2/74 | **Dancing Machine**<br>Jacksons |
| 1/77 | **Dancing Queen**<br>Abba |
| 14/67 | **Dandelion**<br>Rolling Stones |
| 5/66 | **Dandy**<br>Herman's Hermits |
| 7/64 | **Dang Me**<br>Roger Miller |
| 12/55 | **Danger! Heartbreak Ahead**<br>Jaye P. Morgan |
| 25/66 | **Dangling Conversation**<br>Simon & Garfunkel |
| 2/73 | **Daniel**<br>Elton John |
| 13/63 | **Danke Schoen**<br>Wayne Newton |
| 10/59 | **Danny Boy**<br>Conway Twitty |
| 7/73 | **Danny's Song**<br>Anne Murray |
| 15/75 | **Dark Horse**<br>George Harrison |
| 1/74 | **Dark Lady**<br>Cher |
| 4/57<br>6/57 | **Dark Moon**<br>Gale Storm<br>Bonnie Guitar |
| 19/68 | **Darlin'**<br>Beach Boys |
| 15/67 | **Darling Be Home Soon**<br>Lovin' Spoonful |
| 7/55 | **Darling Je Vous Aime Beaucoup**<br>Nat King Cole |

| POS/YR | RECORD TITLE/ARTIST |
|--------|---------------------|
| 13/70 | **Daughter Of Darkness** <br> Tom Jones |
| | **Davy Crockett**...*see: Ballad Of* |
| 3/64 | **Dawn (Go Away)** <br> Four Seasons |
| 36/65 | **Dawn Of Correction** <br> Spokesmen |
| 4/72 | **Day After Day** <br> Badfinger |
| 13/72 | **Day By Day** <br> Godspell |
| 5/72 | **Day Dreaming** <br> Aretha Franklin |
| 35/66 | **Day For Decision** <br> Johnny Sea |
| 23/72 | **Day I Found Myself** <br> Honey Cone |
| 21/69 | **Day Is Done** <br> Peter, Paul & Mary |
| | **Day-O**...*see: Banana Boat* |
| 21/58 <br> 30/58 | **Day The Rains Came** <br> Jane Morgan <br> Raymond Lefevre & His Orchestra |
| 5/66 | **Day Tripper** <br> Beatles |
| 23/77 | **Daybreak** <br> Barry Manilow |
| 39/74 | **Daybreak** <br> Nilsson |
| 2/66 | **Daydream** <br> Lovin' Spoonful |
| 1/67 <br> 12/80 | **Daydream Believer** <br> Monkees <br> Anne Murray |
| 17/79 | **Days Gone Down (Still Got The Light In Your Eyes)** <br> Gerry Rafferty |
| 34/69 | **Days Of Sand And Shovels** <br> Bobby Vinton |
| 26/63 <br> 33/63 | **Days Of Wine And Roses** <br> Andy Williams <br> Henry Mancini & His Orchestra |
| 28/77 | **Daytime Friends** <br> Kenny Rogers |

| POS/YR | RECORD TITLE/ARTIST |
|--------|---------------------|
| 3/77 | **Dazz** <br> Brick |
| 10/81 | **De Do Do Do, De Da Da Da** <br> Police |
| 19/78 | **Deacon Blues** <br> Steely Dan |
| 29/67 | **Dead End Street** <br> Lou Rawls |
| 22/83 | **Dead Giveaway** <br> Shalamar |
| 8/64 | **Dead Man's Curve** <br> Jan & Dean |
| 16/73 | **Dead Skunk** <br> Loudon Wainwright III |
| 24/65 <br> 30/65 | **Dear Heart** <br> Andy Williams <br> Jack Jones |
| 24/62 | **Dear Ivan** <br> Jimmy Dean |
| 9/62 | **Dear Lady Twist** <br> Gary "U.S." Bonds |
| 13/62 | **Dear Lonely Hearts** <br> Nat King Cole |
| 11/62 | **Dear One** <br> Larry Finnegan |
| 1/76 | **December, 1963 (Oh, What A Night)** <br> Four Seasons |
| 7/59 | **Deck Of Cards** <br> Wink Martindale |
| 7/58 | **Dede Dinah** <br> Frankie Avalon |
| 36/66 | **Dedicated Follower Of Fashion** <br> Kinks |
| 3/61 <br> 2/67 | **Dedicated To The One I Love** <br> Shirelles <br> Mamas & The Papas |
| 22/80 | **Deep Inside My Heart** <br> Randy Meisner |
| 20/57 <br> 1/63 <br> 14/76 | **Deep Purple** <br> Billy Ward & His Dominoes <br> Nino Tempo & April Stevens <br> Donny & Marie Osmond |
| 24/70 | **Deeper & Deeper** <br> Freda Payne |

| POS/YR | RECORD TITLE/ARTIST |
|--------|---------------------|
| 11/79 | **Deeper Than The Night**<br>Olivia Newton-John |
| 15/80 | **Deja Vu**<br>Dionne Warwick |
| 22/60 | **Delaware**<br>Perry Como |
| 40/58 | **Delicious!**<br>Jim Backus & Friend |
| 15/68 | **Delilah**<br>Tom Jones |
| | **Delilah Jones**...*see: Man With The Golden Arm* |
| 8/83 | **Delirious**<br>Prince |
| 1/73 | **Delta Dawn**<br>Helen Reddy |
| 10/63 | **Denise**<br>Randy & The Rainbows |
| 25/79 | **Dependin' On You**<br>Doobie Brothers |
| 5/83 | **Der Kommissar**<br>After The Fire |
| 15/62 | **Desafinado**<br>Stan Getz/Charlie Byrd |
| 10/84 | **Desert Moon**<br>Dennis DeYoung |
| 33/63 | **Desert Pete**<br>Kingston Trio |
| 8/71 | **Desiderata**<br>Les Crane |
| 4/80 | **Desire**<br>Andy Gibb |
| 16/78 | **Desiree**<br>Neil Diamond |
| 16/63<br>27/67 | **Detroit City**<br>Bobby Bare<br>Tom Jones |
| 6/60 | **Devil Or Angel**<br>Bobby Vee |
| 3/79 | **Devil Went Down To Georgia**<br>Charlie Daniels Band |
| 4/66 | **Devil With A Blue Dress On**<br>Mitch Ryder & The Detroit Wheels |

| POS/YR | RECORD TITLE/ARTIST |
|--------|---------------------|
| 6/76 | **Devil Woman**<br>Cliff Richard |
| 16/62 | **Devil Woman**<br>Marty Robbins |
| 36/77 | **Devil's Gun**<br>C.J. & Co. |
| 10/58<br>36/78 | **Devoted To You**<br>Everly Brothers<br>Carly Simon & James Taylor |
| 33/74 | **Devotion**<br>Earth, Wind & Fire |
| 24/72 | **Dialogue**<br>Chicago |
| 6/73 | **Diamond Girl**<br>Seals & Crofts |
| 18/60 | **Diamonds And Pearls**<br>Paradons |
| 35/75 | **Diamonds And Rust**<br>Joan Baez |
| 1/57 | **Diana**<br>Paul Anka |
| 10/64 | **Diane**<br>Bachelors |
| 15/72 | **Diary**<br>Bread |
| 14/59 | **Diary, The**<br>Neil Sedaka |
| 9/82 | **Did It In A Minute**<br>Daryl Hall & John Oates |
| 29/76 | **Did You Boogie (With Your Baby)**<br>Flash Cadillac & The Continental Kids |
| 2/66 | **Did You Ever Have To Make Up Your Mind?**<br>Lovin' Spoonful |
| 32/69 | **Did You See Her Eyes**<br>Illusion |
| 10/70 | **Didn't I (Blow Your Mind This Time)**<br>Delfonics |
| 13/68 | **Different Drum**<br>Linda Ronstadt |
| 18/79 | **Different Worlds**<br>Maureen McGovern |
| 2/79 | **Dim All The Lights**<br>Donna Summer |

| POS/YR | RECORD TITLE/ARTIST |
|---|---|
| 11/55 | **Dim, Dim The Lights (I Want Some Atmosphere)** Bill Haley & His Comets |
| 18/60 | **Ding-A-Ling** Bobby Rydell |
| 25/58 | **Ding Dong** McGuire Sisters |
| 36/75 | **Ding Dong; Ding Dong** George Harrison |
| 11/67 | **Ding Dong! The Witch Is Dead** Fifth Estate |
| 6/58 | **Dinner With Drac** John Zacherle |
| 3/83 | **Dirty Laundry** Don Henley |
| 11/66 | **Dirty Water** Standells |
| 12/79 | **Dirty White Boy** Foreigner |
| 36/67 | **Dis-Advantages Of You** Brass Ring featuring Phil Bodner |
| 1/76 | **Disco Duck** Rick Dees & His Cast Of Idiots |
| 11/78 | **Disco Inferno** Trammps |
| 1/76 | **Disco Lady** Johnnie Taylor |
| 24/77 | **Disco Lucy (I Love Lucy Theme)** Wilton Place Street Band |
| 12/79 | **Disco Nights (Rock-Freak)** GQ |
| 28/75 | **Disco Queen** Hot Chocolate |
|  | **(Disco Round)**...see: I Love The Nightlife |
| 28/74 | **Distant Lover** Marvin Gaye |
| 30/66 | **Distant Shores** Chad & Jeremy |
|  | **Dixie**...see: Theme From |
| 30/55 | **Dixie Danny** Laurie Sisters |
| 1/69 | **Dizzy** Tommy Roe |

| POS/YR | RECORD TITLE/ARTIST |
|---|---|
|  | **Do**...also see: Doo |
| 13/82 | **Do I Do** Stevie Wonder |
| 34/64 | **Do I Love You** Ronettes |
| 36/70 | **Do It** Neil Diamond |
| 6/73 | **Do It Again** Steely Dan |
| 20/68 | **Do It Again** Beach Boys |
| 18/67 | **Do It Again A Little Bit Slower** Jon & Robin & The In Crowd |
| 11/75 | **Do It Any Way You Wanna** People's Choice |
| 13/74 | **Do It Baby** Miracles |
| 19/79 | **Do It Or Die** Atlanta Rhythm Section |
| 2/74 | **Do It ('Til You're Satisfied)** B.T. Express |
| 27/62 | **Do-Re-Mi** Lee Dorsey |
| 23/80 | **Do Right** Paul Davis |
| 38/68 | **Do Something To Me** Tommy James & The Shondells |
| 1/80 | **Do That To Me One More Time** Captain & Tennille |
| 10/63 | **Do The Bird** Dee Dee Sharp |
| 36/65 | **Do The Boomerang** Jr. Walker & The All Stars |
| 21/65 | **Do The Clam** Elvis Presley |
| 18/65 | **Do The Freddie** Freddie & The Dreamers *(also see: Let's Do The Freddie)* |
| 28/70 | **Do The Funky Chicken** Rufus Thomas |
| 37/62 | **Do The New Continental** Dovells |

| POS/YR | RECORD TITLE/ARTIST |
|---|---|
| 25/71 | **(Do The) Push And Pull**<br>Rufus Thomas |
| 31/65 | **Do-Wacka-Do**<br>Roger Miller |
| 1/64 | **Do Wah Diddy Diddy**<br>Manfred Mann |
| 37/70 | **Do What You Wanna Do**<br>Five Flights Up |
| 39/76 | **Do What You Want, Be What You Are**<br>Daryl Hall & John Oates |
| 24/77 | **Do Ya**<br>Electric Light Orchestra |
| | **Do Ya Think I'm Sexy?** . . . see: Da Ya |
| 18/77 | **Do Ya Wanna Get Funky With Me**<br>Peter Brown |
| 7/82 | **Do You Believe In Love**<br>Huey Lewis & The News |
| 9/65<br>31/78 | **Do You Believe In Magic**<br>Lovin' Spoonful<br>Shaun Cassidy |
| 10/76 | **Do You Feel Like We Do**<br>Peter Frampton |
| 10/68 | **Do You Know The Way To San Jose**<br>Dionne Warwick |
| 6/71 | **Do You Know What I Mean**<br>Lee Michaels |
| | **Do You Know Where You're Going To** . . . see: Theme From Mahogony |
| 3/62<br>11/64 | **Do You Love Me**<br>Contours<br>Dave Clark Five |
| 30/80 | **Do You Love What You Feel**<br>Rufus featuring Chaka Khan |
| 2/83 | **Do You Really Want To Hurt Me**<br>Culture Club |
| 32/70 | **Do You See My Love (For You Growing)**<br>Jr. Walker & The All Stars |
| 5/77 | **Do You Wanna Make Love**<br>Peter McCann |
| 20/82 | **Do You Wanna Touch Me (Oh Yeah)**<br>Joan Jett & The Blackhearts |
| 5/58<br>12/65<br>17/73 | **Do You Want To Dance**<br>Bobby Freeman<br>Beach Boys<br>Bette Midler |

| POS/YR | RECORD TITLE/ARTIST |
|---|---|
| 2/64 | **Do You Want To Know A Secret**<br>Beatles |
| 39/77 | **Do Your Dance**<br>Rose Royce |
| 11/69 | **Do Your Thing**<br>Charles Wright & The Watts 103rd Street Rhythm Band |
| 30/72 | **Do Your Thing**<br>Isaac Hayes |
| 11/84 | **Doctor! Doctor!**<br>Thompson Twins |
| | **(Doctor, Doctor)** . . . see: Bad Case Of Loving You |
| 28/83 | **Dr. Heckyll & Mr. Jive**<br>Men At Work |
| | **Dr. Kildare** . . . see: Theme From |
| 8/72 | **Doctor My Eyes**<br>Jackson Browne |
| | **Doctor Tarr** . . . see: (System Of) |
| | **Dr. Zhivago** . . . see: Somewhere My Love |
| 11/75 | **Doctor's Orders**<br>Carol Douglas |
| 38/69 | **Does Anybody Know I'm Here**<br>Dells |
| 7/71 | **Does Anybody Really Know What Time It Is?**<br>Chicago |
| 36/83 | **Does It Make You Remember**<br>Kim Carnes |
| 5/61 | **Does Your Chewing Gum Lose It's Flavor (On The Bedpost Over Night)**<br>Lonnie Donegan & His Skiffle Group |
| 29/68 | **Does Your Mama Know About Me**<br>Bobby Taylor & The Vancouvers |
| 19/79 | **Does Your Mother Know**<br>Abba |
| 6/71 | **Doesn't Somebody Want To Be Wanted**<br>Partridge Family |
| 34/79 | **Dog & Butterfly**<br>Heart |
| 30/55 | **Dogface Soldier**<br>Russ Morgan & His Orchestra |

| POS/YR | RECORD TITLE/ARTIST |
|---|---|
| 15/60 | **Doggin' Around** Jackie Wilson |
| 32/69 | **Doggone Right** Miracles |
| 22/73 | **Doing It To Death** J.B.'s |
| 31/60 | **Doll House** Donnie Brooks |
| 13/55 | **Domani (Tomorrow)** Julius LaRosa |
| 1/63 | **Dominique** Singing Nun |
| 9/71 | **Domino** Van Morrison |
| 1/58 | **Don't** Elvis Presley |
| 15/84 | **Don't Answer Me** Alan Parsons Project |
| 19/80 | **Don't Ask Me Why** Billy Joel |
| 25/58 | **Don't Ask Me Why** Elvis Presley |
| 26/63 | **Don't Be Afraid, Little Darlin'** Steve Lawrence |
| 14/55 | **Don't Be Angry** Crew-Cuts |
| 25/55 | Nappy Brown |
| 1/56 | **Don't Be Cruel** Elvis Presley |
| 11/60 | Bill Black's Combo |
| 9/61 | **Don't Bet Money Honey** Linda Scott |
| 20/61 | **Don't Blame Me** Everly Brothers |
| 37/67 | **Don't Blame The Children** Sammy Davis, Jr. |
| 1/62 | **Don't Break The Heart That Loves You** Connie Francis |
| 4/79 | **Don't Bring Me Down** Electric Light Orchestra |
| 12/66 | **Don't Bring Me Down** Animals |
| 9/75 | **Don't Call Us, We'll Call You** Sugarloaf |

| POS/YR | RECORD TITLE/ARTIST |
|---|---|
| | **Don't Cha**. . .also see: Don'tcha |
| 26/74 | **Don't Change Horses (In The Middle Of A Stream)** Tower Of Power |
| 36/71 | **Don't Change On Me** Ray Charles |
| 21/60 | **Don't Come Knockin'** Fats Domino |
| 35/73 | **Don't Cross The River** America |
| 10/83 | **Don't Cry** Asia |
| 39/61 | **Don't Cry, Baby** Etta James |
| 6/70 | **Don't Cry Daddy** Elvis Presley |
| 10/79 | **Don't Cry Out Loud** Melissa Manchester |
| 34/72 | **Don't Do It** The Band |
| 10/80 | **Don't Do Me Like That** Tom Petty & The Heartbreakers |
| 23/72 | **Don't Ever Be Lonely (A Poor Little Fool Like Me)** Cornelius Brothers & Sister Rose |
| 40/79 | **Don't Ever Wanna Lose Ya** New England |
| 8/73 | **Don't Expect Me To Be Your Friend** Lobo |
| 4/80 | **Don't Fall In Love With A Dreamer** Kenny Rogers & Kim Carnes |
| 12/76 | **(Don't Fear) The Reaper** Blue Oyster Cult |
| 17/82 | **Don't Fight It** Kenny Loggins with Steve Perry |
| 1/57 | **Don't Forbid Me** Pat Boone |
| 19/65 | **Don't Forget I Still Love You** Bobbi Martin |
| 29/83 | **Don't Forget To Dance** Kinks |
| 15/69 | **Don't Give In To Him** Gary Puckett & The Union Gap |

| POS/YR | RECORD TITLE/ARTIST |
|--------|---------------------|
| | **Don't Give It Up** |
| 26/81 | Robbie Patton |
| | **Don't Give Up** |
| 37/68 | Petula Clark |
| | **Don't Give Up On Us** |
| 1/77 | David Soul |
| | **Don't Go Breaking My Heart** |
| 1/76 | Elton John & Kiki Dee |
| | **Don't Go Home** |
| 22/58 | Playmates |
| | **Don't Go Near The Indians** |
| 17/62 | Rex Allen |
| | **Don't Go Out Into The Rain (You're Going To Melt)** |
| 18/67 | Herman's Hermits |
| | **Don't Go To Strangers** |
| 38/56 | Vaughn Monroe |
| 36/60 | Etta Jones |
| | **Don't Hang Up** |
| 4/62 | Orlons |
| | **Don't Hold Back** |
| 21/79 | Chanson |
| | **Don't It Make My Brown Eyes Blue** |
| 2/77 | Crystal Gayle |
| | **Don't Just Stand There** |
| 8/65 | Patty Duke |
| | **Don't Knock My Love** |
| 13/71 | Wilson Pickett |
| | **Don't Leave Me This Way** |
| 1/77 | Thelma Houston |
| | **Don't Let Go** |
| 13/58 | Roy Hamilton |
| 18/80 | Isaac Hayes |
| | **Don't Let Go** |
| 38/84 | Wang Chung |
| | **Don't Let Him Go** |
| 24/81 | REO Speedwagon |
| | **Don't Let Him Know** |
| 39/82 | Prism |
| | **Don't Let It End** |
| 6/83 | Styx |
| | **Don't Let Me Be Lonely Tonight** |
| 14/73 | James Taylor |

| POS/YR | RECORD TITLE/ARTIST |
|--------|---------------------|
| | **Don't Let Me Be Misunderstood** |
| 15/65 | Animals |
| 15/78 | Santa Esmeralda |
| | **Don't Let Me Down** |
| 35/69 | Beatles |
| | **Don't Let The Green Grass Fool You** |
| 17/71 | Wilson Pickett |
| | **Don't Let The Joneses Get You Down** |
| 20/69 | Temptations |
| | **Don't Let The Rain Come Down (Crooked Little Man)** |
| 6/64 | Serendipity Singers |
| | **Don't Let The Rain Fall Down On Me** |
| 39/67 | Critters |
| | **Don't Let The Sun Catch You Crying** |
| 4/64 | Gerry & The Pacemakers |
| | **Don't Let The Sun Go Down On Me** |
| 2/74 | Elton John |
| | **Don't Look Back** |
| 4/78 | Boston |
| | **Don't Make Me Over** |
| 21/63 | Dionne Warwick |
| | **Don't Mess Up A Good Thing** |
| 33/65 | Fontella Bass & Bobby McClUre |
| | **Don't Mess With Bill** |
| 7/66 | Marvelettes |
| | **Don't Pay The Ferryman** |
| 34/83 | Chris De Burgh |
| | **Don't Pity Me** |
| 40/59 | Dion & The Belmonts |
| | **Don't Play That Song** |
| 11/62 | Ben E. King |
| 11/70 | Aretha Franklin |
| | **Don't Pull Your Love** |
| 4/71 | Hamilton, Joe Frank & Reynolds |
| 27/76 | Glen Campbell |
| | **Don't Say Goodnight And Mean Goodbye** |
| 26/63 | Shirelles |
| | **Don't Say Goodnight, It's Time For Love** |
| 39/80 | Isley Brothers |
| | **Don't Say Nothin' Bad (About My Baby)** |
| 7/63 | Cookies |
| | **Don't Say You Don't Remember** |
| 15/72 | Beverly Bremers |

| POS/YR | RECORD TITLE/ARTIST |
|---|---|
| 20/63 | **Don't Set Me Free**<br>Ray Charles |
| 5/67 | **Don't Sleep In The Subway**<br>Petula Clark |
| 10/81 | **Don't Stand So Close To Me**<br>Police |
| 3/77 | **Don't Stop**<br>Fleetwood Mac |
| 9/81<br>33/76 | **Don't Stop Believin'**<br>Journey<br>Olivia Newton-John |
| 19/81 | **Don't Stop The Music**<br>Yarbrough & Peoples |
| 1/79 | **Don't Stop 'Til You Get Enough**<br>Michael Jackson |
| 34/76 | **Don't Take Away The Music**<br>Tavares |
| 27/68 | **Don't Take It So Hard**<br>Paul Revere & The Raiders |
| 32/59 | **Don't Take Your Guns To Town**<br>Johnny Cash |
| 37/75 | **Don't Take Your Love**<br>Manhattans |
| 2/82 | **Don't Talk To Strangers**<br>Rick Springfield |
| 27/75 | **Don't Tell Me Goodnight**<br>Lobo |
| 40/83 | **Don't Tell Me You Love Me**<br>Night Ranger |
| 9/63<br>12/65 | **Don't Think Twice, It's All Right**<br>Peter, Paul & Mary<br>Wonder Who? |
| 22/60 | **Don't Throw Away All Those Teardrops**<br>Frankie Avalon |
| 16/64 | **Don't Throw Your Love Away**<br>Searchers |
| 38/69 | **Don't Touch Me**<br>Bettye Swann |
| 26/84 | **Don't Walk Away**<br>Rick Springfield |
| 21/78 | **Don't Want To Live Without It**<br>Pablo Cruise |

| POS/YR | RECORD TITLE/ARTIST |
|---|---|
| 35/81 | **Don't Want To Wait Anymore**<br>Tubes |
| 3/61 | **Don't Worry**<br>Marty Robbins |
| 24/64<br>17/77 | **Don't Worry Baby**<br>Beach Boys<br>B.J. Thomas |
| 29/71 | **(Don't Worry) If There's A Hell Below We're All Going To Go**<br>Curtis Mayfield |
| | **Don't Ya Wanna Play This Game No More . . . see: (Sartorial Eloquence)** |
| | **Don't You . . . also see: Doncha'** |
| 39/62 | **Don't You Believe It**<br>Andy Williams |
| 6/67 | **Don't You Care**<br>Buckinghams |
| 25/83 | **Don't You Get So Mad**<br>Jeffrey Osborne |
| 9/58 | **Don't You Just Know It**<br>Huey "Piano" Smith & The Clowns |
| 2/59 | **Don't You Know**<br>Della Reese |
| 1/82 | **Don't You Want Me**<br>Human League |
| 16/74 | **Don't You Worry 'Bout A Thing**<br>Stevie Wonder |
| | **Don't You Worry 'Bout Me . . . see: Opus 17** |
| 33/79 | **Don't You Write Her Off**<br>McGuinn, Clark & Hillman |
| 15/58 | **Doncha' Think It's Time**<br>Elvis Presley |
| 2/59 | **Donna**<br>Ritchie Valens |
| 6/63 | **Donna The Prima Donna**<br>Dion |
| 15/74 | **Doo Doo Doo Doo Doo (Heartbreaker)**<br>Rolling Stones |
| 6/64 | **Door Is Still Open To My Heart**<br>Dean Martin |
| 35/74 | **Doraville**<br>Atlanta Rhythm Section |

| POS/YR | RECORD TITLE/ARTIST |
|--------|---------------------|
| | **Dose Of Rock 'N' Roll** |
| 26/76 | Ringo Starr |
| | **Dottie** |
| 39/58 | Danny & The Juniors |
| | **Double Barrel** |
| 22/71 | Dave & Ansil Collins |
| | **Double Dutch Bus** |
| 30/81 | Frankie Smith |
| | **Double Lovin'** |
| 14/71 | Osmonds |
| | **Double Shot (Of My Baby's Love)** |
| 17/66 | Swingin' Medallions |
| | **Double Vision** |
| 2/78 | Foreigner |
| | **Down At Lulu's** |
| 33/68 | Ohio Express |
| | **(Down At) Papa Joe's** |
| 9/63 | Dixiebelles |
| | **Down By The Lazy River** |
| 4/72 | Osmonds |
| | **Down By The Station** |
| 13/60 | Four Preps |
| | **Down In The Boondocks** |
| 9/65 | Billy Joe Royal |
| | **Down On The Corner** |
| 3/69 | Creedence Clearwater Revival |
| | **Down The Aisle Of Love** |
| 18/58 | Quin-Tones |
| | **Down The Aisle (Wedding Bells)** |
| 37/63 | Patti LaBelle & The Blue Belles |
| | **Down Under** |
| 1/83 | Men At Work |
| | **Downtown** |
| 1/65 | Petula Clark |
| 40/65 | Allan Sherman (Crazy Downtown) |
| | **Dr.** . . . *see: Doctor* |
| | **Drag City** |
| 10/64 | Jan & Dean |
| | **Draggin' The Line** |
| 4/71 | Tommy James |
| | **Draw Of The Cards** |
| 28/81 | Kim Carnes |
| | **Dream** |
| 19/58 | Betty Johnson |

| POS/YR | RECORD TITLE/ARTIST |
|--------|---------------------|
| | **Dream A Little Dream Of Me** |
| 12/68 | Mama Cass |
| | **Dream Baby (How Long Must I Dream)** |
| 4/62 | Roy Orbison |
| 31/71 | Glen Campbell |
| | **Dream (Hold On To Your Dream)** |
| 37/84 | Irene Cara |
| | **Dream Lover** |
| 2/59 | Bobby Darin |
| | **Dream Merchant** |
| 38/67 | Jerry Butler |
| 36/75 | New Birth |
| | **Dream On** |
| 6/76 | Aerosmith |
| | **Dream On** |
| 32/74 | Righteous Brothers |
| | **Dream On Little Dreamer** |
| 25/65 | Perry Como |
| | **Dream Police** |
| 26/79 | Cheap Trick |
| | **Dream Weaver** |
| 2/76 | Gary Wright |
| | **Dreamer** |
| 15/80 | Supertramp |
| | **Dreamin'** |
| 11/60 | Johnny Burnette |
| | **Dreamin' Is Easy** |
| 30/83 | Steel Breeze |
| | **Dreaming** |
| 10/80 | Cliff Richard |
| | **Dreaming** |
| 27/79 | Blondie |
| | **Dreams** |
| 1/77 | Fleetwood Mac |
| | **Dreams Of The Everyday Housewife** |
| 32/68 | Glen Campbell |
| | **Dreamy Eyes** |
| 35/62 | Johnny Tillotson |
| | **Dreidel** |
| 21/73 | Don McLean |
| | **Drift Away** |
| 5/73 | Dobie Gray |
| | **Drip Drop** |
| 6/63 | Dion |

| POS/YR | RECORD TITLE/ARTIST |
|--------|---------------------|
| 20/63 | **Don't Set Me Free** <br> Ray Charles |
| 5/67 | **Don't Sleep In The Subway** <br> Petula Clark |
| 10/81 | **Don't Stand So Close To Me** <br> Police |
| 3/77 | **Don't Stop** <br> Fleetwood Mac |
| 9/81 | **Don't Stop Believin'** <br> Journey |
| 33/76 | **Don't Stop Believin'** <br> Olivia Newton-John |
| 19/81 | **Don't Stop The Music** <br> Yarbrough & Peoples |
| 1/79 | **Don't Stop 'Til You Get Enough** <br> Michael Jackson |
| 34/76 | **Don't Take Away The Music** <br> Tavares |
| 27/68 | **Don't Take It So Hard** <br> Paul Revere & The Raiders |
| 32/59 | **Don't Take Your Guns To Town** <br> Johnny Cash |
| 37/75 | **Don't Take Your Love** <br> Manhattans |
| 2/82 | **Don't Talk To Strangers** <br> Rick Springfield |
| 27/75 | **Don't Tell Me Goodnight** <br> Lobo |
| 40/83 | **Don't Tell Me You Love Me** <br> Night Ranger |
| 9/63 <br> 12/65 | **Don't Think Twice, It's All Right** <br> Peter, Paul & Mary <br> Wonder Who? |
| 22/60 | **Don't Throw Away All Those Teardrops** <br> Frankie Avalon |
| 16/64 | **Don't Throw Your Love Away** <br> Searchers |
| 38/69 | **Don't Touch Me** <br> Bettye Swann |
| 26/84 | **Don't Walk Away** <br> Rick Springfield |
| 21/78 | **Don't Want To Live Without It** <br> Pablo Cruise |

| POS/YR | RECORD TITLE/ARTIST |
|--------|---------------------|
| 35/81 | **Don't Want To Wait Anymore** <br> Tubes |
| 3/61 | **Don't Worry** <br> Marty Robbins |
| 24/64 <br> 17/77 | **Don't Worry Baby** <br> Beach Boys <br> B.J. Thomas |
| 29/71 | **(Don't Worry) If There's A Hell Below We're All Going To Go** <br> Curtis Mayfield |
|  | **Don't Ya Wanna Play This Game No More**...*see: (Sartorial Eloquence)* |
|  | **Don't You**...*also see: Doncha'* |
| 39/62 | **Don't You Believe It** <br> Andy Williams |
| 6/67 | **Don't You Care** <br> Buckinghams |
| 25/83 | **Don't You Get So Mad** <br> Jeffrey Osborne |
| 9/58 | **Don't You Just Know It** <br> Huey "Piano" Smith & The Clowns |
| 2/59 | **Don't You Know** <br> Della Reese |
| 1/82 | **Don't You Want Me** <br> Human League |
| 16/74 | **Don't You Worry 'Bout A Thing** <br> Stevie Wonder |
|  | **Don't You Worry 'Bout Me**...*see: Opus 17* |
| 33/79 | **Don't You Write Her Off** <br> McGuinn, Clark & Hillman |
| 15/58 | **Doncha' Think It's Time** <br> Elvis Presley |
| 2/59 | **Donna** <br> Ritchie Valens |
| 6/63 | **Donna The Prima Donna** <br> Dion |
| 15/74 | **Doo Doo Doo Doo Doo (Heartbreaker)** <br> Rolling Stones |
| 6/64 | **Door Is Still Open To My Heart** <br> Dean Martin |
| 35/74 | **Doraville** <br> Atlanta Rhythm Section |

| POS/YR | RECORD TITLE/ARTIST |
|--------|---------------------|
| 3/84 | **Drive**<br>Cars |
| 15/79 | **Driver's Seat**<br>Sniff 'n' the Tears |
| 5/80 | **Drivin' My Life Away**<br>Eddie Rabbitt |
| 34/77 | **Drivin' Wheel**<br>Foghat |
| 36/63 | **Drownin' My Sorrows**<br>Connie Francis |
| 11/72 | **Drowning In The Sea Of Love**<br>Joe Simon |
| 29/71 | **Drum, The**<br>Bobby Sherman |
| 29/62 | **Drums Are My Beat**<br>Sandy Nelson |
| 20/67 | **Dry Your Eyes**<br>Brenda & The Tabulations |
| 14/66 | **Duck, The**<br>Jackie Lee |
| 2/73 | **Dueling Banjos**<br>Eric Weissberg & Steve Mandell |
| 1/62 | **Duke Of Earl**<br>Gene Chandler |
|  | **Dukes Of Hazzard**...see: Theme From The |
|  | **Dum-De-Da**...see: She Understands Me |
| 4/61 | **Dum Dum**<br>Brenda Lee |
|  | **(Dum, Dum)**...see: Happy Song |
| 7/56 | **Dungaree Doll**<br>Eddie Fisher |
| 18/77 | **Dusic**<br>Brick |
| 6/78 | **Dust In The Wind**<br>Kansas |
| 30/60 | **Dutchman's Gold**<br>Walter Brennan |
| 15/84 | **Dynamite**<br>Jermaine Jackson |
| 10/75 | **Dynomite**<br>Bazuka [Tony Camillo's] |

# E

| POS/YR | RECORD TITLE/ARTIST |
|--------|---------------------|
| 9/74 | **Earache My Eye Featuring Alice Bowie**<br>Cheech & Chong |
| 12/70 | **Early In The Morning**<br>Vanity Fare |
| 24/58<br>32/58 | **Early In The Morning**<br>Rinky-Dinks<br>Buddy Holly |
| 24/82 | **Early In The Morning**<br>Gap Band |
| 3/55<br>8/55<br>18/55 | **Earth Angel**<br>Crew-Cuts<br>Penguins<br>Gloria Mann |
| 1/63 | **Easier Said Than Done**<br>Essex |
| 27/66 | **East West**<br>Herman's Hermits |
| 4/77 | **Easy**<br>Commodores |
| 9/70 | **Easy Come, Easy Go**<br>Bobby Sherman |
| 39/72 | **Easy Livin**<br>Uriah Heep |
| 17/71 | **Easy Loving**<br>Freddie Hart |
| 4/69 | **Easy To Be Hard**<br>Three Dog Night |
| 36/78 | **Easy To Love**<br>Leo Sayer |
| 12/84 | **Eat It**<br>"Weird Al" Yankovic |
| 25/64<br>5/66 | **Ebb Tide**<br>Lenny Welch<br>Righteous Brothers |
| 1/82 | **Ebony And Ivory**<br>Paul McCartney & Stevie Wonder |
| 8/61 | **Ebony Eyes**<br>Everly Brothers |
| 14/78 | **Ebony Eyes**<br>Bob Welch |

| POS/YR | RECORD TITLE/ARTIST |
|---|---|
| | **Echo Park** |
| 40/69 | Keith Barbour |
| | **Ecstasy** |
| 31/73 | Ohio Players |
| | **Eddie My Love** |
| 11/56 | Fontane Sisters |
| 14/56 | Chordettes |
| 14/56 | Teen Queens |
| | **Edge Of Seventeen (Just Like The White Winged Dove)** |
| 11/82 | Stevie Nicks |
| | **Edge Of The Universe** |
| 26/77 | Bee Gees |
| | **Ego** |
| 34/78 | Elton John |
| | **Eight Days A Week** |
| 1/65 | Beatles |
| | **Eight Miles High** |
| 14/66 | Byrds |
| | **867-5309/Jenny** |
| 4/82 | Tommy Tutone |
| | **Eighteen** |
| 21/71 | Alice Cooper |
| | **Eighteen With A Bullet** |
| 15/75 | Pete Wingfield |
| | **18 Yellow Roses** |
| 10/63 | Bobby Darin |
| | **Ein Schiff Wird Kommen**...*see: Never On Sunday* |
| | **El Condor Pasa** |
| 18/70 | Simon & Garfunkel |
| | **El Matador** |
| 32/60 | Kingston Trio |
| | **El Paso** |
| 1/60 | Marty Robbins |
| | **El Rancho Rock** |
| 30/58 | Champs |
| | **El Watusi** |
| 17/63 | Ray Barretto |
| | **Eleanor Rigby** |
| 11/66 | Beatles |
| 35/68 | Ray Charles |
| 17/69 | Aretha Franklin |
| | **Elected** |
| 26/72 | Alice Cooper |

| POS/YR | RECORD TITLE/ARTIST |
|---|---|
| | **Electric Avenue** |
| 2/83 | Eddy Grant |
| | **Elenore** |
| 6/68 | Turtles |
| | **11th Hour Melody** |
| 21/56 | Al Hibbler |
| 35/56 | Lou Busch & His Orchestra |
| | **Eli's Coming** |
| 10/69 | Three Dog Night |
| | **Eloise** |
| 39/56 | Kay Thompson |
| | **Elusive Butterfly** |
| 5/66 | Bob Lind |
| | **Elvira** |
| 5/81 | Oak Ridge Boys |
| | **Emma** |
| 8/75 | Hot Chocolate |
| | **Emotion** |
| 3/78 | Samantha Sang |
| | **Emotion** |
| 22/75 | Helen Reddy |
| | **Emotional Rescue** |
| 3/80 | Rolling Stones |
| | **Emotions** |
| 7/61 | Brenda Lee |
| | **Empire Strikes Back (Medley)** |
| 18/80 | Meco |
| | **Empty Arms** |
| 13/57 | Teresa Brewer |
| | **Empty Garden (Hey Hey Johnny)** |
| 13/82 | Elton John |
| | **Enchanted** |
| 12/59 | Platters |
| | **Enchanted Island** |
| 12/58 | Four Lads |
| | **Enchanted Sea** |
| 15/59 | Islanders |
| 28/59 | Martin Denny |
| | **End, The** |
| 7/58 | Earl Grant |
| | **End Of Our Road** |
| 15/68 | Gladys Knight & The Pips |
| 40/70 | Marvin Gaye |

| POS/YR | RECORD TITLE/ARTIST |
|---|---|
| 2/63 | **End Of The World**<br>Skeeter Davis |
| 1/81 | **Endless Love**<br>Diana Ross & Lionel Richie |
| 5/58 | **Endless Sleep**<br>Jody Reynolds |
| 12/59 | **Endlessly**<br>Brook Benton |
| 33/74 | **Energy Crisis '74**<br>Dickie Goodman |
| 7/65 | **Engine Engine #9**<br>Roger Miller |
| 14/70 | **Engine Number 9**<br>Wilson Pickett |
| 8/65 | **England Swings**<br>Roger Miller |
| 21/56 | **English Muffins And Irish Stew**<br>Sylvia Syms |
| 6/77 | **Enjoy Yourself**<br>Jacksons |
|  | **Enough Is Enough**. . .*see: No More Tears* |
| 3/74 | **Entertainer, The**<br>Marvin Hamlisch |
| 31/65 | **Entertainer, The**<br>Tony Clarke |
| 34/75 | **Entertainer, The**<br>Billy Joel |
| 19/67 | **Epistle To Dippy**<br>Donovan |
| 9/74 | **Eres Tu (Touch The Wind)**<br>Mocedades |
| 1/79 | **Escape (The Pina Colada Song)**<br>Rupert Holmes |
| 35/71 | **Escape-ism**<br>James Brown |
| 19/62 | **Eso Beso (That Kiss!)**<br>Paul Anka |
| 1/65 | **Eve Of Destruction**<br>Barry McGuire |
| 33/80 | **Even It Up**<br>Heart |
| 12/83 | **Even Now**<br>Bob Seger |

| POS/YR | RECORD TITLE/ARTIST |
|---|---|
| 19/78 | **Even Now**<br>Barry Manilow |
| 36/67 | **Even The Bad Times Are Good**<br>Tremeloes |
| 5/82 | **Even The Nights Are Better**<br>Air Supply |
| 1/77 | **Evergreen**<br>Barbra Streisand |
| 5/78 | **Everlasting Love**<br>Andy Gibb |
| 13/67<br>6/74<br>32/81 | **Everlasting Love**<br>Robert Knight<br>Carl Carlton<br>Rex Smith/Rachel Sweet |
| 16/61 | **Everlovin'**<br>Ricky Nelson |
| 6/61 | **Every Beat Of My Heart**<br>Gladys Knight & The Pips |
| 1/83 | **Every Breath You Take**<br>Police |
|  | **Every Day**. . .*also see: Everyday* |
| 37/56<br>24/72 | **Every Day Of My Life**<br>McGuire Sisters<br>Bobby Vinton |
| 16/78 | **Every Kinda People**<br>Robert Palmer |
| 13/64 | **Every Little Bit Hurts**<br>Brenda Holloway |
| 3/81 | **Every Little Thing She Does Is Magic**<br>Police |
| 39/58 | **Every Night (I Pray)**<br>Chantels |
| 30/63 | **Every Step Of The Way**<br>Johnny Mathis |
| 13/79 | **Every Time I Think Of You**<br>Babys |
| 4/77 | **(Every Time I Turn Around) Back In Love Again**<br>L.T.D. |
| 19/75 | **Every Time You Touch Me (I Get High)**<br>Charlie Rich |
| 30/79 | **Every Which Way But Loose**<br>Eddie Rabbitt |

| POS/YR | RECORD TITLE/ARTIST |
|--------|---------------------|
| 5/81 | **Every Woman In The World**<br>Air Supply |
| 3/63 | **Everybody**<br>Tommy Roe |
| 38/77 | **Everybody Be Dancin'**<br>Starbuck |
| 38/78 | **Everybody Dance**<br>Chic |
| F/70 | **Everybody Is A Star**<br>Sly & The Family Stone |
| 15/64 | **Everybody Knows (I Still Love You)**<br>Dave Clark Five |
| 31/59 | **Everybody Likes To Cha Cha Cha**<br>Sam Cooke |
| 4/65 | **Everybody Loves A Clown**<br>Gary Lewis & The Playboys |
| 6/58<br>19/63 | **Everybody Loves A Lover**<br>Doris Day<br>Shirelles |
| 6/62 | **Everybody Loves Me But You**<br>Brenda Lee |
| 1/64 | **Everybody Loves Somebody**<br>Dean Martin |
| 32/78 | **Everybody Needs Love**<br>Stephen Bishop |
| 39/67 | **Everybody Needs Love**<br>Gladys Knight & The Pips |
| 29/67 | **Everybody Needs Somebody To Love**<br>Wilson Pickett |
| 3/72 | **Everybody Plays The Fool**<br>Main Ingredient |
| 32/82 | **Everybody Wants You**<br>Billy Squier |
| 12/71 | **Everybody's Everything**<br>Santana |
| 20/55 | **Everybody's Got A Home But Me**<br>Eddie Fisher |
| 21/70 | **Everybody's Got The Right To Love**<br>Supremes |
| 18/80 | **Everybody's Got To Learn Sometime**<br>Korgis |
| 26/70 | **Everybody's Out Of Town**<br>B.J. Thomas |

| POS/YR | RECORD TITLE/ARTIST |
|--------|---------------------|
| 1/60 | **Everybody's Somebody's Fool**<br>Connie Francis |
| 6/69 | **Everybody's Talkin'**<br>Nilsson |
| 36/83 | **Everyday I Write The Book**<br>Elvis Costello & The Attractions |
| 1/69<br>37/83 | **Everyday People**<br>Sly & The Family Stone<br>Joan Jett & The Blackhearts |
| 19/69 | **Everyday With You Girl**<br>Classics IV |
| 6/79 | **Every 1's A Winner**<br>Hot Chocolate |
| 17/65 | **Everyone's Gone To The Moon**<br>Jonathan King |
| 5/72 | **Everything I Own**<br>Bread |
| 1/70 | **Everything Is Beautiful**<br>Ray Stevens |
| 10/68 | **Everything That Touches You**<br>Association |
| 16/64 | **Everything's Alright**<br>Newbeats |
| 38/70 | **Everything's Tuesday**<br>Chairmen Of The Board |
| 9/70 | **Evil Ways**<br>Santana |
| 10/76 | **Evil Woman**<br>Electric Light Orchestra |
| 19/70 | **Evil Woman Don't Play Your Games With Me**<br>Crow |
| 2/61<br>31/61<br>36/61 | **Exodus**<br>Ferrante & Teicher<br>Mantovani & His Orchestra<br>Eddie Harris |
| | **Exorcist, Theme From**...*see: Tubular Bells* |
| 14/55 | **Experience Unnecessary**<br>Sarah Vaughan |
| 33/68 | **Explosion In My Soul**<br>Soul Survivors |
| 4/75 | **Express**<br>B.T. Express |

| POS/YR | RECORD TITLE/ARTIST |
|---|---|
| 12/70 | **Express Yourself**<br>Charles Wright & The Watts 103rd Street Rhythm Band |
| 4/67 | **Expressway To Your Heart**<br>Soul Survivors |
| 3/82 | **Eye In The Sky**<br>Alan Parsons Project |
| 1/82 | **Eye Of The Tiger**<br>Survivor |
| 28/68 | **Eyes Of A New York Woman**<br>B.J. Thomas |
| | **Eyes Of Laura Mars**...*see: Love Theme From* |
| 4/84 | **Eyes Without A Face**<br>Billy Idol |

# F

| | |
|---|---|
| 22/78 | **FM (No Static At All)**<br>Steely Dan |
| 29/66 | **Fa-Fa-Fa-Fa-Fa (Sad Song)**<br>Otis Redding |
| 16/57 | **Fabulous**<br>Charlie Gracie |
| 19/56 | **Fabulous Character**<br>Sarah Vaughan |
| 29/68 | **Face It Girl, It's Over**<br>Nancy Wilson |
| 20/81 | **Fade Away**<br>Bruce Springsteen |
| 13/74 | **Fairytale**<br>Pointer Sisters |
| 12/83 | **Faithfully**<br>Journey |
| 35/83 | **Fake Friends**<br>Joan Jett & The Blackhearts |
| 23/67 | **Fakin' It**<br>Simon & Garfunkel |
| 17/83 | **Fall In Love With Me**<br>Earth, Wind & Fire |
| 36/76 | **Fallen Angel**<br>Frankie Valli |

| POS/YR | RECORD TITLE/ARTIST |
|---|---|
| 20/57<br>23/57 | **Fallen Star**<br>Nick Noble<br>Jimmy Newman |
| 30/58 | **Fallin'**<br>Connie Francis |
| 1/75 | **Fallin' In Love**<br>Hamilton, Joe Frank & Reynolds |
| 27/74 | **Fallin' In Love**<br>Souther, Hillman, Furay Band |
| 13/78 | **Falling**<br>Leblanc & Carr |
| 22/63 | **Falling**<br>Roy Orbison |
| 1/75 | **Fame**<br>David Bowie |
| 4/80 | **Fame**<br>Irene Cara |
| 17/60 | **Fame And Fortune**<br>Elvis Presley |
| 1/71 | **Family Affair**<br>Sly & The Family Stone |
| 6/83 | **Family Man**<br>Daryl Hall & John Oates |
| 12/72 | **Family Of Man**<br>Three Dog Night |
| 31/70 | **Fancy**<br>Bobbie Gentry |
| 39/77 | **Fancy Dancer**<br>Commodores |
| 38/60 | **Fannie Mae**<br>Buster Brown |
| 12/76 | **Fanny (Be Tender With My Love)**<br>Bee Gees |
| 23/82 | **Fantasy**<br>Aldo Nova |
| 32/78 | **Fantasy**<br>Earth, Wind & Fire |
| 10/83 | **Far From Over**<br>Frank Stallone |
| 38/84 | **Farewell My Summer Love**<br>Michael Jackson |
| 19/64 | **Farmer John**<br>Premiers |

| POS/YR | RECORD TITLE/ARTIST |
|--------|---------------------|
| | **Fascination** |
| 7/57 | Jane Morgan |
| 15/57 | Dinah Shore |
| 17/57 | Dick Jacobs & His Chorus & Orchestra |
| | **Fat Bottomed Girls** |
| F/79 | Queen |
| | **Feel Like Makin' Love** |
| 1/74 | Roberta Flack |
| | **Feel Like Makin' Love** |
| 10/75 | Bad Company |
| | **Feel So Fine** |
| 14/60 | Johnny Preston |
| 22/67 | Bunny Sigler (medley) |
| | **Feelin' Groovy**...see: 59th Street Bridge |
| | **Feelin' Stronger Every Day** |
| 10/73 | Chicago |
| | **Feeling Alright** |
| 33/72 | Joe Cocker |
| | **Feelings** |
| 6/75 | Morris Albert |
| | **Feels Like The First Time** |
| 4/77 | Foreigner |
| | **Feels So Good** |
| 4/78 | Chuck Mangione |
| | **Feels So Right** |
| 20/81 | Alabama |
| | **Fell In Love On Monday** |
| 32/61 | Fats Domino |
| | **Fernando** |
| 13/76 | Abba |
| | **Ferry Across The Mersey** |
| 6/65 | Gerry & The Pacemakers |
| | **Fever** |
| 24/56 | Little Willie John |
| 8/58 | Peggy Lee |
| 7/65 | McCoys |
| | **Ffun** |
| 23/78 | Con Funk Shun |
| | **Fibbin'** |
| 39/58 | Patti Page |
| | **Fifth Of Beethoven** |
| 1/76 | Walter Murphy & The Big Apple Band |
| | **50 Ways To Leave Your Lover** |
| 1/76 | Paul Simon |

| POS/YR | RECORD TITLE/ARTIST |
|--------|---------------------|
| | **59th Street Bridge Song (Feelin' Groovy)** |
| 13/67 | Harpers Bizarre |
| | **Fight (medley)** |
| 3/79 | Barbra Streisand |
| | **Fight The Power** |
| 4/75 | Isley Brothers |
| | **(Final Acclaim)**...see: You're In My Heart |
| | **Finally Got Myself Together (I'm A Changed Man)** |
| 17/74 | Impressions |
| | **Find Another Fool** |
| 16/82 | Quarterflash |
| | **Find Another Girl** |
| 27/61 | Jerry Butler |
| | **Find Your Way Back** |
| 29/81 | Jefferson Starship |
| | **Fine Fine Day** |
| 22/84 | Tony Carey |
| | **Finger Poppin' Time** |
| 7/60 | Hank Ballard & The Midnighters |
| | **Fingertips** |
| 1/63 | Stevie Wonder |
| | **Fins** |
| 35/79 | Jimmy Buffett |
| | **Fire** |
| 1/75 | Ohio Players |
| | **Fire** |
| 2/68 | Arthur Brown [The Crazy World Of] |
| | **Fire** |
| 2/79 | Pointer Sisters |
| | **Fire And Ice** |
| 17/81 | Pat Benatar |
| | **Fire And Rain** |
| 3/70 | James Taylor |
| | **Fire And Water** |
| 24/72 | Wilson Pickett |
| | **Fire, Baby I'm On Fire** |
| 28/74 | Andy Kim |
| | **Fire In The Morning** |
| 32/80 | Melissa Manchester |
| | **Fire Lake** |
| 6/80 | Bob Seger |

| POS/YR | RECORD TITLE/ARTIST |
|--------|---------------------|
| 38/75 | **Fire On The Mountain**<br>Marshall Tucker Band |
| 20/58 | **Firefly**<br>Tony Bennett |
| 21/77 | **First Cut Is The Deepest**<br>Rod Stewart |
| 25/57 | **First Date, First Kiss, First Love**<br>Sonny James |
| 33/84 | **First Day Of Summer**<br>Tony Carey |
| 20/60 | **First Name Initial**<br>Annette |
| 37/69 | **First Of May**<br>Bee Gees |
| 27/63 | **First Quarrel**<br>Paul & Paula |
| 1/72 | **First Time Ever I Saw Your Face**<br>Roberta Flack |
|  | **(First Time I Was A Fool)**...*see: Third Time Lucky* |
| 38/80 | **First Time Love**<br>Livingston Taylor |
| 25/61 | **Fish, The**<br>Bobby Rydell |
| 26/74 | **Fish Ain't Bitin'**<br>Lamont Dozier |
| 4/66 | **Five O'Clock World**<br>Vogues |
|  | **Five Oaks**...*see: Cinco Robles* |
| 27/78 | **5.7.0.5.**<br>City Boy |
| 11/70 | **5-10-15-20 (25-30 Years Of Love)**<br>Presidents |
| 10/63 | **500 Miles Away From Home**<br>Bobby Bare |
| 14/61 | **Flaming Star**<br>Elvis Presley |
| 28/66 | **Flamingo**<br>Herb Alpert & The Tijuana Brass |
| 16/78 | **Flash Light**<br>Parliament |
| 1/83 | **Flashdance...What A Feeling**<br>Irene Cara |

| POS/YR | RECORD TITLE/ARTIST |
|--------|---------------------|
| 29/84 | **Flesh For Fantasy**<br>Billy Idol |
| 2/77 | **Float On**<br>Floaters |
| 21/56 | **Flowers Mean Forgiveness**<br>Frank Sinatra |
| 4/66 | **Flowers On The Wall**<br>Statler Brothers |
| 16/72 | **Floy Joy**<br>Supremes |
| 7/61 | **Fly, The**<br>Chubby Checker |
| 13/76 | **Fly Away**<br>John Denver |
| 2/77 | **Fly Like An Eagle**<br>Steve Miller Band |
| 14/63 | **Fly Me To The Moon**<br>Joe Harnell & His Orchestra |
| 1/75 | **Fly, Robin, Fly**<br>Silver Convention |
| 38/78 | **Flying High**<br>Commodores |
| 3/56 | **Flying Saucer**<br>Buchanan & Goodman |
| 18/57 | **Flying Saucer The 2nd**<br>Buchanan & Goodman |
|  | **Foggy Mountain Breakdown**...*see: Ballad Of Bonnie & Clyde* |
| 15/62 | **Follow That Dream**<br>Elvis Presley |
| 17/63 | **Follow The Boys**<br>Connie Francis |
| 23/78 | **Follow You Follow Me**<br>Genesis |
| 32/68 | **Folsom Prison Blues**<br>Johnny Cash |
| 7/56 | **Fool, The**<br>Sanford Clark |
| 22/68 | **Fool For You**<br>Impressions |
| 12/78 | **Fool (If You Think It's Over)**<br>Chris Rea |

| POS/YR | RECORD TITLE/ARTIST |
|--------|---------------------|
| 27/60 | **Fool In Love** <br> Ike & Tina Turner |
| 25/81 | **Fool In Love With You** <br> Jim Photoglo |
| 21/80 | **Fool In The Rain** <br> Led Zeppelin |
| 13/64 | **Fool Never Learns** <br> Andy Williams |
| 3/61 | **Fool #1** <br> Brenda Lee |
| 6/68 | **Fool On The Hill** <br> Sergio Mendes & Brasil '66 |
| 2/59 | **Fool Such As I** <br> Elvis Presley |
| 10/76 | **Fool To Cry** <br> Rolling Stones |
| 20/55 | **Fooled** <br> Perry Como |
| 3/76 | **Fooled Around And Fell In Love** <br> Elvin Bishop |
| 28/83 | **Foolin'** <br> Def Leppard |
| 29/78 | **Fooling Yourself (The Angry Young Man)** <br> Styx |
| 4/63 | **Foolish Little Girl** <br> Shirelles |
| 29/59 | **Fools Hall Of Fame** <br> Pat Boone |
| 24/60 <br> 12/63 | **Fools Rush In** <br> Brook Benton <br> Ricky Nelson |
| 25/61 | **Foot Stomping** <br> Flares |
| 1/84 | **Footloose** <br> Kenny Loggins |
| 7/60 | **Footsteps** <br> Steve Lawrence |
| 29/72 | **Footstompin' Music** <br> Grand Funk Railroad |
| 30/76 | **Fopp** <br> Ohio Players |
| 23/59 | **For A Penny** <br> Pat Boone |

| POS/YR | RECORD TITLE/ARTIST |
|--------|---------------------|
| 3/71 | **For All We Know** <br> Carpenters |
| 26/71 | **(For God's Sake) Give More Power To The People** <br> Chi-Lites |
| 30/65 | **For Lovin' Me** <br> Peter, Paul & Mary |
| 28/61 | **For My Baby** <br> Brook Benton |
| 21/58 | **For My Good Fortune** <br> Pat Boone |
| 2/68 | **For Once In My Life** <br> Stevie Wonder |
| 11/71 | **For The Good Times** <br> Ray Price |
| 13/70 | **For The Love Of Him** <br> Bobbi Martin |
| 9/74 | **For The Love Of Money** <br> O'Jays |
| 22/75 | **For The Love Of You** <br> Isley Brothers |
| 7/67 | **For What It's Worth** <br> Buffalo Springfield |
| 6/64 | **For You** <br> Ricky Nelson |
| 4/81 | **For Your Eyes Only** <br> Sheena Easton |
| 6/65 | **For Your Love** <br> Yardbirds |
| 13/58 <br> 20/67 | **For Your Love** <br> Ed Townsend <br> Peaches & Herb |
| 11/58 <br> 26/64 <br> 23/67 | **For Your Precious Love** <br> Jerry Butler <br> Garnet Mimms & The Enchanters <br> Oscar Toney, Jr. |
| 9/60 <br> 25/64 | **Forever** <br> Little Dippers <br> Pete Drake |
| 28/68 | **Forever Came Today** <br> Supremes |
| 35/56 | **Forever Darling** <br> Ames Brothers |
| 20/79 | **Forever In Blue Jeans** <br> Neil Diamond |

| POS/YR | RECORD TITLE/ARTIST |
|--------|---------------------|
| 28/80 | **Forever Mine** <br> O'Jays |
| 4/64 | **Forget Him** <br> Bobby Rydell |
| 12/58 | **Forget Me Not** <br> Kalin Twins |
| 23/82 | **Forget Me Nots** <br> Patrice Rushen |
| 2/80 | **Forgive Me, Girl (medley)** <br> Spinners |
| 21/55 | **Forgive My Heart** <br> Nat King Cole |
| F/69 | **Fortunate Son** <br> Creedence Clearwater Revival |
| 9/59 | **Forty Miles Of Bad Road** <br> Duane Eddy |
| 36/79 | **Found A Cure** <br> Ashford & Simpson |
| 11/57 <br> 15/57 | **Four Walls** <br> Jim Reeves <br> Jim Lowe |
| 36/68 | **1432 Franklin Pike Circle Hero** <br> Bobby Russell |
| 5/76 | **Fox On The Run** <br> Sweet |
| 1/73 | **Frankenstein** <br> Edgar Winter Group |
| 9/59 | **Frankie** <br> Connie Francis |
| 20/61 <br> 14/63 <br> 25/66 | **Frankie And Johnny** <br> Brook Benton <br> Sam Cooke <br> Elvis Presley |
| 36/57 | **Fraulein** <br> Bobby Helms |
|  | **Freddie**...see: Do The & Let's Do The |
| 4/72 | **Freddie's Dead (Theme From "Superfly")** <br> Curtis Mayfield |
| 20/71 | **Free** <br> Chicago |
| 23/56 | **Free** <br> Tommy Leonetti |
| 25/77 | **Free** <br> Deniece Williams |

| POS/YR | RECORD TITLE/ARTIST |
|--------|---------------------|
| 19/75 <br> 38/77 | **Free Bird** <br> Lynyrd Skynyrd <br> Lynyrd Skynyrd (Live) |
| 22/74 | **Free Man In Paris** <br> Joni Mitchell |
| 14/73 | **Free Ride** <br> Edgar Winter Group |
| 33/58 | **Freeze, The** <br> Tony & Joe |
| 4/82 | **Freeze-Frame** <br> J. Geils Band |
| 6/57 <br> 40/57 | **Freight Train** <br> Rusty Draper <br> Chas. McDevitt Skiffle Group |
|  | **(Friday Night)**...see: Livin' It Up |
| 16/67 | **Friday On My Mind** <br> Easybeats |
| 36/66 | **Friday's Child** <br> Nancy Sinatra |
| 5/56 | **Friendly Persuasion (Thee I Love)** <br> Pat Boone |
| 34/71 | **Friends** <br> Elton John |
| 40/73 | **Friends** <br> Bette Midler |
| 38/82 | **Friends In Love** <br> Johnny Mathis & Dionne Warwick |
| 17/69 | **Friendship Train** <br> Gladys Knight & The Pips |
| 32/61 | **Frogg** <br> Brothers Four |
| 6/63 | **From A Jack To A King** <br> Ned Miller |
| 23/64 | **From A Window** <br> Billy J. Kramer with the Dakotas |
| 28/75 | **From His Woman To You** <br> Barbara Mason |
| 39/72 | **From The Beginning** <br> Emerson, Lake & Palmer |
| 11/56 | **From The Candy Store On The Corner To The Chapel On The Hill** <br> Tony Bennett |
| 28/75 | **Full Of Fire** <br> Al Green |

| POS/YR | RECORD TITLE/ARTIST |
|--------|---------------------|
| | Fun . . . see: Ffun |
| | **Fun, Fun, Fun** |
| 5/64 | Beach Boys |
| | **Funky Broadway** |
| 8/67 | Wilson Pickett |
| | **Funky Judge** |
| 39/68 | Bull & The Matadors |
| | **Funky Nassau** |
| 15/71 | Beginning Of The End |
| | **Funky Street** |
| 14/68 | Arthur Conley |
| | **Funky Stuff** |
| 29/73 | Kool & The Gang |
| | **Funky Worm** |
| 15/73 | Ohio Players |
| | **Funkytown** |
| 1/80 | Lipps, Inc. |
| | **Funny** |
| 25/61 | Maxine Brown |
| | **Funny Face** |
| 5/73 | Donna Fargo |
| | **Funny How Time Slips Away** |
| 22/62 | Jimmy Elledge |
| 13/64 | Joe Hinton |
| | **Funny Way Of Laughin'** |
| 10/62 | Burl Ives |
| | **Future Shock** |
| 39/73 | Curtis Mayfield |

# G

| POS/YR | RECORD TITLE/ARTIST |
|--------|---------------------|
| | **G.T.O.** |
| 4/64 | Ronny & The Daytonas |
| | **Galaxy** |
| 39/78 | War |
| | **Gallant Men** |
| 29/67 | Senator Everett McKinley Dirksen |
| | **Galveston** |
| 4/69 | Glen Campbell |
| | **Gambler, The** |
| 16/79 | Kenny Rogers |

| POS/YR | RECORD TITLE/ARTIST |
|--------|---------------------|
| | **Game Of Love** |
| 1/65 | Mindbenders |
| | **Games** |
| 27/71 | Redeye |
| | **Games People Play** |
| 12/69 | Joe South |
| | **Games People Play** |
| 16/81 | Alan Parsons Project |
| | **(Games People Play)** . . . see: They Just Can't Stop It |
| | **Garden Of Eden** |
| 12/56 | Joe Valino |
| | **Garden Party** |
| 6/72 | Ricky Nelson |
| | **Gee, But It's Lonely** |
| 31/58 | Pat Boone |
| | **Gee Whittakers!** |
| 19/56 | Pat Boone |
| | **Gee Whiz** |
| 28/61 | Innocents |
| | **Gee Whiz (Look At His Eyes)** |
| 10/61 | Carla Thomas |
| 31/80 | Bernadette Peters |
| | **Gemini Dream** |
| 12/81 | Moody Blues |
| | **General Hospi-Tale** |
| 33/81 | Afternoon Delights |
| | **Genius Of Love** |
| 31/82 | Tom Tom Club |
| | **Gentle On My Mind** |
| 39/68 | Glen Campbell |
| | **George Jackson** |
| 33/72 | Bob Dylan |
| | **Georgia On My Mind** |
| 1/60 | Ray Charles |
| | **Georgy Girl** |
| 2/67 | Seekers |
| | **Geronimo's Cadillac** |
| 37/72 | Michael Murphey |
| | **Get A Job** |
| 1/58 | Silhouettes |
| 21/58 | Mills Brothers |
| | **Get Back** |
| 1/69 | Beatles |

| POS/YR | RECORD TITLE/ARTIST |
|--------|---------------------|
| 6/76 | **Get Closer** <br> Seals & Crofts |
| 29/82 | **Get Closer** <br> Linda Ronstadt |
| 10/75 | **Get Dancin'** <br> Disco Tex & The Sex-O-Lettes |
| 7/73 | **Get Down** <br> Gilbert O'Sullivan |
| 8/75 | **Get Down, Get Down (Get On The Floor)** <br> Joe Simon |
| 10/82 | **Get Down On It** <br> Kool & The Gang |
| 1/75 | **Get Down Tonight** <br> KC & The Sunshine Band |
| 24/71 | **Get It On** <br> Chase |
| | **(Get It On)**...see: *Bang A Gong* |
| 21/79 | **Get It Right Next Time** <br> Gerry Rafferty |
| 28/73 | **Get It Together** <br> Jacksons |
| 40/67 | **Get It Together** <br> James Brown |
| 27/67 | **Get Me To The World On Time** <br> Electric Prunes |
| 9/78 | **Get Off** <br> Foxy |
| 1/65 | **Get Off Of My Cloud** <br> Rolling Stones |
| 18/72 | **Get On The Good Foot** <br> James Brown |
| 11/67 | **Get On Up** <br> Esquires |
| 29/66 <br> 4/70 | **Get Ready** <br> Temptations <br> Rare Earth |
| 30/76 | **Get The Funk Out Ma Face** <br> Brothers Johnson |
| 31/65 <br> 5/69 | **Get Together** <br> We Five <br> Youngbloods |
| 2/76 | **Get Up And Boogie (That's Right)** <br> Silver Convention |

| POS/YR | RECORD TITLE/ARTIST |
|--------|---------------------|
| | **(Get Up And Dance)**...see: *Bite Your Lip* |
| 34/71 | **Get Up, Get Into It, Get Involved** <br> James Brown |
| | **Get Up I Feel Like A Sex Machine**...see: *Sex Machine* |
| 21/79 | **Get Used To It** <br> Roger Voudouris |
| 12/76 | **Getaway** <br> Earth, Wind & Fire |
| 27/78 | **Gettin' Ready For Love** <br> Diana Ross |
| 18/67 | **Gettin' Together** <br> Tommy James & The Shondells |
| 20/79 | **Getting Closer** <br> Paul McCartney |
| 29/73 | **Ghetto Child** <br> Spinners |
| 30/61 <br> 31/81 | **(Ghost) Riders In The Sky** <br> Ramrods <br> Outlaws |
| 22/56 | **Ghost Town** <br> Don Cherry |
| 1/84 | **Ghostbusters** <br> Ray Parker Jr. |
| 37/83 | **Gimme All Your Lovin'** <br> ZZ Top |
| 9/70 | **Gimme Dat Ding** <br> Pipkins |
| 12/69 | **Gimme Gimme Good Lovin'** <br> Crazy Elephant |
| 9/67 | **Gimme Little Sign** <br> Brenton Wood |
| 7/67 <br> 18/80 | **Gimme Some Lovin'** <br> Spencer Davis Group <br> Blues Brothers |
| 6/62 | **Gina** <br> Johnny Mathis |
| 9/58 | **Ginger Bread** <br> Frankie Avalon |
| 38/61 | **Ginnie Bell** <br> Paul Dino |
| 21/62 | **Ginny Come Lately** <br> Brian Hyland |

| POS/YR | RECORD TITLE/ARTIST |
|---|---|
| 30/65 | **Girl Come Running**<br>Four Seasons |
| 5/64 | **Girl From Ipanema**<br>Stan Getz/Astrud Gilberto |
| 39/67 | **Girl I Knew Somewhere**<br>Monkees |
| 21/66 | **Girl In Love**<br>Outsiders |
| 35/84 | **Girl In Trouble (Is A Temporary Thing)**<br>Romeo Void |
| 2/83 | **Girl Is Mine**<br>Paul McCartney & Michael Jackson |
| 10/67 | **Girl Like You**<br>Rascals |
| 19/61 | **Girl Of My Best Friend**<br>Ral Donner |
| 37/79 | **Girl Of My Dreams**<br>Bram Tchaikovsky |
| 28/66 | **Girl On A Swing**<br>Gerry & The Pacemakers |
| 5/68 | **Girl Watcher**<br>O'Kaysions |
| 26/64 | **Girl (Why You Wanna Make Me Blue)**<br>Temptations |
| 13/57 | **Girl With The Golden Braids**<br>Perry Como |
| 10/67 | **Girl, You'll Be A Woman Soon**<br>Neil Diamond |
| 16/84 | **Girls**<br>Dwight Twilley |
| 34/80 | **Girls Can Get It**<br>Dr. Hook |
| 33/68 | **Girls Can't Do What The Guys Do**<br>Betty Wright |
| 14/62 | **(Girls, Girls, Girls) Made To Love**<br>Eddie Hodges |
| 33/64 | **Girls Grow Up Faster Than Boys**<br>Cookies |
| 39/67 | **Girls In Love**<br>Gary Lewis & The Playboys |
| 2/84 | **Girls Just Want To Have Fun**<br>Cyndi Lauper |
| 33/78 | **Girls' School**<br>Paul McCartney |

| POS/YR | RECORD TITLE/ARTIST |
|---|---|
| 33/84 | **Girls With Guns**<br>Tommy Shaw |
| 8/69 | **Gitarzan**<br>Ray Stevens |
| 15/77 | **Give A Little Bit**<br>Supertramp |
| 18/65 | **Give Him A Great Big Kiss**<br>Shangri-Las |
| 21/72 | **Give Ireland Back To The Irish**<br>Paul McCartney |
| 18/80 | **Give It All You Got**<br>Chuck Mangione |
| 30/73 | **Give It To Me**<br>J. Geils Band |
| 40/81 | **Give It To Me Baby**<br>Rick James |
| 20/74 | **Give It To The People**<br>Righteous Brothers |
| 18/84 | **Give It Up**<br>KC |
| 15/69 | **Give It Up Or Turnit A Loose**<br>James Brown |
| 38/76 | **Give It Up (Turn It Loose)**<br>Tyrone Davis |
| 40/75 | **Give It What You Got**<br>B.T. Express |
| | **Give Me**...*also see: Gimme* |
| 3/70 | **Give Me Just A Little More Time**<br>Chairmen Of The Board |
| 1/73 | **Give Me Love (Give Me Peace On Earth)**<br>George Harrison |
| 4/80 | **Give Me The Night**<br>George Benson |
| 31/73 | **Give Me Your Love**<br>Barbara Mason |
| | **Give More Power To The People**...*see:*<br>*(For God's Sake)* |
| 14/69 | **Give Peace A Chance**<br>John Lennon |
| 30/56 | **Give Us This Day**<br>Joni James |
| 29/65 | **Give Us Your Blessings**<br>Shangri-Las |

| POS/YR | RECORD TITLE/ARTIST |
|--------|---------------------|
| 34/73 | **Give Your Baby A Standing Ovation**<br>Dells |
| 8/81 | **Giving It Up For Your Love**<br>Delbert McClinton |
| 38/64 | **Giving Up**<br>Gladys Knight & The Pips |
| 6/64 | **Glad All Over**<br>Dave Clark Five |
| 19/55 | **Glad Rag Doll**<br>Crazy Otto |
| 26/67 | **Glad To Be Unhappy**<br>Mamas & The Papas |
| 7/84 | **Glamorous Life**<br>Sheila E. |
| 37/75 | **Glasshouse**<br>Temptations |
| 8/56 | **Glendora**<br>Perry Como |
| 2/82 | **Gloria**<br>Laura Branigan |
| 10/66 | **Gloria**<br>Shadows Of Knight |
| 25/77 | **Gloria**<br>Enchantment |
| 34/72 | **Glory Bound**<br>Grass Roots |
| 30/66 | **Go Ahead And Cry**<br>Righteous Brothers |
| 5/72 | **Go All The Way**<br>Raspberries |
| 1/63<br>12/66<br>1/71 | **Go Away Little Girl**<br>Steve Lawrence<br>Happenings<br>Donny Osmond |
| 36/70 | **Go Back**<br>Crabby Appleton |
| 32/71 | **Go Down Gamblin'**<br>Blood, Sweat & Tears |
| 23/84 | **Go Insane**<br>Lindsey Buckingham |
| 5/60 | **Go, Jimmy, Go**<br>Jimmy Clanton |
| 10/65 | **Go Now!**<br>Moody Blues |

| POS/YR | RECORD TITLE/ARTIST |
|--------|---------------------|
| 11/56<br>39/56 | **Go On With The Wedding**<br>Patti Page<br>Kitty Kallen & Georgie Shaw |
| 16/67 | **Go Where You Wanna Go**<br>5th Dimension |
| 10/77 | **Go Your Own Way**<br>Fleetwood Mac |
| 36/59 | **God Bless America**<br>Connie Francis |
| 18/61 | **God, Country And My Baby**<br>Johnny Burnette |
| 22/70 | **God, Love And Rock & Roll**<br>Teegarden & Van Winkle |
| 39/66 | **God Only Knows**<br>Beach Boys |
| | **Godfather**...see: Love Theme From The |
| 17/82 | **Goin' Down**<br>Greg Guidry |
| 36/73 | **Goin' Home**<br>Osmonds |
| 6/64<br>7/68 | **Goin' Out Of My Head**<br>Little Anthony & The Imperials<br>Lettermen |
| 16/57 | **Goin' Steady**<br>Tommy Sands |
| 35/64 | **Going Going Gone**<br>Brook Benton |
| 15/69 | **Going In Circles**<br>Friends Of Distinction |
| 11/66<br>25/82 | **Going To A Go-Go**<br>Miracles<br>Rolling Stones |
| 11/69 | **Going Up The Country**<br>Canned Heat |
| 5/79 | **Gold**<br>John Stewart |
| 29/84 | **Gold**<br>Spandau Ballet |
| 10/76 | **Golden Years**<br>David Bowie |
| 8/65 | **Goldfinger**<br>Shirley Bassey |

| POS/YR | RECORD TITLE/ARTIST |
|---|---|
| 4/57 | **Gone** Ferlin Husky |
| 24/72 | Joey Heatherton |
| 23/75 | **Gone At Last** Paul Simon/Phoebe Snow |
| 31/64 | **Gone, Gone, Gone** Everly Brothers |
| 23/77 | **Gone Too Far** England Dan & John Ford Coley |
| 18/57 | **Gonna Find Me A Bluebird** Marvin Rainwater |
| 1/77 | **Gonna Fly Now (Theme From "Rocky")** Bill Conti |
| 28/77 | Maynard Ferguson |
| 11/56 | **Gonna Get Along Without Ya Now** Patience & Prudence |
| 29/67 | **Gonna Give Her All The Love I've Got** Jimmy Ruffin |
| 36/69 | **Goo Goo Barabajagal (Love Is Hot)** Donovan |
| 17/55 | **Good And Lonesome** Kay Starr |
| | **Good Foot**...see: Get On The |
| 39/79 | **Good Friend** Mary MacGregor |
| 11/79 | **Good Girls Don't** Knack |
| 10/58 | **Good Golly Miss Molly** Little Richard |
| 4/76 | Mitch Ryder & The Detroit Wheels (medley) |
| 25/76 | **Good Hearted Woman** Waylon & Willie |
| 18/63 | **Good Life** Tony Bennett |
| 1/66 | **Good Lovin'** Rascals |
| 30/69 | **Good Lovin' Ain't Easy To Come By** Marvin Gaye & Tammi Terrell |
| 36/75 | **Good Lovin' Gone Bad** Bad Company |
| 1/62 | **Good Luck Charm** Elvis Presley |
| 34/73 | **Good Morning Heartache** Diana Ross |

| POS/YR | RECORD TITLE/ARTIST |
|---|---|
| 3/69 | **Good Morning Starshine** Oliver |
| 11/64 | **Good News** Sam Cooke |
| 21/69 | **Good Old Rock 'N Roll (medley)** Cat Mother & the All Night News Boys |
| 2/68 | **Good, The Bad And The Ugly** Hugo Montenegro & His Orchestra |
| 4/67 | **Good Thing** Paul Revere & The Raiders |
| 11/61 | **Good Time Baby** Bobby Rydell |
| 9/72 | **Good Time Charlie's Got The Blues** Danny O'Keefe |
| 1/79 | **Good Times** Chic |
| 11/64 | **Good Times** Sam Cooke |
| 3/60 | **Good Timin'** Jimmy Jones |
| 40/79 | **Good Timin'** Beach Boys |
| 1/66 | **Good Vibrations** Beach Boys |
| 34/76 | Todd Rundgren |
| 13/69 | **Goodbye** Mary Hopkin |
| 8/59 | **Goodbye Baby** Jack Scott |
| 33/64 | **Goodbye Baby (Baby Goodbye)** Solomon Burke |
| 3/61 | **Goodbye Cruel World** James Darren |
| 15/78 | **Goodbye Girl** David Gates |
| 11/59 | **Goodbye Jimmy, Goodbye** Kathy Linden |
| 31/68 | **Goodbye My Love** James Brown |
| 15/79 | **Goodbye Stranger** Supertramp |
| 7/72 | **Goodbye To Love** Carpenters |

| POS/YR | RECORD TITLE/ARTIST |
|---|---|
| 2/73 | **Goodbye Yellow Brick Road**<br>Elton John |
| 21/65 | **Goodnight**<br>Roy Orbison |
| 32/57<br>32/63<br>27/69 | **Goodnight My Love**<br>McGuire Sisters<br>Fleetwoods<br>Paul Anka |
| 5/79 | **Goodnight Tonight**<br>Paul McCartney |
| 20/57 | **Goody Goody**<br>Frankie Lymon & The Teenagers |
| 37/68 | **Goody Goody Gumdrops**<br>1910 Fruitgum Co. |
| 12/83 | **Goody Two Shoes**<br>Adam Ant |
| 24/60 | **Got A Girl**<br>Four Preps |
| 10/84 | **Got A Hold On Me**<br>Christine McVie |
| 39/58 | **Got A Match?**<br>Daddy-O'S |
| 12/79 | **Got To Be Real**<br>Cheryl Lynn |
| 4/71 | **Got To Be There**<br>Michael Jackson |
| 7/76<br>9/78 | **Got To Get You Into My Life**<br>Beatles<br>Earth, Wind & Fire |
| 22/65 | **Got To Get You Off My Mind**<br>Solomon Burke |
| 1/77 | **Got To Give It Up**<br>Marvin Gaye |
| 21/70 | **Gotta Hold On To This Feeling**<br>Jr. Walker & The All Stars |
| 24/79 | **Gotta Serve Somebody**<br>Bob Dylan |
| 4/59 | **Gotta Travel On**<br>Billy Grammer |
| 16/56<br>17/56 | **Graduation Day**<br>Rover Boys<br>Four Freshmen |
| 34/61 | **Graduation Song...Pomp And Circumstance**<br>Adrian Kimberly |

| POS/YR | RECORD TITLE/ARTIST |
|---|---|
| 39/59 | **Graduation's Here**<br>Fleetwoods |
| 17/63 | **Grass Is Greener**<br>Brenda Lee |
| 9/62 | **Gravy (For My Mashed Potatoes)**<br>Dee Dee Sharp |
| 1/68<br>3/69 | **Grazing In The Grass**<br>Hugh Masekela<br>Friends Of Distinction |
| 1/78 | **Grease**<br>Frankie Valli |
| 20/66 | **Great Airplane Strike**<br>Paul Revere & The Raiders |
| 2/58 | **Great Balls Of Fire**<br>Jerry Lee Lewis |
| | **Great Imposter**...*see: (He's) The* |
| 1/56 | **Great Pretender**<br>Platters |
| | **Greatest American Hero**...*see: Theme From* |
| 34/62 | **Greatest Hurt**<br>Jackie Wilson |
| 24/77 | **Greatest Love Of All**<br>George Benson |
| | **Green Berets**...*see: Ballad Of* |
| 1/56 | **Green Door**<br>Jim Lowe |
| 3/70 | **Green Eyed Lady**<br>Sugarloaf |
| 8/66 | **Green Grass**<br>Gary Lewis & The Playboys |
| 14/63 | **Green, Green**<br>New Christy Minstrels |
| 11/67 | **Green, Green Grass Of Home**<br>Tom Jones |
| 39/68 | **Green Light**<br>American Breed |
| 3/62 | **Green Onions**<br>Booker T. & The Mg's |
| 2/69 | **Green River**<br>Creedence Clearwater Revival |
| 1/68 | **Green Tambourine**<br>Lemon Pipers |

| POS/YR | RECORD TITLE/ARTIST |
|--------|---------------------|
| 21/63 | **Greenback Dollar** <br> Kingston Trio |
| 2/60 | **Greenfields** <br> Brothers Four |
| 7/78 | **Groove Line** <br> Heatwave |
| 6/71 | **Groove Me** <br> King Floyd |
| 1/67 <br> 21/67 | **Groovin'** <br> Rascals <br> Booker T. & The Mg's |
| 30/69 | **Groovy Grubworm** <br> Harlow Wilcox & the Oakies |
| 2/66 | **Groovy Kind Of Love** <br> Mindbenders |
| 12/70 | **Groovy Situation** <br> Gene Chandler |
| 14/76 | **Grow Some Funk Of Your Own** <br> Elton John |
| 9/66 | **Guantanamera** <br> Sandpipers |
| 11/58 | **Guess Things Happen That Way** <br> Johnny Cash |
| 31/59 | **Guess Who** <br> Jesse Belvin |
| 3/81 | **Guilty** <br> Barbra Streisand & Barry Gibb |
| 5/59 | **Guitar Boogie Shuffle** <br> Virtues |
| 11/72 | **Guitar Man** <br> Bread |
| 28/81 | **Guitar Man** <br> Elvis Presley |
|  | **Guitar Man**...see: (Dance With The) |
| 10/55 | **Gum Drop** <br> Crew-Cuts |
| 12/82 | **Gypsy** <br> Fleetwood Mac |
| 24/63 | **Gypsy Cried** <br> Lou Christie |
| 8/73 | **Gypsy Man** <br> War |

| POS/YR | RECORD TITLE/ARTIST |
|--------|---------------------|
| 20/61 <br> 3/70 | **Gypsy Woman** <br> Impressions <br> Brian Hyland |
| 1/71 | **Gypsys, Tramps & Thieves** <br> Cher |

# H

| POS/YR | RECORD TITLE/ARTIST |
|--------|---------------------|
| 2/69 | **Hair** <br> Cowsills |
| 22/66 | **Hair On My Chinny Chin Chin** <br> Sam The Sham & The Pharaohs |
| 1/73 | **Half-Breed** <br> Cher |
| 12/63 | **Half Heaven - Half Heartache** <br> Gene Pitney |
| 15/79 | **Half The Way** <br> Crystal Gayle |
| 39/61 <br> 23/68 | **Halfway To Paradise** <br> Tony Orlando <br> Bobby Vinton |
| 33/71 | **Hallelujah** <br> Sweathog |
| 28/73 | **Hallelujah Day** <br> Jacksons |
|  | **Hand Jive**...see: Willie & The Hand Jive |
| 17/70 | **Hand Me Down World** <br> Guess Who |
| 19/83 | **Hand To Hold On To** <br> John Cougar |
| 2/60 <br> 22/64 <br> 4/77 | **Handy Man** <br> Jimmy Jones <br> Del Shannon <br> James Taylor |
| 9/69 | **Hang 'Em High** <br> Booker T. & The Mg's |
| 20/82 | **Hang Fire** <br> Rolling Stones |
| 8/74 | **Hang On In There Baby** <br> Johnny Bristol |

| POS/YR | RECORD TITLE/ARTIST |
|--------|---------------------|
| | **Hang On Sloopy** |
| 26/64 | Vibrations (My Girl) |
| 1/65 | McCoys |
| 11/65 | Ramsey Lewis |
| | **Hang Up My Rock And Roll Shoes** |
| 24/58 | Chuck Willis |
| | **Hanging Tree** |
| 38/59 | Marty Robbins |
| | **Hanky Panky** |
| 1/66 | Tommy James & The Shondells |
| | **Happening, The** |
| 1/67 | Supremes |
| 32/67 | Herb Alpert & The Tijuana Brass |
| | **Happenings Ten Years Time Ago** |
| 30/66 | Yardbirds |
| | **Happiest Girl In The Whole U.S.A.** |
| 11/72 | Donna Fargo |
| | **Happiness** |
| 30/79 | Pointer Sisters |
| | **Happiness Is Just Around The Bend** |
| 35/74 | Main Ingredient |
| | **Happiness Street** |
| 20/56 | Georgia Gibbs |
| 38/56 | Tony Bennett |
| | **Happy** |
| 22/72 | Rolling Stones |
| | **Happy Anniversary** |
| 16/78 | Little River Band |
| | **Happy Birthday Blues** |
| 30/61 | Kathy Young with The Innocents |
| | **Happy Birthday, Sweet Sixteen** |
| 6/62 | Neil Sedaka |
| | **Happy Days** |
| 5/76 | Pratt & McClain |
| | **Happy-Go-Lucky-Me** |
| 10/60 | Paul Evans |
| | **Happy, Happy Birthday Baby** |
| 5/57 | Tune Weavers |
| | **Happy Heart** |
| 22/69 | Andy Williams |
| | **Happy Jack** |
| 24/67 | Who |
| | **Happy Music** |
| 19/76 | Blackbyrds |

| POS/YR | RECORD TITLE/ARTIST |
|--------|---------------------|
| | **Happy Organ** |
| 1/59 | Dave "Baby" Cortez |
| | **Happy People** |
| 40/75 | Temptations |
| | **Happy Reindeer** |
| 34/59 | Dancer, Prancer & Nervous |
| | **Happy Song (Dum-Dum)** |
| 25/68 | Otis Redding |
| | **Happy Summer Days** |
| 27/66 | Ronnie Dove |
| | **Happy Together** |
| 1/67 | Turtles |
| | **Happy Whistler** |
| 6/56 | Don Robertson |
| | **Harbor Lights** |
| 8/60 | Platters |
| | **Hard Day's Night** |
| 1/64 | Beatles |
| 29/66 | Ramsey Lewis |
| | **Hard Habit To Break** |
| 3/84 | Chicago |
| | **Hard Headed Woman** |
| 1/58 | Elvis Presley |
| | **Hard Luck Woman** |
| 15/77 | Kiss |
| | **Hard Rock Cafe** |
| 30/77 | Carole King |
| | **Hard To Get** |
| 4/55 | Gisele MacKenzie |
| | **Hard To Say** |
| 7/81 | Dan Fogelberg |
| | **Hard To Say I'm Sorry** |
| 1/82 | Chicago |
| | **Harden My Heart** |
| 3/82 | Quarterflash |
| | **Harlem Nocturne** |
| 39/66 | Viscounts |
| | **Harper Valley P.T.A.** |
| 1/68 | Jeannie C. Riley |
| | **Harry Hippie** |
| 31/73 | Bobby Womack |
| | **Harry The Hairy Ape** |
| 17/63 | Ray Stevens |

**Eric Carmen,** a veteran of Ohio power-poppers the Raspberries, started his solo career with a bang, getting three Top 40 hits from his first LP. But he cooled off quickly and is nowhere to be found today.

**David Cassidy** recorded with Beach Boy Bruce Johnston after the cheering stopped. He even cut a version of Johnston's composition "I Write the Songs," but Barry Manilow had the hit.

**Chic** guitarist Nile Rodgers outlived the disco boom to become one of today's most sought-after producers. Among his credits: David Bowie, INXS, Duran Duran, Southside Johnny, Debbie Harry, and Diana Ross.

**Chicago** began as the Big Thing, became Chicago Transit Authority at the suggestion of producer Jim Guercio, and shortened that when the city's administration took umbrage.

**Jimmy Clanton** was not just another pretty face with a weak voice, contrary to appearances. He recorded in New Orleans with some of the best sidemen in r&b, including Dr. John and members of Fats Domino's and Little Richard's bands.

**Joe Cocker** and **Jennifer Warnes** revived their careers (temporarily) with the theme from *An Officer and a Gentleman*. Plus, the song won an Oscar for its composers, Jack Nitzsche, Will Jennings, and Buffy Sainte-Marie.

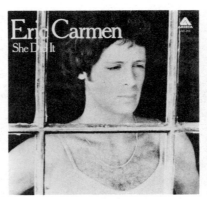

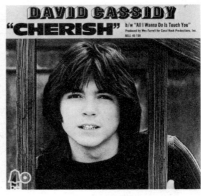

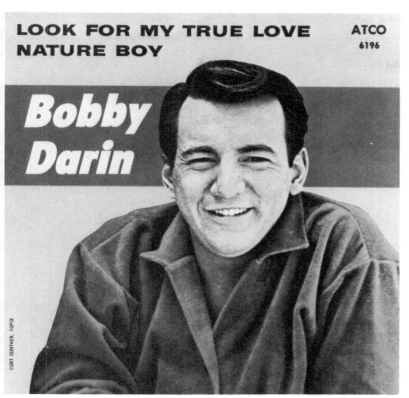

LOOK FOR MY TRUE LOVE
NATURE BOY

ATCO
6196

Bobby Darin

CURT GUNTHER, TOPIX

**Bobby Darin,** born Walden Robert Cassotto, once played an Indian chief with a traveling acting troupe. After his hit records, he got to try his acting skills in movies like *Too Late Blues* and *Come September.*

**Def Leppard** was a seriously abrasive heavy metal band until they sought the assistance of producer Robert John "Mutt" Lange, also known for his work with Graham Parker and the Cars. His expert touch softened their harsh edges and led to multi-platinum sales.

**The DeFranco Family** entered show business at the behest of the editor of *Tiger Beat,* who liked the way young Tony looked. The resemblance to Donny Osmond was just coincidental, of course.

**Dino, Desi and Billy.** Dino was the son of Dean Martin, and Desi of Lucille Ball and Desi Arnaz. Billy's sister later married Carl Wilson of the Beach Boys . . . but the boys were discovered by Frank Sinatra, who signed them to his Reprise record label.

**Donovan.** With his denim cap, curly hair, and harmonica, Donovan Leitch was touted (wrongly) as England's Bob Dylan. Following his hits, he scored the movie *If It's Tuesday, This Must Be Belgium.*

**Tommy Edwards'** biggest hit, "It's All in the Game," was an old pop standard when he recorded it for the second time in 1957. The song's melody was written in 1912 by Charles G. Dawes, U.S. Vice-President from 1925–29, as "Melody in A Major."

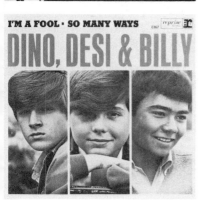

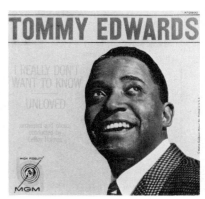

| POS/YR | RECORD TITLE/ARTIST |
|--------|---------------------|
| 13/75 | **Harry Truman**<br>Chicago |
| 5/61 | **Hats Off To Larry**<br>Del Shannon |
| 11/64 | **Haunted House**<br>Gene Simmons |
| 31/62 | **Have A Good Time**<br>Sue Thompson |
| 5/64 | **Have I The Right?**<br>Honeycombs |
| 29/57 | **Have I Told You Lately That I Love You**<br>Ricky Nelson |
| 8/71 | **Have You Ever Seen The Rain**<br>Creedence Clearwater Revival |
| 18/63 | **Have You Heard**<br>Duprees |
| 24/65 | **Have You Looked Into Your Heart**<br>Jerry Vale |
| 1/75 | **Have You Never Been Mellow**<br>Olivia Newton-John |
| 3/71 | **Have You Seen Her**<br>Chi-Lites |
| 9/66 | **Have You Seen Your Mother, Baby, Standing In The Shadow?**<br>Rolling Stones |
| 14/74 | **Haven't Got Time For The Pain**<br>Carly Simon |
| 26/79 | **Haven't Stopped Dancing Yet**<br>Gonzalez |
| 17/62 | **Having A Party**<br>Sam Cooke |
| 4/69 | **Hawaii Five-O**<br>Ventures |
| 33/65 | **Hawaii Tattoo**<br>Waikikis |
| 11/59 | **Hawaiian Wedding Song**<br>Andy Williams |
| 13/66 | **Hazy Shade Of Winter**<br>Simon & Garfunkel |
| 4/55<br>10/55<br>18/66 | **He**<br>Al Hibbler<br>McGuire Sisters<br>Righteous Brothers |

| POS/YR | RECORD TITLE/ARTIST |
|--------|---------------------|
| 7/70<br>20/70 | **He Ain't Heavy, He's My Brother**<br>Hollies<br>Neil Diamond |
| 33/81 | **He Can't Love You**<br>Michael Stanley Band |
| 7/60<br>1/75 | **He Don't Love You (Like I Love You)**<br>Jerry Butler<br>Dawn |
| 34/62 | **He Knows I Love Him Too Much**<br>Paris Sisters |
| | **He Will Break Your Heart**...*see: He Don't Love You* |
| 2/60 | **He'll Have To Go**<br>Jim Reeves |
| 4/60 | **He'll Have To Stay**<br>Jeanne Black |
| 36/76 | **He's A Friend**<br>Eddie Kendricks |
| 30/81 | **He's A Liar**<br>Bee Gees |
| 1/62 | **He's A Rebel**<br>Crystals |
| 1/58 | **He's Got The Whole World (In His Hands)**<br>Laurie London |
| 23/57 | **He's Mine**<br>Platters |
| 14/61 | **(He's My) Dreamboat**<br>Connie Francis |
| 1/63 | **He's So Fine**<br>Chiffons |
| 3/80 | **He's So Shy**<br>Pointer Sisters |
| 11/63 | **He's Sure The Boy I Love**<br>Crystals |
| 30/61 | **(He's) The Great Impostor**<br>Fleetwoods |
| 9/79 | **He's The Greatest Dancer**<br>Sister Sledge |
| 14/79 | **Head Games**<br>Foreigner |
| 11/84 | **Head Over Heels**<br>Go-GO'S |

| POS/YR | RECORD TITLE/ARTIST |
|--------|---------------------|
| 35/80 | **Headed For A Fall**<br>Firefall |
| 14/77 | **Heard It In A Love Song**<br>Marshall Tucker Band |
| 6/55<br>13/55 | **Heart**<br>Eddie Fisher<br>Four Aces |
| 8/83 | **Heart And Soul**<br>Huey Lewis & The News |
| 18/61<br>25/61 | **Heart And Soul**<br>Cleftones<br>Jan & Dean |
| 3/82 | **Heart Attack**<br>Olivia Newton-John |
| 9/65 | **Heart Full Of Soul**<br>Yardbirds |
| 21/80 | **Heart Hotels**<br>Dan Fogelberg |
| 15/62 | **Heart In Hand**<br>Brenda Lee |
| 24/81 | **Heart Like A Wheel**<br>Steve Miller Band |
| 1/79 | **Heart Of Glass**<br>Blondie |
| 1/72 | **Heart Of Gold**<br>Neil Young |
| 6/84 | **Heart Of Rock & Roll**<br>Huey Lewis & The News |
| 19/65 | **Heart Of Stone**<br>Rolling Stones |
| 20/79<br>25/83 | **Heart Of The Night**<br>Poco<br>Juice Newton |
| 15/83 | **Heart To Heart**<br>Kenny Loggins |
| 1/79 | **Heartache Tonight**<br>Eagles |
| 7/61 | **Heartaches**<br>Marcels |
| 1/59<br>35/65 | **Heartaches By The Number**<br>Guy Mitchell<br>Johnny Tillotson |
| 3/73 | **Heartbeat - It's A Lovebeat**<br>DeFranco Family featuring Tony DeFranco |

| POS/YR | RECORD TITLE/ARTIST |
|--------|---------------------|
| 1/56 | **Heartbreak Hotel**<br>Elvis Presley |
| 22/81 | **Heartbreak Hotel**<br>Jacksons |
| 38/60 | **Heartbreak (It's Hurtin' Me)**<br>Little Willie John |
| 39/74 | **Heartbreak Kid**<br>Bo Donaldson & The Heywoods |
| 10/83 | **Heartbreaker**<br>Dionne Warwick |
| 23/80 | **Heartbreaker**<br>Pat Benatar |
| 37/78 | **Heartbreaker**<br>Dolly Parton |
| | **(Heartbreaker)**. . .see: Doo Doo Doo Doo |
| 24/78 | **Heartless**<br>Heart |
| 5/82 | **Heartlight**<br>Neil Diamond |
| 8/81 | **Hearts**<br>Marty Balin |
| 1/55<br>15/55<br>20/61<br>37/73 | **Hearts Of Stone**<br>Fontane Sisters<br>Charms<br>Bill Black's Combo<br>Blue Ridge Rangers |
| 19/81 | **Hearts On Fire**<br>Randy Meisner |
| 4/82 | **Heat Of The Moment**<br>Asia |
| 4/63<br>5/75 | **Heat Wave**<br>Martha & The Vandellas<br>Linda Ronstadt |
| 29/69 | **Heather Honey**<br>Tommy Roe |
| 39/69 | **Heaven**<br>Rascals |
| 9/70 | **Heaven Help Us All**<br>Stevie Wonder |
| 4/79 | **Heaven Knows**<br>Donna Summer |
| 24/69 | **Heaven Knows**<br>Grass Roots |

| POS/YR | RECORD TITLE/ARTIST |
|--------|---------------------|
| 15/76 | **Heaven Must Be Missing An Angel**<br>Tavares |
| 11/79 | **Heaven Must Have Sent You**<br>Bonnie Pointer |
| 39/56 | **Heaven On Earth**<br>Platters |
| 6/77 | **Heaven On The 7th Floor**<br>Paul Nicholas |
| 40/59 | **Heavenly Lover**<br>Teresa Brewer |
| 27/71 | **Heavy Makes You Happy (Sha-Na-Boom Boom)**<br>Staple Singers |
| 33/70 | **Heed The Call**<br>Kenny Rogers & The First Edition |
| 10/74 | **Helen Wheels**<br>Paul McCartney |
| 1/84 | **Hello**<br>Lionel Richie |
| 6/81 | **Hello Again**<br>Neil Diamond |
| 1/64 | **Hello, Dolly!**<br>Louis Armstrong |
| 1/67 | **Hello Goodbye**<br>Beatles |
| 26/63 | **Hello Heartache, Goodbye Love**<br>Little Peggy March |
| 26/67 | **Hello Hello**<br>Sopwith Camel |
| 35/73 | **Hello Hurray**<br>Alice Cooper |
| 1/68 | **Hello, I Love You**<br>Doors |
| 5/73 | **Hello It's Me**<br>Todd Rundgren |
| 9/61 | **Hello Mary Lou**<br>Ricky Nelson |
| 2/63 | **Hello Mudduh, Hello Fadduh! (A Letter From Camp)**<br>Allan Sherman |
| 24/76 | **Hello Old Friend**<br>Eric Clapton |
| 3/63<br>15/77 | **Hello Stranger**<br>Barbara Lewis<br>Yvonne Elliman |

| POS/YR | RECORD TITLE/ARTIST |
|--------|---------------------|
| 12/61 | **Hello Walls**<br>Faron Young |
| 23/60 | **Hello Young Lovers**<br>Paul Anka |
| 1/65 | **Help!**<br>Beatles |
| 14/77 | **Help Is On Its Way**<br>Little River Band |
| 7/74 | **Help Me**<br>Joni Mitchell |
| 29/66<br>37/66 | **Help Me Girl**<br>Animals<br>Outsiders |
| 8/71<br>33/72 | **Help Me Make It Through The Night**<br>Sammi Smith<br>Gladys Knight & The Pips |
| 1/65<br>22/75 | **Help Me, Rhonda**<br>Beach Boys<br>Johnny Rivers |
| 35/68 | **Help Yourself**<br>Tom Jones |
| 6/62 | **Her Royal Majesty**<br>James Darren |
| 11/81 | **Her Town Too**<br>James Taylor & J.D. Souther |
| 23/77 | **Here Come Those Tears Again**<br>Jackson Browne |
| 13/67 | **Here Comes My Baby**<br>Tremeloes |
| 14/59 | **Here Comes Summer**<br>Jerry Keller |
| 15/71 | **Here Comes That Rainy Day Feeling Again**<br>Fortunes |
| 8/68<br>19/68 | **Here Comes The Judge**<br>Shorty Long<br>Pigmeat Markham |
| 24/65 | **Here Comes The Night**<br>Them |
| 4/84 | **Here Comes The Rain Again**<br>Eurythmics |
| 16/71 | **Here Comes The Sun**<br>Richie Havens |
| 10/73 | **Here I Am (Come And Take Me)**<br>Al Green |

| POS/YR | RECORD TITLE/ARTIST |
|--------|---------------------|
| 5/81 | **Here I Am (Just When I Thought I Was Over You)**<br>Air Supply |
| 37/69 | **Here I Go Again**<br>Miracles |
| 27/65 | **Here It Comes Again**<br>Fortunes |
| 15/67 | **Here We Go Again**<br>Ray Charles |
| 3/78 | **Here You Come Again**<br>Dolly Parton |
| 12/67 | **Heroes And Villains**<br>Beach Boys |
| 1/62 | **Hey! Baby**<br>Bruce Channel |
| 12/67 | **Hey Baby (They're Playing Our Song)**<br>Buckinghams |
| 19/72 | **Hey Big Brother**<br>Rare Earth |
| 23/64 | **Hey, Bobba Needle**<br>Chubby Checker |
| 7/78 | **Hey Deanie**<br>Shaun Cassidy |
| 10/63<br>35/68<br>9/72 | **Hey Girl**<br>Freddie Scott<br>Bobby Vee (medley)<br>Donny Osmond |
| 35/73 | **Hey Girl (I Like Your Style)**<br>Temptations |
| 29/64 | **Hey Harmonica Man**<br>Stevie Wonder |
| 3/57 | **Hey! Jealous Lover**<br>Frank Sinatra |
| 32/64 | **Hey Jean, Hey Dean**<br>Dean & Jean |
| 31/66 | **Hey Joe**<br>Leaves |
| 1/68<br>23/69 | **Hey Jude**<br>Beatles<br>Wilson Pickett |
| 35/70 | **Hey Lawdy Mama**<br>Steppenwolf |
| 31/67 | **Hey, Leroy, Your Mama's Callin' You**<br>Jimmy Castor Bunch |

| POS/YR | RECORD TITLE/ARTIST |
|--------|---------------------|
| 20/62 | **Hey, Let's Twist**<br>Joey Dee & The Starliters |
| 4/64 | **Hey Little Cobra**<br>Rip Chords |
| 13/63 | **Hey Little Girl**<br>Major Lance |
| 20/59 | **Hey Little Girl**<br>Dee Clark |
| 29/57 | **Hey! Little Girl**<br>Techniques |
| 38/62 | **Hey! Little Girl**<br>Del Shannon |
| 12/55 | **Hey, Mr. Banjo**<br>Sunnysiders |
| 24/70 | **Hey, Mr. Sun**<br>Bobby Sherman |
| 10/81 | **Hey Nineteen**<br>Steely Dan |
| 1/63 | **Hey Paula**<br>Paul & Paula |
| 27/63<br>2/70<br>31/80 | **Hey There Lonely Girl (Boy)**<br>Ruby & The Romantics<br>Eddie Holman<br>Robert John |
| 16/68 | **Hey, Western Union Man**<br>Jerry Butler |
| 1/75 | **(Hey Won't You Play) Another Somebody Done Somebody Wrong Song**<br>B.J. Thomas |
| 21/75 | **Hey You**<br>Bachman-Turner Overdrive |
| 14/70 | **Hi-De-Ho**<br>Blood, Sweat & Tears |
| 11/64<br>25/68 | **Hi-Heel Sneakers**<br>Tommy Tucker<br>Jose Feliciano |
| 10/73 | **Hi, Hi, Hi**<br>Paul McCartney |
| 33/62 | **Hide & Go Seek**<br>Bunker Hill |
| 29/61 | **Hide Away**<br>Freddy King |
| 20/62 | **Hide 'Nor Hair**<br>Ray Charles |

| POS/YR | RECORD TITLE/ARTIST |
|--------|---------------------|
| 21/58 | **Hideaway**<br>Four Esquires |
| | **High-Heel**...see: Hi-Heel |
| 30/59 | **High Hopes**<br>Frank Sinatra |
| 21/58 | **High School Confidential**<br>Jerry Lee Lewis |
| 17/77 | **High School Dance**<br>Sylvers |
| 28/59 | **High School U.S.A.**<br>Tommy Facenda |
| 37/58 | **High Sign**<br>Diamonds |
| 22/71 | **High Time We Went**<br>Joe Cocker |
| | **Higher & Higher**...see: (Your Love Keeps Lifting Me) |
| 4/73 | **Higher Ground**<br>Stevie Wonder |
| 37/74 | **Higher Plane**<br>Kool & The Gang |
| 26/79 | **Highway Song**<br>Blackfoot |
| 14/75 | **Hijack**<br>Herbie Mann |
| | **Hill Street Blues**...see: Theme From |
| 6/80 | **Him**<br>Rupert Holmes |
| 5/67 | **Him Or Me - What's It Gonna Be?**<br>Paul Revere & The Raiders |
| 31/68 | **Hip City - Pt. 2**<br>Jr. Walker & The All Stars |
| 37/67 | **Hip Hug-Her**<br>Booker T. & The Mg's |
| 24/64 | **Hippy Hippy Shake**<br>Swinging Blue Jeans |
| | **His Latest Flame**...see: Marie's The Name |
| 39/66 | **History Repeats Itself**<br>Buddy Starcher |
| 9/80 | **Hit Me With Your Best Shot**<br>Pat Benatar |
| | **(Hit Record)**...see: Overnight Sensation |

| POS/YR | RECORD TITLE/ARTIST |
|--------|---------------------|
| 1/61<br>40/76 | **Hit The Road Jack**<br>Ray Charles<br>Stampeders |
| 30/63 | **Hitch Hike**<br>Marvin Gaye |
| 34/68 | **Hitch It To The Horse**<br>Fantastic Johnny C |
| 5/70 | **Hitchin' A Ride**<br>Vanity Fare |
| 9/73 | **Hocus Pocus**<br>Focus |
| 35/76 | **Hold Back The Night**<br>Trammps |
| 14/72 | **Hold Her Tight**<br>Osmonds |
| 4/82 | **Hold Me**<br>Fleetwood Mac |
| 3/84 | **Hold Me Now**<br>Thompson Twins |
| 8/65 | **Hold Me, Thrill Me, Kiss Me**<br>Mel Carter |
| 5/68 | **Hold Me Tight**<br>Johnny Nash |
| 40/83 | **Hold Me 'Til The Mornin' Comes**<br>Paul Anka |
| 15/82 | **Hold On**<br>Santana |
| 18/79 | **Hold On**<br>Ian Gomm |
| 38/79 | **Hold On**<br>Triumph |
| 40/80 | **Hold On**<br>Kansas |
| 21/66 | **Hold On! I'm A Comin'**<br>Sam & Dave |
| 27/81 | **Hold On Loosely**<br>38 Special |
| 10/81 | **Hold On Tight**<br>Electric Light Orchestra |
| 10/80 | **Hold On To My Love**<br>Jimmy Ruffin |
| 5/79 | **Hold The Line**<br>Toto |

| POS/YR | RECORD TITLE/ARTIST |
|---|---|
| 5/65 | **Hold What You've Got**<br>Joe Tex |
| 5/72 | **Hold Your Head Up**<br>Argent |
| 37/82 | **Holdin' On**<br>Tane Cain |
| 17/75 | **Holdin' On To Yesterday**<br>Ambrosia |
| 34/84 | **Holding Out For A Hero**<br>Bonnie Tyler |
| 16/67 | **Holiday**<br>Bee Gees |
| 16/84 | **Holiday**<br>Madonna |
| 6/69 | **Holly Holy**<br>Neil Diamond |
| 32/77 | **Hollywood**<br>Rufus featuring Chaka Khan |
| 12/78 | **Hollywood Nights**<br>Bob Seger |
| 6/74 | **Hollywood Swinging**<br>Kool & The Gang |
| 23/66 | **Holy Cow**<br>Lee Dorsey |
| 34/67 | **Homburg**<br>Procol Harum |
| 28/79 | **Home And Dry**<br>Gerry Rafferty |
| 25/65 | **Home Of The Brave**<br>Jody Miller |
| 5/66 | **Homeward Bound**<br>Simon & Garfunkel |
| 28/60 | **Honest I Do**<br>Innocents |
| 32/57 | **Honest I Do**<br>Jimmy Reed |
| 24/79 | **Honesty**<br>Billy Joel |
| 1/68 | **Honey**<br>Bobby Goldsboro |
| 6/55 | **Honey Babe**<br>Art Mooney & His Orchestra |

| POS/YR | RECORD TITLE/ARTIST |
|---|---|
| 11/67 | **Honey Chile**<br>Martha & The Vandellas |
| 19/70 | **Honey Come Back**<br>Glen Campbell |
| 27/74 | **Honey, Honey**<br>Abba |
| 1/57 | **Honeycomb**<br>Jimmie Rodgers |
| 8/72 | **Honky Cat**<br>Elton John |
| 2/56 | **Honky Tonk**<br>Bill Doggett |
| 1/69 | **Honky Tonk Women**<br>Rolling Stones |
| 11/63 | **Honolulu Lulu**<br>Jan & Dean |
| 23/61 | **Hoochi Coochi Coo**<br>Hank Ballard & The Midnighters |
| 17/64 | **Hooka Tooka**<br>Chubby Checker |
| 5/69<br>1/74 | **Hooked On A Feeling**<br>B.J. Thomas<br>Blue Swede |
| 10/82 | **Hooked On Classics**<br>Royal Philharmonic Orchestra |
| 31/82 | **Hooked On Swing (medley)**<br>Larry Elgart |
| 6/66 | **Hooray For Hazel**<br>Tommy Roe |
| 38/63 | **Hootenanny**<br>Glencoves |
| 36/82 | **Hope You Love Me Like You Say You Do**<br>Huey Lewis & The News |
| 13/63 | **Hopeless**<br>Andy Williams |
| 3/78 | **Hopelessly Devoted To You**<br>Olivia Newton-John |
| 2/68 | **Horse, The**<br>Cliff Nobles & Co. |
| 1/72 | **Horse With No Name**<br>America |
| 3/78 | **Hot Blooded**<br>Foreigner |

| POS/YR | RECORD TITLE/ARTIST |
|--------|---------------------|
| 1/78 | **Hot Child In The City** <br> Nick Gilder |
| 1/56 | **Hot Diggity (Dog Ziggity Boom)** <br> Perry Como |
| 2/69 | **Hot Fun In The Summertime** <br> Sly & The Family Stone |
| 11/83 | **Hot Girls In Love** <br> Loverboy |
| 23/82 | **Hot In The City** <br> Billy Idol |
| 28/78 | **Hot Legs** <br> Rod Stewart |
| 5/77 | **Hot Line** <br> Sylvers |
| 31/78 | **Hot Love, Cold World** <br> Bob Welch |
| 21/79 | **Hot Number** <br> Foxy |
| 15/71 | **Hot Pants** <br> James Brown |
| 11/63 | **Hot Pastrami** <br> Dartells |
| 36/63 | **Hot Pastrami With Mashed Potatoes** <br> Joey Dee & The Starliters |
| 15/80 | **Hot Rod Hearts** <br> Robbie Dupree |
| 26/60 <br> 33/60 <br> 9/72 | **Hot Rod Lincoln** <br> Johnny Bond <br> Charlie Ryan <br> Commander Cody |
| 14/69 | **Hot Smoke & Sasafrass** <br> Bubble Puppy |
| 1/79 | **Hot Stuff** <br> Donna Summer |
| 18/79 | **Hot Summer Nights** <br> Night |
| 1/77 | **Hotel California** <br> Eagles |
| 3/63 | **Hotel Happiness** <br> Brook Benton |
| 1/56 | **Hound Dog** <br> Elvis Presley |
| 9/59 | **Hound Dog Man** <br> Fabian |

| POS/YR | RECORD TITLE/ARTIST |
|--------|---------------------|
| 9/55 | **House Of Blue Lights** <br> Chuck Miller |
| 1/64 <br> 7/70 | **House Of The Rising Sun** <br> Animals <br> Frijid Pink |
| 6/68 | **House That Jack Built** <br> Aretha Franklin |
| 20/56 | **House With Love In It** <br> Four Lads |
| 21/65 | **Houston** <br> Dean Martin |
| 33/60 | **How About That** <br> Dee Clark |
| 12/83 | **How Am I Supposed To Live Without You** <br> Laura Branigan |
| 22/58 | **How Are Ya' Fixed For Love?** <br> Frank Sinatra & Keely Smith |
| 12/81 | **How 'Bout Us** <br> Champaign |
| 4/67 <br> 25/72 | **How Can I Be Sure** <br> Rascals <br> David Cassidy |
| 22/73 | **How Can I Tell Her** <br> Lobo |
| 1/71 | **How Can You Mend A Broken Heart** <br> Bee Gees |
| 1/77 | **How Deep Is Your Love** <br> Bee Gees |
| 10/80 | **How Do I Make You** <br> Linda Ronstadt |
| 22/80 | **How Do I Survive** <br> Amy Holland |
| 27/67 | **How Do You Catch A Girl** <br> Sam The Sham & The Pharaohs |
| 8/72 | **How Do You Do** <br> Mouth & MacNeal |
| 9/64 | **How Do You Do It?** <br> Gerry & The Pacemakers |
| 30/80 | **How Does It Feel To Be Back** <br> Daryl Hall & John Oates |
| 7/66 | **How Does That Grab You, Darlin'?** <br> Nancy Sinatra |

| POS/YR | RECORD TITLE/ARTIST |
|---|---|
| | **How Important Can It Be?** |
| 2/55 | Joni James |
| 12/55 | Sarah Vaughan |
| | **(How Little It Matters) How Little We Know** |
| 13/56 | Frank Sinatra |
| | **How Long** |
| 3/75 | Ace |
| | **How Long (Betcha' Got A Chick On The Side)** |
| 20/75 | Pointer Sisters |
| | **How Many Times Can We Say Goodbye** |
| 27/83 | Dionne Warwick & Luther Vandross |
| | **How Much I Feel** |
| 3/78 | Ambrosia |
| | **How Much Love** |
| 17/77 | Leo Sayer |
| | **How Sweet It Is (To Be Loved By You)** |
| 6/65 | Marvin Gaye |
| 18/66 | Jr. Walker & The All Stars |
| 5/75 | James Taylor |
| | **How The Time Flies** |
| 11/58 | Jerry Wallace |
| | **How You Gonna See Me Now** |
| 12/78 | Alice Cooper |
| | **How'd We Ever Get This Way** |
| 21/68 | Andy Kim |
| | **Hucklebuck, The** |
| 14/60 | Chubby Checker |
| | **Hula Hoop Song** |
| 32/58 | Georgia Gibbs |
| 38/58 | Teresa Brewer |
| | **Hula Love** |
| 9/57 | Buddy Knox |
| | **Hully Gully Baby** |
| 25/62 | Dovells |
| | **Human Nature** |
| 7/83 | Michael Jackson |
| | **Human Touch** |
| 18/83 | Rick Springfield |
| | **Hummingbird** |
| 7/55 | Les Paul & Mary Ford |
| 17/55 | Frankie Laine |
| | **Hummingbird** |
| 20/73 | Seals & Crofts |

| POS/YR | RECORD TITLE/ARTIST |
|---|---|
| | **Hundred Pounds Of Clay** |
| 3/61 | Gene McDaniels |
| | **Hungry** |
| 6/66 | Paul Revere & The Raiders |
| | **Hungry For Love** |
| 27/65 | San Remo Golden Strings |
| | **Hungry Heart** |
| 5/80 | Bruce Springsteen |
| | **Hungry Like The Wolf** |
| 3/83 | Duran Duran |
| | **Hunter Gets Captured By The Game** |
| 13/67 | Marvelettes |
| | **Hurdy Gurdy Man** |
| 5/68 | Donovan |
| | **Hurricane** |
| 33/76 | Bob Dylan |
| | **Hurt** |
| 4/61 | Timi Yuro |
| 28/76 | Elvis Presley |
| | **Hurt, The** |
| 31/73 | Cat Stevens |
| | **Hurt So Bad** |
| 10/65 | Little Anthony & The Imperials |
| 12/69 | Lettermen |
| 8/80 | Linda Ronstadt |
| | **Hurting Each Other** |
| 2/72 | Carpenters |
| | **Hurts So Good** |
| 2/82 | John Cougar |
| | **Hurts So Good** |
| 24/73 | Millie Jackson |
| | **Husbands And Wives** |
| 26/66 | Roger Miller |
| | **Hush** |
| 4/68 | Deep Purple |
| | **Hush, Hush, Sweet Charlotte** |
| 8/65 | Patti Page |
| | **Hushabye** |
| 20/59 | Mystics |
| | **Hustle, The** |
| 1/75 | Van McCoy |
| | **Hypnotized** |
| 21/67 | Linda Jones |

| POS/YR | RECORD TITLE/ARTIST |
|--------|---------------------|

**I**

| POS/YR | RECORD TITLE/ARTIST |
|--------|---------------------|
| 26/82 | **I.G.Y. (What A Beautiful World)** <br> Donald Fagen |
| 35/76 | **I.O.U.** <br> Jimmy Dean |
| 25/63 | **I Adore Him** <br> Angels |
| 11/81 | **I Ain't Gonna Stand For It** <br> Stevie Wonder |
| 36/71 | **I Ain't Got Time Anymore** <br> Glass Bottle |
| 24/59 | **I Ain't Never** <br> Webb Pierce |
| 1/56 | **I Almost Lost My Mind** <br> Pat Boone |
| 3/66 | **I Am A Rock** <br> Simon & Garfunkel |
| 4/71 | **I Am...I Said** <br> Neil Diamond |
| 15/75 | **I Am Love (Parts I & II)** <br> Jacksons |
| 39/70 | **I Am Somebody** <br> Johnnie Taylor |
| 1/72 | **I Am Woman** <br> Helen Reddy |
| 8/58 | **I Beg Of You** <br> Elvis Presley |
| 33/64 | **I Believe** <br> Bachelors |
| 33/82 | **I Believe** <br> Chilliwack |
| 22/72 | **I Believe In Music** <br> Gallery |
| 24/80 | **I Believe In You** <br> Don Williams |
| 11/73 | **I Believe In You (You Believe In Me)** <br> Johnnie Taylor |
| 15/75 | **(I Believe) There's Nothing Stronger Than Our Love...** <br> Paul Anka |

| POS/YR | RECORD TITLE/ARTIST |
|--------|---------------------|
| 27/77 | **I Believe You** <br> Dorothy Moore |
| 27/75 | **I Belong To You** <br> Love Unlimited |
| | **I Can Dance**...see: Long Tall Glasses |
| 6/84 | **I Can Dream About You** <br> Dan Hartman |
| 24/69 | **I Can Hear Music** <br> Beach Boys |
| 1/74 | **I Can Help** <br> Billy Swan |
| 32/66 | **I Can Make It With You** <br> Pozo-Seco Singers |
| 6/65 | **I Can Never Go Home Anymore** <br> Shangri-Las |
| 1/72 | **I Can See Clearly Now** <br> Johnny Nash |
| 9/67 | **I Can See For Miles** <br> Who |
| | **(I Can See It In Your Eyes)**...see: Circle Is Small |
| 22/69 | **I Can Sing A Rainbow** <br> Dells |
| 39/81 | **I Can Take Care Of Myself** <br> Billy & The Beaters |
| 22/68 | **I Can Take Or Leave Your Loving** <br> Herman's Hermits |
| 35/73 | **I Can Understand It** <br> New Birth |
| 26/84 | **I Can't Drive 55** <br> Sammy Hagar |
| 1/69 | **I Can't Get Next To You** <br> Temptations |
| 1/65 <br> 31/66 | **(I Can't Get No) Satisfaction** <br> Rolling Stones <br> Otis Redding |
| 1/82 | **I Can't Go For That (No Can Do)** <br> Daryl Hall & John Oates |
| 34/66 | **I Can't Grow Peaches On A Cherry Tree** <br> Just Us |
| 29/76 | **I Can't Hear You No More** <br> Helen Reddy |

| POS/YR | RECORD TITLE/ARTIST |
|--------|---------------------|
| 12/80 | **I Can't Help It**<br>Olivia Newton-John & Andy Gibb |
| 24/62 | **I Can't Help It (If I'm Still In Love With You)**<br>Johnny Tillotson |
| 1/65<br>22/72<br>40/80 | **I Can't Help Myself (Sugar Pie, Honey Bunch)**<br>Four Tops<br>Donnie Elbert<br>Bonnie Pointer |
| 39/60 | **(I Can't Help You) I'm Falling Too**<br>Skeeter Davis<br>*(also see: Please Help Me I'm Falling)* |
| 13/84 | **I Can't Hold Back**<br>Survivor |
| 31/80 | **I Can't Let Go**<br>Linda Ronstadt |
| 22/56 | **I Can't Love You Enough**<br>LaVern Baker |
| 28/69 | **I Can't See Myself Leaving You**<br>Aretha Franklin |
| 10/81 | **I Can't Stand It**<br>Eric Clapton |
| 14/79 | **I Can't Stand It No More**<br>Peter Frampton |
| 28/68 | **I Can't Stand Myself (When You Touch Me)**<br>James Brown |
| 38/73<br>18/78 | **I Can't Stand The Rain**<br>Ann Peebles<br>Eruption |
| 7/63 | **I Can't Stay Mad At You**<br>Skeeter Davis |
| 9/68 | **I Can't Stop Dancing**<br>Archie Bell & The Drells |
| 1/62 | **I Can't Stop Loving You**<br>Ray Charles |
| 35/64 | **I Can't Stop Talking About You**<br>Steve & Eydie |
| 8/80 | **I Can't Tell You Why**<br>Eagles |
| 37/68 | **I Can't Turn You Loose**<br>Chambers Brothers |
| 32/66 | **I Chose To Sing The Blues**<br>Ray Charles |

| POS/YR | RECORD TITLE/ARTIST |
|--------|---------------------|
| 20/56 | **I Could Have Danced All Night**<br>Sylvia Syms |
| 13/68 | **I Could Never Love Another (After Loving You)**<br>Temptations |
| 18/81 | **I Could Never Miss You (More Than I Do)**<br>Lulu |
| 9/66 | **I Couldn't Live Without Your Love**<br>Petula Clark |
| 32/83 | **I Couldn't Say No**<br>Robert Ellis Orrall with Carlene Carter |
| 17/61 | **I Count The Tears**<br>Drifters |
| 6/59 | **I Cried A Tear**<br>LaVern Baker |
| 35/72 | **I Didn't Know I Loved You (Till I Saw You Rock And Roll)**<br>Gary Glitter |
| 9/67 | **I Dig Rock And Roll Music**<br>Peter, Paul & Mary |
| 37/65<br>24/83 | **I Do**<br>Marvelows<br>J. Geils Band |
| 15/76 | **I Do, I Do, I Do, I Do, I Do**<br>Abba |
| 26/65<br>20/79 | **I Do Love You**<br>Billy Stewart<br>GQ |
| | **(I Do The)**...see: *Shimmmy Shimmy* |
| 18/71 | **I Don't Blame You At All**<br>Miracles |
| 39/83 | **I Don't Care Anymore**<br>Phil Collins |
| 13/71<br>28/71 | **I Don't Know How To Love Him**<br>Helen Reddy<br>Yvonne Elliman |
| 23/79 | **I Don't Know If It's Right**<br>Evelyn "Champagne" King |
| 35/82 | **I Don't Know Where To Start**<br>Eddie Rabbitt |
| 12/61 | **I Don't Know Why**<br>Linda Scott |
| 39/69 | **I Don't Know Why**<br>Stevie Wonder |

| POS/YR | RECORD TITLE/ARTIST |
|---|---|
| | **I Don't Know Why** . . . *see: But I Do* |
| 8/75 | **I Don't Like To Sleep Alone**<br>Paul Anka |
| 3/81 | **I Don't Need You**<br>Kenny Rogers |
| 37/64 | **I Don't Wanna Be A Loser**<br>Lesley Gore |
| 35/65 | **I Don't Wanna Lose You Baby**<br>Chad & Jeremy |
| 20/69 | **I Don't Want Nobody To Give Me Nothing**<br>James Brown |
| 22/64 | **I Don't Want To Be Hurt Anymore**<br>Nat King Cole |
| 36/61 | **I Don't Want To Cry**<br>Chuck Jackson |
| 17/71 | **I Don't Want To Do Wrong**<br>Gladys Knight & The Pips |
| 34/64 | **I Don't Want To See Tomorrow**<br>Nat King Cole |
| 16/64 | **I Don't Want To See You Again**<br>Peter & Gordon |
| 39/65 | **I Don't Want To Spoil The Party**<br>Beatles |
| 33/61 | **I Don't Want To Take A Chance**<br>Mary Wells |
| 36/80 | **I Don't Want To Walk Without You**<br>Barry Manilow |
| 9/57 | **I Dreamed**<br>Betty Johnson |
| 20/61 | **I Dreamed Of A Hill-Billy Heaven**<br>Tex Ritter |
| 12/61 | **I Fall To Pieces**<br>Patsy Cline |
| 21/74 | **I Feel A Song (In My Heart)**<br>Gladys Knight & The Pips |
| 1/64 | **I Feel Fine**<br>Beatles |
| 3/84 | **I Feel For You**<br>Chaka Khan |
| 38/57 | **I Feel Good**<br>Shirley & Lee |

| POS/YR | RECORD TITLE/ARTIST |
|---|---|
| F/76 | **I Feel Like A Bullet (In The Gun Of Robert Ford)**<br>Elton John |
| 6/77 | **I Feel Love**<br>Donna Summer |
| 5/61 | **I Feel So Bad**<br>Elvis Presley |
| F/71 | **I Feel The Earth Move**<br>Carole King |
| 9/66 | **I Fought The Law**<br>Bobby Fuller Four |
| 30/65 | **I Found A Girl**<br>Jan & Dean |
| 32/67 | **I Found A Love**<br>Wilson Pickett |
| 31/82 | **I Found Somebody**<br>Glenn Frey |
| 1/64 | **I Get Around**<br>Beach Boys |
| 32/82 | **I Get Excited**<br>Rick Springfield |
| 37/75 | **I Get Lifted**<br>George McCrae |
| 34/68 | **I Get The Sweetest Feeling**<br>Jackie Wilson |
| 7/78 | **I Go Crazy**<br>Paul Davis |
| 9/65 | **I Go To Pieces**<br>Peter & Gordon |
| 10/58 | **I Got A Feeling**<br>Ricky Nelson |
| 25/69 | **I Got A Line On You**<br>Spirit |
| 10/73 | **I Got A Name**<br>Jim Croce |
| 24/59 | **I Got A Wife**<br>Mark IV |
| 20/62 | **I Got A Woman**<br>Jimmy McGriff |
| 27/73 | **I Got Ants In My Pants**<br>James Brown |
| | **I Got Life** . . . *see: Ain't Got No* |

| POS/YR | RECORD TITLE/ARTIST |
|--------|---------------------|
| | **I Got My Mind Made Up (You Can Get It Girl)** |
| 20/79 | Instant Funk |
| | **I Got Rhythm** |
| 3/67 | Happenings |
| | **I Got Stoned And I Missed It** |
| 37/75 | Jim Stafford |
| | **I Got Stung** |
| 8/58 | Elvis Presley |
| | **I Got The Feelin'** |
| 6/68 | James Brown |
| | **I Got The Feelin' (Oh No No)** |
| 16/66 | Neil Diamond |
| | **I Got What I Wanted** |
| 28/63 | Brook Benton |
| | **I Got You Babe** |
| 1/65 | Sonny & Cher |
| | **I Got You (I Feel Good)** |
| 3/65 | James Brown |
| | **I Gotcha** |
| 2/72 | Joe Tex |
| | **I Gotta Dance To Keep From Crying** |
| 35/64 | Miracles |
| | **I Gotta Know** |
| 20/60 | Elvis Presley |
| | **I Guess That's Why They Call It The Blues** |
| 4/84 | Elton John |
| | **I Guess The Lord Must Be In New York City** |
| 34/69 | Nilsson |
| | **I Had A Dream** |
| 17/67 | Paul Revere & The Raiders |
| | **I Had Too Much To Dream (Last Night)** |
| 11/67 | Electric Prunes |
| | **I Have A Boyfriend** |
| 36/64 | Chiffons |
| | **I Hear A Symphony** |
| 1/65 | Supremes |
| | **I Hear Trumpets Blow** |
| 30/66 | Tokens |
| | **I Hear You Knocking** |
| 2/55 | Gale Storm |
| 4/71 | Dave Edmunds |

| POS/YR | RECORD TITLE/ARTIST |
|--------|---------------------|
| | **I Heard It Through The Grapevine** |
| 2/67 | Gladys Knight & The Pips |
| 1/68 | Marvin Gaye |
| | **I Honestly Love You** |
| 1/74 | Olivia Newton-John |
| | **I Just Called To Say I Love You** |
| 1/84 | Stevie Wonder |
| | **I Just Can't Help Believing** |
| 9/70 | B.J. Thomas |
| | **I Just Don't Know** |
| 17/57 | Four Lads |
| | **I Just Don't Know What To Do With Myself** |
| 26/66 | Dionne Warwick |
| | **I Just Don't Understand** |
| 17/61 | Ann-Margret |
| | **I Just Fall In Love Again** |
| 12/79 | Anne Murray |
| | **I Just Wanna Stop** |
| 4/78 | Gino Vannelli |
| | **I Just Want To Be Your Everything** |
| 1/77 | Andy Gibb |
| | **I Just Want To Celebrate** |
| 7/71 | Rare Earth |
| | **I Just Want To Make Love To You** |
| 33/77 | Foghat |
| | **I Keep Forgettin'** |
| 4/82 | Michael McDonald |
| | **I Knew You When** |
| 14/65 | Billy Joe Royal |
| 37/83 | Linda Ronstadt |
| | **I Know A Heartache When I See One** |
| 19/79 | Jennifer Warnes |
| | **I Know A Place** |
| 3/65 | Petula Clark |
| | **(I Know) I'm Losing You** |
| 8/66 | Temptations |
| 7/70 | Rare Earth |
| 24/71 | Rod Stewart |
| | **I Know There's Something Going On** |
| 13/83 | Frida |
| | **I Know (You Don't Love Me No More)** |
| 3/62 | Barbara George |
| | **I Left My Heart In San Francisco** |
| 19/62 | Tony Bennett |

| POS/YR | RECORD TITLE/ARTIST |
|---|---|
| 3/77 | **I Like Dreamin'**<br>Kenny Nolan |
| 17/64 | **I Like It**<br>Gerry & The Pacemakers |
| 31/83 | **I Like It**<br>DeBarge |
| 2/61<br>7/65 | **I Like It Like That**<br>Chris Kenner<br>Dave Clark Five |
| 27/64 | **I Like It Like That**<br>Miracles |
| 25/67 | **I Like The Way**<br>Tommy James & The Shondells |
| 37/77 | **I Like To Do It**<br>KC & The Sunshine Band |
| 28/74 | **I Like To Live The Love**<br>B.B. King |
| 8/57 | **I Like Your Kind Of Love**<br>Andy Williams |
| 38/71 | **I Likes To Do It**<br>People's Choice |
| 12/74 | **I Love**<br>Tom T. Hall |
| 1/81 | **I Love A Rainy Night**<br>Eddie Rabbitt |
| 5/61<br>9/68 | **I Love How You Love Me**<br>Paris Sisters<br>Bobby Vinton |
|  | **I Love Lucy**...see: Disco Lucy |
| 5/76 | **I Love Music**<br>O'Jays |
| 21/57 | **I Love My Baby (My Baby Loves Me)**<br>Jill Corey |
| 24/74 | **I Love My Friend**<br>Charlie Rich |
| 1/82 | **I Love Rock 'N Roll**<br>Joan Jett & The Blackhearts |
| 5/78 | **I Love The Nightlife (Disco 'Round)**<br>Alicia Bridges |
| 9/60 | **I Love The Way You Love**<br>Marv Johnson |
| 12/81 | **I Love You**<br>Climax Blues Band |

| POS/YR | RECORD TITLE/ARTIST |
|---|---|
| 14/68 | **I Love You**<br>People |
| 22/62 | **I Love You**<br>Volume's |
| 37/78 | **I Love You**<br>Donna Summer |
| 3/63 | **I Love You Because**<br>Al Martino |
| 39/63 | **(I Love You) Don't You Forget It**<br>Perry Como |
| 30/66 | **I Love You Drops**<br>Vic Dana |
| 21/71 | **I Love You For All Seasons**<br>Fuzz |
| 17/58 | **(I Love You) For Sentimental Reasons**<br>Sam Cooke |
| 40/60 | **I Love You In The Same Old Way**<br>Paul Anka |
| 28/55 | **I Love You Madly**<br>Four Coins |
| 9/64 | **I Love You More And More Every Day**<br>Al Martino |
| 31/66 | **I Love You One Thousand Times**<br>Platters |
| 38/62 | **I Love You The Way You Are**<br>Bobby Vinton |
| 37/81 | **I Loved 'Em Every One**<br>T.G. Sheppard |
| 18/59 | **I Loves You, Porgy**<br>Nina Simone |
| 10/81 | **I Made It Through The Rain**<br>Barry Manilow |
| 18/67 | **I Make A Fool Of Myself**<br>Frankie Valli |
| 37/68 | **I Met Her In Church**<br>Box Tops |
| 34/57<br>33/59<br>34/65 | **I Miss You So**<br>Chris Connor<br>Paul Anka<br>Little Anthony & The Imperials |
| 19/81 | **I Missed Again**<br>Phil Collins |
| 31/65 | **I Must Be Seeing Things**<br>Gene Pitney |

| POS/YR | RECORD TITLE/ARTIST |
|---|---|
| 28/79 | **I Need A Lover**<br>John Cougar |
| 22/66 | **I Need Somebody**<br>? (Question Mark) & The Mysterians |
| 25/76 | **I Need To Be In Love**<br>Carpenters |
| 9/72 | **I Need You**<br>America |
| 37/82 | **I Need You**<br>Paul Carrack |
| 4/59 | **I Need Your Love Tonight**<br>Elvis Presley |
| 20/62 | **I Need Your Lovin'**<br>Don Gardner & Dee Dee Ford |
| 37/81 | **I Need Your Lovin'**<br>Teena Marie |
| 12/77 | **I Never Cry**<br>Alice Cooper |
| 9/67 | **I Never Loved A Man (The Way I Love You)**<br>Aretha Franklin |
| 11/59<br>18/75 | **I Only Have Eyes For You**<br>Flamingos<br>Art Garfunkel |
| 22/56 | **I Only Know I Love You**<br>Four Aces |
| 12/64<br>12/76 | **I Only Want To Be With You**<br>Dusty Springfield<br>Bay City Rollers |
| 25/71 | **I Play And Sing**<br>Dawn |
| 19/80 | **I Pledge My Love**<br>Peaches & Herb |
| 9/82 | **I Ran (So Far Away)**<br>Flock Of Seagulls |
| 39/82 | **I Really Don't Need No Light**<br>Jeffrey Osborne |
| 18/60<br>22/66<br>21/71 | **I Really Don't Want To Know**<br>Tommy Edwards<br>Ronnie Dove<br>Elvis Presley |
| 29/61 | **I Really Love You**<br>Stereos |
| 5/62 | **I Remember You**<br>Frank Ifield |

| POS/YR | RECORD TITLE/ARTIST |
|---|---|
| 36/64 | **I Rise, I Fall**<br>Johnny Tillotson |
| 5/66 | **I Saw Her Again**<br>Mamas & The Papas |
| 14/64 | **I Saw Her Standing There**<br>Beatles |
| 14/63 | **I Saw Linda Yesterday**<br>Dickey Lee |
| 16/72 | **I Saw The Light**<br>Todd Rundgren |
| 4/67<br>10/68 | **I Say A Little Prayer**<br>Dionne Warwick<br>Aretha Franklin |
| 4/67 | **I Second That Emotion**<br>Miracles |
| 26/66 | **I See The Light**<br>Five Americans |
| 38/74 | **I Shall Sing**<br>Art Garfunkel |
| 1/74 | **I Shot The Sheriff**<br>Eric Clapton |
| 15/62 | **I Sold My Heart To The Junkman**<br>Blue-Belles |
| 6/69 | **I Started A Joke**<br>Bee Gees |
| 12/84 | **I Still Can't Get Over Loving You**<br>Ray Parker Jr. |
| 39/79 | **I Still Have Dreams**<br>Richie Furay |
| 12/67 | **I Take It Back**<br>Sandy Posey |
| 13/67 | **I Thank The Lord For The Night Time**<br>Neil Diamond |
| 9/68<br>34/80 | **I Thank You**<br>Sam & Dave<br>ZZ Top |
| 1/70 | **I Think I Love You**<br>Partridge Family |
| 4/67 | **I Think We're Alone Now**<br>Tommy James & The Shondells |
| 23/69 | **I Turned You On**<br>Isley Brothers |

| POS/YR | RECORD TITLE/ARTIST |
|--------|---------------------|
| | **I Understand (Just How You Feel)** |
| 9/61 | G-Clefs |
| 36/65 | Freddie & The Dreamers |
| | **I Waited Too Long** |
| 33/59 | LaVern Baker |
| | **I Walk The Line** |
| 17/56 | Johnny Cash |
| | **I Wanna Be Around** |
| 14/63 | Tony Bennett |
| | **I Wanna Be Loved** |
| 20/59 | Ricky Nelson |
| | **I Wanna Be Where You Are** |
| 16/72 | Michael Jackson |
| | **I Wanna Be With You** |
| 16/73 | Raspberries |
| | **I Wanna Be Your Lover** |
| 11/80 | Prince |
| | **I Wanna Dance Wit' Choo** |
| 23/75 | Disco Tex & The Sex-O-Lettes |
| | **I Wanna Get Next To You** |
| 10/77 | Rose Royce |
| | **I Wanna Live** |
| 36/68 | Glen Campbell |
| | **I Wanna Love Him So Bad** |
| 9/64 | Jelly Beans |
| | **(I Wanna) Love My Life Away** |
| 39/61 | Gene Pitney |
| | **(I Wanna) Testify** |
| 20/67 | Parliaments |
| 36/69 | Johnnie Taylor |
| | **I Wanna Thank You** |
| 21/61 | Bobby Rydell |
| | **I Want A New Drug** |
| 6/84 | Huey Lewis & The News |
| | **I Want Candy** |
| 11/65 | Strangeloves |
| | **I Want To**...also see: I Wanna & I Want'a |
| | **I Want To Be Wanted** |
| 1/60 | Brenda Lee |
| | **I Want To (Do Everything For You)** |
| 23/65 | Joe Tex |
| | **I Want To Go With You** |
| 36/66 | Eddy Arnold |

| POS/YR | RECORD TITLE/ARTIST |
|--------|---------------------|
| | **I Want To Hold Your Hand** |
| 1/64 | Beatles |
| | **I Want To Stay Here** |
| 28/63 | Steve & Eydie |
| | **I Want To Take You Higher** |
| 34/70 | Ike & Tina Turner |
| 38/70 | Sly & The Family Stone |
| | **I Want To Walk You Home** |
| 8/59 | Fats Domino |
| | **I Want You** |
| 15/76 | Marvin Gaye |
| | **I Want You** |
| 20/66 | Bob Dylan |
| | **I Want You Back** |
| 1/70 | Jacksons |
| | **I Want You, I Need You** |
| 37/81 | Chris Christian |
| | **I Want You, I Need You, I Love You** |
| 1/56 | Elvis Presley |
| | **I Want You To Be My Baby** |
| 14/55 | Georgia Gibbs |
| 18/55 | Lillian Briggs |
| | **I Want You To Be My Girl (Boy)** |
| 13/56 | Frankie Lymon & The Teenagers |
| | **I Want You To Want Me** |
| 7/79 | Cheap Trick |
| | **I Want You Tonight** |
| 19/79 | Pablo Cruise |
| | **I Want Your Love** |
| 7/79 | Chic |
| | **I Want'a Do Something Freaky To You** |
| 15/75 | Leon Haywood |
| | **I Was Checkin' Out She Was Checkin' In** |
| 29/73 | Don Covay |
| | **I Was Kaiser Bill's Batman** |
| 20/67 | Whistling Jack Smith |
| | **I Was Made For Dancin'** |
| 10/79 | Leif Garrett |
| | **I Was Made For Lovin' You** |
| 11/79 | Kiss |
| | **I Was Made To Love Her** |
| 2/67 | Stevie Wonder |
| | **I Was Only Joking** |
| 22/78 | Rod Stewart |

| POS/YR | RECORD TITLE/ARTIST |
|---|---|
| 24/62 | **I Was Such A Fool (To Fall In Love With You)**<br>Connie Francis |
| 19/56 | **I Was The One**<br>Elvis Presley |
| 19/66 | **(I Washed My Hands In) Muddy Water**<br>Johnny Rivers |
| 29/63<br>14/70<br>40/79 | **I (Who Have Nothing)**<br>Ben E. King<br>Tom Jones<br>Sylvester |
| 10/65 | **I Will**<br>Dean Martin |
| 22/68 | **I Will Always Think About You**<br>New Colony Six |
| 30/79 | **I Will Be In Love With You**<br>Livingston Taylor |
| 1/63 | **I Will Follow Him**<br>Little Peggy March |
| 29/78 | **I Will Still Love You**<br>Stonebolt |
| 1/79 | **I Will Survive**<br>Gloria Gaynor |
| 1/77 | **I Wish**<br>Stevie Wonder |
| 32/63 | **I Wish I Were A Princess**<br>Little Peggy March |
| 4/68 | **I Wish It Would Rain**<br>Temptations |
| 16/62 | **I Wish That We Were Married**<br>Ronnie & The Hi-Lites |
| 28/64 | **I Wish You Love**<br>Gloria Lynne |
| 13/71 | **I Woke Up In Love This Morning**<br>Partridge Family |
| 10/83 | **I Won't Hold You Back**<br>Toto |
| 11/74 | **I Won't Last A Day Without You**<br>Carpenters |
| 35/83 | **I Won't Stand In Your Way**<br>Stray Cats |
| 25/63 | **I Wonder**<br>Brenda Lee |
| 8/68 | **I Wonder What She's Doing Tonight**<br>Tommy Boyce & Bobby Hart |

| POS/YR | RECORD TITLE/ARTIST |
|---|---|
| 21/63 | **I Wonder What She's Doing Tonight**<br>Barry & The Tamerlanes |
| 22/58 | **I Wonder Why**<br>Dion & The Belmonts |
| 20/82 | **I Wouldn't Have Missed It For The World**<br>Ronnie Milsap |
| 22/56 | **I Wouldn't Know Where To Begin**<br>Eddy Arnold |
| 36/77 | **I Wouldn't Want To Be Like You**<br>Alan Parsons Project |
| 1/76 | **I Write The Songs**<br>Barry Manilow |
| 7/72<br>13/72 | **I'd Like To Teach The World To Sing (In Perfect Harmony)**<br>New Seekers<br>Hillside Singers |
| 40/71 | **I'd Love To Change The World**<br>Ten Years After |
| 2/72 | **I'd Love You To Want Me**<br>Lobo |
| 38/80 | **I'd Rather Leave While I'm In Love**<br>Rita Coolidge |
| 2/76 | **I'd Really Love To See You Tonight**<br>England Dan & John Ford Coley |
| 15/69 | **I'd Wait A Million Years**<br>Grass Roots |
| 36/73 | **I'll Always Love My Mama**<br>Intruders |
| 35/65 | **I'll Always Love You**<br>Spinners |
| 3/72 | **I'll Be Around**<br>Spinners |
| 8/65 | **I'll Be Doggone**<br>Marvin Gaye |
| 3/76 | **I'll Be Good To You**<br>Brothers Johnson |
| 4/56 | **I'll Be Home**<br>Pat Boone |
| 33/64 | **I'll Be In Trouble**<br>Temptations |
| 20/59 | **I'll Be Satisfied**<br>Jackie Wilson |

| POS/YR | RECORD TITLE/ARTIST |
|---|---|
| 36/74 | **I'll Be The Other Woman**<br>Soul Children |
| 1/70 | **I'll Be There**<br>Jacksons |
| 12/61 | **I'll Be There**<br>Damita Jo |
| 14/65 | **I'll Be There**<br>Gerry & The Pacemakers<br>*(also see: Stand By Me)* |
| 31/59 | **(I'll Be With You In) Apple Blossom Time**<br>Tab Hunter |
| 40/73 | **I'll Be Your Shelter (In Time Of Storm)**<br>Luther Ingram |
| 18/58 | **I'll Come Running Back To You**<br>Sam Cooke |
| 25/64 | **I'll Cry Instead**<br>Beatles |
| 40/75 | **I'll Do For You Anything You Want Me To**<br>Barry White |
| 9/74 | **I'll Have To Say I Love You In A Song**<br>Jim Croce |
| 34/65 | **I'll Keep Holding On**<br>Marvelettes |
| 30/64 | **I'll Keep You Satisfied**<br>Billy J. Kramer with the Dakotas |
| 21/65 | **I'll Make All Your Dreams Come True**<br>Ronnie Dove |
| 9/71 | **I'll Meet You Halfway**<br>Partridge Family |
| 14/62 | **I'll Never Dance Again**<br>Bobby Rydell |
| 6/69 | **I'll Never Fall In Love Again**<br>Tom Jones |
| 6/70 | **I'll Never Fall In Love Again**<br>Dionne Warwick |
| 4/65 | **I'll Never Find Another You**<br>Seekers |
| 5/79 | **I'll Never Love This Way Again**<br>Dionne Warwick |
| 24/57 | **I'll Never Say "Never Again" Again**<br>Dinah Shore |
| 25/61 | **I'll Never Smile Again**<br>Platters |

| POS/YR | RECORD TITLE/ARTIST |
|---|---|
| 13/55 | **I'll Never Stop Loving You**<br>Doris Day |
| 18/75 | **I'll Play For You**<br>Seals & Crofts |
|  | **(I'll Remember)**...*see: In The Still Of The Nite* |
| 23/57 | **I'll Remember Today**<br>Patti Page |
| 34/58 | **I'll Remember Tonight**<br>Pat Boone |
| 22/60 | **I'll Save The Last Dance For You**<br>Damita Jo<br>*(also see: Save The Last Dance For Me)* |
| 32/62 | **I'll See You In My Dreams**<br>Pat Boone |
| 39/67 | **I'll Take Care Of Your Cares**<br>Frankie Laine |
| 30/66 | **I'll Take Good Care Of You**<br>Garnet Mimms |
| 25/63 | **I'll Take You Home**<br>Drifters |
| 1/72 | **I'll Take You There**<br>Staple Singers |
| 25/64 | **I'll Touch A Star**<br>Terry Stafford |
| 40/67 | **I'll Try Anything**<br>Dusty Springfield |
| 39/62<br>25/69 | **I'll Try Something New**<br>Miracles<br>Supremes & Temptations |
| 9/83 | **I'll Tumble 4 Ya**<br>Culture Club |
| 13/84 | **I'll Wait**<br>Van Halen |
| 15/58 | **I'll Wait For You**<br>Frankie Avalon |
| 1/66 | **I'm A Believer**<br>Monkees |
| 38/69 | **I'm A Better Man**<br>Engelbert Humperdinck |
| 17/65 | **I'm A Fool**<br>Dino, Desi & Billy |

| POS/YR | RECORD TITLE/ARTIST |
|--------|---------------------|
| 24/61 | **I'm A Fool To Care**<br>Joe Barry |
| 35/71 | **I'm A Greedy Man**<br>James Brown |
| 36/65 | **I'm A Happy Man**<br>Jive Five |
| 38/59 | **I'm A Hog For You**<br>Coasters |
| 10/67<br>F/71 | **I'm A Man**<br>Spencer Davis Group<br>Chicago |
| 17/65 | **I'm A Man**<br>Yardbirds |
| 31/59 | **I'm A Man**<br>Fabian |
| 24/68 | **I'm A Midnight Mover**<br>Wilson Pickett |
| 20/66 | **(I'm A) Road Runner**<br>Jr. Walker & The All Stars |
| 25/61 | **I'm A Telling You**<br>Jerry Butler |
| 31/74 | **I'm A Train**<br>Albert Hammond |
| 12/75 | **I'm A Woman**<br>Maria Muldaur |
| 16/80 | **I'm Alive**<br>Electric Light Orchestra |
| 35/83 | **I'm Alive**<br>Neil Diamond |
| 34/80 | **I'm Almost Ready**<br>Pure Prairie League |
| 7/80 | **I'm Alright**<br>Kenny Loggins |
| 20/55 | **(I'm Always Hearing) Wedding Bells**<br>Eddie Fisher |
| 9/57 | **I'm Available**<br>Margie Rayburn |
| 19/62 | **I'm Blue (The Gong-Gong Song)**<br>Ikettes |
| 40/71 | **I'm Comin' Home**<br>Tommy James |
| 39/66 | **I'm Comin' Home, Cindy**<br>Trini Lopez |

| POS/YR | RECORD TITLE/ARTIST |
|--------|---------------------|
| 19/61 | **I'm Comin' On Back To You**<br>Jackie Wilson |
| 18/74 | **I'm Coming Home**<br>Spinners |
| 5/80 | **I'm Coming Out**<br>Diana Ross |
| 19/64 | **I'm Crying**<br>Animals |
| 17/73 | **I'm Doin' Fine Now**<br>New York City |
| 17/76 | **I'm Easy**<br>Keith Carradine |
| 21/78 | **I'm Every Woman**<br>Chaka Khan |
| 37/69 | **I'm Free**<br>Who |
| 22/84 | **I'm Free (Heaven Helps The Man)**<br>Kenny Loggins |
|  | **(I'm Gettin')**...*see: Nuttin' For Christmas* |
| 37/60 | **I'm Gettin' Better**<br>Jim Reeves |
| 17/59 | **I'm Gonna Be A Wheel Some Day**<br>Fats Domino |
| 9/64 | **I'm Gonna Be Strong**<br>Gene Pitney |
| 18/63 | **I'm Gonna Be Warm This Winter**<br>Connie Francis |
| 3/59 | **I'm Gonna Get Married**<br>Lloyd Price |
| 12/61 | **I'm Gonna Knock On Your Door**<br>Eddie Hodges |
| 40/76 | **I'm Gonna Let My Heart Do The Walking**<br>Supremes |
| 3/73 | **I'm Gonna Love You Just A Little More Baby**<br>Barry White |
| 26/68<br>2/69 | **I'm Gonna Make You Love Me**<br>Madeline Bell<br>Supremes & Temptations |
| 10/69 | **I'm Gonna Make You Mine**<br>Lou Christie |

| POS/YR | RECORD TITLE/ARTIST |
|--------|---------------------|
| 3/57 | **I'm Gonna Sit Right Down And Write Myself A Letter**<br>Billy Williams |
| 28/78 | **I'm Gonna Take Care Of Everything**<br>Rubicon |
| 27/80 | **I'm Happy That Love Has Found You**<br>Jimmy Hall |
| 1/65 | **I'm Henry VIII, I Am**<br>Herman's Hermits |
| 27/61 | **I'm Hurtin'**<br>Roy Orbison |
| 19/74 | **I'm In Love**<br>Aretha Franklin |
| 40/81 | **I'm In Love**<br>Evelyn "Champagne" King |
| 3/56<br>38/56 | **I'm In Love Again**<br>Fats Domino<br>Fontane Sisters |
| 38/61 | **I'm In The Mood For Love**<br>Chimes |
| 2/77 | **I'm In You**<br>Peter Frampton |
| 13/64<br>38/64 | **I'm Into Something Good**<br>Herman's Hermits<br>Earl-Jean |
| 12/73 | **I'm Just A Singer (In A Rock And Roll Band)**<br>Moody Blues |
| 33/61 | **I'm Learning About Love**<br>Brenda Lee |
| 36/71 | **I'm Leavin'**<br>Elvis Presley |
| 1/63<br>4/74 | **I'm Leaving It Up To You**<br>Dale & Grace<br>Donny & Marie Osmond |
| 10/69 | **I'm Livin' In Shame**<br>Supremes |
| 40/59 | **I'm Movin' On**<br>Ray Charles |
| 37/73 | **I'm Never Gonna Be Alone Anymore**<br>Cornelius Brothers & Sister Rose |
| 36/59 | **I'm Never Gonna Tell**<br>Jimmie Rodgers |
| 27/60 | **I'm Not Afraid**<br>Ricky Nelson |

| POS/YR | RECORD TITLE/ARTIST |
|--------|---------------------|
| 14/78 | **I'm Not Gonna Let It Bother Me Tonight**<br>Atlanta Rhythm Section |
| 2/75 | **I'm Not In Love**<br>10cc |
| 4/75 | **I'm Not Lisa**<br>Jessi Colter |
| 34/70 | **I'm Not My Brothers Keeper**<br>Flaming Ember |
| 20/67 | **(I'm Not Your) Steppin' Stone**<br>Monkees |
| 16/75 | **I'm On Fire**<br>Dwight Twilley |
| 26/75 | **I'm On Fire**<br>5000 Volts |
| 15/64 | **I'm On The Outside (Looking In)**<br>Little Anthony & The Imperials |
| 16/59 | **I'm Ready**<br>Fats Domino |
| 9/66 | **I'm Ready For Love**<br>Martha & The Vandellas |
| 30/82<br>9/84 | **I'm So Excited**<br>Pointer Sisters<br>Pointer Sisters |
| 8/66 | **I'm So Lonesome I Could Cry**<br>B.J. Thomas |
| 14/64 | **I'm So Proud**<br>Impressions |
| 1/60 | **I'm Sorry**<br>Brenda Lee |
| 1/75 | **I'm Sorry**<br>John Denver |
| 11/57 | **I'm Sorry**<br>Platters |
| 36/58 | **I'm Sorry I Made You Cry**<br>Connie Francis |
| 14/57 | **I'm Stickin' With You**<br>Jimmy Bowen |
| 3/72 | **I'm Still In Love With You**<br>Al Green |
| 12/83 | **I'm Still Standing**<br>Elton John |
| 10/72 | **I'm Stone In Love With You**<br>Stylistics |

| POS/YR | RECORD TITLE/ARTIST |
|---|---|
| 1/65 | **I'm Telling You Now**<br>Freddie & The Dreamers |
| 38/62 | **(I'm The Girl On) Wolverton Mountain**<br>Jo Ann Campbell |
| 27/57 | **I'm Waiting Just For You**<br>Pat Boone |
| 4/57<br>17/57 | **I'm Walkin'**<br>Fats Domino<br>Ricky Nelson |
| 12/67 | **I'm Wondering**<br>Stevie Wonder |
| 1/77 | **I'm Your Boogie Man**<br>KC & The Sunshine Band |
| 6/66 | **I'm Your Puppet**<br>James & Bobby Purify |
| 11/65 | **I'm Yours**<br>Elvis Presley |
| 33/59 | **I've Been Around**<br>Fats Domino |
| 35/69 | **I've Been Hurt**<br>Bill Deal & The Rhondels |
| 27/72 | **I've Been Lonely For So Long**<br>Frederick Knight |
| 16/67 | **I've Been Lonely Too Long**<br>Rascals |
| 21/65 | **I've Been Loving You Too Long (To Stop Now)**<br>Otis Redding |
| 9/74 | **(I've Been) Searchin' So Long**<br>Chicago |
| 34/75 | **I've Been This Way Before**<br>Neil Diamond |
| 28/59 | **I've Come Of Age**<br>Billy Storm |
| 8/81 | **I've Done Everything For You**<br>Rick Springfield |
| 5/71 | **I've Found Someone Of My Own**<br>Free Movement |
| 29/76 | **I've Got A Feeling (We'll Be Seeing Each Other Again)**<br>Al Wilson |
| 18/83 | **I've Got A Rock N' Roll Heart**<br>Eric Clapton |
| 39/74 | **I've Got A Thing About You Baby**<br>Elvis Presley |

| POS/YR | RECORD TITLE/ARTIST |
|---|---|
| 25/65 | **I've Got A Tiger By The Tail**<br>Buck Owens |
|  | **I've Got A Woman**...see: I Got A Woman |
| 18/62 | **I've Got Bonnie**<br>Bobby Rydell |
| 5/77 | **I've Got Love On My Mind**<br>Natalie Cole |
| 33/64 | **I've Got Sand In My Shoes**<br>Drifters |
| 32/73 | **I've Got So Much To Give**<br>Barry White |
| 12/74 | **I've Got The Music In Me**<br>Kiki Dee |
|  | **I've Got To**...also see: I've Gotta |
| 38/66 | **I've Got To Be Somebody**<br>Billy Joe Royal |
| 4/74 | **I've Got To Use My Imagination**<br>Gladys Knight & The Pips |
| 9/66 | **I've Got You Under My Skin**<br>Four Seasons |
| 11/69 | **I've Gotta Be Me**<br>Sammy Davis, Jr. |
| 8/68 | **I've Gotta Get A Message To You**<br>Bee Gees |
| 25/78 | **I've Had Enough**<br>Paul McCartney |
| 6/59 | **I've Had It**<br>Bell Notes |
| 32/70 | **I've Lost You**<br>Elvis Presley |
| 4/80 | **I've Loved You For A Long Time (medley)**<br>Spinners |
| 3/82 | **I've Never Been To Me**<br>Charlene |
| 40/68 | **I've Never Found A Girl (To Love Me Like You Do)**<br>Eddie Floyd |
| 17/67 | **I've Passed This Way Before**<br>Jimmy Ruffin |
| 3/61 | **I've Told Every Little Star**<br>Linda Scott |

| POS/YR | RECORD TITLE/ARTIST |
|--------|---------------------|
| 4/71 | **If** <br> Bread |
| 32/62 | **If A Man Answers** <br> Bobby Darin |
| 35/62 | **If A Woman Answers (Hang Up The Phone)** <br> Leroy Van Dyke |
| 14/83 | **If Anyone Falls** <br> Stevie Nicks |
| 7/58 | **If Dreams Came True** <br> Pat Boone |
| 24/78 | **If Ever I See You Again** <br> Roberta Flack |
| 10/84 | **If Ever You're In My Arms Again** <br> Peabo Bryson |
| 12/69 | **If I Can Dream** <br> Elvis Presley |
| 1/78 | **If I Can't Have You** <br> Yvonne Elliman |
| 10/68 | **If I Could Build My Whole World Around You** <br> Marvin Gaye & Tammi Terrell |
| 10/72 | **If I Could Reach You** <br> 5th Dimension |
| 22/59 <br> 30/61 | **If I Didn't Care** <br> Connie Francis <br> Platters |
| 39/75 | **If I Ever Lose This Heaven** <br> Average White Band |
| 34/59 | **If I Give My Heart To You** <br> Kitty Kallen |
| 31/60 | **If I Had A Girl** <br> Rod Lauren |
| 10/62 <br> 3/63 | **If I Had A Hammer** <br> Peter, Paul & Mary <br> Trini Lopez |
| 36/82 | **If I Had My Wish Tonight** <br> David Lasley |
| 23/65 | **If I Loved You** <br> Chad & Jeremy |
| 8/55 | **If I May** <br> Nat King Cole |
| 34/65 | **If I Ruled The World** <br> Tony Bennett |

| POS/YR | RECORD TITLE/ARTIST |
|--------|---------------------|
| 39/79 | **If I Said You Have A Beautiful Body Would You Hold It Against Me** <br> Bellamy Brothers |
| 8/66 <br> 20/68 <br> 36/70 | **If I Were A Carpenter** <br> Bobby Darin <br> Four Tops <br> Johnny Cash & June Carter |
| 9/71 | **If I Were Your Woman** <br> Gladys Knight & The Pips |
| 19/84 | **If I'd Been The One** <br> 38 Special |
| 3/72 <br> 31/79 | **(If Loving You Is Wrong) I Don't Want To Be Right** <br> Luther Ingram <br> Barbara Mandrell |
| 23/63 | **If My Pillow Could Talk** <br> Connie Francis |
| 25/71 | **If Not For You** <br> Olivia Newton-John |
| 28/82 | **If The Love Fits Wear It** <br> Leslie Pearl |
| 6/84 | **If This Is It** <br> Huey Lewis & The News |
| 28/74 | **If We Make It Through December** <br> Merle Haggard |
| 11/68 | **If You Can Want** <br> Miracles |
| 5/71 | **If You Could Read My Mind** <br> Gordon Lightfoot |
| 33/59 | **(If You Cry) True Love, True Love** <br> Drifters |
| 3/72 | **If You Don't Know Me By Now** <br> Harold Melvin & The Blue Notes |
| 40/55 | **If You Don't Want My Love** <br> Jaye P. Morgan |
| 22/62 | **If You Gotta Make A Fool Of Somebody** <br> James Ray |
| 11/76 | **If You Know What I Mean** <br> Neil Diamond |
| 1/76 | **If You Leave Me Now** <br> Chicago |
| 38/72 | **If You Leave Me Tonight I'll Cry** <br> Jerry Wallace |

| POS/YR | RECORD TITLE/ARTIST |
|---|---|
| 8/70 | **(If You Let Me Make Love To You Then) Why Can't I Touch You?**<br>Ronnie Dyson |
| 5/74 | **If You Love Me (Let Me Know)**<br>Olivia Newton-John |
| 37/63 | **If You Need Me**<br>Solomon Burke |
| 8/71 | **If You Really Love Me**<br>Stevie Wonder |
| 17/79 | **If You Remember Me**<br>Chris Thompson & Night |
| 38/80 | **If You Should Sail**<br>Nielsen/Pearson |
| 17/74 | **If You Talk In Your Sleep**<br>Elvis Presley |
| 1/63 | **If You Wanna Be Happy**<br>Jimmy Soul |
| 25/74 | **If You Wanna Get To Heaven**<br>Ozark Mountain Daredevils |
| 37/79 | **If You Want It**<br>Niteflyte |
| 12/73 | **If You Want Me To Stay**<br>Sly & The Family Stone |
| 9/73 | **If You're Ready (Come Go With Me)**<br>Staple Singers |
| 20/65 | **Iko Iko**<br>Dixie Cups |
| 6/60 | **Image Of A Girl**<br>Safaris |
| 7/78 | **Imaginary Lover**<br>Atlanta Rhythm Section |
| 3/71 | **Imagine**<br>John Lennon |
| 22/75 | **Immigrant, The**<br>Neil Sedaka |
| 16/71 | **Immigrant Song**<br>Led Zeppelin |
| 36/72 | **Immigration Man**<br>David Crosby/Graham Nash |
| 35/66 | **Impossible Dream**<br>Jack Jones |
| 17/83 | **In A Big Country**<br>Big Country |

| POS/YR | RECORD TITLE/ARTIST |
|---|---|
| 30/68 | **In-A-Gadda-Da-Vida**<br>Iron Butterfly |
| 31/69 | **In A Moment**<br>Intrigues |
| 27/56 | **In A Shanty In Old Shanty Town**<br>Somethin' Smith & The Redheads |
| 11/80 | **In America**<br>Charlie Daniels Band |
| 9/67 | **In And Out Of Love**<br>Supremes |
| 5/65<br>13/65 | **"In" Crowd**<br>Ramsey Lewis<br>Dobie Gray |
| 7/63 | **In Dreams**<br>Roy Orbison |
| 10/60 | **In My Little Corner Of The World**<br>Anita Bryant |
| 23/63 | **In My Room**<br>Beach Boys |
| 19/81 | **In The Air Tonight**<br>Phil Collins |
| | **In The Chapel In The Moonlight**...*see:*<br>*Chapel* |
| 35/81 | **In The Dark**<br>Billy Squier |
| 3/69 | **In The Ghetto**<br>Elvis Presley |
| 33/67 | **In The Heat Of The Night**<br>Ray Charles |
| 27/61 | **In The Middle Of A Heartache**<br>Wanda Jackson |
| 9/57<br>23/57 | **In The Middle Of An Island**<br>Tony Bennett<br>Tennessee Ernie Ford |
| 11/56<br>20/56 | **In The Middle Of The House**<br>Vaughn Monroe<br>Rusty Draper |
| 21/65<br>30/73 | **In The Midnight Hour**<br>Wilson Pickett<br>Cross Country |
| 19/64 | **In The Misty Moonlight**<br>Jerry Wallace |
| 4/59<br>40/77 | **In The Mood**<br>Ernie Fields Orchestra<br>Henhouse Five Plus Too |

| POS/YR | RECORD TITLE/ARTIST |
|---|---|
| 39/84 | **In The Mood** <br> Robert Plant |
| 3/79 | **In The Navy** <br> Village People |
| 5/72 | **In The Rain** <br> Dramatics |
| 24/56 <br> 38/60 | **In The Still Of The Nite** <br> Five Satins <br> Dion & The Belmonts |
| 3/70 | **In The Summertime** <br> Mungo Jerry |
| 1/69 | **In The Year 2525 (Exordium & Terminus)** <br> Zager & Evans |
| 20/81 | **In Your Letter** <br> REO Speedwagon |
| 1/67 | **Incense And Peppermints** <br> Strawberry Alarm Clock |
| 33/67 | **Indescribably Blue** <br> Elvis Presley |
| 5/69 | **Indian Giver** <br> 1910 Fruitgum Co. |
| 10/68 | **Indian Lake** <br> Cowsills |
| 20/68 <br> 1/71 | **Indian Reservation** <br> Don Fardon <br> Paul Revere & The Raiders |
| 5/70 | **Indiana Wants Me** <br> R. Dean Taylor |
| 6/84 | **Infatuation** <br> Rod Stewart |
| 27/56 <br> 30/56 | **Innamorata** <br> Dean Martin <br> Jerry Vale |
| 9/71 | **Inner City Blues (Make Me Wanna Holler)** <br> Marvin Gaye |
| 10/84 | **Innocent Man** <br> Billy Joel |
| 32/76 | **Inseparable** <br> Natalie Cole |
| 34/66 | **Inside-Looking Out** <br> Animals |
| 3/70 | **Instant Karma** <br> John Lennon |

| POS/YR | RECORD TITLE/ARTIST |
|---|---|
| 29/79 | **Instant Replay** <br> Dan Hartman |
| 11/80 | **Into The Night** <br> Benny Mardones |
| 40/83 | **Invisible Hands** <br> Kim Carnes |
| 15/62 | **Irresistible You** <br> Bobby Darin |
| | **Irving**...see: Ballad Of |
| 35/60 | **Is A Blue Bird Blue** <br> Conway Twitty |
| 34/69 | **Is It Something You've Got** <br> Tyrone Davis |
| 17/64 | **Is It True** <br> Brenda Lee |
| 15/81 | **Is It You** <br> Lee Ritenour |
| 21/79 | **Is She Really Going Out With Him?** <br> Joe Jackson |
| 11/69 | **Is That All There Is** <br> Peggy Lee |
| 31/60 | **Is There Any Chance** <br> Marty Robbins |
| 4/83 | **Is There Something I Should Know** <br> Duran Duran |
| 1/75 | **Island Girl** <br> Elton John |
| 25/57 | **Island In The Sun** <br> Harry Belafonte |
| 37/82 | **Island Of Lost Souls** <br> Blondie |
| 1/83 | **Islands In The Stream** <br> Kenny Rogers with Dolly Parton |
| F/70 | **Isn't It A Pity** <br> George Harrison |
| 13/77 | **Isn't It Time** <br> Babys |
| 29/72 | **Isn't Life Strange** <br> Moody Blues |
| 9/69 | **Israelites** <br> Desmond Dekker & The Aces |
| 17/84 | **It Ain't Enough** <br> Corey Hart |

| POS/YR | RECORD TITLE/ARTIST |
|--------|---------------------|
| 8/65 | **It Ain't Me Babe**<br>Turtles |
| 13/59 | **It Doesn't Matter Anymore**<br>Buddy Holly |
| 4/71 | **It Don't Come Easy**<br>Ringo Starr |
| 10/70 | **It Don't Matter To Me**<br>Bread |
| 29/64 | **It Hurts Me**<br>Elvis Presley |
| 7/64 | **It Hurts To Be In Love**<br>Gene Pitney |
| 23/56 | **It Isn't Right**<br>Platters |
| 23/61 | **It Keeps Rainin'**<br>Fats Domino |
| 3/62 | **It Keeps Right On A-Hurtin'**<br>Johnny Tillotson |
| 37/77 | **It Keeps You Runnin'**<br>Doobie Brothers |
| 11/55 | **It May Sound Silly**<br>McGuire Sisters |
| 22/62 | **It Might As Well Rain Until September**<br>Carole King |
| 25/83 | **It Might Be You**<br>Stephen Bishop |
| 3/67 | **It Must Be Him**<br>Vikki Carr |
| 32/79 | **It Must Be Love**<br>Alton McClain & Destiny |
| 33/83 | **It Must Be Love**<br>Madness |
| 5/72 | **It Never Rains In Southern California**<br>Albert Hammond |
| 38/60 | **It Only Happened Yesterday**<br>Jack Scott |
| 11/56 | **It Only Hurts For A Little While**<br>Ames Brothers |
| 10/75 | **It Only Takes A Minute**<br>Tavares |
| 40/68 | **It Should Have Been Me**<br>Gladys Knight & The Pips |
| 29/62 | **It Started All Over Again**<br>Brenda Lee |

| POS/YR | RECORD TITLE/ARTIST |
|--------|---------------------|
| 27/73 | **It Sure Took A Long, Long Time**<br>Lobo |
| 14/67 | **It Takes Two**<br>Marvin Gaye & Kim Weston |
| 20/66 | **It Tears Me Up**<br>Percy Sledge |
| 28/66 | **It Was A Very Good Year**<br>Frank Sinatra |
| 16/77 | **It Was Almost Like A Song**<br>Ronnie Milsap |
| 11/59 | **It Was I**<br>Skip & Flip |
| 37/77 | **It's A Crazy World**<br>Mac McAnally |
| 3/78 | **It's A Heartache**<br>Bonnie Tyler |
| 20/78 | **It's A Laugh**<br>Daryl Hall & John Oates |
| 28/76 | **It's A Long Way There**<br>Little River Band |
| 28/81 | **It's A Love Thing**<br>Whispers |
| 8/66 | **It's A Man's Man's Man's World**<br>James Brown |
| 12/75 | **It's A Miracle**<br>Barry Manilow |
| 13/84 | **It's A Miracle**<br>Culture Club |
| 6/83 | **It's A Mistake**<br>Men At Work |
| 32/70 | **It's A New Day**<br>James Brown |
| 14/70 | **It's A Shame**<br>Spinners |
| 7/55 | **It's A Sin To Tell A Lie**<br>Somethin' Smith & The Redheads |
| 31/75 | **It's All Down To Goodnight Vienna**<br>Ringo Starr |
| 1/58<br>25/64<br>24/70 | **It's All In The Game**<br>Tommy Edwards<br>Cliff Richard<br>Four Tops |
| 26/64 | **It's All Over Now**<br>Rolling Stones |

**Firefall** was founded by the Flying Burrito Bros.' Rick Roberts, who recruited fellow Burrito/ex-Byrd Michael Clark and Jo Jo Gunne's Mark Andes for his bland enterprise.

**The Floaters** were classic one-hit wonders. The smooth-singing Detroit quintet scored a major hit in 1977 with "Float On," then evaporated into thin air.

**The Four Seasons** struggled for six years as the Four Lovers before coming under the wing of producer Bob Crewe. He brought in a new member, songwriter Bob Gaudio, changed their name to the Four Seasons, and the hits began to roll in.

**Funkadelic.** George Clinton, the brains behind the Parliament-Funkadelic-P. Funk organization, cut his first single as a member of the doo-wop Parliaments way back in 1956.

**Frank Gari,** the son of a New Jersey barber, once headlined a four-week stand at the Waldorf Astoria's Empire Room. He was the youngest male performer ever to accomplish this feat.

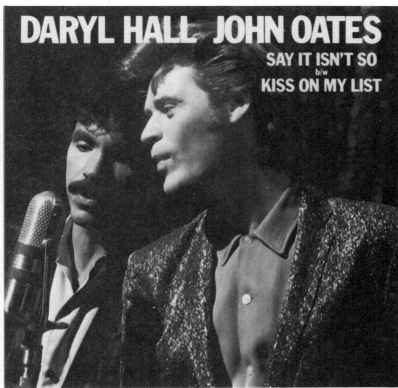

Get Wet, a bubbly New York duo, were one of many minor successes on the late Neil Bogart's Boardwalk Records. The others included Ringo Starr, Chris Christian, Phil Seymour, and Carole Bayer Sager. Bogart's big star was Joan Jett.

Eddy Grant of Guyana first entered Top 40 in 1968 as a member of the Equals, performing the buoyant "Baby Come Back." Britain's punk-rock Clash included the Equals' "Police on My Back" in their Sandanista! album.

Hall & Oates got together in Philadelphia as members of the band Gulliver. Their recording of "She's Gone" was outcharted by Tavares' cover version first time around in '74, but hit the Top Ten when re-released two years later.

Bo Donaldson and the Heywoods snatched their biggest hit right out of another band's hands. Paper Lace had a British hit with "Billy, Don't Be a Hero." Bo and the boys copied it and released their own version first in the States. The Heywoods nailed down Number One; Paper Lace, 96.

Amy Holland's debut LP and hit single were co-produced by Doobie Brother Michael McDonald. Their collaboration went so smoothly that they ended up getting married.

Brenda Holloway's aching ballad "Every Little Bit Hurts," besides being a fine song, was significant because it was the first Motown hit not recorded in Detroit. It was cut in California.

| POS/YR | RECORD TITLE/ARTIST |
|--------|---------------------|
| 4/63 | **It's All Right**<br>Impressions |
| 20/55<br>20/55<br>7/56<br>14/56 | **It's Almost Tomorrow**<br>David Carroll & His Orchestra<br>Snooky Lanson<br>Dream Weavers<br>Jo Stafford |
| 31/65 | **It's Alright**<br>Adam Faith |
| 20/58 | **(It's Been A Long Time) Pretty Baby**<br>Gino & Gina |
| 4/77 | **It's Ecstasy When You Lay Down Next To Me**<br>Barry White |
| 30/69 | **It's Getting Better**<br>Mama Cass |
| 12/72 | **It's Going To Take Some Time**<br>Carpenters |
| 23/65 | **It's Gonna Be Alright**<br>Gerry & The Pacemakers |
| 10/82 | **It's Gonna Take A Miracle**<br>Deniece Williams |
| 14/61 | **It's Gonna Work Out Fine**<br>Ike & Tina Turner |
| 18/65 | **It's Growing**<br>Temptations |
| 10/71 | **It's Impossible**<br>Perry Como |
|  | **It's In His Kiss**...see: *Shoop Shoop Song* |
| 38/83 | **It's Inevitable**<br>Charlie |
| 3/59 | **It's Just A Matter Of Time**<br>Brook Benton |
| 9/59 | **It's Late**<br>Ricky Nelson |
| 23/66 | **It's My Life**<br>Animals |
| 31/84 | **It's My Life**<br>Talk Talk |
| 1/63 | **It's My Party**<br>Lesley Gore |
| 9/81 | **It's My Turn**<br>Diana Ross |
| 5/57 | **It's Not For Me To Say**<br>Johnny Mathis |

| POS/YR | RECORD TITLE/ARTIST |
|--------|---------------------|
| 10/65 | **It's Not Unusual**<br>Tom Jones |
| 1/60<br>14/81 | **It's Now Or Never**<br>Elvis Presley<br>John Schneider |
| 23/67 | **It's Now Winters Day**<br>Tommy Roe |
| 29/76 | **It's O.K.**<br>Beach Boys |
| 20/72 | **It's One Of Those Nights (Yes Love)**<br>Partridge Family |
| 31/66 | **It's Only Love**<br>Tommy James & The Shondells |
| 1/58<br>10/70 | **It's Only Make Believe**<br>Conway Twitty<br>Glen Campbell |
| 16/74 | **It's Only Rock 'N Roll (But I Like It)**<br>Rolling Stones |
| 9/64 | **It's Over**<br>Roy Orbison |
| 37/66 | **It's Over**<br>Jimmie Rodgers |
| 38/76 | **It's Over**<br>Boz Scaggs |
| 11/82 | **It's Raining Again**<br>Supertramp |
| 21/77 | **It's Sad To Belong**<br>England Dan & John Ford Coley |
| 5/77 | **It's So Easy**<br>Linda Ronstadt |
| 1/80 | **It's Still Rock And Roll To Me**<br>Billy Joel |
| 5/65<br>35/78 | **It's The Same Old Song**<br>Four Tops<br>KC & The Sunshine Band |
| 4/59 | **It's Time To Cry**<br>Paul Anka |
| 1/71 | **It's Too Late**<br>Carole King |
| 23/66 | **It's Too Late**<br>Bobby Goldsboro |
| 11/58 | **It's Too Soon To Know**<br>Pat Boone |

| POS/YR | RECORD TITLE/ARTIST |
|--------|---------------------|
| 6/63 | **It's Up To You**<br>Ricky Nelson |
| 20/68 | **It's Wonderful**<br>Rascals |
| 22/57 | **It's You I Love**<br>Fats Domino |
| 33/78 | **It's You That I Need**<br>Enchantment |
| 2/69 | **It's Your Thing**<br>Isley Brothers |
| 25/56 | **Italian Theme**<br>Cyril Stapleton & His Orchestra |
| 25/58 | **Itchy Twitchy Feeling**<br>Bobby Hendricks |
| 16/68 | **Itchycoo Park**<br>Small Faces |
| 1/60 | **Itsy Bitsy Teenie Weenie Yellow Polkadot Bikini**<br>Brian Hyland |
| 2/56<br>6/56<br>11/56 | **Ivory Tower**<br>Cathy Carr<br>Gale Storm<br>Charms |
| 18/57 | **Ivy Rose**<br>Perry Como |

# J

| POS/YR | RECORD TITLE/ARTIST |
|--------|---------------------|
| 1/82 | **Jack & Diane**<br>John Cougar |
| 8/78 | **Jack And Jill**<br>Ray Parker Jr. & Raydio |
| 3/75 | **Jackie Blue**<br>Ozark Mountain Daredevils |
| 14/67 | **Jackson**<br>Nancy Sinatra & Lee Hazlewood |
| 1/57 | **Jailhouse Rock**<br>Elvis Presley |
| 29/62 | **Jam, The**<br>Bobby Gregg & His Friends |
| 8/70 | **Jam Up Jelly Tight**<br>Tommy Roe |

| POS/YR | RECORD TITLE/ARTIST |
|--------|---------------------|
| 14/57 | **Jamaica Farewell**<br>Harry Belafonte |
| 30/62<br>16/73 | **Jambalaya (On The Bayou)**<br>Fats Domino<br>Blue Ridge Rangers |
| 17/62 | **James (Hold The Ladder Steady)**<br>Sue Thompson |
| 30/62 | **Jamie**<br>Eddie Holland |
| 14/80 | **Jane**<br>Jefferson Starship |
| 4/64 | **Java**<br>Al Hirt |
| | **Jaws**...see: Theme From & Mr. Jaws |
| 2/74 | **Jazzman**<br>Carole King |
| 20/69 | **Jealous Kind Of Fella**<br>Garland Green |
| 19/60 | **Jealous Of You**<br>Connie Francis |
| 2/69 | **Jean**<br>Oliver |
| 17/77 | **Jeans On**<br>David Dundas |
| 8/58 | **Jennie Lee**<br>Jan & Arnie |
| 40/68 | **Jennifer Eccles**<br>Hollies |
| 26/68 | **Jennifer Juniper**<br>Donovan |
| 36/70 | **Jennifer Tomkins**<br>Street People |
| | **Jenny**...see: 867-5309 |
| 10/57 | **Jenny, Jenny**<br>Little Richard |
| 10/66 | **Jenny Take A Ride!**<br>Mitch Ryder & The Detroit Wheels |
| 2/83 | **Jeopardy**<br>Greg Kihn Band |
| 35/61 | **Jeremiah Peabody's Poly Unsaturated Pills**<br>Ray Stevens |

| POS/YR | RECORD TITLE/ARTIST |
|--------|---------------------|
| 7/65 | **Jerk, The** <br> Larks |
| 11/80 | **Jesse** <br> Carly Simon |
| 30/73 | **Jesse** <br> Roberta Flack |
| 1/81 | **Jessie's Girl** <br> Rick Springfield |
| | **Jesus Christ Superstar** . . . *see: Superstar* |
| 28/69 | **Jesus Is A Soul Man** <br> Lawrence Reynolds |
| 35/73 | **Jesus Is Just Alright** <br> Doobie Brothers |
| 7/74 | **Jet** <br> Paul McCartney |
| 8/77 | **Jet Airliner** <br> Steve Miller Band |
| 17/57 <br> 25/74 | **Jim Dandy** <br> LaVern Baker <br> Black Oak Arkansas |
| 33/73 | **Jimmy Loves Mary-Anne** <br> Looking Glass |
| 10/67 | **Jimmy Mack** <br> Martha & The Vandellas |
| 25/61 | **Jimmy's Girl** <br> Johnny Tillotson |
| 6/57 <br> 35/58 <br> 36/60 <br> 21/61 | **Jingle Bell Rock** <br> Bobby Helms <br> Bobby Helms <br> Bobby Helms <br> Bobby Rydell & Chubby Checker |
| 10/70 | **Jingle Jangle** <br> Archies |
| 1/75 | **Jive Talkin'** <br> Bee Gees |
| 19/58 | **Jo-Ann** <br> Playmates |
| 17/80 | **JoJo** <br> Boz Scaggs |
| 2/84 | **Joanna** <br> Kool & The Gang |
| 21/70 | **Joanne** <br> Michael Nesmith |
| 28/71 | **Jody's Got Your Girl And Gone** <br> Johnnie Taylor |

| POS/YR | RECORD TITLE/ARTIST |
|--------|---------------------|
| | **John And Yoko** . . . *see: Ballad Of* |
| 1/62 | **Johnny Angel** <br> Shelley Fabares |
| 8/58 | **Johnny B. Goode** <br> Chuck Berry |
| 7/62 | **Johnny Get Angry** <br> Joanie Sommers |
| 21/62 | **Johnny Jingo** <br> Hayley Mills |
| 21/62 | **Johnny Loves Me** <br> Shelley Fabares |
| 35/62 | **Johnny Will** <br> Pat Boone |
| 17/72 | **Join Together** <br> Who |
| 1/74 | **Joker, The** <br> Steve Miller Band |
| 22/57 <br> 25/57 | **Joker (That's What They Call Me)** <br> Hilltoppers <br> Billy Myles |
| 20/66 | **Joker Went Wild** <br> Brian Hyland |
| 4/65 | **Jolly Green Giant** <br> Kingsmen |
| 39/81 | **Jones Vs. Jones** <br> Kool & The Gang |
| 18/60 | **Josephine** <br> Bill Black's Combo |
| 26/78 | **Josie** <br> Steely Dan |
| 16/68 | **Journey To The Center Of The Mind** <br> Amboy Dukes |
| 6/72 | **Joy** <br> Apollo 100 featuring Tom Parker |
| 30/74 | **Joy** <br> Isaac Hayes |
| 1/71 | **Joy To The World** <br> Three Dog Night |
| 26/65 | **Ju Ju Hand** <br> Sam The Sham & The Pharaohs |
| 22/58 | **Judy** <br> Frankie Vaughan |
| | **Judy Blue Eyes** . . . *see: Suite* |

| POS/YR | RECORD TITLE/ARTIST |
|--------|---------------------|
| 1/68 | **Judy In Disguise (With Glasses)** John Fred & His Playboy Band |
| 33/75 | **Judy Mae** Boomer Castleman |
| 5/63 | **Judy's Turn To Cry** Lesley Gore |
| 10/56 | **Juke Box Baby** Perry Como |
| 26/82 | **Juke Box Hero** Foreigner |
| 5/70 | **Julie, Do Ya Love Me** Bobby Sherman |
| 1/84 | **Jump** Van Halen |
| 3/84 | **Jump (For My Love)** Pointer Sisters |
| 27/72 | **Jump Into The Fire** Nilsson |
| 28/60 | **Jump Over** Freddy Cannon |
| 24/82 | **Jump To It** Aretha Franklin |
| 3/68 | **Jumpin' Jack Flash** Rolling Stones |
| 21/57 | **June Night** Jimmy Dorsey Orchestra & Chorus |
| 4/74 | **Jungle Boogie** Kool & The Gang |
| 8/72 | **Jungle Fever** Chakachas |
| 23/77 | **Jungle Love** Steve Miller Band |
| 3/75 | **Junior's Farm** Paul McCartney |
| 9/76 | **Junk Food Junkie** Larry Groce |
| 37/61 | **Jura (I Swear I Love You)** Les Paul & Mary Ford |
| 4/58 | **Just A Dream** Jimmy Clanton |
| 8/65 | **Just A Little** Beau Brummels |
| 40/60 | **Just A Little** Brenda Lee |

| POS/YR | RECORD TITLE/ARTIST |
|--------|---------------------|
| 39/65 | **Just A Little Bit** Roy Head |
| 7/65 | **Just A Little Bit Better** Herman's Hermits |
| 23/75 | **Just A Little Bit Of You** Michael Jackson |
| 9/59 | **Just A Little Too Much** Ricky Nelson |
| 7/77 | **Just A Song Before I Go** Crosby, Stills & Nash |
| 32/59 24/68 | **Just As Much As Ever** Bob Beckham Bobby Vinton |
| 7/59 | **Just Ask Your Heart** Frankie Avalon |
| 19/64 | **Just Be True** Gene Chandler |
| 29/57 | **Just Because** Lloyd Price |
| 8/57 | **Just Between You And Me** Chordettes |
| 21/81 | **Just Between You And Me** April Wine |
| 12/57 | **Just Born (To Be Your Baby)** Perry Como |
| 38/82 | **Just Can't Win 'Em All** Stevie Woods |
| 35/60 | **Just Come Home** Hugo & Luigi Chorus |
| 10/74 | **Just Don't Want To Be Lonely** Main Ingredient |
| 5/68 | **Just Dropped In (To See What Condition My Condition Was In)** Kenny Rogers & The First Edition |
| 20/61 | **Just For Old Time's Sake** McGuire Sisters |
| 36/83 | **Just Got Lucky** JoBoxers |
| 18/59 | **Just Keep It Up** Dee Clark |
| 33/66 | **Just Like A Woman** Bob Dylan |
| 11/66 | **Just Like Me** Paul Revere & The Raiders |

| POS/YR | RECORD TITLE/ARTIST |
|---|---|
| 6/64 | **(Just Like) Romeo & Juliet**<br>Reflections |
| 1/80 | **(Just Like) Starting Over**<br>John Lennon |
| 26/58 | **Just Married**<br>Marty Robbins |
| 1/71 | **Just My Imagination**<br>Temptations |
| 17/81 | **Just Once**<br>James Ingram |
| 9/65 | **Just Once In My Life**<br>Righteous Brothers |
| 10/63 | **Just One Look**<br>Doris Troy |
| 29/60 | **Just One Time**<br>Don Gibson |
| 24/61 | **Just Out Of Reach (Of My Two Open Arms)**<br>Solomon Burke |
| 11/77 | **Just Remember I Love You**<br>Firefall |
| 40/71 | **Just Seven Numbers (Can Straighten Out My Life)**<br>Four Tops |
| 39/81 | **Just So Lonely**<br>Get Wet |
| 2/81 | **Just The Two Of Us**<br>Grover Washington, Jr. |
| 3/78 | **Just The Way You Are**<br>Billy Joel |
| 7/76 | **Just To Be Close To You**<br>Commodores |
| 26/57 | **Just To Hold My Hand**<br>Clyde McPhatter |
| 30/75 | **Just Too Many People**<br>Melissa Manchester |
| 2/56 | **Just Walking In The Rain**<br>Johnnie Ray |
| 27/78 | **Just What I Needed**<br>Cars |
| 4/79 | **Just When I Needed You Most**<br>Randy Vanwarmer |
| 20/65 | **Just You**<br>Sonny & Cher |

| POS/YR | RECORD TITLE/ARTIST |
|---|---|
| 27/76 | **Just You And I**<br>Melissa Manchester |
| 4/73 | **Just You 'N' Me**<br>Chicago |

# K

| POS/YR | RECORD TITLE/ARTIST |
|---|---|
| 39/71 | **K-Jee**<br>Nite-Liters |
| 24/56<br>35/56<br>38/56 | **Ka-Ding-Dong**<br>G-Clefs<br>Diamonds<br>Hilltoppers |
| 1/59<br>23/64 | **Kansas City**<br>Wilbert Harrison<br>Trini Lopez |
| 31/65 | **Kansas City Star**<br>Roger Miller |
| 1/84 | **Karma Chameleon**<br>Culture Club |
| 16/58 | **Kathy-O**<br>Diamonds |
| 16/69 | **Keem-O-Sabe**<br>Electric Indian |
| 8/57 | **Keep A Knockin'**<br>Little Richard |
| 8/83 | **(Keep Feeling) Fascination**<br>Human League |
| 2/77 | **Keep It Comin' Love**<br>KC & The Sunshine Band |
| 37/77 | **Keep Me Cryin'**<br>Al Green |
| 4/65 | **Keep On Dancing**<br>Gentrys |
| 24/68 | **Keep On Lovin' Me Honey**<br>Marvin Gaye & Tammi Terrell |
| 1/81 | **Keep On Loving You**<br>REO Speedwagon |
| 10/64 | **Keep On Pushing**<br>Impressions |
| 15/74 | **Keep On Singing**<br>Helen Reddy |

| POS/YR | RECORD TITLE/ARTIST |
|---|---|
| 10/74 | **Keep On Smilin'** <br> Wet Willie |
| 1/73 | **Keep On Truckin'** <br> Eddie Kendricks |
| 9/65 | **Keep Searchin'** <br> Del Shannon |
| 14/67 | **Keep The Ball Rollin'** <br> Jay & The Techniques |
| 36/80 | **Keep The Fire** <br> Kenny Loggins |
| 7/82 | **Keep The Fire Burnin'** <br> REO Speedwagon |
| | **Keep Your Eye On The Sparrow**...*see:* <br> *Baretta's Theme* |
| 12/62 | **Keep Your Hands Off My Baby** <br> Little Eva |
| 10/73 | **Keeper Of The Castle** <br> Four Tops |
| 20/55 | **Kentuckian Song** <br> Hilltoppers |
| 16/70 | **Kentucky Rain** <br> Elvis Presley |
| 22/67 <br> 38/68 | **Kentucky Woman** <br> Neil Diamond <br> Deep Purple |
| 6/58 | **Kewpie Doll** <br> Perry Como |
| 8/82 | **Key Largo** <br> Bertie Higgins |
| 4/66 | **Kicks** <br> Paul Revere & The Raiders |
| 33/84 | **Kid's American** <br> Matthew Wilder |
| 7/60 | **Kiddio** <br> Brook Benton |
| 25/82 | **Kids In America** <br> Kim Wilde |
| 16/63 | **Killer Joe** <br> Rocky Fellers |
| 12/75 | **Killer Queen** <br> Queen |
| 28/81 | **Killin' Time** <br> Fred Knoblock & Susan Anton |

| POS/YR | RECORD TITLE/ARTIST |
|---|---|
| 1/73 | **Killing Me Softly With His Song** <br> Roberta Flack |
| 30/77 | **Killing Of Georgie** <br> Rod Stewart |
| 1/67 | **Kind Of A Drag** <br> Buckinghams |
| 17/63 | **Kind Of Boy You Can't Forget** <br> Raindrops |
| 40/72 | **King Heroin** <br> James Brown |
| 13/77 | **King Is Gone** <br> Ronnie McDowell |
| 3/83 | **King Of Pain** <br> Police |
| 36/80 | **King Of The Hill** <br> Oak |
| 4/65 | **King Of The Road** <br> Roger Miller <br> *(also see: Queen Of The House)* |
| 30/62 | **King Of The Whole Wide World** <br> Elvis Presley |
| 17/78 | **King Tut** <br> Steve Martin |
| 31/74 | **Kings Of The Party** <br> Brownsville Station |
| 21/72 | **Kiss An Angel Good Mornin'** <br> Charley Pride |
| 1/76 | **Kiss And Say Goodbye** <br> Manhattans |
| 25/65 | **Kiss Away** <br> Ronnie Dove |
| 37/79 | **Kiss In The Dark** <br> Pink Lady |
| 30/56 | **Kiss Me Another** <br> Georgia Gibbs |
| 15/68 | **Kiss Me Goodbye** <br> Petula Clark |
| 37/80 | **Kiss Me In The Rain** <br> Barbra Streisand |
| 34/64 | **Kiss Me Quick** <br> Elvis Presley |
| 29/64 | **Kiss Me Sailor** <br> Diane Renay |

| POS/YR | RECORD TITLE/ARTIST |
|--------|---------------------|
| 1/81 | **Kiss On My List**<br>Daryl Hall & John Oates |
| 25/83 | **Kiss The Bride**<br>Elton John |
| 1/78 | **Kiss You All Over**<br>Exile |
| 3/57 | **Kisses Sweeter Than Wine**<br>Jimmie Rodgers |
| 12/64 | **Kissin' Cousins**<br>Elvis Presley |
| 35/61 | **Kissin' On The Phone**<br>Paul Anka |
| 11/59 | **Kissin' Time**<br>Bobby Rydell |
| 31/73 | **Kissing My Love**<br>Bill Withers |
| 16/57 | **Knee Deep In The Blues**<br>Guy Mitchell |
| 15/67 | **Knight In Rusty Armour**<br>Peter & Gordon |
| 28/66<br>30/67<br>1/79 | **Knock On Wood**<br>Eddie Floyd<br>Otis & Carla<br>Amii Stewart |
| 1/71 | **Knock Three Times**<br>Dawn |
| 12/73 | **Knockin' On Heaven's Door**<br>Bob Dylan |
| 14/77 | **Knowing Me, Knowing You**<br>Abba |
| 2/55<br>6/55 | **Ko Ko Mo (I Love You So)**<br>Perry Como<br>Crew-Cuts |
| 2/73 | **Kodachrome**<br>Paul Simon |
| 4/59 | **Kookie, Kookie (Lend Me Your Comb)**<br>Edward Byrnes |
| 40/74 | **Kung Fu**<br>Curtis Mayfield |
| 1/74 | **Kung Fu Fighting**<br>Carl Douglas |

**L**

| POS/YR | RECORD TITLE/ARTIST |
|--------|---------------------|
| 22/59 | **La Bamba**<br>Ritchie Valens |
| 9/58 | **La Dee Dah**<br>Billy & Lillie |
| 32/58 | **La-Do-Dada**<br>Dale Hawkins |
| 9/70 | **La La La (If I Had You)**<br>Bobby Sherman |
| 4/68 | **La-La Means I Love You**<br>Delfonics |
| 30/74 | **La La Peace Song**<br>Al Wilson |
| | **La Mer**...*see: Beyond The Sea* |
| 20/58 | **La Paloma**<br>Billy Vaughn & His Orchestra |
| 8/80 | **Ladies Night**<br>Kool & The Gang |
| 1/80 | **Lady**<br>Kenny Rogers |
| 6/75 | **Lady**<br>Styx |
| 10/79 | **Lady**<br>Little River Band |
| 28/80 | **Lady**<br>Whispers |
| 39/67 | **Lady**<br>Jack Jones |
| 20/67 | **Lady Bird**<br>Nancy Sinatra & Lee Hazlewood |
| 14/75 | **Lady Blue**<br>Leon Russell |
| 6/66 | **Lady Godiva**<br>Peter & Gordon |
| 24/66 | **Lady Jane**<br>Rolling Stones |
| 24/78 | **Lady Love**<br>Lou Rawls |

| POS/YR | RECORD TITLE/ARTIST |
|--------|---------------------|
| 30/83 | **Lady Love Me (One More Time)** <br> George Benson |
| 14/60 | **Lady Luck** <br> Lloyd Price |
| 4/68 | **Lady Madonna** <br> Beatles |
| 1/75 | **Lady Marmalade** <br> Patti LaBelle & The Blue Belles |
| 2/68 | **Lady Willpower** <br> Gary Puckett & The Union Gap |
| 8/81 | **Lady (You Bring Me Up)** <br> Commodores |
| 33/68 | **Lalena** <br> Donovan |
| | **Lament Of Cherokee** . . . see: *Indian Reservation* |
| 29/66 | **Land Of Milk And Honey** <br> Vogues |
| 30/65 <br> 6/66 | **Land Of 1000 Dances** <br> Cannibal & The Headhunters <br> Wilson Pickett |
| 13/84 | **Language Of Love** <br> Dan Fogelberg |
| 32/61 | **Language Of Love** <br> John D. Loudermilk |
| | **Lara's Theme** . . . see: *Somewhere My Love* |
| 13/65 | **Last Chance To Turn Around** <br> Gene Pitney |
| 21/76 | **Last Child** <br> Aerosmith |
| 3/78 | **Last Dance** <br> Donna Summer |
| 2/60 <br> 21/60 | **Last Date** <br> Floyd Cramer <br> Lawrence Welk <br> *(also see: My Last Date (With You))* |
| 19/75 | **Last Farewell** <br> Roger Whittaker |
| 18/75 | **Last Game Of The Season (A Blind Man In The Bleachers)** <br> David Geddes |
| 2/64 <br> 34/74 | **Last Kiss** <br> J. Frank Wilson & The Cavaliers <br> Wednesday |

| POS/YR | RECORD TITLE/ARTIST |
|--------|---------------------|
| 3/61 | **Last Night** <br> Mar-Keys |
| 8/72 | **(Last Night) I Didn't Get To Sleep At All** <br> 5th Dimension |
| 3/73 | **Last Song** <br> Edward Bear |
| 9/65 | **Last Time** <br> Rolling Stones |
| 40/84 | **Last Time I Made Love** <br> Joyce Kennedy & Jeffrey Osborne |
| 14/74 | **Last Time I Saw Him** <br> Diana Ross |
| 1/66 | **Last Train To Clarksville** <br> Monkees |
| 39/80 | **Last Train To London** <br> Electric Light Orchestra |
| 25/67 | **Last Waltz** <br> Engelbert Humperdinck |
| 40/66 | **Last Word In Lonesome Is Me** <br> Eddy Arnold |
| 27/57 | **Lasting Love** <br> Sal Mineo |
| 6/80 | **Late In The Evening** <br> Paul Simon |
| 10/65 | **Laugh At Me** <br> Sonny |
| 15/65 | **Laugh, Laugh** <br> Beau Brummels |
| 10/69 | **Laughing** <br> Guess Who |
| 15/63 | **Laughing Boy** <br> Mary Wells |
| 1/75 | **Laughter In The Rain** <br> Neil Sedaka |
| 14/65 | **Laurie (Strange Things Happen)** <br> Dickey Lee |
| 3/59 | **Lavender-Blue** <br> Sammy Turner |
| | **Laverne & Shirley Theme** . . . see: *Making Our Dreams Come True* |
| 13/83 | **Lawyers In Love** <br> Jackson Browne |

| POS/YR | RECORD TITLE/ARTIST |
|---|---|
| 11/70 | **Lay A Little Lovin' On Me**<br>Robin McNamara |
| 6/70 | **Lay Down (Candles In The Rain)**<br>Melanie |
| 3/78 | **Lay Down Sally**<br>Eric Clapton |
| 16/56 | **Lay Down Your Arms**<br>Chordettes |
| 7/69 | **Lay Lady Lay**<br>Bob Dylan |
| 10/72 | **Layla**<br>Derek & The Dominos |
| 14/67 | **Lazy Day**<br>Spanky & Our Gang |
| 40/64 | **Lazy Elsie Molly**<br>Chubby Checker |
| 12/58 | **Lazy Mary**<br>Lou Monte |
| 14/61 | **Lazy River**<br>Bobby Darin |
| 21/58 | **Lazy Summer Night**<br>Four Preps |
| 1/78 | **Le Freak**<br>Chic |
| 5/79 | **Lead Me On**<br>Maxine Nightingale |
| 9/82 | **Leader Of The Band**<br>Dan Fogelberg |
| 19/65 | **Leader Of The Laundromat**<br>Detergents |
| 1/64 | **Leader Of The Pack**<br>Shangri-Las |
| 25/62 | **Leah**<br>Roy Orbison |
| 1/72 | **Lean On Me**<br>Bill Withers |
| 9/66 | **Leaning On The Lamp Post**<br>Herman's Hermits |
| 1/55 | **Learnin' The Blues**<br>Frank Sinatra |
| 6/82 | **Leather And Lace**<br>Stevie Nicks |
| 27/84 | **Leave A Tender Moment Alone**<br>Billy Joel |

| POS/YR | RECORD TITLE/ARTIST |
|---|---|
| 24/84 | **Leave It**<br>Yes |
| 3/73 | **Leave Me Alone (Ruby Red Dress)**<br>Helen Reddy |
| 21/73 | **Leaving Me**<br>Independents |
| 1/69 | **Leaving On A Jet Plane**<br>Peter, Paul & Mary |
| 9/58 | **Left Right Out Of Your Heart**<br>Patti Page |
| | **Legend Of Billy Jack**...*see: One Tin Soldier* |
| 31/80 | **Legend Of Wooley Swamp**<br>Charlie Daniels Band |
| 8/84 | **Legs**<br>ZZ Top |
| 35/62<br>20/65 | **Lemon Tree**<br>Peter, Paul & Mary<br>Trini Lopez |
| 25/58 | **Leroy**<br>Jack Scott |
| 31/68 | **Les Bicyclettes De Belsize**<br>Engelbert Humperdinck |
| 34/68 | **Lesson, The**<br>Vikki Carr |
| 21/69<br>40/70 | **Let A Man Come In And Do The Popcorn**<br>James Brown (Part One)<br>James Brown (Part Two) |
| 36/69 | **Let A Woman Be A Woman - Let A Man Be A Man**<br>Dyke & The Blazers |
| 3/76 | **Let 'Em In**<br>Paul McCartney |
| 10/76 | **Let Her In**<br>John Travolta |
| 1/70 | **Let It Be**<br>Beatles |
| 7/60<br>5/64<br>36/69<br>40/82 | **Let It Be Me**<br>Everly Brothers<br>Jerry Butler & Betty Everett<br>Glen Campbell & Bobbie Gentry<br>Willie Nelson |
| 12/67 | **Let It Out (Let It All Hang Out)**<br>Hombres |

| POS/YR | RECORD TITLE/ARTIST |
|--------|---------------------|
| 23/74 | **Let It Ride**<br>Bachman-Turner Overdrive |
| 30/76 | **Let It Shine**<br>Olivia Newton-John |
| 5/82 | **Let It Whip**<br>Dazz Band |
| 23/67 | **Let Love Come Between Us**<br>James & Bobby Purify |
| 20/69 | **Let Me**<br>Paul Revere & The Raiders |
| 29/65 | **Let Me Be**<br>Turtles |
| 31/80 | **Let Me Be The Clock**<br>Smokey Robinson |
| 6/74 | **Let Me Be There**<br>Olivia Newton-John |
| 21/80 | **Let Me Be Your Angel**<br>Stacy Lattisaw |
| 1/57 | **(Let Me Be Your) Teddy Bear**<br>Elvis Presley |
| 20/61 | **Let Me Belong To You**<br>Brian Hyland |
| 38/82 | **Let Me Go**<br>Ray Parker Jr. |
| 35/80 | **Let Me Go, Love**<br>Nicolette Larson |
| 1/55<br>6/55<br>8/55<br>17/55 | **Let Me Go, Lover!**<br>Joan Weber<br>Teresa Brewer<br>Patti Page<br>Sunny Gale |
| 32/70 | **Let Me Go To Him**<br>Dionne Warwick |
| 4/62 | **Let Me In**<br>Sensations |
| 36/73 | **Let Me In**<br>Osmonds |
| 10/80 | **Let Me Love You Tonight**<br>Pure Prairie League |
| 17/73 | **Let Me Serenade You**<br>Three Dog Night |
| 18/82 | **Let Me Tickle Your Fancy**<br>Jermaine Jackson |
| 9/80 | **Let My Love Open The Door**<br>Pete Townshend |

| POS/YR | RECORD TITLE/ARTIST |
|--------|---------------------|
| 18/58 | **Let The Bells Keep Ringing**<br>Paul Anka |
| 29/57<br>15/61 | **Let The Four Winds Blow**<br>Roy Brown<br>Fats Domino |
| 20/56<br>22/67 | **Let The Good Times Roll**<br>Shirley & Lee<br>Bunny Sigler |
| 7/60 | **Let The Little Girl Dance**<br>Billy Bland |
| 8/84 | **Let The Music Play**<br>Shannon |
| 32/76 | **Let The Music Play**<br>Barry White |
| 1/69 | **Let The Sunshine In (medley)**<br>5th Dimension |
| | **Let Them**...see: *Let 'Em* |
| 7/61 | **Let There Be Drums**<br>Sandy Nelson |
| 27/74 | **Let Your Hair Down**<br>Temptations |
| 1/76 | **Let Your Love Flow**<br>Bellamy Brothers |
| 28/71 | **Let Your Love Go**<br>Bread |
| 36/78 | **Let's All Chant**<br>Michael Zager Band |
| 1/83 | **Let's Dance**<br>David Bowie |
| 4/62 | **Let's Dance**<br>Chris Montez |
| 1/75 | **Let's Do It Again**<br>Staple Singers |
| 40/65 | **Let's Do The Freddie**<br>Chubby Checker<br>*(also see: Do The Freddie)* |
| 21/67 | **Let's Fall In Love**<br>Peaches & Herb |
| 1/73 | **Let's Get It On**<br>Marvin Gaye |
| 32/74 | **Let's Get Married**<br>Al Green |
| 9/80 | **Let's Get Serious**<br>Jermaine Jackson |

| POS/YR | RECORD TITLE/ARTIST |
|---|---|
| 8/61 | **Let's Get Together**<br>Hayley Mills |
| | **Let's Get Together**...*see: Get Together* |
| 14/79 | **Let's Go**<br>Cars |
| 19/62 | **Let's Go**<br>Routers |
| 39/61 | **Let's Go Again**<br>Hank Ballard & The Midnighters |
| 1/84 | **Let's Go Crazy**<br>Prince |
| 30/83 | **Let's Go Dancin' (Ooh La, La, La)**<br>Kool & The Gang |
| 31/66 | **Let's Go Get Stoned**<br>Ray Charles |
| 6/60 | **Let's Go, Let's Go, Let's Go**<br>Hank Ballard & The Midnighters |
| 26/63 | **Let's Go Steady Again**<br>Neil Sedaka |
| 3/81 | **Let's Groove**<br>Earth, Wind & Fire |
| 3/65<br>32/82 | **Let's Hang On!**<br>Four Seasons<br>Barry Manilow |
| 37/60 | **Let's Have A Party**<br>Wanda Jackson |
| 1/84 | **Let's Hear It For The Boy**<br>Deniece Williams |
| 38/63 | **Let's Kiss And Make Up**<br>Bobby Vinton |
| 20/63 | **Let's Limbo Some More**<br>Chubby Checker |
| 8/67 | **Let's Live For Today**<br>Grass Roots |
| 35/76 | **Let's Live Together**<br>Road Apples |
| 11/65 | **Let's Lock The Door**<br>Jay & The Americans |
| 35/73 | **Let's Pretend**<br>Raspberries |
| 18/74 | **Let's Put It All Together**<br>Stylistics |
| 20/66 | **Let's Start All Over Again**<br>Ronnie Dove |

| POS/YR | RECORD TITLE/ARTIST |
|---|---|
| 1/72<br>26/84 | **Let's Stay Together**<br>Al Green<br>Tina Turner |
| 31/74 | **Let's Straighten It Out**<br>Latimore |
| 7/60 | **Let's Think About Living**<br>Bob Luman |
| 20/63 | **Let's Turkey Trot**<br>Little Eva |
| 8/61 | **Let's Twist Again**<br>Chubby Checker |
| 26/70<br>32/70 | **Let's Work Together**<br>Canned Heat<br>Wilbert Harrison |
| 1/67<br>20/69<br>7/70 | **Letter, The**<br>Box Tops<br>Arbors<br>Joe Cocker |
| 25/64 | **Letter From Sherry**<br>Dale Ward |
| 19/62 | **Letter Full Of Tears**<br>Gladys Knight & The Pips |
| | **Letter Song**...*see: S.Y.S.L.J.F.M.* |
| 25/58 | **Letter To An Angel**<br>Jimmy Clanton |
| 33/73 | **Letter To Myself**<br>Chi-Lites |
| 39/75 | **Letting Go**<br>Paul McCartney |
| 24/72 | **Levon**<br>Elton John |
| 7/71 | **Liar**<br>Three Dog Night |
| 12/65 | **Liar, Liar**<br>Castaways |
| 14/68 | **Licking Stick - Licking Stick**<br>James Brown |
| 11/77 | **Lido Shuffle**<br>Boz Scaggs |
| 13/62 | **Lie To Me**<br>Brook Benton |
| 16/57 | **Liechtensteiner Polka**<br>Will Glahe & His Orchestra |

| POS/YR | RECORD TITLE/ARTIST |
|--------|---------------------|
| 20/66 | **Lies** <br> Knickerbockers |
| 30/83 | **Lies** <br> Thompson Twins |
| 11/77 | **Life In The Fast Lane** <br> Eagles |
| 8/74 | **Life Is A Rock (But The Radio Rolled Me)** <br> Reunion |
| 34/81 | **Life Of Illusion** <br> Joe Walsh |
| 12/78 | **Life's Been Good** <br> Joe Walsh |
| 1/67 <br> 3/68 | **Light My Fire** <br> Doors <br> Jose Feliciano |
| 1/66 | **Lightnin' Strikes** <br> Lou Christie |
| 24/67 | **Lightning's Girl** <br> Nancy Sinatra |
| 12/84 | **Lights Out** <br> Peter Wolf |
| 11/67 | **(Lights Went Out In) Massachusetts** <br> Bee Gees |
| 27/66 | **Like A Baby** <br> Len Barry |
| 2/65 | **Like A Rolling Stone** <br> Bob Dylan |
| 36/76 | **Like A Sad Song** <br> John Denver |
| 40/78 | **Like A Sunday In Salem (The Amos & Andy Song)** <br> Gene Cotton |
| 24/67 | **Like An Old Time Movie** <br> Scott McKenzie |
| 38/61 | **Like, Long Hair** <br> Paul Revere & The Raiders |
| 22/60 | **Like Strangers** <br> Everly Brothers |
| 17/68 | **Like To Get To Know You** <br> Spanky & Our Gang |
| 2/62 <br> 40/62 | **Limbo Rock** <br> Chubby Checker <br> Champs |

| POS/YR | RECORD TITLE/ARTIST |
|--------|---------------------|
| 28/63 | **Linda** <br> Jan & Dean |
| 26/55 <br> 28/55 | **Ling, Ting, Tong** <br> Charms <br> Five Keys |
| 1/61 <br> 3/72 | **Lion Sleeps Tonight** <br> Tokens <br> Robert John |
| 17/57 | **Lips Of Wine** <br> Andy Williams |
| 15/56 | **Lipstick And Candy And Rubbersole Shoes** <br> Julius LaRosa |
| 5/59 | **Lipstick On Your Collar** <br> Connie Francis |
| 1/56 <br> 19/56 | **Lisbon Antigua** <br> Nelson Riddle & His Orchestra <br> Mitch Miller & His Orchestra |
| 3/66 | **Listen People** <br> Herman's Hermits |
| 11/72 | **Listen To The Music** <br> Doobie Brothers |
| 1/75 | **Listen To What The Man Said** <br> Paul McCartney |
| | **Little**...*also see: Lil'* |
| 16/68 | **Little Arrows** <br> Leapy Lee |
| 21/63 | **Little Band Of Gold** <br> James Gilreath |
| 2/67 | **Little Bit Me, A Little Bit You** <br> Monkees |
| 11/76 | **Little Bit More** <br> Dr. Hook |
| 16/65 | **Little Bit Of Heaven** <br> Ronnie Dove |
| 12/61 <br> 34/79 | **Little Bit Of Soap** <br> Jarmels <br> Nigel Olsson |
| 2/67 | **Little Bit O'Soul** <br> Music Explosion |
| 19/60 | **Little Bitty Girl** <br> Bobby Rydell |

| POS/YR | RECORD TITLE/ARTIST |
|--------|---------------------|
| | **Little Bitty Pretty One** |
| 6/57 | Thurston Harris |
| 25/62 | Clyde McPhatter |
| 13/72 | Jacksons |
| | **Little Bitty Tear** |
| 9/62 | Burl Ives |
| | **Little Black Book** |
| 29/62 | Jimmy Dean |
| | **Little Blue Man** |
| 17/58 | Betty Johnson |
| | **Little Boy Sad** |
| 17/61 | Johnny Burnette |
| | **Little Children** |
| 7/64 | Billy J. Kramer with the Dakotas |
| | **Little Coco Palm** |
| 36/60 | Jerry Wallace |
| | **Little Darlin'** |
| 2/57 | Diamonds |
| | **Little Deuce Coupe** |
| 15/63 | Beach Boys |
| | **Little Devil** |
| 11/61 | Neil Sedaka |
| | **Little Diane** |
| 8/62 | Dion |
| | **Little Dipper** |
| 30/59 | Mickey Mozart Quintet |
| | **Little Drummer Boy** |
| 13/58 | Harry Simeone Chorale |
| 15/59 | Harry Simeone Chorale |
| 24/60 | Harry Simeone Chorale |
| 22/61 | Harry Simeone Chorale |
| 28/62 | Harry Simeone Chorale |
| | **Little Egypt (Ying-Yang)** |
| 23/61 | Coasters |
| | **Little Girl** |
| 8/66 | Syndicate Of Sound |
| | **Little Girl I Once Knew** |
| 20/66 | Beach Boys |
| | **Little Green Apples** |
| 2/68 | O.C. Smith |
| 39/68 | Roger Miller |
| | **Little Green Bag** |
| 21/70 | George Baker Selection |
| | **Little Honda** |
| 9/64 | Hondells |

| POS/YR | RECORD TITLE/ARTIST |
|--------|---------------------|
| | **Little In Love** |
| 17/81 | Cliff Richard |
| | **Little Jeannie** |
| 3/80 | Elton John |
| | **Little Latin Lupe Lu** |
| 17/66 | Mitch Ryder & The Detroit Wheels |
| | **Little Love Can Go A Long, Long Way** |
| 33/56 | Dream Weavers |
| | **Little Man** |
| 21/66 | Sonny & Cher |
| | **Little More Love** |
| 3/79 | Olivia Newton-John |
| | **Little Old Lady (From Pasadena)** |
| 3/64 | Jan & Dean |
| | **Little Old Wine Drinker, Me** |
| 38/67 | Dean Martin |
| | **Little Ole Man (Uptight-Everything's Alright)** |
| 4/67 | Bill Cosby |
| | **Little Red Corvette** |
| 6/83 | Prince |
| | **Little Red Rented Rowboat** |
| 23/62 | Joe Dowell |
| | **Lil' Red Riding Hood** |
| 2/66 | Sam The Sham & The Pharaohs |
| | **Little Red Rooster** |
| 11/63 | Sam Cooke |
| | **Little Sandy Sleighfoot** |
| 32/57 | Jimmy Dean |
| | **Little Sister** |
| 5/61 | Elvis Presley |
| | **Little Space Girl** |
| 20/59 | Jesse Lee Turner |
| | **Little Star** |
| 1/58 | Elegants |
| | **Little Things** |
| 13/65 | Bobby Goldsboro |
| | **Little Things Mean A Lot** |
| 35/60 | Joni James |
| | **Little Too Late** |
| 20/83 | Pat Benatar |
| | **Little Town Flirt** |
| 12/63 | Del Shannon |

| POS/YR | RECORD TITLE/ARTIST |
|---|---|
| 25/57 | **Little White Lies**<br>Betty Johnson |
| 3/73 | **Little Willy**<br>Sweet |
| 3/69 | **Little Woman**<br>Bobby Sherman |
| 2/73 | **Live And Let Die**<br>Paul McCartney |
| 20/76 | **Livin' For The Weekend**<br>O'Jays |
| 19/74 | **Livin' For You**<br>Al Green |
| 31/84 | **Livin' In Desperate Times**<br>Olivia Newton-John |
| 40/77 | **Livin' In The Life**<br>Isley Brothers |
| 15/79 | **Livin' It Up (Friday Night)**<br>Bell & James |
| 13/77 | **Livin' Thing**<br>Electric Light Orchestra |
| 22/63 | **Living A Lie**<br>Al Martino |
| 37/75 | **Living A Little, Laughing A Little**<br>Spinners |
| 30/59 | **Living Doll**<br>Cliff Richard |
| 8/74 | **Living For The City**<br>Stevie Wonder |
| 23/81 | **Living In A Fantasy**<br>Leo Sayer |
| 22/72 | **Living In A House Divided**<br>Cher |
| 11/73 | **Living In The Past**<br>Jethro Tull |
| 6/81 | **Living Inside Myself**<br>Gino Vannelli |
| 25/77 | **Living Next Door To Alice**<br>Smokie |
| 32/73 | **Living Together, Growing Together**<br>5th Dimension |
| 37/75 | **Lizzie And The Rainman**<br>Tanya Tucker |
| 14/69 | **Lo Mucho Que Te Quiero**<br>Rene & Rene |

| POS/YR | RECORD TITLE/ARTIST |
|---|---|
| F/78 | **Load-Out, The**<br>Jackson Browne |
| 1/62<br>1/74 | **Loco-Motion**<br>Little Eva<br>Grand Funk Railroad |
| 12/63 | **Loddy Lo**<br>Chubby Checker |
| 6/79 | **Logical Song**<br>Supertramp |
| 9/70 | **Lola**<br>Kinks |
| 2/58<br>20/58 | **Lollipop**<br>Chordettes<br>Ronald & Ruby |
| 39/78 | **London Town**<br>Paul McCartney |
| 14/67 | **(Loneliness Made Me Realize) It's You That I Need**<br>Temptations |
| 22/65 | **L-O-N-E-L-Y**<br>Bobby Vinton |
| 6/60 | **Lonely Blue Boy**<br>Conway Twitty |
| 1/59<br>F/72 | **Lonely Boy**<br>Paul Anka<br>Donny Osmond |
| 7/77 | **Lonely Boy**<br>Andrew Gold |
| 6/62 | **Lonely Bull**<br>Herb Alpert & The Tijuana Brass |
| 3/71 | **Lonely Days**<br>Bee Gees |
| 24/59 | **Lonely For You**<br>Gary Stites |
| 26/58 | **Lonely Island**<br>Sam Cooke |
| 32/61 | **Lonely Man**<br>Elvis Presley |
| 3/76 | **Lonely Night (Angel Face)**<br>Captain & Tennille |
| 23/59 | **Lonely One**<br>Duane Eddy |
| 5/75 | **Lonely People**<br>America |

| POS/YR | RECORD TITLE/ARTIST |
|--------|---------------------|
| 5/59 | **Lonely Street**<br>Andy Williams |
| 39/63 | **Lonely Surfer**<br>Jack Nitzsche |
| 7/59 | **Lonely Teardrops**<br>Jackie Wilson |
| 12/60 | **Lonely Teenager**<br>Dion |
| 22/60 | **Lonely Weekends**<br>Charlie Rich |
| 6/79 | **Lonesome Loser**<br>Little River Band |
| 7/58 | **Lonesome Town**<br>Ricky Nelson |
| 31/71 | **Long Ago And Far Away**<br>James Taylor |
| 1/70 | **Long And Winding Road**<br>Beatles |
| 2/72 | **Long Cool Woman (In A Black Dress)**<br>Hollies |
| 26/72 | **Long Dark Road**<br>Hollies |
| 38/72 | **Long Haired Lover From Liverpool**<br>Little Jimmy Osmond |
| 33/66 | **Long Live Our Love**<br>Shangri-Las |
| 17/65 | **Long Lonely Nights**<br>Bobby Vinton |
| 20/70 | **Long Lonesome Highway**<br>Michael Parks |
| 25/70 | **Long Long Time**<br>Linda Ronstadt |
| 20/78 | **Long, Long Way From Home**<br>Foreigner |
| | **(Long Nights)**...see: Blue Collar Man |
| 8/80 | **Long Run**<br>Eagles |
| 9/75 | **Long Tall Glasses (I Can Dance)**<br>Leo Sayer |
| 6/56<br>8/56 | **Long Tall Sally**<br>Little Richard<br>Pat Boone |
| 22/77 | **Long Time**<br>Boston |

| POS/YR | RECORD TITLE/ARTIST |
|--------|---------------------|
| 8/73 | **Long Train Runnin'**<br>Doobie Brothers |
| 2/80 | **Longer**<br>Dan Fogelberg |
| 14/84 | **Longest Time**<br>Billy Joel |
| 6/55 | **Longest Walk**<br>Jaye P. Morgan |
| 5/74 | **Longfellow Serenade**<br>Neil Diamond |
| 39/75 | **Look At Me (I'm In Love)**<br>Moments |
| 16/60<br>19/60<br>26/60<br>29/60 | **Look For A Star**<br>Garry Miles<br>Billy Vaughn & His Orchestra<br>Garry Mills<br>Deane Hawley |
| 36/57 | **Look Homeward Angel**<br>Johnnie Ray |
| 14/61 | **Look In My Eyes**<br>Chantels |
| 11/75 | **Look In My Eyes Pretty Woman**<br>Dawn |
| 22/67<br>4/68 | **Look Of Love**<br>Dusty Springfield<br>Sergio Mendes & Brasil '66 |
| 27/65 | **Look Of Love**<br>Lesley Gore |
| 18/83 | **Look Of Love (Part One)**<br>ABC |
| 32/66 | **Look Through Any Window**<br>Hollies |
| 24/66 | **Look Through My Window**<br>Mamas & The Papas |
| 14/70 | **Look What They've Done To My Song Ma**<br>New Seekers |
| 4/72 | **Look What You Done For Me**<br>Al Green |
| 32/67 | **Look What You've Done**<br>Pozo-Seco Singers |
| 14/80 | **Look What You've Done To Me**<br>Boz Scaggs |

| POS/YR | RECORD TITLE/ARTIST |
|---|---|
| 39/72 | **Lookin' For A Love** J. Geils Band |
| 10/74 | Bobby Womack |
| 5/80 | **Lookin' For Love** Johnny Lee |
| 2/70 | **Lookin' Out My Back Door** Creedence Clearwater Revival |
| 16/72 | **Lookin' Through The Windows** Jacksons |
| 5/58 | **Looking Back** Nat King Cole |
| 39/83 | **Looking For A Stranger** Pat Benatar |
| 29/76 | **Looking For Space** John Denver |
| 28/65 | **Looking Through The Eyes Of Love** Gene Pitney |
| 39/73 | Partridge Family |
| 1/77 | **Looks Like We Made It** Barry Manilow |
| 4/63 | **Loop De Loop** Johnny Thunder |
| 4/74 | **Lord's Prayer** Sister Janet Mead |
| 27/76 | **Lorelei** Styx |
| 6/63 | **Losing You** Brenda Lee |
| 34/80 | **Lost Her In The Sun** John Stewart |
| 3/80 | **Lost In Love** Air Supply |
| 35/61 | **Lost Love** H.B. Barnum |
| 9/77 | **Lost Without Your Love** Bread |
| 8/79 | **Lotta Love** Nicolette Larson |
| 13/57 | **Lotta Lovin'** Gene Vincent & His Blue Caps |
| 2/63 | **Louie Louie** Kingsmen |
| 30/66 | Sandpipers |
| 13/75 | **L-O-V-E (Love)** Al Green |

| POS/YR | RECORD TITLE/ARTIST |
|---|---|
| 5/55 | **Love And Marriage** Frank Sinatra |
| 20/55 | Dinah Shore |
| 20/76 | **Love Ballad** L.T.D. |
| 18/79 | George Benson |
| | **Love Being Your Fool**...*see:* (Shu-Doo-Pa-Poo-Poop) |
| 25/67 | **Love Bug Leave My Heart Alone** Martha & The Vandellas |
| 10/62 | **Love Came To Me** Dion |
| 2/69 | **Love (Can Make You Happy)** Mercy |
| 1/68 | **Love Child** Supremes |
| 17/82 | **Love Come Down** Evelyn "Champagne" King |
| 32/79 | **Love Don't Live Here Anymore** Rose Royce |
| 15/74 | **Love Don't Love Nobody** Spinners |
| 15/67 | **Love Eyes** Nancy Sinatra |
| 30/76 | **Love Fire** Jigsaw |
| 5/70 | **Love Grows (Where My Rosemary Goes)** Edison Lighthouse |
| 1/76 | **Love Hangover** Diana Ross |
| 11/71 | **Love Her Madly** Doors |
| 8/76 | **Love Hurts** Nazareth |
| 7/73 | **Love I Lost** Harold Melvin & The Blue Notes |
| 20/67 | **Love I Saw In You Was Just A Mirage** Miracles |
| 36/77 | **Love In 'C' Minor** Cerrone |
| 22/83 | **Love In Store** Fleetwood Mac |
| 15/82 | **Love In The First Degree** Alabama |

| POS/YR | RECORD TITLE/ARTIST |
|---|---|
| 16/76 | **Love In The Shadows**<br>Neil Sedaka |
| 5/83 | **Love Is A Battlefield**<br>Pat Benatar |
| 10/57 | **Love Is A Golden Ring**<br>Frankie Laine |
| 13/66 | **Love Is A Hurtin' Thing**<br>Lou Rawls |
| 1/55<br>26/55 | **Love Is A Many-Splendored Thing**<br>Four Aces<br>Don Cornell |
| F/75 | **Love Is A Rose**<br>Linda Ronstadt |
| 23/83 | **Love Is A Stranger**<br>Eurythmics |
| 2/76 | **Love Is Alive**<br>Gary Wright |
| 7/68 | **Love Is All Around**<br>Troggs |
| 15/58 | **Love Is All We Need**<br>Tommy Edwards |
| 20/82 | **Love Is Alright Tonite**<br>Rick Springfield |
| 1/68<br>22/69 | **Love Is Blue**<br>Paul Mauriat & His Orchestra<br>Dells (medley) |
| 1/67 | **Love Is Here And Now You're Gone**<br>Supremes |
| 10/82 | **Love Is In Control (Finger On The Trigger)**<br>Donna Summer |
| 7/78 | **Love Is In The Air**<br>John Paul Young |
| 26/68 | **(Love Is Like A) Baseball Game**<br>Intruders |
| 37/82 | **Love Is Like A Rock**<br>Donnie Iris |
| 9/66 | **Love Is Like An Itching In My Heart**<br>Supremes |
| 8/78 | **Love Is Like Oxygen**<br>Sweet |
| 11/57<br>13/67 | **Love Is Strange**<br>Mickey & Sylvia<br>Peaches & Herb |

| POS/YR | RECORD TITLE/ARTIST |
|---|---|
| 10/79 | **Love Is The Answer**<br>England Dan & John Ford Coley |
| 30/76 | **Love Is The Drug**<br>Roxy Music |
| 7/56 | **(Love Is) The Tender Trap**<br>Frank Sinatra |
| 1/78 | **(Love Is) Thicker Than Water**<br>Andy Gibb |
| 16/73 | **Love Jones**<br>Brighter Side Of Darkness<br>*(also see: Basketball Jones)* |
| 16/70 | **Love Land**<br>Charles Wright & The Watts 103rd Street Rhythm Band |
| 5/62<br>19/66 | **Love Letters**<br>Ketty Lester<br>Elvis Presley |
| 1/57 | **Love Letters In The Sand**<br>Pat Boone |
| 30/56<br>30/56 | **Love, Love, Love**<br>Clovers<br>Diamonds |
| 1/76 | **Love Machine**<br>Miracles |
| 15/68 | **Love Makes A Woman**<br>Barbara Acklin |
| 33/58<br>26/63<br>11/66 | **Love Makes The World Go Round**<br>Perry Como<br>Paul Anka<br>Deon Jackson |
| 2/57 | **Love Me**<br>Elvis Presley |
| 14/76 | **Love Me**<br>Yvonne Elliman |
| 1/64 | **Love Me Do**<br>Beatles |
| 10/74 | **Love Me For A Reason**<br>Osmonds |
| 24/57<br>25/57 | **Love Me Forever**<br>Eydie Gorme<br>Four Esquires |
| 19/55<br>20/55 | **Love Me Or Leave Me**<br>Lena Horne<br>Sammy Davis, Jr. |

| POS/YR | RECORD TITLE/ARTIST |
|--------|---------------------|
| | **Love Me Tender** |
| 1/56 | Elvis Presley |
| 21/62 | Richard Chamberlain |
| 40/67 | Percy Sledge |
| | **Love Me To Pieces** |
| 11/57 | Jill Corey |
| | **Love Me Tomorrow** |
| 22/82 | Chicago |
| | **Love Me Tonight** |
| 13/69 | Tom Jones |
| | **Love Me Two Times** |
| 25/68 | Doors |
| | **Love Me Warm And Tender** |
| 12/62 | Paul Anka |
| | **Love Me With All Your Heart** |
| 3/64 | Ray Charles Singers |
| 38/66 | Bachelors |
| | **Love Means (You Never Have To Say You're Sorry)** |
| 39/71 | Sounds Of Sunshine |
| | **Love Of My Life** |
| 40/58 | Everly Brothers |
| | **Love Of My Man** |
| 21/63 | Theola Kilgore |
| | **Love On A Two-Way Street** |
| 3/70 | Moments |
| 26/81 | Stacy Lattisaw |
| | **Love On The Rocks** |
| 2/81 | Neil Diamond |
| | **Love Or Leave** |
| 36/76 | Spinners |
| | **Love Or Let Me Be Lonely** |
| 6/70 | Friends Of Distinction |
| 40/82 | Paul Davis |
| | **Love Or Something Like It** |
| 32/78 | Kenny Rogers |
| | **Love Pains** |
| 34/79 | Yvonne Elliman |
| | **Love Plus One** |
| 37/82 | Haircut One Hundred |
| | **Love Potion Number Nine** |
| 23/59 | Clovers |
| 3/65 | Searchers |
| | **Love Power** |
| 22/68 | Sandpebbles |

| POS/YR | RECORD TITLE/ARTIST |
|--------|---------------------|
| | **Love Really Hurts Without You** |
| 22/76 | Billy Ocean |
| | **Love Rollercoaster** |
| 1/76 | Ohio Players |
| | **Love She Can Count On** |
| 31/63 | Miracles |
| | **Love So Fine** |
| 40/63 | Chiffons |
| | **Love So Right** |
| 3/76 | Bee Gees |
| | **Love Somebody** |
| 5/84 | Rick Springfield |
| | **Love Song** |
| 12/74 | Anne Murray |
| | **Love Stinks** |
| 38/80 | J. Geils Band |
| | **Love Story**...see: *Theme From* |
| | **Love Takes Time** |
| 11/79 | Orleans |
| | **Love The One You're With** |
| 14/71 | Stephen Stills |
| 18/71 | Isley Brothers |
| | **Love The World Away** |
| 14/80 | Kenny Rogers |
| | **Love Theme From "One On One"**...see: *My Fair Share* |
| | **Love Theme From Eyes Of Laura Mars (Prisoner)** |
| 21/78 | Barbra Streisand |
| | **Love Theme From Footloose**...see: *Almost Paradise* |
| | **Love Theme From One Eyed Jacks** |
| 37/61 | Ferrante & Teicher |
| | **Love Theme From Romeo & Juliet** |
| 1/69 | Henry Mancini & His Orchestra |
| | **Love Theme From The Godfather** |
| 34/72 | Andy Williams |
| | **Love To Love You Baby** |
| 2/76 | Donna Summer |
| | **Love Train** |
| 1/73 | O'Jays |
| | **Love Walked In** |
| 30/60 | Dinah Washington |

| POS/YR | RECORD TITLE/ARTIST |
|---|---|
| 30/71 | **Love We Had (Stays On My Mind)** <br> Dells |
| 6/78 | **Love Will Find A Way** <br> Pablo Cruise |
| 40/69 | **Love Will Find A Way** <br> Jackie DeShannon |
| 1/75 | **Love Will Keep Us Together** <br> Captain & Tennille |
| 30/84 | **Love Will Show Us How** <br> Christine McVie |
| 13/82 | **Love Will Turn You Around** <br> Kenny Rogers |
| 5/75 | **Love Won't Let Me Wait** <br> Major Harris |
| 1/79 | **Love You Inside Out** <br> Bee Gees |
| 24/81 | **Love You Like I Never Loved Before** <br> John O'Banion |
| 26/58 | **Love You Most Of All** <br> Sam Cooke |
| 1/70 | **Love You Save** <br> Jacksons |
| 7/60 | **Love You So** <br> Ron Holden with The Thunderbirds |
| 7/82 | **Love's Been A Little Bit Hard On Me** <br> Juice Newton |
| 20/77 | **Love's Grown Deep** <br> Kenny Nolan |
| 19/71 | **Love's Lines, Angles And Rhymes** <br> 5th Dimension |
| 26/66 | **Love's Made A Fool Of You** <br> Bobby Fuller Four |
| 1/74 | **Love's Theme** <br> Love Unlimited Orchestra |
| 30/78 | **Lovely Day** <br> Bill Withers |
| 12/80 | **Lovely One** <br> Jacksons |
| 20/56 | **Lovely One** <br> Four Voices |
| 7/62 | **Lover Please** <br> Clyde McPhatter |
| 2/65 | **Lover's Concerto** <br> Toys |

| POS/YR | RECORD TITLE/ARTIST |
|---|---|
| 31/68 | **Lover's Holiday** <br> Peggy Scott & Jo Jo Benson |
| 40/80 | **Lover's Holiday** <br> Change |
| 31/61 | **Lover's Island** <br> Blue Jays |
| 6/59 | **Lover's Question** <br> Clyde McPhatter |
| 36/62 | **Lovers By Night, Strangers By Day** <br> Fleetwoods |
| 3/62 | **Lovers Who Wander** <br> Dion |
| 2/73 | **Loves Me Like A Rock** <br> Paul Simon |
| 25/61 | **Lovey Dovey** <br> Buddy Knox |
| 16/79 | **Lovin', Touchin', Squeezin'** <br> Journey |
| 1/75 | **Lovin' You** <br> Minnie Riperton |
| 32/67 | **Lovin' You** <br> Bobby Darin |
| 26/71 | **Loving Her Was Easier (Than Anything I'll Ever Do Again)** <br> Kris Kristofferson |
| 20/57 | **Loving You** <br> Elvis Presley |
| 29/72 | **Loving You Just Crossed My Mind** <br> Sam Neely |
| 7/75 | **Low Rider** <br> War |
| 3/76 | **Lowdown** <br> Boz Scaggs |
| 35/71 | **Lowdown** <br> Chicago |
|  | **Lt. Calley** . . . see: Battle Hymn Of |
| 5/77 | **Lucille** <br> Kenny Rogers |
| 21/57 <br> 21/60 | **Lucille** <br> Little Richard <br> Everly Brothers |
| 25/77 | **Luckenbach, Texas** <br> Waylon Jennings |

| POS/YR | RECORD TITLE/ARTIST |
|--------|---------------------|
| 25/60 | **Lucky Devil**<br>Carl Dobkins, Jr. |
| 14/59 | **Lucky Ladybug**<br>Billy & Lillie |
| 25/57 | **Lucky Lips**<br>Ruth Brown |
| 20/84 | **Lucky One**<br>Laura Branigan |
| 4/84 | **Lucky Star**<br>Madonna |
| 29/70 | **Lucretia Mac Evil**<br>Blood, Sweat & Tears |
| 1/75 | **Lucy In The Sky With Diamonds**<br>Elton John |
| 16/56 | **Lullaby Of Birdland**<br>Blue Stars |
| 23/61 | **Lullaby Of Love**<br>Frank Gari |
| 2/75 | **Lyin' Eyes**<br>Eagles |

| POS/YR | RECORD TITLE/ARTIST |
|--------|---------------------|
| 15/59 | **M.T.A.**<br>Kingston Trio |
| 5/70 | **Ma Belle Amie**<br>Tee Set |
| 2/68<br>38/71<br>1/78 | **Mac Arthur Park**<br>Richard Harris<br>Four Tops<br>Donna Summer |
| 22/74 | **Machine Gun**<br>Commodores |
| 25/78 | **Macho Man**<br>Village People |
| 8/56<br>11/56<br>17/56<br>20/56<br>37/56<br>1/59<br>27/60 | **Mack The Knife**<br>Dick Hyman Trio<br>Richard Hayman & Jan August<br>Lawrence Welk<br>Louis Armstrong<br>Billy Vaughn & His Orchestra<br>Bobby Darin<br>Ella Fitzgerald |
| | **Made To Love**...*see: (Girls, Girls, Girls)* |

| POS/YR | RECORD TITLE/ARTIST |
|--------|---------------------|
| 36/76 | **Mademoiselle**<br>Styx |
| 23/60 | **Madison, The**<br>Al Brown's Tunetoppers |
| 30/60 | **Madison Time**<br>Ray Bryant |
| 1/71 | **Maggie May**<br>Rod Stewart |
| 1/80 | **Magic**<br>Olivia Newton-John |
| 5/75 | **Magic**<br>Pilot |
| 12/84 | **Magic**<br>Cars |
| 25/68 | **Magic Bus**<br>Who |
| 3/68 | **Magic Carpet Ride**<br>Steppenwolf |
| 9/76 | **Magic Man**<br>Heart |
| 4/58 | **Magic Moments**<br>Perry Como |
| 21/66 | **Magic Town**<br>Vogues |
| 39/77 | **Magical Mystery Tour**<br>Ambrosia |
| 8/78 | **Magnet And Steel**<br>Walter Egan |
| 35/61 | **Magnificent Seven**<br>Al Caiola & His Orchestra |
| | **Magnum P.I.**...*see: Theme From* |
| | **Mahogany**...*see: Theme From* |
| 3/79 | **Main Event**<br>Barbra Streisand |
| | **Main Theme From Exodus**...*see: Exodus* |
| | **Main Title And Molly-O**...*see: Man With The Golden Arm* |
| 24/77 | **Mainstreet**<br>Bob Seger |
| 36/61 | **Majestic, The**<br>Dion |
| 14/83 | **Major Tom (Coming Home)**<br>Peter Schilling |

| POS/YR | RECORD TITLE/ARTIST |
|--------|---------------------|
| 25/80 | **Make A Little Magic**<br>Nitty Gritty Dirt Band |
| 5/82 | **Make A Move On Me**<br>Olivia Newton-John |
| 28/69 | **Make Believe**<br>Wind |
| 30/82 | **Make Believe**<br>Toto |
| 20/62<br>16/65<br>37/70 | **Make It Easy On Yourself**<br>Jerry Butler<br>Walker Bros.<br>Dionne Warwick |
| 22/71 | **Make It Funky**<br>James Brown |
| 1/70 | **Make It With You**<br>Bread |
| 29/83 | **Make Love Stay**<br>Dan Fogelberg |
| 16/58 | **Make Me A Miracle**<br>Jimmie Rodgers |
| 28/66 | **Make Me Belong To You**<br>Barbara Lewis |
| 9/70 | **Make Me Smile**<br>Chicago |
| 27/72 | **Make Me The Woman That You Go Home To**<br>Gladys Knight & The Pips |
| 11/65 | **Make Me Your Baby**<br>Barbara Lewis |
| 21/67 | **Make Me Yours**<br>Bettye Swann |
| 24/63<br>6/65 | **Make The World Go Away**<br>Timi Yuro<br>Eddy Arnold |
| 36/69 | **Make Your Own Kind Of Music**<br>Mama Cass |
| 6/55<br>26/55<br>30/55 | **Make Yourself Comfortable**<br>Sarah Vaughan<br>Andy Griffith<br>Peggy King |
| 5/79 | **Makin' It**<br>David Naughton |
| 20/59 | **Makin' Love**<br>Floyd Robinson |
| 31/67 | **Making Every Minute Count**<br>Spanky & Our Gang |

| POS/YR | RECORD TITLE/ARTIST |
|--------|---------------------|
| 13/82 | **Making Love**<br>Roberta Flack |
| 2/83 | **Making Love Out Of Nothing At All**<br>Air Supply |
| 35/67 | **Making Memories**<br>Frankie Laine |
| 25/76 | **Making Our Dreams Come True**<br>Cyndi Grecco |
| 8/60 | **Mama**<br>Connie Francis |
| 22/66 | **Mama**<br>B.J. Thomas |
|  | **Mama**...*also see: Mamma* |
| 9/79 | **Mama Can't Buy You Love**<br>Elton John |
| 14/63 | **Mama Didn't Lie**<br>Jan Bradley |
| 11/56 | **Mama From The Train**<br>Patti Page |
| 11/57 | **Mama Look At Bubu**<br>Harry Belafonte |
| 4/61 | **Mama Said**<br>Shirelles |
| 32/62<br>38/62 | **Mama Sang A Song**<br>Stan Kenton<br>Walter Brennan |
| 34/56 | **Mama, Teach Me To Dance**<br>Eydie Gorme |
| 1/70 | **Mama Told Me (Not To Come)**<br>Three Dog Night |
| 30/82 | **Mama Used To Say**<br>Junior |
| 2/71 | **Mama's Pearl**<br>Jacksons |
| 17/55 | **Mambo Rock**<br>Bill Haley & His Comets |
| 19/66 | **Mame**<br>Herb Alpert & The Tijuana Brass |
| 32/76 | **Mamma Mia**<br>Abba |
| 16/55 | **Man Chases A Girl**<br>Eddie Fisher |

| POS/YR | RECORD TITLE/ARTIST |
|--------|---------------------|

**Man I'll Never Be**
31/79 Boston

**Man In The Raincoat**
14/55 Marion Marlowe
16/55 Priscilla Wright

**Man On The Corner**
40/82 Genesis

**Man On Your Mind**
14/82 Little River Band

**(Man Who Shot) Liberty Valance**
4/62 Gene Pitney

**Man With The Golden Arm (Main Title/Molly-O/Delilah Jones)**
14/56 Richard Maltby & his Orchestra
16/56 Elmer Bernstein & Orchestra
22/56 Dick Jacobs & His Chorus & Orchestra
37/56 McGuire Sisters

**Man Without Love**
19/68 Engelbert Humperdinck

**Mandy**
1/75 Barry Manilow

**Maneater**
1/82 Daryl Hall & John Oates

**Mangos**
10/57 Rosemary Clooney

**Manhattan Spiritual**
10/59 Reg Owen & His Orchestra

**Maniac**
1/83 Michael Sembello

**Many Tears Ago**
7/60 Connie Francis

**March From The River Kwai And Colonel Bogey**
20/58 Mitch Miller & His Orchestra

**Margaritaville**
8/77 Jimmy Buffett

**Maria Elena**
6/63 Los Indios Tabajaras

**Marianne**
3/57 Hilltoppers
4/57 Terry Gilkyson & The Easy Riders

**Marie**
15/65 Bachelors

**(Marie's the Name) His Latest Flame**
4/61 Elvis Presley

| POS/YR | RECORD TITLE/ARTIST |
|--------|---------------------|

**Marina**
31/59 Rocco Granata

**Marlena**
36/63 Four Seasons

**Marrakesh Express**
28/69 Crosby, Stills & Nash

**Married Men**
40/79 Bette Midler

**Martian Hop**
16/63 Ran-Dells

**Mary Ann Regrets**
39/62 Burl Ives

**Mary Had A Little Lamb**
28/72 Paul McCartney

**Mary In The Morning**
27/67 Al Martino

**Mary Lou**
26/59 Ronnie Hawkins & The Hawks

**Mary's Boy Child**
12/56 Harry Belafonte

**Mary's Little Lamb**
39/62 James Darren

**Mashed Potato Time**
2/62 Dee Dee Sharp

**Massachusetts**...*see: (Lights Went Out)*

**Master Blaster (Jammin')**
5/80 Stevie Wonder

**Master Jack**
18/68 Four Jacks And A Jill

**Master Of Eyes**
33/73 Aretha Franklin

**Masterpiece**
7/73 Temptations

**Matador, The**
20/64 Major Lance

**Matchbox**
17/64 Beatles

**May I**
39/69 Bill Deal & The Rhondels

**May The Bird Of Paradise Fly Up Your Nose**
15/65 "Little" Jimmy Dickens

| POS/YR | RECORD TITLE/ARTIST |
|--------|---------------------|
| | **May You Always** |
| 11/59 | McGuire Sisters |
| | **Maybe** |
| 15/58 | Chantels |
| 29/70 | Three Degrees |
| | **Maybe Baby** |
| 17/58 | Crickets |
| | **Maybe I Know** |
| 14/64 | Lesley Gore |
| | **Maybe I'm A Fool** |
| 22/79 | Eddie Money |
| | **Maybe I'm Amazed** |
| 10/77 | Paul McCartney |
| | **Maybe Tomorrow** |
| 20/71 | Jacksons |
| | **Maybellene** |
| 5/55 | Chuck Berry |
| 12/64 | Johnny Rivers |
| | **Me And Baby Brother** |
| 15/74 | War |
| | **Me And Bobby McGee** |
| 1/71 | Janis Joplin |
| 40/72 | Jerry Lee Lewis |
| | **Me And Julio Down By The Schoolyard** |
| 22/72 | Paul Simon |
| | **Me And Mrs. Jones** |
| 1/72 | Billy Paul |
| | **Me And My Arrow** |
| 34/71 | Nilsson |
| | **Me And You And A Dog Named Boo** |
| 5/71 | Lobo |
| | **Me (Without You)** |
| 40/81 | Andy Gibb |
| | **Mean Woman Blues** |
| 5/63 | Roy Orbison |
| | **Mecca** |
| 12/63 | Gene Pitney |
| | **"Medic" Theme**...see: *Blue Star* |
| | **Medicine Man** |
| 22/69 | Buchanan Brothers |
| | **Mellow Yellow** |
| 2/66 | Donovan |
| | **Melodie D'Amour** |
| 5/57 | Ames Brothers |

| POS/YR | RECORD TITLE/ARTIST |
|--------|---------------------|
| | **Melody Of Love** |
| 2/55 | Billy Vaughn & His Orchestra |
| 3/55 | Four Aces |
| 8/55 | David Carroll & His Orchestra |
| 19/55 | Frank Sinatra & Ray Anthony |
| 30/55 | Leo Diamond |
| | **Memories** |
| 35/69 | Elvis Presley |
| | **Memories Are Made Of This** |
| 1/56 | Dean Martin |
| 5/56 | Gale Storm |
| | **Memories Of You** |
| 22/55 | Four Coins |
| 20/56 | Benny Goodman Trio with Rosemary Clooney |
| | **Memory** |
| 39/83 | Barry Manilow |
| | **Memphis** |
| 5/63 | Lonnie Mack |
| 2/64 | Johnny Rivers |
| | **Memphis Soul Stew** |
| 33/67 | King Curtis |
| | **Men**...see: *Theme From The* |
| | **Men Are Gettin' Scarce** |
| 33/68 | Joe Tex |
| | **Men In My Little Girl's Life** |
| 6/66 | Mike Douglas |
| | **Mendocino** |
| 27/69 | Sir Douglas Quintet |
| | **Mercy** |
| 30/69 | Ohio Express |
| | **Mercy, Mercy** |
| 35/64 | Don Covay |
| | **Mercy Mercy Me (The Ecology)** |
| 4/71 | Marvin Gaye |
| | **Mercy, Mercy, Mercy** |
| 5/67 | Buckinghams |
| 11/67 | Cannonball Adderley Quintet |
| | **Mess Of Blues** |
| 32/60 | Elvis Presley |
| | **Message To Michael** |
| 8/66 | Dionne Warwick |
| | **Mexican Hat Rock** |
| 16/58 | Applejacks |
| | **Mexico** |
| 7/61 | Bob Moore & His Orchestra |

| POS/YR | RECORD TITLE/ARTIST |
|---|---|
| 1/61 | **Michael** <br> Highwaymen |
| 18/66 | **Michelle** <br> David & Jonathan |
| 1/82 | **Mickey** <br> Toni Basil |
| 8/63 | **Mickey's Monkey** <br> Miracles |
| 19/84 | **Middle Of The Road** <br> Pretenders |
| 6/74 | **Midnight At The Oasis** <br> Maria Muldaur |
| 6/75 | **Midnight Blue** <br> Melissa Manchester |
| 5/68 | **Midnight Confessions** <br> Grass Roots |
| 10/70 | **Midnight Cowboy** <br> Ferrante & Teicher |
| | **Midnight Hour**...see: In The |
| 2/62 | **Midnight In Moscow** <br> Kenny Ball & His Jazzmen |
| 10/64 | **Midnight Mary** <br> Joey Powers |
| 27/72 <br> 19/74 | **Midnight Rider** <br> Joe Cocker <br> Gregg Allman |
| 24/80 | **Midnight Rocks** <br> Al Stewart |
| 16/60 <br> 20/65 | **Midnight Special** <br> Paul Evans <br> Johnny Rivers |
| 35/59 | **Midnight Stroll** <br> Revels |
| 1/73 | **Midnight Train To Georgia** <br> Gladys Knight & The Pips |
| 28/79 | **Midnight Wind** <br> John Stewart |
| 34/71 | **Mighty Clouds Of Joy** <br> B.J. Thomas |
| 38/59 | **Mighty Good** <br> Ricky Nelson |
| 20/74 | **Mighty Love** <br> Spinners |

| POS/YR | RECORD TITLE/ARTIST |
|---|---|
| 29/74 | **Mighty Mighty** <br> Earth, Wind & Fire |
| 10/68 | **Mighty Quinn (Quinn The Eskimo)** <br> Manfred Mann |
| 33/64 | **Miller's Cave** <br> Bobby Bare |
| 5/60 <br> 23/73 | **Million To One** <br> Jimmy Charles & The Revelletts <br> Donny Osmond |
| 26/69 | **Mind, Body And Soul** <br> Flaming Ember |
| 18/73 | **Mind Games** <br> John Lennon |
| 38/69 | **Minotaur, The** <br> Dick Hyman & His Electric Eclectics |
| 14/79 | **Minute By Minute** <br> Doobie Brothers |
| 18/56 | **Miracle Of Love** <br> Eileen Rodgers |
| 3/75 | **Miracles** <br> Jefferson Starship |
| 40/83 | **Miracles** <br> Stacy Lattisaw |
| 10/67 | **Mirage** <br> Tommy James & The Shondells |
| 30/83 | **Mirror Man** <br> Human League |
| 8/82 | **Mirror, Mirror** <br> Diana Ross |
| 22/73 | **Misdemeanor** <br> Foster Sylvers |
| 5/84 | **Miss Me Blind** <br> Culture Club |
| 14/81 | **Miss Sun** <br> Boz Scaggs |
| 1/78 | **Miss You** <br> Rolling Stones |
| 1/84 | **Missing You** <br> John Waite |
| 23/82 | **Missing You** <br> Dan Fogelberg |
| 29/61 | **Missing You** <br> Ray Peterson |

| POS/YR | RECORD TITLE/ARTIST |
|--------|---------------------|
| | **Mission Bell** |
| 7/60 | Donnie Brooks |
| | **Mississippi** |
| 32/70 | John Phillips |
| | **Mississippi Queen** |
| 21/70 | Mountain |
| | **Mister**...see: Mr. |
| | **Misty** |
| 12/59 | Johnny Mathis |
| 21/63 | Lloyd Price |
| 14/75 | Ray Stevens |
| | **Misty Blue** |
| 3/76 | Dorothy Moore |
| | **Misunderstanding** |
| 14/80 | Genesis |
| | **Mixed-Up, Shook-Up, Girl** |
| 37/64 | Patty & The Emblems |
| | **Mocking Bird, The** |
| 32/58 | Four Lads |
| | **Mockingbird** |
| 7/63 | Inez Foxx |
| 5/74 | Carly Simon & James Taylor |
| | **Model Girl** |
| 20/61 | Johnny Maestro |
| | **Modern Day Delilah** |
| 22/84 | Van Stephenson |
| | **Modern Girl** |
| 18/81 | Sheena Easton |
| | **Modern Love** |
| 14/83 | David Bowie |
| | **Mohair Sam** |
| 21/65 | Charlie Rich |
| | **Molly-O**...see: Man With The Golden Arm |
| | **Moments To Remember** |
| 2/55 | Four Lads |
| | **Mona Lisa** |
| 25/59 | Carl Mann |
| 29/59 | Conway Twitty |
| | **Monday, Monday** |
| 1/66 | Mamas & The Papas |
| | **Money** |
| 13/73 | Pink Floyd |
| | **Money Honey** |
| 9/76 | Bay City Rollers |

| POS/YR | RECORD TITLE/ARTIST |
|--------|---------------------|
| | **Money (That's What I Want)** |
| 23/60 | Barrett Strong |
| 16/64 | Kingsmen |
| | **Money Tree** |
| 20/56 | Margaret Whiting |
| | **Monkey Time** |
| 8/63 | Major Lance |
| | **Monster** |
| 39/70 | Steppenwolf |
| | **Monster Mash** |
| 1/62 | Bobby (Boris) Pickett |
| 10/73 | Bobby (Boris) Pickett |
| | **Monsters' Holiday** |
| 30/62 | Bobby (Boris) Pickett |
| | **Montego Bay** |
| 8/70 | Bobby Bloom |
| | **Monterey** |
| 15/68 | Animals |
| | **Mony Mony** |
| 3/68 | Tommy James & The Shondells |
| | **Moody Blue** |
| 31/77 | Elvis Presley |
| | **Moody River** |
| 1/61 | Pat Boone |
| | **Moody Woman** |
| 24/69 | Jerry Butler |
| | **Moon River** |
| 11/61 | Jerry Butler |
| 11/61 | Henry Mancini & His Orchestra |
| | **Moon Shadow** |
| 30/71 | Cat Stevens |
| | **Moon Talk** |
| 28/58 | Perry Como |
| | **Moonflight** |
| 38/69 | Vik Venus |
| | **Moonglow And Theme From "Picnic"** |
| 1/56 | Morris Stoloff |
| 4/56 | George Cates |
| 13/56 | McGuire Sisters (Picnic) |
| | **Moonlight Feels Right** |
| 3/76 | Starbuck |
| | **Moonlight Gambler** |
| 3/57 | Frankie Laine |

| POS/YR | RECORD TITLE/ARTIST |
|--------|---------------------|
| | **Moonlight Swim** |
| 24/57 | Tony Perkins |
| 37/57 | Nick Noble |
| | **More** |
| 4/56 | Perry Como |
| | **More** |
| 8/63 | Kai Winding & Orchestra |
| | **More I See You** |
| 16/66 | Chris Montez |
| | **More Love** |
| 23/67 | Miracles |
| 10/80 | Kim Carnes |
| | **More Money For You And Me** |
| 17/61 | Four Preps |
| | **More, More, More** |
| 4/76 | Andrea True Connection |
| | **More Than A Feeling** |
| 5/76 | Boston |
| | **More Than A Woman** |
| 32/78 | Tavares |
| | **More Than I Can Say** |
| 2/80 | Leo Sayer |
| | **More Than Just The Two Of Us** |
| 34/82 | Sneaker |
| | **More Today Than Yesterday** |
| 12/69 | Spiral Starecase |
| | **Morgen** |
| 13/59 | Ivo Robic |
| | **Moritat**...see: Mack The Knife |
| | **Mornin'** |
| 21/83 | Al Jarreau |
| | **Mornin' Beautiful** |
| 14/75 | Dawn |
| | **Morning After** |
| 1/73 | Maureen McGovern |
| | **Morning Dance** |
| 24/79 | Spyro Gyra |
| | **Morning Girl** |
| 17/69 | Neon Philharmonic |
| | **Morning Has Broken** |
| 6/72 | Cat Stevens |
| | **Morning Side Of The Mountain** |
| 27/59 | Tommy Edwards |
| 8/75 | Donny & Marie Osmond |

| POS/YR | RECORD TITLE/ARTIST |
|--------|---------------------|
| | **Morning Train (Nine To Five)** |
| 1/81 | Sheena Easton* |
| | **Most Beautiful Girl** |
| 1/73 | Charlie Rich |
| | **Most Of All** |
| 14/55 | Don Cornell |
| | **Most Of All** |
| 38/71 | B.J. Thomas |
| | **Most People Get Married** |
| 27/62 | Patti Page |
| | **Mostly Martha** |
| 31/56 | Crew-Cuts |
| | **Mother And Child Reunion** |
| 4/72 | Paul Simon |
| | **Mother Freedom** |
| 37/71 | Bread |
| | **Mother-In-Law** |
| 1/61 | Ernie K-Doe |
| | **Mother Popcorn** |
| 11/69 | James Brown |
| | **Mothers Little Helper** |
| 8/66 | Rolling Stones |
| | **Motorcycle Mama** |
| 12/72 | Sailcat |
| | **Mountain Of Love** |
| 21/60 | Harold Dorman |
| 9/64 | Johnny Rivers |
| | **Mountain's High** |
| 2/61 | Dick & DeeDee |
| | **Move Over** |
| 31/69 | Steppenwolf |
| | **Movin'** |
| 14/76 | Brass Construction |
| | **Movin' On** |
| 19/75 | Bad Company |
| | **Movin' Out (Anthony's Song)** |
| 17/78 | Billy Joel |
| | **Mr. Bass Man** |
| 16/63 | Johnny Cymbal |
| | **Mr. Big Stuff** |
| 2/71 | Jean Knight |
| | **Mr. Blue** |
| 1/59 | Fleetwoods |

**Julio Iglesias** and *Willie Nelson* are an undeniably odd couple, but the result of this collaboration was stranger still. The duet with country music's outlaw gave the Latin balladeer the edge he needed to crack the U.S. market, after years of trying. (Love that headband, Julio!)

**INXS,** pronounced "in excess," got together at a recording session for a steel guitar player. At home in Australia, they were first billed as the Farriss Bros. since there were three siblings in the band.

**Michael Jackson.** Just the facts: Michael Jackson's *Thriller* LP spent 37 weeks in the Number One spot, a feat surpassed only by *South Pacific* (69 weeks) and *West Side Story* (54 weeks).

**Michael Jackson** cleaned up at the 1984 Grammy Awards. Out of a record 12 nominations, he walked away with eight, including album of the year and best pop male vocal.

Julio Iglesias & Willie Nelson
To All The Girls I've Loved Before

Michael Jackson
Taken from the #1 Epic Lp "Thriller" (QE 38112)

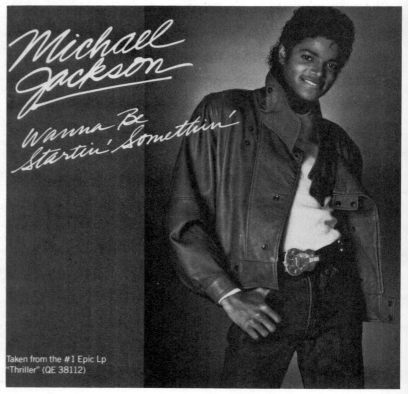

Michael Jackson
Wanna Be Startin' Somethin'

Taken from the #1 Epic Lp "Thriller" (QE 38112)

**Jay and the Techniques** came from Allentown, Pennsylvania, and liked songs with food in the title, such as "Apples, Peaches, Pumpkin Pie" and "Strawberry Shortcake."

**Michael Johnson.** Prior to going solo, Johnson sang in a trio with John Denver and David Biose (who?). Their satiric single "The '68 Nixon" was not a hit.

**Jerry Keller** created one of the great warm-weather singles when he wrote "Here Comes Summer" in 1959. The next year, he tried again with "White for You and Blues for Me," but missed.

**Andy Kim** charted with respectable remakes of two Ronettes classics, "Baby, I Love You" and "Be My Baby," but will be best remembered for co-authoring the Archies' "Sugar, Sugar" with Jeff Barry.

**Billy J. Kramer and the Dakotas** shared manager Brian Epstein with the Beatles. They received a number of Lennon-McCartney songs the Fab Four didn't cut: "I'll Keep You Satisfied," "From a Window," "I'll Be on My Way," and "Bad to Me."

**Rod Lauren.** When Elvis Presley was drafted by the army, Lauren was drafted by RCA to help fill the void. Number 31 was as high as he got.

**Gary Lewis and the Playboys** cut "This Diamond Ring," their first single, after labelmate Bobby Vee rejected the song. They came away with a big Number One for their troubles.

**Little River Band** took their name from a sign by the side of an Australian outback road. Rustic connotations notwithstanding, their hits are harmonic pop not unlike Crosby, Stills and Nash.

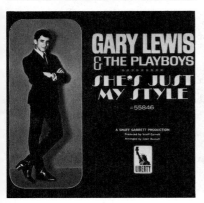

| POS/YR | RECORD TITLE/ARTIST |
|---|---|
| 35/78 | **Mr. Blue Sky** Electric Light Orchestra |
| 9/71 | **Mr. Bojangles** Nitty Gritty Dirt Band |
| 28/68 | **Mr. Businessman** Ray Stevens |
| 38/72 | **Mr. Can't You See** Buffy Sainte-Marie |
| 1/60 | **Mr. Custer** Larry Verne |
| 17/66 | **Mr. Dieingly Sad** Critters |
| | **Mr. Dream Merchant**...see: Dream Merchant |
| 4/75 | **Mr. Jaws** Dickie Goodman |
| 6/57 | **Mr. Lee** Bobbettes |
| 1/64 | **Mr. Lonely** Bobby Vinton |
| 21/60 | **Mr. Lucky** Henry Mancini & His Orchestra |
| 3/83 | **Mr. Roboto** Styx |
| 37/81 | **Mr. Sandman** Emmylou Harris |
| 36/66 | **Mr. Spaceman** Byrds |
| 18/69 | **Mr. Sun, Mr. Moon** Paul Revere & The Raiders |
| 1/65 | **Mr. Tambourine Man** Byrds |
| 13/56 14/56 18/56 | **Mr. Wonderful** Sarah Vaughan Peggy Lee Teddi King |
| 1/65 | **Mrs. Brown You've Got A Lovely Daughter** Herman's Hermits |
| 1/68 37/69 | **Mrs. Robinson** Simon & Garfunkel Booker T. & The Mg's |
| | **Ms.**...see: Miss |
| | **Muhammad Ali**...see: Black Superman |

| POS/YR | RECORD TITLE/ARTIST |
|---|---|
| 5/60 | **Mule Skinner Blues** Fendermen |
| 30/62 | **Multiplication** Bobby Darin |
| 39/59 | **Mummy, The** Bob McFadden & Dor |
| 39/82 | **Murphy's Law** Cheri |
| 10/82 | **Muscles** Diana Ross |
| 39/67 | **Museum** Herman's Hermits |
| 3/79 | **Music Box Dancer** Frank Mills |
| 40/84 | **Music Time** Styx |
| 15/67 34/67 | **Music To Watch Girls By** Bob Crewe Generation Andy Williams |
| 4/76 | **Muskrat Love** Captain & Tennille |
| 12/75 | **Must Of Got Lost** J. Geils Band |
| 8/66 | **Must To Avoid** Herman's Hermits |
| 23/66 | **Mustang Sally** Wilson Pickett |
| 21/56 | **Mutual Admiration Society** Teresa Brewer |
| 13/78 | **My Angel Baby** Toby Beau |
| 13/65 | **My Baby** Temptations |
| | **(My Baby Don't Love Me)**...see: No More |
| 31/56 | **My Baby Left Me** Elvis Presley |
| 13/70 | **My Baby Loves Lovin'** White Plains |
| 22/66 | **My Baby Loves Me** Martha & The Vandellas |
| 17/68 | **My Baby Must Be A Magician** Marvelettes |

| POS/YR | RECORD TITLE/ARTIST |
|---|---|
| 30/67 | **My Back Pages**<br>Byrds |
| 35/78 | **My Best Friend's Girl**<br>Cars |
| 21/56 | **My Blue Heaven**<br>Fats Domino |
| 26/64 | **My Bonnie**<br>Beatles<br>*(also see: Bonnie Came Back)* |
| 11/55 | **My Bonnie Lassie**<br>Ames Brothers |
| 21/62 | **My Boomerang Won't Come Back**<br>Charlie Drake |
| 20/75 | **My Boy**<br>Elvis Presley |
| 16/55<br>39/55 | **My Boy - Flat Top**<br>Dorothy Collins<br>Boyd Bennett & His Rockets |
| 2/64 | **My Boy Lollipop**<br>Millie Small |
| 1/63 | **My Boyfriend's Back**<br>Angels |
| 18/58 | **My Bucket's Got A Hole In It**<br>Ricky Nelson |
| 4/69 | **My Cherie Amour**<br>Stevie Wonder |
| 18/63<br>20/63 | **My Coloring Book**<br>Kitty Kallen<br>Sandy Stewart |
| 8/67 | **My Cup Runneth Over**<br>Ed Ames |
| 6/63 | **My Dad**<br>Paul Petersen |
| 34/60 | **My Dearest Darling**<br>Etta James |
| 1/72 | **My Ding-A-Ling**<br>Chuck Berry<br>*(also see: Ding-A-Ling)* |
| 24/57 | **My Dream**<br>Platters |
| 9/61 | **My Empty Arms**<br>Jackie Wilson |
| 29/84 | **My Ever Changing Moods**<br>Style Council |

| POS/YR | RECORD TITLE/ARTIST |
|---|---|
| 1/75 | **My Eyes Adored You**<br>Frankie Valli |
| 28/77 | **My Fair Share**<br>Seals & Crofts |
| 1/65<br>35/68 | **My Girl**<br>Temptations<br>Bobby Vee |
| 25/82 | **My Girl**<br>Donnie Iris |
| 12/74 | **My Girl Bill**<br>Jim Stafford |
| 22/81 | **My Girl (Gone, Gone, Gone)**<br>Chilliwack |
| 14/65 | **My Girl Has Gone**<br>Miracles |
| 14/60<br>29/67 | **My Girl Josephine**<br>Fats Domino<br>Jerry Jaye |
|  | **My Girl Sloopy**...*see: Hang On Sloopy* |
| 1/64<br>23/82 | **My Guy**<br>Mary Wells<br>Sister Sledge |
| 2/59 | **My Happiness**<br>Connie Francis |
| 4/77 | **My Heart Belongs To Me**<br>Barbra Streisand |
| 9/64 | **My Heart Belongs To Only You**<br>Bobby Vinton |
| 38/64 | **My Heart Cries For You**<br>Ray Charles |
| 1/60 | **My Heart Has A Mind Of Its Own**<br>Connie Francis |
| 3/59 | **My Heart Is An Open Book**<br>Carl Dobkins, Jr. |
|  | **My Heart Reminds Me**...*see: And That Reminds Me* |
|  | **My Heart Sings**...*see: (All Of A Sudden)* |
| 13/66 | **My Heart's Symphony**<br>Gary Lewis & The Playboys |
| 8/60 | **My Home Town**<br>Paul Anka |
| 18/61 | **My Kind Of Girl**<br>Matt Monro |

| POS/YR | RECORD TITLE/ARTIST |
|---|---|
| 31/83 | **My Kind Of Lady**<br>Supertramp |
| 26/61<br>38/61 | **My Last Date (With You)**<br>Skeeter Davis<br>Joni James<br>*(also see: Last Date)* |
| 3/79 | **My Life**<br>Billy Joel |
| 24/56 | **My Little Angel**<br>Four Lads |
| 9/75 | **My Little Town**<br>Simon & Garfunkel |
| 1/66 | **My Love**<br>Petula Clark |
| 1/73 | **My Love**<br>Paul McCartney |
| 5/83 | **My Love**<br>Lionel Richie |
| 16/65 | **My Love, Forgive Me**<br>Robert Goulet |
| 13/67 | **My Mammy**<br>Happenings |
| 9/73 | **My Maria**<br>B.W. Stevenson |
| 26/59 | **My Melancholy Baby**<br>Tommy Edwards |
| 3/74 | **My Melody Of Love**<br>Bobby Vinton |
| 19/74 | **My Mistake (Was To Love You)**<br>Marvin Gaye & Diana Ross |
| 39/81 | **My Mother's Eyes**<br>Bette Midler |
| 16/73 | **My Music**<br>Loggins & Messina |
| 37/84 | **My Oh My**<br>Slade |
| 24/55<br>28/57 | **My One Sin**<br>Nat King Cole<br>Four Coins |
| 33/59<br>13/62 | **My Own True Love**<br>Jimmy Clanton<br>Duprees |
| 21/57 | **My Personal Possession**<br>Nat King Cole |

| POS/YR | RECORD TITLE/ARTIST |
|---|---|
| 14/69 | **My Pledge Of Love**<br>Joe Jeffrey Group |
| 1/56 | **My Prayer**<br>Platters |
| 1/79 | **My Sharona**<br>Knack |
| 31/69 | **My Song**<br>Aretha Franklin |
| 7/57<br>7/68 | **My Special Angel**<br>Bobby Helms<br>Vogues |
| 16/63 | **My Summer Love**<br>Ruby & The Romantics |
| 17/74<br>32/77 | **My Sweet Lady**<br>Cliff DeYoung<br>John Denver |
| 1/70 | **My Sweet Lord**<br>George Harrison |
| 29/74 | **My Thang**<br>James Brown |
| 39/83 | **My Town**<br>Michael Stanley Band |
| 32/65 | **My Town, My Guy And Me**<br>Lesley Gore |
| 31/56 | **My Treasure**<br>Hilltoppers |
| 22/63 | **My True Confession**<br>Brook Benton |
| 3/58 | **My True Love**<br>Jack Scott |
| 3/61 | **My True Story**<br>Jive Five |
| 27/69<br>22/77 | **My Way**<br>Frank Sinatra<br>Elvis Presley |
| 9/69 | **My Whole World Ended (The Moment You Left Me)**<br>David Ruffin |
| 24/63 | **My Whole World Is Falling Down**<br>Brenda Lee |
| 12/59 | **My Wish Came True**<br>Elvis Presley |
| 16/72 | **My World**<br>Bee Gees |

| POS/YR | RECORD TITLE/ARTIST |
|--------|---------------------|
| 5/66 | **My World Is Empty Without You** <br> Supremes |
| 33/65 | **Mystic Eyes** <br> Them |

**N**

| POS/YR | RECORD TITLE/ARTIST |
|--------|---------------------|
| 1/69 | **Na Na Hey Hey Kiss Him Goodbye** <br> Steam |
| 8/76 | **Nadia's Theme (The Young And The Restless)** <br> Barry Devorzon & Perry Botkin, Jr. |
| 23/64 | **Nadine (Is It You?)** <br> Chuck Berry |
| 25/61 | **"Nag"** <br> Halos |
| 3/65 | **Name Game** <br> Shirley Ellis |
| 12/78 | **Name Of The Game** <br> Abba |
| 8/67 | **Nashville Cats** <br> Lovin' Spoonful |
| 16/71 | **Nathan Jones** <br> Supremes |
| 21/78 | **Native New Yorker** <br> Odyssey |
| 38/60 | **Natural Born Lover** <br> Fats Domino |
| 10/73 | **Natural High** <br> Bloodstone |
| 17/71 | **Natural Man** <br> Lou Rawls |
| 8/67 | **Natural Woman** <br> Aretha Franklin |
| 40/68 | **Naturally Stoned** <br> Avant-Garde |
| 40/61 | **Nature Boy** <br> Bobby Darin |
| 3/55 <br> 17/55 | **Naughty Lady Of Shady Lane** <br> Ames Brothers <br> Archie Bleyer |

| POS/YR | RECORD TITLE/ARTIST |
|--------|---------------------|
| 6/64 | **Navy Blue** <br> Diane Renay |
| 22/70 | **Neanderthal Man** <br> Hotlegs |
| 10/58 | **Near You** <br> Roger Williams |
| 40/58 | **Nee Nee Na Na Na Na Nu Nu** <br> Dicky Doo & The Don'ts |
| 11/74 | **Need To Be** <br> Jim Weatherly |
| 31/64 | **Need To Belong** <br> Jerry Butler |
| 25/58 | **Need You** <br> Donnie Owens |
| 13/64 | **Needles And Pins** <br> Searchers |
| 2/73 | **Neither One Of Us (Wants To Be The First To Say Goodbye)** <br> Gladys Knight & The Pips |
| | **Nel Blu Dipinto Di Blu** . . . *see: Volare* |
| 24/67 | **Neon Rainbow** <br> Box Tops |
| 6/59 | **Never Be Anyone Else But You** <br> Ricky Nelson |
| 15/80 | **Never Be The Same** <br> Christopher Cross |
| 28/82 | **Never Been In Love** <br> Randy Meisner |
| 5/72 | **Never Been To Spain** <br> Three Dog Night |
| 2/71 <br> 22/71 <br> 9/75 | **Never Can Say Goodbye** <br> Jacksons <br> Isaac Hayes <br> Gloria Gaynor |
| 13/71 | **Never Ending Song Of Love** <br> Delaney & Bonnie & Friends |
| 20/68 | **Never Give You Up** <br> Jerry Butler |
| 11/76 | **Never Gonna Fall In Love Again** <br> Eric Carmen |
| 4/83 | **Never Gonna Let You Go** <br> Sergio Mendes |
| 26/70 | **Never Had A Dream Come True** <br> Stevie Wonder |

| POS/YR | RECORD TITLE/ARTIST |
|--------|---------------------|
| 6/80 | **Never Knew Love Like This Before**<br>Stephanie Mills |
| 29/75 | **Never Let Her Go**<br>David Gates |
| 2/67<br>12/71<br>7/74 | **Never My Love**<br>Association<br>5th Dimension<br>Blue Swede |
| 7/74 | **Never, Never Gonna Give Ya Up**<br>Barry White |
| 19/60<br>13/61 | **Never On Sunday**<br>Don Costa & His Orchestra<br>Chordettes |
| 33/81 | **Never Too Much**<br>Luther Vandross |
| 22/56 | **Never Turn Back**<br>Al Hibbler |
| 37/64 | **New Girl In School**<br>Jan & Dean |
| 1/77 | **New Kid In Town**<br>Eagles |
| | **New Lovers**...see: (Welcome) |
| 36/63 | **New Mexican Rose**<br>Four Seasons |
| 10/84 | **New Moon On Monday**<br>Duran Duran |
| 6/60 | **New Orleans**<br>Gary "U.S." Bonds |
| 39/80 | **New Romance (It's A Mystery)**<br>Spider |
| 27/84 | **New Song**<br>Howard Jones |
| 21/82 | **New World Man**<br>Rush |
| 13/79 | **New York Groove**<br>Ace Frehley |
| 14/67 | **New York Mining Disaster 1941 Have You See My Wife Mr. Jones**<br>Bee Gees |
| | **New York, New York**...see: Theme From |
| 27/77 | **New York, You Got Me Dancing**<br>Andrea True Connection |
| 32/65 | **New York's A Lonely Town**<br>Trade Winds |

| POS/YR | RECORD TITLE/ARTIST |
|--------|---------------------|
| 5/62 | **Next Door To An Angel**<br>Neil Sedaka |
| 17/67 | **Next Plane To London**<br>Rose Garden |
| F/70 | **Next Step Is Love**<br>Elvis Presley |
| 37/82 | **Nice Girls**<br>Eye To Eye |
| 30/76 | **Nice 'N' Naasty**<br>Salsoul Orchestra |
| 4/72 | **Nice To Be With You**<br>Gallery |
| 35/72 | **Nickel Song**<br>Melanie |
| 39/81 | **Nicole**<br>Point Blank |
| 4/60 | **Night**<br>Jackie Wilson |
| 1/74 | **Night Chicago Died**<br>Paper Lace |
| 1/78 | **Night Fever**<br>Bee Gees |
| 3/63 | **Night Has A Thousand Eyes**<br>Bobby Vee |
| 11/56 | **Night Lights**<br>Nat King Cole |
| 4/77 | **Night Moves**<br>Bob Seger |
| 6/81 | **Night Owls**<br>Little River Band |
| 1/73 | **Night The Lights Went Out In Georgia**<br>Vicki Lawrence |
| 3/71 | **Night They Drove Old Dixie Down**<br>Joan Baez |
| 30/66 | **Night Time**<br>Strangeloves |
| 35/62 | **Night Train**<br>James Brown |
| 33/84 | **Nightbird**<br>Stevie Nicks |
| 9/75 | **Nightingale**<br>Carole King |

| POS/YR | RECORD TITLE/ARTIST |
|--------|---------------------|
| 10/76 | **Nights Are Forever Without You**<br>England Dan & John Ford Coley |
| 2/72 | **Nights In White Satin**<br>Moody Blues |
| 7/75 | **Nights On Broadway**<br>Bee Gees |
| 23/67 | **Niki Hoeky**<br>P.J. Proby |
| 1/81 | **9 To 5**<br>Dolly Parton |
| 2/66 | **19th Nervous Breakdown**<br>Rolling Stones |
| 1/66 | **96 Tears**<br>? (Question Mark) & The Mysterians |
| 7/67 | **98.6**<br>Keith |
| 26/80 | **99**<br>Toto |
| 2/84 | **99 Luftballons**<br>Nena |
| 11/57 | **Ninety-Nine Ways**<br>Tab Hunter |
| 23/56 | **Ninety-Nine Years (Dead Or Alive)**<br>Guy Mitchell |
| 33/71 | **1900 Yesterday**<br>Liz Damon's Orient Express |
| 12/83 | **1999**<br>Prince |
| 8/64<br>19/69 | **Nitty Gritty**<br>Shirley Ellis<br>Gladys Knight & The Pips |
| 23/55<br>26/55<br>27/65 | **No Arms Can Ever Hold You**<br>Georgie Shaw<br>Pat Boone<br>Bachelors |
| 39/74 | **No Charge**<br>Melba Montgomery |
| 23/58 | **No Chemise, Please**<br>Gerry Granahan |
| | **No Gettin' Over Me**...see: (There's) |
| 40/60 | **No If's - No And's**<br>Lloyd Price |
| 16/71 | **No Love At All**<br>B.J. Thomas |
| 21/58 | **No Love (But Your Love)**<br>Johnny Mathis |
| 8/70 | **No Matter What**<br>Badfinger |
| 3/66 | **No Matter What Shape (Your Stomach's In)**<br>T-Bones |
| 31/69 | **No Matter What Sign You Are**<br>Supremes |
| 35/67 | **No Milk Today**<br>Herman's Hermits |
| 6/55<br>17/55 | **No More**<br>De John Sisters<br>McGuire Sisters |
| 6/84 | **No More Lonely Nights**<br>Paul McCartney |
| 25/73 | **No More Mr. Nice Guy**<br>Alice Cooper |
| 1/79 | **No More Tears (Enough Is Enough)**<br>Barbra Streisand & Donna Summer |
| 23/84 | **No More Words**<br>Berlin |
| 23/80 | **No Night So Long**<br>Dionne Warwick |
| 3/75 | **No No Song**<br>Ringo Starr |
| 2/56<br>34/69 | **No, Not Much!**<br>Four Lads<br>Vogues |
| 34/61<br>21/63 | **No One**<br>Connie Francis<br>Ray Charles |
| 19/58 | **No One Knows**<br>Dion & The Belmonts |
| 36/72 | **No One To Depend On**<br>Santana |
| | **No Other Arms**...see: No Arms Can Ever Hold You |
| 27/59 | **No Other Arms, No Other Lips**<br>Chordettes |
| 10/64 | **No Particular Place To Go**<br>Chuck Berry |
| 29/81 | **No Reply At All**<br>Genesis |

| POS/YR | RECORD TITLE/ARTIST |
|--------|---------------------|
| F/70 | **No Sugar Tonight**<br>Guess Who |
| 14/79 | **No Tell Lover**<br>Chicago |
| 5/70 | **No Time**<br>Guess Who |
| 33/83 | **No Time For Talk**<br>Christopher Cross |
| 23/84 | **No Way Out**<br>Jefferson Starship |
| 15/82 | **Nobody**<br>Sylvia |
| 8/68 | **Nobody But Me**<br>Human Beinz |
| 21/59 | **Nobody But You**<br>Dee Clark |
| 40/69 | **Nobody But You Babe**<br>Clarence Reid |
| 2/77 | **Nobody Does It Better**<br>Carly Simon |
| 12/64 | **Nobody I Know**<br>Peter & Gordon |
| 30/60 | **Nobody Loves Me Like You**<br>Flamingos |
| 18/82 | **Nobody Said It Was Easy**<br>Le Roux |
| 5/84 | **Nobody Told Me**<br>John Lennon |
| 29/73 | **Nobody Wants You When You're Down And Out**<br>Bobby Womack |
| 21/81 | **Nobody Wins**<br>Elton John |
| 39/59 | **Nola**<br>Billy Williams |
| 3/62 | **Norman**<br>Sue Thompson |
| 4/60 | **North To Alaska**<br>Johnny Horton |
| 12/63 | **Not Me**<br>Orlons |
| 16/60 | **Not One Minute More**<br>Della Reese |

| POS/YR | RECORD TITLE/ARTIST |
|--------|---------------------|
| 25/65 | **Not The Lovin' Kind**<br>Dino, Desi & Billy |
| 34/69 | **Nothing But A Heartache**<br>Flirtations |
| 11/65 | **Nothing But Heartaches**<br>Supremes |
| 12/62 | **Nothing Can Change This Love**<br>Sam Cooke |
| 18/65 | **Nothing Can Stop Me**<br>Gene Chandler |
| | **Nothing For Xmas**...see: Nuttin' |
| 1/74 | **Nothing From Nothing**<br>Billy Preston |
| 20/66 | **Nothing's Too Good For My Baby**<br>Stevie Wonder |
| 25/58 | **Now And For Always**<br>George Hamilton IV |
| | **(Now And Then) A**...see: Fool Such As I |
| 3/66 | **Nowhere Man**<br>Beatles |
| 8/65 | **Nowhere To Run**<br>Martha & The Vandellas |
| 9/75 | **#9 Dream**<br>John Lennon |
| 22/73 | **Nutbush City Limits**<br>Ike & Tina Turner |
| 23/62 | **Nutrocker**<br>B. Bumble & The Stingers |
| | **Nuttin' For Christmas** |
| 6/55 | Barry Gordon |
| 20/55 | Joe Ward |
| 21/55 | Ricky Zahnd & The Blue Jeaners |
| 36/55 | Fontane Sisters |

| POS/YR | RECORD TITLE/ARTIST |
|--------|---------------------|
| 10/60 | **O Dio Mio**<br>Annette |
| 35/84 | **Obscene Phone Caller**<br>Rockwell |

| POS/YR | RECORD TITLE/ARTIST |
|--------|---------------------|
| | **Ode To Billie Joe** |
| 1/67 | Bobbie Gentry |
| 28/67 | King Curtis |
| | **Off The Wall** |
| 10/80 | Michael Jackson |
| | **Oh**. . .*also see: O* |
| | **Oh, Babe, What Would You Say?** |
| 3/73 | Hurricane Smith |
| | **Oh Baby Don't You Weep** |
| 23/64 | James Brown |
| | **Oh, Boy!** |
| 10/58 | Crickets |
| | **Oh! Carol** |
| 9/59 | Neil Sedaka |
| | **Oh! Darling** |
| 15/78 | Robin Gibb |
| | **Oh Girl** |
| 1/72 | Chi-Lites |
| | **Oh Happy Day** |
| 4/69 | Edwin Hawkins Singers |
| 40/70 | Glen Campbell |
| | **Oh How Happy** |
| 12/66 | Shades Of Blue |
| | **Oh Julie** |
| 5/58 | Crescendos |
| 23/58 | Sammy Salvo |
| | **Oh Julie** |
| 38/82 | Barry Manilow |
| | **Oh La De Da** |
| 33/73 | Staple Singers |
| | **Oh, Little One** |
| 34/60 | Jack Scott |
| | **Oh Lonesome Me** |
| 7/58 | Don Gibson |
| | **Oh Me Oh My (I'm A Fool For You Baby)** |
| 22/70 | Lulu |
| | **Oh My My** |
| 5/74 | Ringo Starr |
| | **Oh No** |
| 4/81 | Commodores |
| | **Oh No, Not My Baby** |
| 24/65 | Maxine Brown |
| | **Oh Oh, I'm Falling In Love Again** |
| 7/58 | Jimmie Rodgers |

| POS/YR | RECORD TITLE/ARTIST |
|--------|---------------------|
| | **Oh, Pretty Woman** |
| 1/64 | Roy Orbison |
| 12/82 | Van Halen |
| | **Oh Sherrie** |
| 3/84 | Steve Perry |
| | **Oh! Susanna** |
| 22/55 | Singing Dogs |
| | **Oh Very Young** |
| 10/74 | Cat Stevens |
| | **Oh Well** |
| 30/79 | Rockets |
| | **Oh, What A Night** |
| 10/69 | Dells |
| | **Oh, What A Night**. . .*see: December, 1963* |
| | **Oh What A Night For Dancing** |
| 24/78 | Barry White |
| | **Oh Yeah** |
| 39/66 | Shadows Of Knight |
| | **Ohio** |
| 14/70 | Crosby, Stills, Nash & Young |
| | **Old Cape Cod** |
| 3/57 | Patti Page |
| | **Old Days** |
| 5/75 | Chicago |
| | **Old Fashion Love** |
| 20/80 | Commodores |
| | **Old Fashioned Boy (You're The One)** |
| 37/77 | Stallion |
| | **Old Fashioned Love Song** |
| 4/71 | Three Dog Night |
| | **Old Lamplighter** |
| 5/60 | Browns |
| | **Old MacDonald** |
| 25/60 | Frank Sinatra |
| | **Old Man** |
| 31/72 | Neil Young |
| | **Old Philosopher** |
| 34/56 | Eddie Lawrence |
| | **Old Rivers** |
| 5/62 | Walter Brennan |
| | **Old Songs** |
| 15/81 | Barry Manilow |

| POS/YR | RECORD TITLE/ARTIST |
|--------|---------------------|
| 28/79 | **Old Time Rock & Roll**<br>Bob Seger |
| 25/61 | **Ole Buttermilk Sky**<br>Bill Black's Combo |
| 11/67 | **On A Carousel**<br>Hollies |
| 5/74 | **On And On**<br>Gladys Knight & The Pips |
| 11/77 | **On And On**<br>Stephen Bishop |
| 9/63<br>7/78 | **On Broadway**<br>Drifters<br>George Benson |
| 38/56 | **On London Bridge**<br>Jo Stafford |
| 20/57 | **On My Word Of Honor**<br>Platters |
| 7/84 | **On The Dark Side**<br>John Cafferty |
| 26/83 | **On The Loose**<br>Saga |
| 5/80 | **On The Radio**<br>Donna Summer |
| 4/61 | **On The Rebound**<br>Floyd Cramer |
| 16/68 | **On The Road Again**<br>Canned Heat |
| 20/80 | **On The Road Again**<br>Willie Nelson |
| 38/78 | **On The Shelf**<br>Donny & Marie Osmond |
| 4/56<br>18/56<br>28/64 | **On The Street Where You Live**<br>Vic Damone<br>Eddie Fisher<br>Andy Williams |
| 27/82 | **On The Way To The Sky**<br>Neil Diamond |
| 29/82 | **On The Wings Of Love**<br>Jeffrey Osborne |
| 14/63 | **On Top Of Spaghetti**<br>Tom Glazer |
| 11/61 | **Once In Awhile**<br>Chimes |
| 19/64 | **Once Upon A Time**<br>Marvin Gaye & Mary Wells |

| POS/YR | RECORD TITLE/ARTIST |
|--------|---------------------|
| 26/61 | **Once Upon A Time**<br>Rochell & The Candles |
| 10/75 | **Once You Get Started**<br>Rufus featuring Chaka Khan |
| 23/72 | **Once You Understand**<br>Think |
| 5/69 | **One**<br>Three Dog Night |
| 1/71 | **One Bad Apple**<br>Osmonds |
| 11/63 | **One Broken Heart For Sale**<br>Elvis Presley |
| 37/74 | **One Day At A Time**<br>Marilyn Sellars |
| 34/65 | **One Dyin' And A Buryin'**<br>Roger Miller |
| | **One Eyed Jacks**...see: Love Theme From |
| 5/63<br>12/80 | **One Fine Day**<br>Chiffons<br>Carole King |
| 24/71 | **One Fine Morning**<br>Lighthouse |
| 13/66 | **One Has My Name (The Other Has My Heart)**<br>Barry Young |
| 11/74 | **One Hell Of A Woman**<br>Mac Davis |
| 14/82 | **One Hundred Ways**<br>James Ingram |
| 31/57 | **One In A Million**<br>Platters |
| 37/84 | **One In A Million**<br>Romantics |
| 9/80 | **One In A Million You**<br>Larry Graham |
| 14/65 | **One Kiss For Old Times' Sake**<br>Ronnie Dove |
| 35/79 | **One Last Kiss**<br>J. Geils Band |
| 2/70 | **One Less Bell To Answer**<br>5th Dimension |
| 37/73 | **One Less Set Of Footsteps**<br>Jim Croce |

| POS/YR | RECORD TITLE/ARTIST |
|--------|---------------------|
| 25/76 | **One Love In My Lifetime**<br>Diana Ross |
| 19/71 | **One Man Band**<br>Three Dog Night |
| 28/73 | **One Man Band (Plays All Alone)**<br>Ronnie Dyson |
| 7/75 | **One Man Woman/One Woman Man**<br>Paul Anka |
| 8/61 | **One Mint Julep**<br>Ray Charles |
| 15/72 | **One Monkey Don't Stop No Show**<br>Honey Cone |
| 29/66 | **One More Heartache**<br>Marvin Gaye |
| | **One More Sunrise**...*see: Morgen* |
| 32/65 | **One More Time**<br>Ray Charles Singers |
| 28/78 | **One Nation Under A Groove**<br>Funkadelic |
| 4/58 | **One Night**<br>Elvis Presley |
| 11/73 | **One Of A Kind (Love Affair)**<br>Spinners |
| 1/75 | **One Of These Nights**<br>Eagles |
| 31/60 | **One Of Us (Will Weep Tonight)**<br>Patti Page |
| 7/83 | **One On One**<br>Daryl Hall & John Oates |
| | **One On One, Love Theme From**...*see:*<br>*My Fair Share* |
| 29/76 | **One Piece At A Time**<br>Johnny Cash |
| 24/81 | **One Step Closer**<br>Doobie Brothers |
| 7/58<br>22/61 | **One Summer Night**<br>Danleers<br>Diamonds |
| 1/81 | **One That You Love**<br>Air Supply |
| 30/83 | **One Thing**<br>Inxs |
| 4/83 | **One Thing Leads To Another**<br>Fixx |

| POS/YR | RECORD TITLE/ARTIST |
|--------|---------------------|
| 34/70<br>26/71 | **One Tin Soldier (The Legend Of Billy Jack)**<br>Original Caste<br>Coven |
| 10/71 | **One Toke Over The Line**<br>Brewer & Shipley |
| 9/61 | **One Track Mind**<br>Bobby Lewis |
| 40/80 | **One-Trick Pony**<br>Paul Simon |
| 2/65 | **1-2-3**<br>Len Barry |
| 5/68 | **1,2,3, Red Light**<br>1910 Fruitgum Co. |
| 24/79 | **One Way Or Another**<br>Blondie |
| 8/62 | **One Who Really Loves You**<br>Mary Wells |
| 15/82 | **One You Love**<br>Glenn Frey |
| 36/80 | **Only A Lonely Heart Sees**<br>Felix Cavaliere |
| 25/63 | **Only In America**<br>Jay & The Americans |
| 2/62 | **Only Love Can Break A Heart**<br>Gene Pitney |
| 33/70 | **Only Love Can Break Your Heart**<br>Neil Young |
| 28/76 | **Only Love Is Real**<br>Carole King |
| 33/57 | **Only One Love**<br>George Hamilton IV |
| 28/59<br>6/76 | **Only Sixteen**<br>Sam Cooke<br>Dr. Hook |
| 24/78 | **Only The Good Die Young**<br>Billy Joel |
| 2/60 | **Only The Lonely**<br>Roy Orbison |
| 9/82 | **Only The Lonely**<br>Motels |
| 4/69 | **Only The Strong Survive**<br>Jerry Butler |

| POS/YR | RECORD TITLE/ARTIST |
|--------|---------------------|
| 17/82 | **Only Time Will Tell**<br>Asia |
| 34/84 | **Only When You Leave**<br>Spandau Ballet |
| 12/75 | **Only Women**<br>Alice Cooper |
| 4/75 | **Only Yesterday**<br>Carpenters |
| | **Only You** |
| 5/55 | Platters |
| 8/55 | Hilltoppers |
| 9/59 | Franck Pourcel's French Fiddles |
| 6/75 | Ringo Starr |
| 20/71 | **Only You Know And I Know**<br>Delaney & Bonnie & Friends |
| 23/65 | **Oo Wee Baby, I Love You**<br>Fred Hughes |
| 34/67 | **Oogum Boogum Song**<br>Brenton Wood |
| 25/73 | **Ooh Baby**<br>Gilbert O'Sullivan |
| | **Ooh Baby Baby** |
| 16/65 | Miracles |
| 7/79 | Linda Ronstadt |
| 8/70 | **O-o-h Child**<br>Five Stairsteps |
| 31/58 | **Ooh! My Soul**<br>Little Richard |
| 28/60 | **Ooh Poo Pah Doo**<br>Jessie Hill |
| 2/82 | **Open Arms**<br>Journey |
| 10/67 | **Open Letter To My Teenage Son**<br>Victor Lundberg |
| 27/66 | **Open The Door To Your Heart**<br>Darrell Banks |
| 8/55 | **Open Up Your Heart (And Let The Sunshine In)**<br>Cowboy Church Sunday School |
| 22/75 | **Operator**<br>Manhattan Transfer |
| 17/72 | **Operator (That's Not The Way It Feels)**<br>Jim Croce |
| 13/66 | **Opus 17 (Don't You Worry 'Bout Me)**<br>Four Seasons |

| POS/YR | RECORD TITLE/ARTIST |
|--------|---------------------|
| 11/83 | **Other Guy**<br>Little River Band |
| 31/67 | **Other Man's Grass Is Always Greener**<br>Petula Clark |
| 4/82 | **Other Woman**<br>Ray Parker Jr. |
| | **Our Day Will Come** |
| 1/63 | Ruby & The Romantics |
| 11/75 | Frankie Valli |
| 7/83 | **Our House**<br>Madness |
| 30/70 | **Our House**<br>Crosby, Stills, Nash & Young |
| 20/81 | **Our Lips Are Sealed**<br>Go-GO'S |
| 10/78 | **Our Love**<br>Natalie Cole |
| | **Our Love Affair**...see: Affair To Remember |
| 9/78 | **(Our Love) Don't Throw It All Away**<br>Andy Gibb |
| 9/63 | **Our Winter Love**<br>Bill Pursell |
| 39/67 | **Out & About**<br>Tommy Boyce & Bobby Hart |
| 19/80 | **Out Here On My Own**<br>Irene Cara |
| 15/70 | **Out In The Country**<br>Three Dog Night |
| 3/64 | **Out Of Limits**<br>Marketts |
| 24/63 | **Out Of My Mind**<br>Johnny Tillotson |
| 24/64 | **Out Of Sight**<br>James Brown |
| 23/56 | **Out Of Sight, Out Of Mind**<br>Five Keys |
| 17/73 | **Out Of The Question**<br>Gilbert O'Sullivan |
| 1/84 | **Out Of Touch**<br>Daryl Hall & John Oates |
| 21/82 | **Out Of Work**<br>Gary "U.S." Bonds |

| POS/YR | RECORD TITLE/ARTIST |
|---|---|
| 2/72 | **Outa-Space** <br> Billy Preston |
| 28/60 | **Outside My Window** <br> Fleetwoods |
| 34/74 | **Outside Woman** <br> Bloodstone |
| 1/65 | **Over And Over** <br> Dave Clark Five |
| 20/76 | **Over My Head** <br> Fleetwood Mac |
| 8/57 <br> 21/63 | **Over The Mountain; Across The Sea** <br> Johnnie & Joe <br> Bobby Vinton |
| 16/60 | **Over The Rainbow** <br> Demensions |
| 13/66 | **Over Under Sideways Down** <br> Yardbirds |
| 7/68 | **Over You** <br> Gary Puckett & The Union Gap |
| 3/83 | **Overkill** <br> Men At Work |
| 18/74 | **Overnight Sensation (Hit Record)** <br> Raspberries |
| 16/70 | **Overture From Tommy (A Rock Opera)** <br> Assembled Multitude |
| 1/84 | **Owner Of A Lonely Heart** <br> Yes |
| 13/71 | **Oye Como Va** <br> Santana |

# P

| POS/YR | RECORD TITLE/ARTIST |
|---|---|
| 10/64 | **P.S. I Love You** <br> Beatles |
| 8/62 | **P.T. 109** <br> Jimmy Dean |
| 10/83 | **P.Y.T. (Pretty Young Thing)** <br> Michael Jackson |
| 9/82 | **Pac-Man Fever** <br> Buckner & Garcia |
| 13/58 | **Padre** <br> Toni Arden |

| POS/YR | RECORD TITLE/ARTIST |
|---|---|
| 1/66 | **Paint It, Black** <br> Rolling Stones |
| | **Paint Me A Picture** . . . *see: You Don't Have To* |
| 34/74 | **Painted Ladies** <br> Ian Thomas |
| 15/63 | **Painted, Tainted Rose** <br> Al Martino |
| | **Paladin** . . . *see: Ballad Of* |
| 3/62 | **Palisades Park** <br> Freddy Cannon |
| 26/76 | **Paloma Blanca** <br> George Baker Selection |
| 13/84 | **Panama** <br> Van Halen |
| 35/66 | **Pandora's Golden Heebie Jeebies** <br> Association |
| 31/74 | **Papa Don't Take No Mess** <br> James Brown |
| | **Papa Joe's** . . . *see: (Down At)* |
| 1/72 | **Papa Was A Rollin' Stone** <br> Temptations |
| 8/65 <br> 21/69 | **Papa's Got A Brand New Bag** <br> James Brown <br> Otis Redding |
| 34/67 | **Paper Cup** <br> 5th Dimension |
| 5/60 <br> 5/73 | **Paper Roses** <br> Anita Bryant <br> Marie Osmond |
| 23/65 | **Paper Tiger** <br> Sue Thompson |
| 1/66 | **Paperback Writer** <br> Beatles |
| 32/82 | **Paperlate** <br> Genesis |
| 39/78 | **Paradise By The Dashboard Light** <br> Meat Loaf |
| 38/58 | **Part Of Me** <br> Jimmy Clanton |
| 31/75 | **Part Of The Plan** <br> Dan Fogelberg |

| POS/YR | RECORD TITLE/ARTIST |
|---|---|
| 19/63 | **Part Time Love**<br>Little Johnny Taylor |
| 22/78 | **Part-Time Love**<br>Elton John |
| 22/75 | **Part Time Love**<br>Gladys Knight & The Pips |
| 1/57<br>5/57 | **Party Doll**<br>Buddy Knox<br>Steve Lawrence |
| 5/62 | **Party Lights**<br>Claudine Clark |
| 34/81 | **Party's Over (Hopelessly In Love)**<br>Journey |
| 10/83 | **Pass The Dutchie**<br>Musical Youth |
| 5/81 | **Passion**<br>Rod Stewart |
| 12/67 | **Pata Pata**<br>Miriam Makeba |
| 4/70 | **Patches**<br>Clarence Carter |
| 6/62 | **Patches**<br>Dickey Lee |
| 1/58 | **Patricia**<br>Perez Prado & His Orchestra |
| 13/71 | **Pay To The Piper**<br>Chairmen Of The Board |
| 28/67 | **Pay You Back With Interest**<br>Hollies |
| 26/74 | **Payback, The**<br>James Brown |
| 39/68 | **Paying The Cost To Be The Boss**<br>B.B. King |
| 38/77 | **Peace Of Mind**<br>Boston |
| 31/75 | **Peace Pipe**<br>B.T. Express |
| 7/71 | **Peace Train**<br>Cat Stevens |
| 32/70 | **Peace Will Come (According To Plan)**<br>Melanie |
| 12/73 | **Peaceful**<br>Helen Reddy |

| POS/YR | RECORD TITLE/ARTIST |
|---|---|
| 22/73 | **Peaceful Easy Feeling**<br>Eagles |
| 36/65 | **Peaches "N" Cream**<br>Ikettes |
| 20/61 | **Peanut Butter**<br>Marathons |
| 22/57 | **Peanuts**<br>Little Joe & The Thrillers |
| 28/59 | **Peek-A-Boo**<br>Cadillacs |
| 11/78 | **Peg**<br>Steely Dan |
| 3/57 | **Peggy Sue**<br>Buddy Holly |
| 18/64 | **Penetration**<br>Pyramids |
| 24/60 | **Pennies From Heaven**<br>Skyliners |
| 33/82 | **Penny For Your Thoughts**<br>Tavares |
| 1/67 | **Penny Lane**<br>Beatles |
| 8/84 | **Penny Lover**<br>Lionel Richie |
| 5/64<br>39/68 | **People**<br>Barbra Streisand<br>Tymes |
| 12/67 | **People Are Strange**<br>Doors |
| 14/65 | **People Get Ready**<br>Impressions |
| 1/68 | **People Got To Be Free**<br>Rascals |
| 22/74 | **People Gotta Move**<br>Gino Vannelli |
| 40/77 | **People In Love**<br>10cc |
| 25/72 | **People Make The World Go Round**<br>Stylistics |
| 23/79 | **People Of The South Wind**<br>Kansas |
| 12/64 | **People Say**<br>Dixie Cups |

| POS/YR | RECORD TITLE/ARTIST |
|---|---|
| 18/61 | **"Pepe"**<br>Duane Eddy |
| 5/63 | **Pepino The Italian Mouse**<br>Lou Monte |
| 12/55 | **Pepper-Hot Baby**<br>Jaye P. Morgan |
| 1/62 | **Peppermint Twist**<br>Joey Dee & The Starliters |
| 10/62 | **Percolator (Twist)**<br>Billy Joe & The Checkmates |
| 15/60 | **Perfidia**<br>Ventures |
| 2/59 | **Personality**<br>Lloyd Price |
| 19/82 | **Personally**<br>Karla Bonoff |
| 8/59<br>27/60 | **Peter Gunn**<br>Ray Anthony & His Orchestra<br>Duane Eddy |
| 5/59 | **Petite Fleur**<br>Chris Barber's Jazz Band |
| 16/56 | **Petticoats Of Portugal**<br>Dick Jacobs & His Chorus & Orchestra |
| 1/75 | **Philadelphia Freedom**<br>Elton John |
| 26/58 | **Philadelphia U.S.A.**<br>Nu Tornados |
| 32/66 | **Phoenix Love Theme**<br>Brass Ring featuring Phil Bodner |
| 1/73 | **Photograph**<br>Ringo Starr |
| 12/83 | **Photograph**<br>Def Leppard |
| 1/81 | **Physical**<br>Olivia Newton-John |
| 25/74 | **Piano Man**<br>Billy Joel |
| 1/75 | **Pick Up The Pieces**<br>Average White Band |
| 27/68 | **Pickin' Wild Mountain Berries**<br>Peggy Scott & Jo Jo Benson |
| | **Picnic**...see: Moonglow |
| 12/68 | **Pictures Of Matchstick Men**<br>Status Quo |

| POS/YR | RECORD TITLE/ARTIST |
|---|---|
| 12/68 | **Piece Of My Heart**<br>Big Brother & The Holding Company |
| 19/73 | **Pieces Of April**<br>Three Dog Night |
| 31/83 | **Pieces Of Ice**<br>Diana Ross |
| 4/66 | **Pied Piper**<br>Crispian St. Peters |
| 3/73 | **Pillow Talk**<br>Sylvia |
| 13/80 | **Pilot Of The Airwaves**<br>Charlie Dore |
| | **(Pina Colada Song)**...see: Escape |
| 19/69<br>29/73 | **Pinball Wizard**<br>Who<br>New Seekers |
| 11/60 | **Pineapple Princess**<br>Annette |
| 8/84 | **Pink Houses**<br>John Cougar |
| 31/64 | **Pink Panther Theme**<br>Henry Mancini & His Orchestra |
| 3/59 | **Pink Shoe Laces**<br>Dodie Stevens |
| | **Piove**...see: Ciao, Ciao Bambina |
| 4/63 | **Pipeline**<br>Chantay's |
| 9/66 | **Place In The Sun**<br>Stevie Wonder |
| 38/59 | **Plain Jane**<br>Bobby Darin |
| 19/55 | **Plantation Boogie**<br>Lenny Dee |
| 40/73 | **Plastic Man**<br>Temptations |
| 11/72 | **Play Me**<br>Neil Diamond |
| 6/55 | **Play Me Hearts And Flowers (I Wanna Cry)**<br>Johnny Desmond |
| 33/74 | **Play Something Sweet (Brickyard Blues)**<br>Three Dog Night |

| POS/YR | RECORD TITLE/ARTIST |
|---|---|
| 1/76 | **Play That Funky Music** <br> Wild Cherry |
| 17/82 | **Play The Game Tonight** <br> Kansas |
| 7/62 | **Playboy** <br> Marvelettes |
| 17/68 | **Playboy** <br> Gene & Debbe |
| 2/73 | **Playground In My Mind** <br> Clint Holmes |
| 21/57 | **Playing For Keeps** <br> Elvis Presley |
| 3/67 | **Pleasant Valley Sunday** <br> Monkees |
| 18/78 | **Please Come Home For Christmas** <br> Eagles |
| 5/74 | **Please Come To Boston** <br> Dave Loggins |
| 15/62 | **Please Don't Ask About Barbara** <br> Bobby Vee |
| 1/80 | **Please Don't Go** <br> KC & The Sunshine Band |
| 39/61 | **Please Don't Go** <br> Ral Donner |
| 24/79 | **Please Don't Leave** <br> Lauren Wood |
| 31/63 | **Please Don't Talk To The Lifeguard** <br> Diane Ray |
| 8/60 | **Please Help Me, I'm Falling** <br> Hank Locklin <br> *(also see: (I Can't Help It))* |
| 12/61 <br> 6/67 | **Please Love Me Forever** <br> Cathy Jean & The Roommates <br> Bobby Vinton |
| 3/75 | **Please Mr. Please** <br> Olivia Newton-John |
| 1/61 <br> 1/75 | **Please Mr. Postman** <br> Marvelettes <br> Carpenters |
| 11/59 | **Please Mr. Sun** <br> Tommy Edwards |
| 3/64 | **Please Please Me** <br> Beatles |
| 26/68 | **Please Return Your Love To Me** <br> Temptations |

| POS/YR | RECORD TITLE/ARTIST |
|---|---|
| 14/61 | **Please Stay** <br> Drifters |
| 20/61 | **Please Tell Me Why** <br> Jackie Wilson |
| 28/66 | **Please Tell Me Why** <br> Dave Clark Five |
| 12/57 <br> 25/57 | **Pledge Of Love** <br> Ken Copeland <br> Mitchell Torok |
| 17/55 <br> 17/55 | **Pledging My Love** <br> Johnny Ace <br> Teresa Brewer |
| 34/62 | **Pocketful Of Miracles** <br> Frank Sinatra |
| 2/60 | **Poetry In Motion** <br> Johnny Tillotson |
| 5/75 | **Poetry Man** <br> Phoebe Snow |
| 37/70 | **Point It Out** <br> Miracles |
| 28/78 | **Point Of Know Return** <br> Kansas |
| 21/62 | **Point Of No Return** <br> Gene McDaniels |
| 25/83 | **Poison Arrow** <br> ABC |
| 7/59 | **Poison Ivy** <br> Coasters |
| 24/84 | **Politics Of Dancing** <br> Re-Flex |
| 8/69 | **Polk Salad Annie** <br> Tony Joe White |
| | **Pomp & Circumstance** . . . *see: Graduation Song* |
| 1/61 | **Pony Time** <br> Chubby Checker |
| 17/58 | **Poor Boy** <br> Royaltones |
| 24/57 | **Poor Boy** <br> Elvis Presley |
| 38/62 | **Poor Fool** <br> Ike & Tina Turner |
| 22/59 | **Poor Jenny** <br> Everly Brothers |

| POS/YR | RECORD TITLE/ARTIST |
|--------|---------------------|
| 1/58 | **Poor Little Fool**<br>Ricky Nelson |
| 27/63 | **Poor Little Rich Girl**<br>Steve Lawrence |
| 14/57 | **Poor Man's Roses (Or A Rich Man's Gold)**<br>Patti Page |
| 33/81 | **Poor Man's Son**<br>Survivor |
| 1/56<br>17/56<br>19/56 | **Poor People Of Paris**<br>Les Baxter & His Orchestra<br>Lawrence Welk<br>Russ Morgan & His Orchestra |
| 31/78 | **Poor Poor Pitiful Me**<br>Linda Ronstadt |
| 1/66 | **Poor Side Of Town**<br>Johnny Rivers |
| 35/82 | **Pop Goes The Movies**<br>Meco |
| 1/79 | **Pop Muzik**<br>M |
| 35/62 | **Pop Pop Pop-Pie**<br>Sherrys |
| 24/72 | **Pop That Thang**<br>Isley Brothers |
| 9/72 | **Popcorn**<br>Hot Butter |
| 30/69 | **Popcorn, The**<br>James Brown |
| 14/55 | **Popcorn Song**<br>Cliffie Stone & His Orchestra |
| 10/62 | **Popeye The Hitchhiker**<br>Chubby Checker |
| 21/66 | **Popsicle**<br>Jan & Dean |
| 3/64 | **Popsicles And Icicles**<br>Murmaids |
| 20/56 | **Port Au Prince**<br>Nelson Riddle & His Orchestra |
| 9/61<br>36/67 | **Portrait Of My Love**<br>Steve Lawrence<br>Tokens |
| 19/56 | **Portuguese Washerwomen**<br>Joe "Fingers" Carr |
|  | **Poseidon Adventure**...see: *Morning After* |

| POS/YR | RECORD TITLE/ARTIST |
|--------|---------------------|
| 7/65 | **Positively 4th Street**<br>Bob Dylan |
| 24/78 | **Power Of Gold**<br>Dan Fogelberg/Tim Weisberg |
| 11/72 | **Power Of Love**<br>Joe Simon |
| 11/71 | **Power To The People**<br>John Lennon |
| 3/72 | **Precious And Few**<br>Climax |
| 19/79 | **Precious Love**<br>Bob Welch |
| 30/71 | **Precious, Precious**<br>Jackie Moore |
| 22/81 | **Precious To Me**<br>Phil Seymour |
| 20/82 | **Pressure**<br>Billy Joel |
| 15/67 | **Pretty Ballerina**<br>Left Banke |
| 9/60 | **Pretty Blue Eyes**<br>Steve Lawrence |
| 29/66 | **Pretty Flamingo**<br>Manfred Mann |
| 39/79 | **Pretty Girls**<br>Melissa Manchester |
| 36/59 | **Pretty Girls Everywhere**<br>Eugene Church & The Fellows |
| 7/61 | **Pretty Little Angel Eyes**<br>Curtis Lee |
| 25/65 | **Pretty Little Baby**<br>Marvin Gaye |
| 15/64 | **Pretty Paper**<br>Roy Orbison |
| 10/63 | **Pride And Joy**<br>Marvin Gaye |
| 34/84 | **Prime Time**<br>Alan Parsons Project |
| 8/59 | **Primrose Lane**<br>Jerry Wallace |
| 30/61 | **Princess**<br>Frank Gari |

| POS/YR | RECORD TITLE/ARTIST |
|---|---|
| 37/65 | **Princess In Rags**<br>Gene Pitney |
| 20/56 | **Priscilla**<br>Eddie Cooley & The Dimples |
| | **(Prisoner)**...see: Love Theme From "Eyes Of Laura Mars" |
| 18/63 | **Prisoner Of Love**<br>James Brown |
| 27/78 | **Prisoner Of Your Love**<br>Player |
| 1/81 | **Private Eyes**<br>Daryl Hall & John Oates |
| 2/58 | **Problems**<br>Everly Brothers |
| 17/58 | **Promise Me, Love**<br>Andy Williams |
| 14/74 | **Promised Land**<br>Elvis Presley |
| 9/79 | **Promises**<br>Eric Clapton |
| 38/81 | **Promises In The Dark**<br>Pat Benatar |
| 11/83 | **Promises, Promises**<br>Naked Eyes |
| 19/68 | **Promises, Promises**<br>Dionne Warwick |
| 29/63 | **Proud**<br>Johnny Crawford |
| 2/69<br>4/71 | **Proud Mary**<br>Creedence Clearwater Revival<br>Ike & Tina Turner |
| 22/75 | **Proud One**<br>Osmonds |
| | **Proud Ones**...see: Theme From |
| 33/78 | **Prove It All Night**<br>Bruce Springsteen |
| 7/70 | **Psychedelic Shack**<br>Temptations |
| 5/66 | **Psychotic Reaction**<br>Count Five |
| 31/67 | **Pucker Up Buttercup**<br>Jr. Walker & The All Stars |
| 2/63 | **Puff The Magic Dragon**<br>Peter, Paul & Mary |

| POS/YR | RECORD TITLE/ARTIST |
|---|---|
| 20/62 | **Punish Her**<br>Bobby Vee |
| 24/70<br>26/71 | **Puppet Man**<br>5th Dimension<br>Tom Jones |
| 14/65 | **Puppet On A String**<br>Elvis Presley |
| 2/60<br>3/72 | **Puppy Love**<br>Paul Anka<br>Donny Osmond |
| 38/64 | **Puppy Love**<br>Barbara Lewis |
| 1/58 | **Purple People Eater**<br>Sheb Wooley |
| 2/84 | **Purple Rain**<br>Prince |
| 27/62 | **Push And Kick**<br>Mark Valentino |
| 36/67 | **Pushin' Too Hard**<br>Seeds |
| 25/63 | **Pushover**<br>Etta James |
| 17/58 | **Pussy Cat**<br>Ames Brothers |
| 8/58 | **Put A Light In The Window**<br>Four Lads |
| 4/69 | **Put A Little Love In Your Heart**<br>Jackie DeShannon |
| 32/58 | **Put A Ring On My Finger**<br>Les Paul & Mary Ford |
| 40/83 | **Put It In A Magazine**<br>Sonny Charles |
| 2/71 | **Put Your Hand In The Hand**<br>Ocean |
| 10/74 | **Put Your Hands Together**<br>O'Jays |
| 2/59 | **Put Your Head On My Shoulder**<br>Paul Anka |
| 4/83 | **Puttin' On The Ritz**<br>Taco |

| POS/YR | RECORD TITLE/ARTIST |
|---|---|

# Q

| POS/YR | RECORD TITLE/ARTIST |
|---|---|
| 1/61 | **Quarter To Three**<br>Gary "U.S." Bonds |
| 2/56 | **Que Sera, Sera (Whatever Will Be, Will Be)**<br>Doris Day |
| 2/81 | **Queen Of Hearts**<br>Juice Newton |
| 40/76 | **Queen Of My Soul**<br>Average White Band |
| 34/83 | **Queen Of The Broken Hearts**<br>Loverboy |
| 9/58 | **Queen Of The Hop**<br>Bobby Darin |
| 12/65 | **Queen Of The House**<br>Jody Miller<br>*(also see: King Of The Road)* |
| 39/57 | **Queen Of The Senior Prom**<br>Mills Brothers |
| 13/69 | **Quentin's Theme**<br>Charles Randolph Grean Sounde |
| 19/60 | **Question**<br>Lloyd Price |
| 21/70 | **Question**<br>Moody Blues |
| 37/68 | **Question Of Temperature**<br>Balloon Farm |
| 24/71 | **Questions 67 And 68**<br>Chicago |
| 25/68 | **Quick Joey Small (Run Joey Run)**<br>Kasenetz-Katz Singing Orchestral Circus |
| 8/64 | **Quicksand**<br>Martha & The Vandellas |
| 4/59 | **Quiet Village**<br>Martin Denny |
| 27/61 | **Quite A Party**<br>Fireballs |

# R

| POS/YR | RECORD TITLE/ARTIST |
|---|---|
| 15/65 | **Race Is On**<br>Jack Jones |
| 13/74 | **Radar Love**<br>Golden Earring |
| 16/84 | **Radio Ga-Ga**<br>Queen |
| 1/64 | **Rag Doll**<br>Four Seasons |
| F/71 | **Rags To Riches**<br>Elvis Presley |
| 16/59 | **Ragtime Cowboy Joe**<br>Chipmunks |
| 23/66 | **Rain**<br>Beatles |
| 19/71 | **Rain Dance**<br>Guess Who |
| 10/66 | **Rain On The Roof**<br>Lovin' Spoonful |
| 12/62 | **Rain Rain Go Away**<br>Bobby Vinton |
| 2/67 | **Rain, The Park & Other Things**<br>Cowsills |
| 4/57 | **Rainbow**<br>Russ Hamilton |
| 25/79 | **Rainbow Connection**<br>Kermit |
| 2/61 | **Raindrops**<br>Dee Clark |
| 1/70 | **Raindrops Keep Fallin' On My Head**<br>B.J. Thomas |
| 34/61 | **Rainin' In My Heart**<br>Slim Harpo |
| 31/66 | **Rains Came**<br>Sir Douglas Quintet |
| 26/75 | **Rainy Day People**<br>Gordon Lightfoot |
| 2/66 | **Rainy Day Women #12 & 35**<br>Bob Dylan |

| POS/YR | RECORD TITLE/ARTIST |
|--------|---------------------|
| 2/71 | **Rainy Days And Mondays** <br> Carpenters |
| 4/70 | **Rainy Night In Georgia** <br> Brook Benton |
| 29/61 | **Ram-Bunk-Shush** <br> Ventures |
| 21/61 | **Rama Lama Ding Dong** <br> Edsels |
| 17/69 | **Ramblin' Gamblin' Man** <br> Bob Seger |
| 2/73 | **Ramblin' Man** <br> Allman Brothers Band |
| 2/62 | **Ramblin' Rose** <br> Nat King Cole |
| 27/58 | **Ramrod** <br> Duane Eddy |
| 2/70 | **Rapper, The** <br> Jaggerz |
| 36/80 | **Rapper's Delight** <br> Sugarhill Gang |
| 1/81 | **Rapture** <br> Blondie |
| 2/57 <br> 4/57 <br> 10/57 | **Raunchy** <br> Bill Justis <br> Ernie Freeman <br> Billy Vaughn & His Orchestra |
| 37/58 | **Rave On** <br> Buddy Holly |
| 23/59 | **Raw-Hide** <br> Link Wray & His Ray Men |
| 24/69 | **Ray Of Hope** <br> Rascals |
| 15/55 | **Razzle-Dazzle** <br> Bill Haley & His Comets |
| 20/70 | **Reach Out And Touch (Somebody's Hand)** <br> Diana Ross |
| 20/64 | **Reach Out For Me** <br> Dionne Warwick |
| 1/66 <br> 29/71 | **Reach Out I'll Be There** <br> Four Tops <br> Diana Ross |
| 10/68 | **Reach Out Of The Darkness** <br> Friend And Lover |

| POS/YR | RECORD TITLE/ARTIST |
|--------|---------------------|
| 18/84 | **Read 'Em And Weep** <br> Barry Manilow |
| 26/75 | **Ready** <br> Cat Stevens |
| 35/69 | **Ready Or Not Here I Come (Can't Hide From Love)** <br> Delfonics |
| 11/78 | **Ready To Take A Chance Again** <br> Barry Manilow |
| 5/80 | **Real Love** <br> Doobie Brothers |
| 16/81 | **Really Wanna Know You** <br> Gary Wright |
| | **Reaper**...see: (Don't Fear) The |
| 6/58 | **Rebel-'Rouser** <br> Duane Eddy |
| 28/69 | **Reconsider Me** <br> Johnny Adams |
| 37/66 | **Recovery** <br> Fontella Bass |
| 34/84 | **Red Red Wine** <br> UB40 |
| 5/59 | **Red River Rock** <br> Johnny & The Hurricanes |
| 37/59 | **Red River Rose** <br> Ames Brothers |
| 10/65 <br> 11/65 <br> 23/65 | **Red Roses For A Blue Lady** <br> Vic Dana <br> Bert Kaempfert & His Orchestra <br> Wayne Newton |
| 2/66 | **Red Rubber Ball** <br> Cyrkle |
| 36/60 <br> 35/63 | **Red Sails In The Sunset** <br> Platters <br> Fats Domino |
| 23/65 <br> 27/73 | **Reelin' And Rockin'** <br> Dave Clark Five <br> Chuck Berry |
| 11/73 | **Reeling In The Years** <br> Steely Dan |
| 2/67 | **Reflections** <br> Supremes |
| 10/70 | **Reflections Of My Life** <br> Marmalade |

| POS/YR | RECORD TITLE/ARTIST |
|--------|---------------------|
| 1/84 | **Reflex, The**<br>Duran Duran |
| 15/80 | **Refugee**<br>Tom Petty & The Heartbreakers |
| 39/73 | **Relay, The**<br>Who |
| 8/62<br>4/67 | **Release Me**<br>Little Esther Phillips<br>Engelbert Humperdinck |
| 39/63 | **Remember Diana**<br>Paul Anka |
| 16/71 | **Remember Me**<br>Diana Ross |
| 26/64 | **Remember Me**<br>Rita Pavone |
| 32/65 | **(Remember Me) I'm The One Who Loves You**<br>Dean Martin |
| 33/77 | **(Remember The Days Of The) Old Schoolyard**<br>Cat Stevens |
| 36/84 | **Remember The Nights**<br>Motels |
| 24/63 | **Remember Then**<br>Earls |
| 5/64 | **Remember (Walkin' In The Sand)**<br>Shangri-Las |
| 25/75 | **Remember What I Told You To Forget**<br>Tavares |
| 6/57 | **Remember You're Mine**<br>Pat Boone |
| 3/78 | **Reminiscing**<br>Little River Band |
| 26/75 | **Rendezvous**<br>Hudson Brothers |
| 16/79 | **Renegade**<br>Styx |
| 39/76 | **Renegade**<br>Michael Murphey |
| 4/65 | **Rescue Me**<br>Fontella Bass |
| 35/65<br>1/67 | **Respect**<br>Otis Redding<br>Aretha Franklin |

| POS/YR | RECORD TITLE/ARTIST |
|--------|---------------------|
| 12/71 | **Respect Yourself**<br>Staple Singers |
| 15/66 | **Respectable**<br>Outsiders |
| F/71<br>40/71 | **Resurrection Shuffle**<br>Tom Jones<br>Ashton, Gardner & Dyke |
| 15/67 | **Return Of The Red Baron**<br>Royal Guardsmen |
| 4/58 | **Return To Me**<br>Dean Martin |
| 2/62 | **Return To Sender**<br>Elvis Presley |
|  | **Reuben**...see: *Ruben* |
| 1/79 | **Reunited**<br>Peaches & Herb |
| 25/59 | **Reveille Rock**<br>Johnny & The Hurricanes |
| 15/62 | **Revenge**<br>Brook Benton |
| 8/63 | **Reverend Mr. Black**<br>Kingston Trio |
| 12/68 | **Revolution**<br>Beatles |
| 16/66 | **Rhapsody In The Rain**<br>Lou Christie |
| 11/76 | **Rhiannon (Will You Ever Win)**<br>Fleetwood Mac |
| 1/75 | **Rhinestone Cowboy**<br>Glen Campbell |
| 24/64 | **Rhythm**<br>Major Lance |
| 3/63 | **Rhythm Of The Rain**<br>Cascades |
| 1/77 | **Rich Girl**<br>Daryl Hall & John Oates |
| 5/62 | **Ride!**<br>Dee Dee Sharp |
| 25/65 | **Ride Away**<br>Roy Orbison |
| 4/70 | **Ride Captain Ride**<br>Blues Image |

| POS/YR | RECORD TITLE/ARTIST |
|---|---|
| 23/75 | **Ride 'Em Cowboy**<br>Paul Davis |
| 2/80 | **Ride Like The Wind**<br>Christopher Cross |
| 37/67 | **Ride, Ride, Ride**<br>Brenda Lee |
| 16/64 | **Ride The Wild Surf**<br>Jan & Dean |
| 28/65 | **Ride Your Pony**<br>Lee Dorsey |
| | **Riders In The Sky**...*see:Ghost* |
| 14/71 | **Riders On The Storm**<br>Doors |
| 2/76 | **Right Back Where We Started From**<br>Maxine Nightingale |
| 29/84 | **Right By Your Side**<br>Eurythmics |
| 12/78 | **Right Down The Line**<br>Gerry Rafferty |
| 23/71 | **Right On The Tip Of My Tongue**<br>Brenda & The Tabulations |
| 29/61<br>14/64 | **Right Or Wrong**<br>Wanda Jackson<br>Ronnie Dove |
| 9/73 | **Right Place Wrong Time**<br>Dr. John |
| 17/73 | **Right Thing To Do**<br>Carly Simon |
| 6/77 | **Right Time Of The Night**<br>Jennifer Warnes |
| 4/74 | **Rikki Don't Lose That Number**<br>Steely Dan |
| 32/59 | **Ring-A-Ling-A-Lario**<br>Jimmie Rodgers |
| 33/65 | **Ring Dang Doo**<br>Sam The Sham & The Pharaohs |
| 1/79 | **Ring My Bell**<br>Anita Ward |
| 17/63 | **Ring Of Fire**<br>Johnny Cash |
| 31/72 | **Ring The Living Bell**<br>Melanie |
| 1/64 | **Ringo**<br>Lorne Greene |

| POS/YR | RECORD TITLE/ARTIST |
|---|---|
| 17/71 | **Rings**<br>Cymarron |
| 10/62 | **Rinky Dink**<br>Dave "Baby" Cortez |
| 14/83 | **Rio**<br>Duran Duran |
| 17/56<br>25/56 | **Rip It Up**<br>Little Richard<br>Bill Haley & His Comets |
| 36/64 | **Rip Van Winkle**<br>Devotions |
| 1/79 | **Rise**<br>Herb Alpert |
| 14/71 | **River Deep - Mountain High**<br>Supremes & Four Tops |
| 31/69 | **River Is Wide**<br>Grass Roots |
| | **River Kwai March**...*see: March From* |
| 33/74 | **River's Risin'**<br>Edgar Winter Group |
| 30/78 | **Rivers Of Babylon**<br>Boney M |
| 25/59 | **Robbin' The Cradle**<br>Tony Bellus |
| 16/56 | **R-O-C-K**<br>Bill Haley & His Comets |
| 10/57 | **Rock-A-Billy**<br>Guy Mitchell |
| 10/56<br>37/61 | **Rock-A-Bye Your Baby With A Dixie Melody**<br>Jerry Lewis<br>Aretha Franklin |
| 23/62 | **Rock-A-Hula Baby**<br>Elvis Presley |
| 7/72 | **Rock And Roll**<br>Gary Glitter |
| | **Rock And Roll**...*also see: Rock 'N' Roll, & Rockin' Roll* |
| 12/76 | **Rock And Roll All Nite**<br>Kiss |
| 32/81 | **Rock And Roll Dreams Come Through**<br>Jim Steinman |
| 3/74 | **Rock And Roll Heaven**<br>Righteous Brothers |

| POS/YR | RECORD TITLE/ARTIST |
|--------|---------------------|
| 23/74 | **Rock And Roll, Hoochie Koo** <br> Rick Derringer |
| 19/58 | **Rock And Roll Is Here To Stay** <br> Danny & The Juniors |
| 28/76 | **Rock And Roll Love Letter** <br> Bay City Rollers |
| 15/72 | **Rock And Roll Lullaby** <br> B.J. Thomas |
| 8/57 <br> 5/76 | **Rock And Roll Music** <br> Chuck Berry <br> Beach Boys |
| 1/56 | **Rock And Roll Waltz** <br> Kay Starr |
| 1/55 <br> 39/74 | **Rock Around The Clock** <br> Bill Haley & His Comets <br> Bill Haley & His Comets |
| 8/56 | **Rock Island Line** <br> Lonnie Donegan & His Skiffle Group |
| 13/55 | **Rock Love** <br> Fontane Sisters |
| 10/69 | **Rock Me** <br> Steppenwolf |
| 34/64 | **Rock Me Baby** <br> B.B. King |
| 38/72 | **Rock Me Baby** <br> David Cassidy |
| 1/74 | **Rock Me Gently** <br> Andy Kim |
| 15/84 | **Rock Me Tonite** <br> Billy Squier |
| | **Rock 'N' Roll** . . . *also see: Rock And Roll, &* <br> *Rockin' Roll* |
| 13/79 | **Rock 'N' Roll Fantasy** <br> Bad Company |
| 30/78 | **Rock 'N' Roll Fantasy** <br> Kinks |
| 15/75 | **Rock 'N' Roll (I Gave You The Best** <br> **Years Of My Life)** <br> Mac Davis |
| 19/83 | **Rock 'N' Roll Is King** <br> Electric Light Orchestra |
| 29/72 | **Rock 'N' Roll Soul** <br> Grand Funk Railroad |
| 16/83 | **Rock Of Ages** <br> Def Leppard |

| POS/YR | RECORD TITLE/ARTIST |
|--------|---------------------|
| 5/74 | **Rock On** <br> David Essex |
| 36/56 | **Rock Right** <br> Georgia Gibbs |
| 9/71 | **Rock Steady** <br> Aretha Franklin |
| 1/74 | **Rock The Boat** <br> Hues Corporation |
| 8/83 | **Rock The Casbah** <br> Clash |
| 9/82 | **Rock This Town** <br> Stray Cats |
| 1/80 | **Rock With You** <br> Michael Jackson |
| 25/84 | **Rock You Like A Hurricane** <br> Scorpions |
| 1/74 | **Rock Your Baby** <br> George McCrae |
| 17/57 | **Rock Your Little Baby To Sleep** <br> Buddy Knox |
| 38/59 | **Rocka-Conga** <br> Applejacks |
| 6/72 | **Rocket Man** <br> Elton John |
| 39/78 | **Rocket Ride** <br> Kiss |
| 10/75 | **Rockford Files** <br> Mike Post |
| 27/75 | **Rockin' All Over The World** <br> John Fogerty |
| 14/60 | **Rockin' Around The Christmas Tree** <br> Brenda Lee |
| 9/75 | **Rockin' Chair** <br> Gwen McCrae |
| 7/60 | **Rockin' Good Way (To Mess Around** <br> **And Fall In Love)** <br> Brook Benton & Dinah Washington |
| 22/60 | **Rockin' Little Angel** <br> Ray Smith |
| 1/76 | **Rockin' Me** <br> Steve Miller Band |
| 6/73 | **Rockin' Pneumonia And The Boogie** <br> **Woogie Flu** <br> Johnny Rivers |

| POS/YR | RECORD TITLE/ARTIST |
|---|---|
| | **Rockin' Robin** |
| 2/58 | Bobby Day |
| 2/72 | Michael Jackson |
| | **Rockin' Roll**...also see: Rock 'N' Roll, & Rock And Roll |
| | **Rockin' Roll Baby** |
| 14/73 | Stylistics |
| | **Rockin' Soul** |
| 18/74 | Hues Corporation |
| | **Rocky** |
| 9/75 | Austin Roberts |
| | **Rocky Mountain High** |
| 9/73 | John Denver |
| | **Rocky Mountain Way** |
| 23/73 | Joe Walsh |
| | **Rocky, Theme From**...see: Gonna Fly Now |
| | **Rolene** |
| 30/79 | Moon Martin |
| | **Roll Me Away** |
| 27/83 | Bob Seger |
| | **Roll On Down The Highway** |
| 14/75 | Bachman-Turner Overdrive |
| | **Roll Over Beethoven** |
| 29/56 | Chuck Berry |
| | **Roller** |
| 34/79 | April Wine |
| | **Rollin' Stone** |
| 13/55 | Fontane Sisters |
| | **Romancing The Stone** |
| 26/84 | Eddy Grant |
| | **Romeo & Juliet**...see: Love Theme & (Just Like) |
| | **Romeo's Tune** |
| 11/80 | Steve Forbert |
| | **Ronnie** |
| 6/64 | Four Seasons |
| | **Rosanna** |
| 2/82 | Toto |
| | **Rose, The** |
| 3/80 | Bette Midler |
| | **Rose And A Baby Ruth** |
| 6/56 | George Hamilton IV |

| POS/YR | RECORD TITLE/ARTIST |
|---|---|
| | **Rose Garden** |
| 3/71 | Lynn Anderson |
| | **Roses And Roses**...see: And Roses |
| | **Roses Are Red (My Love)** |
| 1/62 | Bobby Vinton |
| | **Rosie Lee** |
| 24/57 | Mello-Tones |
| | **Rotation** |
| 30/80 | Herb Alpert |
| | **Round And Round** |
| 1/57 | Perry Como |
| | **Round And Round** |
| 12/84 | Ratt |
| | **Round Every Corner** |
| 21/65 | Petula Clark |
| | **Roundabout** |
| 13/72 | Yes |
| | **Route 66 Theme** |
| 30/62 | Nelson Riddle & His Orchestra |
| | **Route 101** |
| 37/82 | Herb Alpert |
| | **Roxanne** |
| 32/79 | Police |
| | **Rub It In** |
| 16/74 | Billy "Crash" Craddock |
| | **Rubber Ball** |
| 6/61 | Bobby Vee |
| | **Rubber Biscuit** |
| 37/79 | Blues Brothers |
| | **Rubber Duckie** |
| 16/70 | Ernie |
| | **Rubberband Man** |
| 2/76 | Spinners |
| | **Ruben James** |
| 26/69 | Kenny Rogers & The First Edition |
| | **Ruby** |
| 28/60 | Ray Charles |
| | **Ruby Ann** |
| 18/62 | Marty Robbins |
| | **Ruby Baby** |
| 2/63 | Dion |
| 33/75 | Billy "Crash" Craddock |

| POS/YR | RECORD TITLE/ARTIST |
|---|---|
| 6/69 | **Ruby, Don't Take Your Love To Town**<br>Kenny Rogers & The First Edition |
| 30/60 | **Ruby Duby Du**<br>Tobin Mathews & Co. |
| | **Ruby Red Dress**...see: Leave Me Alone |
| 1/67 | **Ruby Tuesday**<br>Rolling Stones |
| 21/60 | **Rudolph The Red-Nosed Reindeer**<br>Chipmunks |
| 34/56 | **Rudy's Rock**<br>Bill Haley & His Comets |
| 16/58 | **Rumble**<br>Link Wray & His Ray Men |
| 12/62 | **Rumors**<br>Johnny Crawford |
| 6/69 | **Run Away Child, Running Wild**<br>Temptations |
| 12/65 | **Run, Baby Run (Back Into My Arms)**<br>Newbeats |
| 33/78 | **Run For Home**<br>Lindisfarne |
| 18/82 | **Run For The Roses**<br>Dan Fogelberg |
| 4/75 | **Run Joey Run**<br>David Geddes |
| 36/60 | **Run Red Run**<br>Coasters |
| 25/66 | **Run, Run, Look And See**<br>Brian Hyland |
| 27/72 | **Run Run Run**<br>Jo Jo Gunne |
| 20/84 | **Run Runaway**<br>Slade |
| 28/60 | **Run Samson Run**<br>Neil Sedaka |
| 2/61 | **Run To Him**<br>Bobby Vee |
| 16/72 | **Run To Me**<br>Bee Gees |
| 23/60 | **Runaround**<br>Fleetwoods |
| 28/61 | **Runaround**<br>Regents |

| POS/YR | RECORD TITLE/ARTIST |
|---|---|
| 1/61 | **Runaround Sue**<br>Dion |
| 13/78 | Leif Garrett |
| 1/61 | **Runaway**<br>Del Shannon |
| 12/78 | **Runaway**<br>Jefferson Starship |
| 39/84 | **Runaway**<br>Bon Jovi |
| 22/84 | **Runner**<br>Manfred Mann's Earth Band |
| 23/72 | **Runnin' Away**<br>Sly & The Family Stone |
| 1/60 | **Running Bear**<br>Johnny Preston |
| 11/78 | **Running On Empty**<br>Jackson Browne |
| 1/61 | **Running Scared**<br>Roy Orbison |
| 7/84 | **Running With The Night**<br>Lionel Richie |
| 39/72 | **Runway, The**<br>Grass Roots |
| 33/65 | **Rusty Bells**<br>Brenda Lee |

# S

| POS/YR | RECORD TITLE/ARTIST |
|---|---|
| 15/75 | **S.O.S.**<br>Abba |
| | **S.W.A.T.**...see: Theme From |
| 39/66 | **S.Y.S.L.J.F.M. (The Letter Song)**<br>Joe Tex |
| 20/61 | **Sacred**<br>Castells |
| 1/79 | **Sad Eyes**<br>Robert John |
| 29/60 | **Sad Mood**<br>Sam Cooke |
| 5/61 | **Sad Movies (Make Me Cry)**<br>Sue Thompson |

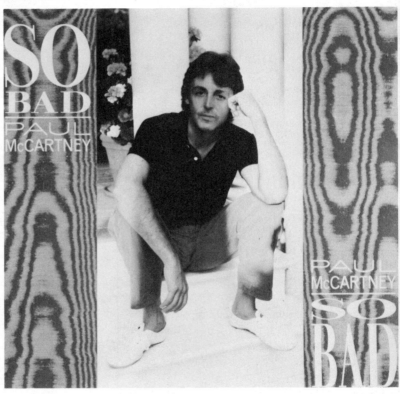

**Loverboy** are a market researcher's dream, blending the most appealing elements of pop and heavy metal into a surefire commercial alloy. Endless critical barbs aside, they're doing just fine, thank you.

**Lulu.** The former Marie Lawrie is best known for "To Sir With Love." In the early seventies, she recorded David Bowie's "The Man Who Sold the World" with Bowie himself producing. Weird, but not a hit.

**M,** also known as Robin Scott, was a more thoughtful musician than his only hit would indicate. He later recorded an engaging LP with the Yellow Magic Orchestra's synthesizer player Riuichi Sakamoto as proof.

**Paul McCartney's** solo career has been a remarkably varied if inconsistent affair, from politics ("Give Ireland Back to the Irish") to nursery rhymes ("Mary Had a Little Lamb"); from a mellow duet with Stevie Wonder ("Ebony and Ivory") to a hot one with Michael Jackson ("Say Say Say").

**The McGuire Sisters** and **Lawrence Welk.** The son of German immigrants, Welk never did like his bands to get too rowdy. In fact, young Harry James once failed an audition with Welk because he played too loud.

**Guy Mitchell** was born Al Cernik in Detroit. Winning an Arthur Godfrey talent competition in 1949, he went on to a decade of light pop hits, including "Singing the Blues" (featuring Ray Conniff) and "Heartaches by the Number."

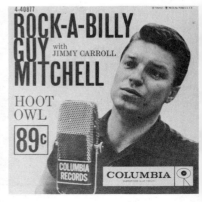

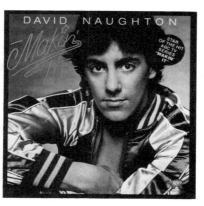

**Anne Murray** had to give up a job teaching physical education on Canada's Prince Edward Island to become a full-time singer. Hit records made the transition easier.

**David Naughton** has all the angles covered. He sang the theme of the Bill Murray movie *Meatballs,* danced up a storm in a Dr. Pepper commercial, and played a student turned monster in the horror movie *An American Werewolf in London.*

**Rick Nelson.** Name the *two* TV series Nelson starred in. The first, of course, was "The Adventures of Ozzie and Harriet." The second? "Malibu U," a 1967 variety series featuring host Rick as the "Dean of the Drop-Ins."

**Night Ranger** evolved from Rubicon, a funk band headed by Jerry Martini, ex-Sly and the Family Stone.

**Gilbert O'Sullivan** once performed in an art-school band with Richard Davies of Supertramp. He scored his hits under the tutelage of Gordon Mills, manager of Tom Jones and Englebert Humperdinck.

| POS/YR | RECORD TITLE/ARTIST |
|---|---|
| 27/65 | **Sad, Sad Girl**<br>Barbara Mason |
| 5/84 | **Sad Songs (Say So Much)**<br>Elton John |
| 14/75 | **Sad Sweet Dreamer**<br>Sweet Sensation |
| 3/83 | **Safety Dance**<br>Men Without Hats |
| 5/58 | **Sail Along Silvery Moon**<br>Billy Vaughn & His Orchestra |
| 4/79 | **Sail On**<br>Commodores |
| 1/80 | **Sailing**<br>Christopher Cross |
| 5/60 | **Sailor (Your Home Is The Sea)**<br>Lolita |
| | **Saint**...*see: St.* |
| | **Saints Rock 'N Roll**...*see: When The Saints Go Marchin' In* |
| 39/75 | **Sally G**<br>Paul McCartney |
| 2/63 | **Sally, Go 'Round The Roses**<br>Jaynetts |
| 36/83 | **Salt In My Tears**<br>Martin Briley |
| 20/77 | **Sam**<br>Olivia Newton-John |
| 9/81 | **Same Old Lang Syne**<br>Dan Fogelberg |
| 13/55 | **Same Old Saturday Night**<br>Frank Sinatra |
| 16/60 | **Same One**<br>Brook Benton |
| 8/61 | **San Antonio Rose**<br>Floyd Cramer |
| 9/67 | **San Franciscan Nights**<br>Animals |
| 4/67 | **San Francisco (Be Sure To Wear Flowers In Your Hair)**<br>Scott McKenzie |
| 23/55 | **Sand And The Sea**<br>Nat King Cole |
| 15/60 | **Sandy**<br>Larry Hall |

| POS/YR | RECORD TITLE/ARTIST |
|---|---|
| 21/63 | **Sandy**<br>Dion |
| 27/66 | **Sandy**<br>Ronny & The Daytonas |
| 32/57 | **Santa & The Satellite**<br>Buchanan & Goodman |
| 23/62 | **Santa Claus Is Coming To Town**<br>Four Seasons |
| 7/80 | **Sara**<br>Fleetwood Mac |
| 4/76 | **Sara Smile**<br>Daryl Hall & John Oates |
| 39/80 | **(Sartorial Eloquence) Don't Ya Wanna Play This Game No More?**<br>Elton John |
| 23/66 | **Satin Pillows**<br>Bobby Vinton |
| 28/73 | **Satin Sheets**<br>Jeanne Pruett |
| 22/75 | **Satin Soul**<br>Love Unlimited Orchestra |
| 39/66 | **Satisfied Mind**<br>Bobby Hebb |
| 3/72 | **Saturday In The Park**<br>Chicago |
| 28/71 | **Saturday Morning Confusion**<br>Bobby Russell |
| 1/76 | **Saturday Night**<br>Bay City Rollers |
| 29/63 | **Saturday Night**<br>New Christy Minstrels |
| 18/64 | **Saturday Night At The Movies**<br>Drifters |
| 27/75 | **Saturday Night Special**<br>Lynyrd Skynyrd |
| 34/79 | **Saturday Night, Sunday Morning**<br>Thelma Houston |
| 12/73 | **Saturday Night's Alright For Fighting**<br>Elton John |
| 21/77 | **Saturday Nite**<br>Earth, Wind & Fire |
| 35/79 | **Saturdaynight**<br>Herman Brood |

| POS/YR | RECORD TITLE/ARTIST |
|--------|---------------------|
| 25/81 | **Sausalito Summernight**<br>Diesel |
| 34/80 | **Savannah Nights**<br>Tom Johnston |
| 22/77 | **Save It For A Rainy Day**<br>Stephen Bishop |
| 10/64 | **Save It For Me**<br>Four Seasons |
| 27/70 | **Save The Country**<br>5th Dimension |
| 1/60<br>18/74 | **Save The Last Dance For Me**<br>Drifters<br>DeFranco Family featuring Tony DeFranco<br>*(also see: I'll Save The Last Dance)* |
| 2/65 | **Save Your Heart For Me**<br>Gary Lewis & The Playboys |
| 27/76 | **Save Your Kisses For Me**<br>Brotherhood Of Man |
| 37/61 | **Saved**<br>LaVern Baker |
| 20/83 | **Saved By Zero**<br>Fixx |
| 17/81 | **Say Goodbye To Hollywood**<br>Billy Joel |
| 3/73 | **Say, Has Anybody Seen My Sweet Gypsy Rose**<br>Dawn |
| 21/66 | **Say I Am (What I Am)**<br>Tommy James & The Shondells |
| 2/83 | **Say It Isn't So**<br>Daryl Hall & John Oates |
| 10/68 | **Say It Loud - I'm Black And I'm Proud**<br>James Brown |
| 20/59 | **Say Man**<br>Bo Diddley |
| 1/83 | **Say Say Say**<br>Paul McCartney & Michael Jackson |
| 22/65 | **Say Something Funny**<br>Patty Duke |
| 32/81 | **Say What**<br>Jesse Winchester |
| 40/64 | **Say You**<br>Ronnie Dove |

| POS/YR | RECORD TITLE/ARTIST |
|--------|---------------------|
| 11/76 | **Say You Love Me**<br>Fleetwood Mac |
| 20/81 | **Say You'll Be Mine**<br>Christopher Cross |
| 15/77 | **Say You'll Stay Until Tomorrow**<br>Tom Jones |
| 39/65 | **(Say) You're My Girl**<br>Roy Orbison |
| 11/68<br>16/68 | **Scarborough Fair**<br>Simon & Garfunkel<br>Sergio Mendes & Brasil '66 |
| 13/59 | **Scarlet Ribbons (For Her Hair)**<br>Browns |
| 33/75 | **School Boy Crush**<br>Average White Band |
| 3/57 | **School Day**<br>Chuck Berry |
| 28/61 | **School Is In**<br>Gary "U.S." Bonds |
| 5/61 | **School Is Out**<br>Gary "U.S." Bonds |
| 7/72 | **School's Out**<br>Alice Cooper |
| 6/72 | **Scorpio**<br>Dennis Coffey & The Detroit Guitar Band |
| 14/59 | **Sea Cruise**<br>Frankie Ford |
| 21/61 | **Sea Of Heartbreak**<br>Don Gibson |
| 2/59<br>33/82<br>3/85 | **Sea Of Love**<br>Phil Phillips with The Twilights<br>Del Shannon<br>Honeydrippers |
| 3/62<br>19/68<br>19/72 | **Sealed With A Kiss**<br>Brian Hyland<br>Gary Lewis & The Playboys<br>Bobby Vinton |
| 3/57 | **Searchin'**<br>Coasters |
| 27/66 | **Searching For My Love**<br>Bobby Moore & The Rhythm Aces |
| 1/74 | **Seasons In The Sun**<br>Terry Jacks |
| 38/69 | **Seattle**<br>Perry Como |

| POS/YR | RECORD TITLE/ARTIST |
|--------|---------------------|
| 34/74 | **Second Avenue**<br>Art Garfunkel |
| 40/56 | **Second Fiddle**<br>Kay Starr |
| 7/62 | **Second Hand Love**<br>Connie Francis |
| 32/66 | **Second Hand Rose**<br>Barbra Streisand |
| 8/80 | **Second Time Around**<br>Shalamar |
| 18/58 | **Secret, The**<br>Gordon MacRae |
| 3/66 | **Secret Agent Man**<br>Johnny Rivers |
| 29/66<br>20/75 | **Secret Love**<br>Billy Stewart<br>Freddy Fender |
| 3/58 | **Secretly**<br>Jimmie Rodgers |
| 35/68 | **Security**<br>Etta James |
| 28/80 | **Seduction**<br>James Last |
| 27/69 | **See**<br>Rascals |
| 12/70<br>29/73 | **See Me, Feel Me**<br>Who<br>New Seekers (medley) |
| 14/68 | **See Saw**<br>Aretha Franklin |
| 25/56 | **See Saw**<br>Moonglows |
| | **See See**...*see: C.C.* |
| 9/64 | **See The Funny Little Clown**<br>Bobby Goldsboro |
| 23/59<br>3/66 | **See You In September**<br>Tempos<br>Happenings |
| 6/56 | **See You Later, Alligator**<br>Bill Haley & His Comets |
| 4/84 | **Self Control**<br>Laura Branigan |
| 11/64 | **Selfish One**<br>Jackie Ross |

| POS/YR | RECORD TITLE/ARTIST |
|--------|---------------------|
| 6/57 | **Send For Me**<br>Nat King Cole |
| 23/83 | **Send Her My Love**<br>Journey |
| 36/75<br>19/77 | **Send In The Clowns**<br>Judy Collins<br>Judy Collins |
| 29/84 | **Send Me An Angel**<br>Real Life |
| 13/63 | **Send Me Some Lovin'**<br>Sam Cooke |
| 17/62<br>22/65 | **Send Me The Pillow You Dream On**<br>Johnny Tillotson<br>Dean Martin |
| 4/79 | **Send One Your Love**<br>Stevie Wonder |
| 8/78 | **Sentimental Lady**<br>Bob Welch |
| 20/73 | **Separate Ways**<br>Elvis Presley |
| 8/83 | **Separate Ways (Worlds Apart)**<br>Journey |
| 8/79 | **September**<br>Earth, Wind & Fire |
| 23/61 | **September In The Rain**<br>Dinah Washington |
| 17/80 | **September Morn'**<br>Neil Diamond |
| 23/80 | **Sequel**<br>Harry Chapin |
| 13/78 | **Serpentine Fire**<br>Earth, Wind & Fire |
| 23/65 | **Set Me Free**<br>Kinks |
| 27/80 | **Set Me Free**<br>Utopia |
| 33/66 | **7 And 7 Is**<br>Love |
| 21/81 | **Seven Bridges Road**<br>Eagles |
| 27/62 | **Seven Day Weekend**<br>Gary "U.S." Bonds |

| POS/YR | RECORD TITLE/ARTIST |
|---|---|
| | **Seven Days** |
| 17/56 | Dorothy Collins |
| 18/56 | Crew-Cuts |
| | **"7-11" (Mambo No. 5)** |
| 30/58 | Gone All Stars |
| | **Seven Little Girls Sitting In The Back Seat** |
| 9/59 | Paul Evans |
| | **7 Rooms Of Gloom** |
| 14/67 | Four Tops |
| | **Seven Year Ache** |
| 22/81 | Rosanne Cash |
| | **Seventh Son** |
| 7/65 | Johnny Rivers |
| | **Seventeen** |
| 3/55 | Fontane Sisters |
| 5/55 | Boyd Bennett & His Rockets |
| 18/55 | Rusty Draper |
| | **17** |
| 36/84 | Rick James |
| | **Sex Machine** |
| 15/70 | James Brown |
| | **Sexual Healing** |
| 3/83 | Marvin Gaye |
| | **Sexy Eyes** |
| 5/80 | Dr. Hook |
| | **Sexy Girl** |
| 20/84 | Glenn Frey |
| | **Sexy Mama** |
| 17/74 | Moments |
| | **Sha-La-La** |
| 12/65 | Manfred Mann |
| | **Sha-La-La (Make Me Happy)** |
| 7/74 | Al Green |
| | **Shadow Dancing** |
| 1/78 | Andy Gibb |
| | **Shadows In The Moonlight** |
| 25/79 | Anne Murray |
| | **Shadows Of The Night** |
| 13/82 | Pat Benatar |
| | **Shadrack** |
| 19/62 | Brook Benton |
| | **Shaft**...see: *Theme From* |
| | **Shaggy Dog** |
| 38/64 | Mickey Lee Lane |

| POS/YR | RECORD TITLE/ARTIST |
|---|---|
| | **Shake** |
| 7/65 | Sam Cooke |
| | **Shake A Tail Feather** |
| 25/67 | James & Bobby Purify |
| | **Shake And Fingerpop** |
| 29/65 | Jr. Walker & The All Stars |
| | **Shake It** |
| 13/79 | Ian Matthews |
| | **Shake It Up** |
| 4/82 | Cars |
| | **Shake Me, Wake Me (When It's Over)** |
| 18/66 | Four Tops |
| | **Shake, Rattle & Roll** |
| 31/67 | Arthur Conley |
| | **Shake! Shake! Shake!** |
| 33/63 | Jackie Wilson |
| | **(Shake, Shake, Shake) Shake Your Booty** |
| 1/76 | KC & The Sunshine Band |
| | **Shake Your Body (Down To The Ground)** |
| 7/79 | Jacksons |
| | **Shake Your Groove Thing** |
| 5/79 | Peaches & Herb |
| | **Shake Your Rump To The Funk** |
| 23/77 | Bar-Kays |
| | **Shakedown Cruise** |
| 31/79 | Jay Ferguson |
| | **Shakey Ground** |
| 26/75 | Temptations |
| | **Shakin' All Over** |
| 22/65 | Guess Who |
| | **Shambala** |
| 3/73 | Three Dog Night |
| | **Shame** |
| 9/78 | Evelyn "Champagne" King |
| | **Shame On Me** |
| 23/62 | Bobby Bare |
| | **Shame On The Moon** |
| 2/83 | Bob Seger |
| | **Shame, Shame** |
| 29/68 | Magic Lanterns |
| | **Shame, Shame, Shame** |
| 12/75 | Shirley and Company |

| POS/YR | RECORD TITLE/ARTIST |
|--------|---------------------|
| 31/82 | **Shanghai Breezes**<br>John Denver |
| 11/57<br>15/64<br>27/64 | **Shangri-La**<br>Four Coins<br>Robert Maxwell His Harp & Orchestra<br>Vic Dana |
| 6/76 | **Shannon**<br>Henry Gross |
| 22/68 | **Shape Of Things To Come**<br>Max Frost & The Troopers |
| 11/66 | **Shapes Of Things**<br>Yardbirds |
| 10/70 | **Share The Land**<br>Guess Who |
| 13/69<br>14/81 | **Share Your Love With Me**<br>Aretha Franklin<br>Kenny Rogers |
| 6/79 | **Sharing The Night Together**<br>Dr. Hook |
| 15/62 | **Sharing You**<br>Bobby Vee |
| 31/79 | **Shattered**<br>Rolling Stones |
| 30/75 | **Shaving Cream**<br>Benny Bell |
| 23/70 | **She**<br>Tommy James & The Shondells |
| 5/79 | **She Believes In Me**<br>Kenny Rogers |
| 33/70 | **She Belongs To Me**<br>Ricky Nelson |
| 5/83 | **She Blinded Me With Science**<br>Thomas Dolby |
| 3/84 | **She Bop**<br>Cyndi Lauper |
| 30/70 | **She Came In Through The Bathroom Window**<br>Joe Cocker |
| 19/62 | **She Can't Find Her Keys**<br>Paul Petersen |
| 5/62 | **She Cried**<br>Jay & The Americans |
| 23/77 | **She Did It**<br>Eric Carmen |

| POS/YR | RECORD TITLE/ARTIST |
|--------|---------------------|
| 27/67 | **She Is Still A Mystery**<br>Lovin' Spoonful |
| 1/64 | **She Loves You**<br>Beatles |
| 18/59 | **She Say (Oom Dooby Doom)**<br>Diamonds |
| 31/64<br>40/66 | **She Understands Me**<br>Johnny Tillotson<br>Bobby Vinton (Dum-De-Da) |
| 27/58 | **She Was Only Seventeen (He Was One Year More)**<br>Marty Robbins |
| 3/83 | **She Works Hard For The Money**<br>Donna Summer |
| 3/67 | **She'd Rather Be With Me**<br>Turtles |
| 22/81 | **She's A Bad Mama Jama (She's Built, She's Stacked)**<br>Carl Carlton |
| 10/83 | **She's A Beauty**<br>Tubes |
| 5/63 | **She's A Fool**<br>Lesley Gore |
| 16/68 | **She's A Heartbreaker**<br>Gene Pitney |
| 2/71 | **She's A Lady**<br>Tom Jones |
| 25/68 | **She's A Rainbow**<br>Rolling Stones |
| 4/64 | **She's A Woman**<br>Beatles |
| 13/65 | **She's About A Mover**<br>Sir Douglas Quintet |
| 39/71 | **She's All I Got**<br>Freddie North |
| 17/78 | **She's Always A Woman**<br>Billy Joel |
| 18/62 | **She's Everything (I Wanted You To Be)**<br>Ral Donner |
| 7/76 | **She's Gone**<br>Daryl Hall & John Oates |
| 23/82 | **She's Got A Way**<br>Billy Joel |

| POS/YR | RECORD TITLE/ARTIST |
|--------|---------------------|
| 14/62 | **She's Got You**<br>Patsy Cline |
| 3/66 | **She's Just My Style**<br>Gary Lewis & The Playboys |
| 15/68 | **She's Lookin' Good**<br>Wilson Pickett |
| 21/84 | **She's Mine**<br>Steve Perry |
| 14/67 | **She's My Girl**<br>Turtles |
| 38/58 | **She's Neat**<br>Dale Wright |
| 11/71 | **She's Not Just Another Woman**<br>8th Day |
| 2/64<br>27/77 | **She's Not There**<br>Zombies<br>Santana |
| 5/62 | **She's Not You**<br>Elvis Presley |
| 10/80 | **She's Out Of My Life**<br>Michael Jackson |
| 5/83 | **(She's) Sexy + 17**<br>Stray Cats |
| 26/80 | **She's So Cold**<br>Rolling Stones |
| 33/64 | **She's The One**<br>Chartbusters |
| 1/62 | **Sheila**<br>Tommy Roe |
| 17/64 | **Shelter Of Your Arms**<br>Sammy Davis, Jr. |
| 1/62 | **Sherry**<br>Four Seasons |
| 3/55<br>5/55 | **Shifting, Whispering Sands**<br>Rusty Draper<br>Billy Vaughn & His Orchestra |
| 24/70 | **Shilo**<br>Neil Diamond |
| 37/60 | **Shimmy Shimmy**<br>Bobby Freeman |
| 24/60 | **Shimmy, Shimmy, Ko-Ko-Bop**<br>Little Anthony & The Imperials |
| 8/79 | **Shine A Little Love**<br>Electric Light Orchestra |

| POS/YR | RECORD TITLE/ARTIST |
|--------|---------------------|
| 40/81 | **Shine On**<br>L.T.D. |
| 37/84 | **Shine Shine**<br>Barry Gibb |
| 11/74 | **Shinin' On**<br>Grand Funk Railroad |
| 1/75 | **Shining Star**<br>Earth, Wind & Fire |
| 5/80 | **Shining Star**<br>Manhattans |
| 9/79 | **Ships**<br>Barry Manilow |
| 10/57 | **Shish-Kebab**<br>Ralph Marterie & His Orchestra |
| 29/83 | **Shock The Monkey**<br>Peter Gabriel |
| 18/75 | **Shoeshine Boy**<br>Eddie Kendricks |
| 9/68 | **Shoo-Be-Doo-Be-Doo-Da-Day**<br>Stevie Wonder<br>*(also see: Shu)* |
| 6/64 | **Shoop Shoop Song (It's In His Kiss)**<br>Betty Everett |
| 31/68 | **Shoot'em Up, Baby**<br>Andy Kim |
| 2/61<br>4/76 | **Shop Around**<br>Miracles<br>Captain & Tennille |
| 5/57 | **Short Fat Fannie**<br>Larry Williams |
| 2/78 | **Short People**<br>Randy Newman |
| 3/58 | **Short Shorts**<br>Royal Teens |
| 4/65 | **Shotgun**<br>Jr. Walker & The All Stars |
| 13/82 | **Should I Do It**<br>Pointer Sisters |
| 19/80 | **Should've Never Let You Go**<br>Neil & Dara Sedaka |
| 6/62 | **Shout**<br>Joey Dee & The Starliters |
| 31/76 | **Shout It Out Loud**<br>Kiss |

| POS/YR | RECORD TITLE/ARTIST |
|---|---|
| 6/62 | **Shout! Shout! (Knock Yourself Out)** <br> Ernie Maresca |
| 1/74 | **Show And Tell** <br> Al Wilson |
| 28/84 | **Show Me** <br> Pretenders |
| 35/67 | **Show Me** <br> Joe Tex |
| 6/76 | **Show Me The Way** <br> Peter Frampton |
| 4/74 | **Show Must Go On** <br> Three Dog Night |
| 28/77 | **Show You The Way To Go** <br> Jacksons |
| 22/76 | **Shower The People** <br> James Taylor |
| 38/75 | **(Shu-Doo-Pa-Poo-Poop) Love Being Your Fool** <br> Travis Wammack |
| 32/61 | **Shu Rah** <br> Fats Domino |
| 23/63 | **Shut Down** <br> Beach Boys |
| 24/63 | **Shutters And Boards** <br> Jerry Wallace |
| 22/58 | **Sick And Tired** <br> Fats Domino |
| 8/74 | **Sideshow** <br> Blue Magic |
| 25/64 | **Sidewalk Surfin** <br> Jan & Dean |
| 32/84 | **Sign Of Fire** <br> Fixx |
| 11/66 | **Sign Of The Times** <br> Petula Clark |
| 18/77 | **Signed, Sealed, Delivered (I'm Yours)** <br> Peter Frampton |
| 3/70 | **Signed, Sealed, Delivered I'm Yours** <br> Stevie Wonder |
| 3/71 | **Signs** <br> Five Man Electrical Band |
| 11/67 | **Silence Is Golden** <br> Tremeloes |

| POS/YR | RECORD TITLE/ARTIST |
|---|---|
| | **Silhouettes** |
| 3/57 | Rays |
| 10/57 | Diamonds |
| 5/65 | Herman's Hermits |
| 1/76 | **Silly Love Songs** <br> Paul McCartney |
| 25/70 | **Silver Bird** <br> Mark Lindsay |
| 20/55 | **Silver Dollar** <br> Teresa Brewer |
| 38/76 | **Silver Star** <br> Four Seasons |
| 20/62 | **Silver Threads And Golden Needles** <br> Springfields |
| 4/68 | **Simon Says** <br> 1910 Fruitgum Co. |
| | **Since I Don't Have You** |
| 12/59 | Skyliners |
| 23/81 | Don McLean |
| 4/63 | **Since I Fell For You** <br> Lenny Welch |
| 17/65 | **Since I Lost My Baby** <br> Temptations |
| | **Since I Met You Baby** |
| 12/56 | Ivory Joe Hunter |
| 34/57 | Mindy Carson |
| 32/67 | **Since You Showed Me How To Be Happy** <br> Jackie Wilson |
| 38/59 | **Since You've Been Gone** <br> Clyde McPhatter |
| | **Since You've Been Gone**...see: *(Sweet Sweet Baby)* |
| | **Sincerely** |
| 1/55 | McGuire Sisters |
| 20/55 | Moonglows |
| 3/73 | **Sing** <br> Carpenters |
| 5/76 | **Sing A Song** <br> Earth, Wind & Fire |
| 24/58 | **Sing Boy Sing** <br> Tommy Sands |
| | **Singing The Blues** |
| 1/56 | Guy Mitchell |
| 17/56 | Marty Robbins |

| POS/YR | RECORD TITLE/ARTIST |
|---|---|
| 12/66 | **Single Girl**<br>Sandy Posey |
| 3/60 | **Sink The Bismarck**<br>Johnny Horton |
| 1/77 | **Sir Duke**<br>Stevie Wonder |
| 5/84 | **Sister Christian**<br>Night Ranger |
| 1/75 | **Sister Golden Hair**<br>America |
| 24/74 | **Sister Mary Elephant (Shudd-Up!)**<br>Cheech & Chong |
| 36/67 | **Sit Down, I Think I Love You**<br>Mojo Men |
| 37/71 | **Sit Yourself Down**<br>Stephen Stills |
| 18/57<br>38/57 | **Sittin' In The Balcony**<br>Eddie Cochran<br>Johnny Dee (Loudermilk) |
| 1/68 | **(Sittin' On) The Dock Of The Bay**<br>Otis Redding |
| 16/73 | **Sitting**<br>Cat Stevens |
| 27/83 | **Sitting At The Wheel**<br>Moody Blues |
| 24/65 | **Sitting In The Park**<br>Billy Stewart |
| 32/63 | **Six Days On The Road**<br>Dave Dudley |
| 28/59 | **Six Nights A Week**<br>Crests |
| 18/67 | **Six O'Clock**<br>Lovin' Spoonful |
| 13/66 | **634-5789 (Soulsville, U.S.A.)**<br>Wilson Pickett<br>(also see: Beechwood 4-5789) |
| 2/59 | **16 Candles**<br>Crests |
| 3/60 | **Sixteen Reasons**<br>Connie Stevens |
| 1/55<br>17/55 | **Sixteen Tons**<br>Tennessee Ernie Ford<br>Johnny Desmond |
| 6/82 | **'65 Love Affair**<br>Paul Davis |

| POS/YR | RECORD TITLE/ARTIST |
|---|---|
| 13/74 | **Skin Tight**<br>Ohio Players |
| 10/67 | **Skinny Legs And All**<br>Joe Tex |
| 22/58 | **Skinny Minnie**<br>Bill Haley & His Comets |
| 25/68 | **Skip A Rope**<br>Henson Cargill |
| 3/75 | **Sky High**<br>Jigsaw |
| 14/68 | **Sky Pilot**<br>Animals |
| 35/64 | **Slaughter On Tenth Avenue**<br>Ventures |
| 13/60 | **Sleep**<br>Little Willie John |
| 1/59 | **Sleep Walk**<br>Santo & Johnny |
|  | **Sleeping Beauty**...see: To A |
| 32/77 | **Slide**<br>Slave |
| 6/68 | **Slip Away**<br>Clarence Carter |
| 5/78 | **Slip Slidin' Away**<br>Paul Simon |
| 33/56 | **Slipin' And Slidin'**<br>Little Richard |
| 19/75 | **Slippery When Wet**<br>Commodores |
| 16/72 | **Slippin' Into Darkness**<br>War |
| 39/83 | **Slipping Away**<br>Dave Edmunds |
| 3/66 | **Sloop John B**<br>Beach Boys |
| 20/77 | **Slow Dancin' Don't Turn Me On**<br>Addrisi Brothers |
| 10/77 | **Slow Dancing (Swayin' To The Music)**<br>Johnny Rivers |
| 25/64 | **Slow Down**<br>Beatles |
| 2/81 | **Slow Hand**<br>Pointer Sisters |

| POS/YR | RECORD TITLE/ARTIST |
|---|---|
| 20/76 | **Slow Ride** Foghat |
| 3/62 | **Slow Twistin'** Chubby Checker |
| 17/56 | **Slow Walk** Sil Austin |
| 26/57 | Bill Doggett |
| 34/77 | **Slowdown** John Miles |
| 30/70 | **Sly, Slick, And The Wicked** Lost Generation |
| 29/72 | **Small Beginnings** Flash |
| 21/62 | **Small Sad Sam** Phil McLean |
| 20/59 | **Small World** Johnny Mathis |
| 5/69 | **Smile A Little Smile For Me** Flying Machine |
| 34/83 | **Smile Has Left Your Eyes** Asia |
| 21/55 | **Smiles** Crazy Otto |
| 3/71 | **Smiling Faces Sometimes** Undisputed Truth |
| 9/77 | **Smoke From A Distant Fire** Sanford/Townsend Band |
| 1/59 | **Smoke Gets In Your Eyes** Platters |
| 27/73 | Blue Haze |
| 4/73 | **Smoke On The Water** Deep Purple |
| 17/60 | **Smokie** Bill Black's Combo |
| 3/74 | **Smokin' In The Boy's Room** Brownsville Station |
| 24/81 | **Smoky Mountain Rain** Ronnie Milsap |
| 12/62 | **Smoky Places** Corsairs |
| 27/68 | **Snake, The** Al Wilson |
| 8/62 | **Snap Your Fingers** Joe Henderson |

| POS/YR | RECORD TITLE/ARTIST |
|---|---|
| 31/69 | **Snatching It Back** Clarence Carter |
| 2/66 | **Snoopy Vs. The Red Baron** Royal Guardsmen *(also see: Return Of The Red Baron)* |
| 8/70 | **Snowbird** Anne Murray |
| 23/84 | **So Bad** Paul McCartney |
| 38/59 | **So Close** Brook Benton |
| 40/83 | **So Close** Diana Ross |
| 14/71 | **So Far Away** Carole King |
| 11/59 | **So Fine** Fiestas |
| 30/79 | **So Good, So Right** Brenda Russell |
| 36/69 | **So Good Together** Andy Kim |
| 39/69 | **So I Can Love You** Emotions |
| 7/77 | **So In To You** Atlanta Rhythm Section |
| 28/61 | **So Long Baby** Del Shannon |
| 6/59 | **So Many Ways** Brook Benton |
| 1/63 | **So Much In Love** Tymes |
| 2/57 | **So Rare** Jimmy Dorsey Orchestra & Chorus |
| 7/60 | **So Sad (To Watch Good Love Go Bad)** Everly Brothers |
| 21/62 | **So This Is Love** Castells |
| 17/73 | **So Very Hard To Go** Tower Of Power |
| 30/83 | **So Wrong** Patrick Simmons |
| 21/74 | **So You Are A Star** Hudson Brothers |

| POS/YR | RECORD TITLE/ARTIST |
|---|---|
| 29/67 | **So You Want To Be A Rock 'N' Roll Star**<br>Byrds |
| 31/77 | **So You Win Again**<br>Hot Chocolate |
| 14/67 | **Society's Child (Baby I've Been Thinking)**<br>Janis Ian |
| 6/67 | **Sock It To Me-Baby!**<br>Mitch Ryder & The Detroit Wheels |
| 35/57 | **Soft**<br>Bill Doggett |
| 11/56<br>34/56 | **Soft Summer Breeze**<br>Eddie Heywood<br>Diamonds |
| 27/64 | **Softly, As I Leave You**<br>Frank Sinatra |
| 29/72 | **Softly Whispering I Love You**<br>English Congregation |
| 1/62 | **Soldier Boy**<br>Shirelles |
| 7/83 | **Solitaire**<br>Laura Branigan |
| 17/75 | **Solitaire**<br>Carpenters |
| 21/70 | **Solitary Man**<br>Neil Diamond |
| 34/64 | **Some Day We're Gonna Love Again**<br>Searchers |
| 36/81 | **Some Days Are Diamonds (Some Days Are Stone)**<br>John Denver |
| 13/65 | **Some Enchanted Evening**<br>Jay & The Americans |
| 39/73<br>10/84 | **Some Guys Have All The Luck**<br>Persuaders<br>Rod Stewart |
| 37/59 | **Some Kind-A Earthquake**<br>Duane Eddy |
| 26/83 | **Some Kind Of Friend**<br>Barry Manilow |
| 3/75 | **Some Kind Of Wonderful**<br>Grand Funk Railroad |
| 32/61 | **Some Kind Of Wonderful**<br>Drifters |

| POS/YR | RECORD TITLE/ARTIST |
|---|---|
| 30/68 | **Some Things You Never Get Used To**<br>Supremes |
| 26/68 | **Some Velvet Morning**<br>Nancy Sinatra & Lee Hazlewood |
| 5/67 | **Somebody To Love**<br>Jefferson Airplane |
| 13/77 | **Somebody To Love**<br>Queen |
| 22/58 | **Somebody Touched Me**<br>Buddy Knox |
| 18/56 | **Somebody Up There Likes Me**<br>Perry Como |
| 7/82 | **Somebody's Baby**<br>Jackson Browne |
| 8/70 | **Somebody's Been Sleeping**<br>100 Proof Aged In Soul |
| 33/76 | **Somebody's Gettin' It**<br>Johnnie Taylor |
| 13/81 | **Somebody's Knockin'**<br>Terri Gibbs |
| 2/84 | **Somebody's Watching Me**<br>Rockwell |
| 32/71 | **Somebody's Watching You**<br>Little Sister |
| | **Someday**...*also see: Some Day* |
| 25/72 | **Someday Never Comes**<br>Creedence Clearwater Revival |
| 36/82 | **Someday, Someway**<br>Marshall Crenshaw |
| 1/69 | **Someday We'll Be Together**<br>Supremes |
| 35/59 | **Someone**<br>Johnny Mathis |
| 15/82 | **Someone Could Lose A Heart Tonight**<br>Eddie Rabbitt |
| 4/75 | **Someone Saved My Life Tonight**<br>Elton John |
| 21/80 | **Someone That I Used To Love**<br>Natalie Cole |
| 13/55 | **Someone You Love**<br>Nat King Cole |
| 37/77 | **Somethin' 'Bout 'Cha**<br>Latimore |

| POS/YR | RECORD TITLE/ARTIST |
|--------|---------------------|
| 1/67 | **Somethin' Stupid**<br>Nancy & Frank Sinatra |
| 1/69 | **Something**<br>Beatles |
| 19/65 | **Something About You**<br>Four Tops |
| 13/75 | **Something Better To Do**<br>Olivia Newton-John |
| 28/76 | **Something He Can Feel**<br>Aretha Franklin |
| 37/69 | **Something In The Air**<br>Thunderclap Newman |
| 11/70 | **Something's Burning**<br>Kenny Rogers & The First Edition |
| 37/62 | **Something's Got A Hold On Me**<br>Etta James |
| 5/55<br>9/55 | **Something's Gotta Give**<br>McGuire Sisters<br>Sammy Davis, Jr. |
| 12/72 | **Something's Wrong With Me**<br>Austin Roberts |
| 31/77 | **Sometimes**<br>Facts Of Life |
| 36/80 | **Sometimes A Fantasy**<br>Billy Joel |
| 3/78 | **Sometimes When We Touch**<br>Dan Hill |
| 19/64 | **Somewhere**<br>Tymes |
| 26/66 | **Somewhere**<br>Len Barry |
| 21/82 | **Somewhere Down The Road**<br>Barry Manilow |
| 19/76<br>9/79 | **Somewhere In The Night**<br>Helen Reddy<br>Barry Manilow |
| 32/65 | **Somewhere In Your Heart**<br>Frank Sinatra |
| 9/66 | **Somewhere, My Love**<br>Ray Conniff |
| 32/66 | **Somewhere There's A Someone**<br>Dean Martin |
| 10/69 | **Son Of A Preacher Man**<br>Dusty Springfield |

| POS/YR | RECORD TITLE/ARTIST |
|--------|---------------------|
| 40/68 | **Son Of Hickory Holler's Tramp**<br>O.C. Smith |
| 28/74 | **Son Of Sagittarius**<br>Eddie Kendricks |
| 8/56 | **Song For A Summer Night**<br>Mitch Miller & His Orchestra |
| 14/70 | **Song Of Joy**<br>Miguel Rios<br>*(also see: Joy)* |
| 11/55 | **Song Of The Dreamer**<br>Eddie Fisher |
| 29/79 | **Song On The Radio**<br>Al Stewart |
| 1/72 | **Song Sung Blue**<br>Neil Diamond |
| 25/78 | **Songbird**<br>Barbra Streisand |
| 30/70 | **Soolaimon (African Trilogy II)**<br>Neil Diamond |
| 9/71 | **Sooner Or Later**<br>Grass Roots |
| 34/69 | **Sophisticated Cissy**<br>Meters |
| 25/76 | **Sophisticated Lady (She's A Different Lady)**<br>Natalie Cole |
| 2/59 | **Sorry (I Ran All The Way Home)**<br>Impalas |
| 6/76 | **Sorry Seems To Be The Hardest Word**<br>Elton John |
| | **Soul Coaxing**...*see: Ame Caline* |
| 18/69 | **Soul Deep**<br>Box Tops |
| 17/67 | **Soul Finger**<br>Bar-Kays |
| 17/68 | **Soul Limbo**<br>Booker T. & The Mg's |
| 35/73 | **Soul Makossa**<br>Manu Dibango |
| 2/67<br>14/79 | **Soul Man**<br>Sam & Dave<br>Blues Brothers |
| 29/71 | **Soul Power**<br>James Brown |

| POS/YR | RECORD TITLE/ARTIST |
|--------|---------------------|
| 23/68 | **Soul Serenade**<br>Willie Mitchell |
| 37/69 | **Soul Shake**<br>Peggy Scott & Jo Jo Benson |
| 37/73 | **Soul Song**<br>Joe Stampley |
| 17/62 | **Soul Twist**<br>King Curtis |
| 3/69 | **Soulful Strut**<br>Young-Holt Unlimited |
| 23/83 | **Souls**<br>Rick Springfield |
| 36/67 | **Sound Of Love**<br>Five Americans |
| 1/66 | **Sounds Of Silence**<br>Simon & Garfunkel |
| 3/63 | **South Street**<br>Orlons |
| 29/75 | **South's Gonna Do It**<br>Charlie Daniels Band |
| 18/82 | **Southern Cross**<br>Crosby, Stills & Nash |
| 1/77 | **Southern Nights**<br>Glen Campbell |
| 15/64 | **Southtown, U.S.A.**<br>Dixiebelles |
| 30/83 | **Space Age Love Song**<br>Flock Of Seagulls |
| 15/73 | **Space Oddity**<br>David Bowie |
| 4/73 | **Space Race**<br>Billy Preston |
| 23/72 | **Spaceman**<br>Nilsson |
| 15/66 | **Spanish Eyes**<br>Al Martino |
| 27/66 | **Spanish Flea**<br>Herb Alpert & The Tijuana Brass |
| 10/61<br>2/71 | **Spanish Harlem**<br>Ben E. King<br>Aretha Franklin |
| 31/62 | **Spanish Lace**<br>Gene McDaniels |

| POS/YR | RECORD TITLE/ARTIST |
|--------|---------------------|
|  | **(Speak Softly Love)**...see: Love Theme<br>From "The Godfather" |
| 14/72 | **Speak To The Sky**<br>Rick Springfield |
| 38/69 | **Special Delivery**<br>1910 Fruitgum Co. |
| 5/80 | **Special Lady**<br>Ray, Goodman & Brown |
| 26/68 | **Special Occasion**<br>Miracles |
| 17/56 | **Speedo**<br>Cadillacs |
| 6/62 | **Speedy Gonzales**<br>Pat Boone |
| 40/83 | **Spice Of Life**<br>Manhattan Transfer |
| 3/74 | **Spiders & Snakes**<br>Jim Stafford |
| 3/70 | **Spill The Wine**<br>Eric Burdon & War |
| 2/69 | **Spinning Wheel**<br>Blood, Sweat & Tears |
| 40/66 | **Spinout**<br>Elvis Presley |
| 23/70 | **Spirit In The Dark**<br>Aretha Franklin |
| 40/77 | **Spirit In The Night**<br>Manfred Mann's Earth Band |
| 3/70 | **Spirit In The Sky**<br>Norman Greenbaum |
| 35/75 | **Spirit Of The Boogie**<br>Kool & The Gang |
| 11/82 | **Spirits In The Material World**<br>Police |
| 3/58 | **Splish Splash**<br>Bobby Darin |
| 3/68<br>17/79 | **Spooky**<br>Classics IV<br>Atlanta Rhythm Section |
| 39/77 | **Spring Rain**<br>Silvetti |
| 37/76 | **Springtime Mama**<br>Henry Gross |

| POS/YR | RECORD TITLE/ARTIST |
|--------|---------------------|
| 16/76 | **Squeeze Box**<br>Who |
| 13/56 | **St. Therese Of The Roses**<br>Billy Ward & His Dominoes |
| 1/59<br>22/67<br>25/71 | **Stagger Lee**<br>Lloyd Price<br>Wilson Pickett<br>Tommy Roe |
| 9/60 | **Stairway To Heaven**<br>Neil Sedaka |
| 22/69 | **Stand!**<br>Sly & The Family Stone |
| 5/83 | **Stand Back**<br>Stevie Nicks |
| 4/61<br>12/67<br>20/75<br>22/80 | **Stand By Me**<br>Ben E. King<br>Spyder Turner<br>John Lennon<br>Mickey Gilley<br>*(also see: I'll Be There)* |
| 19/69<br>24/70 | **Stand By Your Man**<br>Tammy Wynette<br>Candi Staton |
| 10/77 | **Stand Tall**<br>Burton Cummings |
| 37/74 | **Standing At The End Of The Line**<br>Lobo |
| 6/67 | **Standing In The Shadows Of Love**<br>Four Tops |
| 3/56<br>22/56 | **Standing On The Corner**<br>Four Lads<br>Dean Martin |
| 29/74 | **Star**<br>Stealers Wheel |
| 39/74 | **Star Baby**<br>Guess Who |
|  | **Star Is Born, Love Theme From A**...*see:*<br>*Evergreen* |
| 1/77<br>10/77 | **Star Wars Theme**<br>Meco<br>John Williams |
| 25/60 | **Starbright**<br>Johnny Mathis |
| 12/57<br>32/64 | **Stardust**<br>Billy Ward & His Dominoes<br>Nino Tempo & April Stevens |

| POS/YR | RECORD TITLE/ARTIST |
|--------|---------------------|
| 1/81 | **Stars On 45 [Medley]**<br>Stars On 45 |
| 28/82 | **Stars On 45 III**<br>Stars On 45 |
| 2/81 | **Start Me Up**<br>Rolling Stones |
| 9/57 | **Start Movin' (In My Direction)**<br>Sal Mineo |
| 19/72 | **Starting All Over Again**<br>Mel & Tim |
|  | **Starting Over**...*see: (Just Like)* |
| 36/80 | **Starting Over Again**<br>Dolly Parton |
| 3/84 | **State Of Shock**<br>Jacksons |
| 1/60<br>16/64<br>20/78 | **Stay**<br>Maurice Williams & The Zodiacs<br>Four Seasons<br>Jackson Browne |
| 38/78 | **Stay**<br>Rufus featuring Chaka Khan |
| 7/71 | **Stay Awhile**<br>Bells |
| 38/64 | **Stay Awhile**<br>Dusty Springfield |
| 10/68 | **Stay In My Corner**<br>Dells |
| 16/84 | **Stay The Night**<br>Chicago |
| 17/72 | **Stay With Me**<br>Faces |
| 30/84 | **Stay With Me Tonight**<br>Jeffrey Osborne |
| 1/78 | **Stayin' Alive**<br>Bee Gees |
| 33/61 | **Stayin' In**<br>Bobby Vee |
| 37/81 | **Staying With It**<br>Firefall |
| 17/64<br>37/70 | **Steal Away**<br>Jimmy Hughes<br>Johnnie Taylor |
| 6/80 | **Steal Away**<br>Robbie Dupree |

| POS/YR | RECORD TITLE/ARTIST |
|--------|---------------------|
| 25/81 | **Steal The Night** Stevie Woods |
| 17/73 | **Steamroller Blues** Elvis Presley |
| 13/62 | **Steel Guitar And A Glass Of Wine** Paul Anka |
| 5/81 | **Step By Step** Eddie Rabbitt |
| 14/60 | **Step By Step** Crests |
| 37/73 | **Step By Step** Joe Simon |
| 24/67 | **Step Out Of Your Mind** American Breed |
| 39/78 | **Steppin' In A Slide Zone** Moody Blues |
| 6/82 | **Steppin' Out** Joe Jackson |
| 36/76 | **Steppin' Out** Neil Sedaka |
| 7/74 | **Steppin' Out (Gonna Boogie Tonight)** Dawn |
| 35/63 | **Stewball** Peter, Paul & Mary |
| 25/61 | **Stick Shift** Duals |
| 11/71 | **Stick-Up** Honey Cone |
| 40/60 | **Sticks And Stones** Ray Charles |
| 1/79 | **Still** Commodores |
| 8/63 | **Still** Bill Anderson |
| 40/76 | **Still Crazy After All These Years** Paul Simon |
| 22/82 | **Still In Saigon** Charlie Daniels Band |
| 28/81 | **Still Right Here In My Heart** Pure Prairie League |
| 5/76 | **Still The One** Orleans |
| 4/78 | **Still The Same** Bob Seger |

| POS/YR | RECORD TITLE/ARTIST |
|--------|---------------------|
| 19/82 | **Still They Ride** Journey |
| 11/70 | **Still Water (Love)** Four Tops |
| 12/73 | **Stir It Up** Johnny Nash |
| 7/80 | **Stomp!** Brothers Johnson |
| 36/78 | **Stone Blue** Foghat |
| 40/82 | **Stone Cold** Rainbow |
| 7/70 | **Stoned Love** Supremes |
| 30/73 | **Stoned Out Of My Mind** Chi-Lites |
| 3/68 | **Stoned Soul Picnic** 5th Dimension |
| 14/71 | **Stones** Neil Diamond |
| 6/71 | **Stoney End** Barbra Streisand |
| 2/58 | **Stood Up** Ricky Nelson |
| 9/74 | **Stop And Smell The Roses** Mac Davis |
| 8/64 | **Stop And Think It Over** Dale & Grace |
| 3/81 | **Stop Draggin' My Heart Around** Stevie Nicks |
| 1/65 29/83 | **Stop! In The Name Of Love** Supremes Hollies |
| 39/71 | **Stop, Look, Listen (To Your Heart)** Stylistics |
| 7/66 | **Stop Stop Stop** Hollies |
| 36/62 | **Stop The Music** Shirelles |
| 26/71 | **Stop The War Now** Edwin Starr |
| 34/62 | **Stop The Wedding** Etta James |

| POS/YR | RECORD TITLE/ARTIST |
|--------|---------------------|
| 5/68 | **Stormy**<br>Classics IV |
| 32/79 | Santana |
| 23/71 | **Story In Your Eyes**<br>Moody Blues |
| 15/58 | **Story Of My Life**<br>Marty Robbins |
| 16/61 | **Story Of My Love**<br>Paul Anka |
| 28/59 | **Story Of My Love**<br>Conway Twitty |
| 16/55 | **Story Untold**<br>Crew-Cuts |
| 10/83 | **Straight From The Heart**<br>Bryan Adams |
| 39/81 | **Straight From The Heart**<br>Allman Brothers Band |
| 36/68 | **Straight Life**<br>Bobby Goldsboro |
| 15/78 | **Straight On**<br>Heart |
| 29/74 | **Straight Shootin' Woman**<br>Steppenwolf |
| 15/56 | **Stranded In The Jungle**<br>Cadets |
| 18/56 | Jayhawks |
| 39/56 | Gadabouts |
| 14/76 | **Strange Magic**<br>Electric Light Orchestra |
| 11/78 | **Strange Way**<br>Firefall |
| 23/83 | **Stranger In My House**<br>Ronnie Milsap |
| 30/65 | **Stranger In Town**<br>Del Shannon |
| 1/62 | **Stranger On The Shore**<br>Mr. Acker Bilk |
| 38/62 | Andy Williams |
| 1/66 | **Strangers In The Night**<br>Frank Sinatra |
| 8/67 | **Strawberry Fields Forever**<br>Beatles |
| 5/77 | **Strawberry Letter 23**<br>Brothers Johnson |

| POS/YR | RECORD TITLE/ARTIST |
|--------|---------------------|
| 39/68 | **Strawberry Shortcake**<br>Jay & The Techniques |
| 3/83 | **Stray Cat Strut**<br>Stray Cats |
| 1/74 | **Streak, The**<br>Ray Stevens |
| 30/78 | **Street Corner Serenade**<br>Wet Willie |
| 36/79 | **Street Life**<br>Crusaders |
| 27/76 | **Street Singin'**<br>Lady Flash |
| 39/60 | **String Along**<br>Fabian |
| 25/63 | Ricky Nelson |
| 1/62 | **Stripper, The**<br>David Rose & His Orchestra |
| 17/81 | **Stroke**<br>Billy Squier |
| 4/58 | **Stroll, The**<br>Diamonds |
| 30/81 | **Stronger Than Before**<br>Carole Bayer Sager |
| 40/84 | **Strung Out**<br>Steve Perry |
| 7/84 | **Strut**<br>Sheena Easton |
| 22/75 | **Struttin'**<br>Billy Preston |
| 6/73 | **Stuck In The Middle With You**<br>Stealers Wheel |
| 1/60 | **Stuck On You**<br>Elvis Presley |
| 3/84 | **Stuck On You**<br>Lionel Richie |
| 21/78 | **Stuff Like That**<br>Quincy Jones |
| 4/79 | **Stumblin' In**<br>Suzi Quatro & Chris Norman |
| 14/58 | **Stupid Cupid**<br>Connie Francis |
| 18/72 | **Suavecito**<br>Malo |

| POS/YR | RECORD TITLE/ARTIST |
|--------|---------------------|
| 39/65 | **Subterranean Homesick Blues**<br>Bob Dylan |
| 16/64 | **Such A Night**<br>Elvis Presley |
| 26/79 | **Such A Woman**<br>Tycoon |
| 11/65 | **(Such An) Easy Question**<br>Elvis Presley |
| 20/81 | **Suddenly**<br>Olivia Newton-John & Cliff Richard |
| 9/83 | **Suddenly Last Summer**<br>Motels |
| | **Suddenly There's A Valley** |
| 9/55 | Gogi Grant |
| 13/55 | Jo Stafford |
| 20/55 | Julius LaRosa |
| 37/74 | **Sugar Baby Love**<br>Rubettes |
| 10/72 | **Sugar Daddy**<br>Jacksons |
| 36/84 | **Sugar Don't Bite**<br>Sam Harris |
| 32/65 | **Sugar Dumpling**<br>Sam Cooke |
| 30/64 | **Sugar Lips**<br>Al Hirt |
| 5/58 | **Sugar Moon**<br>Pat Boone |
| 22/69 | **Sugar On Sunday**<br>Clique |
| 1/63 | **Sugar Shack**<br>Jimmy Gilmer & The Fireballs |
| | **Sugar, Sugar** |
| 1/69 | Archies |
| 25/70 | Wilson Pickett |
| 5/66 | **Sugar Town**<br>Nancy Sinatra |
| 1/58 | **Sugartime**<br>McGuire Sisters |
| 21/69 | **Suite: Judy Blue Eyes**<br>Crosby, Stills & Nash |
| | **Sukiyaki** |
| 1/63 | Kyu Sakamoto |
| 3/81 | Taste Of Honey |

| POS/YR | RECORD TITLE/ARTIST |
|--------|---------------------|
| 4/79 | **Sultans Of Swing**<br>Dire Straits |
| 7/76 | **Summer**<br>War |
| 6/72 | **Summer Breeze**<br>Seals & Crofts |
| 1/66 | **Summer In The City**<br>Lovin' Spoonful |
| | **Summer Night**...*see: Song For A* |
| 5/78 | **Summer Nights**<br>Olivia Newton-John & John Travolta |
| 24/65 | **Summer Nights**<br>Marianne Faithfull |
| | **Summer Of '42**...*see: Theme From* |
| | **Summer Place**...*see: Theme From A* |
| 14/68 | **Summer Rain**<br>Johnny Rivers |
| 26/66 | **Summer Samba (So Nice)**<br>Walter Wanderley |
| 33/71 | **Summer Sand**<br>Dawn |
| 30/60 | **Summer Set**<br>Monty Kelly & His Orchestra |
| 7/64 | **Summer Song**<br>Chad & Jeremy |
| 21/73 | **Summer (The First Time)**<br>Bobby Goldsboro |
| 25/66 | **Summer Wind**<br>Frank Sinatra |
| 11/60 | **Summer's Gone**<br>Paul Anka |
| 10/66 | **Summertime**<br>Billy Stewart |
| | **Summertime Blues** |
| 8/58 | Eddie Cochran |
| 14/68 | Blue Cheer |
| 27/70 | Who |
| | **Summertime, Summertime** |
| 26/58 | Jamies |
| 38/62 | Jamies |
| 13/66 | **Sun Ain't Gonna Shine (Anymore)**<br>Walker Bros. |

| POS/YR | RECORD TITLE/ARTIST |
|--------|---------------------|
| 18/65 | **Sunday And Me** <br> Jay & The Americans |
| 31/67 | **Sunday For Tea** <br> Peter & Gordon |
| 30/68 <br> 35/69 | **Sunday Mornin'** <br> Spanky & Our Gang <br> Oliver |
| 9/67 | **Sunday Will Never Be The Same** <br> Spanky & Our Gang |
| 1/74 | **Sundown** <br> Gordon Lightfoot |
| 39/77 | **Sunflower** <br> Glen Campbell |
| 7/84 | **Sunglasses At Night** <br> Corey Hart |
| 2/66 | **Sunny** <br> Bobby Hebb |
| 14/66 | **Sunny Afternoon** <br> Kinks |
| 34/72 | **Sunny Days** <br> Lighthouse |
| 34/76 | **Sunrise** <br> Eric Carmen |
| 4/72 | **Sunshine** <br> Jonathan Edwards |
| 20/67 | **Sunshine Girl** <br> Parade |
| 13/65 | **Sunshine, Lollipops And Rainbows** <br> Lesley Gore |
| 5/68 | **Sunshine Of Your Love** <br> Cream |
| 1/74 | **Sunshine On My Shoulders** <br> John Denver |
| 1/66 | **Sunshine Superman** <br> Donovan |
| 13/70 | **Super Bad** <br> James Brown |
| 31/73 | **Super Fly Meets Shaft** <br> John & Ernest |
| 16/81 | **Super Freak** <br> Rick James |
| 8/73 | **Superfly** <br> Curtis Mayfield <br> *(also see: Freddie's Dead)* |

| POS/YR | RECORD TITLE/ARTIST |
|--------|---------------------|
| 26/79 | **Superman** <br> Herbie Mann |
| 5/75 | **Supernatural Thing** <br> Ben E. King |
| 2/71 | **Superstar** <br> Carpenters |
| 14/71 | **Superstar - Jesus Christ Superstar** <br> Murray Head With The Trinidad Singers |
| 35/76 | **Superstar** <br> Paul Davis |
| 18/71 | **Superstar (Remember How You Got Where You Are)** <br> Temptations |
| 1/73 | **Superstition** <br> Stevie Wonder |
| 33/72 | **Superwoman (Where Were You When I Needed You)** <br> Stevie Wonder |
| 16/74 | **Sure As I'm Sittin' Here** <br> Three Dog Night |
| 9/66 | **Sure Gonna Miss Her** <br> Gary Lewis & The Playboys |
| 1/63 | **Surf City** <br> Jan & Dean |
| 7/63 | **Surfer Girl** <br> Beach Boys |
| 31/62 | **Surfer's Stomp** <br> Marketts |
| 4/64 | **Surfin' Bird** <br> Trashmen |
| 14/62 | **Surfin' Safari** <br> Beach Boys |
| 3/63 <br> 36/74 <br> 20/77 | **Surfin' U.S.A.** <br> Beach Boys <br> Beach Boys <br> Leif Garrett |
| 1/61 | **Surrender** <br> Elvis Presley |
| 38/71 | **Surrender** <br> Diana Ross |
| 11/68 | **Susan** <br> Buckinghams |
| 5/58 <br> 35/62 | **Susie Darlin'** <br> Robin Luke <br> Tommy Roe |

| POS/YR | RECORD TITLE/ARTIST |
|--------|---------------------|
| 3/64 | **Suspicion** Terry Stafford |
| 13/79 | **Suspicions** Eddie Rabbitt |
| 1/69 | **Suspicious Minds** Elvis Presley |
| 27/57 | **Suzie-Q** Dale Hawkins |
| 11/68 | Creedence Clearwater Revival |
| 39/73 | **Swamp Witch** Jim Stafford |
| 34/57 | **Swanee River Rock (Talkin' 'Bout That River)** Ray Charles |
| 14/60 | **Sway** Bobby Rydell |
| 6/75 | **Swearin' To God** Frankie Valli |
| 10/55 | **Sweet And Gentle** Alan Dale |
| 12/55 | Georgia Gibbs |
| 7/71 | **Sweet And Innocent** Donny Osmond |
| 19/81 | **Sweet Baby** Stanley Clarke/George Duke |
| 13/68 | **Sweet Blindness** 5th Dimension |
| 4/69 | **Sweet Caroline (Good Times Never Seemed So Good)** Neil Diamond |
| 7/69 | **Sweet Cherry Wine** Tommy James & The Shondells |
| 8/71 | **Sweet City Woman** Stampeders |
| 28/69 | **Sweet Cream Ladies, Forward March** Box Tops |
| 5/82 | **Sweet Dreams** Air Supply |
| 15/66 | **Sweet Dreams** Tommy McLain |
| 1/83 | **Sweet Dreams (Are Made of This)** Eurythmics |
| 36/75 | **Sweet Emotion** Aerosmith |

| POS/YR | RECORD TITLE/ARTIST |
|--------|---------------------|
| 6/71 | **Sweet Hitch-Hiker** Creedence Clearwater Revival |
| 8/74 | **Sweet Home Alabama** Lynyrd Skynyrd |
| 18/68 | **Sweet Inspiration** Sweet Inspirations |
| 37/72 | Barbra Streisand |
| 17/78 | **Sweet Life** Paul Davis |
| 2/58 | **Sweet Little Sixteen** Chuck Berry |
| 5/76 | **Sweet Love** Commodores |
| 36/79 | **Sweet Lui-Louise** Ironhorse |
| 7/71 | **Sweet Mary** Wadsworth Mansion |
| 40/75 | **Sweet Maxine** Doobie Brothers |
| 4/60 | **Sweet Nothin's** Brenda Lee |
| 7/56 | **Sweet Old Fashioned Girl** Teresa Brewer |
| 8/66 | **Sweet Pea** Tommy Roe |
| 9/72 | **Sweet Seasons** Carole King |
| 2/67 | **Sweet Soul Music** Arthur Conley |
| 33/75 | **Sweet Sticky Thing** Ohio Players |
| 13/75 | **Sweet Surrender** John Denver |
| 15/72 | **Sweet Surrender** Bread |
| 5/68 | **(Sweet Sweet Baby) Since You've Been Gone** Aretha Franklin |
| 10/66 | **Sweet Talkin' Guy** Chiffons |
| 17/78 | **Sweet Talkin' Woman** Electric Light Orchestra |
| 5/76 | **Sweet Thing** Rufus featuring Chaka Khan |

| POS/YR | RECORD TITLE/ARTIST |
|--------|---------------------|
| 26/82 | **Sweet Time**<br>REO Speedwagon |
| 33/73 | **Sweet Understanding Love**<br>Four Tops |
| 40/64 | **Sweet William**<br>Millie Small |
| 29/66 | **Sweet Woman Like You**<br>Joe Tex |
| 9/59 | **Sweeter Than You**<br>Ricky Nelson |
| 7/82 | **Sweetest Thing (I've Ever Known)**<br>Juice Newton |
| 32/67 | **Sweetest Thing This Side Of Heaven**<br>Chris Bartley |
| 10/81 | **Sweetheart**<br>Franke & The Knockouts |
| 16/61 | **Sweets For My Sweet**<br>Drifters |
| 19/84 | **Swept Away**<br>Diana Ross |
| 39/60 | **Swingin' On A Rainbow**<br>Frankie Avalon |
| 13/62 | **Swingin' Safari**<br>Billy Vaughn & His Orchestra |
| 5/60 | **Swingin' School**<br>Bobby Rydell |
| 23/58 | **Swingin' Shepherd Blues**<br>Moe Koffman Quartette |
| 38/63 | **Swinging On A Star**<br>Big Dee Irwin |
| 17/77 | **Swingtown**<br>Steve Miller Band |
| 26/61 | **Switch-A-Roo**<br>Hank Ballard & The Midnighters |
| 5/72 | **Sylvia's Mother**<br>Dr. Hook |
| 16/83 | **Synchronicity II**<br>Police |
| 37/76 | **(System Of) Doctor Tarr And Professor Fether**<br>Alan Parsons Project |

| POS/YR | RECORD TITLE/ARTIST |
|--------|---------------------|
| | **T** |
| | **T.L.C.**....*see: Tender, Love and Care* |
| 1/74 | **TSOP (The Sound Of Philadelphia)**<br>MFSB featuring The Three Degrees |
| 23/60 | **Ta Ta**<br>Clyde McPhatter |
| 8/82 | **Tainted Love**<br>Soft Cell |
| 3/78 | **Take A Chance On Me**<br>Abba |
| 2/69 | **Take A Letter Maria**<br>R.B. Greaves |
| 15/80 | **Take A Little Rhythm**<br>Ali Thomson |
| 30/72 | **Take A Look Around**<br>Temptations |
| | **Take A Look At Me Now**...*see: Against All Odds* |
| 16/59 | **Take A Message To Mary**<br>Everly Brothers |
| 20/69 | **Take Care Of Your Homework**<br>Johnnie Taylor |
| 25/61 | **Take Five**<br>Dave Brubeck Quartet |
| 7/61 | **Take Good Care Of Her**<br>Adam Wade |
| 1/61<br>33/68 | **Take Good Care Of My Baby**<br>Bobby Vee<br>Bobby Vinton |
| 10/82 | **Take It Away**<br>Paul McCartney |
| 12/72 | **Take It Easy**<br>Eagles |
| 10/82 | **Take It Easy On Me**<br>Little River Band |
| 33/76 | **Take It Like A Man**<br>Bachman-Turner Overdrive |
| 5/81 | **Take It On The Run**<br>REO Speedwagon |

| POS/YR | RECORD TITLE/ARTIST |
|--------|---------------------|
| 4/76 | **Take It To The Limit** <br> Eagles |
| 16/65 | **Take Me Back** <br> Little Anthony & The Imperials |
| 18/82 | **Take Me Down** <br> Alabama |
| 38/68 | **Take Me For A Little While** <br> Vanilla Fudge |
| 8/79 | **Take Me Home** <br> Cher |
| 2/71 | **Take Me Home, Country Roads** <br> John Denver |
| 11/75 | **Take Me In Your Arms (Rock Me)** <br> Doobie Brothers |
| 14/83 | **Take Me To Heart** <br> Quarterflash |
| 26/79 | **Take Me To The River** <br> Talking Heads |
| 17/81 | **Take My Heart (You Can Have It If You Want It)** <br> Kool & The Gang |
| 16/82 | **Take Off** <br> Bob & Doug McKenzie |
| 10/79 | **Take The Long Way Home** <br> Supertramp |
| 11/76 | **Take The Money And Run** <br> Steve Miller Band |
| 8/63 | **Take These Chains From My Heart** <br> Ray Charles |
| 11/68 | **Take Time To Know Her** <br> Percy Sledge |
| 3/80 | **Take Your Time (Do It Right)** <br> S.O.S. Band |
| 12/74 | **Takin' Care Of Business** <br> Bachman-Turner Overdrive |
| 13/76 | **Takin' It To The Streets** <br> Doobie Brothers |
| 7/64 | **Talk Back Trembling Lips** <br> Johnny Tillotson |
| 15/67 | **Talk Talk** <br> Music Machine |
| 34/60 | **Talk That Talk** <br> Jackie Wilson |

| POS/YR | RECORD TITLE/ARTIST |
|--------|---------------------|
| 38/59 | **Talk To Me** <br> Frank Sinatra |
| 20/58 <br> 11/63 | **Talk To Me, Talk To Me** <br> Little Willie John <br> Sunny & The Sunglows |
| 20/57 | **Talkin' To The Blues** <br> Jim Lowe |
| 12/64 | **Talking About My Baby** <br> Impressions |
| 3/84 | **Talking In Your Sleep** <br> Romantics |
| 18/78 | **Talking In Your Sleep** <br> Crystal Gayle |
| 27/72 | **Talking Loud And Saying Nothing** <br> James Brown |
| 36/59 <br> 38/64 | **Tall Cool One** <br> Wailers <br> Wailers |
| 7/59 | **Tall Paul** <br> Annette |
| 6/59 | **Tallahassee Lassie** <br> Freddy Cannon |
| 1/57 <br> 5/57 | **Tammy** <br> Debbie Reynolds <br> Ames Brothers |
| 18/76 | **Tangerine** <br> Salsoul Orchestra |
| 31/75 | **Tangled Up In Blue** <br> Bob Dylan |
| 34/68 | **Tapioca Tundra** <br> Monkees |
| 38/66 | **Tar And Cement** <br> Verdelle Smith |
| 7/65 | **Taste Of Honey** <br> Herb Alpert & The Tijuana Brass |
| 18/72 | **Taurus** <br> Dennis Coffey & The Detroit Guitar Band |
| 24/72 | **Taxi** <br> Harry Chapin |
| 7/58 | **Tea For Two** <br> Tommy Dorsey Orchestra |
| 25/62 | **Teach Me Tonight** <br> George Maharis |

| POS/YR | RECORD TITLE/ARTIST |
|---|---|
| 16/70 | **Teach Your Children** Crosby, Stills, Nash & Young |
| 21/58 | **Teacher, Teacher** Johnny Mathis |
| 25/84 | **Teacher Teacher** 38 Special |
| 31/61 | **Tear, A** Gene McDaniels |
| 23/59 | **Tear Drop** Santo & Johnny |
| 20/57 | **Tear Drops** Lee Andrews & The Hearts |
| 5/56 | **Tear Fell** Teresa Brewer |
| 15/76 | **Tear The Roof Off The Sucker (Give Up The Funk)** Parliament |
| 20/64 | **Tears And Roses** Al Martino |
| 1/70 | **Tears Of A Clown** Miracles |
| 4/58 | **Tears On My Pillow** Little Anthony & The Imperials |
| 39/59 | **Teasin'** Quaker City Boys |
| 17/60 | **Teddy** Connie Francis |
| 40/76 | **Teddy Bear** Red Sovine |
| 32/73 | **Teddy Bear Song** Barbara Fairchild |
| | **Teen Age**...also see: Teenage |
| 2/57 | **Teen Age Crush** Tommy Sands |
| 5/62 | **Teen Age Idol** Ricky Nelson |
| 6/56 | **Teen Age Prayer** Gale Storm |
| 19/56 | Gloria Mann |
| 1/60 | **Teen Angel** Mark Dinning |
| 4/59 | **Teen Beat** Sandy Nelson |

| POS/YR | RECORD TITLE/ARTIST |
|---|---|
| 29/59 | **Teen Commandments** Paul Anka-George Hamilton IV-Johnny Nash |
| | **Teenage Queen**...see: Ballad Of |
| 5/59 | **Teenager In Love** Dion & The Belmonts |
| 2/57 | **Teenager's Romance** Ricky Nelson |
| 9/83 | **Telefone (Long Distance Love Affair)** Sheena Easton |
| 7/77 | **Telephone Line** Electric Light Orchestra |
| 18/77 | **Telephone Man** Meri Wilson |
| 1/83 | **Tell Her About It** Billy Joel |
| 6/65 | **Tell Her No** Zombies |
| 27/83 | Juice Newton |
| 40/73 | **Tell Her She's Lovely** El Chicano |
| 4/63 | **Tell Him** Exciters |
| 8/59 | **Tell Him No** Travis & Bob |
| 17/70 | **Tell It All Brother** Kenny Rogers & The First Edition |
| 2/67 | **Tell It Like It Is** Aaron Neville |
| 8/81 | Heart |
| 33/64 | **Tell It On The Mountain** Peter, Paul & Mary |
| 10/67 | **Tell It To The Rain** Four Seasons |
| 7/60 | **Tell Laura I Love Her** Ray Peterson |
| 23/68 | **Tell Mama** Etta James |
| 22/62 | **Tell Me** Dick & DeeDee |
| 21/74 | **Tell Me A Lie** Sami Jo |

| POS/YR | RECORD TITLE/ARTIST |
|--------|---------------------|
| 3/74 | **Tell Me Something Good**<br>Rufus featuring Chaka Khan |
| 37/67 | **Tell Me To My Face**<br>Keith |
| 33/82 | **Tell Me Tomorrow**<br>Smokey Robinson |
| 13/64 | **Tell Me Why**<br>Bobby Vinton |
| 18/61 | **Tell Me Why**<br>Belmonts |
| 33/66 | **Tell Me Why**<br>Elvis Presley |
| 24/64 | **Tell Me (You're Coming Back)**<br>Rolling Stones |
| 1/62 | **Telstar**<br>Tornadoes |
| 39/70 | **Temma Harbour**<br>Mary Hopkin |
| 27/61 | **Temptation**<br>Everly Brothers |
| 15/71 | **Temptation Eyes**<br>Grass Roots |
| 22/58 | **Ten Commandments Of Love**<br>Harvey & The Moonglows<br>*(also see: Teen Commandments)* |
| 38/84 | **10-9-8**<br>Face To Face |
| 25/83 | **Tender Is The Night**<br>Jackson Browne |
| 24/60 | **Tender Love And Care (T.L.C.)**<br>Jimmie Rodgers |
|  | **Tender Trap**. . .*see: (Love Is)* |
| 31/61 | **Tenderly**<br>Bert Kaempfert & His Orchestra |
| 23/70 | **Tennessee Bird Walk**<br>Jack Blanchard & Misty Morgan |
| 35/64 | **Tennessee Waltz**<br>Sam Cooke |
| 1/58<br>20/58 | **Tequila**<br>Champs<br>Eddie Platt & His Orchestra |
|  | **Testify**. . .*see: (I Wanna)* |
| 1/75 | **Thank God I'm A Country Boy**<br>John Denver |

| POS/YR | RECORD TITLE/ARTIST |
|--------|---------------------|
| 22/78 | **Thank God It's Friday**<br>Love & Kisses |
| 1/70 | **Thank You (Falettinme Be Mice Elf Agin)**<br>Sly & The Family Stone |
| 25/78 | **Thank You For Being A Friend**<br>Andrew Gold |
| 35/64 | **Thank You Girl**<br>Beatles |
| 16/59 | **Thank You Pretty Baby**<br>Brook Benton |
| 37/74 | **Thanks For Saving My Life**<br>Billy Paul |
| 4/82 | **That Girl**<br>Stevie Wonder |
| 22/80 | **That Girl Could Sing**<br>Jackson Browne |
| 6/73 | **That Lady**<br>Isley Brothers |
| 20/64 | **That Lucky Old Sun**<br>Ray Charles |
| 13/55<br>18/58<br>21/61 | **That Old Black Magic**<br>Sammy Davis, Jr.<br>Louis Prima & Keely Smith<br>Bobby Rydell |
| 21/81 | **That Old Song**<br>Ray Parker Jr. & Raydio |
| 28/62 | **That Stranger Used To Be My Girl**<br>Trade Martin |
| 12/63 | **That Sunday, That Summer**<br>Nat King Cole |
| 1/57<br>11/76 | **That'll Be The Day**<br>Crickets<br>Linda Ronstadt |
| 6/84 | **That's All**<br>Genesis |
| 17/56 | **That's All**<br>Tennessee Ernie Ford |
| 3/55 | **That's All I Want From You**<br>Jaye P. Morgan |
| 16/56 | **That's All There Is To That**<br>Nat King Cole |
| 6/60 | **That's All You Gotta Do**<br>Brenda Lee |

| POS/YR | RECORD TITLE/ARTIST |
|--------|---------------------|
| 40/63 | **That's How Heartaches Are Made**<br>Baby Washington |
| 39/58 | **That's How Much I Love You**<br>Pat Boone |
| 31/61 | **That's It-I Quit-I'm Movin' On**<br>Sam Cooke |
| 4/66 | **That's Life**<br>Frank Sinatra |
| 28/83 | **That's Love**<br>Jim Capaldi |
| 9/62 | **That's Old Fashioned (That's The Way Love Should Be)**<br>Everly Brothers |
| 3/77 | **That's Rock 'N' Roll**<br>Shaun Cassidy |
| 12/64 | **That's The Way Boys Are**<br>Lesley Gore |
| 27/72 | **That's The Way I Feel About Cha**<br>Bobby Womack |
| 1/75 | **That's The Way (I Like It)**<br>KC & The Sunshine Band |
| 10/71 | **That's The Way I've Always Heard It Should Be**<br>Carly Simon |
| 7/69 | **That's The Way Love Is**<br>Marvin Gaye |
| 33/63 | **That's The Way Love Is**<br>Bobby Bland |
| 12/75 | **That's The Way Of The World**<br>Earth, Wind & Fire |
| 27/61 | **That's What Girls Are Made For**<br>Spinners |
| 35/64 | **That's What Love Is Made Of**<br>Miracles |
| 27/75 | **That's When The Music Takes Me**<br>Neil Sedaka |
| 29/70 | **That's Where I Went Wrong**<br>Poppy Family featuring Susan Jacks |
| 27/76 | **That's Where The Happy People Go**<br>Trammps |
| 13/59 | **That's Why (I Love You So)**<br>Jackie Wilson |
| 35/60 | **Theme For Young Lovers**<br>Percy Faith & His Orchestra |

| POS/YR | RECORD TITLE/ARTIST |
|--------|---------------------|
| 1/60<br>16/65 | **Theme From A Summer Place**<br>Percy Faith & His Orchestra<br>Lettermen |
| 28/62 | **Theme From Ben Casey**<br>Valjean |
| 18/73 | **Theme From Cleopatra Jones**<br>Joe Simon |
| 13/78<br>25/78 | **Theme From Close Encounters**<br>John Williams<br>Meco |
| 39/61 | **Theme From Dixie**<br>Duane Eddy |
| 10/62 | **Theme From Dr. Kildare (Three Stars Will Shine Tonight)**<br>Richard Chamberlain |
|  | **Theme From Exorcist**...see: Tubular Bells |
| 2/81 | **Theme From Greatest American Hero (Believe It Or Not)**<br>Joey Scarbury |
| 10/81 | **Theme From Hill Street Blues**<br>Mike Post |
| 32/75 | **Theme From Jaws (Main Title)**<br>John Williams |
| 9/71<br>13/71<br>31/71 | **Theme From Love Story**<br>Andy Williams (Where Do I Begin)<br>Henry Mancini & His Orchestra<br>Francis Lai & His Orchestra |
| 25/82 | **Theme From Magnum P.I.**<br>Mike Post |
| 1/76 | **Theme From Mahogany (Do You Know Where You're Going To)**<br>Diana Ross |
| 32/80 | **Theme From New York, New York**<br>Frank Sinatra |
|  | **Theme From Picnic**...see: Moonglow |
|  | **Theme From Pink Panther**...see: Pink Panther Theme |
|  | **Theme From Rocky**...see: Gonna Fly Now |
| 1/76 | **Theme From S.W.A.T.**<br>Rhythm Heritage |
| 1/71 | **Theme From Shaft**<br>Isaac Hayes |
| 21/71 | **Theme From Summer Of '42**<br>Peter Nero |

| POS/YR | RECORD TITLE/ARTIST |
|---|---|
| | **Theme From Superfly**...*see: Freddie's Dead* |
| 10/60 | **Theme From The Apartment**<br>Ferrante & Teicher |
| 21/80 | **Theme From The Dukes Of Hazzard (Good Ol' Boys)**<br>Waylon Jennings |
| | **Theme From The Man With The Golden Arm**...*see: Man With The Golden Arm* |
| 38/72 | **Theme From The Men**<br>Isaac Hayes |
| 39/56 | **Theme From The Proud Ones**<br>Nelson Riddle & His Orchestra |
| | **Theme From The Three Penny Opera**...*see: Mack The Knife* |
| 27/60 | **Theme From The Unforgiven (The Need For Love)**<br>Don Costa & His Orchestra |
| 2/68 | **Theme From Valley Of The Dolls**<br>Dionne Warwick |
| 21/78 | **Theme From Which Way Is Up**<br>Stargard |
| 35/78 | **Themes From The Wizard Of Oz**<br>Meco |
| 1/74 | **Then Came You**<br>Dionne Warwick & Spinners |
| 6/63 | **Then He Kissed Me**<br>Crystals |
| 6/67<br>27/76 | **Then You Can Tell Me Goodbye**<br>Casinos<br>Glen Campbell (medley) |
| 34/75 | **There Goes Another Love Song**<br>Outlaws |
| 2/59<br>21/84 | **There Goes My Baby**<br>Drifters<br>Donna Summer |
| 20/67<br>F/71 | **There Goes My Everything**<br>Engelbert Humperdinck<br>Elvis Presley |
| 19/58 | **There Goes My Heart**<br>Joni James |
| 1/64 | **There! I've Said It Again**<br>Bobby Vinton |
| 20/68 | **There Is**<br>Dells |

| POS/YR | RECORD TITLE/ARTIST |
|---|---|
| 11/67 | **There Is A Mountain**<br>Donovan |
| | **There Is Love**...*see: Wedding Song* |
| 32/73 | **There It Is**<br>Tyrone Davis |
| 33/59 | **There Must Be A Way**<br>Joni James |
| 26/61 | **There She Goes**<br>Jerry Wallace |
| 23/60 | **(There Was A) Tall Oak Tree**<br>Dorsey Burnette |
| 36/68 | **There Was A Time**<br>James Brown |
| 33/66 | **There Will Never Be Another You**<br>Chris Montez |
| 18/74 | **There Won't Be Anymore**<br>Charlie Rich |
| 25/57 | **(There'll Be) Peace In The Valley (For Me)**<br>Elvis Presley |
| 26/69 | **There'll Come A Time**<br>Betty Everett |
| 36/78 | **There'll Never Be**<br>Switch |
| 20/57 | **There's A Gold Mine In The Sky**<br>Pat Boone |
| 4/67<br>12/76 | **There's A Kind Of Hush (All Over The World)**<br>Herman's Hermits<br>Carpenters |
| 3/61 | **There's A Moon Out Tonight**<br>Capris |
| 27/70<br>8/83 | **(There's) Always Something There To Remind Me**<br>R.B. Greaves<br>Naked Eyes |
| 21/69 | **There's Gonna Be A Showdown**<br>Archie Bell & The Drells |
| 34/67 | **There's Got To Be A Word!**<br>Innocence |
| 5/81 | **(There's) No Gettin' Over Me**<br>Ronnie Milsap |
| 20/62 | **There's No Other (Like My Baby)**<br>Crystals |

| POS/YR | RECORD TITLE/ARTIST |
|---|---|
| | **There's Nothing Stronger Than Our Love**...see: I Believe |
| 10/58 | **There's Only One Of You**<br>Four Lads |
| 31/60 | **There's Something On Your Mind**<br>Bobby Marchan |
| 1/66 | **These Boots Are Made For Walkin'**<br>Nancy Sinatra |
| 6/69<br>16/69 | **These Eyes**<br>Guess Who<br>Jr. Walker & The All Stars |
| 8/84 | **They Don't Know**<br>Tracey Ullman |
| 5/75 | **They Just Can't Stop It the (Games People Play)**<br>Spinners |
| 1/70 | **(They Long To Be) Close To You**<br>Carpenters |
| 3/66 | **They're Coming To Take Me Away, Ha-Haaa!**<br>Napoleon XIV |
| 15/71 | **Thin Line Between Love & Hate**<br>Persuaders |
| 3/62 | **Things**<br>Bobby Darin |
| 23/67 | **Things I Should Have Said**<br>Grass Roots |
| 16/69 | **Things I'd Like To Say**<br>New Colony Six |
| 5/77 | **Things We Do For Love**<br>10cc |
| 7/68 | **Think**<br>Aretha Franklin |
| 25/64 | **Think**<br>Brenda Lee |
| 33/60 | **Think**<br>James Brown |
| 20/80 | **Think About Me**<br>Fleetwood Mac |
| 30/66 | **Think I'll Go Somewhere And Cry Myself To Sleep**<br>Al Martino |
| 16/82 | **Think I'm In Love**<br>Eddie Money |

| POS/YR | RECORD TITLE/ARTIST |
|---|---|
| 27/58 | **Think It Over**<br>Crickets |
| 34/78 | **Think It Over**<br>Cheryl Ladd |
| 9/84 | **Think Of Laura**<br>Christopher Cross |
| 11/61 | **Think Twice**<br>Brook Benton |
| 18/73 | **Thinking Of You**<br>Loggins & Messina |
| 14/75 | **Third Rate Romance**<br>Amazing Rhythm Aces |
| 23/80 | **Third Time Lucky (First Time I Was A Fool)**<br>Foghat |
| 24/60 | **This Bitter Earth**<br>Dinah Washington |
| 1/65 | **This Diamond Ring**<br>Gary Lewis & The Playboys |
| 12/66 | **This Door Swings Both Ways**<br>Herman's Hermits |
| 12/59 | **This Friendly World**<br>Fabian |
| 9/69 | **This Girl Is A Woman Now**<br>Gary Puckett & The Union Gap |
| 1/68<br>7/69 | **This Guy's (Girl's) In Love With You**<br>Herb Alpert<br>Dionne Warwick |
| 24/74 | **This Heart**<br>Gene Redding |
| 26/59 | **This I Swear**<br>Skyliners |
| 11/80 | **This Is It**<br>Kenny Loggins |
| 35/78 | **This Is Love**<br>Paul Anka |
| 25/69 | **This Is My Country**<br>Impressions |
| 3/67 | **This Is My Song**<br>Petula Clark |
| 39/77 | **This Is The Way That I Feel**<br>Marie Osmond |
| 32/65 | **This Little Bird**<br>Marianne Faithfull |

| POS/YR | RECORD TITLE/ARTIST |
|---|---|
| 11/81 | **This Little Girl**<br>Gary "U.S." Bonds |
| 21/63 | **This Little Girl**<br>Dion |
| 26/58 | **This Little Girl Of Mine**<br>Everly Brothers |
| 24/58 | **This Little Girl's Gone Rockin'**<br>Ruth Brown |
| 16/60<br>6/69 | **This Magic Moment**<br>Drifters<br>Jay & The Americans |
| 33/82 | **This Man Is Mine**<br>Heart |
| 10/76 | **This Masquerade**<br>George Benson |
| 19/79 | **This Night Won't Last Forever**<br>Michael Johnson |
| 12/66 | **This Old Heart Of Mine**<br>Isley Brothers |
| 29/76 | **This One's For You**<br>Barry Manilow |
| 20/59 | **This Should Go On Forever**<br>Rod Bernard |
| 25/77 | **This Song**<br>George Harrison |
| 6/61 | **This Time**<br>Troy Shondell |
| 24/83 | **This Time**<br>Bryan Adams |
| 27/80 | **This Time**<br>John Cougar |
| 10/78 | **This Time I'm In It For Love**<br>Player |
| 6/75 | **This Will Be**<br>Natalie Cole |
| 23/84 | **This Woman**<br>Kenny Rogers |
| 38/72 | **This World**<br>Staple Singers |
| 6/63 | **Those Lazy-Hazy-Crazy Days Of Summer**<br>Nat King Cole |
| 9/61 | **Those Oldies But Goodies (Remind Me Of You)**<br>Little Caesar & The Romans |

| POS/YR | RECORD TITLE/ARTIST |
|---|---|
| 2/68 | **Those Were The Days**<br>Mary Hopkin |
| 13/65 | **Thou Shalt Not Steal**<br>Dick & DeeDee |
| 3/60 | **Thousand Stars**<br>Kathy Young with The Innocents |
| 1/59<br>23/59 | **Three Bells**<br>Browns<br>Dick Flood |
| 35/61 | **Three Hearts In A Tangle**<br>Roy Drusky |
| 24/67 | **Three Little Fishes (medley)** *<br>Mitch Ryder & The Detroit Wheels |
| 15/60 | **Three Nights A Week**<br>Fats Domino |
| 33/65 | **Three O'Clock In The Morning**<br>Bert Kaempfert & His Orchestra |
| | **Three Penny Opera**...*see: Mack The Knife* |
| 36/74 | **Three Ring Circus**<br>Blue Magic |
| 11/59 | **Three Stars**<br>Tommy Dee |
| 1/78 | **Three Times A Lady**<br>Commodores |
| 19/80 | **Three Times In Love**<br>Tommy James |
| 28/64 | **Three Window Coupe**<br>Rip Chords |
| 15/70 | **Thrill Is Gone**<br>B.B. King |
| 4/84 | **Thriller**<br>Michael Jackson |
| 13/82 | **Through The Years**<br>Kenny Rogers |
| 17/72 | **Thunder And Lightning**<br>Chi Coltrane |
| 38/77 | **Thunder In My Heart**<br>Leo Sayer |
| 9/78 | **Thunder Island**<br>Jay Ferguson |
| 25/66 | **Thunderball**<br>Tom Jones |

**Elvis Presley.** Del Shannon actually recorded "(Marie's the Name) His Latest Flame" before the King, but didn't like the song and never released it as a single. For Presley, it was just one of an incredible *nine* Top entries in 1961.

**Real Life's** Australian dance-rock sounds more European or English than anything else. On one tour Down Under, the band actually advertised that they came from Australia to be sure they drew crowds.

**Jim Reeves,** a soothing voice if there ever was one, was a promising baseball player at the University of Texas in the forties. Actually signed by the St. Louis Cardinals, he suffered an ankle injury that brought his sports career to an early end.

**Mike Reno** and **Ann Wilson.** When Ann Wilson's Heart played bars in the Pacific Northwest, they were nicknamed "Little Led Zeppelin." More recently, they've appeared in coffee commercials.

**Lionel Richie** and two friends formed the Mystics while attending Alabama's Tuskeegee Institute. The group later expanded, became the Commodores, and made pop music history.

**Rolling Stones.** If Mick Jagger had pursued his studies at the London School of Economics, instead of going off to sing the blues, both rock'n'roll and the British economy would surely be poorer today.

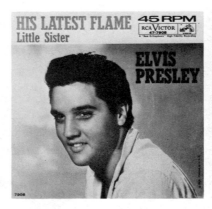

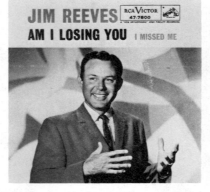

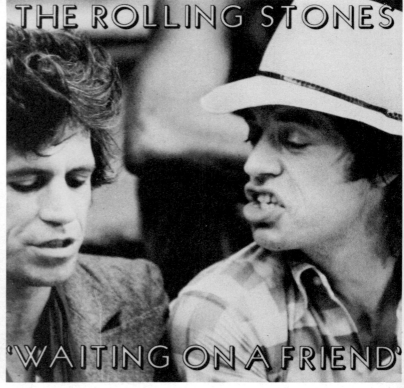

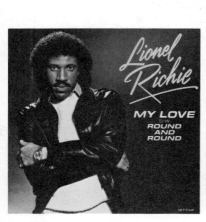

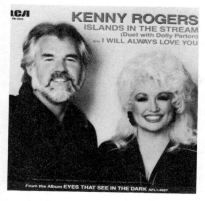

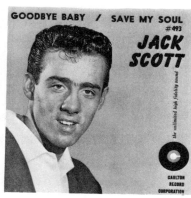

**Kenny Rogers** and **Dolly Parton** together. How could they miss? They couldn't. "Islands in the Stream" became a platinum single in December 1983, a feat not duplicated until Prince's "When Doves Cry" eight months later.

**The Scorpions** have been criticized—not without cause—for degrading women on their album covers. The suggestive cover shot for *Love at First Sting,* by big-time fashion photographer Helmut Newton, had to be replaced with an innocuous pic of the band before some stores would carry the LP.

**Jack Scott's** first single, "Leroy," reached its chart peak at number 25 in July of 1958. Just one month later, the flip side, "My True Love," shot to number 3, and Scott gained national recognition.

**Shalamar's** first records were performed by Los Angeles session musicians, but when concert promoter Dick Griffey needed a touring act, he recruited Jeffrey Daniels and Jody Watley from TV's "Solid Gold." Howard Hewlett joined them later.

**Joe Simon** is a gifted soul singer who's never received the widespread recognition he deserves. Highly respected by those in the know, however, he was chosen by the Redding family to sing at Otis' funeral.

**Patti Smith,** already a published poet when she signed with Arista Records, co-wrote her hit single "Because the Night" with fellow New Jerseyite Bruce Springsteen.

| POS/YR | RECORD TITLE/ARTIST |
|--------|---------------------|
| 1/65 | **Ticket To Ride**<br>Beatles |
| 1/81 | **Tide Is High**<br>Blondie |
| 1/73 | **Tie A Yellow Ribbon Round The Ole Oak Tree**<br>Dawn |
| 3/63 | **Tie Me Kangaroo Down, Sport**<br>Rolf Harris |
| 38/83 | **Tied Up**<br>Olivia Newton-John |
| 37/60 | **Ties That Bind**<br>Brook Benton |
| 3/59 | **Tiger**<br>Fabian |
| 11/72 | **Tight Rope**<br>Leon Russell |
| 1/68 | **Tighten Up**<br>Archie Bell & The Drells |
| 7/70 | **Tighter, Tighter**<br>Alive & Kicking |
| 12/59 | **Tijuana Jail**<br>Kingston Trio |
| 38/66 | **Tijuana Taxi**<br>Herb Alpert & The Tijuana Brass |
| 4/59 | **('Til) I Kissed You**<br>Everly Brothers |
| 32/75 | **Til The World Ends**<br>Three Dog Night |
| 22/57 | **Till**<br>Roger Williams |
| 14/62 | Angels |
| 27/68 | Vogues |
| 26/62 | **Till Death Do Us Part**<br>Bob Braun |
| 20/63 | **Till Then**<br>Classics |
| 30/59 | **Till There Was You**<br>Anita Bryant |
| 15/81 | **Time**<br>Alan Parsons Project |
| 1/84 | **Time After Time**<br>Cyndi Lauper |
| 36/66 | **Time After Time**<br>Chris Montez |

| POS/YR | RECORD TITLE/ARTIST |
|--------|---------------------|
| 30/60 | **Time And The River**<br>Nat King Cole |
| 2/83 | **Time (Clock Of The Heart)**<br>Culture Club |
| 32/74 | **Time For Livin'**<br>Sly & The Family Stone |
| 39/68 | **Time For Livin'**<br>Association |
|  | **Time For Us**...*see: Romeo & Juliet* |
| 11/68 | **Time Has Come Today**<br>Chambers Brothers |
| 1/73 | **Time In A Bottle**<br>Jim Croce |
| 6/64 | **Time Is On My Side**<br>Rolling Stones |
| 6/69 | **Time Is Tight**<br>Booker T. & The Mg's |
| 15/81 | **Time Is Time**<br>Andy Gibb |
| 3/69 | **Time Of The Season**<br>Zombies |
| 22/81 | **Time Out Of Mind**<br>Steely Dan |
| 7/78 | **Time Passages**<br>Al Stewart |
| 33/73 | **Time To Get Down**<br>O'Jays |
|  | **Time To Time To Cry**...*see: Petite Fleur* |
| 18/84 | **Time Will Reveal**<br>DeBarge |
| 5/66 | **Time Won't Let Me**<br>Outsiders |
| 7/76 | **Times Of Your Life**<br>Paul Anka |
| 17/71 | **Timothy**<br>Buoys |
| 4/74 | **Tin Man**<br>America |
| 5/55 | **Tina Marie**<br>Perry Como |
| 17/68 | **Tip-Toe Thru' The Tulips With Me**<br>Tiny Tim |

| POS/YR | RECORD TITLE/ARTIST |
|--------|---------------------|
| 11/71 | **Tired Of Being Alone**<br>Al Green |
| 8/80 | **Tired Of Toein' The Line**<br>Rocky Burnette |
| 6/65 | **Tired Of Waiting For You**<br>Kinks |
| | **To**. . .*also see: Too* |
| 26/62 | **To A Sleeping Beauty**<br>Jimmy Dean |
| 5/84 | **To All The Girls I've Loved Before**<br>Julio Iglesias & Willie Nelson |
| 22/58 | **To Be Loved**<br>Jackie Wilson |
| 21/60 | **To Each His Own**<br>Platters |
| 29/68 | **To Give (The Reason I Live)**<br>Frankie Valli |
| 1/58<br>24/65<br>34/69 | **To Know Him Is To Love Him**<br>Teddy Bears<br>Peter & Gordon<br>Bobby Vinton |
| 38/73 | **To Know You Is To Love You**<br>B.B. King |
| 17/67 | **To Love Somebody**<br>Bee Gees |
| 1/67 | **To Sir With Love**<br>Lulu |
| 35/69 | **To Susan On The West Coast Waiting**<br>Donovan |
| 25/57 | **To The Aisle**<br>Five Satins |
| 17/75 | **To The Door Of The Sun (Alle Porte Del Sole)**<br>Al Martino |
| 25/56 | **To The Ends Of The Earth**<br>Nat King Cole |
| 27/56 | **To You, My Love**<br>Nick Noble |
| 20/71 | **Toast And Marmalade For Tea**<br>Tin Tin |
| 14/64 | **Tobacco Road**<br>Nashville Teens |
| 17/64 | **Today**<br>New Christy Minstrels |

| POS/YR | RECORD TITLE/ARTIST |
|--------|---------------------|
| 39/63 | **(Today I Met) The Boy I'm Gonna Marry**<br>Darlene Love |
| 23/76 | **Today's The Day**<br>America |
| 6/61 | **Together**<br>Connie Francis |
| 18/81 | **Together**<br>Tierra |
| 19/66 | **Together Again**<br>Ray Charles |
| 37/72 | **Together Let's Find Love**<br>5th Dimension |
| 26/60 | **Togetherness**<br>Frankie Avalon |
| 20/63 | **Tom Cat**<br>Rooftop Singers |
| 1/58 | **Tom Dooley**<br>Kingston Trio |
| 29/59 | **Tomboy**<br>Perry Como |
| 23/68 | **Tomorrow**<br>Strawberry Alarm Clock |
| 8/61 | **Tonight**<br>Ferrante & Teicher |
| 13/84 | **Tonight**<br>Kool & The Gang |
| 26/61 | **Tonight (Could Be The Night)**<br>Velvets |
| 16/83 | **Tonight, I Celebrate My Love**<br>Peabo Bryson/Roberta Flack |
| 15/61 | **Tonight I Fell In Love**<br>Tokens |
| 20/82 | **Tonight I'm Yours (Don't Hurt Me)**<br>Rod Stewart |
| 13/61 | **Tonight My Love, Tonight**<br>Paul Anka |
| 4/56<br>15/56 | **Tonight You Belong To Me**<br>Patience & Prudence<br>Lennon Sisters |
| 39/60 | **Tonight's The Night**<br>Shirelles |
| 28/65 | **Tonight's The Night**<br>Solomon Burke |

| POS/YR | RECORD TITLE/ARTIST |
|---|---|
| 1/76 | **Tonight's The Night (Gonna Be Alright)** <br> Rod Stewart |
| 4/69 | **Too Busy Thinking About My Baby** <br> Marvin Gaye |
| 39/56 | **Too Close For Comfort** <br> Eydie Gorme |
| 5/80 | **Too Hot** <br> Kool & The Gang |
| 24/78 | **Too Hot Ta Trot** <br> Commodores |
| 2/72 | **Too Late To Turn Back Now** <br> Cornelius Brothers & Sister Rose |
| 25/65 <br> 24/67 | **Too Many Fish In The Sea** <br> Marvelettes <br> Mitch Ryder & The Detroit Wheels |
| 13/65 | **Too Many Rivers** <br> Brenda Lee |
| 1/57 | **Too Much** <br> Elvis Presley |
| 1/79 | **Too Much Heaven** <br> Bee Gees |
| 35/67 | **Too Much Of Nothing** <br> Peter, Paul & Mary |
| 19/68 | **Too Much Talk** <br> Paul Revere & The Raiders |
| 30/60 | **Too Much Tequila** <br> Champs |
| 9/81 | **Too Much Time On My Hands** <br> Styx |
| 1/78 | **Too Much, Too Little, Too Late** <br> Johnny Mathis & Deniece Williams |
| 5/83 | **Too Shy** <br> Kajagoogoo |
| | **Too Soon To Know**...see: It's Too Soon |
| 40/81 | **Too Tight** <br> Con Funk Shun |
| 13/69 | **Too Weak To Fight** <br> Clarence Carter |
| 13/72 | **Too Young** <br> Donny Osmond |
| 21/56 | **Too Young To Go Steady** <br> Nat King Cole |
| 30/78 | **Took The Last Train** <br> David Gates |

| POS/YR | RECORD TITLE/ARTIST |
|---|---|
| 1/73 | **Top Of The World** <br> Carpenters |
| 27/58 | **Topsy I** <br> Cozy Cole |
| 3/58 | **Topsy II** <br> Cozy Cole |
| 18/58 <br> 21/58 | **Torero** <br> Renato Carosone <br> Julius LaRosa |
| 1/77 | **Torn Between Two Lovers** <br> Mary MacGregor |
| 39/59 | **Torquay** <br> Fireballs |
| 17/84 | **Torture** <br> Jacksons |
| 20/62 | **Torture** <br> Kris Jensen |
| 1/61 | **Tossin' And Turnin'** <br> Bobby Lewis |
| 1/83 | **Total Eclipse Of The Heart** <br> Bonnie Tyler |
| 23/74 | **Touch A Hand, Make A Friend** <br> Staple Singers |
| 37/80 | **Touch And Go** <br> Cars |
| 3/69 | **Touch Me** <br> Doors |
| 19/74 | **Touch Me** <br> Fancy |
| 1/73 | **Touch Me In The Morning** <br> Diana Ross |
| 16/81 | **Touch Me When We're Dancing** <br> Carpenters |
| | **Touch The Wind**...see: Eres Tu |
| 5/61 | **Tower Of Strength** <br> Gene McDaniels |
| 13/62 | **Town Without Pity** <br> Gene Pitney |
| 24/56 | **Tra La La** <br> Georgia Gibbs |
| 35/64 | **Tra La La La Suzy** <br> Dean & Jean |

| POS/YR | RECORD TITLE/ARTIST |
|---|---|
| 2/69 | **Traces**<br>Classics IV |
| 16/65<br>10/67<br>25/76 | **Tracks Of My Tears**<br>Miracles<br>Johnny Rivers<br>Linda Ronstadt |
| 9/69 | **Tracy**<br>Cuff Links |
| 13/60 | **Tracy's Theme**<br>Spencer Ross |
| 5/59<br>10/61 | **Tragedy**<br>Thomas Wayne<br>Fleetwoods |
| 1/79 | **Tragedy**<br>Bee Gees |
| 23/80 | **Train In Vain (Stand By Me)**<br>Clash |
| 36/60 | **Train Of Love**<br>Annette |
| 27/74 | **Train Of Thought**<br>Cher |
| 38/79 | **Train, Train**<br>Blackfoot |
| 22/66 | **Trains And Boats And Planes**<br>Dionne Warwick |
| 26/67 | **Tramp**<br>Otis & Carla |
| 38/75 | **Trampled Under Foot**<br>Led Zeppelin |
| 8/56 | **Transfusion**<br>Nervous Norvus |
| 35/61 | **Transistor Sister**<br>Freddy Cannon |
| 13/71 | **Trapped By A Thing Called Love**<br>Denise LaSalle |
| 2/70 | **Travelin' Band**<br>Creedence Clearwater Revival |
| 1/61 | **Travelin' Man**<br>Ricky Nelson |
| 32/67 | **Travlin' Man**<br>Stevie Wonder |
| 16/56 | **Treasure Of Love**<br>Clyde McPhatter |
| 26/58 | **Treasure Of Your Love**<br>Eileen Rodgers |

| POS/YR | RECORD TITLE/ARTIST |
|---|---|
| 3/71 | **Treat Her Like A Lady**<br>Cornelius Brothers & Sister Rose |
| 2/65 | **Treat Her Right**<br>Roy Head |
| 18/57 | **Treat Me Nice**<br>Elvis Presley |
| 18/81 | **Treat Me Right**<br>Pat Benatar |
| 29/61 | **Triangle**<br>Janie Grant |
| 25/57 | **Tricky**<br>Ralph Marterie & His Orchestra |
| 6/72 | **Troglodyte (Cave Man)**<br>Jimmy Castor Bunch |
| 9/82 | **Trouble**<br>Lindsey Buckingham |
| 35/75 | **T-R-O-U-B-L-E**<br>Elvis Presley |
| 20/60 | **Trouble In Paradise**<br>Crests |
| 33/63 | **Trouble Is My Middle Name**<br>Bobby Vinton |
| 7/73 | **Trouble Man**<br>Marvin Gaye |
| 4/83 | **True**<br>Spandau Ballet |
| 35/69 | **True Grit**<br>Glen Campbell |
| 3/56<br>15/56 | **True Love**<br>Bing Crosby & Grace Kelly<br>Jane Powell |
| 21/63 | **True Love Never Runs Smooth**<br>Gene Pitney |
| | **True Love, True Love**...*see: (If You Cry)* |
| 14/65 | **True Love Ways**<br>Peter & Gordon |
| 1/82 | **Truly**<br>Lionel Richie |
| 30/61 | **Trust In Me**<br>Etta James |
| 23/69 | **Try A Little Kindness**<br>Glen Campbell |

| POS/YR | RECORD TITLE/ARTIST |
|--------|---------------------|
| | **Try A Little Tenderness** |
| 25/67 | Otis Redding |
| 29/69 | Three Dog Night |
| | **Try Again** |
| 23/83 | Champaign |
| | **Try It Baby** |
| 15/64 | Marvin Gaye |
| | **Try The Impossible** |
| 33/58 | Lee Andrews & The Hearts |
| | **Try To Remember (medley)** |
| 11/75 | Gladys Knight & The Pips |
| | **Try Too Hard** |
| 12/66 | Dave Clark Five |
| | **Tryin' To Get The Feeling Again** |
| 10/76 | Barry Manilow |
| | **Tryin' To Live My Life Without You** |
| 5/81 | Bob Seger |
| | **Tryin' To Love Two** |
| 10/77 | William Bell |
| | **Trying To Hold On To My Woman** |
| 15/74 | Lamont Dozier |
| | **Trying To Make A Fool Of Me** |
| 40/70 | Delfonics |
| | **Tubular Bells** |
| 7/74 | Mike Oldfield |
| | **Tucumcari** |
| 32/59 | Jimmie Rodgers |
| | **Tuesday Afternoon (Forever Afternoon)** |
| 24/68 | Moody Blues |
| | **Tuff** |
| 17/62 | Ace Cannon |
| | **Tulsa Time** |
| 30/80 | Eric Clapton |
| | **Tumbling Dice** |
| 7/72 | Rolling Stones |
| 32/78 | Linda Ronstadt |
| | **Tumbling Tumbleweeds** |
| 30/58 | Billy Vaughn & His Orchestra |
| | **Turn Around** |
| 27/64 | Dick & DeeDee |
| | **Turn Around, Look At Me** |
| 7/68 | Vogues |
| | **Turn Back The Hands Of Time** |
| 3/70 | Tyrone Davis |

| POS/YR | RECORD TITLE/ARTIST |
|--------|---------------------|
| | **Turn Down Day** |
| 16/66 | Cyrkle |
| | **Turn Me Loose** |
| 9/59 | Fabian |
| | **Turn Me Loose** |
| 35/81 | Loverboy |
| | **Turn On Your Love Light** |
| 28/62 | Bobby Bland |
| | **Turn The Beat Around** |
| 10/76 | Vicki Sue Robinson |
| | **Turn To Stone** |
| 13/78 | Electric Light Orchestra |
| | **Turn To You** |
| 32/84 | Go-GO'S |
| | **Turn! Turn! Turn!** |
| 1/65 | Byrds |
| | **Turn Your Love Around** |
| 5/82 | George Benson |
| | **Turning Japanese** |
| 36/80 | Vapors |
| | **Turvy II** |
| 36/58 | Cozy Cole |
| | **Tush** |
| 20/75 | ZZ Top |
| | **Tusk** |
| 8/79 | Fleetwood Mac |
| | **Tutti' Frutti** |
| 12/56 | Pat Boone |
| 17/56 | Little Richard |
| | **Tweedlee Dee** |
| 2/55 | Georgia Gibbs |
| 14/55 | LaVern Baker |
| | **Twelfth Of Never** |
| 9/57 | Johnny Mathis |
| 8/73 | Donny Osmond |
| | **Twelve Thirty (Young Girls Are Coming To The Canyon)** |
| 20/67 | Mamas & The Papas |
| | **Twenty Miles** |
| 15/63 | Chubby Checker |
| | **20-75** |
| 31/64 | Willie Mitchell |
| | **Twenty Four Hours From Tulsa** |
| 17/63 | Gene Pitney |

| POS/YR | RECORD TITLE/ARTIST |
|---|---|
| 6/69 | **Twenty-Five Miles**<br>Edwin Starr |
| 4/70 | **25 Or 6 To 4**<br>Chicago |
| 2/58 | **26 Miles (Santa Catalina)**<br>Four Preps |
| 38/81 | **Twilight**<br>Electric Light Orchestra |
| 1/58 | **Twilight Time**<br>Platters |
| 10/83 | **Twilight Zone**<br>Golden Earring |
| 30/80 | **Twilight Zone/Twilight Tone**<br>Manhattan Transfer |
| 14/65 | **Twine Time**<br>Alvin Cash & The Crawlers |
| 39/66 | **Twinkle Toes**<br>Roy Orbison |
| 1/60<br>28/60<br>1/62 | **Twist**<br>Chubby Checker<br>Hank Ballard & The Midnighters<br>Chubby Checker |
| 17/62<br>2/64 | **Twist And Shout**<br>Isley Brothers<br>Beatles |
| 26/62 | **Twist-Her**<br>Bill Black's Combo |
| 25/63 | **Twist It Up**<br>Chubby Checker |
| 5/84 | **Twist Of Fate**<br>Olivia Newton-John |
| 9/62 | **Twist, Twist Senora**<br>Gary "U.S." Bonds |
| 22/62 | **Twistin' Matilda**<br>Jimmy Soul |
| 34/62 | **Twistin' Postman**<br>Marvelettes |
| 9/62 | **Twistin' The Night Away**<br>Sam Cooke |
| 27/60 | **Twistin' U.S.A.**<br>Danny & The Juniors |
|  | **Twistin' White Silver Sands**...see: *White Silver Sands* |
| 17/59 | **Twixt Twelve And Twenty**<br>Pat Boone |

| POS/YR | RECORD TITLE/ARTIST |
|---|---|
| 11/56 | **Two Different Worlds**<br>Don Rondo |
| 16/71 | **Two Divided By Love**<br>Grass Roots |
| 19/78 | **Two Doors Down**<br>Dolly Parton |
| 6/63 | **Two Faces Have I**<br>Lou Christie |
| 33/75 | **Two Fine People**<br>Cat Stevens |
| 16/55 | **Two Hearts**<br>Pat Boone |
| 40/81 | **Two Hearts**<br>Stephanie Mills & Teddy Pendergrass |
| 38/83 | **Two Less Lonely People In The World**<br>Air Supply |
| 31/68 | **Two Little Kids**<br>Peaches & Herb |
| 18/55 | **Two Lost Souls**<br>Perry Como & Jaye P. Morgan |
| 7/63 | **Two Lovers**<br>Mary Wells |
| 11/78 | **Two Out Of Three Ain't Bad**<br>Meat Loaf |
| 30/80 | **Two Places At The Same Time**<br>Ray Parker Jr. & Raydio |
| 38/84 | **Two Sides Of Love**<br>Sammy Hagar |
| 22/78 | **Two Tickets To Paradise**<br>Eddie Money |
| 32/63 | **Two Tickets To Paradise**<br>Brook Benton |
|  | **2001 Space Odyssey**...see: *Also Sprach Zarathustra* |

# U

| | |
|---|---|
| 28/68 | **U.S. Male**<br>Elvis Presley |
| 14/59 | **Uh! Oh!**<br>Nutty Squirrels |

| POS/YR | RECORD TITLE/ARTIST |
|--------|---------------------|
| 5/64 | **Um, Um, Um, Um, Um, Um**<br>Major Lance |
| 9/62 | **Unchain My Heart**<br>Ray Charles |
| | **Unchained Melody** |
| 1/55 | Les Baxter & His Orchestra |
| 3/55 | Al Hibbler |
| 6/55 | Roy Hamilton |
| 29/55 | June Valli |
| 4/65 | Righteous Brothers |
| 1/71 | **Uncle Albert/Admiral Halsey**<br>Paul McCartney |
| 29/82 | **Under Pressure**<br>Queen & David Bowie |
| 4/64 | **Under The Boardwalk**<br>Drifters |
| 35/66 | **Under Your Spell Again**<br>Johnny Rivers |
| 1/77 | **Undercover Angel**<br>Alan O'Day |
| 9/83 | **Undercover Of The Night**<br>Rolling Stones |
| 35/64 | **Understand Your Man**<br>Johnny Cash |
| 22/69 | **Undun**<br>Guess Who |
| 9/73 | **Uneasy Rider**<br>Charlie Daniels Band |
| 17/59 | **Unforgettable**<br>Dinah Washington |
| | **Unforgiven**...see: *Theme From The* |
| 33/70 | **Ungena Za Ulimwengu (Unite The World)**<br>Temptations |
| 7/68 | **Unicorn, The**<br>Irish Rovers |
| 24/76 | **Union Man**<br>Cate Bros. |
| 3/83 | **Union Of The Snake**<br>Duran Duran |
| 13/70 | **United We Stand**<br>Brotherhood Of Man |
| 39/68 | **Unknown Soldier**<br>Doors |

| POS/YR | RECORD TITLE/ARTIST |
|--------|---------------------|
| 40/72 | **Until It's Time For You To Go**<br>Elvis Presley |
| 3/74 | **Until You Come Back To Me (That's What I'm Gonna Do)**<br>Aretha Franklin |
| | **Up A Lazy River**...see: *Lazy River* |
| 4/70 | **Up Around The Bend**<br>Creedence Clearwater Revival |
| 16/75 | **Up In A Puff Of Smoke**<br>Polly Brown |
| 25/70 | **Up On Cripple Creek**<br>The Band |
| | **Up On The Roof** |
| 5/63 | Drifters |
| 28/79 | James Taylor |
| 10/70 | **Up The Ladder To The Roof**<br>Supremes |
| 7/67 | **Up-Up And Away**<br>5th Dimension |
| 1/82 | **Up Where We Belong**<br>Joe Cocker & Jennifer Warnes |
| 22/67 | **Ups And Downs**<br>Paul Revere & The Raiders |
| 1/80 | **Upside Down**<br>Diana Ross |
| 3/66 | **Uptight (Everything's Alright)**<br>Stevie Wonder<br>*(also see: Little Ole Man)* |
| 13/62 | **Uptown**<br>Crystals |
| 25/77 | **Uptown Festival (Motown Medley)**<br>Shalamar |
| 3/83 | **Uptown Girl**<br>Billy Joel |
| 4/81 | **Urgent**<br>Foreigner |
| 2/72 | **Use Me**<br>Bill Withers |
| 4/78 | **Use Ta Be My Girl**<br>O'Jays |
| 34/65 | **Use Your Head**<br>Mary Wells |
| | **Utopia**<br>Frank Gari |

| POS/YR | RECORD TITLE/ARTIST |
|--------|---------------------|

# V

|  |  |
|--------|---------------------|
| 8/82 | **Vacation** <br> Go-GO'S |
| 9/62 | **Vacation** <br> Connie Francis |
| 3/68 | **Valleri** <br> Monkees |
| 32/82 | **Valley Girl** <br> Frank Zappa |
| 6/57 | **Valley Of Tears** <br> Fats Domino |
|  | **Valley Of The Dolls**...see: Theme From |
| 2/70 | **Vehicle** <br> Ides Of March |
| 8/72 | **Ventura Highway** <br> America |
| 1/59 | **Venus** <br> Frankie Avalon |
| 1/70 | **Venus** <br> Shocking Blue |
| 12/75 | **Venus And Mars Rock Show** <br> Paul McCartney |
| 7/62 | **Venus In Blue Jeans** <br> Jimmy Clanton |
| 23/58 | **Very Precious Love** <br> Ames Brothers |
| 20/58 <br> 23/58 | **Very Special Love** <br> Debbie Reynolds <br> Johnny Nash |
| 11/74 | **Very Special Love Song** <br> Charlie Rich |
| 26/64 | **Very Thought Of You** <br> Ricky Nelson |
| 31/79 | **Victim Of Love** <br> Elton John |
| 40/79 | **Video Killed The Radio Star** <br> Buggles |
| 22/62 | **Village Of Love** <br> Nathaniel Mayer & The Fabulous Twilights |

| POS/YR | RECORD TITLE/ARTIST |
|--------|---------------------|
| 7/60 | **Village Of St. Bernadette** <br> Andy Williams |
| 12/72 | **Vincent** <br> Don McLean |
| 29/64 | **Viva Las Vegas** <br> Elvis Presley |
| 28/70 | **Viva Tirado** <br> El Chicano |
| 15/81 | **Voice** <br> Moody Blues |
| 32/80 | **Voices** <br> Cheap Trick |
| 1/58 <br> 12/58 <br> 4/60 <br> 33/75 | **Volare (Nel Blu Dipinto Di Blu)** <br> Domenico Modugno <br> Dean Martin <br> Bobby Rydell <br> Al Martino |
| 27/65 | **Voodoo Woman** <br> Bobby Goldsboro |
| 29/82 | **Voyeur** <br> Kim Carnes |

# W

|  |  |
|--------|---------------------|
| 36/74 | **W-O-L-D** <br> Harry Chapin |
| 40/67 | **Wack Wack** <br> Young-Holt Unlimited |
| 19/66 <br> 37/67 | **Wade In The Water** <br> Ramsey Lewis <br> Herb Alpert & The Tijuana Brass |
| 2/62 | **Wah Watusi** <br> Orlons |
| 37/61 | **Wait A Minute** <br> Coasters |
| 23/57 | **Wait And See** <br> Fats Domino |
| 18/80 | **Wait For Me** <br> Daryl Hall & John Oates |
| 37/60 | **Wait For Me** <br> Playmates |
| 26/63 | **Wait Til' My Bobby Gets Home** <br> Darlene Love |

| POS/YR | RECORD TITLE/ARTIST |
|--------|---------------------|
| 18/58 | **Waitin' In School**<br>Ricky Nelson |
| 19/81 | **Waiting**<br>Tom Petty & The Heartbreakers |
| 2/81 | **Waiting For A Girl Like You**<br>Foreigner |
| 13/82 | **Waiting On A Friend**<br>Rolling Stones |
| 1/84 | **Wake Me Up Before You Go-Go**<br>Wham! |
| 5/55<br>13/55 | **Wake The Town And Tell The People**<br>Les Baxter & His Orchestra<br>Mindy Carson |
| 12/76 | **Wake Up Everybody**<br>Harold Melvin & The Blue Notes |
| 1/57<br>27/82 | **Wake Up Little Susie**<br>Everly Brothers<br>Simon & Garfunkel |
| 7/58 | **Walk, The**<br>Jimmy McCracklin |
| 12/70 | **Walk A Mile In My Shoes**<br>Joe South |
| 23/65 | **Walk Away**<br>Matt Monro |
| 36/80 | **Walk Away**<br>Donna Summer |
| 9/76 | **Walk Away From Love**<br>David Ruffin |
| 5/66<br>14/68 | **Walk Away Renee**<br>Left Banke<br>Four Tops |
| 2/60<br>8/64 | **Walk Don't Run**<br>Ventures<br>Ventures ('64) |
| 10/56 | **Walk Hand In Hand**<br>Tony Martin |
| 12/65 | **Walk In The Black Forest**<br>Horst Jankowski |
| 1/63 | **Walk Like A Man**<br>Four Seasons |
| 19/74 | **Walk Like A Man**<br>Grand Funk Railroad |
| 5/61 | **Walk On By**<br>Leroy Van Dyke |

| POS/YR | RECORD TITLE/ARTIST |
|--------|---------------------|
| 6/64<br>30/69 | **Walk On By**<br>Dionne Warwick<br>Isaac Hayes |
| 16/73 | **Walk On The Wild Side**<br>Lou Reed |
| 21/62 | **Walk On The Wild Side**<br>Jimmy Smith |
| 17/72 | **Walk On Water**<br>Neil Diamond |
| 7/61 | **Walk Right Back**<br>Everly Brothers |
| 1/63 | **Walk Right In**<br>Rooftop Singers |
| 10/77 | **Walk This Way**<br>Aerosmith |
| 12/57 | **Walkin' After Midnight**<br>Patsy Cline |
| 23/64<br>19/70 | **Walkin' In The Rain**<br>Ronettes<br>Jay & The Americans |
| 14/72 | **Walkin' In The Rain With The One I Love**<br>Love Unlimited |
| | **Walkin' In The Sand**...see: Remember |
| 37/67 | **Walkin' In The Sunshine**<br>Roger Miller |
| 12/63 | **Walkin' Miracle**<br>Essex |
| 22/66 | **Walkin' My Cat Named Dog**<br>Norma Tanega |
| 29/58 | **Walking Along**<br>Diamonds |
| 6/75 | **Walking In Rhythm**<br>Blackbyrds |
| 18/84 | **Walking On A Thin Line**<br>Huey Lewis & The News |
| 26/63 | **Walking Proud**<br>Steve Lawrence |
| 10/63 | **Walking The Dog**<br>Rufus Thomas |
| | **Walking The Floor**...see: I'm Walking |
| 6/60 | **Walking To New Orleans**<br>Fats Domino |

| POS/YR | RECORD TITLE/ARTIST |
|--------|---------------------|
| 32/80 | **Walks Like A Lady**<br>Journey |
| 2/62 | **Wanderer, The**<br>Dion |
| 3/80 | **Wanderer, The**<br>Donna Summer |
| 5/83 | **Wanna Be Startin' Somethin'**<br>Michael Jackson |
| 1/71 | **Want Ads**<br>Honey Cone |
| 38/56 | **Wanting You**<br>Roger Williams |
| 1/70 | **War**<br>Edwin Starr |
| 17/84 | **War Song**<br>Culture Club |
| 17/66 | **Warm And Tender Love**<br>Percy Sledge |
| 39/78 | **Warm Ride**<br>Rare Earth |
| 25/62 | **Warmed Over Kisses (Left Over Love)**<br>Brian Hyland |
| 7/84 | **Warrior, The**<br>Scandal featuring Patty Smyth |
| 2/63 | **Washington Square**<br>Village Stompers |
| 37/81 | **Wasn't That A Party**<br>Irish Rovers |
| 8/75 | **Wasted Days And Wasted Nights**<br>Freddy Fender |
| 9/82 | **Wasted On The Way**<br>Crosby, Stills & Nash |
| 40/79 | **Watch Out For Lucy**<br>Eric Clapton |
| 30/67 | **Watch The Flowers Grow**<br>Four Seasons |
| 11/71 | **Watching Scotty Grow**<br>Bobby Goldsboro |
| 10/81 | **Watching The Wheels**<br>John Lennon |
| 40/61 | **Water Boy**<br>Don Shirley Trio |
| 4/59 | **Waterloo**<br>Stonewall Jackson |

| POS/YR | RECORD TITLE/ARTIST |
|--------|---------------------|
| 6/74 | **Waterloo**<br>Abba |
| 10/63 | **Watermelon Man**<br>Mongo Santamaria |
| 25/61 | **Watusi, The**<br>Vibrations<br>*(also see: El Watusi and Wah Watusi)* |
| 18/77 | **Way Down**<br>Elvis Presley |
| 3/60 | **Way Down Yonder In New Orleans**<br>Freddy Cannon |
| 40/83 | **Way He Makes Me Feel**<br>Barbra Streisand |
| 24/78 | **Way I Feel Tonight**<br>Bay City Rollers |
| 35/59 | **Way I Walk**<br>Jack Scott |
| 4/75 | **Way I Want To Touch You**<br>Captain & Tennille |
| 7/72 | **Way Of Love**<br>Cher |
| 1/74<br>11/75 | **Way We Were**<br>Barbra Streisand<br>Gladys Knight & The Pips |
| 11/64<br>20/78 | **Way You Do The Things You Do**<br>Temptations<br>Rita Coolidge |
| 13/61 | **Way You Look Tonight**<br>Lettermen |
| 24/58 | **Ways Of A Woman In Love**<br>Johnny Cash |
| 1/56<br>28/56 | **Wayward Wind**<br>Gogi Grant<br>Tex Ritter |
| 5/67 | **(We Ain't Got) Nothin' Yet**<br>Blues Magoos |
| | **We All Shine On**...*see: Instant Karma* |
| 2/79 | **We Are Family**<br>Sister Sledge |
| 4/78 | **We Are The Champions**<br>Queen |
| 25/84 | **We Are The Young**<br>Dan Hartman |

| POS/YR | RECORD TITLE/ARTIST |
|---|---|
| 5/85 | **We Belong** <br> Pat Benatar |
| 32/58 | **We Belong Together** <br> Robert & Johnny |
| 21/68 | **We Can Fly** <br> Cowsills |
| 1/66 <br> 13/71 | **We Can Work It Out** <br> Beatles <br> Stevie Wonder |
| 36/76 | **We Can't Hide It Anymore** <br> Larry Santos |
| 7/80 | **We Don't Talk Anymore** <br> Cliff Richard |
| 6/59 | **We Got Love** <br> Bobby Rydell |
| 35/69 | **We Got More Soul** <br> Dyke & The Blazers |
| 2/82 | **We Got The Beat** <br> Go-GO'S |
| 13/65 | **We Gotta Get Out Of This Place** <br> Animals |
| 20/71 | **We Gotta Get You A Woman** <br> Todd Rundgren |
| 12/77 | **We Just Disagree** <br> Dave Mason |
| 27/80 | **We Live For Love** <br> Pat Benatar |
| 39/64 | **We Love You Beatles** <br> Carefrees |
| 21/73 | **We May Never Pass This Way (Again)** <br> Seals & Crofts |
| 22/83 | **We Two** <br> Little River Band |
| 31/80 | **We Were Meant To Be Lovers** <br> Jim Photoglo |
| F/78 | **We Will Rock You** <br> Queen |
| 9/78 | **We'll Never Have To Say Goodbye Again** <br> England Dan & John Ford Coley |
| 4/64 | **We'll Sing In The Sunshine** <br> Gale Garnett |
| 14/68 | **We're A Winner** <br> Impressions |

| POS/YR | RECORD TITLE/ARTIST |
|---|---|
| 7/77 | **We're All Alone** <br> Rita Coolidge |
| 1/73 | **We're An American Band** <br> Grand Funk Railroad |
| 40/72 | **We're Free** <br> Beverly Bremers |
| 34/74 | **We're Getting Careless With Our Love** <br> Johnnie Taylor |
|  | **(We're Gonna)** . . . see: *Rock Around The Clock* |
| 25/65 | **We're Gonna Make It** <br> Little Milton |
| 15/81 | **We're In This Love Together** <br> Al Jarreau |
| 21/84 | **We're Not Gonna Take It** <br> Twisted Sister |
| 25/72 | **We've Got To Get It On Again** <br> Addrisi Brothers |
| 13/79 <br> 6/83 | **We've Got Tonite** <br> Bob Seger <br> Kenny Rogers & Sheena Easton |
| 2/70 | **We've Only Just Begun** <br> Carpenters |
| 2/58 | **Wear My Ring Around Your Neck** <br> Elvis Presley |
| 23/67 | **Wear Your Love Like Heaven** <br> Donovan |
| 32/56 | **Weary Blues** <br> McGuire Sisters |
| 10/65 | **Wedding, The** <br> Julie Rogers |
| 1/69 | **Wedding Bell Blues** <br> 5th Dimension |
|  | **Wedding Bells** . . . see: *(I'm Always Hearing)* |
| 24/71 | **Wedding Song (There Is Love)** <br> Paul Stookey <br> *(also see: Down The Aisle)* |
| 35/58 | **Week End** <br> Kingsmen |
| 29/79 | **Weekend** <br> Wet Willie |
| 10/77 | **Weekend In New England** <br> Barry Manilow |

| POS/YR | RECORD TITLE/ARTIST |
|--------|---------------------|
| 19/69 | **Weight, The**<br>Aretha Franklin |
| 1/76 | **Welcome Back**<br>John Sebastian |
| 22/62 | **Welcome Home Baby**<br>Shirelles |
| 18/60 | **(Welcome) New Lovers**<br>Pat Boone |
| 24/83 | **Welcome To Heartlight**<br>Kenny Loggins |
| 29/61 | **Well, I Told You**<br>Chantels |
| 13/66 | **Well Respected Man**<br>Kinks |
| 21/78 | **Werewolves Of London**<br>Warren Zevon |
| 37/62 | **West Of The Wall**<br>Miss Toni Fisher |
| 24/70 | **Westbound # 9**<br>Flaming Ember |
| 8/58 | **Western Movies**<br>Olympics |
| 5/67 | **Western Union**<br>Five Americans |
| 24/63 | **Wham!**<br>Lonnie Mack |
| 16/76 | **Wham Bam (Shang-A-Lang)**<br>Silver |
|  | **What A Beautiful World**...*see: I.G.Y.* |
| 8/59<br>20/75 | **What A Diff'rence A Day Makes**<br>Dinah Washington<br>Little Esther Phillips |
| 1/79 | **What A Fool Believes**<br>Doobie Brothers |
| 22/61 | **What A Party**<br>Fats Domino |
| 22/61 | **What A Price**<br>Fats Domino |
| 33/61 | **What A Surprise**<br>Johnny Maestro |
| 31/67 | **What A Woman In Love Won't Do**<br>Sandy Posey |
|  | **(What A) Wonderful World**...*see:*<br>*Wonderful World* |

| POS/YR | RECORD TITLE/ARTIST |
|--------|---------------------|
| 15/84 | **What About Me**<br>Kenny Rogers with Kim Carnes & James Ingram |
| 29/83 | **What About Me**<br>Moving Pictures |
| 39/72 | **What Am I Crying For?**<br>Classics IV |
| 35/83 | **What Am I Gonna Do (I'm So In Love With You)**<br>Rod Stewart |
| 8/75 | **What Am I Gonna Do With You**<br>Barry White |
| 9/58<br>26/60 | **What Am I Living For**<br>Chuck Willis<br>Conway Twitty |
| 14/81 | **What Are We Doin' In Love**<br>Dottie West |
| 39/71 | **What Are You Doing Sunday**<br>Dawn |
| 7/66 | **What Becomes Of The Brokenhearted**<br>Jimmy Ruffin |
|  | **What Cha**...*see: Whatcha* |
| 38/65 | **What Color (Is A Man)**<br>Bobby Vinton |
| 4/69 | **What Does It Take (To Win Your Love)**<br>Jr. Walker & The All Stars |
| 29/65 | **What Have They Done To The Rain**<br>Searchers |
| 39/84 | **(What) In The Name Of Love**<br>Naked Eyes |
| 5/60 | **What In The World's Come Over You**<br>Jack Scott |
| 10/71 | **What Is Life**<br>George Harrison |
| 15/59 | **What Is Love?**<br>Playmates |
| 33/84 | **What Is Love?**<br>Howard Jones |
| 19/70 | **What Is Truth**<br>Johnny Cash |
| 10/81 | **What Kind Of Fool**<br>Barbra Streisand & Barry Gibb |
| 17/62 | **What Kind Of Fool Am I**<br>Sammy Davis, Jr. |

| POS/YR | RECORD TITLE/ARTIST |
|--------|---------------------|
| | **What Kind Of Fool Am I** |
| 21/82 | Rick Springfield |
| | **What Kind Of Fool Do You Think I Am** |
| 9/64 | Tams |
| 23/69 | Bill Deal & The Rhondels |
| | **What Kind Of Love Is This** |
| 18/62 | Joey Dee & The Starliters |
| | **What Now** |
| 40/65 | Gene Chandler |
| | **What Now My Love** |
| 14/66 | Sonny & Cher |
| 24/66 | Herb Alpert & The Tijuana Brass |
| 30/67 | Mitch Ryder & The Detroit Wheels |
| | **What The World Needs Now Is Love** |
| 7/65 | Jackie DeShannon |
| 8/71 | Tom Clay |
| | **What Will Mary Say** |
| 9/63 | Johnny Mathis |
| | **What You**...also see: Whatcha |
| | **What You Won't Do For Love** |
| 9/79 | Bobby Caldwell |
| | **What'd I Say** |
| 6/59 | Ray Charles |
| 30/61 | Jerry Lee Lewis |
| 24/62 | Bobby Darin |
| 21/64 | Elvis Presley |
| | **What's A Matter Baby** |
| 12/62 | Timi Yuro |
| | **What's Easy For Two Is So Hard For One** |
| 29/64 | Mary Wells |
| | **What's Forever For** |
| 19/82 | Michael Murphey |
| | **What's Going On** |
| 2/71 | Marvin Gaye |
| | **What's Love Got To Do With It** |
| 1/84 | Tina Turner |
| | **What's New Pussycat?** |
| 3/65 | Tom Jones |
| | **What's So Good About Good-By** |
| 35/62 | Miracles |
| | **What's The Matter With You Baby** |
| 17/64 | Marvin Gaye & Mary Wells |
| | **What's The Use Of Breaking Up** |
| 20/69 | Jerry Butler |

| POS/YR | RECORD TITLE/ARTIST |
|--------|---------------------|
| | **What's Your Name** |
| 7/62 | Don & Juan |
| | **What's Your Name** |
| 13/78 | Lynyrd Skynyrd |
| | **Whatcha Gonna Do** |
| 6/77 | Pablo Cruise |
| | **Whatcha Gonna Do With My Lovin'** |
| 22/79 | Stephanie Mills |
| | **Whatcha See Is Whatcha Get** |
| 9/71 | Dramatics |
| | **Whatever Gets You Thru The Night** |
| 1/74 | John Lennon |
| | **Whatever Lola Wants** |
| 6/55 | Sarah Vaughan |
| 12/55 | Dinah Shore |
| | **Whatever Will Be, Will Be**...see: Que Sera, Sera |
| | **Whatever You Got, I Want** |
| 38/74 | Jacksons |
| | **Wheel Of Hurt** |
| 26/66 | Margaret Whiting |
| | **Wheels** |
| 3/61 | String-A-Longs |
| 28/61 | Billy Vaughn & His Orchestra |
| | **When** |
| 5/58 | Kalin Twins |
| | **When A Man (Woman) Loves A Woman (Man)** |
| 1/66 | Percy Sledge |
| 35/80 | Bette Midler |
| | **When All Is Said And Done** |
| 27/82 | Abba |
| | **When Doves Cry** |
| 1/84 | Prince |
| | **When He Shines** |
| 30/82 | Sheena Easton |
| | **When I Die** |
| 18/69 | Motherlode |
| | **When I Fall In Love** |
| 7/62 | Lettermen |
| | **When I Grow Up (To Be A Man)** |
| 9/64 | Beach Boys |
| | **When I Need You** |
| 1/77 | Leo Sayer |

| POS/YR | RECORD TITLE/ARTIST |
|--------|---------------------|
| 29/57 | **When I See You** <br> Fats Domino |
| 20/80 | **When I Wanted You** <br> Barry Manilow |
| 15/67 | **When I Was Young** <br> Animals |
| 25/65 | **When I'm Gone** <br> Brenda Holloway |
| 26/82 | **When It's Over** <br> Loverboy |
| 18/66 | **When Liking Turns To Loving** <br> Ronnie Dove |
| 19/56 | **When My Blue Moon Turns To Gold Again** <br> Elvis Presley |
| 14/56 | **When My Dreamboat Comes Home** <br> Fats Domino |
| 28/62 | **When My Little Girl Is Smiling** <br> Drifters |
| 37/66 | **(When She Needs Good Lovin') She Comes To Me** <br> Chicago Loop |
| 11/81 | **When She Was My Girl** <br> Four Tops |
| 10/62 | **When The Boy In Your Arms (Is The Boy In Your Heart)** <br> Connie Francis |
| 19/58 | **When The Boys Talk About The Girls** <br> Valerie Carr |
| 37/83 | **When The Lights Go Out** <br> Naked Eyes |
| 23/64 | **When The Lovelight Starts Shining Through His Eyes** <br> Supremes |
| 18/56 | **When The Saints Go Marching In** <br> Bill Haley & His Comets |
| 12/56 <br> 18/56 | **When The White Lilacs Bloom Again** <br> Helmut Zacharias <br> Billy Vaughn & His Orchestra |
| 10/61 | **When We Get Married** <br> Dreamlovers |
| 8/60 <br> 2/75 | **When Will I Be Loved** <br> Everly Brothers <br> Linda Ronstadt |

| POS/YR | RECORD TITLE/ARTIST |
|--------|---------------------|
| 2/74 | **When Will I See You Again** <br> Three Degrees |
| 14/84 | **When You Close Your Eyes** <br> Night Ranger |
| 33/56 | **When You Dance** <br> Turbans |
| 32/72 | **When You Say Love** <br> Sonny & Cher |
| 35/64 | **When You Walk In The Room** <br> Searchers |
| 30/60 | **When You Wish Upon A Star** <br> Dion & The Belmonts |
| 9/71 | **When You're Hot, You're Hot** <br> Jerry Reed |
| 6/79 | **When You're In Love With A Beautiful Woman** <br> Dr. Hook |
| 23/67 | **When You're Young And In Love** <br> Marvelettes |
| 39/64 | **Whenever He (She) Holds You** <br> Bobby Goldsboro |
| 5/78 | **Whenever I Call You "Friend"** <br> Kenny Loggins |
| 38/76 | **Whenever I'm Away From You** <br> John Travolta |
| 32/60 | **Where Are You** <br> Frankie Avalon |
| 36/62 | **Where Are You** <br> Dinah Washington |
| 1/64 <br> 15/71 | **Where Did Our Love Go** <br> Supremes <br> Donnie Elbert |
| 33/71 | **Where Did They Go, Lord** <br> Elvis Presley |
| | **(Where Do I Begin)** . . . see: *Theme From Love Story* |
| 25/65 | **Where Do You Go** <br> Cher |
| 21/62 <br> 26/65 | **Where Have All The Flowers Gone** <br> Kingston Trio <br> Johnny Rivers |
| 5/72 | **Where Is The Love** <br> Roberta Flack & Donny Hathaway |

| POS/YR | RECORD TITLE/ARTIST |
|--------|---------------------|
| 3/60 | **Where Or When**<br>Dion & The Belmonts |
| 28/73 | **Where Peaceful Waters Flow**<br>Gladys Knight & The Pips |
| | **Where The Action Is**...see: Action |
| 4/61 | **Where The Boys Are**<br>Connie Francis |
| 23/59 | **Where Were You (On Our Wedding Day)?**<br>Lloyd Price |
| 28/66 | **Where Were You When I Needed You**<br>Grass Roots |
| 23/79 | **Where Were You When I Was Falling In Love**<br>Lobo |
| 21/67 | **Where Will The Words Come From**<br>Gary Lewis & The Playboys |
| 40/71<br>37/72 | **Where You Lead**<br>Barbra Streisand<br>Barbra Streisand (medley) |
| 26/69 | **Where's The Playground Susie**<br>Glen Campbell |
| | **Which Way Is Up**...see: Theme From |
| 2/70 | **Which Way You Goin' Billy?**<br>Poppy Family featuring Susan Jacks |
| 7/81 | **While You See A Chance**<br>Steve Winwood |
| 14/80 | **Whip It**<br>Devo |
| 28/83 | **Whirly Girl**<br>Oxo |
| 37/84 | **Whisper To A Scream (Birds Fly)**<br>Icicle Works |
| 11/64<br>27/77 | **Whispering**<br>Nino Tempo & April Stevens<br>Dr. Buzzard's Original "Savannah" Band |
| 9/57 | **Whispering Bells**<br>Dell-Vikings |
| 11/66 | **Whispers (Gettin' Louder)**<br>Jackie Wilson |

| POS/YR | RECORD TITLE/ARTIST |
|--------|---------------------|
| 7/55<br>34/57<br>26/60<br>12/61<br>38/62 | **White Christmas**<br>Bing Crosby<br>Bing Crosby<br>Bing Crosby<br>Bing Crosby<br>Bing Crosby |
| 26/84 | **White Horse**<br>Laid Back |
| 19/76 | **White Knight**<br>Cledus Maggard & The Citizen's Band |
| 28/72 | **White Lies, Blue Eyes**<br>Bullet |
| 9/64 | **White On White**<br>Danny Williams |
| 8/67 | **White Rabbit**<br>Jefferson Airplane |
| 6/68 | **White Room**<br>Cream |
| 7/57<br>18/57<br>22/57<br>9/60 | **White Silver Sands**<br>Don Rondo<br>Owen Bradley Quintet<br>Dave Gardner<br>Bill Black's Combo |
| 2/57 | **White Sport Coat (And A Pink Carnation)**<br>Marty Robbins |
| 36/83 | **White Wedding**<br>Billy Idol |
| 5/67 | **Whiter Shade Of Pale**<br>Procol Harum |
| 21/66 | **Who Am I**<br>Petula Clark |
| 14/78 | **Who Are You**<br>Who |
| 33/64 | **Who Can I Turn To**<br>Tony Bennett |
| 1/82 | **Who Can It Be Now?**<br>Men At Work |
| 25/64 | **Who Do You Love**<br>Sapphires |
| 15/74 | **Who Do You Think You Are**<br>Bo Donaldson & The Heywoods |
| 40/81 | **Who Do You Think You're Foolin'**<br>Donna Summer |

| POS/YR | RECORD TITLE/ARTIST |
|---|---|
| 33/68 | **Who Is Gonna Love Me?**<br>Dionne Warwick |
| 3/75 | **Who Loves You**<br>Four Seasons |
| 9/57 | **Who Needs You**<br>Four Lads |
| 7/61 | **Who Put The Bomp (In The Bomp, Bomp, Bomp)**<br>Barry Mann |
| 16/84 | **Who Wears These Shoes?**<br>Elton John |
| 19/68 | **Who Will Answer?**<br>Ed Ames |
| 18/76 | **Who'd She Coo?**<br>Ohio Players |
| 29/80 | **Who'll Be The Fool Tonight**<br>Larsen/Feiten Band |
| 34/65 | **Who'll Be The Next In Line**<br>Kinks |
| F/70 | **Who'll Stop The Rain**<br>Creedence Clearwater Revival |
| 4/81 | **Who's Crying Now**<br>Journey |
| 27/73 | **Who's In The Strawberry Patch With Sally**<br>Dawn |
| 5/68<br>39/81 | **Who's Making Love**<br>Johnnie Taylor<br>Blues Brothers |
| 4/58<br>40/75 | **Who's Sorry Now**<br>Connie Francis<br>Marie Osmond |
| 21/84 | **Who's That Girl?**<br>Eurythmics |
| 40/70 | **Who's Your Baby?**<br>Archies |
| 22/77 | **Whodunit**<br>Tavares |
| 3/57 | **Whole Lot Of Shakin' Going On**<br>Jerry Lee Lewis |
| 4/70 | **Whole Lotta Love**<br>Led Zeppelin |
| 6/59 | **Whole Lotta Loving**<br>Fats Domino |

| POS/YR | RECORD TITLE/ARTIST |
|---|---|
| 1/59<br>13/72 | **Why**<br>Frankie Avalon<br>Donny Osmond |
| 5/57 | **Why Baby Why**<br>Pat Boone |
| 6/75 | **Why Can't We Be Friends?**<br>War |
| 3/73 | **Why Can't We Live Together**<br>Timmy Thomas |
| 6/56<br>9/56<br>12/56<br>7/81 | **Why Do Fools Fall In Love**<br>Frankie Lymon & The Teenagers<br>Gale Storm<br>Diamonds<br>Diana Ross |
| 38/63 | **Why Do Lovers Break Each Other's Heart?**<br>Bob B. Soxx & The Blue Jeans |
| 10/58 | **Why Don't They Understand**<br>George Hamilton IV |
| 37/63 | **Why Don't You Believe Me**<br>Duprees |
| 13/83 | **Why Me**<br>Irene Cara |
| 16/73 | **Why Me**<br>Kris Kristofferson |
| 26/80 | **Why Me**<br>Styx |
| 18/80 | **Why Not Me**<br>Fred Knoblock |
| 3/69 | **Wichita Lineman**<br>Glen Campbell |
| 22/63 | **Wiggle Wobble**<br>Les Cooper & The Soul Rockers |
| 33/63 | **Wild!**<br>Dee Dee Sharp |
| 2/84 | **Wild Boys**<br>Duran Duran |
| 29/56 | **Wild Cherry**<br>Don Cherry |
| 31/67 | **Wild Honey**<br>Beach Boys |
| 28/71 | **Wild Horses**<br>Rolling Stones |
| 26/61 | **Wild In The Country**<br>Elvis Presley |

| POS/YR | RECORD TITLE/ARTIST |
|--------|---------------------|
| 22/57 | **Wild Is The Wind** <br> Johnny Mathis |
| 28/71 | **Wild Night** <br> Van Morrison |
| 2/60 | **Wild One** <br> Bobby Rydell |
| 34/65 | **Wild One** <br> Martha & The Vandellas |
| 1/66 <br> 20/67 <br> 14/74 | **Wild Thing** <br> Troggs <br> Senator Bobby <br> Fancy |
| 8/63 | **Wild Weekend** <br> Rebels |
| 11/71 | **Wild World** <br> Cat Stevens |
| 3/75 | **Wildfire** <br> Michael Murphey |
| 9/73 | **Wildflower** <br> Skylark |
| 17/63 | **Wildwood Days** <br> Bobby Rydell |
| 7/74 | **Wildwood Weed** <br> Jim Stafford |
| 1/73 | **Will It Go Round In Circles** <br> Billy Preston |
| 32/69 | **Will You Be Staying After Sunday** <br> Peppermint Rainbow |
| 1/61 <br> 24/68 <br> 39/78 | **Will You Love Me Tomorrow** <br> Shirelles <br> Four Seasons <br> Dave Mason |
| 9/58 <br> 26/74 | **Willie And The Hand Jive** <br> Johnny Otis Show <br> Eric Clapton |
| 15/65 | **Willow Weep For Me** <br> Chad & Jeremy |
| 22/58 | **Win Your Love For Me** <br> Sam Cooke |
| 1/66 | **Winchester Cathedral** <br> New Vaudeville Band |
| 31/69 | **Windmills Of Your Mind** <br> Dusty Springfield |
| 32/67 | **Windows Of The World** <br> Dionne Warwick |

| POS/YR | RECORD TITLE/ARTIST |
|--------|---------------------|
| 38/83 | **Winds Of Change** <br> Jefferson Starship |
| 1/67 | **Windy** <br> Association |
| 12/61 | **Wings Of A Dove** <br> Ferlin Husky |
| 8/81 | **Winner Takes It All** <br> Abba |
| 21/76 | **Winners And Losers** <br> Hamilton, Joe Frank & Reynolds |
| 17/81 | **Winning** <br> Santana |
| 16/70 | **Winter World Of Love** <br> Engelbert Humperdinck |
| 2/63 <br> 16/66 | **Wipe Out** <br> Surfaris <br> Surfaris |
| 35/57 | **Wisdom Of A Fool** <br> Five Keys |
| 17/64 | **Wish Someone Would Care** <br> Irma Thomas |
| 38/67 | **Wish You Didn't Have To Go** <br> James & Bobby Purify |
| 6/64 | **Wishin' And Hopin'** <br> Dusty Springfield |
| 18/58 | **Wishing For Your Love** <br> Voxpoppers |
| 26/83 | **Wishing (If I Had A Photograph Of You)** <br> Flock Of Seagulls |
| 11/74 | **Wishing You Were Here** <br> Chicago |
| 1/58 | **Witch Doctor** <br> David Seville |
| 21/72 | **Witch Queen Of New Orleans** <br> Redbone |
| 6/58 | **Witchcraft** <br> Frank Sinatra |
| 32/63 | **Witchcraft** <br> Elvis Presley |
| 9/72 | **Witchy Woman** <br> Eagles |
| 29/66 | **With A Girl Like You** <br> Troggs |

| POS/YR | RECORD TITLE/ARTIST |
|---|---|
| 1/78 | **With A Little Luck** <br> Paul McCartney |
| 15/57 | **With All My Heart** <br> Jodie Sands |
| 39/59 | **With Open Arms** <br> Jane Morgan |
| 35/69 | **With Pen In Hand** <br> Vikki Carr |
| 21/59 | **With The Wind And The Rain In Your Hair** <br> Pat Boone |
| 27/65 | **With These Hands** <br> Tom Jones |
| 14/67 | **With This Ring** <br> Platters |
| 4/80 | **With You I'm Born Again** <br> Billy Preston & Syreeta |
| 30/57 | **With You On My Mind** <br> Nat King Cole |
| 12/76 | **With Your Love** <br> Jefferson Starship |
| 28/58 | **With Your Love** <br> Jack Scott |
| 19/57 <br> 29/63 <br> 5/70 | **Without Love (There Is Nothing)** <br> Clyde McPhatter <br> Ray Charles <br> Tom Jones |
| 1/72 | **Without You** <br> Nilsson |
| 7/61 | **Without You** <br> Johnny Tillotson |
| 24/82 | **Without You (Not Another Lonely Night)** <br> Franke & The Knockouts |
| 20/80 | **Without Your Love** <br> Roger Daltrey |
| 14/64 | **Wives And Lovers** <br> Jack Jones |
| | **Wizard Of Oz**...see: Themes From The |
| 40/75 | **Wolf Creek Pass** <br> C.W. McCall |
| 6/62 | **Wolverton Mountain** <br> Claude King <br> (also see: (I'm The Girl On)) |
| 2/81 | **Woman** <br> John Lennon |

| POS/YR | RECORD TITLE/ARTIST |
|---|---|
| 14/66 | **Woman** <br> Peter & Gordon |
| 15/60 | **Woman, A Lover, A Friend** <br> Jackie Wilson |
| 14/55 <br> 19/55 | **Woman In Love** <br> Four Aces <br> Frankie Laine |
| 1/80 | **Woman In Love** <br> Barbra Streisand |
| 33/83 | **Woman In Me** <br> Donna Summer |
| 24/83 | **Woman In You** <br> Bee Gees |
| 4/81 | **Woman Needs Love (Just Like You Do)** <br> Ray Parker Jr. & Raydio |
| 22/74 | **Woman To Woman** <br> Shirley Brown |
| 4/68 | **Woman, Woman** <br> Gary Puckett & The Union Gap |
| 29/65 | **Woman's Got Soul** <br> Impressions |
| 36/71 | **Women's Love Rights** <br> Laura Lee |
| 15/71 | **Won't Get Fooled Again** <br> Who |
| 19/60 | **Won't You Come Home Bill Bailey** <br> Bobby Darin |
| 11/61 | **Wonder Like You** <br> Ricky Nelson |
| 25/59 <br> 9/70 | **Wonder Of You** <br> Ray Peterson <br> Elvis Presley |
| 22/62 | **Wonderful Dream** <br> Majors |
| 14/63 | **Wonderful Summer** <br> Robin Ward |
| 4/58 | **Wonderful Time Up There** <br> Pat Boone |
| 16/78 | **Wonderful Tonight** <br> Eric Clapton |
| 14/57 <br> 7/63 | **Wonderful! Wonderful!** <br> Johnny Mathis <br> Tymes <br> (also see: Wun'erful Wun'erful) |

| POS/YR | RECORD TITLE/ARTIST |
|--------|---------------------|
| | **Wonderful World** |
| 12/60 | Sam Cooke |
| 4/65 | Herman's Hermits |
| 17/78 | Art Garfunkel with James Taylor & Paul Simon |
| | **Wonderful World, Beautiful People** |
| 25/70 | Jimmy Cliff |
| | **Wonderful You** |
| 40/59 | Jimmie Rodgers |
| | **Wondering** |
| 12/57 | Patti Page |
| | **Wondering Where The Lions Are** |
| 21/80 | Bruce Cockburn |
| | **Wonderland** |
| 25/80 | Commodores |
| | **Wonderland By Night** |
| 1/61 | Bert Kaempfert & His Orchestra |
| 15/61 | Louis Prima |
| 18/61 | Anita Bryant |
| | **Woo-Hoo** |
| 16/59 | Rock-A-Teens |
| | **Wooden Heart** |
| 1/61 | Joe Dowell |
| | **Woodstock** |
| 11/70 | Crosby, Stills, Nash & Young |
| 23/71 | Matthews' Southern Comfort |
| | **Wooly Bully** |
| 2/65 | Sam The Sham & The Pharaohs |
| | **Words** |
| 11/67 | Monkees |
| | **Words** |
| 15/68 | Bee Gees |
| | **Words Of Love** |
| 5/67 | Mamas & The Papas |
| | **Words Of Love** |
| 13/57 | Diamonds |
| | **Work Song** |
| 18/66 | Herb Alpert & The Tijuana Brass |
| | **Workin' At The Car Wash Blues** |
| 32/74 | Jim Croce |
| | **Workin' For The Man** |
| 33/62 | Roy Orbison |
| | **Workin' On A Groovy Thing** |
| 20/69 | 5th Dimension |

| POS/YR | RECORD TITLE/ARTIST |
|--------|---------------------|
| | **Working For The Weekend** |
| 29/82 | Loverboy |
| | **Working In The Coal Mine** |
| 8/66 | Lee Dorsey |
| | **Working My Way Back To You** |
| 9/66 | Four Seasons |
| 2/80 | Spinners |
| | **Workout Stevie, Workout** |
| 33/63 | Stevie Wonder |
| | **World** |
| 37/69 | James Brown |
| | **World Is A Ghetto** |
| 7/73 | War |
| | **World Of Our Own** |
| 19/65 | Seekers |
| | **World Outside** |
| 21/58 | Four Coins |
| | **World We Knew (Over And Over)** |
| 30/67 | Frank Sinatra |
| | **World Without Love** |
| 1/64 | Peter & Gordon |
| | **Worried Guy** |
| 37/64 | Johnny Tillotson |
| | **Worried Man** |
| 20/59 | Kingston Trio |
| | **Worst That Could Happen** |
| 3/69 | Brooklyn Bridge |
| | **Wouldn't It Be Nice** |
| 8/66 | Beach Boys |
| | **Wrack My Brain** |
| 38/81 | Ringo Starr |
| | **Wrapped Around Your Finger** |
| 8/84 | Police |
| | **Wreck Of The Edmund Fitzgerald** |
| 2/76 | Gordon Lightfoot |
| | **Wringle, Wrangle** |
| 12/57 | Fess Parker |
| 33/57 | Bill Hayes |
| | **Writing On The Wall** |
| 5/61 | Adam Wade |
| | **Wrong For Each Other** |
| 34/64 | Andy Williams |

| POS/YR | RECORD TITLE/ARTIST |
|---|---|
| 32/57 | **Wun'erful, Wun'erful!** <br> Stan Freberg |

**X**

| | |
|---|---|
| 8/80 | **Xanadu** <br> Olivia Newton-John/Electric Light Orchestra |

**Y**

| POS/YR | RECORD TITLE/ARTIST |
|---|---|
| 2/79 | **Y.M.C.A.** <br> Village People |
| 7/61 | **Ya Ya** <br> Lee Dorsey |
| 19/84 | **Yah Mo B There** <br> James Ingram |
| 35/63 | **Yakety Sax (Axe)** <br> Boots Randolph |
| 1/58 | **Yakety Yak** <br> Coasters |
| 8/77 | **Year Of The Cat** <br> Al Stewart |
| 35/80 | **Years** <br> Wayne Newton |
| 37/61 | **Years From Now** <br> Jackie Wilson |
| 21/65 | **Yeh, Yeh** <br> Georgie Fame |
| 25/67 | **Yellow Balloon** <br> Yellow Balloon |
| 4/61 | **Yellow Bird** <br> Arthur Lyman Group |
| 23/70 | **Yellow River** <br> Christie |
| 1/55 <br> 3/55 <br> 16/55 | **Yellow Rose Of Texas** <br> Mitch Miller & His Orchestra <br> Johnny Desmond <br> Stan Freberg |

| POS/YR | RECORD TITLE/ARTIST |
|---|---|
| 2/66 | **Yellow Submarine** <br> Beatles |
| 30/59 | **"Yep!"** <br> Duane Eddy |
| 5/65 <br> 2/80 | **Yes, I'm Ready** <br> Barbara Mason <br> Teri DeSario with K.C. |
| 34/60 | **Yes Sir, That's My Baby** <br> Ricky Nelson |
| 12/57 | **Yes Tonight, Josephine** <br> Johnnie Ray |
| 11/73 | **Yes We Can Can** <br> Pointer Sisters |
| 31/68 | **Yester Love** <br> Miracles |
| 7/69 | **Yester-Me, Yester-You, Yesterday** <br> Stevie Wonder |
| 1/65 <br> 25/67 | **Yesterday** <br> Beatles <br> Ray Charles |
| 2/73 | **Yesterday Once More** <br> Carpenters |
| 19/69 | **Yesterday, When I Was Young** <br> Roy Clark |
| 21/64 | **Yesterday's Gone** <br> Chad & Jeremy |
| 11/82 | **Yesterday's Songs** <br> Neil Diamond |
| 3/71 | **Yo-Yo** <br> Osmonds |
| 8/60 | **Yogi** <br> Ivy Three |
| 20/75 | **You** <br> George Harrison |
| 21/58 | **You** <br> Aquatones |
| 25/78 | **You** <br> Rita Coolidge |
| 34/68 | **You** <br> Marvin Gaye |
| 1/74 | **You Ain't Seen Nothing Yet** <br> Bachman-Turner Overdrive |
| 12/61 | **You Always Hurt The One You Love** <br> Clarence "Frogman" Henry |

| POS/YR | RECORD TITLE/ARTIST |
|---|---|
| 7/83 | **You And I**<br>Eddie Rabbitt & Crystal Gayle |
| 13/78 | **You And I**<br>Rick James |
| 9/77 | **You And Me**<br>Alice Cooper |
| 9/74 | **You And Me Against The World**<br>Helen Reddy |
| 4/83 | **You Are**<br>Lionel Richie |
| 9/72 | **You Are Everything**<br>Stylistics |
| 26/62 | **You Are Mine**<br>Frankie Avalon |
| 7/58 | **You Are My Destiny**<br>Paul Anka |
| 6/55 | **You Are My Love**<br>Joni James |
| 27/76 | **You Are My Starship**<br>Norman Connors |
| 7/62 | **You Are My Sunshine**<br>Ray Charles |
| 5/75 | **You Are So Beautiful**<br>Joe Cocker |
| 25/61 | **You Are The Only One**<br>Ricky Nelson |
| 1/73 | **You Are The Sunshine Of My Life**<br>Stevie Wonder |
| 9/76 | **You Are The Woman**<br>Firefall |
| 20/66 | **You Baby**<br>Turtles |
| 9/62 | **You Beat Me To The Punch**<br>Mary Wells |
| 6/78 | **You Belong To Me**<br>Carly Simon |
| 7/62 | **You Belong To Me**<br>Duprees |
| 37/59 | **You Better Know It**<br>Jackie Wilson |
| 24/62 | **You Better Move On**<br>Arthur Alexander |
| 20/66 | **You Better Run**<br>Rascals |

| POS/YR | RECORD TITLE/ARTIST |
|---|---|
| 9/67 | **You Better Sit Down Kids**<br>Cher |
| 18/81 | **You Better You Bet**<br>Who |
| 6/61 | **You Can Depend On Me**<br>Brenda Lee |
| 37/79 | **You Can Do It**<br>Dobie Gray |
| 8/82 | **You Can Do Magic**<br>America |
| 12/61<br>34/74 | **You Can Have Her (Him)**<br>Roy Hamilton<br>Sam Neely |
| 36/58 | **You Can Make It If You Try**<br>Gene Allison |
| 18/63 | **You Can Never Stop Me Loving You**<br>Johnny Tillotson |
| 9/79 | **You Can't Change That**<br>Ray Parker Jr. & Raydio |
| 15/84 | **You Can't Get What You Want (Till You Know What You Want)**<br>Joe Jackson |
| 1/66<br>10/83 | **You Can't Hurry Love**<br>Supremes<br>Phil Collins |
| 40/66 | **You Can't Roller Skate In A Buffalo Herd**<br>Roger Miller |
| 20/56 | **You Can't Run Away From It**<br>Four Aces |
| 29/61<br>3/63 | **You Can't Sit Down**<br>Philip Upchurch Combo<br>Dovells |
| 12/77 | **You Can't Turn Me Off (In The Middle Of Turning Me On)**<br>High Inergy |
| 12/58 | **You Cheated**<br>Shields |
| 32/72 | **You Could Have Been A Lady**<br>April Wine |
| 15/82 | **You Could Have Been With Me**<br>Sheena Easton |
| 32/81 | **You Could Take My Heart Away**<br>Silver Condor |

| POS/YR | RECORD TITLE/ARTIST |
|--------|---------------------|
| 7/79 | **You Decorated My Life** <br> Kenny Rogers |
| 10/66 | **You Didn't Have To Be So Nice** <br> Lovin' Spoonful |
| 1/78 | **You Don't Bring Me Flowers** <br> Barbra Streisand & Neil Diamond |
| 3/63 | **You Don't Have To Be A Baby To Cry** <br> Caravelles |
| 1/77 | **You Don't Have To Be A Star (To Be In My Show)** <br> Marilyn McCoo & Billy Davis, Jr. |
| 15/66 | **You Don't Have To Paint Me A Picture** <br> Gary Lewis & The Playboys |
| 4/66 <br> 11/70 | **You Don't Have To Say You Love Me** <br> Dusty Springfield <br> Elvis Presley |
| 11/64 | **(You Don't Know) How Glad I Am** <br> Nancy Wilson |
| 14/56 <br> 2/62 | **You Don't Know Me** <br> Jerry Vale <br> Ray Charles |
| 4/61 | **You Don't Know What You've Got (Until You Lose It)** <br> Ral Donner |
| 8/72 | **You Don't Mess Around With Jim** <br> Jim Croce |
| 10/57 | **You Don't Owe Me A Thing** <br> Johnnie Ray |
| 2/64 | **You Don't Own Me** <br> Lesley Gore |
| 16/82 | **You Don't Want Me Anymore** <br> Steel Breeze |
| 31/82 | **You Dropped A Bomb On Me** <br> Gap Band |
| 24/69 | **You Gave Me A Mountain** <br> Frankie Laine |
| 38/79 | **You Gonna Make Me Love Somebody Else** <br> Jones Girls |
| 20/83 | **You Got Lucky** <br> Tom Petty & The Heartbreakers |
| 11/74 | **You Got The Love** <br> Rufus featuring Chaka Khan |
| 18/67 | **You Got To Me** <br> Neil Diamond |

| POS/YR | RECORD TITLE/ARTIST |
|--------|---------------------|
| 10/60 <br> 7/67 | **You Got What It Takes** <br> Marv Johnson <br> Dave Clark Five |
| 40/69 | **You Got Yours And I'll Get Mine** <br> Delfonics |
| 1/74 | **You Haven't Done Nothin** <br> Stevie Wonder |
| 24/69 | **You, I** <br> Rugbys |
| 1/66 <br> 6/68 | **You Keep Me Hangin' On** <br> Supremes <br> Vanilla Fudge |
| 25/68 | **(You Keep Me) Hangin' On** <br> Joe Simon |
| 38/82 | **You Keep Runnin' Away** <br> 38 Special |
| 19/67 | **You Keep Running Away** <br> Four Tops |
| 35/80 | **You Know That I Love You** <br> Santana |
| 12/67 | **You Know What I Mean** <br> Turtles |
| 1/77 | **You Light Up My Life** <br> Debby Boone |
| 12/74 | **You Little Trustmaker** <br> Tymes |
| 22/63 | **You Lost The Sweetest Boy** <br> Mary Wells |
| 10/77 | **You Made Me Believe In Magic** <br> Bay City Rollers |
| 9/77 | **You Make Loving Fun** <br> Fleetwood Mac |
| 2/74 | **You Make Me Feel Brand New** <br> Stylistics |
| 1/77 | **You Make Me Feel Like Dancing** <br> Leo Sayer |
| 36/79 | **You Make Me Feel Mighty Real** <br> Sylvester |
| 5/81 | **You Make My Dreams** <br> Daryl Hall & John Oates |
| 7/80 | **You May Be Right** <br> Billy Joel |
| 17/60 | **You Mean Everything To Me** <br> Neil Sedaka |

| POS/YR | RECORD TITLE/ARTIST |
|--------|---------------------|
| 35/68 | **You Met Your Match**<br>Stevie Wonder |
| 7/84 | **You Might Think**<br>Cars |
| 15/64 | **You Must Believe Me**<br>Impressions |
| 5/61<br>35/67 | **You Must Have Been A Beautiful Baby**<br>Bobby Darin<br>Dave Clark Five |
| 40/79 | **You Need A Woman Tonight**<br>Captain & Tennille |
| 11/58 | **You Need Hands**<br>Eydie Gorme |
| 25/70 | **You Need Love Like I Do (Don't You)**<br>Gladys Knight & The Pips |
| 1/78 | **You Needed Me**<br>Anne Murray |
| 14/64 | **You Never Can Tell**<br>Chuck Berry |
| 10/78 | **You Never Done It Like That**<br>Captain & Tennille |
| 3/72 | **You Ought To Be With Me**<br>Al Green |
|  | **You Really Got A Hold On Me**...*see:*<br>*You've Really* |
| 7/64<br>36/78 | **You Really Got Me**<br>Kinks<br>Van Halen |
| 27/65 | **You Really Know How To Hurt A Guy**<br>Jan & Dean |
| 37/81 | **You Saved My Soul**<br>Burton Cummings |
| 1/57<br>8/57 | **You Send Me**<br>Sam Cooke<br>Teresa Brewer |
| 3/76 | **You Sexy Thing**<br>Hot Chocolate |
| 35/80 | **You Shook Me All Night Long**<br>AC/DC |
| 1/76 | **You Should Be Dancing**<br>Bee Gees |
| 39/64 | **You Should Have Seen The Way He Looked At Me**<br>Dixie Cups |

| POS/YR | RECORD TITLE/ARTIST |
|--------|---------------------|
| 5/82 | **You Should Hear How She Talks About You**<br>Melissa Manchester |
| 6/69 | **You Showed Me**<br>Turtles |
| 10/79 | **You Take My Breath Away**<br>Rex Smith |
| 3/60 | **You Talk Too Much**<br>Joe Jones |
| 38/65 | **You Tell Me Why**<br>Beau Brummels |
| 40/79 | **You Thrill Me**<br>Exile |
| 39/79 | **You Took The Words Right Out Of My Mouth**<br>Meat Loaf |
| 8/65 | **You Turn Me On**<br>Ian Whitcomb |
| 25/73 | **You Turn Me On, I'm A Radio**<br>Joni Mitchell |
| 36/72 | **You Want It, You Got It**<br>Detroit Emeralds |
| 13/72 | **You Wear It Well**<br>Rod Stewart |
| 12/60 | **(You Were Made For) All My Love**<br>Jackie Wilson |
| 21/65 | **You Were Made For Me**<br>Freddie & The Dreamers |
| 39/58 | **You Were Made For Me**<br>Sam Cooke |
| `21/59 | **You Were Mine**<br>Fireflies |
| 3/65<br>36/67 | **You Were On My Mind**<br>We Five<br>Crispian St. Peters |
| 30/65 | **You Were Only Fooling (While I Was Falling In Love)**<br>Vic Damone |
| 22/62 | **You Win Again**<br>Fats Domino |
| 8/74 | **You Won't See Me**<br>Anne Murray |
| 22/65 | **You'd Better Come Home**<br>Petula Clark |

| POS/YR | RECORD TITLE/ARTIST |
|--------|---------------------|
| 14/80 | **You'll Accomp'ny Me**<br>Bob Seger |
| 8/62<br>32/76 | **You'll Lose A Good Thing**<br>Barbara Lynn<br>Freddy Fender |
| 2/76 | **You'll Never Find Another Love Like Mine**<br>Lou Rawls |
| 34/64<br>23/73 | **You'll Never Get To Heaven (If You Break My Heart)**<br>Dionne Warwick<br>Stylistics |
| 11/56 | **You'll Never Never Know**<br>Platters |
| 34/64 | **You'll Never Walk Alone**<br>Patti LaBelle & The Blue Belles |
|  | **You're**...*also see: Your* |
| 36/78 | **You're A Part Of Me**<br>Gene Cotton with Kim Carnes |
| 12/73 | **You're A Special Part Of Me**<br>Marvin Gaye & Diana Ross |
| 15/64 | **You're A Wonderful One**<br>Marvin Gaye |
| 7/68<br>19/71<br>34/75 | **You're All I Need To Get By**<br>Marvin Gaye & Tammi Terrell<br>Aretha Franklin<br>Dawn |
| 25/57 | **You're Cheatin' Yourself (If You're Cheatin' On Me)**<br>Frank Sinatra |
| 35/83 | **You're Driving Me Out Of My Mind**<br>Little River Band |
| 39/66 | **(You're Gonna) Hurt Yourself**<br>Frankie Valli |
| 34/59 | **You're Gonna Miss Me**<br>Connie Francis |
| 1/74 | **(You're) Having My Baby**<br>Paul Anka |
| 4/78 | **You're In My Heart (The Final Acclaim)**<br>Rod Stewart |
| 16/76 | **You're My Best Friend**<br>Queen |
| 6/67 | **You're My Everything**<br>Temptations |

| POS/YR | RECORD TITLE/ARTIST |
|--------|---------------------|
| 27/81 | **You're My Girl**<br>Franke & The Knockouts |
|  | **You're My Girl**...*see: (Say)* |
| 14/57 | **You're My One And Only Love**<br>Ricky Nelson |
| 1/66<br>38/78 | **(You're My) Soul And Inspiration**<br>Righteous Brothers<br>Donny & Marie Osmond |
| 26/64<br>18/77 | **You're My World**<br>Cilla Black<br>Helen Reddy |
| 1/75 | **You're No Good**<br>Linda Ronstadt |
| 25/65 | **You're Nobody Till Somebody Loves You**<br>Dean Martin |
| 7/79 | **You're Only Lonely**<br>J.D. Souther |
| 8/60<br>1/74 | **You're Sixteen**<br>Johnny Burnette<br>Ringo Starr |
| 17/59 | **You're So Fine**<br>Falcons |
| 1/73 | **You're So Vain**<br>Carly Simon |
| 29/72 | **You're Still A Young Man**<br>Tower Of Power |
| 34/80 | **You're Supposed To Keep Your Love For Me**<br>Jermaine Jackson |
| 3/63 | **(You're The) Devil In Disguise**<br>Elvis Presley |
| 2/75 | **You're The First, The Last, My Everything**<br>Barry White |
| 18/78 | **You're The Love**<br>Seals & Crofts |
| 4/65 | **You're The One**<br>Vogues |
| 22/70 | **You're The One**<br>Little Sister |
| 1/78 | **You're The One That I Want**<br>Olivia Newton-John & John Travolta |
| 13/80 | **You're The Only Woman (You & I)**<br>Ambrosia |

**Rex Smith** and **Rachel Sweet.** There must be something strange in the water of Akron, Ohio. Musicians produced by the city include Rachel Sweet, Devo, the Pretenders' Chrissie Hynde, and the Waitresses.

**Rick Springfield.** Before he set hearts aflutter in the TV series "General Hospital", before he starred in the movie *Hard to Hold,* Rick Springfield was a teen idol in his native Australia, playing in a band called Zoot.

**Styx** have been consistently lambasted by critics for their mild-mannered synthesis of art bands like Yes and Genesis. But nobody raised an eyebrow when some members admitted voting for Ronald Reagan in 1980.

**38 Special.** Lead singer Donnie Van Zant, brother of the late Ronnie Van Zant of Lynyrd Skynyrd, employs an unusual gimmick on stage. Aided by wires, he soars above the audience like Peter Pan. Not what you'd expect from a boogie band.

**Bonnie Tyler,** a Rod Stewart sound-alike, was a forgotten one-hit wonder until she resurfaced via the *Footloose* soundtrack and a collaboration with Jim Steinman of Meat Loaf fame.

**The Tymes** were more elegant than their Cameo-Parkway labelmates of the mid-sixties (who were primarily noisy dance-music makers like Dee Dee Sharp, Chubby Checker, and the Orlons).

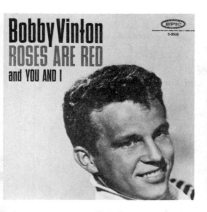

**Bobby Vinton** was a bandleader from Pennsylvania who had cut two flop albums of instrumental music when he decided to try a vocal. The song was "Roses are Red" and his career was saved.

**Andy Williams** hosted variety shows on all three networks between 1958 and 1971. Among the talents he presented were Ray Stevens, Jonathan Winters, the New Christy Minstrels, and the Osmond Brothers. Quite a range.

**Wang Chung's** first album was issued under the name Huang Chung, a reference to perfect pitch, pronounced just the same. Either way, there's not a trace of the Oriental in their music.

**War** took part in a novel promotional gimmick shortly after splitting from Eric Burdon. They joined labelmates Sugarloaf, Canned Heat, and the Nitty Gritty Dirt Band for a 99-cents-a-seat show at the Hollywood Bowl—17,000 showed.

**Larry Williams** was a valet to r&b giant Lloyd Price before he cut Price's "Just Because" in 1957. The Beatles acknowledged his influence by covering "Slow Down" and "Dizzy, Miss Lizzy."

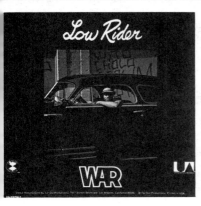

| POS/YR | RECORD TITLE/ARTIST |
|---|---|
| 11/61 | **You're The Reason**<br>Bobby Edwards |
| 3/63 | **You're The Reason I'm Living**<br>Bobby Darin |
| 33/66 | **You've Been Cheatin'**<br>Impressions |
| 36/65 | **You've Been In Love Too Long**<br>Martha & The Vandellas |
| | **(You've Got)**...see: Personality |
| 1/71<br>29/71 | **You've Got A Friend**<br>James Taylor<br>Roberta Flack & Donny Hathaway |
| 38/70 | **(You've Got Me) Dangling On A String**<br>Chairmen Of The Board |
| 33/77 | **You've Got Me Runnin'**<br>Gene Cotton |
| 4/56 | **(You've Got) The Magic Touch**<br>Platters |
| 28/71 | **You've Got To Crawl (Before You Walk)**<br>8th Day |
| 10/65 | **You've Got To Hide Your Love Away**<br>Silkie |
| 20/60 | **(You've Got To) Move Two Mountains**<br>Marv Johnson |
| | **(You've Got What It Takes)**...see: Baby |
| 7/65 | **You've Got Your Troubles**<br>Fortunes |
| 1/65<br>16/69<br>12/80 | **You've Lost That Lovin' Feelin'**<br>Righteous Brothers<br>Dionne Warwick<br>Daryl Hall & John Oates |
| 39/67<br>2/69 | **You've Made Me So Very Happy**<br>Brenda Holloway<br>Blood, Sweat & Tears |
| 22/73 | **You've Never Been This Far Before**<br>Conway Twitty |
| 8/63 | **You've Really Got A Hold On Me**<br>Miracles |
| 25/55 | **Young Abe Lincoln**<br>Don Cornell |
| 28/75 | **Young Americans**<br>David Bowie |
| 17/63 | **Young And In Love**<br>Dick & DeeDee |

| POS/YR | RECORD TITLE/ARTIST |
|---|---|
| | **Young And The Restless**...see: Nadia's Theme |
| 23/58 | **Young And Warm And Wonderful**<br>Tony Bennett |
| 8/57<br>20/76 | **Young Blood**<br>Coasters<br>Bad Company |
| 40/79 | **Young Blood**<br>Rickie Lee Jones |
| 12/60 | **Young Emotions**<br>Ricky Nelson |
| 2/68 | **Young Girl**<br>Gary Puckett & The Union Gap |
| 20/76 | **Young Hearts Run Free**<br>Candi Staton |
| 1/57<br>1/57<br>17/57<br>F/73 | **Young Love**<br>Tab Hunter<br>Sonny James<br>Crew-Cuts<br>Donny Osmond |
| 38/82 | **Young Love**<br>Air Supply |
| 6/63 | **Young Lovers**<br>Paul & Paula |
| | **Young Lovers**...see: Theme For |
| 5/81 | **Young Turks**<br>Rod Stewart |
| 5/62 | **Young World**<br>Ricky Nelson |
| | **Your**...also see: You're |
| 24/75 | **Your Bulldog Drinks Champagne**<br>Jim Stafford |
| 29/62 | **Your Cheatin' Heart**<br>Ray Charles |
| 34/61 | **Your Friends**<br>Dee Clark |
| 18/69 | **Your Good Thing (Is About To End)**<br>Lou Rawls |
| 33/82 | **Your Imagination**<br>Daryl Hall & John Oates |
| 15/77 | **Your Love**<br>Marilyn McCoo & Billy Davis, Jr. |
| 38/75 | **Your Love**<br>Graham Central Station |

| POS/YR | RECORD TITLE/ARTIST |
|--------|---------------------|
| 13/83 | **Your Love Is Driving Me Crazy**<br>Sammy Hagar |
| 6/67<br>2/77 | **(Your Love Keeps Lifting Me) Higher And Higher**<br>Jackie Wilson<br>Rita Coolidge |
| 24/61 | **Your Ma Said You Cried In Your Sleep Last Night**<br>Kenny Dino |
| 4/73 | **Your Mama Don't Dance**<br>Loggins & Messina |
| 40/71 | **Your Move**<br>Yes |
| 14/62 | **Your Nose Is Gonna Grow**<br>Johnny Crawford |
| 40/63 | **Your Old Stand By**<br>Mary Wells |
| 40/61 | **Your One And Only Love**<br>Jackie Wilson |
| 28/63 | **Your Other Love**<br>Connie Francis |
| 5/67 | **Your Precious Love**<br>Marvin Gaye & Tammi Terrell<br>*(also see: For Your Precious Love)* |
| 20/77 | **Your Smiling Face**<br>James Taylor |
| 8/71 | **Your Song**<br>Elton John |
| 40/71 | **Your Time To Cry**<br>Joe Simon |
| 33/67 | **Your Unchanging Love**<br>Marvin Gaye |
| 32/63 | **Your Used To Be**<br>Brenda Lee |
| 20/57 | **Your Wild Heart**<br>Joy Layne |
|  | **(Yowsah, Yowsah, Yowsah)**...*see: Dance, Dance, Dance* |
| 4/68 | **Yummy Yummy Yummy**<br>Ohio Express |

| POS/YR | RECORD TITLE/ARTIST |
|--------|---------------------|
|  | **Z** |
| 8/63 | **Zip-A-Dee Doo-Dah**<br>Bob B. Soxx & The Blue Jeans |
| 36/67 | **Zip Code**<br>Five Americans |
| 16/57 | **Zip Zip**<br>Diamonds |
| 11/66 | **Zorba The Greek**<br>Herb Alpert & The Tijuana Brass |
| 17/58 | **Zorro**<br>Chordettes |

# THE RECORD HOLDERS

## HOLDERS

TOP ARTIST AND RECORD ACHIEVEMENTS

| | WEEKS | | | | THE TOP 100 RECORDS 1955-1984 |
|---|---|---|---|---|---|
| YR | T10 | T40 | CHR | #1 | TITLE/ARTIST |
| 56 | 21 | 24 | 28 | 11 | 1. DON'T BE CRUEL/HOUND DOG  Elvis Presley |
| 55 | 20 | 26 | 26 | 10 | 2. CHERRY PINK AND APPLE BLOSSOM WHITE  Perez Prado |
| 56 | 17 | 22 | 26 | 10 | 3. SINGING THE BLUES  Guy Mitchell |
| 81 | 15 | 21 | 26 | 10 | 4. PHYSICAL  Olivia Newton-John |
| 77 | 14 | 21 | 25 | 10 | 5. YOU LIGHT UP MY LIFE  Debby Boone |
| 55 | 18 | 21 | 21 | 10 | 6. SINCERELY  McGuire Sisters |
| 57 | 15 | 22 | 30 | 9 | 7. ALL SHOOK UP  Elvis Presley |
| 81 | 13 | 19 | 27 | 9 | 8. ENDLESS LOVE  Diana Ross & Lionel Richie |
| 59 | 16 | 22 | 26 | 9 | 9. MACK THE KNIFE  Bobby Darin |
| 81 | 14 | 20 | 26 | 9 | 10. BETTE DAVIS EYES  Kim Carnes |
| 60 | 12 | 17 | 21 | 9 | 11. THE THEME FROM "A SUMMER PLACE"  Percy Faith |
| 68 | 14 | 19 | 19 | 9 | 12. HEY JUDE  Beatles |
| 55 | 19 | 25 | 38 | 8 | 13. ROCK AROUND THE CLOCK  Bill Haley & His Comets |
| 56 | 16 | 22 | 37 | 8 | 14. THE WAYWARD WIND  Gogi Grant |
| 56 | 15 | 22 | 27 | 8 | 15. HEARTBREAK HOTEL  Elvis Presley |
| 76 | 11 | 17 | 23 | 8 | 16. TONIGHT'S THE NIGHT (GONNA BE ALRIGHT)  Rod Stewart |
| 83 | 13 | 20 | 22 | 8 | 17. EVERY BREATH YOU TAKE  Police |
| 55 | 16 | 19 | 22 | 8 | 18. SIXTEEN TONS  Tennessee Ernie Ford |
| 78 | 13 | 18 | 20 | 8 | 19. NIGHT FEVER  Bee Gees |
| 57 | 17 | 24 | 34 | 7 | 20. LOVE LETTERS IN THE SAND  Pat Boone |
| 57 | 15 | 19 | 27 | 7 | 21. JAILHOUSE ROCK  Elvis Presley |
| 78 | 12 | 19 | 25 | 7 | 22. SHADOW DANCING  Andy Gibb |
| 57 | 14 | 18 | 25 | 7 | 23. (LET ME BE YOUR) TEDDY BEAR  Elvis Presley |
| 83 | 11 | 17 | 24 | 7 | 24. BILLIE JEAN  Michael Jackson |
| 61 | 12 | 17 | 23 | 7 | 25. TOSSIN' AND TURNIN'  Bobby Lewis |
| 58 | 12 | 18 | 21 | 7 | 26. AT THE HOP  Danny & The Juniors |
| 82 | 12 | 16 | 20 | 7 | 27. I LOVE ROCK 'N ROLL  Joan Jett & The Blackhearts |
| 82 | 12 | 15 | 19 | 7 | 28. EBONY AND IVORY  Paul McCartney & Stevie Wonder |
| 68 | 11 | 15 | 15 | 7 | 29. I HEARD IT THROUGH THE GRAPEVINE  Marvin Gaye |
| 64 | 12 | 14 | 15 | 7 | 30. I WANT TO HOLD YOUR HAND  Beatles |
| 66 | 12 | 13 | 15 | 7 | 31. I'M A BELIEVER  Monkees |
| 57 | 14 | 19 | 26 | 6 | 32. APRIL LOVE  Pat Boone |
| 56 | 16 | 20 | 25 | 6 | 33. ROCK AND ROLL WALTZ  Kay Starr |
| 83 | 14 | 20 | 25 | 6 | 34. FLASHDANCE . . . WHAT A FEELING  Irene Cara |
| 82 | 12 | 20 | 25 | 6 | 35. CENTERFOLD  J. Geils Band |

YR : Year record reached its peak position
T10 : Total weeks charted in the Top 10
T40 : Total weeks charted in the Top 40
CHR: Total weeks charted
#1 : Total weeks record held the #1 position

Records are ranked according to the number of weeks they held the #1 position. Ties are broken in the following order:
1. Total weeks charted
2. Total weeks in the Top 40
3. Total weeks in the Top 10

This ranking system is identical to the one used in compiling our *Top 1000 1955–1984* book. However, the above ranking takes into account all singles from 1955, whereas the "Top 1000" ranking begins when "Rock Around The Clock" peaked at position #1 on July 9, 1955.

| | WEEKS | | | THE TOP 100 RECORDS 1955-1984 |
|---|---|---|---|---|
| YR | T10 | T40 | CHR | #1 | TITLE/ARTIST |

| YR | T10 | T40 | CHR | #1 | TITLE/ARTIST |
|---|---|---|---|---|---|
| 78 | 15 | 19 | 25 | 6 | 36. LE FREAK   Chic |
| 80 | 13 | 19 | 25 | 6 | 37. LADY   Kenny Rogers |
| 80 | 12 | 19 | 25 | 6 | 38. CALL ME   Blondie |
| 82 | 15 | 18 | 25 | 6 | 39. EYE OF THE TIGER   Survivor |
| 56 | 15 | 20 | 24 | 6 | 40. THE POOR PEOPLE OF PARIS   Les Baxter & His Orchestra |
| 56 | 15 | 19 | 24 | 6 | 41. MEMORIES ARE MADE OF THIS   Dean Martin |
| 58 | 12 | 19 | 22 | 6 | 42. IT'S ALL IN THE GAME   Tommy Edwards |
| 83 | 13 | 18 | 22 | 6 | 43. SAY SAY SAY   Paul McCartney & Michael Jackson |
| 79 | 12 | 16 | 22 | 6 | 44. MY SHARONA   Knack |
| 55 | 17 | 21 | 21 | 6 | 45. LOVE IS A MANY-SPLENDORED THING   Four Aces |
| 59 | 13 | 18 | 21 | 6 | 46. THE BATTLE OF NEW ORLEANS   Johnny Horton |
| 57 | 13 | 17 | 21 | 6 | 47. YOUNG LOVE   Tab Hunter |
| 55 | 16 | 19 | 19 | 6 | 48. THE YELLOW ROSE OF TEXAS   Mitch Miller |
| 72 | 11 | 15 | 18 | 6 | 49. THE FIRST TIME EVER I SAW YOUR FACE   Roberta Flack |
| 72 | 11 | 15 | 18 | 6 | 50. ALONE AGAIN (NATURALLY)   Gilbert O'Sullivan |
| 69 | 11 | 16 | 17 | 6 | 51. AQUARIUS/LET THE SUNSHINE IN   5th Dimension |
| 71 | 11 | 15 | 17 | 6 | 52. JOY TO THE WORLD   Three Dog Night |
| 60 | 11 | 14 | 16 | 6 | 53. ARE YOU LONESOME TO-NIGHT?   Elvis Presley |
| 58 | 10 | 14 | 14 | 6 | 54. THE PURPLE PEOPLE EATER   Sheb Wooley |
| 70 | 10 | 13 | 14 | 6 | 55. BRIDGE OVER TROUBLED WATER   Simon & Garfunkel |
| 69 | 9 | 12 | 12 | 6 | 56. IN THE YEAR 2525 (EXORDIUM & TERMINUS)   Zager & Evans |
| 57 | 16 | 23 | 31 | 5 | 57. TAMMY   Debbie Reynolds |
| 56 | 14 | 20 | 23 | 5 | 58. MY PRAYER   Platters |
| 56 | 15 | 19 | 23 | 5 | 59. LOVE ME TENDER   Elvis Presley |
| 77 | 12 | 17 | 23 | 5 | 60. BEST OF MY LOVE   Emotions |
| 80 | 14 | 19 | 22 | 5 | 61. (JUST LIKE) STARTING OVER   John Lennon |
| 84 | 11 | 16 | 21 | 5 | 62. WHEN DOVES CRY   Prince |
| 84 | 10 | 15 | 21 | 5 | 63. JUMP   Van Halen |
| 55 | 16 | 20 | 20 | 5 | 64. THE BALLAD OF DAVY CROCKETT   Bill Hayes |
| 60 | 11 | 16 | 20 | 5 | 65. IT'S NOW OR NEVER   Elvis Presley |
| 58 | 10 | 16 | 20 | 5 | 66. DON'T   Elvis Presley |
| 79 | 10 | 15 | 20 | 5 | 67. BAD GIRLS   Donna Summer |
| 58 | 12 | 16 | 19 | 5 | 68. ALL I HAVE TO DO IS DREAM   Everly Brothers |
| 58 | 11 | 16 | 19 | 5 | 69. TEQUILA   Champs |
| 76 | 11 | 15 | 19 | 5 | 70. SILLY LOVE SONGS   Wings |
| 68 | 10 | 15 | 18 | 5 | 71. LOVE IS BLUE   Paul Mauriat |
| 62 | 11 | 14 | 18 | 5 | 72. I CAN'T STOP LOVING YOU   Ray Charles |
| 71 | 11 | 15 | 17 | 5 | 73. MAGGIE MAY   Rod Stewart |
| 71 | 10 | 15 | 17 | 5 | 74. IT'S TOO LATE   Carole King |
| 67 | 9 | 15 | 17 | 5 | 75. TO SIR WITH LOVE   Lulu |
| 59 | 10 | 14 | 17 | 5 | 76. VENUS   Frankie Avalon |
| 60 | 9 | 13 | 17 | 5 | 77. CATHY'S CLOWN   Everly Brothers |
| 70 | 11 | 16 | 16 | 5 | 78. I'LL BE THERE   Jackson 5 |
| 62 | 10 | 14 | 16 | 5 | 79. BIG GIRLS DON'T CRY   Four Seasons |
| 61 | 10 | 13 | 16 | 5 | 80. BIG BAD JOHN   Jimmy Dean |

| | WEEKS | | | | THE TOP 100 RECORDS 1955-1984 |
|---|---|---|---|---|---|
| YR | T10 | T40 | CHR | #1 | TITLE/ARTIST |
| 58 | 10 | 13 | 16 | 5 | 81. NEL BLU DIPINTO DI BLU (VOLARE)   Domenico Modugno |
| 73 | 9 | 13 | 16 | 5 | 82. KILLING ME SOFTLY WITH HIS SONG   Roberta Flack |
| 63 | 10 | 13 | 15 | 5 | 83. SUGAR SHACK   Jimmy Gilmer & The Fireballs |
| 68 | 10 | 13 | 15 | 5 | 84. HONEY   Bobby Goldsboro |
| 71 | 9 | 12 | 15 | 5 | 85. ONE BAD APPLE   Osmonds |
| 68 | 9 | 13 | 14 | 5 | 86. PEOPLE GOT TO BE FREE   Rascals |
| 62 | 7 | 12 | 14 | 5 | 87. SHERRY   Four Seasons |
| 66 | 9 | 11 | 13 | 5 | 88. THE BALLAD OF THE GREEN BERETS   SSgt Barry Sadler |
| 69 | 9 | 12 | 12 | 5 | 89. GET BACK   Beatles |
| 64 | 6 | 9 | 10 | 5 | 90. CAN'T BUY ME LOVE   Beatles |
| 77 | 16 | 23 | 31 | 4 | 91. I JUST WANT TO BE YOUR EVERYTHING   Andy Gibb |
| 56 | 17 | 24 | 29 | 4 | 92. LISBON ANTIGUA   Nelson Riddle |
| 83 | 11 | 18 | 29 | 4 | 93. TOTAL ECLIPSE OF THE HEART   Bonnie Tyler |
| 80 | 14 | 17 | 29 | 4 | 94. UPSIDE DOWN   Diana Ross |
| 57 | 13 | 23 | 28 | 4 | 95. HONEYCOMB   Jimmie Rodgers |
| 58 | 6 | 13 | 28 | 4 | 96. THE CHIPMUNK SONG   Chipmunks |
| 78 | 13 | 22 | 27 | 4 | 97. STAYIN' ALIVE   Bee Gees |
| 55 | 18 | 26 | 26 | 4 | 98. AUTUMN LEAVES   Roger Williams |
| 57 | 11 | 20 | 26 | 4 | 99. WAKE UP LITTLE SUSIE   Everly Brothers |
| 80 | 12 | 19 | 25 | 4 | 100. ANOTHER BRICK IN THE WALL (PART II)   Pink Floyd |

# RECORDS OF LONGEVITY

Records making the top 40 for 22 or more weeks

| YR | POS | WKS | TITLE/ARTIST |
|----|-----|-----|--------------|
| 60 | 1 | 33 | 1. THE TWIST   Chubby Checker |
| 55 | 2 | 27 | 2. MELODY OF LOVE   Billy Vaughn |
| 55 | 1 | 26 | 3. CHERRY PINK AND APPLE BLOSSOM WHITE   Perez Prado |
| 55 | 1 | 26 | 4. AUTUMN LEAVES   Roger Williams |
| 77 | 1 | 26 | 5. HOW DEEP IS YOUR LOVE   Bee Gees |
| 57 | 2 | 26 | 6. SO RARE   Jimmy Dorsey |
| 55 | 1 | 25 | 7. ROCK AROUND THE CLOCK   Bill Haley & His Comets |
| 55 | 2 | 25 | 8. MOMENTS TO REMEMBER   Four Lads |
| 78 | 7 | 25 | 9. I GO CRAZY   Paul Davis |
| 56 | 1 | 24 | 10. DON'T BE CRUEL/HOUND DOG   Elvis Presley |
| 57 | 1 | 24 | 11. LOVE LETTERS IN THE SAND   Pat Boone |
| 56 | 1 | 24 | 12. LISBON ANTIGUA   Nelson Riddle |
| 62 | 1 | 24 | 13. MONSTER MASH   Bobby "Boris" Pickett & The Crypt-Kickers |
| 57 | 1 | 23 | 14. TAMMY   Debbie Reynolds |
| 77 | 1 | 23 | 15. I JUST WANT TO BE YOUR EVERYTHING   Andy Gibb |
| 57 | 1 | 23 | 16. HONEYCOMB   Jimmie Rodgers |
| 56 | 2 | 23 | 17. CANADIAN SUNSET   Hugo Winterhalter and Eddie Heywood |
| 56 | 2 | 23 | 18. JUST WALKING IN THE RAIN   Johnnie Ray |
| 57 | 5 | 23 | 19. IT'S NOT FOR ME TO SAY   Johnny Mathis |
| 55 | 7 | 23 | 20. IT'S A SIN TO TELL A LIE   Somethin' Smith & The Redheads |
| 56 | 1 | 22 | 21. SINGING THE BLUES   Guy Mitchell |
| 57 | 1 | 22 | 22. ALL SHOOK UP   Elvis Presley |
| 59 | 1 | 22 | 23. MACK THE KNIFE   Bobby Darin |
| 56 | 1 | 22 | 24. THE WAYWARD WIND   Gogi Grant |
| 56 | 1 | 22 | 25. HEARTBREAK HOTEL   Elvis Presley |
| 78 | 1 | 22 | 26. STAYIN' ALIVE   Bee Gees |
| 56 | 1 | 22 | 27. MOONGLOW AND THEME FROM "PICNIC"   Morris Stoloff |
| 56 | 1 | 22 | 28. THE GREEN DOOR   Jim Lowe |
| 81 | 1 | 22 | 29. JESSIE'S GIRL   Rick Springfield |
| 78 | 1 | 22 | 30. (LOVE IS) THICKER THAN WATER   Andy Gibb |
| 57 | 1 | 22 | 31. CHANCES ARE   Johnny Mathis |
| 76 | 1 | 22 | 32. A FIFTH OF BEETHOVEN   Walter Murphy & The Big Apple Band |
| 80 | 1 | 22 | 33. DO THAT TO ME ONE MORE TIME   Captain & Tennille |
| 82 | 2 | 22 | 34. HURTS SO GOOD   John Cougar |
| 57 | 2 | 22 | 35. BYE BYE LOVE   Everly Brothers |
| 82 | 2 | 22 | 36. GLORIA   Laura Branigan |
| 56 | 2 | 22 | 37. HONKY TONK (PARTS 1 & 2)   Bill Doggett |
| 56 | 2 | 22 | 38. WHATEVER WILL BE, WILL BE (QUE SERA, SERA)   Doris Day |
| 56 | 2 | 22 | 39. ALLEGHENY MOON   Patti Page |
| 56 | 3 | 22 | 40. TRUE LOVE   Bing Crosby & Grace Kelly |

1. Re-charted '62 (Pos #1)
7. Re-charted '74 (Pos #39)
13. Re-charted '73 (Pos #10)

YR  : Year of peak popularity
POS : Highest position reached
WKS : Total weeks in top 40

Ties are broken by the following criteria:
1. Highest charted position
2. Weeks at highest position
3. Weeks on Hot 100

# THE TOP 100 ARTISTS 1955-1984

| ARTISTS | POINTS | ARTISTS | POINTS |
|---------|--------|---------|--------|
| 1. ELVIS PRESLEY | 5131 | 26. DIANA ROSS | 1359 |
| 2. BEATLES | 2940 | 27. DARYL HALL & JOHN OATES | 1297 |
| 3. STEVIE WONDER | 2302 | 28. JACKSONS | 1290 |
| 4. ROLLING STONES | 2082 | 29. BOBBY VINTON | 1267 |
| 5. PAT BOONE | 1986 | 30. RAY CHARLES | 1258 |
| 6. ELTON JOHN | 1971 | 31. DIONNE WARWICK | 1255 |
| 7. RICKY NELSON | 1887 | 32. FRANK SINATRA | 1249 |
| 8. SUPREMES | 1885 | 33. BARRY MANILOW | 1229 |
| 9. PAUL McCARTNEY | 1857 | 34. CARPENTERS | 1224 |
| 10. NEIL DIAMOND | 1803 | 35. MICHAEL JACKSON | 1221 |
| 11. TEMPTATIONS | 1776 | 36. SAM COOKE | 1217 |
| 12. CONNIE FRANCIS | 1687 | 37. THREE DOG NIGHT | 1203 |
| 13. BEE GEES | 1662 | 38. MIRACLES | 1178 |
| 14. ARETHA FRANKLIN | 1648 | 39. NAT KING COLE | 1171 |
| 15. MARVIN GAYE | 1646 | 40. GLADYS KNIGHT & THE PIPS | 1134 |
| 16. BEACH BOYS | 1619 | 41. FOUR TOPS | 1131 |
| 17. PAUL ANKA | 1545 | 42. BROOK BENTON | 1125 |
| 18. OLIVIA NEWTON-JOHN | 1540 | 43. BILLY JOEL | 1112 |
| 19. FATS DOMINO | 1528 | 44. DONNA SUMMER | 1108 |
| 20. FOUR SEASONS | 1506 | 45. CHUBBY CHECKER | 1094 |
| 21. CHICAGO | 1445 | 46. KENNY ROGERS | 1092 |
| 22. PERRY COMO | 1444 | 47. NEIL SEDAKA | 1078 |
| 23. JAMES BROWN | 1416 | 48. PLATTERS | 1077 |
| 24. BRENDA LEE | 1402 | 49. ANDY WILLIAMS | 1077 |
| 25. EVERLY BROTHERS | 1382 | 50. BOBBY DARIN | 1047 |

Artist's points are calculated using the following formula:

1. Each artist's top 40 records are given points based on their highest charted position (#1 = 40 points; #2 = 39 points, etc.) and added together.
2. Bonus points are added to each record based on its highest charted position (#1-5 = 25 points; #6-10 = 20 points; #11-20 = 15 points, #21-30 = 10 points; #31-40 = 5 points).
3. Total weeks charted are added in.
4. Total weeks an artist held the #1 position are also added in.

When two artists combine for one hit record (Ex.: Paul McCartney/Michael Jackson; Supremes/Temptations) the full point value is given to each artist.

Artists such as 'Simon and Garfunkel,' 'Sonny & Cher,' 'Marvin Gaye & Tammi Terrell' and 'Loggins & Messina' are considered regular recording teams and their points are not shared by either of the artists individually.

# THE TOP 100 ARTISTS 1955-1984

| ARTISTS | POINTS | ARTISTS | POINTS |
|---|---|---|---|
| 51. BARBRA STREISAND | 1031 | 76. DRIFTERS | 766 |
| 52. ROY ORBISON | 995 | 77. POINTER SISTERS | 762 |
| 53. HERMAN'S HERMITS | 992 | 78. KOOL & THE GANG | 744 |
| 54. ROD STEWART | 982 | 79. PAUL REVERE & THE RAIDERS | 741 |
| 55. BOBBY RYDELL | 980 | 80. GLEN CAMPBELL | 737 |
| 56. EAGLES | 979 | 81. PETULA CLARK | 737 |
| 57. 5TH DIMENSION | 952 | 82. JOHN DENVER | 729 |
| 58. JOHNNY MATHIS | 941 | 83. TOMMY JAMES & THE | |
| 59. JACKIE WILSON | 941 | SHONDELLS | 722 |
| 60. DAVE CLARK FIVE | 917 | 84. FOREIGNER | 719 |
| | | 85. IMPRESSIONS | 711 |
| 61. LINDA RONSTADT | 896 | | |
| 62. ELECTRIC LIGHT ORCHESTRA | 894 | 86. AL GREEN | 706 |
| 63. JOHNNY RIVERS | 882 | 87. ABBA | 705 |
| 64. COMMODORES | 880 | 88. LIONEL RICHIE | 705 |
| 65. SIMON & GARFUNKEL | 874 | 89. DAWN | 703 |
| 66. SPINNERS | 873 | 90. DEAN MARTIN | 701 |
| 67. EARTH, WIND & FIRE | 829 | 91. GENE PITNEY | 701 |
| 68. TOM JONES | 824 | 92. STYX | 701 |
| 69. JOHN LENNON | 803 | 93. CHUCK BERRY | 700 |
| 70. BOB SEGER | 792 | 94. LITTLE RIVER BAND | 699 |
| | | 95. JAN & DEAN | 686 |
| 71. CREEDENCE CLEARWATER | | | |
| REVIVAL | 784 | 96. RICK SPRINGFIELD | 686 |
| 72. DION | 781 | 97. BOBBY VEE | 682 |
| 73. PATTI PAGE | 780 | 98. JAMES TAYLOR | 680 |
| 74. FLEETWOOD MAC | 774 | 99. RASCALS | 677 |
| 75. HELEN REDDY | 767 | 100. GARY LEWIS & THE PLAYBOYS | 673 |

# TOP ARTISTS BY DECADE

| ARTISTS | POINTS | ARTISTS | POINTS |
|---|---|---|---|
| **FIFTIES ('55-'59)** | | **SEVENTIES ('70-'79)** | |
| 1. ELVIS PRESLEY | 1996 | 1. ELTON JOHN | 1433 |
| 2. PAT BOONE | 1725 | 2. PAUL McCARTNEY | 1352 |
| 3. PERRY COMO | 1232 | 3. BEE GEES | 1227 |
| 4. RICKY NELSON | 1044 | 4. CHICAGO | 1195 |
| 5. FATS DOMINO | 1013 | 5. CARPENTERS | 1175 |
| 6. NAT KING COLE | 851 | 6. JACKSON 5 | 1079 |
| 7. PLATTERS | 842 | 7. STEVIE WONDER | 1076 |
| 8. FRANK SINATRA | 765 | 8. THREE DOG NIGHT | 967 |
| 9. EVERLY BROTHERS | 695 | 9. OLIVIA NEWTON-JOHN | 944 |
| 10. FOUR LADS | 671 | 10. BARRY MANILOW | 905 |
| 11. JOHNNY MATHIS | 671 | 11. NEIL DIAMOND | 878 |
| 12. PATTI PAGE | 670 | 12. EAGLES | 812 |
| 13. McGUIRE SISTERS | 615 | 13. ELVIS PRESLEY | 798 |
| 14. DIAMONDS | 590 | 14. GLADYS KNIGHT & THE PIPS | 780 |
| 15. BILL HALEY & HIS COMETS | 579 | 15. HELEN REDDY | 767 |
| 16. PAUL ANKA | 577 | 16. DIANA ROSS | 730 |
| 17. TERESA BREWER | 558 | 17. DONNA SUMMER | 723 |
| 18. ANDY WILLIAMS | 532 | 18. ARETHA FRANKLIN | 715 |
| 19. FRANKIE AVALON | 530 | 19. AL GREEN | 706 |
| 20. JIMMIE RODGERS | 522 | 20. DAWN | 703 |
| 21. CONNIE FRANCIS | 504 | 21. EARTH, WIND & FIRE | 701 |
| 22. FONTANE SISTERS | 504 | 22. JOHN DENVER | 695 |
| 23. SARAH VAUGHAN | 484 | 23. SPINNERS | 675 |
| 24. CREW-CUTS | 467 | 24. BREAD | 661 |
| 25. AMES BROTHERS | 457 | 25. MARVIN GAYE | 660 |
| **SIXTIES ('60-'69)** | | **EIGHTIES ('80-'84)** | |
| 1. BEATLES | 2666 | 1. DARYL HALL & JOHN OATES | 987 |
| 2. ELVIS PRESLEY | 2309 | 2. MICHAEL JACKSON | 833 |
| 3. SUPREMES | 1554 | 3. KENNY ROGERS | 781 |
| 4. BRENDA LEE | 1402 | 4. LIONEL RICHIE | 705 |
| 5. BEACH BOYS | 1400 | 5. BILLY JOEL | 699 |
| 6. FOUR SEASONS | 1338 | 6. AIR SUPPLY | 649 |
| 7. TEMPTATIONS | 1222 | 7. RICK SPRINGFIELD | 635 |
| 8. CONNIE FRANCIS | 1183 | 8. DIANA ROSS | 629 |
| 9. RAY CHARLES | 1146 | 9. OLIVIA NEWTON-JOHN | 596 |
| 10. BOBBY VINTON | 1096 | 10. KOOL & THE GANG | 547 |
| 11. CHUBBY CHECKER | 1084 | 11. POLICE | 542 |
| 12. ROLLING STONES | 1059 | 12. CULTURE CLUB | 540 |
| 13. ROY ORBISON | 995 | 13. ELTON JOHN | 538 |
| 14. HERMAN'S HERMITS | 992 | 14. JOURNEY | 528 |
| 15. DAVE CLARK FIVE | 917 | 15. SHEENA EASTON | 522 |
| 16. MARVIN GAYE | 908 | 16. POINTER SISTERS | 505 |
| 17. MIRACLES | 901 | 17. PAUL McCARTNEY | 505 |
| 18. ARETHA FRANKLIN | 900 | 18. DURAN DURAN | 500 |
| 19. JAMES BROWN | 892 | 19. PAT BENATAR | 497 |
| 20. SAM COOKE | 886 | 20. PRINCE | 487 |
| 21. BOBBY RYDELL | 857 | 21. JOHN COUGAR | 479 |
| 22. DIONNE WARWICK | 813 | 22. CHRISTOPHER CROSS | 479 |
| 23. STEVIE WONDER | 796 | 23. DAN FOGELBERG | 474 |
| 24. BROOK BENTON | 795 | 24. NEIL DIAMOND | 451 |
| 25. DION | 781 | 25. STEVIE WONDER | 430 |

# TOP ARTIST ACHIEVEMENTS

## MOST CHARTED RECORDS

| | | |
|---|---|---|
| 1. | ELVIS PRESLEY | 107 |
| 2. | BEATLES | 48 |
| 3. | JAMES BROWN | 43 |
| 4. | STEVIE WONDER | 40 |
| 5. | PAT BOONE | 38 |
| 6. | ROLLING STONES | 37 |
| 7. | NEIL DIAMOND | 37 |
| 8. | TEMPTATIONS | 37 |
| 9. | ELTON JOHN | 36 |
| 10. | FATS DOMINO | 36 |
| 11. | RICKY NELSON | 35 |
| 12. | CONNIE FRANCIS | 35 |
| 13. | SUPREMES | 33 |
| 14. | ARETHA FRANKLIN | 33 |
| 15. | MARVIN GAYE | 33 |
| 16. | PAUL ANKA | 33 |
| 17. | PAUL McCARTNEY | 32 |
| 18. | BEACH BOYS | 32 |
| 19. | RAY CHARLES | 32 |
| 20. | BOBBY VINTON | 30 |
| 21. | FOUR SEASONS | 29 |
| 22. | PERRY COMO | 29 |
| 23. | BRENDA LEE | 29 |
| 24. | DIONNE WARWICK | 29 |
| 25. | SAM COOKE | 29 |
| 26. | MIRACLES | 29 |

## MOST #1 RECORDS

| | | |
|---|---|---|
| 1. | BEATLES | 21 |
| 2. | ELVIS PRESLEY | 18 |
| 3. | SUPREMES | 12 |
| 4. | PAUL McCARTNEY | 9 |
| 5. | BEE GEES | 9 |
| 6. | STEVIE WONDER | 8 |
| 7. | ROLLING STONES | 8 |
| 8. | PAT BOONE | 6 |
| 9. | ELTON JOHN | 6 |
| 10. | DIANA ROSS | 6 |
| 11. | DARYL HALL & JOHN OATES | 6 |
| 12. | MICHAEL JACKSON | 6 |
| 13. | OLIVIA NEWTON-JOHN | 5 |
| 14. | FOUR SEASONS | 5 |
| 15. | BARBRA STREISAND | 5 |
| 16. | EAGLES | 5 |
| 17. | KC & THE SUNSHINE BAND | 5 |
| 18. | TEMPTATIONS | 4 |
| 19. | EVERLY BROTHERS | 4 |
| 20. | JACKSON 5 | 4 |
| 21. | BOBBY VINTON | 4 |
| 22. | DONNA SUMMER | 4 |
| 23. | PLATTERS | 4 |
| 24. | JOHN DENVER | 4 |
| 25. | LIONEL RICHIE | 4 |
| 26. | BLONDIE | 4 |

## MOST TOP 10 RECORDS

| | | |
|---|---|---|
| 1. | ELVIS PRESLEY | 38 |
| 2. | BEATLES | 33 |
| 3. | STEVIE WONDER | 25 |
| 4. | ROLLING STONES | 21 |
| 5. | PAUL McCARTNEY | 21 |
| 6. | SUPREMES | 20 |
| 7. | ELTON JOHN | 19 |
| 8. | RICKY NELSON | 18 |
| 9. | PAT BOONE | 16 |
| 10. | CONNIE FRANCIS | 16 |
| 11. | TEMPTATIONS | 15 |
| 12. | OLIVIA NEWTON-JOHN | 15 |
| 13. | FOUR SEASONS | 15 |
| 14. | EVERLY BROTHERS | 15 |
| 15. | MICHAEL JACKSON | 15 |
| 16. | BEE GEES | 14 |
| 17. | ARETHA FRANKLIN | 14 |
| 18. | MARVIN GAYE | 14 |
| 19. | BEACH BOYS | 14 |
| 20. | CHICAGO | 14 |
| 21. | DARYL HALL & JOHN OATES | 14 |
| 22. | DONNA SUMMER | 13 |
| 23. | NEIL DIAMOND | 13 |
| 24. | PAUL ANKA | 12 |
| 25. | BRENDA LEE | 12 |
| 26. | CARPENTERS | 12 |

## MOST WEEKS HELD #1 POSITION

| | | |
|---|---|---|
| 1. | ELVIS PRESLEY | 80 |
| 2. | BEATLES | 59 |
| 3. | PAUL McCARTNEY | 30 |
| 4. | BEE GEES | 27 |
| 5. | SUPREMES | 22 |
| 6. | MICHAEL JACKSON | 22 |
| 7. | PAT BOONE | 21 |
| 8. | STEVIE WONDER | 20 |
| 9. | DIANA ROSS | 20 |
| 10. | OLIVIA NEWTON-JOHN | 18 |
| 11. | FOUR SEASONS | 18 |
| 12. | ROLLING STONES | 17 |
| 13. | ROD STEWART | 17 |
| 14. | LIONEL RICHIE | 17 |
| 15. | ELTON JOHN | 15 |
| 16. | EVERLY BROTHERS | 15 |
| 17. | DARYL HALL & JOHN OATES | 14 |
| 18. | McGUIRE SISTERS | 14 |
| 19. | DONNA SUMMER | 13 |
| 20. | BARBRA STREISAND | 13 |
| 21. | ANDY GIBB | 13 |
| 22. | BOBBY VINTON | 12 |
| 23. | MONKEES | 12 |
| 24. | ROBERTA FLACK | 12 |
| 25. | GUY MITCHELL | 12 |

# THE TOP RECORDS—BY DECADE

| YR | T10 | T40 | CHR | #1 | TITLE/ARTIST |
|---|---|---|---|---|---|
| | WEEKS | | | | **FIFTIES ('55–'59)** |
| 56 | 21 | 24 | 28 | 11 | 1. DON'T BE CRUEL/HOUND DOG   Elvis Presley |
| 55 | 20 | 26 | 26 | 10 | 2. CHERRY PINK AND APPLE BLOSSOM WHITE   Perez Prado |
| 56 | 17 | 22 | 26 | 10 | 3. SINGING THE BLUES   Guy Mitchell |
| 55 | 18 | 21 | 21 | 10 | 4. SINCERELY   McGuire Sisters |
| 57 | 15 | 22 | 30 | 9 | 5. ALL SHOOK UP   Elvis Presley |
| 59 | 16 | 22 | 26 | 9 | 6. MACK THE KNIFE   Bobby Darin |
| 55 | 19 | 25 | 38 | 8 | 7. ROCK AROUND THE CLOCK   Bill Haley & His Comets |
| 56 | 16 | 22 | 37 | 8 | 8. THE WAYWARD WIND   Gogi Grant |
| 56 | 15 | 22 | 27 | 8 | 9. HEARTBREAK HOTEL   Elvis Presley |
| 55 | 16 | 19 | 22 | 8 | 10. SIXTEEN TONS   Tennessee Ernie Ford |
| 57 | 17 | 24 | 34 | 7 | 11. LOVE LETTERS IN THE SAND   Pat Boone |
| 57 | 15 | 19 | 27 | 7 | 12. JAILHOUSE ROCK   Elvis Presley |
| 57 | 14 | 18 | 25 | 7 | 13. (LET ME BE YOUR) TEDDY BEAR   Elvis Presley |
| 58 | 12 | 18 | 21 | 7 | 14. AT THE HOP   Danny & The Juniors |
| 57 | 14 | 19 | 26 | 6 | 15. APRIL LOVE   Pat Boone |
| 56 | 16 | 20 | 25 | 6 | 16. ROCK AND ROLL WALTZ   Kay Starr |
| 56 | 15 | 20 | 24 | 6 | 17. THE POOR PEOPLE OF PARIS   Les Baxter |
| 56 | 15 | 19 | 24 | 6 | 18. MEMORIES ARE MADE OF THIS   Dean Martin |
| 58 | 12 | 19 | 22 | 6 | 19. IT'S ALL IN THE GAME   Tommy Edwards |
| 55 | 17 | 21 | 21 | 6 | 20. LOVE IS A MANY-SPLENDORED THING   Four Aces |
| 59 | 13 | 18 | 21 | 6 | 21. THE BATTLE OF NEW ORLEANS   Johnny Horton |
| 57 | 13 | 17 | 21 | 6 | 22. YOUNG LOVE   Tab Hunter |
| 55 | 16 | 19 | 19 | 6 | 23. THE YELLOW ROSE OF TEXAS   Mitch Miller |
| 58 | 10 | 14 | 14 | 6 | 24. THE PURPLE PEOPLE EATER   Sheb Wooley |
| 57 | 16 | 23 | 31 | 5 | 25. TAMMY   Debbie Reynolds |
| | | | | | **SIXTIES ('60–'69)** |
| 60 | 12 | 17 | 21 | 9 | 1. THE THEME FROM "A SUMMER PLACE"   Percy Faith |
| 68 | 14 | 19 | 19 | 9 | 2. HEY JUDE   Beatles |
| 61 | 12 | 17 | 23 | 7 | 3. TOSSIN' AND TURNIN'   Bobby Lewis |
| 68 | 11 | 15 | 15 | 7 | 4. I HEARD IT THROUGH THE GRAPEVINE   Marvin Gaye |
| 64 | 12 | 14 | 15 | 7 | 5. I WANT TO HOLD YOUR HAND   Beatles |
| 66 | 12 | 13 | 15 | 7 | 6. I'M A BELIEVER   Monkees |
| 69 | 11 | 16 | 17 | 6 | 7. AQUARIUS/LET THE SUNSHINE IN   5th Dimension |
| 60 | 11 | 14 | 16 | 6 | 8. ARE YOU LONESOME TO-NIGHT?   Elvis Presley |
| 69 | 9 | 12 | 12 | 6 | 9. IN THE YEAR 2525 (EXORDIUM & TERMINUS)   Zager & Evans |
| 60 | 11 | 16 | 20 | 5 | 10. IT'S NOW OR NEVER   Elvis Presley |
| 68 | 10 | 15 | 18 | 5 | 11. LOVE IS BLUE   Paul Mauriat |
| 62 | 11 | 14 | 18 | 5 | 12. I CAN'T STOP LOVING YOU   Ray Charles |
| 67 | 9 | 15 | 17 | 5 | 13. TO SIR WITH LOVE   Lulu |
| 60 | 9 | 13 | 17 | 5 | 14. CATHY'S CLOWN   Everly Brothers |
| 62 | 10 | 14 | 16 | 5 | 15. BIG GIRLS DON'T CRY   Four Seasons |
| 61 | 10 | 13 | 16 | 5 | 16. BIG BAD JOHN   Jimmy Dean |
| 63 | 10 | 13 | 15 | 5 | 17. SUGAR SHACK   Jimmy Gilmer & The Fireballs |
| 68 | 10 | 13 | 15 | 5 | 18. HONEY   Bobby Goldsboro |
| 68 | 9 | 13 | 14 | 5 | 19. PEOPLE GOT TO BE FREE   Rascals |
| 62 | 7 | 12 | 14 | 5 | 20. SHERRY   Four Seasons |
| 66 | 9 | 11 | 13 | 5 | 21. THE BALLAD OF THE GREEN BERETS   SSgt Barry Sadler |
| 69 | 9 | 12 | 12 | 5 | 22. GET BACK   Beatles |
| 64 | 6 | 9 | 10 | 5 | 23. CAN'T BUY ME LOVE   Beatles |
| 69 | 12 | 18 | 22 | 4 | 24. SUGAR, SUGAR   Archies |
| 67 | 9 | 12 | 20 | 4 | 25. ODE TO BILLIE JOE   Bobbie Gentry |

# THE TOP RECORDS—BY DECADE

| | WEEKS | | | | TITLE/ARTIST |
|---|---|---|---|---|---|
| YR | T10 | T40 | CHR | #1 | SEVENTIES ('70-'79) |
| 77 | 14 | 21 | 25 | 10 | 1. YOU LIGHT UP MY LIFE  Debby Boone |
| 76 | 11 | 17 | 23 | 8 | 2. TONIGHT'S THE NIGHT (GONNA BE ALRIGHT)  Rod Stewart |
| 78 | 13 | 18 | 20 | 8 | 3. NIGHT FEVER  Bee Gees |
| 78 | 12 | 19 | 25 | 7 | 4. SHADOW DANCING  Andy Gibb |
| 78 | 15 | 19 | 25 | 6 | 5. LE FREAK  Chic |
| 79 | 12 | 16 | 22 | 6 | 6. MY SHARONA  Knack |
| 72 | 11 | 15 | 18 | 6 | 7. THE FIRST TIME EVER I SAW YOUR FACE  Roberta Flack |
| 72 | 11 | 15 | 18 | 6 | 8. ALONE AGAIN (NATURALLY)  Gilbert O'Sullivan |
| 71 | 11 | 15 | 17 | 6 | 9. JOY TO THE WORLD  Three Dog Night |
| 70 | 10 | 13 | 14 | 6 | 10. BRIDGE OVER TROUBLED WATER  Simon & Garfunkel |
| 77 | 12 | 17 | 23 | 5 | 11. BEST OF MY LOVE  Emotions |
| 79 | 10 | 15 | 20 | 5 | 12. BAD GIRLS  Donna Summer |
| 76 | 11 | 15 | 19 | 5 | 13. SILLY LOVE SONGS  Wings |
| 71 | 11 | 15 | 17 | 5 | 14. MAGGIE MAY  Rod Stewart |
| 71 | 10 | 15 | 17 | 5 | 15. IT'S TOO LATE  Carole King |
| 70 | 11 | 16 | 16 | 5 | 16. I'LL BE THERE  Jackson 5 |
| 73 | 9 | 13 | 16 | 5 | 17. KILLING ME SOFTLY WITH HIS SONG  Roberta Flack |
| 71 | 9 | 12 | 15 | 5 | 18. ONE BAD APPLE  Osmonds |
| 77 | 16 | 23 | 31 | 4 | 19. I JUST WANT TO BE YOUR EVERYTHING  Andy Gibb |
| 78 | 13 | 22 | 27 | 4 | 20. STAYIN' ALIVE  Bee Gees |
| 78 | 13 | 17 | 23 | 4 | 21. KISS YOU ALL OVER  Exile |
| 73 | 11 | 17 | 23 | 4 | 22. TIE A YELLOW RIBBON ROUND THE OLE OAK TREE  Dawn featuring Tony Orlando |
| 75 | 6 | 16 | 23 | 4 | 23. LOVE WILL KEEP US TOGETHER  Captain & Tennille |
| 79 | 10 | 15 | 23 | 4 | 24. REUNITED  Peaches & Herb |
| 70 | 13 | 19 | 22 | 4 | 25. RAINDROPS KEEP FALLIN' ON MY HEAD  B.J. Thomas |
| | | | | | EIGHTIES ('80-'84) |
| 81 | 15 | 21 | 26 | 10 | 1. PHYSICAL  Olivia-Newton John |
| 81 | 13 | 19 | 27 | 9 | 2. ENDLESS LOVE  Diana Ross & Lionel Richie |
| 81 | 14 | 20 | 26 | 9 | 3. BETTE DAVIS EYES  Kim Carnes |
| 83 | 13 | 20 | 22 | 8 | 4. EVERY BREATH YOU TAKE  Police |
| 83 | 11 | 17 | 24 | 7 | 5. BILLIE JEAN  Michael Jackson |
| 82 | 12 | 16 | 20 | 7 | 6. I LOVE ROCK 'N ROLL  Joan Jett & The Blackhearts |
| 82 | 12 | 15 | 19 | 7 | 7. EBONY AND IVORY  Paul McCartney & Stevie Wonder |
| 83 | 14 | 20 | 25 | 6 | 8. FLASHDANCE . . . WHAT A FEELING  Irene Cara |
| 82 | 12 | 20 | 25 | 6 | 9. CENTERFOLD  J. Geils Band |
| 80 | 13 | 19 | 25 | 6 | 10. LADY  Kenny Rogers |
| 80 | 12 | 19 | 25 | 6 | 11. CALL ME  Blondie |
| 82 | 15 | 18 | 25 | 6 | 12. EYE OF THE TIGER  Survivor |
| 83 | 13 | 18 | 22 | 6 | 13. SAY SAY SAY  Paul McCartney & Michael Jackson |
| 80 | 14 | 19 | 22 | 5 | 14. (JUST LIKE) STARTING OVER  John Lennon |
| 84 | 11 | 16 | 21 | 5 | 15. WHEN DOVES CRY  Prince |
| 84 | 10 | 15 | 21 | 5 | 16. JUMP  Van Halen |
| 83 | 11 | 18 | 29 | 4 | 17. TOTAL ECLIPSE OF THE HEART  Bonnie Tyler |
| 80 | 14 | 17 | 29 | 4 | 18. UPSIDE DOWN  Diana Ross |
| 80 | 12 | 19 | 25 | 4 | 19. ANOTHER BRICK IN THE WALL (PART II)  Pink Floyd |
| 83 | 10 | 19 | 25 | 4 | 20. DOWN UNDER  Men At Work |
| 80 | 9 | 19 | 24 | 4 | 21. ROCK WITH YOU  Michael Jackson |
| 83 | 13 | 17 | 24 | 4 | 22. ALL NIGHT LONG (ALL NIGHT)  Lionel Richie |
| 82 | 13 | 17 | 23 | 4 | 23. MANEATER  Daryl Hall & John Oates |
| 80 | 9 | 16 | 23 | 4 | 24. MAGIC  Olivia Newton-John |
| 80 | 9 | 15 | 23 | 4 | 25. FUNKYTOWN  Lipps, Inc. |

The following 2 songs each had
4 versions make the top 10:

UNCHAINED MELODY
Les Baxter 1/55
Al Hibbler 3/55
Righteous Brothers 4/65
Roy Hamilton 6/55

ONLY YOU
Platters 5/55
Ringo Starr 6/74
Hilltoppers 8/55
Franck Pourcel 9/59

The following song had 7
versions make the top 40:

MACK THE KNIFE
(Moritat - A Theme From "The Threepenny Opera")
Bobby Darin 1/59
Dick Hyman Trio 8/56
Richard Hayman & Jan August 11/56
Lawrence Welk 17/56
Louis Armstrong 20/56
Ella Fitzgerald 27/60
Billy Vaughn 37/56

The songs highest position and year are shown after the artist's name.

Not including medleys, there have been 20 songs that have had at least four versions to make the top 40 since 1955.

# #1 RECORDS LISTED CHRONOLOGICALLY 1955-1982

For the years 1955 through 1958, when more than one pop chart was published each week, special columns are shown here to show the weeks each #1 record spent on each of these pop charts.

The date shown is the earliest date that a record hit #1 on any of the four pop charts. The weeks column (next to date) is the most total weeks each record held the #1 position from any *one* of the four charts. This total is *not* a combined total from the four charts.

Because of the four charts used in my research, some dates are duplicated, as different records peaked at #1 on the same week on different charts. *Billboard* also showed ties at #1 on some of these charts, therefore the total weeks for each year may calculate out to more than 52.

Lines are drawn in on the charts column to show when any of the four pop charts were not published. See the introduction of this book for more details about researching the four pop charts.

DATE: Date record first hit the #1 position.
WKS : Total weeks record held the #1 position.
\* : Consensus #1 record - hit #1 on all pop charts published ('55-'58)
† : Indicates record hit #1, dropped down, then returned to the #1 spot.

CHARTS COLUMN:
BS : Best Sellers
JY : Jockeys
JB : Juke Box
TP : Top 100
HT : Hot 100

592 records have hit the #1 position on *Billboard's* pop charts from 1955 through 1982. "The Twist", even though it hit #1 in 1960 and again in 1962, is counted only once. There have been 526 #1 records since the Hot 100 chart began in 1958.

| DATE | WKS | RECORD TITLE | ARTIST | CHARTS | | | | |
|------|-----|--------------|--------|----|----|----|----|----|
| | | **1955** | | BS | JY | JB | TP | HT |
| 1/1 | 4 | * 1. LET ME GO LOVER | Joan Weber | 2 | 4† | 4 | — | — |
| 2/5 | 3 | 2. HEARTS OF STONE | Fontane Sisters | 1 | — | 3 | — | — |
| 2/12 | 10 | * 3. SINCERELY | McGuire Sisters | 6 | 10 | 7 | — | — |
| 3/26 | 5 | * 4. THE BALLAD OF DAVY CROCKETT | Bill Hayes | 5 | 3 | 3 | — | — |
| 4/30 | 10 | * 5. CHERRY PINK AND APPLE BLOSSOM WHITE | Perez Prado | 10 | 6† | 8 | — | — |
| 5/14 | 2 | 6. UNCHAINED MELODY | Les Baxter | — | 2† | — | — | — |
| 5/14 | 3 | 7. DANCE WITH ME HENRY | Georgia Gibbs | — | — | 3 | — | — |
| 7/9 | 2 | 8. LEARNIN' THE BLUES | Frank Sinatra | — | 2† | — | — | — |
| 7/9 | 8 | * 9. ROCK AROUND THE CLOCK | Bill Haley & His Comets | 8 | 6† | 7 | — | — |
| 9/3 | 6 | *10. THE YELLOW ROSE OF TEXAS | Mitch Miller | 6† | 6 | 6 | — | — |
| 9/17 | 2 | 11. AIN'T THAT A SHAME | Pat Boone | — | — | 2 | — | — |
| 10/8 | 6 | *12. LOVE IS A MANY-SPLENDORED THING | Four Aces | 2† | 6 | 3 | 3 | — |
| 10/29 | 4 | 13. AUTUMN LEAVES | Roger Williams | 4 | — | — | — | — |
| 11/26 | 8 | *14. SIXTEEN TONS | Tennessee Ernie Ford | 7 | 6 | 8 | 6 | — |
| | | **1956** | | | | | | |
| 1/7 | 6 | * 1. MEMORIES ARE MADE OF THIS | Dean Martin | 5 | 6 | 4 | 5 | — |
| 2/18 | 2 | 2. THE GREAT PRETENDER | Platters | — | 2 | 1 | 2 | — |
| 2/18 | 6 | * 3. ROCK AND ROLL WALTZ | Kay Starr | 1 | 1 | 6 | 4 | — |
| 2/25 | 4 | 4. LISBON ANTIGUA | Nelson Riddle | 4 | 2† | — | — | — |
| 3/17 | 6 | * 5. THE POOR PEOPLE OF PARIS | Les Baxter | 4 | 6† | 3 | 6 | — |
| 4/21 | 8 | * 6. HEARTBREAK HOTEL | Elvis Presley | 8 | 3 | 8 | 7 | — |
| 5/5 | 1 | 7. HOT DIGGITY | Perry Como | — | 1 | — | — | — |
| 6/2 | 3 | 8. MOONGLOW AND THEME FROM "PICNIC" | Morris Stoloff | — | 3 | — | — | — |

| DATE | WKS | RECORD TITLE | ARTIST | CHARTS | | | | |
|---|---|---|---|---|---|---|---|---|

## 1956 CONTINUED

| DATE | WKS | RECORD TITLE | ARTIST | BS | JY | JB | TP | HT |
|---|---|---|---|---|---|---|---|---|
| 6/16 | 8 | * 9. THE WAYWARD WIND | Gogi Grant | 6 | 8 | 4 | 7 | — |
| 7/28 | 1 | 10. I WANT YOU, I NEED YOU, I LOVE YOU | Elvis Presley | 1 | — | — | — | — |
| 7/28 | 4 | 11. I ALMOST LOST MY MIND | Pat Boone | — | — | 4 | 2 | — |
| 8/4 | 5 | *12. MY PRAYER | Platters | 2 | 3 | 1 | 5 | — |
| 8/18 | 11 | *13. DON'T BE CRUEL/ 14. HOUND DOG | Elvis Presley | 11 | 8 | 11 | 7 | — |
| 11/3 | 3 | 15. THE GREEN DOOR | Jim Lowe | — | — | 3 | 3 | — |
| 11/3 | 5 | *16. LOVE ME TENDER | Elvis Presley | 5 | 5 | 1 | 4† | — |
| 12/8 | 10 | *17. SINGING THE BLUES | Guy Mitchell | 9 | 9 | 10 | 9 | — |

## 1957

| DATE | WKS | RECORD TITLE | ARTIST | BS | JY | JB | TP | HT |
|---|---|---|---|---|---|---|---|---|
| 2/9 | 1 | 1. DON'T FORBID ME | Pat Boone | — | — | 1 | 1 | — |
| 2/9 | 3 | 2. TOO MUCH | Elvis Presley | 3 | — | 1 | — | — |
| 2/9 | 1 | 3. YOUNG LOVE | Sonny James | — | 1 | — | — | — |
| 2/16 | 6 | * 4. YOUNG LOVE | Tab Hunter | 4 | 6 | 5† | 6 | — |
| 3/30 | 1 | 5. PARTY DOLL | Buddy Knox | 1 | — | — | — | — |
| 3/30 | 3 | 6. BUTTERFLY | Andy Williams | — | 2 | — | 3 | — |
| 4/6 | 2 | 7. BUTTERFLY | Charlie Gracie | — | — | 2 | — | — |
| 4/6 | 2 | 8. ROUND AND ROUND | Perry Como | 1 | 2 | — | 1 | — |
| 4/13 | 9 | * 9. ALL SHOOK UP | Elvis Presley | 8 | 7 | 9 | 8 | — |
| 6/3 | 7 | *10. LOVE LETTERS IN THE SAND | Pat Boone | 5 | 7 | — | 5 | — |
| 7/8 | 7 | *11. LET ME BE YOUR TEDDY BEAR | Elvis Presley | 7 | 3 | — | 7 | — |
| 8/19 | 5 | *12. TAMMY | Debbie Reynolds | 3† | 5 | — | 5 | — |
| 9/9 | 1 | 13. DIANA | Paul Anka | 1 | — | — | — | — |
| 9/23 | 1 | 14. THAT'LL BE THE DAY | Crickets | 1 | — | — | — | — |
| 9/23 | 4 | *15. HONEYCOMB | Jimmie Rodgers | 2 | 4 | — | 2 | — |
| 10/14 | 4 | *16. WAKE UP LITTLE SUSIE | Everly Brothers | 1 | 4 | — | 2 | — |
| 10/21 | 1 | 17. CHANCES ARE | Johnny Mathis | — | 1 | — | — | — |
| 10/21 | 7 | *18. JAILHOUSE ROCK | Elvis Presley | 7† | 2 | — | 6 | — |
| 12/2 | 3 | *19. YOU SEND ME | Sam Cooke | 2 | 1 | — | 3 | — |
| 12/16 | 6 | *20. APRIL LOVE | Pat Boone | 2 | 6 | — | 1 | — |

## 1958

| DATE | WKS | RECORD TITLE | ARTIST | BS | JY | JB | TP | HT |
|---|---|---|---|---|---|---|---|---|
| 1/6 | 7 | * 1. AT THE HOP | Danny & The Juniors | 5 | 3 | — | 7 | — |
| 2/10 | 5 | * 2. DON'T | Elvis Presley | 5 | 1 | — | 1 | — |
| 2/17 | 4 | 3. SUGARTIME | McGuire Sisters | — | 4 | — | — | — |
| 2/24 | 2 | 4. GET A JOB | Silhouettes | — | — | — | 2 | — |
| 3/17 | 5 | * 5. TEQUILA | Champs | 5 | 2 | — | 5 | — |
| 3/24 | 1 | 6. CATCH A FALLING STAR | Perry Como | — | 1 | — | — | — |
| 4/14 | 4 | 7. HE'S GOT THE WHOLE WORLD IN HIS HANDS | Laurie London | — | 4 | — | — | — |
| 4/21 | 1 | * 8. TWILIGHT TIME | Platters | 1 | 1 | — | 1 | — |
| 4/28 | 3 | 9. WITCH DOCTOR | David Seville | 2 | — | — | 3 | — |
| 5/12 | 5 | *10. ALL I HAVE TO DO IS DREAM | Everly Brothers | 4 | 5 | — | 3 | — |
| 6/9 | 6 | *11. THE PURPLE PEOPLE EATER | Sheb Wooley | 6 | 4 | — | 6 | — |
| 7/21 | 1 | 12. YAKETY YAK | Coasters | — | — | — | 1 | — |
| 7/21 | 2 | 13. HARD HEADED WOMAN | Elvis Presley | 2 | 1 | — | — | — |
| 7/28 | 1 | 14. PATRICIA | Perez Prado | — | 1 | — | 1 | — |
| 8/4 | 2 | *15. POOR LITTLE FOOL | Ricky Nelson | 2 | — | — | — | 2 |

| DATE | WKS | RECORD TITLE | ARTIST | CHARTS | | | | |
|------|-----|--------------|--------|--------|--|--|--|--|
| | | **1958 CONTINUED** | | BS | JY | JB | TP | HT |
| 8/18 | 5 | * 16. NEL BLU DIPINTO DI BLUE (VOLARE) | Domenico Modugno | 5† | — | — | — | 5† |
| 8/25 | 1 | 17. BIRD DOG | Everly Brothers | 1 | — | — | — | — |
| 8/25 | 1 | 18. LITTLE STAR | Elegants | — | — | — | — | 1 |
| 9/29 | 6 | * 19. IT'S ALL IN THE GAME | Tommy Edwards | 3 | — | — | — | 6 |
| 11/10 | 2 | 20. IT'S ONLY MAKE BELIEVE | Conway Twitty | — | — | — | — | 2† |
| 11/17 | 1 | 21. TOM DOOLEY | Kingston Trio | — | — | — | — | 1 |
| 12/1 | 3 | 22. TO KNOW HIM, IS TO LOVE HIM | Teddy Bears | — | — | — | — | 3 |
| 12/22 | 4 | 23. THE CHIPMUNK SONG | Chipmunks | — | — | — | — | 4 |

| DATE | WKS | RECORD TITLE | ARTIST |
|------|-----|--------------|--------|
| | | **1959** | |
| 1/19 | 3 | 1. SMOKE GETS IN YOUR EYES | Platters |
| 2/9 | 4 | 2. STAGGER LEE | Lloyd Price |
| 3/9 | 5 | 3. VENUS | Frankie Avalon |
| 4/13 | 4 | 4. COME SOFTLY TO ME | Fleetwoods |
| 5/11 | 1 | 5. THE HAPPY ORGAN | Dave 'Baby' Cortez |
| 5/18 | 2 | 6. KANSAS CITY | Wilbert Harrison |
| 6/1 | 6 | 7. THE BATTLE OF NEW ORLEANS | Johnny Horton |
| 7/13 | 4 | 8. LONELY BOY | Paul Anka |
| 8/10 | 2 | 9. A BIG HUNK O' LOVE | Elvis Presley |
| 8/24 | 4 | 10. THE THREE BELLS | Browns |
| 9/21 | 2 | 11. SLEEP WALK | Santo & Johnny |
| 10/5 | 9 | 12. MACK THE KNIFE | Bobby Darin† |
| 11/16 | 1 | 13. MR. BLUE | Fleetwoods |
| 12/14 | 2 | 14. HEARTACHES BY THE NUMBER | Guy Mitchell |
| 12/28 | 1 | 15. WHY | Frankie Avalon |
| | | **1960** | |
| 1/4 | 2 | 1. EL PASO | Marty Robbins |
| 1/18 | 3 | 2. RUNNING BEAR | Johnny Preston |
| 2/8 | 2 | 3. TEEN ANGEL | Mark Dinning |
| 2/22 | 9 | 4. THE THEME FROM "A SUMMER PLACE" | Percy Faith |
| 4/25 | 4 | 5. STUCK ON YOU | Elvis Presley |
| 5/23 | 5 | 6. CATHY'S CLOWN | Everly Brothers |
| 6/27 | 2 | 7. EVERYBODY'S SOMEBODY'S FOOL | Connie Francis |
| 7/11 | 1 | 8. ALLEY-OOP | Hollywood Argyles |
| 7/18 | 3 | 9. I'M SORRY | Brenda Lee |
| 8/8 | 1 | 10. ITSY BITSY TEENIE WEENIE YELLOW POLKADOT BIKINI | Brian Hyland |
| 8/15 | 5 | 11. IT'S NOW OR NEVER | Elvis Presley |
| 9/19 | 1 | 12. THE TWIST (re-entered #1 on 1/13/62) | Chubby Checker |
| 9/26 | 2 | 13. MY HEART HAS A MIND OF ITS OWN | Connie Francis |
| 10/10 | 1 | 14. MR. CUSTER | Larry Verne |
| 10/17 | 3 | 15. SAVE THE LAST DANCE FOR ME | Drifters† |
| 10/24 | 1 | 16. I WANT TO BE WANTED | Brenda Lee |
| 11/14 | 1 | 17. GEORGIA ON MY MIND | Ray Charles |
| 11/21 | 1 | 18. STAY | Maurice Williams & The Zodiacs |
| 11/28 | 6 | 19. ARE YOU LONESOME TO-NIGHT? | Elvis Presley |

| DATE | WKS | RECORD TITLE | ARTIST |
|------|-----|--------------|--------|
| | | **1961** | |
| 1/9 | 3 | 1. WONDERLAND BY NIGHT | Bert Kaempfert |
| 1/30 | 2 | 2. WILL YOU LOVE ME TOMORROW | Shirelles |
| 2/13 | 2 | 3. CALCUTTA | Lawrence Welk |
| 2/27 | 3 | 4. PONY TIME | Chubby Checker |
| 3/20 | 2 | 5. SURRENDER | Elvis Presley |
| 4/3 | 3 | 6. BLUE MOON | Marcels |
| 4/24 | 4 | 7. RUNAWAY | Del Shannon |
| 5/22 | 1 | 8. MOTHER-IN-LAW | Ernie K-Doe |
| 5/29 | 2 | 9. TRAVELIN' MAN | Ricky Nelson† |
| 6/5 | 1 | 10. RUNNING SCARED | Roy Orbison |
| 6/19 | 1 | 11. MOODY RIVER | Pat Boone |
| 6/26 | 2 | 12. QUARTER TO THREE | U.S. Bonds |
| 7/10 | 7 | 13. TOSSIN' AND TURNIN' | Bobby Lewis |
| 8/28 | 1 | 14. WOODEN HEART | Joe Dowell |
| 9/4 | 2 | 15. MICHAEL | Highwaymen |
| 9/18 | 3 | 16. TAKE GOOD CARE OF MY BABY | Bobby Vee |
| 10/9 | 2 | 17. HIT THE ROAD JACK | Ray Charles |
| 10/23 | 2 | 18. RUNAROUND SUE | Dion |
| 11/6 | 5 | 19. BIG BAD JOHN | Jimmy Dean |
| 12/11 | 1 | 20. PLEASE MR. POSTMAN | Marvelettes |
| 12/18 | 3 | 21. THE LION SLEEPS TONIGHT | Tokens |
| | | **1962** | |
| 1/13 | 2 | 1. THE TWIST (formerly #1 on 9/19/60) | Chubby Checker |
| 1/27 | 3 | 2. PEPPERMINT TWIST | Joey Dee & The Starliters |
| 2/17 | 3 | 3. DUKE OF EARL | Gene Chandler |
| 3/10 | 3 | 4. HEY! BABY | Bruce Channel |
| 3/31 | 1 | 5. DON'T BREAK THE HEART THAT LOVES YOU | Connie Francis |
| 4/7 | 2 | 6. JOHNNY ANGEL | Shelley Fabares |
| 4/21 | 2 | 7. GOOD LUCK CHARM | Elvis Presley |
| 5/5 | 3 | 8. SOLDIER BOY | Shirelles |
| 5/26 | 1 | 9. STRANGER ON THE SHORE | Mr. Acker Bilk |
| 6/2 | 5 | 10. I CAN'T STOP LOVING YOU | Ray Charles |
| 7/7 | 1 | 11. THE STRIPPER | David Rose |
| 7/14 | 4 | 12. ROSES ARE RED | Bobby Vinton |
| 8/11 | 2 | 13. BREAKING UP IS HARD TO DO | Neil Sedaka |
| 8/25 | 1 | 14. THE LOCO-MOTION | Little Eva |
| 9/1 | 2 | 15. SHEILA | Tommy Roe |
| 9/15 | 5 | 16. SHERRY | 4 Seasons |
| 10/20 | 2 | 17. MONSTER MASH | Bobby "Boris" Pickett & The Crypt Kickers |
| 11/3 | 2 | 18. HE'S A REBEL | Crystals |
| 11/17 | 5 | 19. BIG GIRLS DON'T CRY | 4 Seasons |
| 12/22 | 3 | 20. TELSTAR | Tornadoes |

| DATE | WKS | RECORD TITLE | ARTIST |
|---|---|---|---|
| **1963** | | | |
| 1/12 | 2 | 1. GO AWAY LITTLE GIRL | Steve Lawrence |
| 1/26 | 2 | 2. WALK RIGHT IN | Rooftop Singers |
| 2/9 | 3 | 3. HEY PAULA | Paul & Paula |
| 3/2 | 3 | 4. WALK LIKE A MAN | 4 Seasons |
| 3/23 | 1 | 5. OUR DAY WILL COME | Ruby & The Romantics |
| 3/30 | 4 | 6. HE'S SO FINE | Chiffons |
| 4/27 | 3 | 7. I WILL FOLLOW HIM | Little Peggy March |
| 5/18 | 2 | 8. IF YOU WANNA BE HAPPY | Jimmy Soul |
| 6/1 | 2 | 9. IT'S MY PARTY | Lesley Gore |
| 6/15 | 3 | 10. SUKIYAKI | Kyu Sakamoto |
| 7/6 | 2 | 11. EASIER SAID THAN DONE | Essex |
| 7/20 | 2 | 12. SURF CITY | Jan & Dean |
| 8/3 | 1 | 13. SO MUCH IN LOVE | Tymes |
| 8/10 | 3 | 14. FINGERTIPS - PT 2 | Little Stevie Wonder |
| 8/31 | 3 | 15. MY BOYFRIEND'S BACK | Angels |
| 9/21 | 3 | 16. BLUE VELVET | Bobby Vinton |
| 10/12 | 5 | 17. SUGAR SHACK | Jimmy Gilmer & The Fireballs |
| 11/16 | 1 | 18. DEEP PURPLE | Nino Tempo & April Stevens |
| 11/23 | 2 | 19. I'M LEAVING IT UP TO YOU | Dale & Grace |
| 12/7 | 4 | 20. DOMINIQUE | Singing Nun |
| **1964** | | | |
| 1/4 | 4 | 1. THERE! I'VE SAID IT AGAIN | Bobby Vinton |
| 2/1 | 7 | 2. I WANT TO HOLD YOUR HAND | Beatles |
| 3/21 | 2 | 3. SHE LOVES YOU | Beatles |
| 4/4 | 5 | 4. CAN'T BUY ME LOVE | Beatles |
| 5/9 | 1 | 5. HELLO, DOLLY! | Louis Armstrong |
| 5/16 | 2 | 6. MY GUY | Mary Wells |
| 5/30 | 1 | 7. LOVE ME DO | Beatles |
| 6/6 | 3 | 8. CHAPEL OF LOVE | Dixie Cups |
| 6/27 | 1 | 9. A WORLD WITHOUT LOVE | Peter & Gordon |
| 7/4 | 2 | 10. I GET AROUND | Beach Boys |
| 7/18 | 2 | 11. RAG DOLL | 4 Seasons |
| 8/1 | 2 | 12. A HARD DAY'S NIGHT | Beatles |
| 8/15 | 1 | 13. EVERYBODY LOVES SOMEBODY | Dean Martin |
| 8/22 | 2 | 14. WHERE DID OUR LOVE GO | Supremes |
| 9/5 | 3 | 15. THE HOUSE OF THE RISING SUN | Animals |
| 9/26 | 3 | 16. OH, PRETTY WOMAN | Roy Orbison |
| 10/17 | 2 | 17. DO WAH DIDDY DIDDY | Manfred Mann |
| 10/31 | 4 | 18. BABY LOVE | Supremes |
| 11/28 | 1 | 19. LEADER OF THE PACK | Shangri-Las |
| 12/5 | 1 | 20. RINGO | Lorne Greene |
| 12/12 | 1 | 21. MR. LONELY | Bobby Vinton |
| 12/19 | 2 | 22. COME SEE ABOUT ME | Supremes† |
| 12/26 | 3 | 23. I FEEL FINE | Beatles |

| DATE | WKS | RECORD TITLE | ARTIST |
|---|---|---|---|
| | | **1965** | |
| 1/23 | 2 | 1. DOWNTOWN | Petula Clark |
| 2/6 | 2 | 2. YOU'VE LOST THAT LOVIN' FEELIN' | Righteous Brothers |
| 2/20 | 2 | 3. THIS DIAMOND RING | Gary Lewis & The Playboys |
| 3/6 | 1 | 4. MY GIRL | Temptations |
| 3/13 | 2 | 5. EIGHT DAYS A WEEK | Beatles |
| 3/27 | 2 | 6. STOP! IN THE NAME OF LOVE | Supremes |
| 4/10 | 2 | 7. I'M TELLING YOU NOW | Freddie & The Dreamers |
| 4/24 | 1 | 8. GAME OF LOVE | Wayne Fontana & The Mindbenders |
| 5/1 | 3 | 9. MRS. BROWN YOU'VE GOT A LOVELY DAUGHTER | Herman's Hermits |
| 5/22 | 1 | 10. TICKET TO RIDE | Beatles |
| 5/29 | 2 | 11. HELP ME, RHONDA | Beach Boys |
| 6/12 | 1 | 12. BACK IN MY ARMS AGAIN | Supremes |
| 6/19 | 2 | 13. I CAN'T HELP MYSELF | Four Tops† |
| 6/26 | 1 | 14. MR. TAMBOURINE MAN | Byrds |
| 7/10 | 4 | 15. (I CAN'T GET NO) SATISFACTION | Rolling Stones |
| 8/7 | 1 | 16. I'M HENRY VIII, I AM | Herman's Hermits |
| 8/14 | 3 | 17. I GOT YOU BABE | Sonny & Cher |
| 9/4 | 3 | 18. HELP! | Beatles |
| 9/25 | 1 | 19. EVE OF DESTRUCTION | Barry McGuire |
| 10/2 | 1 | 20. HANG ON SLOOPY | McCoys |
| 10/9 | 4 | 21. YESTERDAY | Beatles |
| 11/6 | 2 | 22. GET OFF MY CLOUD | Rolling Stones |
| 11/20 | 2 | 23. I HEAR A SYMPHONY | Supremes |
| 12/4 | 3 | 24. TURN! TURN! TURN! | Byrds |
| 12/25 | 1 | 25. OVER AND OVER | Dave Clark Five |
| | | **1966** | |
| 1/1 | 2 | 1. THE SOUNDS OF SILENCE | Simon & Garfunkel† |
| 1/8 | 3 | 2. WE CAN WORK IT OUT | Beatles† |
| 2/5 | 2 | 3. MY LOVE | Petula Clark |
| 2/19 | 1 | 4. LIGHTNIN' STRIKES | Lou Christie |
| 2/26 | 1 | 5. THESE BOOTS ARE MADE FOR WALKIN' | Nancy Sinatra |
| 3/5 | 5 | 6. THE BALLAD OF THE GREEN BERETS | Ssgt. Barry Sadler |
| 4/9 | 3 | 7. (YOU'RE MY) SOUL AND INSPIRATION | Righteous Brothers |
| 4/30 | 1 | 8. GOOD LOVIN' | Young Rascals |
| 5/7 | 3 | 9. MONDAY, MONDAY | Mama's & Papa's |
| 5/28 | 2 | 10. WHEN A MAN LOVES A WOMAN | Percy Sledge |
| 6/11 | 2 | 11. PAINT IT, BLACK | Rolling Stones |
| 6/25 | 2 | 12. PAPERBACK WRITER | Beatles† |
| 7/2 | 1 | 13. STRANGERS IN THE NIGHT | Frank Sinatra |
| 7/16 | 2 | 14. HANKY PANKY | Tommy James & The Shondells |
| 7/30 | 2 | 15. WILD THING | Troggs |
| 8/13 | 3 | 16. SUMMER IN THE CITY | Lovin' Spoonful |
| 9/3 | 1 | 17. SUNSHINE SUPERMAN | Donovan |
| 9/10 | 2 | 18. YOU CAN'T HURRY LOVE | Supremes |
| 9/24 | 3 | 19. CHERISH | Association |
| 10/15 | 2 | 20. REACH OUT I'LL BE THERE | Four Tops |

| DATE | WKS | RECORD TITLE | ARTIST |
|---|---|---|---|
| | | **1966 continued** | |
| 10/29 | 1 | 21. 96 TEARS | ? (Question Mark) & The Mysterians |
| 11/5 | 1 | 22. LAST TRAIN TO CLARKSVILLE | Monkees |
| 11/12 | 1 | 23. POOR SIDE OF TOWN | Johnny Rivers |
| 11/19 | 2 | 24. YOU KEEP ME HANGIN' ON | Supremes |
| 12/3 | 3 | 25. WINCHESTER CATHEDRAL | New Vaudeville Band† |
| 12/10 | 1 | 26. GOOD VIBRATIONS | Beach Boys |
| 12/31 | 7 | 27. I'M A BELIEVER | Monkees |
| | | **1967** | |
| 2/18 | 2 | 1. KIND OF A DRAG | Buckinghams |
| 3/4 | 1 | 2. RUBY TUESDAY | Rolling Stones |
| 3/11 | 1 | 3. LOVE IS HERE AND NOW YOU'RE GONE | Supremes |
| 3/18 | 1 | 4. PENNY LANE | Beatles |
| 3/25 | 3 | 5. HAPPY TOGETHER | Turtles |
| 4/15 | 4 | 6. SOMETHIN' STUPID | Nancy Sinatra & Frank Sinatra |
| 5/13 | 1 | 7. THE HAPPENING | Supremes |
| 5/20 | 4 | 8. GROOVIN' | Young Rascals† |
| 6/3 | 2 | 9. RESPECT | Aretha Franklin |
| 7/1 | 4 | 10. WINDY | Association |
| 7/29 | 3 | 11. LIGHT MY FIRE | Doors |
| 8/19 | 1 | 12. ALL YOU NEED IS LOVE | Beatles |
| 8/26 | 4 | 13. ODE TO BILLY JOE | Bobbie Gentry |
| 9/23 | 4 | 14. THE LETTER | Box Tops |
| 10/21 | 5 | 15. TO SIR WITH LOVE | Lulu |
| 11/25 | 1 | 16. INCENSE AND PEPPERMINTS | Strawberry Alarm Clock |
| 12/2 | 4 | 17. DAYDREAM BELIEVER | Monkees |
| 12/30 | 3 | 18. HELLO GOODBYE | Beatles |
| | | **1968** | |
| 1/20 | 2 | 1. JUDY IN DISGUISE (WITH GLASSES) | John Fred & His Playboy Band |
| 2/3 | 1 | 2. GREEN TAMBOURINE | Lemon Pipers |
| 2/10 | 5 | 3. LOVE IS BLUE | Paul Mauriat |
| 3/16 | 4 | 4. (SITTIN' ON) THE DOCK OF THE BAY | Otis Redding |
| 4/13 | 5 | 5. HONEY | Bobby Goldsboro |
| 5/18 | 2 | 6. TIGHTEN UP | Archie Bell & The Drells |
| 6/1 | 3 | 7. MRS. ROBINSON | Simon & Garfunkel |
| 6/22 | 4 | 8. THIS GUY'S IN LOVE WITH YOU | Herb Alpert |
| 7/20 | 2 | 9. GRAZING IN THE GRASS | Hugh Masekela |
| 8/3 | 2 | 10. HELLO, I LOVE YOU | Doors |
| 8/17 | 5 | 11. PEOPLE GOT TO BE FREE | Rascals |
| 9/21 | 1 | 12. HARPER VALLEY P.T.A. | Jeannie C. Riley |
| 9/28 | 9 | 13. HEY JUDE | Beatles |
| 11/30 | 2 | 14. LOVE CHILD | Diane Ross & The Supremes |
| 12/14 | 7 | 15. I HEARD IT THROUGH THE GRAPEVINE | Marvin Gaye |

| DATE | WKS | RECORD TITLE | ARTIST |
|------|-----|--------------|--------|
| | | **1969** | |
| 2/1 | 2 | 1. CRIMSON AND CLOVER | Tommy James & The Shondells |
| 2/15 | 4 | 2. EVERYDAY PEOPLE | Sly & The Family Stone |
| 3/15 | 4 | 3. DIZZY | Tommy Roe |
| 4/12 | 6 | 4. AQUARIUS / LET THE SUNSHINE IN | 5th Dimension |
| 5/24 | 5 | 5. GET BACK | Beatles |
| 6/28 | 2 | 6. LOVE THEME FROM ROMEO & JULIET | Henry Mancini |
| 7/12 | 6 | 7. IN THE YEAR 2525 | Zager & Evans |
| 8/23 | 4 | 8. HONKY TONK WOMEN | Rolling Stones |
| 9/20 | 4 | 9. SUGAR, SUGAR | Archies |
| 10/18 | 2 | 10. I CAN'T GET NEXT TO YOU | Temptations |
| 11/1 | 1 | 11. SUSPICIOUS MINDS | Elvis Presley |
| 11/8 | 3 | 12. WEDDING BELL BLUES | 5th Dimension |
| 11/29 | 1 | 13. COME TOGETHER/SOMETHING | Beatles |
| 12/6 | 2 | 14. NA NA HEY HEY KISS HIM GOODBYE | Steam |
| 12/20 | 1 | 15. LEAVING ON A JET PLANE | Peter, Paul & Mary |
| 12/27 | 1 | 16. SOMEDAY WE'LL BE TOGETHER | Diana Ross & The Supremes |
| | | **1970** | |
| 1/3 | 4 | 1. RAINDROPS KEEP FALLIN' ON MY HEAD | B. J. Thomas |
| 1/31 | 1 | 2. I WANT YOU BACK | Jackson 5 |
| 2/7 | 1 | 3. VENUS | Shocking Blue |
| 2/14 | 2 | 4. THANK YOU FALETTINME BE MICE ELF AGIN | Sly & The Family Stone |
| 2/28 | 6 | 5. BRIDGE OVER TROUBLED WATER | Simon & Garfunkel |
| 4/11 | 2 | 6. LET IT BE | Beatles |
| 4/25 | 2 | 7. ABC | Jackson 5 |
| 5/9 | 3 | 8. AMERICAN WOMAN | Guess Who |
| 5/30 | 2 | 9. EVERYTHING IS BEAUTIFUL | Ray Stevens |
| 6/13 | 2 | 10. THE LONG AND WINDING ROAD | Beatles |
| 6/27 | 2 | 11. THE LOVE YOU SAVE | Jackson 5 |
| 7/11 | 2 | 12. MAMA TOLD ME (NOT TO COME) | Three Dog Night |
| 7/25 | 4 | 13. (THEY LONG TO BE) CLOSE TO YOU | Carpenters |
| 8/22 | 1 | 14. MAKE IT WITH YOU | Bread |
| 8/29 | 3 | 15. WAR | Edwin Starr |
| 9/19 | 3 | 16. AIN'T NO MOUNTAIN HIGH ENOUGH | Diana Ross |
| 10/10 | 1 | 17. CRACKLIN' ROSIE | Neil Diamond |
| 10/17 | 5 | 18. I'LL BE THERE | Jackson 5 |
| 11/21 | 3 | 19. I THINK I LOVE YOU | Partridge Family |
| 12/12 | 2 | 20. THE TEARS OF A CLOWN | Smokey Robinson & The Miracles |
| 12/26 | 4 | 21. MY SWEET LORD | George Harrison |

| DATE | WKS | RECORD TITLE | ARTIST |
|---|---|---|---|
| **1971** | | | |
| 1/23 | 3 | 1. KNOCK THREE TIMES | Dawn |
| 2/13 | 5 | 2. ONE BAD APPLE | Osmonds |
| 3/20 | 2 | 3. ME AND BOBBY McGEE | Janis Joplin |
| 4/3 | 2 | 4. JUST MY IMAGINATION (RUNNING AWAY WITH ME) | Temptations |
| 4/17 | 6 | 5. JOY TO THE WORLD | Three Dog Night |
| 5/29 | 2 | 6. BROWN SUGAR | Rolling Stones |
| 6/12 | 1 | 7. WANT ADS | Honey Cone |
| 6/19 | 5 | 8. IT'S TOO LATE | Carole King |
| 7/24 | 1 | 9. INDIAN RESERVATION | Raiders |
| 7/31 | 1 | 10. YOU'VE GOT A FRIEND | James Taylor |
| 8/7 | 4 | 11. HOW CAN YOU MEND A BROKEN HEART | Bee Gees |
| 9/4 | 1 | 12. UNCLE ALBERT / ADMIRAL HALSEY | Paul & Linda McCartney |
| 9/11 | 3 | 13. GO AWAY LITTLE GIRL | Donny Osmond |
| 10/2 | 5 | 14. MAGGIE MAY | Rod Stewart |
| 11/6 | 2 | 15. GYPSYS, TRAMPS, & THIEVES | Cher |
| 11/20 | 2 | 16. THEME FROM SHAFT | Isaac Hayes |
| 12/4 | 3 | 17. FAMILY AFFAIR | Sly & The Family Stone |
| 12/25 | 3 | 18. BRAND NEW KEY | Melanie |
| **1972** | | | |
| 1/15 | 4 | 1. AMERICAN PIE | Don McLean |
| 2/12 | 1 | 2. LET'S STAY TOGETHER | Al Green |
| 2/19 | 4 | 3. WITHOUT YOU | Nilsson |
| 3/18 | 1 | 4. HEART OF GOLD | Neil Young |
| 3/25 | 3 | 5. A HORSE WITH NO NAME | America |
| 4/15 | 6 | 6. THE FIRST TIME EVER I SAW YOUR FACE | Roberta Flack |
| 5/27 | 1 | 7. OH GIRL | Chi-Lites |
| 6/3 | 1 | 8. I'LL TAKE YOU THERE | Staple Singers |
| 6/10 | 3 | 9. THE CANDY MAN | Sammy Davis, Jr. |
| 7/1 | 1 | 10. SONG SUNG BLUE | Neil Diamond |
| 7/8 | 3 | 11. LEAN ON ME | Bill Withers |
| 7/29 | 6 | 12. ALONE AGAIN (NATURALLY) | Gilbert O'Sullivan† |
| 8/26 | 1 | 13. BRANDY (YOU'RE A FINE GIRL) | Looking Glass |
| 9/16 | 1 | 14. BLACK & WHITE | Three Dog Night |
| 9/23 | 3 | 15. BABY DON'T GET HOOKED ON ME | Mac Davis |
| 10/14 | 1 | 16. BEN | Michael Jackson |
| 10/21 | 2 | 17. MY DING-A-LING | Chuck Berry |
| 11/4 | 4 | 18. I CAN SEE CLEARLY NOW | Johnny Nash |
| 12/2 | 1 | 19. PAPA WAS A ROLLING STONE | Temptations |
| 12/9 | 1 | 20. I AM WOMAN | Helen Reddy |
| 12/16 | 3 | 21. ME AND MRS. JONES | Billy Paul |

| DATE | WKS | RECORD TITLE | ARTIST |
|------|-----|-------------|--------|
| | | **1973** | |
| 1/6 | 3 | 1. YOU'RE SO VAIN | Carly Simon |
| 1/27 | 1 | 2. SUPERSTITION | Stevie Wonder |
| 2/3 | 3 | 3. CROCODILE ROCK | Elton John |
| 2/24 | 5 | 4. KILLING ME SOFTLY WITH HIS SONG | Roberta Flack† |
| 3/24 | 1 | 5. LOVE TRAIN | O'Jays |
| 4/7 | 2 | 6. THE NIGHT THE LIGHTS WENT OUT IN GEORGIA | Vicki Lawrence |
| 4/21 | 4 | 7. TIE A YELLOW RIBBON ROUND THE OLE OAK TREE | Dawn |
| 5/19 | 1 | 8. YOU ARE THE SUNSHINE OF MY LIFE | Stevie Wonder |
| 5/26 | 1 | 9. FRANKENSTEIN | Edgar Winter Group |
| 6/2 | 4 | 10. MY LOVE | Paul McCartney & Wings |
| 6/30 | 1 | 11. GIVE ME LOVE (GIVE ME PEACE ON EARTH) | George Harrison |
| 7/7 | 2 | 12. WILL IT GO ROUND IN CIRCLES | Billy Preston |
| 7/21 | 2 | 13. BAD, BAD LEROY BROWN | Jim Croce |
| 8/4 | 2 | 14. THE MORNING AFTER (SONG FROM THE POSEIDON ADVENTURE) | Maureen McGovern |
| 8/18 | 1 | 15. TOUCH ME IN THE MORNING | Diana Ross |
| 8/25 | 2 | 16. BROTHER LOUIE | Stories |
| 9/8 | 2 | 17. LET'S GET IT ON | Marvin Gaye† |
| 9/15 | 1 | 18. DELTA DAWN | Helen Reddy |
| 9/29 | 1 | 19. WE'RE AN AMERICAN BAND | Grand Funk |
| 10/6 | 2 | 20. HALF-BREED | Cher |
| 10/20 | 1 | 21. ANGIE | Rolling Stones |
| 10/27 | 2 | 22. MIDNIGHT TRAIN TO GEORGIA | Gladys Knight & The Pips |
| 11/10 | 2 | 23. KEEP ON TRUCKIN' | Eddie Kendricks |
| 11/24 | 1 | 24. PHOTOGRAPH | Ringo Starr |
| 12/1 | 2 | 25. TOP OF THE WORLD | Carpenters |
| 12/15 | 2 | 26. THE MOST BEAUTIFUL GIRL | Charlie Rich |
| 12/29 | 2 | 27. TIME IN A BOTTLE | Jim Croce |

| DATE | WKS | RECORD TITLE | ARTIST |
|---|---|---|---|
| | | **1974** | |
| 1/12 | 1 | 1. THE JOKER | Steve Miller Band |
| 1/19 | 1 | 2. SHOW AND TELL | Al Wilson |
| 1/26 | 1 | 3. YOU'RE SIXTEEN | Ringo Starr |
| 2/2 | 3 | 4. THE WAY WE WERE | Barbra Streisand† |
| 2/9 | 1 | 5. LOVE'S THEME | Love Unlimited Orchestra |
| 3/2 | 3 | 6. SEASONS IN THE SUN | Terry Jacks |
| 3/23 | 1 | 7. DARK LADY | Cher |
| 3/30 | 1 | 8. SUNSHINE ON MY SHOULDERS | John Denver |
| 4/6 | 1 | 9. HOOKED ON A FEELING | Blue Swede |
| 4/13 | 1 | 10. BENNIE AND THE JETS | Elton John |
| 4/20 | 2 | 11. TSOP (THE SOUND OF PHILADELPHIA) | MFSB featuring The Three Degrees |
| 5/4 | 2 | 12. THE LOCO-MOTION | Grand Funk |
| 5/18 | 3 | 13. THE STREAK | Ray Stevens |
| 6/8 | 1 | 14. BAND ON THE RUN | Paul McCartney & Wings |
| 6/15 | 2 | 15. BILLY, DON'T BE A HERO | Bo Donaldson & The Heywoods |
| 6/29 | 1 | 16. SUNDOWN | Gordon Lightfoot |
| 7/6 | 1 | 17. ROCK THE BOAT | Hues Corporation |
| 7/13 | 2 | 18. ROCK YOUR BABY | George McCrae |
| 7/27 | 2 | 19. ANNIE'S SONG | John Denver |
| 8/10 | 1 | 20. FEEL LIKE MAKIN' LOVE | Roberta Flack |
| 8/17 | 1 | 21. THE NIGHT CHICAGO DIED | Paper Lace |
| 8/24 | 3 | 22. (YOU'RE) HAVING MY BABY | Paul Anka |
| 9/14 | 1 | 23. I SHOT THE SHERIFF | Eric Clapton |
| 9/21 | 1 | 24. CAN'T GET ENOUGH OF YOUR LOVE, BABE | Barry White |
| 9/28 | 1 | 25. ROCK ME GENTLY | Andy Kim |
| 10/5 | 2 | 26. I HONESTLY LOVE YOU | Olivia Newton-John |
| 10/19 | 1 | 27. NOTHING FROM NOTHING | Billy Preston |
| 10/26 | 1 | 28. THEN CAME YOU | Dionne Warwicke & Spinners |
| 11/2 | 1 | 29. YOU HAVEN'T DONE NOTHIN | Stevie Wonder |
| 11/9 | 1 | 30. YOU AIN'T SEEN NOTHING YET | Bachman-Turner Overdrive |
| 11/16 | 1 | 31. WHATEVER GETS YOU THRU THE NIGHT | John Lennon with the Plastic Ono Nuclear Band |
| 11/23 | 2 | 32. I CAN HELP | Billy Swan |
| 12/7 | 2 | 33. KUNG FU FIGHTING | Carl Douglas |
| 12/21 | 1 | 34. CAT'S IN THE CRADLE | Harry Chapin |
| 12/28 | 1 | 35. ANGIE BABY | Helen Reddy |

| DATE | WKS | RECORD TITLE | ARTIST |
|------|-----|-------------|--------|
| | | **1975** | |
| 1/4 | 2 | 1. LUCY IN THE SKY WITH DIAMONDS | Elton John |
| 1/18 | 1 | 2. MANDY | Barry Manilow |
| 1/25 | 1 | 3. PLEASE MR. POSTMAN | Carpenters |
| 2/1 | 1 | 4. LAUGHTER IN THE RAIN | Neil Sedaka |
| 2/8 | 1 | 5. FIRE | Ohio Players |
| 2/15 | 1 | 6. YOU'RE NO GOOD | Linda Ronstadt |
| 2/22 | 1 | 7. PICK UP THE PIECES | AWB |
| 3/1 | 1 | 8. BEST OF MY LOVE | Eagles |
| 3/8 | 1 | 9. HAVE YOU NEVER BEEN MELLOW | Olivia Newton-John |
| 3/15 | 1 | 10. BLACK WATER | Doobie Brothers |
| 3/22 | 1 | 11. MY EYES ADORED YOU | Frankie Valli |
| 3/29 | 1 | 12. LADY MARMALADE | Labelle |
| 4/5 | 1 | 13. LOVIN' YOU | Minnie Riperton |
| 4/12 | 2 | 14. PHILADELPHIA FREEDOM | Elton John Band |
| 4/26 | 1 | 15. (HEY WON'T YOU PLAY) ANOTHER SOMEBODY DONE SOMEBODY WRONG SONG | B. J. Thomas |
| 5/3 | 3 | 16. HE DON'T LOVE YOU (LIKE I LOVE YOU) | Tony Orlando & Dawn |
| 5/24 | 1 | 17. SHINING STAR | Earth, Wind & Fire |
| 5/31 | 1 | 18. BEFORE THE NEXT TEARDROP FALLS | Freddy Fender |
| 6/7 | 1 | 19. THANK GOD I'M A COUNTRY BOY | John Denver |
| 6/14 | 1 | 20. SISTER GOLDEN HAIR | America |
| 6/21 | 4 | 21. LOVE WILL KEEP US TOGETHER | Captain & Tennille |
| 7/19 | 1 | 22. LISTEN TO WHAT THE MAN SAID | Wings |
| 7/26 | 1 | 23. THE HUSTLE | Van McCoy & The Soul City Symphony |
| 8/2 | 1 | 24. ONE OF THESE NIGHTS | Eagles |
| 8/9 | 2 | 25. JIVE TALKIN' | Bee Gees |
| 8/23 | 1 | 26. FALLIN' IN LOVE | Hamilton, Joe Frank & Reynolds |
| 8/30 | 1 | 27. GET DOWN TONIGHT | K.C. & The Sunshine Band |
| 9/6 | 2 | 28. RHINESTONE COWBOY | Glen Campbell |
| 9/20 | 2 | 29. FAME | David Bowie† |
| 9/27 | 1 | 30. I'M SORRY | John Denver |
| 10/11 | 3 | 31. BAD BLOOD | Neil Sedaka |
| 11/1 | 3 | 32. ISLAND GIRL | Elton John |
| 11/22 | 2 | 33. THAT'S THE WAY (I LIKE IT) | K.C. & The Sunshine Band† |
| 11/29 | 3 | 34. FLY, ROBIN, FLY | Silver Convention |
| 12/27 | 1 | 35. LET'S DO IT AGAIN | Staple Singers |

| DATE | WKS | RECORD TITLE | ARTIST |
|---|---|---|---|
| | | **1976** | |
| 1/3 | 1 | 1. SATURDAY NIGHT | Bay City Rollers |
| 1/10 | 1 | 2. CONVOY | C. W. McCall |
| 1/17 | 1 | 3. I WRITE THE SONGS | Barry Manilow |
| 1/24 | 1 | 4. THEME FROM MAHOGANY (DO YOU KNOW WHERE YOU'RE GOING TO) | Diana Ross |
| 1/31 | 1 | 5. LOVE ROLLERCOASTER | Ohio Players |
| 2/7 | 3 | 6. 50 WAYS TO LEAVE YOUR LOVER | Paul Simon |
| 2/28 | 1 | 7. THEME FROM S.W.A.T. | Rhythm Heritage |
| 3/6 | 1 | 8. LOVE MACHINE (PART 1) | Miracles |
| 3/13 | 3 | 9. DECEMBER, 1963 (OH, WHAT A NIGHT) | Four Seasons |
| 4/3 | 4 | 10. DISCO LADY | Johnnie Taylor |
| 5/1 | 1 | 11. LET YOUR LOVE FLOW | Bellamy Brothers |
| 5/8 | 1 | 12. WELCOME BACK | John Sebastian |
| 5/15 | 1 | 13. BOOGIE FEVER | Sylvers |
| 5/22 | 5 | 14. SILLY LOVE SONGS | Wings† |
| 5/29 | 2 | 15. LOVE HANGOVER | Diana Ross |
| 7/10 | 2 | 16. AFTERNOON DELIGHT | Starland Vocal Band |
| 7/24 | 2 | 17. KISS AND SAY GOODBYE | Manhattans |
| 8/7 | 4 | 18. DON'T GO BREAKING MY HEART | Elton John & Kiki Dee |
| 9/4 | 1 | 19. YOU SHOULD BE DANCING | Bee Gees |
| 9/11 | 1 | 20. (SHAKE, SHAKE, SHAKE) SHAKE YOUR BOOTY | KC & The Sunshine Band |
| 9/18 | 3 | 21. PLAY THAT FUNKY MUSIC | Wild Cherry |
| 10/9 | 1 | 22. A FIFTH OF BEETHOVEN | Walter Murphy & The Big Apple Band |
| 10/16 | 1 | 23. DISCO DUCK (PART 1) | Rick Dees & His Cast Of Idiots |
| 10/23 | 2 | 24. IF YOU LEAVE ME NOW | Chicago |
| 11/6 | 1 | 25. ROCK'N ME | Steve Miller |
| 11/13 | 7 | 26. TONIGHT'S THE NIGHT (GONNA BE ALRIGHT) | Rod Stewart |
| | | **1977** | |
| 1/8 | 1 | 1. YOU DON'T HAVE TO BE A STAR (TO BE IN MY SHOW) | Marilyn McCoo & Billy Davis, Jr. |
| 1/15 | 1 | 2. YOU MAKE ME FEEL LIKE DANCING | Leo Sayer |
| 1/22 | 1 | 3. I WISH | Stevie Wonder |
| 1/29 | 1 | 4. CAR WASH | Rose Royce |
| 2/5 | 2 | 5. TORN BETWEEN TWO LOVERS | Mary MacGregor |
| 2/19 | 1 | 6. BLINDED BY THE LIGHT | Manfred Mann's Earth Band |
| 2/26 | 1 | 7. NEW KID IN TOWN | Eagles |
| 3/5 | 3 | 8. LOVE THEME FROM "A STAR IS BORN" (EVERGREEN) | Barbra Streisand |
| 3/26 | 2 | 9. RICH GIRL | Daryl Hall & John Oates |

| DATE | WKS | RECORD TITLE | ARTIST |
|------|-----|-------------|--------|
| | | **1977 CONTINUED** | |
| 4/9 | 1 | 10. DANCING QUEEN | Abba |
| 4/16 | 1 | 11. DON'T GIVE UP ON US | David Soul |
| 4/23 | 1 | 12. DON'T LEAVE ME THIS WAY | Thelma Houston |
| 4/30 | 1 | 13. SOUTHERN NIGHTS | Glen Campbell |
| 5/7 | 1 | 14. HOTEL CALIFORNIA | Eagles |
| 5/14 | 1 | 15. WHEN I NEED YOU | Leo Sayer |
| 5/21 | 3 | 16. SIR DUKE | Stevie Wonder |
| 6/11 | 1 | 17. I'M YOUR BOOGIE MAN | KC & The Sunshine Band |
| 6/18 | 1 | 18. DREAMS | Fleetwood Mac |
| 6/25 | 1 | 19. GOT TO GIVE IT UP | Marvin Gaye |
| 7/2 | 1 | 20. GONNA FLY NOW (THEME FROM "ROCKY") | Bill Conti |
| 7/9 | 1 | 21. UNDERCOVER ANGEL | Alan O'Day |
| 7/16 | 1 | 22. DA DOO RON RON | Shaun Cassidy |
| 7/23 | 1 | 23. LOOKS LIKE WE MADE IT | Barry Manilow |
| 7/30 | 4 | 24. I JUST WANT TO BE YOUR EVERYTHING | Andy Gibb† |
| 8/20 | 5 | 25. BEST OF MY LOVE | Emotions† |
| 10/1 | 2 | 26. STAR WARS THEME/CANTINA BAND | Meco |
| 10/15 | 10 | 27. YOU LIGHT UP MY LIFE | Debby Boone |
| 12/24 | 3 | 28. HOW DEEP IS YOUR LOVE | Bee Gees |
| | | **1978** | |
| 1/14 | 3 | 1. BABY COME BACK | Player |
| 2/4 | 4 | 2. STAYIN' ALIVE | Bee Gees |
| 3/4 | 2 | 3. (LOVE IS) THICKER THAN WATER | Andy Gibb |
| 3/18 | 8 | 4. NIGHT FEVER | Bee Gees |
| 5/13 | 1 | 5. IF I CAN'T HAVE YOU | Yvonne Elliman |
| 5/20 | 2 | 6. WITH A LITTLE LUCK | Wings |
| 6/3 | 1 | 7. TOO MUCH, TOO LITTLE, TOO LATE | Johnny Mathis/ Deniece Williams |
| 6/10 | 1 | 8. YOU'RE THE ONE THAT I WANT | John Travolta & Olivia Newton-John |
| 6/17 | 7 | 9. SHADOW DANCING | Andy Gibb |
| 8/5 | 1 | 10. MISS YOU | Rolling Stones |
| 8/12 | 2 | 11. THREE TIMES A LADY | Commodores |
| 8/26 | 2 | 12. GREASE | Frankie Valli |
| 9/9 | 3 | 13. BOOGIE OOGIE OOGIE | Taste Of Honey |
| 9/30 | 4 | 14. KISS YOU ALL OVER | Exile |
| 10/28 | 1 | 15. HOT CHILD IN THE CITY | Nick Gilder |
| 11/4 | 1 | 16. YOU NEEDED ME | Anne Murray |
| 11/11 | 3 | 17. MacARTHUR PARK | Donna Summer |
| 12/2 | 2 | 18. YOU DON'T BRING ME FLOWERS | Barbra Streisand & Neil Diamond† |
| 12/9 | 5 | 19. LE FREAK | Chic† |

| DATE | | RECORD TITLE | ARTIST |
|---|---|---|---|
| **1979** | | | |
| 1/6 | 2 | 1. TOO MUCH HEAVEN | Bee Gees |
| 2/10 | 4 | 2. DA YA THINK I'M SEXY? | Rod Stewart |
| 3/10 | 3 | 3. I WILL SURVIVE | Gloria Gaynor† |
| 3/24 | 2 | 4. TRAGEDY | Bee Gees |
| 4/14 | 1 | 5. WHAT A FOOL BELIEVES | Doobie Brothers |
| 4/21 | 1 | 6. KNOCK ON WOOD | Amili Stewart |
| 4/28 | 1 | 7. HEART OF GLASS | Blondie |
| 5/5 | 4 | 8. REUNITED | Peaches & Herb |
| 6/2 | 3 | 9. HOT STUFF | Donna Summer† |
| 6/9 | 1 | 10. LOVE YOU INSIDE OUT | Bee Gees |
| 6/30 | 2 | 11. RING MY BELL | Anita Ward |
| 7/14 | 5 | 12. BAD GIRLS | Donna Summer |
| 8/18 | 1 | 13. GOOD TIMES | Chic |
| 8/25 | 6 | 14. MY SHARONA | The Knack |
| 10/6 | 1 | 15. SAD EYES | Robert John |
| 10/13 | 1 | 16. DON'T STOP 'TIL YOU GET ENOUGH | Michael Jackson |
| 10/20 | 2 | 17. RISE | Herb Alpert |
| 11/3 | 1 | 18. POP MUZIK | M |
| 11/10 | 1 | 19. HEARTACHE TONIGHT | Eagles |
| 11/17 | 1 | 20. STILL | Commodores |
| 11/24 | 2 | 21. NO MORE TEARS (ENOUGH IS ENOUGH) | Barbra Streisand/ Donna Summer |
| 12/8 | 2 | 22. BABE | Styx |
| 12/22 | 2 | 23. ESCAPE (THE PINA COLADA SONG) | Rupert Holmes† |
| **1980** | | | |
| 1/5 | 1 | 1. PLEASE DON'T GO | KC & The Sunshine Band |
| 1/19 | 4 | 2. ROCK WITH YOU | Michael Jackson |
| 2/16 | 1 | 3. DO THAT TO ME ONE MORE TIME | Captain & Tennille |
| 2/23 | 4 | 4. CRAZY LITTLE THING CALLED LOVE | Queen |
| 3/22 | 4 | 5. ANOTHER BRICK IN THE WALL (PART II) | Pink Floyd |
| 4/19 | 6 | 6. CALL ME | Blondie |
| 5/31 | 4 | 7. FUNKYTOWN | Lipps, Inc. |
| 6/28 | 3 | 8. COMING UP (LIVE AT GLASGOW) | Paul McCartney & Wings |
| 7/19 | 2 | 9. IT'S STILL ROCK AND ROLL TO ME | Billy Joel |
| 8/2 | 4 | 10. MAGIC | Olivia Newton-John |
| 8/30 | 1 | 11. SAILING | Christopher Cross |
| 9/6 | 4 | 12. UPSIDE DOWN | Diana Ross |
| 10/4 | 3 | 13. ANOTHER ONE BITES THE DUST | Queen |
| 10/25 | 3 | 14. WOMAN IN LOVE | Barbra Streisand |
| 11/15 | 6 | 15. LADY | Kenny Rogers |
| 12/27 | 5 | 16. (JUST LIKE) STARTING OVER | John Lennon |

| DATE | WKS | RECORD TITLE | ARTIST |
|---|---|---|---|
| | | **1981** | |
| 1/31 | 1 | 1. THE TIDE IS HIGH | Blondie |
| 2/7 | 2 | 2. CELEBRATION | Kool & The Gang |
| 2/21 | 2 | 3. 9 TO 5 | Dolly Parton† |
| 2/28 | 2 | 4. I LOVE A RAINY NIGHT | Eddie Rabbitt |
| 3/21 | 1 | 5. KEEP ON LOVING YOU | REO Speedwagon |
| 3/28 | 2 | 6. RAPTURE | Blondie |
| 4/11 | 3 | 7. KISS ON MY LIST | Daryl Hall & John Oates |
| 5/2 | 2 | 8. MORNING TRAIN (NINE TO FIVE) | Sheena Easton |
| 5/16 | 9 | 9. BETTE DAVIS EYES | Kim Carnes† |
| 6/20 | 1 | 10. STARS ON 45 MEDLEY | Stars on 45 |
| 7/25 | 1 | 11. THE ONE THAT YOU LOVE | Air Supply |
| 8/1 | 2 | 12. JESSIE'S GIRL | Rick Springfield |
| 8/15 | 9 | 13. ENDLESS LOVE | Diana Ross & Lionel Richie |
| 10/17 | 3 | 14. ARTHUR'S THEME (BEST THAT YOU CAN DO) | Christopher Cross |
| 11/7 | 2 | 15. PRIVATE EYES | Daryl Hall & John Oates |
| 11/21 | 10 | 16. PHYSICAL | Olivia Newton-John |
| | | **1982** | |
| 1/30 | 1 | 1. I CAN'T GO FOR THAT (NO CAN DO) | Daryl Hall & John Oates |
| 2/6 | 6 | 2. CENTERFOLD | J. Geils Band |
| 3/20 | 7 | 3. I LOVE ROCK 'N ROLL | Joan Jett & The Blackhearts |
| 5/8 | 1 | 4. CHARIOTS OF FIRE — TITLES | Vangelis |
| 5/15 | 7 | 5. EBONY AND IVORY | Paul McCartney/ Stevie Wonder |
| 6/19 | 3 | 6. DON'T YOU WANT ME | Human League |
| 7/24 | 6 | 7. EYE OF THE TIGER | Survivor |
| 9/4 | 2 | 8. ABRACADABRA | Steve Miller Band† |
| 9/11 | 2 | 9. HARD TO SAY I'M SORRY | Chicago |
| 9/18 | 4 | 10. JACK & DIANE | John Cougar |
| 10/30 | 1 | 11. WHO CAN IT BE NOW? | Men At Work |
| 11/6 | 3 | 12. UP WHERE WE BELONG | Joe Cocker & Jennifer Warnes |
| 11/27 | 2 | 13. TRULY | Lionel Richie |
| 12/11 | 1 | 14. MICKEY | Toni Basil |
| 12/18 | 4 | 15. MANEATER | Daryl Hall & John Oates |

| DATE | WKS | RECORD TITLE | ARTIST |
|---|---|---|---|
| **1983** | | | |
| 1/15 | 4 | 1. DOWN UNDER | Men At Work† |
| 2/5 | 1 | 2. AFRICA | Toto |
| 2/19 | 2 | 3. BABY, COME TO ME | Patti Austin & James Ingram |
| 3/5 | 7 | 4. BILLIE JEAN | Michael Jackson |
| 4/23 | 1 | 5. COME ON EILEEN | Dexys Midnight Runners |
| 4/30 | 3 | 6. BEAT IT | Michael Jackson |
| 5/21 | 1 | 7. LET'S DANCE | David Bowie |
| 5/28 | 6 | 8. FLASHDANCE . . . WHAT A FEELING | Irene Cara |
| 7/9 | 8 | 9. EVERY BREATH YOU TAKE | Police |
| 9/3 | 1 | 10. SWEET DREAMS (ARE MADE OF THIS) | Eurythmics |
| 9/10 | 2 | 11. MANIAC | Michael Sembello |
| 9/24 | 1 | 12. TELL HER ABOUT IT | Billy Joel |
| 10/1 | 4 | 13. TOTAL ECLIPSE OF THE HEART | Bonnie Tyler |
| 10/29 | 2 | 14. ISLANDS IN THE STREAM | Kenny Rogers with Dolly Parton |
| 11/12 | 4 | 15. ALL NIGHT LONG (ALL NIGHT) | Lionel Richie |
| 12/10 | 6 | 16. SAY SAY SAY | Paul McCartney & Michael Jackson |
| **1984** | | | |
| 1/21 | 2 | 1. OWNER OF A LONELY HEART | Yes |
| 2/4 | 3 | 2. KARMA CHAMELEON | Culture Club |
| 2/25 | 5 | 3. JUMP | Van Halen |
| 3/31 | 3 | 4. FOOTLOOSE | Kenny Loggins |
| 4/21 | 3 | 5. AGAINST ALL ODDS (TAKE A LOOK AT ME NOW) | Phil Collins |
| 5/12 | 2 | 6. HELLO | Lionel Richie |
| 5/26 | 2 | 7. LET'S HEAR IT FOR THE BOY | Deniece Williams |
| 6/9 | 2 | 8. TIME AFTER TIME | Cyndi Lauper |
| 6/23 | 2 | 9. THE REFLEX | Duran Duran |
| 7/7 | 5 | 10. WHEN DOVES CRY | Prince |
| 8/11 | 3 | 11. GHOSTBUSTERS | Ray Parker Jr. |
| 9/1 | 3 | 12. WHAT'S LOVE GOT TO DO WITH IT | Tina Turner |
| 9/22 | 1 | 13. MISSING YOU | John Waite |
| 9/29 | 2 | 14. LET'S GO CRAZY | Prince |
| 10/13 | 3 | 15. I JUST CALLED TO SAY I LOVE YOU | Stevie Wonder |
| 11/3 | 2 | 16. CARIBBEAN QUEEN (NO MORE LOVE ON THE RUN) | Billy Ocean |
| 11/17 | 3 | 17. WAKE ME UP BEFORE YOU GO-GO | Wham! |
| 12/8 | 2 | 18. OUT OF TOUCH | Daryl Hall & John Oates |
| 12/22 | 6 | 19. LIKE A VIRGIN | Madonna |